CIVIL RIGHTS AND CONSTITUTIONAL LITIGATION

CASES AND MATERIALS

Fifth Edition

■ ■ ■

By

Charles F. Abernathy

Professor of Law
Georgetown University Law Center

AMERICAN CASEBOOK SERIES®

WEST®
A Thomson Reuters business

Mat #41062455

American Casebook Series is a trademark registered in the U.S. Patent and Trademark Office.

COPYRIGHT © 1980, 1992 WEST PUBLISHING CO.
© West, a Thomson business, 2000, 2006
© 2012 Thomson Reuters
    610 Opperman Drive
    St. Paul, MN 55123
    1–800–313–9378
Printed in the United States of America

ISBN: 978–0–314–26787–0

for Chip and Julia

PREFACE TO THE FIFTH EDITION

This edition aims to retain the look and feel of prior editions while substantially updating the material with new cases and concepts. The overall goal remains that of introducing interested and motivated students to one of the most challenging areas of modern federal law.

This edition continues the statute-centered organization that makes civil rights law more readily accessible to and easily organized by students. At the same time, greater effort has been made in this edition to connect themes running among statutes—constitutional issues (such as Congressional competence to enact civil rights laws and its limits), analytical issues (such as intent and impact analysis and pertinent defenses), and social issues (emerging claims to protection and emerging dissents to expansion). As the Court and Congress have evolved over time, the task of presenting this material in an evenhanded manner that will interest and challenge all students has grown more difficult, but it continues to motivate my work. Moreover, these evolutions have also introduced increasing complexity and conflict into civil rights law, making it more difficult to present the law as a comprehensive and intelligible whole. The response in this edition has been to reduce unnecessary complexity, especially in the Notes following cases, while maintaining the richness of the underlying evolution in law.

Professors new to teaching will notice some significant differences between this edition and other casebooks. This book uses the familiar organization of principal cases and Notes that follow. But as in past editions, the Notes ask fewer open-ended questions than many casebooks and provide more organization, leading the student through a critique of the more difficult cases. The Notes also raise significant additional issues only hinted at or not presented by the principal cases. (Practical issues, such as relevant procedural devices or appellate permutations on the Supreme Court's announced doctrines, not only highlight the frailty of some precedents but also allow students to see that major precedents can, in the real world, be severely limited or have an impact different from that apparently foreseen by the Court.) The Notes also push students to consider the several dimensions of civil rights law, from cases and rules, to doctrine and theory, to legal realism. (Generally, the Notes progress in numerical order to greater levels of complexity, allowing the professor to cut off reading at the point considered appropriate for the degree of detail permitted by class hours.)

Although my name appears alone on this volume, it is in fact the work of a large group of people, primarily my students who constantly bring me new insights and the research assistants who have done far more than merely "assist" me over the years. Special thanks go to Stephanie Jeane, Terri Taylor, Rachel Paul, Chris Mishler, Consuelo Kendall, Ryan Hart, and Phoebe

Taubman. I have also benefitted enormously from colleagues who teach in the same or related fields and who educate me regularly. Special thanks for this edition go to Robert Schwemm at the University of Kentucky, who stretched my knowledge of fair housing law.

Finally, and most importantly, I have once again been blessed with generous supporters. I thank my enormously talented and tolerant spouse and children who have allowed me the time to produce this edition. I am also happy to offer a lifetime of special thanks to the editors at Thomson/West Publishing, particularly Louis Higgins, who have supported the many of us who want to provide teaching materials to students in courses that often seem too specialized to warrant the investment. Family, friends, colleagues, and students, I thank you all.

CHARLES F. ABERNATHY

September, 2011
Washington, DC

PREFACE TO THE FOURTH EDITION

This edition remains committed to the original vision of the first edition—treatment of civil rights legislation as a "major body of federal law as sophisticated and as important as Labor Law, Securities Regulation, or Taxation." As a part of the original effort, a primary goal was to induce students to see that there are connections between apparently unrelated statutes and that these inter-relations tell us something important about civil-rights policy—and our national and personal values.

This edition includes updating material throughout the volume, but the unifying theme of the Fourth Edition is to highlight more clearly the "families" of civil rights statutes. Long-time users of the book will notice the first effect of this theme in the creation of three new "Parts" for the volume—

Part I, which emphasizes the connections between civil rights statutes (primarily § 1983) and constitutional law and judicial policymaking,

Part II, which highlights the quasi-constitutional status of some statutes in the sense that they raise complex questions of congressional power to expand or enforce constitutional norms,

Part III, which continues, as before, to focus on modern statutes that are policy-driven and often pragmatic products of the political process.

Part II presents some especially interesting developments because it discusses two civil rights statutes that have largely failed, 42 U.S.C. § 1985(3) and the Violence Against Women Act. The lessons of these statutes are especially important because they demonstrate that some significant provisions of older civil rights legislation, which are widely revered in modern life as embodying virtually constitutional values, actually rest on secondary assumptions about the extent of congressional power to enforce constitutional values that are themselves much narrower.

Other than this major realignment of emphasis, the other substantial changes that have occurred throughout the area of civil rights law have been integrated almost seamlessly into the existing third edition. Major cases remain as major cases, without a self-conscious attempt to change principal cases just for the sake of change. When new principal cases have been added, it is because the changes were sufficiently dramatic that students can best understand the law by reading the new case before hearing of an older one in the Notes. The Notes continue, as in the past, to direct students to a historical and contextual consideration of developments, with a light hand on judgmental issues that leaves professors and students free to pursue a structured but open-ended discussion. As before, the book continues a more demanding style that asks students to think more deeply—not unpolitically, but more-than-politically—about the roles of Congress, regulators, and courts.

* * *

I have been incredibly fortunate to teach some of the very best students in the world, people who have made my life in civil rights law exciting, fun, and inspiring. I have tried to return the favor, as I am sure all professors do every time we take to the podium. I am sure that I join my colleagues in thanking our students for giving us the splendid opportunity to discuss and consider civil rights each day of our lives. I also thank especially Jason Elstor, who has served as my research assistant during the last year and who gave generously of his time and energy to support this project. Thanks also to Georgetown's in-house editing team, Anna Selden and Zinta Saulkalns, who have also read and commented on drafts, often on short notice, and to my editors at West Group, especially Louis Higgins. Of course, despite the help of these and many other colleagues, I regret that mistakes will probably remain; they are mine alone.

Finally, I thank my wife Kathleen, who despite a very demanding legal position of her own, has continued to support my time-consuming (and humor-consuming) writing projects. My son Chip (my bocce ball and hiking partner and political sounding board) has been a source of education and inspiration, and Julia (now ten years old and already a star student and athlete) has kept her father young even as his eyes glow red before the computer monitor. Friends and family, I thank you.

Charles F. Abernathy

Washington, DC, 2006

PREFACE TO THE THIRD EDITION

As this book has evolved over the years, I have tried to stay true to the original vision of the first edition. These materials should make it possible for a professor to teach a Civil Rights or Constitutional Litigation course that "would treat the area as a major body of federal law as sophisticated and as important as Labor Law, Securities Regulation, or Taxation." In practical terms this means that the materials have needed to serve two goals, one focusing largely on litigation of constitutional claims under § 1983 and its cohorts and another focusing on policy-based modern statutes, such as Titles VI and VII and the Americans With Disabilities Act, that are products of legislative compromise rather than, in some respects, constitutional command. From this broad coverage, one may create a course in constitutional litigation alone (Part One), a course in civil rights policy or statutory enforcement of civil rights (Part Two), or a course examining the intersection of constitutional litigation and legislative policy on civil rights (selecting from Parts One and Two).

Judicial development of the older civil rights statutes has led to some significant additions to Part One in this third edition. The Supreme Court, for example, has created a new doctrine of general "back-up" due process which makes actionable under § 1983 a potentially broad range of state and local activities that were previously covered only by specific constitutional provisions or were covered not at all. The Court has also reintroduced the concept that state common law may prescribe the elements that a plaintiff must prove to sustain a claim under § 1983, at least in suits by prisoners challenging their convictions. Despite these new developments, however, the long-term themes identified in the first edition remain: the tension between statutory and constitutional sources of law, the search for the relevance of state law in federal civil rights claims, and the role of courts in interpreting civil rights law when so many potential sources lie about begging for attention. The traditional user of this text will feel at home despite the updating.

Even greater changes have occurred in the topics covered in Part Two of this third edition, reflecting new activity flowing from passage of the Civil Rights Act of 1991 and the Americans With Disabilities Act of 1990. There has also been significant judicial activity in developing remedies under these and the other more traditional civil rights statutes that are pure creatures of legislative policy. Nevertheless, the themes found in Part Two of previous editions continue to dominate the scene: the wisdom and clarity of Congressional policy choices, the role of administrative agencies in interpretation and enforcement, and the judicial implication of remedies that subtly transfer more interpretive power to the courts by bringing such claims into widespread, privately-initiated litigation. These are exciting new times for policy-based civil rights, but the creativity is within the limits of long-relevant and long-established parameters.

Because most "modern" civil rights legislation now goes back over half a century to taskforce reports of the late 1940's, and since many of the basic judicial disputes over interpretation go back almost forty years to the mid–1960's, Civil Rights law has become something of a stale middle- aged baby boomer in law. Therefore, this third edition makes a special effort, especially in Part Two, to stimulate students to question the results achieved so far, with an eye toward considering new and different solutions, ones that cannot be labeled liberal, conservative, or progressive. (As in the earlier editions, among the positions offered for dissection and criticism are ones that I litigated or on which I consulted, reflecting my belief that we should learn to second-guess not only our opponents, but also ourselves.) More consciously than before, this third edition, even while trying to provide more cases, more information, and more analysis, encourages the student to test what is given in order to stimulate greater creativity and experimentation.

* * *

In terms of pedagogy, this third edition proceeds with a more demanding style and focus that provides more information to students and expects more from them. The reading level required to master the Notes has been raised, and the questions go several steps beyond those presented in previous editions. I have also adopted a more argumentative tone in order to try to challenge students to produce more. I have also infused the Notes with many of the more intractable and ironic issues that I had previously raised only in my own classes at Georgetown. These changes have been stimulated by recognition that our students in law schools are better than any I have seen during my lifetime.

Despite its more demanding tone and style, this third edition remains user-friendly for professors. Although there are many questions followed by case citations, these citations now, more often than not, reveal the cited court's ruling, making it easier for professors and students to read the materials—and not incidentally, leaving more time for thinking about the issues raised. This edition is also structured so that a professor can pick and choose from among different chapters or sub-chapters in order to create his or her own course. Although Notes continue to make cross-references to other Chapters, they are now given with more context so that reading the entire other chapter is unnecessary.

Professors will notice one substantial pedagogical decision reflected in this edition. I have substantially restricted the number of citations to law review articles and books in order to reflect the Supreme Court's deemphasis on such materials. Now, citations to law reviews are largely restricted to showing some historical position or to provide contemporaneous descriptions of how courts treated a particular issue at some point along its evolutionary path. This decision to de-emphasize secondary sources in the textbook makes room for professors who wish to use secondary materials to do so by adoption or creation of anthologies which can be much more focused than I could provide in such a topically broad textbook. It also allows professors to choose the kind of anthology which allows individualizing the course to accentuate each professors area of interest. (I myself use an anthology of sociological readings about race, sex, and other timely issues, one which supplements the textbook with cutting-edge sociological research rather than strictly legal developments.)

* * *

In the past few years while I have taught this course at Georgetown, I have benefitted greatly from the magnificent diversity of students who have used this book. Committed progressives and Federalist Society members, feminists and racial radicals, old line liberals and conservatives, peace activists and police officers in search of a second career, and many others—all have contributed substantially to my understanding of civil rights law, and I thank them all. I also thank my research assistants who have worked with me on this third edition, Erica Salmon, Emily Friedman, Rhonda McKitten, Kenneth Terrell, Zhonette Brown, and Michelle Butler. I am much indebted to all my students here at Georgetown who have made teaching an enjoyable, central part of my professorial career.

Most professors would consider themselves sufficiently blessed to be as well supported and challenged by students as I have been. (They are, I realize more each day, not really my students but my future colleagues.) I am additionally fortunate because I have had the constancy of family support as well. Kathleen, bar association president and national leader in her field of law, has found time to be my faithful spouse and best friend. Charles, who was Chip when the first edition of this book appeared (and remains so for me), is now a happy and well-adjusted attorney, no small achievement, who is also his father's confidant and principal advisor. And Julia—*inteligente* and *bella* Julia—has brought a twinkle to the eyes of her middle-aged father, with a promise of more excitement to come. Friends and family, I thank you.

CHARLES F. ABERNATHY

Washington, D.C.

PREFACE TO THE SECOND EDITION

Those familiar with the first edition of this book will notice a short addition to the title of the second edition. It is now Civil Rights *and Constitutional Litigation*. This represents neither a change of goals nor a change of emphasis, but only a more accurate description of the course or courses that can be taught from these materials.

The goal of the materials as a whole remains to demonstrate and highlight the fascinating interplay between statutory sources of civil rights law and constitutional sources. Given the structure of government and law in the United States, this could also be called the interplay between congressional and judicial sources of civil rights. To a much greater extent than the normal course in constitutional law, therefore, a course in civil rights discloses the tension between majoritarian solutions to community conflicts and judicial solutions.

The overall goal of the materials may be pursued in at least three different ways. First, the book as a whole offers broad coverage of the main themes of all major civil rights legislation, allowing students to see the connection between judicially developed themes and legislatively developed themes, for example, the difference between the intent test for racial discrimination in § 1983 cases involving the Fourteenth Amendment and the impact and intent tests for racial discrimination used under Title VII as well as the Voting Rights Act. The fuller picture also gives the student a more reassuring knowledge of how civil rights laws fit together as a whole to accomplish more finely detailed or sophisticated solutions: if § 1983's " 'under color' of law" test does not reach all discrimination, it can be supplemented by legislation such as Title VI or the Rehabilitation Act.

Two other courses may also be taught from these materials. First, the first chapter—in essence the first half of the book—provides the basis for a self-contained course in constitutional litigation under 42 USC § 1983, the basic civil rights act that enforces the Fourteenth Amendment against state and local governments. Sometimes called "constitutional torts," this area involves more than a synthesis of constitutional law and torts; it may in fact show why synthesis is not completely possible. (Assignment of the materials on §§ 1981, 1982, and 1985 would valuably supplement coverage of § 1983.) Second, these materials may also be used as the shell around which many topical courses in civil rights may be built using the individual professor's own experiences. The professor who wants to try something new but is daunted by the prospect of assembling all the basic material is hereby invited to innovate, building on these foundation materials.

Napoleon reportedly asked his prospective generals not whether they were good, but whether they were lucky. He thought that good fortune played a strong role in life. I am unsure about the cosmic truth of Napoleon's views, but I know that I have been extraordinarily lucky to have the faculty, student, and family support that have made my life immensely rewarding and enjoyable. A chance meeting made possible a short, untraditional clerkship that confirmed my interest in civil rights. My son's illness in Cambridge, England, brought me back to the United States and led to work with two civil rights lawyers, to the founding of a public interest law firm, and to the opportunity to engage in a wealth of test-cases litigation before I entered teaching at age 27. The chance retirement of a treasured founder of the study of civil rights, Chester Antieau, made it possible for me to start at Georgetown, where I have always been challenged by intelligent and highly motivated students. Dean David Wilmot has joined me in teaching this course for over fifteen years, vastly expanding my understanding of civil rights. I feel very lucky.

I would like to thank the excellent research assistants whom fortune has brought my way. Bobbi Kienast and Marjorie Nicol provided valuable support in early research, and Kathleen Bender and Kelly Ramsdell helped me finish the materials and took me through the production process. I also thank the staff at West Publishing Company for their courteous and professional efforts. And to the users of the first edition, who have encouraged me to present this second edition, I express my sincere appreciation.

This may be a particularly difficult time to prepare materials for a course in civil rights, but I do it with enthusiasm. I have sought to write about fundamental and enduring themes that will prepare students for this volatile area of law; I have sought to provoke thoughts, without being merely provocative—to let truth speak for itself to each one of us. This has been a major challenge, for our vocabulary is changing at a time when many are re-emphasizing the value of vocabulary: Congress has been caught in the change as it moved from laws protecting "handicapped" persons to those protecting persons with "disabilities," and I write in these materials about both "blacks" and "African–Americans." It is my hope that the basic value of these materials—like the civil rights laws themselves—will survive, accommodate, and thrive on the changes that are coming.

Yet, even as I write this preface to the second edition, I am impressed by how constant the educational values in civil rights law have been. Many of the themes that I mentioned in that first preface, such as the goal of making the study of civil rights law as sophisticated and demanding as other fields, have endured and are now being pursued by many dedicated and talented professors. And I am similarly impressed by how constant my family's support and understanding have been. My son, Chip, has grown to be a mature adult, and my spouse, Kathleen, has not only achieved her own career goals, she has also helped me meet one of my important goals, to grow older with her. Colleagues, friends, and family, I thank you.

CHARLES F. ABERNATHY

Washington, D.C.
December, 1991

PREFACE TO THE FIRST EDITION

As with most publication efforts, these materials began with the search for a book which did not exist. As a new professor preparing to teach civil rights, I found excellent casebooks on constitutional law and challenging new works on topical issues such as race and sex discrimination. Along with these grand books on substance I also considered the grand book of federal practice and procedure, Hart and Wechsler's, The Federal Courts and the Federal System.

None of these superior books, prepared for other courses, fit my conception of what a book for a course in civil rights ought to be. Civil rights is more than constitutional law because statutory considerations play such an important role. Civil rights is broader than race or sex discrimination, broader of course, in the topical sense, especially with Congress' newer legislation. More importantly, focusing on a single topic fails to disclose the similarities which many civil rights topics share—and the pertinent differences which so shape policies and decisions. The topical approach also sometimes produces students long on policy but short on the skills necessary to implement policy, and if there is anything the civil rights area needs it is attorneys as skilled as they are committed. Procedural skills alone, however, even the specialized knowledge of federal practice which serves a civil rights attorney so well, cannot win a case when substantive knowledge is lacking.

The civil rights course I wanted to teach would treat the area as a major body of federal law as sophisticated and as important as Labor Law, Securities Regulation, or Taxation. At the core of those courses, and at the core of this book, are major statutory frameworks around which issues of interpretation and policy swirl. Civil rights, moreover, is even more complex because the statutes interplay so often with constitutional considerations, yielding a much more overtly active judicial role than can be found in other areas of federal law.

The apparent statutory focus of these materials may therefore be grossly misleading. It does, however, serve real pedagogical purposes. The statutes provide a comfortable framework for orienting the subject matter because they give students a clear set of choices on how to proceed when they encounter a civil rights case. More importantly, however, each statute raises certain specific constitutional and policy issues that the statutory framework creates its own parallel constitutional framework. The division of statutes between Part One and Part Two also shows clearly the respective active roles of the Judiciary and Congress in promoting civil rights.

I should perhaps add a few points relating to use of this book in teaching. First, I realize that many of us who teach in this area are for mer civil rights attorneys or persons with specific experiences in civil rights. The materials which many of us have privately assembled in the past show substantial personal experience and commitment. I do not deny the value of the contribution made by such experiences: this book searches for common elements in our respective experiences so that we may begin to convey systematically and more certainly our knowledge of civil rights. I have planned the book to encourage individual professors to go beyond this common and systematic foundation. The statutory framework of the book lends itself to supplementation, and I have regularly in the past handed out problem sets to my classes on specific topical problems on which I have worked, including prisoner's rights, sex discrimination, and school desegregation.

Second, the statutory framework of this book, especially the division into Parts One and Two, makes it possible to teach only part of the material in a course. Several persons with whom I have shared these materials in the past have used Part One to teach a course in traditional civil rights which emphasizes the importance of the judicial role in lawmaking. One person has used Chapter 1 alone as the core material for a course on § 1983 and litigation against state officials. Of course you may want to use the entire book: I have five times taught almost the entire set of materials to dedicated—and challenged—classes at Georgetown, usually for only two credits.

Third, I have tried to eliminate as much bias as possible from these materials, even to the point of occasionally suggesting that holdings I supported—or even litigated—as an attorney may have been wrongly decided. My goal was not particularly to accommodate conservative students or professors, although I believe that every law student should learn civil rights law regardless of his political persuasion. Rather I firmly believe that civil rights law can be advanced permanently and regularly only when we bring the same rigor, the same willingness to ask hard questions, the same hardheadedness to this area of law as we apply in all others. The whirring of active minds is to be preferred over the click of knees jerking in unison.

I wish to thank my research assistants who have for four years hunted cases, cut and pasted them, and helped me catch my repeated mistakes: Ellen Miyasato, Pamela Perry, Kathy Russo, Jim Conner, and Carrie Schnelker. Also, I thank Tony Taylor, Judy Byrd, and Teri Jackson for their valuable proofreading. Joaquin Avila (University of Texas) and Paul Bender (Pennsylvania) as well as my colleagues here at Georgetown, Chester Antieau, Fred Dorsey, and David Wilmot, deserve my appreciation for having used and commented helpfully on earlier versions of these materials. My colleague Bob Schoshinski told me jokes funny enough to keep me sane while I was in the library. All of these persons are hereby credited with any contributions which this work may make and are absolved of all liabilities—some of their advice I refused to take.

Finally, there was a small set of friends who ensured that this book finally went to press. My family, especially my son Chip, gave me valuable psychological strength and much understanding. My mother and father watched for me as though I were thirty years younger, especially during the last nine months when I grew thirty years older. Pat Allred shepherded this project, painstakingly transforming my manuscript into material perfectly prepared for the printer. And Laura Glassman, a skilled Washington lawyer, gave time which she did not have to read and criticize my final draft. My friends, I thank you.

CHARLES F. ABERNATHY

Washington, D.C.
December, 1979

INTRODUCTION

This book is organized around the non-criminal statutes that Congress has enacted to protect the civil rights of Americans. Part One covers the section of the 1871 Civil Rights Act, § 1983, that gave rise to most modern constitutional litigation, especially after it was resurrected by an activist Supreme Court a century later. Part Three deals with modern legislation adopted during Second Reconstruction, the civil rights revolution which began in the 1950's and continues today. Sandwiched between is Part Two, which covers important transitional issues where constitutional law and legislative policy mix and collide. Few cases in any Part predate 1960. Most of the decisions have been handed down in the last twenty years.

From an ignored backwater in 1961, civil rights has since that year emerged into a bustling metropolis of issues, disputes, and concerns, as timely, as sophisticated, and as interesting as any major area of federal legislation. In that sense the materials in this book should be as challenging and intriguing as courses in Securities Regulation, Labor Law, and Federal Taxation were in the early decades after these statutory schemes were set in place. And if Congress' recent pace of activity is a guide, civil rights should remain an area as dynamic as any of those others throughout the remainder of this century.

In presenting civil rights as a major area of federal legislative concern, this book will on one level focus on the usual issues attorneys must face in dealing with statutes: what is the meaning of ambiguous terms? How do related or similar pieces of legislation fit together? What recurring patterns emerge, suggesting long-standing Congressional policies or phobias? This statutory focus will, of course, involve some inquiry into the courts' role in interpreting and applying statutes, their power to rewrite and reshape legislation.

Although they are constructed on a statutory framework, it would be a mistake to assume that these materials cover only mundane topics of statutory interpretation. Because civil rights has long been a topic of peculiar federal judicial concern in the United States, federal courts have taken an especially active role—beyond that of mere statutory interpretation—in molding civil rights legislation to respond to the judicially declared terms of the Constitution. Sometimes it is impossible to determine which aspects of a holding are statutorily based and which constitutionally derived as the courts mesh the two together. At other times the two concerns may be artificially separated, with the Court arguing that the applicability of a statutory principle permits it to avoid a decision of constitutional significance. Finally, fluidity also works with sophistication in another direction, as a Congressionally adopted technique or practice will occasionally so commend itself to the courts that it will be adopted as constitutional doctrine.

The interplay between statutory and constitutional considerations, moreover, takes place on two different planes. On the plane discussed above, federal courts see civil rights legislation as interacting with constitutional safeguards for individual rights. For example, a statute protecting minority interests might parallel Fourteenth Amendment notions of equal protection, and the courts might act to bring the statute and Amendment into harmony. On a different plane, however, courts will be concerned with another set of constitutional considerations, those of a structural or federal nature: in our nation of limited central governmental power, what legislation is Congress constitutionally empowered to enact? What sources of authority may Congress call upon to enact civil rights legislation? The federal courts, in short, must also be concerned that Congress, in pursuit of a good cause, does not arrogate to itself power our Constitution has sought, for the safety of all citizens, to diffuse between Congress and Judiciary, between federal government and state government.

As we shall see throughout these materials, the two constitutional planes of individual rights and structural power are not wholly separate, and indeed most often intersect. Decision on a structural constitutional issue of Congressional power will almost necessarily enhance or impair the effectiveness of federal superintendence of constitutional rights of the individual, and every decision in the area of individual rights will surely affect the constitutional balance of federal and state powers.

In addition to the statutory and constitutional issues raised in this book, there is also a third set of concerns: not what Congress wants the law to be or what the courts perceive or demand that it be, but what in your policy judgment the law ought to be. The statutes covered in this book represent only the archtypes of federal civil rights legislation, with Congress writing new analogous legislation each session. To what extent have the archtypes been successful in promoting individual rights? Have they failed to provide guidance to courts or defendants? Has success been won at a cost too great to bear in the future? When new legislation needs to be drafted or old legislation reformed through legislative or judicial amendment, how should it be done?

In short, this book does not answer the old conundrum "what is the difference between constitutional rights and civil rights" by saying that the latter are statutory rights. This introduction suggests, and the materials here should show, that if there is an answer to the old question, it is a much more complex one than we have heretofore considered.

Summary of Contents

TABLE OF CONTENTS

PART TWO. SEMI–CONSTITUTIONAL STATUTES: THE POWER OF CONGRESS TO EXPAND CONSTITUTION–BASED RIGHTS

TABLE OF CASES

The principal cases are in bold type. Cases cited or discussed in the text are in roman type. References are to pages. Cases cited in principal cases and within other quoted materials are not included.

CIVIL RIGHTS
AND CONSTITUTIONAL
LITIGATION

PART ONE

THE ORIGINAL CIVIL RIGHTS STATUTES AND CONSTITUTIONAL LITIGATION

■ ■ ■

CHAPTER 1

SECTION 1983—STATE INTERFERENCE WITH CIVIL RIGHTS

■ ■ ■

A. INTRODUCTION

MONROE v. PAPE

Supreme Court of the United States, 1961.
365 U.S. 167, 81 S.Ct. 473, 5 L.Ed.2d 492.

MR. JUSTICE DOUGLAS delivered the opinion of the Court.

This case presents important questions concerning the construction of * * * 42 U.S.C. § 1983, * * * which reads as follows:

"Every person who, under color of any statute, ordinance, regulation, custom or usage, of any State or Territory, subjects, or causes to be subjected, any citizen of the United States or other person within the jurisdiction thereof to the deprivation of any rights, privileges, or immunities secured by the Constitution and laws, shall be liable to the party injured in an action at law, suit in equity, or other proper proceeding for redress."

The complaint alleges that 13 Chicago police officers broke into petitioners' home in the early morning, routed them from bed, made them stand naked in the living room, and ransacked every room, emptying drawers and ripping mattress covers. It further alleges that Mr. Monroe was then taken to the police station and detained on "open" charges for 10 hours, while he was interrogated about a two-day-old murder, that he was not taken before a magistrate, though one was accessible, that he was not permitted to call his family or attorney, that he was subsequently released without criminal charges being preferred against him. It is alleged that the officers had no search warrant and no arrest warrant and that they acted "under color of the statutes, ordinances, regulations, customs and usages" of Illinois and of the City of Chicago. * * *

The City of Chicago moved to dismiss the complaint on the ground that it is not liable under the Civil Rights Acts or for acts committed in performance of its governmental functions. All defendants moved to dismiss, alleging that the complaint alleged no cause of action under those

Acts or under the Federal Constitution. The District Court dismissed the complaint. The Court of Appeals affirmed. . . .

I.

Petitioners claim that the invasion of their home and the subsequent search without a warrant and the arrest and detention of Mr. Monroe without a warrant and without arraignment constituted a deprivation of their "rights, privileges, or immunities secured by the Constitution" within the meaning of [§ 1983].

Section [1983] came onto the books as § 1 of the Ku Klux Act of April 20, 1871. 17 Stat. 13. It was one of the means whereby Congress exercised the power vested in it by § 5 of the Fourteenth Amendment to enforce the provisions of that Amendment. Senator Edmunds, Chairman of the Senate Committee on the Judiciary, said concerning this section:

> "The first section is one that I believe nobody objects to, as defining the rights secured by the Constitution of the United States when they are assailed by any State law or under color of any State law, and it is merely carrying out the principles of the civil rights bill, which has since become a part of the Constitution," viz., the Fourteenth Amendment.

Its purpose is plain from the title of the legislation, "An Act to enforce the Provisions of the Fourteenth Amendment to the Constitution of the United States, and for other Purposes." 17 Stat. 13. Allegation of facts constituting a deprivation under color of state authority of a right guaranteed by the Fourteenth Amendment satisfies to that extent the requirement of [§ 1983]. So far petitioners are on solid ground. For the guarantee against unreasonable searches and seizures contained in the Fourth Amendment has been made applicable to the States by reason of the Due Process Clause of the Fourteenth Amendment. Wolf v. People of State of Colorado, 338 U.S. 25, 69 S.Ct. 1359, 93 L.Ed. 1782.

II.

There can be no doubt at least since Ex parte Virginia, 100 U.S. 339, 346–347, 25 L.Ed. 676, that Congress has the power to enforce provisions of the Fourteenth Amendment against those who carry a badge of authority of a State and represent it in some capacity, whether they act in accordance with their authority or misuse it. See Home Tel. & Tel. Co. v. City of Los Angeles, 227 U.S. 278, 287–296, 33 S.Ct. 312, 314, 318, 57 L.Ed. 510. The question with which we now deal is the narrower one of whether Congress, in enacting [§ 1983], meant to give a remedy to parties deprived of constitutional rights, privileges and immunities by an official's abuse of his position. Cf. Williams v. United States, 341 U.S. 97, 71 S.Ct. 576, 95 L.Ed. 774; Screws v. United States, 325 U.S. 91, 65 S.Ct. 1031, 89 L.Ed. 1495; United States v. Classic, 313 U.S. 299, 61 S.Ct. 1031, 85 L.Ed. 1368. We conclude that it did so intend.

It is argued that "under color of" enumerated state authority excludes acts of an official or policeman who can show no authority under state law, state custom, or state usage to do what he did. In this case it is said that these policemen, in breaking into petitioners' apartment, violated the Constitution[6] and laws of Illinois. It is pointed out that under Illinois law a simple remedy is offered for that violation and that, so far as it appears, the courts of Illinois are available to give petitioners that full redress which the common law affords for violence done to a person; and it is earnestly argued that no "statute, ordinance, regulation, custom or usage" of Illinois bars that redress.

The legislation—in particular the section with which we are now concerned—had several purposes. There are threads of many thoughts running through the debates. One who reads them in their entirety sees that the present section had three main aims.

First, it might, of course, override certain kinds of state laws.

Second, it provided a remedy where state law was inadequate.

But the purposes were much broader. The *third* aim was to provide a federal remedy where the state remedy, though adequate in theory, was not available in practice.

This Act of April 20, 1871, sometimes called "the third 'force bill,' " was passed by a Congress that had the Klan "particularly in mind." The debates are replete with references to the lawless conditions existing in the South in 1871. There was available to the Congress during these debates a report, nearly 600 pages in length, dealing with the activities of the Klan and the inability of the state governments to cope with it. This report was drawn on by many of the speakers. It was not the unavailability of state remedies but the failure of certain States to enforce the laws with an equal hand that furnished the powerful momentum behind this "force bill."

* * *

The debates were long and extensive. It is abundantly clear that one reason the legislation was passed was to afford a federal right in federal courts because, by reason of prejudice, passion, neglect, intolerance or otherwise, state laws might not be enforced and the claims of citizens to the enjoyment of rights, privileges, and immunities guaranteed by the Fourteenth Amendment might be denied by the state agencies.

* * *

Although the legislation was enacted because of the conditions that existed in the South at that time, it is cast in general language and is as applicable to Illinois as it is to the States whose names were mentioned

---

6. Illinois Const., Art. II, § 6, S.H.A. Const., provides: "The right of the people to be secure in their persons, houses, paper and effects, against unreasonable searches and seizures, shall not be violated; and no warrant shall issue without probable cause, supported by affidavit, particularly describing the place to be searched, and the persons or things to be seized." Respondents also point to Ill.Rev.Stat., c. 38, §§ 252, 449.1; Chicago, Illinois, Municipal Code, §§ 11–40.

over and again in the debates. It is no answer that the State has a law which if enforced would give relief. The federal remedy is supplementary to the state remedy, and the latter need not be first sought and refused before the federal one is invoked. Hence the fact that Illinois by its constitution and laws outlaws unreasonable searches and seizures is no barrier to the present suit in the federal court.

We had before us in United States v. Classic, supra, § 20 of the Criminal Code, 18 U.S.C. § 242, which provides a criminal punishment for anyone who "under color of any law, statute, ordinance, regulation, or custom" subjects any inhabitant of a State to the deprivation of "any rights, privileges, or immunities secured or protected by the Constitution or laws of the United States." * * * In an opinion written by Mr. Justice (later Chief Justice) Stone, in which Mr. Justice Roberts, Mr. Justice Reed, and Mr. Justice Frankfurter joined, the Court ruled, "Misuse of power, possessed by virtue of state law and made possible only because the wrongdoer is clothed with the authority of state law, is action taken 'under color of' state law." [There was no dissent on this issue.]

That view of the meaning of the words "under color of" state law was reaffirmed in Screws v. United States, supra. The acts there complained of were committed by state officers in performance of their duties, viz., making an arrest effective. It was urged there, as it is here, that "under color of" state law should not be construed to duplicate in federal law what was an offense under state law. It was said there, as it is here, that the ruling in the Classic case as to the meaning of "under color of" state law was not in focus and was ill-advised. It was argued there, as it is here, that "under color of" state law included only action taken by officials pursuant to state law. We rejected that view. We [noted that, as statutory construction, Congress was free to change our interpretation if they disagreed. We also reached the same conclusion in Williams v. United States, supra.]

[Since the legislative history of § 1983 shows that it was modeled on § 242's use of "under color of" law,] it is beyond doubt that this phrase should be accorded the same construction in both statutes * * *.

Since the Screws and Williams decisions, Congress has had several pieces of civil rights legislation before it [in which it adopted the " 'under color of' law" of §§ 1983 and 242. Committee reports in each instance cited the Screws language.]

If the results of our construction of "under color of" law were as horrendous as now claimed, if they were as disruptive of our federal scheme as now urged, if they were such an unwarranted invasion of States' rights as pretended, surely the voice of the opposition would have been heard in those Committee reports. Their silence and the new uses to which "under color of" law have recently been given reinforce our conclusion that our prior decisions were correct on this matter of construction.

We conclude that the meaning given "under color of" law in the Classic case and in the Screws and Williams cases was the correct one; and we adhere to it. In the Screws case we dealt with a statute that imposed criminal penalties for acts "willfully" done. We construed that word in its setting to mean the doing of an act with "a specific intent to deprive a person of a federal right." 325 U.S. at 103. We do not think that gloss should be placed on [§ 1983] which we have here. The word "willfully" does not appear in [§ 1983]. Moreover, [§ 1983] provides a civil remedy, while in the Screws case we dealt with a criminal law challenged on the ground of vagueness. Section [1983] should be read against the background of tort liability that makes a man responsible for the natural consequences of his actions.

So far, then, the complaint states a cause of action. There remains to consider only a defense peculiar to the City of Chicago.

III.

The City of Chicago asserts that it is not liable under [§ 1983]. We do not stop to explore the whole range of questions tendered us on this issue at oral argument and in the briefs. For we are of the opinion that Congress did not undertake to bring municipal corporations within the ambit of [§ 1983]. When the bill that became the Act of April 20, 1871, was being debated in the Senate, Senator Sherman of Ohio proposed an amendment which would have made "the inhabitants of the county, city, or parish" in which certain acts of violence occurred liable "to pay full compensation" to the person damaged or his widow or legal representative.[38] The amendment was adopted by the Senate. The House, however, rejected it. The Conference Committee reported another version, [which, after some alteration,] dropped out all provision for municipal liability and extended liability in damages to "any person or persons, having knowledge that any" of the specified wrongs are being committed. * * *

* * *

It is said that doubts should be resolved in favor of municipal liability because private remedies against officers for illegal searches and seizures

---

38. Cong., Globe, 42d Cong., 1st Sess., p. 663. The proposed amendment read:

"That if any house, tenement, cabin, shop, building, barn, or granary shall be unlawfully or feloniously demolished, pulled down, burned, or destroyed, wholly or in part, by any persons riotously and tumultuously assembled together; or if any person shall unlawfully and with force and violence be whipped, scourged, wounded, or killed by any persons riotously and tumultuously assembled together; and if such offense was committed to deprive any person of any right conferred upon him by the Constitution and laws of the United States, or to deter him or punish him for exercising such right, or by reason of his race, color, or previous condition of servitude, in every such case the inhabitants of the county, city, or parish in which any of the said offenses shall be committed shall be liable to pay full compensation to the person or persons damnified by such offense if living, or to his widow or legal representative if dead; and such compensation may be recovered by such person or his representative by a suit in any court of the United States of competent jurisdiction * * *. And execution may be issued on a judgment rendered in such suit and may be levied upon any property, real or personal, of any person in said county, city, or parish, and the said county, city, or parish may recover the full amount of such judgment, costs and interest, from any person or persons engaged as principal or accessory in such riot in an action in any court of competent jurisdiction."

are conspicuously ineffective, and because municipal liability will not only afford plaintiffs responsible defendants but cause those defendants to eradicate abuses that exist at the police level. We do not reach those policy considerations. Nor do we reach the constitutional question whether Congress has the power to make municipalities liable for acts of its officers that violate the civil rights of individuals.

The response of the Congress to the proposal to make municipalities liable for certain actions being brought within federal purview by [§ 1983] was so antagonistic that we cannot believe that the word "person" was used in this particular Act to include them. Accordingly we hold that the motion to dismiss the complaint against the City of Chicago was properly granted. But since the complaint should not have been dismissed against the officials the judgment must be and is reversed.

Reversed.

MR. JUSTICE HARLAN, whom MR. JUSTICE STEWART joins, concurring.

Were this case here as one of first impression, I would find the "under color of any statute" issue very close indeed. However, in Classic and Screws this Court considered a substantially identical statutory phrase to have a meaning which, unless we now retreat from it, requires that issue to go for the petitioners here.

From my point of view, the policy of stare decisis, as it should be applied in matters of statutory construction and, to a lesser extent, the indications of congressional acceptance of this Court's earlier interpretation, require that it appear beyond doubt from the legislative history of the 1871 statute that Classic and Screws misapprehended the meaning of the controlling provision, before a departure from what was decided in those cases would be justified. Since I can find no such justifying indication in that legislative history, I join the opinion of the Court. * * *

* * *

MR. JUSTICE FRANKFURTER, dissenting except insofar as the Court holds that this action cannot be maintained against the City of Chicago.

* * * [I]nsofar as the Court undertakes to demonstrate—as the bulk of its opinion seems to do—that [§ 1983] was meant to reach some instances of action not specifically authorized by the avowed, apparent, written law inscribed in the statute books of the States, the argument knocks at an open door. No one would or could, deny this, for by its express terms the statute comprehends deprivations of federal rights under color of any "statute, ordinance, regulation, *custom, or usage*" of a State. (Emphasis added.) The question is, what class of cases other than those involving state statute law were meant to be reached. * * * Congress—made keenly aware by the post-bellum conditions in the South that States through their authorities could sanction offenses against the individual by settled practice which established state law as truly as written codes—designed [§ 1983] to reach, as well, official conduct which, because engaged in "permanently and as a rule," or "systematically," came

through acceptance by law-administering officers to constitute "custom, or usage" having the cast of law. They do not indicate an attempt to reach, nor does the statute by its terms include, instances of acts in defiance of state law and which no settled state practice, no systematic pattern of official action or inaction, no "custom, or usage, of any State," insulates from effective and adequate reparation by the State's authorities.

* * * This purpose, manifested even by the so-called "Radical" Reconstruction Congress in 1871, accords with the presuppositions of our federal system. The jurisdiction which Article III of the Constitution conferred on the national judiciary reflected the assumption that the state courts, not the federal courts, would remain the primary guardians of that fundamental security of person and property which the long evolution of the common law had secured to one individual as against other individuals. The Fourteenth Amendment did not alter this basic aspect of our federalism.

* * *

Since the federal courts went out of the business of making "general law," Erie R.R. Co. v. Tompkins, 304 U.S. 64, 58 S.Ct. 817, 82 L.Ed. 1188, such decisions of local policy have admittedly been the exclusive province of state lawmakers. * * * To extend Civil Rights Act liability [as the majority wishes] is to interfere in areas of state policymaking where Congress has not determined to interfere.

* * *

Relevant also are the effects upon the institution of federal constitutional adjudication of sustaining under [§ 1983] damage actions for relief against conduct allegedly violative of federal constitutional rights, but plainly violative of state law. Permitting such actions necessitates the immediate decision of federal constitutional issues despite the admitted availability of state-law remedies which would avoid those issues. This would make inroads, throughout a large area, upon the principle of federal judicial self-limitation which has become a significant instrument in the efficient functioning of the national judiciary. See Railroad Commission of Texas v. Pullman Co., 312 U.S. 496, 61 S.Ct. 643, 85 L.Ed. 971, and cases following. Self-limitation is not a matter of technical nicety, nor judicial timidity. It reflects the recognition that to no small degree the effectiveness of the legal order depends upon the infrequency with which it solves its problems by resorting to determinations of ultimate power. * * *

Of course, these last considerations would be irrelevant to our duty if Congress had demonstrably meant to reach by [§ 1983] activities like those of respondents in this case. But where it appears that Congress plainly did not have that understanding, respect for principles which this Court has long regarded as critical to the most effective functioning of our federalism should avoid extension of a statute beyond its manifest area of operation into applications which invite conflict with the administration of local policies. Such an extension makes the extreme limits of federal constitutional power a law to regulate the quotidian business of every traffic policeman, every registrar of elections, every city inspector or investigator, every clerk in every municipal licensing bureau in this country. * * *

* * *

NOTE ON THE "PERSONAL LIABILITY" MODEL FOR § 1983

1. What is the relation between § 1983 and the Fourteenth Amendment? When a state employs its judicial machinery to affect a person's legal status or other interests, as in a criminal prosecution or state-initiated civil proceeding, the Fourteenth Amendment applies of its own force without need for additional federal statutory enactment or supplementation of constitutional law. See, e.g., MLB v. SLJ, 519 U.S. 102, 117 S.Ct. 555, 136 L.Ed.2d 473 (1996) (Fourteenth Amendment forbids excessive bond requirement that precludes indigent parent's appeal of state-initiated suit terminating parental rights); Texas v. Johnson, 491 U.S. 397, 109 S.Ct. 2533, 105 L.Ed.2d 342 (1989) (flag-burning cannot be punished in state court because it is free speech protected by the First and Fourteenth Amendments). Similarly, when a private party initiates litigation in state courts on any ground permitted under state law, the Constitution of its own force applies to govern the state court's decision in the proceeding. See, e.g., Stop the Beach Renourishment, Inc. v. Florida Dept. of Environmental Protection, 560 U.S. ___, 130 S.Ct. 2592, 177 L.Ed.2d 184 (2010) (state court suit and claimed property rights); Palmore v. Sidoti, 466 U.S. 429, 104 S.Ct. 1879, 80 L.Ed.2d 421 (1984) (state court adoption case); Evans v. Newton, 382 U.S. 296, 86 S.Ct. 486, 15 L.Ed.2d 373 (1966) (estate administration). The Fourteenth Amendment thus acts as a shield to protect against state action.

(a) As the Court held in Monroe, § 1983 adds to these self-executing properties of the Fourteenth Amendment by authorizing persons whose constitutional rights are violated by state officials to sue in federal court—giving them a sword as well as a shield, a tort-like remedy to redress their grievances. Shapo, *Constitutional Tort*: Monroe v. Pape *and the Frontiers Beyond*, 60 NW. U. L. REV. 277, 322 (1965). (A separate statute, 28 U.S.C. § 1343, provides for federal district-court jurisdiction for § 1983 claims.)

(b) When the U.S. Supreme Court overturns a state court's unconstitutional ruling, the case is usually remanded with the requirement that the Fourteenth Amendment be obeyed—but the victim usually receives no compensation beyond the correction of the specific constitutional mistake. See, e.g., Evans v. Abney, 396 U.S. 435, 90 S.Ct. 628, 24 L.Ed.2d 634 (1970) (on remand of the *Newton* case, *supra*, alternative state ruling still results in loss for appellant). To what degree does § 1983, this provision of an additional federal civil mechanism for enforcing the Fourteenth Amendment, change the dynamics of constitutional law by (i) providing remedies (damages, injunctions) that might otherwise be unavailable; (ii) providing federal judges and factfinders; or (iii) providing, as suggested by Justice Frankfurter's dissenting opinion in *Monroe,* simply many more occasions for the interpretation and enforcement of the Fourteenth Amendment?

(c) The defendant officers in *Monroe* sought to narrow the scope of § 1983 by having the Court read the statute to provide no federal civil remedy when an officer disobeys applicable state law. This would have left Mr. Monroe, as Justice Frankfurter notes, with only a civil remedy in state court. Why would a federal defendant admit to conduct—the violation of state law— that would expose him to civil liability in state court under state law? Has the federal defendant jumped from the frying pan into the fire?

2. The *Monroe* Court solves the problem of potential state-court favoritism toward state and local officials by interpreting "under color of law" in § 1983 to cover all unconstitutional actions by state and local officials, both those actions authorized by state law and those actions violative of state law.

(a) Consider the three reasons given by Justice Douglas for the Court's broad interpretation of § 1983 as a freely available remedy independent of state common law. Do these three reasons support the Court's reasoning? Is not Justice Frankfurter's narrower interpretation also consistent with those three factors? Has Justice Douglas stretched § 1983 beyond what its drafters intended?

(b) Consider as a preliminary matter the potential analytical problems created when the Court seeks to apply the Fourteenth Amendment to official conduct, such as that in *Monroe*, which violates state law. Fourteenth Amendment analysis typically balances state and citizen interests through some inquiry such as the "compelling state interest test" or the "rational basis test." See Roe v. Wade, 410 U.S. 113, 93 S.Ct. 705, 35 L.Ed.2d 147 (1973) (compelling interest test applies to review state statute punishing abortion); John Nowak and Ronald Rotunda, CONSTITUTIONAL LAW § 14.3 (8th ed. 2010) (reviewing such tests for Equal Protection cases). How can such tests be applied when, by definition, the state has no detectable interest because the state official is violating state law?

(c) Justice Frankfurter's dissent argues that § 1983 should be interpreted to cover only violations so widespread and "systematic[]" that they "constitute[d] 'custom, or usage' having the cast of law." How does that solve the problem of applying traditional constitutional law in § 1983 cases? Might there not be other ways to solve the problem—by developing a greater variety of constitutional tests than just the basic ones covered in a first course in constitutional law?

3. Is § 1983 a mere procedural vehicle for enforcing Fourteenth Amendment rights, or does it alter the scope of coverage of constitutional law? Consider the two major issues in *Monroe*, the coverage of errant police officials and the non-coverage of municipal governments, in answering this pair of questions: Can Congress by statute expand the Fourteenth Amendment to make additional conduct illegal? Can Congress by statute narrow the effective scope of the Fourteenth Amendment by providing a damage remedy that covers less than all unconstitutional actions?

(a) The principal defense contention in *Monroe*, that official action violative of state law cannot be deemed action "under color of" state law for purposes of § 1983, had been rejected as a constitutional proposition for almost a half-century prior to *Monroe*, most recently the year before *Monroe* was decided. Home Telephone & Telegraph Co. v. City of Los Angeles, 227

U.S. 278, 33 S.Ct. 312, 57 L.Ed. 510 (1913); United States v. Raines, 362 U.S. 17, 80 S.Ct. 519, 4 L.Ed.2d 524 (1960). In rejecting the notion that local action could be "state action" under the Fourteenth Amendment only if authorized or approved by the state's highest court, the *Home Telephone* case set up a functional test: a state or local government official will be deemed to be acting for the state for Fourteenth Amendment purposes, if his "act be one which there would not be opportunity to perform but for the possession of some state authority." 227 U.S. at 289, 33 S.Ct. at 315. Is *Monroe*'s interpretation of "under color of" law coterminous with *Home Telephone*'s state action ruling? Could Congress have used § 1983 to reach private persons who might have ransacked Monroe's home? See Morrison v. United States, Chapter 3D, infra (no).

(b) The *Monroe* Court's holding that § 1983 does not cover municipalities and other local government units departs from the constitutional interpretation of the Fourteenth Amendment itself, which has been interpreted to apply directly, of its own force, to local governments. Avery v. Midland County, 390 U.S. 474, 88 S.Ct. 1114, 20 L.Ed.2d 45 (1968); Ward v. Board of County Commissioners of Love County, 253 U.S. 17, 40 S.Ct. 419, 64 L.Ed. 751 (1920). Can Congress constitutionally exempt some persons or entities from the proscriptions of the Constitution? Is that what Congress has done with § 1983 as interpreted in *Monroe*? Is a failure to provide for a civil remedy in federal court a negation of the Constitution? Cf. Chapter 4B, infra.

4. What is the relationship between "constitutional torts" under § 1983 and state common-law torts? *Monroe* foresees a regime in which § 1983 claims would be equally available alternatives to filing suits under state law: § 1983 is "supplementary to the state remedy, and the latter need not first be sought and refused before the federal one is invoked."

(a) *Monroe* is often cited for the proposition that "exhaustion of state judicial remedies" is not required in § 1983 actions. See Chapter 1G, infra. How would such an exhaustion doctrine have worked? Normally, res judicata rules prevent relitigation of the same claims in state and federal court, even constitutional claims. See Chapter 1E, infra. Would there have to be an exception made for § 1983 cases if exhaustion of state remedies had been required in *Monroe*?

(b) Much of Justice Frankfurter's dissent is devoted to arguments about federalism and respect for state courts. Would an exhaustion doctrine have led to less friction between state and federal courts, or more? Is that why Frankfurter argued for a narrow construction of § 1983 ("systematic" constitutional violations only) instead of a simple exhaustion doctrine? But does his approach really avoid such friction? What would be the consequences for federal-state relations if a federal judge were to declare that Monroe could sue because Chicago officials "systematically" deny citizens' constitutional rights?

5. Should constitutional torts under § 1983 be coterminous with state-law torts? Why might standards under the two sources of law be different?

(a) Section 1983, with its state action limitation, regulates state-citizen relationships, whereas tort law is made mostly to govern relationships between two private parties. Might the rules made to superintend state-citizen relationships be different from those made to superintend private-private relationships? Why—because the state represents a weightier collective interest? Because the state is capable of greater harm?

(b) Justice Douglas writes in *Monroe* that § 1983 "should be read against the background of tort liability that makes a man responsible for the natural consequences of his actions." Does that mean state officials are liable under § 1983 when they commit state-law torts? Elsewhere Justice Douglas notes that § 1983 should be available where "by reason of prejudice, passion, *neglect,* intolerance or otherwise, state laws might not be enforced ..." [emphasis added]. Does this mean that § 1983 covers negligent constitutional deprivations? Negligent deprivations of state-law rights?

6. When one puts together the two parts of the *Monroe* decision, coverage of errant officers and non-coverage of local governments, it appears that the Court has adopted a model of personal liability for § 1983. Later cases specifically hold that the damages paid in such § 1983 cases require payment by the officer in his or her "personal capacity," that is, from the officer's own bank account. See Hafer v. Melo, 502 U.S. 21, 112 S.Ct. 358, 116 L.Ed.2d 301 (1991); Kentucky v. Graham, 473 U.S. 159, 105 S.Ct. 3099, 87 L.Ed.2d 114 (1985).[1] Is this "personal liability model" the best approach to protecting constitutional rights, or would it be better to require governments to pay some or all damage awards arising from their officers' constitutional violations?

(a) Would a governmental-liability model make § 1983 more consistent with constitutional theory? Reconsider the constitutional law briefly reviewed in ¶ 2(b) *supra,* with its traditional emphasis on governmental interests and balancing. Should local governments at least be held liable when an officer is acting in obedience to state law? Does personal liability lead to greater deterrence because the officers will be required to pay for their own mistakes?

(b) Would a governmental-liability model be a preferable policy choice? As the Court reconsidered the *Monroe* model in the 1970's, several social policy considerations loomed large in the debate. What factors favor municipal liability? See Kates and Kouba, *Liability of Public Entities under Section 1983 of the Civil Rights Act,* 45 S.Cal.L.Rev. 131, 133, 136–37 (1972) (noting that under *Monroe* plaintiffs are often left with a judgment and a judgment-proof defendant official). What policy factors make local government liability undesirable? See City of Kenosha v. Bruno, 412 U.S. 507, 517–20, 93 S.Ct. 2222, 2228–30, 37 L.Ed.2d 109 (1973) (Douglas, J., dissenting in part) (financial impact on local treasuries if government held responsible for misbehaving officials).

MONELL v. DEPARTMENT OF SOCIAL SERVICES OF THE CITY OF NEW YORK

Supreme Court of the United States, 1978.
436 U.S. 658, 98 S.Ct. 2018, 56 L.Ed.2d 611.

MR. JUSTICE BRENNAN delivered the opinion of the Court.

Petitioners, a class of female employees of the Department of Social Services and of the Board of Education of the city of New York, com-

---

1. In some cases it is possible to control the officer's conduct through an injunction that effectively regulates governmental policy, and these are sometimes called "official capacity" suits. See Chapter 1H infra. But under the terms of the *Monroe* decision, a local government could not be held liable for damages.

menced this action under 42 U.S.C. § 1983 in July 1971. The gravamen of the complaint was that the Board and the Department had as a matter of official policy compelled pregnant employees to take unpaid leaves of absence before such leaves were required for medical reasons. Cf. Cleveland Board of Education v. LaFleur, 414 U.S. 632, 94 S.Ct. 791, 39 L.Ed.2d 52 (1974). The suit sought injunctive relief and backpay for periods of unlawful forced leave [,which plaintiffs sought to have paid from the city treasury. The District Court held the city's conduct unconstitutional but refused to hold the city liable based on our precedent in the *Monroe* case. We granted review.]

I

In Monroe v. Pape, we held that "Congress did not undertake to bring municipal corporations within the ambit of [§ 1983]." 365 U.S., at 187, 81 S.Ct. at 484. The sole basis for this conclusion was an inference drawn from Congress' rejection of the "Sherman Amendment" to the bill which became the Civil Rights Act of 1871, [which] would have held a municipal corporation liable for damage done to the person or property of its inhabitants by *private* persons "riotously and tumultuously assembled."[8] Cong. Globe, 42d Cong., 1st Sess., 749 (1871) (hereinafter Globe). [The Court here discussed the legislative history of the 1871 Act, drawing a distinction between Congress' attitude toward § 1 of the bill—now codified as § 1983—and § 7—the rejected Sherman Amendment. Section 1 only required state and local governments to obey the Constitution as they carried out their existing governmental functions, thus raising no constitutional problems. Congress saw the Sherman Amendment, on the other hand, as raising several thorny constitutional law issues. First, the amendment made local governments responsible for private lawlessness, not the lawlessness of its own officials, as § 1 did. Second, state law of the 1870's generally delegated local governments no authority over police functions, and the Sherman Amendment therefore imposed new federal duties on local governments. Third, federal constitutional doctrine of the 1870's forbade the federal government to impose new duties on local officials who had no such duties under state law. Congress did not see § 1 as creating these same constitutional problems, however, because it only required local governments to exercise in a constitutional manner the power already held under state law.]

* * *

C. DEBATE ON § 1 OF THE CIVIL RIGHTS BILL

From the foregoing discussion, it is readily apparent that nothing said in debate on the Sherman Amendment would have prevented holding a

---

8. We expressly declined to consider "policy considerations" for or against municipal liability. See 365 U.S., at 191.

municipality liable under § 1 of the Civil Rights Act for its own violations of the Fourteenth Amendment. The question remains, however, whether the general language describing those to be liable under § 1—"any person"—covers more than natural persons. An examination of the debate on § 1 and application of appropriate rules of construction show unequivocally that § 1 was intended to cover legal as well as natural persons.

* * *

In both Houses, statements of the supporters of § 1 corroborated that Congress, in enacting § 1, intended to give a broad remedy for violations of federally protected civil rights. Moreover, since municipalities through their official acts could, equally with natural persons, create the harms intended to be remedied by § 1, and, further, since Congress intended § 1 to be broadly construed, there is no reason to suppose that municipal corporations would have been excluded from the sweep of § 1. One need not rely on this inference alone, however, for the debates show that Members of Congress understood "persons" to include municipal corporations.

* * *

Representative Bingham, for example, in discussing § 1 of the bill, explained that he had drafted § 1 of the Fourteenth Amendment with the case of Barron v. Mayor of Baltimore, 7 Pet. 243, 8 L.Ed. 672 (1833), especially in mind. "In [that] case the *city* had taken private property for public use, without compensation . . ., and there was no redress for the wrong . . ." Globe App. 04 (emphasis added). Bingham's further remarks clearly indicate his view that such takings by cities, as had occurred in Barron, would be redressable under § 1 of the bill. See Globe App. 85. . . .

* * *

That the "usual" meaning of the word "person" would extend to municipal corporations is also evidenced by an Act of Congress which had been passed only months before the Civil Rights Act was passed. This Act provided that "in all acts hereafter passed . . . the word 'person' may extend and be applied to bodies politic and corporate . . . unless the context shows that such words were intended to be used in a more limited sense." Act of Feb. 25, 1871, § 2, 16 Stat. 431.

Municipal corporations in 1871 were included within the phrase "bodies politic and corporate"[51] and, accordingly, the "plain meaning" of § 1 is that local government bodies were to be included within the ambit of the persons who could be sued under § 1 of the Civil Rights Act. Indeed, a Circuit Judge, writing in 1873 in what is apparently the first

---

51. See Northwestern Fertilizing Co. v. Hyde Park, 18 Fed.Cas. pp. 393, 394 (No. 10,336) (CC ND Ill.1873); 2 J. Kent, Commentaries on American Law 2 *278–*279 (12th O.W. Holmes ed. 1873). See also United States v. Maurice, 26 Fed.Cas. No. 15,747, 2 Brock. 96, 109 (CC Va.1823) (Marshall, C.J.) ("The United States is a government, and, consequently, a body politic and corporate"); Apps. D and E to Brief for Petitioners in Monroe v. Pape, O.T.1960, No. 39 (collecting state statutes which, in 1871, defined municipal corporations as bodies politic and corporate).

reported case under § 1, read the Dictionary Act in precisely this way in a case involving a corporate plaintiff and a municipal defendant. See Northwestern Fertilizing Co. v. Hyde Park, 18 F.Cas. 393, 394 (No. 10,336) (CC ND Ill.1873).[53]

II

Our analysis of the legislative history of the Civil Rights Act of 1871 compels the conclusion that Congress did intend municipalities and other local government units to be included among those persons to whom § 1983 applies. Local governing bodies, therefore, can be sued directly under § 1983 for monetary, declaratory, or injunctive relief where, as here, the action that is alleged to be unconstitutional implements or executes a policy statement, ordinance, regulation, or decision officially adopted and promulgated by that body's officers. Moreover, although the touchstone of the § 1983 action against a government body is an allegation that official policy is responsible for a deprivation of rights protected by the Constitution, local governments, like every other § 1983 "person," by the very terms of the statute, may be sued for constitutional deprivations visited pursuant to governmental "custom" even though such a custom has not received formal approval through the body's official decisionmaking channels. * * *

On the other hand, the language of § 1983, read against the background of the same legislative history, compels the conclusion that Congress did not intend municipalities to be held liable unless action pursuant to official municipal policy of some nature caused a constitutional tort. In particular, we conclude that a municipality cannot be held liable solely because it employs a tortfeasor—or, in other words, a municipality cannot be held liable under § 1983 on a respondeat superior theory.

* * *

We conclude, therefore, that a local government may not be sued under § 1983 for an injury inflicted solely by its employees or agents. Instead, it is when execution of a government's policy or custom, whether made by its lawmakers or by those whose edicts or acts may fairly be said to represent official policy, inflicts the injury that the government as an entity is responsible under § 1983. Since this case unquestionably involves official policy as the moving force of the constitutional violation found by the District Court, we must reverse the judgment below. In so doing, we have no occasion to address, and do not address, what the full contours of municipal liability under § 1983 may be. * * *

---

53. In considering the effect of the Act of Feb. 25, 1871, in Monroe, however, Mr. Justice Douglas, apparently focusing on the word "may," stated: "[T]his definition [of person] is merely an allowable, not a mandatory, one." 365 U.S., at 191, 81 S.Ct., at 486. A review of the legislative history of the Dictionary Act shows this conclusion to be incorrect. * * * Such a mandatory use of the extended meanings of the words defined by the Act is also required for it to perform its intended function—to be a guide to "rules of construction" of Acts of Congress. Were the defined words "allowable, [but] not mandatory" constructions, as Monroe suggests, there would be no "rules" at all.

III

Although we have stated that stare decisis has more force in statutory analysis than in constitutional adjudication because, in the former situation, Congress can correct our mistakes through legislation, we have never applied stare decisis mechanically to prohibit overruling our earlier decisions determining the meaning of statutes. Nor is this a case where we should "place on the shoulders of Congress the burden of the Court's own error," Girouard v. United States, 328 U.S. 61, 70, 66 S.Ct. 826, 90 L.Ed. 1084 (1946)[, because not only was *Monroe*'s immunization of municipalities a departure from prior case law, it would also undermine long-recognized suits against school boards.]

Finally, even under the most stringent test for the propriety of overruling a statutory decision proposed by Mr. Justice Harlan in *Monroe*[55]—"that it appear beyond doubt from the legislative history of the 1871 statute that [*Monroe*] misapprehended the meaning of the [section]"—the overruling of Monroe insofar as it holds that local governments are not "persons" who may be defendants in § 1983 suits is clearly proper. * * *

* * *

For the reasons stated above, the judgment of the Court of Appeals is Reversed.

MR. JUSTICE POWELL, concurring.

* * *

This Court traditionally has been hesitant to overrule prior constructions of statutes or interpretations of common-law rules. "Stare decisis is usually the wise policy," Burnet v. Coronado Oil & Gas Co., 285 U.S. 393, 406, 52 S.Ct. 443, 447, 76 L.Ed. 815 (1932) (Brandeis, J., dissenting), but this cautionary principle must give way to countervailing considerations in appropriate circumstances. * * *

In Monroe and its progeny, we have answered a question that was never actually briefed or argued in this Court—whether a municipality is liable in damages for injuries that are the direct result of its official policies. "The theory of the complaint [in *Monroe* was] that under the circumstances [t]here alleged the City [was] liable for the acts of its police officers, by virtue of respondeat superior." Brief for Petitioners, O.T.1960, No. 39, p. 21. * * * Thus the ground of decision in *Monroe* [—the blanket exclusion of all liability of municipalities—] was not advanced by either party and was broader than necessary to resolve the contentions made in that case.[6]

---

55. We note, however, that Mr. Justice Harlan's test has not been expressly adopted by this Court. Moreover, that test is based on two factors: stare decisis and "indications of congressional acceptance of this Court's earlier interpretation [of the statute in question]." 365 U.S., at 192, 81 S.Ct., at 487. As we have explained, the second consideration is not present in this case.

6. The doctrine of stare decisis advances two important values of a rational system of law: (i) the certainty of legal principles and (ii) the wisdom of the conservative vision that existing rules

MR. JUSTICE STEVENS, concurring in part. [Omitted]

MR. JUSTICE REHNQUIST, with whom THE CHIEF JUSTICE joins, dissenting.

Seventeen years ago, in Monroe v. Pape, this Court held that the 42d Congress did not intend to subject a municipal corporation to liability as a "person" within the meaning of 42 U.S.C. § 1983. Since then, the Congress has remained silent, but this Court has reaffirmed that holding on at least three separate occasions. Aldinger v. Howard, 427 U.S. 1, 96 S.Ct. 2413, 49 L.Ed.2d 276 (1976); City of Kenosha v. Bruno, 412 U.S. 507, 93 S.Ct. 2222, 37 L.Ed.2d 109 (1973); Moor v. County of Alameda, 411 U.S. 693, 93 S.Ct. 1785, 36 L.Ed.2d 596 (1973). Today, the Court abandons this long and consistent line of precedents, offering in justification only an elaborate canvass of the same legislative history which was before the Court in 1961.

I

As this Court has repeatedly recognized, considerations of stare decisis are at their strongest when this Court confronts its previous constructions of legislation. In all cases, private parties shape their conduct according to this Court's settled construction of the law, but the Congress is at liberty to correct our mistakes of statutory construction, unlike our constitutional interpretations, whenever it sees fit. The controlling principles were best stated by Mr. Justice Brandeis:

"Stare decisis is usually the wise policy, because in most matters it is more important that the applicable rule of law be settled than that it be settled right.... This is commonly true even where the error is a matter of serious concern, provided correction can be had by legislation. But in cases involving the Federal Constitution, where correction through legislative action is practically impossible, this court has often overruled its earlier decisions." Burnet v. Coronado Oil & Gas Co., 285 U.S. 393, 406–407, 52 S.Ct. 443, 447, 76 L.Ed. 815 (1932) (dissenting opinion) (footnotes omitted).

Only the most compelling circumstances can justify this Court's abandonment of such firmly established statutory precedents. * * *

The Court does not demonstrate that any exception to this general rule is properly applicable here. [Justice Rehnquist here observed that no case prior to Monroe had ruled on the issue of coverage of municipalities, and thus it could not be maintained that Monroe was a departure from prior practice. Moreover, Congress never later expressed the view that municipalities should be suable under § 1983.]

---

should be presumed rational and not subject to modification "at any time a new thought seems appealing," dissenting opinion of Mr. Justice Rehnquist, post; cf. O. Holmes, The Common Law 36 (1881). But, at the same time, the law has recognized the necessity of change, lest rules "simply persis[t] from blind imitation of the past." Holmes, The Path of the Law, 10 Harv.L.Rev. 457, 469 (1897). Any overruling of prior precedent, whether of a constitutional decision or otherwise, deserves to some extent the value of certainty. But I think we owe somewhat less deference to a decision that was rendered without benefit of a full airing of all the relevant considerations. * * *

* * * Since *Monroe,* municipalities have had the right to expect that they would not be held liable retroactively for their officers' failure to predict this Court's recognition of new constitutional rights. No doubt innumerable municipal insurance policies and indemnity ordinances have been founded on this assumption, which is wholly justifiable under established principles of stare decisis. * * *

I cannot agree with Mr. Justice Powell's view that "[w]e owe somewhat less deference to a decision that was rendered without benefit of a full airing of all the relevant considerations." Private parties must be able to rely upon explicitly stated holdings of this Court without being obliged to peruse the briefs of the litigants to predict the likelihood that this Court might change its mind. To cast such doubt upon each of our cases, from Marbury v. Madison, 1 Cranch 137, 2 L.Ed. 60 (1803), forward, in which the explicit ground of decision "was never actually briefed or argued," would introduce intolerable uncertainty into the law. Indeed, in Marbury itself, the argument of Charles Lee on behalf of the applicants * * * devotes not a word to the question of whether this Court has the power to invalidate a statute duly enacted by the Congress.

Thus, our only task is to discern the intent of the 42d Congress. That intent was first expounded in Monroe, and it has been followed consistently ever since. This is not some esoteric branch of the law in which congressional silence might reasonably be equated with congressional indifference. Indeed, this very year, the Senate has been holding hearings on a bill, S. 35, 95th Cong., 1st Sess. (1977), which would [overturn this aspect of] *Monroe.* 124 Cong.Rec. D117 (daily ed. Feb. 8, 1978). In these circumstances, it cannot be disputed that established principles of stare decisis require this Court to pay the highest degree of deference to its prior holdings. * * * *

NOTE ON THE "GOVERNMENTAL LIABILITY" MODEL FOR § 1983

1. The *Monell* majority interprets the word "person" in § 1983 to include municipalities and other local governments. How persuasive is the Court's opinion?

(a) The legislative history of the Sherman Amendment, which seemed so dispositive to Justice Douglas in *Monroe,* is explained away in *Monell*: Proposed § 7 would have imposed on municipalities liability for the acts of private citizens, and congressional rejection therefore only signified a rejection of such vicarious liability for acts by private persons. Rejection of § 7, therefore, fails to imply a rejection of municipal liability for its own officials' actions. Elsewhere, the legislative history affirmatively shows, says Justice Brennan, that Congress wanted to hold governments liable for their officer's unconstitutional actions. Are you persuaded?

(b) The Dictionary Act allows Justice Brennan to make an argument about the facial meaning of the word "person": Congress specifically defined it to include local government entities in a statute enacted earlier by the same

Congress. Are you persuaded?[1]

2. While the Court in *Monell* held that municipalities and other local governments are "persons" suable under § 1983, it rejected the respondeat superior theory that would have established automatic governmental liability for all unconstitutional acts by municipal employees. What part of § 1983 supports such limited or occasional liability for cities? Is this part of the Court's ruling a judicial reading of the text of § 1983 or its legislative history? Does it come from a political deal crafted by Justice Brennan?

(a) *Monell* notes that local governments will be held responsible for their own actions, that is, the ordinances and regulations adopted by the city council and other lawmaking bodies. Systematic local practices rising to the level of "custom" may also make the city liable. On the other hand, later cases, see Chapter 1H.1 infra, make explicit the idea that a city will not ordinarily be held liable when an employee violates city policy. Why should this be so? Because "the city" is not at fault in such situations? Has the Court implicitly held that a city is only liable for *its* actions, not those of an employee? (Who is "the city"?)

(b) Considering that a "city" (like any corporation or other incorporeal entity) has no physical existence, what acts are those of the city and what acts are those of its employees? The operative result of municipal liability is to make citizens—or perhaps more exactly, city taxpayers—liable for the acts of a city officer. Is it fair for taxpayers to pick up the check in those circumstances identified by Justice Brennan? Why (not)?

3. Note the intellectual connections between *Monroe* and *Monell*. *Monroe* holds that compliance or non-compliance with city policy is irrelevant to assessing whether action is "under color of" law, and thus an individual officer is herself liable under § 1983 regardless of whether she obeyed local law. *Monell* appears to say that exactly the opposite is true for municipal liability—the city is liable only when an individual officer has acted to enforce city law or custom.

(a) In some respects *Monell* appears to adopt—for municipal liability—the standard proposed by the dissent in *Monroe* for personal liability: liability follows only when an act is done in obedience to local law or in conformity with a widespread or "systematic" practice of violations. Why is the theory that was rejected for individual liability so persuasive to the Court in the context of municipal liability?

(b) Does *Monell*'s adoption of the governmental liability model for § 1983 supplant or supplement *Monroe*'s model of personal liability? Supplementation appears to be the rule. When an employee acts in compliance with an unconstitutional local law or custom, and the city is held responsible under *Monell,* later cases hold that the individual officer remains co-liable with the government to pay any judgment. See Chapter 1D infra. Is this fair? Is joint

---

1. "Person" appears twice in § 1983, once in referring to potential defendants as in *Monroe* and *Monell*, and again later referring to the victim or plaintiff (where "party" is also used). Under Justice Brennan's view of the Dictionary Act, could a municipality also be a plaintiff? Who is a "person" under § 1983 for purposes of initiating a claim? See Inyo County v. Paiute–Shoshone Indians of the Bishop Community, 538 U.S. 701, 123 S.Ct. 1887, 155 L.Ed.2d 933 (2003) (Native–American Indian tribe is not a "person" and cannot sue local county to enforce claimed tribal rights). See paragraph 4 infra.

and several liability between the municipality and the tortfeasor no practical problem for the individual officer because plaintiffs will seek to satisfy their judgment solely from the city's coffers?

4. *Monell* dealt solely with local governments' liability under § 1983. In **Will v. Michigan Department of State Police**, 491 U.S. 58, 109 S.Ct. 2304, 105 L.Ed.2d 45 (1989), the Supreme Court held that neither a state nor a state-level entity is a "person" suable under § 1983. The decision leaves in place individual liability for state-level officers, but precludes naming the state as a defendant or otherwise obtaining a damage award against the state treasury. The Supreme Court has, therefore, refused to extend the governmental liability model of § 1983 liability to state governments.

(a) Is *Will* consistent with the Dictionary Act, cited in *Monell*? What accounts for the different treatment accorded state versus local governments? The language of § 1983 also covers federal territories and the District of Columbia; should they be considered state governments or local governments? See Ngiraingas v. Sanchez, 495 U.S. 182, 110 S.Ct. 1737, 109 L.Ed.2d 163 (1990) (although language covers officers of Territory of Guam for their own actions, § 1983 does not cover "Territory itself," citing *Will*; *Monell* distinguished as involving "municipalities"). Reconsider footnote 1 supra.

(b) What is the dividing line between state-level government entities and local government entities? Should a county sheriff or county prosecutor, both often constitutionally specified officeholders in many states' constitutions, be deemed officers of the state—thus making their office budgets untouchable under *Will*—or of the county in which they serve—thus making their budgets or the county's budget subject to *Monell*? See McMillian v. Monroe County, 520 U.S. 781, 117 S.Ct. 1734, 138 L.Ed.2d 1 (1997) (Alabama sheriff, though locally elected, is a state officer as shown by constitutional law of Alabama and distribution of power by Alabama law: enforcement authority is from state, not local government).

(c) If state-level entities are not suable under § 1983, may a state protect its various governmental bodies by simply designating all local-and state-level bodies as state entities? May the state add other, further protections for local governments not contemplated by § 1983? See Howlett v. Rose, 496 U.S. 356, 110 S.Ct. 2430, 110 L.Ed.2d 332 (1990) ("Federal law makes governmental defendants that are not arms of the state, such as municipalities, liable for their constitutional violations"; to uphold Florida's immunizing of such entities would leave states "free to nullify for their own people the legislative decisions that Congress has made on behalf of all the people").

5. In **Los Angeles County v. Humphries**, ___ U.S. ___, 131 S.Ct. 447, 178 L.Ed.2d 460 (2010), the Court made plain what was implicit in *Monell*: the ruling applies to both damages and prospective injunctive relief. In *Humphries* the plaintiffs had been erroneously placed on a state registry of child-abuse perpetrators, even though they had been exonerated. The Ninth Circuit ordered the county to remove their names, even though it conceded that the error had been made at the state level. The Supreme Court reversed and specifically rejected the idea that failure to hold the county liable would leave the plaintiffs with no effective remedy. Why? Is it because the "personal liability model" would still hold the individual state and local officers liable?

Is the personal liability model therefore a necessary element for § 1983's effectiveness? Cf. Brown v. Plata, ___ U.S. ___, 131 S.Ct. 1910 (2011) (Court upholds injunction against to state officers of California to reduce unconstitutional overcrowding of prisons).

NOTE ON STARE DECISIS AND THE JUDICIARY'S LEGISLATIVE ROLE

1. All sides appear to agree in *Monell* that the pertinent issue is one of statutory interpretation, but are there not substantial parallel issues of constitutional significance intertwined with the statutory language? Section 1983, after all, makes constitutional violations actionable in federal court.

(a) The Court has repeatedly held that § 1983 itself does "not provide for any substantive rights," but "only gives a remedy" for rights found elsewhere, ordinarily in the Constitution, but occasionally in other federal statutes. Chapman v. Houston Welfare Rights Organization, 441 U.S. 600, 617–18, 99 S.Ct. 1905, 1915–16, 60 L.Ed.2d 508 (1979). Is this holding consistent with the justices' various approaches in *Monell*? Would it not be more accurate to say that some standards applicable in § 1983 actions derive from the statute's own language, as in *Monell*, while others are imported from other sources of law?

(b) If § 1983 is a hybrid of statutory and constitutional law, what should be the Court's role in interpreting § 1983? Should it treat its § 1983 rulings as entitled to the strength of statutory-style stare decisis? Or is § 1983 a peculiar province of judicial authority because it is so interwoven with constitutional law? Some professors have recently argued for "dynamic interpretation" of statutes, signaling a desire for relaxed rules of stare decisis. See, e.g., William Eskridge, *Dynamic Statutory Interpretation*, 135 U. PA. L. REV. 1479 (1987). Is Professor Eskridge's theory of dynamic statutory interpretation especially appropriate for § 1983 cases because the statute melds constitutional and legislative themes? Especially inappropriate because an expanded power of statutory interpretation, when joined with expansive power of constitutional interpretation, gives the Court too much power?

(c) Justice Rehnquist's dissenting opinion in *Monell* mentions a pending Senate Bill that would have specified with some certainty the circumstances under which local governments would be liable under § 1983. If you were writing such legislation, what should the rules be? Is deterrence of unconstitutional conduct best accomplished by a personal liability model of liability or a governmental model of liability?

2. What should be Congress' role with respect to § 1983? Should it treat the statute as sacrosanct because it is semi-constitutional? Or should Congress freely amend § 1983 to overturn undesired Supreme Court interpretations?

(a) An unreproduced part of Justice Rehnquist's dissent in *Monell* obliquely predicted that Congress would override *Monell*, but in fact Congress has left § 1983 almost untouched, even as it has regularly amended other modern civil rights legislation.[2] Why? Because federal legislators are uncon-

---

2. A 1979 amendment overturned District of Columbia v. Carter, 409 U.S. 418, 93 S.Ct. 602, 34 L.Ed.2d 613 (1973), and included D.C. as a potential defendant entity in a failed bid to

cerned with problems of their constituents' local governments? Because civil rights groups are potent lobbyists before the federal Congress, even though they may lack power in some local areas around the country?

(b) Although Congress has not meaningfully altered section 1983's blanket coverage of constitutional claims, it has substantially narrowed the scope of one specific class of claims, those by prisoners. See Chapter 1G.1, infra. Should we view § 1983 as the general, catch-all provision for litigating constitutional claims against state officials—but one that may have some specific exceptions or exemptions? Does the Court's willingness to continue a partial exemption for municipalities in *Monell* indicate that the other exemptions must also be constitutionally permissible?

3. If Congress and the Courts are free to play some substantial political role in altering § 1983, what remains of the simple notions that constitutional rights are fundamental and that they merit special protection by the federal courts? What is the difference between "civil rights" and "constitutional rights"?

B. ELEMENTS OF A PLAINTIFF'S § 1983 CLAIM—DEPRIVATIONS OF CONSTITUTIONAL RIGHTS

The Supreme Court has held that there are only "two essential elements" that a plaintiff must prove in order to state a claim under § 1983, **Parratt v. Taylor**, 451 U.S. 527, 535, 101 S.Ct. 1908, 68 L.Ed.2d 420 (1981):

[1] "[that] the conduct complained of was committed by a person acting under color of state law, and

[2] [that] this conduct deprived a person of rights, privileges, or immunities secured by the Constitution or laws of the United States."

Accord, West v. Atkins, 487 U.S. 42, 108 S.Ct. 2250, 101 L.Ed.2d 40 (1988). Courts often say that the plaintiff who proves these two elements has established a prima facie case of § 1983 liability, which means that the plaintiff is entitled to recover, should his facts be believed, unless the defendant brings forward a recognized defense. This sub-chapter and the one following discuss the two essential elements of the prima facie case; the succeeding sub-chapter treats defenses.

1. STANDARDS OF CARE APPLICABLE IN § 1983 SUITS—GENERAL APPROACH: SOURCES OF LAW

Justice Douglas' opinion in Monroe v. Pape, Chapter 1A supra, urged lower courts to read § 1983 "against the background of tort liability that

---

promote statehood. See Pub.L. 96–170, § 1, Dec. 29, 1979, 93 Stat. 1284. A 1996 amendment concerned the extremely rare issue of relief against judicial defendants. See Pub.L. 104–317, Title III, § 309(c), Oct. 19, 1996, 110 Stat. 3853.

makes a man responsible for the natural consequences of his actions."
Monroe also adopted a personal liability model for enforcing § 1983 that
made individual defendants responsible for paying compensatory damages
for the harms they caused, an approach that also seemed to emulate the
common law of torts. The common law, rich in intentional torts, negli-
gence-based torts, and even various versions of strict-liability torts, provides a detailed background of liability rules. To what extent does § 1983
impose duties that are analogous to those found in such common-law
torts? Should § 1983 be interpreted to incorporate by reference these
traditional standards?

WHIRL v. KERN

United States Court of Appeals, Fifth Circuit, 1968.
407 F.2d 781.

GOLDBERG, CIRCUIT JUDGE:

We review here * * * the custodial derelictions of a Texas sheriff. The
sheriff is accused of wrongfully overextending to an inmate of his jail the
hospitality of his hostelry and the pleasure of his cuisine. The jury in the
court below found for the sheriff. We reverse.

The evidence in this case is largely undisputed. On September 9,
1962, the appellant, William Whirl, was arrested on suspicion of felony
theft by the City of Houston police and placed in the Houston city jail.
Two days later Whirl was transferred to the Harris County jail where he
was booked, identified and deprived of the use of his artificial leg. On
September 20, 1962, an examining trial was held and Whirl was bound
over to the Harris County Grand Jury. Some weeks later the Grand Jury
returned two indictments against him, one for burglary and one for theft.

On November 4, 1962, on the motion of the Harris County District
Attorney, the indictments pending against Whirl were dismissed by a
judge of the Criminal District Court of Harris County, Texas. The District
Attorney had sought and obtained dismissal of the indictments on the
grounds that the evidence against Whirl was "insufficient to obtain and
sustain a conviction." The minutes of the court for November 5, 1962,
recited the dismissal of the indictments, and a list of dismissals was then
sent to the Sheriff's office, but the Sheriff who keeps the county jail
testified that he was not apprised of these proceedings. As a result, Whirl
languished in jail for almost nine months after all charges against him
were dismissed, and was not restored to his freedom until July 25, 1963.
[Following his release, Whirl filed this claim against the sheriff under
§ 1983. The jury, responding to special interrogatories, found the sheriff
"not negligent," and the trial court entered a judgment for the sheriff.]

* * *

I.

Turning first to appellees' contention that [§ 1983 of the Civil Rights
Act of 1871] is limited in scope to reprehensible conduct, we note that

some courts have so construed it. However, in our view the trend of recent decisions and the language of the Statute itself cannot be reconciled with so restrictive an interpretation.

* * * The Civil Rights Act, we are told, should be read "against the background of tort liability that makes a man responsible for the natural consequences of his actions." Monroe v. Pape. We do not find in this language or in the language of the Act itself any intimation that an invasion of constitutional rights unaccompanied by an improper motive lies beyond the reach of the Statute. * * *

* * * Of course, when an essential element of the wrong itself under well established principles of tort law includes the demonstration of an improper motive as in malicious prosecution, then such principle becomes a part of sec. 1983. But the origin of such a requirement is in the common law of torts, not in the Civil Rights Act. In cases where tort law imposes no such burden upon the plaintiff, we are not persuaded that the burden should be judicially imposed under sec. 1983. We think it inconsistent to say in one and the same breath that a man is "responsible for the natural consequences of his actions," Monroe v. Pape, supra, and that he is responsible only if his actions are improperly motivated.

* * *

II.

[Turning to the common law, then, Whirl's] argument in brief is that neither the common law of false imprisonment nor the Civil Rights Act requires that a jailer have actual knowledge that his prisoner's incarceration is contrary to law. Whirl contends that negligence is not an element of false imprisonment or of liability under § 1983, and that the "good faith" of a jailer is neither a defense to nor a justification for an unlawful restraint. In evaluating these contentions, we are beaconed by the nascent case of Monroe v. Pape [which can be analogized to a common law action for false arrest rather than one for false imprisonment.]

* * * While it is certainly true that false arrest cases are often denominated actions for false imprisonment, false imprisonment deriving from an arrest and false imprisonment where no arrest has occurred are in substance quite different. Cf. Restatement of Torts, Second, 35–45 and 112–139. Admittedly, a person who is falsely arrested is at the same time falsely imprisoned, Fox v. McCurnin, 1928, 205 Iowa 752, 218 N.W. 499, yet "it is not necessary, to commit false imprisonment, either to intend to make an arrest or actually to make an arrest." 32 Am.Jur.2d, False Imprisonment, 2 (1968); Titus v. Montgomery Ward & Co., 232 Mo.App. 987, 123 S.W.2d 574; McGlone v. Landreth, 1948, 200 Okl. 425, 195 P.2d 268. "False arrest is merely one means of committing a false imprisonment." Harrer v. Montgomery Ward & Co., 1950, 124 Mont. 295, 221 P.2d 428, 433.

* * *

Appellees urge that [jailers should be given wide discretion, as are police in making arrests, and they see this] rule as their shield and protection. However, the breadth of a peace officer's privilege in an arrest situation is not necessarily the test of the breadth of a jailer's privilege in the context of a false imprisonment. There is no privilege in a jailer to keep a prisoner in jail beyond the period of his lawful sentence. Birdsall v. Lewis, 1936, 246 App.Div. 132, 285 N.Y.S. 146; Waterman v. State, 1957, 2 N.Y.2d 803, 159 N.Y.S.2d 702, 140 N.E.2d 551; Cohen v. State, 1965, 47 Misc.2d 470, 262 N.Y.S.2d 980, reversed on other grounds, 25 A.D.2d 339, 269 N.Y.S.2d 498; Weigel v. McCloskey, 1914, 113 Ark. 1, 166 S.W. 944; 46 A.L.R. 806. While a jailer cannot be held liable for errors in a warrant of commitment fair and valid on its face, Francis v. Lyman, 1 Cir.1954, 216 F.2d 583; Peterson v. Lutz, 1942, 212 Minn. 307, 3 N.W.2d 489, it is also the law that where a prisoner is held in jail without a court order or written mittimus, the jailer is liable for false imprisonment. Garvin v. Muir, Ky.1957, 306 S.W.2d 256. The fact that the jailer is without personal knowledge that the prisoner is held unlawfully does not constitute a defense to an action for false imprisonment. Garvin v. Muir, supra; Ulvestad v. Dolphin, 1929, 152 Wash. 580, 278 P. 681; Great American Indemnity Co. v. Beverly, M.D.Ga.1956, 150 F.Supp. 134, 141. In fact, "[a]n illegal imprisonment must be treated as a wrong from its very inception, and it matters not on what date knowledge of such illegality is acquired." Emanuele v. State, 1964, 43 Misc.2d 135, 250 N.Y.S.2d 361, 366.

The case at bar is not, as appellees would have us view it, a case of justifiable reliance upon a warrant of commitment valid on its face. The sheriff relied on nothing[10] and his actions were not informed actions. Nor is this a situation where the dismissal of an indictment by a grand jury still leaves questions for judicial determination. Cf. Lowry v. Thompson, 1936, 53 Ga.App. 71, 184 S.E. 891. Proceedings against Whirl were terminated by the actions of a court of competent jurisdiction. While not easily characterized, the case at bar seems to us closest to the situation where the jailer keeps a prisoner beyond the lawful term of his sentence. In such circumstance, as in the one before us, ignorance of the law is no excuse.

* * * The tort of false imprisonment is an intentional tort. Restatement of Torts, Second, 44. It is committed when a man intentionally deprives another of his liberty without the other's consent and without adequate legal justification. Roberts v. Hecht Co., D.Md.1968, 280 F.Supp. 639, 640; Browning v. Pay–Less Self Service Shoes, Inc., Tex.Civ.App. 1963, 373 S.W.2d 71 (no writ); 32 Am.Jur.2d, False Imprisonment 1 (1968). Failure to know of a court proceeding terminating all charges against one held in custody is not, as a matter of law, adequate legal

---

10. The indictments against Whirl and the arrest warrant were rendered functus officio by the nolle prosequi. A nolle prosequi terminates a prosecution, and there is no longer any legal authority to detain the accused in custody. Venters v. State, 1885, 18 Tex.App. 198; Ex parte Minus, 1931, 118 Tex.Cr.R. 170, 37 S.W.2d 1040. Appellees' reliance upon the arrest warrant and the indictments is thus misplaced.

justification for an unauthorized restraint. Were the law otherwise, Whirl's nine months could easily be nine years, and those nine years, ninety-nine years, and still as a matter of law no redress would follow. The law does not hold the value of a man's freedom in such low regard.

The sheriff, of course, must have some protection too. His duty to his prisoner is not breached until the expiration of a reasonable time for the proper ascertainment of the authority upon which his prisoner is detained. We are not to be interpreted as holding that a sheriff commits an instant tort at the moment when his prisoner should have been released. However, in the present case what is or is not a reasonable time is not at issue. It may safely be said that Kern's ignorance for nine long months after the termination of all proceedings against Whirl was, as a matter of law, ignorance for an unreasonable time.

* * * The district court should have granted plaintiff's motion for directed verdict as to liability, and left for the jury only the issue of damages. * * *

NOTE ON TORT LAW ANALOGIES AND EARLY APPROACHES TO DEFINING § 1983 STANDARDS

1. The *Whirl* court suggests that the standard of care applicable in a § 1983 suit can be found by analogizing the constitutional tort to a common law tort; the standard (intent, negligence, strict liability) used in that state tort-law analogue is then read into § 1983. This approach is typical of those used in some early § 1983 cases.

(a) Under the *Whirl* approach how should courts find common law? By reference to the "rules prevailing in the states in which they sit"? Cf. Klaxon Co. v. Stentor Elec. Mfg. Co., Inc., 313 U.S. 487, 61 S.Ct. 1020, 85 L.Ed. 1477 (1941) (rule applicable to diversity cases). The benefit of such a rule would be the certainty and the simplicity of demands placed on defendants, as a single standard of care would be applied in both § 1983 cases and state-tort cases within a given state. Of course, there would be potential lack of uniformity across the states, as § 1983 would mimic Montana law in Montana, Georgia law in Georgia, etc. Is this non-uniformity objectionable?

(b) Alternatively, should courts after *Whirl* analogize not to a given state's common law, but to the general common law of the various Restatements and Corpus Juris Secundum? This would provide nationwide uniformity, would it not? Is this impossible, however, because there is no "general tort law"? Cf. Erie Railroad Co. v. Tompkins, 304 U.S. 64, 58 S.Ct. 817, 82 L.Ed. 1188 (1938) (diversity case). There is, nevertheless, a "majority rule" for many torts, is there not? What would happen to standards applicable under § 1983 if the majority rule changed? Who would ultimately control the law applied in § 1983 cases under this approach?

(c) Which of these approaches does the *Whirl* court implicitly adopt? What sources does it cite?

2. The *Whirl* court, analogizing to the common law of false imprisonment, eventually adopted a standard somewhat similar to strict liability. The

technique of analogizing to the common law, however, would permit a variety of standards to be adopted from torts, depending upon what torts seemed pertinent to the facts of the § 1983 claim. See, e.g., Madison v. Manter, 441 F.2d 537 (1st Cir.1971) (by analogy to common law, negligence in obtaining search warrant held not to be unconstitutional search); Aldridge v. Mullins, 377 F.Supp. 850 (M.D.Tenn.1972), aff'd, 474 F.2d 1189 (6th Cir.1973) (officer liable for shooting by analogy to Tennessee law when no "reasonable" necessity for such force).

(a) What should a court do when it can find no state tort law analogue? Consider a claim of racial discrimination in a state where the common law does not forbid such discrimination. In **Hawkins v. Town of Shaw**, 437 F.2d 1286 (5th Cir.1971), aff'd en banc, 461 F.2d 1171 (1972), the Fifth Circuit faced a claim that a Mississippi town had discriminated on the basis of race in providing public services to its citizens. Against a backdrop of highly segregated housing and good public services for white areas, the court found 97% of streets in black neighborhoods unpaved, 0% of streets adequately lighted, and only 20% of black citizens served with sanitary sewers. With no Mississippi tort analogue to which it could turn, the court derived a test directly from constitutional law. Its rule outlawed not only intentional discrimination, but also "arbitrary * * * thoughtlessness" that produced "discriminatory results." Compare Norwalk CORE v. Norwalk Redev. Agency, 395 F.2d 920 (2d Cir.1968).[1] Is this approach preferable to that used in *Whirl*?

(b) If the courts are to make standards of care from constitutional cloth, where are these standards to be found? Does the Constitution speak of "negligence," "intent," or "strict liability"?

3. The Supreme Court's rejection of the *Whirl* approach came in stages and almost intuitively, but it was most evident in a pair of 1976 decisions written by one of the Court's leading liberals and by its leading conservative.

(a) In **Paul v. Davis**, 424 U.S. 693, 96 S.Ct. 1155, 47 L.Ed.2d 405 (1976), Justice Rehnquist's majority opinion characterized the case as essentially a state law defamation suit against a police officer who had circulated a flyer labeling the plaintiff a "known shoplifter." Reviewing *Monroe*'s statements about § 1983 and similar statements about § 1983's criminal counterpart, Justice Rehnquist noted that Congress did not intend to "make all torts of state officials" civil rights violations. Rather only violations of constitutional rights are actionable under § 1983. Compare Baker v. McCollan, 443 U.S. 137, 99 S.Ct. 2689, 61 L.Ed.2d 433 (1979) (misidentification leading to arrest of the wrong person is not a violation of arrestee's due process rights; mere false arrest is not a constitutional violation).

(b) In **Estelle v. Gamble**, 429 U.S. 97, 97 S.Ct. 285, 50 L.Ed.2d 251 (1976), discussed in detail later, Justice Marshall wrote for the Court in rejecting a prisoner's claim that a prison doctor's negligence stated a claim under § 1983. "[A] complaint that a physician has been negligent in diagnosing or treating a medical condition does not state a valid" § 1983 claim, wrote

---

1. The Supreme Court later rejected the constitutional test adopted in this line of circuit cases, but it ultimately adopted their focus on Constitution-based norms. See Village of Arlington Heights v. Metropolitan Housing Dev. Corp., 429 U.S. 252, 97 S.Ct. 555, 50 L.Ed.2d 450 (1977), discussed in Chapter 1B.5 infra.

Marshall; "[m]edical malpractice does not become a constitutional violation merely because the victim is a prisoner."

(c) What is the appropriate standard for § 1983 cases? Should the same standard apply in both *Paul* and *Estelle*? Might negligence be applicable to some § 1983 claims but not to others? See Parratt v. Taylor, 451 U.S. 527, 101 S.Ct. 1908, 68 L.Ed.2d 420 (1981) (prisoner's allegation that guard lost his hobby kit through "negligence" states a claim under § 1983) (per Rehnquist, J.).

DANIELS v. WILLIAMS

Supreme Court of the United States, 1986.
474 U.S. 327, 106 S.Ct. 662, 88 L.Ed.2d 662.

JUSTICE REHNQUIST delivered the opinion of the Court.

* * *

In this § 1983 action, petitioner seeks to recover damages for back and ankle injuries allegedly sustained when he fell on a prison stairway. He claims that, while an inmate at the city jail in Richmond, Virginia, he slipped on a pillow negligently left on the stairs by respondent, a correctional deputy stationed at the jail. Respondent's negligence, the argument runs, "deprived" petitioner of his "liberty" interest in freedom from bodily injury * * * without "due process of law." [The lower courts rejected Daniels' claim despite the Court's decision in Parratt v. Taylor, 451 U.S. 527, 101 S.Ct. 1908, 68 L.Ed.2d 420 (1981), which held that negligent takings of property state a claim under § 1983.]

* * *

In Parratt v. Taylor we granted certiorari, as we had twice before, "to decide whether mere negligence will support a claim for relief under § 1983." After examining the language, legislative history and prior interpretations of the statute, we concluded that § 1983, unlike its criminal counterpart, 18 U.S.C. § 242, contains no state-of-mind requirement independent of that necessary to state a violation of the underlying constitutional right. We adhere to that conclusion. But in any given § 1983 suit, the plaintiff must still prove a violation of the underlying constitutional right; and depending on the right, merely negligent conduct may not be enough to state a claim. See Estelle v. Gamble, 429 U.S. 97, 105, 97 S.Ct. 285, 291, 50 L.Ed.2d 251 (1976) ("deliberate indifference" to prisoner's serious illness or injury sufficient to constitute cruel and unusual punishment under the Eighth Amendment).

In *Parratt* * * * we said that the loss of the prisoner's hobby kit, "even though negligently caused, amounted to a deprivation [under the Due Process Clause]." * * * Upon reflection, we * * * overrule *Parratt* to the extent that it states that mere lack of due care by a state official may "deprive" an individual of life, liberty or property under the Fourteenth Amendment.

The Due Process Clause of the Fourteenth Amendment provides: "[N]or shall any State deprive any person of life, liberty, or property, without due process of law." Historically, this guarantee of due process has been applied to deliberate decisions of government officials to deprive a person of life, liberty or property. E.g., Davidson v. New Orleans, 96 U.S. 97, 24 L.Ed. 616 (1878) (assessment of real estate); Rochin v. California, 342 U.S. 165, 72 S.Ct. 205, 96 L.Ed. 183 (1952) (stomach-pumping); Bell v. Burson, 402 U.S. 535, 91 S.Ct. 1586, 29 L.Ed.2d 90 (1971) (suspension of driver's license); Ingraham v. Wright, 430 U.S. 651, 97 S.Ct. 1401, 51 L.Ed.2d 711 (1977) (paddling student); Hudson v. Palmer, supra (intentional destruction of inmate's property). No decision of this Court before Parratt supported the view that negligent conduct by a state official, even though causing injury, constitutes a deprivation under the Due Process Clause. This history reflects the traditional and common-sense notion that the Due Process Clause, like its forebear in the Magna Carta, see Corwin, The Doctrine of Due Process of Law Before the Civil War, 24 Harv.L.Rev. 366, 368 (1911), was " 'intended to secure the individual from the arbitrary exercise of the powers of government,' " Hurtado v. California, 110 U.S. 516, 527, 4 S.Ct. 111, 116, 28 L.Ed. 232 (1884). By requiring the government to follow appropriate procedures when its agents decide to "deprive any person of life, liberty, or property," the Due Process Clause promotes fairness in such decisions. And by barring certain government actions regardless of the fairness of the procedures used to implement them, e.g., *Rochin*, supra, it serves to prevent governmental power from being "used for purposes of oppression," Murray's Lessee v. Hoboken Land & Improvement Co., 18 How. (59 U.S.) 272, 277, 15 L.Ed. 372 (1856) (discussing Due Process Clause of Fifth Amendment).

We think that the actions of prison custodians in leaving a pillow on the prison stairs, or mislaying an inmate's property, are quite remote from the concerns just discussed. Far from an abuse of power, lack of due care suggests no more than a failure to measure up to the conduct of a reasonable person. To hold that injury caused by such conduct is a deprivation within the meaning of the Fourteenth Amendment would trivialize the centuries-old principle of due process of law.

The Fourteenth Amendment is a part of a constitution generally designed to allocate governing authority among the branches of the Federal Government and between that Government and the States, and to secure certain individual rights against both State and Federal Government. When dealing with a claim that such a document creates a right in prisoners to sue a government official because he negligently created an unsafe condition in the prison, we bear in mind Chief Justice Marshall's admonition that "we must never forget, that it is *a constitution* we are expounding," McCulloch v. Maryland, 4 Wheat. (17 U.S.) 316, 407, 4 L.Ed. 579 (1819) (emphasis in original). Our Constitution deals with the large concerns of the governors and the governed, but it does not purport to supplant traditional tort law in laying down rules of conduct to regulate liability for injuries that attend living together in society. We have previously rejected reasoning that "would make of the Fourteenth Amendment a font of tort law to be superimposed upon whatever systems may already be administered by the States," Paul v. Davis.

The only tie between the facts of this case and anything governmental in nature is the fact that respondent was a sheriff's deputy at the Richmond city jail and petitioner was an inmate confined in that jail. But while the Due Process Clause of the Fourteenth Amendment obviously speaks to some facets of this relationship, see, e.g., Wolff v. McDonnell, 418 U.S. 539, 94 S.Ct. 2963, 41 L.Ed.2d 935 (1974) [concerning length of confinement], we do not believe its protections are triggered by lack of due care by prison officials. "Medical malpractice does not become a constitutional violation merely because the victim is a prisoner," Estelle v. Gamble, and "false imprisonment does not become a violation of the Fourteenth Amendment merely because the defendant is a state official." Baker v. McCollan. * * *

That injuries inflicted by governmental negligence are not addressed by the United States Constitution is not to say that they may not raise significant legal concerns and lead to the creation of protectible legal interests. The enactment of tort claim statutes, for example, reflects the view that injuries caused by such negligence should generally be redressed. It is no reflection on either the breadth of the United States Constitution or the importance of traditional tort law to say that they do not address the same concerns.

In support of his claim that negligent conduct can give rise to a due process "deprivation," petitioner makes several arguments, none of which we find persuasive. He states for example, that "it is almost certain that some negligence claims are within § 1983," * * * [b]ut we need not rule out the possibility that there are other constitutional provisions that would be violated by mere lack of care in order to hold, as we do, that such conduct does not implicate the Due Process Clause of the Fourteenth Amendment.

Petitioner also suggests that * * * requiring complainants to allege something more than negligence would raise serious questions about what "more" than negligence—intent, recklessness or "gross negligence"—is required,[3] and indeed about what these elusive terms mean. But even if accurate, petitioner's observations do not carry the day. In the first place, many branches of the law abound in nice distinctions that may be troublesome but have been thought nonetheless necessary:

"I do not think we need trouble ourselves with the thought that my view depends upon differences of degree. The whole law does so as soon as it is civilized." LeRoy Fibre Co. v. Chicago, M. & St. P.R. Co.,

---

3. Despite his claim about what he might have pleaded, petitioner concedes that respondent was at most negligent. Accordingly, this case affords us no occasion to consider whether something less than intentional conduct, such as recklessness or "gross negligence," is enough to trigger the protections of the Due Process Clause.

232 U.S. 340, 354, 34 S.Ct. 415, 418, 58 L.Ed. 631 (1914) (Holmes, J., partially concurring).

More important, the difference between one end of the spectrum—negligence—and the other—intent—is abundantly clear. See O. Holmes, The Common Law 3 (1923). In any event, we decline to trivialize the Due Process Clause in an effort to simplify constitutional litigation.

Finally, citing South v. Maryland, 18 How. (59 U.S.) 396, 15 L.Ed. 433 (1855), petitioner argues that respondent's conduct, even if merely negligent, breached a sheriff's "special duty of care" for those in his custody. * * * We read [this precedent, however, as] an action brought under federal diversity jurisdiction on a Maryland sheriff's bond, [and] as stating no more than what this Court thought to be the principles of common law and Maryland law applicable to that case; it is not cast at all in terms of constitutional law, and indeed could not have been, since at the time it was rendered there was no due process clause applicable to the States.

* * * Jailers may owe a special duty of care to those in their custody under state tort law, see Restatement (Second) of Torts § 314A(4) (1965), but for the reasons previously stated we reject the contention that the Due Process Clause of the Fourteenth Amendment embraces such a tort law concept. Petitioner alleges that he was injured by the negligence of respondent, a custodial official at the city jail. Whatever other provisions of state law or general jurisprudence he may rightly invoke, the Fourteenth Amendment to the United States Constitution does not afford him a remedy.

Affirmed.

JUSTICE MARSHALL concurs in the result.

JUSTICE BLACKMUN, concurring in the judgment. [Omitted]

NOTE ON THE SOURCE OF STANDARDS FOR § 1983 CLAIMS

1. *Daniels'* approach for defining the standard of care for § 1983 cases focuses on two distinct concepts: the role of § 1983 itself and the role of constitutional law.

(a) *Daniels* first holds that § 1983, as a statute, contains no single standard of care that would apply to all claims brought under it. Section 1983 may thus be seen as a clear—and empty—glass that takes on its color—its standards of care—depending upon the constitutional right that the plaintiff pours into the glass. This aspect of *Daniels'* holding is consistent with Whirl v. Kern, is it not?

(b) Whereas *Whirl* gave content to § 1983 by referring to state tort law, *Daniels* finds content by referring to constitutional law. Do you find Justice Rehnquist's reasoning persuasive? Note that, as with *Whirl*, a variety of standards might apply to the panoply of § 1983 claims—potentially a different one for each identifiable constitutional right that could be enforced through § 1983. But all claims would have one thing in common—their standards would derive from constitutional law, not from state tort law. See, e.g., Baker

v. McCollan, 443 U.S. 137, 99 S.Ct. 2689, 61 L.Ed.2d 433 (1979) (on facts remarkably similar to those in *Whirl*, the Court finds state tort law irrelevant and relies on constitutional rules).

2. Looking at the constitutional provision invoked by the plaintiff, the Due Process Clause, the Court holds that negligent deprivations are not actionable; only "deliberate decisions" are covered. Is this an adequate test to identify a standard for reviewing an official's acts? In **Davidson v. Cannon**, 474 U.S. 344, 106 S.Ct. 668, 88 L.Ed.2d 677 (1986), decided the same day as *Daniels*, Justice Rehnquist lost the unanimous support of the other Justices, and delivered an opinion for a 6–3 majority. In *Davidson* the plaintiff contended that, following an altercation with a fellow inmate, he wrote a note to a prison administrator explaining the situation; the administrator saw no pressing need to protect the plaintiff and passed the note to a subordinate who, charged with other matters, forgot about the note. The plaintiff was later savagely beaten by a fellow inmate. Did the prison administrator make a "deliberate decision" in failing to protect the plaintiff from the subsequent attack?

(a) Justice Rehnquist thought not and wrote a short opinion stating that the case was controlled by *Daniels:* "Respondent's lack of due care in this case led to a serious injury, but that lack of care simply does not approach the sort of abusive conduct that the Due Process Clause was designed to prevent." Was there no abuse because defendant was only negligent in failing to protect the prisoner? Exactly what duty or level of care does the Constitution impose on jailors regarding protection of their prisoners?

(b) Justice Blackmun, joined by Brennan and Marshall, dissented in *Davidson:* "When the State incarcerated Daniels it left intact his own faculties for avoiding a slip and fall. But the State prevented Davidson from defending himself and therefore assumed some responsibility to protect him [—a responsibility undercut] by the negligence of prison officials." Do you agree? Would Blackmun's argument have been stronger if Davidson's note had specifically requested protection? Would the case be harder or easier if the facts showed that the overworked defendant simply made a difficult choice about which prison problems deserved his attention, in the process sending guards elsewhere than to protect Davidson? Would the case be harder or easier if the guard admitted that he simply forgot about Davidson's note?

3. What is a "standard of care" for a constitutional tort claim under § 1983? As noted above, the *Daniels* opinion appears to be a focus on the mental element of deliberateness—but deliberateness with respect to what? See William Burnham, *Separating Constitutional and Common–Law Torts,* 73 MINN.L.REV. 515 (1989) (arguing that *Daniels* speaks to only one of two relevant analytical issues). In **Collins v. City of Harker Heights**, 503 U.S. 115, 112 S.Ct. 1061, 117 L.Ed.2d 261 (1992), a municipal worker died of asphyxiation while working in a sewer, and his estate brought a claim under § 1983 alleging that the death violated the worker's Due Process rights. Justice Stevens' opinion for a unanimous Court focused on the second issue, the question of what duty the Fourteenth Amendment imposes on government, and concluded that "[n]either the text nor the history of the Due Process Clause supports [plaintiff's] claim that the governmental employer's

duty to provide its employees with a safe working environment is a substantive component of the Due Process Clause." Interpreting the surviving spouse's claim as a "fairly typical state law tort claim," Justice Stevens observed that "we have previously rejected claims that the Due Process Clause should be interpreted to impose federal duties that are analogous to those traditionally imposed by state tort law." 503 U.S. at 128, 112 S.Ct. at 1070.

(a) What constitutionally-imposed duty was at issue in *Daniels*? Does the Constitution impose any duties on prison guards?

(b) If the Constitution imposes no duty on a state actor, does the defendant's state-of-mind thereafter become irrelevant? Consider these statements. (i) Any constitutionally-imposed duty states the maximum action that is required of a state actor; the mental element necessarily attenuates that maximum. (ii) The mental element of a constitutional claim may greatly alter a constitutional duty because it describes the degree of mental attentiveness that a state actor must pay to a duty.

4. In later cases, particularly **Wilson v. Seiter**, 501 U.S. at 300, 111 S.Ct. at 2326 (1991), excerpted more fully in Chapter 1B.2 infra, the Court developed a vocabulary to describe the two aspects of a standard of care underlying a plaintiff's § 1983 claim: it referred to the duty as the "objective component" and to the mental element as the "subjective component" of any standard.

(a) In what sense is a duty "objective"—because it is an issue of law for judges? In what sense is a mental element "subjective"—because it looks at the variable state-of-mind of each particular defendant? Will jury factfinding be necessary for both components?

(b) How many "packages" of duties and attendant mental elements can the Court create through constitutional interpretation? Justice Rehnquist's statement in *Daniels*—"depending on the right," there may be different mental elements—suggests that there could be several constitutional contexts where different packages of duties and mental elements will apply.

5. The early cases discussed in this sub-chapter mark the beginning of the Supreme Court's exploration of Constitution-based standards for § 1983 cases. (As you will soon learn below, for example, the early decision in Davidson v. Cannon, ¶ 2(b) supra, is superseded by a more detailed constitutional standard founded on a different constitutional provision.) As the Court evolves constitutional standards of care for § 1983 cases, where should it look to find the relevant duties and mental elements? Consider the many textual constitutional sources for such Court-made standards:

• Procedural Due Process—the right to notice and a hearing in some contexts;

• "Selectively Incorporated Rights" of Substantive Due Process—state observance of rights originally binding only upon the federal government under (primarily) the First, Second, Fourth, Fifth, Sixth, and Eighth Amendments (thus potentially yielding multiple textual sources for rights);

● "Fundamental Rights" of Substantive Due Process—state observance of judicially-identified non-textual rights, such as the right to procreational choice, right to marry, right to privacy, etc.(again potential yielding multiple non-textual rights);

● Equal Protection Rights—state observance of restrictions on classifications by race, sex, national origin, etc.

(a) If both *Daniels* (subjective component—mental aspect of a claim) and *Harker* (objective component—duty aspect of a claim) are relevant to defining what must be proved in a constitutional case under § 1983, then every claim noted above should be analyzed for both components. As you read the subsequent cases in this sub-chapter, try to identify with particularity the duties and mental elements outlined by the Court for each constitutional right.

(b) Using the Court's new vocabulary, what is a constitutional "right"? Only the expectation that a state official will observe a particular duty with a particular degree of mental attentiveness? Does this trivialize constitutional rights? Or is it a practical and even necessary way of managing judicial protection of Constitution-based rights? Is it only necessary because the Court in *Monroe* permitted suits to be brought directly against errant governmental officials?

2. EIGHTH AMENDMENT STANDARDS AND CARE OF PRISONERS

ESTELLE v. GAMBLE

Supreme Court of the United States, 1976.
429 U.S. 97, 97 S.Ct. 285, 50 L.Ed.2d 251.

MR. JUSTICE MARSHALL delivered the opinion of the Court.

Respondent J.W. Gamble, an inmate of the Texas Department of Corrections, was injured on November 9, 1973, while performing a prison work assignment. On February 11, 1974, he instituted this civil rights action under 42 U.S.C. § 1983, complaining of the treatment he received after the injury. [Gamble alleged that a 600–pound bale of cotton fell on him during a work detail, giving him severe back pain and rendering him unable to work during the succeeding three months. The prison doctor and other health personnel prescribed several pain relievers and muscle relaxants, as well as bed rest, but Gamble continued to report pain too great to allow him to resume work. Gamble's further refusals to work led to follow-up diagnostic tests and treatment for apparently unrelated heart problems. When defendants later ordered Gamble disciplined for continued refusal to work, Gamble sued the prison warden, the prison doctor, and several other officials, alleging that the doctor's treatment did not relieve his pain. The federal district court dismissed the complaint, but the appellate court reversed.] We granted certiorari.

II

The gravamen of respondent's § 1983 complaint is that petitioners have subjected him to cruel and unusual punishment in violation of the

Eighth Amendment, made applicable to the States by the Fourteenth.[4] See Robinson v. California, 370 U.S. 660, 82 S.Ct. 1417, 8 L.Ed.2d 758 (1962). We therefore base our evaluation of respondent's complaint on those Amendments and our decisions interpreting them.

The history of the constitutional prohibition of "cruel and unusual punishments" has been recounted at length in prior opinions of the Court and need not be repeated here. See, e.g., Gregg v. Georgia, 428 U.S. 153, 169–173, 96 S.Ct. 2909, 2923, 49 L.Ed.2d 859 (1976) (joint opinion of Stewart, Powell, and Stevens, JJ. (hereinafter joint opinion)); see also Granucci, Nor Cruel and Unusual Punishment Inflicted: The Original Meaning, 57 Calif.L.Rev. 839 (1969). It suffices to note that the primary concern of the drafters was to proscribe "torture[s]" and other "barbar[ous]" methods of punishment. Id., at 842. Accordingly, this Court first applied the Eighth Amendment by comparing challenged methods of execution to concededly inhuman techniques of punishment. See Wilkerson v. Utah, 99 U.S. 130, 136, 25 L.Ed. 345 (1879) ("(I)t is safe to affirm that punishments of torture ... and all others in the same line of unnecessary cruelty, are forbidden by that amendment ..."); In re Kemmler, 136 U.S. 436, 447, 10 S.Ct. 930, 933, 34 L.Ed. 519 (1890) ("Punishments are cruel when they involve torture or a lingering death ...").

Our more recent cases, however, have held that the Amendment proscribes more than physically barbarous punishments. See, e.g., Gregg v. Georgia, supra, at 171, 96 S.Ct. at 2924 (joint opinion) [death penalty case]. The Amendment embodies "broad and idealistic concepts of dignity, civilized standards, humanity, and decency ...," Jackson v. Bishop, 404 F.2d 571, 579 (C.A.8 1968), against which we must evaluate penal measures. Thus, we have held repugnant to the Eighth Amendment punishments which are incompatible with "the evolving standards of decency that mark the progress of a maturing society," Trop v. Dulles, [356 U.S. 86, 101, 78 S.Ct. 590, 598, 2 L.Ed.2d 630 (1958)]; or which "involve the unnecessary and wanton infliction of pain," Gregg v. Georgia, supra, at 173, 96 S.Ct. at 2925 (joint opinion).

These elementary principles establish the government's obligation to provide medical care for those whom it is punishing by incarceration. An inmate must rely on prison authorities to treat his medical needs; if the authorities fail to do so, those needs will not be met. In the worst cases, such a failure may actually produce physical "torture or a lingering death," In re Kemmler, supra, the evils of most immediate concern to the drafters of the Amendment. In less serious cases, denial of medical care may result in pain and suffering which no one suggests would serve any penological purpose. Cf. Gregg v. Georgia, supra, at 173, 96 S.Ct. at 2924–25 (joint opinion). The infliction of such unnecessary suffering is inconsistent with contemporary standards of decency as manifested in modern

---

4. The Eighth Amendment provides: "Excessive bail shall not be required, nor excessive fines imposed, nor cruel and unusual punishments inflicted." * * *

[state] legislation [and model legislation] codifying the common-law view that "(i)t is but just that the public be required to care for the prisoner, who cannot by reason of the deprivation of his liberty, care for himself."

We therefore conclude that deliberate indifference to serious medical needs of prisoners constitutes the "unnecessary and wanton infliction of pain," Gregg v. Georgia, supra, at 182–183, 96 S.Ct. at 2925 (joint opinion), proscribed by the Eighth Amendment. This is true whether the indifference is manifested by prison doctors in their response to the prisoner's needs[10] or by prison guards in intentionally denying or delaying access to medical care or intentionally interfering with the treatment once prescribed. Regardless of how evidenced, deliberate indifference to a prisoner's serious illness or injury states a cause of action under § 1983.

This conclusion does not mean, however, that every claim by a prisoner that he has not received adequate medical treatment states a violation of the Eighth Amendment. An accident, although it may produce added anguish, is not on that basis alone to be characterized as wanton infliction of unnecessary pain. In Louisiana ex rel. Francis v. Resweber, 329 U.S. 459, 67 S.Ct. 374, 91 L.Ed. 422 (1947), for example, the Court concluded that it was not unconstitutional to force a prisoner to undergo a second effort to electrocute him after a mechanical malfunction had thwarted the first attempt. Writing for the plurality, Mr. Justice Reed reasoned that the second execution would not violate the Eighth Amendment because the first attempt was an "unforeseeable accident." Id., at 464, 67 S.Ct. 376. Mr. Justice Frankfurter's concurrence, based solely on the Due Process Clause of the Fourteenth Amendment, concluded that since the first attempt had failed because of "an innocent misadventure," id., at 470, 67 S.Ct. at 379, the second would not be " 'repugnant to the conscience of mankind,' " id., at 471, 67 S.Ct. at 380, quoting Palko v. Connecticut, 302 U.S. 319, 323, 58 S.Ct. 149, 150, 82 L.Ed. 288.

Similarly, in the medical context, an inadvertent failure to provide adequate medical care cannot be said to constitute "an unnecessary and wanton infliction of pain" or to be "repugnant to the conscience of mankind." Thus, a complaint that a physician has been negligent in diagnosing or treating a medical condition does not state a valid claim of medical mistreatment under the Eighth Amendment. Medical malpractice does not become a constitutional violation merely because the victim is a prisoner. In order to state a cognizable claim, a prisoner must allege acts or omissions sufficiently harmful to evidence deliberate indifference to

---

10. See, e.g., Williams v. Vincent, 508 F.2d 541 (C.A.2 1974) (doctor's choosing the "easier and less efficacious treatment" of throwing away the prisoner's ear and stitching the stump may be attributable to "deliberate indifference ... rather than an exercise of professional judgment"); Thomas v. Pate, 493 F.2d 151, 158 (C.A.7), cert. denied sub nom. Thomas v. Cannon, 419 U.S. 879, 95 S.Ct. 143, 42 L.Ed.2d 119 (1974) (injection of penicillin with knowledge that prisoner was allergic, and refusal of doctor to treat allergic reaction); Jones v. Lockhart, 484 F.2d 1192 (C.A.8 1973) (refusal of paramedic to provide treatment); Martinez v. Mancusi, 443 F.2d 921 (C.A.2 1970), cert. denied, 401 U.S. 983, 91 S.Ct. 1202, 28 L.Ed.2d 335 (1971) (prison physician refuses to administer the prescribed pain killer and renders leg surgery unsuccessful by requiring prisoner to stand despite contrary instructions of surgeon).

serious medical needs. It is only such indifference that can offend "evolving standards of decency" in violation of the Eighth Amendment.

III

Against this backdrop, we now consider whether respondent's complaint states a cognizable § 1983 claim. The handwritten pro se document is to be liberally construed. * * *

Even applying these liberal standards, however, Gamble's claims against [the prison doctor who repeatedly saw Gamble and prescribed his treatment] are not cognizable under § 1983. * * * Respondent contends that more should have been done by way of diagnosis and treatment, and suggests a number of options that were not pursued. The Court of Appeals agreed, stating: "Certainly an x-ray of (Gamble's) lower back might have been in order and other tests conducted that would have led to appropriate diagnosis and treatment for the daily pain and suffering he was experiencing." But the question whether an x-ray or additional diagnostic techniques or forms of treatment is indicated is a classic example of a matter for medical judgment. A medical decision not to order an x-ray, or like measures, does not represent cruel and unusual punishment. At most it is medical malpractice, and as such the proper forum is the state court under the Texas Tort Claims Act. The Court of Appeals was in error in holding that the alleged insufficiency of the medical treatment required reversal and remand. That portion of the judgment of the District Court should have been affirmed.[16] [Claims against the other defendants are to be reconsidered on remand.]

It is so ordered.

MR. JUSTICE BLACKMUN concurs in the judgment of the Court.

MR. JUSTICE STEVENS, dissenting. [Omitted; see footnote 16 in the majority opinion.]

NOTE ON CONSTITUTIONAL STANDARDS FOR PRISON MEDICAL CARE

1. Typical appellate cases refer to *Estelle*'s "objective" component as involving a duty relating to meeting "serious medical needs." See Self v. Crum, 439 F.3d 1227 (10th Cir. 2006) (referring to objective and subjective components of a claim); Chance v. Armstrong, 143 F.3d 698 (2d Cir.1998). In *Estelle* itself, the Court had no occasion to discuss this component. What is a serious medical need?

(a) Many cases discuss particular maladies or needs and characterize them as serious or not. See, e.g., Schaub v. VonWald, 638 F.3d 905 (8th Cir. 2011) (infected bed sores of paraplegic prisoner serious, sustaining $964

---

16. Contrary to Mr. Justice Stevens' assertion in dissent, this case signals no retreat from Haines v. Kerner, 404 U.S. 519, 92 S.Ct. 594, 30 L.Ed.2d 652 (1972). In contrast to the general allegations in Haines, Gamble's complaint provides a detailed factual accounting of the treatment he received. By his exhaustive description he renders speculation unnecessary. It is apparent from his complaint that he received extensive medical care and that the doctors were not indifferent to his needs.

damage award); Pinkston v. Madry, 440 F.3d 879 (7th Cir. 2006) ("puffy" lip and swollen side of face due to fight not serious medical needs). Some cases also adopt a particular approach to defining the issue. For example, in Wynn v. Southward, 251 F.3d 588 (7th Cir. 2001), the Court said that serious medical needs are simply those that are "so obvious that even a lay person would easily recognize the necessity for a doctor's attention." In Chance v. Armstrong, 143 F.3d 698 (2d Cir. 1998), the Second Circuit tried to summarize the difficulty of the decision it had to make:

> "The standard for Eighth Amendment violations contemplates "a condition of urgency" that may result in "degeneration" or "extreme pain." A prisoner who nicks himself shaving obviously does not have a constitutional right to cosmetic surgery [, but a five-inch gash would be different]. Compare Arce v. Banks, 913 F.Supp. 307, 309–10 (S.D.N.Y.1996) (small cyst-like growth on forehead not sufficiently serious), with Gutierrez v. Peters, 111 F.3d 1364, 1373–74 (7th Cir.1997) (large cyst that had become infected was a serious medical condition). * * * Factors that have been considered include "[t]he existence of an injury that a reasonable doctor or patient would find important and worthy of comment or treatment; the presence of a medical condition that significantly affects an individual's daily activities; or the existence of chronic and substantial pain." We agree * * * that "[i]t is a far easier task to identify a few exemplars of conditions so plainly trivial and insignificant as to be outside the domain of Eighth Amendment concern than it is to articulate a workable standard for determining 'seriousness' at the pleading stage." [143 F.3d at 702–03]

(b) In what sense is this component of the test "objective"? Does it rely on objective medical judgment? See Camberos v. Branstad, 73 F.3d 174 (8th Cir.1995) ("A serious medical need is 'one that has been diagnosed by a physician as requiring treatment,' or one that is so obvious that even a layperson would easily recognize the necessity for a doctor's attention"). Or does a judge decide the issue in some normative way? Should a jury decide the issue?

(c) *Estelle* concerned an immediate condition that arose during confinement. Should prisons be required to treat pre-existing conditions by providing medicine and dental care for long-term problems that antedated the inmate's incarceration? See Plemmons v. Roberts, 439 F.3d 818 (8th Cir. 2006) (prior heart disease resulting in heart attack); Koehl v. Dalsheim, 85 F.3d 86 (2d Cir.1996) (prescription eyeglasses required). What rationale would support these decisions?

(d) Consider possible special situations. With so many prisoners serving long sentences, would you expect in the future to see new claims related to an aging prison population? See Norfleet v. Webster, 439 F.3d 392 (7th Cir. 2006) (long-term inmate with ten-year history of arthritis pain). Are self-inflicted medical issues, such as those caused by a hunger strike, legitimate medical needs? See Owens v. Hinsley, 635 F.3d 950 (7th Cir. 2011) (not when weight loss and discomfort are the consequences). Is a claimed gender disorder such a need? See Konitzer v. Frank, 711 F.Supp. 2d 874 (E.D. Wis. 2010) (yes).

Should the identification of a medical need as serious necessarily relate to what the court may see as the necessity of future medical treatment?

2. Should *Estelle*'s duty also cover foreseeable future medical needs? In **Helling v. McKinney**, 509 U.S. 25, 113 S.Ct. 2475, 125 L.Ed.2d 22 (1993), an inmate double-celled with a five-pack-a-day smoker claimed that the practice violated his Eighth Amendment rights under the *Estelle* standard. The Court granted certiorari to consider whether "the health risk posed by involuntary exposure of a prison inmate to environmental tobacco smoke [TBS or 'second-hand smoking']" implicates the duty described in *Estelle*. The Court ruled for the plaintiff, observing, "[t]hat the Eighth Amendment covers future harm to inmates is not a novel proposition * * *. It would be odd to deny [relief] to inmates who plainly proved an unsafe, life-threatening condition in their prison on the ground that nothing yet had happened to them." A claim has been stated, added the Court, when an inmate is exposed to "an unreasonable risk of serious damage to his future health." 509 U.S. at 31, 113 S.Ct. at 2480–81. On the narrow question of whether "second-hand smoke" posed such a risk, the Court remanded for a trial that would take into account the exposure suffered by plaintiff and the medical risk involved. Id.

(a) After *Helling*, would it be more accurate to say that the Eighth Amendment requires attention not only to serious medical needs but also serious medical "risks"? How immediate must the risk be? See LaBounty v. Coughlin, 137 F.3d 68 (2d Cir.1998) (asbestos is serious risk). How substantial must the risk be? See Coleman v. Rahija, 114 F.3d 778 (8th Cir.1997) (normal pregnancy not a risky situation but pregnant inmate's labor complications presented a serious risk).

(b) If the duty recognized in *Estelle*—for both existing medical needs and future risks—derives from a state's incarceration of the § 1983 plaintiff, can the state escape its duty by simply releasing the prisoner from custody? Does the duty continue, with respect to needs or risks developed in prison, even after a jail term had ended and custody has been relinquished? See Jailed Sisters Are Released for Kidney Transplant, http://www.nytimes.com/2011/01/08/us/08sisters.html?_r=1&scp=1&sq=sisters+kidney+donate+prison&st=nyt (Jan. 7, 2011) (imprisoned sisters released as one donates kidney to other); cf. Johnson v. Quinones, 145 F.3d 164 (4th Cir.1998) (inmate who lost sight after release claims inadequate treatment during incarceration).

(c) *Estelle* creates an affirmative duty to provide medical care to prisoners in some circumstances. Is there a complementary right in prisoners to refuse medical care? Compare Cruzan v. Director, Missouri Dept. of Health, 497 U.S. 261, 110 S.Ct. 2841, 111 L.Ed.2d 224 (1990) (private person's right to refuse medical treatment "may be inferred from our prior cases") with Washington v. Harper, 494 U.S. 210, 110 S.Ct. 1028, 108 L.Ed.2d 178 (1990) (inmate may be treated against his will with antipsychotic drug where he poses a danger to himself or others). Does the "socialistic" concern on which *Estelle* is based—that the state has a duty to care for its charges—preordain the result in *Washington*? Or is it possible to recognize prisoners as dependent for some purposes and independent for others?

3. The *Estelle* case is widely cited for the component of its test that focuses on "deliberate indifference." What does the term mean? It is defined

in detail in the Court's subsequent opinion in Farmer v. Brennan, this subsection *infra*, involving inmate safety, but consider here the special difficulty attendant to distinguishing between non-actionable "mere negligence" and actionable "deliberate indifference" in the medical context.

(a) Prison health facilities are often rudimentary and resources in lower supply than private hospitals. Does a prison doctor's decision to choose a simpler and less efficient cure constitute deliberate indifference? See Williams v. Vincent, 508 F.2d 541 (2d Cir.1974) (conscious choice of "an easier and less efficacious" treatment plan; doctor closed wound where inmates ear had been severed in knife fight instead of attempting to reattach the ear); Chance v. Armstrong, 143 F.3d 698 (2d Cir.1998) (extraction of teeth rather than filling). Does the "deliberate indifference" standard require that prison hospitals be raised to ordinary professional levels available in private hospitals? Close to them? Compare Schaub v. VonWald, 638 F.3d 905 (8th Cir. 2011) (some medical needs will require outside expert proof before deliberate indifference can be shown; some do not), with Norfleet v. Webster, 439 F.3d 392 (7th Cir. 2006) (medical "decision must be so far afield of accepted professional standards as to raise the inference that it was not actually based on a medical judgment").

(b) Misdiagnosis based on poor medical skill, inadequate information, or overwork—a common problem in medical malpractice litigation—also appears in Eighth Amendment litigation. Is an improper diagnosis by definition not deliberate indifference? See Franklin v. Zain, 152 F.3d 783 (8th Cir.1998) (urinary tract infection misdiagnosed as cervical cancer); Johnson v. Quinones, 145 F.3d 164 (4th Cir. 1998) (failure to diagnose tumor). Is action based on inadequate information not deliberate indifference, or does the test require a doctor or jailor to obtain necessary information? Compare Schaub v. VonWald, supra (failure to recognize bed sores is deliberate indifferent in light of smells that give notice of their existence), with Jolly v. Badgett, 144 F.3d 573 (8th Cir.1998) (guards unaware that medication was needed). Cf. Clark–Murphy v. Foreback, 439 F.3d 280 (6th Cir. 2006) (death of prisoner from dehydration because no one noticed prisoner's need for water).

(c) Several cases involve not medical decisions as such but administrative policies that delay or deny medical care. See, e.g., Plemmons v. Roberts, 439 F.3d 818 (8th Cir. 2006) (alleged policy of requiring jailors to notify chief personally before calling an ambulance; heart attack not treated for over an hour); Norfleet v. Webster, 439 F.3d 392 (7th Cir. 2006) ("low-level prison employee" follows policy of requiring inmate to wait ten days for prescription refill). Is the refusal to consider in a timely manner a request for treatment "deliberate indifference"?

(d) Should the subjective component of a prison medical claim always be tried before a jury because it reflects defendants' state of mind? Should appellate courts defer to the decisions of factfinders (trial judge or jury) as to whether a particular medical need is serious? Do you agree with the statement in Schaub v. VonWald, supra: "Whether an inmate's condition is a serious medical need and whether an official was deliberately indifferent to the inmate's serious medical need are questions of fact" that cannot be overruled if "plausible"?

4. The "deliberate indifference" component formulated in *Estelle* cannot be found in the text of the Eighth Amendment. How does the Court derive this standard?

(a) Although the phrase is a familiar one from torts, the *Estelle* Court finds the phrase to be mandated by constitutional law. Are you persuaded that this phrase captures the spirit of the underlying Eighth Amendment cases from which the Court derived it?

(b) Why would the Court choose to use a second-hand torts phrase to capture constitutional notions? Why not use the constitutional phrase itself, "cruel and unusual punishment"? Because these § 1983 cases are "constitutional torts" necessitating a torts-like standard? Because these cases will possibly go to a jury trial, and courts are confident of the results likely to be produced when juries are charged in tort-like language?

(c) Can the Court's resort to choice of a torts-like phrase be explained in a simpler way: educated in the common law tradition, the Justices' thoughts naturally turn to the common law's torts-based phrases when they seek to create constitutional standards?

5. The Court in *Estelle* notes that the Eighth Amendment is the appropriate source of law in this case because the plaintiff is incarcerated following a conviction. Other cases continue the theme that the Eighth Amendment applies only to convicted persons held in custody, see Whitley v. Albers, following this Note.

(a) Would you expect to see a different standard applied for arrestees, pretrial detainees, and others held in custody but not yet convicted? See Block v. Rutherford, 468 U.S. 576, 104 S.Ct. 3227, 82 L.Ed.2d 438 (1984) (for pretrial detainees, restrictions for the "purpose of punishment" forbidden; "absent proof of intent to punish," no liability); Woloszyn v. County of Lawrence, 396 F.3d 314 (3d Cir. 2005) (stating the run-away circuit view that Eighth Amendment standards also apply to pre-trial detainees, applying *Estelle* and subsequent cases); Cooper v. Dyke, 814 F.2d 941 (4th Cir.1987) (same). If the standard is the same, without regard to status of conviction, does the standard really grow from the Eighth Amendment?

(b) Is there a duty to provide medical care to persons civilly institutionalized without their consent? See Youngberg v. Romeo, 457 U.S. 307, 102 S.Ct. 2452, 73 L.Ed.2d 28 (1982) (yes). Should such a duty be greater in scope than that applicable to prisoners? The same? What is the constitutional source for such a duty if the Eighth Amendment provides rights only for persons convicted of crimes?

WHITLEY v. ALBERS

Supreme Court of the United States, 1986.
475 U.S. 312, 106 S.Ct. 1078, 89 L.Ed.2d 251.

JUSTICE O'CONNOR delivered the opinion of the Court.

This case requires us to decide what standard governs a prison inmate's claim that prison officials subjected him to cruel and unusual punishment by shooting him during the course of their attempt to quell a prison riot.

I

At the time he was injured, respondent Gerald Albers was confined in * * * the Oregon State Penitentiary. [A few prisoners at the facility, agitated that guards had forcefully moved inebriated prisoners into segregation, took a guard hostage and assumed control of the cellblock where Albers and 200 other prisoners were confined. Whitley, the "prison security manager," negotiated with the leader of the disturbance, one Klenk, to permit four inmate emissaries to visit the segregated prisoners to confirm that they had not been harmed, but this did not end the disturbance. When Klenk later moved the hostage to a more secure location, threatened to kill him, and informed Whitley that one inmate had already been killed, Whitley organized an assault on the cellblock to restore control. Meanwhile, Albers, an apparent inmate by-stander during the disturbance, took steps to safeguard some elderly inmates in case of violence.]

Whitley next consulted with his superiors, [who] agreed that forceful intervention was necessary to protect the life of the hostage and the safety of the inmates who were not rioting, and ruled out tear gas as an unworkable alternative. Cupp ordered Whitley to take a squad armed with shotguns into [the] cellblock[, although he also ordered them first to fire a warning shot and to shoot low at any prisoners who rushed to the area where the hostage was held. As Whitley prepared to enter the cellblock, Albers asked for a key to the area where the elderly inmates were being held so that he could care for them.] Whitley replied "No," clambered over the barricade, yelled "shoot the bastards," and ran toward the stairs after Klenk, who had been standing in the open areaway along with a number of other inmates. [One guard] fired a warning shot into the wall opposite the cellblock entrance as he followed Whitley over the barricade. He then fired a second shot that struck a post near the stairway. Meanwhile, Whitley chased Klenk up the stairs, and shortly thereafter [Albers] started up the stairs. [The guard] fired a third shot that struck respondent in the left knee. [The guards subsequently restored order, and Albers brought this claim against Whitley and others under § 1983, alleging that they had violated his Eighth Amendment rights by showing deliberate indifference to his circumstances during their efforts to restore order.]

[At trial, many] of the facts were stipulated, but both sides also presented testimony from witnesses to the disturbance and the rescue attempt, as well as from expert witnesses with backgrounds in prison discipline and security. At the conclusion of trial, the District Judge directed a verdict for petitioners. * * * [The Court of Appeals reversed, holding that the *Whitley* standard of deliberate indifference created a jury issue on these facts.]

II

The language of the Eighth Amendment, "[e]xcessive bail shall not be required, nor excessive fines imposed, nor cruel and unusual punishments inflicted," manifests "an intention to limit the power of those entrusted

with the criminal-law function of government." Ingraham v. Wright, 430
U.S. 651, 664, 97 S.Ct. 1401, 1408, 51 L.Ed.2d 711 (1977). The Cruel and
Unusual Punishments Clause "was designed to protect those convicted of
crimes," ibid., and consequently the Clause applies "only after the State
has complied with the constitutional guarantees traditionally associated
with criminal prosecutions." Id., at 671 n. 40, 97 S.Ct., at 1412 n. 40. An
express intent to inflict unnecessary pain is not required, Estelle v.
Gamble, and "conditions of confinement" may constitute cruel and unusual punishment because such conditions "are part of the penalty that
criminal offenders pay for their offenses against society." Rhodes v.
Chapman, 452 U.S. 337, 347, 101 S.Ct. 2392, 2399, 69 L.Ed.2d 59 (1981).

Not every governmental action affecting the interests or well-being of
a prisoner is subject to Eighth Amendment scrutiny, however. "After
incarceration, only the 'unnecessary and wanton infliction of pain' . . .
constitutes cruel and unusual punishment forbidden by the Eighth
Amendment." Ingraham v. Wright, supra. To be cruel and unusual
punishment, conduct that does not purport to be punishment at all must
involve more than ordinary lack of due care for the prisoner's interests or
safety. This reading of the Clause underlies our decision in Estelle v.
Gamble. * * * It is obduracy and wantonness, not inadvertence or error in
good faith, that characterize the conduct prohibited by the Cruel and
Unusual Punishments Clause, whether that conduct occurs in connection
with establishing conditions of confinement, supplying medical needs, or
restoring official control over a tumultuous cellblock. The infliction of pain
in the course of a prison security measure, therefore, does not amount to
cruel and unusual punishment simply because it may appear in retrospect
that the degree of force authorized or applied for security purposes was
unreasonable, and hence unnecessary in the strict sense.

The general requirement that an Eighth Amendment claimant allege
and prove the unnecessary and wanton infliction of pain should also be
applied with due regard for differences in the kind of conduct against
which an Eighth Amendment objection is lodged. The deliberate indifference standard articulated in *Estelle* was appropriate in the context presented in that case because the State's responsibility to attend to the
medical needs of prisoners does not ordinarily clash with other equally
important governmental responsibilities. Consequently, "deliberate indifference to a prisoner's serious illness or injury" can typically be established or disproved without the necessity of balancing competing institutional concerns for the safety of prison staff or other inmates. But, in
making and carrying out decisions involving the use of force to restore
order in the face of a prison disturbance, prison officials undoubtedly must
take into account the very real threats the unrest presents to inmates and
prison officials alike, in addition to the possible harms to inmates against
whom force might be used. As we said in Hudson v. Palmer, 468 U.S. 517,
526–527, 104 S.Ct. 3194, 3200, 82 L.Ed.2d 393 (1984), prison administrators are charged with the responsibility of ensuring the safety of the
prison staff, administrative personnel, and visitors, as well as the "obli-

gation to take reasonable measures to guarantee the safety of the inmates themselves." In this setting, a deliberate indifference standard does not adequately capture the importance of such competing obligations, or convey the appropriate hesitancy to critique in hindsight decisions necessarily made in haste, under pressure, and frequently without the luxury of a second chance.

Where a prison security measure is undertaken to resolve a disturbance, such as occurred in this case, that indisputably poses significant risks to the safety of inmates and prison staff, we think the question whether the measure taken inflicted unnecessary and wanton pain and suffering ultimately turns on "whether force was applied in a good faith effort to maintain or restore discipline or maliciously and sadistically for the very purpose of causing harm." Johnson v. Glick, 481 F.2d 1028, 1033 (CA2) (Friendly, J.), cert. denied sub nom. John v. Johnson, 414 U.S. 1033, 94 S.Ct. 462, 38 L.Ed.2d 324 (1973). As the District Judge correctly perceived, "such factors as the need for the application of force, the relationship between the need and the amount of force that was used, [and] the extent of injury inflicted," ibid., are relevant to that ultimate determination. From such considerations inferences may be drawn as to whether the use of force could plausibly have been thought necessary, or instead evinced such wantonness with respect to the unjustified infliction of harm as is tantamount to a knowing willingness that it occur. See Duckworth v. Franzen, 780 F.2d 645, 654 (C.A.7 1985) (equating "deliberate indifference", in an Eighth Amendment case involving security risks, with "recklessness in criminal law," which "implies an act so dangerous that the defendant's knowledge of the risk can be inferred"); cf. Block v. Rutherford, 468 U.S. 576, 584, 104 S.Ct. 3227, 82 L.Ed.2d 438 (1984) (requiring pretrial detainees claiming that they were subjected to "punishment" without due process to prove intent to punish or show that the challenged conduct is not "reasonably related to a legitimate goal," from which an intent to punish may be inferred). But equally relevant are such factors as the extent of the threat to the safety of staff and inmates, as reasonably perceived by the responsible officials on the basis of the facts known to them, and any efforts made to temper the severity of a forceful response.

When the "ever-present potential for violent confrontation and conflagration," Jones v. North Carolina Prisoners' Labor Union, Inc., 433 U.S. 119, 132, 97 S.Ct. 2532, 2541, 53 L.Ed.2d 629 (1977), ripens into actual unrest and conflict, the admonition that "a prison's internal security is peculiarly a matter normally left to the discretion of prison administrators," Rhodes v. Chapman, 452 U.S., at 349, n. 14, 101 S.Ct., at 2400, n. 14, carries special weight. "Prison administrators . . . should be accorded wide-ranging deference in the adoption and execution of policies and practices that in their judgment are needed to preserve internal order and discipline and to maintain institutional security." Bell v. Wolfish, 441 U.S., at 547, 99 S.Ct., at 1878. That deference extends to a prison security measure taken in response to an actual confrontation with riotous inmates, just as it does to prophylactic or preventive measures intended to reduce the incidence of these or any other breaches of prison discipline. It does not insulate from review actions taken in bad faith and for no legitimate purpose, but it requires that neither judge nor jury freely substitute their judgment for that of officials who have made a considered choice. Accordingly, in ruling on a motion for a directed verdict in a case such as this, courts must determine whether the evidence goes beyond a mere dispute over the reasonableness of a particular use of force or the existence of arguably superior alternatives. Unless it appears that the evidence, viewed in the light most favorable to the plaintiff, will support a reliable inference of wantonness in the infliction of pain under the standard we have described, the case should not go to the jury.

III

* * *

[On the facts presented here, there was insufficient evidence to send the case to the jury.] Respondent's expert testimony[, which tended to show that the experts thought other less-lethal means could have been used to put down the riot or that the rioters could have been waited out,] is likewise unavailing. * * * At most, this evidence, which was controverted by petitioners' experts, establishes that prison officials arguably erred in judgment when they decided on a plan that employed potentially deadly force. It falls far short of a showing that there was no plausible basis for the officials' belief that this degree of force was necessary. Indeed, any such conclusion would run counter to common sense, in light of the risks to the life of the hostage and the safety of inmates that demonstrably persisted notwithstanding repeated attempts to defuse the situation. An expert's after-the-fact opinion that danger was not "imminent" in no way establishes that there was no danger, or that a conclusion by the officers that it was imminent would have been wholly unreasonable.

* * * To be sure, the plan was not adapted to take into account the appearance of respondent on the scene, and, on the facts * * *, Whitley was aware that respondent was present on the [scene] for benign reasons. Conceivably, Whitley could have added a proviso exempting respondent from his order to shoot any prisoner climbing the stairs. But such an oversight simply does not rise to the level of an Eighth Amendment violation. Officials cannot realistically be expected to consider every contingency or minimize every risk, and it was far from inevitable that respondent would react as he did. * * * While respondent had not been actively involved in the riot and indeed had attempted to help matters, there is no indication that [the guard who shot him] knew this, nor any claim that he acted vindictively or in retaliation. * * * Under these circumstances, the actual shooting was part and parcel of a good faith effort to restore prison security. As such, it did not violate respondent's Eighth Amendment right to be free from cruel and unusual punishments.

* * *

The judgment of the Court of Appeals is

Reversed.

JUSTICE MARSHALL, with whom JUSTICE BRENNAN, JUSTICE BLACKMUN, and JUSTICE STEVENS join, dissenting.

* * *

The Court properly begins by acknowledging that, for a prisoner attempting to prove a violation of the Eighth Amendment, "[a]n express intent to inflict unnecessary pain is not required, Estelle v. Gamble." Rather, our cases have established that the "unnecessary and wanton" infliction of pain on prisoners constitutes cruel and unusual punishment prohibited by the Eighth Amendment, even in the absence of intent to harm. Ibid. Having correctly articulated the teaching of our cases on this issue, however, the majority inexplicably arrives at the conclusion that a constitutional violation in the context of a prison uprising can be established only if force was used "maliciously and sadistically for the very purpose of causing harm," thus requiring the very "express intent to inflict unnecessary pain" that it had properly disavowed.[1]

The Court imposes its heightened version of the "unnecessary and wanton" standard only when the injury occurred in the course of a "disturbance" that "poses significant risks." But those very questions— whether a disturbance existed and whether it posed a risk—are likely to be hotly contested. It is inappropriate, to say the least, to condition the choice of a legal standard, the purpose of which is to determine whether to send a constitutional claim to the jury, upon the court's resolution of factual disputes that in many cases should themselves be resolved by the jury. * * *

* * *

The majority suggests that the existence of more appropriate alternative measures for controlling prison disturbances is irrelevant to the constitutional inquiry, but surely it cannot mean what it appears to say. For if prison officials were to drop a bomb on a cellblock in order to halt a fistfight between two inmates, for example, I feel confident that the Court would have difficulty concluding, as a matter of law, that such an action was not sufficiently wanton to present a jury question, even though concededly taken in an effort to restore order in the prison. Thus, the question of wantonness in the context of prison disorder, as with other claims of mistreatment under the Eighth Amendment, is a matter of degree. And it is precisely in cases like this one, when shading the facts one way or the other can result in different legal conclusions, that a jury should be permitted to do its job. Properly instructed, a jury would take into account the petitioners' legitimate need to protect security, the extent

---

1. This intent standard ostensibly derives from an opinion of Judge Friendly in Johnson v. Glick. That opinion, however, considered maliciousness not as a prerequisite to a constitutional violation, but rather as a factor that, if present, could enable a plaintiff to survive a motion to dismiss when otherwise the facts might be insufficient to make out a claim. 481 F.2d, at 1033.

of the danger presented, and the reasonableness of force used, in assessing liability. * * *

NOTE ON CONTEXTUAL STANDARDS OF CARE

1. It might be structurally satisfying to find that each amendment incorporated into the Due Process Clause, such as the Eighth Amendment, has its own single standard of care, but *Whitley* appears to hold that there can be more than one standard for each amendment and that the standard varies by context. The Court focuses primarily on the mental element that plaintiff must prove, rejecting *Estelle*'s test in the prison riot context.

(a) How does the Court derive the standard that it adopts in *Whitley*? From the text of the Eighth Amendment? From Eighth Amendment case law? From balancing? Compare *Whitley*'s discussion of the interests that influence its decision with that of the Court in New York Times Co. v. Sullivan, 376 U.S. 254, 84 S.Ct. 710, 11 L.Ed.2d 686 (1964) (libel and free speech concerns produce the "actual malice" rule).

(b) Reconsider Part III of the majority opinion, in which Justice O'Connor applies the rule she has announced. Is it significantly more favorable to the defendant than the verbal formulation alone implies? What does this part of the opinion add? If experts' opinions are irrelevant, is it because experts cannot be trusted, or that second-guessing of defendants is not permitted?

2. In **Hudson v. McMillian**, 503 U.S. 1, 112 S.Ct. 995, 117 L.Ed.2d 156 (1992), the Court extended *Whitley* to cover claims of use of excessive force in prison, reasoning that "[m]any of the concerns underlying our holding in *Whitley* arise whenever guards use force to keep order" because "[b]oth situations may require prison officials to act quickly and decisively," and "both implicate the principle that '[p]rison administrators * * * should be accorded wide-ranging deference in the adoption and execution of policies and practices that in their judgment are needed to preserve internal order and discipline and to maintain institutional security.'" Does this eliminate Justice Marshall's concern?

(a) Is *Hudson* a new context (use of force by guards) that happens to have the same mental element or subjective component as *Whitley* (riot control), or are *Hudson* and *Whitley* the same context (use of force by guards)and so have the same objective and subjective components? Does it matter?

(b) Following the Court's decision in *Hudson*, some lower court's dismissed claims of excessive force based solely on the observation that the resultant injuries were "de minimis," but the Supreme Court reversed that automatic practice in Wilkins v. Gaddy, ___ U.S. ___, 130 S.Ct. 1175, 175 L.Ed.2d 995 (2010). The Court noted *Hudson*'s focus on the malicious or sadistic use of "force," not resultant "injury." Nevertheless, the Court seemed to stress that its objection was only with the automatic nature of the lower courts' action: de minimis injury remains "one factor" that influences a court's decision as to whether "force" was used or whether its use was considered in good faith to be "necessary." Does *Wilkins* simply warn lower courts to slow down? (The *Wilkins* Court cross-cited *Whitley* in its discussion; reconsider ¶ 2(b).)

(c) Recall that *Estelle*'s standard for medical care applies only to "serious medical needs," presumably more than "de minimis" medical needs, whereas *Hudson* potentially covers even minor medical problems resulting from un-justified use of force. Is it possible that the *Whitley–Hudson* standard, though less generous to plaintiffs on the subjective mental element, is actually more generous on the objective duty imposed? If so, how can a single constitutional provision, the Eighth Amendment, yield such odd and inconsistent couplings of objective duties and subjective mental elements?

3.   Try to re-conceptualize the *Whitley* standard using the Court's later two-part vocabulary of duties and mental elements: for example, the objective component (or duty) could be characterized as the duty not to harm, and the subjective component (or mental element) might be characterized as mali-ciousness. As a two-part package, the *Whitley* test admonishes a prison guard not to harm prisoners, at least not maliciously or sadistically.

(a) How could a plaintiff prove maliciousness? Would it be necessary to show that a guard had selected the plaintiff individually for infliction of harm or pain? In other contexts where this test is used, see ¶ 3 infra, such proof is often required. See, e.g., Hayes v. Marriott, 70 F.3d 1144 (10th Cir.1995) (strip search conducted before 100 persons, including secretaries and manag-ers, may state a claim by male prisoner that he was intentionally humiliated and harmed). Recall that in *Whitley*, the defendant shouted an expletive at Albers and other prisoners while ordering his guards to shoot. Why was that not evidence of maliciousness?

(b) Justice O'Connor juxtaposes "maliciousness" with a "good faith" effort to carry out prison duties, suggesting that a good faith purpose of restoring order necessarily precludes a finding of malicious intent to harm. Again, in analogous contexts, the lower courts regularly adopt this approach. See Peckham v. Wisconsin Dept. of Corrections, 141 F.3d 694 (7th Cir.1998) (strip searches in prison ordinarily upheld if for the penological purpose of safety); Harris v. Ostrout, 65 F.3d 912 (11th Cir.1995) (upholding searches of closely supervised inmates upon leaving a cell "for any reason" based on a "presumption of reasonableness which we must attach to such prison security regulations"). Although the mental element adopted in *Whitley* is labeled as "maliciousness," does the juxtaposed "good faith" test effectively convert the standard into a low-level reasonableness or rational basis test? Does this always favor defendants? See Beard v. Whitmore Lake School Dist., 402 F.3d 598 (6th Cir. 2005) (strip search of body cavities of all students in gym following reported theft of money is a violation).

4.   Consider the other contexts that might call for standards developed under the Eighth Amendment. Some appear to adopt the *Whitley* approach, or a close variant, and uphold prison regulatory policies if they are not malicious-ly enforced but rather serve legitimate penological needs.

(a) The Supreme Court permitted substantial restrictions on Substantive Due Process rights that prisoners seek to exercise in prison in **Turner v. Safley**, 482 U.S. 78, 107 S.Ct. 2254, 96 L.Ed.2d 64 (1987). There the Court held that prison restrictions on the non-textual right to marry will be upheld if they are "reasonably related to legitimate penological interests." See Estate of O'Lone v. Shabazz, 482 U.S. 342, 107 S.Ct. 2400, 96 L.Ed.2d 282 (1987) (less drastic means test normally applied to fundamental right to religion not applicable in prison context; legitimate penological needs suffice to uphold limitations). Is this standard really a variant of the *Whitley* standard?

(b) Strip searches in prisons are also routinely upheld in the lower courts unless the inmate can show an intent to harm as opposed to a legitimate penological need for the search.[1] In upholding a particularly intrusive body-cavity search, the Seventh Circuit declared in Del Raine v. Williford, 32 F.3d 1024, 1038 (7th Cir.1994):

> "By its very nature, a rectal search is likely to be an unpleasant, uncomfortable, and degrading experience. Digital rectal searches are not condemned per se, however, and until a kinder, gentler method of satisfying the particular security concern is devised, they will be conducted. Absent evidence that a rectal search is performed in a cruel, unsanitary, unprofessional, or injurious manner, there is no basis for a reasonable inference the [defendant] gratuitously inflicted pain for the purpose of causing harm."

The requirement that there be a legitimate penological interest to support prison decisions often leads administrators to adopt across-the-board policies, often expanding the number of searches of or limitations on prisoners. See, e.g., Peckham v. Wisconsin Dept. of Corrections, 141 F.3d 694 (7th Cir.1998) (strip searches justified after virtually any prisoner movement or at random). Does the difficulty of proving maliciousness and the deferential ease of establishing a penological interest insufficiently protect prisoners from degrading circumstances? Or does it protect orderly prisoners from the random violence perpetrated by fellow prisoners?

5. The recognition of a second Eighth–Amendment-based test in *Whitley*, along side *Estelle*'s original test, has led to some confusion in deciding which standard might govern in yet-to-be-recognized Eighth Amendment contexts. In **Wilson v. Seiter**, 501 U.S. 294, 111 S.Ct. 2321, 115 L.Ed.2d 271 (1991), for example, the Supreme Court faced a claim that conditions of confinement violated the Eight Amendment. The Court had previously wrestled with the question of what conditions are so degrading as to amount to unconstitutional punishment. See, e.g., Rhodes v. Chapman, 452 U.S. 337, 101 S.Ct. 2392, 69 L.Ed.2d 59 (1981) (only conditions falling below "the minimal civilized measure of life's necessities" are unconstitutional). The inmates in *Wilson* argued that the very existence of such conditions (strict liability) amounted to a violation, at least when the conditions were long-term; the jailers argued that such conditions were only unconstitutional if they had a "culpable state of mind." The Court sided with the jailers, though it adopted *Estelle*'s deliberate indifference test rather than the pro-defendant test from *Whitley*.

(a) Justice Scalia's majority opinion said that prior cases such as *Rhodes* dealt with the "objective component of an Eighth Amendment [conditions-of-confinement] claim (was the deprivation sufficiently serious?), and [so] we did

---

1. These cases rely heavily on the Supreme Court decision in Bell v. Wolfish, 441 U.S. 520, 99 S.Ct. 1861, 60 L.Ed.2d 447 (1979), which applied the same test to pretrial detainees.

not consider the subjective component (did the officials act with a sufficiently culpable state of mind?)" [parentheses in original]. In addressing the subjective component for the first time, Justice Scalia justified the "deliberate indifference" test from *Estelle* on the ground that it is appropriate for circumstances where hasty decisions are not necessary and immediate constraints do not face prison officials. 501 U.S. at 300, 111 S.Ct. at 2326. Are decisions regarding conditions of confinement the same as ones regarding medical care?

(b) Justice Scalia rationalized the differing mental elements in the various Eighth Amendment cases by noting that the Eighth Amendment forbids "wanton" infliction of pain and that this word "must be determined with 'due regard for the differences in the kind of conduct against which an Eighth Amendment objection is lodged.' " 509 U.S. at 300, 111 S.Ct. at 2326. What does "wanton" mean? Can it carry the weight the Court places on it?

(c) Looking at the line-up of cases, *Estelle* and *Wilson* on one hand (deliberate indifference) and *Whitley* and *Hudson* on the other (maliciousness), is it so easy to say that the distinguishing feature is whether the defendants have time to consider their judgments? Might one say that there are only two Eighth Amendment contexts, one for situations involving prison order and other prison conditions of confinement?[2]

6. *Estelle* and *Whitley* adopt standards of care that rely on words or phrases from tort law, even though the Court emphasizes that it uses those words and phrases to reflect underlying constitutional law principles. Why does the Court—even Justice Scalia, normally a stickler for following constitutional text—resort to tort-style words and phrases to reflect such underlying constitutional concerns? Why not use the underlying constitutional concepts themselves?

(a) Why not perform some version of structured scrutiny such as is seen in traditional equal protection or due process cases? It might be suggested that tort-like phrases are adopted because the Court foresees that most cases will involve aberrant conduct by individual officers, as in Monroe v. Pape, Chapter 1A supra, or at least ad hoc, nonstatutory governmental policies. Is that true of all these Eighth Amendment cases?

(b) Are the torts phrases useful for instructing juries? In Baskerville v. Mulvaney, 411 F.3d 45 (2d Cir. 2005), the trial judge instructed the jury virtually verbatim using the language of "objective" and "subjective" components, supplemented by these statements: "To satisfy the objective requirement the plaintiff must prove that the violation is sufficiently serious or harmful enough by objective standards." The objective component is "context specific, turning upon 'contemporary standards of decency.' " Can juries understand these terms? Is a plaintiff entitled to an instruction that he should automatically win if maliciousness is proved, or must he also prove that the circumstances for use of force were objectively unreasonable? See id. (maliciousness ordinarily not enough because "force" used may be de minimis). Cf. Wilkins v. Gaddy, ¶ 2(b) supra.

---

2. What other contextual rights for prisoners might exist under the Eighth Amendment? And what duties and mental elements might be created to govern those contexts? See Burgin v. Nix, 899 F.2d 733 (8th Cir.1990) (food for prisoner).

FARMER v. BRENNAN

United States Supreme Court, 1994.
511 U.S. 825, 114 S.Ct. 1970, 128 L.Ed.2d 811.

JUSTICE SOUTER delivered the opinion of the Court.

A prison official's "deliberate indifference" to a substantial risk of serious harm to an inmate violates the Eighth Amendment. See Helling v. McKinney; Wilson v. Seiter; Estelle v. Gamble. This case requires us to define the term "deliberate indifference," as we do by requiring a showing that the official was subjectively aware of the risk.

I

* * * Petitioner, who is serving a federal sentence for credit card fraud, has been diagnosed by medical personnel of the Bureau of Prisons as a transsexual, one who has "[a] rare psychiatric disorder in which a person feels persistently uncomfortable about his or her anatomical sex," and who typically seeks medical treatment, including hormonal therapy and surgery, to bring about a permanent sex change. American Medical Association, Encyclopedia of Medicine 1006 (1989). For several years before being convicted and sentenced in 1986 at the age of 18, petitioner, who is biologically male, wore women's clothing (as petitioner did at the 1986 trial), underwent estrogen therapy, received silicone breast implants, and submitted to unsuccessful "black market" testicle-removal surgery. Petitioner's precise appearance in prison is unclear from the record before us, but petitioner claims to have continued hormonal treatment while incarcerated by using drugs smuggled into prison, and apparently wears clothing in a feminine manner, as by displaying a shirt "off one shoulder." The parties agree that petitioner "projects feminine characteristics."

The practice of federal prison authorities is to incarcerate preoperative transsexuals with prisoners of like biological sex, and over time authorities housed petitioner in several federal facilities, sometimes in the general male prison population but more often in segregation. [After being transferred to a higher-security prison, Farmer was raped by another inmate in his own cell. Farmer then initiated this suit claiming that authorities had violated his Eighth Amendment rights by mixing him with male prisoners "despite knowledge that the penitentiary had a violent environment and a history of inmate assaults, and despite knowledge that petitioner, as a transsexual who 'projects feminine characteristics,' would be particularly vulnerable to sexual attack by some [male] inmates." The trial court granted summary judgment to the defendants on the ground that their conduct did not amount to deliberate indifference. The Court of Appeals affirmed.]

II

A

The Constitution "does not mandate comfortable prisons," Rhodes v. Chapman, 452 U.S. 337 (1981), but neither does it permit inhumane ones, and it is now settled that "the treatment a prisoner receives in prison and the conditions under which he is confined are subject to scrutiny under the Eighth Amendment." * * *

In particular, as the lower courts have uniformly held, and as we have assumed, "[p]rison officials have a duty ... to protect prisoners from violence at the hands of other prisoners." Cortes–Quinones v. Jimenez–Nettleship, 842 F.2d 556, 558 (CA1). Having incarcerated "persons [with] demonstrated proclivit[ies] for antisocial criminal, and often violent, conduct," having stripped them of virtually every means of self-protection and foreclosed their access to outside aid, the government and its officials are not free to let the state of nature take its course. Cf. *Estelle*, supra. * * * Being violently assaulted in prison is simply not "part of the penalty that criminal offenders pay for their offenses against society." *Rhodes*, supra.

It is not, however, every injury suffered by one prisoner at the hands of another that translates into constitutional liability for prison officials responsible for the victim's safety. Our cases have held that a prison official violates the Eighth Amendment only when two requirements are met. First, the deprivation alleged must be, objectively, "sufficiently serious," [and thus for a claim like the one here] based on a failure to prevent harm, the inmate must show that he is incarcerated under conditions posing a substantial risk of serious harm. See *Helling*, supra.

The second requirement follows from the principle that "only the unnecessary and wanton infliction of pain implicates the Eighth Amendment." *Wilson*. To violate the Cruel and Unusual Punishments Clause, a prison official must have a "sufficiently culpable state of mind." Ibid. In prison-conditions cases that state of mind is one of "deliberate indifference" to inmate health or safety, *Wilson*, supra; *Estelle*, supra, a standard the parties agree governs the claim in this case. The parties disagree, however, on the proper test for deliberate indifference, which we must therefore undertake to define.

B

1

* * *

While *Estelle* establishes that deliberate indifference entails something more than mere negligence, the cases are also clear that it is satisfied by something less than acts or omissions for the very purpose of causing harm or with knowledge that harm will result. That point underlies the ruling that "application of the deliberate indifference standard is inappropriate" in one class of prison cases: when "officials stand accused of using excessive physical force." Hudson v. McMillian, [supra]; *Whitley*, supra. In such situations, * * * an Eighth Amendment claimant must show * * * that officials applied force "maliciously and sadistically for the very purpose of causing harm." * * *

With deliberate indifference lying somewhere between the poles of negligence at one end and purpose or knowledge at the other, the Courts of Appeals have routinely equated deliberate indifference with recklessness. [Citations omitted.] It is, indeed, fair to say that acting or failing to act with deliberate indifference to a substantial risk of serious harm to a prisoner is the equivalent of recklessly disregarding that risk.

That does not, however, fully answer the pending question about the level of culpability deliberate indifference entails, for the term recklessness is not self-defining. The civil law generally calls a person reckless who acts or (if the person has a duty to act) fails to act in the face of an unjustifiably high risk of harm that is either known or so obvious that it should be known. See Prosser and Keeton § 34, pp. 213–214; Restatement (Second) of Torts § 500 (1965). The criminal law, however, generally permits a finding of recklessness only when a person disregards a risk of harm of which he is aware. See R. Perkins & R. Boyce, Criminal Law 850–851 (3d ed. 1982); J. Hall, General Principles of Criminal Law 115–116, 120, 128 (2d ed. 1960) (hereinafter Hall); American Law Institute, Model Penal Code § 2.02(2)(c), and Comment 3 (1985); but see Commonwealth v. Pierce, 138 Mass. 165, 175–178 (1884) (Holmes, J.) (adopting an objective approach to criminal recklessness). The standards proposed by the parties in this case track the two approaches (though the parties do not put it that way): petitioner asks us to define deliberate indifference as what we have called civil-law recklessness, and respondents urge us to adopt an approach consistent with recklessness in the criminal law.

We reject petitioner's invitation to adopt an objective test for deliberate indifference. We hold instead that a prison official cannot be found liable under the Eighth Amendment for denying an inmate humane conditions of confinement unless the official knows of and disregards an excessive risk to inmate health or safety; the official must both be aware of facts from which the inference could be drawn that a substantial risk of serious harm exists, and he must also draw the inference. This approach comports best with the text of the Amendment as our cases have interpreted it. The Eighth Amendment does not outlaw cruel and unusual "conditions"; it outlaws cruel and unusual "punishments." An act or omission unaccompanied by knowledge of a significant risk of harm might well be something society wishes to discourage, and if harm does result society might well wish to assure compensation. The common law reflects such concerns when it imposes tort liability on a purely objective basis. See Prosser and Keeton §§ 2, 34, pp. 6, 213–214. But an official's failure to alleviate a significant risk that he should have perceived but did not, while no cause for commendation, cannot under our cases be condemned as the infliction of punishment.

* * *

2

* * * Under the test we adopt today, an Eighth Amendment claimant need not show that a prison official acted or failed to act believing that

harm actually would befall an inmate; it is enough that the official acted or failed to act despite his knowledge of a substantial risk of serious harm. We doubt that a subjective approach will present prison officials with any serious motivation "to take refuge in the zone between 'ignorance of obvious risks' and 'actual knowledge of risks.' " Brief for Petitioner 27. Whether a prison official had the requisite knowledge of a substantial risk is a question of fact subject to demonstration in the usual ways, including inference from circumstantial evidence ([thus avoiding] "confusing a mental state with the proof of its existence"), and a factfinder may conclude that a prison official knew of a substantial risk from the very fact that the risk was obvious. Cf. LaFave & Scott § 3.7 ("[I]f the risk is obvious, so that a reasonable man would realize it, we might well infer that [the defendant] did in fact realize it; but the inference cannot be conclusive, for we know that people are not always conscious of what reasonable people would be conscious of"). For example, if an Eighth Amendment plaintiff presents evidence showing that a substantial risk of inmate attacks was "longstanding, pervasive, well-documented, or expressly noted by prison officials in the past, and the circumstances suggest that the defendant-official being sued had been exposed to information concerning the risk and thus 'must have known' about it, then such evidence could be sufficient to permit a trier of fact to find that the defendant-official had actual knowledge of the risk." Brief for Respondents 22.[8]

Nor may a prison official escape liability for deliberate indifference by showing that, while he was aware of an obvious, substantial risk to inmate safety, he did not know that the complainant was especially likely to be assaulted by the specific prisoner who eventually committed the assault. The question under the Eighth Amendment is whether prison officials, acting with deliberate indifference, exposed a prisoner to a sufficiently substantial "risk of serious damage to his future health," *Helling*, and it does not matter whether the risk comes from a single source or multiple sources, any more than it matters whether a prisoner faces an excessive risk of attack for reasons personal to him or because all prisoners in his situation face such a risk. See Brief for Respondents 15 (stating that a prisoner can establish exposure to a sufficiently serious risk of harm "by showing that he belongs to an identifiable group of prisoners who are frequently singled out for violent attack by other inmates"). If, for example, prison officials were aware that inmate "rape was so common and uncontrolled that some potential victims dared not sleep [but] instead

---

8. While the obviousness of a risk is not conclusive and a prison official may show that the obvious escaped him, he would not escape liability if the evidence showed that he merely refused to verify underlying facts that he strongly suspected to be true, or declined to confirm inferences of risk that he strongly suspected to exist (as when a prison official is aware of a high probability of facts indicating that one prisoner has planned an attack on another but resists opportunities to obtain final confirmation; or when a prison official knows that some diseases are communicable and that a single needle is being used to administer flu shots to prisoners but refuses to listen to a subordinate who he strongly suspects will attempt to explain the associated risk of transmitting disease). When instructing juries in deliberate indifference cases with such issues of proof, courts should be careful to ensure that the requirement of subjective culpability is not lost. It is not enough merely to find that a reasonable person would have known, or that the defendant should have known, and juries should be instructed accordingly.

... would leave their beds and spend the night clinging to the bars nearest the guards' station," it would obviously be irrelevant to liability that the officials could not guess beforehand precisely who would attack whom. Cf. *Helling*, supra, (observing that the Eighth Amendment requires a remedy for exposure of inmates to "infectious maladies" such as hepatitis and venereal disease "even though the possible infection might not affect all of those exposed").

Because, however, prison officials who lacked knowledge of a risk cannot be said to have inflicted punishment, it remains open to the officials to prove that they were unaware even of an obvious risk to inmate health or safety. That a trier of fact may infer knowledge from the obvious, in other words, does not mean that it must do so. Prison officials charged with deliberate indifference might show, for example, that they did not know of the underlying facts indicating a sufficiently substantial danger and that they were therefore unaware of a danger, or that they knew the underlying facts but believed (albeit unsoundly) that the risk to which the facts gave rise was insubstantial or nonexistent.

In addition, prison officials who actually knew of a substantial risk to inmate health or safety may be found free from liability if they responded reasonably to the risk, even if the harm ultimately was not averted. A prison official's duty under the Eighth Amendment is to ensure "reasonable safety," *Helling*, supra, a standard that incorporates due regard for prison officials' "unenviable task of keeping dangerous men in safe custody under humane conditions." Whether one puts it in terms of duty or deliberate indifference, prison officials who act reasonably cannot be found liable under the Cruel and Unusual Punishments Clause.

We address, finally, petitioner's argument that a subjective deliberate indifference test will unjustly require prisoners to suffer physical injury before obtaining court-ordered correction of objectively inhumane prison conditions. [This is not a problem because our] subjective approach to deliberate indifference does not require a prisoner seeking "a remedy for unsafe conditions [to] await a tragic event [such as an] actua[l] assaul[t] before obtaining relief." *Helling*, supra. [Consequently, if a trial court] finds the Eighth Amendment's subjective and objective requirements satisfied, it may grant appropriate injunctive relief. See Hutto v. Finney (upholding order designed to halt "an ongoing violation" in prison conditions that included extreme overcrowding, rampant violence, insufficient food, and unsanitary conditions). Of course, a district court should approach issuance of injunctive orders with the usual caution, see Bell v. Wolfish (warning courts against becoming "enmeshed in the minutiae of prison conditions"), and may, for example, exercise its discretion if appropriate by giving prison officials time to rectify the situation before issuing an injunction.

* * *

The judgment of the Court of Appeals is vacated, and the case is remanded for further proceedings consistent with this opinion.

So ordered.

JUSTICE BLACKMUN, concurring. [Omitted.]

JUSTICE THOMAS, concurring in the judgment.

* * * "Punishment," from the time of the Founding through the present day, "has always meant a 'fine, penalty, or confinement inflicted upon a person by the authority of the law and the judgment and sentence of a court, for some crime or offense committed by him.' " Conditions of confinement are not punishment in any recognized sense of the term, unless imposed as part of a sentence. As an original matter, therefore, this case would be an easy one for me: because the unfortunate attack that befell petitioner was not part of his sentence, it did not constitute "punishment" under the Eighth Amendment. [But because the standard adopted today is among the highest known to constitutional law, I concur.]

NOTE ON "DELIBERATE INDIFFERENCE" IN EIGHTH AMENDMENT CASES

1.   The *Farmer* case, specifically emphasizing the objective and subjective components that form the standard of care in Eighth Amendment cases, articulates a "duty" (objective component) and a "state of mind" or "mental element" (subjective component) that inhere in the constitutional right that the plaintiff seeks to enforce by a § 1983 action. The case focuses primarily on the mental element, but first notice the duty that the Court finds implicit in the Eighth Amendment.

(a) How does the Court identify the duty in *Farmer*? Is this case consistent with the Court's earlier decision in Davidson v. Cannon, Chapter 1B.1 supra? In that case the Court held that prison officials were not liable for an inmate's beating at the hands of fellow prisoners, interpreting the "Due Process Clause" generally. How does the text of the Eighth Amendment, as well as the precedents accumulated after *Estelle v. Gamble*, change the Court's approach here?

(b) The opening of the *Farmer* opinion emphasizes that the duty to protect the safety of prisoners extends only to harms that are "sufficiently serious," but the later discussion pointedly expands the duty by noting that it extends not only to actual completed harms, but also to the "risk" of serious harm. Recall the similar focus on seriousness and risk in the medical-care cases arising under the Eighth Amendment. See the Note on Constitutional Standard for Prison Medical Care Cases, this sub-section supra. Is the use of the "risk" notion inappropriate in the safety context—precisely because everything in prison is a safety risk or threat? If the "risk" notion is broad, is it narrowed by limiting it to "serious" risks, or are all risks in prison serious?

(c) If the Eighth Amendment imposed no duty regarding inmate safety, there would be no need to discuss a mental element (subjective component). See Collins v. City of Harker Heights, Chapter 1B.1 supra. Does that make the existence of an objective component of a right more important than the subjective component? But once a duty is announced, as shown in *Farmer*, the subjective component may greatly attenuate or lessen the duty apparently imposed. So is the subjective component then more important than the objective component? In what sense are the two components a single package that is more important than either component alone?

2. The *Estelle* and *Whitley* cases discussed two different mental elements that might apply under the Eighth Amendment, depending on the context or duty at issue. The *Farmer* case identifies "deliberate indifference," as in *Estelle*, as the relevant subjective component in the safety context and proceeds to define the term.

(a) What position did the plaintiff take in suggesting a definition for deliberate indifference? Was his approach inherently flawed because he wanted to define this "subjective" element of his claim "objectively"? Was his approach just a clever way to redefine deliberate indifference as negligence? The plaintiff could theoretically have argued that *Estelle*'s mental element applies in medical-care cases, that *Whitley*'s mental element applies to use of force in prison, and that a completely different mental element applies in prison safety context—perhaps strict liability. Was that argument doomed to failure?

(b) Turning to a subjective definition of deliberate indifference, the Court in effect defines it doubly subjectively, does it not? Notice the Court's language: "the official must both be aware of facts from which the inference could be drawn that a substantial risk of serious harm exists, and he must also draw the inference." Why is there such double emphasis on the defendant's subjective state of mind?

(c) How do you interpret footnote 8? Does it add to the subjectivity—making it triply subjective—or is the Court attempting to give the "should have known" idea more play? Must a jury believe a jailor's claim that he knew nothing or drew no conclusions from what he knew?

(d) Does *Farmer*'s definition of deliberate indifference invite guards to know nothing? Assuming they know something factually, does the standard encourage them not to think about what they know? See Perkins v. Grimes, 161 F.3d 1127 (8th Cir.1998) (guards' denials of rape or detainee's proclivity for it leads to finding in their favor, even though they admitted that rapist was well known as an "easily provoked" person). Does *Farmer*'s standard effectively insulate higher prison administrators from liability for any particular failure in providing for inmate safety? Compare Steidl v. Gramley, 151 F.3d 739 (7th Cir.1998) (warden not liable for attack because he had no "actual knowledge" of the safety risk), with Schaub v. VonWald, 638 F.3d 905 (8th Cir. 2011) (supervisor liable because he admittedly personally knew of risks and failed to respond).

3. After defining deliberate indifference the *Farmer* Court appears to recognize that the doubly subjective definition presents substantial problems of proof for plaintiffs, and it suggests how a successful case might be proved circumstantially. In what way does the Court's discussion of proof re-introduce objective considerations that had been ruled out in defining the deliberate indifference subjectively?

(a) The subjective appreciation of a risk may be inferred if the risk was obvious or longstanding, says the Court. Why is it reasonable for a factfinder to conclude that a prison administrator likely knew of and appreciated the risk of an existing, longstanding danger? Does the assumption depend upon a related assumption of training and professionalism among administrators? Notice that such evidence of obviousness merely "may" authorize a finding of deliberate indifference. Re-read footnote 8 again. Should the Court have said "must" instead of "may"?

(b) Even if the plaintiff is able to present circumstantial evidence of the defendant's deliberate indifference, says the Court, that evidence may be trumped or rebutted by the defendant's testimony about what he actually knew or appreciated. Must the factfinder believe the defendant's denials? Is footnote 8 simply about circumstantial evidence?

(c) Presumably, if the answer to all these questions of proof is that a factfinder is the ultimate decisionmaker, then every such case must go to trial and await a jury verdict. Cf. Jensen v. Clarke, 94 F.3d 1191, 1197 (8th Cir.1996) ("[e]ach stage of [*Farmer*'s doubly subjective] analysis is fact-intensive"). If this is so, does the uncertainty of outcome lessen the pressure on the defendant to protect prisoner safety or increase the pressure? Given the litigiousness of prisoners, does the possibility of a jury trial in all such cases expose defendants to unfair litigation costs, even should they ultimately prevail at trial?[1]

(d) The Court's discussion of deliberate indifference includes a refined description of the safety duty, one which notes (i) that the risk need not be clearly foreseen for a particular inmate and (ii) that reasonable responses to risks of safety may show lack of deliberate indifference, even if the risk is ultimately realized. Do these refinements favor the plaintiff or the defendant? How would you describe the ultimate package of liability rules—objective and subjective components—created by the Court?

4. Presumably, the Court's definition of deliberate indifference applies to all Eighth Amendment claims that use this mental element, regardless of the context. See Schaub v. VonWald, supra (medical care); Martinez v. Garden, 430 F.3d 1302 (10th Cir. 2005) (same); Tesch v. County of Green Lake, 157 F.3d 465 (7th Cir.1998) (citing *Farmer* as controlling disabled inmates conditions-of-confinement claim).

(a) How will the Court's definition in *Farmer* affect these other types of Eighth Amendment cases in which the mental element of deliberate indifference applies? Will they be more difficult for plaintiffs to prove? If an inmate is prescient enough to complain and put his jailers on notice of his medical condition or of prison conditions of confinement, does *Farmer* actually make his case easier to win? See Frost v. Agnos, 152 F.3d 1124 (9th Cir.1998) (jailed disabled person complained of inaccessibility of showers). But see Schaub v. VonWald, supra (no need to inform jailor of specific needs where condition is brought to attention of authorities).

(b) Presumably *Farmer* has no application to *Whitley*-style claims of excessive force, which require proof of malicious or sadistic intent to impose harm. Yet given *Farmer*'s doubly subjective definition of deliberate indiffer-

---

1. Should courts require prisoner plaintiff's to prove their cases by "clear and convincing evidence," rather than the usual civil standard of "preponderance of the evidence," in order to prevent frivolous claims of bad intent from harassing prison administrators? See Crawford–El v. Britton, 523 U.S. 574, 118 S.Ct. 1584, 140 L.Ed.2d 759 (1998) (no; 5–4 opinion).

ence, how different is the subjective element of deliberate indifference from the mental element defined in *Whitley*? What is the difference between wanting to harm an inmate and not caring if others harm him?

5. In **Hope v. Pelzer,** 536 U.S. 730, 122 S.Ct. 2508, 153 L.Ed.2d 666 (2002), the Court considered a claim by a prisoner who had been handcuffed to Alabama's infamous "hitching post," arms at face height for seven hours burning in the sun shirtless. Even though the harm had been imposed by guards, not fellow prisoners, the Court proceeded to apply *Farmer* because the case involved prisoner "safety"—defendants had "knowingly subjected him to a substantial risk of physical harm." The Court held that the defendants had violated the Eighth Amendment because the punishment and harm were "obvious" under *Farmer*.

(a) Did the case not fit the *Whitley* mold—requiring proof of maliciousness-because there was no disorder to quell? Actually, the defendants argued that they had acted to restore order and punish the plaintiff to maintain order after he got into a scuffle with another prisoner and overslept instead of performing his chain-gang duties. See 536 U.S. at 734, 122 S.Ct. at 2512–13. Do you read *Hope* as holding that all "safety" cases are subject to *Farmer*'s standard? All "risk of harm" cases? Why—because the guards (or the rule-makers in Alabama's prisons) had time to reflect on their decisions, and "deliberate indifference" is the appropriate standard for such circumstances? Because the pattern of other inmates suffering at the hitching post showed that the guards actually knew of the suffering it caused?

(b) Applying the *Farmer* test, the Court found that *Farmer*'s doubly subjective standard had been met because the danger and harm to Hope had been "obvious." The Court considered no evidence regarding whether the guards knew that their actions harmed Hope? Was this a misapplication of *Farmer*'s footnote 8? Or on the facts—the policy was admittedly to use the hitching post as "punishment"—was it the very purpose of the hitching post to cause pain? Is every form of corporal punishment unconstitutional after *Hope*?[2] Should this new "obviousness" test, if the Court chooses to follow it, also apply to other Eighth Amendment claims where "deliberate indifference" is the subjective mental element? Cf. Schaub v. VonWald, 638 F.3d 905 (8th Cir. 2011) (visible condition of inmate's serious wounds, which grew worse over time, satisfied subjective component by making it "obvious" that supervisor was aware of medical needs and ignored them).

(c) Does *Hope* show the limit of the objective and subjective components for defining Eighth Amendment violations? Unlike *Farmer*, *Whitley*, and *Estelle*, which involved individual employee decisions that can harm a prisoner, the conduct in *Hope* was officially sanctioned and made policy by prison authorities and enforced as a meaningful punishment. If the hitching post in fact harmed prisoners by causing them to have wrists cut from handcuffs and backs burned in the sun, does it make any difference whether defendants foresaw or failed to appreciate these specific harms? Isn't the hitching post

---

2. Compare the harm in *Hope*—risk of pain from a sunburn and handcuffs cutting into wrists as the prisoner grew tired; are these harms not far less than some ignored by courts in the medical care context? See the Note following *Estelle* supra. Should those appellate case be re-examined now?

unconstitutional for the same reason that other bizarre and uncivilized punishments are forbidden—precisely because they are disproportionate and cruel, regardless of whether they are so intended? See Kennedy v. Louisiana, 554 U.S. 407, 128 S.Ct. 2641, 171 L.Ed.2d 525 (2008) (death penalty unconstitutional for murder of child; collecting cases); Weems v. United States, 217 U.S. 349, 30 S.Ct. 544, 54 L.Ed. 793 (1910) (twelve years at hard labor in irons imposed by U.S. territory of the Philippines is cruel and unusual). Should cases that involve conscious governmental policies be analyzed differently from cases involving errant action by individual officials? Cf. Clark–Murphy v. Foreback, 439 F.3d 280 (6th Cir. 2006) (prison guards designated to watch inmate in confinement allow him to die of dehydration; *Farmer* standard applies).

(d) If *Hope* extends *Farmer* to situations where the guards themselves are threats to prisoner's safety, what other circumstances will *Farmer* control? Is inmate suicide, where the inmate presents a danger of harm to himself—controlled by *Farmer*? See Short v. Smoot, 436 F.3d 422 (4th Cir. 2006) (*Farmer* applies; once risk is appreciated, reasonable response to the risk satisfies *Farmer*); Woloszyn v. County of Lawrence, 396 F.3d 314 (3d Cir. 2005) (*Farmer* applies, so liability only when jailor appreciated risk of suicide).

6.   The standards developed under the Eighth Amendment apply only to prisoners (and by analogy to pretrial detainees held in jail). What standards should apply to free citizens who encounter police?

3.   FOURTH AMENDMENT STANDARDS AND POLICE MISCONDUCT

In early decisions, the Supreme Court suggested that there were two contexts governing police use of force against ordinary citizens, one for deadly force and another for non-lethal use of force. More recently the two standards appear to have merged.

TENNESSEE v. GARNER

Supreme Court of the United States, 1985.
471 U.S. 1, 105 S.Ct. 1694, 85 L.Ed.2d 1.

JUSTICE WHITE delivered the opinion of the Court.

This case requires us to determine the constitutionality of the use of deadly force to prevent the escape of an apparently unarmed suspected felon. We conclude that such force may not be used unless it is necessary to prevent the escape and the officer has probable cause to believe that the suspect poses a significant threat of death or serious physical injury to the officer or others.

I

At about 10:45 p.m. on October 3, 1974, Memphis Police Officers Elton Hymon and Leslie Wright were dispatched to answer a "prowler inside call." Upon arriving at the scene they saw a woman standing on her porch and gesturing toward the adjacent house. She told them she had heard glass breaking and that "they" or "someone" was breaking in next door. While Wright radioed the dispatcher to say that they were on the scene, Hymon went behind the house. He heard a door slam and saw someone run across the backyard. The fleeing suspect, who was appellee-respondent's decedent, Edward Garner, stopped at a 6–feet–high chain link fence at the edge of the yard. With the aid of a flashlight, Hymon was able to see Garner's face and hands. He saw no sign of a weapon, and, though not certain, was "reasonably sure" and "figured" that Garner was unarmed. He thought Garner was 17 or 18 years old and about 5'5" or 5'7" tall.[2] While Garner was crouched at the base of the fence, Hymon called out "police, halt" and took a few steps toward him. Garner then began to climb over the fence. Convinced that if Garner made it over the fence he would elude capture, Hymon shot him. The bullet hit Garner in the back of the head. Garner was taken by ambulance to a hospital, where he died on the operating table. Ten dollars and a purse taken from the house were found on his body.

In using deadly force to prevent the escape, Hymon was acting under the authority of a Tennessee statute and pursuant to Police Department policy. The statute provides that "[i]f, after notice of the intention to arrest the defendant, he either flee or forcibly resist, the officer may use all the necessary means to effect the arrest." Tenn. Code Ann. § 40–7–108 (1982).[5] The Department policy was slightly more restrictive than the statute, but still allowed the use of deadly force in cases of burglary. * * *

Garner's father then brought this action in the Federal District Court for the Western District of Tennessee, seeking damages under 42 U.S.C. § 1983 for asserted violations of Garner's constitutional rights. The complaint alleged that the shooting violated the Fourth, Fifth, Sixth, Eighth, and Fourteenth Amendments of the United States Constitution. [After a bench trial the district court entered judgment for defendants, finding that the decedent had by his attempted escape "assum[ed] the risk of being fired upon." The Court of Appeals ultimately reversed, and the Supreme Court then agreed to review the case.]

* * *

II

Whenever an officer restrains the freedom of a person to walk away, he has seized that person. United States v. Brignoni–Ponce, 422 U.S. 873, 878, 95 S.Ct. 2574, 2578, 45 L.Ed.2d 607 (1975). While it is not always clear just when minimal police interference becomes a seizure, see United States v. Mendenhall, 446 U.S. 544, 100 S.Ct. 1870, 64 L.Ed.2d 497 (1980), there can be no question that apprehension by the use of deadly force is a

---

2. In fact, Garner, an eighth-grader, was 15. He was 5'4" tall and weighed somewhere around 100 or 110 pounds.

5. Although the statute does not say so explicitly, Tennessee law forbids the use of deadly force in the arrest of a misdemeanant. See Johnson v. State, 173 Tenn. 134, 114 S.W.2d 819 (1938).

seizure subject to the reasonableness requirement of the Fourth Amendment.

A

A police officer may arrest a person if he has probable cause to believe that person committed a crime. E.g., United States v. Watson, 423 U.S. 411, 96 S.Ct. 820, 46 L.Ed.2d 598 (1976). Petitioners and appellant argue that if this requirement is satisfied the Fourth Amendment has nothing to say about how that seizure is made. This submission ignores the many cases in which this Court, by balancing the extent of the intrusion against the need for it, has examined the reasonableness of the manner in which a search or seizure is conducted. To determine the constitutionality of a seizure "[w]e must balance the nature and quality of the intrusion on the individual's Fourth Amendment interests against the importance of the governmental interests alleged to justify the intrusion." United States v. Place, 462 U.S. 696, 703, 103 S.Ct. 2637, 2642, 77 L.Ed.2d 110 (1983). * * * Because one of the factors is the extent of the intrusion, it is plain that reasonableness depends on not only when a seizure is made, but also how it is carried out. Terry v. Ohio, 392 U.S. 1, 28–29, 88 S.Ct. 1868, 1883–1884, 20 L.Ed.2d 889 (1968).

Applying these principles to particular facts, the Court has held that governmental interests did not support a lengthy detention of luggage, [surgery to obtain evidence, or fingerprinting without probable cause.] On the other hand, under the same approach it has upheld the taking of fingernail scrapings from a suspect, an unannounced entry into a home to prevent the destruction of evidence, administrative housing inspections without probable cause to believe that a code violation will be found, and a blood test of a drunken-driving suspect. [Citations omitted.] In each of these cases, the question was whether the totality of the circumstances justified a particular sort of search or seizure.

B

The same balancing process applied in the cases cited above demonstrates that, notwithstanding probable cause to seize a suspect, an officer may not always do so by killing him. The intrusiveness of a seizure by means of deadly force is unmatched. The suspect's fundamental interest in his own life need not be elaborated upon. The use of deadly force also frustrates the interest of the individual, and of society, in judicial determination of guilt and punishment. Against these interests are ranged governmental interests in effective law enforcement.[8] It is argued that overall

---

8. The dissent emphasizes that subsequent investigation cannot replace immediate apprehension. We recognize that this is so; indeed, that is the reason why there is any dispute. If subsequent arrest were assured, no one would argue that use of deadly force was justified. * * * In lamenting the inadequacy of later investigation, the dissent relies on the report of the President's Commission on Law Enforcement and Administration of Justice. It is worth noting that, notwithstanding its awareness of this problem, the Commission itself proposed a policy for use of deadly force arguably even more stringent than the formulation we adopt today. See President's Commission on Law Enforcement and Administration of Justice, Task Force Report: The Police 189 (1967). The Commission proposed that deadly force be used only to apprehend

violence will be reduced by encouraging the peaceful submission of suspects who know that they may be shot if they flee. Effectiveness in making arrests requires the resort to deadly force, or at least the meaningful threat thereof. "Being able to arrest such individuals is a condition precedent to the state's entire system of law enforcement." Brief for Petitioners 14.

Without in any way disparaging the importance of these goals, we are not convinced that the use of deadly force is a sufficiently productive means of accomplishing them to justify the killing of nonviolent suspects. The use of deadly force is a self-defeating way of apprehending a suspect and so setting the criminal justice mechanism in motion. If successful, it guarantees that that mechanism will not be set in motion. And while the meaningful threat of deadly force might be thought to lead to the arrest of more live suspects by discouraging escape attempts, the presently available evidence does not support this thesis.[9] The fact is that a majority of police departments in this country have forbidden the use of deadly force against nonviolent suspects. If those charged with the enforcement of the criminal law have abjured the use of deadly force in arresting nondangerous felons, there is a substantial basis for doubting that the use of such force is an essential attribute of the arrest power in all felony cases. * * *

The use of deadly force to prevent the escape of all felony suspects, whatever the circumstances, is constitutionally unreasonable. It is not better that all felony suspects die than that they escape. Where the suspect poses no immediate threat to the officer and no threat to others, the harm resulting from failing to apprehend him does not justify the use of deadly force to do so. It is no doubt unfortunate when a suspect who is in sight escapes, but the fact that the police arrive a little late or are a little slower afoot does not always justify killing the suspect. A police officer may not seize an unarmed, nondangerous suspect by shooting him dead. The Tennessee statute is unconstitutional insofar as it authorizes the use of deadly force against such fleeing suspects.

It is not, however, unconstitutional on its face. Where the officer has probable cause to believe that the suspect poses a threat of serious physical harm, either to the officer or to others, it is not constitutionally unreasonable to prevent escape by using deadly force. Thus, if the suspect threatens the officer with a weapon or there is probable cause to believe that he has committed a crime involving the infliction or threatened

"perpetrators who, in the course of their crime threatened the use of deadly force, or if the officer believes there is a substantial risk that the person whose arrest is sought will cause death or serious bodily harm if his apprehension is delayed." In addition, the officer would have "to know, as a virtual certainty, that the suspect committed an offense for which the use of deadly force is permissible." Ibid.

9. See Sherman, Reducing Police Gun Use, in Control in the Police Organization 98, 120–123 (M. Punch ed. 1983); Fyfe, Observations on Police Deadly Force, 27 Crime & Delinquency 376, 378–381 (1981); W. Geller & K. Karales, Split–Second Decisions 67 (1981); App. 84 (affidavit of William Bracey, Chief of Patrol, New York City Police Department). See generally Brief for Police Foundation et al. as Amici Curiae.

infliction of serious physical harm, deadly force may be used if necessary to prevent escape, and if, where feasible, some warning has been given. As applied in such circumstances, the Tennessee statute would pass constitutional muster.

III

It is insisted that the Fourth Amendment must be construed in light of the common-law rule, which allowed the use of whatever force was necessary to effect the arrest of a fleeing felon, though not a misdemeanant. [But this antiquated rule arose in the days when all felonies were punishable by death and that label marked the relative dangerousness of felons. It was said that shooting a fleeing felon simply accelerated the death penalty he would receive at law. The extreme variability among states in classifying misdemeanors and felonies no longer makes this line sufficiently clear to define the difference between life and death.]

There is an additional reason why the common-law rule cannot be directly translated to the present day. The common-law rule developed at a time when weapons were rudimentary. Deadly force could be inflicted almost solely in a hand-to-hand struggle during which, necessarily, the safety of the arresting officer was at risk. Handguns were not carried by police officers until the latter half of the last century. L. Kennett & J. Anderson, The Gun in America 150–151 (1975). Only then did it become possible to use deadly force from a distance as a means of apprehension. As a practical matter, the use of deadly force under the standard articulation of the common-law rule has an altogether different meaning—and harsher consequences—now than in past centuries. See Wechsler & Michael, A Rationale for the Law of Homicide: I, 37 COLUM.L.REV. 701, 741 (1937).

* * *

In evaluating the reasonableness of police procedures under the Fourth Amendment, we have also looked to prevailing rules in individual jurisdictions. [The states are currently split, with 23 continuing to follow some version of the common law rule. Although there has been no recent movement in the states rejecting the common law rule, the historical trend is against it.]

This trend is more evident and impressive when viewed in light of the policies adopted by the police departments themselves. Overwhelmingly, these are more restrictive than the common-law rule. [The FBI and others have adopted standards similar to those we adopt today.] Overall, only 7.5% of departmental and municipal policies explicitly permit the use of deadly force against any felon; 86.8% explicitly do not. K. Matulia, A Balance of Forces: A Report of the International Association of Chiefs of Police 161 (1982). In light of the rules adopted by those who must actually administer them, the older and fading common-law view is a dubious indicium of the constitutionality of the Tennessee statute now before us. [The Police Foundation, as Amicus Curia, has assured the Court that the practice of shooting all fleeing felons is unnecessary to protect citizens and officers or to deter crime.]

* * *

The judgment of the Court of Appeals is affirmed, and the case is remanded for further proceedings consistent with this opinion.

So ordered.

JUSTICE O'CONNOR, with whom THE CHIEF JUSTICE and JUSTICE REHN-QUIST join, dissenting.

* * * By disregarding the serious and dangerous nature of residential burglaries and the longstanding practice of many States, the Court effectively creates a Fourth Amendment right allowing a burglary suspect to flee unimpeded from a police officer who has probable cause to arrest, who has ordered the suspect to halt, and who has no means short of firing his weapon to prevent escape. I do not believe that the Fourth Amendment supports such a right, and I accordingly dissent.

* * *

[A]pprehension of fleeing criminal suspects requires instantaneous police response, and the] clarity of hindsight cannot provide the standard for judging the reasonableness of police decisions made in uncertain and often dangerous circumstances. Moreover, I am far more reluctant than is the Court to conclude that the Fourth Amendment proscribes a police practice that was accepted at the time of the adoption of the Bill of Rights and has continued to receive the support of many state legislatures. Although the Court has recognized that the requirements of the Fourth Amendment must respond to the reality of social and technological change, fidelity to the notion of constitutional—as opposed to purely judicial—limits on governmental action requires us to impose a heavy burden on those who claim that practices accepted when the Fourth Amendment was adopted are now constitutionally impermissible. * * *

NOTE ON STANDARDS OF CARE USING CONSTITUTION-BASED WORDS AND PHRASES

1. Notice the similarity and distinctiveness of *Garner* and *Whitley v. Albers*. Both use interest analysis in creating constitutional law, both yielding standards of care for constitutional torts. But whereas *Whitley* adopts a tort-like phrase to capture its constitutional notions ("malicious intent to harm"), *Garner* uses more traditional Constitution-based words and phrases, specifically, "reasonableness" and "probable cause" found in the text of the Fourth Amendment. Why does the Court sometimes use tort phrases in declaring constitutional standards and at other times Constitution-based phrases?

(a) Fourth Amendment jurisprudence is richly developed, primarily in a set of cases involving criminal prosecutions in which the Fourth Amendment is raised as a defense at a suppression hearing presided over by a judge without a jury. Note that *Garner* cites many such cases. Is Fourth–Amendment law so deeply embedded in judges' psyches that its words and phrases survive even when transplanted from the usual criminal-defense context to § 1983 suits?

(b) Notice that the plaintiff in *Garner* attacked a state statute authorizing the use of deadly force. The case thus falls into the traditional constitutional mold (challenge to state or local statute) rather than into the mold of Monroe v. Pape (challenge to official action that violates state law). Yet *Garner* refuses to hold the Tennessee law unconstitutional on its face but only as applied. Does that mean that the *Monroe* factor—whether an officer acts consistently with or in violation of state law—is not important in affecting the Court's choice of constitutional standards?

(c) Does it matter whether a given standard is made from Constitution-based words and phrases or tort-like language? Is one preferable to the other? Since § 1983 suits for damages are actions at law, they will often be tried before a jury, a jury which must be charged concerning the law it is to apply. Is a tort-like charge more easily understood by the jury?

2.   Consider the actual rule *Garner* creates to enforce the Fourth Amendment—the relevant Constitutional provision because a shooting is a "seizure."[1] While the Court uses the Fourth–Amendment—based word "reasonable," it in fact abandons the general concept of reasonableness and gives a more precise definition applicable in cases of use of deadly force against fleeing suspects. A jury would not be allowed to second-guess an officer's action by gauging its general "reasonableness," but would instead focus on whether (i) the officer had "probable cause" to believe that (ii) the fleeing felon presented "the threat of serious physical harm" to the officer or others. Consider first "probable cause."

(a) Probable cause is usually a standard employed by judges sitting at preliminary (charging) hearings or suppression hearings or by grand juries greatly controlled by prosecutors. Yet the classic definition of the term points toward common sense and ordinary understandings:

> "In dealing with probable cause, however, as the very name implies, we deal with probabilities. These are not technical; they are the factual and practical considerations of everyday life on which reasonable and prudent men, not legal technicians, act. . . . Probable cause exists where the facts and circumstances within [the officers] knowledge and of which they had reasonably trustworthy information [are] sufficient in themselves to warrant a man of reasonable caution in the belief that an offense has been or is being committed." Brinegar v. United States, 338 U.S. 160, 69 S.Ct. 1302, 93 L.Ed. 1879 (1949).[2]

Should an instruction phrased in these terms be given to the jury?

(b) Police encounters with suspects often occur rapidly and under stress. Assuming that an automobile is a dangerous weapon went directed at an officer, does an officer have probable cause to believe that such a danger is

---

1. Regarding seizures, see Note on Police Misconduct Litigation Under the Fourth Amendment, following the next principal case in this section.

2. For quite similar recent restatements, see the Note on Other Fourth Amendment Cases and Their Relation to Garner and Graham, *infra* in this section.

present when he sees a suspect drive rapidly in his general direction? Does "probable cause" allow him to err and believe there may be a danger, even though the suspect may in fact not be aiming his car at the officer or a bystander? See Sigley v. City of Parma Heights, 437 F.3d 527 (6th Cir. 2006) (collecting cases and holding that on disputed facts issue is for a jury to decide); Untalan v. City of Lorain, 430 F.3d 312 (6th Cir. 2005): "Within a few seconds of reasonably perceiving a sufficient danger, officers may use deadly force even if in hindsight the facts show that the persons threatened could have escaped unharmed." Cf. Los Angeles County v. Rettele, 550 U.S. 609, 127 S.Ct. 1989, 167 L.Ed.2d 974 (2007) (for warranted searches, "probable cause, a standard well short of absolute certainty," means that police may "search the innocent," who will "unfortunately bear the cost").

(c) In the arrest context, the Supreme Court has ruled that "an arresting officer's state of mind (except for facts that he knows) is irrelevant to probable cause," **Devenpeck v. Alford**, 543 U.S. 146, 125 S.Ct. 588, 160 L.Ed.2d 537 (2004), and therefore an officer's decision to arrest on one charge is valid even if he actually wanted to arrest for another violation. See Whren v. United States, 517 U.S. 806, 812–815, 116 S.Ct. 1769, 135 L.Ed.2d 89 (1996) (sham stop/arrest on one charge when officer wanted to catch suspect on a different charge). Can an officer shoot to kill a hated suspect, based on probable cause to believe there is a danger, even though he would not have shot any other person under the same circumstances? Is "probable cause" for police shootings the same as "probable cause" in all other Fourth Amendment contexts?

3. Now consider the second part of *Garner*'s test—"threat of serious physical harm, either to the officer or to others." The actual holding in *Garner* simply affirms that "mere flight" cannot be such a danger, and therefore the Court has no occasion to discuss what its test actually means.

(a) Is any fleeing suspect automatically a threat if he has himself used force earlier in the encounter? Compare Hemphill v. Schott, 141 F.3d 412 (2d Cir.1998) (heinousness of violent crime does not justify all subsequent uses of deadly force), with Montoute v. Carr, 114 F.3d 181 (11th Cir.1997) (fleeing with shotgun in hand may be such a threat). Is the word "threat" like the word "risk" in the Eighth Amendment cases discussed in the previous section? A "threat of serious physical harm" is less of a showing than certainty or actual danger, is it not? Is this term as loose as the term "probable cause"?

(b) In the years after *Garner* several circuits held that the threat is to be appraised from the point of view of the officer in the situation because "[r]econsideration [of events] will nearly always reveal that something different could have been done if ... the future [were completely predictable] before it occurred." Carr v. Tatangelo, 338 F.3d 1259 (11th Cir. 2003). See Graham v. Connor, infra (next principal case, warning against review by "20–20 hindsight"). See Robinson v. Arrugueta, 415 F.3d 1252 (11th Cir. 2005) (2.7–second reaction time means officer who fears he will be crushed can shoot immediately before determining if victim intended to hurt him). Does this show that Garner's "threat" of harm is much broader than the harm itself?

(c) Although *Garner* involves fleeing felons, lower courts typically applied Fourth Amendment standards to any purposeful shooting regardless of whether the person shot has committed a crime. See Ciminillo v. Streicher, 434 F.3d 461 (6th Cir. 2006) (person "not a suspect" when shot during a riot; shooting itself is seizure regardless of whether person otherwise seized or arrested). Cf. Scott v. Harris, infra in this subsection. But should the test for dangerousness be ratcheted up if the person shot is not even a suspect, one who presents a danger only to himself? See Sova v. City of Mt. Pleasant, 142 F.3d 898 (6th Cir.1998) (officers shoot suicidal son after he stabs himself with knives).

4. Most cases tried under the *Garner* standard involve the injured party's use of traditional weapons, usually a gun or knife (or what the officer had reason to believe was such a weapon), while a few involve an unconventional weapon, such as an automobile used to run down an officer. Few cases concern alleged naked, cold-blooded responsive shootings, but see Harris v. Roderick, 126 F.3d 1189 (9th Cir.1997) (in "Ruby Ridge massacre" plaintiff alleges shooting to kill and cover-up conspiracy). Most contain a claim by the officer of some threat of current danger. What is a sufficient threat? Are there many factors involved?

(a) In gun cases, how much observation is necessary in order to establish under the probable-cause standard that a suspect had a weapon in his possession? Is a glint of metal or the "distinctive sound" of a bullet being chambered enough? See Carr v. Tatangelo, 338 F.3d 1259 (11th Cir. 2003) (yes). Might a "furtive gesture" be the act of reaching inside the pocket for a gun or even refusing to show one's hands while exiting a vehicle? See Carnaby v. City of Houston, 636 F.3d 183 (5th Cir. 2011) (hiding hands); Hemphill v. Schott, 141 F.3d 412 (2d Cir.1998) (plaintiff "furtively" crouched and reached toward chest pocket); Ting v. United States, 927 F.2d 1504 (9th Cir.1991) (lunging from subdued position toward a dark closet). Consider the risk of being shot that an officer assumes by waiting to see if there is a gun; does shifting the risk of harm to the officer virtually guarantee that she will be shot sometime during the course of her career? See McLenagan v. Karnes, 27 F.3d 1002 (4th Cir.1994) ("we do not think it wise to require a police officer, in all instances, to actually detect the presence of an object in a suspect's hands before firing on him"). Cf. Elliott v. Leavitt, 105 F.3d 174 (4th Cir.1997) (Wilkins, J., dissenting from rehearing en banc: "So it has come to this—my dissenting colleagues would require police officers to gamble with their lives in order to avoid civil liability [by requiring that they] actually await the bullet").

(b) What item or weapon must the defendant be using or suspected of using in order to pose a threat of serious physical injury to the officer or others? A gun satisfies the test, see supra, and so does a knife. Untalan v. City of Lorain, 430 F.3d 312 (6th Cir. 2005). What other implements qualify? Smith v. Cupp, 430 F.3d 766 (6th Cir. 2005) (stolen police car, if aimed at officer). Can conduct alone, even absent the existence of a weapon, establish that a person presents a sufficient threat? See Blossom v. Yarbrough, 429 F.3d 963 (10th Cir. 2005) (loud and boisterous threats to take officer's gun and use it on him is a sufficient threat, even discounting any evidence that victim actually lunged for the knife).

(c) Starting from the opposite end of the analytical spectrum, are there some circumstances where courts can say with assurance that there is no threat of harm to the officer or others? See Ciminillo v. Streicher, 434 F.3d 461 (6th Cir. 2006) (approaching officer with hands up in the "surrender position"); Russo v. City of Cincinnati, 953 F.2d 1036 (6th Cir.1992) (police shoot schizophrenic several minutes after he has dropped his knife). Shooting an unarmed fleeing suspect in the back may be an easier case, see Whitfield v. Melendez–Rivera, 431 F.3d 1 (1st Cir. 2005) (jury verdict for plaintiff), but is the case still easy if the suspect remains armed while fleeing? See Troupe v. Sarasota County, 419 F.3d 1160 (11th Cir. 2005) (victim tries to flee while reportedly armed and is shot after he passes SWAT team).

5. Judging by the dissent's arguments, one might think that the *Garner* standard over-protects suspects. Might it actually be under-protective? Might it paradoxically encourage police to use greater force? Should *Garner*'s test be altered?

(a) Consider that the only evidence contrary to the officer's version of events may be that of the shooting victim. Does this encourage officers to shoot to kill or to cover up their shootings? Cf. Blossom v. Yarbrough, 429 F.3d 963, 968–69 (10th Cir. 2005) (concurring opinion) (majority rejected dead man's mother's argument for her son because she had no first-hand knowledge, but only remaining witness was an "interested" party—the shooter). Does *Garner* authorize shootings when there is no need because it permits deadly force to be used based upon a mere threat and even when a suspect will be captured soon anyway? See Forrett v. Richardson, 112 F.3d 416 (9th Cir.1997) ("suspect need not be armed or pose an immediate threat to the officers or others at the time of the shooting" to permit use of deadly force against him).

(b) Should an officer be authorized to shoot under *Garner* where his own conduct has precipitated or provoked the victim's threatening reaction? In Blossom v. Yarbrough, 429 F.3d 963 (10th Cir. 2005), the Court stated that it must consider "whether the officer's own reckless or deliberate conduct during the seizure unreasonably created the need to use such force," though it noted that merely negligent conduct by the officer is irrelevant. What is reckless precipitating conduct? See Sevier v. City of Lawrence, 60 F.3d 695 (10th Cir. 1995) (perhaps "confronting [victim] in the manner that they did after knowing that he was armed and distraught over problems he was having with his girlfriend"); Estate of Starks v. Enyart, 5 F.3d 230 (7th Cir.1993) (officer who steps in front of unarmed suspect's fleeing car cannot argue that he is protecting himself from victim's threat of harm). Do you agree?

6. What role did common law play in the *Garner* majority's decision? In Whirl v. Kern, supra, it was assumed that common law standards would be more protective (of plaintiffs) than those of constitutional law, but does not *Garner*'s result show that this is sometimes untrue? Is *Garner* the definitive rejection of *Whirl*'s theory that § 1983 incorporates by reference state-tort standards of care?

GRAHAM v. CONNOR

Supreme Court of the United States, 1989.
490 U.S. 386, 109 S.Ct. 1865, 104 L.Ed.2d 443.

CHIEF JUSTICE REHNQUIST delivered the opinion of the Court.

This case requires us to decide what constitutional standard governs a free citizen's claim that law enforcement officials used excessive force in the course of making an arrest, investigatory stop, or other "seizure" of his person. We hold that such claims are properly analyzed under the Fourth Amendment's "objective reasonableness" standard, rather than under a substantive due process standard.

* * * On November 12, 1984, Graham, a diabetic, felt the onset of an insulin reaction. [His hurried exit from a convenience store led suspicious officers to follow him and make an investigative stop. When Graham subsequently suffered a "sugar reaction" and started acting strangely, officers cuffed him, thinking him to be drunk. They subsequently threw him against a police car, breaking his foot and injuring his wrists, forehead, and shoulders. They soon releasing him when others officers reported that nothing had occurred at the convenience store. Graham subsequently filed this suit under § 1983. A trial court's directed judgment for defendants was affirmed on appeal.]

Fifteen years ago, in Johnson v. Glick, 481 F.2d 1028 (CA2), cert. denied, 414 U.S. 1033, 94 S.Ct. 462, 38 L.Ed.2d 324 (1973), the Court of Appeals for the Second Circuit addressed a § 1983 damages claim filed by a pretrial detainee who claimed that a guard had assaulted him without justification. In evaluating the detainee's claim, Judge Friendly applied neither the Fourth Amendment nor the Eighth, the two most textually obvious sources of constitutional protection against physically abusive governmental conduct. Instead, he looked to "substantive due process," holding that "quite apart from any 'specific' of the Bill of Rights, application of undue force by law enforcement officers deprives a suspect of liberty without due process of law." 481 F.2d, at 1032. * * * Judge Friendly went on to set forth four factors to guide courts in determining "whether the constitutional line has been crossed" by a particular use of force—the same four factors relied upon by the courts below in this case. [These four factors were the following: "(1) the need for the application of force; (2) the relationship between that need and the amount of force that was used; (3) the extent of the injury inflicted; and (4) [w]hether the force was applied in a good faith effort to maintain and restore discipline or maliciously and sadistically for the very purpose of causing harm" (internal quotations omitted).]

[Lower courts have followed Judge Friendly's generic approach to Due Process] without considering whether the particular application of force might implicate a more specific constitutional right governed by a different standard. Indeed, many courts have seemed to assume, as did the courts below in this case, that there is a generic "right" to be free from excessive force, grounded not in any particular constitutional provision but rather in "basic principles of § 1983 jurisprudence."

We reject this notion that all excessive force claims brought under § 1983 are governed by a single generic standard. As we have said many times, § 1983 "is not itself a source of substantive rights," but merely provides "a method for vindicating federal rights elsewhere conferred." Baker v. McCollan, 443 U.S. 137, 144, n. 3, 99 S.Ct. 2689, 2694, n. 3, 61 L.Ed.2d 433 (1979). In addressing an excessive force claim brought under § 1983, analysis begins by identifying the specific constitutional right allegedly infringed by the challenged application of force. See id., at 140, 99 S.Ct., at 2692 ("The first inquiry in any § 1983 suit" is "to isolate the precise constitutional violation with which [the defendant] is charged"). In most instances, that will be either the Fourth Amendment's prohibition against unreasonable seizures of the person, or the Eighth Amendment's ban on cruel and unusual punishments, which are the two primary sources of constitutional protection against physically abusive governmental conduct. The validity of the claim must then be judged by reference to the specific constitutional standard which governs that right, rather than to some generalized "excessive force" standard. See Tennessee v. Garner; Whitley v. Albers.

Where, as here, the excessive force claim arises in the context of an arrest or investigatory stop of a free citizen, it is most properly characterized as one invoking the protections of the Fourth Amendment, which guarantees citizens the right "to be secure in their persons . . . against unreasonable . . . seizures" of the person. This much is clear from our decision in Tennessee v. Garner. * * * Today we make explicit what was implicit in Garner's analysis, and hold that all claims that law enforcement officers have used excessive force—deadly or not—in the course of an arrest, investigatory stop, or other "seizure" of a free citizen should be analyzed under the Fourth Amendment and its "reasonableness" standard, rather than under a "substantive due process" approach. Because the Fourth Amendment provides an explicit textual source of constitutional protection against this sort of physically intrusive governmental conduct, that Amendment, not the more generalized notion of "substantive due process," must be the guide for analyzing these claims.[10]

---

10. A "seizure" triggering the Fourth Amendment's protections occurs only when government actors have, "by means of physical force or show of authority, . . . in some way restrained the liberty of a citizen," Terry v. Ohio, 392 U.S. 1, 19, n. 16, 88 S.Ct. 1868, 1879, n. 16, 20 L.Ed.2d 889 (1968).

Our cases have not resolved the question whether the Fourth Amendment continues to provide individuals with protection against the deliberate use of excessive physical force beyond the point at which arrest ends and pretrial detention begins, and we do not attempt to answer that question today. It is clear, however, that the Due Process Clause protects a pretrial detainee from the use of excessive force that amounts to punishment. See Bell v. Wolfish, 441 U.S. 520, 535–539, 99 S.Ct. 1861, 1871–1874, 60 L.Ed.2d 447 (1979). After conviction, the Eighth Amendment "serves as the primary source of substantive protection . . . in cases . . . where the deliberate use of force is challenged as excessive and unjustified." Whitley v. Albers. Any protection that "substantive due process" affords convicted prisoners against excessive force is, we have held, at best redundant of that provided by the Eighth Amendment. Ibid.

Determining whether the force used to effect a particular seizure is "reasonable" under the Fourth Amendment requires a careful balancing of " 'the nature and quality of the intrusion on the individual's Fourth Amendment interests' " against the countervailing governmental interests at stake. [Tennessee v. Garner.] Our Fourth Amendment jurisprudence has long recognized that the right to make an arrest or investigatory stop necessarily carries with it the right to use some degree of physical coercion or threat thereof to effect it. See Terry v. Ohio, 392 U.S., at 22–27, 88 S.Ct., at 1880–1883. Because "[t]he test of reasonableness under the Fourth Amendment is not capable of precise definition or mechanical application," however, its proper application requires careful attention to the facts and circumstances of each particular case, including the severity of the crime at issue, whether the suspect poses an immediate threat to the safety of the officers or others, and whether he is actively resisting arrest or attempting to evade arrest by flight. The "reasonableness" of a particular use of force must be judged from the perspective of a reasonable officer on the scene, rather than with the 20/20 vision of hindsight. See Terry v. Ohio. The Fourth Amendment is not violated by an arrest based on probable cause, even though the wrong person is arrested, Hill v. California, 401 U.S. 797, 91 S.Ct. 1106, 28 L.Ed.2d 484 (1971), nor by the mistaken execution of a valid search warrant on the wrong premises, Maryland v. Garrison, 480 U.S. 79, 107 S.Ct. 1013, 94 L.Ed.2d 72 (1987). With respect to a claim of excessive force, the same standard of reasonableness at the moment applies: "Not every push or shove, even if it may later seem unnecessary in the peace of a judge's chambers," Johnson v. Glick, violates the Fourth Amendment. The calculus of reasonableness must embody allowance for the fact that police officers are often forced to make split-second judgments—in circumstances that are tense, uncertain, and rapidly evolving—about the amount of force that is necessary in a particular situation.

As in other Fourth Amendment contexts, however, the "reasonableness" inquiry in an excessive force case is an objective one: the question is whether the officers' actions are "objectively reasonable" in light of the facts and circumstances confronting them, without regard to their underlying intent or motivation. See Scott v. United States, 436 U.S. 128, 137–139, 98 S.Ct. 1717, 1723–1724, 56 L.Ed.2d 168 (1978). An officer's evil intentions will not make a Fourth Amendment violation out of an objectively reasonable use of force; nor will an officer's good intentions make an objectively unreasonable use of force constitutional.

Because petitioner's excessive force claim is one arising under the Fourth Amendment, the Court of Appeals erred in analyzing it under the four-part Johnson v. Glick test. That test, which requires consideration of whether the individual officers acted in "good faith" or "maliciously and sadistically for the very purpose of causing harm," is incompatible with a proper Fourth Amendment analysis. We do not agree with the Court of Appeals' * * * conclusion that because the subjective motivations of the individual officers are of central importance in deciding whether force used against a convicted prisoner violates the Eighth Amendment, see Whitley v. Albers,[11] [they are also relevant] in deciding whether force used against a suspect or arrestee violates the Fourth Amendment. Differing standards under the Fourth and Eighth Amendments are hardly surprising: the terms "cruel" and "punishment" clearly suggest some inquiry into subjective state of mind, whereas the term "unreasonable" does not. Moreover, the less protective Eighth Amendment standard applies "only after the State has complied with the constitutional guarantees traditionally associated with criminal prosecutions." Ingraham v. Wright, 430 U.S. 651, 671, n. 40, 97 S.Ct. 1401, 1412, n. 40, 51 L.Ed.2d 711 (1977). The Fourth Amendment inquiry is one of "objective reasonableness" under the circumstances, and subjective concepts like "malice" and "sadism" have no proper place in that inquiry.[12]

Because the Court of Appeals reviewed the District Court's ruling on the motion for directed verdict under an erroneous view of the governing substantive law, its judgment must be vacated and the case remanded to that court for reconsideration of that issue under the proper Fourth Amendment standard.

It is so ordered. [Concurring opinion omitted.]

NOTE ON POLICE MISCONDUCT LITIGATION UNDER THE FOURTH AMENDMENT

1. A major theme of Justice Rehnquist's opinion in *Graham* appears to be the need to analyze § 1983 claims by reference not only to constitutional norms, recall Daniels v. Williams, section B.1 of this Chapter, supra, but by reference to the most specific applicable constitutional norm—a theme also found in Justice O'Connor's majority opinion in Whitley v. Albers, section B2 of this Chapter, supra.[1] When Justice Rehnquist distinguishes between the

---

11. In *Whitley*, we addressed a § 1983 claim brought by a convicted prisoner, who claimed that prison officials had violated his Eighth Amendment rights by shooting him in the knee during a prison riot. We [held that] when prison officials use physical force against an inmate "to restore order in the face of a prison disturbance, ... the question whether the measure taken inflicted unnecessary and wanton pain ... ultimately turns on 'whether the force was applied in a good faith effort to maintain or restore discipline or maliciously and sadistically for the very purpose of causing harm,'" quoting Johnson v. Glick. We also suggested that the other prongs of the Johnson v. Glick test might be useful in analyzing excessive force claims brought under the Eighth Amendment. But we made clear that this was so not because Judge Friendly's four-part test is some talismanic formula generally applicable to all excessive force claims, but because its four factors help to focus the central inquiry in the Eighth Amendment context, which is whether the particular use of force amounts to the "unnecessary and wanton infliction of pain." Our endorsement of the Johnson v. Glick test in *Whitley* thus had no implications beyond the Eighth Amendment context.

12. Of course, in assessing the credibility of an officer's account of the circumstances that prompted the use of force, a fact-finder may consider, along with other factors, evidence that the officer may have harbored ill-will toward the citizen. See Scott v. United States, 436 U.S. 128, 139, n. 13, 98 S.Ct. 1717, 56 L.Ed.2d 168 (1978). * * *

1. In *Whitley* the plaintiff had used § 1983 to invoke both his Eighth Amendment and Substantive Due Process rights. After ruling against him on the specific Amendment, the Court quickly rejected the backup claim as redundant: "We think the Eighth Amendment, which is specifically concerned with the unnecessary and wanton infliction of pain in penal institutions, serves as the primary source of substantive protection to convicted prisoners in cases such as this one, where the deliberate use of force is challenged as excessive and unjustified." 475 U.S. at 327, 106 S.Ct. at 1078.

"substantive due process right" and the Fourth Amendment right, he apparently means to distinguish between non-textual substantive due process rights (such as that found in Johnson v. Glick) and incorporated due process rights (such as the Fourth Amendment).[2] Justice Rehnquist's majority prefers the more specific text-based standard.

(a) In Roe v. Wade, 410 U.S. 113, 93 S.Ct. 705, 35 L.Ed.2d 147 (1973), Justice Rehnquist dissented from the Court's recognition of an abortion right as a part of the general right to privacy. In doing so he echoed a theme seen in *Graham*, arguing that "the 'privacy' that the Court finds here is a distant relative of the freedom from searches and seizures protected by the Fourth Amendment" and the right created "apparently completely unknown to the drafters" of the Due Process Clause. Is the majority's opinion in *Graham* a continuation of the constitutional disagreement over the power of the Supreme Court to create non-textual constitutional rights? How does the approach of tying § 1983 cases to specific textual provisions serve Rehnquist's side of that argument?

(b) Note that Justice Rehnquist's majority opinion states only that "in most instances" specific amendments will govern police misconduct cases and that the Fourth and Eighth Amendments are only the "primary" sources of standards in such cases. Cf. footnote 1 supra in this Note, quoting Whitley v. Albers. Why does Justice Rehnquist leave himself some wiggle room? Is he opposed to all non-textual constitutional rights, or does he just oppose what he views as the activist creation of too many rights? Cf. Cruzan v. Director, Missouri Dept. of Health, 497 U.S. 261, 110 S.Ct. 2841, 111 L.Ed.2d 224 (1990) (recognizing a non-textual right to refuse medical treatment) (per Rehnquist, J.).

(c) Apart from constitutional technique, does Justice Rehnquist prefer the Fourth Amendment because its rules are more pro-defendant? Do the *Johnson v. Glick* factors favor plaintiffs? Compare Martin v. Gentile, 849 F.2d 863, 868 & n. 6 (4th Cir.1988) (Fourth Amendment standard more favorable to plaintiff), with Martin v. Malhoyt, 830 F.2d 237 (D.C.Cir.1987) (under Fourth Amendment objective test, evidence of malice—helpful to defendant under general Due Process—cannot be considered).

2. The *Graham* majority calls its standard an "objective" one, apparently in comparison to the element in *Johnson v. Glick* that focuses on the subjective intent of the officer. Consider the factors on the Court's list of relevant issues in *Graham*. They appear to be somewhat similar to the factors cited in *Johnson v. Glick*, excluding the factor of malice. Do the factors in *Graham* point to only one essential question—whether there was an objective need to use force? Cf. United States v. Ramirez, 523 U.S. 65, 118 S.Ct. 992, 140 L.Ed.2d 191 (1998) (per Rehnquist, C.J.: "Excessive or unnecessary destruction of property in the course of a search may violate the Fourth Amendment, even though the entry itself is lawful"). If need and proportion-

---

2. Of course, the Fourth Amendment applies to the states only by virtue of its selective incorporation into the Fourteenth Amendment, as noted in Monroe v. Pape, Chapter 1A, supra. To that extent, both the right recognized in Johnson v. Glick and the Fourth Amendment right are "substantive due process rights." The relevant difference thus appears to be between text-based incorporated due process rights (such as what the majority calls "Fourth Amendment" rights) and non-textual rights (called "substantive Due Process" rights in the majority opinion).

ality of response are the keys, would it not be more accurate to say that officers are permitted by *Graham* to use a little more than proportionate force, i.e., equal counter-force plus sufficiently more to exercise control?

(a) The rejection of a "subjective" approach also suggests that the officer alone does not decide the issue of whether the force used was proportional (or proportional-plus zone). Who is an objectively reasonable officer—a "reasonable person" from negligence law who is dressed in a uniform? Alternatively, should expert testimony be accepted on the issue of how much force a reasonable police officer would have used under the circumstances? See Abdullahi v. City of Madison, 423 F.3d 763 (7th Cir. 2005) (expert testimony concerning standard police practices relevant); Carter v. Fenner, 136 F.3d 1000 (5th Cir.1998) (expert testifies as to violent proclivities of inebriated person and need for force). Given that professionally trained judges often see the work of police officers, should judges decide the ultimate issue of whether excessive force was used? See Mellott v. Heemer, 161 F.3d 117 (3d Cir.1998) (panel splits over particular facts; majority holds that placing gun at person's head, accompanied by much pushing and threats of death, is not unreasonable and case may not go to jury).

(b) Would it be fair to say that the *Graham* standard is not "subjective" in the sense it avoids inquiry into the officer's subjective intent, but is "subjective" in the sense that it leaves much leeway to a judge or jury hearing in particular case? Compare Guite v. Wright, 147 F.3d 747 (8th Cir.1998) (whether grabbing arm and shoving amounted to reasonable force in light of slight need is for the jury), with Boyd v. Benton County, 374 F.3d 773 (9th Cir. 2004) (police use of "flash-bang device," or stun grenade, is unreasonably excessive use of force when used against apartment where some residents are not suspects).

3.   Although *Graham* was remanded for determination on the merits, the Supreme Court has subsequently decided several cases that establish boundaries for the reasonable use of force by police officers. In **Muehler v. Mena**, 544 U.S. 93, 125 S.Ct. 1465, 161 L.Ed.2d 299 (2005), for example, the Supreme Court rejected an excessive force claim by a woman held in handcuffs for two hours while her home was searched, overturning a jury verdict for the plaintiff. The Court observed that "governmental interests in not only detaining, but using handcuffs, are at their maximum when, as here, a warrant authorizes a search for weapons and a wanted gang member resides on the premises." Similarly, in **Los Angeles County v. Rettele**, 550 U.S. 609, 127 S.Ct. 1989, 167 L.Ed.2d 974 (2007), the Court overruled a lower court finding that police acted unreasonably in detaining a Caucasian couple nude in their bedroom while they searched for an African–American suspect in the same house. The Court observed that the persons briefly detained might have been concealing weapons in their bed and that the officers reasonably needed time to secure the premises to avoid such a danger. That the officers had searched the wrong house was deemed irrelevant because probable cause does not require certainty: "the innocent," therefore, must "unfortunately bear the cost" of "resulting frustration, embarrassment, and humiliation."

(a) The handcuffing in *Mena* endured for 2–3 hours, a fact that apparently influenced the jury, but the Court pointed out that it did not last any longer than the search itself. In *Rettele* the nude detention lasted no longer than the time necessary to secure the bedroom. Are these "objective" standards? But is any search that is time-limited and based on probable cause constitutional after *Rettele*, regardless of the other circumstances? The Court has also rejected that view. In **Safford v. Redding**, ___ U.S. ___, 129 S.Ct. 2633, 174 L.Ed.2d 354 (2009), involving school searches rather than police misconduct, the Court ruled that a principal's reasonable suspicion that student was carrying contraband made search of backpack reasonable, but not search of underwear where principal claimed she could have secreted drugs. If time is irrelevant in *Safford*, is there an "objective" line beyond which a search or seizure may not reasonably pass? See Mlodzinski v. Lewis, 648 F.3d 24, 2011 WL 2150741 (1st Cir. 2011) (holding 15–year–old daughter in handcuffs for half hour after suspect, her father, was removed from premises, and aiming assault rifle at her head, were unreasonable acts of force).

(b) Does *Graham* inherently leave lower courts to their own devices in considering the myriad range of other potential interactions between citizens and police? In the infamous Rodney King case, cf. United States v. Koon, 833 F.Supp. 769 (C.D.Cal.1993) (sentencing determination disclosing facts constituting denial of King's rights in criminal prosecution under § 242, the criminal counterpart to § 1983), the trial judge found that King had violated traffic laws, led police on a wild chase, appeared inebriated and refused to submit to an order to remain prone after arrest, and actively resisted arrest. The police responded with a series of measures of escalating force, including nightsticks and tasers. The trial judge found that the use of force was "initially" constitutional but that somewhere along the course of "ambiguous" events, the use of force became unconstitutionally excessive. The court claimed to find the well-known videotape of the event somewhat unpersuasive because it did not show all events. Compare Moore v. Novak, 146 F.3d 531 (8th Cir.1998) (judgment for police who arrest inebriated citizen then, after resistance to arrest, strike him with batons and shoot him with "stun gun"; surveillance videotape of the event was mysteriously lost), with Lamont v. New Jersey, 637 F.3d 177 (3d. Cir. 2011) (initial conduct was reasonable but continuing violence may have been unreasonable; remanded). See also Untalan v. City of Lorain, 430 F.3d 312 (6th Cir. 2005) (long standoff with several encounters resulting in final shooting).[3]

4. The *Graham* majority takes special care to distinguish Eighth Amendment claims, in which an intent inquiry is relevant, from Fourth Amendment claims of excessive force, which must be measured by an objective standard. What is the dividing line between the two? Justice Rehnquist in *Graham* states that the Fourth Amendment applies to a "free citizen," even ones briefly handcuffed and detained as Graham was, and the Eighth Amendment as developed in *Whitley* applies only to persons convicted of crimes.

---

3. See also Haugen v. Brosseau, 351 F.3d 372, 375 (9th Cir. 2003) (Tallman, J., dissenting from rehearing en banc) (escalating force is reasonable response and courts should not look at end conduct only), rev'd on other grounds, 543 U.S. 194, 125 S.Ct. 596, 160 L.Ed.2d 583 (2004) (discussed in Chapter 1D.2 infra).

(a) What statuses exist between these two situations? Is a citizen who is taken into custody and beaten in the back seat of the police cruiser a "free citizen"? Is a person detained at the police station a "free citizen"? See Taylor v. McDuffie, 155 F.3d 479 (4th Cir.1998) (collecting cases from other circuits). Are there any policy considerations that suggest how the line should be drawn? What line should be drawn between Fourth Amendment violations and other unconstitutional conduct by police that is an improper use of force? See Rogers v. City of Little Rock, 152 F.3d 790 (8th Cir.1998) (officer follows woman home and rapes her).

(b) Note that in *Graham*'s footnote 12 the Court permits evidence of the officer's subjective state-of-mind to be used as proof of the objective need for force. Recall that in Farmer v. Brennan, section B.2 of this Chapter, supra, the Court permitted objective evidence to be used as inferential proof of a prison guard's subjective state of mind. Is there really a difference in Fourth and Eighth Amendment cases? Compare Hudson v. McMillian, 503 U.S. 1, 112 S.Ct. 995, 117 L.Ed.2d 156 (1992) (*Whitley*'s "deliberate indifference" standard applies to all use-of-force claims in prison; prisoner need not prove serious injury in order to recover), with Petta v. Rivera, 143 F.3d 895 (5th Cir.1998) (*Hudson*'s decision not to require proof of serious injury for Eighth Amendment claims should also apply to Fourth Amendment claims of excessive force).

5.   Though the Supreme Court referred to its standard in *Graham* as an "objective" one, that may be misleading in that it covers only half of Fourth Amendment analysis. While the measure of "reasonableness" under the Fourth Amendment is objective, the question of whether there has been a "seizure" so as to activate the reasonableness inquiry appears to be a subjective one. In **Brower v. Inyo County**, 489 U.S. 593, 109 S.Ct. 1378, 103 L.Ed.2d 628 (1989), police placed an 18–wheel tractor-trailer astride both lanes of a two-lane highway in order to block the path of a person who had led police on a 20–mile high-speed chase in a stolen car. The driver subsequently died from crashing into the obstacle. Justice Scalia's opinion for the Court held that a seizure had occurred: "Violation of the Fourth Amendment requires an intentional acquisition of physical control. A seizure occurs even when an unintended person or thing is the object of the detention or taking, but the detention or taking itself must be willful." On the other hand, in **California v. Hodari D.**, 499 U.S. 621, 111 S.Ct. 1547, 113 L.Ed.2d 690 (1991), the Court ruled that no seizure occurred from the mere fact of pursuit (for seizure "requires either physical force ... or, where that is absent, submission to the assertion of authority"), at least where the defendant had eluded the officer's grasp at the time he threw away contraband. Thus a seizure appears to occur only when the officer has a subjective desire to acquire physical control and control has been established.[4]

(a) In **County of Sacramento v. Lewis**, Chapter 1B.4 infra, the Court clarified the interaction between *Brower* and *Hodari* in a case involving a high-speed motorcycle chase in which the cyclist lost control and the officer ran over and killed the cyclist's passenger. *Brower* had suggested that the

---

4. See Ohio v. Robinette, 519 U.S. 33, 117 S.Ct. 417, 136 L.Ed.2d 347 (1996) (Fourth Amendment does not require per se rule that person be advised that he is "free to go" when he is requested to consent voluntarily to a police search).

officer's intent to seize one person transferred to third parties inadvertently seized, but *Sacramento* read *Hodari* to preclude a finding of seizure when there had only been a pursuit. That the officer had in fact taken control of the passenger by killing him, cf. Tennessee v. Garner, was deemed irrelevant because the hitting was an unintended accident. Has a seizure occurred when two teams of police chase a fleeing suspect on foot, and the suspect jumps a fence onto an expressway—where he is struck and killed by a car? See Cameron v. City of Pontiac, 813 F.2d 782 (6th Cir.1987) (no). Would the result in these cases be different if the police more actively directed the suspect toward a known danger, as in *Brower*, such as by shooting at him until he jumps off a bridge?

(b) Assume that the suspect in *Brower* had ricocheted off the tractor-trailer and struck an innocent bystander. Would the bystander have been "seized" by the police? See Apodaca v. Rio Arriba County Sheriff's Dept., 905 F.2d 1445 (10th Cir.1990). If the police shoot a fleeing felon in violation of *Garner* and the felon crashes his car into an innocent bystander, has the bystander been "seized"? If they shoot into a car hitting one person, have the other persons been seized too? See Vaughan v. Cox, 343 F.3d 1323 (11th Cir. 2003) (yes, even when the other person is the driver who continues to flee). Do "third parties" have Fourth Amendment rights?

(c) Is "acquisition of physical control" limited to literal physical touchings? In **Michigan Dep't of State Police v. Sitz**, 496 U.S. 444, 110 S.Ct. 2481, 110 L.Ed.2d 412 (1990), the Court held that a "sobriety checkpoint" constituted a seizure because of the intent to stop and the intrusiveness of the effectuated stop, though on the facts the seizure was found reasonable. When is the degree of control sufficient to amount to a seizure? See Soldal v. Cook County, 506 U.S. 56, 113 S.Ct. 538, 121 L.Ed.2d 450 (1992) ("meaningful interference" test for seizure; towing away of mobile home is a seizure).[5] Does the same test for seizure apply to persons and property? Do these cases suggest that a shooting where the suspect continues to elude police may nevertheless be a seizure because police have begun to exercise some degree of control over the fleeing person? Compare Brooks v. Gaenzle, 614 F.3d 1213 (10th Cir. 2010) (no seizure when suspect continues to flee), with Carr v. Tatangelo, 338 F.3d 1259 (11th Cir. 2003) (seizure even when flight occurs). Conversely, might some use of guns less than actual shooting might be considered seizures? See Mellott v. Heemer, 161 F.3d 117 (3d Cir.1998) (pointing gun at suspect's head to threaten him).

6. When the Supreme Court directs appellate courts away from a previous approach and mandates a new one, as in *Garner* and *Graham,* should the new standard be retroactively applied to all pending cases? Compare Mitchell v. City of Sapulpa, 857 F.2d 713 (10th Cir.1988) (new Fourth Amendment standards "certainly" not retroactive) (collecting cases), with Davis v. Little, 851 F.2d 605, 608–11 (2d Cir.1988) (new Fourth Amendment standards "clearly" retroactive) (discussing standards and collecting cases).

---

5. In United States v. Mendenhall, 446 U.S. 544, 554, 100 S.Ct. 1870, 64 L.Ed.2d 497 (1980), the Court said that "a person has been 'seized' within the meaning of the Fourth Amendment only if, in view of all of the circumstances surrounding the incident, a reasonable person would have believed that he was not free to leave."

SCOTT v. HARRIS

Supreme Court of the United States, 2007
550 U.S. 372, 127 S.Ct. 1769, 167 L.Ed.2d 686

JUSTICE SCALIA delivered the opinion of the Court.

[Police detected Harris speeding and pursued him to give him a ticket. Finally, after a ten-mile chase, Deputy Scott attempted to bump Harris's vehicle to bring him to a halt. The bump caused Harris to lose control, and he suffered substantial injuries that left him a quadriplegic. Harris thereafter sued Scott under 1983, claiming that the bump and subsequent crash constituted an unreasonable seizure. The lower courts ruled that the claim could go to trial on the view that the plaintiff's version of the facts, if proved, constituted "deadly use of force" when there was no danger of threat to others or the officer. Yet, because the record contains a videotape showing the high-speed nature of the chase, we need not restrict ourselves to plaintiff's facts: we must take these recorded facts as the starting point for determining whether a claim can be maintained.]

The videotape tells quite a different story [from the plaintiff's claim that he presented no threat to others]. There we see respondent's vehicle racing down narrow, two-lane roads in the dead of night at speeds that are shockingly fast. We see it swerve around more than a dozen other cars, cross the double-yellow line, and force cars traveling in both directions to their respective shoulders to avoid being hit. We see it run multiple red lights and travel for considerable periods of time in the occasional center left-turn-only lane, chased by numerous police cars forced to engage in the same hazardous maneuvers just to keep up. Far from being the cautious and controlled driver the lower court depicts [based on plaintiff's mere complaint], what we see on the video more closely resembles a Hollywood-style car chase of the most frightening sort, placing police officers and innocent bystanders alike at great risk of serious injury.[6]

* * *

Respondent urges us to analyze this case as we analyzed *Garner*. We must first decide, he says, whether the actions Scott took constituted "deadly force." (He defines "deadly force" as "any use of force which creates a substantial likelihood of causing death or serious bodily injury.") If so, respondent claims that Garner prescribes certain preconditions that must be met before Scott's actions can survive Fourth Amendment scrutiny: (1) The suspect must have posed an immediate threat of serious physical harm to the officer or others; (2) deadly force must have been necessary to prevent escape;[9] and (3) where feasible, the officer must have

---

6. This is not to say that each and every factual statement made by the Court of Appeals is inaccurate. For example, the videotape validates the court's statement that when Scott rammed respondent's vehicle it was not threatening any other vehicles or pedestrians. (Undoubtedly Scott *waited* for the road to be clear before executing his maneuver.)

9. Respondent, like the Court of Appeals, defines this second precondition as " 'necessary to prevent escape,' " But that quote from Garner is taken out of context. The necessity described in

given the suspect some warning. Since these Garner preconditions for using deadly force were not met in this case, [claims respondent,] Scott's actions were per se unreasonable.

Respondent's argument falters at its first step; *Garner* did not establish a magical on/off switch that triggers rigid preconditions whenever an officer's actions constitute "deadly force." *Garner* was simply an application of the Fourth Amendment's "reasonableness" test to the use of a particular type of force in a particular situation. *Garner* held that it was unreasonable to kill a "young, slight, and unarmed" burglary suspect by shooting him "in the back of the head" while he was running away on foot, and when the officer "could not reasonably have believed that [the suspect] . . . posed any threat," and "never attempted to justify his actions on any basis other than the need to prevent an escape." Whatever *Garner* said about the factors that *might have* justified shooting the suspect in that case, such "preconditions" have scant applicability to this case, which has vastly different facts. "*Garner* had nothing to do with one car striking another or even with car chases in general. A police car's bumping a fleeing car is, in fact, not much like a policeman's shooting a gun so as to hit a person." Adams v. St. Lucie County Sheriff's Dept., 962 F.2d 1563, 1577 (C.A.11 1992) (Edmondson, J., dissenting), adopted by 998 F.2d 923 (C.A.11 1993) (en banc) (per curiam). Nor is the threat posed by the flight on foot of an unarmed suspect even remotely comparable to the extreme danger to human life posed by respondent in this case. Although respondent's attempt to craft an easy-to-apply legal test in the Fourth Amendment context is admirable, in the end we must still slosh our way through the factbound morass of "reasonableness." Whether or not Scott's actions constituted application of "deadly force," all that matters is whether Scott's actions were reasonable.

In determining the reasonableness of the manner in which a seizure is effected, "[w]e must balance the nature and quality of the intrusion on the individual's Fourth Amendment interests against the importance of the governmental interests alleged to justify the intrusion." United States v. Place, 462 U.S. 696 (1983). Scott defends his actions by pointing to the paramount governmental interest in ensuring public safety, and respondent nowhere suggests this was not the purpose motivating Scott's behavior. Thus, in judging whether Scott's actions were reasonable, we must consider the risk of bodily harm that Scott's actions posed to respondent in light of the threat to the public that Scott was trying to eliminate. Although there is no obvious way to quantify the risks on either side, it is clear from the videotape that respondent posed an actual and imminent

---

Garner was, in fact, the need to prevent "serious physical harm, either to the officer or to others." By way of example only, Garner hypothesized that deadly force may be used "if necessary to prevent escape" when the suspect is known to have "committed a crime involving the infliction or threatened infliction of serious physical harm," so that his mere being at large poses an inherent danger to society. Respondent did not pose that type of inherent threat to society, since (prior to the car chase) he had committed only a minor traffic offense and, as far as the police were aware, had no prior criminal record. But in this case, unlike in Garner, it was respondent's flight itself (by means of a speeding automobile) that posed the threat of "serious physical harm . . . to others."

threat to the lives of any pedestrians who might have been present, to other civilian motorists, and to the officers involved in the chase. It is equally clear that Scott's actions posed a high likelihood of serious injury or death to respondent—though not the near *certainty* of death posed by, say, shooting a fleeing felon in the back of the head, or pulling alongside a fleeing motorist's car and shooting the motorist. So how does a court go about weighing the perhaps lesser probability of injuring or killing numerous bystanders against the perhaps larger probability of injuring or killing a single person? We think it appropriate in this process to take into account not only the number of lives at risk, but also their relative culpability. It was respondent, after all, who intentionally placed himself and the public in danger by unlawfully engaging in the reckless, high-speed flight that ultimately produced the choice between two evils that Scott confronted. Multiple police cars, with blue lights flashing and sirens blaring, had been chasing respondent for nearly 10 miles, but he ignored their warning to stop. By contrast, those who might have been harmed had Scott not taken the action he did were entirely innocent. We have little difficulty in concluding it was reasonable for Scott to take the action that he did.

But wait, says respondent: Couldn't the innocent public equally have been protected, and the tragic accident entirely avoided, if the police had simply ceased their pursuit? We think the police need not have taken that chance and hoped for the best. Whereas Scott's action—ramming respondent off the road—was *certain* to eliminate the risk that respondent posed to the public, ceasing pursuit was not. First of all, there would have been no way to convey convincingly to respondent that the chase was off, and that he was free to go. Had respondent looked in his rearview mirror and seen the police cars deactivate their flashing lights and turn around, he would have had no idea whether they were truly letting him get away, or simply devising a new strategy for capture. * * * Given such uncertainty, respondent might have been just as likely to respond by continuing to drive recklessly as by slowing down and wiping his brow.

Second, we are loath to lay down a rule requiring the police to allow fleeing suspects to get away whenever they drive *so recklessly* that they put other people's lives in danger. It is obvious the perverse incentives such a rule would create: Every fleeing motorist would know that escape is within his grasp, if only he accelerates to 90 miles per hour, crosses the double-yellow line a few times, and runs a few red lights. The Constitution assuredly does not impose this invitation to impunity-earned-by-recklessness. Instead, we lay down a more sensible rule: A police officer's attempt to terminate a dangerous high-speed car chase that threatens the lives of innocent bystanders does not violate the Fourth Amendment, even when it places the fleeing motorist at risk of serious injury or death.

[Reversed.] [Concurring opinions omitted.]

JUSTICE STEVENS, dissenting.

* * * Whether a person's actions have risen to a level warranting deadly force is a question of fact best reserved for a jury. * * *

NOTE ON THE COURT'S [NEW?] UNIFIED APPROACH
TO FOURTH AMENDMENT CASES

1. As discussed in the previous Notes in this subsection, most lower courts had after *Garner* and *Graham* assumed that there were two contextual standards applied to § 1983 cases presenting Fourth Amendment claims—one for uses of "deadly force," with its per se test regarding probable cause to believe the suspect presented a danger to the officer or others, and another for uses of more ordinary force, with its test regarding proportionality-plus. The *Scott* case abjures that bifurcation. It emphasizes that all Fourth Amendment claims are subject to the same reasonableness test that looks at the totality of the circumstances.

(a) Or does it? The Court rejects the idea that "deadly force" cases involve a "per se" test that operates as an "on-off switch." But do you read that paragraph as rejecting a separate test for deadly-force cases? If *Garner* is still good law, then isn't its test still an accurate statement of what would be "reasonable"—and thus still applicable to similar cases involving use of guns? Or does the great factual detail that Justice Scalia attaches to *Garner* indicate that the category of *Garner*-test cases consists of only *Garner* itself? (Notice the emphasis on the facts that Garner was a "young, slight, unarmed" person.)[1]

(b) If *Scott* rejects *Garner* as a self-contained category of Fourth Amendment cases with its own test, then is it correct to say that the only test for Fourth Amendment claims regarding the use of any force is *Graham*'s test? If so, do all cases involving the use of force include *Graham*'s "proportionality-plus" principle, i.e., the idea that an objectively defined officer may reasonably use a bit more than force equal to the suspect's force? See Penley v. Eslinger, 605 F.3d 843 (11th Cir. 2010) (*Graham*'s proportionality-plus principle cited in police shooting case to excuse shooting even though suspect had not aimed gun at police). Does Scott also use the proportionality-plus principle? Is that what the officer did when he not only drove as quickly as his fleeing suspect but also bumped him off the road? That is the Court's holding, is it not?

(c) The Court holds that respondent's argument fails at his first step. But what about the other two steps for which he argued? Does the Court reject them? Consider especially footnote 9: does it reject a "necessity", or less drastic means, inquiry? Is consideration of whether less force would have accomplished the officer's goals an inherent component of deciding whether the force used was reasonable? Or is reasonableness a broad zone that might

---

1. If a separate category remains for deadly use of force, what constitutes such force? See Abdullahi v. City of Madison, 423 F.3d 763 (7th Cir. 2005) (crushing of back with leg producing death); Gutierrez v. City of San Antonio, 139 F.3d 441 (5th Cir.1998) ("hog-tying" a suspect who dies in the process); Estate of Phillips v. City of Milwaukee, 123 F.3d 586, 593–94 (7th Cir.1997) (restraint in a prone position); Quintanilla v. City of Downey, 84 F.3d 353, 357 (9th Cir.1996) (police dog unleashed); In re City of Philadelphia Litigation, 49 F.3d 945, 966 (3d Cir.1995) (bomb dropped on house).

include many uses of force that are not necessary but nevertheless are within the reasonable range? Reconsider the proportionality-plus idea.

2. Although the Court claims to steer clear of "per se" test in favor of its individualistic inquiry, nevertheless the Court appears to announce several principles that guide its judgment in the *Scott* case. For example, the Court declares that (1) weighing of culpability is appropriate, including the appropriateness of under-weighting the suspect's interest when he has caused the danger that an officer seeks to eliminate; and (2) discontinuance of a pursuit is not required in order to satisfy a reasonableness inquiry. This presents a somewhat esoteric question: should the fact-specific reasonableness inquiry depend on generic principles that may apply across different factual circumstances, or do the values on which the facts are to be weighed for reasonable also change with the factual situations? See, e.g., Penley v. Eslinger, supra (taking the view that values remain constant: "This Court has distilled from Supreme Court jurisprudence several factors to aid our effort to "slosh ... through the factbound morass of [this] 'reasonableness' analysis"); Espinosa v. City and County of San Francisco, 598 F.3d 528 (9th Cir. 2010) (relative culpabilities is "a" factor to consider).

(a) After *Scott*, would the weighing of culpabilities justify a police use of force against a hostage-taker, based on the view that he had culpably endangered innocents? Compare Penley v. Eslinger, supra (police kill teenage boy during hostage negotiations fearing he posed threat to other students; "weighty interest in protecting members of the public"), with Estate of Escobedo v. Bender, 600 F.3d 770 (7th Cir. 2010) (use of tear gas and flash devices that killed suicidal person barricaded without hostages is excessive).

(b) Some courts have held that if an officer intentionally provokes a confrontation, such as by entering a home without a warrant, the officer may not rely on the homeowner's use of a gun to justify shooting the person. See, e.g., Espinosa v. City and County of San Francisco 598 F.3d 528 (9th Cir. 2010) (collecting cases). Is this circuit practice consistent with *Scott*? Yes because it is a principle directing how to weigh individual factual situations? No because it creates a per se rule?

3. Even though *Scott* seems to reject per se rules for Fourth Amendment cases, does it not in the end create such a per se rule? Note the concluding paragraph's statement: "we lay down a more sensible rule: A police officer's attempt to terminate a dangerous high-speed car chase that threatens the lives of innocent bystanders does not violate the Fourth Amendment, even when it places the fleeing motorist at risk of serious injury or death."

(a) Compare this statement to the conclusion in *Garner*: "Where the officer has probable cause to believe that the suspect poses a threat of serious physical harm, either to the officer or to others, it is not constitutionally unreasonable to prevent escape by using deadly force." Are not both rules "per se" in the sense that they are categorical—when their terms are met, a dictated result follows? Are the two rules acceptable because they mark the outer boundaries of non-liability (constitutionality), leaving other circumstances not fitting their categories to be decided by the "totality of the circumstances"?

(b) In a concurring opinion not reproduced above, Justice Ginsburg joined the Court because "I do not read today's decision as articulating a mechanical, per se rule." 550 U.S. at 386, 127 S.Ct. at 1779. If such cases literally use no preconceived standards, why is not every case for the jury, as Justice Stevens argues in dissent, on the theory that small variations in the facts might affect the weighing of all circumstances? Does the Court's footnote 7 show that there may be some facts established and some still open?

NOTE ON OTHER FOURTH AMENDMENT CASES AND THE WIDER INFLUENCE OF FOURTH AMENDMENT CONCEPTS

1.   In a series of cases arising during the nation's war on drugs, the Court applied the same "reasonableness" inquiry at issue in the seizure cases, and generally supported the power of police to conduct drug searches outside the home. All the cases arose in civil constitutional tort cases, not in the criminal context.

(a) Three cases concerned public or highly regulated employment. In O'Connor v. Ortega, 480 U.S. 709, 107 S.Ct. 1492, 94 L.Ed.2d 714 (1987), the Court found the warrantless search of a government worker's office, even though not supported by the usual probable cause, to be constitutionally reasonable if undertaken for an administrative rather than criminal or penal purpose. Soon afterwards, in Skinner v. Railway Labor Executives' Ass'n, 489 U.S. 602, 109 S.Ct. 1402, 103 L.Ed.2d 639 (1989), the Court upheld federal regulations requiring warrantless drug testing for rail engineers involved in major accidents, even absent probable cause to believe that drugs were involved in the accident.[2] More recently, in Ontario v. Quon, ___ U.S. ___, 130 S.Ct. 2619, 177 L.Ed.2d 216 (2010), the Court upheld the warrantless search of a police officer's wireless text pager that turned up costly non-official use of the device, including sexually explicit messages. In all three cases the Court claimed to be interpreting the word "reasonable" in the Fourth Amendment. Does the word mean whatever the Court wants it to mean? Or is it that government workers have a lesser expectation of privacy than private workers? Or that as an employer the government can assert a non-criminal, work-related purpose for its searches?

(b) In Michigan Dept. of State Police v. Sitz, 496 U.S. 444, 110 S.Ct. 2481, 110 L.Ed.2d 412 (1990), and Vernonia School Dist. 47J v. Acton, 515 U.S. 646, 115 S.Ct. 2386, 132 L.Ed.2d 564 (1995), the Court moved outside the public employment context. In *Sitz* the Court upheld random sobriety checkpoints of automobile drivers, admittedly a seizure, again using its balancing test to determine reasonableness and dispensing with the ordinary requirements of probable cause and a warrant. In *Acton* the Court upheld a school's random urinalysis testing of athletes, an admitted seizure, again finding the search reasonable in light of the dangers involved. More recently, in Safford v. Redding, ___ U.S. ___, 129 S.Ct. 2633, 174 L.Ed.2d 354 (2009), the Court upheld a principal's search of a student's backpack (though it found a follow-

---

2.   On the same day, in National Treasury Employees Union v. Von Raab, 489 U.S. 656, 109 S.Ct. 1384, 103 L.Ed.2d 685 (1989), the Court upheld federal regulations requiring certain customs workers involved in drug interdiction to submit to warrantless searches, again unsupported by probable cause.

up search of her underwear unreasonable). In these cases the Court has finally confronted ordinary citizens' encounter with police. Do you interpret these cases to offer substantially less protection in the drug search context as compared to the context of seizures under *Garner* and *Graham*? Are greater restraints on police appropriate in the seizure context because personal security is at issue? Whose security? Cf. United States v. Ramirez, 523 U.S. 65, 118 S.Ct. 992, 140 L.Ed.2d 191 (1998) ("no-knock" searches that destroy property not unreasonable if officers have a reasonable suspicion that announcement will cause danger to officer).

2. The Fourth Amendment also plays a role in § 1983 cases presenting claims of an unconstitutional arrest, claims analogous to false arrest at common law, see Whirl v. Kern, Chapter 1B.1 supra. Under Fourth Amendment analysis, the cases turn on the existence of probable cause for the arrests. In **Hartman v. Moore**, 547 U.S. 250, 126 S.Ct. 1695, 164 L.Ed.2d 441 (2006), the Supreme court faced the issue of probable cause in the context of a claimed "malicious prosecution." Following its practice of looking to constitutional norms to supply the elements for a plaintiff's claim, the Court held that in order to prevail a plaintiff would need to prove the absence of probable cause to initiate the prosecution: "want of probable cause must be alleged and proven."[3]

(a) The Court has repeatedly emphasized that the probable cause that an officer must possess is substantially less than would be necessary for a conviction. In **Maryland v. Pringle**, 540 U.S. 366, 124 S.Ct. 795, 157 L.Ed.2d 769 (2003), the officer found cocaine in a car during a valid search and arrested the driver on the spot; the question was whether he had probable cause to believe that the driver was actually in possession of the illegal cocaine. The Court overturned the state court's finding against the officer, 540 U.S. at 371, 124 S.Ct. at 800, noting that it had often

> "reiterated that the probable-cause standard is a 'practical, nontechnical conception' that deals with 'the factual and practical considerations of everyday life on which reasonable and prudent men, not legal technicians, act.' [P]robable cause is a fluid concept—turning on the assessment of probabilities in particular factual contexts—not readily, or even usefully, reduced to a neat set of legal rules.' "

> "The probable-cause standard is incapable of precise definition or quantification into percentages because it deals with probabilities and depends on the totality of the circumstances. We have stated, however, that '[t]he substance of all the definitions of probable cause is a reasonable ground for belief of guilt,' and that the belief of guilt must be particularized with respect to the person to be searched or seized. [But we have also noted that 'finely] tuned standards such as proof beyond a reasonable doubt or by a preponderance of the evidence, useful in formal trials, have no place in the [probable-cause] decision.' To determine whether an officer had probable cause to arrest an individual, we examine the events leading up

---

3. Said the Court, 125 S.Ct. at 1702–06, "[a]s for the invitation to rely on common-law parallels, we certainly are ready to look at the elements of common-law torts when we think about elements of actions for constitutional violations, see Carey v. Piphus, [Chapter 1F.1 infra], but the common law is best understood here more as a source of inspired examples than of prefabricated components."

to the arrest, and then decide 'whether these historical facts, viewed from the standpoint of an objectively reasonable police officer, amount to 'probable cause.' ''

Does *Pringle* make it very unlikely that an officer will lack probable cause? In dissent in *Hartman*, supra, Justice Ginsburg complained that "only entirely 'baseless prosecutions' would be checked," 547 U.S. at 267. See Tatum v. City and County of San Francisco, 441 F.3d 1090 (9th Cir. 2006) (evidence of minor crime, kicking door at police station, supplies "fair probability" of possible crime and thus probable cause to arrest); Lyons v. City of Xenia, 417 F.3d 565 (6th Cir. 2005) (officer arrests for obstruction and assault of officer herself). Cf. Askew v. City of Chicago, 440 F.3d 894 (7th Cir. 2006) (officer has probable cause to arrest when he acts on information given by apparently disinterested witnesses, without need independently to ascertain facts; later recanting irrelevant). Do the Court's pro-police constitutional decisions in the war on drugs necessarily affect the scope of § 1983?

(b) In Devenpeck v. Alford, 543 U.S. 146, 125 S.Ct. 588, 160 L.Ed.2d 537 (2004) (§ 1983 case), the Court lessened the required connection between probable cause and a first-suspected crime by permitting probable cause to arrest on one crime to support charges filed on another. It has also permitted officers to arrest on secondary charges when they actually were motivated to conduct a search for other suspected violations for which they did not have probable cause. See Whren v. United States, 517 U.S. 806, 812–815, 116 S.Ct. 1769, 135 L.Ed.2d 89 (1996) (arresting officer's state of mind (except for facts that he knows) is irrelevant to probable cause). Do these cases make probable cause a much less relevant concept in the arrest and search contexts?

3. Claims of retaliatory arrest for speech protected under the First Amendment have also been subjected to Fourth Amendment principles, albeit indirectly. In Hartman v. Moore, ¶ 2 supra, the plaintiff added a claim that he, a private citizen, had been arrested in retaliation for speaking out against practices of the U.S. Postal Service. Conceding that such a claim would ordinarily call for the application of First Amendment principles, the Court nevertheless added a requirement that plaintiff prove lack of probable cause for the prosecution when the alleged method of suppressing speech was by an unfounded criminal prosecution. The lengthy and somewhat convoluted opinion by Justice Souter makes unclear the exact source of law for the Court's ruling, but it seems must likely to be merely a judicially crafted rule of evidence. See 547 U.S. at 265 (lack of probable cause has "obvious evidentiary value" in making a "prima facie inference").

(a) In Rothgery v. Gillespie County, 554 U.S. 191, 128 S.Ct. 2578, 171 L.Ed.2d 366 (2008), the Court held that a § 1983 suit could be filed for failure of state courts to appoint counsel promptly after the hearing at which probable cause was found to hold him for trial. The Court did not decide any other details applicable to the claim, merely remanding for further consideration. On remand, should the plaintiff be required to prove lack of probable cause for holding him? Does *Hartman* have any application to such Fifth Amendment claims?[4]

---

4. Cf. Chavez v. Martinez, 538 U.S. 760, 123 S.Ct. 1994, 155 L.Ed.2d 984 (2003). In that case police allegedly shot, then coercively questioned a suspect without giving *Miranda* warnings. He

(b) In parts of the *Hartman* opinion, the Court refers to constitutional principles, but it candidly admits that in "defining [of] the elements of the tort" of retaliatory prosecution, its decision has been dictated by practical considerations of proof of causation. If the Court's rule is not constitutionally based, then we have now seen at least one situation where an element of at least one constitutional claim is not grounded in constitutional law. (Cf. Parratt v. Taylor, Chapter 1B (introduction) supra) "essential elements" of § 1983 claims are based in constitutional law). Does *Hartman* implicitly hold that the Court may add other non-essential elements to constitutional torts based on its own policy determinations? If so, then this may not be an incorporation of state common law, but it is an act of creation of federal common law, is it not?

4. SUBSTANTIVE DUE PROCESS AND THE "BACKGROUND OF TORT LIABILITY"

Although the Fourteenth Amendment has only one Due Process Clause limiting state power, the Court has interpreted the clause to have two distinctive components, "procedural due process" and "substantive due process." For reasons covered in section G.3 of this Chapter, Procedural Due Process has not had a great impact in § 1983 litigation. Substantive Due Process, on the other hand, has been at the core of § 1983's development. To understand its role, one may conceive of substantive due process as an umbrella concept that includes three different sources of rights.

1) *Incorporated Provisions of the Bill of Rights (Amendments 1–8)*: To the extent that the substantive component of the Due Process Clause selectively incorporates the Bill of Rights and applies it to the states, all of the Eighth Amendment and Fourth Amendment cases brought against state officials, previously covered in this Chapter, are "substantive due process" cases. The same may be said of cases brought under the First Amendment or any other of the Amendments in the Bill of Rights that have been made applicable to the states. See, e.g., McDonald v. Chicago, 561 U.S. ___, 130 S.Ct. 3020, 177 L.Ed.2d 894 (2010) (Second Amendment's right to bear arms is incorporated into Due Process and applies to the states).

2) *Non-textual Fundamental Rights*: All of the non-textual "fundamental rights" discussed in most courses in constitutional law, such as the right of privacy, give rise to a "substantive due process" claim. See, e.g., Roe v. Wade, 410 U.S. 113, 93 S.Ct. 705, 35 L.Ed.2d 147 (1973) (right to choose abortion is non-textual component of Due Process Clause's general protection for "liberty").

---

brought a § 1983 suit against the officers for the coercive questioning, alleging a violation of the Fifth Amendment. A badly divided Court rejected the claim, commonly ruling only that no violation occurs under the Fifth Amendment unless the fruits of an otherwise unconstitutional interrogation are used against the person at trial. Is this a variation on *Hartman*'s causation principle?

3) *General, Back-up Substantive Due Process*: The Substantive Due Process Clause may act as a general back-up provision authorizing courts to create tort-like liability for state officials even in the absence of a specific incorporated right (category 1 supra) or a specific, non-textual fundamental right (category 2 supra). Cf. Johnson v. Glick, discussed in Graham v. Connor, Chapter 1B.3 supra.

Claims brought under the first and second categories above are not conceptually difficult in the context of a § 1983 action: § 1983, according to currently prevailing doctrine, primarily adopts the standards of the constitutional right that the plaintiff seeks to enforce. For "incorporated rights," this often means a richly tailored set of provisions that reflect the complexities of the particular Amendment in the Bill of Rights which is at issue. See Chapter 1B.2 & 1B.3 supra. For "fundamental rights," this often means the use of "strict scrutiny" as discussed in most major courses in constitutional law. See e.g., Roe v. Wade, supra (strict scrutiny originally applied).

This sub-section takes up the third aspect of the Substantive Due Process Clause. It is central to the development of § 1983 because it once again raises the specter of the Court straying away from the text or implied meaning of the text to create judge-made tort-like standards that bind state officials. Is the creation of this general backup role for the Substantive Due Process Clause a valid act of *constitutional* interpretation, or is it backsliding into the realm of *common-law* tort-making? Does this third branch of the Substantive Due Process Clause authorize the Justices to declare illegal anything that offends a majority of them?

COUNTY OF SACRAMENTO v. LEWIS

Supreme Court of the United States, 1998.
523 U.S. 833, 118 S.Ct. 1708, 140 L.Ed.2d 1043.

JUSTICE SOUTER delivered the opinion of the Court.

The issue in this case is whether a police officer violates the Fourteenth Amendment's guarantee of substantive due process by causing death through deliberate or reckless indifference to life in a high-speed automobile chase aimed at apprehending a suspected offender. We answer no, and hold that in such circumstances only a purpose to cause harm unrelated to the legitimate object of arrest will satisfy the element of arbitrary conduct shocking to the conscience, necessary for a due process violation.

I

[A Sacramento County deputy sheriff (Smith) saw a motorcycle operated at high speed by a young man with a passenger (Lewis) aboard. When his warning to stop produced no result, the deputy gave chase with siren and lights for 75 seconds over residential streets at speeds approaching 100 mph. After 1.3 miles the cyclist lost control and the deputy, unable to stop at high speed, ran over the cyclist's passenger. Representatives of the passenger's estate brought this action under § 1983. The trial court dismissed the claim, but the Court of Appeals for the Ninth Circuit reversed.]

We granted certiorari to resolve a conflict among the Circuits over the standard of culpability on the part of a law enforcement officer for violating substantive due process in a pursuit case * * *. We now reverse.

II

Our prior cases have held [the Due Process Clause] to guarantee more than fair process and to cover a substantive sphere as well, "barring certain government actions regardless of the fairness of the procedures used to implement them," Daniels v. Williams; see also Zinermon v. Burch, [section G.2 of this Chapter, infra] (noting that substantive due process violations are actionable under § 1983). The allegation here that Lewis was deprived of his right to life in violation of substantive due process amounts to such a claim, that under the circumstances described earlier, Smith's actions in causing Lewis's death were an abuse of executive power so clearly unjustified by any legitimate objective of law enforcement as to be barred by the Fourteenth Amendment. Cf. Collins v. Harker Heights.

[R]espondents face two principal objections to their claim.[5] The first is that its subject is necessarily governed by a more definite provision of the Constitution (to the exclusion of any possible application of substantive due process); the second, that in any event the allegations are insufficient to state a substantive due process violation through executive abuse of power. Respondents can meet the first objection, but not the second.

A

Because we have "always been reluctant to expand the concept of substantive due process," Collins v. Harker Heights, supra, we held in Graham v. Connor that "[w]here a particular amendment provides an explicit textual source of constitutional protection against a particular sort of government behavior, that Amendment, not the more generalized notion of substantive due process, must be the guide for analyzing these claims." Albright v. Oliver, 510 U.S. 266, 273, 114 S.Ct. 807, 813, 127 L.Ed.2d 114 (1994) (plurality opinion of REHNQUIST, C.J.) (quoting Graham v. Connor). Given the rule in Graham, we were presented at oral argument with the threshold issue raised in several amicus briefs, whether facts involving a police chase aimed at apprehending suspects can ever support a [generalized] due process claim. The argument runs that in chasing the motorcycle, Smith was attempting to make a seizure within the meaning of the Fourth Amendment, and, perhaps, even that he succeeded when Lewis was stopped by the fatal collision. Hence, any liability must turn on an application of the reasonableness standard governing searches and seizures, not the due process standard of liability

5. As in any action under § 1983, the first step is to identify the exact contours of the underlying right said to have been violated. See Graham v. Connor. [Repositioned footnote.]

for constitutionally arbitrary executive action. See Graham v. Connor ("all claims that law enforcement officers have used excessive force—deadly or not—in the course of an arrest, investigatory stop, or other 'seizure' of a free citizen should be analyzed under the Fourth Amendment and its 'reasonableness' standard, rather than under a 'substantive due process' approach"). One Court of Appeals has indeed applied the rule of Graham to preclude the application of principles of generalized substantive due process to a motor vehicle passenger's claims for injury resulting from reckless police pursuit. See Mays v. East St. Louis, 123 F.3d 999, 1002–1003 (C.A.7 1997).

The argument is unsound. Just last Term, we explained that *Graham* "does not hold that all constitutional claims relating to physically abusive government conduct must arise under either the Fourth or Eighth Amendments; rather, *Graham* simply requires that if a constitutional claim is covered by a specific constitutional provision, such as the Fourth or Eighth Amendment, the claim must be analyzed under the standard appropriate to that specific provision, not under the rubric of substantive due process." United States v. Lanier, [noted in section D.3 of this Chapter, infra]. Substantive due process analysis is therefore inappropriate in this case only if respondents' claim is "covered by" the Fourth Amendment. It is not.

The Fourth Amendment covers only "searches and seizures," U.S. Const., Amdt. 4, neither of which took place here. No one suggests that there was a search, and our cases foreclose finding a seizure. We held in California v. Hodari D., that a police pursuit in attempting to seize a person does not amount to a "seizure" within the meaning of the Fourth Amendment. And in Brower v. County of Inyo, we explained "that a Fourth Amendment seizure does not occur whenever there is a governmentally caused termination of an individual's freedom of movement * * * but only when there is a governmental termination of freedom of movement through means intentionally applied." We illustrated the point by saying that no Fourth Amendment seizure would take place where a "pursuing police car sought to stop the suspect only by the show of authority represented by flashing lights and continuing pursuit," but accidentally stopped the suspect by crashing into him. That is exactly this case. Graham's more-specific-provision rule is therefore no bar to respondents' suit.[7]

B

* * *

---

7. Several amici suggest that, for the purposes of *Graham*, the Fourth Amendment should cover not only seizures, but also failed attempts to make a seizure. This argument is foreclosed by California v. Hodari D., in which we explained that "neither usage nor common-law tradition makes an attempted seizure a seizure. The common law may have made an attempted seizure unlawful in certain circumstances; but it made many things unlawful, very few of which were elevated to constitutional proscriptions." Attempted seizures of a person are beyond the scope of the Fourth Amendment.

We have emphasized time and again that "[t]he touchstone of due process is protection of the individual against arbitrary action of government," whether the fault lies in a denial of fundamental procedural fairness, or in the exercise of power without any reasonable justification in the service of a legitimate governmental objective, see, e.g., Daniels v. Williams. While due process protection in the substantive sense limits what the government may do in both its legislative, and its executive capacities, see, e.g., Rochin v. California, 342 U.S. 165, 72 S.Ct. 205, 96 L.Ed. 183 (1952), criteria to identify what is fatally arbitrary differ depending on whether it is legislation or a specific act of a governmental officer that is at issue.

* * *

[F]or half a century now we have spoken of the cognizable level of executive abuse of power as that which shocks the conscience. We first put the test this way in Rochin v. California, supra, where we found the forced pumping of a suspect's stomach enough to offend due process as conduct "that shocks the conscience" and violates the "decencies of civilized conduct." In the intervening years we have repeatedly adhered to Rochin's benchmark. [Citations omitted.] Most recently, in Collins v. Harker Heights, we said again that the substantive component of the Due Process Clause is violated by executive action only when it "can properly be characterized as arbitrary, or conscience shocking, in a constitutional sense." While the measure of what is conscience-shocking is no calibrated yard stick, it does, as Judge Friendly put it, "poin[t] the way." Johnson v. Glick, 481 F.2d 1028, 1033 (C.A.2), cert. denied, 414 U.S. 1033, 94 S.Ct. 462, 38 L.Ed.2d 324 (1973).[8]

---

8. As Justice Scalia has explained before, he fails to see "the usefulness of 'conscience shocking' as a legal test," Herrera v. Collins, 506 U.S. 390, 428, 113 S.Ct. 853, 875, 122 L.Ed.2d 203 (1993), and his independent analysis of this case is therefore understandable. He is, however, simply mistaken in seeing our insistence on the shocks-the-conscience standard as an atavistic return to a scheme of due process analysis rejected by the Court in Washington v. Glucksberg, 521 U.S. 702, 117 S.Ct. 2258, 138 L.Ed.2d 772 (1997).

Glucksberg presented a disagreement about the significance of historical examples of protected liberty in determining whether a given statute could be judged to contravene the Fourteenth Amendment. The differences of opinion turned on the issues of how much history indicating recognition of the asserted right, viewed at what level of specificity, is necessary to support the finding of a substantive due process right entitled to prevail over state legislation.

As we explain in the text, a case challenging executive action on substantive due process grounds, like this one, presents an issue antecedent to any question about the need for historical examples of enforcing a liberty interest of the sort claimed. For executive action challenges raise a particular need to preserve the constitutional proportions of constitutional claims, lest the Constitution be demoted to what we have called a font of tort law. Thus, in a due process challenge to executive action, the threshold question is whether the behavior of the governmental officer is so egregious, so outrageous, that it may fairly be said to shock the contemporary conscience. That judgment may be informed by a history of liberty protection, but it necessarily reflects an understanding of traditional executive behavior, of contemporary practice, and of the standards of blame generally applied to them. Only if the necessary condition of egregious behavior were satisfied would there be a possibility of recognizing a substantive due process right to be free of such executive action, and only then might there be a debate about the sufficiency of historical examples of enforcement of the right claimed, or its recognition in other ways. In none of our prior cases have we considered the necessity for such examples, and no such question is raised in this case.

In sum, the difference of opinion in *Glucksberg* was about the need for historical examples of recognition of the claimed liberty protection at some appropriate level of specificity. In an

It should not be surprising that the constitutional concept of conscience-shocking duplicates no traditional category of common-law fault, but rather points clearly away from liability, or clearly toward it, only at the ends of the tort law's spectrum of culpability. Thus, we have made it clear that the due process guarantee does not entail a body of constitutional law imposing liability whenever someone cloaked with state authority causes harm. In Paul v. Davis, for example, we explained that the Fourteenth Amendment is not a "font of tort law to be superimposed upon whatever systems may already be administered by the States," and in Daniels v. Williams, we reaffirmed the point that "[o]ur Constitution deals with the large concerns of the governors and the governed, but it does not purport to supplant traditional tort law in laying down rules of conduct to regulate liability for injuries that attend living together in society." We have accordingly rejected the lowest common denominator of customary tort liability as any mark of sufficiently shocking conduct, and have held that the Constitution does not guarantee due care on the part of state officials; liability for negligently inflicted harm is categorically beneath the threshold of constitutional due process. See Daniels v. Williams; see also Davidson v. Cannon. It is, on the contrary, behavior at the other end of the culpability spectrum that would most probably support a substantive due process claim; conduct intended to injure in some way unjustifiable by any government interest is the sort of official action most likely to rise to the conscience-shocking level. See Daniels v. Williams ("Historically, this guarantee of due process has been applied to *deliberate* decisions of government officials to deprive a person of life, liberty, or property.") (emphasis in original).

Whether the point of the conscience-shocking is reached when injuries are produced with culpability falling within the middle range, following from something more than negligence but "less than intentional conduct, such as recklessness or 'gross negligence,' " is a matter for closer calls.[9] To be sure, we have expressly recognized the possibility that some official acts in this range may be actionable under the Fourteenth Amendment, and our cases have compelled recognition that such conduct is egregious enough to state a substantive due process claim in at least one instance. We held in City of Revere v. Massachusetts Gen. Hospital, 463 U.S. 239, 103 S.Ct. 2979, 77 L.Ed.2d 605 (1983), that "the due process rights of a [pretrial detainee] are at least as great as the Eighth Amendment protections available to a convicted prisoner" [thus leading us to apply the "deliberate indifference" standard of the Eighth Amendment].

Rules of due process are not, however, subject to mechanical application in unfamiliar territory. Deliberate indifference that shocks in one

---

executive action case, no such issue can arise if the conduct does not reach the degree of the egregious.

9. In Rochin v. California, the case in which we formulated and first applied the shocks-the-conscience test [in 1952], it was not the ultimate purpose of the government actors to harm the plaintiff, but they apparently acted with full appreciation of what the Court described as the brutality of their acts. *Rochin*, of course, was decided long before Graham v. Connor, and today would be treated under the Fourth Amendment, albeit with the same result.

environment may not be so patently egregious in another, and our concern with preserving the constitutional proportions of substantive due process demands an exact analysis of circumstances before any abuse of power is condemned as conscience-shocking * * *. Thus, attention to the markedly different circumstances of normal pretrial custody and high-speed law enforcement chases shows why the deliberate indifference that shocks in the one case is less egregious in the other (even assuming that it makes sense to speak of indifference as deliberate in the case of sudden pursuit). As the very term "deliberate indifference" implies, the standard is sensibly employed only when actual deliberation is practical, see Whitley v. Albers, and in the custodial situation of a prison, forethought about an inmate's welfare is not only feasible but obligatory under a regime that incapacitates a prisoner to exercise ordinary responsibility for his own welfare * * *.

But [we have adopted higher demands of plaintiffs when deliberation is not feasible, even in the Eighth Amendment cases, such as Whitley v. Albers, which involved prompt action during a prison disturbance.] We accordingly held that a much higher standard of fault than deliberate indifference has to be shown for officer liability in a prison riot. In those circumstances, liability should turn on "whether force was applied in a good faith effort to maintain or restore discipline or maliciously and sadistically for the very purpose of causing harm." Id. The analogy to sudden police chases (under the Due Process Clause) would be hard to avoid.

Like prison officials facing a riot, the police on an occasion calling for fast action have obligations that tend to tug against each other. Their duty is to restore and maintain lawful order, while not exacerbating disorder more than necessary to do their jobs. They are supposed to act decisively and to show restraint at the same moment, and their decisions have to be made "in haste, under pressure, and frequently without the luxury of a second chance." Id.; cf. Graham v. Connor ("police officers are often forced to make split-second judgments—in circumstances that are tense, uncertain, and rapidly evolving"). A police officer deciding whether to give chase must balance on one hand the need to stop a suspect and show that flight from the law is no way to freedom, and, on the other, the high-speed threat to everyone within stopping range, be they suspects, their passengers, other drivers, or bystanders.

To recognize a substantive due process violation in these circumstances when only mid-level fault has been shown would be to forget that liability for deliberate indifference to inmate welfare rests upon the luxury enjoyed by prison officials of having time to make unhurried judgments, upon the chance for repeated reflection, largely uncomplicated by the pulls of competing obligations. When such extended opportunities to do better are teamed with protracted failure even to care, indifference is truly shocking. But when unforeseen circumstances demand an officer's instant judgment, even precipitate recklessness fails to inch close enough to harmful purpose to spark the shock that implicates "the large concerns of the governors and the governed." Daniels v. Williams. Just as a purpose to cause harm is needed for Eighth Amendment liability in a riot case, so it ought to be needed for Due Process liability in a pursuit case. Accordingly, we hold that high-speed chases with no intent to harm suspects physically or to worsen their legal plight do not give rise to liability under the Fourteenth Amendment, redressible by an action under § 1983.

The fault claimed on [the deputy's] part in this case accordingly fails to meet the shocks-the-conscience test [for, at most, only "conscious disregard" was claimed in this case]. [The deputy] was faced with a course of lawless behavior for which the police were not to blame. They had done nothing to cause [the motorcyclist's] high-speed driving in the first place, nothing to excuse his flouting of the commonly understood law enforcement authority to control traffic, and nothing (beyond a refusal to call off the chase) to encourage him to race through traffic at breakneck speed forcing other drivers out of their travel lanes. [The motorcyclist's] outrageous behavior was practically instantaneous, and so was Smith's instinctive response. While prudence would have repressed the reaction, the officer's instinct was to do his job as a law enforcement officer, not to induce ... lawlessness [by the cyclist], or to terrorize, cause harm, or kill. Prudence, that is, was subject to countervailing enforcement considerations, and while Smith exaggerated their demands, there is no reason to believe that they were tainted by an improper or malicious motive on his part.

Regardless whether Smith's behavior offended the reasonableness held up by tort law or the balance struck in law enforcement's own codes of sound practice, it does not shock the conscience, and petitioners are not called upon to answer for it under § 1983. The judgment below is accordingly reversed.

It is so ordered.

CHIEF JUSTICE REHNQUIST, concurring.

I join the opinion of the Court in this case. [The County's petition for writ of certiorari did not pose the question of what legal standard to apply—Fourth Amendment or general Substantive Due Process—but instead assumed that Due Process applies and asked us to choose between two phrases reflective of Due Process standards—either the "shocks the conscience" test or the "deliberate indifference" test.] The assumption was surely not without foundation in our case law, as the Court makes clear. The Court is correct in concluding that "shocks the conscience" is the right choice among the alternatives posed in the question presented, and correct in concluding that this demanding standard has not been met here.

JUSTICE KENNEDY, with whom JUSTICE O'CONNOR joins, concurring.

* * *

The Court decides this case by applying the "shocks the conscience" test first recognized in Rochin v. California, and reiterated in subsequent decisions. The phrase has the unfortunate connotation of a standard laden with subjective assessments. In that respect, it must be viewed with considerable skepticism. * * *

[I]t must be added that history and tradition are the starting point, but not in all cases the ending point, of the substantive due process inquiry. There is room as well for an objective assessment of the necessities of law enforcement, in which the police must be given substantial latitude and discretion, acknowledging, of course, the primacy of the interest in life which the State, by the Fourteenth Amendment, is bound to respect. I agree with the Court's assessment of the State's interests in this regard. Absent intent to injure, the police, in circumstances such as these, may conduct a dangerous chase of a suspect who disobeys a lawful command to stop when they determine it is appropriate to do so. * * * [A]ny suggestion that suspects may ignore a lawful command to stop and then sue for damages sustained in an ensuing chase might cause suspects to flee more often, increasing accidents of the kind which occurred here.

* * *

Jᴜsᴛɪᴄᴇ Sᴄᴀʟɪᴀ, with whom Jᴜsᴛɪᴄᴇ Tʜᴏᴍᴀs joins, concurring in the judgment.

* * *

Just last Term, in Washington v. Glucksberg, 521 U.S. 702, 117 S.Ct. 2258, 2267–2269, 138 L.Ed.2d 772 (1997), the Court specifically rejected the method of substantive-due-process analysis employed by Justice Souter in his concurrence in that case, which is the very same method employed by Justice Souter in his opinion for the Court today. To quote the opinion in *Glucksberg*:

"Our established method of substantive-due-process analysis has two primary features: First, we have regularly observed that the Due Process Clause specially protects those fundamental rights and liberties which are, objectively, 'deeply rooted in this Nation's history and tradition,' ... and 'implicit in the concept of ordered liberty'.... Second, we have required in substantive-due-process cases a 'careful description' of the asserted fundamental liberty interest.... Our Nation's history, legal traditions, and practices thus provide the crucial 'guideposts for responsible decisionmaking,' ... that direct and restrain our exposition of the Due Process Clause....."

"Justice Souter * * * would largely abandon this restrained methodology, and instead ask 'whether [Washington's] statute sets up one of those 'arbitrary impositions' or 'purposeless restraints' at odds with the Due Process Clause.... In our view, however, the development of this Court's substantive-due-process jurisprudence ... has been a process whereby the outlines of the 'liberty' specially protected by the Fourteenth Amendment ... have at least been carefully refined by concrete examples involving fundamental rights found to be deeply rooted in our legal tradition. This approach tends to rein in the subjective elements that are necessarily present in due-process judicial review."

[I]f anything, today's opinion is even more of a throw-back to highly subjective substantive-due-process methodologies than the concurrence in *Glucksberg* was. Whereas the latter said merely that substantive due process prevents "arbitrary impositions" and "purposeless restraints" (without any objective criterion as to what is arbitrary or purposeless), today's opinion resuscitates the ... subjectivity, th' ol' "shocks-the-conscience" test * * *.

Adhering to our decision in *Glucksberg*, rather than ask whether the police conduct here at issue shocks my unelected conscience, I would ask whether our Nation has traditionally protected the right respondents assert. [That right, described by plaintiffs as a right to be free from "deliberate or reckless indifference to life in a high-speed automobile chase aimed at apprehending a suspected offender," cannot be found in our constitutional text, history, or traditions. To recognize such a right would make " 'the Fourteenth Amendment a font of tort law to be superimposed upon whatever systems may already be administered by the States.' " *Daniels*, supra, quoting Paul v. Davis.]

I would reverse the judgment of the Ninth Circuit, not on the ground that petitioners have failed to shock my still, soft voice within, but on the ground that respondents offer no textual or historical support for their alleged due process right. Accordingly, I concur in the judgment of the Court.

NOTE ON THE ORIGIN AND USES OF THE "SHOCKS THE CONSCIENCE" TEST

1. The opening discussion in *Sacramento* establishes an apparently simple rule of priority for analyzing different types of Due Process claims: "[w]here a particular amendment provides an explicit textual source of constitutional protection against a particular sort of government behavior, that Amendment, not the more generalized notion of substantive due process, must be the guide for analyzing these claims." The Court restated the rule: "if a constitutional claim is covered by a specific constitutional provision, such as the Fourth or Eighth Amendment, the claim must be analyzed under the standard appropriate to that specific provision, not under the rubric of substantive due process." The rule appears to reflect the familiar theme from Graham v. Connor, Chapter 1B.3 supra, that more specific provisions are to be preferentially applied over more general ones. Consider first the ordinary analytical difficulties in applying the Court's ruling in the police-pursuit context.

(a) The Court holds that the Fourth Amendment does not apply in this case because it controls only "seizures" of persons—and there was no seizure in this case. Ordinarily, under the *Brower* case, intent to acquire control is necessary to establish a seizure, and under *Hodari* the intended effort must be effective (events prior to taking control not a seizure). Why was there no seizure in the *Sacramento* case? Even assuming that the display of flashing lights was no seizure, when the officer's police cruiser struck and killed the motorcycle passenger, at least then was the passenger not as completely controlled as the fleeing suspect in Tennessee v. Garner? Was it the accidental nature of the crash that led the Court to declare that there had been no seizure?

(b) Apparently, if the officer in *Sacramento* had intended to seize a fleeing driver, the Fourth Amendment would have applied, so that an officer who intentionally rams, cuts off, or otherwise controls a fleeing vehicle would have his conduct reviewed under the Fourth Amendment. See Harris v. Coweta County, 433 F.3d 807 (11th Cir. 2005) (officer rams suspect's car to attempt to end chase; Fourth Amendment applies). What is the dividing line between Fourth Amendment analysis and General Substantive Due Process analysis—whether the officer both intends to take control and actually accomplishes it? See Hawkins v. City of Farmington, 189 F.3d 695 (8th Cir.1999) (officer who "maneuvered his vehicle into [plaintiff's] path in his effort to stop or to slow him down and, in fact, stopped him" caused a seizure).[1]

(c) Assuming Fourth Amendment analysis applies to an intentional seizure, a seizure is deemed unconstitutional only if it is "unreasonable" under the circumstances, as discussed in Graham v. Connor and Tennessee v. Garner, see Chapter 1B.3 supra. Think tactically: would a police officer prefer to have his actions reviewed under the reasonableness test announced in *Graham* or the "shocks the conscience" test announced in *Sacramento*? Who is benefitted by Justice Souter's distinction between Fourth Amendment cases and Due Process cases, plaintiff citizens or defendant officers? Is the textual standard, Fourth Amendment here, always more protective of the citizen than the general Due Process standard?

2.   Now consider *Sacramento*'s distinction between specific and general standards at a more theoretical level. To be workable, the principle would need to establish exactly the topic as to which the more specific amendment is specific (and thus exclusive). The issue could arise in any context where a plaintiff might consider a specific Due Process claim (based on an "incorporated right" or a "fundamental right") as well as a general Due Process claim.

(a) The Fourth Amendment itself shows the problem. Is it the exclusive mode of analysis for all "seizures," or only for all "unreasonable seizures"? If the Court in *Sacramento* had found that there was an intended seizure, but that it was reasonable, could the plaintiff have then pressed his general Due Process argument by saying that the Fourth Amendment was "inapplicable"? Compare Whitley v. Albers, 475 U.S. 312, 106 S.Ct. 1078, 89 L.Ed.2d 251 (1986) (after rejecting Eighth Amendment claim, Court also considers general Due Process claim). Or is it intuitively clear that "seizure" is the exclusive topic of the Fourth Amendment and "reasonableness" is the analysis performed for that topic? See Conn v. Gabbert, 526 U.S. 286, 119 S.Ct. 1292, 143 L.Ed.2d 399 (1999) (attorney claimed that an unreasonable search, timed to prevent him from meeting and advising a client, violated his right to substantive due process): "Challenges to the reasonableness of a search by govern-

---

1. Note that the same problem can arise in the context of searches because the term "search" does not have self-evident contours. See B.C. v. Plumas Unified School Dist., 192 F.3d 1260 (9th Cir.1999) (noting conflict among the circuits as to whether a "dog sniff" for drugs is a "search").

ment agents clearly fall under the Fourth Amendment, and not the Four-teenth."

(b) The Court faced the exclusiveness issue once again after *Sacramento*, in **Chavez v. Martinez**, 538 U.S. 760, 123 S.Ct. 1994, 155 L.Ed.2d 984 (2003), where a fractured Court found no Fifth Amendment violation and remanded the case to the lower courts to determine if there had been a violation under *Sacramento*'s general Substantive Due Process. But *Chavez* involved a bright-line rule—no violation absent the use of a coerced statement at a suspect's trial. Lower courts have faced the issue in other contexts with more limited success. Some judges will perform the analysis required by specific constitutional provisions, then additionally perform "shocks the con-science" analysis. See, e.g., Flaim v. Medical College of Ohio, 418 F.3d 629 (6th Cir. 2005) (plaintiff loses on Procedural Due Process analysis, and court also considers and rejects shocks-the-conscience claim); Morris v. Dearborne, 181 F.3d 657 (5th Cir.1999) (parents whose child was taken after teacher's fabrication of child abuse may assert both fundamental due process right to family status as well as general due process right to be free of "conscience-shocking" conduct).[2]

(c) In one of the few cases to discuss the exclusivity issue specifically, the Fourth Circuit in Edwards v. City of Goldsboro, 178 F.3d 231, 248 n. 11 (4th Cir.1999), stated that the more specific provisions of the First Amendment, not the "shocks the conscience" approach, apply when the general Due Process claim "fully overlaps [the] free speech claim." Cf. American Federa-tion of Labor and Congress of Indus. Organizations v. City of Miami, 637 F.3d 1178 (11th Cir. 2011) (where plaintiffs asserted rights under specific constitu-tional amendments, it was error for trial court to move to shocks the conscience test). Is this approach more protective of plaintiff's interests or less?

3. Moving to the claim based on a generalized Due Process guarantee, the *Sacramento* majority holds that "conscience-shocking" acts may violate general Due Process safeguards. Should the Court perform this form of analysis? Is it a legitimate form of judicial reform or mere judicial activism?

(a) The phrase "shocks-the-conscience" originated in Rochin v. Califor-nia, as discussed in *Sacramento*. When *Rochin* was decided in 1952, it was one of many opinions highlighting the "incorporation controversy"—the dispute between Justices (led by Hugo Black) who would read the Due Process Clause to adopt and apply the Bill of Rights to the states and Justices (led by Felix Frankfurter, author of *Rochin*) who would independently decide whether specific state action was so shocking as to violate Due Process. While Black's approach looked more mechanical (and perhaps conservative to modern sensi-bilities), it would have broadly protected virtually all rights found in the first eight amendments. Justice Frankfurter's approach, while using expansive language (thus appearing more liberal to modern sensibilities), actually pro-

---

2. Other cases show variations that are possible with other overlapping rights. See, e.g., Whiteland Woods v. Township of West Whiteland, 193 F.3d 177 (3d Cir.1999) (refusal to allow videotaping of council meetings; First Amendment and "shocks the conscience"); Khan v. Gallitano, 180 F.3d 829, 836 (7th Cir.1999) (Contracts Clause claim and "shocks the conscience" claim). Cf. Natale v. Town of Ridgefield, 170 F.3d 258 (2d Cir. 1999) (taking of property and "shocks the conscience" claim) (zoning context).

duced more conservative results—decisions that applied less than all of the Bill of Rights to the states. See, e.g., Adamson v. California, 332 U.S. 46, 67 S.Ct. 1672, 91 L.Ed. 1903 (1947) (aspects of self incrimination) (Frankfurter, J., concurring).[3] Did the *Sacramento* majority rip the "shocks the conscience" test from its historical moorings? Which was more important, the limiting historical use of the "shocks the conscience" test or its liberating language?

(b) In McDonald v. Chicago, 561 U.S. ___, 130 S.Ct. 3020, 177 L.Ed.2d 894 (2010), the majority used the incorporation principle to apply the Second Amendment's text to the States. The core of the dissenters (Justices Stevens, Ginsburg, and Breyer) were the same Justices who in *Sacramento* had created the non-textual "shocks the conscience" test. Justice Scalia noted with some irony that their desire to create non-textual rights but refusal to apply textual ones could only be explained by their personal prejudices. ___ U.S. at ___, 130 S.Ct. at 3051. Is this fair criticism?[4]

(c) Consider the factors that the majority balances to reach its judgment about what amounts to conscience-shocking behavior in the police-pursuit context. Is the balancing process different from that of a common-law court trying to define liability under state tort law? Is the Court's reliance on Whitley v. Albers misplaced because that was an Eighth Amendment case— and thus the Court had *constitutional* standards to inform its judgment? What are the constitutional standards here? Should courts always keep in mind that they should not be readily displacing state tort law with a federalized policy judgment? See Moore v. Guthrie, 438 F.3d 1036 (10th Cir. 2006) ("the overarching need [under *Sacramento* is] for deference to local policy-making bodies [so that these cases do not] become a substantial and unnecessary substitute to state tort law"); Perez v. Unified Government of Wyandotte County/Kansas City, 432 F.3d 1163 (10th Cir. 2005) (noting that *Sacramento* must be paired with traditional view that "the Fourteenth Amendment is not a 'font of tort law to be superimposed upon whatever systems may already be administered by the States' ").

4. After admitting that the "shocks the conscience" phrase has no precise contour, the majority tries to give it some definition in the specific situation of police-pursuit cases, and it concludes by deciding that only "a purpose to cause harm unrelated to the legitimate object of arrest" meets the standard in this context.[5]

3. *Rochin* involved police recruitment of medical personnel to pump the stomach of a drug suspect who had swallowed capsules later determined to be morphine. The Court declined to hold that the stomach-pumping was an unreasonable search (because it found the Fourth Amendment inapplicable to the states), but it independently determined that it violated sensibilities inherent in the Due Process Clause of the Fourteenth Amendment.

4. Note Chief Justice Rehnquist's tentative concurring opinion and the concurring opinions of Justices Kennedy and Scalia, both of which seem to reject some or all of Justice Souter's openended balancing. Was there no majority in *Sacramento*?

5. The *Sacramento* Court treats the motorcycle passenger as an object of the pursuit, not as a third party. Should true bystanders—other motorists or pedestrians collaterally injured during a pursuit—fall into the same categorical context, with their claims analyzed by the same standard as that applied to pursued suspects? See Onossian v. Block, 175 F.3d 1169 (9th Cir.1999) (yes). Would a bystander injured by all other police enforcement actions be treated the same? See Moreland v. Las Vegas Met. Police Dept., 159 F.3d 365 (9th Cir.1998) (bystander injured in a shooting).

(a) What is a "purpose to cause harm unrelated to the legitimate object of arrest" in the context of a police chase of a motorist? In Whitley v. Albers, the phrase is contrasted with its supposed opposite, the good-faith desire to restore order in prison. What is the opposite reference point here? The good-faith desire to enforce the traffic laws? In the real world an officer might act for a legitimate law-enforcement purpose, but only after being prompted to action by a motorist who has disrespectfully irritated the officer. Does the irritation amount to a "purpose to cause harm"? In Davis v. Township of Hillside, 190 F.3d 167 (3d Cir.1999) (concurring opinion), the concurring judge opined that a desire "to teach [the motorist] a lesson" or to "get even" amounts to a "purpose to cause harm." Do you agree?[6]

(b) Does the "intent to harm" test render Justice Souter's test self-defeating for plaintiffs? If an officer intends to cause harm and actually accomplishes it by hitting and later controlling the motorist by running him of the road, has the officer not accomplishes a "seizure" under *Brower* and *Hodari*? If he has accomplished a seizure, then Fourth Amendment analysis would apply pursuant to the exclusivity ruling discussed in ¶ 1 supra, correct? To eliminate the problem, one must assume that any crash or injury resulting from an intent to harm does not amount to a "seizure." Is that consistent with Tennessee v. Garner (culmination of shooting is seizure even when suspect lies dead)?

(c) Alternatively, has Justice Souter strained mightily, relying on the majestic expansiveness of the phrase "shocks the conscience," only to give birth to a gnat? How could a plaintiff prove that he had been chased and hit for the very purpose of causing harm? Would not an officer deny such a motive? How could the denial be disproved? Does the test have practical application only in circumstances where the officer and the chased suspect have a history of bad blood, a history that might give rise to an inference of an intent to harm? How often will these circumstances arise? Note the similar criticism raised against the same test in Whitley v. Albers, Chapter B.2 supra. See Perez v. Unified Government of Wyandotte County/Kansas City, 432 F.3d 1163 (10th Cir. 2005) (no intent to harm or shock the conscience where emergency responder proceeds through intersection, even recklessly, and kills motorist).

5. The "intent to harm" formulation, according to the *Sacramento* majority, captures the essence of the "shocks the conscience" test only in the context of police chases. What formulation might courts create in other contexts?

(a) In Hart v. City of Little Rock, 432 F.3d 801 (8th Cir. 2005), the city released personnel records of two police officers to the attorney for a suspect whom they had arrested and who was now standing trial—thus disclosing all their private information to a person who might have reason to harm them. The Court applied a "deliberate indifference" test because the city had time to reflect before disclosing the information. See Brown v. Nationsbank Corp., 188 F.3d 579 (5th Cir.1999) ("deliberate indifference" test applies to claim by

---

6. The *Sacramento* Court extends the "intent to harm" formulation at one point in the opinion by noting that it covers an intent to harm "physically or to worsen [the suspect's] legal plight." What did the Court intend to cover with the expanded idea?

innocent business owner that his business was destroyed by police who had time to consider how to set up sting operation).[7] Some courts have adopted what they call a "recklessness" standard for some circumstances. See, e.g., Cooper v. Martin, 634 F.3d 477 (8th Cir. 2011) (striking failure to investigate case before filing charges was only act of negligence, not recklessness). In Miller v. City of Philadelphia, 174 F.3d 368 (3d Cir.1999), the court considered claims against a social worker for abusively removing a child from her parents. The court settled on an intermediate standard: "a social worker need not have acted with the 'purpose to cause harm,' but the standard of culpability ... must exceed both negligence and deliberate indifference, and reach a level of gross negligence or arbitrariness." Does *Sacramento*'s recognition that actual standards may vary from context to context open the door to a Tower of Babel as lower courts create a welter of standards for different contexts?

(b) Might there be some circumstances in which the "shocks the conscience" test is applied directly, without translation into some other sub-test such as "intent to harm" or "deliberate indifference"? See Evans v. Secretary Pennsylvania Dept. of Corrections, 645 F.3d 650, 2011 WL 1833237 (3d Cir. 2011) (jailor's correction of clerical error that set earlier release date does not shock conscience); Moore v. Guthrie, 438 F.3d 1036 (10th Cir. 2006) (decision to have police recruits wear less than full gear during training exercise is just "negligence [and] is not sufficient to shock the conscience"); Morris v. Dearborne, 181 F.3d 657 (5th Cir.1999) (teacher's alleged acts of guiding illiterate four-year-old to type messages accusing her father of sexual abuse may shock). Does leaving the shocks-the-conscience test at a general level invite inconsistent or unpredictable results? See Evans, supra ("What is shocking to the conscience inevitably depends to a degree on whose conscience is being tested; so, to put it mildly, the standard has some give in it").

(c) Are some acts so trivial that they cannot possibly be conscience-shocking, regardless of the state official's intent to harm? See T.W. ex rel. Wilson v. School Bd. of Seminole County, 610 F.3d 588 (11th Cir. 2010) ("it is inconceivable that tripping a student and causing the student to stumble, without more, violates the Constitution").

(d) Some courts have created a "state-created danger" doctrine, which they apply when a state official has created an unreasonable danger, or enhanced a danger, and the conduct "shocks the conscience" of the court. See Estate of Smith v. Marasco, 430 F.3d 140 (3d Cir. 2005); Hart v. City of Little Rock, 432 F.3d 801 (8th Cir. 2005). Is this just another name for a claim under *Sacramento*, or is it a different animal?

6. What do you think of Justice Souter's distinction in *Sacramento* between executive acts and legislative acts? Does the "shocks the conscience" test apply only to executive acts, not to legislation? See City of Cuyahoga Falls v. Buckeye Community Hope Foundation, 538 U.S. 188, 123 S.Ct. 1389, 155 L.Ed.2d 349 (2003) (city engineer's refusal to issue the permits during pendency of referendum on building proposal "in no sense constituted egre-

---

7. See also O'Connor v. Pierson, 426 F.3d 187 (2d Cir. 2005) (school board's demand for teacher's medical records may shock conscience after further facts developed).

gious or arbitrary government conduct" under *Sacramento*; ambiguously noting that he was only following city charter).

(a) If a city council by ordinance requires its police to perform in a manner that can be deemed "conscience shocking," is the analysis nevertheless inapplicable because "legislative" rather than "executive" action is at issue? Cf. Whiteland Woods v. Township of West Whiteland, 193 F.3d 177 (3d Cir.1999) (police officer's effort to enforce city's ordinance against videotaping meetings not actionable under "shocks the conscience" test). If a city directs its officers to chase and harm motorists whom the city leaders dislike, is it not actionable under *Sacramento*?

(b) What is the relation between Justice Souter's idea and Monroe v. Pape? If Souter is correct, is a "shocks the conscience" claim a strange creature, one that requires violation of a local law? At least actions not authorized by local law?

7. In **Village of Willowbrook v. Olech**, 528 U.S. 562, 120 S.Ct. 1073, 145 L.Ed.2d 1060 (2000), the Supreme Court held that the Equal Protection Clause also protects against an intent to harm aimed at a "class of one." The plaintiff alleged that the village council demanded a double-wide easement from him to supply water and that the excessive demand "was motivated solely by a spiteful effort to 'get' " her because of prior successful lawsuits against the village. A short two-page per curiam opinion explained that it is not the size of the class that is relevant, but the motivation for governmental action, 528 U.S. at 564, 120 S.Ct. at 1074–75:

> "Our cases have recognized successful equal protection claims brought by a 'class of one' [or more], where the plaintiff alleges that she has been intentionally treated differently from others similarly situated and that there is no rational basis for the difference in treatment. In so doing, we have explained that '[t]he purpose of the equal protection clause of the Fourteenth Amendment is to secure every person within the State's jurisdiction against intentional and arbitrary discrimination, whether occasioned by express terms of a statute or by its improper execution through duly constituted agents.' "

(a) As the Court explained in Lawrence v. Texas, 539 U.S. 558, 123 S.Ct. 2472, 156 L.Ed.2d 508 (2003) (state law punishing homosexual sex implicates the fundamental right to choose sexual partners and fulfillment), moral disagreement or a mere desire to harm someone is an unacceptable reason for action when a fundamental right is at stake, but should the same be true when only low-level scrutiny applies? Government typically taxes or criminalizes much activity simply because it disagrees with the action or finds it morally reprehensible. Why should courts get involved in cases of mere ill will and spite, as in *Olech*? Was *Olech* a mistake? See Engquist v. Oregon Department of Agriculture, 553 U.S. 591, 128 S.Ct. 2146, 170 L.Ed.2d 975 (2008): "Ratifying a class-of-one theory of equal protection in the context of public employment would impermissibly 'constitutionalize the employee grievance.' " Isn't the same true for all ordinary grievances by citizens?

(b) Is *Olech* a low-level "shocks the conscience" test, with ill-will or maliciousness always shocking the Court's conscience? See Lauth v. McCollum, 424 F.3d 631, 633 (7th Cir.2005):

"The paradigmatic 'class of one' case, more sensibly conceived, is one in which a public official, with no conceivable basis for his action other than spite or some other improper motive (improper because unrelated to his public duties), comes down hard on a hapless private citizen. Perhaps he is the holder of a license from the state to operate a bar or restaurant or other business, and the official deprives him of a valuable property right that identically situated citizens toward whom the official bears no ill will are permitted the unfettered enjoyment of. As one moves away from the paradigmatic case, the sense of a wrong of constitutional dignity, and of a need for a federal remedy, attenuates."

Is this also true of "shocks the conscience" cases? See Lingle v. Chevron U.S.A. Inc., 544 U.S. 528, 125 S.Ct. 2074, 161 L.Ed.2d 876 (2005) (summarily citing *Sacramento* as holding that "arbitrary or irrational [governmental action] runs afoul of the Due Process Clause").

DeSHANEY v. WINNEBAGO COUNTY DEPT. OF SOCIAL SERVICES

Supreme Court of the United States, 1989.
489 U.S. 189, 109 S.Ct. 998, 103 L.Ed.2d 249.

CHIEF JUSTICE REHNQUIST delivered the opinion of the Court.

Petitioner is a boy who was beaten and permanently injured by his father, with whom he lived. The respondents are social workers and other local officials who received complaints that petitioner was being abused by his father and had reason to believe that this was the case, but nonetheless did not act to remove petitioner from his father's custody. Petitioner sued respondents claiming that their failure to act deprived him of his liberty in violation of the Due Process Clause of the Fourteenth Amendment to the United States Constitution. We hold that it did not.

I

The facts of this case are undeniably tragic. Petitioner Joshua DeShaney was born in 1979. [The following year his parents divorced, and custody was awarded to Joshua's father, who thereafter moved to Winnebago County.]

The Winnebago County authorities first learned that Joshua DeShaney might be a victim of child abuse in January 1982, when his father's second wife complained to the police, at the time of their divorce, that he had previously "hit the boy causing marks and [was] a prime case for child abuse." The Winnebago County Department of Social Services (DSS) interviewed the father, but he denied the accusations, and DSS did not pursue them further. In January 1983, Joshua was admitted to a local hospital with multiple bruises and abrasions. The examining physician suspected child abuse and notified DSS, which immediately obtained an order from a Wisconsin juvenile court placing Joshua in the temporary custody of the hospital. Three days later, the county convened an ad hoc "Child Protection Team"—consisting of a pediatrician, a psychologist, a police detective, the county's lawyer, several DSS caseworkers, and various hospital personnel—to consider Joshua's situation. At this meeting, the Team decided that there was insufficient evidence of child abuse to retain Joshua in the custody of the court. The Team did, however, decide to recommend several measures to protect Joshua, including enrolling him in a preschool program, providing his father with certain counseling services, and encouraging his father's girlfriend to move out of the home. Randy DeShaney entered into a voluntary agreement with DSS in which he promised to cooperate with them in accomplishing these goals.

Based on the recommendation of the Child Protection Team, the juvenile court dismissed the child protection case and returned Joshua to the custody of his father. A month later, emergency room personnel called the DSS caseworker handling Joshua's case to report that he had once again been treated for suspicious injuries. The caseworker concluded that there was no basis for action. For the next six months, the caseworker made monthly visits to the DeShaney home, during which she observed a number of suspicious injuries on Joshua's head; she also noticed that he had not been enrolled in school and that the girlfriend had not moved out. The caseworker dutifully recorded these incidents in her files, along with her continuing suspicions that someone in the DeShaney household was physically abusing Joshua, but she did nothing more. In November 1983, the emergency room notified DSS that Joshua had been treated once again for injuries that they believed to be caused by child abuse. On the caseworker's next two visits to the DeShaney home, she was told that Joshua was too ill to see her. Still DSS took no action. In March 1984, Randy DeShaney beat 4–year–old Joshua so severely that he fell into a life-threatening coma. Emergency brain surgery revealed a series of hemorrhages caused by traumatic injuries to the head inflicted over a long period of time. Joshua did not die, but he suffered brain damage so severe that he is expected to spend the rest of his life confined to an institution for the profoundly retarded. Randy DeShaney was subsequently tried and convicted of child abuse.

Joshua and his mother brought this action under 42 U.S.C. § 1983 [alleging] that respondents had deprived Joshua of his liberty without due process of law, in violation of his rights under the Fourteenth Amendment, by failing to intervene to protect him against a risk of violence at his father's hands of which they knew or should have known. [Lower courts dismissed the claim.]

II

The Due Process Clause of the Fourteenth Amendment provides that "[n]o State shall ... deprive any person of life, liberty, or property, without due process of law." Petitioners contend that the State deprived Joshua of his liberty interest in "free[dom] from ... unjustified intrusions on personal security," see Ingraham v. Wright, 430 U.S. 651, 673, 97 S.Ct. 1401, 1413, 51 L.Ed.2d 711 (1977), by failing to provide him with adequate protection against his father's violence. The claim is one invoking the substantive rather than procedural component of the Due Process Clause; petitioners do not claim that the State denied Joshua protection without according him appropriate procedural safeguards, see Morrissey v. Brewer, 408 U.S. 471, 481, 92 S.Ct. 2593, 2600, 33 L.Ed.2d 484 (1972), but that it was categorically obligated to protect him in these circumstances, see Youngberg v. Romeo, 457 U.S. 307, 309, 102 S.Ct. 2452, 2454, 73 L.Ed.2d 28 (1982).

But nothing in the language of the Due Process Clause itself requires the State to protect the life, liberty, and property of its citizens against invasion by private actors. The Clause is phrased as a limitation on the State's power to act, not as a guarantee of certain minimal levels of safety and security. It forbids the State itself to deprive individuals of life, liberty, or property without "due process of law," but its language cannot fairly be extended to impose an affirmative obligation on the State to ensure that those interests do not come to harm through other means. Nor does history support such an expansive reading of the constitutional text. Like its counterpart in the Fifth Amendment, the Due Process Clause of the Fourteenth Amendment was intended to prevent government "from abusing [its] power, or employing it as an instrument of oppression," Davidson v. Cannon; see also Daniels v. Williams. Its purpose was to protect the people from the State, not to ensure that the State protected them from each other. The Framers were content to leave the extent of governmental obligation in the latter area to the democratic political processes.

Consistent with these principles, our cases have recognized that the Due Process Clauses generally confer no affirmative right to governmental aid, even where such aid may be necessary to secure life, liberty, or property interests of which the government itself may not deprive the individual. See, e.g., Harris v. McRae, 448 U.S. 297, 317–318, 100 S.Ct. 2671, 2688–2689, 65 L.Ed.2d 784 (1980) (no obligation to fund abortions or other medical services) (discussing Due Process Clause of Fifth Amendment); Lindsey v. Normet, 405 U.S. 56, 74, 92 S.Ct. 862, 874, 31 L.Ed.2d 36 (1972) (no obligation to provide adequate housing) (discussing Due Process Clause of Fourteenth Amendment); see also Youngberg v. Romeo, supra, 457 U.S., at 317, 102 S.Ct., at 2458 ("As a general matter, a State is under no constitutional duty to provide substantive services for those within its border"). As we said in Harris v. McRae, "[a]lthough the liberty protected by the Due Process Clause affords protection against unwarranted *government* interference . . . , it does not confer an entitlement to such [governmental aid] as may be necessary to realize all the advantages of that freedom." 448 U.S., at 317–318, 100 S.Ct., at 2688–2689 (emphasis added). If the Due Process Clause does not require the State to provide its citizens with particular protective services, it follows that the State cannot be held liable under the Clause for injuries that could have been averted had it chosen to provide them.[8] As a general matter, then, we conclude

---

8. The State may not, of course, selectively deny its protective services to certain disfavored minorities without violating the Equal Protection Clause. See Yick Wo v. Hopkins, 118 U.S. 356, 6 S.Ct. 1064, 30 L.Ed. 220 (1886). But no such argument has been made here.

that a State's failure to protect an individual against private violence simply does not constitute a violation of the Due Process Clause.

Petitioners contend, however, that even if the Due Process Clause imposes no affirmative obligation on the State to provide the general public with adequate protective services, such a duty may arise[, as here,] out of certain "special relationships" created or assumed by the State with respect to particular individuals. * * *

We reject this argument. It is true that in certain limited circumstances the Constitution imposes upon the State affirmative duties of care and protection with respect to particular individuals. [The Court cited Estelle v. Gamble and its duty to provide medical care to prisoners; Youngberg v. Romeo and its duty[6] to provide involuntarily committed mental patients with such services as are necessary to ensure their "reasonable safety" from themselves and others; and Revere v. Massachusetts General Hospital, 463 U.S. 239, 244, 103 S.Ct. 2979, 2983, 77 L.Ed.2d 605 (1983), and its duty to provide medical care to injured arrestees.]

But these cases afford petitioners no help. Taken together, they stand only for the proposition that when the State takes a person into its custody and holds him there against his will, the Constitution imposes upon it a corresponding duty to assume some responsibility for his safety and general well-being. The rationale for this principle is simple enough: when the State by the affirmative exercise of its power so restrains an individual's liberty that it renders him unable to care for himself, and at the same time fails to provide for his basic human needs—e.g., food, clothing, shelter, medical care, and reasonable safety—it transgresses the substantive limits on state action set by the Eighth Amendment and the Due Process Clause. The affirmative duty to protect arises not from the State's knowledge of the individual's predicament or from its expressions of intent to help him, but from the limitation which it has imposed on his freedom to act on his own behalf. In the substantive due process analysis, it is the State's affirmative act of restraining the individual's freedom to act on his own behalf—through incarceration, institutionalization, or other similar restraint of personal liberty—which is the "deprivation of liberty" triggering the protections of the Due Process Clause, not its failure to act to protect his liberty interests against harms inflicted by other means.[8]

The *Estelle–Youngberg* analysis simply has no applicability in the present case. Petitioners concede that the harms Joshua suffered did not

---

6. The Eighth Amendment applies "only after the State has complied with the constitutional guarantees traditionally associated with criminal prosecutions.... [T]he State does not acquire the power to punish with which the Eighth Amendment is concerned until after it has secured a formal adjudication of guilt in accordance with due process of law." Ingraham v. Wright, 430 U.S. 651, 671–672, n. 40, 97 S.Ct. 1401, 1412–1413, n. 40, 51 L.Ed.2d 711 (1977).

8. Of course, the protections of the Due Process Clause, both substantive and procedural, may be triggered when the State, by the affirmative acts of its agents, subjects an involuntarily confined individual to deprivations of liberty which are not among those generally authorized by his confinement. See, e.g., Whitley v. Albers.

occur while he was in the State's custody, but while he was in the custody of his natural father, who was in no sense a state actor.[9] While the State may have been aware of the dangers that Joshua faced in the free world, it played no part in their creation, nor did it do anything to render him any more vulnerable to them. That the State once took temporary custody of Joshua does not alter the analysis, for when it returned him to his father's custody, it placed him in no worse position than that in which he would have been had it not acted at all; the State does not become the permanent guarantor of an individual's safety by having once offered him shelter. Under these circumstances, the State had no constitutional duty to protect Joshua.

It may well be that, by voluntarily undertaking to protect Joshua against a danger it concededly played no part in creating, the State acquired a duty under state tort law to provide him with adequate protection against that danger. See Restatement (Second) of Torts § 323 (1965) (one who undertakes to render services to another may in some circumstances be held liable for doing so in a negligent fashion); see generally W. Keeton, D. Dobbs, R. Keeton, & D. Owen, Prosser and Keeton on the Law of Torts § 56 (5th ed. 1984) (discussing "special relationships" which may give rise to affirmative duties to act under the common law of tort). But the claim here is based on the Due Process Clause of the Fourteenth Amendment, which, as we have said many times, does not transform every tort committed by a state actor into a constitutional violation. See Daniels v. Williams; Paul v. Davis. A State may, through its courts and legislatures, impose such affirmative duties of care and protection upon its agents as it wishes. But not "all common-law duties owed by government actors were ... constitutionalized by the Fourteenth Amendment." Daniels v. Williams. Because, as explained above, the State had no constitutional duty to protect Joshua against his father's violence, its failure to do so—though calamitous in hindsight—simply does not constitute a violation of the Due Process Clause.[10]

Judges and lawyers, like other humans, are moved by natural sympathy in a case like this to find a way for Joshua and his mother to receive adequate compensation for the grievous harm inflicted upon them. But before yielding to that impulse, it is well to remember once again that the harm was inflicted not by the State of Wisconsin, but by Joshua's father. The most that can be said of the state functionaries in this case is that

---

9. * * * Had the State by the affirmative exercise of its power removed Joshua from free society and placed him in a foster home operated by its agents, we might have a situation sufficiently analogous to incarceration or institutionalization to give rise to an affirmative duty to protect. Indeed, several Courts of Appeals have held, by analogy to *Estelle* and *Youngberg*, that the State may be held liable under the Due Process Clause for failing to protect children in foster homes from mistreatment at the hands of their foster parents. See Doe v. New York City Dept. of Social Services, 649 F.2d 134, 141–142 (C.A.2 1981), Taylor ex rel. Walker v. Ledbetter, 818 F.2d 791, 794–797 (C.A.11 1987) (en banc). We express no view on the validity of this analogy, however, as it is not before us in the present case.

10. Because we conclude that the Due Process Clause did not require the State to protect Joshua from his father, we need not address respondents' alternative argument that the individual state actors lacked the requisite "state of mind" to make out a due process violation. See Daniels v. Williams, 474 U.S., at 334, n. 3. * * *

they stood by and did nothing when suspicious circumstances dictated a more active role for them. In defense of them it must also be said that had they moved too soon to take custody of the son away from the father, they would likely have been met with charges of improperly intruding into the parent-child relationship, charges based on the same Due Process Clause that forms the basis for the present charge of failure to provide adequate protection.

The people of Wisconsin may well prefer a system of liability which would place upon the State and its officials the responsibility for failure to act in situations such as the present one. They may create such a system, if they do not have it already, by changing the tort law of the State in accordance with the regular law-making process. But they should not have it thrust upon them by this Court's expansion of the Due Process Clause of the Fourteenth Amendment.

Affirmed.

JUSTICE BRENNAN, with whom JUSTICE MARSHALL and JUSTICE BLACKMUN join, dissenting.

* * * It may well be, as the Court decides, that the Due Process Clause as construed by our prior cases creates no general right to basic governmental services. That, however, is not the question presented here * * *. No one * * * has asked the Court to proclaim that, as a general matter, the Constitution safeguards positive as well as negative liberties. This is more than a quibble over dicta; it is a point about perspective, having substantive ramifications. In a constitutional setting that distinguishes sharply between action and inaction, one's characterization of the misconduct alleged under § 1983 may effectively decide the case. Thus, by leading off with a discussion (and rejection) of the idea that the Constitution imposes on the States an affirmative duty to take basic care of their citizens, the Court foreshadows—perhaps even preordains—its conclusion that no duty existed even on the specific facts before us. * * *

* * *

I would begin from the opposite direction. I would focus first on the action that Wisconsin has taken with respect to Joshua and children like him, rather than on the actions that the State failed to take[, citing *Estelle* and *Youngberg*]. Cases from the lower courts also recognize that a State's actions can be decisive in assessing the constitutional significance of subsequent inaction. For these purposes, moreover, actual physical restraint is not the only State action that has been considered relevant. See, e.g., White v. Rochford, 592 F.2d 381 (C.A.7 1979) (police officers violated due process when, after arresting the guardian of three young children, they abandoned the children on a busy stretch of highway at night).

Because of the Court's initial fixation on the general principle that the Constitution does not establish positive rights[, it artificially narrowly construes *Youngberg* and *Estelle*]. I would not, however, give *Youngberg* and *Estelle* such a stingy scope. I would recognize, as the Court apparently cannot, that "the State's knowledge of [an] individual's predicament [and] its expressions of intent to help him" can amount to a "limitation of his freedom to act on his own behalf" or to obtain help from others. Thus, I would read *Youngberg* and *Estelle* to stand for the much more generous proposition that, if a State cuts off private sources of aid and then refuses aid itself, it cannot wash its hands of the harm that results from its inaction.

* * *

Wisconsin has established a child-welfare system specifically designed to help children like Joshua. Wisconsin law places upon the local departments of social services such as respondent (DSS or Department) a duty to investigate reported instances of child abuse. See Wis.Stat.Ann. § 48.981(3) (1987 and Supp. 1988–1989). While other governmental bodies and private persons are largely responsible for the reporting of possible cases of child abuse, see § 48.981(2), Wisconsin law channels all such reports to the local departments of social services for evaluation and, if necessary, further action. * * * In this way, Wisconsin law invites— indeed, directs—citizens and other governmental entities to depend on local departments of social services such as respondent to protect children from abuse. * * *

In these circumstances, a private citizen, or even a person working in a government agency other than DSS, would doubtless feel that her job was done as soon as she had reported her suspicions of child abuse to DSS. Through its child-welfare program, in other words, the State of Wisconsin has relieved ordinary citizens and governmental bodies other than the Department of any sense of obligation to do anything more than report their suspicions of child abuse to DSS. If DSS ignores or dismisses these suspicions, no one will step in to fill the gap. Wisconsin's child-protection program thus effectively confined Joshua DeShaney within the walls of Randy DeShaney's violent home until such time as DSS took action to remove him. Conceivably, then, children like Joshua are made worse off by the existence of this program when the persons and entities charged with carrying it out fail to do their jobs. It simply belies reality, therefore, to contend that the State "stood by and did nothing" with respect to Joshua. Through its child-protection program, the State actively intervened in Joshua's life and, by virtue of this intervention, acquired ever more certain knowledge that Joshua was in grave danger. These circumstances, in my view, plant this case solidly within the tradition of cases like *Youngberg* and *Estelle*.

* * * *Youngberg*'s deference to a decisionmaker's professional judgment ensures that once a caseworker has decided, on the basis of her professional training and experience, that one course of protection is preferable for a given child, or even that no special protection is required, she will not be found liable for the harm that follows. * * * Moreover, that the Due Process Clause is not violated by merely negligent conduct, see Daniels [v. Williams], means that a social worker who simply makes a

mistake of judgment under what are admittedly complex and difficult conditions will not find herself liable in damages under § 1983.

* * * My disagreement with the Court arises from its failure to see that inaction can be every bit as abusive of power as action, that oppression can result when a State undertakes a vital duty and then ignores it. Today's opinion construes the Due Process Clause to permit a State to displace private sources of protection and then, at the critical moment, to shrug its shoulders and turn away from the harm that it has promised to try to prevent. Because I cannot agree that our Constitution is indifferent to such indifference, I respectfully dissent.

JUSTICE BLACKMUN, dissenting. [Omitted.]

NOTE ON AFFIRMATIVE DUTIES, THIRD PARTIES, AND THE LINE BETWEEN Sacramento AND DeShaney

1.   The argument that government should be constitutionally required to provide basic services to citizens has been remarkably unsuccessful in the Supreme Court. As the *DeShaney* majority notes, from housing to education to welfare subsistence, the Court has rejected virtually every claim for constitutionally mandatory, judicially supervised provision of government services. Indeed, even Justice Brennan's dissenting opinion does not make the argument. Why not?

(a) Justice Rehnquist finds one justification in text: the negatively phrased Fourteenth Amendment restrains government; it mandates nothing positive. Consider Judge Posner's opinion for the Seventh Circuit in Jackson v. City of Joliet, 715 F.2d 1200 (7th Cir.1983), in which plaintiffs claimed a right to be rescued by police officers who came upon a wrecked automobile:

"[T]he Constitution is a charter of negative rather than positive liberties. The men who wrote the Bill of Rights were not concerned that government might do too little for the people but that it might do too much to them. The Fourteenth Amendment, adopted in 1868 at the height of laissez-faire thinking, sought to protect Americans from oppression by state government, not to secure them basic governmental services. * * * The modern expansion of government has led to proposals for reinterpreting the Fourteenth Amendment to guarantee the provision of basic services such as education, poor relief, and, presumably, police protection, even if they are not being withheld discriminatorily. See, e.g., Michelman, *Foreword: On Protecting the Poor Through the Fourteenth Amendment,* 83 Harv.L.Rev. 7 (1979). To adopt these proposals, however, would be more than an extension of traditional conceptions of the due process clause. It would turn the clause on its head. It would change it from a protection against coercion by state government to a command that the state use its taxing power to coerce some of its citizens to provide services to others. The Supreme Court[, with few exceptions,] has refused to go so far, see, e.g., San Antonio Independent School Dist. v. Rodriguez, 411 U.S. 1, 93 S.Ct. 1278, 36 L.Ed.2d 16 (1973). * * * [T]he difference between harming and failing to help is just the difference noted earlier between negative liberty—being let alone by the state—and positive liberty—being helped by the state."

Do you agree? For criticism of the distinction, see Currie, *Positive and Negative Constitutional Rights,* 53 U.CHI.L.REV. 864 (1986).

(b) To what extent is *DeShaney* compelled not by the language of the Fourteenth Amendment but by the Court's traditional reluctance to reorder state spending priorities? Consider Dollar v. Haralson County, 704 F.2d 1540 (11th Cir.1983), in which plaintiffs posited a duty on the state to build a bridge, thus eliminating a flooded stream crossing that had killed children in an automobile: if the Court had recognized a duty to build bridges to protect children, from what source would the funding come? If tax dollars are spent on bridges, how much would be left for Joshua DeShaney and reform of a state's child-protection system? Does the spending concern dovetail with textual concerns? Because, even though recognition of negative rights may lead to some judicial control of spending, see Missouri v. Jenkins, Chapter F.2 infra (taxes necessary to complete school desegregation remedy), recognition of a broad range of positive rights would open the floodgates?

(c) The distinction between positive and negative rights essentially seeks to show that the government has been inactive and thus is not the cause of the harm to the plaintiff. That idea is reinforced by the *DeShaney* Court's insistence that the harm to Joshua was done not by Joshua himself or by the state, but by a "third party"—Joshua's father. Can government be expected to protect every citizen from all other citizens? See Bryson v. City of Edmond, 905 F.2d 1386 (10th Cir.1990) (survivors of mass-murder in post office sue local officials for allowing murders to take place). Would a rule subjecting police to liability lead to unrestrained enforcement of all penal laws? See Saenz v. Heldenfels Bros., 183 F.3d 389 (5th Cir.1999) (police sued for failure to arrest drunken driver).

2. What is the dividing line between those situations in which the government is an affirmative actor—thus giving rise to potential Due Process liability—and those in which it has been inactive and/or third parties have caused harm? The majority in *DeShaney* recognizes only one explicit situation, that in which states have custody of persons. Cf. Estelle v. Gamble, Chapter B.2, supra (duty to provide some medical services). Why should that situation lead to an affirmative duty on the state? What other circumstances might be similar?

(a) In Justice Rehnquist's state of nature, each person cares for himself, and the government becomes a guarantor only when it incarcerates a citizen and thereby disables the citizen from caring for himself. Is anyone other than a prisoner in this situation?

(b) Why was baby Joshua not in custody of the state? Because the state had relinquished custody back to his father? Would the result have been different if Joshua's harm had occurred while in the state's custody or control? See S.S. v. McMullen, 186 F.3d 1066 (8th Cir.1999) (child returned temporarily to father and known pedophile). Was the social worker in *DeShaney* in an untenable situation because she feared a potential § 1983 suit by Joshua's father for violating his parental rights? See Tenenbaum v. Williams,

193 F.3d 581 (2d Cir.1999) (suit by parents denied custody of child); Miller v. City of Philadelphia, 174 F.3d 368 (3d Cir.1999) (similar).

3. Building on the *DeShaney* Court's discussion of custody situations, lower courts have recognized "two exceptions [under which government may be liable for acts of third parties]: the 'special relationship' theory and the 'state-created danger' theory. Under the former, the state has a duty to protect an individual under its care, custody, or control when the state has removed one's ability to care for oneself. Under the [latter] theory of liability, a duty to protect emerges after the state affirmatively places an individual in a position of danger that the individual would not otherwise have faced." S.S. v. McMullen, 186 F.3d 1066 (8th Cir.1999) (collecting cases). As you review these exceptions, consider what they have in common. Are they simply attempts to try to define circumstances where the state itself has significantly acted to cause the plaintiff's harm?

(a) What relationship, other than close penal custody, is so special that a person is prevented from caring for herself? Is state-mandated compulsory education such a situation? See Hasenfus v. LaJeunesse, 175 F.3d 68 (1st Cir.1999) (noting that argument is usually rejected, but that in context of school suicides the position may not be absolute) (collecting cases); McQueen v. Beecher Community Schools, 433 F.3d 460 (6th Cir. 2006) (more recent case rejecting liability of teacher where student shoots another student in school).[1] See also White v. Lemacks, 183 F.3d 1253 (11th Cir.1999) (nurses attacked by prisoners inside prison infirmary; only "involuntary confinement" creates a special relationship). Claims are generally limited and unsuccessful. See Laura Oren, *Safari into the Snake Pit: The State Created Danger Doctrine*, 13 WM. & MARY BILL RTS. J. 1165 (2005): "Under the new, 'custodial' version of special relationships, very few relationships qualified outside of the obvious contexts of incarceration or civil commitment."

(b) "The 'danger creation' doctrine generally provides that state officials may be liable for injuries caused by a private actor where those officials created [or enhanced] the danger that led to the harm." Sutton v. Utah State School for the Deaf and Blind, 173 F.3d 1226 (10th Cir.1999) (bathroom assault at school by co-students; no liability because defendant school official only failed to act and did not act "affirmatively" to increase danger). Accord, McQueen v. Beecher Community Schools, 433 F.3d 460 (6th Cir. 2006) (noting that every circuit recognizes the state-created danger doctrine, but finding failure to supervise students does not increase danger). Are the following two cases different—Wood v. Ostrander, 879 F.2d 583 (9th Cir.1989) (police who left woman in car alone after arresting her friend/driver can be liable for subsequent assault on woman), and Ross v. United States, 910 F.2d 1422 (7th Cir.1990) (officers who do not merely stand by but actively prevent citizens from rescuing drowning swimmer may be liable for his subsequent death). Does failure to arrest a person imminently capable of causing harm to others constitute a state-created danger? See Saenz v. Heldenfels Bros., supra (drunken driver not arrested, no § 1983 liability for subsequent accident). Does the exception have the potential of swallowing the *DeShaney* rule if it is

---

1. Cf. Vernonia Sch. Dist. v. Acton, 515 U.S. 646, 655, 115 S.Ct. 2386, 132 L.Ed.2d 564 (1995) (in drug-search case, Court observes students are not ordinarily in custody).

used to label all governmental failures as state-created dangers?[2] See Laura Oren, *Safari into the Snake Pit: The State Created Danger Doctrine*, 13 WM. & MARY BILL RTS. J. 1165 (2005) (recording notable limitations on claims).

(c) Are the "special relationship" theory and the "state-created danger" theory nothing more than guidelines for establishing when state officials have acted sufficiently affirmatively so that Due Process standards attach? Is the "state-created danger" theory consistent with the majority's ruling in *DeShaney*? Did the state create or enhance the danger to Joshua by returning him to his parent? Or was the state merely returning matters to the status quo ante of parental supervision?

4.   What is the connection between *DeShaney* and the *Sacramento* case? One possibility is that *Sacramento* holds the potential for displacing (or overriding the result in) *DeShaney*: the theory is that conduct that is not covered because of *DeShaney* may nevertheless "shock the conscience" under *Sacramento*. The other possibility is that *Sacramento* adds other requirements to any claim viable under the *DeShaney* exceptions: the theory is that state-created dangers and such must additionally shock the conscience of the court under *Sacramento*.

(a) While it is possible to find a few cases holding state officers liable for their own direct actions under *Sacramento*, see, e.g., Neal v. Fulton County Bd. of Educ., 229 F.3d 1069, 1076 (11th Cir.2000) (coach strikes player causing permanent blindness), there appear to be few, if any, cases that actually reject *DeShaney* liability, then find for the plaintiff under *Sacramento*. Why is this so? Do all the arguments against affirmative duties still apply even when courts only impose affirmative duties episodically with a shocks-the-conscience test?

(b) Cases running in the opposite direction—holding that state-created danger claims must additionally meet *Sacramento*'s conscience-shocking test—can be found in the topical area of state-created dangers, reversing the pre-*Sacramento* approach of applying the state-created danger doctrine pristinely. See, e.g., Kallstrom v. City of Columbus, 136 F.3d 1055 (6th Cir. 1998). Soon after *Sacramento*, in Hasenfus v. LaJeunesse, 175 F.3d 68 (1st Cir.1999), the court assumed that in some circumstances there might be an "obligation of the school or school employees to render aid to a student in peril," but even so, the subsequent "basic due process constraint" is only "against behavior so extreme as to 'shock the conscience'" under *Sacramento*. The Court found that standard not met in the context of a school official who failed to prevent an attempted suicide by a pupil chastised at school. Cases since then have often adopted the same approach. See McQueen v. Beecher Community Schools, 433 F.3d 460 (6th Cir. 2006) (noting that its previous *Kallstrom* decision has been "clarified" to include *Sacramento*'s conscience-shocking test). Several circuits have adopted a multi-part test for state-created danger

---

2. Does Justice Brennan's theory undermine its own liberal impulse? Consider the case of Archie v. City of Racine, 847 F.2d 1211 (7th Cir.1988) (en banc) (pre-*DeShaney;* city creates emergency 911 telephone number for medical care but inadequately provides such care). If government becomes liable for a special relationship whenever it creates a public program, will governments create such programs? Can it pay for both the programs and the resulting § 1983 judgments based on failure to implement the programs effectively? Is government permitted to undertake a program only when it can do so perfectly?

claims that specifically require proof of conscience-shocking under *Sacramento*. See, e.g., Bright v. Westmoreland County, 443 F.3d 276 (3d Cir. 2006) (second element of four-part test); Hart v. City of Little Rock, 432 F.3d 801 (8th Cir. 2005) (last step in a five-part test); Sutton v. Utah State School for the Deaf and Blind, 173 F.3d 1226 (10th Cir.1999) (additional factor after *DeShaney*). But see Kennedy v. City of Ridgefield, 439 F.3d 1055 (9th Cir. 2006) (explaining that circuit's refusal to join the parade). What do you think of this development?

(c) Presumably, when a court reaches the *Sacramento* issue after finding a state-created danger under *DeShaney*, it would imitate *Sacramento* with a process that might yield the "intent to harm" standard in some contexts, a "deliberate indifference" standard in another context, or possibly some other formulation. See Sutton v. Utah State School for the Deaf and Blind, 173 F.3d 1226 (10th Cir.1999) ("deliberate indifference" formulation adopted for failure to provide safe environment for disabled school child). Does this mean that the *DeShaney* precedent keeps the *Sacramento* inquiry in check? Or does the demanding *Sacramento* inquiry keep *DeShaney*'s state-created-danger exception in check?

5. Can Procedural Due Process accomplish what Substantive Due Process failed to do in *DeShaney*?[3] In **Town of Castle Rock v. Gonzales**, 545 U.S. 748, 125 S.Ct. 2796, 162 L.Ed.2d 658 (2005), a wife had obtained a protective order against her husband requiring him to stay away from the family home. Police officers failed to enforce the order, and the husband took her daughters and murdered them. The Court of Appeals ruled that the restraining order gave her entitlements under state law that made the protections of Procedural Due Process attach, noting that unless federal courts gave protection, such orders would be "valueless." The Supreme Court disagreed, found no entitlement (because of a tradition of police discretion in enforcement), and noted that the value of the restraining order was its potential for enforcement in state courts at the behest of the state. The Court concluded, 545 U.S. at 768, 125 S.Ct. at 2810:

> "In light of today's decision and that in *DeShaney*, the benefit that a third party may receive from having someone else arrested for a crime generally does not trigger protections under the Due Process Clause, neither in its procedural nor in its 'substantive' manifestations. This result reflects our continuing reluctance to treat the Fourteenth Amendment as 'a font of tort law,' Parratt v. Taylor, [Chapter 1G.3 infra], but it does not mean States are powerless to provide victims with personally enforceable remedies. Although the framers of the Fourteenth Amendment and [§ 1983] did not create a system by which police departments are generally held financially accountable for crimes that better policing might have prevented, the people of Colorado are free to craft such a system under state law."

(a) The concluding statement seems to be as important as the remainder of the Court's decision, which drew only two dissenters. Note the last

---

3. As discussed in Chapter 1G.3 infra, Procedural Due Process protects state-created "liberty" and "property" interests. Once these are created, federal courts will enforce certain procedural safeguards to ensure that these interests are not taken away without a hearing.

sentence quoted supra. If Colorado had created an entitlement, why didn't plaintiff seek to enforce it in state court? Was it because Colorado law might have given remedies against the husband but not against the police officers? Was the plaintiff, then, trying to leverage her state-law interests to get a remedy from third parties, as in *DeShaney*?

(b) Why do plaintiffs seem to prefer federal court for these types of claims? If state courts are unreceptive, does that prove that there is no entitlement under state law to which Procedural Due Process attaches? Or does that just prove the need for federal protection? Is the Supreme Court unsympathetic, or does it worry about the role federal courts can play in these situations? Does it worry that a decision to the contrary could make federal courts domestic-relations courts? See U.S. v. Morrison, Chapter 5 infra. Is that the driving force behind *DeShaney* as well?

5. EQUAL PROTECTION: RACIAL AND GENDER CLASSIFICATIONS (AND OTHER DISCRIMINATION MERITING HIGH–LEVEL SCRUTINY)

In some early cases from the modern era of the civil rights movement, courts flirted with the proposition that neutral state rules having a disparate effect or impact on black citizens would immediately give rise to strict scrutiny to determine if the differential impacts were constitutionally justifiable. In **Hawkins v. Town of Shaw**, 437 F.2d 1286 (5th Cir. 1971), aff'd en banc, 461 F.2d 1171 (5th Cir.1972), the old Fifth Circuit faced a situation in which areas of town inhabited by blacks consistently received lesser public services than the neighborhoods inhabited by whites. The plaintiffs offered overwhelming evidence to show that the disparity existed, but no direct evidence that the difference was racially motivated. The court observed that

> "it may be argued that this result was not intended. That is to say, the record contains no direct evidence aimed at establishing bad faith, ill will or an evil motive on the part of the Town of Shaw and its public officials. We feel, however, that the law on this point is clear. In a civil rights suit alleging racial discrimination in contravention of the Fourteenth Amendment, actual intent or motive need not be directly proved, for 'equal protection of the laws means more than merely the absence of governmental action designed to discriminate; * * * we now firmly recognize that the arbitrary quality of thoughtlessness can be as disastrous and unfair to private rights and the public interest as the perversity of a willful scheme.' "

The principal intellectual competitor to the *Hawkins* approach came from judges who thought that the better approach would be to use the statistical disparity as circumstantial evidence of an intent to discriminate. Only if the factfinder ultimately found intentional discrimination would the court move on to perform strict scrutiny. See id. at 1294 (Bell, J. [later Attorney General for President Carter], concurring specially). Judge Bell voted in the *Hawkins* case to overturn the trial court's factual determination of no intentional racial discrimination, labeling it clearly erroneous in light of the statistical disparity and substantial proof that the town's neutral, non-racial explanations for the disparity were a lie. This approach had a long and distinguished record in the Supreme Court, albeit mostly limited to cases involving racial discrimination in the selection of jurors. There it became known as the "statistical prima facie case."

The assumptions and rules of the "statistical prima facie case" may be succinctly stated:

(1) If jury lists are compiled without discrimination, one would not expect blacks to be totally excluded, and indeed one would expect blacks under a fair selection procedure to be represented in approximately the same proportion as they represent in the population area in which the selection occurred. Whitus v. Georgia, 385 U.S. 545, 87 S.Ct. 643, 17 L.Ed.2d 599 (1967). If statistics show that blacks are underrepresented, the Court will infer that intentional racial discrimination produced the skewed results. See, Castaneda v. Partida, 430 U.S. 482, 97 S.Ct. 1272, 51 L.Ed.2d 498 (1977) (Hispanic–Americans).

(2) This inference will shift the burden of proof to defendants, requiring them to "justify such an exclusion as having been brought about by some reason other than racial discrimination," Patton v. Mississippi, 332 U.S. 463, 466, 68 S.Ct. 184, 92 L.Ed. 76 (1947), or suffer a directed verdict.

(3) Defendants' mere denials of having employed racial considerations cannot rebut the prima facie case, nor can the state meet its burden by simply posing a set of theories that might account for the statistical disparity. Rather, they must offer direct evidence to show the factfinder that some factor other than race caused the underrepresentation at issue. Patton v. Mississippi, supra; Coleman v. Alabama, 389 U.S. 22, 23, 88 S.Ct. 2, 19 L.Ed.2d 22 (1967).

Whether one believes that disparate impact should give rise to an inference of racial discrimination or should itself be immediately subjected to strict scrutiny may depend on the pervasiveness that one detects in racial discrimination.[4] Or it may depend upon whether one believes that judges understand the science of statistics sufficiently to make informed judgments about their use in particular cases. Compare Castaneda v. Partida, supra, 430 U.S. at 496 n. 17 (judges know statistics), with Craig v. Boren, supra, 429 U.S. at 203 n. 16, 97 S.Ct. at 460 n. 16 (state legislators cannot be trusted to understand statistics; statistics are not as important as normative judgments by judges). Scholarly opinion in the early period was as split as the approaches of judges. See Ely, *Legislative and Adminis-*

---

4. One might, for example, believe that racism is pervasive at a subconscious level. See Lawrence, *The Id, the Ego, and Equal Protection: Reckoning with Unconscious Racism*, 39 STAN. L. REV. 317 (1987). If courts should always be suspicious of covert intentional discrimination by race when African–Americans are adversely affected, do the same suspicions arise when Asian–Americans or women are adversely affected? White males? Cf. Matsuda, *Public Response to Racist Speech: Considering the Victim's Story,* 87 MICH. L. REV. 2320 (1989) (only statements harmful to minorities and women should be closely scrutinized).

trative Motivation in Constitutional Law, 79 YALE L.J. 1205 (1970) (statistical prima facie case of adverse impact should only raise a factual inference of racial discrimination); Brest, Palmer v. Thompson: *An Approach to the Problem of Unconstitutional Legislative Motivation,* 1971 SUP.CT.REV. 95 (adverse impact standing alone triggers strict scrutiny); Perry, *Disproportionate Impact Theory of Racial Discrimination,* 125 U.PA.L.REV. 540 (1977) (disproportionate impact triggers sliding scale of scrutiny depending on topic).

VILLAGE OF ARLINGTON HEIGHTS v. METROPOLITAN HOUSING DEVELOPMENT CORP.

Supreme Court of the United States, 1977.
429 U.S. 252, 97 S.Ct. 555, 50 L.Ed.2d 450.

MR. JUSTICE POWELL delivered the opinion of the Court. * * *

I

Arlington Heights is a suburb of Chicago, located about 26 miles northwest of the downtown Loop area. Most of the land in Arlington Heights is zoned for detached single-family homes, and this is in fact the prevailing land use. The Village experienced substantial growth during the 1960's, but, like other communities in northwest Cook County, its population of racial minority groups remained quite low. According to the 1970 census, only 27 of the Village's 64,000 residents were black.

The Clerics of St. Viator, a religious order (Order), own an 80–acre parcel just east of the center of Arlington Heights. Part of the site is occupied by the Viatorian high school, and part by the Order's three-story novitiate building, which houses dormitories and a Montessori school. Much of the site, however, remains vacant. Since 1959, when the Village first adopted a zoning ordinance, all the land surrounding the Viatorian property has been zoned R–3, a single-family specification with relatively small minimum lot-size requirements. On three sides of the Viatorian land there are single-family homes just across a street; to the east the Viatorian property directly adjoins the backyards of other single-family homes.

The Order decided in 1970 to devote some of its land to low-and moderate-income housing. Investigation revealed that the most expeditious way to build such housing was to work through a nonprofit developer experienced in the use of federal housing subsidies under § 236 of the National Housing Act, 48 Stat. 1246, as added and amended, 12 U.S.C. § 1715z–1.

MHDC is such a developer. [MHDC and the Order negotiated a lease-purchase agreement for 15 acres of the Viatorian property on which MHDC would build "Lincoln Green," a development comprising 20 two-story buildings and a total of 190 units, each with a private entrance.]

The planned development did not conform to the Village's zoning ordinance and could not be built unless Arlington Heights rezoned the parcel to R–5, its multiple-family housing classification. Accordingly, MHDC filed with the Village Plan Commission a petition for rezoning, accompanied by supporting materials describing the development and specifying that it would be subsidized under § 236. The materials made clear that one requirement under § 236 is an affirmative marketing plan designed to assure that a subsidized development is racially integrated. * * *

During the spring of 1971, the Plan Commission considered the proposal at a series of three public meetings, which drew large crowds. Although many of those attending were quite vocal and demonstrative in opposition to Lincoln Green, a number of individuals and representatives of community groups spoke in support of rezoning. Some of the comments, both from opponents and supporters, addressed what was referred to as the "social issue," the desirability or undesirability of introducing at this location in Arlington Heights low-and moderate-income housing, housing that would probably be racially integrated.

Many of the opponents, however, focused on the zoning aspects of the petition, stressing two arguments. First, the area always had been zoned single-family, and the neighboring citizens had built or purchased there in reliance on that classification. Rezoning threatened to cause a measurable drop in property value for neighboring sites. Second, the Village's apartment policy, adopted by the Village Board in 1962 and amended in 1970, called for R–5 zoning primarily to serve as a buffer between single-family development and land uses thought incompatible, such as commercial or manufacturing districts. Lincoln Green did not meet this requirement, as it adjoined no commercial or manufacturing district. [The Planning Commission recommended rejection of MHDC's proposal, and the Village government thereafter denied the rezoning request. MHDC, joined by three prospective black tenants then filed this suit, challenging the decision as racially discriminatory. The District Court ruled for defendants after finding no intentional discrimination, but the Court of Appeals reversed, finding that the "historical content and ultimate effect" of the refusal to re-zone would be to fence blacks outside the Village.]

* * *

III

Our decision last Term in Washington v. Davis, 426 U.S. 229, 96 S.Ct. 2040, 48 L.Ed.2d 597 (1976), made it clear that official action will not be held unconstitutional solely because it results in a racially disproportionate impact. "Disproportionate impact is not irrelevant, but it is not the sole touchstone of an invidious racial discrimination." Id., at 242, 96 S.Ct., at 2049. Proof of racially discriminatory intent or purpose is required to show a violation of the Equal Protection Clause. Although some contrary indications may be drawn from some of our cases, the holding in *Davis* reaffirmed a principle well established in a variety of contexts. E.g., Keyes v. School Dist. No. 1, Denver, Colo., 413 U.S. 189, 208, 93 S.Ct. 2686,

2697, 37 L.Ed.2d 548 (1973) (schools); Wright v. Rockefeller, 376 U.S. 52, 56–57, 84 S.Ct. 603, 605, 11 L.Ed.2d 512 (1964) (election districting); Akins v. Texas, 325 U.S. 398, 403–404, 65 S.Ct. 1276, 1279, 89 L.Ed. 1692 (1945) (jury selection).

Davis does not require a plaintiff to prove that the challenged action rested solely on racially discriminatory purposes. Rarely can it be said that a legislature or administrative body operating under a broad mandate made a decision motivated solely by a single concern, or even that a particular purpose was the "dominant" or "primary" one.[11] In fact, it is because legislators and administrators are properly concerned with balancing numerous competing considerations that courts refrain from reviewing the merits of their decisions, absent a showing of arbitrariness or irrationality. But racial discrimination is not just another competing consideration. When there is a proof that a discriminatory purpose has been a motivating factor in the decision, this judicial deference is no longer justified.

Determining whether invidious discriminatory purpose was a motivating factor demands a sensitive inquiry into such circumstantial and direct evidence of intent as may be available. The impact of the official action whether it "bears more heavily on one race than another," Washington v. Davis, may provide an important starting point. Sometimes a clear pattern, unexplainable on grounds other than race, emerges from the effect of the state action even when the governing legislation appears neutral on its face. Yick Wo v. Hopkins, 118 U.S. 356, 6 S.Ct. 1064, 30 L.Ed. 220 (1886); Gomillion v. Lightfoot, 364 U.S. 339, 81 S.Ct. 125, 5 L.Ed.2d 110 (1960). The evidentiary inquiry is then relatively easy.[13] But such cases are rare. Absent a pattern as stark as that in *Gomillion* or *Yick Wo*, impact alone is not determinative,[14] and the Court must look to other evidence.[15]

The historical background of the decision is one evidentiary source, particularly if it reveals a series of official actions taken for invidious purposes. The specific sequence of events leading up to the challenged

11. In McGinnis v. Royster, 410 U.S. 263, 276–277, 93 S.Ct. 1055, 1063, 35 L.Ed.2d 282 (1973), in a somewhat different context, we observed: "The search for legislative purpose is often elusive enough, Palmer v. Thompson, 403 U.S. 217, 91 S.Ct. 1940, 29 L.Ed.2d 438 (1971), without a requirement that primacy be ascertained. Legislation is frequently multipurposed: the removal of even a 'subordinate' purpose may shift altogether the consensus of legislative judgment supporting the statute."

13. Several of our jury-selection cases fall into this category. Because of the nature of the jury-selection task, however, we have permitted a finding of constitutional violation even when the statistical pattern does not approach the extremes of *Yick Wo* or *Gomillion*. See, e.g., Turner v. Fouche, 396 U.S. 346, 359, 90 S.Ct. 532, 539, 24 L.Ed.2d 567 (1970); Sims v. Georgia, 389 U.S. 404, 407, 88 S.Ct. 523, 525, 19 L.Ed.2d 634 (1967).

14. This is not to say that a consistent pattern of official racial discrimination is a necessary predicate to a violation of the Equal Protection Clause. A single invidiously discriminatory governmental act in the exercise of the zoning power as elsewhere would not necessarily be immunized by the absence of such discrimination in the making of other comparable decisions. See City of Richmond v. United States, 422 U.S. 358, 378, 95 S.Ct. 2296, 2307, 45 L.Ed.2d 245 (1975).

15. In many instances, to recognize the limited probative value of disproportionate impact is merely to acknowledge the "heterogeneity" of the Nation's population. Jefferson v. Hackney, 406 U.S. 535, 548, 92 S.Ct. 1724, 1732, 32 L.Ed.2d 285 (1972).

decision also may shed some light on the decisionmaker's purposes. Reitman v. Mulkey, 387 U.S. 369, 373–376, 87 S.Ct. 1627, 1629–1631, 18 L.Ed.2d 830 (1967). For example, if the property involved here always had been zoned R–5 but suddenly was changed to R–3 when the town learned of MHDC's plans to erect integrated housing,[16] we would have a far different case. Departures from the normal procedural sequence also might afford evidence that improper purposes are playing a role. Substantive departures too may be relevant, particularly if the factors usually considered important by the decisionmaker strongly favor a decision contrary to the one reached.[17]

The legislative or administrative history may be highly relevant, especially where there are contemporary statements by members of the decisionmaking body, minutes of its meetings, or reports. In some extraordinary instances the members might be called to the stand at trial to testify concerning the purpose of the official action, although even then such testimony frequently will be barred by privilege. See Tenney v. Brandhove, 341 U.S. 367, 71 S.Ct. 783, 95 L.Ed. 1019 (1951); United States v. Nixon, 418 U.S. 683, 705, 94 S.Ct. 3090, 3106, 41 L.Ed.2d 1039 (1974); 8 J. Wigmore, Evidence § 2371 (McNaughton rev. ed. 1961).[18]

The foregoing summary identifies, without purporting to be exhaustive, subjects of proper inquiry in determining whether racially discriminatory intent existed. With these in mind, we now address the case before us.

IV

This case was tried in the District Court and reviewed in the Court of Appeals before our decision in Washington v. Davis, supra. The respondents proceeded on the erroneous theory that the Village's refusal to rezone carried a racially discriminatory effect and was, without more, unconstitutional. But both courts below understood that at least part of their function was to examine the purpose underlying the decision. In making its findings on this issue, the District Court noted that some of the opponents of Lincoln Green who spoke at the various hearings might have been motivated by opposition to minority groups. The court held, however, that the evidence "does not warrant the conclusion that this motivated the defendants." 373 F.Supp., at 211.

---

16. See, e.g., Progress Development Corp. v. Mitchell, 286 F.2d 222 (C.A.7 1961) (park board allegedly condemned plaintiffs' land for a park upon learning that the homes plaintiffs were erecting there would be sold under a marketing plan designed to assure integration). * * *

17. See Dailey v. City of Lawton, 425 F.2d 1037 (C.A.10 1970). [The city refused to rezone a pocket of land even though all surrounding parcels were so classified], and both the present and the former planning director for the city testified that there was no reason "from a zoning standpoint" why the land should not be [rezoned].

18. This Court has recognized, ever since Fletcher v. Peck, 6 Cranch 87, 130–131, 3 L.Ed. 162 (1810), that judicial inquiries into legislative or executive motivation represent a substantial intrusion into the workings of other branches of government. Placing a decisionmaker on the stand is therefore "usually to be avoided." Citizens to Preserve Overton Park v. Volpe, 401 U.S. 402, 420, 91 S.Ct. 814, 825, 28 L.Ed.2d 136 (1971). * * *

On appeal the Court of Appeals focused primarily on respondents' claim that the Village's buffer policy had not been consistently applied and was being invoked with a strictness here that could only demonstrate some other underlying motive. The court concluded that the buffer policy, though not always applied with perfect consistency, had on several occasions formed the basis for the Board's decision to deny other rezoning proposals. "The evidence does not necessitate a finding that Arlington Heights administered this policy in a discriminatory manner." 517 F.2d, at 412. The Court of Appeals therefore approved the District Court's findings concerning the Village's purposes in denying rezoning to MHDC.

We also have reviewed the evidence. The impact of the Village's decision does arguably bear more heavily on racial minorities. Minorities constitute 18% of the Chicago area population, and 40% of the income groups said to be eligible for Lincoln Green. But there is little about the sequence of events leading up to the decision that would spark suspicion. The area around the Viatorian property has been zoned R–3 since 1959, the year when Arlington Heights first adopted a zoning map. Single-family homes surround the 80–acre site, and the Village is undeniably committed to single-family homes as its dominant residential land use. The rezoning request progressed according to the usual procedures. The Plan Commission even scheduled two additional hearings, at least in part to accommodate MHDC and permit it to supplement its presentation with answers to questions generated at the first hearing.

* * *

In sum, the evidence does not warrant overturning the concurrent findings of both courts below. Respondents simply failed to carry their burden of proving that discriminatory purpose was a motivating factor in the Village's decision.[21] This conclusion ends the constitutional inquiry. The Court of Appeals' further finding that the Village's decision carried a discriminatory "ultimate effect" is without independent constitutional significance.

V

Respondents' complaint also alleged that the refusal to rezone violated the Fair Housing Act of 1968, 42 U.S.C. § 3601 et seq. * * * We remand the case for further consideration of respondents' statutory claims.

Reversed and remanded.

---

21. Proof that the decision by the Village was motivated in part by a racially discriminatory purpose would not necessarily have required invalidation of the challenged decision. Such proof would, however, have shifted to the Village the burden of establishing that the same decision would have resulted even had the impermissible purpose not been considered. If this were established, the complaining party in a case of this kind no longer fairly could attribute the injury complained of to improper consideration of a discriminatory purpose. In such circumstances, there would be no justification for judicial interference with the challenged decision. But in this case respondents failed to make the required threshold showing. See Mt. Healthy City School Dist. Bd. of Education v. Doyle, 429 U.S. 274, 97 S.Ct. 568, 50 L.Ed.2d 471.

MR. JUSTICE STEVENS took no part in the consideration or decision of this case.

MR. JUSTICE MARSHALL, with whom MR. JUSTICE BRENNAN joins, concurring in part and dissenting in part.

I concur in Parts I–III of the Court's opinion. However, I believe the proper result would be to remand this entire case to the Court of Appeals for further proceedings consistent with Washington v. Davis, and today's opinion. * * *

MR. JUSTICE WHITE, dissenting. [Omitted.]

NOTE ON INTENT AND CAUSATION IN DISCRIMINATION CASES

1. Only intentional discrimination by race or other suspect classification activates strict scrutiny and violates the Equal Protection Clause, says the Court in *Arlington Heights*. How does one know when such intent is present? Statutes, regulations, and other laws that make racial distinctions or classifications "on their face" are deemed to be racial classifications. See Loving v. Virginia, 388 U.S. 1, 87 S.Ct. 1817, 18 L.Ed.2d 1010 (1967) (statute barring inter-racial marriage). The same is true for other classifications meriting higher scrutiny. See United States v. Virginia, 518 U.S. 515, 116 S.Ct. 2264, 135 L.Ed.2d 735 (1996) (facial gender distinction immediately subjected to mid-level review requiring an "exceedingly persuasive justification"). No additional proof of a bad motive is necessary to have the classification deemed to be race-based, sex-based, etc.[1] But since "facial" discrimination based on a suspect classification usually succumbs to judicial scrutiny, most governmental decisionmakers either do not make race-based decisions or claim that they do not. See, e.g., Hunt v. Cromartie, 526 U.S. 541, 119 S.Ct. 1545, 143 L.Ed.2d 731 (1999) (redistricting case). *Arlington Heights* deals with this group of cases. How does the Court suggest that such covert intent be proved?

(a) Covert intent may be proven by direct evidence, i.e., a confession or testimony that a defendant has admitted his true motive. Such cases are rare. But see Miller v. Johnson, 515 U.S. 900, 917, 115 S.Ct. 2475, 2489, 132 L.Ed.2d 762 (1995) (racially discriminatory intent admitted in districting case).

(b) More often only circumstantial evidence will be available to prove that the defendant covertly intended to classify by race, sex/gender, etc. What would be reliable objective indicators of the defendant's true intent? What factors are listed by the Court? Which factors are more important? See Church of Lukumi Babalu Aye, Inc. v. City of Hialeah, 508 U.S. 520, 113 S.Ct. 2217, 124 L.Ed.2d 472 (1993) (proof that neutral anti-animal-sacrifice ordinance was actually intentional discrimination based on religion; history of

---

1. Some race-based and gender-based classifications may nevertheless pass constitutional muster because they meet the Court's demanding level of review, though this is rare. See Johnson v. California, 543 U.S. 499, 125 S.Ct. 1141, 160 L.Ed.2d 949 (2005) (preliminary racial segregation in prison must meet strict scrutiny, not lower test usually applied to prison decisions); United States v. Virginia, 518 U.S. 515, 116 S.Ct. 2264, 135 L.Ed.2d 735 (ratcheted-up middle-level scrutiny applies to sex-based classifications). This approach now generally applies to affirmative action programs, as well. City of Richmond v. J.A. Croson Co., 488 U.S. 469, 109 S.Ct. 706, 102 L.Ed.2d 854 (1989). See Chapter 7D infra.

adoption of ordinance is persuasive of intentional discrimination). How persuasive must be the proof of intent to discriminate on a forbidden basis? See Crawford–El v. Britton, 523 U.S. 574, 118 S.Ct. 1584, 140 L.Ed.2d 759 (1998) (in inmate's suit against jailor for intentionally misdirecting his mail in violation of First Amendment, where proof of motive/intent is required, plaintiff need not adduce "clear and convincing evidence"; normal preponderance standard applies).

(c) Does the Court additionally approve of use of the "statistical prima facie case" to prove intent? The Court notes that sometimes a decision would have such an adverse impact on one group that such adverse impact alone would be probative of an intent to classify on that group basis. This was the case in Yick Wo v. Hopkins, cited in *Arlington Heights* (ordinance ostensibly banning wooden laundries in fact applies virtually without exception to Chinese laundries), but the Court says that such cases are "rare." Do you agree? See Castaneda v. Partida, 430 U.S. 482, 97 S.Ct. 1272, 51 L.Ed.2d 498 (1977) (post-*Arlington Heights* approval of statistical prima facie case).[2] Might there be other evidence than statistics that could raise an inference of discrimination? See Miller v. Johnson, supra (irregularly drawn election districts).

2.   In **City of Cuyahoga Falls v. Buckeye Community Hope Foundation**, 538 U.S. 188, 123 S.Ct. 1389, 155 L.Ed.2d 349 (2003), the trial court granted summary judgment after finding no racial discrimination in sending a proposed low-rent housing development to a referendum for approval. The court of appeals reversed and remanded for trial (with Judge Nathaniel R. Jones, a former civil rights lawyer, writing for the court). The Supreme Court reversed in turn. It emphasized that the factors found relevant in *Arlington Heights* were irrelevant to this case because all the city had required was a referendum; it had not made a decision denying the project. Turning to the referendum itself, the Court found no evidence of racial intent by the city, 538 U.S. at 195–96, 123 S.Ct. at 1394–95:

> "[T]o establish discriminatory intent, respondents and the Sixth Circuit both rely heavily on evidence of allegedly discriminatory voter sentiment. But statements made by private individuals in the course of a citizen-driven petition drive, while sometimes relevant to equal protection analysis, do not, in and of themselves, constitute state action [attributable to the city itself because] respondents put forth no evidence that the 'private motives [that] triggered' the referendum drive can fairly be attributed to the State.'

> "In fact, by adhering to charter procedures, city officials enabled public debate on the referendum to take place, thus advancing significant First Amendment interests. In assessing the referendum as a 'basic instrument of democratic government,' we have observed that '[p]rovisions for referendums demonstrate devotion to democracy, not to bias, discrimination, or prejudice.' "

---

2. The Court has adopted a similar approach of rebuttable inference in the context of challenges to jury selection under its *Batson* precedent. See Hernandez v. New York, 500 U.S. 352, 111 S.Ct. 1859, 114 L.Ed.2d 395 (1991) (inference rebutted).

(a) In not automatically tying private and official motivation together, the Court echoes themes that it also found relevant in U.S. v. Morrison, Chapter 5 infra (private sex-based discrimination cannot be attributed to state officials, federal Violence Against Women Act unconstitutional). But it would be a mistake to assume that the Court is always unreceptive to proofs of claims of intentional discrimination. In **Miller–El v. Dretke**, 545 U.S. 231, 125 S.Ct. 2317, 162 L.Ed.2d 196 (2005), a 6–3 majority overrode the appellate and trial court's determination that there had been no intentional racial discrimination in jury selection, even applying the "clear and convincing evidence" standard. The Court noted that the prosecutors had not only stricken a disproportionately high percentage of potential black members from the jury, it had also given explanations of its differential treatment that were not applicable equally to blacks and whites. Under *Arlington Heights* does each claim of racial discrimination turn on its own facts? Does that mean that the Court thinks that non-discrimination is the rule of American life and discrimination the exception?

(b) Is there a competition between the Equal Protection Clause and the First Amendment, or does *City of Cuyahoga Falls* in fact try to rationalize them? In Grutter v. Bollinger, Chapter 6E infra, Justice O'Connor, also the author of *City of Cuyahoga Falls*, permitted an affirmative action plan in education by pointing to the university's significant First–Amendment interest in a diverse classroom. Does *Grutter* show that the First Amendment cuts both ways?

3. *Arlington Heights* focuses primarily on the methods for proving intent. The Court had already rejected the broader proposition that an adverse impact or effect on blacks—without regard to the defendant's intent—should lead to high-level scrutiny. That came in **Washington v. Davis**, 426 U.S. 229, 96 S.Ct. 2040, 48 L.Ed.2d 597 (1976). The Court explained its position succinctly in text and footnote:

> "[Adoption of an impact standard] would be far-reaching and would raise serious questions about, and perhaps invalidate, a whole range of tax, welfare, public service, regulatory, and licensing statutes that may be more burdensome to the poor and the average black than to the more affluent white.[14]"

(a) If Footnote 14 is correct, is it not a damning indictment of continued racial and economic segregation in American society? If every economics-based decision produces a disparate impact on African–Americans, should we not do something to solve this problem? Should that "something" be to change constitutional law? Or statutory law? Are the social and economic factors cited in footnote 14 still true?

---

14. "Goodman, *De Facto School Segregation: A Constitutional and Empirical Analysis*, 60 Calif.L.Rev. 275, 300 (1972), suggests that disproportionate impact analysis might invalidate 'tests and qualifications for voting, draft deferment, public employment, jury service, and other government-conferred benefits and opportunities * * *, [s]ales taxes, bail schedules, utility rates, bridge tolls, license fees, and other state-imposed charges.' It has also been argued that minimum wage and usury laws as well as professional licensing requirements would require major modifications in light of the unequal-impact rule. Silverman, *Equal Protection, Economic Legislation, and Racial Discrimination*, 25 Vand.L.Rev. 1183 (1972). See also Demetz, *Minorities in the Market Place*, 43 N.C.L.Rev. 271 (1965)." [Footnote by the Court]

(b) By requiring proof of intent in each individual circumstance where blacks are adversely affected, see ¶ 2 supra, the Court appears to presume that racial disparities are not predominantly the result of intentional discrimination, but may be caused by other factors. Allowing defendants to rebut a presumption of discrimination allows each case to be judged individually. Will this not lead to extremely variable results? Is that exactly the point—results should vary depending on whether intent to classify by race is proved? See Hearne v. Board of Educ. of Chicago, 185 F.3d 770 (7th Cir.1999) (state regulation that affected only Chicago claimed to be intentionally racially discriminatory): "There are substantial numbers of African Americans in many other cities in the state, and it is simply too great a stretch to say that the population represented by the Chicago school system is such a good proxy for African Americans that the ostensibly neutral classification [by size of city] is 'an obvious pretext for racial discrimination.'"

(c) Is there a larger picture to be seen? Compare the Court's rejection of an impact test for equal protection cases with its decision in DeShaney v. Winnebago County Dep't of Social Services, Chapter 1B.4, *supra*, rejecting an affirmative duty to protect third parties under the Due Process Clause. Is the common theme to these cases that American society is individualistic and opportunity-oriented? Is *Arlington Heights* justified because it only adopts an intent standard for constitutional law, but leaves Congress free to adopt an impact test as a matter of statutory law? See Metropolitan Housing Dev. Corp. v. Arlington Heights, 558 F.2d 1283 (7th Cir.1977), and Chapter 8 infra.

4. In a few post-*Arlington Heights* cases courts tried to limit the decision by holding that intent should be measured by "the natural, probable, and foreseeable results" of one's actions. See, e.g., Arthur v. Nyquist, 573 F.2d 134, 140–43 (2d Cir.1978), but that line of cases did not survive. In **Personnel Administrator of Massachusetts v. Feeney**, 442 U.S. 256, 99 S.Ct. 2282, 60 L.Ed.2d 870 (1979), a woman challenged the state's veterans-preference rule for government employment, alleging it to be intentionally sex biased because the legislature knew it to hurt females because of limitations on women serving in the armed forces. In ruling against the plaintiff the Court stated, 442 U.S. at 279, 99 S.Ct. at 2296:

> "'[D]iscriminatory purpose' * * * implies more than intent as volition or intent as awareness of consequences. It implies that the decisionmaker * * * selected or reaffirmed a particular course at least in part 'because of,' not merely 'in spite of,' its adverse effects upon an identifiable group."

(a) Is *Feeney* compelled by the same considerations that led to the decision in *Arlington Heights*? See Hearne v. Board of Educ. of Chicago, 185 F.3d 770 (7th Cir.1999) (citing *Feeney* to minimize proof that some legislators knew that they were harming blacks but did not seek to regulate Chicago teachers for the very purpose of harming blacks).

(b) Is *Feeney* more credible as a statement about causation? Consider this statement: when an official has not intended to harm because of race or gender, but harm has nevertheless resulted because of social divisions in society, then the official's action did not cause the harm; the pre-existing social divisions caused the harm. This argument that private action caused the plaintiff's harm may be persuasive for many situations, but is it persuasive for the circumstances presented in *Feeney* itself?

5.   In Footnote 21 in *Arlington Heights*, the Court notes that even after intent is proved, there is a defense available to state officials if they can show that they acted for mixed motives. The scope of this so-called "mixed-motive" defense is more fully developed in a companion case decided the same day, **Mt. Healthy City School District Board of Education v. Doyle**, 429 U.S. 274, 97 S.Ct. 568, 50 L.Ed.2d 471 (1977). Doyle had been fired from his teaching job for complex reasons, some relating to his exercise of free speech rights and some relating to other, constitutionally permissible considerations. The Court held that Doyle had proved the requisite intent to hurt him because of his political speech, thus showing a constitutional violation, but the Court nevertheless reversed and remanded the case. Showing unconstitutional motivation, wrote Justice Rehnquist for the Court, 429 U.S. at 287, 97 S.Ct. at 576, does not end the case, for the defendants can avoid liability by proving that they "would have reached the same decision" based solely on the other permissible considerations that motivated their action.

(a) *Mt. Healthy* appears to be based on a theory of causation: if the school district would have fired Doyle anyway for the independent reason that he was a bad teacher, then he would have suffered the same ultimate harm as if there were no constitutional violation. The constitutional violation, in essence, "caused" Doyle no harm beyond what he would have received anyway. Do you agree with this theory of causation? Does it offend you because it allows unconstitutional intent (either to discriminate based on race or for First–Amendment-prohibited reasons) to go unpunished and thus undeterred?

(b) Virtually all commentators from the early civil rights era, see the introduction to this sub-chapter, view this issue as one of dichotomous choice: one either adopts the intent standard or the impact standard. But *Mt. Healthy* suggests a wholly different idea: that courts must consider not one or the other, but both intent and impact (at least impact on plaintiff, if not his entire class). See, e.g., Burton v. City of Belle Glade, 178 F.3d 1175 (11th Cir. 1999) (refusal to annex predominantly black area; plaintiffs must show challenged "decision or act had a discriminatory purpose and effect"). Where intent to discriminate causes no impact on the plaintiff, says this interpretation of *Mt. Healthy*, there is no constitutional violation. Does this idea help to explain such cases as Palmer v. Thompson, 403 U.S. 217, 91 S.Ct. 1940, 29 L.Ed.2d 438 (1971) (swimming pool closings do not violate equal protection where both blacks and whites affected by closures)? Is the argument persuasive?

(c) Can the *Mt. Healthy* defense be better understood as part of a judicial horse trade? Note that *Arlington Heights* does not require plaintiff to prove that intentional racial discrimination was the sole cause for his harm, but only that it was "a motivating factor." If the plaintiff need only prove that race was "a * * * factor," is it not appropriate to allow the defendant to prove that it was not an important factor? Is that what *Mount Healthy*'s mixed-motive defense does?

6.   What are the contours of the *Mt. Healthy* defense? Given the social and economic disparities between different groups in American society, can defendants always conjure up a neutral post-hoc explanation for intentionally

discriminatory actions? Who bears the burden of proof on the issues raised? Does the defense apply to both damages claims and cases involving injunctive relief?

(a) *Mt. Healthy* posits the existence of a separate permissible motive, and appears to place the burden on the defendant of proving the existence of this motive.[3] Must this motive have been extant at the time the original decision was made, or is it sufficient for the defendant to find and adopt a second neutral motive through subsequent inquiry? In **Hunter v. Underwood**, 471 U.S. 222, 105 S.Ct. 1916, 85 L.Ed.2d 222 (1985), the Court appeared to demand that the second motive actually be a basis for the original decision. The 1901 Alabama constitutional convention had adopted a provision limiting the vote for certain criminals, a provision that was covertly aimed at disenfranchising blacks in violation of the Fifteenth Amendment's ban on intentional racial discrimination in voting. The state claimed that even if its law was racially discriminatory when adopted, it could be justified today on non-discriminatory ground that such criminals did not deserve to vote. Justice Rehnquist's opinion for the Court rejected the offer of proof, noting that the provision at "its original enactment was motivated by a desire to discriminate against blacks on account of race and continues to this day to have that effect." 471 U.S. at 233, 105 S.Ct. at 1922. Does *Hunter* support the thesis that the *Mt. Healthy* principle is all about causation?

(b) Is the *Mt. Healthy* defense relevant when a plaintiff challenges the operation of an on-going governmental program rather than a discrete prior decision? In **Texas v. Lesage**, 528 U.S. 18, 120 S.Ct. 467, 145 L.Ed.2d 347 (1999), in a brief per curiam opinion the Court applied the mixed-motive defense to uphold a university's claim for summary judgment based on uncontroverted proof that the applicant for admission, though subjected to a questionable affirmative action program, was also rejected because he was totally unqualified. The Court suggested that an amended complaint challenging the on-going maintenance of the program and its repeated application might present a different claim, however, because the injury in such a circumstance is not the loss of admission itself but the " 'inability to compete on an equal footing' " because of the allegedly invalid affirmative action program. Does *Lesage* suggest that *Mt. Healthy* applies only in damages cases and not to those eligible for injunctive relief? Or does *Lesage* turn on a special definition of injury for affirmative action cases, leaving *Mt. Healthy* otherwise generally applicable to both claims at law and in equity?

FINAL NOTE ON METHODOLOGY OF § 1983 AND ITS RELATION TO CONSTITUTIONAL LAW

1. Once intent to discriminate or classify on a forbidden basis has been proved, governmental action usually fails because of the strict scrutiny that is

---

3. The Court also adopted this position in other areas of discrimination law that use the mixed-motive defense. See Price Waterhouse v. Hopkins, 490 U.S. 228, 109 S.Ct. 1775, 104 L.Ed.2d 268 (1989) (same rules applied to Title VII actions). Interestingly, Congress has subsequently changed the defense so that it only prevents certain relief rather than defeating the plaintiff's case altogether. See Chapter 7A.2.b infra. Should that also be the rule in Equal Protection cases? Would that deter racial intentions more effectively?

given to discrimination under the Equal Protection Clause or the First Amendment. This means that in the real world where discrimination is usually covert, proof of intent to discriminate is usually the dispositive issue in the case. See Church of Lukumi Babalu Aye, Inc. v. City of Hialeah, 508 U.S. 520, 113 S.Ct. 2217, 124 L.Ed.2d 472 (1993) (proof of intentional discrimination against a religious group); Gratz v. Bollinger, 539 U.S. 244, 123 S.Ct. 2411, 156 L.Ed.2d 257 (2003) (intentional discrimination in affirmative action; racial balancing as only goal); Miller v. Johnson, 515 U.S. 900, 917, 115 S.Ct. 2475, 2489, 132 L.Ed.2d 762 (1995) (covert intent in affirmative action; redistricting).

(a) Recall the issues discussed earlier in this Chapter with regard to tort-like standards that appear in Due Process cases. Is the same now true for discrimination cases as well?

(b) In the Due Process area it appeared that the application of § 1983 to individual officials placed pressure on the Court to find constitutional standards that could be applied to individual—rather than institutional—acts of wrongdoing. Is the same true in the discrimination context?

2. Review the methodology that the Court has adopted for determining the "standards of care" applicable in all constitutional cases brought under § 1983. See Abernathy, *Section 1983 and Constitutional Torts*, 77 GEO. L.J. 1441 (1989):

> ["The methodology of finding § 1983's standards of care now seems firmly established, thanks to the Court's decisions in Daniels v. Williams, Chapter 1B.1, and Davidson v. Cannon, Chapter 1B.1, supra.] Both cases involved plaintiffs who had suffered injuries in prison, Davidson in a prison brawl (of the type portrayed on late night television programs) and Daniels in a classic slip-and-fall case (beloved by lawyers who advertise on late-night television programs). Justice Rehnquist [stated in *Daniels*] that § 1983 'contains no state of mind requirement independent of that necessary to state a violation of the underlying constitutional right. [Rather,] in any given § 1983 suit, the plaintiff must still prove a violation of the underlying constitutional right; and depending on right, merely negligent conduct may not be enough to state a claim....' In retrospect, [this two-part approach] explains a great number of cases, whether based on equal protection, incorporated rights, or general substantive due process, in which the Court never thought it relevant to explain whether § 1983 was the basis for the constitutional claim at issue. * * * The *Daniels* approach leaves each intact for use under § 1983."

(a) Prior to the *Daniels* and *Williams* decisions some academics had argued quite powerfully that § 1983's standards should be found by reference to either state tort law or evolving federalized common law. See Eisenburg, *State Law in Federal Civil Rights Cases: The Proper Scope of Section 1988*, 128 U.PA.L.REV. 499, 528 (1980) (arguing that § 1983's companion statute, 42 U.S.C. § 1988, requires use of state-law standards of care); Kreimer, *The Source of Law in Civil Rights Actions: Some Old Light on Section 1988*, 133 U.PA.L.REV. 601, 630 (1985) (arguing that § 1988 requires courts to create an evolving federal common law free from state interpretation).

(b) Some cases still occasionally find that § 1983 should find some of its standards by reference to common-law tort concepts. Consider footnote 7 in **Malley v. Briggs**, 475 U.S. 335, 344–45, 106 S.Ct. 1092, 89 L.Ed.2d 271 (1986), a case in which a police officer unconstitutionally sought a warrant and the state judge approved his application:

> "Petitioner has not pressed the argument that in a case like this the officer should not be liable because the judge's decision to issue the warrant breaks the causal chain between the application for the warrant and the improvident arrest. It should be clear, however, that the District Court's 'no causation' rationale in this case is inconsistent with our interpretation of § 1983. As we stated in Monroe v. Pape, § 1983 'should be read against the background of tort liability that makes a man responsible for the natural consequences of his actions.' Since the common law recognized the causal link between the submission of a complaint and an ensuing arrest, we read § 1983 as recognizing the same causal link."

Similarly, in **Heck v. Humphrey**, Chapter 1G.1 infra, the Court stated that "we first look to the common law" and imposed a rule against collaterallly attacking convictions in a § 1983 suit—mimicking the same tort rule at common law. But more recently, in **Hartman v. Moore**, 547 U.S. 250, 126 S.Ct. 1695, 164 L.Ed.2d 441 (2006), the Court noted that "the common law is best understood 'more as a source of inspired examples than of prefabricated components.'" Is *Hartman* the more sophisticated view?

3.   Under the prevailing *Daniels–Davidson* approach, constitutional law gives § 1983 its meaning. Is it not possible that very subtly the reverse has occurred? See Abernathy, supra, at 1441–45:

> "We have long recognized that the resurrection of § 1983 converted the Fourteenth Amendment from a sword into a shield by providing a civil action for vindication of constitutional rights, and to the extent that damages have gradually become the usual authorized remedy for § 1983 violations, we have easily come to think of such actions as 'constitutional torts'—civil damage remedies for violation of constitutionally defined rights. There is, however a subtler and greater reality to what has transpired, for the mere procedural vehicle of constitutional enforcement has, in retrospect, changed the substance of constitutional law itself. Section 1983 has not merely served as a vehicle for enforcing constitutional law, it has led to the making of a new constitutional law as the Court has adjusted constitutional norms to permit their enforcement under § 1983.... The Supreme Court decisions that create standards of care for § 1983 actions share the striking feature that they [often] force the Court to use tort-like phrases in defining constitutional law."

Is this especially true after Sacramento v. Lewis, Chapter 1B.4 supra? Is it especially true in constitutional cases involving discrimination, because the Court wants to individualize the results through use of the intent test?

C. ELEMENTS OF A PLAINTIFF'S § 1983 CLAIM—ACTION "UNDER COLOR OF" LAW

1. METHODOLOGY: "UNDER COLOR OF" LAW AND THE FOURTEENTH AMENDMENT'S STATE–ACTION REQUIREMENT

WEST v. ATKINS

Supreme Court of the United States, 1988.
487 U.S. 42, 108 S.Ct. 2250, 101 L.Ed.2d 40.

JUSTICE BLACKMUN delivered the opinion of the Court.

This case presents the question whether a physician who is under contract with the State to provide medical services to inmates at a state-prison hospital on a part-time basis acts "under color of state law," within the meaning of 42 U.S.C. § 1983, when he treats an inmate.

I

Petitioner, Quincy West, tore his left Achilles tendon in 1983 while playing volleyball [and was transferred to the state's Central Prison Hospital for medical care]. Central Prison Hospital has one full-time staff physician, and obtains additional medical assistance under "Contracts for Professional Services" between the State and area physicians.

Respondent, Samuel Atkins, M.D., a private physician, provided orthopedic services to inmates pursuant to one such contract. Under it, Doctor Atkins was paid approximately $52,000 annually to operate two "clinics" each week at Central Prison Hospital, with additional amounts for surgery.[3] Over a period of several months, he treated West's injury by placing his leg in a series of casts. West alleges that although the doctor acknowledged that surgery would be necessary, he refused to schedule it, and that he eventually discharged West while his ankle was still swollen and painful, and his movement still impeded. [Believing that the physician had been "deliberately indifferent" to his "serious medical needs," West filed this suit against the doctor under § 1983. The District Court dismissed his claim, and the Fourth Circuit, sitting en banc, affirmed on the ground that those persons who act "within the bounds of traditional

---

3. Doctor Atkins' contractual duties included the following: to provide two orthopedic clinics per week; to see all orthopedic and neurological referrals; to perform orthopedic surgery as scheduled; to conduct rounds as often as necessary for his surgical and other orthopedic patients; to coordinate with the Physical Therapy Department; to request the assistance of neurosurgical consultants on spinal surgical cases; and to provide emergency on-call orthopedic services 24 hours per day. His contract required him to furnish two days of professional service each week in fulfillment of these duties. Atkins also had supervisory authority over Department of Correction nurses and physician's assistants, who were subject to his orders.

Apparently, respondent maintained a private practice apart from his work at the prison. Atkins' submissions on his motion for summary judgment, however, do not reflect the extent of his nonprison practice or the extent to which he depended upon the prison work for his livelihood.

professional discretion and judgment," do not act under color of state law for purposes of § 1983.]

II

To state a claim under § 1983, a plaintiff must allege the violation of a right secured by the Constitution and laws of the United States, and must show that the alleged deprivation was committed by a person acting under color of state law. Daniels v. Williams. Petitioner West sought to fulfill the first requirement by alleging a violation of his rights secured by the Eighth Amendment under Estelle v. Gamble. * * * The adequacy of West's allegation and the sufficiency of his showing on this element of his § 1983 cause of action are not contested here. The only issue before us is whether petitioner has established the second essential element—that respondent acted under color of state law in treating West's injury.

A

The traditional definition of acting under color of state law requires that the defendant in a § 1983 action have exercised power "possessed by virtue of state law and made possible only because the wrongdoer is clothed with the authority of state law." United States v. Classic, 313 U.S. 299, 326, 61 S.Ct. 1031, 1043, 85 L.Ed. 1368 (1941). Accord, Monroe v. Pape (adopting *Classic* standard for purposes of § 1983). In Lugar v. Edmondson Oil Co., [457 U.S. 922, 102 S.Ct. 2744, 73 L.Ed.2d 482 (1982)], the Court made clear that if a defendant's conduct satisfies the state-action requirement of the Fourteenth Amendment, "that conduct [is] also action under color of state law and will support a suit under § 1983." Accord, Rendell–Baker v. Kohn, 457 U.S. 830, 838, 102 S.Ct. 2764, 2769, 73 L.Ed.2d 418 (1982); United States v. Price, 383 U.S. 787, 794, n. 7, 86 S.Ct. 1152, 1157, n. 7, 16 L.Ed.2d 267 (1966). In such circumstances, the defendant's alleged infringement of the plaintiff's federal rights is "fairly attributable to the State." *Lugar.*

* * *

Reversed.

JUSTICE SCALIA, concurring in part and concurring in judgment. [Omitted.]

NOTE ON RELATION OF "UNDER COLOR OF LAW" TO STATE ACTION

1.   *West*'s discussion of "under color of law" drew the Court's unanimous vote, and the principle that the case adopts can be traced back to at least 1966. See United States v. Price, 383 U.S. 787, 794 n. 7, 86 S.Ct. 1152, 1157 n. 7, 16 L.Ed.2d 267 (1966) (interpreting same language in § 1983's criminal law counterpart). Yet there were suggestions made periodically in the years between *Price* and *West* that revealed that some members of the Court wanted § 1983 to be interpreted either more broadly or more narrowly than the Fourteenth Amendment.

(a) In **Adickes v. S.H. Kress & Co.**, 398 U.S. 144, 90 S.Ct. 1598, 26 L.Ed.2d 142 (1970), Ms. Adickes sued the variety store under § 1983 after she and her black students conducted a "sit-in" at its segregated lunch-counter which led to her arrest. A Supreme Court majority remanded the case for trial after suggesting some theories by which plaintiff might prove state action, but Justice Brennan wrote separately to suggest that § 1983's use of the word "custom" made the statute more inclusive than the state action concept alone. "A custom," he wrote, "can have the effect or force of law even where it is not backed by the force of the State. [Italics omitted.]" 398 U.S. at 225, 90 S.Ct. at 1638. What would be the practical effect if § 1983 were construed to provide a remedy against more persons than are covered by the state action doctrine of the Fourteenth Amendment? Would such a construction render § 1983 unconstitutional?

(b) In **Polk County v. Dodson**, 454 U.S. 312, 102 S.Ct. 445, 70 L.Ed.2d 509 (1981), Justice Powell's majority opinion intimated that the statutory requirement of action "under color of law" should be decided before reaching the constitutional issue of state action, thus obliquely suggesting that § 1983's "under color of law" concept might be narrower than the state action doctrine. See also Lugar v. Edmondson Oil Co., 457 U.S. 922, 102 S.Ct. 2744, 73 L.Ed.2d 482 (1982) (Powell, J., dissenting) (majority "undermines fundamental distinctions * * * between the legal concepts of 'state action' and private action 'under color of law' "); Flagg Bros., Inc. v. Brooks, 436 U.S. 149, 98 S.Ct. 1729, 56 L.Ed.2d 185 (1978) (both majority and dissent indicate that state action and "under color of law" are separate inquiries). What would be the practical effect of construing § 1983's language to cover fewer persons than are covered by the Fourteenth Amendment's state action doctrine? Would § 1983 be constitutional if so construed?

(c) How did *West* come to be unanimously decided only six years after *Lugar?*

2.   Recall Monroe v. Pape's holding that "under color of law" covers both action in violation of state law and action in compliance with state law, a decision also making "under color of law" synonymous with the interpretation given the state action doctrine. See the Note on the Personal Liability Model for § 1983, ¶ 1, Chapter 1 supra. Why is there such a strong urge to construe the statute and the Fourteenth Amendment coterminously? Is it because of the paucity of sources for interpreting § 1983 differently? But see *Monroe,* supra. Is it because the statutory language seems so wedded to the constitutional language?

3.   Recall that the other element of a plaintiff's § 1983 claim has also been read to adopt constitutional standards. See Daniels v. Williams, Chapter 1B.1 supra. Do *West* and *Daniels* together make § 1983 completely coterminous with the Fourteenth Amendment? If so, then there is one enormous practical advantage: cases not based on § 1983 but calling for a construction of the state action doctrine, see, e.g., Burton v. Wilmington Parking Auth., infra, are now equally authoritative precedents for interpreting § 1983. What should be the scope of the Constitution's state action doctrine?[4]

---

4. Courts occasionally note that although "conduct qualifying as state action under the Fourteenth Amendment also counts as acting under the color of state law for the purposes of

2. SCOPE OF THE STATE ACTION DOCTRINE: STATE AND LOCAL GOVERNMENT EMPLOYEES

WEST v. ATKINS

Supreme Court of the United States, 1988.
487 U.S. 42, 108 S.Ct. 2250, 101 L.Ed.2d 40.

JUSTICE BLACKMUN delivered the opinion of the Court.

* * *

[II]

[A]

To constitute state action, "the deprivation must be caused by the exercise of some right or privilege created by the State ... or by a person for whom the State is responsible," and "the party charged with the deprivation must be a person who may fairly be said to be a state actor." [Lugar v. Edmondson Oil Co.] "[S]tate employment is generally sufficient to render the defendant a state actor." Id., at 936, n. 18. It is firmly established that a defendant in a § 1983 suit acts under color of state law [even] when he abuses the position given to him by the State. See Monroe v. Pape. Thus, generally, a public employee acts under color of state law while acting in his official capacity or while exercising his responsibilities pursuant to state law.

Indeed, Polk County v. Dodson, 454 U.S. 312, 102 S.Ct. 445, 70 L.Ed.2d 509 (1981), relied upon by the Court of Appeals, is the only case in which this Court has determined that a person who is employed by the State and who is sued under § 1983 for abusing his position in the performance of his assigned tasks was not acting under color of state law. The Court held that "a public defender does not act under color of state law when performing a lawyer's traditional functions as counsel to a defendant in a criminal proceeding." In this capacity, the Court noted, a public defender differs from the typical government employee and state actor. While performing his duties, the public defender retains all of the essential attributes of a private attorney, including, most importantly, his "professional independence," which the State is constitutionally obliged to respect. * * * The Court accordingly concluded that when representing an indigent defendant in a state criminal proceeding, the public defender does not act under color of state law for purposes of § 1983 because he "is not acting on behalf of the State; he is the State's adversary."

B.

We disagree with the Court of Appeals and respondent that *Polk County* dictates a conclusion that respondent did not act under color of

§ 1983, [] the reverse is not necessarily true," Abraham v. Raso, 183 F.3d 279 (3d Cir. 1999), citing Groman v. Township of Manalapan, 47 F.3d 628, 638 n. 15 (3d Cir.1995). How can this be true? Does this suggest that while state action cases may be used to meet the "under color of law" standard, "under color of law" cases may not be cited to show state action?

state law in providing medical treatment to petitioner. In contrast to the public defender, Doctor Atkins' professional and ethical obligation to make independent medical judgments did not set him in conflict with the State and other prison authorities. Indeed, his relationship with other prison authorities was cooperative. "Institutional physicians assume an obligation to the mission that the State, through the institution, attempts to achieve." *Polk County*. The Manual governing prison health care in North Carolina's institutions, which Doctor Atkins was required to observe, declares: "The provision of health care is a joint effort of correctional administrators and health care providers, and can be achieved only through mutual trust and cooperation." Similarly, the American Medical Association Standards for Health Services in Prisons (1979) provide that medical personnel and other prison officials are to act in " 'close cooperation and coordination' " in a " 'joint effort,' " Preface at I; Standard 102 & Discussion. Doctor Atkins' professional obligations certainly did not oblige him to function as "the State's adversary." *Polk County*. We thus find the proffered analogy between respondent and the public defender in Polk County unpersuasive.

* * * [The Court of Appeals] appears to have misread *Polk County* as establishing the general principle that professionals do not act under color of state law when they act in their professional capacities. The court considered a professional not to be subject to suit under § 1983 unless he was exercising "custodial or supervisory" authority. To the extent this Court in *Polk County* relied on the fact that the public defender is a "professional" in concluding that he was not engaged in state action, the case turned on the particular professional obligation of the criminal defense attorney to be an adversary of the State, not on the independence and integrity generally applicable to professionals as a class. Indeed, the Court of Appeals' reading would be inconsistent with cases, decided before and since *Polk County*, in which this Court either has identified professionals as state actors, see, e.g., Tower v. Glover, 467 U.S. 914, 104 S.Ct. 2820, 81 L.Ed.2d 758 (1984) (state public defenders), or has assumed that professionals are state actors in § 1983 suits, see, e.g., Estelle v. Gamble (medical director of state prison who was also the treating physician). Defendants are not removed from the purview of § 1983 simply because they are professionals acting in accordance with professional discretion and judgment.[10]

---

10. We do not suggest that this factor is entirely irrelevant to the state-action inquiry. Where the issue is whether a private party is engaged in activity that constitutes state action, it may be relevant that the challenged activity turned on judgments controlled by professional standards, where those standards are not established by the State. The Court has held that "a State normally can be held responsible for a private decision only when it has exercised coercive power or has provided such significant encouragement, either overt or covert, that the choice must in law be deemed to be that of the State." Blum v. Yaretsky, 457 U.S. 991, 1004, 102 S.Ct. 2777, 73 L.Ed.2d 534 (1982) (decisions of physicians and administrators of privately owned and operated nursing home to transfer Medicaid patients not state action); Rendell–Baker v. Kohn, 457 U.S. 830, 840, 102 S.Ct. 2764, 2770–2771, 73 L.Ed.2d 418 (1982) (discharge decisions of privately owned and operated school not state action). * * * Thus, the requisite "nexus" to the State was absent [in those cases].

Court of Appeals' approach to determining who is subject to suit under § 1983, wholeheartedly embraced by respondent, cannot be reconciled with this Court's decision in *Estelle*, which demonstrates that custodial and supervisory functions are irrelevant to an assessment whether the particular action challenged was performed under color of state law. * * *

C

We now make explicit what was implicit in our holding in *Estelle*: Respondent, as a physician employed by North Carolina to provide medical services to state prison inmates, acted under color of state law for purposes of § 1983 when undertaking his duties in treating petitioner's injury. Such conduct is fairly attributable to the State.

The Court recognized in *Estelle*: "An inmate must rely on prison authorities to treat his medical needs; if the authorities fail to do so, those needs will not be met." In light of this, the Court held that the State has a constitutional obligation, under the Eighth Amendment, to provide adequate medical care to those whom it has incarcerated. North Carolina employs physicians, such as respondent, and defers to their professional judgment, in order to fulfill this obligation. By virtue of this relationship, effected by state law, Doctor Atkins is authorized and obliged to treat prison inmates, such as West. He does so "clothed with the authority of state law." United States v. Classic. He is "a person who may fairly be said to be a state actor." Lugar v. Edmondson Oil Co. It is only those physicians authorized by the State to whom the inmate may turn. Under state law, the only medical care West could receive for his injury was that provided by the State. If Doctor Atkins misused his power by demonstrating deliberate indifference to West's serious medical needs, the resultant deprivation was caused, in the sense relevant for state-action inquiry, by the State's exercise of its right to punish West by incarceration and to deny him a venue independent of the State to obtain needed medical care.

The fact that the State employed respondent pursuant to a contractual arrangement that did not generate the same benefits or obligations applicable to other "state employees" does not alter the analysis. It is the physician's function within the state system, not the precise terms of his employment, that determines whether his actions can fairly be attributed to the State. Whether a physician is on the state payroll or is paid by contract, the dispositive issue concerns the relationship among the State, the physician, and the prisoner. Contracting out prison medical care does not relieve the State of its constitutional duty to provide adequate medical treatment to those in its custody, and it does not deprive the State's

---

This determination cannot be transformed into the proposition that no person acts under color of state law where he is exercising independent professional judgment. "[T]he exercise of ... independent professional judgment" is not, as the Court of Appeals suggested, "the primary test." 815 F.2d at 995, n. 1. And *Blum* and *Rendell–Baker* provide no support for respondent's argument that a physician, employed by the State to fulfill the State's constitutional obligations, does not act under color of state law merely because he renders medical care in accordance with professional obligations.

prisoners of the means to vindicate their Eighth Amendment rights. The State bore an affirmative obligation to provide adequate medical care to West; the State delegated that function to respondent Atkins; and respondent voluntarily assumed that obligation by contract.

Nor does the fact that Doctor Atkins' employment contract did not require him to work exclusively for the prison make him any less a state actor than if he performed those duties as a full-time, permanent member of the state prison medical staff. It is the physician's function while working for the State, not the amount of time he spends in performance of those duties or the fact that he may be employed by others to perform similar duties, that determines whether he is acting under color of state law.[15] * * *

III

For the reasons stated above, we conclude that respondent's delivery of medical treatment to West was state action fairly attributable to the State, and that respondent therefore acted under color of state law for purposes of § 1983. Accordingly, we reverse the judgment of the Court of Appeals and remand the case for further proceedings consistent with this opinion. It is so ordered.

JUSTICE SCALIA, concurring in part and concurring in judgment. [Omitted]

NOTE ON STATE EMPLOYEES AND OFFICIALS AS STATE ACTORS

1. Since the state is a legal or philosophical creation lacking a corporeal existence of its own, the real question in state action cases is, what persons will be deemed to be the state? If one conceives of state action as identifying not simply two categories (state action and private action), but a range of situations in which persons may be state or private actors, state employees probably fall at the end of the spectrum most intuitively perceptible as state actors: a state may only act through its employees and officials.

(a) Do you agree with the Court that there should be no "white-collar professional" exception for state actors? What would be the limits of such an exception? Does a state Secretary of Health exercise professional judgment? Does a secretary who types letters for the Secretary exercise professional judgment? Would a "white collar" exception leave the most powerful state employees outside § 1983's coverage?

---

15. Contrary to respondent's intimations, the fact that a state employee's role parallels one in the private sector is not, by itself, reason to conclude that the former is not acting under color of state law in performing his duties. "If an individual is possessed of state authority and purports to act under that authority, his action is state action. It is irrelevant that he might have taken the same action had he acted in a purely private capacity...." Griffin v. Maryland, 378 U.S. 130, 135, 84 S.Ct. 1770, 1773, 12 L.Ed.2d 754 (1964).

Moreover, although the provision of medical services is a function traditionally performed by private individuals, the context in which respondent performs these services for the State (quite apart from the source of remuneration) distinguishes the relationship between respondent and West from the ordinary physician-patient relationship. * * * Unlike the situation confronting free patients, the nonmedical functions of prison life inevitably influence the nature, timing, and form of medical care provided to inmates such as West. * * *

(b) The case that created an opening for the Fourth Circuit's exception was Polk County v. Dodson, discussed in *West*. Was *Polk County* properly decided? Are you persuaded that public defenders uniquely represent a private interest and so cannot be state actors? If nine doctors sat as our Supreme Court Justices, would the case results have been reversed, with doctors being viewed as uniquely representing a private interest?

(c) Was *Polk County* indefensible result-oriented jurisprudence? Did the Court find public defenders not to be state actors just to dam a flood of convicted defendants' claims against their court-appointed attorneys? If so, did the Court achieve its goal? See Tower v. Glover, 467 U.S. 914, 104 S.Ct. 2820, 81 L.Ed.2d 758 (1984).

2. Justice Blackmun emphasizes that the state is under an affirmative duty to provide medical care to prisoners, citing Estelle v. Gamble, Chapter 1B.2 supra, and he appears to rely heavily on this factor to show state action.

(a) Is this factor relevant? Or is it merely relevant that a constitutional violation was committed, regardless of whether it involved prisoners and affirmative duties? Was *West* unanimously decided on a very simple ground—that to rule otherwise would reverse *Estelle* as a practical matter? See American Mfrs. Mut. Ins. Co. v. Sullivan, 526 U.S. 40, 119 S.Ct. 977, 143 L.Ed.2d 130 (1999) (which follows this Note): "[In *West*] the State was constitutionally obligated to provide medical treatment to injured inmates, and the delegation of that traditionally exclusive public function to a private physician gave rise to a finding of state action." Does that mean that if the doctor had been providing healthcare at a state welfare office he would not have been a state actor?

(b) The holding in *West* appears to bring to a sharp halt any idea that a state could avoid its affirmative duties to prisoners by contracting out the provision of prison services to private companies or persons. What should happen in those states where the governmental unit completely shuts down its prison and sends inmates to a privately constructed facility? See Ira Robbins, *The Legal Dimensions of Private Incarceration*, 38 AM.U.L.REV. 531 (1989).

(c) Should privatized governmental services fall outside the state-action doctrine? Only if they are not core governmental functions such as incarceration of prisoners?

3. What are the limits of the concept of state contractual agents as state actors? In 1982 the Supreme Court decided companion cases that seem at least superficially at odds with *West*. In **Rendell–Baker v. Kohn**, 457 U.S. 830, 838, 102 S.Ct. 2764, 73 L.Ed.2d 418 (1982), the Court held, in a suit under § 1983, that a private school was not a state actor even though most of its students had been referred to the school under a state contract that paid for the education of maladjusted students. In **Blum v. Yaretsky**, 457 U.S. 991, 102 S.Ct. 2777, 73 L.Ed.2d 534 (1982), the Court refused to find a nursing home to be a state actor in its decisions regarding Medicaid patients whose stays were paid by the state.[1] What is the difference between the

---

1. Would *Rendell–Baker* have been decided differently had the suit been brought by students receiving state aid rather than, as it was, by teachers who taught both aided and unaided students? See *Blum*.

contractors who were held not to be state actors in *Rendell–Baker* and *Blum* and the contractor who was held to be a state actor in *West?*

(a) Does Justice Blackmun persuasively distinguish these cases in footnote 10? Is the affirmative-duty concept important only in this narrow class of state action cases—those involving contractors? Were the 1982 cases correctly decided because any duty arose from state, not federal constitutional, law?

(b) Consider this quandary: All state employees are state actors, but state contractors are not state actors. Are not state employees just persons who contract with the state to provide services? So what is the difference between contractors and employees? Whether the services are performed on state property at state offices or at private offices? Is the location of the work constitutionally significant? See Moose Lodge No. 107 v. Irvis, 407 U.S. 163, 92 S.Ct. 1965, 32 L.Ed.2d 627 (1972).

4. Are state employees still state actors when they go off duty? A police officer is a state actor even when she misuses her authority, *Monroe,* but is she still a state actor when she stops at a bar and beats a patron? See Stengel v. Belcher, 522 F.2d 438 (6th Cir.1975), cert. dismissed, 429 U.S. 118, 97 S.Ct. 514, 50 L.Ed.2d 269 (1976) (state action found, given local rules requiring officer to carry gun off-duty); cf. Griffin v. Maryland, 378 U.S. 130, 84 S.Ct. 1770, 12 L.Ed.2d 754 (1964) (off-duty officer moonlighting at amusement park).

(a) If an officer goes home and shoots a spouse with a weapon other than his service revolver, is he a state actor at the time of the shooting? See Gulledge v. Smart, 691 F.Supp. 947 (D.S.C.1988), aff'd, 878 F.2d 379 (4th Cir.1989). Compare Gibson v. City of Chicago, 910 F.2d 1510 (7th Cir.1990) (officer previously declared mentally unfit and placed on leave). Are off-duty officers who work as mall security guards or as off-duty security officers acting under color of state law? See Parks v. City of Columbus, 395 F.3d 643 (6th Cir. 2005) (off-duty officer in uniform with badge is "purport[ing]" to be state actor and is); Abraham v. Raso, 183 F.3d 279 (3d Cir. 1999) (similar) (collecting cases). But see Zambrana–Marrero v. Suarez–Cruz, 172 F.3d 122 (1st Cir.1999) (collecting cases): "No single, easily determinable factor will control whether a police officer was acting under state law. While certain factors will certainly be relevant—for example, a police officer's garb, an officer's duty status, the officer's use of a service revolver, and the location of the incident—these factors must not be assessed mechanically."

(b) If a local sanitation worker leaves work for the day, gets in his automobile, and runs down a pedestrian on the drive home, is he a state actor at the time of the incident? Cf. Pena v. DePrisco, 432 F.3d 98 (2d Cir. 2005) (absence of viable claim against drunk officer prompts suit against fellow officers for condoning drunkenness and permitting incident to occur). Are some government workers be considered always "on duty"? How would you define this class of officials?

(c) A public official properly respects his assistant on the job, but he pursues her relentlessly after work and demands sexual attention from her at her home, but never takes any action against her on the job. Is his sexual harassment done as a state actor or a private actor? If a police officer argues with a motorist on the job, then goes to the motorist's home while off-duty and beats the motorist, is the officer a state actor at the time of the beating? Cf. Andrews v. City of Philadelphia, 895 F.2d 1469 (3d Cir.1990) (on-duty and off-duty harassment, state action assumed).

5. If state employees are state actors, there remains another problem: what is the "state"? The usual institutions and entities comprising state government, including cities, counties, and local governments, are part of the "state." See, e.g., Monroe v. Pape, Chapter 1A supra; Ward v. Love County, 253 U.S. 17, 40 S.Ct. 419, 64 L.Ed. 751 (1920). Other entities present more problematic situations.

(a) State employees may unionize in some states and later engage in collective bargaining or similar concerted activity that makes contracts for the employees. Are employee unions part of the "state" because their members are state actors? See Messman v. Helmke, 133 F.3d 1042 (7th Cir.1998) (restrictions on speech and association in contract signed by union).

(b) Governments sometimes establish corporate entities as a vehicle for carrying out public policies. Are these entities part of the "state," or should they be treated like other corporate entities which are typically deemed private entities? See Lebron v. National R.R. Passenger Corp., 513 U.S. 374, 115 S.Ct. 961, 130 L.Ed.2d 902 (1995) ("corporate form" is not important; control through appointment of directors is). Would a corporation be a state actor if it, like most private corporations, had independently-chosen directors?

(c) Can a state circumvent the holding in *Lebron* by allying itself with private persons, businesses, or corporations? Would both private persons and private corporations be state actors if they joined together? See Brentwood Academy v. Tennessee Secondary School Athletic Ass'n, 531 U.S. 288, 121 S.Ct. 924, 148 L.Ed.2d 807 (2001).

3. SCOPE OF THE STATE ACTION DOCTRINE: PRIVATE ACTORS WHO JOIN WITH STATE ACTORS

SAN FRANCISCO ARTS & ATHLETICS, INC. v. UNITED STATES OLYMPIC COMMITTEE

Supreme Court of the United States, 1987.
483 U.S. 522, 107 S.Ct. 2971, 97 L.Ed.2d 427.

JUSTICE POWELL delivered the opinion of the Court.

In this case, we consider the scope and constitutionality of a provision of the Amateur Sports Act of 1978 that authorizes the United States Olympic Committee [USOC] to prohibit certain commercial and promotional uses of the word "Olympic." [This suit was brought by Petitioner San Francisco Arts & Athletics, Inc. (SFAA), a nonprofit California corporation, that planned to conduct the "Gay Olympic Games," paying for the venture with the sale of promotional items bearing the logo "Gay Olympics Games." The USOC, exercising its veto power granted by law, requested the SFAA to terminate its use of the word "Olympic" in its promotions. When the SFAA refused, the USOC brought this suit in federal court to enjoin further infringing conduct by SFAA. The lower courts granted the injunction, and the SFAA sought review in the Supreme Court, alleging that the statutory grant of exclusive use to the USOC violate its rights under the First Amendment. The Court first held that the Act did in fact grant the USOC exclusive rights to the word "Olympic" and that this trademark-like right did not violated the First Amendment. The Court then faced the SFAA's final issue: whether the USOC's enforcement of its interest in the term was discriminatory against homosexuals in violation of Equal Protection principles.]

IV

The SFAA argues that even if the exclusive use granted by [federal statute] does not violate the First Amendment, the USOC's enforcement of that right is discriminatory in violation of the Fifth Amendment.[1] The fundamental inquiry is whether the USOC is a governmental actor to whom the prohibitions of the Constitution apply.[2] The USOC is a "private corporation established under Federal law." 36 U.S.C. § 1101(46).[3] In the Act, Congress granted the USOC a corporate charter, imposed certain requirements on the USOC, and provided for some USOC funding through exclusive use of the Olympic words and symbols and through direct grants.

The fact that Congress granted it a corporate charter does not render the USOC a Government agent. All corporations act under charters granted by a government, usually by a State. They do not thereby lose their essentially private character. Even extensive regulation by the government does not transform the actions of the regulated entity into those of the government. See Jackson v. Metropolitan Edison Co., 419 U.S. 345,

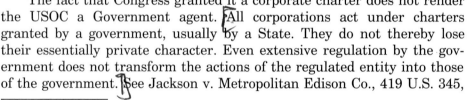

---

1. The SFAA invokes the Fourteenth Amendment for its discriminatory enforcement claim. The Fourteenth Amendment applies to actions by a State. The claimed association in this case is between the USOC and the Federal Government. Therefore, the Fourteenth Amendment does not apply. The Fifth Amendment, however, does apply to the Federal Government and contains an equal protection component. Bolling v. Sharpe, 347 U.S. 497, 499, 74 S.Ct. 693, 694, 98 L.Ed. 884 (1954). "This Court's approach to Fifth Amendment equal protection claims has ... been precisely the same as to equal protection claims under the Fourteenth Amendment." Weinberger v. Wiesenfeld, 420 U.S. 636, 638, n. 2, 95 S.Ct. 1225, 1228, n. 2, 43 L.Ed.2d 514 (1975). * * * Accordingly, we address the claim as one under the Fifth Amendment.

2. Because we find no governmental action, we need not address the merits of the SFAA's discriminatory enforcement claim. We note, however, that the SFAA's claim of discriminatory enforcement is far from compelling [because the USOC has regularly enforced its trademark against others who have sought to use it, including a shoe company, a bus company, and the March of Dimes. It has licensed use to the "Special Olympics" for disabled persons.] The record before us strongly indicates that the USOC has acted strictly in accord with its charter and that there has been no actionable discrimination.

3. As such, the USOC is listed with 69 other federally created private corporations such as the American Legion, Big Brothers–Big Sisters of America, Daughters of the American Revolution, Veterans of Foreign Wars of the United States, the National Academy of Sciences, and the National Ski Patrol System, Inc. 36 U.S.C. § 1101. It hardly need be said that if federally created private corporations were to be viewed as governmental rather than private actors, the consequences would be far reaching. Apart from subjecting these private entities to suits under the equal protection component of the Due Process Clause of the Fifth Amendment, presumably—by analogy—similar types of nonprofit corporations established under state law could be viewed as governmental actors subject to such suits under the Equal Protection Clause of the Fourteenth Amendment.

95 S.Ct. 449, 42 L.Ed.2d 477 (1974). Nor is the fact that Congress has granted the USOC exclusive use of the word "Olympic" dispositive. All enforceable rights in trademarks are created by some governmental act, usually pursuant to a statute or the common law. The actions of the trademark owners nevertheless remain private. Moreover, the intent on the part of Congress to help the USOC obtain funding does not change the analysis. The Government may subsidize private entities without assuming constitutional responsibility for their actions. Blum v. Yaretsky, 457 U.S. 991, 1011, 102 S.Ct. 2777, 2789, 73 L.Ed.2d 534 (1982); Rendell–Baker v. Kohn, 457 U.S. 830, 840, 102 S.Ct. 2764, 2770, 73 L.Ed.2d 418 (1982).

* * *

Most fundamentally, this Court has held that a government "normally can be held responsible for a private decision only when it has exercised coercive power or has provided such significant encouragement, either overt or covert, that the choice must in law be deemed to be that of the [government]." Blum v. Yaretsky, supra; Moose Lodge No. 107 v. Irvis, 407 U.S. 163, 173, 92 S.Ct. 1965, 1971, 32 L.Ed.2d 627 (1972). The USOC's choice of how to enforce its exclusive right to use the word "Olympic" simply is not a governmental decision. There is no evidence that the Federal Government coerced or encouraged the USOC in the exercise of its right. At most, the Federal Government, by failing to supervise the USOC's use of its rights, can be said to exercise "[m]ere approval of or acquiescence in the initiatives" of the USOC. Blum v. Yaretsky. This is not enough to make the USOC's actions those of the Government.[9] Because the USOC is not a governmental actor, the SFAA's claim that the USOC has enforced its rights in a discriminatory manner must fail.

V

Accordingly, we affirm the judgment of the Court of Appeals for the Ninth Circuit.

It is so ordered.

JUSTICE BRENNAN, with whom JUSTICE MARSHALL joins, dissenting. [JUSTICES O'CONNOR and BLACKMUN also joined the part of the opinion quoted below.]

* * *

* * * At a minimum, this case, like Burton v. Wilmington Parking Authority, 365 U.S. 715, 81 S.Ct. 856, 6 L.Ed.2d 45 (1961), is one in which

---

9. For all of the same reasons indicated above, we reject the SFAA's argument that the United States Government should be viewed as a "joint participant" in the USOC's efforts to enforce its right to use the word "Olympic." See Burton v. Wilmington Parking Authority. The SFAA has failed to demonstrate that the Federal Government can or does exert any influence over the exercise of the USOC's enforcement decisions. Absent proof of this type of "close nexus between the [Government] and the challenged action of the [USOC]," the challenged action may not be "fairly treated as that of the [Government] itself." Jackson v. Metropolitan Edison Co.

the Government "has so far insinuated itself into a position of interdependence with [the USOC] that it must be recognized as a joint participant in the challenged activity."

* * *

The USOC and the Federal Government exist in a symbiotic relationship sufficient to provide a nexus between the USOC's challenged action and the Government. First, as in *Burton*, the relationship here confers a variety of mutual benefits. [T]he Act gave the USOC authority and responsibilities that no private organization in this country had ever held. The Act also conferred substantial financial resources on the USOC [and gave it] unprecedented power to control the use of the word "Olympic" and related emblems to raise additional funds. As a result of the Act, the United States obtained, for the first time in its history, an exclusive and effective organization to coordinate and administer all amateur athletics related to international competition, and to represent that program abroad.

Second, in the eye of the public,[14] both national and international, the connection between the decisions of the United States Government and those of the United States Olympic Committee is profound. The President of the United States has served as the Honorary President of the USOC. The national flag flies both literally and figuratively over the central product of the USOC, the United States Olympic Team. [All athletes know that they are competing for the "United States of America."]

Even more importantly, there is a close financial and legislative link between the USOC's alleged discriminatory exercise of its word-use authority and the financial success of both the USOC and the Government. It would certainly be "irony amounting to grave injustice" if, to finance the team that is to represent the virtues of our political system, the USOC were free to employ Government-created economic leverage to prohibit political speech. * * *

If petitioner is correct in its allegation that the USOC has used its discretion to discriminate against certain groups, then the situation here, as in *Burton*, is that "profits earned by discrimination not only contribute to, but also are indispensable elements in, the financial success of a governmental agency." *Burton*. Indeed, the required nexus between the challenged action and the Government appears even closer here than in *Burton*. While in *Burton* the restaurant was able to pursue a policy of discrimination because the State had failed to impose upon it a policy of nondiscrimination, the USOC could pursue its alleged policy of selective enforcement only because Congress affirmatively granted it power that it

---

14. In *Burton*, the Court also found significant evidence that would link the two actors in the public's eye. There was "the obvious fact that the restaurant is operated as an integral part of a public building devoted to a public parking service," and the fact that "the Authority located at appropriate places [on the facility] official signs indicating the public character of the building, and flew from mastheads on the roof both the state and national flags." This evident interdependence created public perceptions of "grave injustice" that the Court could not ignore. [Repositioned footnote.]

would not otherwise have to control the use of the word "Olympic." I conclude, then, that the close nexus between the Government and the challenged action compels a finding of Government action.

[The portion of the opinion finding a violation of the First Amendment, joined only by Justice Marshall, is omitted.]

AMERICAN MANUFACTURERS MUTUAL INSURANCE COMPANY v. SULLIVAN

Supreme Court of the United States, 1999.
526 U.S. 40, 119 S.Ct. 977, 143 L.Ed.2d 130.

CHIEF JUSTICE REHNQUIST delivered the opinion of the Court.

[Pennsylvania has a "Workers' Compensation Law" that repeals the usual tort rules for suits by employees against employers for injuries on the job and replaces it with a system by which workers recover automatically for reasonable expenses for work-related injuries. Most employers comply by purchasing insurance. The system initially proved to be expensive, especially a provision that required insurers to pay benefits within 30 days, a feature that sometimes resulted in payments of unjustified claims to persons from whom the payments could not be later recouped. To solve the problem, Pennsylvania amended its law to permit insurers to decline to pay in the required time if they notified the state and promptly sought private arbitration. An insurer's refusal to pay a justified claim was actionable under state law.]

[Some employees denied benefits by an insurer sued the insurer and the state under § 1983, claiming that the delay occasioned by state-permitted arbitral decision violated their constitutional rights. They argued that the heavy state regulation of workers' compensation converted the private insurance company's decisions regarding healthcare into joint private-state decisions, making the insurer also a state actor. The Third Circuit accepted the argument, citing the Supreme Court's holding in Burton v. Wilmington Parking Authority, discussed in the preceding case. The Supreme Court agreed to the insurer's request to review the decision.]

II

To state a claim for relief in an action brought under § 1983, respondents must establish that they were deprived of a right secured by the Constitution or laws of the United States, and that the alleged deprivation was committed under color of state law. Like the state-action requirement of the Fourteenth Amendment, the under-color-of-state-law element of § 1983 excludes from its reach " 'merely private conduct, no matter how discriminatory or wrongful,' " Blum v. Yaretsky.

* * *

* * * All agree that the public officials responsible for administering the workers' compensation system [are] state actors. Thus, the issue we address, in accordance with our cases, is whether a private insurer's decision to withhold payment for disputed medical treatment may be fairly attributable to the State so as to subject insurers to the constraints of the Fourteenth Amendment. Our answer to that question is "no."

In cases involving extensive state regulation of private activity, we have consistently held that "[t]he mere fact that a business is subject to state regulation does not by itself convert its action into that of the State for purposes of the Fourteenth Amendment." Jackson v. Metropolitan Edison Co; see Blum [v. Yaretsky] Faithful application of the state-action requirement in these cases ensures that the prerogative of regulating private business remains with the States and the representative branches, not the courts. Thus, the private insurers in this case will not be held to constitutional standards unless "there is a sufficiently close nexus between the State and the challenged action of the regulated entity so that the latter may be fairly treated as that of the State itself." Ibid. Whether such a "close nexus" exists, our cases state, depends on whether the State "has exercised coercive power or has provided such significant encouragement, either overt or covert, that the choice must in law be deemed to be that of the State." Ibid. Action taken by private entities with the mere approval or acquiescence of the State is not state action. Blum, supra.

Here, respondents do not assert that the decision to [seek arbitration of a disputed claim] should be attributed to the State because the State compels or is directly involved in that decision. Obviously the State is not so involved. It authorizes, but does not require, insurers to withhold payments for disputed medical treatment. The decision to withhold payment, like the decision to transfer Medicaid patients to a lower level of care in Blum, is made by concededly private parties, and "turns on ... judgments made by private parties" without "standards ... established by the State."

Respondents do assert, however, that the decision to withhold payment to providers may be fairly attributable to the State because the State has "authorized" and "encouraged" it. Respondents' primary argument in this regard is that, in amending the Act to provide for [arbitration] and to grant insurers an option they previously did not have, the State purposely "encouraged" insurers to withhold payments for disputed medical treatment. This argument reads too much into the State's reform, and in any event cannot be squared with our cases.

We do not doubt that the State's decision to provide insurers the option of deferring payment for unnecessary and unreasonable treatment pending review can in some sense be seen as encouraging them to do just that. But, as petitioners note, this kind of subtle encouragement is no more significant than that which inheres in the State's creation or modification of any legal remedy. We have never held that the mere availability of a remedy for wrongful conduct, even when the private use of that remedy serves important public interests, so significantly encourages the private activity as to make the State responsible for it. See Tulsa

Professional Collection Services, Inc. v. Pope, 485 U.S. 478, 485, 108 S.Ct. 1340, 99 L.Ed.2d 565 (1988) ["Private use of state-sanctioned private remedies or procedures does not rise to the level of state action"] [While it is true that an insurer must file a notice form with the state, the state does not approve or deny such forms. The state is merely engaged in "paper shuffling."] It bears repeating that a finding of state action on this basis would be contrary to the "essential dichotomy" between public and private acts that our cases have consistently recognized.

Rule [margin annotation]

* * *

The Court of Appeals, in response to the various arguments advanced by respondents, seems to have figuratively thrown up its hands and fallen back on language in our decision in Burton v. Wilmington Parking Authority. The Pennsylvania system, that court said, "inextricably entangles the insurance companies in a partnership with the Commonwealth such that they become an integral part of the state in administering the statutory scheme." Relying on Burton, respondents urge us to affirm the Court of Appeals' holding under a "joint participation" theory of state action.

Burton was one of our early cases dealing with "state action" under the Fourteenth Amendment, and later cases have refined the vague "joint participation" test embodied in that case. Blum and Jackson, in particular, have established that "privately owned enterprises providing services that the State would not necessarily provide, even though they are extensively regulated, do not fall within the ambit of Burton." Blum. Here, workers' compensation insurers are at least as extensively regulated as the private nursing facilities in Blum [yet as in Blum], the state statutory and regulatory scheme leaves the challenged decisions to the judgment of insurers.

joint participation test [margin annotation]

Rule [margin annotation]

* * *

We conclude that an insurer's decision to withhold payment and seek [arbitration] of the reasonableness and necessity of particular medical treatment is not fairly attributable to the State. Respondents have therefore failed to satisfy an essential element of their § 1983 claim [against the insurer].

[Reversed.]

[Concurring opinions omitted; opinion of Justice Stevens dissenting in part omitted.]

NOTE ON PRIVATE PERSONS AS STATE ACTORS

1. When the Fourteenth Amendment was adopted in 1868, the modern American bureaucratic state had not yet been created. Although states and private entities occasionally joined for a perceived common good, as in road building or public works, see Proprietors of Charles River Bridge v. Proprietors of Warren Bridge, 36 U.S. (11 Pet.) 420, 9 L.Ed. 773 (1837), governmen-

tal regulation and private-public joint ventures had not blurred the distinction between governmental and private activity. The Fourteenth Amendment's direction that "No State shall" violate its proscriptions thus accorded with an intuitive contemporary notion that the amendment covered state action, but not private action. See The Civil Rights Cases, 109 U.S. 3, 3 S.Ct. 18, 27 L.Ed. 835 (1883). Since that day, of course, categories that seemed then as distinct as Boston and Washington, Los Angeles and San Diego, and Dallas and Ft. Worth, have grown together as much as those cities have.

(a) The end points for the state action continuum remain relatively distinct: the state, in the form of its employees exercising their governmental authority, is virtually always a state actor, see West v. Atkins, supra, while private persons acting without governmental sanction are not state actors, see Flagg Bros., Inc. v. Brooks, infra.

(b) It is the intervening set of government-private relationships that presents problems for the modern courts. How should the Court give continued meaning to a distinction that was once bright but now is blurred? As you read the remainder of this Note, consider whether the following sub-categories of cases give predictable modern meaning to the once-clear state-private distinction.

2. *Conspiracy Cases.* When state and private actors conspire together to achieve a joint goal, the private person takes on the mantle of the state actor and becomes one himself, as the Court held in **United States v. Price**, 383 U.S. 787, 86 S.Ct. 1152, 16 L.Ed.2d 267 (1966), involving the infamous murder of civil rights workers in Philadelphia, Mississippi, by a gang of private persons who joined police officers. See Adickes v. S.H. Kress & Co., 398 U.S. 144, 90 S.Ct. 1598, 26 L.Ed.2d 142 (1970) (if store manager and police conspire to have civil rights worker arrested, both are state actors); Dennis v. Sparks, 449 U.S. 24, 101 S.Ct. 183, 66 L.Ed.2d 185 (1980) ("corrupt conspiracy involving bribery of the judge"; private briber is state actor, too). Are these not easy cases because the private person has become a "de facto deputy," helping the state actor in the misuse of his state power?

(a) Why cannot the majority in the two principal cases see the USOC and the insurance companies as conspirators with the lawmakers or executives? Because then everyone who seeks to influence government—and wins—would be a state actor? Are the two cases different? Is the insurance company less of a state actor because it sought and won less government-private interaction or regulation than previously existed? Is a lobbyist for less government, ironically, a state actor? What makes a "conspiracy" a "conspiracy"—a motive to corrupt an existing law by other than the usual lawmaking process? See Tower v. Glover, 467 U.S. 914, 104 S.Ct. 2820, 81 L.Ed.2d 758 (1984) (public defender, a private actor under *Polk County*, is state actor when conspiring with covered prosecutor or judge); United Steelworkers v. Phelps Dodge Corp., 865 F.2d 1539 (9th Cir.1989) (en banc) (potential conspiracy between employer and police to break strike by arresting strikers).

(b) In the conspiracy cases, should it matter who initiates the unconstitutional acts? If a sheriff recruits a private person, then the private person becomes a deputy. But if the private person goes to the sheriff and proposes corruption, why is the private person then a state actor? See United States v.

Price, supra. Is it because either way the private person takes on more power than she would otherwise have?

3. *Joint–Participation Cases.* If the conspiracy cases represent the situation where state and private persons act together to pursue a specific and common non-legislative goal, the more ordinary joint participation cases represent those situations where government and private persons act together, but for somewhat differing goals. In **Burton v. Wilmington Parking Auth.**, 365 U.S. 715, 81 S.Ct. 856, 6 L.Ed.2d 45 (1961), a city sought to derive more revenue from a municipally constructed parking garage by renting space in the structure to a private restaurant. The local government sought its self-interest; the restaurant lessee rented space to make a profit in its self-interest. In **National Collegiate Athletic Ass'n v. Tarkanian**, 488 U.S. 179, 109 S.Ct. 454, 102 L.Ed.2d 469 (1988), the Court rejected a "joint participant" argument in a case in which a college coach challenged sanctions imposed on him and his school by the NCAA: "[T]he state and private parties' relevant interests do not coincide, as they did in *Burton*; rather, they have clashed throughout the investigation, the attempt to discipline Tarkanian, and this litigation. [The coach's employer, a state university,] and the NCAA were antagonists, not joint participants, and the NCAA may not be deemed a state actor on this ground."

(a) Methodologically, the Court has referred to several tests, beginning with *Burton*'s command that courts "sift the facts and weigh the circumstances" to decide if there was state action—an admitted attempt to accrete case-by-case results from which the Court could in the future deduce doctrine. See 365 U.S. at 722, 81 S.Ct. at 860. A passing line indicating that "any involvement" might suffice to show state action did not survive. In later cases the Court suggested a "nexus" inquiry, asking alternatively whether the state had put its "imprimatur" on the private conduct or had created a "symbiotic relationship" so as to make both the state and private entities culpable. Moose Lodge No. 107 v. Irvis, 407 U.S. 163, 176, 92 S.Ct. 1965, 32 L.Ed.2d 627 (1972). What concerns lie beneath these verbal formulations? Is the Court asking whether, in the public's perception, there is a joint goal? Why does Justice Brennan like, and want to stay with, these older tests in his opinion in the *San Francisco Arts & Athletics* case? Do they make findings of state action more malleable than in the later tests noted below?

(b) Verbal formulations aside, some later cases appear to turn on mundane distinctions between which spaces are perceived as private and which public. See *Moose Lodge*, 407 U.S. at 175, 92 S.Ct. at 1972 (club's discrimination on private property distinguishes case from *Burton* where discrimination took place in publicly owned parking structure; private club does not "hold itself out" as serving the public at large); Gilmore v. City of Montgomery, 417 U.S. 556, 573–74, 94 S.Ct. 2416, 2426–27, 41 L.Ed.2d 304 (1974) (city property used by private segregationist clubs makes "this case more like *Burton* than *Moose Lodge*," but fact that others can use parks freely shows that use of parks does not connote governmental approval of clubs); Norwood v. Harrison, 413 U.S. 455, 93 S.Ct. 2804, 37 L.Ed.2d 723 (1973) (lending free textbooks to private segregated schools links schools and state because textbooks are "a basic educational tool," and connotes more state involvement than provision of "generalized" public services such as police protection or electricity).

(c) The most recent test used in "joint participation" cases is that applied by the majorities in *San Francisco Arts & Athletics* and in *American Manufacturers*. This approach developed primarily in cases involving state regulation of private business activity. See Reitman v. Mulkey, 387 U.S. 369, 87 S.Ct. 1627, 18 L.Ed.2d 830 (1967) (state law "encouraged" private racial discrimination in housing transactions); Lombard v. Louisiana, 373 U.S. 267, 83 S.Ct. 1122, 10 L.Ed.2d 338 (1963) (city officials "coerced" lunchcounter operators to enforce segregation). The test appeared to be a convincing way of explaining why general business regulation, without command involvement in all business decisions, does not give rise to state action. Notice how the majority in *San Francisco Arts & Athletics* ruled that a governmentally granted charter, or "[e]ven extensive regulation" of a private group by the state, does not make the otherwise private entity a governmental actor. Indeed, the "Government may subsidize private entities without assuming constitutional responsibility for their actions."

(d) Should there be an exception for especially heavily regulated monopolies? Because of their unique power, may they be considered state actors? See Jackson v. Metropolitan Edison Co., 419 U.S. 345, 349, 95 S.Ct. 449, 452, 42 L.Ed.2d 477 (1974) (utility is not state actor absent state compulsion to act; business decisions not required by state law are not state action) (per Marshall, J.).[1] Why? Because there is no mechanism for separating "heavily regulated" businesses and all other businesses that are partly regulated? Is the "encouragement" test the only way to prevent all private businesses from being labeled state actors, thus destroying the dichotomy between state and private action?

(e) In **Lebron v. National R.R. Passenger Corp.**, 513 U.S. 374, 115 S.Ct. 961, 130 L.Ed.2d 902 (1995), the Court found that AMTRAC is a state actor because a majority of its board of directors is controlled by governmental appointees. Is this a bright-line rule in an area often devoid of them? Is a corporation whose board is dominated by the government just another government agency, albeit a thinly disguised one?

4. *Government "Contractors and Grantees" Cases.* In **Rendell–Baker v. Kohn**, 457 U.S. 830, 838, 102 S.Ct. 2764, 2769, 73 L.Ed.2d 418 (1982), and Blum v. Yaretsky, 457 U.S. 991, 102 S.Ct. 2777, 73 L.Ed.2d 534 (1982), the Supreme Court held that contractors and grantees are not, by virtue of the contract or grant alone, state actors. See the Note on State Employees and Officials as State Actors, preceding the *American Manufacturers* case, supra.

(a) Contractors and grantees virtually by definition carry out state functions. Why are they not jointly involved with the state so as to be deemed state actors? Is it because so many citizens are state (or federal) contractors and grantees at any given moment—recipients of social security, guaranteed

---

1. For earlier attempts to make the case for an affirmative response, see Lombard v. Louisiana, supra, at 274–83, 83 S.Ct. at 1129–1130 (Douglas, J., concurring) (citing the first Justice Harlan, argues that businesses that open themselves to the public become state actors and must serve all); Bell v. Maryland, 378 U.S. 226, 245–46, 259, 278–81, 84 S.Ct. 1814, 1824–25, 1832, 1842–45, 12 L.Ed.2d 822 (1964) (Douglas, J., dissenting) (corporations).

student loans, crop subsidies, highway subsidies—that everyone would thereby become a state actor? If a particular rule would label everyone a state actor, is it untenable because it thus destroys the "essential dichotomy" between state and private action? Was the USOC in *San Francisco Arts & Athletics* more than a mere grantee of government funds? Was the insurer not a state actor because it was not even a grantee of state funds?

(b) Are there any affirmative benefits from leaving persons outside the state action doctrine, and thus unrestricted by the requirements of the Fourteenth Amendment? How does the majority in *American Manufacturers* perceive those benefits? Though a state may not restrict marriages based on race, Loving v. Virginia, 388 U.S. 1, 87 S.Ct. 1817, 18 L.Ed.2d 1010 (1967), is there a positive benefit to allowing private persons to decide to limit their marriage choices based on race? If procedural due process requires prior notice and a hearing to restrict arbitrary government decisionmaking, Cleveland Board of Education v. Loudermill, 470 U.S. 532, 105 S.Ct. 1487, 84 L.Ed.2d 494 (1985), is there an affirmative benefit to leaving a person free to purchase pink pumps or fuchsia sneakers without hearing all sellers' views? See Columbia Broadcasting System v. Democratic National Committee, 412 U.S. 94, 93 S.Ct. 2080, 36 L.Ed.2d 772 (1973) (plurality opinion by Chief Justice Burger) (free-speech constitutional standards that aid society by restricting government harm society when applied to restrict private persons).

(c) The state action doctrine has substantially declined in recent years as a topic of academic and judicial interest, at least for those persons interested in racial equality. This is because other civil rights statutes allow the pursuit of these claims, based on statutes derived from the Thirteenth Amendment, without proof of state action. See Chapter 2 infra. Does that leave some topics, those not covered by the Thirteenth Amendment, still of concern? See Chapter 3 infra.

5. As you read the next group of cases, consider whether there is a "grand unification" theory that would explain all state-action cases involving state employees and private persons. Ostensibly, the next class of cases deals with state inaction and neutrality. Are they really different from the "joint participation" cases? Are the tests used there different from the "compulsion" and "encouragement" tests discussed in this sub-section?

4. SCOPE OF THE STATE ACTION DOCTRINE: STATE INACTION OR NEUTRALITY

FLAGG BROS., INC. v. BROOKS

Supreme Court of the United States, 1978.
436 U.S. 149, 98 S.Ct. 1729, 56 L.Ed.2d 185.

MR. JUSTICE REHNQUIST delivered the opinion of the Court.

The question presented by this litigation is whether a warehouseman's proposed sale of goods entrusted to him for storage, as permitted by New York Uniform Commercial Code § 7–210 (McKinney 1964), is an action properly attributable to the State of New York. The District Court found that the warehouseman's conduct was not that of the State, and dismissed this suit[, but the court of appeals disagreed.] We agree with the District Court, and we therefore reverse.

I

According to her complaint, the allegations of which we must accept as true, respondent Shirley Brooks and her family were evicted from their apartment in Mount Vernon, N.Y., on June 13, 1973. The City Marshal arranged for Brooks' possessions to be stored by petitioner, Flagg Brothers, Inc., in its warehouse. Brooks was informed of the cost of moving and storage, and she instructed the workmen to proceed, although she found the price too high. On August 25, 1973, after a series of disputes over the validity of the charges being claimed by petitioner Flagg Brothers, Brooks received a letter demanding that her account be brought up to date within 10 days "or your furniture will be sold." A series of subsequent letters from respondent and her attorneys produced no satisfaction.

Brooks thereupon initiated this class action in the District Court under 42 U.S.C. § 1983, seeking damages, an injunction against the threatened sale of her belongings, and the declaration that such a sale pursuant to § 7–210 would violate the Due Process and Equal Protection Clauses of the Fourteenth Amendment. [Although Flagg Brothers had never sold Brooks' belongings, the Court held that the suit was still live based on the plaintiff's claim for damages. Another party, Jones, later joined in Ms. Brooks' suit, alleging that she had never authorized the removal and storage of her property.] * * *

II

* * *

Respondents allege in their complaints that "the threatened sale of the goods pursuant to New York Uniform Commercial Code § 7–210" is an action under color of state law. * * * It must be noted that respondents have named no public officials as defendants in this action. The City Marshal, who supervised their evictions, was dismissed from the case by the consent of all the parties. This total absence of overt official involvement plainly distinguishes this case from earlier decisions imposing procedural restrictions on creditors' remedies such as North Georgia Finishing, Inc. v. Di–Chem, Inc., 419 U.S. 601, 95 S.Ct. 719, 42 L.Ed.2d 751 (1975); Fuentes v. Shevin, 407 U.S. 67, 92 S.Ct. 1983, 32 L.Ed.2d 556 (1972); Sniadach v. Family Finance Corp., 395 U.S. 337, 89 S.Ct. 1820, 23 L.Ed.2d 349 (1969)[, where state officials were named as defendants].

III

Respondents' primary contention is that New York has delegated to Flagg Brothers a power "traditionally exclusively reserved to the State." Jackson [v. Metropolitan Edison Co.]. They argue that the resolution of private disputes is a traditional function of civil government, and that the State in § 7–210 has delegated this function to Flagg Brothers. Respondents, however, have read too much into the language of our previous cases. While many functions have been traditionally performed by governments, very few have been "exclusively reserved to the State." One such area has been elections. While the Constitution protects private rights of association and advocacy with regard to the election of public officials, our cases make it clear that the conduct of the elections themselves is an exclusively public function. This principle was established by a series of cases challenging the exclusion of blacks from participation in primary elections in Texas. Terry v. Adams, 345 U.S. 461, 73 S.Ct. 809, 97 L.Ed. 1152 (1953); Smith v. Allwright, 321 U.S. 649, 64 S.Ct. 757, 88 L.Ed. 987 (1944); Nixon v. Condon, 286 U.S. 73, 52 S.Ct. 484, 76 L.Ed. 984 (1932). Although the rationale of these cases may be subject to some dispute, their scope is carefully defined. The doctrine does not reach to all forms of private political activity, but encompasses only state-regulated elections or elections conducted by organizations which in practice produce "the uncontested choice of public officials." Terry, supra, 345 U.S. at 484, 73 S.Ct. at 820 (Clark, J., concurring). As Mr. Justice Black described the situation in Terry, supra, at 469, 73 S.Ct. at 813: "The only election that has counted in this Texas county for more than fifty years has been that held by the Jaybirds from which Negroes were excluded."

A second line of cases under the public-function doctrine originated with Marsh v. Alabama, 326 U.S. 501, 66 S.Ct. 276, 90 L.Ed. 265 (1946). Just as the Texas Democratic Party in *Smith* and the Jaybird Democratic Association in *Terry* effectively performed the entire public function of selecting public officials, so too the Gulf Shipbuilding Corp. performed all the necessary municipal functions in the town of Chickasaw, Ala., which it owned. Under those circumstances, the Court concluded it was bound to recognize the right of a group of Jehovah's Witnesses to distribute religious literature on its streets. The Court expanded this municipal-function theory in Amalgamated Food Employees Union v. Logan Valley Plaza, Inc., 391 U.S. 308, 88 S.Ct. 1601, 20 L.Ed.2d 603 (1968), to encompass the activities of a private shopping center[, but it later overruled this extension in Hudgens v. NLRB, 424 U.S. 507, 96 S.Ct. 1029, 47 L.Ed.2d 196 (1976), limiting Marsh to the situation where the private entity functioned with all the physical traditional attributes of a town].

These two branches of the public-function doctrine have in common the feature of exclusivity.[8] Although the elections held by the Democratic Party and its affiliates were the only meaningful elections in Texas, and the streets owned by the Gulf Shipbuilding Corp. were the only streets in Chickasaw, the proposed sale by Flagg Brothers under § 7–210 is not the only means of resolving this purely private dispute. Respondent Brooks

---

8. Respondents also contend that Evans v. Newton, 382 U.S. 296, 86 S.Ct. 486, 15 L.Ed.2d 373 (1966), establishes that the operation of a park for recreational purposes is an exclusively public function. We doubt that *Newton* intended to establish any such broad doctrine in the teeth of the experience of several American entrepreneurs who amassed great fortunes by operating parks for recreational purposes. We think *Newton* rests on a finding of ordinary state action under extraordinary circumstances. The Court's opinion emphasizes that the record showed "no change in the municipal maintenance and concern over this facility," id., at 301, 86 S.Ct. at 489, after the transfer of title to private trustees. That transfer had not been shown to have eliminated the actual involvement of the city in the daily maintenance and care of the park.

has never alleged that state law barred her from seeking a waiver of Flagg Brothers' right to sell her goods at the time she authorized their storage. Presumably, respondent Jones, who alleges that she never authorized the storage of her goods, could have sought to replevy her goods at any time under state law. See N.Y.Civ.Prac.L. & R. § 7101 et seq. (McKinney 1963). The challenged statute itself provides a damages remedy against the warehouseman for violations of its provisions. N.Y.U.C.C. § 7–210(9) (McKinney 1964). This system of rights and remedies, recognizing the traditional place of private arrangements in ordering relationships in the commercial world,[9] can hardly be said to have delegated to Flagg Brothers an exclusive prerogative of the sovereign.[10]

This situation is clearly distinguishable from cases such as North Georgia Finishing, Inc. v. Di–Chem, Inc., 419 U.S. 601, 95 S.Ct. 719, 42 L.Ed.2d 751 (1975); Fuentes v. Shevin, 407 U.S. 67, 92 S.Ct. 1983, 32 L.Ed.2d 556 (1972); and Sniadach v. Family Finance Corp., 395 U.S. 337, 89 S.Ct. 1820, 23 L.Ed.2d 349 (1969)[, where a private claimant invoked the state court's processes to obtain aid in securing property and relied upon court orders that effectuated] the affirmative command of the law of [the state].

Whatever the particular remedies available under New York law, we do not consider a more detailed description of them necessary to our conclusion that the settlement of disputes between debtors and creditors is not traditionally an exclusive public function.[11] Creditors and debtors have had available to them historically a far wider number of choices than has one who would be an elected public official, or a member of Jehovah's Witnesses who wished to distribute literature in Chickasaw, Ala., at the time Marsh was decided. Our analysis requires no parsing of the difference between various commercial liens and other remedies to support the

---

9. Unlike the parade of horribles suggested by our Brother Stevens in dissent, post, at 1740, this case does not involve state authorization of private breach of the peace.

10. It is undoubtedly true, as our Brother Stevens says in dissent, that "respondents have a property interest in the possessions that the warehouseman proposes to sell." But that property interest is not a monolithic, abstract concept hovering in the legal stratosphere. It is a bundle of rights in personalty, the metes and bounds of which are determined by the decisional and statutory law of the State of New York. The validity of the property interest in these possessions which respondents previously acquired from some other private person depends on New York law, and the manner in which that same property interest in these same possessions may be lost or transferred to still another private person likewise depends on New York law. It would intolerably broaden, beyond the scope of any of our previous cases, the notion of state action under the Fourteenth Amendment to hold that the mere existence of a body of property law in a State, whether decisional or statutory, itself amounted to "state action" even though no process or state officials were ever involved in enforcing that body of law.

11. It may well be, as my Brother Stevens' dissent contends, that "[t]he power to order legally binding surrenders of property and the constitutional restrictions on that power are necessary correlatives in our system." But here New York, unlike Florida in *Fuentes*, Georgia in *North Georgia Finishing*, and Wisconsin in *Sniadach*, has not ordered respondents to surrender any property whatever. It has merely enacted a statute which provides that a warehouseman conforming to the provisions of the statute may convert his traditional lien into good title. There is no reason whatever to believe that either Flagg Brothers or respondents could not, if they wished, seek resort to the New York courts in order to either compel or prevent the "surrenders of property" to which that dissent refers, and that the compliance of Flagg Brothers with applicable New York property law would be reviewed after customary notice and hearing in such a proceeding. * * *

conclusion that this entire field of activity is outside the scope of *Terry* and *Marsh*.[12] This is true whether these commercial rights and remedies are created by statute or decisional law. To rely upon the historical antecedents of a particular practice would result in the constitutional condemnation in one State of a remedy found perfectly permissible in another.[13]

Thus, even if we were inclined to extend the sovereign-function doctrine outside of its present carefully confined bounds, the field of private commercial transactions would be a particularly inappropriate area into which to expand it. We conclude that our sovereign-function cases do not support a finding of state action here. Our holding today impairs in no way the precedential value of such cases as Norwood v. Harrison, 413 U.S. 455, 93 S.Ct. 2804, 37 L.Ed.2d 723 (1973), or Gilmore v. City of Montgomery, 417 U.S. 556, 94 S.Ct. 2416, 41 L.Ed.2d 304 (1974), which arose in the context of state and municipal programs which benefited private schools engaging in racially discriminatory admissions practices following judicial decrees desegregating public school systems. And we would be remiss if we did not note that there are a number of state and municipal functions not covered by our election cases or governed by the reasoning of *Marsh* which have been administered with a greater degree of exclusivity by States and municipalities than has the function of so-called "dispute resolution." Among these are such functions as education, fire and police protection, and tax collection. We express no view as to the extent, if any, to which a city or State might be free to delegate to private parties the performance of such functions and thereby avoid the strictures of the Fourteenth Amendment. The mere recitation of these possible permutations and combinations of factual situations suffices to caution us that their resolution should abide the necessity of deciding them.

IV

Respondents further urge that Flagg Brothers' proposed action is properly attributable to the State because the State has authorized and encouraged it in enacting § 7–210. Our cases state "that a State is responsible for the ... act of a private party when the State, by its law, has compelled the act." *Adickes*. This Court, however, has never held that a State's mere acquiescence in a private action converts that action into that of the State. The Court rejected a similar argument in Jackson [v. Metropolitan Edison]:

---

12. * * * Self-help of the type involved in this case is not significantly different from creditor remedies generally, whether created by common law or enacted by legislatures. New York's statute has done nothing more than authorize (and indeed limit)—without participation by any public official—what Flagg Brothers would tend to do, even in the absence of such authorization, i.e., dispose of respondents' property in order to free up its valuable storage space. The proposed sale pursuant to the lien in this case is not a significant departure from traditional private arrangements.

13. See also Davis v. Richmond, 512 F.2d 201, 203 (C.A.1 1975): "[W]e are disinclined to decide the issue of state involvement on the basis of whether a particular class of creditor did or did not enjoy the same freedom to act in Elizabethan or Georgian England."

"Approval by a state utility commission of such a request from a regulated utility, where the commission has not put its own weight on the side of the proposed practice by ordering it, does not transmute a practice initiated by the utility and approved by the commission into 'state action.' " (Emphasis added.)

The clearest demonstration of this distinction appears in Moose Lodge No. 107 v. Irvis, 407 U.S. 163, 92 S.Ct. 1965, 32 L.Ed.2d 627 (1972), which held that the Commonwealth of Pennsylvania, although not responsible for racial discrimination voluntarily practiced by a private club, could not by law require the club to comply with its own discriminatory rules. These cases clearly rejected the notion that our prior cases permitted the imposition of Fourteenth Amendment restraints on private action by the simple device of characterizing the State's inaction as "authorization" or "encouragement." See id., at 190, 92 S.Ct. at 1979 (Brennan, J., dissenting).

It is quite immaterial that the State has embodied its decision not to act in statutory form. If New York had no commercial statutes at all, its courts would still be faced with the decision whether to prohibit or to permit the sort of sale threatened here the first time an aggrieved bailor came before them for relief. A judicial decision to deny relief would be no less an "authorization" or "encouragement" of that sale than the legislature's decision embodied in this statute. It was recognized in the earliest interpretations of the Fourteenth Amendment "that a State may act through different agencies—either by its legislative, its executive, or its judicial authorities; and the prohibitions of the amendment extend to all action of the State" infringing rights protected thereby. Virginia v. Rives, 100 U.S. 313, 318, 25 L.Ed. 667 (1880). If the mere denial of judicial relief is considered sufficient encouragement to make the State responsible for those private acts, all private deprivations of property would be converted into public acts whenever the State, for whatever reason, denies relief sought by the putative property owner. Not only is this notion completely contrary to that "essential dichotomy," Jackson, supra, 419 U.S. at 349, 95 S.Ct. at 452, between public and private acts, but it has been previously rejected by this Court. In Evans v. Abney, 396 U.S. 435, 458, 90 S.Ct. 628, 640, 24 L.Ed.2d 634 (1970), our Brother Brennan in dissent contended that a Georgia statutory provision authorizing the establishment of trusts for racially restricted parks conferred a "special power" on testators taking advantage of the provision. The Court nevertheless concluded that the State of Georgia was in no way responsible for the purely private choice involved in that case. By the same token, the State of New York is in no way responsible for Flagg Brothers' decision, a decision which the State in § 7–210 permits but does not compel, to threaten to sell these respondents' belongings.

Here, the State of New York has not compelled the sale of a bailor's goods, but has merely announced the circumstances under which its courts will not interfere with a private sale. Indeed, the crux of respondents' complaint is not that the State has acted, but that it has refused to act. This statutory refusal to act is no different in principle from an ordinary statute of limitations whereby the State declines to provide a remedy for private deprivations of property after the passage of a given period of time.

We conclude that the allegations of these complaints do not establish a violation of these respondents' Fourteenth Amendment rights by either petitioner Flagg Brothers or the State of New York. The District Court properly concluded that their complaints failed to state a claim for relief under 42 U.S.C. § 1983. The judgment of the Court of Appeals holding otherwise is

Reversed.

MR. JUSTICE BRENNAN took no part in the consideration or decision of these cases.

MR. JUSTICE MARSHALL, dissenting.

* * * I cannot remain silent as the Court demonstrates, not for the first time, an attitude of callous indifference to the realities of life for the poor. See, e.g., Beal v. Doe, 432 U.S. 438, 454–457, 97 S.Ct. 2366, 2394, 2395–2396, 53 L.Ed.2d 464 (1977) (Marshall, J., dissenting); United States v. Kras, 409 U.S. 434, 458–460, 93 S.Ct. 631, 644–645, 34 L.Ed.2d 626 (1973) (Marshall, J., dissenting). While the Court is technically correct that respondent "could have sought" replevin [which required posting of a large bond at the commencement of the action], it is also true that, given adequate funds, respondent could have paid her rent and remained in her apartment, thereby avoiding eviction and the seizure of her household goods by the warehouseman. * * *

I am also troubled by the Court's cavalier treatment of the place of historical factors in the "state action" inquiry. While we are, of course, not bound by what occurred centuries ago in England, the test adopted by the Court itself requires us to decide what functions have been "traditionally exclusively reserved to the State," Jackson v. Metropolitan Edison Co. Such an issue plainly cannot be resolved in a historical vacuum. New York's highest court has stated that "[i]n [New York] the execution of a lien ... traditionally has been the function of the Sheriff." Blye v. Globe–Wernicke Realty Co., 33 N.Y.2d 15, 20, 347 N.Y.S.2d 170, 175, 300 N.E.2d 710, 713–714 (1973). Numerous other courts, in New York and elsewhere, have reached a similar conclusion. By ignoring this history, the Court approaches the question before us as if it can be decided without reference to the role that the State has always played in lien execution by forced sale. In so doing, the Court treats the State as if it were, to use the Court's words, "a monolithic, abstract concept hovering in the legal stratosphere." Ante, at n. 10. The state-action doctrine, as developed in our past cases, requires that we come down to earth and decide the issue here with careful attention to the State's traditional role.

I dissent.

MR. JUSTICE STEVENS, with whom MR. JUSTICE WHITE and MR. JUSTICE MARSHALL join, dissenting.

* * *

There is no question in this case but that respondents have a property interest in the possessions that the warehouseman proposes to sell. It is also clear that, whatever power of sale the warehouseman has, it does not derive from the consent of the respondents. The claimed power derives solely from the State, and specifically from § 7–210 of the New York Uniform Commercial Code. * * *

In determining that New York's statute cannot be scrutinized under the Due Process Clause, the Court reasons that the warehouseman's proposed sale is solely private action because the state statute "permits but does not compel" the sale, and because the warehouseman has not been delegated a power "exclusively reserved to the State." Under this approach a State could enact laws authorizing private citizens to use self-help in countless situations without any possibility of federal challenge. A state statute could authorize the warehouseman to retain all proceeds of the lien sale, even if they far exceeded the amount of the alleged debt; it could authorize finance companies to enter private homes to repossess merchandise; or indeed, it could authorize "any person with sufficient physical power," to acquire and sell the property of his weaker neighbor. An attempt to challenge the validity of any such outrageous statute would be defeated by the reasoning the Court uses today: The Court's rationale would characterize action pursuant to such a statute as purely private action, which the State permits but does not compel, in an area not exclusively reserved to the State.

As these examples suggest, the distinctions between "permission" and "compulsion" on the one hand, and "exclusive" and "nonexclusive," on the other, cannot be determinative factors in state-action analysis. There is no great chasm between "permission" and "compulsion" requiring particular state action to fall within one or the other definitional camp. * * * In this case, the State of New York, by enacting § 7–210 of the Uniform Commercial Code, has acted in the most effective and unambiguous way a State can act. This section specifically authorizes petitioner Flagg Brothers to sell respondents' possessions; it details the procedures that petitioner must follow; and it grants petitioner the power to convey good title to goods that are now owned by respondents to a third party. [My view is buttressed by the fact that this is a traditional state function.]

[Cases such as Fuentes v. Shevin, Sniadach v. Family Finance Corp. and North Georgia Finishing, Inc. v. Di–Chem, Inc., cited by the majority,] must be viewed as reflecting this Court's recognition of the significance of the State's role in defining and controlling the debtor-creditor relationship. * * * And it is clear that what was of concern in *Shevin* was the private use of state power to achieve a nonconsensual resolution of a commercial dispute. The state statutes placed the state power to repossess property in the hands of an interested private party, just as the state statute in this case places the state power to conduct judicially binding sales in satisfaction of a lien in the hands of the warehouseman. * * *

* * * Yet the very defect that made the statutes in *Shevin* and *North Georgia Finishing* unconstitutional—lack of state control—is, under today's decision, the factor that precludes constitutional review of the state statute. The Due Process Clause cannot command such incongruous results. If it is unconstitutional for a State to allow a private party to exercise a traditional state power because the state supervision of that power is purely mechanical, the State surely cannot immunize its actions from constitutional scrutiny by removing even the mechanical supervision.

* * *

It is important to emphasize that, contrary to the Court's apparent fears, this conclusion does not even remotely suggest that "all private deprivations of property [will] be converted into public acts whenever the State, for whatever reason, denies relief sought by the putative property owner." The focus is not on the private deprivation but on the state authorization. "[W]hat is always vital to remember is that it is the *state's* conduct, whether action or inaction, not the *private* conduct, that gives rise to constitutional attack." Friendly, The Dartmouth College Case and The Public–Private Penumbra, 12 Texas Quarterly, No. 2, p. 17 (1969) (Supp.) (emphasis in original). The State's conduct in this case takes the concrete form of a statutory enactment, and it is that statute that may be challenged. [Thus, while private parties' deviations from the state-prescribed procedure are not actionable, challenges to the statute are challenges to state action.]

* * *

NOTE ON STATE INACTION AND THE PUBLIC FUNCTION DOCTRINE

1. *Flagg Brothers* seems at one level merely to clarify the limits of the previously discussed "compulsion cases," see the preceding Note, supra, and to raise a narrow new issue—the circumstances under which concededly private persons, not involved with the state, may be treated as though they are the state because they are serving a traditional state function. As you read this Note, however, notice how these discrete issues merge with a more all-encompassing social and philosophical problem: Which topics in American society are considered private and which governmental?

2. With respect to the "compulsion cases," Justice Rehnquist's majority opinion states that they must be limited to those situations where the private party truly acts as the agent of the state in carrying out the state's goals. Mere authority, "acquiescence," or permission from the state does not convert private action into state action—or, as Justice Rehnquist puts it, state inaction does not make subsequent private acts state action.

(a) A walks his dog on the lawn of B, where the dog converts B's property to his own natural uses. State caselaw deems this otherwise-trespassory conduct de minimis and provides no cause of action. Is A a state actor? Is the state non-law that permits private use of another's property a taking without just compensation? Similarly, C strikes D in the nose after D insulted C; state caselaw provides no compensation for D because it recognizes an insult as an affirmative defense to battery. Similarly, E kills F in self-defense after F tried to kill E. If state law recognizes the usual pleas of defense, has state law taken D's nose or F's life? Is *Flagg Brothers* distinguishable from these cases? (Does it matter whether state law is statutory or case law?)

(b) Is it the "no-liability" aspect of New York's law that makes the warehouse owner's conduct private rather than state conduct? If a state prescribes a rule of liability, its rule is state action, see, e.g., New York Times Co. v. Sullivan, 376 U.S. 254, 84 S.Ct. 710, 11 L.Ed.2d 686 (1964), but if it prescribes a rule of no-liability, is all resulting conduct private? Is all resulting conduct state-sanctioned conduct? If you wipe your hands of your neighbor's infidelity to a spouse, are you complicit in the infidelity? If you wipe your hands of your neighbors' abuse of their child, are you complicit in the abuse?

3. Essential to the state action concept is its opposite—that private conduct lies outside the proscriptions of the Fourteenth Amendment. Yet, there may be occasions when private persons, though not incorporated as a local government or as a state entity, so monopolize power that they will be deemed to be the state because they have taken over a "public function." The so-called "white primary" cases and the so-called "company town" case, cited by Justice Rehnquist, are the original cases in which this idea was developed. What is the proper scope of this idea?

(a) Do you agree with Justice Rehnquist that only traditionally "exclusive" governmental functions are covered by the public-function doctrine? In a portion of his dissenting opinion in **San Francisco Arts & Athletics, Inc. v. USOC**, supra, Justice Brennan argued that foreign policy was a traditional governmental function which had been promoted by the creation of the USOC. 483 U.S. at 550, 107 S.Ct. at 2988. Would home-building be such a function? Assistance to hungry people? If liberal government assumes a wider range of governmental programs, do they thereby become traditional governmental functions, so that all who take government money to assist in the effort become state actors? Note that labeling an action "state action" brings it under potential judicial control through constitutional law. Must the "state function" exception be confined narrowly to traditional state functions precisely so that liberal *legislatures* will be allowed leeway in creating new social policies?

(b) Were the white primary cases and the company town case properly decided? Should there be any public-function doctrine at all? Did not white voters have an associational right to exclude black voters from their membership? Did not the landowner have a First Amendment right to refuse to receive information? Is the very existence of the public-function doctrine a threat to privacy rights? Or is it just a practical admission that the line between public and private, as Justice Stevens argues, is not crystal clear—thus implicitly authorizing the Court to look broadly at even non-exclusive exercises of a public function?

(c) Is the public-function doctrine inherently incapable of application because, like the "traditional governmental functions" test once used in commerce clause cases, National League of Cities v. Usery, 426 U.S. 833, 96 S.Ct. 2465, 49 L.Ed.2d 245 (1976), overruled, Garcia v. San Antonio Metropolitan Transit Auth., 469 U.S. 528, 105 S.Ct. 1005, 83 L.Ed.2d 1016 (1985), it provides no judicially manageable standard? Or have Justices Rehnquist and Stevens, in their separate ways, given the concepts a discernible meaning?

4. Although the opinions in *Flagg Brothers* are constructed around the two precise topics discussed earlier in this Note, they seem to wrestle with a greater philosophical issue—in a modern complex society, what is the core dividing line between private and governmental action? Notice how Justice Rehnquist's opinion, especially, seems to rehearse themes he will later use in DeShaney v. Winnebago County Dep't of Social Services, Chapter 1B.4 supra: affirmative (action) versus negative (inaction) and, more importantly, the concept of a "state of nature" in which events occur in the absence of government.

(a) It is sometimes said of European code-based legal systems, especially socialist ones, that "everything that is not permitted by law is prohibited"—in stark contrast to the American social conception that "everything that is not prohibited is permitted." Is the concept labeled "American" an accurate description of how Americans feel about their society? If so, does the social conception prove that the action at issue in *Flagg Brothers* was private? Has Justice Rehnquist prevailed because his view is American and the dissent's is socialist?

(b) The major intellectual competitor to Justice Rehnquist's notion is one that posits that all or virtually all arrangements in modern society are the result of government ordering of our lives through what government regulates, taxes, approves—especially what it permits the powerful to do. See generally Brest, *State Action and Liberal Theory: A Case Note on* Flagg Brothers v. Brooks, 130 U. PA. L. REV. 1296 (1982); Goodman, *Professor Brest on State Action and Liberal Theory, and a Postscript to Professor Stone,* 130 U. PA. L. REV. 1331 (1982); Sunstein, *Public Values, Private Interests, and the Equal Protection Clause,* 1982 SUP. CT. REV. 127.

(c) How does Justice Stevens seek to avoid the thrust of Justice Rehnquist's vision of society? Does he argue that all action is governmental action? Or does he try to develop a view that is as traditionally American as Justice Rehnquist's? And how would you classify Justice Marshall's position?

5. Has *Flagg Brothers* brought this debate to a close? Note the manner in which its themes dominated the later decision in San Francisco Arts & Athletics, Inc. v. United States Olympic Committee and in American Manufacturers Mutual Insurance Company v. Sullivan, both excerpted earlier in this sub-chapter. In both cases the government appears to have arranged the law so as to permit one set of private persons to have greater power than another. Are those cases as much about state inaction as they are about "joint participation"?

(a) Does *San Francisco Arts & Athletics* fit as neatly into Justice Rehnquist's "state of nature" as *Flagg Brothers* did? Was the former case an "action" case rather than an "inaction" case?

(b) Note Justice Brennan's reliance on the affirmative-negative distinction in the dissent in *San Francisco Arts & Athletics.* The USOC is a government actor because "Congress *affirmatively* granted it power that it would not otherwise have to control the use of the word 'Olympic' " (emphasis in original). Is this the same affirmative-negative concept on which Justice Rehnquist previously relied? Or is it Justice Stevens' idea from *Flagg Brothers,* albeit stated in different words? Is even Justice Brennan resorting to the "state of nature" argument without acknowledging it?

(c) Are the "compulsion" test and the "government inaction" theory two sides of the same coin? Is "compulsion" simply the opposite of "inaction," so that the two lines of cases are inquiring about the same issue? Is state neutrality, discussed in the following case, also the same issue?

EVANS v. ABNEY

Supreme Court of the United States, 1970.
396 U.S. 435, 90 S.Ct. 628, 24 L.Ed.2d 634.

MR. JUSTICE BLACK delivered the opinion of the Court.

Once again this Court must consider the constitutional implications of the 1911 will of United States Senator A. O. Bacon of Georgia which conveyed property in trust to Senator Bacon's home city of Macon for the creation of a public park for the exclusive use of the white people of that city. As a result of our earlier decision in this case which held that the park, Baconsfield, could not continue to be operated on a racially discriminatory basis, Evans v. Newton, 382 U.S. 296, 86 S.Ct. 486, 15 L.Ed.2d 373 (1966), the Supreme Court of Georgia ruled that Senator Bacon's intention to provide a park for whites only had become impossible to fulfill and that accordingly the trust had failed and the parkland and other trust property had reverted by operation of Georgia law to the heirs of the Senator. Petitioners, the same Negro citizens of Macon who have sought in the courts to integrate the park, contend that this termination of the trust violates their rights to equal protection and due process under the Fourteenth Amendment. * * * For the reasons to be stated, we are of the opinion that the judgment of the Supreme Court of Georgia should be, and it is, affirmed.

The early background of this litigation was summarized by Mr. Justice Douglas in his opinion for the Court in Evans v. Newton:

"In 1911 United States Senator Augustus O. Bacon executed a will that devised to the Mayor and Council of the City of Macon, Georgia, a tract of land which, after the death of the Senator's wife and daughters, was to be used as 'a park and pleasure ground' for white people only, the Senator stating in the will that while he had only the kindest feeling for the Negroes he was of the opinion that 'in their social relations the two races (white and negro) should be forever separate.' The will provided that the park should be under the control of a Board of Managers of seven persons, all of whom were to be white. The city kept the park segregated for some years but in time let Negroes use it, taking the position that the park was a public facility which it could not constitutionally manage and maintain on a segregated basis.

"Thereupon, individual members of the Board of Managers of the park brought this suit in a state court against the City of Macon and the trustees of certain residuary beneficiaries of Senator Bacon's estate, asking that the city be removed as trustee and that the court appoint new trustees, to whom title to the park would be transferred. The city answered, alleging it could not legally enforce racial segregation in the park. The other defendants admitted the allegation and requested that the city be removed as trustee.

"Several Negro citizens of Macon intervened, alleging that the racial limitation was contrary to the laws and public policy of the United States, and asking that the court refuse to appoint private trustees. [After the city resigned as trustee and Bacon's heirs intervened to seek reversion of the property, the trial court appointed three new trustees who were expected, as the Georgia Supreme Court noted in approving their appointment, to continue the segregationist desires of Senator Bacon.]"

The Court in Evans v. Newton, supra, went on to reverse the judgment of the Georgia Supreme Court and to hold that the public character of Baconsfield "requires that it be treated as a public institution subject to the command of the Fourteenth Amendment, regardless of who now has title under state law." [In subsequent proceedings the heirs succeeded in persuading the Georgia courts that the purpose of the trust had failed, as judged by ordinary rules of the law of trusts, and that the land should therefore revert to them.]

We are of the opinion that in ruling as they did the Georgia courts did no more than apply well-settled general principles of Georgia law to determine the meaning and effect of a Georgia will. At the time Senator Bacon made his will Georgia cities and towns were, and they still are, authorized to accept devises of property for the establishment and preservation of "parks and pleasure grounds" and to hold the property thus received in charitable trust for the exclusive benefit of the class of persons named by the testator. Ga.Code Ann., c. 69–5 (1967); Ga.Code Ann. §§ 108–203, 108–207 (1959). These provisions of the Georgia Code explicitly authorized the testator to include, if he should choose, racial restrictions such as those found in Senator Bacon's will. The city accepted the trust with these restrictions in it. When this Court in Evans v. Newton, supra, held that the continued operation of Baconsfield as a segregated park was unconstitutional, the particular purpose of the Baconsfield trust as stated in the will failed under Georgia law. The question then properly before the Georgia Supreme Court was whether as a matter of state law the doctrine of cy pres should be applied to prevent the trust itself from failing. Petitioners urged that the cy pres doctrine allowed the Georgia courts to strike the racially restrictive clauses in Bacon's will so that the terms of the trust could be fulfilled without violating the Constitution.

* * * The Georgia courts have held that the fundamental purpose of these cy pres provisions is to allow the court to carry out the general charitable intent of the testator where this intent might otherwise be thwarted by the impossibility of the particular plan or scheme provided by the testator. Moss v. Youngblood, 187 Ga. 188, 200 S.E. 689 (1938). But this underlying logic of the cy pres doctrine implies that there is a certain class of cases in which the doctrine cannot be applied. Professor Scott in his treatise on trusts states this limitation on the doctrine of cy pres which is common to many States as follows:

> "It is not true that a charitable trust never fails where it is impossible to carry out the particular purpose of the testator. In some cases ... it appears that the accomplishment of the particular purpose and only that purpose was desired by the testator and that he had no more general charitable intent and that he would presumably have preferred to have the whole trust fail if the particular purpose is impossible of accomplishment. In such a case the cy pres doctrine is not applicable." 4 A. Scott, The Law of Trusts § 399, p. 3085 (3d ed. 1967).

In this case, Senator Bacon provided an unusual amount of information in his will from which the Georgia courts could determine the limits of his charitable purpose. Immediately after specifying that the park should be for "the sole, perpetual and unending, use, benefit and enjoyment of the white women, white girls, white boys and white children of the City of Macon," the Senator stated that "the said property under no circumstances ... (is) to be ... at any time for any reason devoted to any other purpose or use excepting so far as herein specifically authorized." And the Senator continued:

> "I take occasion to say that in limiting the use and enjoyment of this property perpetually to white people, I am not influenced by any unkindness of feeling or want of consideration for the Negroes, or colored people. On the contrary I have for them the kindest feeling, and for many of them esteem and regard, while for some of them I have sincere personal affection.

> "I am, however, without hesitation in the opinion that in their social relations the two races ... should be forever separate and that they should not have pleasure or recreation grounds to be used or enjoyed, together and in common."

The Georgia courts, construing Senator Bacon's will as a whole, Yerbey v. Chandler, 194 Ga. 263, 21 S.E.2d 636 (1942), concluded from this and other language in the will that the Senator's charitable intent was not "general" but extended only to the establishment of a segregated park for the benefit of white people. The Georgia trial court found that "Senator Bacon could not have used language more clearly indicating his intent that the benefits of Baconsfield should be extended to white persons only, or more clearly indicating that this limitation was an essential and indispensable part of his plan for Baconsfield." Since racial separation was found to be an inseparable part of the testator's intent, the Georgia courts held that the State's cy pres doctrine could not be used to alter the will to permit racial integration. See Ford v. Thomas, 111 Ga. 493, 36 S.E. 841 (1900); Adams v. Bass, 18 Ga. 130 (1855). The Baconsfield trust was therefore held to have failed, and, under Georgia law, "(w)here a trust is expressly created, but (its) uses ... fail from any cause, a resulting trust is implied for the benefit of the grantor, or testator, or his heirs." Ga. Code Ann. § 108–106(4) (1959). The Georgia courts concluded, in effect, that Senator Bacon would have rather had the whole trust fail than have Baconsfield integrated.

When a city park is destroyed because the Constitution requires it to be integrated, there is reason for everyone to be disheartened. [Here, however,] any harshness that may have resulted from the state court's decision can be attributed solely to its intention to effectuate as nearly as possible the explicit terms of Senator Bacon's will.

[T]he Georgia Supreme Court, as we read its opinion, interpreted Senator Bacon's will as embodying a preference for termination of the park rather than its integration. Given this, the Georgia court had no alternative under its relevant trust laws, which are long standing and neutral with regard to race, but to end the Baconsfield trust and return the property to the Senator's heirs.

[P]etitioners stress the similarities between this case and the case in which a city holds an absolute fee simple title to a public park and then closes that park of its own accord solely to avoid the effect of a prior court order directing that the park be integrated as the Fourteenth Amendment commands. Yet, assuming arguendo that the closing of the park would in those circumstances violate the Equal Protection Clause, that case would be clearly distinguishable from the case at bar because there it is the State and not a private party which is injecting the racially discriminatory motivation. In the case at bar there is not the slightest indication that any of the Georgia judges involved were motivated by racial animus or discriminatory intent of any sort in construing and enforcing Senator Bacon's will. Nor is there any indication that Senator Bacon in drawing up his will was persuaded or induced to include racial restrictions by the fact that such restrictions were permitted by the Georgia trust statutes. * * * On the contrary, the language of the Senator's will shows that the racial restrictions were solely the product of the testator's own full-blown social philosophy. Similarly, the situation presented in this case is also easily distinguishable from that presented in Shelley v. Kraemer, 334 U.S. 1, 68 S.Ct. 836, 92 L.Ed. 1161 (1948), where we held unconstitutional state judicial action which had affirmatively enforced a private scheme of discrimination against Negroes. Here the effect of the Georgia decision eliminated all discrimination against Negroes in the park by eliminating the park itself, and the termination of the park was a loss shared equally by the white and Negro citizens of Macon since both races would have enjoyed a constitutional right of equal access to the park's facilities had it continued.

* * * What remains of petitioners' argument is the idea that the Georgia courts had a constitutional obligation in this case to resolve any doubt about the testator's intent in favor of preserving the trust. Thus stated, we see no merit in the argument. The only choice the Georgia courts either had or exercised in this regard was their judicial judgment in construing Bacon's will to determine his intent, and the Constitution imposes no requirement upon the Georgia courts to approach Bacon's will any differently than they would approach any will creating any charitable trust of any kind. Surely the Fourteenth Amendment is not violated where, as here, a state court operating in its judicial capacity fairly applies its normal principles of construction to determine the testator's true intent in establishing a charitable trust and then reaches a conclusion with regard to that intent which, because of the operation of neutral and nondiscriminatory state trust laws, effectively denies everyone, whites as well as Negroes, the benefits of the trust.

* * *

Petitioners also advance a number of considerations of public policy in opposition to the conclusion which we have reached. In particular, they regret, as we do, the loss of the Baconsfield trust to the City of Macon, and they are concerned lest we set a precedent under which other charitable trusts will be terminated. It bears repeating that our holding today reaffirms the traditional role of the States in determining whether or not to apply their cy pres doctrines to particular trusts. Nothing we have said here prevents a state court from applying its cy pres rule in a case where the Georgia court, for example, might not apply its rule. More fundamentally, however, the loss of charitable trusts such as Baconsfield is part of the price we pay for permitting deceased persons to exercise a continuing control over assets owned by them at death. This aspect of freedom of testation, like most things, has it advantages and disadvantages. The responsibility of this Court, however, is to construe and enforce the Constitution and laws of the land as they are and not to legislate social policy on the basis of our own personal inclinations.

* * *

The judgment is Affirmed.

MR. JUSTICE MARSHALL took no part in the consideration or decision of this case.

MR. JUSTICE DOUGLAS, dissenting.

* * *

The purpose of the will was to dedicate the land for some municipal use. That is still possible. Whatever that use, Negroes will of course be admitted, for such is the constitutional command. But whites will also be admitted. Letting both races share the facility is closer to a realization of

Bacon's desire than a complete destruction of the will and the abandonment of Bacon's desire that the property be used for some municipal purpose.

* * *

The Georgia decision, which we today approve, can only be a gesture toward a state-sanctioned segregated way of life, now passe. It therefore should fail as the imposition of a penalty for obedience to a principle of national supremacy.

MR. JUSTICE BRENNAN, dissenting.

* * *

I have no doubt that a public park may constitutionally be closed down because it is too expensive to run or has become superfluous, or for some other reason, strong or weak, or for no reason at all. But under the Equal Protection Clause a State may not close down a public facility solely to avoid its duty to desegregate that facility. In Griffin v. County School Board, 377 U.S. 218, 231, 84 S.Ct. 1226, 1233, 12 L.Ed.2d 256 (1964), we said, "Whatever nonracial grounds might support a State's allowing a county to abandon public schools, the object must be a constitutional one, and grounds of race and opposition to desegregation do not qualify as constitutional." In this context what is true of public schools is true of public parks. When it is as starkly clear as it is in this case that a public facility would remain open but for the constitutional command that it be operated on a non-segregated basis, the closing of that facility conveys an unambiguous message of community involvement in racial discrimination. Its closing for the sole and unmistakable purpose of avoiding desegregation, like its operation as a segregated park, "generates (in Negroes) a feeling of inferiority as to their status in the community that may affect their hearts and minds in a way unlikely ever to be undone." Brown v. Board of Education, 347 U.S. 483, 494, 74 S.Ct. 686, 691, 98 L.Ed. 873 (1954). * * *

The Court, however, affirms the judgment of the Georgia Supreme Court on the ground that the closing of Baconsfield did not involve state action. * * * I need emphasize only three elements of the state action present here.

* * * Shelley v. Kraemer, 334 U.S. 1, 68 S.Ct. 836, 92 L.Ed. 1161 (1948), stands at least for the proposition that where parties of different races are willing to deal with one another a state court cannot keep them from doing so by enforcing a privately devised racial restriction. Nothing in the record suggests that after our decision in Evans v. Newton, supra, the City of Macon retracted its previous willingness to manage Baconsfield on a nonsegregated basis, or that the white beneficiaries of Senator Bacon's generosity were unwilling to share it with Negroes, rather than have the park revert to his heirs. * * * Thus, so far as the record shows, this is a case of a state court's enforcement of a racial restriction to prevent willing parties from dealing with one another. The decision of the

Georgia courts thus, under Shelley v. Kraemer, constitutes state action denying equal protection.

* * *

NOTE ON STATE NEUTRALITY AS STATE ACTION

1. The "state neutrality" cases present an analytical—or perhaps only semantic—dilemma. They typically involve, as in *Abney,* state-court judges who have invoked state rules of general applicability. Of course, the orders of state-court judges constitute state action as much as the orders of state executive officials, Virginia v. Rives, 100 U.S. (10 Otto) 313, 318, 25 L.Ed. 667 (1879) (state judges are state actors), but the judges themselves have not acted for an unconstitutional reason. At most, they are aware of the resulting adverse impact of their decisions, but they have not acted (as the records show) for the purpose of obtaining such unconstitutional results. Cf. Personnel Administrator of Massachusetts v. Feeney, 442 U.S. 256, 99 S.Ct. 2282, 60 L.Ed.2d 870 (1979). On the other hand, in this class of cases it is shown that private parties have ends or motives that would be constitutionally forbidden were they state actors. The real question is whether the state actors and private parties are so related that the private person's ends or motives may be attributable to the state official.

(a) Are these cases simply misclassified when courts speak of them as state action cases? Should they rather be treated simply as cases of potential covert discrimination where the pertinent issue is to discern whether such intent is actually present? Compare Crawford v. Board of Educ., 458 U.S. 527, 102 S.Ct. 3211, 73 L.Ed.2d 948 (1982) (state amendment requiring judicial inaction in face of non-intentional school segregation—the rule of the Fourteenth Amendment—is not intentional classification by race), with Washington v. Seattle School Dist. No. 1, 458 U.S. 457, 102 S.Ct. 3187, 73 L.Ed.2d 896 (1982) (state amendment designed to eliminate busing to achieve school integration is intentional racial discrimination because it structures the government system to harm blacks).

(b) Are state "inaction" cases, see the preceding Note, simply a variation on the state "neutrality" cases? In **Reitman v. Mulkey**, 387 U.S. 369, 87 S.Ct. 1627, 18 L.Ed.2d 830 (1967), California voters adopted a state constitutional amendment that required state neutrality in housing discrimination by repealing the state's fair housing laws. The California Supreme Court held that the amendment, in historical context, had the immediate objective of promoting racial discrimination. The U.S. Supreme Court affirmed, saying that the proper approach in such cases was to look for the "purpose, scope, and operative effect" of the legislation.

(c) Are both the state "inaction" and "neutrality" cases merely variations on the original "compulsion and encouragement" cases, see the Note on Private Persons as State Actors, in this sub-Chapter, supra, because the Court looks in all cases to determine the impetus for the private persons' acts? Does the Court hold that only if the state has encouraged the private actor to resort to state court for discriminatory reasons will the private action be intertwined with state action?

2. Perhaps the biggest non-event of the 1960's was the Supreme Court's failure to declare court action against sit-in demonstrators—both in the civil and legal contexts—to be discriminatory and unconstitutional. In cases such as **Peterson v. City of Greenville**, 373 U.S. 244, 83 S.Ct. 1119, 10 L.Ed.2d 323 (1963), **Lombard v. Louisiana**, 373 U.S. 267, 83 S.Ct. 1122, 10 L.Ed.2d 338 (1963), and **Bell v. Maryland**, 378 U.S. 226, 84 S.Ct. 1814, 12 L.Ed.2d 822 (1964), the Court never adopted the broad-based proposition that a private discriminator's resort to a state court legal process yielded a package of state-private discriminatory state action.

(a) **Shelley v. Kraemer**, cited by Justice Brennan and sometimes understood to equate private resort to courts with state action, apparently no longer stands for that broad proposition after *Abney*. The case involved a covenantor's suit to enforce the racially restrictive covenant on the sale of housing. *Shelley* was one of several in which the Court pushed the envelope of state-action doctrine after a government had transferred its functions to a private entity. In Buchanan v. Warley, 245 U.S. 60, 38 S.Ct. 16, 18, 62 L.Ed. 149 (1917), the Court had forbidden city-adopted racially restrictive covenants, and *Shelley* may be seen as an attempt to evade the Court's earlier ruling. In a similar vein, the Court carried on a running battle with Texas's desire to prevent blacks from voting, and even though Texas twice delegated power over elections to the Democratic Party or subparts of it, the Court continued to enforce its orders against the private groups on the ground that they were acting on behalf of an evasive and recalcitrant state government. See Nixon v. Condon, 286 U.S. 73, 52 S.Ct. 484, 76 L.Ed. 984 (1932); Terry v. Adams, 345 U.S. 461, 73 S.Ct. 809, 97 L.Ed. 1152 (1953). Does *Shelley* stand not for the proposition that any resort to state courts is state action, but for the narrower proposition that a state may not evade its constitutional duty by intentionally seeking to enable private litigants to come to its courts to achieve the same purpose? Does Evans v. Abney run afoul of even the narrower interpretation of *Shelley*?

(b) When a government is subject to a previously entered injunction requiring desegregation, the Court has held that it no longer suffices constitutionally for the entity to be neutral; rather it is then under an affirmative duty to see that private parties do not seek its aid to promote segregation. See Gilmore v. City of Montgomery, 417 U.S. 556, 94 S.Ct. 2416, 41 L.Ed.2d 304 (1974) (city under court-ordered decree requiring desegregation must ensure that its facilities are not used by private school groups to enhance their position as alternative educational providers). In Evans v. Abney Justice Black alludes to the idea that would later be adopted in *Gilmore* and tries to distinguish it. Is he successful? Why is the *Gilmore* principle inapplicable—because there had been no injunction issued after the decision in Evans v. Newton, the original appeal of the case? Should that make a difference? Cf. Dayton Board of Educ. v. Brinkman, 439 U.S. 1066, 99 S.Ct. 831, 59 L.Ed.2d 31 (1979) (suggesting duty to eliminate continuing segregative effects of constitutional violation once violation becomes known).

(c) Is *Abney* the case that affirmatively rejects the argument that "any" resort to courts creates state action?

3.   Is there an affirmative social good that flows from leaving courts free to enforce neutral state laws without having them ask the plaintiff's purpose for seeking judicial relief? Does it prevent resort to self-help remedies? Does it encourage respect for legal solutions to solve the many other non-constitutional problems of life?

(a) Assume that a homeowner sues her neighbor for making loud noises that ruin her enjoyment of her home, in violation of state nuisance laws or residential zoning laws. The neighbor raises as a defense that the plaintiff does not like members of his racial group or gender group and argues that the plaintiff should be forbidden to exploit the state courts to achieve her discriminatory goals. Should the courts be open only to those pure of heart?

(b) If there existed a separate federal statute that outlawed private discrimination in wills and trusts, would you be less receptive to the claim of state action in *Abney*? Is a desire to eradicate all racial discrimination driving Justices Douglas' and Brennan's views? How would their ideas apply in a due process rather than an equal protection case? See ¶ 6 infra.

4.   In **Palmore v. Sidoti**, 466 U.S. 429, 104 S.Ct. 1879, 80 L.Ed.2d 421 (1984), a father (white) who had lost custody of his child upon divorce later sought an order awarding him the child on the ground that the mother (white), who now lived with a black man, was no longer fit. The trial court, although expressly declining to find the mother unfit, ruled for the father:

> "The father's evident resentment of the mother's choice of a black partner is not sufficient to wrest custody from the mother. It is of some significance, however, that the mother did see fit to bring a man into her home and carry on a sexual relationship with him without being married to him. Such action tended to place gratification of her own desires ahead of her concern for the child's future welfare. This Court feels that despite the strides that have been made in bettering relations between the races in this country, it is inevitable that [this child] will, if allowed to remain in her present situation and attains school age and thus more vulnerable to peer pressures, suffer from the social stigmatization that is sure to come."

The U.S. Supreme Court unanimously reversed in a short opinion by Chief Justice Burger. He observed that the trial "court was entirely candid and made no effort to place its holding on any ground other than race. Taking the court's findings and rationale at face value, it is clear that the outcome would have been different had petitioner married a Caucasian male of similar respectability." Thus, the state court had made a race-based decision that could only be justified by a compelling state interest. Had the Florida court simply made a neutral, non-race-specific ruling based on the best interests of the child, would the outcome have been different?

(a) The *Palmore* Court resolved the state-action issue with a single sentence in Footnote 1: "The actions of state courts and judicial officers in their official capacity have long been held to be state action governed by the Fourteenth Amendment. Shelley v. Kraemer; Ex parte Virginia, 100 U.S. (10 Otto) 339, 346–347, 25 L.Ed. 676 (1880)." Can *Palmore* be distinguished from *Abney*? Did the Florida court go beyond neutrality by merely considering society's views about race?

(b) Assume that the trial court in *Palmore* had before it actual evidence that the child's black or white playmates were taunting her because of her mother's interracial relationship. Would that change the outcome of the case? Note the Court's observation in *Palmore:*

> "Private biases may be outside the reach of the law, but the law cannot, directly or indirectly, give them effect. Public officials sworn to uphold the Constitution may not avoid a constitutional duty by bowing to the hypothetical effects of private racial prejudice that they assume to be both widely and deeply held."

Is "hypothetical" a key qualifying idea or stray dictum? Would not a change of custody based on actual harm give effect to private discrimination? Now assume that the mother's new husband taunted the child because of her race; should that provoke a change in custody? Can a court *never* recognize the harmful effects of private discrimination in order to protect a child?

5. In Equal Protection cases involving private parties' resort to state court, there is often the suspicion that the state judges desire the same end as the plaintiff—that they share the same unconstitutionally discriminatory intent. Are Due Process cases different? In general, the Court has held that state-action analysis should be the same for both classes of cases under the Fourteenth Amendment, see Jackson v. Metropolitan Edison Co., 419 U.S. 345, 95 S.Ct. 449, 42 L.Ed.2d 477 (1974), but should that be true in the context of state-neutrality cases?

(a) For Procedural Due Process, a substantial line of cases holds that ordinarily private litigants may not constitutionally invoke state-court processes of automatic prejudgment attachment. See Sniadach v. Family Finance Corp., 395 U.S. 337, 89 S.Ct. 1820, 23 L.Ed.2d 349 (1969) (failure of state law to require notice and a hearing before attachment violates procedural due process). But these cases are usually understood to be examples of situations where the state itself has unconstitutionally structured its trial processes, and the interesting question is whether the private state-court plaintiffs who invoke such statutes are acting "under color of law" for purposes of § 1983. See Lugar v. Edmondson Oil Co., 457 U.S. 922, 102 S.Ct. 2744, 73 L.Ed.2d 482 (1982). In effect, the state judges are not state actors because the private litigants have done something unconstitutional; rather the private litigants are state actors because the judges (and legislators) have done something unconstitutional. Should the private state-court plaintiffs be deemed co-liable state actors for unwittingly enforcing the state's unconstitutional mistake? See id. (yes).

(b) In the Substantive Due Process arena, results are more problematic because generally there is no requirement of an intent to harm in order to establish a violation. Rather a sufficiently restrictive effect alone may trigger strict constitutional inquiry. See, e.g., Planned Parenthood of Southeastern Pennsylvania v. Casey, 505 U.S. 833, 112 S.Ct. 2791, 120 L.Ed.2d 674 (1992) ("undue burden" on abortion right); Dunn v. Blumstein, 405 U.S. 330, 92 S.Ct. 995, 31 L.Ed.2d 274 (1972) ("penalty" on exercise of right). Typically, most judicial decrees that burden a right are deemed state action subject to Due Process analysis, even when the underlying case was initiated by a private party. See, e.g., New York Times Co. v. Sullivan, 376 U.S. 254, 84

S.Ct. 710, 11 L.Ed.2d 686 (1964) (sheriff's suit to enforce neutral libel law protecting all private citizens); cf. Schenck v. Pro–Choice Network Of Western New York, 519 U.S. 357, 117 S.Ct. 855, 137 L.Ed.2d 1 (1997) (clinic's suit under state law to bar intrusive anti-abortion demonstrators results in injunction grounded in state law that violated constitutional rights of defendants). Does the *Abney* principle apply only to Equal Protection cases (or at least only to constitutional provisions that have an equality component requiring proof of intent)?

6.   What should be the remedy in a case when state action is found in an Equal Protection case? Should the federal court order a breaking of the bond between the state and the private actor, or should the state-private partnership be ordered to obey the Fourteenth Amendment? In Evans v. Newton, the prior appeal in the *Abney* case, the Court had issued no order requiring future operation of the park in a racially non-discriminatory manner. It only remanded for further proceedings in the Georgia courts, resulting in the disposition at issue in Evans v. Abney. Should a desegregation order have been entered?

(a) In **Moose Lodge No. 107 v. Irvis**, 407 U.S. 163, 92 S.Ct. 1965, 32 L.Ed.2d 627 (1972), the Court found state action in one small aspect of the relationship between a racially discriminatory private club and the state liquor licensing agency: that was in the state's requirement that the club follow its by-laws, which in turn required exclusion of blacks. As relief the Court ordered that the state be directed not to enforce its rule. Should the Court instead have ordered desegregation of the club?

(b) In Smith v. Young Men's Christian Ass'n, 462 F.2d 634 (5th Cir. 1972), the court found city-private cooperation in segregated operation of recreational facilities in the city. It approved a detailed district court order requiring desegregation. Is this the better approach?

(c) Should the relief depend upon which party was the impetus for the unconstitutional joint action? If the private party initiates the partnership, breaking the partnership is appropriate; if the state initiates the partnership, then a court decree against the partnership is correct? Should the remedy depend upon how much harm the partners caused while engaged in their association, with an injunction appropriate until effects of the union are remedied?

D.   OFFICIAL IMMUNITY FROM LIABILITY FOR DAMAGES

1.   METHODOLOGY: A ROLE FOR STATE COMMON LAW?

PIERSON v. RAY

Supreme Court of the United States, 1967.
386 U.S. 547, 87 S.Ct. 1213, 18 L.Ed.2d 288.

MR. CHIEF JUSTICE WARREN delivered the opinion of the Court.

These cases present issues involving the liability of local police officers and judges under § 1983. Petitioners * * * were members of a group of 15 white and Negro Episcopal clergymen who attempted to use segregated facilities at an interstate bus terminal in Jackson, Mississippi, in 1961. [Acting as "Freedom Riders," the clergymen traveled through southern cities seeking peacefully to use public facilities segregated by local law, thereby establishing their right to equal access without regard to race.] They were arrested by respondents Ray, Griffith, and Nichols, policemen of the City of Jackson, and charged with violating § 2087.5 of the Mississippi Code, which makes guilty of a misdemeanor anyone who congregates with others in a public place under circumstances such that a breach of the peace may be occasioned thereby, and refuses to move on when ordered to do so by a police officer. Petitioners waived a jury trial and were convicted of the offense by respondent Spencer, a municipal police justice[, despite the police officers' concession that the clergymen had been peaceful when an angry crowd assembled around them]. They were each given the maximum sentence of four months in jail and a fine of $200. On appeal petitioner Jones was accorded a trial de novo in the County Court, and after the city produced its evidence the court granted his motion for a directed verdict. The cases against the other petitioners were then dropped. [All then filed § 1983 suits against the arresting officers and the police justice. They suffered adverse jury verdicts, but won partial new trials on appeal. They sought further review to achieve wider rights on retrial.]

* * *

We find no difficulty in agreeing with the Court of Appeals that Judge Spencer is immune from liability for damages for his role in these convictions. The record is barren of any proof or specific allegation that Judge Spencer played any role in these arrests and convictions other than to adjudge petitioners guilty when their cases came before his court. Few doctrines were more solidly established at common law than the immunity of judges from liability for damages for acts committed within their judicial jurisdiction, as this Court recognized when it adopted the doctrine, in Bradley v. Fisher, 13 Wall. 335, 20 L.Ed. 646 (1872). This immunity applies even when the judge is accused of acting maliciously and corruptly, and it "is not for the protection or benefit of a malicious or corrupt judge, but for the benefit of the public, whose interest it is that the judges should be at liberty to exercise their functions with independence and without fear of consequences." (Scott v. Stansfield, L.R. 3 Ex. 220, 223 (1868), quoted in Bradley v. Fisher, supra, 349, note, at 350.) It is a judge's duty to decide all cases within his jurisdiction that are brought before him, including controversial cases that arouse the most intense feelings in the litigants. His errors may be corrected on appeal, but he should not have to fear that unsatisfied litigants may hound him with litigation charging malice or corruption. Imposing such a burden on judges would contribute not to principled and fearless decisionmaking but to intimidation.

We do not believe that this settled principle of law was abolished by § 1983, which makes liable "every person" who under color of law deprives another person of his civil rights. The legislative record gives no clear indication that Congress meant to abolish wholesale all common-law immunities. Accordingly, this Court held in Tenney v. Brandhove, 341 U.S. 367, 71 S.Ct. 783, 95 L.Ed. 1019 (1951), that the immunity of legislators for acts within the legislative role was not abolished. The immunity of judges for acts within the judicial role is equally well established, and we presume that Congress would have specifically so provided had it wished to abolish the doctrine.

The common law has never granted police officers an absolute and unqualified immunity, and the officers in this case do not claim that they are entitled to one. Their claim is rather that they should not be liable if they acted in good faith and with probable cause in making an arrest under a statute that they believed to be valid. Under the prevailing view in this country a peace officer who arrests someone with probable cause is not liable for false arrest simply because the innocence of the suspect is later proved. Restatement, Second, Torts § 121 (1965); 1 Harper & James, The Law of Torts § 3.18, at 277–278 (1956); State of Missouri ex rel. and to Use of, Ward v. Fidelity & Deposit Co. of Maryland, 179 F.2d 327 (C.A.8th 1950). A policeman's lot is not so unhappy that he must choose between being charged with dereliction of duty if he does not arrest when he has probable cause, and being mulcted in damages if he does. Although the matter is not entirely free from doubt, the same consideration would seem to require excusing him from liability for acting under a statute that he reasonably believed to be valid but that was later held unconstitutional on its face or as applied.

The Court of Appeals held that the officers had such a limited privilege under the common law of Mississippi, and indicated that it would have recognized a similar privilege under § 1983 except that it felt compelled to hold otherwise by our decision in Monroe v. Pape. [But that case presented no claim of immunity, and even spoke approvingly of the "tort background" against which § 1983 should be read.] Part of the background of tort liability, in the case of police officers making an arrest, is the defense of good faith and probable cause.

We hold that the defense of good faith and probable cause, which the Court of Appeals found available to the officers in the common-law action for false arrest and imprisonment, is also available to them in the action under § 1983. This holding does not, however, mean that the count based thereon should be dismissed. The Court of Appeals ordered dismissal * * * on the theory that the police officers were not required to predict our decision in Thomas v. Mississippi, 380 U.S. 524, 85 S.Ct. 1327, 14 L.Ed.2d 265 (1965)[, which guaranteed free access to facilities of interstate travel]. We agree that a police officer is not charged with predicting the future course of constitutional law. But the petitioners in this case did not simply argue that they were arrested under a statute later held unconstitutional. They claimed and attempted to prove that the police officers arrested them solely for attempting to use the "White Only" waiting room, that no crowd was present, and that no one threatened violence or seemed about to cause a disturbance. The officers did not defend on the theory that [segregation laws are constitutional but instead on the ground that they were faithfully enforcing anti-violence laws. This creates an issue for the jury.] Accordingly, the case must be remanded to the trial court for a new trial.

It is necessary to decide what importance should be given at the new trial to the substantially undisputed fact that the petitioners went to Jackson expecting to be illegally arrested. We do not agree with the Court of Appeals that they somehow consented to the arrest because of their anticipation that they would be illegally arrested, even assuming that they went to the Jackson bus terminal for the sole purpose of testing their rights to unsegregated public accommodations. The case contains no proof or allegation that they in any way tricked or goaded the officers into arresting them. The petitioners had the right to use the waiting room of the Jackson bus terminal, and their deliberate exercise of that right in a peaceful, orderly, and inoffensive manner does not disqualify them from seeking damages under § 1983.

The judgment of the Court of Appeals is affirmed in part and reversed in part, and the cases are remanded for further proceedings consistent with this opinion.

It is so ordered.

MR. JUSTICE DOUGLAS, dissenting.

I do not think that all judges, under all circumstances, no matter how outrageous their conduct are immune from suit under § 1983. * * *

The position that Congress did not intend to change the common-law rule of judicial immunity ignores the fact that every member of Congress who spoke to the issue assumed that the words of the statute meant what they said and that judges would be liable. Many members of Congress objected to the statute because it imposed liability on members of the judiciary. [Quotations from the legislative history omitted.]

Yet despite the repeated fears of its opponents, and the explicit recognition that the section would subject judges to suit, the section remained as it was proposed: it applied to "any person." There was no exception for members of the judiciary. In light of the sharply contested nature of the issue of judicial immunity it would be reasonable to assume that the judiciary would have been expressly exempted from the wide sweep of the section, if Congress had intended such a result.

* * *

This is not to say that a judge who makes an honest mistake should be subjected to civil liability. It is necessary to exempt judges from liability for the consequences of their honest mistakes.[4] The judicial function

---

4. Other justifications for the doctrine of absolute immunity have been advanced: (1) preventing threat of suit from influencing decision; (2) protecting judges from liability for honest mistakes; (3) relieving judges of the time and expense of defending suits; (4) removing an impediment to responsible men entering the judiciary; (5) necessity of finality; (6) appellate

involves an informed exercise of judgment. It is often necessary to choose between differing versions of fact, to reconcile opposing interests, and to decide closely contested issues. Decisions must often be made in the heat of trial. A vigorous and independent mind is needed to perform such delicate tasks. It would be unfair to require a judge to exercise his independent judgment and then to punish him for having exercised it in a manner which, in retrospect, was erroneous. Imposing liability for mistaken, though honest judicial acts, would curb the independent mind and spirit needed to perform judicial functions. Thus, a judge who sustains a conviction on what he forthrightly considers adequate evidence should not be subjected to liability when an appellate court decides that the evidence was not adequate. Nor should a judge who allows a conviction under what is later held an unconstitutional statute.

But that is far different from saying that a judge shall be immune from the consequences of any of his judicial actions, and that he shall not be liable for the knowing and intentional deprivation of a person's civil rights. What about the judge who conspires with local law enforcement officers to "railroad" a dissenter? What about the judge who knowingly turns a trial into a "kangaroo" court? Or one who intentionally flouts the Constitution in order to obtain a conviction? Congress, I think, concluded that the evils of allowing intentional, knowing deprivations of civil rights to go unredressed far outweighed the speculative inhibiting effects which might attend an inquiry into a judicial deprivation of civil rights.

* * *

NOTE ON SOURCES OF AND LIMITS ON OFFICIAL IMMUNITIES

1. The Court's thesis in *Pierson* is rather straight-forward: because Congress showed no affirmative desire in § 1983 to overturn long-standing immunities available at common law, § 1983's silence should be read as adopting and preserving those immunities. In **Imbler v. Pachtman**, 424 U.S. 409, 96 S.Ct. 984, 47 L.Ed.2d 128 (1976), the Court refined its approach in an opinion by Justice White. The immunities available "are not products of judicial fiat that officials in different branches of government" merit different defenses, said the Court. Rather each immunity recognized by the Court is "predicated upon a considered inquiry into the immunity historically accorded the relevant official at common law and the interests behind it." The Court proceeded to give a prosecutor sued for withholding evidence at trial an absolute immunity because (i) such officers received absolute immunity from malicious prosecution actions at common law, citing cases from 1896 to 1935, and (ii) the "public policy that underlie[s] the common law rule likewise countenance[s] absolute immunity under § 1983."

(a) Consider *Imbler*'s two-part methodology. If the relevant theory is that the 1871 Congress that adopted § 1983 approved common law immunities,

---

review is satisfactory remedy; (7) the judge's duty is to the public and not to the individual; (8) judicial self-protection; (9) separation of powers. See generally Jennings, *Tort Liability of Administrative Officers*, 21 MINN. L. REV. 263, 271–72 (1937). [Repositioned footnote.]

should the relevant period of inquiry be the common law of 1871 or the evolving common law? In other words, did the 1871 Congress intend to adopt the process of the common law or the set of results used by the common law in 1871? See Mitchell v. Forsyth, 472 U.S. 511, 105 S.Ct. 2806, 86 L.Ed.2d 411 (1985) ("we have generally looked for a *historical or* common law basis" to justify an immunity) (emphasis added); Smith v Wade, 461 U.S. 30, 34 n. 2, 103 S.Ct. 1625, 75 L.Ed.2d 632 (1983) (reprinted in Chapter 1F.1 infra).

(b) After some flirtation with the idea that the Court itself determined who should receive official immunities, see Forrester v. White, which follows this Note ("we examine the nature of the functions" and "we seek to evaluate the effect" of liability on the official's actions), later cases have staunchly followed the *Pierson–Imbler* line and have specifically pledged themselves to reflect the common law of 1871, albeit with recognition that the policies of the common law must be consistent with the purposes of § 1983. See, e.g., Bogan v. Scott–Harris, 523 U.S. 44, 118 S.Ct. 966, 140 L.Ed.2d 79 (1998) ("Because the common law accorded local legislators [absolute immunity] and because the rationales for such immunity are fully applicable" to local legislators, immunity recognized); Buckley v. Fitzsimmons, 509 U.S. 259, 113 S.Ct. 2606, 125 L.Ed.2d 209 (1993): "Although we have found immunities in § 1983 that do not appear on the face of the statute, [w]e do not have a license to establish immunities * * * in the interests of what we judge to be sound public policy. [O]ur role is to interpret the intent of Congress in enacting § 1983, not to make a freewheeling policy choice" (internal citations and quotation marks omitted). Do cases like *Bogan* and *Buckley* necessarily end speculation that references to "common law" may mean "evolutionary process of common law"?

(c) Some cases state the second *Imbler* factor more forcefully and independently. For example, in **Wyatt v. Cole**, 504 U.S. 158, 112 S.Ct. 1827, 118 L.Ed.2d 504 (1992), the Court noted its practice of referring to 1871 common law, then added this line: "Additionally, irrespective of the common law support, we will not recognize an immunity available at common law if § 1983's history or purpose counsel against applying it in § 1983 actions." Only one case has in fact exercised this independent judgment, see Owen v. City of Independence, Chapter 1H.1.b infra, and then only in the context of a municipal entity, not a real person. Is the second factor defensible? No, because it gives modern federal judges exactly the power they claim to abjure? Yes, because it can only be used to limit an implied immunity, not to expand one?[5]

2. The reality of § 1983 litigation is that every governmental official can invoke either an "absolute immunity" (quite favorable to the defendant, but not as absolute as the name implies) or a "qualified immunity" (a less complete, but still helpful, defense). The *Imbler* approach is primarily used only to determine whether a defendant receives the greater of the two immunities: if common law accorded an immunity in 1871, the defendant receives absolute immunity under § 1983.

---

5. Is this last statement an accurate reading of *Imbler*? See Richardson v. McKnight, ¶ 4(b) infra.

(a) If you were able to determine the issue without reference to pre-existing common law, would you give absolute immunity to judges? Are you persuaded that police officers should receive the lesser immunity? Recall County of Sacramento v. Lewis, Chapter 1B.4 supra, and its emphasis on the need for police officers to make prompt judgments. Is it not paradoxical that judges, with the benefit of law books and time to reflect on their decisions, receive greater immunity than police who must act quickly? Or have courts already taken account of police officers' predicament by making laxer liability rules for them, as in *Sacramento*?

(b) Is there a class bias, or perhaps a "lawyer class" bias, in the awarding of absolute immunity to judges? Although *Imbler* holds that absolute immunity is not limited to judges, most of those receiving the immunity are closely linked to the judicial process—judges (*Pierson*), prosecutors (*Imbler*), and indeed any officer when acting as a witness in court (Briscoe v. LaHue, 460 U.S. 325, 103 S.Ct. 1108, 75 L.Ed.2d 96 (1983)). If there is such a bias, then why do legislators receive absolute immunity? See Tenney v. Brandhove, 340 U.S. 903, 71 S.Ct. 279, 95 L.Ed. 653 (1950).

(c) As you will soon read, absolute immunity applies to fewer than all acts by a judge or prosecutor. When deciding which acts warrant absolute immunity, the Court often discusses the policy bases for immunity. See, e.g., Van de Kamp v. Goldstein, 555 U.S. 335, 129 S.Ct. 855, 172 L.Ed.2d 706 (2009) (citing twin reasons for absolute immunity for judges—i) better " 'to leave unredressed the wrongs done by dishonest officers than to subject those who try to do their duty to the constant dread of retaliation' " and ii) sheer volume of cases brought by disgruntled criminal defendants against judges and prosecutors). Are the Justices in fact making policy judgments, only claiming to follow common-law precedents regarding immunity? Even if the Court is only deciding the scope of absolute immunity, not which officers receive it, isn't the power to define scope the power to grant or withhold the immunity itself?

3. How should the Court discover immunities in those cases where the defendant holds an office or performs a governmental task that did not exist in 1871? Should the Court analogize the modern official's tasks to ones undertaken in 1871 and award the relevant immunity? Yes and no, the Court appears to have said in **Cleavinger v. Saxner**, 474 U.S. 193, 106 S.Ct. 496, 88 L.Ed.2d 507 (1985), a case involving prison disciplinary committee members who argued that they should receive the same absolute immunity accorded judges. Describing its approach as "functional," the Court refused to look simplistically at whether the defendants worked as judges; instead it looked at the entire context of the defendants' activities to determine whether the system bore the hallmarks of a judicial decisionmaking process. Some later cases, such as **Antoine v. Byers & Anderson, Inc.**, 508 U.S. 429, 113 S.Ct. 2167, 124 L.Ed.2d 391 (1993), offer less overt balancing of factors and instead merely ask whether the modern officer performs functions analogous to those of a judge in 1871. In *Antoine* the Court rejected the analogy between a modern court reporter transcribing the trial verbatim and the older practice of judicial note-taking during a trial.

(a) *Cleavinger* focused on six factors: "(i) the need to assure that the individual [defendant] can perform his functions without harassment or intimidation; (ii) the presence of safeguards that reduce the need for private damages actions as a means of controlling unconstitutional conduct; (iii) insulation from political influence; (iv) the importance of precedent; (v) the adversary nature of the process; and (vi) the correctability of error on appeal." Is the Court asking whether the defendant is functionally a judge? Or simply whether there is, in the Court's subjective opinion, a need for absolute immunity? See Malley v. Briggs, 475 U.S. 335, 106 S.Ct. 1092, 89 L.Ed.2d 271 (1986): "We intend no disrespect to the officer [who asked to be analogized to a judge when sued for seeking a defective warrant] by observing that his action, while a vital part of the administration of criminal justice, is further removed from the judicial phase * * * than the act of a prosecutor seeking an indictment." Is *Antoine*'s simpler reference to analogous functions more obedient to the concept that the Court should be reflecting 1871 common law, not making new law?

(b) Based on the *Cleavinger* and *Antoine* approaches, which immunity should be accorded to a child welfare caseworker, especially one engaged in judicial proceedings to protect children? See Pittman v. Cuyahoga County Dept. of Children and Family Services, 640 F.3d 716 (6th Cir. 2011) (no). C.A.6 (Ohio),2011. Parole or probation officers? See Swift v. California, 384 F.3d 1184 (9th Cir. 2004). Members of state boards regulating professional conduct? See Guzman–Rivera v. Lucena–Zabala, 642 F.3d 92 (1st Cir. 2011) (accounting board, yes). Since so many offices extant in government today did not exist in 1871, do both *Cleavinger*'s "functional" approach and *Antoine*'s "analogy" approach effectively give courts the power to choose which immunity should be accorded to most officials?

(c) In *Cleavinger* the official's offices and duties did not exist in 1871. A variation on that problem may arise even when the defendant's office existed in 1871 but the common law recognized no equivalent claim against the officeholder. Should the common law's failure to recognize a claim be treated functionally as the equivalent of failure to recognize an immunity? Or should the Court stick literally to the 1871 law and find no immunity? In *Imbler* for example, there was no claim recognized for suppression of evidence and no immunity recognized because there was no possibility of a claim. In Buckley v. Fitzsimmons, supra, the Court described *Imbler* as a case in which it had looked not only at the holdings of the common law, but also at its "policies" in order to determine if they were also applicable to modern § 1983 claims not recognized at common law. Does this give the Court effective power to determine whether or not an immunity should be recognized? See also Kalina v. Fletcher, Chapter 1D.3 infra (Scalia, J., concurring).

4. Recall that private persons may be sued under § 1983 if their conduct amounts to state action. See Chapter 1C.3 supra. Should such private persons also be eligible to receive an official immunity? In **Dennis v. Sparks**, 449 U.S. 24, 101 S.Ct. 183, 66 L.Ed.2d 185 (1980), plaintiff alleged that private persons conspired with a judge to enter a corrupt state court injunction that deprived them of their property. Although the judge was entitled to an absolute immunity, the Supreme Court declined to extend a derivative immunity to the private joint conspirators, holding that no such immunity could be

found for co-conspirators at common law and that no derivative immunity was necessary to protect the judge himself.

(a) Should *Dennis* be treated as a general rule applicable to all private parties who find themselves as defendants under § 1983? **Wyatt v. Cole**, 504 U.S. 158, 112 S.Ct. 1827, 118 L.Ed.2d 504 (1992), concerned a claim against a private person who had invoked an unconstitutional state attachment process. The private person was deemed a state actor under Lugar v. Edmondson Oil Co., Chapter 1C.4 supra, but claimed an immunity derived from common law. In a detailed opinion, the Court first determined the most analogous common law tort ("malicious prosecution and abuse of process"). It then noted that only judges, not complaining witnesses, were entitled to absolute immunity for these torts at common law and, moreover, that "the rationales mandating [an official] immunity for public officials are not applicable to private parties." Does *Wyatt* rule out an immunity for all private persons suable under § 1983?

(b) The Court rejected the apparently categorical approach of *Dennis* and *Wyatt* in **Richardson v. McKnight**, 521 U.S. 399, 117 S.Ct. 2100, 138 L.Ed.2d 540 (1997) (5–4 vote), involving a § 1983 claim against guards at a private company that operated a prison under state contract. It rejected both the argument that no private actor is ever entitled to immunity and the argument that any private person performing a governmental function should receive the same immunity as his governmental equivalent. It held that the correct methodology is to look to the common law of 1871 to determine if such private persons had qualified immunity at common law under similar circumstances, then determine whether the common law result is consistent with the purposes of § 1983. It found no historical practice to support an immunity for privately retained jailors and no current need for immunity. Does the *Richardson* approach show more fidelity to the original *Pierson* rationale for official immunity? Or does it sow seeds of uncertainty?

5. Although called "official immunity," that name for the concept developed in *Pierson* can be quite misleading in two respects. First, it protects not the governmental entity or office which employs the defendant but rather the defendant's own wallet: it protects the defendant from personal liability. See Hafer v. Melo, 502 U.S. 21, 112 S.Ct. 358, 116 L.Ed.2d 301 (1991) (official immunity is not for all officers, but only those meriting it after the prescribed official immunity analysis). Second, official immunity protects an officer only from liability for damages and erects no bar against injunctive or declaratory relief—or the award of attorneys fees that would accompany such relief. See Pulliam v. Allen, 466 U.S. 522, 104 S.Ct. 1970, 80 L.Ed.2d 565 (1984) (5–4 vote). The *Pulliam* dissenters argued for an extension to bar all relief, but only for defendants who could claim absolute immunity.

(a) In one important caveat to *Pulliam,* the Supreme Court has held that persons acting in a state legislative capacity are insulated from both damages liability and injunctive liability. See Supreme Court of Virginia v. Consumers Union of the United States, Inc., 446 U.S. 719, 731–34, 100 S.Ct. 1967, 1974–76, 64 L.Ed.2d 641 (1980). Why should legislators receive an all-encompassing immunity? Is this immunity meaningless for plaintiffs seeking relief in light of *Pierson*, which refuses to extend such blanket immunity to administrative personnel who enforce the statutes legislators enact?

(b) Several doctrines applicable in § 1983 litigation severely limit the injunctive relief that might theoretically be available against state judges and prosecutors. See Chapter 1G infra. Do those doctrines yield a practical result not far from the position desired by the *Pulliam* dissenters?

(c) Should courts extend official immunity so that it protects not only against damages awards but also against injunctions? Would such a step stop the federal courts' constitutional enforcement in its tracks? Are injunctions necessary simply to ensure that the Constitution is obeyed? See Nowicki v. Cooper, 56 F.3d 782 (7th Cir.1995) (paralegal unconstitutionally excluded from court gets no damages from judge but is entitled to injunctive relief barring continuation of his acts). Is direct review of the judge's acts in state court sufficient to protect § 1983 plaintiffs?

2. ABSOLUTE IMMUNITY: JUDICIAL, PROSECU-TORIAL, AND LEGISLATIVE FUNCTIONS

FORRESTER v. WHITE

Supreme Court of the United States, 1988.
484 U.S. 219, 108 S.Ct. 538, 98 L.Ed.2d 555.

JUSTICE O'CONNOR delivered the opinion of the Court.

This case requires us to decide whether a state-court judge has absolute immunity from a suit for damages under 42 U.S.C. § 1983 for his decision to dismiss a subordinate court employee. The employee, who had been a probation officer, alleged that she was demoted and discharged on account of her sex, in violation of the Equal Protection Clause of the Fourteenth Amendment. We conclude that the judge's decisions were not judicial acts for which he should be held absolutely immune.

I

Respondent Howard Lee White served as Circuit Judge of the Seventh Judicial Circuit of the State of Illinois and Presiding Judge of the Circuit Court in Jersey County. Under Illinois law, Judge White had the authority to hire adult [and juvenile] probation officers, who were removable in his discretion * * * In April 1977, Judge White hired petitioner Cynthia A. Forrester as an adult and juvenile probation officer. Forrester prepared presentence reports for Judge White in adult offender cases, and recommendations for disposition and placement in juvenile cases. She also supervised persons on probation and recommended revocation when necessary. In July 1979, Judge White appointed Forrester as Project Supervisor of the Jersey County Juvenile Court Intake and Referral Services Project, a position that carried increased supervisory responsibilities. Judge White demoted Forrester to a nonsupervisory position in the summer of 1980. He discharged her on October 1, 1980. Forrester filed this lawsuit in the United States District Court for the Southern District of Illinois in July 1982. She alleged violations of * * * 42 U.S.C. § 1983. A jury found that Judge White had discriminated against Forrester on account of her sex, in violation of the Equal Protection Clause of the

Fourteenth Amendment. The jury awarded her $81,818.80 in compensatory damages under § 1983. * * *

[The trial court set aside the judgment on the ground that the defendant was entitled to absolute immunity in his capacity as a state-court judge. The Court of Appeals affirmed by a divided vote.]

II

Suits for monetary damages are meant to compensate the victims of wrongful actions and to discourage conduct that may result in liability. Special problems arise, however, when government officials are exposed to liability for damages. To the extent that the threat of liability encourages these officials to carry out their duties in a lawful and appropriate manner, and to pay their victims when they do not, it accomplishes exactly what it should. By its nature, however, the threat of liability can create perverse incentives that operate to inhibit officials in the proper performance of their duties. In many contexts, government officials are expected to make decisions that are impartial or imaginative, and that above all are informed by considerations other than the personal interests of the decisionmaker. Because government officials are engaged by definition in governing, their decisions will often have adverse effects on other persons. When officials are threatened with personal liability for acts taken pursuant to their official duties, they may well be induced to act with an excess of caution or otherwise to skew their decisions in ways that result in less than full fidelity to the objective and independent criteria that ought to guide their conduct. In this way, exposing government officials to the same legal hazards faced by other citizens may detract from the rule of law instead of contributing to it.

Such considerations have led to the creation of various forms of immunity from suit for certain government officials. Aware of the salutary effects that the threat of liability can have, however, as well as the undeniable tension between official immunities and the ideal of the rule of law, this Court has been cautious in recognizing claims that government officials should be free of the obligation to answer for their acts in court. Running through our cases, with fair consistency, is a "functional" approach to [this issue that sometimes grants absolute immunity and sometimes qualified immunity.]

III

As a class, judges have long enjoyed a comparatively sweeping form of immunity, though one not perfectly well-defined. Judicial immunity apparently originated, in medieval times, as a device for discouraging collateral attacks and thereby helping to establish appellate procedures as the standard system for correcting judicial error. See Block, Stump v. Sparkman and the History of Judicial Immunity, 1980 Duke L.J. 879. More recently, this Court found that judicial immunity was "the settled doctrine of the English courts for many centuries, and has never been denied, that we are aware of, in the courts of this country." Bradley v. Fisher, 13 Wall.

335, 347, 20 L.Ed. 646 (1872). Besides protecting the finality of judgments or discouraging inappropriate collateral attacks, the *Bradley* Court concluded, judicial immunity also protected judicial independence by insulating judges from vexatious actions prosecuted by disgruntled litigants.

In the years since *Bradley* was decided, this Court has not been quick to find that federal legislation was meant to diminish the traditional common law protections extended to the judicial process. See, e.g., Pierson v. Ray. On the contrary, these protections have been held to extend to executive branch officials who perform quasi-judicial functions, see Butz v. Economou [438 U.S. 478, 98 S.Ct. 2894, 57 L.Ed.2d 895 (1978) (administrative law judge in executive department)], or who perform prosecutorial functions that are "intimately associated with the judicial phase of the criminal process," Imbler v. Pachtman, 424 U.S. 409, 430, 96 S.Ct. 984, 47 L.Ed.2d 128 (1976). The common law's rationale for these decisions— freeing the judicial process of harassment or intimidation—has been thought to require absolute immunity even for advocates and witnesses. See Briscoe v. La Hue, 460 U.S. 325, 103 S.Ct. 1108, 75 L.Ed.2d 96 (1983).

* * *

The purposes served by judicial immunity from liability in damages have been variously described. In Bradley v. Fisher, supra, and again in Pierson v. Ray, the Court emphasized that the nature of the adjudicative function requires a judge frequently to disappoint some of the most intense and ungovernable desires that people can have. As Judge Posner pointed out in his dissenting opinion below, this is the principal characteristic that adjudication has in common with legislation and with criminal prosecution, which are the two other areas in which absolute immunity has most generously been provided. 792 F.2d, at 660. If judges were personally liable for erroneous decisions, the resulting avalanche of suits, most of them frivolous but vexatious, would provide powerful incentives for judges to avoid rendering decisions likely to provoke such suits. The resulting timidity would be hard to detect or control, and it would manifestly detract from independent and impartial adjudication. Nor are suits against judges the only available means through which litigants can protect themselves from the consequences of judicial error. Most judicial mistakes or wrongs are open to correction through ordinary mechanisms of review, which are largely free of the harmful side-effects inevitably associated with exposing judges to personal liability.

When applied to the paradigmatic judicial acts involved in resolving disputes between parties who have invoked the jurisdiction of a court, the doctrine of absolute judicial immunity has not been particularly controversial. Difficulties have arisen primarily in attempting to draw the line between truly judicial acts, for which immunity is appropriate, and acts that simply happen to have been done by judges. Here, as in other contexts, immunity is justified and defined by the functions it protects and serves, not by the person to whom it attaches.

This Court has never undertaken to articulate a precise and general definition of the class of acts entitled to immunity. The decided cases, however, suggest an intelligible distinction between judicial acts and the administrative, legislative, or executive functions that judges may on occasion be assigned by law to perform. Thus, for example, the informal and ex parte nature of a proceeding has not been thought to imply that an act otherwise within a judge's lawful jurisdiction was deprived of its judicial character. See Stump v. Sparkman, 435 U.S. 349, 363, n. 12, 98 S.Ct. 1099, 1108, n. 12, 55 L.Ed.2d 331 (1978). Similarly, acting to disbar an attorney as a sanction for contempt of court, by invoking a power "possessed by all courts which have authority to admit attorneys to practice," does not become less judicial by virtue of an allegation of malice or corruption of motive. Bradley v. Fisher, supra. * * *

Administrative decisions, even though they may be essential to the very functioning of the courts, have not similarly been regarded as judicial acts. In Ex Parte Virginia, 100 U.S. (10 Otto) 339, 25 L.Ed. 676 (1880), for example, this Court declined to extend immunity to a county judge who had been charged in a criminal indictment with discriminating on the basis of race in selecting trial jurors for the county's courts. The Court reasoned: "Whether the act done by him was judicial or not is to be determined by its character, and not by the character of the agent. Whether he was a county judge or not is of no importance. The duty of selecting jurors might as well have been committed to a private person as to one holding the office of a judge.... That the jurors are selected for a court makes no difference. So are court-criers, tipstaves, sheriffs, & c. Is their election or their appointment a judicial act?" Id., at 348.

Although this case involved a criminal charge against a judge, the reach of the Court's analysis was not in any obvious way confined by that circumstance. Likewise, judicial immunity has not been extended to judges acting to promulgate a code of conduct for attorneys. Supreme Court of Virginia v. Consumers Union of United States, Inc., 446 U.S. 719, 100 S.Ct. 1967, 64 L.Ed.2d 641 (1980). In explaining why legislative, rather than judicial, immunity furnished the appropriate standard, we said: "Although it is clear that under Virginia law the issuance of the Bar Code was a proper function of the Virginia Court, propounding the Code was not an act of adjudication but one of rulemaking." Similarly, in the same case, we held that judges acting to enforce the Bar Code would be treated like prosecutors, and thus would be amenable to suit for injunctive and declaratory relief. Cf. Pulliam v. Allen, 466 U.S. 522, 104 S.Ct. 1970, 80 L.Ed.2d 565 (1984). Once again, it was the nature of the function performed, not the identity of the actor who performed it, that informed our immunity analysis.

IV

In the case before us, we think it clear that Judge White was acting in an administrative capacity when he demoted and discharged Forrester. Those acts—like many others involved in supervising court employees and overseeing the efficient operation of a court—may have been quite important in providing the necessary conditions of a sound adjudicative system. The decisions at issue, however, were not themselves judicial or adjudicative. As Judge Posner pointed out below, a judge who hires or fires a probation officer cannot meaningfully be distinguished from a district attorney who hires and fires assistant district attorneys, or indeed from any other executive branch official who is responsible for making such employment decisions. Such decisions, like personnel decisions made by judges, are often crucial to the efficient operation of public institutions (some of which are at least as important as the courts), yet no one suggests that they give rise to absolute immunity from liability in damages under § 1983.

The majority below thought that the threat of vexatious lawsuits by disgruntled ex-employees could interfere with the quality of a judge's decisions:

> "The evil to be avoided is the following: A judge loses confidence in his probation officer, but hesitates to fire him because of the threat of litigation. He then retains the officer, in which case the parties appearing before the court are the victims, because the quality of the judge's decision-making will decline." 792 F.2d, at 658.

There is considerable force in this analysis, but it in no way serves to distinguish judges from other public officials who hire and fire subordinates. Indeed, to the extent that a judge is less free than most executive branch officials to delegate decisionmaking authority to subordinates, there may be somewhat less reason to cloak judges with absolute immunity from such suits than there would be to protect such other officials. This does not imply that qualified immunity, like that available to executive branch officials who make similar discretionary decisions, is unavailable to judges for their employment decisions. See, e.g., Scheuer v. Rhodes, 416 U.S. 232, 94 S.Ct. 1683, 40 L.Ed.2d 90 (1974). Absolute immunity, however, is "strong medicine, justified only when the danger of [officials' being] deflect[ed from the effective performance of their duties] is very great." 792 F.2d, at 660 (Posner, J., dissenting). The danger here is not great enough. Nor do we think it significant that, under Illinois law, only a judge can hire or fire probation officers. To conclude that, because a judge acts within the scope of his authority, such employment decisions are brought within the court's "jurisdiction," or converted into "judicial acts," would lift form above substance. Under Virginia law, only that State's judges could promulgate and enforce a Bar Code, but we nonetheless concluded that neither function was judicial in nature. See Supreme Court of Virginia v. Consumers Union, supra. We conclude that Judge White was not entitled to absolute immunity for his decisions to demote and discharge Forrester. In so holding, we do not decide whether Judge White is entitled to a new trial, or whether he may be able to claim a qualified immunity for the acts complained of in Forrester's suit. The judgment of the Court of Appeals is reversed and the case is remanded for further proceedings consistent with this opinion.

It is so ordered.

NOTE ON THE SCOPE OF ABSOLUTE IMMUNITY FOR JUDICIAL ACTS

1.   As the Court holds in *Forrester,* absolute immunity applies to particular functions—"judicial functions"—rather than to particular offices—"judge." But how does the Court know which functions are "judicial"? What methodology is appropriate?

(a) The Court rejects the idea that the law of the state in which the judge sits should be the guide as to what functions are judicial. Do you agree? Is this part of the Court's opinion dictated by the fundamental decision to take a "functional" approach to defining immunities? Or does it reflect a concern that states not be able to negate § 1983 by placing many ordinary administrative functions in the hands of judges?

(b) Should Justice O'Connor have looked to the common law of 1871 to guide her decision as to what acts are "judicial"? If, under *Pierson,* the common law is the touchstone for deciding which immunity is applicable, should it also be the touchstone for the scope of the duties that merit the immunity? Justice O'Connor suggests that the accretion of case law will draw the line between judicial and administrative functions. Would this necessarily be federal common law as defined by the Justices? What considerations are appropriate to making this federal law?

(c) Does Justice O'Connor play on your intuitive sense that employment decisions are "administrative" and not "judicial" decisions? In **Van de Kamp v. Goldstein**, 555 U.S. 335, 129 S.Ct. 855, 172 L.Ed.2d 706 (2009), a case involving similar prosecutorial absolute immunity, the plaintiff tried to play on *Forrester*'s dichotomy by suing not the prosecutor for his misconduct but the supervising prosecutor for misconduct in failing to train the errant prosecutor. Were the acts of mis-training "administrative"? The Court ruled that, though administrative, the conduct was close enough to the core of prosecutorial functions to require absolute immunity. Is *Forrester* now a weak precedent?

2.   The Supreme Court has twice faced decisions that appeared to be outrageous, but which were performed by a judge by court order. In **Stump v. Sparkman**, 435 U.S. 349, 98 S.Ct. 1099, 55 L.Ed.2d 331 (1978), a married adult sued after discovering that her mother had secretly procured her court-ordered sterilization when she was a minor. The mother had filed a petition with a state court judge, claiming that her daughter was a "somewhat retarded" minor, and the judge approved the petition, endorsing his name and stating his office on the petition—but the petition had not been filed with the court clerk and the judge had opened no formal case file, had appointed no guardian ad litem for the minor, and had held no hearing before authorizing the sterilization. In **Mireles v. Waco**, 502 U.S. 9, 112 S.Ct. 286, 116 L.Ed.2d 9 (1991), the plaintiff, an attorney, alleged that the defendant judge had intentionally ordered police to arrest and beat the plaintiff for failing to appear in court. The Court found absolute judicial immunity to bar a claim for damages in each case.

(a) In *Mireles*, the Court stated that the allegations must be judged against the generic background of the judge's action, not the particular excessiveness alleged. Said the Court:

> "Of course, a judge's direction to police officers to carry out a judicial order with excessive force is not a function normally performed by a judge. But if only the particular act in question were to be scrutinized, then any mistake of a judge in excess of his authority would become a 'nonjudicial' act, because an improper or erroneous act cannot be said to be normally performed by a judge. * * * In other words, we look to the particular act's relation to a general function normally performed by a judge, in this case the function of directing police officers to bring counsel in a pending case before the court[, which we find to be a traditional act of a judge]." 502 U.S. at 12–13, 112 S.Ct. at 288–89.

Do you agree? If the *Mireles* position is not adopted, could every plaintiff easily circumvent judicial immunity by simply alleging that the defendant judge maliciously harmed the plaintiff? Is *Mireles* dictated by *Pierson*'s holding that judges cannot be sued for even malicious acts?

(b) Justice Stewart dissented in *Stump* on the ground that absolute immunity attaches only to " 'judicial acts,' and I think what Judge Stump did * * * was beyond the pale of anything that could sensibly be called a judicial act." 435 U.S. at 365, 98 S.Ct. at 1109. Has *Forrester* adopted Justice Stewart's dissenting position, implicitly overruling *Stump*? Or is any order issued "in open court" or in a pending case a judicial function? See Antoine v. Byers & Anderson, Inc., 508 U.S. 429, 113 S.Ct. 2167, 124 L.Ed.2d 391 (1993) (the "touchstone" for absolute judicial immunity is the "performance of the function of resolving disputes between parties, or of authoritatively adjudicating private rights"; absolute immunity for court reporter rejected).

3.   How should the following cases be decided on an assertion of absolute judicial immunity?

(a) On facts remarkably similar to those in Whirl v. Kern, Chapter 1B.1 supra, a trial judge's revocation of probation is reversed on appeal but the judge fails to follow through and have a release order sent and enforced. The plaintiff sits in jail for months. Is the conduct administrative or judicial? See Dawson v. Newman, 419 F.3d 656 (7th Cir. 2005) (among other factors, court looks at particular issue and asks "whether the parties dealt with the judge as judge" regarding that issue).

(b) A juvenile court judge threatens an applicant for a job in his office that he will award custody of her daughter in a pending case to her parents unless she submits to his request for sexual favors. He rapes another employee "in his chambers" and threatens to rule against her in her child custody case. Is he entitled to judicial immunity, especially in light of *Mireles*? See Archie v. Lanier, 95 F.3d 438 (6th Cir.1996) ("The fact that, regrettably, Lanier happened to be a judge when he committed these reprehensible acts is not relevant to the question of whether he is entitled to immunity [because c]learly he is not"). Ex-husband goes to ex-wife's job in order to make overdue child support payments, but unfortunately for him she works for a judge at the courthouse. A fellow judge overhears ex-husband's request to meet ex-wife, sends for their closed divorce case file, swears in ex-husband in his chambers (while seated at a secretary's desk) and summarily holds ex-husband in contempt of court. Does the judge merit absolute immunity? See Harper v. Merckle, 638 F.2d 848 (5th Cir.1981). Are acts in the judge's private office never judicial acts? Does that make legal research a non-judicial act? Does it matter what he was doing in his office? Cf. Clinton v. Jones, infra (sexual dalliances were not official acts).

(c) Judge, angry that party continues to argue his case after judgment is entered, descends from bench and personally throws litigant from the court-room rather than ordering bailiff to do so. Does the judge merit absolute immunity? See Gregory v. Thompson, 500 F.2d 59 (9th Cir.1974). Is *Mireles* distinguishable because issuing an order is judicial but carrying it out is not? Or is *Gregory* simply a case where the judge's judicial functions ended with the expiration of the case? After litigation in her court a judge gives a press conference to explain her position. Are statements to the media part of the judicial function? See Barrett v. Harrington, 130 F.3d 246 (6th Cir.1997).

(d) A judge, learning that transsexual has given false information to take out a marriage license and later seek probate benefits in his court, has the person prosecuted by swearing out a warrant against him. Is the initiation of charges a judicial function? Judge, angry at passing motorist, puts a flashing light atop his automobile and stops motorist, later having him arrested; judge prosecutes him while court is closed. Compare Brookings v. Clunk, 389 F.3d 614 (6th Cir. 2004) (by 2–1 vote), with Malina v. Gonzales, 994 F.2d 1121 (5th Cir.1993). Can the results be distinguished? See also Barnes v. Winchell, 105 F.3d 1111 (6th Cir.1997) (misdemeanor court judge advised complainants how to prosecute cases) (collecting cases).

4. In **Mireles v. Waco**, supra, the Court added another factor not discussed in Forrester v. White. Even if an act is deemed "judicial," there may be limitations on a judge's ability to invoke absolute immunity because:

> "the immunity is overcome in only two sets of circumstances. First, a judge is not immune from liability for nonjudicial actions, i.e., actions not taken in the judge's judicial capacity. Forrester v. White. Second, a judge is not immune for actions, though judicial in nature, taken in the complete absence of all jurisdiction." 502 U.S. at 11–12, 112 S.Ct. at 288.

(a) Why is jurisdiction relevant to the analysis of whether an action is "judicial" in nature? Notice the anomaly: the judge in *Stump* would be performing judicial acts even though he wantonly fails to open a case file, appoint a guardian, or hold a hearing—but if he makes a mistake about the scope of his jurisdiction, he loses his immunity? Does this make the technical issue of jurisdiction more important than the merits?

(b) What would be an act in "the complete absence of all jurisdiction"? See *Stump*, supra (judge of court of general jurisdiction acted within his jurisdiction even if no law authorized the action he took on the merits); Ireland v. Tunis, 113 F.3d 1435 (6th Cir.1997) (issuance of arrest warrant is judicial act; since issuing judge sat on a court of general jurisdiction, and no law specifically forbade his act, he did not act in complete absence of jurisdiction). One court has described the demarcation line as this: "Where there is clearly no jurisdiction over the subject-matter any authority exercised is a usurped authority, [but] where jurisdiction over the subject-matter is invested by law in the judge, or in the court which he holds, the manner and extent in which the jurisdiction shall be exercised are generally as much questions for his determination as any other questions involved in the case." Tucker v. Outwater, 118 F.3d 930 (2d Cir. 1997). Is the jurisdictional exception applicable only to low-level judges in courts of limited jurisdiction? But see Duty v. City of Springdale, 42 F.3d 460 (8th Cir.1994) (even limited-jurisdiction municipal court judge is entitled to immunity when he acts in excess of his jurisdiction).

5. The inquiry into "judicial functions" appeared to narrow the availability of absolute judicial immunity in *White*, where a titular judge was denied immunity. Does the concept also expand the range of persons entitled to absolute judicial immunity? The Supreme Court held in **Butz v. Economou**, 438 U.S. 478, 515, 98 S.Ct. 2894, 2915, 57 L.Ed.2d 895 (1978), that even executive department officials, such as administrative law judges, may be entitled to absolute judicial immunity if they perform judicial functions, thus foreshadowing *White*'s focus on the judicial functions of an official rather than the title of judge in ruling on a claim of official immunity.

(a) *Butz* seems to fit comfortably with *White*'s notion that judicial immunity is not an act of obeisance to the judicial branch of government, but of respect for traditional judicial functions. What other officers in the executive branch perform judicial functions? Consider the great number of licensing boards, review boards, and professional-fitness boards that operate in the modern regulatory bureaucracy. Do all the members of these boards receive absolute immunity when they are resolving individual cases brought within their regulatory purview? Or are they merely one more set of law-enforcers like sheriffs and police officers? See Mishler v. Clift, 191 F.3d 998 (9th Cir.1999) (medical licensing and disciplinary board is covered for its quasi-judicial acts, but not for ministerial acts; detailed discussion of what makes an act functionally similar to a judicial act, concluding that destruction of evidence at hearing is included within quasi-judicial acts) (collecting cases); Crenshaw v. Baynerd, 180 F.3d 866 (7th Cir.1999) (state civil rights commission entitled to quasi-judicial absolute immunity in reviewing civil rights complaints filed before it).

(b) Judicial immunity may also be expanded by extending it to persons who execute the orders of judges, provided the order being enforced entitled the judge to absolute judicial immunity. See Martin v. Hendren, 127 F.3d 720 (8th Cir.1997) (officer enforcing judge's order to handcuff unruly courtroom visitor enjoys "absolute quasi-judicial immunity for actions 'specifically ordered by the trial judge and related to the judicial function' "); Bush v. Rauch, 38 F.3d 842 (6th Cir.1994) (administrative officer of court was not exercising judicial functions in making placements for juvenile offenders, but he was executing judge's lawful orders and therefore was "an arm of the judicial officer" and entitled to quasi-judicial immunity). Would the ordinary actions of police officers become protected quasi-judicial acts if they were directed by proper judicial order? See Mays v. Sudderth, 97 F.3d 107 (5th Cir.1996) (execution of bench warrant entitles sheriff to judge's absolute immunity as executor of court order). Does quasi-judicial immunity destroy the distinction between absolute immunity for judicial functions and qualified immunity for ordinary administrative functions?

(c) Finally, consider the possibly unique status of parole officials, from parole board members to parole officers who work with individual parolees. Given the broad range of decision that such persons make—all affecting the duration of a person's confinement, the traditional province of judicial sentencing—should the actions of all parole officials be treated as functionally judicial decisions? Of some that are merely administrative, how should the line be drawn? See Dawson v. Newman, 419 F.3d 656 (7th Cir. 2005) ("parole officials are entitled to absolute immunity 'for their activities that are analogous to those performed by judges,'" such as grant or revocation of parole, but not for "day-today duties" of supervising parolees); Swift v. California, 384 F.3d 1184 (9th Cir. 2004) (no immunity for low-level parole officials who recommend termination of parole).

6. In **Clinton v. Jones**, 520 U.S. 681, 117 S.Ct. 1636, 137 L.Ed.2d 945 (1997), the President faced a § 1983 action for untoward sexual overtures claimed to have occurred when he was a state actor, the governor of Arkansas. The Supreme Court refused to accord the defendant, now the sitting president who would normally receive absolute immunity for acts in office, immunity in the case. In a broadly, if ambiguously worded statement, the Court noted that all forms of official immunity are designed to protect officers in the performance of their official duties, and that "[t]his reasoning provides no support for an immunity for *unofficial* conduct" for "we have never suggested that [an immunity claimant] has an immunity that extends beyond the scope of any action taken in an official capacity" (emphasis in original).

(a) Was the Court's reference to conduct outside the president's "official capacity" a reference to the fact that the events occurred before he was president? Or was it a reference to the alleged sexual misconduct, distinguishing between functions performed for the job and personal functions performed while at work? If the latter, then the defendant in the *Lanier* case, supra, would have received no judicial immunity even if he had coerced the parties in a court order, correct? Is *Clinton* a rather simple case: neither a judge nor a president is immune for everything he might do (such as defaulting on a contract), only for his official acts?

(b) In those cases in which a president or judge is not entitled to absolute immunity, does that end the immunity discussion? Only if the functions are "official functions"? Can a judge nevertheless assert qualified immunity for non-judicial but nevertheless official functions? See Nunez v. Davis, 169 F.3d 1222 (9th Cir.1999) (judge who exercised administrative power over employment may assert qualified immunity). Does this give judges two bites at the apple of immunity? Or only one bite for each type of function that may be exercised?

KALINA v. FLETCHER

United States Supreme Court, 1997.
522 U.S. 118, 118 S.Ct. 502, 139 L.Ed.2d 471.

JUSTICE STEVENS delivered the opinion of the Court.

The question presented is whether 42 U.S.C. S 1983 creates a damages remedy against a prosecutor for making false statements of fact in an affidavit supporting an application for an arrest warrant, or whether, as she contends, such conduct is protected by "the doctrine of absolute prosecutorial immunity."

I

Petitioner is a Deputy Prosecuting Attorney for King County, Washington. Following customary practice, on December 14, 1992, she commenced a criminal proceeding against respondent by filing three documents in the King County Superior Court. Two of those documents—an information charging respondent with burglary and a motion for an arrest warrant—were unsworn pleadings. The burglary charge was based on an alleged theft of computer equipment from a school. Washington Criminal Rules require that an arrest warrant be supported by an affidavit or "sworn testimony establishing the grounds for issuing the warrant." To satisfy that requirement, petitioner supported her motion with a third document—a "Certification for Determination of Probable Cause"—that summarized the evidence supporting the charge. She personally vouched for the truth of the facts set forth in the certification under penalty of perjury. Based on petitioner's certification, the trial court found probable cause and ordered that an arrest warrant be issued.

[Kalina's Certification contained two important inaccuracies: 1) one statement claimed that evidence of Fletcher's fingerprints at the school was inculpatory because he had no connection with the school, when in fact Fletcher had previously worked at the school; and 2) another statement claimed that Fletcher had been identified as the perpetrator from a photo line-up, when in fact no such identification had occurred. Based on the certification, Fletcher was arrested. The charges were dismissed a month later, and this § 1983 suit alleging violation of Fourth Amendment rights ensued. Kalina invoked her absolute immunity, but the lower courts rejected her claim. The Supreme Court then agreed to review that decision.]

III

* * *

In Imbler v. Pachtman we held that a former prisoner whose conviction had been set aside in collateral proceedings could not maintain a § 1983 action against the prosecutor who had litigated the charges against him. Relying in part on common-law precedent, and perhaps even more importantly on the policy considerations underlying that precedent, we concluded that "a state prosecuting attorney who acted within the scope of his duties in initiating and pursuing a criminal prosecution" was not amenable to suit under § 1983.

Liberally construed, Imbler's complaint included not only a charge that the prosecution had been wrongfully commenced, but also a charge that false testimony had been offered as well as a charge that exculpatory evidence had been suppressed. His constitutional claims were thus broader than any specific common-law antecedent. Nevertheless, relying on common-law decisions providing prosecutors with absolute immunity from tort actions based on claims that the decision to prosecute was malicious and unsupported by probable cause, as well as from actions for defamation based on statements made during trial, we concluded that [§ 1983] should be construed to provide an analogous defense against the claims asserted by Imbler. The policy considerations that justified the common-law decisions affording absolute immunity to prosecutors when performing traditional functions applied equally to statutory claims based on the conduct of the same functions.

Those [policy] considerations included both the interest in protecting the prosecutor from harassing litigation that would divert his time and attention from his official duties and the interest in enabling him to exercise independent judgment when "deciding which suits to bring and in conducting them in court." The former interest would lend support to an immunity from all litigation against the occupant of the office whereas the latter is applicable only when the official is performing functions that require the exercise of prosecutorial discretion. Our later cases have made it clear that it is the interest in protecting the proper functioning of the office, rather than the interest in protecting its occupant, that is of primary importance.

In *Imbler*, we did not attempt to define the outer limits of the prosecutor's absolute immunity, but we did recognize that our rationale would not encompass some of his official activities. Thus, while we concluded that Pachtman's "activities were intimately associated with the judicial phase of the criminal process, and thus were functions to which the reasons for absolute immunity apply with full force," we put to one side "those aspects of the prosecutor's responsibility that cast him in the role of an administrator or investigative officer rather than that of advocate." Subsequent cases have confirmed the importance [of the prosecutor's adversarial role in the judicial process as the touchstone of prosecutorial immunity]. Thus, in Burns v. Reed, 500 U.S. 478, 111 S.Ct. 1934, 114 L.Ed.2d 547 (1991), * * * we held that the prosecutor's appearance in court in support of an application for a search warrant and the presentation of evidence at that hearing were protected by absolute immunity. And in Buckley [v. Fitzsimmons, 509 U.S. 259, 113 S.Ct. 2606, 125 L.Ed.2d 209 (1993)], we categorically stated that "acts undertaken by a prosecutor in preparing for the initiation of judicial proceedings or for trial, and which occur in the course of his role as an advocate for the State, are entitled to the protections of absolute immunity."

In both of those cases, however, we found the defense unavailable when the prosecutor was performing a different function. In *Burns*, the provision of legal advice to the police during their pretrial investigation of the facts was protected only by qualified, rather than absolute, immunity. Similarly, in *Buckley*, the prosecutor was not acting as an advocate either when he held a press conference, or when he allegedly fabricated evidence concerning an unsolved crime. With reference to the latter holding, we explained:

> "There is a difference between the advocate's role in evaluating evidence and interviewing witnesses as he prepares for trial, on the one hand, and the detective's role in searching for the clues and corroboration that might give him probable cause to recommend that a suspect be arrested, on the other hand. When a prosecutor performs the investigative functions normally performed by a detective or police officer, it is 'neither appropriate nor justifiable that, for the same act, immunity should protect the one and not the other.' Thus, if a prosecutor plans and executes a raid on a suspected weapons cache, he 'has no greater claim to complete immunity than activities of police officers allegedly acting under his direction.'"

* * *

These cases[, as well as our decision in Malley v. Briggs, 475 U.S. 335, 106 S.Ct. 1092, 89 L.Ed.2d 271 (1986), where we noted that a police officer has no absolute immunity as a complaining witness because complaining witnesses "were not absolutely immune at common law,"] make it quite clear that petitioner's activities in connection with the preparation and filing of two of the three charging documents—the information and the motion for an arrest warrant—are protected by absolute immunity. Indeed, except for her act in personally attesting to the truth of the averments in the certification, it seems equally clear that the preparation and filing of the third document in the package was part of the advocate's function as well. The critical question, however, is whether she was acting as a complaining witness rather than a lawyer when she executed the certification "[u]nder penalty of perjury." We now turn to that question.

IV

The Fourth Amendment requires that arrest warrants be based "upon probable cause, supported by Oath or affirmation"—a requirement that may be satisfied by an indictment returned by a grand jury, but not by the mere filing of criminal charges in an unsworn information signed by the prosecutor. Gerstein v. Pugh, 420 U.S. 103, 117, 95 S.Ct. 854, 864–865, 43 L.Ed.2d 54 (1975). [Washington, like some other western states which avoid grand juries, meets the *Gerstein* requirement by commencing prosecutions based on an "Information" supported by either a sworn affidavit or a sworn "Certification for Determination of Probable Cause" containing facts sufficient to establish probable cause. In Washington, this certification may be sworn to by a witness or a prosecutor acting as complaining witness, so "petitioner performed an act that any competent witness might have performed * * * Indeed, tradition, as well as the ethics of our profession, generally instruct counsel to avoid the risks associated with participating as both advocate and witness in the same proceeding."]

Nevertheless, petitioner argues that the execution of the certificate was just one incident in a presentation that, viewed as a whole, was the work of an advocate and was integral to the initiation of the prosecution. That characterization is appropriate for her drafting of the certification, her determination that the evidence was sufficiently strong to justify a probable-cause finding, her decision to file charges, and her presentation of the information and the motion to the court. Each of those matters involved the exercise of professional judgment; indeed, even the selection of the particular facts to include in the certification to provide the evidentiary support for the finding of probable cause required the exercise of the judgment of the advocate. But that judgment could not affect the truth or falsity of the factual statements themselves. Testifying about facts is the function of the witness, not of the lawyer. No matter how brief or succinct it may be, the evidentiary component of an application for an arrest warrant is a distinct and essential predicate for a finding of probable cause. Even when the person who makes the constitutionally required "Oath or affirmation" is a lawyer, the only function that she performs in giving sworn testimony is that of a witness.

* * *

Accordingly, the judgment of the Court of Appeals for the Ninth Circuit is

Affirmed.

JUSTICE SCALIA, with whom JUSTICE THOMAS joins, concurring.

I agree that Ms. Kalina performed essentially the same "function" in the criminal process as the police officers in Malley v. Briggs, and so I join the opinion of the Court. I write separately because it would be a shame if our opinions did not reflect the awareness that our "functional" approach to 42 U.S.C. § 1983 immunity questions has produced some curious inversions of the common law as it existed in 1871, when § 1983 was enacted. A conscientious prosecutor reading our cases should now conclude that there is absolute immunity for the decision to seek an arrest warrant after filing an information, but only qualified immunity for testimony as a witness in support of that warrant. The common-law rule was, in a sense, exactly opposite. [Extended discussion of common law torts and defenses omitted.]

The Court's long road to what is, superficially at least, the opposite result in today's opinion, began with Imbler v. Pachtman, which granted prosecutors absolute immunity for the "function" of initiating a criminal prosecution. Then, in Briscoe v. LaHue, 460 U.S. 325, 103 S.Ct. 1108, 75 L.Ed.2d 96 (1983), the Court extended a similar absolute immunity to the "function" of serving as a witness. And in Malley v. Briggs it recognized the additional "functional category" of "complaining witness," [which it held to merit only qualified immunity. This distinction between ordinary "witnesses" and "complaining witnesses" had no basis in the common law of immunities, but it did at least partially reflect the common law's actual results if one looked at the limited, specific torts made actionable at common law. The "functional approach" is therefore more a matter of labeling our results to show their consistency with common law than it is an accurate reflection of immunities that existed in 1871.]

[At common law Kalina would have been liable for falsely initiating a prosecution, not just for testifying in the moving documents. So in this context the "functional analysis" produces a result inconsistent with the common law.] *Imbler*'s principle of absolute prosecutorial immunity, and the "functional categories" approach to immunity questions * * * make faithful adherence to the common law embodied in § 1983 very difficult. But both Imbler and the "functional" approach are so deeply embedded in our § 1983 jurisprudence that, for reasons of stare decisis, I would not abandon them now. Given those concessions, *Malley*'s distortion of the term "complaining witness" may take us as close to the right answer as we are likely to get. Because Kalina's conduct clearly places her in that functional category, I agree with the Court that she is not entitled to absolute immunity under our precedents.

NOTE ON THE SCOPE OF PROSECUTORIAL IMMUNITY

1. While in theory both judges and prosecutors receive absolute immunity for their functions, it appears that the rather generous version accorded judges under § 1983 gives way to a somewhat more parsimonious application for prosecutors. Although the court excused a judge's alleged complicity in a physical attack in the *Mireles* case, the prosecutor in *Kalina* receives no immunity for the act of swearing to a document to be filed in Court. Compare Stump v. Sparkman (low-level judge protected for sterilization order handed out without benefit of litigation process), discussed in the preceding Note, with Mitchell v. Forsyth, 472 U.S. 511, 105 S.Ct. 2806, 86 L.Ed.2d 411 (1985) (Attorney General, the highest federal prosecutor, receives no absolute immunity even when engaged in national defense functions). What explains the difference? Is there really a difference?

(a) One view might posit that, as the Court explained in *Kalina*, absolute immunity for prosecutors is based on a subordinating view of the prosecutorial role: prosecutors are protected not for their own work, but for the role they play in the judicial process. See also **Van de Kamp v. Goldstein**, 555 U.S. 335, 129 S.Ct. 855, 172 L.Ed.2d 706 (2009) (immunity for "prosecutorial actions that are 'intimately associated with the judicial phase of the criminal process' "). Does this mean that prosecutors are protected only because of their closeness to judges? Cynically, after all, who has the power to make the official immunity rules—judges or prosecutors? In Buckley v. Fitzsimmons, infra, the Court noted that prosecutorial immunity does not turn on the "location" of the prosecutor's acts and the resulting injury, but on the prosecutor's closeness to the judicial process. Nevertheless, as you read this Note, ask whether physical proximity to the courthouse and the judge is the best predictor of whether absolute immunity will be accorded a prosecutor.

(b) Alternatively, perhaps the difference in treatment between judges and prosecutors represents no subordinating view of prosecutors. Absolute immunity keys on the "judicial process," not "judges" (see Forrester v. White, supra) or "prosecutors" (as in Kalina v. Fletcher, supra). Under this view, it is simply a fact of life that most states assign judges few functions outside the judicial process—thus making them less likely to lose their immunity; on the other hand, many states assign prosecutors functions outside the judicial process—thus making them more likely to lose their immunity. The danger to prosecutors of losing their absolute immunity results from their multiple roles, not their lack of power in the judicial process. See Van de Kamp, supra ("other tasks" than as "officer of the court" receive no immunity).

2. Consider the *Kalina* decision in the context of the two principal cases on which it relies. In **Burns v. Reed**, 500 U.S. 478, 111 S.Ct. 1934, 114 L.Ed.2d 547 (1991), police hypnotized a defendant, inducing her to "confess" to a crime. The state prosecutor gave legal advice to the police on how to proceed and falsely represented the "confession" as truth at a probable cause hearing for a warrant to search at the defendant's home which resulted in the defendant's indictment. She later sued the prosecutor under § 1983 after the trial court learned of the hypnosis and dismissed all charges. In **Buckley v. Fitzsimmons**, 509 U.S. 259, 113 S.Ct. 2606, 125 L.Ed.2d 209 (1993), the prosecutor allegedly fabricated evidence of a bootprint placing defendant at the scene of a sensational crime (murder of an eleven-year-old child) and used it to procure the defendant's indictment; he also later gave a press conference implicating the defendant. All charges were subsequently dismissed, and the suspect then sued the prosecutor under § 1983.

(a) As described in *Kalina*, the *Burns* Court ruled that the act of giving legal advice to police falls outside the advocacy functions of a prosecutor, while the presentation of evidence at a probable cause hearing falls inside the envelope of his functions in the judicial process. Where did the prosecutor cross the line? Appearance in court cannot be the threshold, at least not after *Kalina*, where even an in-court presentation is deemed unprotected. Note also *Kalina*'s holding that even some out-of-court functions will be deemed prosecutorial functions (preparing the charging document, excluding the sworn certification).[1] Why are some trial-preparation activities protected (evaluating evidence, preparing charges) and some not (advising police as to whether there is sufficient evidence to charge)? Why are some trial-preparation activities covered and some in-court activities not (presenting a sworn statement)?

(b) As described in *Kalina*, the *Buckley* Court ruled that the act of fabricating evidence falls outside the functions of a prosecutor, as does the act of giving a press conference. On the other hand, the act of presenting even fabricated evidence to an investigative grand jury is within the prosecutor's advocacy role. Here is the problem: the act of fabrication is investigative only; the acts of "professional evaluation" and presentation of the fabricated evidence are part of the prosecutorial process. Where does fabrication cross the line into professional evaluation that is a part of advocacy? The *Buckley* Court held that a "prosecutor neither is, nor should consider himself to be, an

---

1. Compare Imbler v. Pachtman, discussed in a preceding Note: The "duties of the prosecutor in his role as advocate for the State involve actions preliminary to the initiation of a prosecution and actions apart from the courtroom," 424 U.S. at 431, n. 33, 96 S.Ct., at 995, n. 33; moreover, an out-of-court "effort to control the presentation of [a] witness' testimony" is also "fairly within [the prosecutor's] function as an advocate," id. at 430, n. 32, 96 S.Ct. at 995, n. 32.

advocate before he has probable cause to have anyone arrested." 509 U.S. at 274, 113 S.Ct. at 2616. Given the elusiveness of the concept of probable cause, how is it possible to apply this dividing line?[2]

(c) After considering the holdings in *Kalina, Burns,* and *Buckley,* would it be more accurate to say that prosecutors receive absolute immunity only for acts that can be performed *exclusively* by advocates in judicial proceedings? See Van de Kamp v. Goldstein, supra (protection for "administrative obligation [of] a kind that itself is directly connected with the conduct of a trial"). Any official can conduct a search, give a press conference, be a complaining witness, or even fabricate evidence, but only a trained prosecutor can appear at trial, at probable-cause hearings, or before grand juries—and only prosecutors can make an "exercise of professional judgment" to evaluate the evidence to be presented and train their underlings to follow constitutional procedures in judicial proceedings. Does this explain the results? (Do you believe it is true?)

(d) The circuit cases are richer in detail concerning the range of decisions that prosecutors may play. In Lacey v. Maricopa County, 649 F.3d 1118 (9th Cir. 2011), a prosecutor appointed a special prosecutor to handle a specific case; later both were sued under § 1983. Does either receive prosecutorial immunity? Also consider three perhaps simpler cases. In Lampton v. Diaz, 639 F.3d 223 (5th Cir. 2011), a judge who had been acquitted of tax evasion sued his prosecutor after the prosecutor later sent the judge's confidential tax records to the state ethics commission. In Botello v. Gammick, 413 F.3d 971 (9th Cir. 2005), prosecutors developed a disrespect for a police officer and thereafter demanded that he be barred from conducting investigations, refused to prosecute any charges he filed, and tried to sabotage his efforts to get a new job. In Shmueli v. City of New York, 424 F.3d 231 (2d Cir. 2005), plaintiff alleged that prosecutors conspired to have her charged with harassment, then had her held for an excessive length of time without bail, then allowed the charges to languish without prosecution—all because of an improper relation between prosecutors and the person allegedly harassed. Which actions, if any, receive absolute prosecutorial immunity?

3. The initial discussion in *Kalina* restates in a more cursory manner the two parts of the original *Imbler* test for determining official immunity—the initial inquiry into the 1871 common law and the subsequent inquiry as to whether the policy goals of the common law are consistent with § 1983. Notice also Justice Stevens' concession that, because of the paucity of claims available at common law, the actual decision in *Imbler* may have been more a product of the policy determination than of the inquiry into common law.

---

2. In *Buckley* the prosecutor had not yet impaneled a grand jury at the time of the fabrication, thus allowing the Court to find that the "probable cause" line had not been crossed. 509 U.S. at 274, 113 S.Ct. at 2616. Does this suggest that the line refers to probable cause as officially determined by a court or grand jury? Or can a prosecutor show that he had probable cause even though it had not yet been officially declared? To make matters somewhat more problematic, after fixing the dividing line at the moment of "probable cause," the *Buckley* Court added a footnote admitting that if the prosecutor resumed an "investigation" after the determination of probable cause, he would once again be treated as acting outside his advocacy role. Id. at n. 5. Does this suggest that association with police activity is a more reliable determinant of the line between functions than is the determination of probable cause?

(a) One primary ingredient of the policy decision in these cases, as revealed in *Kalina*, is the determination of whether a finding of no immunity would, under the circumstances, leave the prosecutor subject to "harassing litigation that would divert his time and attention from his official duties." Does this explain why the Court always grants immunity against claims of fabricated or suppressed evidence—because if it did not, every dissatisfied defendant could subject a prosecutor to suit by merely claiming that he had mishandled evidence? Is the protection for prosecutors who have allegedly fabricated and suppressed evidence therefore analogous to the protection afforded judges, see Mireles v. Waco, excerpted earlier in this sub-chapter, who have allegedly acted maliciously or outrageously during court proceedings? Why then are not press conferences protected? Because the prosecutor can easily protect himself by keeping his mouth shut—and easily prove at trial that he did so?

(b) The other primary ingredient of the policy decision in these cases is "the interest in enabling [the prosecutor] to exercise independent judgment when 'deciding which suits to bring and in conducting them in court.' " The interest apparently promotes zealous advocacy. Is the presentation of fabricated evidence at trial a desirable part of zealous advocacy? Why is the signing of a false affidavit outside the bounds of zealous advocacy but the presentation of that affidavit in court within bounds?

(c) Is the result in *Kalina* foreordained by the holding in Malley v. Briggs that "complaining witnesses" are not entitled to absolute immunity? Yet, in **Briscoe v. LaHue**, 460 U.S. 325, 103 S.Ct. 1108, 75 L.Ed.2d 96 (1983), the Court held that any witness at the actual trial is accorded absolute immunity. What is the difference between mere witnesses (protected under *LaHue*) and "complaining witnesses" (left unprotected by *Malley* and *Kalina*)? The historical accident of which was deemed within the bounds of zealous advocacy in 1871? The policy choice that mere witnesses must appear in court, where their potential misconduct can be exposed? The complaining witness is outside the courtroom? Under any of these explanations, is the line between complaining witness and witness at least easy for courts to apply? See Todd v. Weltman, Weinberg & Reis Co., L.P.A. 434 F.3d 432 (6th Cir. 2006) ("complaining witness" initiates suits). Might there be some problems: is a prosecutor who commits a constitutional violation because of a close relationship with the complaining witness treated as a prosecutor or as an adjunct to the complaining witness? See Shmueli v. City of New York, 424 F.3d 231 (2d. Cir. 2005).

4. The Court has also held that absolute immunity extends to legislative acts, even to local-government legislators when they exercise "legislative functions." In **Bogan v. Scott–Harris**, 523 U.S. 44, 118 S.Ct. 966, 140 L.Ed.2d 79 (1998), the plaintiff alleged that in passing the annual budget the city council members had eliminated his city job because they wanted to punish him for exercising his free-speech rights. The Court noted that common law protected both local and state legislators for their "legislative activities," and it found this immunity consistent with the policies underlying § 1983:

"Regardless of the level of government, the exercise of legislative discretion should not be inhibited by judicial interference or distorted by the fear of personal liability. Furthermore, the time and energy required to defend against a lawsuit are of particular concern at the local level, where the part-time citizen-legislator remains commonplace. And the threat of liability may significantly deter service in local government, where prestige and pecuniary rewards may pale in comparison to the threat of civil liability. Moreover, certain deterrents to legislative abuse may be greater at the local level than at other levels of government. Municipalities themselves can be held liable for constitutional violations, whereas States and the Federal Government are often protected by sovereign immunity. And, of course, the ultimate check on legislative abuse—the electoral process—applies with equal force at the local level, where legislators are often more closely responsible to the electorate." 523 U.S. at 49, 118 S.Ct. at 971–72.

(a) The same problems that courts face in determining the limits of judicial and prosecutorial immunity are also present in the context of legislative immunity. In **Supreme Court of Virginia v. Consumers Union of United States, Inc.**, 446 U.S. 719, 100 S.Ct. 1967, 64 L.Ed.2d 641 (1980), extensively discussed in Forrester v. White, excerpted in this sub-chapter, the Court held that a state court's adoption of its code of professional responsibility was an act of "general application," making it legislative in character and entitling the court to legislative immunity. Nevertheless, ruled the Supreme Court, since the state court also had power to enforce its Bar rules against attorneys, it could be sued for exercising its "enforcement powers," which is an administrative rather than legislative act. Is the line between "general application" and "specific application" the line between legislative acts and administrative acts? If the court's decisions were "specific," why did it not receive judicial immunity? What is the difference between administrative and judicial acts? See Forrester v. White, excerpted earlier in this sub-chapter.

(b) Are the following actions legislative functions or administrative? A state legislative committee carries out an investigation of the governor, trying to implicate him in a politically motivated murder: Romero–Barcelo v. Hernandez–Agosto, 75 F.3d 23 (1st Cir.1996). Legislative caucus leaders discharge their press officer and he alleges that they forced him out for exercise of his free-speech rights: Chateaubriand v. Gaspard, 97 F.3d 1218 (9th Cir.1996). A county legislative body bars a speaker from attending any of its future meetings: Kamplain v. Curry County Bd. of Com'rs, 159 F.3d 1248 (10th Cir.1998). Can courts in § 1983 actions distinguish between acts of zoning legislation, which often involve specific street-by-street zoning plats, and acts of a local government hearing appeals on zoning decisions? See Biblia Abierta v. Banks, 129 F.3d 899 (7th Cir.1997) (specific-use zoning); Haskell v. Washington Township, 864 F.2d 1266 (6th Cir.1988) (local government legislators entitled to absolute immunity in making rules of general application, but not for administrative zoning decisions involving single person).

5. If an officer, normally entitled to absolute immunity, is found to be exercising functions that disentitle him to absolute immunity, should he be able to claim qualified immunity as a backup protection? If a judge steps outside her functions and acts as a prosecutor, would she still receive absolute

immunity because prosecutors are entitled to claim it? Or no immunity because she is serving no lawful role? See Supreme Court of Virginia v. Consumers Union of U.S., Inc., 446 U.S. 719, 100 S.Ct. 1967, 64 L.Ed.2d 641 (1980) (judges serving dual roles); Sevier v. Turner, 742 F.2d 262 (6th Cir.1984) (judge who stepped outside his role and acted as prosecutor to collect child-support payments denied immunity).

3. QUALIFIED IMMUNITY

When the Supreme Court first recognized qualified immunity in Pierson v. Ray, supra, it equated the defense with a showing of "good faith and probable cause," at least in the context of a police officer effectuating an arrest. Eight years later the Supreme Court attempted to formulate a more general definition of the defense. In **Wood v. Strickland,** 420 U.S. 308, 95 S.Ct. 992, 43 L.Ed.2d 214 (1975), a case involving high school students who claimed that their due process rights were violated when the school board suspended them from school for spiking the punch at a school party, the Court ruled that administrators should not bear the "burden of mistakes made in good faith." It went on to consider how "good faith" should be measured:

> "The disagreement between the Court of Appeals and the District Court over the immunity standard in this case has been put in terms of an 'objective' versus a 'subjective' test of good faith. As we see it, the appropriate standard necessarily contains elements of both. The official himself must be acting sincerely and with a belief that he is doing right, but an act violating a student's constitutional rights can be no more justified by ignorance or disregard of settled, indisputable law on the part of one entrusted with supervision of students' daily lives than by the presence of actual malice. * * * Therefore, [a] * * * compensatory award will be appropriate only if the school board member has acted with such an impermissible motivation or with such disregard of the student's clearly established constitutional rights that his action cannot reasonably be characterized as being in good faith."

Wood's two-part test survived less than a decade. Its two parts meant that public officials were required to prove both that they had not violated "settled, indisputable law" and that they had acted without an "impermissible motivation." The second issue usually involved a question of fact and often overlapped with the merits. Therefore, even if a defendant prevailed, it was only after a costly trial.

In the case that follows involving constitutional claims against federal officers, the Court reconstituted the qualified immunity and held that, as reformulated, it also applied in § 1983 actions. Since 1982, the phrase "good faith immunity," popularized after Wood as a synonym for qualified immunity, has passed into disuse at the Supreme Court.

HARLOW v. FITZGERALD

Supreme Court of the United States, 1982.
457 U.S. 800, 102 S.Ct. 2727, 73 L.Ed.2d 396.

Justice Powell delivered the opinion of the Court.

The issue in this case is the scope of the immunity available to the senior aides and advisers of the President of the United States in a suit for damages based upon their official acts.

I

In this suit for civil damages petitioners Bryce Harlow and Alexander Butterfield are alleged to have participated in a conspiracy to violate the constitutional and statutory rights of the respondent A. Ernest Fitzgerald. Respondent avers that petitioners entered the conspiracy in their capacities as senior White House aides to former President Richard M. Nixon. [Fitzgerald claimed that the defendants caused his discharge from government employment, in violation of his First Amendment rights, in retaliation for his having "blown the whistle" on Defense Department overspending in testimony before a Congressional Committee. Extensive discovery turned up scant evidence of a conspiracy, and the defendants averred that they had taken all adverse personnel decisions against Fitzgerald "in good faith." The trial court rejected the defendants' claims of official immunity.]

Independently of former President Nixon, petitioners invoked the collateral order doctrine and appealed the denial of their immunity defense to the Court of Appeals for the District of Columbia Circuit. The Court of Appeals dismissed the appeal without opinion. Never having determined the immunity available to the senior aides and advisers of the President of the United States, we granted certiorari.

II

[O]ur decisions consistently have held that government officials are entitled to some form of immunity from suits for damages. As recognized at common law, public officers require this protection to shield them from undue interference with their duties and from potentially disabling threats of liability.

Our decisions have recognized immunity defenses of two kinds. For officials whose special functions or constitutional status requires complete protection from suit, we have recognized the defense of "absolute immunity." The absolute immunity of legislators, in their legislative functions, and of judges, in their judicial functions, now is well settled. Our decisions also have extended absolute immunity to certain officials of the Executive Branch. These include prosecutors and similar officials, see Butz v. Economou, 438 U.S. 478, 508–512, 98 S.Ct. 2894, 2911–2916, 57 L.Ed.2d 895 (1978), executive officers engaged in adjudicative functions, id., at 513–

517, 98 S.Ct., at 2914–2916, and the President of the United States, see Nixon v. Fitzgerald, 457 U.S. 731, 102 S.Ct. 2690, 73 L.Ed.2d 349 [(1982)].

For executive officials in general, however, our cases make plain that qualified immunity represents the norm. In Scheuer v. Rhodes, 416 U.S. 232, 94 S.Ct. 1683, 40 L.Ed.2d 90 (1974), we acknowledged that high officials require greater protection than those with less complex discretionary responsibilities. Nonetheless, we held that a governor and his aides could receive the requisite protection from qualified or good-faith immunity. In Butz v. Economou, supra, we extended the approach of *Scheuer* to high federal officials of the Executive Branch. Discussing in detail the considerations that also had underlain our decision in *Scheuer*, we explained that the recognition of a qualified immunity defense for high executives reflected an attempt to balance competing values: not only the importance of a damages remedy to protect the rights of citizens, but also "the need to protect officials who are required to exercise their discretion and the related public interest in encouraging the vigorous exercise of official authority." Without discounting the adverse consequences of denying high officials an absolute immunity from private lawsuits alleging constitutional violations[,] we emphasized our expectation that insubstantial suits need not proceed to trial: "Insubstantial lawsuits can be quickly terminated by federal courts alert to the possibilities of artful pleading. Unless the complaint states a compensable claim for relief . . ., it should not survive a motion to dismiss. Moreover, the Court recognized in *Scheuer* that damages suits concerning constitutional violations need not proceed to trial, but can be terminated on a properly supported motion for summary judgment based on the defense of immunity. . . . In responding to such a motion, plaintiffs may not play dog in the manger; and firm application of the Federal Rules of Civil Procedure will ensure that federal officials are not harassed by frivolous lawsuits."

* * *

IV

[The defendants' argument that they are entitled to absolute immunity cannot be accepted. They fit no category generally entitled to absolute immunity, and, as with virtually all executive department officials exercising discretionary, non-judicial functions, there is no need to create for them an absolute immunity.] Even if they cannot establish that their official functions require absolute immunity, petitioners assert that public policy at least mandates an application of the qualified immunity standard that would permit the defeat of insubstantial claims without resort to trial. We agree.

A

The resolution of immunity questions inherently requires a balance between the evils inevitable in any available alternative. In situations of abuse of office, an action for damages may offer the only realistic avenue for vindication of constitutional guarantees. Butz v. Economou, supra; see Bivens v. Six Unknown Fed. Narcotics Agents, [Chapter 4B infra]. It is this recognition that has required the denial of absolute immunity to most public officers. At the same time, however, it cannot be disputed seriously that claims frequently run against the innocent as well as the guilty—at a cost not only to the defendant officials, but to society as a whole.[22] These social costs include the expenses of litigation, the diversion of official energy from pressing public issues, and the deterrence of able citizens from acceptance of public office. Finally, there is the danger that fear of being sued will "dampen the ardor of all but the most resolute, or the most irresponsible [public officials], in the unflinching discharge of their duties." Gregoire v. Biddle, 177 F.2d 579, 581 (C.A.2 1949), cert. denied, 339 U.S. 949, 70 S.Ct. 803, 94 L.Ed. 1363 (1950).

In identifying qualified immunity as the best attainable accommodation of competing values, we [have] relied on the assumption that this standard would permit "[i]nsubstantial lawsuits [to] be quickly terminated." [Butz v. Economou.][23] Yet petitioners advance persuasive arguments that the dismissal of insubstantial lawsuits without trial—a factor presupposed in the balance of competing interests struck by our prior cases— requires an adjustment of the "good faith" standard established by our decisions.

B

Qualified or "good faith" immunity is an affirmative defense that must be pleaded by a defendant official. Gomez v. Toledo, 446 U.S. 635, 100 S.Ct. 1920, 64 L.Ed.2d 572 (1980). Decisions of this Court have established that the "good faith" defense has both an "objective" and a "subjective" aspect. The objective element involves a presumptive knowledge of and respect for "basic, unquestioned constitutional rights." Wood v. Strickland. The subjective component refers to "permissible intentions." Ibid. * * *[25]

The subjective element of the good-faith defense frequently has proved incompatible with our admonition in *Butz* that insubstantial claims should not proceed to trial. Rule 56 of the Federal Rules of Civil Procedure provides that disputed questions of fact ordinarily may not be decided on motions for summary judgment. And an official's subjective good faith has

---

22. See generally Schuck, Suing Our Servants: The Court, Congress, and the Liability of Public Officials for Damages, 1980 S.Ct. Rev. 281, 324–327.

23. The importance of this consideration hardly needs emphasis. This Court has noted the risk imposed upon political officials who must defend their actions and motives before a jury. See Tenney v. Brandhove, 341 U.S. 367, 377–378, 71 S.Ct. 783, 788–789, 95 L.Ed. 1019 (1951). As the Court observed in Tenney: "In times of political passion, dishonest or vindictive motives are readily attributed . . . and as readily believed." Id., at 378, 71 S.Ct., at 789.

25. In Wood the Court explicitly limited its holding to the circumstances in which a school board member, "in the specific context of school discipline," would be stripped of claimed immunity in an action under § 1983. Subsequent cases, however, have quoted the Wood formulation as a general statement of the qualified immunity standard. See, e.g., Procunier v. Navarette, 434 U.S. 555, 562–563, 566, 98 S.Ct. 855, 859–860, 862, 55 L.Ed.2d 24 (1978).

been considered to be a question of fact that some courts have regarded as inherently requiring resolution by a jury.

In the context of *Butz'* attempted balancing of competing values, it now is clear that substantial costs attend the litigation of the subjective good faith of government officials. Not only are there the general costs of subjecting officials to the risks of trial—distraction of officials from their governmental duties, inhibition of discretionary action, and deterrence of able people from public service. There are special costs to "subjective" inquiries of this kind. Immunity generally is available only to officials performing discretionary functions. In contrast with the thought processes accompanying "ministerial" tasks, the judgments surrounding discretionary action almost inevitably are influenced by the decisionmaker's experiences, values, and emotions. These variables explain in part why questions of subjective intent so rarely can be decided by summary judgment. Yet they also frame a background in which there often is no clear end to the relevant evidence. Judicial inquiry into subjective motivation therefore may entail broad-ranging discovery and the deposing of numerous persons, including an official's professional colleagues. Inquiries of this kind can be peculiarly disruptive of effective government.

Consistently with the balance at which we aimed in *Butz*, we conclude today that bare allegations of malice should not suffice to subject government officials either to the costs of trial or to the burdens of broad-reaching discovery. We therefore hold that government officials performing discretionary functions generally are shielded from liability for civil damages insofar as their conduct does not violate clearly established statutory or constitutional rights of which a reasonable person would have known. Wood v. Strickland, 420 U.S. at 322, 95 S.Ct. at 1001.[30]

Reliance on the objective reasonableness of an official's conduct, as measured by reference to clearly established law, should avoid excessive disruption of government and permit the resolution of many insubstantial claims on summary judgment. On summary judgment, the judge appropriately may determine, not only the currently applicable law, but whether that law was clearly established at the time an action occurred.[32] If the law at that time was not clearly established, an official could not reasonably be expected to anticipate subsequent legal developments, nor could he fairly be said to "know" that the law forbade conduct not previously identified as unlawful. Until this threshold immunity question is resolved, discovery should not be allowed. If the law was clearly established, the immunity defense ordinarily should fail, since a reasonably competent public official should know the law governing his conduct. Nevertheless, if

---

30. This case involves no issue concerning the elements of the immunity available to state officials sued for constitutional violations under 42 U.S.C. § 1983. We have found previously, however, that it would be "untenable to draw a distinction for purposes of immunity law between suits brought against state officials under § 1983 and suits brought directly under the Constitution against federal officials." Butz v. Economou. * * *

32. [W]e need not define here the circumstances under which "the state of the law" should be "evaluated by reference to the opinions of this Court, of the Courts of Appeals, or of the local District Court."

the official pleading the defense claims extraordinary circumstances and can prove that he neither knew nor should have known of the relevant legal standard, the defense should be sustained. But again, the defense would turn primarily on objective factors.

By defining the limits of qualified immunity essentially in objective terms, we provide no license to lawless conduct. The public interest in deterrence of unlawful conduct and in compensation of victims remains protected by a test that focuses on the objective legal reasonableness of an official's acts. Where an official could be expected to know that certain conduct would violate statutory or constitutional rights, he should be made to hesitate; and a person who suffers injury caused by such conduct may have a cause of action. But where an official's duties legitimately require action in which clearly established rights are not implicated, the public interest may be better served by action taken "with independence and without fear of consequences." Pierson v. Ray.

* * *

The judgment of the Court of Appeals is vacated, and the case is remanded for further action consistent with this opinion.

So ordered.

JUSTICE BRENNAN, with whom JUSTICE MARSHALL and JUSTICE BLACKMUN join, concurring.

I agree with the substantive standard announced by the Court today, imposing liability when a public-official defendant "knew or should have known" of the constitutionally violative effect of his actions. This standard would not allow the official who actually knows that he was violating the law to escape liability for his actions, even if he could not "reasonably have been expected" to know what he actually did know. Thus the clever and unusually well-informed violator of constitutional rights will not evade just punishment for his crimes. I also agree that this standard applies "across the board," to all "government officials performing discretionary functions." I write separately only to note that given this standard, it seems inescapable to me that some measure of discovery may sometimes be required to determine exactly what a public-official defendant did "know" at the time of his actions.

[A second concurring opinion by the same justice—a rarity—is omitted. A separate concurring statement by Justice Rehnquist is also omitted. Chief Justice Burger dissented on the ground that absolute immunity would have been appropriate for these officials.]

NOTE ON QUALIFIED IMMUNITY AND "SETTLED CONSTITUTIONAL LAW"

1. The *Harlow* Court appears to say that the subjective component of qualified immunity must be rejected because it undercuts the underlying goal

of the immunity—quickly ending unnecessary or inappropriate litigation.[1] But was a subjective inquiry into good faith ever a good idea in its own right?

(a) What did "good faith" mean? In Wood v. Strickland the Court said that it meant acting "sincerely." What does that mean? One possible interpretation of "good faith" is reliance upon state statutory or common law, even though it is later held unconstitutional in the § 1983 case. This interpretation was apparently rejected in the original *Pierson* case. Why so? Should defendants be released from liability if they were "just following [state law] orders"? Who is favored by jettisoning the subjective component from qualified immunity, plaintiffs or defendants? Why would Justice Brennan want to retain some inquiry into subjective knowledge of the defendant? (Recall that Justice Brennan and liberal colleagues had argued against intent requirements under the Equal Protection Clause.) See Chapter 1B.5 supra. See also Chapter 7A infra (opposing intent requirement in employment discrimination cases).

(b) Does *Harlow*'s changing of the very content of qualified immunity alter *Pierson*'s original rationale that the immunities are derived from common law? See **Anderson v. Creighton**, 483 U.S. 635, 644–45, 107 S.Ct. 3034, 3041–42, 97 L.Ed.2d 523 (1987):

> "Although it is true that we have observed that our determinations as to the scope of official immunity are made in the light of the 'common-law tradition,' we have never suggested that the precise contours of official immunity can and should be slavishly derived from the often arcane rules of the common law. That notion is plainly contradicted by *Harlow*, where the Court completely reformulated qualified immunity along principles not at all embodied in the common law, replacing the inquiry into subjective malice so frequently required at common law with an objective inquiry into the legal reasonableness of the official action."

Would it be fair to say that 1871 common law has influenced the decision as to whether an official receives absolute or qualified immunity, but it has not affected the content of qualified immunity? Is that just another way of saying that qualified immunity is entirely the creation of the Court? Does the Court have power to create qualified immunity because it, after all, resurrected § 1983 in Monroe v. Pape?[2]

2. In **Mitchell v. Forsyth**, 472 U.S. 511, 105 S.Ct. 2806, 86 L.Ed.2d 411 (1985), another suit against a federal official that adopted § 1983's defense of official immunity, the Court reinforced a basic principle noted in *Harlow*—the time element in judging qualified immunity's "settled constitutional law" test. At issue was a claim that Attorney General Mitchell had violated the Fourth Amendment in ordering warrantless national security wiretaps. The taps had occurred one year before the Supreme Court issued an

---

1. In later cases the Supreme Court noted that *Harlow* had focused qualified immunity on an objective inquiry, "purging" it of any subjective components. See, e.g., Mitchell v. Forsyth, infra, 472 U.S. at 516, 105 S.Ct. at 2810.

2. *Harlow* was a case involving federal officials, where the right to sue for damages is court-created; no statutory equivalent of § 1983 exists for federal officials. Given that the Court has applied qualified immunity in an "identical" manner regardless of whether state or federal officials are sued, does it not follow that the defense grows from some other source than § 1983? See Wilson v. Layne, infra.

opinion specifically outlawing the practice. In upholding the claim of qualified immunity the Court stressed that the appropriate time frame of its inquiry was the date on which the defendant acted:

"The District Court's conclusion that Mitchell is not immune because he gambled and lost on the resolution of this open question departs from the principles of *Harlow*. Such hindsight-based reasoning on immunity issues is precisely what *Harlow* rejected. The decisive fact is not that Mitchell's position turned out to be incorrect, but that the question was open at the time he acted." 472 U.S. at 535, 105 S.Ct. at 2820.

Mitchell shows that § 1983 defendants are generally excused from developments in the law that occurred after they acted. See Wilson v. Layne, 526 U.S. 603, 119 S.Ct. 1692, 143 L.Ed.2d 818 (1999) (decision in 1999 inquires into the case law as it existed in 1992 when defendants acted; if judges "disagree on a constitutional question, it is unfair [later] to subject the police to money damages for picking the losing side of the controversy").[3]

(a) Usually in the Anglo–American common law, when a judge "clarifies" the law (or, more likely, makes new law), the new rule applies not only to future litigants but to the parties before the Court. *Mitchell* therefore departs from traditional legal practice in the extreme: it not only excuses the defendants from rules announced in a pending case, it even excuses them from the application of any legal rules that have developed in the years since they acted. What policies dictate that officeholders should be excepted from common practice in constitutional law cases for damages? Is *Mitchell* a "conservative" opinion? Or is *Mitchell* actually a "liberal" decision, favoring the creation of new common law—because it frees a judge from worrying about the immediate monetary consequences of making new law?

(b) Does *Mitchell* conclusively reject Justice Brennan's concurring position in *Harlow*? How can an official "actually know[] that he was violating the law," as Justice Brennan posited, if the law was in fact unsettled? Was Justice Brennan's idea just a relic of a notion he claimed to reject—*Wood*'s focus on subjective motive and good faith? Compare Conn v. Gabbert, 526 U.S. 286, 119 S.Ct. 1292, 143 L.Ed.2d 399 (1999) (overturning court of appeals view that there should be no immunity because "the intended result" of the defendant's conduct was to violate constitutional rights; no such right found).

3. If defendants can invoke qualified immunity when pertinent principles of constitutional law are unsettled, and thereby prevail on this complete defense, how does constitutional law become settled? How is the uncertainty of constitutional law eliminated by a decisive announcement of the law? The Supreme Court noted the problem in Justice Souter's majority opinion in **County of Sacramento v. Lewis**, 523 U.S. 833, 841 n. 5, 118 S.Ct. 1708, 1714 n. 5, 140 L.Ed.2d 1043 (1998):

"In practical terms, escape from uncertainty would require the [constitutional] issue to arise in a suit to enjoin future conduct [because immunities are applicable only in damages actions], in an action against a

---

3. Should defendants receive an additional period following the settlement of a constitutional issue so as to reflect the amount of time necessary for a reasonable person to learn newly settled law? See Fields v. City of Omaha, 810 F.2d 830 (8th Cir.1987) (no knowledge when Supreme Court precedent only 6 weeks old).

municipality [because they have no immunity], or in litigating a suppression motion in a criminal proceeding; in none of these instances would qualified immunity be available to block a determination of law. But these avenues would not necessarily be open, and therefore the better approach is to determine the [constitutional] right before determining whether it was previously established with clarity."

The Court therefore developed a somewhat venerable practice of first deciding the merits of the constitutional issue before then turning (if liability had been found) to the issue of qualified immunity. See Saucier v. Katz, 533 U.S. 194, 121 S.Ct. 2151, 150 L.Ed.2d 272 (2001) (right to be free from unnecessary use of force, but this right not settled on the facts presented); Wilson v. Layne, 526 U.S. 603, 119 S.Ct. 1692, 143 L.Ed.2d 818 (1999) (police may not constitutionally take media into a searched house; but this right not settled).

(a) The two-step sequence, merits-then-immunity, drew criticism from a consistent group of dissenting justices, see Bunting v. Mellen, 541 U.S. 1019, 124 S.Ct. 1750, 158 L.Ed.2d 636 (2004) (opinion of Justice Stevens, joined by Ginsburg and Breyer, on dismissal of certiorari) (referring to it as an "unwise judge-made rule"), as well as from federal appellate judges forced to implement the practice, see Lyons v. City of Xenia, 417 F.3d 565 (6th Cir. 2005) (Sutton and Gibbons, JJ., "concurring" on this issue) (admitting that "there is a risk that some constitutional guarantees would never become established" but nevertheless objecting to an inflexible rule requiring decision on the merits of "all cases, no matter the costs, no matter the ease with which the second question might be answered"). They even drew support from progressive, plaintiff-oriented academics who noted that the need to decide cases on the merits usually resulted in judgments against plaintiffs, setting precedents and settling constitutional law unfavorably to plaintiffs. See Nancy Leong, *The Saucier Qualified Immunity Experiment: An Empirical Analysis*, 36 PEPP. L. REV. 667, 676–84 (2009) (although originally supported as a mechanism for settling law so that qualified immunity would apply less often, an empirical study of the two-step approach showed an increase in finding no violation on the merits).

(b) Finally, in **Pearson v. Callahan**, 555 U.S. 223, 129 S.Ct. 808, 172 L.Ed.2d 565 (2009), Justice Alito's appointment to the Court shifted momentum against the mandatory sequencing of merits-then-immunity. The resultant compromise was to find sequencing "often appropriate, [but] no longer * * * regarded as mandatory." The Court pointed to several problems caused by mandatory requirement to decide the merits: wasted judicial and litigation resources, inability to make meaningful precedents at such an early stage of litigation, poor judicial decisionmaking because of inadequate briefing (presumably as attorneys inadequately briefed the merits because they knew they would lose anyway on the immunity issue), and contravention of the long-standing practice of avoiding unnecessary decision of constitutional issues, citing Ashwander v. TVA, 297 U.S. 288, 347, 56 S.Ct. 466, 80 L.Ed. 688 (1936) (Brandeis, J., concurring) ("The Court will not pass upon a constitutional question although properly presented by the record, if there is also present some other ground upon which the case may be disposed of"). How much will *Pearson* actually change things? Does it invite judges to be more tactical or political? See See Karen M. Blum, Section 1983 Litigation: Post–*Pearson* and

Post–*Iqbal*, 26 TOURO L. REV. 433, 434 (2010) (surveying variety of reactions in the circuits).

4. What is "settled" constitutional law? In **Anderson v. Creighton**, 483 U.S. 635, 639, 107 S.Ct. 3034, 3038–39, 97 L.Ed.2d 523 (1987), involving the search of a home without a warrant, the Court tried to shed some light on its standard:

> "The operation of this standard * * * depends substantially upon the level of generality at which the relevant 'legal rule' is to be identified. For example, the right to due process of law is quite clearly established by the Due Process Clause, and thus there is a sense in which any action that violates that Clause (no matter how unclear it may be that the particular action is a violation) violates a clearly established right. * * * But if the test of 'clearly established law' were to be applied at this level of generality, it would bear no relationship to the 'objective legal reasonableness' that is the touchstone of *Harlow* * * * [O]ur cases establish that the right the official is alleged to have violated must have been 'clearly established' in a more particularized, and hence more relevant, sense: The contours of the right must be sufficiently clear that a reasonable official would understand that what he is doing violates that right. This is not to say that an official action is protected by qualified immunity unless the very action in question has previously been held unlawful, but it is to say that in the light of preexisting law the unlawfulness must be apparent."

Does *Anderson* provide sufficient guidance as to what is settled law? Consider subsequent cases that apply the standard.

(a) In **United States v. Lanier**, 520 U.S. 259, 117 S.Ct. 1219, 137 L.Ed.2d 432 (1997), decided in a context analogous to § 1983 and cross-citing qualified immunity precedents,[4] the Court faced a defendant judge who claimed that he was entitled to exemption because there existed no precedents declaring that a judge who raped and demanded sexual favors from defendants and their loved one violated their constitutional rights. The Court easily rejected the argument: "[Even] general statements of the law are not inherently incapable of giving fair and clear warning [without need of a specific precedent. As one judge has noted, 'just because there] has never been . . . a section 1983 case accusing welfare officials of selling foster children into slavery, it does not follow that if such a case arose, the officials would be immune from damages.'" Similarly, in **Hope v. Pelzer,** 536 U.S. 730, 122 S.Ct. 2508, 153 L.Ed.2d 666 (2002), the Supreme Court struck down Alabama's "hitching post" technique for punishing inmates in prison, declaring it an Eighth Amendment violation. In the course of its decision, the Court interpreted Farmer v. Brennan, Chapter 1B.1 supra, as permitting "deliberate indifference" to be found from the "obviousness" of the technique's harm to prisoners—then it used that finding of obviousness to deny qualified immuni-

---

4. The case involved a prosecution under the criminal law analogue to § 1983 discussed in Monroe v. Pape, Chapter 1A supra. As the Court would later say in Hope v. Pelzer, infra, "[o]fficers sued in a civil action for damages under 42 U.S.C. § 1983 have the same right to fair notice as do defendants charged with the criminal offense defined in 18 U.S.C. § 242 [because of the latter's 'willfulness' requirement]."

ty. The Court noted that there were similar prison mistreatment cases also outlawing corporal punishment. Are these such easy cases? Why?

(b) On the other hand, in another shocking case the Court held that a warrantless search of a 15–year–old schoolgirl's underwear was unconstitutional—but then ruled that the principal could not have known this because there was no precedent settling the "reasonableness" of such a search. **Safford Unified School Dist. No. 1 v. Redding**, ___ U.S. ___, 129 S.Ct. 2633, 174 L.Ed.2d 354 (2009). Just how shocking must conduct be to run afoul of a foreseeable general rule? In **Brosseau v. Haugen**, 543 U.S. 194, 125 S.Ct. 596, 160 L.Ed.2d 583 (2004), the Court granted qualified immunity to a police officer who shot a fleeing felon in the back, despite its long-time precedent of Tennessee v. Garner, Chapter 1B.3 supra. The Court noted that *Garner* allowed shootings when there was a danger to the officer and that some lower courts had permitted shootings of persons in cars. Was the Court influenced by the "obvious" dangerousness of a fast-driving, fleeing felon?[5]

(c) Consider this issue from a greater distance. Is it an inevitable by-product of the fact that some constitutional rules are more clear-cut and easier to apply than others? Some constitutional principles are inherently nebulous, especially those that require balancing of competing interests or an appreciation of factual variations. See, e.g., Connick v. Myers, 461 U.S. 138, 103 S.Ct. 1684, 75 L.Ed.2d 708 (1983) (free speech analysis requires balancing when public employee claims right to criticize supervisors). How should settled law be determined in such a context? Compare Lytle v. Wondrash, 182 F.3d 1083 (9th Cir.1999) ("we must decide whether the outcome of the [*Connick*] balancing test so clearly favored [plaintiff] that it would have been patently unreasonable for [defendants] to conclude that their actions were lawful"); with Coady v. Steil, 187 F.3d 727 (7th Cir.1999) ("because [*Connick*] balancing always involves fact specific balancing, if plaintiffs had to point to a case on all fours with their own, defendants would nearly always be entitled to qualified immunity [so] we have rejected that argument").[6] Other constitutional principles may have a clear enough rule, but its application may be highly fact specific or contextual, as in Brosseau v. Haugen, supra ("probable cause" and "threat of serious harm"). There is also the possibility that cultural norms simply make some conduct beyond the pale even when the law applicable to it is nebulous. See *Lanier*, supra; Markham v. White, 172 F.3d 486 (7th Cir.1999) ("[c]ontrary to the defendants' argument, the fact that neither this court nor any other has ever dealt with a situation involving [crotch-grabbing at] a short training seminar conducted for narcotics officers" does not make applicable legal rules unsettled).

5.   Of course, the Supreme Court is not the only court that may decide constitutional cases. Many constitutional issues are decided, or decided with more factual specificity, only by the accumulation of cases in lower courts. May these be considered in deciding whether law is settled? In other words, at

---

5.   Unlike its usual practice of deciding the constitutional issue first, the Court decided only the qualified immunity issue, excusing itself on the ground that the procedure at issue was a "summary reversal" by a per curiam Court. Was the issue just tool hard to decide? Is that the reason that lower-court judges also want power to avoid the merits? See ¶ 3(a) supra.

6.   But see Evans–Marshall v. Board of Educ. of Tipp City Exempted Village School Dist., 428 F.3d 223 (6th Cir. 2005) (finding settled law in similar *Pickering* balancing context).

what level of the judicial system must the principle have been decided in order to put defendants on notice?

(a) Courts should look beyond Supreme Court decisions, the Supreme Court held in United States v. Lanier, supra ("universe of relevant interpretive decisions is [not] confined to our opinions"; circuit opinions may be used) and demonstrated in Hope v. Pelzer, supra, where all applicable precedents were within the circuit. Do cases from other circuits count? See Pearson v. Callahan, 555 U.S. 223, 129 S.Ct. 808, 172 L.Ed.2d 565 (2009) (defendants entitled to rely on cases outside their circuit announcing a pro-defendant rule when their circuit was silent). Cf. Wilson v. Layne, supra (looking at state, district court, and federal appellate decisions, and finding them conflicting).

(b) Is settled *state* law—not state-court decisions on constitutional issues, but decisions on comparable state-law issues—relevant to deciding whether constitutional law is settled? The classic answer is, no. Davis v. Scherer, 468 U.S. 183, 104 S.Ct. 3012, 82 L.Ed.2d 139 (1984) (that defendant's act may have violated clear state law is irrelevant to whether he violated clearly settled constitutional law). See Wilson v. Layne, supra (that state law authorized certain conduct is relevant to reasonableness when other indicators show constitutional law is unsettled; but state law "could not make reasonable [conduct] that was contrary to a decided body of case law").

(c) Are administrative rulings or statements from the federal executive branch relevant? In *Hope*, supra, the Court included in its discussion repeated references to the fact that the federal Department of Justice had issued a memorandum warning that the specific practice of using "hitching posts" as punishment is unconstitutional. If there had been no judicial precedents, would this have been enough? Cf. Groh v. Ramirez, 540 U.S. 551, 124 S.Ct. 1284, 157 L.Ed.2d 1068 (2004) (citing federal agency instructions applicable to one of its own agent's claiming immunity).

6. Does the *Anderson* standard, ¶ 4 supra concerning fact-specific constitutional tests, necessarily mean that a court must not only decide whether legal doctrine is settled, it must also decide whether the law is sufficiently settled as applied to the facts in the case before the court? Consider the case that follows.

MALLEY v. BRIGGS

Supreme Court of the United States, 1986.
475 U.S. 335, 106 S.Ct. 1092, 89 L.Ed.2d 271.

JUSTICE WHITE delivered the opinion of the Court.

This case presents the question of the degree of immunity accorded a defendant police officer in a damages action under 42 U.S.C. § 1983 when it is alleged that the officer caused the plaintiffs to be unconstitutionally arrested by presenting a judge with a complaint and a supporting affidavit which failed to establish probable cause. [We reject a claim to absolute immunity and rule that qualified immunity adequately protects the officer seeking a warrant.]

I

In December 1980, the Rhode Island State Police were conducting a court-authorized wiretap on the telephone of one Paul Driscoll, an acquaintance of the respondents' daughter. On December 20, the police intercepted a call to Driscoll from an unknown individual who identified himself as "Dr. Shogun." The police logsheet summarizes the call as follows: "General conversation re. [sic] a party they went to last night— caller says I can't believe I was token [sic] in front of Jimmy Briggs— caller states he passed it to Louisa ... Paul says Nancy was sitting in his lap rolling her thing." Petitioner Edward Malley was the Rhode Island state trooper in charge of the investigation of Driscoll. After reviewing the logsheet for December 20, Petitioner decided that the call from "Dr. Shogun" was incriminating, because in drug parlance "toking" means smoking marihuana and "rolling her thing" refers to rolling a marihuana cigarette. Petitioner also concluded that another call monitored the same day showed that the party discussed by Driscoll and "Dr. Shogun" took place at respondents' house. On the basis of these two calls, petitioner drew up felony complaints charging that respondents and Paul Driscoll "did unlawfully conspire to violate the uniform controlled substance act of the State of Rhode Island by having [marijuana] in their possession...." These complaints were presented to a State District Court judge in February 1981, after the wiretap of Driscoll's phone had been terminated. Accompanying the complaints were unsigned warrants for each respondent's arrest, and supporting affidavits describing the two intercepted calls and petitioner's interpretation of them. [The judge signed the warrants, and Briggs was arrested amid considerable unfavorable publicity, but the grand jury refused to indict him. This suit, alleging a violation of the Fourth Amendment, followed. The District Court entered a directed verdict for the defendants, but the First Circuit reinstated the claims.]

II

* * *

As the qualified immunity defense has evolved, it provides ample protection to all but the plainly incompetent or those who knowingly violate the law. At common law, in cases where probable cause to arrest was lacking, a complaining witness's immunity turned on the issue of malice, which was a jury question. Under the *Harlow* standard, on the other hand, an allegation of malice is not sufficient to defeat immunity if the defendant acted in an objectively reasonable manner. The *Harlow* standard is specifically designed to "avoid excessive disruption of government and permit the resolution of many insubstantial claims on summary judgment," and we believe it sufficiently serves this goal. Defendants will not be immune if, on an objective basis, it is obvious that no reasonably competent officer would have concluded that a warrant should issue; but if officers of reasonable competence could disagree on this issue, immunity should be recognized.

* * *

In the case of the officer applying for a warrant, it is our judgment that the judicial process will on the whole benefit from a rule of qualified rather than absolute immunity. We do not believe that the *Harlow* standard, which gives ample room for mistaken judgments, will frequently deter an officer from submitting an affidavit when probable cause to make an arrest is present. True, an officer who knows that objectively unreasonable decisions will be actionable may be motivated to reflect, before submitting a request for a warrant, whether he has a reasonable basis for believing that his affidavit establishes probable cause. But such reflection is desirable, because it reduces the likelihood that the officer's request for a warrant will be premature. Premature requests for warrants are at best a waste of judicial resources; at worst, they lead to premature arrests, which may injure the innocent or, by giving the basis for a suppression motion, benefit the guilty.

Furthermore, it would be incongruous to test police behavior by the "objective reasonableness" standard in a suppression hearing, see United States v. Leon, 468 U.S. 897, 104 S.Ct. 3405, 82 L.Ed.2d 677 (1984), while exempting police conduct in applying for an arrest or search warrant from any scrutiny whatsoever in a § 1983 damages action.[7] While we believe the exclusionary rule serves a necessary purpose, it obviously does so at a considerable cost to society as a whole, because it excludes evidence probative of guilt. On the other hand, a damages remedy for an arrest following an objectively unreasonable request for a warrant imposes a cost directly on the officer responsible for the unreasonable request, without the side effect of hampering a criminal prosecution. Also, in the case of the § 1983 action, the likelihood is obviously greater than at the suppression hearing that the remedy is benefiting the victim of police misconduct one would think most deserving of a remedy—the person who in fact has done no wrong, and has been arrested for no reason, or a bad reason.

Accordingly, we hold that the same standard of objective reasonableness that we applied in the context of a suppression hearing in *Leon,* supra, defines the qualified immunity accorded an officer whose request for a warrant allegedly caused an unconstitutional arrest.[8] Only where the warrant application is so lacking in indicia of probable cause as to render official belief in its existence unreasonable, will the shield of immunity be lost.

---

7. Although the case before us only concerns a damages action for an officer's part in obtaining an allegedly unconstitutional arrest warrant, the distinction between a search warrant and an arrest warrant would not make a difference in the degree of immunity accorded the officer who applied for the warrant.

8. Petitioner has not pressed the argument that in a case like this the officer should not be liable because the judge's decision to issue the warrant breaks the causal chain between the application for the warrant and the improvident arrest. It should be clear, however, that the District Court's "no causation" rationale in this case is inconsistent with our interpretation of § 1983. As we stated in Monroe v. Pape, § 1983 "should be read against the background of tort liability that makes a man responsible for the natural consequences of his actions." Since the common law recognized the causal link between the submission of a complaint and an ensuing arrest, we read § 1983 as recognizing the same causal link.

III

We also reject petitioner's argument that if an officer is entitled to only qualified immunity in cases like this, he is nevertheless shielded from damages liability because the act of applying for a warrant is per se objectively reasonable, provided that the officer believes that the facts alleged in his affidavit are true. Petitioner insists that he is entitled to rely on the judgment of a judicial officer in finding that probable cause exists and hence issuing the warrant. This view of objective reasonableness is at odds with our development of that concept in *Harlow* and *Leon.* In *Leon,* we stated that "our good-faith inquiry is confined to the objectively ascertainable question whether a reasonably well-trained officer would have known that the search was illegal despite the magistrate's authorization." The analogous question in this case is whether a reasonably well-trained officer in petitioner's position would have known that his affidavit failed to establish probable cause and that he should not have applied for the warrant.[9] If such was the case, the officer's application for a warrant was not objectively reasonable, because it created the unnecessary danger of an unlawful arrest. It is true that in an ideal system an unreasonable request for a warrant would be harmless, because no judge would approve it. But ours is not an ideal system, and it is possible that a magistrate, working under docket pressures, will fail to perform as a magistrate should. We find it reasonable to require the officer applying for the warrant to minimize this danger by exercising reasonable professional judgment.[10]

The judgment of the Court of Appeals is affirmed, and the case is remanded for further proceedings consistent with this opinion.

It is so ordered.

JUSTICE POWELL, with whom JUSTICE REHNQUIST joins, concurring in part and dissenting in part.

* * *

[I agree with the Court's general approach, but I would grant the officer summary judgment in this case rather than remand for further proceedings.] In my view, in the light of the logs of the duly authorized wiretap, a reasonably competent officer could have believed that a warrant should issue. It is undisputed that wiretaps initiated as part of a drug

---

9. The question is not presented to us, nor do we decide, whether petitioner's conduct in this case was in fact objectively reasonable. That issue must be resolved on remand.

10. Notwithstanding petitioner's protestations, the rule we adopt in no way "requires the police officer to assume a role even more skilled ... than the magistrate." Brief for Petitioner 33. It is a sound presumption that "the magistrate is more qualified than the police officer to make a probable cause determination," Ibid., and it goes without saying that where a magistrate acts mistakenly in issuing a warrant but within the range of professional competence of a magistrate, the officer who requested the warrant cannot be held liable. But it is different if no officer of reasonable competence would have requested the warrant, i.e., his request is outside the range of the professional competence expected of an officer. If the magistrate issues the warrant in such a case, his action is not just a reasonable mistake, but an unacceptable error indicating gross incompetence or neglect of duty. The officer then cannot excuse his own default by pointing to the greater incompetence of the magistrate.

investigation revealed that respondents had attended a party where marihuana was being smoked, that a marihuana cigarette may have been passed to Mrs. Briggs, and that another party—at least inferentially of a similar type—was to be held in respondents' home. Under the *Harlow* standard, we need not consider whether this information would be viewed by every reasonable officer as sufficient evidence of probable cause for the issuance of a warrant. Police often operate "in the midst and haste of a criminal investigation," and they have to make judgment calls over which reasonable officers could differ. In this case, the logs from the wiretaps at least arguably implicated respondents in unlawful activities. Under these circumstances, an officer of reasonable competence could have believed that the wiretaps provided probable cause to arrest respondents.

* * *

The police, where they have reason to believe probable cause exists, should be encouraged to submit affidavits to judicial officers. I therefore believe that in a suit such as this, the Court should expressly hold that the decision by the magistrate is entitled to substantial evidentiary weight.[8] A more restrictive standard will discourage police officers from seeking warrants out of fear of litigation and possible personal liability. The specter of personal liability for a mistake in judgment may cause a prudent police officer to close his eyes to facts that should at least be brought to the attention of the judicial officer authorized to make the decision whether a warrant should issue. Law enforcement is ill-served by this in terrorem restraint.

NOTE ON *QUALIFIED IMMUNITY AND CIVIL PROCEDURE*

1. *Malley* contains a lengthy discussion of not only the advisability of making officers accept only qualified immunity, but also how it would work in probable cause cases.

(a) *Malley* refuses to allow the police to excuse their conduct by pointing to the magistrate's probable cause ruling. Is that fair? Do probable-cause determinations present special problems for officers where they peculiarly need legal assistance? If they obtain legal advice that tells them the law is unsettled, may they use such advice to show that their action was "reasonable"? See Womack v. City of Bellefontaine Neighbors, 193 F.3d 1028 (8th Cir.1999). The magistrate will be relieved of liability, under absolute immunity for judicial functions, regardless of his attentiveness to the law, correct?

(b) *Malley* also appears to add a refinement to *Harlow*, further particularizing the inquiry that courts should make in ruling on qualified immunity, at least in the context of Fourth Amendment claims. Though generally

---

8. There will, of course, be instances where "it is plainly evident that a magistrate or judge ha[s] no business issuing a warrant." Illinois v. Gates, 462 U.S. 213, 264, 103 S.Ct. 2317, 2346, 76 L.Ed.2d 527 (1983) (White, J., concurring in judgment). If the magistrate has wholly abandoned his judicial role in the manner condemned in Lo–Ji Sales, Inc. v. New York, 442 U.S. 319, 99 S.Ct. 2319, 60 L.Ed.2d 920 (1979), then the magistrate's approval of a warrant would not necessarily be probative of whether an officer's request for a warrant was objectively reasonable. [Repositioned footnote]

favorable to plaintiffs, the Court allows—commands—trial judges to go be-yond the legal rules to look at how "reasonably well-trained officer *in petitioner's position* would have known that his affidavit failed to establish probable cause" (emphasis added). Does this not require that the trial court look at the actual facts of the case, even the facts as they are known to the defendant? Any doubt that this would involve a closer judicial inspection of the facts was removed the following Term in **Anderson v. Creighton**, 483 U.S. 635, 107 S.Ct. 3034, 97 L.Ed.2d 523 (1987), in a context involving "probable cause": "the determination whether it was objectively legally reasonable to conclude that a given search was supported by probable cause or exigent circumstances will often require examination of the information possessed by the searching officials. * * * [The judge must ask] the objective (albeit fact-specific) question whether a reasonable officer could have believed [this defendant's] warrantless search to be lawful, in light of clearly estab-lished law and the information the searching officers possessed."

2. The Court creates in *Malley* the "reasonable officer"—the hypotheti-cally objectively reasonable person who would make the correct decision under the facts presented. In **Saucier v. Katz**, 533 U.S. 194, 121 S.Ct. 2151, 150 L.Ed.2d 272 (2001), the Court considered a claim of excessive force claim brought by a heckler demonstrating at a public event, a type of case that had produced some confusion in the lower courts because both the excessive force claim and the qualified immunity defense ostensibly turn on how an "objec-tively reasonable police officer" would act under the circumstances. Compare *Malley* with Graham v. Connor, Chapter 1B.3 supra. The Ninth Circuit held that the two issues merge into one that should be decided by the trier of fact. The Supreme Court reversed, observing that this approach, by requiring all immunity claims to go to trial, negates the central idea of qualified immunity: it is " 'an immunity from suit' rather than a mere defense to liability; and ... it is effectively lost if a case is erroneously permitted to go to trial." In trying to explain the difference between the "reasonable officer" inquiry in the two contexts, the Court first noted that *Graham* requires consideration of several objective factors. It continued, 533 U.S. at 205–06, 121 S.Ct. at 2158–59:

> "The qualified immunity inquiry, on the other hand, has a further dimension. The concern of the immunity inquiry is to acknowledge that reasonable mistakes can be made as to the legal constraints on particular police conduct. It is sometimes difficult for an officer to determine how the relevant legal doctrine, here excessive force, will apply to the factual situation the officer confronts. An officer might correctly perceive all of the relevant facts but have a mistaken understanding as to whether a particular amount of force is legal in those circumstances. If the officer's mistake as to what the law requires is reasonable, however, the officer is entitled to the immunity defense."

> "*Graham* does not always give a clear answer as to whether a particular application of force will be deemed excessive by the courts. This is the nature of a test which must accommodate limitless factual circumstances [and] must be elaborated from case to case. Qualified immunity operates in this case, then, just as it does in others, to protect officers from the sometimes 'hazy border between excessive and accept-

able force,' and to ensure that before they are subjected to suit, officers are on notice their conduct is unlawful.''

* * * Officers can have reasonable, but mistaken, beliefs as to the facts establishing the existence of probable cause or exigent circumstances, for example, and in those situations courts will not hold that they have violated the Constitution. Yet, even if a court were to hold that the officer violated the Fourth Amendment by conducting an unreasonable, warrantless search, *Anderson* still operates to grant officers immunity for reasonable mistakes as to the legality of their actions.''

Does *Saucier* stand for the proposition that even reasonable officers may occasionally behave unreasonably? Does it simply add another layer of deference that reviewing courts owe to police officers?

(b) Turning to the very case before it, the Court determined that the "gratuitously violent shove" that the officer applied to the plaintiff was insufficient: "[a] reasonable officer in petitioner's position could have believed that hurrying respondent away from the scene * * * was within the bounds of appropriate police responses" given that the officer "did not know the full extent of the threat [the plaintiff heckler] posed or how many other persons there might be who, in concert with respondent, posed a threat to" the speaker being heckled. The Court also referred to the "urgency" of the situation. 533 U.S. at 209–10, 121 S.Ct. at 2159–60. Does *Saucier*'s application of its new approach show that the Court has in fact returned to the pre-*Harlow* test of "good faith"? Is the test now "good faith" in light of clearly established law? Is the qualified immunity issue only different from the merits because of the introduction of this element?[1]

(c) The Court's *Malley* approach of asking whether law is settled as to the specific facts of the pending case has spread beyond the confines of the Fourth Amendment. See, e.g., Hope v. Pelzer, 536 U.S. 730, 122 S.Ct. 2508, 153 L.Ed.2d 666 (2002) (involving an Eighth Amendment claim and carefully showing that the facts of the hitching post matched other favorable precedents, not unfavorable ones); Conn v. Gabbert, 526 U.S. 286, 119 S.Ct. 1292, 143 L.Ed.2d 399 (1999) (Substantive Due Process "right to engage in a calling" not applicable to alleged facts). Cf. United States v. Lanier, 520 U.S. 259, 117 S.Ct. 1219, 137 L.Ed.2d 432 (1997) (substantive Due Process claim); Tenenbaum v. Williams, 193 F.3d 581 (2d Cir.1999) (substantive due process claim to family privacy).

3. To the extent that *Malley* and *Saucier* may give judges a role in making an early determination of the merits of a claim, it has been accentuated by another development—the characterization of official immunity as not simply an affirmative defense, but an "immunity from suit," **Mitchell v.**

---

1. Does the issue of the "clarity" of constitutional law necessarily, see the preceding Note, require some appreciation of the facts of the pending case—regardless of the area of constitutional law—so that a judge will know with respect to what acts the law is settled? See Markham v. White, 172 F.3d 486 (7th Cir.1999) (case law generally shows different treatment based on sex is unconstitutional in educational setting; "[c]ontrary to the defendants' argument, the fact that neither this court nor any other has ever dealt with a situation involving [crotch-grabbing at] a short training seminar conducted for narcotics officers" does not make applicable legal rules unsettled). Was the *Saucier* approach not new, but rather always implicit in *Harlow*'s "settled law" standard?

Forsyth, 472 U.S. 511, 105 S.Ct. 2806, 86 L.Ed.2d 411 (1985). There the Court explained that denial of some immunity claims is reviewable by interlocutory appeal because ordinary appeal comes too late to protect official's interest in avoiding not just liability but the very burden of standing trial. Reconsider *Harlow*'s policy basis for changing the terms of the qualified immunity defense. Was the idea of a immunity from the burden of defending suit also implicit there? Do *Harlow* and *Saucier* subtly push judges into deciding the facts and the merits of the plaintiff's claim, denying the right to jury trial in cases where the qualified immunity is accepted?[2]

4.   In **City of Monterey v. Del Monte Dunes, Ltd.**, 526 U.S. 687, 119 S.Ct. 1624, 143 L.Ed.2d 882 (1999), the Supreme Court held that "a § 1983 suit seeking legal relief is an action at law within the meaning of the Seventh Amendment" and that "[d]amages for a constitutional violation are a legal remedy." The practical result is that the Seventh Amendment right to jury trial attaches to § 1983 cases. Moreover, significant provisions in the Federal Rules of Civil Procedure seek to preserve the right to jury trial (or at least to a full adversary trial before the judge in a non-jury case) by preventing the entry of judgment in cases where there are disputed issues of fact outstanding. See FRCP 12(b)(6) (dismissal for failure to state a claim), 56 (summary judgment). Cf. FRCP 50 (judgment as a matter of law at and after trail). How does qualified immunity work in the context of these constitutional and FRCP-based rules?

(a) *Rule 8(c)*. The Court has held that qualified immunity is an affirmative defense to be pled by the defendant, see Gomez v. Toledo, 446 U.S. 635, 100 S.Ct. 1920, 64 L.Ed.2d 572 (1980), but raising the issue by pleading under FRCP 8(c) merely preserves it for trial—a point too late to protect the claimant against the time and expense of trial.[3] What mechanisms are open to the defendant for a quick resolution of his qualified immunity defense? In Behrens v. Pelletier, 516 U.S. 299, 116 S.Ct. 834, 133 L.Ed.2d 773 (1996), the Supreme Court noted that primarily Rules 12 and 56 of the Federal Rules of Civil Procedure would provide the desired mechanisms.

(b) *Rule 12(b)(6)*. A motion to dismiss under FRCP 12(b)(6) accepts the opponent's allegations and associated inferences as true, for purposes of the motion. See Conley v. Gibson, 355 U.S. 41, 78 S.Ct. 99, 2 L.Ed.2d 80 (1957). Such motions to dismiss appear to be helpful in asserting the qualified immunity defense only in the simplest cases involving inartful pleading. Where the plaintiff alleges facts that would state a violation of settled law if believed, this device cannot not be used to advance the defendant's qualified immunity defense. See Evans–Marshall v. Board of Educ. of Tipp City Exempted Village School Dist., 428 F.3d 223 (6th Cir. 2005) (allegations satisfy elements of offence under First–Amendment balancing test); McSherry

---

2. What is the difference between the merits of a Fourth Amendment claim under Graham v. Connor, Chapter 1B.3 supra, and the merits of an official immunity defense if both use an objective test of reasonableness? See Katz v. United States, 194 F.3d 962 (9th Cir.1999). See Urbonya, *Problematic Standards of Reasonableness: Qualified Immunity in Section 1983 Action for a Police Officer's Use of Excessive Force*, 62 TEMPLE L. REV. 61 (1989).

3. Some courts have a "heightened pleading" requirement for plaintiffs who encounter a qualified immunity defense, but while this raises the barrier for plaintiff, it does not guarantee the dismissal of the complaint. See Anderson v. Pasadena Independent School Dist., 184 F.3d 439 (5th Cir.1999) (collecting cases).

v. City of Long Beach, 423 F.3d 1015 (9th Cir. 2005) (since plaintiff's facts must be accepted as true, when plaintiff pleads sufficient facts, the goal of allowing the defendant to avoid all expenses of trial cannot be accomplished).[4] Typical of the cases is this statement from Jones v. Hunt, 410 F.3d 1221, 1231 n.7: "[w]e emphasize that our disposition of this case is largely dictated by the Rule 12(b)(6) standard. Jones' complaint effectively portrays the encounter at issue as an unjustified seizure in light of clearly established law, and we must accept her allegations as true."

(c) *Rule 56*. A party may go behind the pleadings by use of a motion for summary judgment under FRCP 56. Such a motion may be made and supported by the movant's affidavit, and when so made, the opposing party may not rest on her allegations but must come forward with responsive factual evidence to show that a material issue of fact exists. Only if there is no disputed material issue may the judge grant summary judgment. See FED. R. CIV. P. 56(c & e); Celotex Corp. v. Catrett, 477 U.S. 317, 106 S.Ct. 2548, 91 L.Ed.2d 265 (1986). This appears to be the most useful vehicle for raising qualified immunity claims in the *Malley* context, where facts beyond those in the complaint may be necessary for the defendant to show his version of the facts. See Brosseau v. Haugen, 543 U.S. 194, 125 S.Ct. 596, 160 L.Ed.2d 583 (2004) (extensive evidence supplied by defendant and other officers to show circumstances of shooting), discussed in the previous Note. Yet even here, if there is indeed a disputed issue of fact, the plaintiff's version and all inferences favorable to her will prevail, and this may well preclude summary judgment. See Groh v. Ramirez, 540 U.S. 551, 124 S.Ct. 1284, 157 L.Ed.2d 1068 (2004) (position taken by agent might prevail if true, but it is contradicted by plaintiff's evidence in opposition to summary judgment, which must be accepted for purposes of Rule 56). In the circuit courts, award of immunity often turns on whether facts sufficient to state a claim, based on settled law, remain at the summary judgment stage. Compare Abdullahi v. City of Madison, 423 F.3d 763 (7th Cir. 2005) (no summary judgment on qualified immunity because factual disputes adequate to support plaintiff remain), with McCormick v. City of Fort Lauderdale, 333 F.3d 1234 (11th Cir. 2003) (no facts in dispute after deposition of plaintiff; probable cause established).

5. Now consider the interaction between the motions considered above and the other procedural issues raised by qualified immunity, discovery and interlocutory appeals. *Harlow* held that discovery should normally be stayed while the trial court rules on a claim of qualified immunity. The staying of discovery also serves the goal of protecting the defendant from the time and expense of trial.

(a) Staying discovery would seem possible if the only issue were the simple one envisioned in *Harlow*—whether, on the facts alleged, constitutional law is settled. But when a defendant moves under Rule 56 to add further

---

4. Would the same be true for claims asserting *absolute* immunity defenses? For example, if the complaint alleged that "D, acting as a member of the ABC Review Board, entered an order denying my right to build a house," would it be subject to dismissal under Rule 12(b)(6) based on absolute immunity? See Buckles v. King County, 191 F.3d 1127 (9th Cir.1999) (illustrating facts used in considering motion to dismiss).

facts, is it fair to halt discovery? After all, under *Celotex*, the plaintiff must respond with countervailing affidavits or discovery to show that there exists a dispute over the facts. Is not discovery required in these circumstances? Should the discovery be limited to the facts related to the qualified immunity claim? See Anderson v. Creighton, 483 U.S. 635, 646 n. 6, 107 S.Ct. 3034, 3042 n. 6, 97 L.Ed.2d 523 (1987) (some discovery may be necessary where factual basis for immunity claim is uncertain). For example, an officer may assert sufficient facts that a reasonable officer would have thought that he had probable cause; a plaintiff may need to discover whether the officer actually knew those facts when the warrant was sought. See, e.g., Carr v. Tatangelo, 338 F.3d 1259 (11th Cir. 2003) (officers establish probable cause with their own unrebutted statements that they heard "distinctive sound" of chambering of bullet in victim's gun, thus giving probable cause to believe there was a danger).

(b) In addition to restrictions on discovery, *Harlow*'s progeny have also permitted an immediate interlocutory appeal by an immunity claimant dissatisfied with a trial court's refusal to accord him qualified immunity. See Mitchell v. Forsyth, 472 U.S. 511, 105 S.Ct. 2806, 86 L.Ed.2d 411 (1985).[5] In **Johnson v. Jones**, 515 U.S. 304, 313–19, 115 S.Ct. 2151, 132 L.Ed.2d 238 (1995), a police misconduct case, the Court revisited the issue of interlocutory appeals and once again noted the difference between immunity appeals based on undisputed facts and those in which there remained factual contests precluding summary judgment. About the latter, it held that a trial court's "determination that the summary judgment record in this case raised a genuine issue of fact concerning [the defendant's actual conduct] in the alleged beating of respondent was not a 'final decision'" subject to immediate appeal. Only an issue of law relating to whether constitutional law was settled, "not a district court's determination about what factual issues are 'genuine,'" qualifies for *Mitchell*'s immediate appeals. Why? Does *Johnson* "threaten[] to undercut the very policy (protecting public officials from lawsuits)" that *Mitchell* sought to achieve?[6]

6. The inability of usual procedural rules to accommodate the interests served by qualified immunity apparently has led the Supreme Court to try another approach—more closely scrutinizing whether a § 1983 plaintiff has even stated a claim for relief on which the claim may proceed. In **Ashcroft v. Iqbal**, ___ U.S. ___, 129 S.Ct. 1937, 173 L.Ed.2d 868 (2009), the Court faced a claim by a Pakistani Muslim that he had been detained by order of top government officials, including the Attorney General and Director of the FBI, based solely on his religion and race. (He also charged lower officials with

---

5. Does the right to interlocutory review apply when the § 1983 claim is brought in state courts that have no interlocutory review? Do any of the aspects of qualified immunity discussed in this Note apply in state courts that have different procedural rules? See Johnson v. Fankell, 520 U.S. 911, 117 S.Ct. 1800, 138 L.Ed.2d 108 (1997). If yes, is it because the immunity is a substantive component of § 1983 that state courts must enforce?

6. If an appellate court rejects an appeal under *Johnson* because the facts remain in dispute (or because the facts not in dispute are insufficient to show that the defendant acted in the absence of settled constitutional law), it is possible that after further discovery those facts may become undisputed. May the defendant appeal once again, this time properly within *Mitchell*? See Behrens v. Pelletier, 516 U.S. 299, 116 S.Ct. 834, 133 L.Ed.2d 773 (1996).

excessive use of force, but those claims were not before the Court.) Admitting the difficulty in applying the usual procedural mechanisms to a qualified immunity defense, the Court turned its attention to the basic pleading requirements of Rule 8(a), which requires a "short and plain statement of the claim showing that the pleader is entitled to relief." Amplifying on a recent precedent regarding antitrust conspiracies, the Court found the plaintiff's complaint wanting, 129 S.Ct. at 1949–50:

> First, * * * [t]hreadbare recitals of the elements of a cause of action, supported by mere conclusory statements, do not suffice. * * * Rule 8 marks a notable and generous departure from the hyper-technical, code-pleading regime of a prior era, but it does not unlock the doors of discovery for a plaintiff armed with nothing more than conclusions. Second, only a complaint that states a plausible claim for relief survives a motion to dismiss. Determining whether a complaint states a plausible claim for relief will, as the Court of Appeals observed, be a context-specific task that requires the reviewing court to draw on its judicial experience and common sense.

Applying these tenets, the Court found Iqbal's complaint inadequate because it merely restated boilerplate elements of claims of discrimination, devoid of factual context connecting the high officials to the policies he claimed had been adopted.

(a) How specific would a claim need to be to meet the Court's pleading requirements? In Erickson v. Pardus, 551 U.S. 89, 127 S.Ct. 2197, 167 L.Ed.2d 1081 (2007) (pre-*Iqbal* but applying the same standards), the Court upheld as adequate a complaint by a prisoner that he had been denied medical care in violation of the Eighth Amendment. The complaint named the disease, prior treatment, withdrawal of treatment, and the harm that withdrawal would do to the plaintiff. What more could Iqbal have alleged that would have provided such equivalent specificity? Does *Iqbal* in effect preclude constitutional (especially discrimination) claims when a plaintiff has only a suspicion of misconduct but no actual facts to back up his suspicions? See Suzette M. Malveaux, *Front Loading and Heavy Lifting: How Pre–Dismissal Discovery Can Address the Detrimental Effect of* Iqbal *on Civil Rights Cases*, 14 Lewis & Clark L. Rev. 65, 82 (2010) ("At this early juncture in the litigation, legal conclusions may be the best a plaintiff can offer when the requisite proof of plausibility is in the exclusive possession of the defendant and can only be revealed via discovery"). Does *Iqbal* in effect create a special immunity for higher government officials?

(b) Does the plausibility factor from *Iqbal* give trial judges too much discretion in deciding which cases may stay in court? See Malveaux, supra, at 92: "Where a judge has only his 'judicial experience and common sense' to guide him when determining the plausibility of an intentional discrimination claim pre-discovery, there is the risk of unpredictability, lack of uniformity, and confusion."

E. STATE–LAW DEFENSES AND SECTIONS 1988 AND 1738

WILSON v. GARCIA

Supreme Court of the United States, 1985.
471 U.S. 261, 105 S.Ct. 1938, 85 L.Ed.2d 254.

JUSTICE STEVENS delivered the opinion of the Court.

In this case we must determine the most appropriate state statute of limitations to apply to claims enforceable under § 1 of the Civil Rights Act of 1871, which is codified in its present form as 42 U.S.C. § 1983.

On January 28, 1982, respondent brought this § 1983 action in the United States District Court for the District of New Mexico seeking "money damages to compensate him for the deprivation of his civil rights guaranteed by the Fourth, Fifth and Fourteenth Amendments to the United States Constitution and for the personal injuries he suffered which were caused by the acts and omissions of the [petitioners] acting under color of law." App. 4. The complaint alleged that on April 27, 1979, petitioner Wilson, a New Mexico State Police Officer, unlawfully arrested the respondent, "brutally and viciously" beat him, and sprayed his face with tear gas; that petitioner Vigil, the Chief of the New Mexico State Police, had notice of Officer Wilson's allegedly "violent propensities," and had failed to reprimand him for committing other unprovoked attacks on citizens; and that Vigil's training and supervision of Wilson was seriously deficient.

The respondent's complaint was filed two years and nine months after the claim purportedly arose. Petitioners moved to dismiss on the ground that the action was barred by the 2–year statute of limitations contained in § 41–4–15(A) of the New Mexico Tort Claims Act. The petitioners' motion was supported by a decision of the New Mexico Supreme Court which squarely held that the Tort Claims Act provides "the most closely analogous state cause of action" to § 1983, and that its two-year statute of limitations is therefore applicable to actions commenced under § 1983 in the state courts. DeVargas v. New Mexico, 97 N.M. 563, 642 P.2d 166 (1982). In addition to the 2–year statute of limitations in the Tort Claims Act, two other New Mexico statutes conceivably could apply to § 1983 claims: § 37–1–8, which provides a 3–year limitation period for actions "for an injury to the person or reputation of any person"; and § 37–1–4, which provides a 4–year limitation period for "all other actions not herein otherwise provided for." If either of these longer statutes applies to the respondent's § 1983 claim, the complaint was timely filed.

[The District Court and Court of Appeals found the shorter time period inapplicable.]

I

The Reconstruction Civil Rights Acts do not contain a specific statute of limitations governing § 1983 actions—"a void which is commonplace in federal statutory law." Board of Regents v. Tomanio, 446 U.S. 478, 483, 100 S.Ct. 1790, 1794, 64 L.Ed.2d 440 (1980). When Congress has not established a time limitation for a federal cause of action, the settled practice has been to adopt a local time limitation as federal law if it is not inconsistent with federal law or policy to do so. In 42 U.S.C. § 1988, Congress has implicitly endorsed this approach with respect to claims enforceable under the Reconstruction Civil Rights Acts.

The language of § 1988,[13] directs the courts to follow "a three-step process" in determining the rules of decision applicable to civil rights claims:

> "First, courts are to look to the laws of the United States 'so far as such laws are suitable to carry [the civil and criminal civil rights statutes] into effect.' [42 U.S.C. § 1988.] If no suitable federal rule exists, courts undertake the second step by considering application of state 'common law, as modified and changed by the constitution and statutes' of the forum state. A third step asserts the predominance of the federal interest: courts are to apply state law only if it is not 'inconsistent with the Constitution and laws of the United States.' " Burnett v. Grattan, 468 U.S. [42, 48,] 104 S.Ct. 2924, 2929, 82 L.Ed.2d 36 (1984).

This case principally involves the second step in the process: the selection of "the most appropriate," or "the most analogous" state statute of limitations to apply to this § 1983 claim.

In order to determine the most "most appropriate" or "most analogous" New Mexico statute to apply to the respondent's claim, we must answer three questions. We must first consider whether state law or federal law governs the characterization of a § 1983 claim for statute of limitations purposes. If federal law applies, we must next decide whether all § 1983 claims should be characterized in the same way, or whether they should be evaluated differently depending upon the varying factual circumstances and legal theories presented in each individual case. Finally, we must characterize the essence of the claim in the pending case, and decide which state statute provides the most appropriate limiting principle. Although the text of neither § 1983 nor § 1988 provides a pellucid answer to any of these questions, all three parts of the inquiry are, in final analysis, questions of statutory construction.

---

13. Title 42 U.S.C. § 1988 provides, in relevant part:

"The jurisdiction in civil and criminal matters conferred on the district courts by the provisions of this Title, and of Title 'CIVIL RIGHTS,' and of Title 'CRIMES,' for the protection of all persons in the United States in their civil rights, and for their vindication, shall be exercised and enforced in conformity with the laws of the United States, so far as such laws are suitable to carry the same into effect; but in all cases where they are not adapted to the object, or are deficient in the provisions necessary to furnish suitable remedies and punish offenses against law, the common law, as modified and changed by the constitution and statutes of the State wherein the court having jurisdiction of such civil or criminal cause is held, so far as the same is not inconsistent with the Constitution and laws of the United States, shall be extended to and govern the said courts in the trial and disposition of the cause...."

II

Our identification of the correct source of law properly begins with the text of § 1988. Congress' first instruction in the statute is that the law to be applied in adjudicating civil rights claims shall be in "conformity with the laws of the United States, so far as such laws are suitable." 42 U.S.C. § 1988. This mandate implies that resort to state law—the second step in the process—should not be undertaken before principles of federal law are exhausted. The characterization of § 1983 for statute of limitations purposes is derived from the elements of the cause of action, and Congress' purpose in providing it. These, of course, are matters of federal law. Since federal law is available to decide the question, the language of § 1988 directs that the matter of characterization should be treated as a federal question. Only the length of the limitations period, and closely related questions of tolling and application, are to be governed by state law.

This interpretation is also supported by Congress' third instruction in § 1988: state law shall only apply "so far as the same is not inconsistent with" federal law. This requirement emphasizes "the predominance of the federal interest" in the borrowing process, taken as a whole. Burnett v. Grattan. Even when principles of state law are borrowed to assist in the enforcement of this federal remedy, the state rule is adopted as "a federal rule responsive to the need whenever a federal right is impaired." Sullivan v. Little Hunting Park, Inc., 396 U.S. 229, 240, 90 S.Ct. 400, 406, 24 L.Ed.2d 386 (1969). The importation of the policies and purposes of the States on matters of civil rights is not the primary office of the borrowing provision in § 1988; rather, the statute is designed to assure that neutral rules of decision will be available to enforce the civil rights actions, among them § 1983. Congress surely did not intend to assign to state courts and legislatures a conclusive role in the formative function of defining and characterizing the essential elements of a federal cause of action.

* * * So here, the federal interest in uniformity and [clearly ascertainable rules supports] the conclusion that Congress intended the characterization of § 1983 to be measured by federal rather than state standards. The Court of Appeals was therefore correct in concluding that it was not bound by the New Mexico Supreme Court's holding in *DeVargas*.

III

A federal cause of action "brought at any distance of time" would be "utterly repugnant to the genius of our laws." Adams v. Woods, [6 U.S. (2 Cranch)] 336, 341, 2 L.Ed. 297 (1805). Just determinations of fact cannot be made when, because of the passage of time, the memories of witnesses have faded or evidence is lost. In compelling circumstances, even wrongdoers are entitled to assume that their sins may be forgotten.

The borrowing of statutes of limitations for § 1983 claims serves these policies of repose. Of course, the application of *any* statute of limitations would promote repose. By adopting the statute governing an analogous cause of action under state law, federal law incorporates the State's judgment on the proper balance between the policies of repose and the substantive policies of enforcement embodied in the state cause of action. However, when the federal claim differs from the state cause of action in fundamental respects, the State's choice of a specific period of limitation is, at best, only a rough approximation of "the point at which the interests in favor of protecting valid claims are outweighed by the interests in prohibiting the prosecution of stale ones." Johnson v. Railway Express Agency, Inc., 421 U.S. 454, 463–464, 95 S.Ct. 1716, 1721–1722, 44 L.Ed.2d 295 (1975).

Thus, in considering whether all § 1983 claims should be characterized in the same way for limitations purposes, it is useful to recall that § 1983 provides "a uniquely federal remedy against incursions under the claimed authority of state law upon rights secured by the Constitution and laws of the Nation." Mitchum v. Foster, 407 U.S. 225, 239, 92 S.Ct. 2151, 2160, 32 L.Ed.2d 705 (1972). The high purposes of this unique remedy make it appropriate to accord the statute "a sweep as broad as its language." Because the § 1983 remedy is one that can "override certain kinds of state laws," Monroe v. Pape, and is, in all events, "supplementary to any remedy any State might have," it can have no precise counterpart in state law. Monroe v. Pape (Harlan, J., concurring). Therefore, it is "the purest coincidence," *ibid.*, when state statutes or the common law provide for equivalent remedies; any analogies to those causes of action are bound to be imperfect.[23]

* * *

When § 1983 was enacted, it is unlikely that Congress actually foresaw the wide diversity of claims that the new remedy would ultimately embrace. The simplicity of the admonition in § 1988 is consistent with the assumption that Congress intended the identification of the appropriate statute of limitations to be an uncomplicated task for judges, lawyers and litigants, rather than a source of uncertainty, and unproductive and ever increasing litigation. Moreover, the legislative purpose to create an effective remedy for the enforcement of federal civil rights is obstructed by uncertainty in the applicable statute of limitations, for scarce resources must be dissipated by useless litigation on collateral matters.

Although the need for national uniformity "has not been held to warrant the displacement of state statutes of limitations for civil rights actions," Board of Regents v. Tomanio, uniformity within each State is entirely consistent with the borrowing principle contained in § 1988. We conclude that the statute is fairly construed as a directive to select, in each State, the one most appropriate statute of limitations for all § 1983 claims. The federal interests in uniformity, certainty, and the minimiza-

---

23. For this reason the adoption of one analogy rather than another will often be somewhat arbitrary; in such a case, the losing party may "infer that the choice of a limitations period in his case was result oriented, thereby undermining his belief that he has been dealt with fairly."

tion of unnecessary litigation all support the conclusion that Congress favored this simple approach.

IV

After exhaustively reviewing the different ways that § 1983 claims have been characterized in every Federal Circuit, the Court of Appeals concluded that the tort action for the recovery of damages for personal injuries is the best alternative available.

* * *

Finally, we are satisfied that Congress would not have characterized § 1983 as providing a cause of action analogous to state remedies for wrongs committed by public officials. It was the very ineffectiveness of state remedies that led Congress to enact the Civil Rights Acts in the first place. Congress therefore intended that the remedy provided in § 1983 be independently enforceable whether or not it duplicates a parallel state remedy. Monroe v. Pape. The characterization of all § 1983 actions as involving claims for personal injuries minimizes the risk that the choice of a state statute of limitations would not fairly serve the federal interests vindicated by § 1983. General personal injury actions, sounding in tort, constitute a major part of the total volume of civil litigation in the state courts today, and probably did so in 1871 when § 1983 was enacted. It is most unlikely that the period of limitations applicable to such claims ever was, or ever would be, fixed in a way that would discriminate against federal claims, or be inconsistent with federal law in any respect.

V

In view of our holding that § 1983 claims are best characterized as personal injury actions, the Court of Appeals correctly applied the 3–year statute of limitations governing actions "for an injury to the person or reputation of any person." N.M.Stat.Ann. § 37–1–8 (1978). The judgment of the Court of Appeals is affirmed.

It is so ordered.

JUSTICE POWELL took no part in the consideration or decision of this case.

JUSTICE O'CONNOR, dissenting. [Omitted]

NOTE ON SECTION 1988 AND PERMISSIBLE RESORT TO STATE LAW

1.   The supplementation of § 1983 with state-law rules ordinarily occurs in the context of defenses, since the language of the statute appears to be deficient primarily with respect to defenses. Liability issues appear to be rather fully covered by the statute's allusions to constitutional or other federal law, with some analytical problems. See Chapter 1A–C supra. *Wilson* holds that in some circumstances, the supplementation should occur by resort to state law, yet even when that occurs, federal concerns with uniformity and evenhandedness can influence the choice of the appropriate supplementary state law.

(a) The Court assumes that § 1983 is "deficient" because it has no statute of limitations of its own. How does the Court know that this is a deficiency? Why does the Court not simply leave § 1983 with no statute of limitations, relying solely on some type of laches principle to rule out seriously stale cases? Note the citation to the 1805 decision in Adams v. Woods. Is the Court reading a state statute of limitations into § 1983 because the Justices want the security of having an easily determinable standard? Does this suggest that the Court would have resorted to state law even in the absence of § 1988?

(b) The Court holds that every § 1983 action should be analogized to a single statute of limitation in each state, primarily in order to settle easily the question of an applicable limitations period. What should happen when the state has multiple statutes of limitations for personal injury actions? To which should a court turn? See Owens v. Okure, 488 U.S. 235, 109 S.Ct. 573, 102 L.Ed.2d 594 (1989) (noting its choice was between "the intentional torts approach and the general or residual personal injury approach"). When that problem is solved and uniformity is gained, it is uniformity only within the state, is it not? The statute of limitations applicable to § 1983 claims will still vary from state to state, will it not? Why is this state-to-state variation not a major concern? Would it be better policy to legislate a specific federal statute of limitations for all § 1983 claims? See 28 U.S.C. § 1658 (four-year limitations period for all federal-question claims based on statutes passed after 1991).

(c) The question of whether to resort to state law is under *Wilson* a federal question. Similarly, the issue of which state law to choose is a federal question. Does this double-barreled federal control over resort to state law ensure that federal concerns will not be lost when state law is adopted? Or does labeling these two issues "federal questions" create the mere illusion of federal protection: since there are no clear standards to apply in deciding these questions, a Court disposed to abandoning federal interests may easily do so?

2. Viewed more generically, *Wilson* provides a two-step (perhaps three-step) analysis. First, the Court may make a federal common law to control an issue, if appropriate. Second, if no federal law if found or made, § 1988 permits resort to state law to fill any deficiency. Third (or perhaps as a qualification inherent in step two), the court may yet turn away from any particular state law if that law is somehow inappropriate. Consider the following standard defense issues; should each be controlled by creating federal common law or adopting state law?

(a) *Wilson* holds that the limitations period should be governed by state law, but should the same be true for tolling rules? See Board of Regents v. Tomanio, cited in *Wilson*, (state tolling rules apply).

(b) The date on which the statute of limitations begins to run is the accrual date. It is controlled by federal law without reference to state law. Wallace v. Kato, 549 U.S. 384, 127 S.Ct. 1091, 166 L.Ed.2d 973 (2007). Yet in Wallace the Court referred repeated to torts treatises and deciding the case by analogizing the plaintiff's § 1983 claim to the most similar common-law tort, then adopting the common-law rule for accrual of such claims. Is the "federal rule" that of adopting the general common law? If so, is the real difference between tolling and accrual rules the difference between a specific state's tolling rule and the general common law's accrual rule? Might a purer federal rule be better? See Chardon v. Fernandez, 454 U.S. 6, 102 S.Ct. 28, 70 L.Ed.2d 6 (1981) (claim accrual governed by federal law; under it the limitations period begins to run when plaintiff learns of harm; in employment context that is on day of notification of discharge, not on last day of work).

(c) Should survivorship of claims—the continuation of claims when the plaintiff dies during the course of litigation for reasons not related to his claim—be governed by federal or state law? See Robertson v. Wegmann, 436 U.S. 584, 98 S.Ct. 1991, 56 L.Ed.2d 554 (1978) (unusual Louisiana rule extinguishing claims upon plaintiff's death applied).

3.   Does resort to § 1988 invariably help defendants by expanding their defenses? Or might some state rules actually assist plaintiffs? Consider the following issues.

(a) Some states provide special tolling rules for prisoners on the theory that their incarceration makes it more difficult to meet state limitations periods for filing suits. Should these apply to § 1983 actions by prisoners? See Hardin v. Straub, 490 U.S. 536, 109 S.Ct. 1998, 104 L.Ed.2d 582 (1989) (yes).

(b) Section 1988 has also aided plaintiffs with wrongful death claims, claims that are not specifically authorized by § 1983. These are deemed resurrected when state wrongful death statutory doctrines are read into § 1983. See Brazier v. Cherry, 293 F.2d 401 (5th Cir.1961). When the state law concepts are so adopted, defendants often argue that the plaintiff should be required to "take the bitter with the sweet"—and thus that any state-law limitations on recovery should also be adopted. Should any attendant limitations attached to the state law, such as a ceiling on the amount of recovery, also apply to the § 1983 claim? See Bell v. Milwaukee, 746 F.2d 1205, 1234–41 (7th Cir.1984) (state wrongful death statute may extend deceased's § 1983 claim, but burdensome limitations not applicable).

(c) Section 1983 is apparently silent with respect to municipal indemnification of officers found liable. If state law authorizes and requires indemnification, should that law be read into § 1983? See Graham v. Sauk Prairie Police Commission, 915 F.2d 1085 (7th Cir.1990). If so, is this an adoption favorable to the defendant or to the plaintiff? If state law simply applies collaterally (by, for example, giving the officer a claim against her employer municipality), may the federal court incorporate that idea into the federal judgment? See DiSorbo v. Hoy, 343 F.3d 172 (2d Cir. 2003) (actual provisions of state law govern, including any state court rulings concerning indemnification in the instant case). How should courts resolve third-party claims against insurance companies for indemnification? See Coleman v. School Bd. of Richland Parish, 418 F.3d 511 (5th Cir. 2005) (policy provisions apply as ordinary contract).

4.   If state law is to be presumptively adopted under § 1988, when should courts reject it, see step the third step in ¶ 2 supra, because it is inconsistent with the goals of § 1983? See, Burnett v. Grattan, 468 U.S. 42, 104 S.Ct. 2924, 82 L.Ed.2d 36 (1984) (state limitations law not followed if it contains too-short administrative time limit). How short is too short?

5. Does the principle captured in § 1988 reflect concerns similar to those seen in other aspects of federal litigation? Recall, for example, that in diversity litigation in federal courts we have since 1938 followed a refined version of the proposition that state law should govern "substance," while federal law may govern "procedure." See Erie R.R. Co. v. Tompkins, 304 U.S. 64, 58 S.Ct. 817, 82 L.Ed. 1188 (1938). Are the roles simply reversed when it is a federally created claim that is being enforced?

(a) Which rules are ones of "substance"? Of "procedure"? The *Erie* doctrine was considerably refined in later cases to emphasize whether state law would "discriminate" against some litigants or whether failure to follow them would lead to state-federal forum-shopping. See Hanna v. Plumer, 380 U.S. 460, 85 S.Ct. 1136, 14 L.Ed.2d 8 (1965). Are those—or similar—concerns applicable in the decision whether to supplement § 1983 with state law?

(b) State courts of general jurisdiction are also open to § 1983 claims. See Howlett v. Rose, 496 U.S. 356, 110 S.Ct. 2430, 110 L.Ed.2d 332 (1990). Does § 1988 (or the Supremacy Clause) also compel state courts to follow federal law relating to § 1983? Must state courts follow the federalized version of state law in § 1983 suits filed in state court? Or do these become state law questions when the action is filed in state court?

FELDER v. CASEY

Supreme Court of the United States, 1988.
487 U.S. 131, 108 S.Ct. 2302, 101 L.Ed.2d 123.

JUSTICE BRENNAN delivered the opinion of the Court.

A Wisconsin statute provides that before suit may be brought in state court against a state or local governmental entity or officer, the plaintiff must notify the governmental defendant of the circumstances giving rise to the claim, the amount of the claim, and his or her intent to hold the named defendant liable. The statute further requires that, in order to afford the defendant an opportunity to consider the requested relief, the claimant must refrain from filing suit for 120 days after providing such notice. Failure to comply with these requirements constitutes grounds for dismissal of the action. In the present case, the Supreme Court of Wisconsin held that this notice-of-claim statute applies to federal civil rights actions brought in state court under 42 U.S.C. § 1983. Because we conclude that these requirements are preempted as inconsistent with federal law, we reverse.

I

[Felder's § 1983 claim arose from an altercation with police that resulted in the alleged excessive use of force. His suit in state court was dismissed for failure to comply with the state's notice-of-claims statute, the state supreme court ruling that the statute comprised a mere procedural rule that did not limit any substantive federal rights.]

II

No one disputes the general and unassailable proposition relied upon by the Wisconsin Supreme Court below that States may establish the rules of procedure governing litigation in their own courts. By the same token, however, where state courts entertain a federally created cause of action, the "federal right cannot be defeated by the forms of local practice." Brown v. Western Railway of Alabama, 338 U.S. 294, 296, 70 S.Ct. 105, 106, 94 L.Ed. 100 (1949). The question before us today, therefore, is essentially one of preemption: is the application of the State's notice-of-claim provision to § 1983 actions brought in state courts consistent with the goals of the federal civil rights laws, or does the enforcement of such a requirement instead " 'stan[d] as an obstacle to the accomplishment and execution of the full purposes and objectives of Congress' "? Perez v. Campbell, 402 U.S. 637, 649, 91 S.Ct. 1704, 1711, 29 L.Ed.2d 233 (1971) (quoting Hines v. Davidowitz, 312 U.S. 52, 67, 61 S.Ct. 399, 404, 85 L.Ed. 581 (1941)). Under the Supremacy Clause of the Federal Constitution, "[t]he relative importance to the State of its own law is not material when there is a conflict with a valid federal law," for "any state law, however clearly within a State's acknowledged power, which interferes with or is contrary to federal law, must yield." Free v. Bland, 369 U.S. 663, 666, 82 S.Ct. 1089, 1092, 8 L.Ed.2d 180 (1962). Because the notice-of-claim statute at issue here conflicts both in its purpose and effects with the remedial objectives of § 1983, and because its enforcement in such actions will frequently and predictably produce different outcomes in § 1983 litigation based solely on whether the claim is asserted in state or federal court, we conclude that the state law is preempted when the § 1983 action is brought in a state court.

A

Section 1983 creates a species of liability in favor of persons deprived of their federal civil rights by those wielding state authority. As we have repeatedly emphasized, "the central objective of the Reconstruction–Era civil rights statutes ... is to ensure that individuals whose federal constitutional or statutory rights are abridged may recover damages or secure injunctive relief." Burnett v. Grattan, 468 U.S. 42, 55, 104 S.Ct. 2924, 2932, 82 L.Ed.2d 36 (1984). Thus, § 1983 provides "a uniquely federal remedy against incursions ... upon rights secured by the Constitution and laws of the Nation," Mitchum v. Foster, 407 U.S. 225, 239, 92 S.Ct. 2151, 2160, 32 L.Ed.2d 705 (1972), and is to be accorded "a sweep as broad as its language." United States v. Price, 383 U.S. 787, 801, 86 S.Ct. 1152, 1160, 16 L.Ed.2d 267 (1966). Any assessment of the applicability of a state law to federal civil rights litigation, therefore, must be made in light of the purpose and nature of the federal right. This is so whether the question of state-law applicability arises in § 1983 litigation brought in state courts, which possess concurrent jurisdiction over such actions, or in federal-court litigation, where, because the federal civil rights law fail to provide certain rules of decision thought essential to the orderly adjudication of rights, courts are occasionally called upon to borrow state law. See 42 U.S.C. § 1988. Accordingly, we have held that a state law that immunizes government conduct otherwise subject to suit under § 1983 is preempted, even where the federal civil rights litigation takes place in state court, because the application of the state immunity law would thwart the congressional remedy, see Martinez v. California, 444 U.S. 277, 284, 100 S.Ct. 553, 558, 62 L.Ed.2d 481 (1980), which of course already provides certain immunities for state officials. See e.g., Stump v. Sparkman. Similarly, in actions brought in federal courts, we have disapproved the adoption of state statutes of limitation that provide only a truncated period of time within which to file suit, because such statutes inadequately accommodate the complexities of federal civil rights litigation and are thus inconsistent with Congress' compensatory aims. Burnett, supra. And we have directed the lower federal courts in § 1983 cases to borrow the state-law limitations period for personal injury claims because it is "most unlikely that the period of limitations applicable to such claims ever was, or ever would be, fixed [by the forum State] in a way that would discriminate against federal claims, or be inconsistent with federal law in any respect." Wilson v. Garcia.

Although we have never passed on the question, the lower federal courts have all, with but one exception, concluded that notice-of-claim provisions are inapplicable to § 1983 actions brought in federal court. These courts have reasoned that, unlike the lack of statutes of limitations in the federal civil rights laws, the absence of any notice-of-claim provision is not a deficiency requiring the importation of such statutes into the federal civil rights scheme. Because statutes of limitation are among the universally familiar aspects of litigation considered indispensable to any scheme of justice, it is entirely reasonable to assume that Congress did not intend to create a right enforceable in perpetuity. Notice-of-claim provisions, by contrast, are neither universally familiar nor in any sense indispensable prerequisites to litigation, and there is thus no reason to suppose that Congress intended federal courts to apply such rules, which "significantly inhibit the ability to bring federal actions."

While we fully agree with this near unanimous consensus of the federal courts, that judgment is not dispositive here, where the question is not one of adoption but of preemption. Nevertheless, this determination that notice-of-claim statutes are inapplicable to federal-court § 1983 litigation informs our analysis in two crucial respects. First, it demonstrates that the application of the notice requirement burdens the exercise of the federal right by forcing civil rights victims who seek redress in state courts to comply with a requirement that is entirely absent from civil rights litigation in federal courts. This burden, as we explain below, is inconsistent in both design and effect with the compensatory aims of the federal civil rights laws. Second, it reveals that the enforcement of such statutes in § 1983 actions brought in state court will frequently and predictably produce different outcomes in federal civil rights litigation based solely on whether that litigation takes place in state or federal court. States may not apply such an outcome-determinative law when entertaining substantive federal rights in their courts.

B

* * *

[The state's statute was drafted primarily as part of a package that allowed local governments to be sued, but limited the manner in which such claims could be pursued.] The decision to subject state subdivisions to liability for violations of federal rights, however, was a choice that Congress, not the Wisconsin legislature, made, and it is a decision that the State has no authority to override. Thus, however understandable or laudable the State's interest in controlling liability expenses might otherwise be, it is patently incompatible with the compensatory goals of the federal legislation, as are the means the State has chosen to effectuate it.

* * *

This burdening of a federal right, moreover, is not the natural or permissible consequence of an otherwise neutral, uniformly applicable state rule. Although it is true that the notice-of-claim statute does not discriminate between state and federal causes of action against local governments, the fact remains that the law's protection extends only to governmental defendants and thus conditions the right to bring suit against the very persons and entities Congress intended to subject to liability. We therefore cannot accept the suggestion that this requirement is simply part of "the vast body of procedural rules, rooted in policies unrelated to the definition of any particular substantive cause of action, that forms no essential part of 'the cause of action' as applied to any given plaintiff." Brief for International City Management Association et al. as Amici Curiae (Brief for Amici Curiae) 22. On the contrary, the notice-of-claim provision is imposed only upon a specific class of plaintiffs—those who sue governmental defendants—and, as we have seen, is firmly rooted in policies very much related to, and to a large extent directly contrary to, the substantive cause of action provided those plaintiffs. This defendant-specific focus of the notice requirement serves to distinguish it, rather starkly, from rules uniformly applicable to all suits, such as rules governing service of process or substitution of parties, which respondents cite as examples of procedural requirements that penalize noncompliance through dismissal. That state courts will hear the entire § 1983 cause of action once a plaintiff complies with the notice-of-claim statute, therefore, in no way alters the fact that the statute discriminates against the precise type of claim Congress has created.

C

* * *

* * * Federal law takes state courts as it finds them only insofar as those courts employ rules that do not "impose unnecessary burdens upon rights of recovery authorized by federal laws." Brown v. Western R. Co. of Alabama, 338 U.S., at 298–299, 70 S.Ct., at 108; see also Monessen Southwestern R. Co. v. Morgan, 486 U.S. 330, 336, 108 S.Ct. 1837, 100

L.Ed.2d 349 (1988) (state rule designed to encourage settlement cannot limit recovery in federally created action).

* * * As we have seen, enforcement of the notice-of-claim statute in § 1983 actions brought in state court so interferes with and frustrates the substantive right Congress created that, under the Supremacy Clause, it must yield to the federal interest. This interference, however, is not the only consequence of the statute that renders its application in § 1983 cases invalid. In a State that demands compliance with such a statute before a § 1983 action may be brought or maintained in its courts, the outcome of federal civil rights litigation will frequently and predictably depend on whether it is brought in state or federal court. Thus, the very notions of federalism upon which respondents rely dictate that the State's outcome-determinative law must give way when a party asserts a federal right in state court.

Under Erie R. Co. v. Tompkins, 304 U.S. 64, 58 S.Ct. 817, 82 L.Ed. 1188 (1938), when a federal court exercises diversity or pendent jurisdiction over state-law claims, "the outcome of the litigation in the federal court should be substantially the same, so far as legal rules determine the outcome of a litigation, as it would be if tried in a State court." Guaranty Trust Co. v. York, 326 U.S. 99, 109, 65 S.Ct. 1464, 1470, 89 L.Ed. 2079 (1945). Accordingly, federal courts entertaining state-law claims against Wisconsin municipalities are obligated to apply the notice-of-claim provision. See Orthmann v. Apple River Campground, Inc., 757 F.2d 909, 911 (C.A.7 1985). Just as federal courts are constitutionally obligated to apply state law to state claims, so too the Supremacy Clause imposes on state courts a constitutional duty "to proceed in such manner that all the substantial rights of the parties under controlling federal law [are] protected." Garrett v. Moore–McCormack, 317 U.S. 239, 245, 63 S.Ct. 246, 251, 87 L.Ed. 239 (1942).

* * * The state notice-of-claim statute is more than a mere rule of procedure: as we discussed above, the statute is a substantive condition on the right to sue governmental officials and entities, and the federal courts have therefore correctly recognized that the notice statute governs the adjudication of state-law claims in diversity actions. *Orthmann*, supra, at 911. In Guaranty Trust, supra, we held that, in order to give effect to a State's statute of limitations, a federal court could not hear a state-law action that a state court would deem time-barred. Conversely, a state court may not decline to hear an otherwise properly presented federal claim because that claim would be barred under a state law requiring timely filing of notice. State courts simply are not free to vindicate the substantive interests underlying a state rule of decision at the expense of the federal right.

* * *

Accordingly, the judgment of the Supreme Court of Wisconsin is reversed, and the case is remanded for further proceedings not inconsistent with this opinion.

It is so ordered.

JUSTICE WHITE, concurring. [Omitted]

JUSTICE O'CONNOR, with whom CHIEF JUSTICE REHNQUIST joins, dissenting.

"A state statute cannot be considered 'inconsistent' with federal law merely because the statute causes the plaintiff to lose the litigation." Robertson v. Wegmann, 436 U.S. 584, 593, 98 S.Ct. 1991, 56 L.Ed.2d 554 (1978). Disregarding this self-evident principle, the Court today holds that Wisconsin's notice of claim statute is pre-empted by federal law as to actions under 42 U.S.C. § 1983 filed in state court. This holding is not supported by the statute whose preemptive force it purports to invoke, or by our precedents. Relying only on its own intuitions about "the goals of the federal civil rights laws," the Court fashions a new theory of preemption that unnecessarily and improperly suspends a perfectly valid state statute.

* * *

* * * Brown v. Western Railway of Alabama, which is repeatedly quoted by the majority, does not control the present case. In *Brown*, which arose under the Federal Employers' Liability Act (FELA), this Court refused to accept a state court's interpretation of allegations in a complaint asserting a federal statutory right. Concluding that the state court's interpretation of the complaint operated to "detract from 'substantive rights' granted by Congress in FELA cases," the Court "simply h[e]ld that under the facts alleged it was error to dismiss the complaint and that [the claimant] should be allowed to try his case." In the case before us today, by contrast, the statute at issue does not diminish or alter any substantive right cognizable under § 1983. As the majority concedes, the Wisconsin courts "will hear the entire § 1983 cause of action once a plaintiff complies with the notice-of-claim statute."

* * *

The Court also suggests that there is some parallel between this case and cases that are tried in federal court under the doctrine of Erie R. Co. v. Tompkins. Quoting the "outcome-determinative" test of Guaranty Trust Co. v. York, the Court opines today that state courts hearing federal suits are obliged to mirror federal procedures to the same extent that federal courts are obliged to mirror state procedures in diversity suits. This suggestion seems to be based on a sort of upside-down theory of federalism, which the Court attributes to Congress on the basis of no evidence at all. Nor are the implications of this "reverse-*Erie*" theory quite clear. If the Court means the theory to be taken seriously, it should follow that defendants, as well as plaintiffs, are entitled to the benefit of all federal court procedural rules that are "outcome determinative." If, however, the Court means to create a rule that benefits only plaintiffs, then the discussion of *Erie* principles is simply an unsuccessful effort to find some analogy, no matter how attenuated, to today's unprecedented holding. "Borrowing" cases under 42 U.S.C. § 1988, which the Court cites several times, have little more to do with today's decision than does *Erie*. Under that statute and those cases, we are sometimes called upon to fill in gaps in federal law by choosing a state procedural rule for application in § 1983 actions brought in federal court. See, e.g., Wilson v. Garcia. The congressionally imposed necessity of supplementing federal law with state procedural rules might well caution us against supplanting state procedural rules with federal gaps, but it certainly offers no support for what the Court does today.

* * *

As I noted at the outset, the majority correctly characterizes the issue before us as one of statutory preemption. In order to arrive at the result it has chosen, however, the Court is forced to search for "inconsistencies" between Wisconsin's notice of claim statute and some ill-defined federal policy that Congress has never articulated, implied, or suggested, let alone enacted. Nor is there any difficulty in explaining the absence of congressional attention to the problem that the Court wrongly imagines it is solving. A plaintiff who chooses to bring a § 1983 action in state court necessarily rejects the federal courts that Congress has provided. Virtually the only conceivable reason for doing so is to benefit from procedural advantages available exclusively in state court. Having voted with their feet for state procedural systems, such plaintiffs would hardly be in a position to ask Congress for a new type of forum that combines the advantages that Congress gave them in the federal system with those that Congress did not give them, and which are only available in state courts.

* * * I respectfully dissent.

NOTE ON § 1983 IN STATE COURTS

1. Is the answer to the problem posed by *Felder* so difficult because it is essentially based on intuition and subjective factors? Even Justice O'Connor would ask some version of the question whether Wisconsin law is somehow so inconsistent with or so frustrates the scheme of § 1983 that it is to be deemed preempted. Does the answer to the Justices' inquiry turn on legally identifiable concerns, or on one's appreciation of the real experiences of citizens and litigators? The general issue raised by *Felder*, the role of federal law in state court actions invoking § 1983, is exhaustively treated in Steven Steinglass, SECTION 1983 LITIGATION IN STATE COURTS (2010).

(a) Is not Justice Brennan correct in *Felder*? He argues that § 1983 aims to have a certain effectiveness or impact in a neutral procedural system, and therefore the addition of any state rule that would substantially alter the scope of § 1983 under the guise of procedure in effect amends § 1983? Is the important question whether the state-court practice is indeed a significant change?

(b) Do notice-of-claims provisions impair § 1983 claims in any serious way? Is Justice O'Connor correct in stating that such provisions are unimportant because anyone may avoid their impact by simply complying with them? Is a notice-of-claim provisions as unimportant as, for example, a state pleading deadline or a state discovery limitation?

(c) Would Justice O'Connor's argument be stronger if the state law's notice requirement applied to all claims, not simply to claims against government? What role does a notice requirement play? What role does the state want it to play—protecting the courts' resources or protecting the defendant's resources? Should a state be permitted to carry out such a goal when the underlying claim is based on federal rather than state law?

2. The year following the Court's divided action in *Felder,* it unanimously decided **Howlett v. Rose**, 496 U.S. 356, 110 S.Ct. 2430, 110 L.Ed.2d 332 (1990). In that § 1983 case filed in state court, Florida courts had applied a state "sovereign immunity" rule that precluded the plaintiff's constitutional claim against a school board and its officers. Justice Stevens wrote for the Court:

> "[Plaintiff] argues that the [state] court [below] adopted a substantive rule of decision that state agencies are not subject to liability under § 1983. [Defendant], stressing the [state] court's language that it had not 'opened its own courts for federal actions against the state,' argues that the case simply involves the court's refusal to take cognizance of § 1983 actions against state defendants. We conclude that whether the question is framed in pre-emption terms, as [plaintiff] would have it, or in the obligation to assume jurisdiction over a 'federal' cause of action, as [defendant] would have it, the Florida court's refusal to entertain one discrete category of § 1983 claims, when the court entertains similar state law actions against state defendants, violates the Supremacy Clause.

> "If the [state court below] meant to hold that governmental entities subject to § 1983 liability enjoy an immunity over and above those already provided in § 1983, that holding directly violates federal law. The elements of, and the defenses to, a federal cause of action are defined by federal law. A State may not, by statute or common law, create a cause of action under § 1983 against an entity whom Congress has not subjected to liability. Moor v. County of Alameda, 411 U.S. 693, 698–710 (1973). Since this Court has construed the word 'person' in § 1983 to exclude States, neither a federal court or a state court may entertain a § 1983 action against such a defendant. Conversely, since the Court has held that municipal corporations and similar governmental entities are 'persons,' see Monell v. New York City Dept. of Social Services, [Chapter 1A, supra,] a state court entertaining a § 1983 action must adhere to that interpretation. 'Municipal defenses—including an assertion of sovereign immunity—to a federal right of action are, of course, controlled by federal law.' By including municipalities with the class of 'persons' subject to liability for violation of the Federal Constitution and laws, Congress—the supreme sovereign on matters of federal law—abolished whatever vestige of the State's sovereign immunity the municipality possessed."

(a) *Howlett* failed to mention § 1988 and instead relied upon the preemption doctrine. Why? In citing Supremacy Clause ideas, Justice Stevens wrote: "An excuse [for refusal to hear federal claims] that is inconsistent with or violates federal law is not a valid excuse: the Supremacy Clause forbids state courts to dissociate themselves from federal law because of disagreement with its content or a refusal to recognize the superior authority of its source." 496 U.S. at 371, 110 S.Ct. at 2440. Is this the same principle Justice Brennan invoked, albeit with a different label, in *Felder*?

(b) Justice Stevens in *Howlett* also analogized to the "adequate and independent state grounds" doctrine which controls when state procedural rules may be invoked to dismiss an appeal from state court to the U.S. Supreme Court. He expressed "concern that the state court may be evading federal law and discriminating against federal causes of action." Justice Stevens continued: "It therefore is within our province to inquire not only whether the right was denied in express terms, but also whether it was denied in substance and effect, as by putting forward non-federal grounds of decision that were without any fair or substantial support." 496 U.S. at 366, 110 S.Ct. at 2437. Is this the same question Justice Brennan posed in *Felder*?

3. After *Howlett*, New York adopted a statute withdrawing jurisdiction of its state courts for claims based on § 1983—but only those brought against corrections officials for damages. In practical effect the state scheme remitted prisoners to a claim against the state itself in the state's specialty court. A bare 5–4 majority struck down the statute in **Haywood v. Drown**, ___ U.S. ___, 129 S.Ct. 2108, 173 L.Ed.2d 920 (2009), citing *Howlett*, even though the Court admitted that the state practice treated federal and state claims the same, disallowing both.

(a) Justice Stevens again wrote for the majority, striking down the New York law as a violation of the Supremacy Clause, reasoning that states "lack authority to nullify a federal right or cause of action they believe is inconsistent with their local policies," policies that disfavor a damages remedy for prisoners. 129 S.Ct. at 2114–15, 2118 (law "operates more as an immunity-from-damages provision [for corrections officers] than as a jurisdictional rule"; "contrary conclusion would permit a State to withhold a forum for the adjudication of any federal cause of action with which it disagreed as long as the policy took the form of a jurisdictional rule"). Is that true if the statute merely provides an alternative source for the damages—the state as defendant? See 129 S.Ct. 2118 n.9 (intimation that the suit against the state could be brought only under state law, not under § 1983). See Chapter 1H.2 infra.

(b) The dissenters read *Howlett* as merely forbidding states to add defenses to § 1983 claims, saying nothing about the power of states to simply refuse to hear claims. As such, the New York law operated as no adjudication on the merits and left any prospective plaintiff free to choose any other available forum. Why is the majority so concerned about opening state courts if the federal forum remains open to § 1983 plaintiffs?

4. After *Howlett*, should *any* modern state-law defense—that is, state-created defenses recognized by state-created claims—be applied to a § 1983 action in state court? Only those presumptively incorporated by Congress in § 1988? (Is this a circular question?) How does the adoption of official immunity fit this approach of abjuring state-created defenses? Is there no problem because the Court in *Pierson* assumed that Congress wanted to adopt state law?

Note on Res Judicata and Section 1738

1.   In **Migra v. Warren City School District Bd. of Educ.**, 465 U.S. 75, 104 S.Ct. 892, 79 L.Ed.2d 56 (1984), the plaintiff argued that she should be able to relitigate under § 1983 a claim that she had already litigated under state law. More specifically, the plaintiff had filed suit against the defendants under state law in the state courts of Ohio, claiming that their decision to fire her constituted a breach of contract; she won. Thereafter, she filed a different suit under § 1983 alleging that the same events gave rise to a constitutional claim under § 1983. Held the Court, 465 U.S. at 81, 104 S.Ct. at 896:

> "It is now settled that a federal court must give to a state court judgment the same preclusive effect as would be given that judgment under the law of the state in which the judgment was rendered. * * * Accordingly, in the absence of federal law modifying the operation of [28 U.S.C.] § 1738, [the full faith and credit statute,] the preclusive effect in federal court of petitioner's state-court judgment is determined by Ohio law. * * *

> [This conclusion applies to both claim preclusion and issue preclusion.] Having rejected in [our precedents] the view that state-court judgments have no issue preclusive effect in § 1983 suits, we must reject the view that § 1983 prevents the judgment in petitioner's state-court proceeding from creating a claim preclusion bar to this case."

(a) Assume that Ohio follows the "modern" rule of identifying a claim that requires all related claims growing from the same transaction or occurrence to be litigated in the same action and precludes relitigation not only of those theories actually raised, but also those that could have been raised. Would Migra's § 1983 claim be precluded? Assume that Ohio follows an older rule that requires claims to be brought together only when they are based on the same statute or legal wrong; would Migra's claim be precluded? Assume that Ohio follows a different modern rule that requires joinder of all claims arising under different statutes only when the defendant so demands it in the first suit; would Migra's claim be precluded? How do you justify the state-to-state variation in results?

(b) Is state-to-state variation that arises under § 1738 consistent with the state-to-state variation that is permitted under § 1988 (for statutes of limitations, for example), considered in the previous Note? Is not the ability to relitigate a claim a substantial aspect of a case that could change the outcome of the case—as well as change the effectiveness of § 1983? Should § 1738 be amended to adopt a uniform preclusion rule for all § 1983 cases?

2.   *Migra's* ruling on claim preclusion ("merger and bar" in the old res judicata vocabulary) also applies to issue preclusion (roughly collateral estoppel in the old vocabulary), that is, binding a party not only on full claims but also on issues litigated in a previous case in state court. See **Allen v. McCurry**, 449 U.S. 90, 101 S.Ct. 411, 66 L.Ed.2d 308 (1980). *Allen* involved a defendant in a state criminal proceeding who raised a Fourth Amendment defense in the state-court trial and, after losing on that issue, brought suit under § 1983 for a Fourth Amendment violation. Although it was not entirely

clear in *Allen* that the Court applied state law to bar relitigation, the Court in *Migra* so interpreted *Allen*. See 465 U.S. at 81, 104 S.Ct. at 896.

(a) Is use of state law on issue preclusion in § 1983 cases less defensible than use of state law for claim preclusion? If so, why? Because the plaintiff has not had a choice of a federal forum in Allen? If a state court has an affirmative defense rule in civil and criminal litigation that requires all affirmative defenses to be pled in the pending action, then applies claim preclusion, would the result not be to forestall § 1983 suits on the issues raisable by affirmative defense? Only when the state court rules against the defense? In *Migra* the Court responded to this issue by noting that § 1738 "embodies the view that it is more important to give full faith and credit to state-court judgments than to ensure separate forums for federal and state claims." 465 U.S. at 84, 104 S.Ct. at 897. Do you agree?

(b) Note that *Allen* involved prior litigation in the criminal context where habeas corpus would sometimes be available to overturn a state-court conviction and obtain the defendant's release from custody. Does the availability, limited though it may be, of habeas corpus mitigate the problem of lack of a federal forum in relitigated § 1983 cases?

3. Should preclusive effect be given to other bodies than state courts? In **McDonald v. City of West Branch**, 466 U.S. 284, 104 S.Ct. 1799, 80 L.Ed.2d 302 (1984), the Court held that § 1738 did not cover arbitration judgments and refused to give such resolutions preclusive effect. On the other hand, in **University of Tennessee v. Elliott**, 478 U.S. 788, 106 S.Ct. 3220, 92 L.Ed.2d 635 (1986), the Court held that administrative determinations, when made by a quasi-judicial body, would fall under § 1738 and would be given preclusive effect if the courts of the state gave such judgments preclusive effect. Can these results be distinguished?

(a) Assuming that an arbitration judgment has no preclusive effect, should courts nevertheless accord it some evidentiary weight in their consideration of the § 1983 claim? See Alexander v. Gardner–Denver Co., 415 U.S. 36, 60 n. 21, 94 S.Ct. 1011, 1025 n. 21, 39 L.Ed.2d 147 (1974) (court "may" give some arbitral awards great weight in Title VII context of employment discrimination).

(b) Assume that a state court reviews state administrative decisions under an "abuse of discretion" standard or a similar rule allowing only limited review of agency decisions. Should we characterize the state's law as "giving preclusive effect" to the agency decision? Are there any state agency decisions that are literally unreviewable in state court, that is, ones that literally receive preclusive effect in the state's courts? If there are some such agencies, are they not the ones that should be most closely scrutinized when someone claims a constitutional violation? Should it matter whether the § 1983 plaintiff initiated the state agency action?

4. Section 1738 has no application when the prior judicial decision came from another federal court rather than from a state court. In this circumstance, ordinary federal law of res judicata will be applied to determine whether the § 1983 claim remains viable. See Blonder–Tongue Laboratories v. University of Illinois Foundation, 402 U.S. 313, 91 S.Ct. 1434, 28 L.Ed.2d 788

(1971) (demonstrating the practice in a patent case); Clarke v. Redeker, 406 F.2d 883 (8th Cir.1969) (successive constitutional claims).

(a) The inapplicability of § 1738 to prior federal judgments means that the preclusive effect of the outcome in identical suits may be different—because state and federal res judicata rules may be different—based solely upon whether the first suit was brought in federal or state court. Is this fair? Is it consistent with the practice under § 1988 as interpreted in the *Felder* case? If there is a variation, is it explainable as being the by-product of Congress' decision in adopting § 1738?

(b) Section 1738 also has no applicability when a § 1983 claim is first litigated in federal court, followed by litigation involving the same claim or issues in state court. Must the state court then follow the federal res judicata rules? See Jack Friedenthal, Mary Kay Kane, and Arthur Miller, CIVIL PROCEDURE § 14.3 (4th ed. 2005) (yes, by virtue of the Supremacy Clause).

(c) Although the various combinations of possible claims seems confusing, see Semtek Intern. Inc. v. Lockheed Martin Corp., 531 U.S. 497, 121 S.Ct. 1021, 149 L.Ed.2d 32 (2001) (in federal diversity actions federal law applies but federal law adopts law of state in which federal court sat), all relitigation across federal-state system boundaries, or even state-state boundaries, can be explained by one principle—the "full faith and credit" principle that the second court will give a valid first judgment the same preclusive effect as that judgment would be given under the res judicata law of the first court system. See Jack Friedenthal, Mary Kay Kane, and Arthur Miller, CIVIL PROCEDURE § 14.3 (4th ed. 2005). Does this mean that § 1738 is irrelevant? Or only that it fits the pattern of all other res judicata rules?

(d) Does our national willingness to foreclose repetitious federal relitigation of constitutional claims under § 1983 support a similar consensus for limiting relitigation of habeas corpus claims already once heard in federal court? See Antiterrorism and Effective Death Penalty Act of 1996, PL 104–132, §§ 101–108, codified in part at 28 U.S.C. §§ 2244, 2254, 2264–66 (limiting use of habeas corpus and appeals); Rice v. Collins, 546 U.S. 333, 126 S.Ct. 969, 163 L.Ed.2d 824 (2006) (AEDPA prevents habeas challenges to race-based jury selection after state court has heard and determined the challenge); Pace v. DiGuglielmo, 544 U.S. 408, 125 S.Ct. 1807, 161 L.Ed.2d 669 (2005) (no equitable tolling to permit late-filed petitions). See also McCleskey v. Zant, 496 U.S. 904, 110 S.Ct. 2585, 110 L.Ed.2d 266 (1990) (prisoner who has once filed habeas corpus petition ordinarily may not thereafter file additional writs covering claims that could have been joined in the first writ).

F. RELIEF

1. DAMAGES

Courts have long held that a successful plaintiff may recover nominal damages, compensatory damages, and punitive damages under § 1983. How do they know that these various types of damages are available, and when is each appropriate? Compensatory damages are the most-often awarded remedy in § 1983 cases; how do courts know which losses merit compensation when the plaintiff wins her § 1983 case? The cases that follow deal with these two sets of issues.

SMITH v. WADE

Supreme Court of the United States, 1983.
461 U.S. 30, 103 S.Ct. 1625, 75 L.Ed.2d 632.

JUSTICE BRENNAN delivered the opinion of the Court.

We granted certiorari in this case to decide whether the District Court for the Western District of Missouri applied the correct legal standard in instructing the jury that it might award punitive damages under 42 U.S.C. § 1983. The Court of Appeals for the Eighth Circuit sustained the award of punitive damages. We affirm.

I

* * *

Wade brought suit under 42 U.S.C. § 1983 against Smith and four other guards and correctional officials, alleging that his Eighth Amendment rights had been violated [when Smith placed hardened offenders in Wade's cell and subsequently failed to protect Wade from their sexual assaults. Evidence at trial showed that the defendants were aware of the problem and had a free cell that could have been used to protect Wade]. Further, only a few weeks earlier, another inmate had been beaten to death in the same dormitory during the same shift, while Smith had been on duty. Wade asserted that Smith and the other defendants knew or should have known that an assault against him was likely under the circumstances.

During trial, the district judge entered a directed verdict for two of the defendants. He instructed the jury that Wade could make out an Eighth Amendment violation only by showing "physical abuse of such base, inhumane and barbaric proportions as to shock the sensibilities." * * * He reiterated that Wade could not recover on a showing of simple negligence.

The district judge also charged the jury that it could award punitive damages on a proper showing [of "*a reckless or callous disregard of, or indifference to, the rights or safety of others* (emphasis in original), with the amount to be set in the jury's discretion. The jury awarded $25,000 in compensatory damages and $5,000 in punitive damages, and the District Court approved, as did the court of appeals. Smith now challenges only the award of punitive damages."]

II

Section 1983 is derived from § 1 of the Civil Rights Act of 1871, 17 Stat. 13. It was intended to create "a species of tort liability" in favor of persons deprived of federally secured rights. Carey v. Piphus, [which follows this case]; Imbler v. Pachtman. We noted in *Carey* that there was little in the section's legislative history concerning the damages recoverable for this tort liability. In the absence of more specific guidance, we looked first to the common law of torts (both modern and as of 1871), with such modification or adaptation as might be necessary to carry out the purpose and policy of the statute. We have done the same in other contexts arising under § 1983, especially the recurring problem of common-law immunities.[2]

Smith correctly concedes that "punitive damages are available in a 'proper' § 1983 action...." Although there was debate about the theoretical correctness of the punitive damages doctrine in the latter part of the last century, the doctrine was accepted as settled law by nearly all state and federal courts, including this Court. It was likewise generally established that individual public officers were liable for punitive damages for their misconduct on the same basis as other individual defendants. See also Scott v. Donald, 165 U.S. 58, 77–89, 17 S.Ct. 265, 266–68, 41 L.Ed. 632 (1897) (punitive damages for constitutional tort). Further, although the precise issue of the availability of punitive damages under § 1983 has never come squarely before us, we have had occasion more than once to make clear our view that they are available; indeed, we have rested decisions on related questions on the premise of such availability.[5]

Smith argues, nonetheless, that this was not a "proper" case in which to award punitive damages. More particularly, he attacks the instruction that punitive damages could be awarded on a finding of reckless or callous disregard of or indifference to Wade's rights or safety. Instead, he contends that the proper test is one of actual malicious intent—"ill will, spite, or intent to injure."[6] He offers two arguments for this position: first, that

---

2. * * * Justice Rehnquist's dissent faults us for referring to modern tort decisions in construing § 1983. Its argument rests on the unstated and unsupported premise that Congress necessarily intended to freeze into permanent law whatever principles were current in 1871, rather than to incorporate applicable general legal principles as they evolve. The dissents are correct, of course, that when the language of the section and its legislative history provide no clear answer, we have found useful guidance in the law prevailing at the time when § 1983 was enacted; but it does not follow that that law is absolutely controlling, or that current law is irrelevant. On the contrary, if the prevailing view on some point of general tort law had changed substantially in the intervening century (which is not the case here), we might be highly reluctant to assume that Congress intended to perpetuate a now-obsolete doctrine. Indeed, in *Imbler* we recognized a common-law immunity that first came into existence 25 years after § 1983 was enacted. Under the dissents' view, *Imbler* was wrongly decided.

5. * * * [Justice Rehnquist's dissent] points to two other statutes enacted in 1863 and 1870 that provided expressly for punitive remedies[, but these] statutes do not support Justice Rehnquist's speculation that Congress acted expressly when it intended to approve punitive damages, since both statutes created new remedies not available at common law; moreover, they undercut his argument that Congress was hostile to punitive civil remedies in favor of private parties. Finally, Justice Rehnquist argues that Congress would not likely have approved "this often condemned doctrine" in the 1871 Civil Rights Act. This speculation is remarkable, to say the least, given that Congress did approve a punitive civil remedy in an 1870 civil rights act. Act of May 31, 1870, § 2, 16 Stat. 140 (creating private cause of action for fixed penalty on behalf of persons suffering racial discrimination in voting registration). At any rate, the punitive damages debate, though lively, was by no means one-sided, [citing nineteenth century cases upholding punitive damages awards].

6. Smith uses the term "actual malice" to refer to the standard he would apply[, but we avoid using it to prevent ambiguity, since] this Court has used the very term "actual malice" in the defamation context to refer to a recklessness standard. See New York Times Co. v. Sullivan, 376

actual intent is the proper standard for punitive damages in all cases under § 1983; and second, that even if intent is not always required, it should be required here because the threshold for punitive damages should always be higher than that for liability in the first instance. We address these in turn.

III

Smith does not argue that the common law, either in 1871 or now, required or requires a showing of actual malicious intent for recovery of punitive damages. Perhaps not surprisingly, there was significant variation (both terminological and substantive) among American jurisdictions in the latter nineteenth century on the precise standard to be applied in awarding punitive damages—variation that was exacerbated by the ambiguity and slipperiness of such common terms as "malice" and "gross negligence." Most of the confusion, however, seems to have been over the degree of negligence, recklessness, carelessness, or culpable indifference that should be required—not over whether actual intent was essential. On the contrary, the rule in a large majority of jurisdictions was that punitive damages (also called exemplary damages, vindictive damages, or smart money) could be awarded without a showing of actual ill will, spite, or intent to injure.

This Court so stated on several occasions, before and shortly after 1871. * * * The large majority of state and lower federal courts were in agreement that punitive damage awards did not require a showing of actual malicious intent; they permitted punitive awards on variously stated standards of negligence, recklessness, or other culpable conduct short of actual malicious intent.[12]

The same rule applies today. The Restatement (Second) of Torts (1977), for example, states: "Punitive damages may be awarded for conduct that is outrageous, because of the defendant's evil motive or his reckless indifference to the rights of others." Id., § 908(2) (emphasis added); see also id., Comment b. Most cases under state common law,

---

U.S. 254, 280, 84 S.Ct. 710, 726, 11 L.Ed.2d 686 (1964). We note in passing that it appears quite uncertain whether even Justice Rehnquist's dissent ultimately agrees with Smith's view that "ill will, spite, or intent to injure" should be required to allow punitive damages awards. Justice Rehnquist consistently confuses, and attempts to blend together, the quite distinct concepts of intent to cause injury, on one hand, and subjective consciousness of risk of injury (or of unlawfulness) on the other. * * * Consciousness of consequences or of wrongdoing, of course, does not require injurious intent or motive; it is equally consistent with indifference toward or disregard for consequences. This confusion of standards continues throughout the opinion. * * *

12. In the often-cited case of Welch v. Durand, 36 Conn. 182 (1869), for example, the Court held that punitive damages were proper where the defendant's pistol bullet, fired at a target, ricocheted and hit the plaintiff:

"In what cases then may smart money be awarded in addition to the damages? The proper answer to this question ... seems to be, in actions of tort founded on the malicious or wanton misconduct or culpable neglect of the defendant...." In this case the defendant was guilty of wanton misconduct and culpable neglect.... It is an immaterial fact that the injury was unintentional, and that the ball glanced from the intended direction.... [I]f the act is done where there are objects from which the balls may glance and endanger others, the act is wanton, reckless, without due care, and grossly negligent." Id., at 185. [Extensive citation of other cases omitted.]

although varying in their precise terminology, have adopted more or less the same rule, recognizing that punitive damages in tort cases may be awarded not only for actual intent to injure or evil motive, but also for recklessness, serious indifference to or disregard for the rights of others, or even gross negligence. [Citations omitted.]

The remaining question is whether the policies and purposes of § 1983 itself require a departure from the rules of tort common law. * * *

Smith's argument, which he offers in several forms, is that an actual intent standard is preferable to a recklessness standard because it is less vague. [Deterrence, he admits, is the purpose of punitive damages, but such] deterrence, he contends, cannot be achieved unless the standard of conduct sought to be deterred is stated with sufficient clarity to enable potential defendants to conform to the law and to avoid the proposed sanction. * * *

Smith's argument, if valid, would apply to ordinary tort cases as easily as to § 1983 suits; hence, it hardly presents an argument for adopting a different rule under § 1983. In any event, the argument is unpersuasive. While, arguendo, an intent standard may be easier to understand and apply to particular situations than a recklessness standard, we are not persuaded that a recklessness standard is too vague to be fair or useful. * * *

More fundamentally, Smith's argument for certainty in the interest of deterrence overlooks the distinction between a standard for punitive damages and a standard of liability in the first instance. Smith seems to assume that prison guards and other state officials look mainly to the standard for punitive damages in shaping their conduct. We question the premise; we assume, and hope, that most officials are guided primarily by the underlying standards of federal substantive law—both out of devotion to duty, and in the interest of avoiding liability for compensatory damages. At any rate, the conscientious officer who desires clear guidance on how to do his job and avoid lawsuits can and should look to the standard for actionability in the first instance. The need for exceptional clarity in the standard for punitive damages arises only if one assumes that there are substantial numbers of officers who will not be deterred by compensatory damages; only such officers will seek to guide their conduct by the punitive damages standard. The presence of such officers constitutes a powerful argument against raising the threshold for punitive damages.

* * * [W]e are content to adopt the policy judgment of the common law—that reckless or callous disregard for the plaintiff's rights, as well as intentional violations of federal law, should be sufficient to trigger a jury's consideration of the appropriateness of punitive damages.

IV

Smith contends that even if § 1983 does not ordinarily require a showing of actual malicious intent for an award of punitive damages, such a showing should be required in this case. He argues that the deterrent and punitive purposes of punitive damages are served only if the threshold for punitive damages is higher in every case than the underlying standard for liability in the first instance. In this case, while the district judge did not use the same precise terms to explain the standards of liability for compensatory and punitive damages, the parties agree that there is no substantial difference between the showings required by the two instructions; both apply a standard of reckless or callous indifference to Wade's rights. * * * The argument overlooks a key feature of punitive damages— that they are never awarded as of right, no matter how egregious the defendant's conduct. "If the plaintiff proves sufficiently serious misconduct on the defendant's part, the question whether to award punitive damages is left to the jury, which may or may not make such an award." D. Dobbs, Handbook on the Law of Remedies 204 (1973) (footnote omitted). * * *

Moreover, the rules of ordinary tort law are once more against Smith's argument. There has never been any general common-law rule that the threshold for punitive damages must always be higher than that for compensatory liability. On the contrary, both the First and Second Restatements of Torts have pointed out that "in torts like malicious prosecution that require a particular antisocial state of mind, the improper motive of the tortfeasor is both a necessary element in the cause of action and a reason for awarding punitive damages."[16] Accordingly, in situations where the standard for compensatory liability is as high as or higher than the usual threshold for punitive damages, most courts will permit awards of punitive damages without requiring any extra showing. * * *

* * *

[Affirmed.]

JUSTICE REHNQUIST, with whom THE CHIEF JUSTICE and JUSTICE POWELL join, dissenting.

* * * In my view, a forthright inquiry into the intent of the 42d Congress and a balanced consideration of the public policies at issue compel the conclusion that the proper standard for an award of punitive damages under § 1983 requires at least some degree of bad faith or improper motive on the part of the defendant.

[An extensive review of the history of punitive damages awards shows that "in the years preceding and immediately following the enactment of § 1983," federal courts and "a solid majority of [state] jurisdictions" required proof of "ill will" in order to recover punitive damages.]

While fully recognizing that the issue is a complex one, in my judgment the dangers that accompany the vague recklessness standard adopted by the Court far outweigh the deterrence achieved thereby.

---

16. Restatement of Torts § 908, comment c (1939); Restatement (Second) of Torts § 908, comment c (1977). * * *

Recklessness too easily shades into negligence, particularly when the defendant is an unpopular official—whether because of his official actions, or for more invidious reasons. Punitive damages are not bound by a measure of actual damages, so when a jury does act improperly, the harm it may occasion can be great. These threats occur in an area—the provision of governmental services—where it is important to have efficient, competent public servants. I fear that the Court's decision poorly serves this goal, and that in the end, official conduct will be less useful to our citizens, not better.

Moreover, notwithstanding the Court's inability to discern them, there are important distinctions between a right to damages under § 1983 and a similar right under state tort law. A leading rationale seized upon by proponents of punitive damages to justify the doctrine is that "the award is ... a covert response to the legal system's overt refusal to provide financing for litigation." D. Dobbs, Remedies 221 (1973); K. Redden, Punitive Damages § 2.4(c) (1980). Yet, 42 U.S.C. § 1988 provides not just a "covert response" to plaintiffs' litigation expenses but an explicit provision for an award to the prevailing party in a § 1983 action of "a reasonable attorney's fee as part of the costs." By permitting punitive damages as well as attorney's fees, § 1983 plaintiffs, unlike state tort law plaintiffs, get not just one windfall but two—one for them, and one for their lawyer. * * *

* * *

Finally, by unquestioningly transferring the standard of punitive damages in state tort actions to federal § 1983 actions, the Court utterly fails to recognize the fundamental difference that exists between an award of punitive damages by a federal court, acting under § 1983, and a similar award by a state court acting under prevailing local laws. * * * * When federal courts enforce punitive damage awards against local officials they intrude into sensitive areas of sovereignty of coordinate branches of our nation, thus implicating the most basic values of our system of federalism. Moreover, by yet further distorting the incentives that exist for litigating claims against local officials in federal court, as opposed to state courts, the Court's decision makes it even more difficult for state courts to attempt to conform the conduct of state officials to the Constitution. * * *

JUSTICE O'CONNOR, dissenting.

Although I agree with the result reached in Justice Rehnquist's dissent, I write separately because I cannot agree with the approach taken by either the Court or Justice Rehnquist. Both opinions engage in exhaustive, but ultimately unilluminating, exegesis of the common law of the availability of punitive damages in 1871. Although both the Court and Justice Rehnquist display admirable skills in legal research and analysis of great numbers of musty cases, the results do not significantly further the goal of the inquiry: to establish the intent of the 42d Congress. In interpreting § 1983, we have often looked to the common law as it existed in 1871, in the belief that, when Congress was silent on a point, it intended to adopt the principles of the common law with which it was familiar. This approach makes sense when there was a generally prevailing rule of common law, for then it is reasonable to assume that congressmen were familiar with that rule and imagined that it would cover the cause of action that they were creating. But when a significant split in authority existed, it strains credulity to argue that Congress simply assumed that one view rather than the other would govern. [W]e cannot safely infer anything about congressional intent from the divided contemporaneous judicial opinions. The battle of the string citations can have no winner.

Once it is established that the common law of 1871 provides us with no real guidance on this question, we should turn to the policies underlying § 1983 to determine which rule best accords with those policies. [Given the availability of compensatory damages and attorneys fees for the successful § 1983 plaintiff, and the potential chill of unchecked punitive damages against public servants, I find no incremental good accomplished by choosing Justice Brennan's incrementally more pro-plaintiff standard for awarding punitive damages.]

NOTE ON DAMAGES, JURY TRIALS, AND ATTORNEYS FEES AWARDS

1. Consider first the question of what types of damages should be awardable under § 1983. Well-established case law holds that three types of damages are available: nominal damages to vindicate the violation of a right when no actual injury can be shown, compensatory damages which redress injuries by making the victim whole, and punitive damages which deter or punish especially serious violations. How do courts know that these three types of damages are recoverable under § 1983?

(a) Conceptually, this question simply calls for an interpretation of the damages that were implicitly authorized in § 1983's authorization of an "action at law." Is Justice Rehnquist more nearly correct when he says that judicial practice as of 1871 is relevant (because that was the date of § 1983's adoption)? Or is Justice Brennan right in wanting to look to the evolving common law? Should the Justices have looked at the legislative debates to determine which concept Congress intended? If they had looked, what would they have found?

(b) Is Justice O'Connor's approach a better one—even better than she admits? In the absence of a clear Congressional mandate, must not the Court look to general principles and policies? But why look only to modern policy goals in the absence of clarity from Congress? Why not create a complete federal common law of damages? See Basista v. Weir, 340 F.2d 74 (3d Cir.1965) (holding that federal common law controls damages under § 1983).

(c) Is § 1983 "deficient" in its specification of damages so that, under § 1988 as discussed in the preceding subsection, federal courts should look to the law of the states in which they sit for damages doctrines? See Basista v. Weir, supra (rejecting this approach). Why would such an approach be undesirable? Is it any more undesirable than having statutes of limitations periods vary from state to state?

2.   Assuming that punitive damages are one kind of damages recoverable under § 1983, in what circumstances should they be recoverable? That is the subject of the *Smith* case. Do you get the feeling in reading the opinions of the majority and Justice Rehnquist that they had already made their decisions before they ever researched a single Nineteenth Century case?

(a) Did Justice Brennan really believe what he wrote in footnote 2, or was it a fall-back position created after he saw Justice Rehnquist's research? Do the final portions of Justice Rehnquist's opinion reveal far more about the factors affecting his judgment than he is willing to admit? Is Justice O'Connor correct in saying that the Justices should more frankly acknowledge the policy judgments that they must inevitably make?

(b) Can judges be trusted to do legal history? Is there any reason to believe that legal skills aid historical research? Alternatively, has the Court's work in civil rights become so heavily politicized that you simply do not believe the Justices when they represent that they are following neutral norms of law? See the similar issues raised in the Chapter 2A, *infra*.

3.   To the extent that the plaintiff in a § 1983 action requests damages or other remedies available at common law, the Seventh Amendment requires that the right to a jury trial must be preserved. See **City of Monterey v. Del Monte Dunes, Ltd.**, 526 U.S. 687, 119 S.Ct. 1624, 143 L.Ed.2d 882 (1999) ("a § 1983 suit seeking legal relief is an action at law within the meaning of the Seventh Amendment," and "[d]amages for a constitutional violation are a legal remedy"); Curtis v. Loether, 415 U.S. 189, 94 S.Ct. 1005, 39 L.Ed.2d 260 (1974) (same as applied to Fair Housing Act's provision for damages remedy exceeding $20). *Smith* may be seen, in turn, as holding that punitive damages are implicitly included within the remedy "at law" under § 1983, provided the relevant test for awarding such damages is satisfied.

(a) Whatever their merits in other litigation, are punitive damages inappropriate in § 1983 cases? Under what circumstances could a plaintiff realistically expect such an award? Is there an upper limit to punitive damages awards that § 1983 juries may not exceed? See Patterson v. Balsamico, 440 F.3d 104 (2d Cir. 2006) (collecting cases and upholding $100,000 in compensatory damages but finding $20,000 in punitive damages excessive in light of defendant's ability to pay).

(b) The Supreme Court has independently held that excessive punitive damages awards are subject to challenge under Due Process analysis. In **State Farm Mut. Auto. Insurance v. Campbell**, 538 U.S. 408, 123 S.Ct. 1513, 155 L.Ed.2d 585 (2003), the court struck down a Utah jury's award of $145 million in punitive damages tacked onto $1 million in compensatory damages. The Court held that multipliers exceeding ten times actual damages are presumptively excessive. See also BMW of North America, Inc. v. Gore, 517 U.S. 559, 116 S.Ct. 1589, 134 L.Ed.2d 809 (1996) (constitutional restraints on excessive punitive damages).

(c) Are juries likely to impose punitive damages awards only in favor of "majorities" whose constitutional rights are violated? Is a black plaintiff whose free-speech rights were violated in a virtually all-white state likely to recover punitive damages after showing that his anti-white speech was intentionally suppressed? Is a white plaintiff in a virtually all African–American district likely to recover punitive damages after showing that speech against Rev. Martin Luther King, Jr., was intentionally suppressed? Does it bother you that punitive damages are within the discretion of the jury? Is total jury discretion what leads to excessive verdicts as in *State Farm*, supra?

(d) Is some proof of actual damages—actual losses—necessary to support an award of punitive damages? Or will the award of nominal damages for the very loss of the constitutional right support an award of punitive damages? Cf. Doe v. Chao, 540 U.S. 614, 124 S.Ct. 1204, 157 L.Ed.2d 1122 (2004) (under statute protecting privacy and providing for minimum statutory award, with no compensatory damages, no statutory liquidated damages awardable unless plaintiff shows some actual loss; cross-citing non-specific § 1983 precedents).

4. In 1976 Congress amended § 1988 by adding a lengthy provision, called the Civil Rights Attorneys Fees Awards Act, designed to give attorney's fees to "prevailing parties" in suits under several civil rights statutes, including § 1983. The law has been interpreted to give fees, virtually without restriction, to "prevailing" plaintiffs; fees are only rarely awarded to defendants when they can show that the plaintiff's claim was frivolous. Thus the statute serves primarily to shift a significant cost of litigation to defendants when plaintiffs prevail under § 1983. See Hensley v. Eckerhart, 461 U.S. 424, 103 S.Ct. 1933, 76 L.Ed.2d 40 (1983) (plaintiffs ordinarily due an award unless "special circumstances" render it "unjust"); Christiansburg Garment Co. v. EEOC, 434 U.S. 412, 98 S.Ct. 694, 54 L.Ed.2d 648 (1978) (interpreting parallel provisions of Title VII) (defendants rarely due an award).

(a) Under *Hensley* plaintiff's attorney is ordinarily compensated at a "market rate," that is, a standard hourly rate in the community multiplied by the number of hours reasonably spent on the case (often called the "lodestar" factors).[1] Is this a sufficient amount of money to attract competent attorneys to represent plaintiffs in § 1983 actions? No, because attorneys will refuse to take difficult cases since they can only receive fees for winning cases? Yes, because attorneys should exercise professional judgment, as they do in ordinary contingency fee cases, before agreeing to represent a client in a § 1983 case?[2]

(b) Despite Justice Brennan's history in the *Smith* case, the award of punitive damages is rare, and in many cases compensatory damages may be low because actual losses are low (e.g., denial of speech rights), even though the effort of plaintiff's attorney may be high. Should fees be adjusted upwards in such cases? In Perdue v. Kenny A., ___ U.S. ___, 130 S.Ct. 1662, 176

---

1. Different fee provisions apply to prisoner's claims, including limitations on amount of fees. Is this constitutional? See Johnson v. Daley, 339 F.3d 582 (7th Cir. 2003) (noting provisions in Prison Litigation Reform Act, 42 U.S.C. § 1997e(d)(3), and upholding them).

2. Should any expert witness fees also be included in the fee award? See West Virginia University Hospitals, Inc. v. Casey, 499 U.S. 83, 111 S.Ct. 1138, 113 L.Ed.2d 68 (1991) (no). Will this affect incentives to bring some complex cases? The Civil Rights Act of 1991, § 113, see Appendix, overturned *Casey* with respect to some other statutory claims, excluding § 1983. Cf. Stender v. Lucky Stores, Inc., 780 F.Supp. 1302 (N.D.Cal. 1992).

L.Ed.2d 494 (2010), the Court rejected ready enhancement of the lodestar base fee to attract superior counsel to litigate the case, ruling that the "circumstances in which superior attorney performance is not adequately taken into account in the lodestar calculation are 'rare' and 'exceptional.'" Any enhancement must be based on specific identifiable factors reflecting superior performance not already reflected in the attorney's basic hourly rate. (Four Justices wrote separately to state that this was a rare case, one in which extraordinary relief had been obtained in a lengthy class action, for which lawyers had been compensated at an hourly rate lower than that of the average lawyer in the state.)[3]

(c) In many cases attorneys fees awards will far exceed the economic recovery of the plaintiff. Should the Court create a proportionality rule to prevent attorneys from making more in fees from the § 1983 suit than a winning plaintiff would make in damages? Compare City of Riverside v. Rivera, 477 U.S. 561, 106 S.Ct. 2686, 91 L.Ed.2d 466 (1986) (proportionality rule inconsistent with § 1988's goals), with Farrar v. Hobby, 506 U.S. 103, 113 S.Ct. 566, 121 L.Ed.2d 494 (1992) (minor win of one of twenty claims merits no fee). Can an attorney protect herself from a low attorney's fee award by providing in the retainer agreement with her client for a normal contingency fee? Cf. Evans v. Jeff D., infra (assuming that lower court-awarded fee would apply).

(d) Should a plaintiff who provokes a change in government practice, mooting the case, receive award of attorney's fees on the theory that the case was the "catalyst" for change? Has the plaintiff as a practical matter "prevailed" in such cases? See Buckhannon Bd. and Care Home, Inc. v. West Virginia Dept. of Health, 532 U.S. 598, 121 S.Ct. 1835, 149 L.Ed.2d 855 (2001) (plaintiff must obtain either a judgment on merits or court-ordered consent decree to be considered a prevailing party); Sole v. Wyner, 551 U.S. 74, 127 S.Ct. 2188, 167 L.Ed.2d 1069 (2007) (party who prevails on preliminary injunction is not a prevailing party unless she also prevails at final judgment). As a part of any consent decree, can the defendant demand a waiver of plaintiff's attorney's fees? See Evans v. Jeff D., 475 U.S. 717, 106 S.Ct. 1531, 89 L.Ed.2d 747 (1986). Can an offer of judgment under Rule 68 cut off the accrual of attorney's fees? Does an accepted offer preclude a separate fee award? See Marek v. Chesny, 473 U.S. 1, 105 S.Ct. 3012, 87 L.Ed.2d 1 (1985); FRCP 68.

CAREY v. PIPHUS

Supreme Court of the United States, 1978.
435 U.S. 247, 98 S.Ct. 1042, 55 L.Ed.2d 252.

MR. JUSTICE POWELL delivered the opinion of the Court.

In this case, brought under 42 U.S.C.A. § 1983, we consider the elements and prerequisites for recovery of damages by students who were suspended from public elementary and secondary schools without proce-

---

3. Should a successful pro se litigant be awarded fees when she acts as the lawyer in her own § 1983 case? Should the answer vary with whether the plaintiff is an actual attorney or is merely acting as one on her own behalf? See Kay v. Ehrler, 499 U.S. 432, 111 S.Ct. 1435, 113 L.Ed.2d 486 (1991).

dural due process. The Court of Appeals for the Seventh Circuit held that the students are entitled to recover substantial nonpunitive damages even if their suspensions were justified, and even if they do not prove that any other actual injury was caused by the denial of procedural due process. We disagree, and hold that in the absence of proof of actual injury, the students are entitled to recover only nominal damages.

[The principal discovered students smoking what he deemed to be marijuana and ordered the assistant principal to suspend them for 20 days, all without an opportunity to respond to the charges. The district court determined that this violated the students right to procedural due process, returned them to school at a preliminary hearing, but denied their claim for $3,000 in compensatory damages. The Seventh Circuit reversed, holding that damages were available without further proof of economic loss. The only issue for review here is whether compensatory damages can be awarded in these circumstances.]

* * * Rights, constitutional and otherwise, do not exist in a vacuum. Their purpose is to protect persons from injuries to particular interests, and their contours are shaped by the interests they protect.

Our legal system's concept of damages reflects this view of legal rights. "The cardinal principle of damages in Anglo–American law is that of *compensation* for the injury caused to plaintiff by defendant's breach of duty." 2 F. Harper & F. James, Law of Torts § 25.1, p. 1299 (1956) (emphasis in original).

The Members of the Congress that enacted § 1983 did not address directly the question of damages, but the principle that damages are designed to compensate persons for injuries caused by the deprivation of rights hardly could have been foreign to the many lawyers in Congress in 1871. Two other sections of the Civil Rights Act of 1871 appear to incorporate this principle, and no reason suggests itself for reading § 1983 differently. To the extent that Congress intended that awards under § 1983 should deter the deprivation of constitutional rights, there is no evidence that it meant to establish a deterrent more formidable than that inherent in the award of compensatory damages.[11]

* * *

B

It is less difficult to conclude that damages awards under § 1983 should be governed by the principle of compensation than it is to apply this principle to concrete cases. But over the centuries the common law of torts has developed a set of rules to implement the principle that a person should be compensated fairly for injuries caused by the violation of his legal rights. These rules, defining the elements of damages and the

---

11. This is not to say that exemplary or punitive damages might not be awarded in a proper case under § 1983 with the specific purpose of deterring or punishing violations of constitutional rights. Although we imply no approval or disapproval of any of these cases, we note that there is no basis for such an award in this case. * * *

prerequisites for their recovery, provide the appropriate starting point for the inquiry under § 1983 as well.

It is not clear, however, that common-law tort rules of damages will provide a complete solution to the damages issue in every § 1983 case. In some cases, the interests protected by a particular branch of the common law of torts may parallel closely the interests protected by a particular constitutional right. In such cases, it may be appropriate to apply the tort rules of damages directly to the § 1983 action. In other cases, the interests protected by a particular constitutional right may not also be protected by an analogous branch of the common law torts. In those cases, the task will be the more difficult one of adapting common-law rules of damages to provide fair compensation for injuries caused by the deprivation of a constitutional right.

Although this task of adaptation will be one of some delicacy—as this case demonstrates—it must be undertaken. The purpose of § 1983 would be defeated if injuries caused by the deprivation of constitutional rights went uncompensated simply because the common law does not recognize an analogous cause of action. In order to further the purpose of § 1983, the rules governing compensation for injuries caused by the deprivation of constitutional rights should be tailored to the interests protected by the particular right in question—just as the common-law rules of damages themselves were defined by the interests protected in the various branches of tort law. We agree with Mr. Justice Harlan that "the experience of judges in dealing with private [tort] claims supports the conclusion that courts of law are capable of making the types of judgment concerning causation and magnitude of injury necessary to accord meaningful compensation for invasion of [constitutional] rights." Bivens v. Six Unknown Fed. Narcotics Agents, 403 U.S., at 409, 91 S.Ct., at 2011 (Harlan, J., concurring in judgment). With these principles in mind, we now turn to the problem of compensation in the case at hand.

C

The Due Process Clause * * * "raises no impenetrable barrier to the taking of a person's possessions," or liberty, or life. Fuentes v. Shevin, 407 U.S. 67, 81, 92 S.Ct. 1983, 1994, 32 L.Ed.2d 556 (1972). Procedural due process rules are meant to protect persons not from the deprivation, but from the mistaken or unjustified deprivation of life, liberty, or property. * * *

In this case, the Court of Appeals held that if petitioners can prove on remand that "[respondents] would have been suspended even if a proper hearing had been held," then respondents will not be entitled to recover damages to compensate them for injuries caused by the suspensions. The court thought that in such a case, the failure to accord procedural due process could not properly be viewed as the cause of the suspensions. Cf. Mt. Healthy City Board of Ed. v. Doyle * * *. The court suggested that in such circumstances, an award of damages for injuries caused by the suspensions would constitute a windfall, rather than compensation, to respondents. We do not understand the parties to disagree with this conclusion. Nor do we.

The parties do disagree as to the further holding of the Court of Appeals that respondents are entitled to recover substantial—although unspecified—damages to compensate them for "the injury which is 'inherent in the nature of the wrong,'" even if their suspensions were justified and even if they fail to prove that the denial of procedural due process actually caused them some real, if intangible, injury. Respondents, elaborating on this theme, submit that the holding is correct because injury fairly may be "presumed" to flow from every denial of procedural due process. Their argument is that in addition to protecting against unjustified deprivations, the Due Process Clause also guarantees the "feeling of just treatment" by the government. Anti–Fascist Committee v. McGrath, 341 U.S. 123, 162, 71 S.Ct. 624, 643, 95 L.Ed. 817 (1951) (Frankfurter, J., concurring). They contend that the deprivation of protected interests without procedural due process, even where the premise for the deprivation is not erroneous, inevitably arouses strong feelings of mental and emotional distress in the individual who is denied this "feeling of just treatment." They analogize their case to that of defamation *per se,* in which "the plaintiff is relieved from the necessity of producing any proof whatsoever that he has been injured" in order to recover substantial compensatory damages. C. McCormick, Law of Damages § 116, p. 423 (1935).

Petitioners do not deny that a purpose of procedural due process is to convey to the individual a feeling that the government has dealt with him fairly, as well as to minimize the risk of mistaken deprivations of protected interests. They go so far as to concede that, in a proper case, persons in respondents' positions might well recover damages for mental and emotional distress caused by the denial of procedural due process. Petitioners' argument is the more limited one that such injury cannot be presumed to occur, and that plaintiffs at least should be put to their proof on the issue, as plaintiffs are in most tort actions.

We agree with petitioners in this respect. As we have observed in another context, the doctrine of presumed damages in the common law of defamation *per se* "is an oddity of tort law, for it allows recovery of purportedly compensatory damages without evidence of actual loss." Gertz v. Welch, 418 U.S. 323, 349, 94 S.Ct. 2997, 3011–3012, 41 L.Ed.2d 789 (1974). The doctrine has been defended on the grounds that those forms of defamation that are actionable *per se* are virtually certain to cause serious injury to reputation * * * * But these considerations do not support respondents' contention that damages should be presumed to flow from every deprivation of procedural due process.

First, it is not reasonable to assume that every departure from procedural due process, no matter what the circumstances or how minor, inherently is as likely to cause distress as the publication of defamation *per se* is to cause injury to reputation and distress. Where the deprivation of a protected interest is substantively justified but procedures are deficient in some respect, there may well be those who suffer no distress over the procedural irregularities. Indeed, in contrast to the immediately distressing effect of defamation *per se,* a person may not even know that procedures *were* deficient until he enlists the aid of counsel to challenge a perceived substantive deprivation.

Moreover, where a deprivation is justified but procedures are deficient, whatever distress a person feels may be attributable to the justified deprivation rather than to deficiencies in procedure. But as the Court of Appeals held, the injury caused by a justified deprivation, including distress, is not properly compensable under § 1983.[19] This ambiguity in causation, which is absent in the case of defamation *per se,* provides additional need for requiring the plaintiff to convince the trier of fact that he actually suffered distress because of the denial of procedural due process itself.

Finally, we foresee no particular difficulty in producing evidence that mental and emotional distress actually was caused by the denial of procedural due process itself. Distress is a personal injury familiar to the law, customarily proved by showing the nature and circumstances of the wrong and its effect on the plaintiff.[20] In sum, then, although mental and emotional distress caused by the denial of procedural due process itself is compensable under § 1983, we hold that neither the likelihood of such injury nor the difficulty of proving it is so great as to justify awarding compensatory damages without proof that such injury actually was caused.

D

The Court of Appeals believed, and respondents urge, that cases dealing with awards of damages for racial discrimination, the denial of voting rights, and the denial of Fourth Amendment rights, support a presumption of damages where procedural due process is denied. Many of the cases relied upon do not help respondents because they held or implied that some actual, if intangible, injury must be proved before compensatory damages may be recovered. Others simply did not address the issue. More importantly, the elements and prerequisites for recovery of damages appropriate to compensate injuries caused by the deprivation of one constitutional right are not necessarily appropriate to compensate injuries caused by the deprivation of another. As we have said, supra, these issues must be considered with reference to the nature of the interests protected by the particular constitutional right in question. For this reason, and

---

19. In this case, for example, respondents denied the allegations against them. They may well have been distressed that their denials were not believed. They might have been equally distressed if they had been disbelieved only after a full-dress hearing, but in that instance they would have no cause of action against petitioners.

20. We use the term "distress" to include mental suffering or emotional anguish. Although essentially subjective, genuine injury in this respect may be evidenced by one's conduct and observed by others. Juries must be guided by appropriate instructions, and an award of damages must be supported by competent evidence concerning the injury.

without intimating an opinion as to their merits, we do not deem the cases relied upon to be controlling.

III

Even if respondents' suspensions were justified, and even if they did not suffer any other actual injury, the fact remains that they were deprived of their right to procedural due process. * * *

Common-law courts traditionally have vindicated deprivations of certain "absolute" rights that are not shown to have caused actual injury through the award of a nominal sum of money. By making the deprivation of such rights actionable for nominal damages without proof of actual injury, the law recognizes the importance to organized society that those rights be scrupulously observed; but at the same time, it remains true to the principle that substantial damages should be awarded only to compensate actual injury or, in the case of exemplary or punitive damages, to deter or punish malicious deprivations of rights.

Because the right to procedural due process is "absolute" in the sense that it does not depend upon the merits of a claimant's substantive assertions, and because of the importance to organized society that procedural due process be observed, we believe that the denial of procedural due process should be actionable for nominal damages without proof of actual injury. We therefore hold that if, upon remand, the District Court determines that respondents' suspensions were justified, respondents nevertheless will be entitled to recover nominal damages not to exceed one dollar from petitioners.

The judgment of the Court of Appeals is reversed, and the case is remanded for further proceedings consistent with this opinion.

It is so ordered.

NOTE ON THE ELEMENTS OF COMPENSATORY DAMAGES

1. Should *Carey*'s prohibition on recovery of substantial damages for the "mere" violation of a right be read in context with the preceding *Smith* decision? If a jury can award substantial damages in every § 1983 case based simply on the violation of a right, then will not juries have wide discretion to levy awards against defendants even in the absence of proof of "recklessness" under *Smith*? Does not *Carey*, at both a practical and philosophical level, preserve the distinction between compensatory and punitive damages?

2. *Carey* first deals with ordinary compensatory damages: for what losses should damages be awarded? What are the interests protected by § 1983, protected so that the loss of them should be compensated? As to the methodology of determining the losses protected under § 1983, *Carey* states that common law notions should provide the "starting point" for deciding the compensable elements of a § 1983 claim, partly echoing a theme in Smith v. Wade. But *Carey* must be wrong in extending this idea to the losses that are compensable, must it not? Perhaps Congress might want common law to

provide guidance as to the kinds of additional damages awardable under § 1983 (nominal and compensatory, in addition to punitive) and even the standards for making such awards (recklessness for punitive damages), but is there any reason to believe that a novel statute protecting constitutional interests would want to incorporate common law as to losses that are compensable?

(a) Re-read *Carey*'s part B. While the Court starts with common law notions does it not pointedly indicate that these concerns must then be "tailored to the interests protected by the particular right in question"? If this is correct, is the tailoring process of identifying compensable elements of damages under § 1983 like the process of identifying standards for each constitutional right claimed under § 1983? See Chapter 1B supra.

(b) If the interests protected by § 1983 are of constitutional source and dimension, then are the losses to be compensated likewise of constitutional source and dimension? See Memphis Community Sch. Dist. v. Stachura, 477 U.S. 299, 106 S.Ct. 2537, 91 L.Ed.2d 249 (1986), discussed in the next Note. If so, will they then vary, as § 1983's standards of care do, from right to right? See *Carey*'s section D; Dellums v. Powell, 566 F.2d 167 (D.C.Cir.1977) (different claims give rise to different damages; no double recovery); Jeffries, *Damages for Constitutional Violations,* 75 VA. L. REV. 1461 (1989).

(c) Is the process of identifying compensable elements of damages more difficult and problematical than identifying standards for each constitutional right invoked under § 1983? Is common law a useful starting point because it expresses our consensual intuition about what harms flow from an illegal decision? How does one know that lost pay compensates for a lost job? Why not simply award the costs of seeking a new job? Is the humiliation that a person feels compensable when police search her without probable cause or a warrant? If legal culture tells us the answer to these questions, is it legal culture that is grounded in the Constitution—or is it merely a consensus grounded in the common law?

3. If courts are to construct rules on compensable loses according to the right at issue, did the Court create good rules for procedural due process cases in *Carey*? Consider here the Court's two ideas: first, that even if a plaintiff shows a violation of procedural due process, no recovery may be had if the defendant thereafter shows that despite the procedural irregularity the underlying substantive decision (e.g., discharge from employment for cause) was correct; and second, that procedural due process cases allow compensation for emotional distress, but only when such injury is proved by "competent evidence," *Carey* at n. 20.

(a) Is the first rule defensible? Will it not simply encourage federal-court mini-trials on the substantive state law issues, something not the concern of federal Due Process? Should not § 1983 be concerned only with the issue of an adequate and timely hearing? Is this aspect of the *Carey* decision not about losses at all, but about causation of losses? Does it sensibly describe when injuries flow from a hearing denial (and are thus compensable) and when they flow from some non–§ 1983 violation (for which there is no compensation)? Is this a *constitutional* rule? If you think not, review the *Mt. Healthy* case, cited in *Carey*, which is discussed in the Note in Chapter 1B.5 supra (similar causation issue as a negation of intent in constitutional cases).

(b) Assume that an erroneous decision was made because of failure to observe the procedures required by Due Process. What losses are then compensable? In the context where an employee is fired for lack of Procedural Due Process, would lost wages be a compensable loss? Mental anguish from plaintiffs having to search for a new job and support his family while unemployed? See Peterson v. Minidoka County School Dist. No. 331, 118 F.3d 1351 (9th Cir.1997) ($200,000 damages for lost income and $100,000 damages for "mental anguish, humiliation, embarrassment, and emotional distress" based on ample "evidence of [plaintiff's] desperate struggle to survive after" his discharge). Lost pension benefits? Denton v. Morgan, 136 F.3d 1038 (5th Cir.1998) (yes). Lost job satisfaction?

(c) Does this second rule override the first rule discussed above? See footnote 19 and accompanying text. If a plaintiff can show humiliation from lack of a hearing, is it not irrelevant that the correct substantive decision was made? If the defendant offers no claim that it made the correct decision, must the plaintiff nevertheless show some actual humiliation? Is expert testimony required to prove emotional injury (and its source), or would the plaintiff's own testimony be adequate? See Miner v. City of Glens Falls, 999 F.2d 655 (2d Cir.1993) (collecting cases).

(d) *Carey* holds that in an appropriate case the plaintiff who has suffered a constitutional loss may recover substantial damages if she proves some actual—not just presumed—loss. How would she show such a loss? Through her own testimony of emotional distress? Cf. Rodriguez–Garcia v. Miranda–Marin, 610 F.3d 756 (1st Cir. 2010) (unconstitutional demotion for free speech; upholding award of $350,000 in non-economic losses based on her testimony that the demotion made her feel "very bad" and "depressed" and doctor's testimony of her need for treatment). Would her testimony alone have been sufficient?

4. Even in the absence of a compensatory award, the Court in *Carey* holds that nominal damages may be awarded for the vindication of the right at issue.

(a) Are there some cases in which the award of only nominal damages would be inadequate? See Westcott v. Crinklaw, 133 F.3d 658 (8th Cir. 1998) (allowing jury to return a verdict for $1 in nominal damages was plain error given proof of actual losses).

(b) Is this not a greater award to plaintiffs than it first appears? See the preceding Note, ¶ 4 (attorneys fees). Some pre-*Carey* cases appear to hold that some injuries are de minimis and not actionable under § 1983. See, e.g., Bart v. Telford, 677 F.2d 622 (7th Cir.1982); Northern v. Nelson, 448 F.2d 1266 (9th Cir.1971). Are such cases consistent with *Carey*?

5. Procedural Due Process has not produced a great many cases on damages, largely because of the Court's later decision in Parratt v. Taylor, Chapter 1G.3 infra. In order to see *Carey*'s general impact, consider some other constitutional rights and the interests they protect—and thus the losses that might be compensable. How do we know which losses are related to the

loss of the right? What is the role for common law for other constitutional rights?

NIEHUS v. LIBERIO

United States Court of Appeals for the Seventh Circuit, 1992.
973 F.2d 526.

POSNER, CIRCUIT JUDGE.

James Niehus was arrested on suspicion of drunk driving and brought to a police station in Berkeley, Illinois, a suburb of Chicago. He got into an argument with the police, and a fight ensued in the course of which—he testified—officers Liberio and Vittorio kicked him in the face, breaking his left cheekbone, as a consequence of which he suffered brain damage that has caused significant although not totally disabling mental and emotional injury. He sued the officers under 42 U.S.C. S 1983, charging that they had used excessive force against him in violation of his rights under the due process clause of the Fourteenth Amendment[.] The jury awarded Niehus $336,320.59 in damages (all compensatory). [This appeal involves a related claim from his wife, who claimed that the beating of her husband had been so stressful to her that it wrecked their marriage and led to their divorce.]

The unavoidable question raised by the cross-appeal is whether Denise Niehus, who attributes the breakup of her marriage to the psychological consequences of her husband's injury, can recover damages under the Constitution for loss of consortium. * * * For scholarly analysis see Michael S. Bogren, "The Constitutionalization of Consortium Claims," 68 U.Det.L.Rev. 479 (1991). She could have brought a claim under state law for loss of consortium [but did not. Rather she] staked her all on convincing [the federal trial court] that loss of consortium is a deprivation of "liberty" within the meaning of the due process clause.

There would be no novelty in interpreting "liberty" to embrace the right of sexual companionship in marriage. The Supreme Court has placed the freedom to marry in the firmament of liberties protected by the due process clause, Loving v. Virginia, 388 U.S. 1, 12, 87 S.Ct. 1817, 1823, 18 L.Ed.2d 1010 (1967); and the sexual dimension of marriage, one of the principal interests encompassed by the right to consortium, W. Page Keeton et al., Prosser and Keeton on the Law of Torts S 125, at p. 931 (5th ed. 1984), was singled out for constitutional protection in Griswold v. Connecticut, 381 U.S. 479, 85 S.Ct. 1678, 14 L.Ed.2d 510 (1965). * * * Setting prisons to one side, we may assume that if the Village of Berkeley decreed that married couples shall live in separate houses except on weekends it would be invading a form of liberty protected by the due process clause. Cf. Ellis v. Hamilton, 669 F.2d 510, 512 (7th Cir.1982). Other family associations, such as that between parent and child or even grandparent and grandchild, have likewise been held to be aspects of liberty protected by the Fourteenth Amendment. Moore v. City of East Cleveland, 431 U.S. 494, 97 S.Ct. 1932, 52 L.Ed.2d 531 (1977).

Wrongful-death suits brought under section 1983 by domiciliaries of states in which the wrongful-death statute is conceived of as conferring a right on the decedent's survivors rather than on his estate * * * provide a particularly apt analogy to Mrs. Niehus's claim, because the suit is allowed even though the plaintiff was not the target of the wrongful conduct. These cases[, some of which allowed consortium recoveries,] have, it is true, evoked a measure of skepticism in other circuits, especially now that the Supreme Court has held that negligent infliction of harm is not actionable under section 1983. Daniels v. Williams, 474 U.S. 327, 330–31, 106 S.Ct. 662, 664–65, 88 L.Ed.2d 662 (1986). As one of our sister circuits said in a case in which a grandmother was seeking damages for the death of her grandchild as a result of wrongful state action, "Protecting familial relationships does not necessarily entail compensating relatives who suffer a loss as a result of wrongful state conduct, especially when the loss is an indirect result of that conduct." Harpole v. Arkansas Department of Human Services, 820 F.2d 923, 928 (8th Cir.1987). But the common law doctrine of transferred intent, In re EDC, Inc., 930 F.2d 1275, 1279 (7th Cir.1991), [may be viewed as protecting our favorable precedents] from attack based on *Daniels*. If A aims at B, and hits C, C can sue A for battery, even though he was not the intended victim and even though battery is an intentional tort. C can of course still sue A if A hits B as well as C. The plaintiff in a survivor's wrongful-death suit is C, the decedent B, the defendant A—so here Mr. Niehus is B, Mrs. Niehus is C, and the defendants are A.

This extension of [the transferred-intent argument] to consortium is neat and logical but not convincing. Concerned to keep section 1983 from swallowing the whole of the states' law of public-officer torts, the courts have confined "liberty" to the core of personhood. Even bodily integrity is not protected completely; minor assaults and batteries are not actionable as deprivations of constitutional liberty. See cases cited in Cameron v. Internal Revenue Service, 773 F.2d 126, 129 (7th Cir.1985). Turning from body to spirit, we point out that minor interferences with peace of mind are also not actionable, Cameron v. Internal Revenue Service, supra, 773 F.2d at 129—nor all major ones. Though some may be, Wilkins v. May, 872 F.2d 190, 195 (7th Cir.1989), even the shock that a bystander might experience from witnessing a shooting is not, and this even if the bystander is the shooting victim's wife. Coon v. Ledbetter, 780 F.2d 1158, 1160–61 (5th Cir.1986). [Even our cases involving wrongful death thought] a limiting principle necessary, and held that the siblings of the victim could not sue for the loss of his companionship. A grandparent suit was nixed on similar grounds in *Harpole*, and a suit by the mother, stepfather, and siblings of an adult in *Valdivieso Ortiz*.

The relationships that define the nuclear family—relationships that for many people are constitutive of their very identity—are protected, as we have seen, and if consortium were a synonym for marriage Mrs. Niehus would have a stronger claim, though whether strong enough we need not speculate. But consortium is not a synonym for marriage. It is the name of the sexual and other services (apart from financial support) that spouses render to each other. Tribble v. Gregory, 288 So.2d 13, 16 (Miss.1974). A loss of consortium can therefore be as minor and transient as a wife's losing a month's help from her husband in mowing the lawn and washing the dishes and grooming the cat, cf. Blansit v. Hyatt Corp., 874 F.2d 1015, 1018 (5th Cir.1989) (raking leaves); Orlando Regional Medical Center, Inc. v. Chmielewski, 573 So.2d 876, 881 (Fla.App.1990) (dancing), and as major as the loss of all spousal services consequent upon an injury that renders the injured spouse a human vegetable.

Deprivations of the lesser services comprehended in the portmanteau term "consortium" are not deprivations of liberty within the restricted meaning that the term bears in the Constitution. The right to a husband's assistance in raking leaves is not a liberty protected by the Fourteenth Amendment. But Mrs. Niehus does not ask us to confine the constitutional right of consortium to the greater deprivations. She wants us to rule that consortium is liberty, period. We decline the invitation. Nor are we eager on our own to fix a point on the scale from the smallest to the largest loss of consortium and say that above that point the Constitution provides a remedy but below it not. Whether (as here) the plaintiff's marriage actually broke up cannot be the criterion, for that would encourage people to divorce in order to maximize their prospects for bringing a claim for loss of consortium under federal law. We add that the authority newly conferred by Congress [in 28 U.S.C. § 1367] to join a state-law claim for consortium with the spouse's constitutional claim, and thus bring both in federal court, will enable persons similarly situated to the Niehuses to obtain full compensation in a single proceeding. That will make the question whether consortium is a constitutionally protected liberty largely an academic one in future cases.

Affirmed.

NOTE ON INTERESTS PROTECTED BY CONSTITUTIONAL LAW

1. In **Memphis Community Sch. Dist. v. Stachura**, 477 U.S. 299, 106 S.Ct. 2537, 91 L.Ed.2d 249 (1986), the plaintiff teacher had been put on leave with pay after community objection to his method of teaching a part of sex education. He later sued under § 1983 for violation of his First Amendment rights, and was reinstated before trial. Nevertheless, a jury ruled that his rights had been violated and awarded him almost $300,000 in compensatory damages, based at least in part on an instruction that gave the jury power to fix damages for the "abstract value" of the right, based on their "discretion." In reversing, the Court observed,

> "We have repeatedly noted that § 1983 creates 'a species of tort liability' [and accordingly,] when § 1983 plaintiffs seek damages for violations of constitutional rights, the level of damages is ordinarily determined according to principles derived from the common law of torts. * * * [D]amages in tort cases are designed to provide 'compensation for the injury caused to plaintiff by defendant's breach of duty.' 2 F. Harper, F.

James, & O. Gray, Law of Torts S 25.1, p. 490 (2d ed. 1986) (emphasis in original). To that end, compensatory damages may include not only out-of-pocket loss and other monetary harms, but also such injuries as 'impairment of reputation . . ., personal humiliation, and mental anguish and suffering.' Congress adopted this common-law system of recovery when it established liability for 'constitutional torts.' Consequently, 'the basic purpose' of § 1983 damages is 'to compensate persons for injuries that are caused by the deprivation of constitutional rights.' Carey v. Piphus. * * *

"The instructions at issue here cannot be squared with *Carey*, or with the principles of tort damages on which *Carey* and § 1983 are grounded. [The instructions] focus, not on compensation for provable injury, but on the jury's subjective perception of the importance of constitutional rights as an abstract matter. *Carey* establishes that such an approach is impermissible."

(a) What did the *Stachura* Court mean by "the level of damages"? Is it an all-encompassing phrase, designed to direct courts to common law for all damages issues in § 1983 cases, or does it have a more limited scope?

(b) Judge Posner's later opinion in the *Niehus* case takes a more discrete approach, asking what interests are protected by the constitutional right at stake. His judgment is informed by common-law discussions but ultimately rests on constitutional concerns. Is it preferable?

(c) In Hartman v. Moore, 547 U.S. 250, 126 S.Ct. 1695, 164 L.Ed.2d 441 (2006), the Court cast doubt on *Stachura* and seemed to approve *Niehus*, calling common law "a source of inspired examples [more] than of prefabricated components." *Hartman*, however, arose in the context of setting evidentiary rules for proving liability in a § 1983 action. Consider the connection between the issue of elements of damages (here) and the issue of elements of a constitutional claim (Chapter 1B supra). Are the issues the same or is the second controlled by federal common law (or perhaps statutory law) rather than constitutional law?

2. Ms. Niehus' claim might be formulated in two different ways. First, she may been seen as arguing that she herself has a constitutional right to her marriage and that when the police caused the break-up of the marriage, her interest in the marriage was lost, including her consortium interest. Her second possible argument is that her husband's Fourth–Amendment right was violated and that she was consequently injured when his right was invaded. How strong is either argument?

(a) How does Judge Posner answer the first possible argument? Does he think that there is no marriage right or that it is simply impossible to prove whether the beating caused the break-up of the marriage? If the latter, is this simply an issue of "proximate cause"? Is Judge Posner saying that as a matter of constitutional law, a beating of one person cannot cause the infringement of a constitutional right of a separate person?

(b) How does Judge Posner respond to the second possible argument? Does he think that there is no injury or simply that it is unquantifiable? Assume the husband had been rendered impotent by a police bullet, and the wife specifically testified, with ample expert support, that she and her husband had had a wonderful sexual relationship before the shooting that was now non-existent—much to her psychological harm. Would her loss then be compensable?

3. The *Stachura* Court recognizes compensation for a range of relatively unquantifiable interests. Why are these interests compensable? For what amount should compensation be awarded?

(a) Prisoners' claims present a special problem because incarcerated persons have little or no actual monetary resources that can be lost, and their lives are already lived in rather degrading conditions. How should they be compensated for unconstitutional changes in their status? See Trobaugh v. Hall, 176 F.3d 1087 (8th Cir.1999):

> "In our opinion, the $1 compensatory damage award was patently insufficient to compensate Trobaugh for the injury he suffered by being placed in segregation in retaliation for exercising a constitutional right [, citing one case 'upholding $2,000 damage award for paraplegic inmates placed in solitary confinement for thirty-two hours' and another 'suggesting appropriate damage range for unconstitutional segregation is between $25 and $129 per day']. Therefore, we reverse the District Court's $1 award and remand so that the Court may award damages of an appropriate amount, which we believe would be in the vicinity of $100 per day for each of the three days [plaintiff] spent in administrative segregation[, citing case holding that 'compensatory damages of $100 per day of solitary confinement not excessive or arbitrary']."

Do you agree? What is the actual value, not the abstract value, of a day of unwarranted isolation? Would a case of failure to provide medical care be easier? See Roe v. Elyea, 631 F.3d 843 (7th Cir. 2011) (jury award of $20,000 for failure to provide medical care under *Estelle* affirmed on appeal). Why?

(b) Consider the same issue outside the prison context. How much should be awarded as compensatory damages for the resulting emotional distress? Compare Mercado–Berrios v. Cancel–Alegria 611 F.3d 18 (1st Cir. 2010) ($113,000 in lost earnings and $100,000 for emotional distress upheld in case of retaliation for free speech), with Deloughery v. City of Chicago, 422 F.3d 611 (7th Cir. 2005) (remittitur in harassment case to $175,000 upheld). How much is a shooting worth? See Whitfield v. Melendez–Rivera, 431 F.3d 1 (1st Cir. 2005) (overturning $4 million award to defendant shot in the leg in violation of *Garner*; overturning $500,000 awards to parents for emotional loss when no specific expenses). What is the value of an unconstitutionally "rough search" that results in no immediate injury? See Carter v. Chicago Police Officers, 165 F.3d 1071 (7th Cir.1998) ($50,000 for search; yet, later action causing death yields only $50,000 award). What is the value of lost dignity resulting from a rape or other invasion of the right to bodily integrity? Compare Rogers v. City of Little Rock, Ark., 152 F.3d 790 (8th Cir.1998) (upholding verdict of $100,000 for woman raped—denied right to "bodily integrity"—by police officer), with Mathie v. Fries, 121 F.3d 808 (2d Cir.1997) (upholding $250,000 award in similar case, plus $250,000 punitive damages).

(c) Assuming that a certain interest is protected, (e.g., an interest in life or an interest in companionship or continued employment), what losses are sufficiently closely related to that interest to warrant compensation? If a developer is unconstitutionally denied the right to develop his property, is his loss the potential lost profits from the project or only the lost value of the land? See Creek v. Village of Westhaven, 144 F.3d 441 (7th Cir.1998) (land value). If a person is killed by police in violation of the Fourth Amendment, are his funeral expenses recoverable in the § 1983 suit? See Westcott v. Crinklaw, 133 F.3d 658 (8th Cir.1998).

4. Review the role of constitutional law and common law in determining damages.

(a) Are losses "related" to the right that was lost—the "duty" that defendant failed to observe—only when socially we deem there to be a relation? Is the common law relevant, as the Court held in *Stachura*, because it is simply an easily-referenced barometer of what losses society has deemed relevant in certain factual contexts? Do we know what losses to protect in constitutional cases by analogizing the constitutional claim (or distinguishing it from) apparently similar common law claims? If so, which version of common law is relevant—today's or that of 1871?

(b) Some aspects of damages, for example the kinds of damages available (punitive, nominal) appear to be decided by reference to § 1983 itself or by reference to common law. See Smith v. Wade, supra. Other aspects of damages, for example, the losses that are compensable under compensatory damages, appear to be decided by reference to the underlying right that plaintiff seeks to enforce, by common law, or by some mixture of constitutional and common law. Compare *Niehus* supra, with *Stachura*, supra. There may be other aspects of damages, e.g., rules about mitigation of damages. How do courts know which of the above approaches to apply to those other issues?

2. INJUNCTIONS

CITY OF LOS ANGELES v. LYONS

Supreme Court of the United States, 1983.
461 U.S. 95, 103 S.Ct. 1660, 75 L.Ed.2d 675.

JUSTICE WHITE delivered the opinion of the Court.

The issue here is whether respondent Lyons satisfied the prerequisites for seeking injunctive relief in the federal district court.

I

This case began on February 7, 1977, when respondent, Adolph Lyons, filed a complaint for damages, injunction, and declaratory relief in the United States District Court for the Central District of California. The defendants were the City of Los Angeles and four of its police officers. The complaint alleged that on October 6, 1976, at 2 a.m., Lyons was stopped by the defendant officers for a traffic or vehicle code violation and that although Lyons offered no resistance or threat whatsoever, the officers, without provocation or justification, seized Lyons and applied a "chokehold"[1]—either the "bar arm control" hold or the "carotid-artery control" hold or both—rendering him unconscious and causing damage to his larynx. [In addition to damages, the complaint sought] a preliminary and permanent injunction against the City barring the use of the control holds[, based on the allegation that city officers routinely and unnecessarily used chokeholds and that Lyons feared again being victimized, all in a continuing violation of the Fourth Amendment.] Injunctive relief was sought against the use of the control holds "except in situations where the proposed victim of said control reasonably appears to be threatening the immediate use of deadly force." [After an intermediate appeal, the trial court ordered a preliminary injunction as requested, finding the facts to be substantially as alleged by the plaintiff. This order was stayed on appeal and still had not gone into effect as of the date of the Supreme Court's decision here.]

II

Since our grant of certiorari, circumstances pertinent to the case have changed. Originally, Lyons' complaint alleged that at least two deaths had occurred as a result of the application of chokeholds by the police. His first amended complaint alleged that 10 chokehold-related deaths had occurred. By May, 1982, there had been five more such deaths. On May 6, 1982, the Chief of Police in Los Angeles prohibited the use of the bar-arm chokehold in any circumstances. A few days later, on May 12, 1982, the Board of Police Commissioners imposed a six-month moratorium on the use of the carotid-artery chokehold except under circumstances where deadly force is authorized. [The City nevertheless sought to have this Court review the case, overturning the court below. Lyons opposed continued review, asking us to dismiss the case as moot.]

* * *

We agree with the City that the case is not moot, since the moratorium by its terms is not permanent. Intervening events have not "irrevocably eradicated the effects of the alleged violation." County of Los Angeles v. Davis, 440 U.S. 625, 631, 99 S.Ct. 1379, 1383, 59 L.Ed.2d 642 (1979). We nevertheless hold, for another reason, that the federal courts are without jurisdiction to entertain Lyons' claim for injunctive relief.

III

It goes without saying that those who seek to invoke the jurisdiction of the federal courts must satisfy the threshold requirement imposed by Article III of the Constitution by alleging an actual case or controversy. Flast v. Cohen, 392 U.S. 83, 94–101, 88 S.Ct. 1942, 1949–1953, 20 L.Ed.2d 947 (1968). Plaintiffs must demonstrate a "personal stake in the outcome" in order to "assure that concrete adverseness which sharpens the

---

1. * * * The "carotid" hold is capable of rendering the subject unconscious by diminishing the flow of oxygenated blood to the brain. The "bar arm" hold, which is administered similarly, applies pressure at the front of the subject's neck. "Bar arm" pressure causes pain, reduces the flow of oxygen to the lungs, and may render the subject unconscious.

presentation of issues" necessary for the proper resolution of constitutional questions. Baker v. Carr, 369 U.S. 186, 204, 82 S.Ct. 691, 703, 7 L.Ed.2d 663 (1962). Abstract injury is not enough. The plaintiff must show that he "has sustained or is immediately in danger of sustaining some direct injury" as the result of the challenged official conduct and the injury or threat of injury must be both "real and immediate," not "conjectural" or "hypothetical." See, e.g., Golden v. Zwickler, 394 U.S. 103, 109–110, 89 S.Ct. 956, 960, 22 L.Ed.2d 113 (1969).

In O'Shea v. Littleton, 414 U.S. 488, 94 S.Ct. 669, 38 L.Ed.2d 674 (1974), we dealt with a case brought by a class of plaintiffs claiming that they had been subjected to discriminatory enforcement of the criminal law. Among other things, a county magistrate and judge were accused of discriminatory conduct in various respects, such as sentencing members of plaintiff's class more harshly than other defendants. The Court of Appeals reversed the dismissal of the suit by the District Court, ruling that if the allegations were proved, an appropriate injunction could be entered.

We reversed for failure of the complaint to allege a case or controversy. Although it was claimed in that case that particular members of the plaintiff class had actually suffered from the alleged unconstitutional practices, we observed that "[p]ast exposure to illegal conduct does not in itself show a present case or controversy regarding injunctive relief ... if unaccompanied by any continuing, present adverse effects." Past wrongs were evidence bearing on "whether there is a real and immediate threat of repeated injury." But the prospect of future injury rested "on the likelihood that [plaintiffs] will again be arrested for and charged with violations of the criminal law and will again be subjected to bond proceedings, trial, or sentencing before petitioners." Ibid. The most that could be said for plaintiffs' standing was "that if [plaintiffs] proceed to violate an unchallenged law and if they are charged, held to answer, and tried in any proceedings before petitioners, they will be subjected to the discriminatory practices that petitioners are alleged to have followed." We could not find a case or controversy in those circumstances: the threat to the plaintiffs was not "sufficiently real and immediate to show an existing controversy simply because they anticipate violating lawful criminal statutes and being tried for their offenses...." It was to be assumed "that [plaintiffs] will conduct their activities within the law and so avoid prosecution and conviction as well as exposure to the challenged course of conduct said to be followed by petitioners."

We further observed that case or controversy considerations "obviously shade into those determining whether the complaint states a sound basis for equitable relief," and went on to hold that even if the complaint presented an existing case or controversy, an adequate basis for equitable relief against petitioners had not been demonstrated:

"[Plaintiffs] have failed, moreover, to establish the basic requisites of the issuance of equitable relief in these circumstances—the likelihood of substantial and immediate irreparable injury, and the inadequacy of remedies at law. We have already canvassed the necessarily conjectural nature of the threatened injury to which [plaintiffs] are allegedly subjected. And if any of the [plaintiffs] are ever prosecuted and face trial, or if they are illegally sentenced, there are available state and federal procedures which could provide relief from the wrongful conduct alleged." 414 U.S., at 502.

Another relevant decision for present purposes is Rizzo v. Goode, 423 U.S. 362, 96 S.Ct. 598, 46 L.Ed.2d 561 (1976), a case in which plaintiffs alleged widespread illegal and unconstitutional police conduct aimed at minority citizens and against City residents in general. The Court reiterated the holding in *O'Shea* that past wrongs do not in themselves amount to that real and immediate threat of injury necessary to make out a case or controversy. * * *

* * *

IV

No extension of *O'Shea* and *Rizzo* is necessary to hold that respondent Lyons has failed to demonstrate a case or controversy with the City that would justify the equitable relief sought. Lyons' standing to seek the injunction requested depended on whether he was likely to suffer future injury from the use of the chokeholds by police officers. Count V of the complaint alleged the traffic stop and choking incident five months before. That Lyons may have been illegally choked by the police on October 6, 1976, while presumably affording Lyons standing to claim damages against the individual officers and perhaps against the City, does nothing to establish a real and immediate threat that he would again be stopped for a traffic violation, or for any other offense, by an officer or officers who would illegally choke him into unconsciousness without any provocation or resistance on his part. The additional allegation in the complaint that the police in Los Angeles routinely apply chokeholds in situations where they are not threatened by the use of deadly force falls far short of the allegations that would be necessary to establish a case or controversy between these parties.

* * *

Under *O'Shea* and *Rizzo*, these allegations were an insufficient basis to provide a federal court with jurisdiction to entertain Count V of the complaint.[8] * * *

* * *

* * * We agree that Lyons had a live controversy with the City. Indeed, he still has a claim for damages against the City that appears to

---

8. As previously indicated, Lyons alleged that he feared he would be choked in any future encounter with the police. * * * It is the reality of the threat of repeated injury that is relevant to the standing inquiry, not the plaintiff's subjective apprehensions. The emotional consequences of a prior act simply are not a sufficient basis for an injunction absent a real and immediate threat of future injury by the defendant. Of course, emotional upset is a relevant consideration in a damages action.

meet all Article III requirements. Nevertheless, the issue here is not whether that claim has become moot but whether Lyons meets the preconditions for asserting an injunctive claim in a federal forum. The equitable doctrine that cessation of the challenged conduct does not bar an injunction is of little help in this respect, for Lyons' lack of standing does not rest on the termination of the police practice but on the speculative nature of his claim that he will again experience injury as the result of that practice even if continued.

The rule that a claim does not become moot where it is capable of repetition, yet evades review, is likewise inapposite. Lyons' claim that he was illegally strangled remains to be litigated in his suit for damages; in no sense does that claim "evade" review. Furthermore, the capable-of-repetition doctrine applies only in exceptional situations, and generally only where the named plaintiff can make a reasonable showing that he will again be subjected to the alleged illegality. DeFunis v. Odegaard, 416 U.S. 312, 319, 94 S.Ct. 1704, 1707, 40 L.Ed.2d 164 (1974). As we have indicated, Lyons has not made this demonstration.

* * *

V

Lyons fares no better if it be assumed that his pending damages suit affords him Article III standing to seek an injunction as a remedy for the claim arising out of the October 1976 events. The equitable remedy is unavailable absent a showing of irreparable injury, a requirement that cannot be met where there is no showing of any real or immediate threat that the plaintiff will be wronged again—a "likelihood of substantial and immediate irreparable injury." O'Shea v. Littleton. The speculative nature of Lyons' claim of future injury requires a finding that this prerequisite of equitable relief has not been fulfilled. Nor will the injury that Lyons allegedly suffered in 1976 go unrecompensed; for that injury, he has an adequate remedy at law. * * * [I]t is not at all "difficult" under our holding "to see how anyone can ever challenge police or similar administrative practices." The legality of the violence to which Lyons claims he was once subjected is at issue in his suit for damages and can be determined there.

* * *

We decline the invitation to slight the preconditions for equitable relief; for as we have held, recognition of the need for a proper balance between state and federal authority counsels restraint in the issuance of injunctions against state officers engaged in the administration of the states' criminal laws in the absence of irreparable injury which is both great and immediate. O'Shea; Younger v. Harris, 401 U.S. 37, 46, 91 S.Ct. 746, 751, 27 L.Ed.2d 669 (1971) [set out later in this Chapter]. * * * In exercising their equitable powers federal courts must recognize "[t]he special delicacy of the adjustment to be preserved between federal equitable power and State administration of its own law." Stefanelli v. Minard,

342 U.S. 117, 120, 72 S.Ct. 118, 120, 96 L.Ed. 138 (1951). The Court of Appeals failed to apply these factors properly and therefore erred in finding that the District Court had not abused its discretion in entering an injunction in this case.

As we noted in *O'Shea,* withholding injunctive relief does not mean that the "federal law will exercise no deterrent effect in these circumstances." If Lyons has suffered an injury barred by the Federal Constitution, he has a remedy for damages under § 1983. Furthermore, those who deliberately deprive a citizen of his constitutional rights risk conviction under the federal criminal laws. Ibid. Beyond these considerations the state courts need not impose the same standing or remedial requirements that govern federal court proceedings. The individual states may permit their courts to use injunctions to oversee the conduct of law enforcement authorities on a continuing basis. But this is not the role of a federal court absent far more justification than Lyons has proffered in this case.

The judgment of the Court of Appeals is accordingly

Reversed.

JUSTICE MARSHALL, with whom JUSTICE BRENNAN, JUSTICE BLACKMUN and JUSTICE STEVENS join, dissenting.

* * * The Court today holds that a federal court is without power to enjoin the enforcement of the City's policy [favoring chokeholds], no matter how flagrantly unconstitutional it may be. Since no one can show that he will be choked in the future, no one—not even a person who, like Lyons, has almost been choked to death—has standing to challenge the continuation of the policy. The City is free to continue the policy indefinitely as long as it is willing to pay damages for the injuries and deaths that result. I dissent from this unprecedented and unwarranted approach to standing.

There is plainly a "case or controversy" concerning the constitutionality of the City's chokehold policy. The constitutionality of that policy is directly implicated by Lyons' claim for damages * * * Lyons therefore has standing to challenge the City's chokehold policy and to obtain whatever relief a court may ultimately deem appropriate. None of our prior decisions suggests that his requests for particular forms of relief raise any additional issues concerning his standing. Standing has always depended on whether a plaintiff has a "personal stake in the outcome of the controversy," Baker v. Carr, 369 U.S. 186, 204, 82 S.Ct. 691, 703, 7 L.Ed.2d 663 (1962), not on the "precise nature of the relief sought." Jenkins v. McKeithen, 395 U.S. 411, 423, 89 S.Ct. 1843, 1849, 23 L.Ed.2d 404 (1969) (opinion of Marshall, J., joined by Warren, C.J., and Brennan, J.).

* * *

* * * [B]y fragmenting a single claim into multiple claims for particular types of relief and requiring a separate showing of standing for each

form of relief, the decision today departs from this Court's traditional conception of standing and of the remedial powers of the federal courts.

* * *

Apparently because it is unwilling to rely solely on its unprecedented rule of standing, the Court goes on to conclude that, even if Lyons has standing, "[t]he equitable remedy is unavailable." The Court's reliance on this alternative ground is puzzling for [this issue was never raised in the petition for certiorari and is not properly before the Court].

* * *

[In any event, courts] of equity have much greater latitude in granting injunctive relief "in furtherance of the public interest ... than when only private interests are involved." Virginian Ry. Co. v. System Federation No. 40, 300 U.S. 515, 552, 57 S.Ct. 592, 601, 81 L.Ed. 789 (1937). See Wright & Miller, supra, at § 2948; 7 Moore's Federal Practice Pt. 2, at P 65.04[1]. In this case we know that the District Court would have been amply justified in considering the risk to the public, for after the preliminary injunction was stayed, five additional deaths occurred prior to the adoption of a moratorium. Under these circumstances, I do not believe that the District Court abused its discretion. * * *

NOTE ON THE RULES GOVERNING AWARD OF INJUNCTIONS IN § 1983 ACTIONS

1. *Lyons* is a rather typical case in that it demonstrates that both constitutional and non-constitutional considerations are relevant to the decision of whether to grant injunctive relief in § 1983 cases. Consider first the Court's decision on standing.

(a) Who has the better argument: the majority that insists that bifurcated or separate standing must be established for each type of relief requested, or Justice Brennan who argues that standing is a separate initial inquiry which, if passed, gives plaintiff license to request any appropriate relief? Does the majority view really give the defendants the power to continue to violate constitutional rights so long as they are willing to pay for it in damages? Will the certainty of an award of punitive damages against the defendants for successive violations have an impact as powerful as an injunction? Is there any such certainty?

(b) Does the majority's standing ruling have substantial impact in any areas outside police encounters with the general public? Would it prevent a school desegregation injunction in a case like Brown v. Board of Education? Compare Buchwald v. University of New Mexico School of Medicine, 159 F.3d 487 (10th Cir.1998) (standing allowed for plaintiff's request for order granting her own admission to medical school, but no general injunction barring future use of non-racial discriminatory criteria permitted because she will not re-apply after being admitted; non-race case). The court in the preceding case referred to its holding as "paradoxical." Is it that—or just wrong?

(c) Would not standing for an injunction be rather easily established in any situation where (1) plaintiffs have regular, ongoing encounters with the defendants (as in school and voting cases), and (2) the defendants adhere to a scheme that is consistently applied to the plaintiff's detriment? In **County of Riverside v. McLaughlin**, 500 U.S. 44, 50, 111 S.Ct. 1661, 1667, 114 L.Ed.2d 49 (1991), the Court distinguished *Lyons* in a case involving the ongoing practice of allegedly denying prompt probable cause hearings. Is police work different because it involves only episodic, non-repetitive encounters between an officer and any particular citizen? See Simmons v. Poe, 47 F.3d 1370 (4th Cir.1995) (alleged racial motives in rape searches; no standing for "extreme remedy" of injunction).

(d) Should "prudential" considerations also limit standing in a constitutional case under § 1983? In **Elk Grove Unified School Dist. v. Newdow**, 542 U.S. 1, 124 S.Ct. 2301, 159 L.Ed.2d 98 (2004), the non-custodial parent of a minor brought suit, on behalf of himself and his daughter, to challenge a school district's practice of reciting the pledge of allegiance at the start of his daughter's daily classes. After a early win, the custodial parent intervened and represented that only she had legal custody with power to represent the child in legal proceedings. Noting that "our standing jurisprudence contains two strands: Article III standing, which enforces the Constitution's case or controversy requirement, and prudential standing, which embodies 'judicially self-imposed limits on the exercise of federal jurisdiction,'" the Justice Stevens' majority opinion ruled against prudential standing for the father. It rested its decision primarily on its desire not to become entangled in a domestic relations dispute between the father and mother. Are you suspicious that Justice Stevens simply saw a religious thicket and avoided it? Can't prudential standing be used to avoid protecting a constitutional right?

2. Relying on traditional equitable principles, the Court also rules that plaintiffs may not obtain an injunction unless there is no adequate remedy at law. Is this rule appropriate for § 1983's Constitution-based claims?

(a) Should the opposite rule apply—that is, that equitable relief should be the preferred remedy in constitutional cases? Is the purpose of § 1983 and constitutional law to compensate victims or to secure compliance? Of course, it is impossible to reverse time and prevent a violation that has already occurred, but where it is known that violations are continuing, should not courts foremost demand the observance of constitutional norms? Does the now-popular phrase "constitutional tort" have a degrading effect by associating constitutional goals with ordinary tort-law goals? See Nahmod, *Section 1983 Discourse: The Move from Constitution to Tort,* 77 GEO. L. J. 1719 (1989).

(b) Is the equitable basis for *Lyons* potentially even more far-reaching than its decision on standing? Does the "adequate remedy at law" rule forbid most injunctions? Is a damage remedy adequate, absent repetitious conduct for any constitutional violation? In Campbell v. Miller, 373 F.3d 834 (7th Cir. 2004), the court upheld denial of relief by a district judge who had found damages to be an adequate remedy at law in individual strip search case. Judge Easterbrook wrote:

"[Plaintiff] supposes that money never is an adequate remedy for a constitutional wrong. That belief is incorrect. Damages are a normal, and adequate, response to an improper search or seizure, which as a constitutional tort often is analogized to (other) personal-injury litigation. See, e.g., Wilson v. Garcia [involving statute of limitations, Chapter 1E supra]. Erroneous grants of injunctive relief that hamper enforcement of the criminal law have the potential to cause havoc, while erroneous awards (or denials) of damages to a single person have more limited ability to injure the general public."

Do you agree?

(c) Think the unthinkable: is there an adequate remedy at law—damages—for all § 1983 claims, except those involving representational interests (such as voting or office-holding)? Are damages an adequate remedy, for example, in a discrimination case charging failure to hire or promote, or should the plaintiff get damages and an injunction awarding the job? Cf. Webb v. Board of Trustees of Ball State University, 167 F.3d 1146 (7th Cir. 1999) (rejecting preliminary relief for teacher on ground that there are costs to others to be considered; final injunction might be appropriate if "continuing" violation). Should damages be the ordinary remedy even in school segregation cases? If a black student received a truly compensatory award, he could afford to pay tuition at the school of his choice, presumably one where he could avoid many residual racial slights. Would this be the best inducement to schools to carry out their programs in a non-discriminatory manner? See H. Cruse, Plural But Equal (1987). Is money the best remedy? The best revenge?

3. Injunctions come in two sizes—prohibitory relief, which requires the defendant to obey the law in the future, and structural or remedial, which requires changes in behavior that may exceed mere future compliance.

(a) In **Lankford v. Gelston**, 364 F.2d 197 (4th Cir.1966) (en banc), the court ordered the district judge to enter an injunction protecting black families from illegal searches and seizures. The Baltimore police department had conducted wholesale searches in the black community, based on unverifiable anonymous tips, in an attempt to catch two black men charged with shooting a white police officer. Similar events had occurred previously. In ordering the injunction, the court reasoned that the individual police officers were effectively judgment-proof and that "the lesson of experience is that the remote possibility of money damages serves as no deterrent to future police invasions." 364 F.2d at 202. The decree simply forbade future unconstitutional searches. Assuming that the injunction is still valid after *Lyons*, what is its value to plaintiffs? None? What action will a court take if its decree is violated? How is this different from filing a new § 1983 action for damages?

(b) In **Rizzo v. Goode**, 423 U.S. 362, 96 S.Ct. 598, 46 L.Ed.2d 561 (1976), the Court declined to permit injunctive relief in a case where two police officers were charged with repeated police brutality and police superiors with condonation of the brutality. Justice Rehnquist's majority opinion first held the superiors not to be responsible for the underlings' violence; then it found *Lankford* to be "obviously distinguishable" because "the wholesale raids [in that case] were the 'effectuation of a plan conceived by high ranking [police] officials,' * * * as to which 'the danger of repetition has not been removed.'" 423 U.S. at 374 n. 8, 96 S.Ct. at 605 n. 8. Is *Lyons* consistent with

Rizzo? Does *Rizzo* validate *Lankford*? Only on grounds different from those stated by the *Lankford* court?

(c) *Lyons* and *Rizzo* both involved requests for structural decrees that would have required extensive supervision or training of police and extensive judicial supervision of the decree. *Lankford*, on the other hand, involved only a general prohibitory decree. Is this the factor that distinguishes the contrary holdings? If so, then has Justice White in *Lyons* crafted a broader rule than necessary? Should prohibitory injunctions—ones that merely prohibit continuation of unconstitutional activity—be easier to obtain?

4. Does the *Lyons* result present special problems in the context of actions as to which there is no "settled constitutional law"? Assuming that there was no settled law as to use of chokeholds, what would happen to Lyons' claim for damages on remand from the Supreme Court's decision? What role would qualified immunity play? Would Lyons be left remediless? If so, does that make it imperative that municipal governments be held liable in such cases and that they be accorded no qualified immunity defense? See Chapter 1H infra.

5. To what extent is the result in *Lyons* predicated on federalism concerns? If local officials are routinely denying the rights of African–Americans in their community, as was alleged in the *O'Shea* case, who will intervene to protect their rights if not the federal courts? State courts? If federalism concerns make the Court reluctant to intervene too forcefully in these problems, do the same concerns apply to Congress? To the Justice Department in pursuing criminal convictions under § 1983's criminal counterpart, 18 U.S.C. § 242?

MILLIKEN v. BRADLEY (*MILLIKEN II*)

Supreme Court of the United States, 1977.
433 U.S. 267, 97 S.Ct. 2749, 53 L.Ed.2d 745.

MR. CHIEF JUSTICE BURGER delivered the opinion of the Court.

We granted certiorari in this case to consider two questions concerning the remedial powers of federal district courts in school desegregation cases, namely, whether a District Court can, as part of a desegregation decree, order compensatory or remedial educational programs for schoolchildren who have been subjected to past acts of *de jure* segregation, and whether, consistent with the Eleventh Amendment, a federal court can require state officials found responsible for constitutional violations to bear part of the costs of those programs.

I

This case is before the Court for the second time following our remand, Milliken v. Bradley, 418 U.S. 717, 94 S.Ct. 3112, 41 L.Ed.2d 1069 (1974) (*Milliken I*); it marks the culmination of seven years of litigation over *de jure* school segregation in the Detroit Public School System. For almost six years, the litigation has focused exclusively on the appropriate remedy to correct official acts of racial discrimination committed by both the Detroit School Board and the State of Michigan. No challenge is now made by the State or the local school board to the prior findings of *de jure* segregation.[1]

A

In the first stage of the remedy, proceedings which we reviewed in *Milliken I*, supra, the District Court, after reviewing several "Detroit-only" desegregation plans, concluded that an interdistrict plan was required to " 'achieve the greatest degree of actual desegregation * * * [so that] no school, grade or classroom [would be] substantially disproportionate to the overall pupil racial composition.' " [To achieve this goal, the district court needed to pull 54 surrounding districts under its decree. The Sixth Circuit affirmed, but we reversed, citing Swann v. Charlotte–Mecklenburg Board of Educ., 402 U.S. 1, 24, 91 S.Ct. 1267, 1280, 28 L.Ed.2d 554 (1971), and pointed out that the lower courts' mistakes were (i) to believe that "as a matter of substantive constitutional right, [a] particular degree of racial balance" is required," and (ii) to bring uninvolved school districts into the remedy phase.] Proceeding from the *Swann* standard "that the scope of the remedy is determined by the nature and extent of the constitutional violation," we held that, on the record before us, there was no interdistrict violation calling for an interdistrict remedy.

[On remand the district court called for new desegregation plans. The plaintiff's plan proposed extensive busing, while the Detroit Board offered little busing but a substantial increase in "educational components."] These compensatory programs, which were proposed in addition to the plan's provisions for magnet schools and vocational high schools, included three of the four components at issue in this case—in-service training for teachers and administrators, guidance and counseling programs, and revised testing procedures. Pursuant to the District Court's direction, the [defendant] State Department of Education on April 21, 1975, submitted a critique of the Detroit Board's desegregation plan; in its report, the Department opined that, although "[i]t is possible that none of the thirteen 'quality education' components is essential * * * to correct the constitutional violation. * * * ", eight of the 13 proposed programs nonetheless deserved special consideration in the desegregation setting. * * *

After receiving the State Board's critique, the District Court conducted extensive hearings on the two plans over a two-month period. [It concluded that "two components of testing and counseling, as then administered in Detroit's schools, were infected with the discriminatory bias" and further found that "to make desegregation work, it was necessary to

---

1. The violations of the Detroit Board of Education, which included the improper use of optional attendance zones, racially based transportation of schoolchildren, improper creation and alteration of attendance zones, grade structures, and feeder school patterns, are described in the District Court's initial "Ruling on Issue of Segregation." 338 F.Supp. 582, 587–588 (E.D.Mich.

include remedial reading programs and in-service training for teachers and administrators." The court of appeals affirmed.]

II

This Court has not previously addressed directly the question whether federal courts can order remedial education programs as part of a school desegregation decree. However, the general principles governing our resolution of this issue are well settled by the prior decisions of this Court. In the first case concerning federal courts' remedial powers in eliminating *de jure* school segregation, the Court laid down the basic rule which governs to this day: "In fashioning and effectuating the [desegregation] decrees, the courts will be guided by equitable principles." Brown v. Board of Education, 349 U.S. 294, 300, 75 S.Ct. 753, 756, 99 L.Ed. 1083 (1955) (*Brown II*).

A

Application of those "equitable principles," we have held, requires federal courts to focus upon three factors. In the first place, like other equitable remedies, the nature of the desegregation remedy is to be determined by the nature and scope of the constitutional violation. The remedy must therefore be related to "the *condition* alleged to offend the Constitution * * *." *Milliken I,* supra, 418 U.S., at 738, 94 S.Ct., at 3124.[14] Second, the decree must indeed be *remedial* in nature, that is, it must be designed as nearly as possible "to restore the victims of discriminatory conduct to the position they would have occupied in the absence of such conduct." Third, the federal courts in devising a remedy must take into account the interests of state and local authorities in managing their own affairs, consistent with the Constitution. * * *

B

In challenging the order before us, petitioners do not specifically question that the District Court's mandated programs are designed, as nearly as practicable, to restore the schoolchildren of Detroit to a position they would have enjoyed absent constitutional violations by state and local officials. And, petitioners do not contend, nor could they, that the prerogatives of the Detroit School Board have been abrogated by the decree, since of course the Detroit School Board itself proposed incorporation of these programs in the first place. Petitioners' sole contention is that, under *Swann,* the District Court's order exceeds the scope of the constitutional violation. Invoking our holding in *Milliken I,* supra, petitioners claim that, since the constitutional violation found by the District Court was the unlawful segregation of students on the basis of race, the court's decree must be limited to remedying unlawful pupil assignments. This contention

1971). The District Court further found that "[t]he State and its agencies * * * have acted directly to control and maintain the pattern of segregation in the Detroit schools." Id., at 589.

14. Thus, the Court has consistently held that the Constitution is not violated by racial imbalance in the schools, without more. An order contemplating the " 'substantive constitutional right [to a] particular degree of racial balance or mixing' " is therefore infirm as a matter of law.

misconceives the principle petitioners seek to invoke, and we reject their argument.

The well-settled principle that the nature and scope of the remedy is to be determined by the violation means simply that federal court decrees must directly address and relate to the constitutional violation itself. Because of this inherent limitation upon federal judicial authority, federal court decrees exceed appropriate limits if they are aimed at eliminating a condition that does not violate the Constitution or does not flow from such a violation, or if they are imposed upon governmental units that were neither involved in nor affected by the constitutional violation, as in *Milliken I,* supra. But where, as here, a constitutional violation has been found, the remedy does not "exceed" the violation if the remedy is tailored to cure the "*condition* that offends the Constitution." *Milliken I,* supra, 418 U.S., at 738, 94 S.Ct., at 3124. (Emphasis supplied.)

The "condition" offending the Constitution is Detroit's *de jure* segregated school system, which was so pervasively and persistently segregated that the District Court found that the need for the educational components flowed directly from constitutional violations by both state and local officials. These specific educational remedies, although normally left to the discretion of the elected school board and professional educators, were deemed necessary to restore the victims of discriminatory conduct to the position they would have enjoyed in terms of education had these four components been provided in a nondiscriminatory manner in a school system free from pervasive *de jure* racial segregation.

* * *

* * * In a word, discriminatory student assignment policies can themselves manifest and breed other inequalities built into a dual system founded on racial discrimination. Federal courts need not, and cannot, close their eyes to inequalities, shown by the record, which flow from a longstanding segregated system.

* * *

We do not, of course, imply that the order here is a blueprint for other cases. That cannot be; in school desegregation cases, "[t]here is no universal answer to complex problems * * *; there is obviously no plan that will do the job in every case." *Green,* supra, 391 U.S., at 439, 88 S.Ct., at 1695. On this record, however, we are bound to conclude that the decree before us was aptly tailored to remedy the consequences of the constitutional violation. Children who have been thus educationally and culturally set apart from the larger community will inevitably acquire habits of speech, conduct, and attitudes reflecting their cultural isolation. * * *

* * *

Nor do we find any other reason to believe that the broad and flexible equity powers of the court were abused in this case. The established role of local school authorities was maintained inviolate, and the remedy is indeed remedial. * * *

* * *

Affirmed.

NOTE ON THE SCOPE OF REMEDIAL DISCRETION

1. In **Dayton Bd. of Educ. v. Brinkman**, 433 U.S. 406, 97 S.Ct. 2766, 53 L.Ed.2d 851 (1977), the Court overturned a district court's district-wide school desegregation decree. The district court had found a "cumulative violation" of constitutional rights without specifically articulating the defendants' impermissible actions, and the Court ruled that this ambiguous approach made it impossible to determine appropriate relief. This was because if "violations are found, the District Court * * * must determine how much incremental segregative effect these violations had on the racial distribution [in the school system]. The remedy must be designed to redress that difference * * *."

(a) A necessary complement to the *Milliken* and *Dayton* cases must be that if there is no violation, then there is no judicial remedy, correct? See Lopez v. Garriga, 917 F.2d 63 (1st Cir.1990) (no authority to issue injunction for plaintiffs after jury ruled against their claim at damages trial).

(b) Is it also a necessary complement that where there is a violation without an adequate remedy at law, there *must* be an injunctive remedy imposed? For a classic formulation of an affirmative answer, see Louisiana v. United States, 380 U.S. 145, 154, 85 S.Ct. 817, 13 L.Ed.2d 709 (1965). If a past violation has no continuing impact, must there be a remedy? May there be? See Bazemore v. Friday, 478 U.S. 385, 106 S.Ct. 3000, 92 L.Ed.2d 315 (1986) (state dropped rules requiring segregated 4–H and Homemaker Clubs, which thereafter remained racially segregated by voluntary choice of members).

(c) The Court seems to suggest in *Milliken* that the rules governing the scope of courts' injunctive power are based in traditional equitable principles. Do you discern a different basis? Are these norms, even though they mimic equitable phrases, really based in constitutional law?

2. Is *Milliken* consistent with the proportionality rule it purports to apply? Does the Court not order defendants to provide more than would be constitutionally required of them absent litigation? Does the proportionality rule confine courts to prohibitory decrees, or should it properly permit courts to demand super-constitutional efforts from defendants guilty of prior violations?

(a) Assume that "C" represents a constitutional norm. If defendant violates that norm by a factor of "1," she reduces plaintiff to a condition of "C" minus "1" or "C–1." Merely to order defendant to conform again to C would not help plaintiff, who would remain at C–1. Under *Milliken* the court would order the defendant to exceed C by a factor of +1 in order to make the plaintiff whole: violation (C–1) offset by remedy (+1) returns plaintiff to even (C). *Milliken* is representative of a broad group of cases where courts impose on defendants super-constitutional duties that would not be imposed in the absence of a prior constitutional violation. See, e.g., Hutto v. Finney, 437 U.S. 678, 98 S.Ct. 2565, 57 L.Ed.2d 522 (1978) (lengthy punitive solitary confinement not itself a constitutional violation, but where other inhumane violations found, such confinement may be enjoined as a remedy); Gilmore v. City of Montgomery, 417 U.S. 556, 94 S.Ct. 2416, 41 L.Ed.2d 304 (1974) (city ordinarily under no duty to forbid segregated private school groups to use city parks, but where city guilty of prior segregation in parks and schools, such a duty may be imposed as a remedy); Turner v. Fouche, 396 U.S. 346, 90 S.Ct. 532, 24 L.Ed.2d 567 (1970) (with companion case, demonstrating that while there is no right to proportional racial representation on jury absent a showing of racial discrimination, after such a showing court may order proportional representation as a remedy).

(b) Is *Milliken*'s rule, then, nothing but a corollary to rules of proportionality in damages: while a police officer is normally under no duty to pay a citizen $10,000, if he unconstitutionally beats the citizen and causes $10,000 in damages, then courts will impose a super-constitutional requirement to pay plaintiff that amount?

3. For the reasons just stated, the problematic question in this area has not been whether courts can order super-constitutional relief, but what amount of relief is the proper compensatory amount. In the real world the degree of constitutional infraction cannot easily be denominated as C–1 or C–3, with respective corresponding +1 and +3 remedies.

(a) Is it so clear that the remedies ordered in *Milliken* cure the underlying violations? Is it a question of degree? To what degree does the remedy cure the violation? Note the Court's language: "directly address and relate to." Does this demand something more than the well-known "rational basis test"? Should courts be more closely cabined in curing constitutional ills than legislatures are in curing social and economic ills? Why so?

(b) Despite the difficulty of correlating violation and cure, some cases may present bright lines. For example, in an earlier phase of the *Milliken* case ("*Milliken I*," as cited in the excerpts above), the Court reversed a decree ordering relief against school boards not proven guilty of racial discrimination. The remedy, held the Court, must be confined to the boundaries of the entity that committed the violation. How many other such "bright line" cases would you anticipate? Is the bright line in *Milliken I* really so bright?

4. Multiple remedial choices may satisfy *Milliken*'s demand that relief be directly curative of the underlying violation. Should a court have broad discretion to choose among these available remedies? In **Swann v. Charlotte–Mecklenburg Bd. of Educ.**, 402 U.S. 1, 6, 91 S.Ct. 1267, 28 L.Ed.2d 554 (1971), Chief Justice Burger's decision for a unanimous Court suggested that courts would need to consider the "intractable realities" and choose from among competing alternatives the most workable remedial combination.

(a) Does *Swann* authorize a judge, after a violation is shown, to sit as an administrator or legislator in selecting from among permissible remedies? Is this a non-judicial function?

(b) This paragraph assumes that a judge first decides which remedies are permissible, then she selects from among those to find a final remedy or combination of permissible remedies. In reality are the two steps only one? Do judges—should judges—simply look for remedies and ask only if they are effective? As indefinite as the scope of remedial discretion might be under *Milliken,* are there some outside limits beyond which a court may not go?

MISSOURI v. JENKINS (*JENKINS IV*)

United States Supreme Court, 1995.
515 U.S. 70, 115 S.Ct. 2038, 132 L.Ed.2d 63.

CHIEF JUSTICE REHNQUIST delivered the opinion of the Court.

As this school desegregation litigation enters its 18th year, we are called upon again to review the decisions of the lower courts. In this case, the State of Missouri has challenged the District Court's order of salary increases for virtually all instructional and noninstructional staff within the Kansas City, Missouri, School District (KCMSD) and the District Court's order requiring the State to continue to fund remedial "quality education" programs because student achievement levels were still "at or below national norms at many grade levels."[1]

[At this stage of the litigation, the trial court's orders have run up a bill for over $200 million. The capital improvements now exceed $500 million. KCMSD's enrollment is 68% black, so the usual remedies of busing and schools re-assignments have not been used by the trial court. Therefore, not without reason, the] District Court's desegregation plan has been described as the most ambitious and expensive remedial program in the history of school desegregation. The annual cost per pupil at the KCMSD far exceeds that of the neighboring [school districts] or of any school district in Missouri. Nevertheless, the KCMSD, which has pursued a "friendly adversary" relationship with the plaintiffs, has continued to propose ever more expensive programs. As a result, the desegregation costs have escalated and now are approaching an annual cost of $200 million. These massive expenditures have financed "high schools in which every classroom will have air conditioning, an alarm system, and 15 microcomputers; a 2,000–square–foot planetarium; green houses and vi-variums; a 25–acre farm with an air-conditioned meeting room for 104 people; a Model United Nations wired for language translation; broadcast capable radio and television studios with an editing and animation lab; a temperature controlled art gallery; movie editing and screening rooms; a 3,500–square–foot dust-free diesel mechanics room; 1,875–square–foot elementary school animal rooms for use in a zoo project; swimming pools; and numerous other facilities." Not surprisingly, the cost of this remedial

---

1. [In an earlier appeal of the same case, Missouri v. Jenkins (*Jenkins III*), 495 U.S. 33, 110 S.Ct. 1651, 109 L.Ed.2d 31 (1990), the Supreme Court had foreseen a tripling of costs under the trial court's desegregation order. Since the school district could not pay this amount, the Supreme Court approved removal of state caps on local taxes so that the local government could be ordered to raise taxes to pay for the plan. The state was also ordered to bear some costs, upholding a district court order to apportion the costs of remedies between the two culpable defendants, the KCMSD and the state.—Ed.]

plan has "far exceeded KCMSD's budget, or for that matter, its authority to tax." The [co-defendant] State, through the operation of joint-and-several liability, has borne the brunt of these costs. The District Court candidly has acknowledged that it has "allowed the District planners to dream" and "provided the mechanism for th[ose] dreams to be realized." In short, the District Court "has gone to great lengths to provide KCMSD with facilities and opportunities not available anywhere else in the country."

II

With this background, we turn to the present controversy. First, the State has challenged the District Court's requirement that it fund salary increases for KCMSD instructional and noninstructional staff. * * *

Almost 25 years ago, in Swann v. Charlotte–Mecklenburg Bd. of Ed., we dealt with the authority of a district court to fashion remedies for a school district that had been segregated in law in violation of the Equal Protection Clause of the Fourteenth Amendment. Although recognizing the discretion that must necessarily adhere in a district court in fashioning a remedy, we also recognized the limits on such remedial power: "[E]limination of racial discrimination in public schools is a large task and one that should not be retarded by efforts to achieve broader purposes lying beyond the jurisdiction of the school authorities. One vehicle can carry only a limited amount of baggage. It would not serve the important objective of *Brown I* to seek to use school desegregation cases for purposes beyond their scope, although desegregation of schools ultimately will have impact on other forms of discrimination."

[In our later *Milliken* decisions, we "said that a desegregation remedy 'is necessarily designed, as all remedies are, to restore the victims of discriminatory conduct to the position they would have occupied in the absence of such conduct.' *Milliken I*. We responded in *Milliken II* with a "three-part framework derived from our prior cases to guide district courts in the exercise of their remedial authority": the requirements that (i) the nature of the remedy must relate to the nature and scope of the violation; (ii) the remedy must be "remedial" and restore the plaintiff to the "position they would have occupied in the absence of" the violation; and (iii) the trial court must take into account the management interests of local and state authorities.] In applying these principles, we have identified "student assignments, ... 'faculty, staff, transportation, extra-curricular activities and facilities,'" as the most important indicia of a racially segregated school system.

Proper analysis of the District Court's orders challenged here, then, must rest upon their serving as proper means to the end of restoring the victims of discriminatory conduct to the position they would have occupied in the absence of that conduct and their eventual restoration of "state and local authorities to the control of a school system that is operating in compliance with the Constitution." We turn to that analysis.

[The salary supplements required by the district court were crafted to serve the "interdistrict goals" of getting better teachers for KCMSD so as to attract white students from the suburbs; but the district court found only an "intradistrict violation" within Kansas City itself. This remedy thus exceeds the scope of the violation under *Milliken I*.] The proper response to an intradistrict violation is an intradistrict remedy that serves to eliminate the racial identity of the schools within the effected school district by eliminating, as far as practicable, the vestiges of de jure segregation in all facets of their operations.

* * *

[It is true that we have previously approved the use of "magnet schools" as an intradistrict remedy.] The District Court's remedial plan in this case, however, is not designed solely to redistribute the students within the KCMSD in order to eliminate racially identifiable schools within the KCMSD. Instead, its purpose is to attract nonminority students from outside the KCMSD schools. But this interdistrict goal is beyond the scope of the intradistrict violation identified by the District Court. In effect, the District Court has devised a remedy to accomplish indirectly what it admittedly lacks the remedial authority to mandate directly: the interdistrict transfer of students. * * * [In the absence of proof that the State caused "white flight" that would merit an interdistrict remedy, the] District Court's pursuit of "desegregative attractiveness" is beyond the scope of its broad remedial authority.

* * *

The District Court's pursuit of "desegregative attractiveness" cannot be reconciled with our [other] cases placing limitations on a district court's remedial authority. It is certainly theoretically possible that the greater the expenditure per pupil within the KCMSD, the more likely it is that some unknowable number of nonminority students not presently attending schools in the KCMSD will choose to enroll in those schools. Under this reasoning, however, every increased expenditure, whether it be for teachers, noninstructional employees, books, or buildings, will make the KCMSD in some way more attractive, and thereby perhaps induce nonminority students to enroll in its schools. But this rationale is not susceptible to any objective limitation. This case provides numerous examples demonstrating the limitless authority of the District Court operating under this rationale. In short, desegregative attractiveness has been used "as the hook on which to hang numerous policy choices about improving the quality of education in general within the KCMSD."

Nor are there limits to the duration of the District Court's involvement. The expenditures per pupil in the KCMSD currently far exceed those in the neighboring [school districts, over $9,400/pupil versus $2,854 to $5,956 in other districts.] Each additional program ordered by the District Court—and financed by the State—to increase the "desegregative attractiveness" of the school district makes the KCMSD more and more dependent on additional funding from the State; in turn, the greater the KCMSD's dependence on state funding, the greater its reliance on continued supervision by the District Court. But our cases recognize that local autonomy of school districts is a vital national tradition, and that a district court must strive to restore state and local authorities to the control of a school system operating in compliance with the Constitution.

* * *

[The State has also challenged the district court's order of continued operation of certain "quality education" programs. Based on considerations similar to those noted above, we uphold the State's argument. The district court's rationale for continued funding was that "student achievement levels were still 'at or below national norms at many grade levels.' We analyze this issue as a question of whether the State has met its court-imposed desegregation duties under Freeman v. Pitts, 503 U.S. 467, 112 S.Ct. 1430, 118 L.E.2d. 108 (1992).] The basic task of the District Court is to decide whether the reduction in achievement by minority students attributable to prior de jure segregation has been remedied to the extent practicable. Under our precedents, the State and the KCMSD are "entitled to a rather precise statement of [their] obligations under a desegregation decree." Although the District Court has determined that "[s]egregation has caused a system wide reduction in achievement in the schools of the KCMSD," it never has identified the incremental effect that segregation has had on minority student achievement or the specific goals of the quality education programs.

* * * As all the parties agree that improved achievement on test scores is not necessarily required for the State to achieve partial unitary status as to the quality education programs, the District Court should sharply limit, if not dispense with, its reliance on this factor. Just as demographic changes independent of de jure segregation will affect the racial composition of student assignments, so too will numerous external factors beyond the control of the KCMSD and the State affect minority student achievement. So long as these external factors are not the result of segregation, they do not figure in the remedial calculus. Insistence upon academic goals unrelated to the effects of legal segregation unwarrantably postpones the day when the KCMSD will be able to operate on its own.

* * *

The judgment of the Court of Appeals is reversed.

It is so ordered.

JUSTICE O'CONNOR, concurring. [Omitted.]

JUSTICE THOMAS, concurring.

It never ceases to amaze me that the courts are so willing to assume that anything that is predominantly black must be inferior. * * *

Two threads in our jurisprudence have produced this unfortunate situation * * * First, the court has read our cases to support the theory that black students suffer an unspecified psychological harm from segregation that retards their mental and educational development. This approach not only relies upon questionable social science research rather than constitutional principle, but it also rests on an assumption of black inferiority. Second, we have permitted the federal courts to exercise virtually unlimited equitable powers to remedy this alleged constitutional violation. The exercise of this authority has trampled upon principles of federalism and the separation of powers and has freed courts to pursue other agendas unrelated to the narrow purpose of precisely remedying a constitutional harm * * *.

* * *

Given that desegregation has not produced the predicted leaps forward in black educational achievement, there is no reason to think that black students cannot learn as well when surrounded by members of their own race as when they are in an integrated environment. Indeed, it may very well be that what has been true for historically black colleges is true for black middle and high schools. Despite their origins in "the shameful history of state-enforced segregation," these institutions can be " 'both a source of pride to blacks who have attended them and a source of hope to black families who want the benefits of . . . learning for their children.' " United States v. Fordice, 505 U.S. 717, 748, 112 S.Ct. 2727, 2746. Because of their "distinctive histories and traditions," black schools can function as the center and symbol of black communities, and provide examples of independent black leadership, success, and achievement. [We should not believe that "segregation injures blacks because blacks, when left on their own, cannot achieve. To my way of thinking, that conclusion is the result of a jurisprudence based upon a theory of black inferiority."]

* * *

The dissent's approval of the District Court's treatment of salary increases is typical of this Court's failure to place limits on the equitable remedial power[, limits that would "ensure that constitutional remedies are actually targeted toward those who have been injured."] When the standard of review is as vague as whether "Federal-court decrees . . . directly address and relate to the constitutional violation," *Milliken II*, it is difficult to ever find a remedial order "unreasonable." Such criteria provide District Courts with little guidance, and provide appellate courts few principles with which to review trial court decisions. If the standard reduces to what one believes is a "fair" remedy, or what vaguely appears to be a good "fit" between violation and remedy, then there is little hope of imposing the constraints on the equity power that the framers envisioned and that our constitutional system requires. * * *

JUSTICE SOUTER, with whom JUSTICE STEVENS, JUSTICE GINSBURG, and JUSTICE BREYER join, dissenting.

* * *

* * * While the Court suggests otherwise, the District Court did not ground its orders of salary increases solely on the goal of attracting students back to the KCMSD. From the start, the District Court has consistently treated salary increases as an important element in remedying the systemwide reduction in student achievement resulting from segregation in the KCMSD. As noted above, the Court does not question this remedial goal, which we expressly approved in *Milliken II*. The only issue, then, is whether the salary increases ordered by the District Court have been reasonably related to achieving that goal, keeping in mind the broad discretion enjoyed by the District Court in exercising its equitable powers. [Salary supplements certainly would keep the better teachers in the district, teachers better able to provide the remedial programs necessary in a school district under court order to desegregate.]

* * *

* * * There is no dispute that before the District Court's remedial plan was placed into effect the schools in the unreformed segregated system were physically a shambles: "The KCMSD facilities still have numerous health and safety hazards, educational environment hazards, functional impairments, and appearance impairments. The specific problems include: inadequate lighting; peeling paint and crumbling plaster on ceilings, walls and corridors; loose tiles, torn floor coverings; odors resulting from unventilated restrooms with rotted, corroded toilet fixtures; noisy classrooms due to lack of adequate acoustical treatment; lack of off street parking and bus loading for parents, teachers and students; lack of appropriate space for many cafeterias, libraries and classrooms; faulty and antiquated heating and electrical systems; damaged and inoperable lockers; and inadequate fire safety systems. The conditions at Paseo High School are such that even the principal stated that he would not send his own child to that facility." The cost of turning this shambles into habitable schools was enormous, as anyone would have seen long before the District Court ordered repairs. Property tax-paying parents of white children, seeing the handwriting on the wall in 1985, could well have decided that the inevitable cost of clean-up would produce an intolerable tax rate and could have moved to escape it. The District Court's remedial orders had not yet been put in place. Was the white flight caused by segregation or desegregation? * * * My point is only that the Court is on shaky grounds when it assumes that prior segregation and later desegregation are separable in fact as causes of "white flight," that the flight can plausibly be said to result from desegregation alone, and that therefore as a matter of fact the "intradistrict" segregation violation lacked the relevant consequences outside the district required to justify the District Court's magnet concept. With the arguable plausibility of each of these assumptions seriously in question, it is simply rash to reverse the concurrent factual findings of the District Court and the Court of Appeals [that interdistrict white flight is a cause of KCMSD's current problems].

Justice Ginsburg, dissenting. [Omitted]

NOTE ON THE OUTER LIMITS OF INJUNCTIVE RELIEF

1. Consider this argument: Curing past constitutional violations requires an appreciation for the subtle social problems created by that violation; formulating a remedy is, much like the process of legislating in any social arena, a matter of practicality—experimenting, seeing what works, and moving forward incrementally over many years.

(a) Justice Souter, dissenting in *Jenkins IV*, argues that district courts should be accorded power to formulate a package of remedies that "reasonably relate[]" to curing past segregation, an approach that admittedly gives "broad discretion" to the trial judge. Note the similarity of the formula to that used for low-level scrutiny in reviewing legislative enactments. See, e.g., Dandridge v. Williams, 397 U.S. 471, 90 S.Ct. 1153, 25 L.Ed.2d 491 (1970) (due process analysis of social legislation); Williamson v. Lee Optical, 348 U.S. 483, 75 S.Ct. 461, 99 L.Ed. 563 (1955) (equal protection analysis; lax "rational" relation does not require logical consistency). Is Justice Souter suggesting that trial judges should be reviewed for their remedial efforts as legislators are for their problem-solving? Cf. *Williamson* supra: "It is enough that there is an evil at hand for correction, and that it might be thought that the particular [remedial] measure was a rational way to correct it."

(b) The Court has often said that legislation is reviewed laxly because the legislature has special capacities for making policy judgments, capacities that judges lack. See New York City Transit Auth. v. Beazer, 440 U.S. 568, 99 S.Ct. 1355, 59 L.Ed.2d 587 (1979) (drug policy is for legislature). Does this mean that judges should not be treated the same as legislators?

(c) Legislators have general competence, but federal judges have competence, Justice Souter concedes, only to cure constitutional (or other federal statutory) violations. Is the problem with Justice Souter's approach that it permits federal judges to pursue two remedies simultaneously—one constitutional (desegregation) and one policy-based (better schools)? How does Justice Souter respond to this criticism? Is he more realistic that Chief Justice Rehnquist? Is he right?

2. Consider this argument: If the Court had paid serious attention to the district court's over-spending back in *Jenkins III*, see Editor's footnote "a" in *Jenkins IV*, the earlier decision involving courts in a tax increase would have never been necessary. Was Chief Justice Rehnquist correct in *Jenkins III* when he said that unrestrained spending on issues unrelated to desegregation was the crux of the problem?

(a) Consider the remedial items listed by the majority in *Jenkins IV*, particularly the "2,000–square–foot planetarium; green houses and vivariums; [the] 25–acre farm with an air-conditioned meeting room for 104 people; [the] temperature controlled art gallery; [and the] swimming pools." Was the trial judge his own worst enemy? If these facilities are related to desegregation, what is not? If a vacation in the Bahamas would produce more rested and motivated teachers—ones who had seen a functioning majority-black culture—could the trial judge have ordered such vacations for teachers? Could he have done it by labeling the trips as "teacher training"? Cf. *Milliken II*, supra.

(b) Is the problem with the majority opinion in *Jenkins IV* that it gives no standard for dividing what remedies are acceptable and what remedies are forbidden? Chief Justice Rehnquist seizes on the trial judge's statement that he had sought to achieve "desegregative attractiveness," which the majority is able easily to characterize as a forbidden attempt at an interdistrict remedy, one beyond the scope of the school district's violation. See *Milliken II*, supra. If the district judge had never uttered these words, how would the Court have justified its view that the cited remedies exceeded the scope of the violation? Does *Jenkins IV* pack less punch than at first appears? See People Who Care v. Rockford Bd. of Educ., 171 F.3d 1083 (7th Cir.1999) ("We can decide which provisions of the remedial decree are valid and which invalid, but when it comes to the design of specific programs for achieving the objectives of the valid provisions, and to the funding for those programs, we have no practical alternative to deferring broadly to the judgment of the district court").

(c) In **Lewis v. Casey**, 518 U.S. 343, 116 S.Ct. 2174, 135 L.Ed.2d 606 (1996), the Court struck down an injunction reforming the Arizona prison system's methods for providing legal materials to inmates. The Court emphasized that only two inmates had shown any injury from failure to obtain legal materials to assist their preparation of their court cases, then it interpreted its precedents as not calling for law libraries in prisons per se, but as requiring effective access to the courts. Moreover, the Court noted that the two persons affected, one illiterate and the other a non-English speaker, were inadequate to support a system-wide remedy. Does *Lewis* suffer line-drawing problems as in *Jenkins IV*? No, because the number of affected plaintiffs was so low?

3. In **Schenck v. Pro–Choice Network of Western N.Y.**, 519 U.S. 357, 117 S.Ct. 855, 137 L.Ed.2d 1 (1997), the Supreme Court considered a federal court's injunction limiting protests at abortion clinics. The Court unanimously ruled that because of the potential restrictions on protected speech, the district judge could issue no injunction greater than that "necessary to serve a significant governmental interest." Does this provide a model for reviewing creative remedial decrees in all cases? On the other hand in **Grupo Mexicano de Desarrollo S.A. v. Alliance Bond Fund, Inc.**, 527 U.S. 308, 119 S.Ct. 1961, 144 L.Ed.2d 319 (1999), the Court faced an ordinary commercial case involving notes sold to finance a toll road, and talked at length about the desirability of a "dynamic equity jurisprudence" that is "adequate to the social needs," and "possesses an inherent capacity of expansion, so as to keep abreast of each succeeding generation and age." Is that a better model for reviewing these cases?

(a) Is *Schenck*'s higher scrutiny only appropriate because First Amendment speech rights were at stake? Because two rights were at stake—the abortion right and speech rights? Or is it a salutary approach for reviewing all injunctions in order to prevent judicial over-reaching? Compare the similar issues that arise in awarding injunctive relief in the employment context, where courts enforce the duty to return victims of discrimination to their "rightful place" in employment. See Chapter 7C infra.

(b) Do all desegregation decrees also involve competing rights—because the plaintiffs are entitled to be free from race-based decisions, but so are all the school children who would be affected by an overbroad remedial decree? See Capacchione v. Charlotte–Mecklenburg Schools, 57 F.Supp.2d 228 (W.D.N.C.1999) (race-based assignment policies that help blacks but go beyond curing past discrimination constitute forbidden present-day discrimination against whites). Cf. City of Richmond v. J.A. Croson Co., Chapter 7B.5 infra (strict scrutiny for race-based affirmative action). See also Lewis v. Casey, ¶ 2(c) supra (failing to take into account local authorities' needs dooms wide-ranging remedy).

(c) Notice the unusual litigating posture taken by KCMSD in this case. Did it really oppose relief, or was it in silent partnership with the plaintiffs from the beginning to obtain more revenues for local education? Should the courts strictly review all relief that comes from settlements that are non-adversarial? Do they represent a peculiar danger that the trial court's decree may exceed the scope of the violation?

(d) Finally, consider this: are the two approaches actually different? In *Grupo Mexicano*, supra, the Court's opinion, authored by Justice Scalia, cited school desegregation cases as an example of dynamic modern equity jurisprudence, 119 S.Ct. at 1977 n.4. Is it possible that even a "dynamic jurisprudence" has its limits, or was Justice Scalia's statement filled with irony?

4. Now consider the taxing issues raised in *Jenkins III*, 495 U.S. 33, 110 S.Ct. 1651, 109 L.Ed.2d 31 (1990) (discussed in footnote "a" in *Jenkins IV*). It represents the high-water mark for judicial intervention in local affairs in the course of carrying out a remedial decree. Are the tax issues discussed there analytically the same as the issues discussed above, or do they present distinctive problems?

(a) Is the assertion of judicial taxing power, or the power to lift democratically adopted limitations on taxes, a usurpation of state power? Of legislative power? In dissent there, Justice Kennedy noted that the district court lacks the perspective to see the full range of community needs and make sophisticated political and moral judgments necessary in the allocation of public resources. See 495 U.S. at 69, 110 S.Ct. at 1673 ("federal judges have no fear that the competition for scarce public resources could result in a diminution of their salaries[, and it] is not surprising that imposition of taxes by an authority so insulated from public communication or control can lead to deep feelings of frustration, powerlessness, and anger on the part of taxpaying citizens"). If Kansas City's resources are devoted overwhelmingly to educational reform, will there be tax resources left to deal with environmental problems, prison reform, health care delivery, or better training for law enforcement officers? But does not every federal injunctive decree create the same possibility of judicial skewing of local resource-allocation decisions? If a court orders a desegregation program and the defendant "voluntarily" levies a tax to pay for the decree, is not the same resource allocation problem created?

(b) Is the majority in *Jenkins III* driven by the "bad government" view of law? Has it created a remedy that is necessary only because one believes that without the power, a "bad government" could thumb its nose at a federal court's constitutional ruling? See Griffin v. Prince Edward County School Bd., 377 U.S. 218, 233, 84 S.Ct. 1226, 1234, 12 L.Ed.2d 256 (1964) (upholding the remedy in a school desegregation case where the county had tried to avoid relief by shuttering all its schools, black and white).[1]

(c) Is the *Jenkins III* majority's differentiation between ordering a tax and ordering a government to meet its burden (while removing state-level limits on its power to do so) an act of Solomonic wisdom—or just a political shell game? What could occur under the majority's approach that would not occur if the district court were permitted to order a certain tax?

5. Finally, consider how the issues raised in these school desegregation cases play out in other areas of constitutional litigation, particularly ones in which defendants have with steadfast recalcitrance refused to remedy their own constitutional violations.

(a) In **Brown v. Plata**, ___ U.S. ___, 131 S.Ct. 1910, 179 L.Ed.2d 969 (2011), the Court reviewed a lower court order requiring California, absent construction of new facilities, to relieve persistent unconstitutional overcrowding and lack of medical care in its prisons by releasing incarcerated offenders—approximately 46,000 of the total of 156,000 prisoners. The Court emphasized that massive violations had persisted for years and that no other way than release of prisoners had been found to cure the admitted constitutional violations. Said the Court, ___ U.S. at ___, 131 S.Ct. at 1944:

> "Establishing the population at which the State could begin to provide constitutionally adequate medical and mental health care, and the appropriate time frame within which to achieve the necessary reduction, requires a degree of judgment. The inquiry involves uncertain predictions regarding the effects of population reductions, as well as difficult determinations regarding the capacity of prison officials to provide adequate care at various population levels. Courts have substantial flexibility when making these judgments. "Once invoked, 'the scope of a district court's equitable powers . . . is broad, for breadth and flexibility are inherent in equitable remedies.' Hutto; Milliken v. Bradley, Swann v. Charlotte–Mecklenburg Bd. of Ed.[2]"

Justice Scalia's dissent took the view that the "proper outcome is so clearly indicated by tradition and common sense" that the Court should seek to avoid the "judicial travesty" occasioned by the trial court. He specifically noted that "structural injunctions are radically different from the injunctions traditionally issued by courts of equity" because they expand the judicial power over non-constitutional issues, here giving relief to prisoners who themselves may have never been subject to constitutional violations. The choice between curing violations or releasing undeserving prisoners onto an

---

1. Assume that KCMSD had violated the Constitution by levying an impermissible tax, then spent all of the money, then refused to raise alternative taxes to reimburse the persons it had illegally taxed. Would the Court order a tax levy to repay those who suffered this constitutional deprivation? See McKesson Corp. v. Division of Alcoholic Beverages & Tobacco, 496 U.S. 18, 110 S.Ct. 2238, 110 L.Ed.2d 17 (1990) (unanimous opinion) (Due Process Clause requires that state must provide repayment). Is *McKesson* distinguishable because the Court did not specifically order a tax levy—it only told the defendant to repay? But if the defendant had refused to repay, what would the Court have done? Nothing?

2. The Prison Litigation Reform Act of 1995, 18 U.S.C. § 3626, places additional limitations on judicial decrees regulating prison practices, including orders limiting prison populations. The Court found all these to be met.

innocent population seems unbelievably difficult. Which solution is better? Less bad?

(b) In **Spallone v. United States**, 493 U.S. 265, 110 S.Ct. 625, 107 L.Ed.2d 644 (1990), the defendant City of Yonkers had entered into a consent decree settling claims of racial discrimination in public housing, but city council members subsequently refused, repeatedly, to comply with the critical terms of the settlement. Plaintiffs requested a sanction, and the trial court ordered the city to adopt complying legislation. When the city failed to act, the court held the council members in contempt of court. The question for the Supreme Court was whether the contempt fines could be levied against the individual council members or only against the city treasury:

> "Sanctions directed against the city * * * coerce the city legislators and, of course, restrict the freedom of those legislators to act in accordance with their current view of the city's best interests. But we believe there are significant differences between the two types of fines. The imposition of sanctions on individual legislators is designed to cause them to vote, not with a view to the interests of their constituents or of the city, but with a view solely to their own personal interests. * * * Such fines thus encourage legislators, in effect, to declare that they favor an ordinance not in order to avoid bankrupting the city for which they legislate, but in order to avoid bankrupting themselves.

> " * * * Only if [the approach of fining the city first] failed to produce compliance within a reasonable time should the question of imposing contempt sanctions against petitioners have even been considered. 'This limitation accords with the doctrine [in contempt cases] that a court must exercise the least possible power adequate to the end imposed.' "

Is *Spallone* consistent with *Jenkins III*? With *Jenkins IV*? To the extent that fines against a city can bankrupt it, is not a contempt sanction, even though indirect, as great an intrusion on local financial affairs as a court-imposed tax?

(c) The persistent debt crisis facing state and local governments in the United States[3] suggests that such governments may be short of resources necessary to remedy pre-existing institutional violations of the Constitution, just as was California in the *Brown* case. How should federal courts respond to this "new normal" situation?

NOTE ON THE TERMINATION OF INJUNCTIVE SUPERVISION

1. The previous Note concerned the range of options open to a trial court in achieving an end to a proven constitutional violation. The cases assumed that courts must remedy the violation, but there remained the elusive problem of how to measure this end point and for how long the effort must be carried out. This issue has arisen most critically in school desegrega-

---

3. See *State and Local Government Debt: An Analysis*, Congressional Research Service (March 31, 2011), available online at http://www.nasbo.org/LinkClick.aspx?fileticket=4sLYo0HTYI8% 3D & tabid=81 (June 14, 2011): "The fiscal health of many states has been severely strained by the prolonged economic slowdown following the recent recession, even after the official end of the recession in June 2009."

tion cases. The Supreme Court held in Swann v. Charlotte–Mecklenburg Bd. of Education, 402 U.S. 1, 91 S.Ct. 1267, 28 L.Ed.2d 554 (1971), and in Green v. New Kent County School Bd., 391 U.S. 430, 88 S.Ct. 1689, 20 L.Ed.2d 716 (1968) that the burden falls on the defendant to show that it is in compliance with the Constitution. Is the problem otherwise the same as that discussed in the preceding Note?

2.   In **Board of Educ. of Oklahoma City Public Schools v. Dowell**, 498 U.S. 237, 111 S.Ct. 630, 112 L.Ed.2d 715 (1991), the Court reviewed the circumstances under which a federal court should cease its supervision of the city's efforts to desegregate its schools. The litigation had begun in 1961 and had continued through multiple court decrees regulating the city's attempts to dismantle the remaining effects of segregation—a goal described by the Supreme Court as the achievement of "unitary schools." See Green v. New Kent County School Bd., 391 U.S. 430, 436, 88 S.Ct. 1689, 20 L.Ed.2d 716 (1968); Swann v. Charlotte–Mecklenburg Bd. of Educ., 402 U.S. 1, 91 S.Ct. 1267, 28 L.Ed.2d 554 (1971). The Court of Appeals ruled that the relief decree entered by the district court could not be lifted except upon a showing of a "grievous wrong evoked by new and unforeseen conditions," but the Supreme Court found that standard applicable only to consent decrees in which there was a "continuing danger of unlawful[ness]." It was particularly inappropriate in the school desegregation context, said the Court, because "it would condemn a school district, once governed by a board that intentionally discriminated, to judicial tutelage for the indefinite future." The Court then addressed itself to the standard that should govern, 498 U.S. at 249–250, 111 S.Ct. at 638:

> "The District Court should address itself to whether the Board had complied in good faith with the desegregation decree since it was entered, and whether the vestiges of past discrimination had been eliminated to the extent practicable. * * * In considering whether the vestiges of de jure segregation had been eliminated as far as practicable, the District Court should look not only at student assignments, but 'to every facet of school operations—faculty, staff, transportation, extracurricular activities and facilities.' *Green*. See also *Swann*."

(a) Should *Dowell* be read closely as adopting both subjective ("good faith") and objective ("vestiges * * * eliminated") tests for dissolution of a decree? Or should it be read for a more general tone of inquiry, one broadly concerned with whether the effects of past wrongdoing had been eliminated and whether such wrongdoing was unlikely to recur? In Freeman v. Pitts, infra, the Court re-read *Dowell* to ensure that subjective factors are considered. Was it correct to do so?

(b) If *Dowell* merely focuses on the common-sense notion that when a violation is remedied, judicial supervision should end, is not the critical issue the meaning of "remedied"? Justice Marshall's three-vote dissent, for example, noted that he agreed with the majority that the "proper standard" for dissolving a decree was whether its underlying purposes had "been fully achieved." Is there a substantial difference between Justice Rehnquist's formulation for a remedy—"eliminated as far as practicable"—and Justice Marshall's statement—"fully achieved"? Cf. Green v. New Kent County Sch.

Bd., 391 U.S. at 438, 88 S.Ct. at 1694 (duty is to eliminate segregation "root and branch"). How does this ambiguity affect the Court's discussion in *Jenkins IV*?

3. In **Freeman v. Pitts**, 503 U.S. 467, 112 S.Ct. 1430, 118 L.Ed.2d 108 (1992), the Supreme Court returned to treat more systematically the issue of the circumstances under which trial courts should end their supervision of desegregation decrees. As with many large, urban districts, the Atlanta-area district in *Freeman* had undergone substantial demographic change that saw the county largely segregate north to south in housing patterns, while its black student population shifted dramatically upward. In response to the school district's request to be released from judicial supervision, the Court adopted what it called a "practical" approach. The district would be judged by its ability to show that it had integrated its schools to the extent that was possible, but it would not be held responsible for failures of school integration that it had not caused.

(a) As a prelude to its decision, the Court reaffirmed precedents requiring desegregation in six loosely-related topical areas (student assignment, faculty assignment, staff assignment, transportation, extracurricular activities, and facilities) so that there would no longer be "racial identifiability" to the district's schools. Then the Court added that its "practical" approach allowed a school district to be released from judicial supervision in some areas (e.g., teacher assignments) while remaining subject to decree in others (e.g., student assignments) as it could show that it was non-discriminatory in each area. There was no requirement to meet all measures of desegregation simultaneously. Is this a wise weaning of the parties from federal control? Can a school be "racially identifiable" on some criteria and not on others?

(b) Assuming that, as found by the trial court, the housing segregation that occurred in the county came because of blacks moving from downtown Atlanta into the close-in county suburbs, was that a reason for withdrawing federal supervision or for increasing it? The Court held the former, 503 U.S. at 495, 112 S.Ct. at 1448:

> "Where resegregation is a product not of state action but of private choices, it does not have constitutional implications. It is beyond the authority and beyond the practical ability of the federal courts to try to counteract these kinds of continuous and massive demographic shifts. * * * The vestiges of segregation that are the concern of the law in a school case may be subtle and intangible but nonetheless they must be so real that they have a causal link to the de jure violation being remedied. It is simply not always the case that demographic forces causing population change bear any real and substantial relation to a de jure violation. And the law need not proceed on that premise. As the de jure violation becomes more remote in time and these demographic changes intervene, it becomes less likely that a current racial imbalance in a school district is a vestige of the prior de jure system."

Did *Freeman*'s ruling foreordain the result in *Jenkins IV*? Justice Souter concurred in the *Freeman* decision. Is that consistent with his argument dissenting in *Jenkins IV*?[1]

(c) In a concurring opinion, Justice Scalia noted that in some cases, e.g., unconstitutionally collected taxes, the scope of the remedy may be easily calculable, while in others, e.g., school segregation, it is not because of the difficulty of separating the various factors that have caused the segregation. Since "[r]acially imbalanced schools are * * * the product of a blend of public and private actions," he wrote, any judgment about their cause or degree of cause is merely "guesswork." Consequently, the party that bears the burden of proof on the issue will usually lose because of its inability to establish causation. 503 U.S. at 503; 112 S.Ct. at 1452. Does burden-shifting give federal courts too much supervisory power? Does it guarantee that constitutional violations will be over-remedied? Do you agree that, as Justice Scalia concluded, in desegregation cases "the extraordinary presumption of causation simply must dissipate as the de jure system and the school boards who produced it recede further into the past"? See United States v. City of Yonkers, 181 F.3d 301 (2d Cir.1999) (burden-shifting rejected).

(d) If a school district's affirmative action policy has been held unconstitutional, should courts keep the school district under long-term scrutiny to ensure that it does not backslide into more race-based decisions? In other words, should the *Swan–Green* standards be applied symmetrically to all types of race-based decisionmaking? See Tuttle v. Arlington County School Bd., 195 F.3d 698 (4th Cir.1999).

4. Is all over-remediation in desegregation itself a constitutional violation, or is it just surplus relief that should be avoided? If relief is a zero-sum game in which over-remediation is itself a constitutional violation, then every decision prescribing over-remediation will also establish a reciprocal constitutional violation. How do these concepts work in a multi-racial context?

(a) If an affirmative action program in a formerly segregated district is no longer appropriate under *Freeman*, is the same affirmative action program a constitutional violation when inaugurated by a district that has never been under a desegregation order? Compare Tuttle v. Arlington County School Bd., 195 F.3d 698 (4th Cir.1999) (race-based assignments as a remedy), with Eisenberg ex rel. Eisenberg v. Montgomery County Public Schools, 197 F.3d 123 (4th Cir.1999) (voluntary race-based assignments).

(b) *Freeman* involved a universe that seems strange by most modern measures because the school system was composed almost entirely, at the time of the reviewed decree, of only blacks and whites. Do desegregation decrees present special problems in modern cities that have substantial numbers of other minorities? See Ho by Ho v. San Francisco Unified School Dist., 147 F.3d 854 (9th Cir.1998); U.S. v. City of Yonkers, supra; Wessmann v. Gittens, 160 F.3d 790 (1st Cir.1998).

5. *Dowell* and *Freeman*, like the *Jenkins* and *Milliken* cases, involved school desegregation. If there something especially difficult in deciding in this class of cases, as Justice Scalia argued in *Freeman*, what other classes of cases

---

1. Does *Freeman* make too much turn on the facts as found by the trial judge? See, e.g., Lockett v. Board of Educ. of Muscogee County School Dist., Georgia, 111 F.3d 839 (11th Cir.1997) (review of factfinding is by "clearly erroneous" standard).

might present similar problems? Different ones? Are desegregation cases unique?

(a) Consider the following examples and try to decide whether the court will be called upon to play an indefinite supervisory role with an ambiguous endgame, or whether a decree will crisply end litigation without ongoing supervision: reapportionment litigation under Reynolds v. Sims, 377 U.S. 533, 84 S.Ct. 1362, 12 L.Ed.2d 506 (1964); prison conditions cases, under Rhodes v. Chapman, 452 U.S. 337, 101 S.Ct. 2392, 69 L.Ed.2d 59 (1981); police supervision cases that can meet the test of Los Angeles v. Lyons, Chapter 1F.2 supra.

(b) If trial judges have substantial leeway in choosing what efforts are necessary to remedy any violation, is it possible that courts in all cases will naturally begin to confuse means—their decree—with ends—curing the underlying violation? Will judges see full implementation of the decree as itself proof of an adequately achieved remedy? See Mahan v. Howell, 411 U.S. 922, 93 S.Ct. 1475, 36 L.Ed.2d 316 (1973) (non-racial redistricting to meet "one-person, one-vote" rule; the limits of ever-more-refined measures of equal population per district). But what is wrong with that? See Gewirtz, *Remedies and Resistance*, 92 YALE L.J. 585 (1983) (questioning whether "realism" should limit judicial decrees).

(c) Of course, one explanation for the Court's decreasing interest in remedial decrees is that the Court's personnel has changed, the Court becoming more politically conservative in the process. But is there another possible explanation? Has a chastened Supreme Court learned through institutional experience that active supervision of remedial decrees involves risks of spreading judicial resources too thin? That active supervision of judicial decrees may involve local judges too much in local politics? Does excessive remedial power "corrupt" the independence of federal judges?

(d) Can conceptions of proper relief, and termination of relief, be separated from our political views of society? Consider Justice Scalia's withering and caustic criticism of modern approaches to § 1983 litigation of institutional claims, dissenting in **Brown v. Plata**, discussed in the previous Note. Justice Scalia cited two primary concerns. First, class-action status had warped the sensitivities of judges so that they now saw a wide swath of persons as victims, even those who had not in fact suffered a constitutional violation. 131 S.Ct. at 1951–53 (many prisoners benefit from release decree who never suffered constitutional deprivations). Second, and independently, the "structural" decree itself stretched the boundaries of judicial competence by focusing not only single acts of compliance, as traditional prohibitory decrees did, but on complex interactions that will take place in the future—"the sort of predictions regularly made by legislators and executive officials, but inappropriate for the Third Branch." How do you respond?

6. Regardless of the constitutional dimensions of these issues, there remains the simple question of whether the Federal Rules of Civil Procedure, particularly, Rule 60(b), permit reopening of cases containing remedial decrees. In Horne v. Flores, ___ U.S. ___, 129 S.Ct. 2579, 174 L.Ed.2d 406 (2009), the Court opted for a generous reading permitting district courts to

modify or withdraw such decrees. The particular case involved a failure to a statutory obligation to provide educational opportunities to language minorities, and the lower courts had consistently focused on whether the defendant had spent enough on the problem rather than on the more general issue of whether the defendant had by several other means met its overall obligations. The Court reversed the lower courts' narrow focus. With respect to Rule 65(b)'s provision for altering a decree that has become "inequitable," the Court stated, ___ U.S. at ___, 129 S.Ct. at 2593: "Rule 60(b)(5) may not be used to challenge the legal conclusions on which a prior judgment or order rests, but the Rule provides a means by which a party can ask a court to modify or vacate a judgment or order if 'a significant change either in factual conditions or in law' renders continued enforcement 'detrimental to the public interest.' The party seeking relief bears the burden of establishing that changed circumstances warrant relief, but once a party carries this burden, a court abuses its discretion 'when it refuses to modify an injunction or consent decree in light of such changes.' "

(a) The Court, while basing its interpretation of Rule 65(b) on general considerations also noted that it "serves a particularly important function in what we have termed 'institutional reform litigation,' " because decrees may last for many years, implicate serious federalism concerns, and may often involve defendants who acquiesce in judgments because they may become the beneficiaries of increased judicial supervision (in the form of increased funding). Should relief decrees contain "sunset" provisions so that they automatically expire after a set number of years? Cf. Chapter 8A (sunset provisions in Voting Rights Act may reflect recognition that underlying problems have been remedied).

(b) Although couched in terms of Rule 60(b), are the considerations mentioned in the preceding sub-paragraph of constitutional dimension? Would an action brought in state court, with its own distinctive rules of procedure, be subject to the same considerations? Cf. Note on § 1983 in State Courts in section E of this Chapter supra.

G. LIMITATIONS ON RELIEF

1. EXHAUSTION OF REMEDIES AND PRISON REFORM LITIGATION

As a general matter federal courts require neither the exhaustion of state judicial remedies, see Monroe v. Pape, Chapter 1A supra, nor state administrative remedies, see Patsy v. Board of Regents of the State of Florida, 457 U.S. 496, 102 S.Ct. 2557, 73 L.Ed.2d 172 (1982), as a prerequisite to suit under § 1983. In the cases that follow, the Court held that special considerations apply to prisoners' claims relating to release from confinement and challenges against their original convictions. Later legislation expanded the notions to cover prison litigation more generally.

PREISER v. RODRIGUEZ

Supreme Court of the United States, 1973.
411 U.S. 475, 93 S.Ct. 1827, 36 L.Ed.2d 439.

MR. JUSTICE STEWART delivered the opinion of the Court.

The respondents in this case were state prisoners who were deprived of good-conduct-time credits by the New York State Department of Correctional Services as a result of disciplinary proceedings. They then brought actions in a federal district court, pursuant to the Civil Rights Act of 1871, 42 U.S.C.A. § 1983. Alleging that the Department had acted unconstitutionally in depriving them of the credits, they sought injunctive relief to compel restoration of the credits, which in each case would result in their immediate release from confinement in prison. The question before us is whether state prisoners seeking such redress may obtain equitable relief under the Civil Rights Act, even though the federal habeas corpus statute, 28 U.S.C.A. § 2254, clearly provides a specific federal remedy.

The question is of considerable practical importance. For if a remedy under the Civil Rights Act is available, a plaintiff need not first seek redress in a state forum. If, on the other hand, habeas corpus is the exclusive federal remedy in these circumstances, then a plaintiff cannot seek the intervention of a federal court until he has first sought and been denied relief in the state courts, if a state remedy is available and adequate. 28 U.S.C.A. § 2254(b).

[Under New York law Rodriguez's and the other prisoners' indeterminate sentences could be reduced by award of "goodtime" of 10 days per month to be deducted from the maximum sentence. These credits could be reduced, and these prisoners' were, for disciplinary violations. Each of the aggrieved prisoners filed a combined habeas corpus/§ 1983 complaint challenging his loss of credits. The district court treated each as a § 1983 suit not requiring exhaustion. The appellate court reversed, characterizing the complaints as "in fact" petitions for habeas corpus requiring exhaustion of available state remedies. Thereafter the court of appeals sitting en banc reinstated the district court's judgments based on the Supreme Court's holding in Wilwording v. Swenson. We granted certiorari.]

* * *

It is clear, not only from the language of §§ 2241(c)(3) and 2254(a), but also from the common-law history of the writ, that the essence of habeas corpus is an attack by a person in custody upon the legality of that custody, and that the traditional function of the writ is to secure release from illegal custody. By the end of the 16th century, there were in England several forms of habeas corpus, of which the most important and the only one with which we are here concerned was *habeas corpus ad subjiciendum*—the writ used to "inquir[e] into illegal detention with a view to an order releasing the petitioner." Fay v. Noia, 372 U.S. 391, 399 n. 5, 83 S.Ct. 822, 827, 9 L.Ed.2d 837 (1963). * * *

* * *

The original [American] view of a habeas corpus attack upon detention under a judicial order was a limited one. The relevant inquiry was confined to determining simply whether or not the committing court had been possessed of jurisdiction. But, over the years, the writ of habeas corpus evolved as a remedy available to effect discharge from any confinement contrary to the Constitution or fundamental law, even though imposed pursuant to conviction by a court of competent jurisdiction. Thus, whether the petitioner's challenge to his custody is that the statute under which he stands convicted is unconstitutional, that he has been imprisoned prior to trial on account of a defective indictment against him, that he is unlawfully confined in the wrong institution, * * * that he was denied his constitutional rights at trial, that his guilty plea was invalid, that he is being unlawfully detained by the Executive or the military, or that his parole was unlawfully revoked, causing him to be reincarcerated in prison—in each case his grievance is that he is being unlawfully subjected to physical restraint, and in each case habeas corpus has been accepted as the specific instrument to obtain release from such confinement.[7]

In the case before us, the respondents' suits in the District Court fell squarely within this traditional scope of habeas corpus. They alleged that the deprivation of their good-conduct-time credits was causing or would cause them to be in illegal physical confinement, i.e., that once their conditional-release date had passed, any further detention of them in prison was unlawful; and they sought restoration of those good-time credits, which, by the time the District Court ruled on their petitions, meant their immediate release from physical custody.

Even if the restoration of the respondents' credits would not have resulted in their immediate release, but only in shortening the length of their actual confinement in prison, habeas corpus would have been their appropriate remedy. For recent cases have established that habeas corpus relief is not limited to immediate release from illegal custody, but that the writ is available as well to attack future confinement and obtain future releases. [Peyton v. Rowe, 391 U.S. 54, 88 S.Ct. 1549, 20 L.Ed.2d 426 (1968).] * * *

---

7. It was not until quite recently that habeas corpus was made available to challenge less obvious restraints. In 1963, the Court held that a prisoner released on parole from immediate physical confinement was nonetheless sufficiently restrained in his freedom as to be in custody for purposes of federal habeas corpus. Jones v. Cunningham, 371 U.S. 236, 83 S.Ct. 373, 9 L.Ed.2d 285. In Carafas v. LaVallee, 391 U.S. 234, 88 S.Ct. 1556, 20 L.Ed.2d 554 (1968), the Court for the first time decided that once habeas corpus jurisdiction has attached, it is not defeated by the subsequent release of the prisoner. And just this Term, in Hensley v. Municipal Court, 411 U.S. 345, 93 S.Ct. 1571, 36 L.Ed.2d 294 (1973), we held that a person, who, after conviction, is released on bail or on his own recognizance, is "in custody" within the meaning of the federal habeas corpus statute. But those cases marked no more than a logical extension of the traditional meaning and purpose of habeas corpus—to effect release from illegal custody.

[The plaintiffs do not argue that § 2254 is unavailable, but rather claim that they have a choice of either § 2254 or § 1983, reasoning that the literal terms of § 1983 cover their suit. But the] broad language of § 1983, however, is not conclusive of the issue before us. The statute is a general one, and, despite the literal applicability of its terms, the question remains whether the specific federal habeas corpus statute, explicitly and historically designed to provide the means for a state prisoner to attack the validity of his confinement, must be understood to be the exclusive remedy available in a situation like this where it so clearly applies. The respondents' counsel acknowledged at oral argument that a state prisoner challenging his underlying conviction and sentence on federal constitutional grounds in a federal court is limited to habeas corpus. It was conceded that he cannot bring a § 1983 action, even though the literal terms of § 1983 might seem to cover such a challenge, because Congress has passed a more specific act to cover that situation, and, in doing so, has provided that a state prisoner challenging his conviction must first seek relief in a state forum, if a state remedy is available. It is clear to us that the result must be the same in the case of a state prisoner's challenge to the fact or duration of his confinement, based, as here, upon the alleged unconstitutionality of state administrative action. Such a challenge is just as close to the core of habeas corpus as an attack on the prisoner's conviction, for it goes directly to the constitutionality of his physical confinement itself and seeks either immediate release from that confinement or the shortening of its duration.

* * *

In the respondents' view, the whole purpose of the exhaustion requirement, now codified in § 2254(b), is to give state *courts* the first chance at remedying *their own* mistakes, and thereby to avoid "the unseemly spectacle of federal district courts trying the regularity of proceedings had in *courts* of coordinate jurisdiction." Parker, Limiting the Abuse of Habeas Corpus, 8 F.R.D. 171, 172–173 (1948) (emphasis added). This policy, the respondents contend, does not apply when the challenge is not to the action of a state court, but, as here, to the action of a state administrative body. * * *

We cannot agree. The respondents, we think, view the reasons for the exhaustion requirement of § 2254(b) far too narrowly. The rule of exhaustion in federal habeas corpus actions is rooted in considerations of federal-state comity. That principle was defined in Younger v. Harris, 401 U.S. 37, 44, 91 S.Ct. 746, 750, 27 L.Ed.2d 669 (1971), as "a proper respect for state functions," and it has as much relevance in areas of particular state administrative concern as it does where state judicial action is being attacked. * * *

It is difficult to imagine an activity in which a State has a stronger interest, or one that is more intricately bound up with state laws, regulations, and procedures, than the administration of its prisons. The relationship of state prisoners and the state officers who supervise their confinement is far more intimate than that of a State and a private citizen. For state prisoners, eating, sleeping, dressing, washing, working, and playing are all done under the watchful eye of the State, and so the possibilities for litigation under the Fourteenth Amendment are boundless.[10] * * * Since these internal problems of state prisons involve issues so peculiarly within state authority and expertise, the States have an important interest in not being bypassed in the correction of those problems. Moreover, because most potential litigation involving state prisoners arises on a day-to-day basis, it is most efficiently and properly handled by the state administrative bodies and state courts, which are, for the most part, familiar with the grievances of state prisoners and in a better physical and practical position to deal with those grievances. In New York, for example, state judges sit on a regular basis at all but one of the State's correctional facilities * * *.

* * *

[W]hile conceding the availability in the New York courts of an opportunity for equitable relief, the respondents contend that confining state prisoners to federal habeas corpus, after first exhausting state remedies, could deprive those prisoners of any damages remedy to which they might be entitled for their mistreatment, since damages are not available in federal habeas corpus proceedings, and New York provides no damages remedy at all for state prisoners. In the respondents' view, if habeas corpus is the exclusive federal remedy for a state prisoner attacking his confinement, damages might never be obtained, at least where the State makes no provision for them. They argue that even if such a prisoner were to bring a subsequent federal civil rights action for damages, that action could be barred by principles of *res judicata* where the state courts had previously made an adverse determination of his underlying claim, even though a federal habeas court had later granted him relief on habeas corpus.

The answer to this contention is that the respondents here sought no damages, but only equitable relief—restoration of their good-time credits—and our holding today is limited to that situation. If a state prisoner is seeking damages, he is attacking something other than the fact or length of his confinement, and he is seeking something other than immediate or more speedy release—the traditional purpose of habeas corpus. In the case of a damages claim, habeas corpus is *not* an appropriate or available federal remedy. Accordingly, as petitioners themselves

---

10. The dissent argues that the respondents' attacks on the actions of the prison administration here are no different, in terms of the potential for exacerbating federal-state relations, from the attacks made by the petitioners in McNeese v. Board of Education, Damico v. California, and Monroe v. Pape * * * on the various state administrative actions there. Thus, it is said, since exhaustion of state remedies was not required in those cases, it is anomalous to require it here. The answer, of course, is that in those cases, brought pursuant to § 1983, no other, more specific federal statute was involved that might have reflected a different congressional intent. In the present case, however, the respondents' actions fell squarely within the traditional purpose of federal habeas corpus, and Congress has made the specific determination in § 2254(b) that requiring the exhaustion of adequate state remedies in such cases will best serve the policies of federalism. [Repositioned footnote.]

concede, a damages action by a state prisoner could be brought under the Civil Rights Act in federal court without any requirement of prior exhaustion of state remedies. Cf. Ray v. Fritz, 468 F.2d 586 (C.A.2 1972).

The respondents next argue that to require exhaustion of state remedies in a case such as the one at bar would deprive a state prisoner of the speedy review of his grievance which is so often essential to any effective redress. * * *

It is true that exhaustion of state remedies takes time, but there is no reason to assume that state prison administrators or state courts will not act expeditiously. * * * [S]tate judges in New York actually sit in the institutions to hear prisoner complaints. Moreover, once a state prisoner arrives in federal court with his petition for habeas corpus, the federal habeas statute provides for a swift, flexible, and summary determination of his claim. 28 U.S.C.A. § 2243. By contrast, the filing of a complaint pursuant to § 1983 in federal court initiates an original plenary civil action, governed by the full panoply of the Federal Rules of Civil Procedure. That such a proceeding, with its discovery rules and other procedural formalities, can take a significant amount of time, very frequently longer than a federal habeas corpus proceeding, is demonstrated by the respondents' actions[—which the District Court took over ten months to decide].

* * *

Principles of *res judicata* are, of course, not wholly applicable to habeas corpus proceedings. 28 U.S.C.A. § 2254(d). See Salinger v. Loisel, 265 U.S. 224, 230, 44 S.Ct. 519, 68 L.Ed. 989 (1924). Hence, a state prisoner in the respondents' situation who has been denied relief in the state courts is not precluded from seeking habeas relief on the same claims in federal court. On the other hand, *res judicata* has been held to be fully applicable to a civil rights action brought under § 1983. Accordingly, there would be an inevitable incentive for a state prisoner to proceed at once in federal court by way of a civil rights action, lest he lose his right to do so. * * * Federal habeas corpus, on the other hand, serves the important function of allowing the State to deal with these peculiarly local problems on its own, while preserving for the state prisoner an expeditious federal forum for the vindication of his federally protected rights, if the State has denied redress.

The respondents place a great deal of reliance on our recent decisions upholding the right of state prisoners to bring federal civil rights actions to challenge the conditions of their confinement. But none of the state prisoners in those cases was challenging the fact or duration of his physical confinement itself, and none was seeking immediate release or a speedier release from that confinement—the heart of habeas corpus.[14]
* * *

* * *

---

14. If a prisoner seeks to attack both the conditions of his confinement and the fact or length of that confinement, his latter claim, under our decision today, is cognizable only in federal

Reversed.

MR. JUSTICE BRENNAN, with whom MR. JUSTICE DOUGLAS and MR. JUSTICE MARSHALL join, dissenting.

* * *

At the outset, it is important to consider the nature of the line that the Court has drawn. The Court holds today that "when a state prisoner is challenging the very fact or duration of his physical imprisonment, and the relief he seeks is a determination that he is entitled to immediate release or a speedier release from that imprisonment, his sole federal remedy is a writ of habeas corpus." But, even under the Court's approach, there are undoubtedly some instances where a prisoner has the option of proceeding either by petition for habeas corpus or by suit under § 1983. [We have held, for example, that claims regarding conditions of confinement can be pursued under either § 1983 or § 2254.]

Yet even though a prisoner may challenge the conditions of his confinement by petition for writ of habeas corpus, he is not precluded by today's opinion from raising the same or similar claim, without exhaustion of state remedies, by suit under [§ 1983] provided he attacks only the conditions of his confinement and not its fact or duration. To that extent, at least, the Court leaves unimpaired our holdings in Wilwording v. Swenson, supra, and the other cases in which we have upheld the right of prisoners to sue their jailers under § 1983 without exhaustion of state remedies. Accordingly, one can only conclude that some instances remain where habeas corpus provides a supplementary but not an exclusive remedy—or, to put it another way, where an action may properly be brought in habeas corpus, even though it is somehow sufficiently distant from the "core of habeas corpus" to avoid displacing concurrent jurisdiction under [§ 1983]. In such a case, a state prisoner retains the option of foregoing the habeas corpus remedy in favor of suit under § 1983.

[The real issue in this case is on what occasions habeas corpus must be treated as an exclusive rather than supplementary remedy.] Putting momentarily to one side the grave analytic shortcomings of the Court's approach, it seems clear that the scheme's unmanageability is sufficient reason to condemn it. For the unfortunate but inevitable legacy of today's opinion is a perplexing set of uncertainties and anomalies. And the nub of the problem is the definition of the Court's new-found and essentially ethereal concept, the "core of habeas corpus."[9]

* * *

---

habeas corpus, with its attendant requirement of exhaustion of state remedies. But, consistent with our prior decisions, that holding in no way precludes him from simultaneously litigating in federal court, under § 1983, his claim relating to the conditions of his confinement. [Repositioned footnote.]

9. Indeed, one must inevitably wonder whether the "core" of habeas corpus will not prove as intractable to definition as the "core" of another concept that some of us have struggled to define. Cf. Jacobellis v. Ohio, 378 U.S. 184, 197, 84 S.Ct. 1676, 1683, 12 L.Ed.2d 793 (1964) (Stewart, J., concurring).

NOTE ON EXHAUSTION OF JUDICIAL AND ADMINISTRATIVE REMEDIES

1. *Preiser* notes that exhaustion of state judicial remedies is not required of § 1983 plaintiffs, citing Monroe v. Pape, Chapter 1A, supra, but the Court held that § 1983 is only a general civil rights act protecting constitutional deprivations. The question for the Court was whether another more specific statute, requiring exhaustion of state judicial remedies, should supplant § 1983.

(a) Both majority and dissent rely on the general principle that a specific statute with special provisions should displace a general one in order to give effect to the special terms in the specific statute. They disagree on what core functions are covered by § 2254, on what core situations are covered exclusively by the specific habeas corpus statute. Where does each draw the line?

(b) Is Justice Brennan's uncharacteristically personal criticism of Justice Stewart, delivered in footnote 9, fair? (Justice Brennan's reference is to Justice Stewart's acknowledgment that pornography is difficult to define, "but I know it when I see it.") Is Justice Stewart's core of habeas corpus that difficult to define? Do not both majority and dissent see a habeas corpus statute that covers many problems—and covers only some of them exclusively?

(c) In **Wolff v. McDonnell**, 418 U.S. 539, 94 S.Ct. 2963, 41 L.Ed.2d 935 (1974), a prisoner sued for alleged unconstitutional reduction of good-conduct-time credits and asked damages and declaratory relief. The Court permitted the suit under § 1983 without exhaustion of remedies. Is *Wolff* compelled by *Preiser*? Does judgment for the prisoner in the federal damages action have res judicata effect in a subsequent suit in state court demanding release? See Embry v. Palmer, 107 U.S. 3, 2 S.Ct. 25, 27 L.Ed. 346 (1883); Degnan, *Federalized Res Judicata*, 85 YALE L. J. 741 (1976). Does this reduce *Preiser* to a nullity?

(d) The line between the exclusive remedy of habeas corpus and § 1983 has been further refined after *Wolff.* In Wilkinson v. Dotson, 544 U.S. 74, 125 S.Ct. 1242, 161 L.Ed.2d 253 (2005), a near-unanimous Court permitted a suit under § 1983 where the plaintiff only sought an order directing defendants to consider him for parole, reasoning that the order did not necessarily hasten his release from confinement. Similarly, in Hill v. McDonough, 547 U.S. 573, 126 S.Ct. 2096, 165 L.Ed.2d 44 (2006), the Court allowed § 1983 to be used to challenge the method of his execution because no release was sought. And in Skinner v. Switzer, ___ U.S. ___, 131 S.Ct. 1289, 179 L.Ed.2d 233 (2011), the Court held that § 1983 can be used to challenge state processes by which a district attorney's refused to test crime-scene evidence for DNA that might exonerate the person convicted of the crime. (It ruled that had testing already been done and produced exculpatory results, that would undermine the conviction, result in release, and call for exclusive use of habeas corpus.)[1] Is this line clear or meandering?

---

1. The plaintiff's victory in *Skinner* appears ephemeral because the Court had previously ruled that there is no constitutional right of access to and DNA-testing of crime-scene evidence.

2. In the Civil Rights of Institutionalized Persons Act, 42 U.S.C. § 1997(e), later amended by the Prison Litigation Reform Act, Pub.L. 104–134, 110 Stat. 1321 (1996), Congress provided for exhaustion of state administrative remedies even in cases relating to "conditions of confinement." The statute has had a dramatic impact, as discussed by the Supreme Court in **Crawford–El v. Britton**, 523 U.S. 574, 118 S.Ct. 1584, 140 L.Ed.2d 759 (1998):

> "The Prison Litigation Reform Act contains provisions that should discourage prisoners from filing claims that are unlikely to succeed. Among the many new changes relating to civil suits, the statute requires all inmates to pay filing fees; denies in forma pauperis status to prisoners with three or more prior 'strikes' (dismissals because a filing is frivolous, malicious, or fails to state a claim upon which relief may be granted) unless the prisoner is 'under imminent danger of serious physical injury'; bars suits for mental or emotional injury unless there is a prior showing of physical injury; limits attorney's fees; directs district courts to screen prisoners' complaints before docketing and authorizes the court on its own motion to dismiss 'frivolous,' 'malicious,' or meritless actions; permits the revocation of good time credits for federal prisoners who file malicious or false claims; and encourages hearings by telecommunication or in prison facilities to make it unnecessary for inmate plaintiffs to leave prison for pretrial proceedings. See 28 U.S.C. §§ 1346(b)(2), 1915, 1915A, 1932; 42 U.S.C.A. § 1997e (Supp.1997). Recent statistics suggest that the Act is already having its intended effect." 523 U.S. at 596–97, 118 S.Ct. at 1596.

(a) In a succeeding footnote 18, the Court described the impact: "Despite the continuing rise in the state and federal prison populations, the number of prisoner civil rights suits filed in federal court dropped from 41,215 in fiscal year 1996 to 28,635 in fiscal year 1997, a decline of 31 percent. Administrative Office of the United States Courts, L. Mecham, Judicial Business of the United States Courts: 1997 Report of the Director 131–132 (Table C–2A)." Was the Act overkill? Must you know the number of non-meritorious claims filed in the past in order to answer that question?

(b) In **Porter v. Nussle,** 534 U.S. 516, 122 S.Ct. 983, 152 L.Ed.2d 12 (2002), a unanimous Court ruled that "conditions of confinement" claims to which exhaustion now applies are not limited to the similarly named subset of all Eighth Amendment cases, see Chapter 1B.2 supra. Justice Ginsburg's opinion stated that the phrase simply connotes prisoners' claims while in confinement, even those for excessive use of force. Do you agree? Does lowering the quantity of prisoners' cases allow the court to improve the quality of its work? See id.

(c) Another provision in the Prison Litigation Reform Act caps attorneys fees in order to limit the incentive of attorneys to work on such cases (and possibly also to preserve money to spend on the prison conditions themselves). See Martin v. Hadix, 527 U.S. 343, 119 S.Ct. 1998, 144 L.Ed.2d 347 (1999); Johnson v. Daley, 339 F.3d 582 (7th Cir. 2003) (noting provisions in Prison

District Attorney's Office for Third Judicial Dist. v. Osborne, ___ U.S. ___, 129 S.Ct. 2308, 174 L.Ed.2d 38 (2009).

Litigation Reform Act, 42 U.S.C. § 1997e(d)(3), and finding them constitutional). Is this a better or a worse way to solve the perceived problem of too much prison litigation?

(d) Is exhaustion of state administrative remedies a desirable approach to solving state violations of federal rights? If Congress wants exhaustion of some administrative process in order to keep federal judges from meddling in prison affairs, would it be better to adopt a federal omsbudsman system for state prisoners who claim their constitutional rights have been violated? Or is federalism the greater concern?

3. Prisoners are not the only group to have had an exhaustion requirement imposed on them in § 1983 litigation. Perhaps oddly, the other most-affected group is landowners who challenge zoning laws, usually under the Just Compensation Clause of the Fifth Amendment, and their exhaustion rule was created by the Court. Notwithstanding the *Patsy* ruling against administrative exhaustion, the Court has enforced a "ripeness doctrine" that requires one who seeks a benefit under a zoning law to stay with the complete process until it has finally determined his request. In **Williamson County Regional Planning Comm'n v. Hamilton Bank**, 473 U.S. 172, 105 S.Ct. 3108, 87 L.Ed.2d 126 (1985), the Court required a developer who challenged a zoning decision to initiate a request for a variance or exception; only after denial of his administrative request by the full administrative body was he permitted to file a constitutional claim under § 1983.

(a) If a developer can show that resort to the state administrative scheme would be futile, is his claim immediately "ripe," i.e., no resort to the process is required? See Suitum v. Tahoe Regional Planning Agency, 520 U.S. 725, 117 S.Ct. 1659, 137 L.Ed.2d 980 (1997) (decision of planning agency against development of property is final when agency has no discretion to grant variance). If a plaintiff exhausts by going to state court, is he thereafter subject to a res judicata defense when he returns to federal court? See San Remo Hotel, L.P. v. City and County of San Francisco, Cal., 545 U.S. 323, 125 S.Ct. 2491, 162 L.Ed.2d 315 (2005).

(b) Should exhaustion, in the guise of administrative ripeness, apply to other contexts than land use, or is it a special rule designed to give flexibility to state administrative organs in this difficult and sensitive area? See Hall v. City of Santa Barbara, 833 F.2d 1270 (9th Cir.1986) (rent control). Compare Burford v. Sun Oil Co., 319 U.S. 315, 63 S.Ct. 1098, 87 L.Ed. 1424 (1943) (abstention may be required where complex state regulatory scheme implicated).

HECK v. HUMPHREY

United States Supreme Court, 1994.
512 U.S. 477, 114 S.Ct. 2364, 129 L.Ed.2d 383.

JUSTICE SCALIA delivered the opinion of the Court.

This case presents the question whether a state prisoner may challenge the constitutionality of his conviction in a suit for damages under 42 U.S.C. § 1983.

Petitioner Roy Heck was convicted in Indiana state court of voluntary manslaughter for the killing of Rickie Heck, his wife, and is serving a 15–

year sentence in an Indiana prison. While the appeal from his conviction was pending, petitioner, proceeding pro se, filed this suit in Federal District Court under 42 U.S.C. § 1983, [claiming that defendants knowingly destroyed evidence and unconstitutionally procured his conviction. Plaintiff requested damages only, foregoing any claim for release from prison.]

* * *

Preiser v. Rodriguez considered the potential overlap between [the habeas corpus statute and § 1983], and held that habeas corpus is the exclusive remedy for a state prisoner who challenges the fact or duration of his confinement and seeks immediate or speedier release, even though such a claim may come within the literal terms of § 1983. We emphasize that *Preiser* did not create an exception to the "no exhaustion" rule of § 1983; it merely held that certain claims by state prisoners are not cognizable under that provision, and must be brought in habeas corpus proceedings, which do contain an exhaustion requirement.

This case is clearly not covered by the holding of *Preiser*, for petitioner seeks not immediate or speedier release, but monetary damages [which are unavailable under the habeas statute].

* * *

[*Preiser* has no application in the present case because plaintiff sought damages, a remedy not available under the habeas corpus statute. Wolff v. McDonnell. Indeed], the question posed by § 1983 damage claims that do call into question the lawfulness of conviction or confinement remains open. To answer that question correctly, we see no need to abandon * * * our teaching that § 1983 contains no exhaustion requirement beyond what Congress has provided. The issue with respect to monetary damages challenging conviction is not, it seems to us, exhaustion; but rather, the same as the issue was with respect to injunctive relief challenging conviction in *Preiser*: whether the claim is cognizable under § 1983 at all. We conclude that it is not.

"We have repeatedly noted that 42 U.S.C. § 1983 creates a species of tort liability." Memphis Community School Dist. v. Stachura, [Chapter 1F supra]. "[O]ver the centuries the common law of torts has developed a set of rules to implement the principle that a person should be compensated fairly for injuries caused by the violation of his legal rights. These rules, defining the elements of damages and the prerequisites for their recovery, provide the appropriate starting point for the inquiry under § 1983 as well." Carey v. Piphus, [Chapter 1F supra]. Thus, to determine whether there is any bar to the present suit, we look first to the common law of torts.

The common-law cause of action for malicious prosecution provides the closest analogy to claims of the type considered here because, unlike the related cause of action for false arrest or imprisonment, it permits damages for confinement imposed pursuant to legal process. * * *

One element that must be alleged and proved in a malicious prosecution action is termination of the prior criminal proceeding in favor of the
accused. [Prosser and Keeton on the Law of Torts]. This requirement
"avoids parallel litigation over the issues of probable cause and guilt . . .
and it precludes the possibility of the claimant [sic] succeeding in the tort
action after having been convicted in the underlying criminal prosecution,
in contravention of a strong judicial policy against the creation of two
conflicting resolutions arising out of the same or identical transaction." 8
S. Speiser, C. Krause, & A. Gans, American Law of Torts s 28:5, p. 24
(1991). Furthermore, "to permit a convicted criminal defendant to proceed
with a malicious prosecution claim would permit a collateral attack on the
conviction through the vehicle of a civil suit." This Court has long
expressed similar concerns for finality and consistency and has generally
declined to expand opportunities for collateral attack, see Parke v. Raley
(1992) [in which the Court denied the use of habeas corpus to attack a
guilty plea]. We think the hoary principle that civil tort actions are not
appropriate vehicles for challenging the validity of outstanding criminal
judgments applies to § 1983 damages actions that necessarily require the
plaintiff to prove the unlawfulness of his conviction or confinement, just
as it has always applied to actions for malicious prosecution.

We hold that, in order to recover damages for allegedly unconstitutional conviction or imprisonment, or for other harm caused by actions
whose unlawfulness would render a conviction or sentence invalid, a
§ 1983 plaintiff must prove that the conviction or sentence has been
reversed on direct appeal, expunged by executive order, declared invalid by
a state tribunal authorized to make such determination, or called into
question by a federal court's issuance of a writ of habeas corpus, 28 U.S.C.
§ 2254. A claim for damages bearing that relationship to a conviction or
sentence that has not been so invalidated is not cognizable under § 1983.
Thus, when a state prisoner seeks damages in a s 1983 suit, the district
court must consider whether a judgment in favor of the plaintiff would
necessarily imply the invalidity of his conviction or sentence; if it would,
the complaint must be dismissed unless the plaintiff can demonstrate that
the conviction or sentence has already been invalidated. But if the district
court determines that the plaintiff's action, even if successful, will not
demonstrate the invalidity of any outstanding criminal judgment against
the plaintiff, the action should be allowed to proceed, in the absence of
some other bar to the suit.

* * *

[In today's case we do] not engraft an exhaustion requirement upon
§ 1983, but rather deny the existence of a cause of action. Even a prisoner
who has fully exhausted available state remedies has no cause of action
under § 1983 unless and until the conviction or sentence is reversed,
expunged, invalidated, or impugned by the grant of a writ of habeas
corpus. * * *

Applying these principles to the present action, in which both courts below found that the damage claims challenged the legality of the conviction, we find that the dismissal of the action was correct. The judgment of the Court of Appeals for the Seventh Circuit is

Affirmed.

JUSTICE THOMAS, concurring.

* * *

Given that the Court created the tension between [§ 1983 and the habeas statute by too broadly construing the latter], it is proper for the Court to devise limitations aimed at ameliorating the conflict, provided that it does so in a principled fashion. Because the Court today limits the scope of § 1983 in a manner consistent both with the federalism concerns undergirding the explicit exhaustion requirement of the habeas statute, and with the state of the common law at the time § 1983 was enacted, I join the Court's opinion.

JUSTICE SOUTER, with whom JUSTICE BLACKMUN, JUSTICE STEVENS, and JUSTICE O'CONNOR join, concurring in the judgment.

* * *

While I do not object to referring to the common law when resolving the question this case presents, I do not think that the existence of the tort of malicious prosecution alone provides the answer. Common-law tort rules can provide a "starting point for the inquiry under § 1983," Carey v. Piphus * * *.

* * *

[I would] follow the interpretive methodology employed in Preiser v. Rodriguez. * * * Though in contrast to *Preiser* the state prisoner here seeks damages, not release from custody, the distinction makes no difference when the damages sought are for unconstitutional conviction or confinement. * * * Whether or not a federal-court § 1983 damages judgment against state officials in such an action would have preclusive effect in later litigation against the state, mounting damages against the defendant-officials for unlawful confinement (damages almost certainly to be paid by state indemnification) would, practically, compel the state to release the prisoner. Because allowing a state prisoner to proceed directly with a federal-court § 1983 attack on his conviction or sentence "would wholly frustrate explicit congressional intent" as declared in the habeas exhaustion requirement, *Preiser*, the statutory scheme must be read as precluding such attacks. * * *

That leaves the question of how to implement what statutory analysis requires. It is at this point that the malicious-prosecution tort's favorable-termination requirement becomes helpful, not in dictating the elements of a § 1983 cause of action, but in suggesting a relatively simple way to avoid collisions at the intersection of habeas and § 1983. A state prisoner may seek federal-court § 1983 damages for unconstitutional conviction or confinement, but only if he has previously established the unlawfulness of his conviction or confinement, as on appeal or on habeas. This has the effect of requiring a state prisoner challenging the lawfulness of his confinement to follow habeas's rules before seeking § 1983 damages for unlawful confinement in federal court, and it is ultimately the Court's holding today. * * *

NOTE ON "FALSE EXHAUSTION" FOR PRISONERS' CLAIMS

1. The majority and dissent in *Heck* agree not only on the existence of a problem, they also agree on the necessary solution, albeit with a bit of divergence on how that solution is reached. Justice Souter apparently sees the problem here as one of prisoners who want to circumvent the holding in Preiser v. Rodriguez. The majority bases its interpretation not on the habeas corpus statute, but on § 1983 itself. Does this make a difference? Aren't both the majority and concurring positions grounded in statute?

2. Does the decision in *Heck* amount to an exhaustion decision? Would it be exhaustion of state judicial or administrative remedies? Only state remedies?

(a) *Heck* would force the prospective § 1983 plaintiff to find a way to overturn or set aside his conviction before filing a claim for damages under § 1983. By what methods can this be accomplished?

(b) As the Court later explained again in Edwards v. Balisok, 520 U.S. 641, 117 S.Ct. 1584, 137 L.Ed.2d 906 (1997), "exhaustion" is not required in § 1983 suits, and what *Heck* denies is the availability of a claim at all. In the usual exhaustion context, all that is required of a plaintiff is that he attempted to win in the alternative forum before using the federal forum; losing in the alternative forum is the prerequisite to the federal suit. Is that permitted under *Heck*? While *Heck* has some of the hallmarks of an exhaustion remedy, is it missing the most critical one for the plaintiff—the ultimate opportunity to get into court under § 1983, even if state authorities reject his claim?

(c) *Heck*'s "false exhaustion" requirement appears to prevent the plaintiff from ever gaining a § 1983 forum until he has persuaded the state authorities that their conviction of him was wrong. But in *Heck* Justice Scalia interprets the common law to include any setting aside of the state conviction, whether by a state authority or a federal court on habeas corpus. Is it the availability of the habeas challenge that guarantees that the prisoner will indeed obtain a federal forum? And if he succeeds on the habeas claim, what will follow for his § 1983 claim? Is not *Heck* in reality an exhaustion requirement after all? A "super-exhaustion" requirement—because state remedies must be exhausted before federal habeas and federal habeas before the § 1983 suit for damages?

3. Can the *Heck* principle be applied to other prisoner litigation? U.S. Spencer v. Kemna, 523 U.S. 1, 118 S.Ct. 978, 140 L.Ed.2d 43 (1998) (parole revocation) (if challenged "procedural defect did not necessarily imply the invalidity of the revocation, then *Heck* would have no application all"), with Edwards v. Balisok, 520 U.S. 641, 117 S.Ct. 1584, 137 L.Ed.2d 906 (1997) (disciplinary hearing's punishment challenged; *Heck* applies). In Muhammad

v. Close, 540 U.S. 749, 124 S.Ct. 1303, 158 L.Ed.2d 32 (2004), the Court found that *Heck* is inapplicable to claim of unconstitutional punishment while in prison, noting that the claim did not call into question the inmate's underlying conviction.

(a) Notice the triangulation that results when *Patsy*'s no-exhaustion rule is considered with *Preiser*'s exhaustion rule and *Heck*'s false-exhaustion rule. A plaintiff must avoid *Preiser* by eschewing relief that would result in an earlier release from custody, then must avoid *Heck* by not challenging his underlying conviction, so that he can rely on *Patsy*'s no-exhaustion rule. Several of the cases discussed in the preceding Note, ¶ 1(d) supra, also discuss whether the permissible § 1983 claim is also barred by *Heck*. See, e.g., Hill v. McDonough, 547 U.S. 573, 126 S.Ct. 2096, 165 L.Ed.2d 44 (2006) (*Heck* inapplicable).

2. CERTIFICATION AND ABSTENTION, ESPECIALLY FIRST AMENDMENT CLAIMS

CITY OF HOUSTON v. HILL

Supreme Court of the United States, 1987.
482 U.S. 451, 107 S.Ct. 2502, 96 L.Ed.2d 398.

JUSTICE BRENNAN delivered the opinion of the Court.

This case presents the question whether a municipal ordinance that makes it unlawful to interrupt a police officer in the performance of his or her duties is unconstitutionally overbroad under the First Amendment.

[Plaintiff, a "life-long resident of Houston," a member of the Gay Political Caucus, and Executive Director of the Houston Human Rights League, had an encounter with police on a public street in the "center of gay political and social life in Houston." Police were questioning one of Hill's friends when Hill approached and, "in an admitted attempt to divert" the officers from their interrogation, told the officers, "Why don't you pick on somebody your own size?" One officer replied, "[A]re you interrupting me in my official capacity as a Houston police officer?" Hill answered affirmatively and was immediately arrested under Houston Municipal Code § 34–11(a) for "wilfully or intentionally interrupt[ing] a city policeman ... by verbal challenge during an investigation."]

Houston Municipal Code § 34–11(a) (1984) reads:

"Sec. 34–11. Assaulting or interfering with policemen.

(a) It shall be unlawful for any person to * * * in any manner oppose, molest, abuse or interrupt any policeman in the execution of his duty, or any person summoned to aid in making an arrest."

Following his acquittal in the Charles Hill incident, Hill brought suit in Federal District Court for the Southern District of Texas seeking (1) a declaratory judgment that § 34–11(a) was unconstitutional both on its face and as it had been applied to him, (2) a permanent injunction against any attempt to enforce the ordinance, (3) an order expunging the records of his arrests under the ordinance, and (4) damages and attorney's fees under 42 U.S.C. §§ 1983 and 1988.

[The district court upheld the ordinance but was reversed on appeal to the Fifth Circuit. That court found the ordinance unconstitutional under the First Amendment because of overbreadth, relying on Broadrick v. Oklahoma, 413 U.S. 601, 93 S.Ct. 2908, 37 L.Ed.2d 830 (1973). The Supreme Court affirmed this finding of unconstitutionality, noting that even if the law could be applied to some non-protected activity, on its face it applied to a broad range of protected speech.]

Houston's ordinance criminalizes a substantial amount of constitutionally protected speech, and accords the police unconstitutional discretion in enforcement. The ordinance's plain language is admittedly violated scores of times daily, App. 77, yet only some individuals—those chosen by the police in their unguided discretion—are arrested. Far from providing the "breathing space" that "First Amendment freedoms need . . . to survive," NAACP v. Button, 371 U.S. 415, 433, 83 S.Ct. 328, 9 L.Ed.2d 405 (1963), the ordinance is susceptible of regular application to protected expression. We conclude that the ordinance is substantially overbroad, and that the Court of Appeals did not err in holding it facially invalid.

The City has also urged us not to reach the merits of Hill's constitutional challenge, but rather to abstain for reasons related to those underlying our decision in Railroad Comm'n v. Pullman Co., 312 U.S. 496, 61 S.Ct. 643, 85 L.Ed. 971 (1941). In its view, there are certain limiting constructions readily available to the state courts that would eliminate the ordinance's overbreadth.

Abstention is, of course, the exception and not the rule, Colorado River Water Conservation Dist. v. United States, 424 U.S. 800, 813, 96 S.Ct. 1236, 1244, 47 L.Ed.2d 483 (1976), and we have been particularly reluctant to abstain in cases involving facial challenges based on the First Amendment. We have held that "abstention . . . is inappropriate for cases [where] . . . statutes are justifiably attacked on their face as abridging free expression." Dombrowski v. Pfister, 380 U.S. 479, 489–490, 85 S.Ct. 1116, 1122, 14 L.Ed.2d 22 (1965). "In such case[s] to force the plaintiff who has commenced a federal action to suffer the delay of state-court proceedings might itself effect the impermissible chilling of the very constitutional right he seeks to protect." Zwickler v. Koota, 389 U.S. 241, 252, 88 S.Ct. 391, 397, 19 L.Ed.2d 444 (1967).

Even if this case did not involve a facial challenge under the First Amendment, we would find abstention inappropriate. In cases involving a facial challenge to a statute, the pivotal question in determining whether abstention is appropriate is whether the statute is "fairly subject to an interpretation which will render unnecessary or substantially modify the federal constitutional question." Harman v. Forssenius, 380 U.S. 528, 534–535, 85 S.Ct. 1177, 14 L.Ed.2d 50 (1965); see also Hawaii Housing Authority v. Midkiff, 467 U.S. 229, 236, 104 S.Ct. 2321, 81 L.Ed.2d 186

(1984) (same). If the statute is not obviously susceptible of a limiting construction, then even if the statute has "never [been] interpreted by a state tribunal ... it is the duty of the federal court to exercise its properly invoked jurisdiction." Harmon, supra, at 535; see, e.g., Wisconsin v. Constantineau, 400 U.S. 433, 439, 91 S.Ct. 507, 511, 27 L.Ed.2d 515 (1971) ("Where there is no ambiguity in the state statute, the federal court should not abstain but should proceed to decide the federal constitutional claim").

This ordinance is not susceptible to a limiting construction because, as both courts below agreed, its language is plain and its meaning unambiguous. Its constitutionality cannot "turn upon a choice between one or several alternative meanings." Baggett v. Bullitt, 377 U.S. 360, 378, 84 S.Ct. 1316, 1326, 12 L.Ed.2d 377 (1964); * * * The enforceable portion of this ordinance is a general prohibition of speech that "simply has no core" of constitutionally unprotected expression to which it might be limited. Smith v. Goguen, 415 U.S. at 578, 94 S.Ct., at 1249 (emphasis deleted). The City's proposed constructions are insufficient,[18] and it is doubtful that even "a remarkable job of plastic surgery upon the face of the ordinance" could save it. Shuttlesworth v. Birmingham, 394 U.S. 147, 153, 89 S.Ct. 935, 940, 22 L.Ed.2d 162 (1969). In sum, "[s]ince 'the naked question, uncomplicated by [ambiguous language], is whether the Act on its face is unconstitutional,' Wisconsin v. Constantineau, 400 U.S. 433, 439, 91 S.Ct. 507, 511, 27 L.Ed.2d 515 (1971), abstention from federal jurisdiction is not required." Hawaii Housing Authority, supra, at 237, 104 S.Ct., at 2327.

The City relies heavily on its claim that the state courts have not had an opportunity to construe the statute. Even if true, that factor would not in itself be controlling. As stated above, when a statute is not ambiguous, there is no need to abstain even if state courts have never interpreted the statute. For example, we have declined to abstain from deciding a facial challenge to a state statute when the suit was filed in federal court just four days after the statute took effect. Brockett v. Spokane Arcades, Inc., 472 U.S. 491, 105 S.Ct. 2794, 86 L.Ed.2d 394 (1985). But in any event, the City's claim that state courts have not had an opportunity to construe the statute is misleading. Only the state *appellate* courts appear to have lacked this opportunity. It is undisputed that Houston's Municipal Courts, which have been courts of record in Texas since 1976, have had numerous opportunities to narrow the scope of the ordinance. There is no evidence that they have done so. In fact, the City's primary position throughout

---

18. The City suggests that the statute would be constitutional if construed to apply only to (1) intentional interruptions by (2) "physical, rather than verbal, acts" during (3) an officer's attempts to make "arrests and detentions." Brief for Appellant 30–31. These proposals are either at odds with the ordinance's plain meaning, or do not sufficiently limit its scope. First, speech does not necessarily lose its constitutional protection because the speaker intends it to interrupt an officer, nor would an intent requirement cabin the excessive discretion the ordinance provides to officers. Second, limiting the ordinance to "physical acts" would be equivalent to invalidating it on its face. Third, there is no reasonable way to read the plain language of the ordinance as limited to arrests and detentions; even if there were, such a limitation would not significantly limit its scope.

this litigation has been "to insis[t] on the validity of the ordinance as literally read." 789 F.2d at 1107. We have long recognized that trial court interpretations, such as those given in jury instructions, constitute "a ruling on a question of state law that is as binding on us as though the precise words had been written into the ordinance." Thus, where municipal courts have regularly applied an unambiguous statute, there is certainly no need for a federal court to abstain until state appellate courts have an opportunity to construe it.

The possibility of certification does not change our analysis.[21] The certification procedure is useful in reducing the substantial burdens of cost and delay that abstention places on litigants. Where there is an uncertain question of state law that would affect the resolution of the federal claim, and where delay and expense are the chief drawbacks to abstention, the availability of certification becomes an important factor in deciding whether to abstain. E.g., Bellotti v. Baird, 428 U.S. 132, 96 S.Ct. 2857, 49 L.Ed.2d 844 (1976). Nevertheless, even where we have recognized the importance of certification in deciding whether to abstain, we have been careful to note that the availability of certification is not in itself sufficient to render abstention appropriate. Id., at 151, 96 S.Ct., at 2868. It would be manifestly inappropriate to certify a question in a case where, as here, there is no uncertain question of state law whose resolution might affect the pending federal claim. As we have demonstrated, this ordinance is neither ambiguous nor obviously susceptible of a limiting construction. A federal court may not properly ask a state court if it would care in effect to rewrite a statute.[23] We therefore see no need in this case to abstain pending certification.

* * *

We therefore affirm the judgment of the Court of Appeals.

It is so ordered.

JUSTICE BLACKMUN, concurring. [Omitted]

JUSTICE SCALIA, concurring in the judgment. [Omitted]

JUSTICE POWELL, with whom JUSTICE O'CONNOR joins, and with whom THE CHIEF JUSTICE joins as to Parts I and II, and JUSTICE SCALIA joins as to Parts II and III, concurring in the judgment in part and dissenting in part.

* * *

Pullman abstention is inappropriate unless the state courts "provid[e] the parties with adequate means to adjudicate the controverted state law

---

21. Under Texas law, either this Court or a United States Court of Appeals may certify a question of Texas criminal law "which may be determinative of the cause then pending and as to which it appears to the certifying court that there is no controlling precedent in the decisions of the Court of Criminal Appeals." Tex.Rule App.Proc. 214.

23. It would also be inappropriate for a federal court to certify the entire constitutional challenge to the state court, of course, for certified questions should be confined to uncertain questions of state law. See 17 C. Wright, A. Miller, & E. Cooper, Federal Practice and Procedure § 4248, pp. 529–530 (1978).

issue." Field, Abstention in Constitutional Cases: The Scope of the *Pullman* Abstention Doctrine, 122 U.PA.L.REV. 1071, 1144 (1974). See 17 C. Wright, A. Miller, & E. Cooper, Federal Practice and Procedure § 4242, p. 468 (1978).

It is not clear that Texas law affords a remedy by which Hill could obtain a state court interpretation of the ordinance [because he has been acquitted of criminal charges and because the] Texas Supreme Court has held, with narrow exceptions, that injunctive or declaratory relief against criminal statutes is not available in civil cases. See Texas Liquor Control Board v. Canyon Creek Land Corp., 456 S.W.2d 891, 894–896 (Tex.1970).

* * *

CHIEF JUSTICE REHNQUIST, dissenting. [Omitted]

NOTE ON THE ABSTENTION DOCTRINE AND CERTIFICATION

1. Since its creation in the *Pullman* case,[1] the abstention doctrine has evolved along several strains and applies in a broad range of federal litigation where state law is at issue. In its normal guise, abstention seeks from state courts a construction of an unclear state statute or ordinance in order to clarify or avoid a plaintiff's constitutional claim.

(a) Does Justice Brennan make the abstention decision appear to be more rule-bound than it actually is? Consider footnote 18. Should abstention require a more practical balancing of the likelihood of successful avoidance of unnecessary constitutional adjudication, abstention's goal, against the harm to the plaintiff caused by delay? Does balancing make it too easy for a federal court to justify abstention and avoid protecting the plaintiff? See Lipscomb v. Columbus Mun. Separate Sch. Dist., 145 F.3d 238 (5th Cir. 1998): "[T]he mere presence of an ambiguity in state law and a likelihood of avoiding a constitutional adjudication does not automatically compel *Pullman* abstention[, but only starts] a broad inquiry which should include consideration of the rights at stake and the costs of delay pending state court adjudication."

But does every statute fall neatly into either of two categories, obviously clear or obviously unclear?

(b) Of course, if a state court has already construed the statute at issue, making it plain that the statute is no longer ambiguous, then abstention is no longer appropriate. Why is this so? Because the application to a state court would be futile under its precedents? But cannot the state court overturn its precedents? Is abstention always appropriate because a state may alter its precedent to eliminate a constitutional problem?

2. The Supreme Court described its doctrines of abstention and certification in **Arizonans for Official English v. Arizona**, 520 U.S. 43, 117 S.Ct. 1055, 137 L.Ed.2d 170 (1997), involving a challenge to that state's "official English" law. Justice Ginsburg wrote for the majority:

---

1. The doctrine is thus often called *Pullman*-type abstention to distinguish it from *Younger*-type abstention, discussed separately in subsection 3 infra.

"Certification today covers territory once dominated by a deferral device called 'Pullman abstention,' after the generative Railroad Comm'n of Tex. v. Pullman Co., 312 U.S. 496, 61 S.Ct. 643, 85 L.Ed. 971 (1941). Designed to avoid federal-court error in deciding state-law questions antecedent to federal constitutional issues, the Pullman mechanism remitted parties to the state courts for adjudication of the unsettled state-law issues. If settlement of the state-law question did not prove dispositive of the case, the parties could return to the federal court for decision of the federal issues. Attractive in theory because it placed state-law questions in courts equipped to rule authoritatively on them, Pullman abstention proved protracted and expensive in practice, for it entailed a full round of litigation in the state-court system before any resumption of proceedings in federal court. See generally 17A C. Wright, A. Miller, & E. Cooper, Federal Practice and Procedure §§ 4242, 4243 (2d ed.1988 and Supp. 1996).

"Certification procedure, in contrast, allows a federal court faced with a novel state-law question to put the question directly to the State's highest court, reducing the delay, cutting the cost, and increasing the assurance of gaining an authoritative response. Most States have adopted certification procedures. See generally 17A Wright, Miller & Cooper, supra, § 4248."

(a) Does the ease of resort to certification mean that it should be more regularly used than is abstention? See id. ("[certification] procedures do not entail the delays, expense, and procedural complexity that generally attend abstention decisions").

(b) Every § 1983 action in which the defendant has acted within her statutory authority, and that statute's constitutionality is attacked, will provide an opportunity for certification. In order to prevent certification from becoming routine, should courts restrict its use to "unique circumstances"? See id.: "Novel, unsettled questions of state law, however, not 'unique circumstances,' are necessary before federal courts may avail themselves of state certification procedures." Does *Arizonans for Official English* suggest that certification should be used more readily?

2.   What good comes from abstention or certification? What does the federal court hope that the state court will do when it receives the case? What risks are created for the § 1983 plaintiff?

(a) If the hope is that the state court will give the unclear state law a narrowing interpretation, so as to avoid the constitutional problem presented in the § 1983 suit, should the plaintiff not present his constitutional argument to the state court so as to inform its judgment? See Government & Civic Employees Organizing Committee v. Windsor, 353 U.S. 364, 366, 77 S.Ct. 838, 839, 1 L.Ed.2d 894 (1957). Does the § 1983 plaintiff risk a plea of res judicata upon his return to federal court? See England v. Louisiana State Bd. of Med. Examiners, 375 U.S. 411, 84 S.Ct. 461, 11 L.Ed.2d 440 (1964) (litigant sent to state court may return to federal trial court and present his federal claim after sojourn in state court, or he may seek direct review of the state court judgment in the U.S. Supreme Court). But see San Remo Hotel, L.P. v. City and County of San Francisco, 545 U.S. 323, 125 S.Ct. 2491, 162 L.Ed.2d 315

(2005) (*England* inapplicable to Taking claims, even when lower court has ordered abstention).

(b) Under certification, of course, the federal court retains jurisdiction while awaiting a reply. Should a federal court which decides to abstain stay its proceedings or dismiss the plaintiff's claim? Compare Zwickler v. Koota, 389 U.S. 241, 244 n. 4, 88 S.Ct. 391, 393 n. 4, 19 L.Ed.2d 444 (1967), with Harris County Comm'rs v. Moore, 420 U.S. 77, 88–89, 95 S.Ct. 870, 43 L.Ed.2d 32 (1975). What risks might dismissal pose for plaintiff? See Deakins v. Monaghan, 484 U.S. 193, 108 S.Ct. 523, 98 L.Ed.2d 529 (1988) (parallel problem under *Younger*-type abstention).

3. Certification may present special problems in the context of First Amendment litigation because of the doctrines of "overbreadth" and "vagueness." The two doctrines both enforce the free-speech idea that speakers should not be required to self-censor because of the lack of clear standards in a statute regulating speech. Overbreadth, as in *Hill*, presents the problem of a statute that sweeps so broadly that a speaker cannot know its limits.[1] Vagueness presents the problem of the statute that is so unclear that the speaker cannot know its limits.[2]

(a) *Hill* appears to hold that facial attacks on ordinances that are overbroad under the First Amendment will usually present no cause for abstention. But if such a relatively absolute approach is appropriate for overbreadth cases, should there not be a similar rule virtually requiring abstention or certification when plaintiff attacks an ordinance on void-for-vagueness grounds under the First Amendment? See Procunier v. Martinez, 416 U.S. 396, 401 n. 5, 94 S.Ct. 1800, 1805 n. 5, 40 L.Ed.2d 224 (1974). Does a vagueness claim not inherently involve an ambiguous state statute that may be saved through state-court interpretation?

(b) Should abstention or certification have been ordered in the following cases, both involving First–Amendment based attacks? New Mexico adopts a statutory ban on internet dissemination of material "harmful to minors": American Civil Liberties Union v. Johnson, 194 F.3d 1149 (10th Cir. 1999). North Carolina bans "political action committees" from making certain donations to candidates, even if they are only engaged in protected "issue advocacy": North Carolina Right to Life, Inc. v. Bartlett, 168 F.3d 705 (4th Cir. 1999). Do you need to know the text of the statutes to decide, or can you

---

1. "Under the First Amendment overbreadth doctrine, an individual whose own speech or conduct may be prohibited is permitted to challenge a statute on its face 'because it also threatens others not before the court—those who desire to engage in legally protected expression but who may refrain from doing so rather than risk prosecution or undertake to have the law declared partially invalid.' Brockett v. Spokane Arcades, Inc., 472 U.S. 491, 503, 105 S.Ct. 2794, 86 L.Ed.2d 394 (1985)." Board of Airport Com'rs of City of Los Angeles v. Jews for Jesus, Inc., 482 U.S. 569, 107 S.Ct. 2568, 96 L.Ed.2d 500 (1987) (total ban on "First Amendment activities"; abstention refused also).

2. See Reno v. American Civil Liberties Union, 521 U.S. 844, 117 S.Ct. 2329, 138 L.Ed.2d 874 (1997) (vague statute prohibiting "indecency" on the internet has "obvious chilling effect on free speech"); City of Chicago v. Morales, 527 U.S. 41, 119 S.Ct. 1849, 144 L.Ed.2d 67 (1999) (loitering ordinance that inhibits First Amendment rights): "[E]ven if an enactment does not reach a substantial amount of constitutionally protected conduct, it may be impermissibly vague because it fails to establish standards for the police and public that are sufficient to guard against the arbitrary deprivation of liberty interests."

accept the state's argument that a narrowing construction is possible for any text?

4. Abstention and certification issues outside the First Amendment area carry less danger, according to *Hill*. How should federal courts respond to an abstention request outside the First Amendment area where such special concerns as censorship are not present?

(a) Abstention or certification can in the First Amendment context lead to serious harms befalling the § 1983 plaintiff while she awaits the state court's ruling. Are there any other situations where there might be similar harms? See, e.g., Lake Carriers' Ass'n v. MacMullan, 406 U.S. 498, 92 S.Ct. 1749, 32 L.Ed.2d 257 (1972) (unclear state anti-pollution laws attacked; abstention ordered); Rivera–Feliciano v. Acevedo–Vila, 438 F.3d 50 (1st Cir. 2006) (electronic monitoring; similar litigation in process in state courts); Brooks v. Walker County Hosp. Dist., 688 F.2d 334 (5th Cir.1982) (claim of free medical services under unclear state constitutional provision). Is any novel issue arising under a new state law subject to certification if the state law may be interpreted more narrowly to avoid the constitutional question?

(b) Why must abstention be the "exception and not the rule," as stated in *Hill*? Because every requirement of abstention is a requirement of exhaustion of state judicial remedies in violation of Monroe v. Pape? Is certification also an implicit exhaustion doctrine?

(c) Do abstention and certification favor the conservative or liberal political agendas, or neither? Does the answer depend upon what kinds of claims are presented or what types or parties are usually present in § 1983 actions? If conservative students challenge a liberal university's rules for socially acceptable speech, is abstention to allow attack on the rules on state law grounds appropriate? Is the principal problem with abstention that it allows a judge to postpone justice for a party whose claim she dislikes?

5. In **Askew v. Hargrave**, 401 U.S. 476, 91 S.Ct. 856, 28 L.Ed.2d 196 (1971), the Supreme Court ordered abstention in a § 1983 case challenging Florida's educational funding scheme on equal protection grounds. It limited its holding to the situation where a parallel state proceeding presenting the possibility for relief on state law grounds would possibly obviate the need for federal-court decision on constitutional grounds. But *Askew* was decided at a time before the Court more solidly adopted its no-exhaustion rule for § 1983 in the *Patsy* case, discussed in the preceding Note.

(a) *Askew* is rarely cited, but its theme is occasionally seen. See, e.g., Rivera–Feliciano v. Acevedo–Vila, 438 F.3d 50 (1st Cir. 2006) (electronic monitoring; similar litigation in process in state courts); Ziegler v. Ziegler, 632 F.2d 535, 539 (5th Cir.1980); Finch v. Mississippi State Med. Ass'n, 585 F.2d 765 (5th Cir.1978). Is *Askew* rarely seen because it is a mere fortuity that a parallel state proceeding would dispose of a § 1983 case on state grounds?

(b) Should *Askew* be overturned because it allows federal courts too easily to evade their duty to enforce federal law? Expanded because it is a salutary rule that avoids unnecessary decisions on constitutional issues? See Ashwander v. Tennessee Valley Auth., 297 U.S. 288, 346, 56 S.Ct. 466, 80 L.Ed. 688 (1936) (Brandeis, J., concurring). But an expanded *Askew* case would effectively negate the grant of federal jurisdiction in 28 U.S.C. § 1343, as well as overturn *Monroe,* with the costs there noted, and require exhaustion of state judicial remedies, would it not?[3]

3. THE *PARRATT* DOCTRINE FOR PROCEDURAL DUE PROCESS CASES

PARRATT v. TAYLOR

Supreme Court of the United States, 1981.
451 U.S. 527, 101 S.Ct. 1908, 68 L.Ed.2d 420.

JUSTICE REHNQUIST delivered the opinion of the Court.

The respondent is an inmate at the Nebraska Penal and Correctional Complex who ordered by mail certain hobby materials valued at $23.50. The hobby materials were lost and respondent brought suit under 42 U.S.C. § 1983 to recover their value. At first blush one might well inquire why respondent brought an action in federal court to recover damages of such a small amount for negligent loss of property, but because 28 U.S.C. § 1343, the predicate for the jurisdiction of the United States District Court, contains no minimum dollar limitation, he was authorized by Congress to bring his action under that section if he met its requirements and if he stated a claim for relief under 42 U.S.C. § 1983. Respondent claimed that his property was negligently lost by prison officials in violation of his rights under the Fourteenth Amendment to the United States Constitution. More specifically, he claimed that he had been deprived of property without due process of law.[1]

* * *

* * * Nothing in that Amendment protects against all deprivations of life, liberty, or property by the State. The Fourteenth Amendment protects only against deprivations "without due process of law." Our inquiry therefore must focus on whether the respondent has suffered a deprivation of property without due process of law. In particular, we must decide whether the tort remedies which the State of Nebraska provides as a means of redress for property deprivations satisfy the requirements of procedural due process.

---

3. In Burford v. Sun Oil Co., 319 U.S. 315, 63 S.Ct. 1098, 87 L.Ed. 1424 (1943), the Court authorized abstention in a diversity case where a federal decision of state law would have intruded on a complex state regulatory scheme controlling oil and gas production. Should *Burford* have application to § 1983 suits that raise a federal constitutional challenge to state regulatory schemes? See Chiropractic America v. Lavecchia, 180 F.3d 99 (3rd Cir. 1999) (state insurance licensing; *Burford* applies); New Orleans Public Serv., Inc. v. Council of the City of New Orleans, 491 U.S. 350, 109 S.Ct. 2506, 105 L.Ed.2d 298 (1989) (no abstention where federal claims not entangled with construction of state law).

1. As we explained in Board of Regents v. Roth, 408 U.S. 564, 92 S.Ct. 2701, 33 L.Ed.2d 548 (1972), property interests "are not created by the Constitution. Rather, they are created and their dimensions are defined by existing rules or understandings that stem from an independent source such as state law—rules or understandings that secure certain benefits and that support claims of entitlement to those benefits." Id., at 577, 92 S.Ct., at 2709. It is not contended that under Nebraska law respondent does not enjoy a property interest in the hobby materials here in question.

* * * In some cases this Court has held that due process requires a predeprivation hearing before the State interferes with any liberty or property interest enjoyed by its citizens. In most of these cases, however, the deprivation of property was pursuant to some established state procedure and "process" could be offered before any actual deprivation took place. For example, * * * in Bell v. Burson, 402 U.S. 535, 91 S.Ct. 1586, 29 L.Ed.2d 90 (1971), we reviewed a state statute which provided for the taking of the driver's license and registration of an uninsured motorist who had been involved in an accident. We recognized that a driver's license is often involved in the livelihood of a person and as such could not be summarily taken without a prior hearing. In Fuentes v. Shevin, 407 U.S. 67, 92 S.Ct. 1983, 32 L.Ed.2d 556 (1972), we struck down the Florida prejudgment replevin statute which allowed secured creditors to obtain writs in ex parte proceedings. We held that due process required a prior hearing before the State authorized its agents to seize property in a debtor's possession. See also Boddie v. Connecticut, 401 U.S. 371, 91 S.Ct. 780, 28 L.Ed.2d 113 (1971); Goldberg v. Kelly, 397 U.S. 254, 90 S.Ct. 1011, 25 L.Ed.2d 287 (1970); and Sniadach v. Family Finance Corp., 395 U.S. 337, 89 S.Ct. 1820, 23 L.Ed.2d 349 (1969). In all these cases, deprivations of property were authorized by an established state procedure and due process was held to require predeprivation notice and hearing in order to serve as a check on the possibility that a wrongful deprivation would occur.

We have, however, recognized that postdeprivation remedies made available by the State can satisfy the Due Process Clause. In such cases, the normal predeprivation notice and opportunity to be heard is pretermitted if the State provides a postdeprivation remedy. In North American Cold Storage Co. v. Chicago, 211 U.S. 306, 29 S.Ct. 101, 53 L.Ed. 195 (1908), we upheld the right of a State to seize and destroy unwholesome food without a preseizure hearing. The possibility of erroneous destruction of property was outweighed by the fact that the public health emergency justified immediate action and the owner of the property could recover his damages in an action at law after the incident. In Ewing v. Mytinger & Casselberry, Inc., 339 U.S. 594, 70 S.Ct. 870, 94 L.Ed. 1088 (1950), we upheld under the Fifth Amendment Due Process Clause the summary seizure and destruction of drugs without a preseizure hearing. Similarly, in Fahey v. Mallonee, 332 U.S. 245, 67 S.Ct. 1552, 91 L.Ed. 2030 (1947), we recognized that the protection of the public interest against economic harm can justify the immediate seizure of property without a prior hearing when substantial questions are raised about the competence of a bank's management. In Bowles v. Willingham, 321 U.S. 503, 64 S.Ct. 641, 88 L.Ed. 892 (1944), we upheld in the face of a due process challenge the authority of the Administrator of the Office of Price Administration to issue rent control orders without providing a hearing to landlords before the order or regulation fixing rents became effective. These cases recognize that either the necessity of quick action by the State or the impracticality of providing any meaningful predeprivation process, when coupled with the availability of some meaningful means by which to assess the propriety of the State's action at some time after the initial taking, can satisfy the requirements of procedural due process. As we stated in Mitchell v. W.T. Grant Co., 416 U.S. 600, 94 S.Ct. 1895, 40 L.Ed.2d 406 (1974):

> "Petitioner asserts that his right to a hearing before his possession is in any way disturbed is nonetheless mandated by a long line of cases in this Court * * * [These] cases are said by petitioner to hold that 'the opportunity to be heard must precede any actual deprivation of private property.' Their import, however, is not so clear as petitioner would have it: they merely stand for the proposition that a hearing must be had before one is finally deprived of his property and do not deal at all with the need for a pretermination hearing where a full and immediate post-termination hearing is provided. The usual rule has been '[w]here only property rights are involved, mere postponement of the judicial enquiry is not a denial of due process, if the opportunity given for ultimate judicial determination of liability is adequate.' Phillips v. Commissioner, 283 U.S. 589, 596–597 [51 S.Ct. 608, 611, 75 L.Ed. 1289] (1931)." Id., at 611, 94 S.Ct., at 1902 (footnote omitted).

* * *

The justifications which we have found sufficient to uphold takings of property without any predeprivation process are applicable to a situation such as the present one involving a tortious loss of a prisoner's property as a result of a random and unauthorized act by a state employee. In such a case, the loss is not a result of some established state procedure and the State cannot predict precisely when the loss will occur. It is difficult to conceive of how the State could provide a meaningful hearing before the deprivation takes place. The loss of property, although attributable to the State as action under "color of law," is in almost all cases beyond the control of the State. Indeed, in most cases it is not only impracticable, but impossible, to provide a meaningful hearing before the deprivation. That does not mean, of course, that the State can take property without providing a meaningful postdeprivation hearing. The prior cases which have excused the prior-hearing requirement have rested in part on the availability of some meaningful opportunity subsequent to the initial taking for a determination of rights and liabilities.

* * *

Application of the principles recited above to this case leads us to conclude the respondent has not alleged a violation of the Due Process Clause of the Fourteenth Amendment. Although he has been deprived of property under color of state law, the deprivation did not occur as a result of some established state procedure. Indeed, the deprivation occurred as a result of the unauthorized failure of agents of the State to follow established state procedure. There is no contention that the procedures themselves are inadequate nor is there any contention that it was practicable for the State to provide a predeprivation hearing. Moreover, the State of Nebraska has provided respondent with the means by which he can receive redress for the deprivation. The State provides a remedy to persons who believe they have suffered a tortious loss at the hands of the State. See Neb.Rev.Stat. §§ 81–8,209 et seq. (1976). Through this tort claims procedure the State hears and pays claims of prisoners housed in its penal institutions. * * * Although the state remedies may not provide the respondent with all the relief which may have been available if he could have proceeded under § 1983, that does not mean that the state remedies are not adequate to satisfy the requirements of due process. The remedies provided could have fully compensated the respondent for the property loss he suffered, and we hold that they are sufficient to satisfy the requirements of due process.

* * *

Accordingly, the judgment of the Court of Appeals is

Reversed.

[The concurring opinions are omitted.]

NOTE ON THE SCOPE OF THE *PARRATT* DOCTRINE

1. *Parratt* holds that when *procedural* due process guarantees only a post-deprivation hearing, provision of a right to sue in state court is provision of a hearing; procedural due process need not be tied to an administrative hearing. By its terms, the *Parratt* doctrine has no impact on *substantive* due process cases involving either selectively incorporated rights from the Bill of Rights, see, e.g., Estelle v. Gamble, Chapter 1B.2 supra, or non-textual fundamental rights, see, e.g., Griswold v. Connecticut, 381 U.S. 479, 85 S.Ct. 1678, 14 L.Ed.2d 510 (1965) (right to procreational choice). Similarly, *Parratt* has no application to even procedural due process cases in which a *pre*-deprivation hearing is due, for a hearing in state court given after the fact is not a hearing prior to the deprivation. See Zinermon v. Burch, which follows this Note.

(a) Should *Parratt* be extended to substantive due process rights? See Mann v. City of Tucson, 782 F.2d 790, 794–800 (9th Cir.1986) (Sneed, J., concurring in the result) (proposing that courts "extend *Parratt* to all other constitutional injuries cognizable under section 1983" because the "procedural-substantive due process distinction has no roots in logic"). Judge Sneed quite frankly admits that his approach would substantially overrule Monroe v. Pape's no-exhaustion rule. All circuits refused to take his position. See, e.g., Gilmere v. City of Atlanta, 774 F.2d 1495 (11th Cir. 1985) (en banc). Should it have been adopted?

(b) Does the argument for extension of *Parratt* not undervalue the force of the opinion? Is *Parratt* just an exhaustion doctrine, requiring the plaintiff first to resort to state court before going to federal court? Is the case not much more substantial than that—for when the state provides a hearing in state court, it has provided procedural due process, and thus it has done no constitutional wrong? A dismissal under *Parratt* should be a Rule 12(b)(6) dismissal on the merits, should it not?

(c) Why does *Parratt* have no application to procedural due process cases when due process requires a *pre*-deprivation hearing? Cf. Cleveland Bd. of Educ. v. Loudermill, 470 U.S. 532, 105 S.Ct. 1487, 84 L.Ed.2d 494 (1985); New Windsor Volunteer Ambulance Corps, Inc. v. Meyers, 442 F.3d 101 (2d Cir. 2006). Is Einstein relevant here: time runs in only one direction, so a post-deprivation remedy cannot provide a pre-deprivation hearing?

2. While *Parratt* has not been extended beyond post-deprivation procedural due process cases, it has spread throughout that area. Thus, its thesis has been held to apply to claims based on "liberty" interests as well as those based on "property" interests, Ingraham v. Wright, 430 U.S. 651, 97 S.Ct. 1401, 51 L.Ed.2d 711 (1977) (pre-*Parratt*); and to intentional as well as negligent deprivations, Hudson v. Palmer, 468 U.S. 517, 104 S.Ct. 3194, 82 L.Ed.2d 393 (1984). Indeed, two years following *Hudson,* the Court partially overruled *Parratt* and held that negligent deprivations were not even actionable under the procedural due process clause. Daniels v. Williams, Chapter 1B.1, supra. Is the expansion of *Parratt* throughout the domain of procedural due process an important development?

(a) For substantive due process, the Court itself identifies those rights that are protected, either by selectively incorporating the Bill of Rights (thus applying it to the states) or by recognizing non-textual fundamental rights. As great as the public controversy over recognition of non-textual rights may be, the fact is that the list of incorporated and non-textual rights is very short. Outside the criminal law context, what rights are incorporated from the Bill of Rights? Although the right to an abortion has raised great debate, are not fundamental rights non-composed of only a few controversial familial—apple-pie American—rights?

(b) Rights protected under procedural due process spring primarily from state law, which may create a wide range of liberty and property interests varying from state to state. See Kentucky Dept. of Corrections v. Thompson, 490 U.S. 454, 109 S.Ct. 1904, 104 L.Ed.2d 506 (1989) (whether prisoner has interest in receiving visitors is determined by analysis of state law); Board of Regents v. Roth, 408 U.S. 564, 92 S.Ct. 2701, 33 L.Ed.2d 548 (1972) ("property" interest in state job established by contract). Given the brevity of the list of substantive due process rights, plaintiffs are likely to find "rights," if at all, only under procedural due process.[2]

(c) Finally, even when procedural due process covers a particular state-created right, the only process due will often be post-deprivation process, says the Court in *Parratt.* (If pre-deprivation process is due, rudimentary informal process often suffices. See Cleveland Bd. of Educ. v. Loudermill, supra.) Thus while *Parratt* has application only to procedural due process rights involving post-deprivation procedural rights, that area as anticipated in *Parratt* is probably the most fecund source of rights. If the state provides a state-court

---

2. Of course, *Parratt* only applies when there has been a "deprivation," and there is a rich jurisprudence as to what kinds of losses qualify. See, e.g., Gilbert v. Homar, 520 U.S. 924, 117 S.Ct. 1807, 138 L.Ed.2d 120 (1997) (police officer suspended after his own arrest).

remedy for deprivations of such rights, *Parratt* is presumptively satisfied—and state common law and statutory law often provide for state-court review of such state-created rights, just as in *Parratt*. Is *Parratt*'s reach too great?

3. Given the potential practical impact of the *Parratt* doctrine, and the availability of some state-court process that would satisfy the doctrine, most plaintiffs must attempt to show either that they have a substantive due process right or that they have a procedural due process right meriting pre-deprivation protection.

(a) The neat conceptual division between substantive and procedural due process sometimes unravels in the real world, for the Court has not always been clear in identifying the bases for rights. This is compounded by the fact that many substantive due process cases concern procedural safeguards necessary to show a compelling state interest in overriding the substantive right. See Cruzan by Cruzan v. Director, Missouri Dept. of Health, 497 U.S. 261, 110 S.Ct. 2841, 111 L.Ed.2d 224 (1990) (showing necessary in state court in order to ascertain patient's desire to exercise right to refuse medical treatment); Ohio v. Akron Center for Reproductive Health, 497 U.S. 502, 110 S.Ct. 2972, 111 L.Ed.2d 405 (1990) (judicial bypass procedure for protecting abortion right of minor). Is the liberty interest of a confined mental patient to freedom or effective treatment, recognized in Youngberg v. Romeo, 457 U.S. 307, 102 S.Ct. 2452, 73 L.Ed.2d 28 (1982), a procedural due process right or a substantive due process right?

(b) Is "procedural" due process itself a misnomer? Does procedural due process require that the state reach a substantively just result, or does it merely require that the process be provided? Compare Snowden v. Hughes, 321 U.S. 1, 64 S.Ct. 397, 88 L.Ed. 497 (1944) (mere violation of state law by state official constitutes no Fourteenth Amendment violation), with Regents of the University of Michigan v. Ewing, 474 U.S. 214, 106 S.Ct. 507, 88 L.Ed.2d 523 (1985) (courts should not second-guess school administrators' factual determinations in procedural due process case, but scope of review left open), and Board of Curators of the University of Missouri v. Horowitz, 435 U.S. 78, 98 S.Ct. 948, 55 L.Ed.2d 124 (1978) (open issue of whether courts may review under "arbitrary and capricious" standard ultimate correctness of state's hearing-based determination).

(c) Note also the distinction recognized in *Parratt* between deprivations pursuant to an "established state procedure" as opposed to those resulting from a "random and unauthorized act." Justice Rehnquist says that no pre-deprivation process is due in the latter group of cases, whereas some such process is apparently due in the former cases. How can a plaintiff show that his case falls into the "established state procedure" category, to which *Parratt* does not apply?

ZINERMON v. BURCH

Supreme Court of the United States, 1990.
494 U.S. 113, 110 S.Ct. 975, 108 L.Ed.2d 100.

JUSTICE BLACKMUN delivered the opinion of the Court.

I

Respondent Darrell Burch brought this suit under 42 U.S.C. § 1983 against the 11 petitioners, who are physicians, administrators, and staff members at Florida State Hospital (FSH) in Chattahoochee, and others. Respondent alleges that petitioners deprived him of his liberty, without due process of law, by admitting him to FSH as a "voluntary" mental patient when he was incompetent to give informed consent to his admission. Burch contends that in his case petitioners should have afforded him procedural safeguards required by the Constitution before involuntary commitment of a mentally ill person, and that petitioners' failure to do so violated his due process rights.

Petitioners argue that Burch's complaint failed to state a claim under § 1983 because, in their view, it alleged only a random, unauthorized violation of the Florida statutes governing admission of mental patients. Their argument rests on Parratt v. Taylor, where this Court held that a deprivation of a constitutionally protected property interest caused by a state employee's random, unauthorized conduct does not give rise to a § 1983 procedural due process claim, unless the State fails to provide an adequate postdeprivation remedy.

[The trial court dismissed the claim and was affirmed by the court of appeals, only to be reversed by that court sitting en banc. The Supreme Court granted limited certiorari.]

Because this case concerns the propriety of a Rule 12(b)(6) dismissal, the question before us is a narrow one. We decide only whether the *Parratt* rule necessarily means that Burch's complaint fails to allege any deprivation of due process, because he was constitutionally entitled to nothing more than what he received—an opportunity to sue petitioners in tort for his allegedly unlawful confinement. The broader questions of what procedural safeguards the Due Process Clause requires in the context of an admission to a mental hospital, and whether Florida's statutes meet these constitutional requirements, are not presented in this case. Burch did not frame his action as a challenge to the constitutional adequacy of Florida's mental health statutes. Both before the Eleventh Circuit and in his brief here, he disavowed any challenge to the statutes themselves, and restricted his claim to the contention that petitioners' failure to provide constitutionally adequate safeguards in his case violated his due process rights.

For purposes of review of a Rule 12(b)(6) dismissal, the factual allegations of Burch's complaint are taken as true. Burch's complaint, and the medical records and forms attached to it as exhibits, provide the following factual background:[Burch arrived at the state-sponsored treatment facility in a confused psychotic state. Rather than providing him with a competency hearing that probably would have resulted in his being ordered into custody, the administrators asked the hallucinating Burch to "consent" to treatment. Having diagnosed him as a paranoid schizophrenic, administrators again asked Burch to consent to his voluntary detention and treatment. After five months Burch was released, and soon thereafter he initiated this suit claiming that he should have been accorded a hearing prior to admittance because he was unable to give informed consent. He based his claim on his federal right to "due process of law."]

To understand the background against which this question arises, we return to the interpretation of § 1983 articulated in Monroe v. Pape. In *Monroe,* this Court rejected the view that § 1983 applies only to violations of constitutional rights that are authorized by state law, and does not reach abuses of state authority that are forbidden by the State's statutes or Constitution, or are torts under the State's common law. It explained that § 1983 was intended not only to "override" discriminatory or otherwise unconstitutional state laws, and to provide a remedy for violations of civil rights "where state law was inadequate," but also to provide a federal remedy "where the state remedy, though adequate in theory, was not available in practice." * * * Thus, overlapping state remedies are generally irrelevant to the question of the existence of a cause of action under § 1983. A plaintiff, for example, may bring a § 1983 action for an unlawful search and seizure despite the fact that the search and seizure violated the State's Constitution or statutes, and despite the fact that there are common-law remedies for trespass and conversion. As was noted in *Monroe,* in many cases there is "no quarrel with the state laws on the books," instead, the problem is the way those laws are or are not implemented by state officials.

This general rule applies in a straightforward way to two of the three kinds of § 1983 claims that may be brought against the State under the Due Process Clause of the Fourteenth Amendment. First, the Clause incorporates many of the specific protections defined in the Bill of Rights. A plaintiff may bring suit under § 1983 for state officials' violation of his rights to, e.g., freedom of speech or freedom from unreasonable searches and seizures. Second, the Due Process Clause contains a substantive component that bars certain arbitrary, wrongful government actions "regardless of the fairness of the procedures used to implement them." Daniels v. Williams, 474 U.S. 327, 331, 106 S.Ct. 662, 664, 88 L.Ed.2d 662 (1986). As to these two types of claims, the constitutional violation actionable under § 1983 is complete when the wrongful action is taken. Id., at 338, 106 S.Ct., at 678 (Stevens, J., concurring in judgments). A plaintiff, under Monroe v. Pape, may invoke § 1983 regardless of any state-tort remedy that might be available to compensate him for the deprivation of these rights.

The Due Process Clause also encompasses a third type of protection, a guarantee of fair procedure. A § 1983 action may be brought for a violation of procedural due process, but here the existence of state remedies *is* relevant in a special sense. In procedural due process claims, the deprivation by state action of a constitutionally protected interest in "life, liberty, or property" is not in itself unconstitutional; what is unconstitutional is the deprivation of such an interest *without due process of law. Parratt.* ("Procedural due process rules are meant to protect persons not from the deprivation, but from the mistaken or unjustified deprivation of life, liberty, or property"). The constitutional violation actionable under § 1983 is not complete when the deprivation occurs; it is not complete unless and until the State fails to provide due process. Therefore, to determine whether a constitutional violation has occurred, it is necessary to ask what process the State provided, and whether it was constitutionally adequate. This inquiry would examine the procedural safeguards built into the statutory or administrative procedure of effecting the deprivation, and any remedies for erroneous deprivations provided by statute or tort law.

[Burch raises only the third type of claim, one of procedural due process.]

Due process, as this Court often has said, is a flexible concept that varies with the particular situation. To determine what procedural protections the Constitution requires in a particular case, we weigh several factors:

> "First, the private interest that will be affected by the official action; second, the risk of an erroneous deprivation of such interest through the procedures used, and the probable value, if any, of additional or substitute procedural safeguards; and finally, the Government's interest, including the function involved and the fiscal and administrative burdens that the additional or substitute procedural requirement would entail." Mathews v. Eldridge, 424 U.S. 319, 335, 96 S.Ct. 893, 903, 47 L.Ed.2d 18 (1976).

Applying this test, the Court usually has held that the Constitution requires some kind of a hearing *before* the State deprives a person of liberty or property. See, e.g., Cleveland Board of Education v. Loudermill, 470 U.S. 532, 542, 105 S.Ct. 1487, 1493, 84 L.Ed.2d 494 (1985) (" 'the root requirement' of the Due Process Clause" is "that an individual be given an opportunity for a hearing *before* he is deprived of any significant protected interest"; hearing required before termination of employment (emphasis in original)); Goldberg v. Kelly, 397 U.S. 254, 264, 90 S.Ct. 1011, 1018, 25 L.Ed.2d 287 (1970) (hearing required before termination of welfare benefits).

In some circumstances, however, the Court has held that a statutory provision for a postdeprivation hearing, or a common-law tort remedy for erroneous deprivation, satisfies due process. [Hudson v. Palmer, 468 U.S. 517, 104 S.Ct. 3194, 82 L.Ed.2d 393 (1984) (intentional deprivation)]; Ingraham v. Wright, 430 U.S. 651, 682, 97 S.Ct. 1401, 1418, 51 L.Ed.2d 711 (1977) (hearing not required before corporal punishment of junior high school students). This is where the *Parratt* rule comes into play. *Parratt* and *Hudson* represent a special case of the general Mathews v. Eldridge analysis, in which postdeprivation tort remedies are all the process that is due, simply because they are the only remedies the State could be expected to provide.

[Because the loss in *Parratt* was negligent, it could not have been anticipated; because the prison guard searched and destroyed plaintiff's property on a personal vendetta without authorization in *Hudson,* state officials could not have anticipated and prevented his actions.]

Petitioners argue that the dismissal under Rule 12(b)(6) was proper because, as in *Parratt* and *Hudson,* the State could not possibly have provided predeprivation process to prevent the kind of "random, unauthorized" wrongful deprivation of liberty Burch alleges, so the postdeprivation remedies provided by Florida's statutory and common law necessarily are all the process Burch was due.

* * *

To determine whether, as petitioners contend, the *Parratt* rule necessarily precludes § 1983 liability in this case, we must ask whether predeprivation procedural safeguards could address the risk of deprivations of the kind Burch alleges. To do this, we examine the risk involved. The risk is that some persons who come into Florida's mental health facilities will apparently be willing to sign forms authorizing admission and treatment, but will be incompetent to give the "express and informed consent" required for voluntary placement under [Florida law]. * * * Such a person thus is in danger of being confined indefinitely without benefit of the procedural safeguards of the involuntary placement process, a process specifically designed to protect persons incapable of looking after their own interests.

Persons who are mentally ill and incapable of giving informed consent to admission would not necessarily meet the statutory standard for involuntary placement, which requires either that they are likely to injure themselves or others, or that their neglect or refusal to care for themselves threatens their well-being. The involuntary placement process serves to guard against the confinement of a person who, though mentally ill, is harmless and can live safely outside an institution. Confinement of such a person not only violates Florida law, but also is unconstitutional. O'Connor v. Donaldson, 422 U.S. 563, 575, 95 S.Ct. 2486, 2493, 45 L.Ed.2d 396 (1975) (there is no constitutional basis for confining mentally ill persons involuntarily "if they are dangerous to no one and can live safely in freedom").

* * *

We now consider whether predeprivation safeguards would have any value in guarding against the kind of deprivation Burch allegedly suffered. Petitioners urge that here, as in *Parratt* and *Hudson,* such procedures could have no value at all, because the State cannot prevent its officials from making random and unauthorized errors in the admission process. We disagree.

* * *

Florida chose to delegate to petitioners a broad power to admit patients to FSH, i.e., to effect what, in the absence of informed consent, is a substantial deprivation of liberty. Because petitioners had state authority to deprive persons of liberty, the Constitution imposed on them the State's concomitant duty to see that no deprivation occur without adequate procedural protections.

It may be permissible constitutionally for a State to have a statutory scheme like Florida's, which gives state officials broad power and little guidance in admitting mental patients. But when those officials fail to provide constitutionally required procedural safeguards to a person whom they deprive of liberty, the state officials cannot then escape liability by invoking *Parratt* and *Hudson*. It is immaterial whether the due process violation Burch alleges is best described as arising from petitioners' failure to comply with state procedures for admitting involuntary patients, or from the absence of a specific requirement that petitioners determine whether a patient is competent to consent to voluntary admission. Burch's suit is neither an action challenging the facial adequacy of a State's statutory procedures, nor an action based only on state officials' random and unauthorized violation of state laws. Burch is not simply attempting to blame the State for misconduct by its employees. He seeks to hold state officials accountable for their abuse of their broadly delegated, uncircumscribed power to effect the deprivation at issue.

This case, therefore, is not controlled by *Parratt* and *Hudson,* for three basic reasons:

[First, such an event as this was predictable because, unlike an erring prison guard, the state should have anticipated that this kind of problem would arise. Second, predeprivation process was not impossible here, since the loss did not occur by unforeseeable mistake; the loss was preventable. Third, defendant's acts were not "unauthorized" because they were given broad discretionary authority to act.]

Unlike *Parratt* and *Hudson*, this case does not represent the special instance of the *Mathews* due process analysis where postdeprivation process is all that is due because no predeprivation safeguards would be of use in preventing the kind of deprivation alleged.

We express no view on the ultimate merits of Burch's claim; we hold only that his complaint was sufficient to state a claim under § 1983 for violation of his procedural due process rights.

The judgment of the Court of Appeals is affirmed.

It is so ordered.

JUSTICE O'CONNOR, with whom CHIEF JUSTICE SCALIA and JUSTICE KENNEDY join, dissenting.

* * *

Application of *Parratt* and *Hudson* indicates that respondent has failed to state a claim allowing recovery under 42 U.S.C. § 1983. Petitioners' actions were unauthorized: they are alleged to have wrongly and without license departed from established state practices. Florida officials in a position to establish safeguards commanded that the voluntary admission process be employed only for consenting patients and that the involuntary hearing procedures be used to admit unconsenting patients. Yet it is alleged that petitioners "with willful, wanton and reckless disregard of and indifference to" Burch's rights contravened both commands. As in *Parratt*, the deprivation "occurred as a result of the unauthorized failure of agents of the State to follow established state procedure." The wanton or reckless nature of the failure indicates it to be random. The State could not foresee the particular contravention and was hardly "in a position to provide for predeprivation process," *Hudson*, to ensure that officials bent upon subverting the State's requirements would in fact follow those procedures. For this wrongful deprivation resulting from an unauthorized departure from established state practice, Florida provides adequate postdeprivation remedies, as two courts below concluded, and which the Court and respondent do not dispute. *Parratt* and *Hudson* thus should govern this case and indicate that respondent has failed to allege a violation of the Fourteenth Amendment.

* * *

The Court suggests that additional safeguards surrounding the voluntary admission process would have quite possibly reduced the risk of deprivation. This reasoning conflates the value of procedures for preventing error in the repeated and usual case (evaluated according to the test set forth in Mathews v. Eldridge) with the value of additional predeprivation procedures to forestall deprivations by state actors bent upon departing from or indifferent to complying with established practices.

* * *

Every command to act imparts the duty to exercise discretion in accord with the command and affords the opportunity to abuse that discretion. The *Mathews* test measures whether the State has sufficiently constrained discretion in the usual case, while the *Parratt* doctrine requires the State to provide a remedy for any wrongful abuse. The Court suggests that this case differs from *Parratt* and *Hudson* because petitioners possessed a sort of delegated power. Yet petitioners no more had the delegated power to depart from the admission procedures and requirements than did the guard in *Hudson* to exceed the limits of his established search and seizure authority, or the prison official in *Parratt* wrongfully to withhold or misdeliver mail.

The Court's reliance upon the State's inappropriate delegation of duty also creates enormous line-drawing problems. Today's decision applies to deprivations occasioned by state actors given "little guidance" and "broadly delegated, uncircumscribed power" to initiate required procedures. At some undefined point, the breadth of the delegation of power requires officials to channel the exercise of that power or become liable for its misapplications.

NOTE ON THE LINE BETWEEN PRE-DEPRIVATION AND POST-DEPRIVATION PROCESS

1. *Parratt* had suggested, and the *Zinermon* dissent read it as holding, that the line between pre-deprivation process and post-deprivation process is ascertainable by determining whether the defendants' acts were done pursuant to established state procedure or were random and unauthorized. This fundamental dichotomy, says the dissent, decides the applicability of *Parratt*'s doctrine. What goal does the dichotomy serve? How does the *Zinermon* majority undermine that dichotomy?

(a) *Parratt*'s dichotomy, says the dissent, means that it is relatively easy to decide when a post-deprivation hearing via suit under state law in state court provides due process: (i) if plaintiff's challenge is to a random and unauthorized act, the state court remedies provide procedural due process; (ii) if plaintiff's challenge is to an established state procedure, pre-deprivation process is due and the state court remedies are irrelevant. Reconsider *Parratt*: did the Court there say that every case fits this two-compartment mold? Or did the Court only say that this is a general pattern often seen?

(b) Decisions since *Zinermon* can be rationalized taking the dissent's view as a minimum position. Therefore, in Los Angeles v. David, 538 U.S. 715, 123 S.Ct. 1895, 155 L.Ed.2d 946 (2003), the Court heard a challenge to the city's established procedure of towing vehicles and holding them for 30 days without notifying the owner. No mention was made of the *Parratt* doctrine. (On the merits, the practice was upheld.) Why isn't this adequate to protect procedural interests?

(c) What more does *Zinermon* seek to add to the dissent's formulation? One court has recently sorted out the dispute this way, Brentwood Academy v. Tennessee Secondary Sch. Athletic Ass'n, 442 F.3d 410 (6th Cir. 2006):

"Under circuit precedent, a § 1983 plaintiff can prevail on a procedural due process claim by demonstrating that the property deprivation resulted from either: (1) an 'established state procedure that itself violates due process rights,' or (2) a 'random and unauthorized act' causing a loss for which available state remedies would not adequately compensate the plaintiff. A plaintiff alleging the first element of this test would not need to demonstrate the inadequacy of state remedies. If the plaintiff pursues the second line of argument, he must navigate the rule of Parratt v. Taylor, which holds that a state may satisfy procedural due process with only an adequate postdeprivation procedure when the state action was 'random and unauthorized.' In Zinermon v. Burch, the Supreme Court narrowed the *Parratt* rule to apply only to those situations where predeprivation process would have been impossible or impractical. In this context, an 'unauthorized' state action means that the official in question did not have the power or authority to effect the deprivation, not that the act was contrary to law."

Does this capture the essence of the majority's position? Cf. Silberstein v. City of Dayton, 440 F.3d 306 (6th Cir. 2006) (*Parratt* "applies only where the deprivation complained of is random and unpredictable, such that the state cannot feasibly provide a predeprivation hearing. *Zinermon*.)."

2.   Can one ascribe more to the *Zinermon* majority? They appear to deny that the dichotomy suggested by the dissent even exists. The real distinction, they say, between the cases requiring a pre-deprivation hearing and those requiring only a post-deprivation hearing turns upon a sensitive balancing of interests as demonstrated in the *Mathews* case. While there may be some correlation between results applying this test and the two labels "established state procedure" and "random, unauthorized actions," the majority apparently believes that any such correlation is happenstance and should not detract from the reality of situation-by-situation balancing—at least where the abuse of authority is "foreseeable."

(a)   Does this make the circuit decisions quoted above appear too simple? How far can this concept be pushed? See Armendariz v. Penman, 31 F.3d 860 (9th Cir.1994), rev'd in part on other grounds, Armendariz v. Penman, 75 F.3d 1311 (9th Cir.1996) (en banc) (even acts illegal under state law can be deemed "authorized" if defendants were "those persons who are assigned the duty of interpreting and enforcing" the law; it is "reasonably foreseeable that the deprivation would occur since it was the intent of the defendants for it to occur").

(b)   In **Gilbert v. Homar**, 520 U.S. 924, 117 S.Ct. 1807, 138 L.Ed.2d 120 (1997), where the Court cited the precedent: "This Court has recognized, on many occasions, that where a State must act quickly, or where it would be impractical to provide pre-deprivation process, post-deprivation process satisfies the requirements of the Due Process Clause. *Zinermon*." The Court proceeded with a discussion of the balancing test advocated in *Zinermon* to determine with what kind of process is due. Is *Gilbert* consistent with *Zinermon* or a "clarification" of it? See also Wilkinson v. Austin, 545 U.S. 209, 125 S.Ct. 2384, 162 L.Ed.2d 174 (2005) (proceeding to balancing discussion without citing *Parratt*; pre-deprivation, non-adversary hearing adequate).

3.   Does *Zinermon* replicate within the confines of procedural due process the same conflict between state and federal courts that was at issue for all § 1983 cases in Monroe v. Pape, Chapter 1A supra? When the only issue at stake is procedural due process, and state courts are open for state-law based claims in order to provide such process, cannot state courts be trusted to hear those claims? Is the "random and unauthorized acts" exception to *Parratt* an implicit line for delineating cases where state authorities can be trusted to catch errant state actors? Does it also matter what remedies the state was willing to recognize?

(a)   Is "random and unauthorized act" another way of expressing the idea in Monroe v. Pape that a state actor has "abused" his authority? Can abuses of authority be easily corrected in procedural Due Process cases because, after all, it is the state that has created the liberty of property interest? See Hellenic American Neighborhood Action Committee v. City of New York, 101 F.3d 877 (2d Cir.1996): "The loss of property, although attributable to the State as action under 'color of law,' is ... almost ... [invariably] beyond the control of the State. Indeed, in most cases it is not only impracticable, but impossible, to provide a meaningful hearing before the deprivation." Are local officials' acts that are inconsistent with state law always "random and unauthorized"? See Gudema v. Nassau County, 163 F.3d 717 (2d Cir. 1998) (local police cannot revoke state-granted driver's license).

(b) If an act is "foreseeable," in what sense is it not "random and unauthorized"? Is this another way of saying the majority expects the state to superintend this problem—or the federal courts will do it for them?

4. Is the problem with *Zinermon* that it is not what it appears to be? Did the justices treat this as an ordinary procedural due process case in order to avoid more serious underlying doctrinal conflicts?

(a) Is *Zinermon* really a substantive due process case, particularly that subset of such cases where the Court decides the appropriate procedural devices necessary to show that a compelling state interest is present? Compare Cruzan v. Director, Missouri Dept. of Health, 497 U.S. 261, 110 S.Ct. 2841, 111 L.Ed.2d 224 (1990) (showing necessary in state court in order to ascertain patient's desire to exercise right to refuse medical treatment), with Ohio v. Akron Center for Reproductive Health, 497 U.S. 502, 110 S.Ct. 2972, 111 L.Ed.2d 405 (1990) (judicial bypass procedure for protecting abortion right of minor). If the interest is a federally declared substantive due process interest, should the Court so easily trust state-court procedures?

(b) Is *Zinermon* tortured because it follows a fault line evident in the constitutional doctrine of procedural due process? Recall that procedural due process protects liberty or property interests that are at least primarily bestowed by state law. Are there other procedural due process interests, some irreducible minimum, that are separately, federally bestowed? See Washington v. Harper, 494 U.S. 210, 110 S.Ct. 1028, 108 L.Ed.2d 178 (1990) ("state law recognizes a liberty interest [in refusing treatment with antipsychotic drugs], *also* protected by the Due Process Clause") (emphasis added). Is the interest in physical liberty such an interest? Does the Court's later recognition of a Substantive Due Process right to be free of "conscious-shocking" state action solve the problems that *Parratt* created for the Court's activists?

5. Is *Zinermon* explainable purely in terms of realism? The majority intuitively knows that state hospital officials will try to evade citizens' liberty interests by involuntarily committing persons via their fictitious informed consent. The cure for the problem, given an unvigorous state court, is to create § 1983 liability, and the *Parratt* rules are manipulated to achieve liability. The dissent, less concerned about state courts' unwillingness to solve the problem, manipulates the rules to yield no § 1983 liability. Is the case that simple?

NOTE ON JUST COMPENSATION CASES

1. In **Williamson County Regional Planning Com'n v. Hamilton Bank**, 473 U.S. 172, 105 S.Ct. 3108, 87 L.Ed.2d 126 (1985), the Supreme Court considered a claim for just compensation under the Fifth Amendment (as applied to the states through the Fourteenth Amendment). A developer claimed that the county so regulated its property as effectively to take it for

public use without payment for its value. The Court first rejected the claim because the state administrative machinery had not reached a final decision, see the Note on page 235 supra, but then it added a second ripeness-based concept that inhered in the Fifth Amendment itself, 473 U.S. at 194, 195, 105 S.Ct. at 3120, 3121:

> "A second reason the taking claim is not yet ripe is that respondent did not seek compensation through the procedures the State has provided for doing so.[13] The Fifth Amendment does not proscribe the taking of property; it proscribes taking without just compensation. Nor does the Fifth Amendment require that just compensation be paid in advance of, or contemporaneously with, the taking; all that is required is that a 'reasonable, certain, and adequate provision for obtaining compensation' exist at the time of the taking. If the government has provided an adequate process for obtaining compensation, and if resort to that process 'yield[s] just compensation,' then the property owner 'has no claim against the government for a taking.' * * * [I]f a State provides an adequate procedure for seeking just compensation, the property owner cannot claim a violation of the Just Compensation Clause until it has used the procedure and been denied just compensation.

> "The recognition that a property owner has not suffered a violation of the Just Compensation Clause until the owner has unsuccessfully attempted to obtain just compensation through the procedures provided by the state for obtaining such compensation is analogous to the Court's holding in Parratt v. Taylor. * * *

> " * * * Respondent has not shown that the inverse condemnation procedure is unavailable or inadequate, and until it has utilized that procedure, its taking claim is premature."

(a) Why is the Court's holding in *Williamson County* merely "analogous" to the Court's holding in *Parratt*? Is it because the Just Compensation Clause has a substantive component as well—the requirement of payment at the end of the process?

(b) If a complainant must first seek recovery under state process in state court before her Just Compensation claim is ripe, may a Just Compensation claim ever be tried in federal court under § 1983? Only if the state provides no compensatory remedy? (Would return of the unregulated property be sufficiently compensatory? See First English Evangelical Lutheran Church v. County of Los Angeles, 482 U.S. 304, 107 S.Ct. 2378, 96 L.Ed.2d 250 (1987).)

(c) If a complainant sought to return to federal court under § 1983 after obtaining no compensation for her property in state court, would res judicata (claim preclusion) bar the suit? Is the only form of federal-court protection of the right to Just Compensation direct Supreme Court review of the adverse

---

13. * * * Exhaustion of [administrative] review procedures is not required. Patsy v. Florida Bd. of Regents. As we have explained, however, because the Fifth Amendment proscribes takings *without just compensation,* no constitutional violation occurs until just compensation has been denied. The nature of the constitutional right therefore requires that a property owner utilize procedures for obtaining compensation before bringing a § 1983 action. [Footnote and emphasis by the Court]

state-court judgment? See McKesson Corp. v. Division of Alcoholic Beverages & Tobacco, 496 U.S. 18, 110 S.Ct. 2238, 110 L.Ed.2d 17 (1990).

2. Other "property" claims, of course, may arise under procedural due process. See the preceding Note; Catanzaro v. Weiden, 188 F.3d 56 (2d Cir. 1999) (emergency demolition of damaged buildings); Sullivan v. Town of Salem, 805 F.2d 81 (2d Cir.1986) (no property right in developer to have town accept his roads, but property interest in certificate of occupancy requires procedural due process); Sanderson v. Village of Greenhills, 726 F.2d 284 (6th Cir.1984) (holder of license to use property has property interest under state law qualifying for procedural due process protection). Might there be another version of "property"—an independent due-process-based right not to have property taken at all, regardless of whether the state is willing to pay compensation? See Pennell v. City of San Jose, 485 U.S. 1, 108 S.Ct. 849, 99 L.Ed.2d 1 (1988) (rent control ordinance). If the Court adopts such a theory in the future, would the *Parratt* doctrine make state remedies relevant?

3. The *Williamson County* case discusses only property claims under the Just Compensation Clause. Are there other constitutional claims subject to its analysis? First Amendment licensing claims, for example? See generally FW/PBS, Inc. v. City of Dallas, 493 U.S. 215, 110 S.Ct. 596, 107 L.Ed.2d 603 (1990); Shuttlesworth v. City of Birmingham, 394 U.S. 147, 89 S.Ct. 935, 22 L.Ed.2d 162 (1969) (appeal of state-court conviction after defying injunction); Cox v. New Hampshire, 312 U.S. 569, 61 S.Ct. 762, 85 L.Ed. 1049 (1941) (criminal appeal; only limited challenge permitted).

4. THE *YOUNGER* DOCTRINE

(a) *Younger* and State Criminal Proceedings

YOUNGER v. HARRIS

Supreme Court of the United States, 1971.
401 U.S. 37, 91 S.Ct. 746, 27 L.Ed.2d 669.

MR. JUSTICE BLACK delivered the opinion of the Court.

Appellee, John Harris, Jr., was indicted in a California state court, charged with violation of the California Penal Code §§ 11400 and 11401, known as the California Criminal Syndicalism Act, set out below.[1] He then filed a complaint in the Federal District Court, asking that court to enjoin the appellant, Younger, the District Attorney of Los Angeles County, from prosecuting him, and alleging that the prosecution and even the presence of the Act inhibited him in the exercise of his rights of free speech and press, rights guaranteed him by the First and Fourteenth Amendments. [Others not under prosecution joined as plaintiffs, claiming that indictment of Harris chilled exercise of their First Amendment rights to

---

1. [The Act punished anyone who by "written words or personal conduct advocates, teaches or aids and abets" the commission of acts of violence "as a means of accomplishing a change in industrial ownership or control." The statute had once before reached the Supreme Court in Whitney v. California, 274 U.S. 357, 47 S.Ct. 641, 71 L.Ed. 1095 (1927), occasioning Justice Brandeis' danger test in his concurring opinion.]

organize for the Progressive Labor Party or teach the doctrines of Karl Marx in college. The district court granted the injunction.]

* * * Without regard to the questions raised about Whitney v. California, supra, since overruled by Brandenburg v. Ohio, 395 U.S. 444, 89 S.Ct. 1827, 23 L.Ed.2d 430 (1969), or the constitutionality of the state law, we have concluded that the judgment of the District Court, enjoining appellant Younger from prosecuting under these California statutes, must be reversed as a violation of the national policy forbidding federal courts to stay or enjoin pending state court proceedings except under special circumstances. We express no view about the circumstances under which federal courts may act when there is no prosecution pending in state courts at the time the federal proceeding is begun.

I

Appellee Harris has been indicted, and was actually being prosecuted by California for a violation of its Criminal Syndicalism Act at the time this suit was filed. He thus has an acute, live controversy with the State and its prosecutor. But none of the other parties plaintiff in the District Court * * * has such a controversy. None has been indicted, arrested, or even threatened by the prosecutor. * * * Whatever right Harris, who is being prosecuted under the state syndicalism law may have, [the other plaintiffs] cannot share it with him. * * *

[They] do not claim that they have ever been threatened with prosecution, that a prosecution is likely, or even that a prosecution is remotely possible. They claim the right to bring this suit solely because, in the language of their complaint, they "feel inhibited." We do not think this allegation, even if true, is sufficient to bring the equitable jurisdiction of the federal courts into play to enjoin a pending state prosecution. A federal lawsuit to stop a prosecution in a state court is a serious matter. And persons having no fears of state prosecution except those that are imaginary or speculative, are not to be accepted as appropriate plaintiffs in such cases. Since Harris is actually being prosecuted under the challenged laws, however, we proceed with him as a proper party.

II

Since the beginning of this country's history Congress has, subject to few exceptions, manifested a desire to permit state courts to try state cases free from interference by federal courts [as shown by the Anti–Injunction Act, 28 U.S.C.A. § 2283].

In addition, [to the few congressionally authorized exceptions] a judicial exception to the longstanding policy evidenced by the statute has been made where a person about to be prosecuted in a state court can show that he will, if the proceeding in the state court is not enjoined, suffer irreparable damages.

The precise reasons for this longstanding public policy against federal court interference with state court proceedings * * * are plain. One is the basic doctrine of equity jurisprudence that courts of equity should not act, and particularly should not act to restrain a criminal prosecution, when the moving party has an adequate remedy at law and will not suffer irreparable injury if denied equitable relief. The doctrine [recognizes that in most cases a state-court defendant's litigation of that] single suit would be adequate to protect the rights asserted. This underlying reason for restraining courts of equity from interfering with criminal prosecutions is reinforced by an even more vital consideration, the notion of "comity," that is, a proper respect for state functions, a recognition of the fact that the entire country is made up of a Union of separate state governments, and a continuance of the belief that the National Government will fare best if the States and their institutions are left free to perform their separate functions in their separate ways. This, perhaps for lack of a better and clearer way to describe it, is referred to by many as "Our Federalism," and one familiar with the profound debates that ushered our Federal Constitution into existence is bound to respect those who remain loyal to the ideals and dreams of "Our Federalism." The concept does not mean blind deference to "States' Rights" any more than it means centralization of control over every important issue in our National Government and its courts. The Framers rejected both these courses. What the concept does represent is a system in which there is sensitivity to the legitimate interests of both State and National Governments, and in which the National Government, anxious though it may be to vindicate and protect federal rights and federal interests, always endeavors to do so in ways that will not unduly interfere with the legitimate activities of the States. * * *

This brief discussion should be enough to suggest some of the reasons why it has been perfectly natural for our cases to repeat time and time again that the normal thing to do when federal courts are asked to enjoin pending proceedings in state courts is not to issue such injunctions. In Fenner v. Boykin, 271 U.S. 240, 46 S.Ct. 492, 70 L.Ed. 927 (1926), suit had been brought in the Federal District Court seeking to enjoin state prosecutions under a recently enacted state law that allegedly interfered with the free flow of interstate commerce. The Court, in a unanimous opinion made clear that such a suit, even with respect to state criminal proceedings not yet formally instituted, could be proper only under very special circumstances:

> "Ex parte Young, 209 U.S. 123, 28 S.Ct. 441, [52 L.Ed. 714], and following cases have established the doctrine that when absolutely necessary for protection of constitutional rights, courts of the United States have power to enjoin state officers from instituting criminal actions. But this may not be done except under extraordinary circumstances where the danger of irreparable loss is both great and immediate. Ordinarily, there should be no interference with such officers; primarily, they are charged with the duty of prosecuting offenders against the laws of the State and must decide when and how this is to be done. The accused should first set up and rely upon his defense in the state courts, even though this involves a challenge of the validity

of some statute, unless it plainly appears that this course would not afford adequate protection.''

* * * In addition, however, the Court also made clear that in view of the fundamental policy against federal interference with state criminal prosecutions, even irreparable injury is insufficient unless it is ''both great and immediate.'' *Fenner*, supra. Certain types of injury, in particular, the cost, anxiety, and inconvenience of having to defend against a single criminal prosecution, could not by themselves be considered ''irreparable'' in the special legal sense of that term. Instead, the threat to the plaintiff's federally protected rights must be one that cannot be eliminated by his defense against a single criminal prosecution.

This is where the law stood when the Court decided Dombrowski v. Pfister, 380 U.S. 479, 85 S.Ct. 1116, 14 L.Ed.2d 22 (1965), and held that an injunction against the enforcement of certain state criminal statutes could properly issue under the circumstances presented in that case. In *Dombrowski*, unlike many of the earlier cases denying injunctions, the complaint made substantial allegations that: ''the threats to enforce the statutes against appellants are not made with any expectation of securing valid convictions, but rather are part of a plan to employ arrests, seizures, and threats of prosecution under color of the statutes to harass appellants and discourage them and their supporters from asserting and attempting to vindicate the constitutional rights of Negro citizens of Louisiana.'' The appellants in *Dombrowski* had offered to prove that their offices had been raided and all their files and records seized pursuant to search and arrest warrants that were later summarily vacated by a state judge for lack of probable cause. They also offered to prove that despite the state court order quashing the warrants and suppressing the evidence seized, the prosecutor was continuing to threaten to initiate new prosecutions of appellants under the same statutes, was holding public hearings at which photostatic copies of the illegally seized documents were being used, and was threatening to use other copies of the illegally seized documents to obtain grand jury indictments against the appellants on charges of violating the same statutes. These circumstances, as viewed by the Court sufficiently establish the kind of irreparable injury, above and beyond that associated with the defense of a single prosecution brought in good faith, that had always been considered sufficient to justify federal intervention.

It is against the background of these principles that we must judge the propriety of an injunction under the circumstances of the present case. Here a proceeding was already pending in the state court, affording Harris an opportunity to raise his constitutional claims. There is no suggestion that this single prosecution against Harris is brought in bad faith or is only one of a series of repeated prosecutions to which he will be subjected. In other words, the injury that Harris faces is solely ''that incidental to every criminal proceeding brought lawfully and in good faith,'' *Douglas*, supra, and therefore under the settled doctrine we have already described he is not entitled to equitable relief ''even if such statutes are unconstitutional,'' *Buck*, supra.

The District Court, however, thought that the *Dombrowski* decision substantially broadened the availability of injunctions against state criminal prosecutions and that under that decision the federal courts may give equitable relief, without regard to any showing of bad faith or harassment, whenever a state statute is found "on its face" to be vague or overly broad, in violation of the First Amendment. We recognize that there are some statements in the *Dombrowski* opinion that would seem to support this argument. But, * * * we do not regard the reasons adduced to support this position as sufficient to justify such a substantial departure from the established doctrines regarding the availability of injunctive relief. It is undoubtedly true, as the Court stated in *Dombrowski*, that "[a] criminal prosecution under a statute regulating expression usually involves imponderables and contingencies that themselves may inhibit the full exercise of First Amendment freedoms." But this sort of "chilling effect," as the Court called it, should not by itself justify federal intervention. In the first place, the chilling effect cannot be satisfactorily eliminated by federal injunctive relief. * * *

Moreover, the existence of a "chilling effect," even in the area of First Amendment rights, has never been considered a sufficient basis, in and of itself, for prohibiting state action[, for a state may narrowly construe its statute so as to meet the demands of the Constitution].

Beyond all this is another, more basic consideration. Procedures for testing the constitutionality of a statute "on its face" in the manner apparently contemplated by *Dombrowski*, and for then enjoining all action to enforce the statute until the State can obtain court approval for a modified version, are fundamentally at odds with the function of the federal courts in our constitutional plan. The power and duty of the judiciary to declare laws unconstitutional are in the final analysis derived from its responsibility for resolving concrete disputes brought before the courts for decision; a statute apparently governing a dispute cannot be applied by judges, consistently with their obligations under the Supremacy Clause, when such an application of the statute would conflict with the Constitution. Marbury v. Madison. But this vital responsibility, broad as it is, does not amount to an unlimited power to survey the statute books and pass judgment on laws before the courts are called upon to enforce them. Ever since the Constitutional Convention rejected a proposal for having members of the Supreme Court render advice concerning pending legislation it has been clear that, even when suits of this kind involve a "case or controversy" sufficient to satisfy the requirements of Article III of the Constitution, the task of analyzing a proposed statute, pinpointing its deficiencies, and requiring correction of these deficiencies before the statute is put into effect, is rarely if ever an appropriate task for the judiciary. The combination of the relative remoteness of the controversy, the impact on the legislative process of the relief sought, and above all the speculative and amorphous nature of the required line-by-line analysis of detailed statutes ordinarily results in a kind of case that is wholly unsatisfactory for deciding constitutional questions, whichever way they might be decided. * * *

* * * There may, of course, be extraordinary circumstances in which the necessary irreparable injury can be shown even in the absence of the usual prerequisites of bad faith and harassment. For example, as long ago as the *Buck* case, * * * we indicated:

> "It is of course conceivable that a statute might be flagrantly and patently violative of express constitutional prohibitions in every clause, sentence and paragraph, and in whatever manner and against whomever an effort might be made to apply it." [Watson v. Buck, 313 U.S. 387, 402, 61 S.Ct. 962, 967, 85 L.Ed. 1416 (1941).]

Other unusual situations calling for federal intervention might also arise, but there is no point in our attempting now to specify what they might be. It is sufficient for purposes of the present case to hold, as we do, that the possible unconstitutionality of a statute "on its face" does not in itself justify an injunction against good-faith attempts to enforce it * * *.

The judgment of the District Court is reversed, and the case is remanded for further proceedings not inconsistent with this opinion.

Reversed.

MR. JUSTICE BRENNAN, with whom MR. JUSTICE WHITE and MR. JUSTICE MARSHALL join, concurring in the result.

I agree that the judgment of the District Court should be reversed. Appellee Harris had been indicted for violations of the California Criminal Syndicalism Act before he sued in federal court. He has not alleged that the prosecution was brought in bad faith to harass him. His constitutional contentions may be adequately adjudicated in the state criminal proceeding, and federal intervention at his instance was therefore improper.

* * *

MR. JUSTICE DOUGLAS, dissenting.

The fact that we are in a period of history when enormous extrajudicial sanctions are imposed on those who assert their First Amendment rights in unpopular causes emphasizes the wisdom of Dombrowski v. Pfister. There we recognized that in times of repression, when interests with powerful spokesmen generate symbolic pogroms against nonconformists, the federal judiciary, charged by Congress with special vigilance for protection of civil rights, has special responsibilities to prevent an erosion of the individual's constitutional rights.

* * *

The special circumstances when federal intervention in a state criminal proceeding is permissible are not restricted to bad faith on the part of state officials or the threat of multiple prosecutions. They also exist where for any reason the state statute being enforced is unconstitutional on its face. * * *

* * *

In *Younger,* "criminal syndicalism" is defined so broadly as to jeopardize "teaching" that socialism is preferable to free enterprise.

Harris' "crime" was distributing leaflets advocating change in industrial ownership through political action. The statute under which he was indicted was the one involved in Whitney v. California, a decision we overruled in Brandenburg v. Ohio.

If the "advocacy" which Harris used was an attempt at persuasion through the use of bullets, bombs, and arson, we would have a different case. But Harris is charged only with distributing leaflets advocating political action toward his objective. He tried unsuccessfully to have the state court dismiss the indictment on constitutional grounds. He resorted to the state appellate court for writs of prohibition to prevent the trial, but to no avail. He went to the federal court as a matter of last resort in an effort to keep this unconstitutional trial from being saddled on him.

* * *

Whatever the balance of the pressures of localism and nationalism prior to the Civil War, they were fundamentally altered by the war. The Civil War Amendments made civil rights a national concern. Those Amendments, especially § 5 of the Fourteenth Amendment, cemented the change in American federalism brought on by the war. Congress immediately commenced to use its new powers to pass legislation. Just as the first Judiciary Act, 1 Stat. 73, and the "anti-injunction" statute represented the early views of American federalism, the Reconstruction statutes, including the enlargement of federal jurisdiction, represent a later view of American federalism.

* * *

Decided with *Younger* were two related groups of companion cases which showed in more detail the critical elements of the Court's thinking. Justice Black wrote the opinion for the Court in each case.

In **Boyle v. Landry**, 401 U.S. 77, 91 S.Ct. 758, 27 L.Ed.2d 696 (1971), seven groups of black residents of Chicago sought injunctions against a variety of city and state laws (concerning mob action, resisting arrest, aggravated assault, aggravated battery, and intimidation) which they claimed city officials used to intimidate blacks. Justice Black noted that:

"[T]he complaint contains no mention of any specific threat by any officer or official of Chicago, Cook County, or the State of Illinois to arrest or prosecute any one or more of the plaintiffs under that statute either one time or many times. Rather, it appears from the allegations that those who originally brought this suit made a search of state statutes and city ordinances with a view to picking out certain ones that they thought might possibly be used by the authorities as devices for bad-faith prosecutions against them. There is nothing contained in the allegations of the complaint from which one could infer that any one or more of the citizens who brought this suit is in any jeopardy of suffering irreparable injury if the State is left free to prosecute * * * in the normal manner. * * * [T]he normal course of state criminal prosecutions cannot be disrupted or blocked on the basis of charges which in the last analysis amount to nothing more than speculation about the future." 401 U.S. at 81, 91 S.Ct. at 760.

Samuels v. Mackell, 401 U.S. 66, 91 S.Ct. 764, 27 L.Ed.2d 688 (1971), involved an attempt to abort a trial under New York's criminal anarchy statute not just by enjoining the pending prosecution but also by seeking a declaratory judgment as to the statute's unconstitutionality. Stressing that such judgments were " 'essentially an equitable cause of action,' " the Court held that:

"[T]he propriety of declaratory and injunctive relief should be judged by essentially[1] the same standards. In both situations deeply rooted and long-settled principles of equity have narrowly restricted the scope for federal intervention, and ordinarily a declaratory judgment will result in precisely the same interference with and disruption of state proceedings that the longstanding policy limiting injunctions was designed to avoid. This is true for at least two reasons. In the first place, the Declaratory Judgment Act provides that after a declaratory judgment is issued the district court may enforce it by granting '[f]urther necessary or proper relief,' 28 U.S.C. § 2202, and "therefore a declaratory judgment issued while state proceedings are pending might serve as the basis for a subsequent injunction against those proceedings to 'protect or effectuate' the declaratory judgment, 28 U.S.C. § 2283, and thus result in a clearly improper interference with the state proceedings. Secondly, even if the declaratory judgment is not used as a basis for actually issuing an injunction, the declaratory relief alone has virtually the same practical impact as a formal injunction would. As we said in the *Wycoff* case, 344 U.S. at 247, 73 S.Ct. at 242, 97 L.Ed. at 298: 'Is the declaration contemplated here to be res judicata, so that the [state court] cannot hear evidence and decide any matter for itself? If so, the federal court has virtually lifted the case out of the State [court] before it could be heard. If not, the federal judgment serves no useful purpose as a final determination of rights.' "

---

1. []The Court later explained its use of the adjective "essentially" by opining that in cases where the high *Younger* standards could be met, it might be more appropriate to grant declaratory relief rather than an injunction if the latter, under the circumstances, were deemed too "intrusive or offensive." 401 U.S. at 73, 91 S.Ct. at 768.

"We therefore hold that, in cases where the state criminal prosecution was begun prior to the federal suit, the same equitable principles relevant to the propriety of an injunction must be taken into consideration by federal district courts in determining whether to issue a declaratory judgment, and that where an injunction would be impermissible under these principles, declaratory relief should ordinarily be denied as well." 401 U.S. at 72–73, 91 S.Ct. at 767–768.

NOTE ON *YOUNGER* AND *ITS* COMPANION CASES

1. The Court emphasized in *Younger* that the "irreparable injury" which a plaintiff must show in order to obtain an injunction against prosecution is something substantially greater than that term implies in a normal civil action.

(a) Note the examples which the Court gave as adequate to meet the *Younger* standard. What do they have in common? The inability to defend oneself in one action? That appears to be true of all except, perhaps, the last example given by Justice Black, that of a statute which is "flagrantly" unconstitutional. Is the common feature rather that all the examples involve improper motivation, motivation (on the part of prosecutors or legislators) to accomplish some goal other than impartial law enforcement? But see Palmer v. Thompson, 403 U.S. 217, 91 S.Ct. 1940, 29 L.Ed.2d 438 (1971) (per Black, J.). Did *Younger* simply adopt a rebuttable presumption that state criminal proceedings are ordinarily conducted in good faith and for the public good?

(b) Near the end of the *Younger* opinion Justice Black struck out at a target seemingly unrelated to his specific topic—the Court's practice of striking down statutes on their face, a practice employed by the Court more often in reviewing state judgments than in § 1983 cases. See, e.g., Cox v. Louisiana, 379 U.S. 536, 551, 85 S.Ct. 453, 462, 13 L.Ed.2d 471 (1965) (statute found "unconstitutionally vague in its overly broad scope"). But does Black's idea not have particular relevance in a § 1983 case because of a federal court's constitutional inability to give a narrowing, constitutionally acceptable, construction to state law? Is the *Younger* doctrine not simply a procedural decision which funnels most cases through state courts so that such constructions can be given? Cf. In re Harris, 20 Cal.App.3d 632, 97 Cal.Rptr. 844 (1971) (state court's judgment after *Younger* plaintiff raised his claim in state criminal proceeding).

(c) Reconsider the abstention doctrine discussed in subsection G.2 supra. How does *Younger* differ? Is it narrower or broader in scope?

2. Justice Black refers repeatedly to the conceptions of the "Framers." Who were the "Framers"? Those who drafted the Constitution? Those who drafted the Anti–Injunction Act? Figments of the Court's imagination? What are the implications of choosing one set of drafters over the others?

(a) If the *Younger* doctrine is constitutionally based, why not refer, as Justice Douglas does, to the conceptions of the "Framers" of the later Fourteenth Amendment? Did those drafters not surely intend to alter the balance between federal and state courts? Note the similarity between Justice Black's thinking and that expressed by a majority of the Court in the

Slaughter–House Cases, 83 U.S. (16 Wall.) 36, 82, 21 L.Ed. 394 (1873) (Fourteenth Amendment does not alter "main features of the general system").

(b) If the "Framers" are the drafters of the Anti–Injunction Act, should the Court not inquire more closely into whether suits under § 1983 are excepted from the act, rather than rely on broad generalizations? In Mitchum v. Foster, 407 U.S. 225, 92 S.Ct. 2151, 32 L.Ed.2d 705 (1972), the Court faced the question and found § 1983 to fall within one of the act's exceptions.

(c) If, as the *Mitchum* case held, § 1983 is an exception to the Anti–Injunction Act, is it not clear that in reality the "Framers" are the Justices themselves? Is the *Younger* doctrine one of federal common law which Congress, through appropriate legislation, may change?

3. Was *Younger* rightly decided because procedurally it made sense? As mentioned above, it permits state courts to give saving constructions to their own statutes; did it also avoid complications which could result if federal courts followed a contrary rule? If *Younger* had been decided the opposite way, what kind of injunction would have issued? One perpetually forbidding prosecution? One forbidding prosecution until a narrower construction is obtained from state courts? Did Justice Brennan, who wrote the language in *Dombrowski* "that would seem to support" a wider role for district courts,[1] realize that activism here was simply unmanageable? But do not these same problems arise under *Younger* in those few circumstances where injunctions are permitted?

4. If *Younger* appears to rest on considerations of procedural regularity and respect for state court judges, are those factors important enough to override the individual plaintiff's interest in vindication of his constitutional rights? In **Dombrowski v. Pfister,** the 1965 precedent which was distinguished in *Younger,* the plaintiffs, civil rights workers in Louisiana, sought an injunction to restrain the state's attempt to prosecute them under its communist control law. While noting narrowly that the prosecutions had allegedly been initiated in bad faith and without hope of conviction, the Court also relied on wider grounds, 380 U.S. at 486:

> "A criminal prosecution under a statute regulating expression usually involves imponderables and contingencies that themselves may inhibit the full exercise of First Amendment freedoms. When the statutes also have an overbroad sweep, as is here alleged, the hazard of loss or substantial impairment of those precious rights may be critical. For in such cases, the statutes lend themselves too readily to denial of those rights. The assumption that defense of a criminal prosecution will generally assure ample vindication of constitutional rights is unfounded in such cases. For '[t]he threat of sanctions may deter * * * almost as potently as the actual application of sanctions [].' Because of the sensitive nature of constitutionally protected expression, we have not required that all of those subject to overbroad regulations risk prosecution to test their

---

1. See also Justice Brennan's decision confirming a wider role for district courts in habeas corpus cases, Fay v. Noia, 372 U.S. 391, 83 S.Ct. 822, 9 L.Ed.2d 837 (1963). But see, McCleskey v. Zant, 499 U.S. 467, 111 S.Ct. 1454, 113 L.Ed.2d 517 (1991).

rights. For free expression—of transcendent value to all society, and not merely to those exercising their rights—might be the loser.''

(a) Had the prosecutions in *Dombrowski* not been initiated in bad faith, would the Court's decision have been as persuasive?

(b) Does *Dombrowski* sound suspiciously like Justice Brennan's decision in City of Houston v. Hill, Chapter 1G.2 supra? How did the *Hill* case avoid the *Younger* doctrine?

(c) Are there no criminal prosecutions where *Younger* would not apply? The Double Jeopardy Clause is designed to protect against a second criminal prosecution on the same charge after a first judgment; if the state commences a second charge, can the state-court defendant obtain a federal injunction to protect his right to be free of the second trial? See Nivens v. Gilchrist, 319 F.3d 151 (4th Cir. 2003).

5.   The Court's holding regarding standing may appear initially to be a casual adjunct to *Younger,* a related effort to keep federal courts, as in *Boyle,* supra, from too closely scrutinizing a state's criminal code. On reflection, however, is it not an integral and critical feature of the *Younger* doctrine? Note that those persons who lack standing because they are not yet under indictment cannot be said to have an adequate remedy at law defending a state criminal action, and therefore would not *Younger* be inapplicable? Should the standing rule be loosened? Should *Younger* be extended to cover uninitiated prosecutions?

STEFFEL v. THOMPSON

Supreme Court of the United States, 1974.
415 U.S. 452, 94 S.Ct. 1209, 39 L.Ed.2d 505.

MR. JUSTICE BRENNAN delivered the opinion of the Court.

* * *

This case presents the important question reserved in Samuels v. Mackell, whether declaratory relief is precluded when a state prosecution has been threatened, but is not pending, and a showing of bad-faith enforcement or other special circumstances has not been made.

* * *

The parties stipulated to the relevant facts: On October 8, 1970, while petitioner and other individuals were distributing handbills protesting American involvement in Vietnam on an exterior sidewalk of the North DeKalb Shopping Center, shopping center employees asked them to stop handbilling and leave. They declined to do so, and police officers were summoned. The officers told them that they would be arrested if they did not stop handbilling. The group then left to avoid arrest. Two days later petitioner and a companion returned to the shopping center and again began handbilling. The manager of the center called the police, and petitioner and his companion were once again told that failure to stop their handbilling would result in their arrests. Petitioner left to avoid arrest. His companion stayed, however, continued handbilling, and was arrested and subsequently arraigned on a charge of criminal trespass in violation of § 26–1503³ [of the Georgia Code].

[Steffel and his companion, Sandra Becker, thereafter filed this claim under § 1983 asking for a declaratory judgment and an injunction against Becker's prosecution. The district court denied all relief. On appeal, the demonstrators' counsel conceded the application of *Younger* to Becker's injunction request but argued that Steffel's claim for declaratory relief, because no prosecution was pending against him, stood on a different footing. The Fifth Circuit, quoting the Harvard Law Review's analysis, held that " 'the reasoning in *Younger* [concerning on-the-face attacks and disruption of state interests] would appear to ignore any distinction between pending and threatened proceedings, and make denial of federal relief obligatory in both situations unless bad faith enforcement can be shown.' " 459 F.2d 919, 922 (1972).]

We granted certiorari and now reverse.

I

At the threshold we must consider whether petitioner presents an "actual controversy," a requirement imposed by Art. III of the Constitution and the express terms of the Federal Declaratory Judgment Act, 28 U.S.C.A. § 2201.

Unlike three of the appellees in Younger v. Harris, petitioner has alleged threats of prosecution that cannot be characterized as "imaginary or speculative." He has been twice warned to stop handbilling that he claims is constitutionally protected and has been told by the police that if he again handbills at the shopping center and disobeys a warning to stop he will likely be prosecuted. The prosecution of petitioner's handbilling companion is ample demonstration that petitioner's concern with arrest has not been "chimerical." In these circumstances, it is not necessary that petitioner first expose himself to actual arrest or prosecution to be entitled to challenge a statute that he claims deters the exercise of his constitutional rights. See, e.g., Epperson v. Arkansas, 393 U.S. 97, 89 S.Ct. 266, 21 L.Ed.2d 228 (1968). Moreover, petitioner's challenge is to those specific provisions of state law which have provided the basis for threats of criminal prosecution against him.

Nonetheless, there remains a question as to the *continuing* existence of a live and acute controversy that must be resolved on the remand we order today.¹⁰ * * * Here, petitioner's complaint indicates that his handbilling activities were directed "against the war in Vietnam and the United States, foreign policy in Southeast Asia." Since we cannot ignore the recent developments reducing the Nation's involvement in that part of the world, it will be for the District Court on remand to determine if

---

3. We were advised at oral argument that the trial of petitioner's companion, Sandra Lee Becker, has been stayed pending decision of this case.

10. The rule in federal cases is that an actual controversy must be extant at all stages of review, not merely at the time the complaint is filed.

subsequent events have so altered petitioner's desire to engage in hand-billing at the shopping center that it can no longer be said that this case presents "a substantial controversy, between parties having adverse legal interests, of sufficient immediacy and reality to warrant the issuance of a declaratory judgment."

II

We now turn to the question of whether the District Court and the Court of Appeals correctly found petitioner's request for declaratory relief inappropriate.

Sensitive to principles of equity, comity, and federalism, we recognized in Younger v. Harris that federal courts should ordinarily refrain from enjoining ongoing state criminal prosecutions. We were cognizant that a pending state proceeding, in all but unusual cases, would provide the federal plaintiff with the necessary vehicle for vindicating his constitutional rights, and, in that circumstance, the restraining of an ongoing prosecution would entail an unseemly failure to give effect to the principle that state courts have the solemn responsibility, equally with the federal courts "to guard, enforce, and protect every right granted or secured by the constitution of the United States. * * * " In Samuels v. Mackell, the Court also found that the same principles ordinarily would be flouted by issuance of a federal declaratory judgment when a state proceeding was pending, since the intrusive effect of declaratory relief "will result in precisely the same interference with and disruption of state proceedings that the long-standing policy limiting injunctions was designed to avoid." * * *

Neither *Younger* nor *Samuels*, however, decided the question whether federal intervention might be permissible in the absence of a pending state prosecution. * * *

These reservations anticipated the Court's recognition that the relevant principles of equity, comity, and federalism "have little force in the absence of a pending state proceeding." When no state criminal proceeding is pending at the time the federal complaint is filed, federal intervention does not result in duplicative legal proceedings or disruption of the state criminal justice system; nor can federal intervention, in that circumstance, be interpreted as reflecting negatively upon the state court's ability to enforce constitutional principles. In addition, while a pending state prosecution provides the federal plaintiff with a concrete opportunity to vindicate his constitutional rights, a refusal on the part of the federal courts to intervene when no state proceeding is pending may place the hapless plaintiff between the Scylla of intentionally flouting state law and the Charybdis of forgoing what he believes to be constitutionally protected activity in order to avoid becoming enmeshed in a criminal proceeding.

When no state proceeding is pending and thus considerations of equity, comity, and federalism have little vitality, the propriety of granting federal declaratory relief may properly be considered independently of a request for injunctive relief. Here, the Court of Appeals held that, because injunctive relief would not be appropriate since petitioner failed to demonstrate irreparable injury—a traditional prerequisite to injunctive relief—it followed that declaratory relief was also inappropriate. Even if the Court of Appeals correctly viewed injunctive relief as inappropriate—a question we need not reach today since petitioner has abandoned his request for that remedy, the court erred in treating the requests for injunctive and declaratory relief as a single issue. "[W]hen no state prosecution is pending and the only question is whether declaratory relief is appropriate[,] * * * the congressional scheme that makes the federal courts the primary guardians of constitutional rights, and the express congressional authorization of declaratory relief, afforded because it is a less harsh and abrasive remedy than the injunction, become the factors of primary significance." Perez v. Ledesma, 401 U.S. 82, 104, 91 S.Ct. 674, 686, 27 L.Ed.2d 701 (1971) (separate opinion of Brennan, J.).

The subject matter jurisdiction of the lower federal courts was greatly expanded in the wake of the Civil War. A pervasive sense of nationalism led to enactment of the Civil Rights Act of 1871, empowering the lower federal courts to determine the constitutionality of actions, taken by persons under color of state law, allegedly depriving other individuals of rights guaranteed by the Constitution and federal law, see 42 U.S.C.A. § 1983, 28 U.S.C.A. § 1343(3).[13] Four years later, in the Judiciary Act of March 3, 1875, 18 Stat. 470, Congress conferred upon the lower federal courts, for but the second time in their nearly century-old history, general federal-question jurisdiction subject only to a jurisdictional-amount requirement, see 28 U.S.C.A. § 1331. With this latter enactment, the lower federal courts "ceased to be restricted tribunals of fair dealing between citizens of different states and became the *primary* and powerful reliances for vindicating every right given by the Constitution, the laws, and treaties of the United States." F. Frankfurter & J. Landis, The Business of the Supreme Court 65 (1928) (emphasis added).

[The Court here recounted the impact of its earliest precedent authorizing injunctions against state proceedings; Congress' reaction in adopting the Three–Judge Court Act, 28 U.S.C.A. § 2281; and the later Congressional concern that injunctions were both too difficult for plaintiffs to obtain and yet too intrusive on state interests when granted.]

To dispel these difficulties, Congress in 1934 enacted the Declaratory Judgment Act, 28 U.S.C.A. §§ 2201–2202. That Congress plainly intended declaratory relief to act as an alternative to the strong medicine of the injunction and to be utilized to test the constitutionality of state criminal statutes in cases where injunctive relief would be unavailable is amply

---

13. "Sensitiveness to 'states' rights,' fear of rivalry with state courts and respect for state sentiment, were swept aside by the great impulse of national feeling born of the Civil War. Nationalism was triumphant; in national administration was sought its vindication. The new exertions of federal power were no longer trusted to the enforcement of state agencies." F. Frankfurter & J. Landis, The Business of the Supreme Court 64 (1928).

evidenced by the legislative history of the Act.[18] * * *

[This history makes it clear, said the Court, that "different considerations" are involved when a plaintiff requests a declaratory judgment rather than an injunction.] First, as Congress recognized in 1934, a declaratory judgment will have a less intrusive effect on the administration of state criminal laws. As was observed in Perez v. Ledesma, 401 U.S., at 124–126, 91 S.Ct., at 696–697 (separate opinion of Brennan, J.):

> "Of course, a favorable declaratory judgment may nevertheless be valuable to the plaintiff though it cannot make even an unconstitutional statute disappear. A state statute may be declared unconstitutional *in toto*—that is, incapable of having constitutional applications; or it may be declared unconstitutionally vague or overbroad—that is, incapable of being constitutionally applied to the full extent of its purport. In either case, a federal declaration of unconstitutionality reflects the opinion of the federal court that the statute cannot be fully enforced. If a declaration of total unconstitutionality is affirmed by this Court, it follows that this Court stands ready to reverse any conviction under the statute. If a declaration of partial unconstitutionality is affirmed by this Court, the implication is that this Court will overturn particular applications of the statute, but that if the statute is narrowly construed by the state courts it will not be incapable of constitutional applications. Accordingly, the declaration does not necessarily bar prosecutions under the statute, as a broad injunction would. Thus, where the highest court of a State has had an opportunity to give a statute regulating expression a narrowing or clarifying construction but has failed to do so, and later a federal court declares the statute unconstitutionally vague or overbroad, it may well be open to a state prosecutor, after the federal court decision, to bring a prosecution under the statute if he reasonably believes that the defendant's conduct is not constitutionally protected and that the state courts may give the statute a construction so as to yield a constitutionally valid conviction. Even where a declaration of unconstitutionality is not reviewed by this Court, the declaration may still be able to cut down the deterrent effect of an unconstitutional state statute. The persuasive force of the court's opinion and judgment may lead state prosecutors, courts, and legislators to reconsider

---

18. As Professor Borchard, a principal proponent and author of the Federal Declaratory Judgment Act, said in a written statement introduced at the hearings on the Act:

"It often happens that courts are unwilling to grant injunctions to restrain the enforcement of penal statutes or ordinances, and relegate the plaintiff to his option, either to violate the statute and take his chances in testing constitutionality on a criminal prosecution, or else to [forgo], in the fear of prosecution, the exercise of his claimed rights. Into this dilemma no civilized legal system operating under a constitution should force any person. The court, in effect, by refusing an injunction informs the prospective victim that the only way to determine whether the suspect is a mushroom or a toadstool, is to eat it. Assuming that the plaintiff has a vital interest in the enforcement of the challenged statute or ordinance, there is no reason why a declaratory judgment should not be issued, instead of compelling a violation of the statute as a condition precedent to challenging its constitutionality." Hearings on H.R. 5623 before a Subcommittee of the Senate Committee on the Judiciary, 70th Cong., 1st Sess., 75–76 (1928). [Repositioned footnote.]

their respective responsibilities toward the statute. Enforcement policies or judicial construction may be changed, or the legislature may repeal the statute and start anew. Finally, the federal court judgment may have some *res judicata* effect, though this point is not free from difficulty and the governing rules remain to be developed with a view to the proper workings of a federal system. What is clear, however, is that even though a declaratory judgment has the 'force and effect of a final judgment,' 28 U.S.C. § 2201, it is a much milder form of relief than an injunction. Though it may be persuasive, it is not ultimately coercive; noncompliance with it may be inappropriate, but is not contempt."[19] (Footnote omitted.)

Second, engrafting upon the Declaratory Judgment Act a requirement that all of the traditional equitable prerequisites to the issuance of an injunction be satisfied before the issuance of a declaratory judgment is considered would defy Congress' intent to make declaratory relief available in cases where an injunction would be inappropriate.

"Were the law to be that a plaintiff could not obtain a declaratory judgment that a local ordinance was unconstitutional when no state prosecution is pending unless he could allege and prove circumstances justifying a federal injunction of an existing state prosecution, the Federal Declaratory Judgment Act would have been *pro tanto* repealed." Wulp v. Corcoran, 454 F.2d 826, 832 (CA1 1972) (Coffin, J.).

* * * In the instant case, principles of federalism not only do not preclude federal intervention, they compel it. Requiring the federal courts totally to step aside when no state criminal prosecution is pending against the federal plaintiff would turn federalism on its head. When federal claims are premised on 42 U.S.C.A. § 1983 and 28 U.S.C.A. § 1343(3)—as they are here—we have not required exhaustion of state judicial or administrative remedies, recognizing the paramount role Congress has assigned to the federal courts to protect constitutional rights. But exhaustion of state remedies is precisely what would be required if both federal injunctive and declaratory relief were unavailable in a case where no state prosecution had been commenced.

III

Respondents, however, relying principally upon our decision in Cameron v. Johnson, 390 U.S. 611, 88 S.Ct. 1335, 20 L.Ed.2d 182 (1968), argue that, although it may be appropriate to issue a declaratory judgment when no state criminal proceeding is pending and the attack is upon the *facial validity* of a state criminal statute, such a step would be improper where, as here, the attack is merely upon the constitutionality of the statute as

---

19. The public prosecution of petitioner's handbilling companion does not affect petitioner's action for declaratory relief. In Roe v. Wade, 410 U.S. 113, 93 S.Ct. 705, 35 L.Ed.2d 147 (1973), while the pending prosecution of Dr. Hallford under the Texas Abortion law was found to render his action for declaratory and injunctive relief impermissible, this did not prevent our granting plaintiff Roe, against whom no action was pending, a declaratory judgment that the statute was unconstitutional.

applied. [The Court distinguished *Cameron* as involving a pending prosecution.]

Indeed, the State's concern with potential interference in the administration of its criminal laws is of lesser dimension when an attack is made upon the constitutionality of a state statute as applied. A declaratory judgment of a lower federal court that a state statute is invalid *in toto*—and therefore incapable of any valid application—or is overbroad or vague—and therefore no person can properly be convicted under the statute until it is given a narrowing or clarifying construction—will likely have a more significant potential for disruption of state enforcement policies than a declaration specifying a limited number of impermissible applications of the statute. While the federal interest may be greater when a state statute is attacked on its face, since there exists the potential for eliminating any broad-ranging deterrent effect on would-be actors, we do not find this consideration controlling. The solitary individual who suffers a deprivation of his constitutional rights is no less deserving of redress than one who suffers together with others.[21]

We therefore hold that, regardless of whether injunctive relief may be appropriate, federal declaratory relief is not precluded when no state prosecution is pending and a federal plaintiff demonstrates a genuine threat of enforcement of a disputed state criminal statute, whether an attack is made on the constitutionality of the statute on its face or as applied. The judgment of the Court of Appeals is reversed, and the case is remanded for further proceedings consistent with this opinion.

Reversed and remanded.

[Justice Stewart, joined by Chief Justice Burger, concurred, noting that *Steffel* had surpassed the standing hurdle of Boyle v. Landry. Such cases, said Stewart, are "exceedingly rare."]

Mr. Justice White, concurring.

I offer the following few words in light of Mr. Justice Rehnquist's concurrence in which he discusses the impact on a pending federal action of a later filed criminal prosecution against the federal plaintiff, whether a federal court may enjoin a state criminal prosecution under a statute the federal court has earlier declared unconstitutional at the suit of the defendant now being prosecuted, and the question whether that declaratory judgment is res judicata in such a later filed state criminal action.

It should be noted, first, that his views on these issues are neither expressly nor impliedly embraced by the Court's opinion filed today. Second, my own tentative views on these questions are somewhat contrary to my Brother's.

---

21. Abstention, a question "entirely separate from the question of granting declaratory or injunctive relief," Lake Carriers' Assn. v. MacMullan, might be more appropriate when a challenge is made to the state statute as applied, rather than upon its face, since the reach of an uncertain state statute might, in that circumstance, be more susceptible of a limiting or clarifying construction that would avoid the federal constitutional question.

At this writing at least, I would anticipate that a final declaratory judgment entered by a federal court holding particular conduct of the federal plaintiff to be immune on federal constitutional grounds from prosecution under state law should be accorded res judicata effect in any later prosecution of that very conduct. There would also, I think, be additional circumstances in which the federal judgment should be considered as more than a mere precedent bearing on the issue before the state court.

Neither can I at this stage agree that the federal court, having rendered a declaratory judgment in favor of the plaintiff, could not enjoin a later state prosecution for conduct that the federal court has declared immune. The Declaratory Judgment Act itself provides that a "declaration shall have the force and effect of a final judgment or decree," 28 U.S.C.A. § 2201; eminent authority anticipated that declaratory judgments would be res judicata, and there is every reason for not reducing declaratory judgments to mere advisory opinions.

Finally, I would think that a federal suit challenging a state criminal statute on federal constitutional grounds could be sufficiently far along so that ordinary consideration of economy would warrant refusal to dismiss the federal case solely because a state prosecution has subsequently been filed and the federal question may be litigated there.

MR. JUSTICE REHNQUIST, with whom THE CHIEF JUSTICE joins, concurring.

* * *

* * * I do not believe that today's decision can properly be raised to support the issuance of a federal injunction based upon a favorable declaratory judgment. The Court's description of declaratory relief as " 'a milder alternative to the injunction remedy,' " having a "less intrusive effect on the administration of state criminal laws" than an injunction, indicates to me critical distinctions which make declaratory relief appropriate where injunctive relief would not be. It would all but totally obscure these important distinctions if a successful application for declaratory relief came to be regarded, not as the conclusion of a lawsuit, but as a giant step toward obtaining an injunction against a subsequent criminal prosecution. The availability of injunctive relief must be considered with an eye toward the important policies of federalism which this Court has often recognized.

* * *

A declaratory judgment is simply a statement of rights, not a binding order supplemented by continuing sanctions. State authorities may choose to be guided by the judgment of a lower federal court, but they are not compelled to follow the decision by threat of contempt or other penalties. If the federal plaintiff pursues the conduct for which he was previously threatened with arrest and is in fact arrested, he may not return the controversy to federal court, although he may, of course, raise the federal declaratory judgment in the state court for whatever value it may prove to have. In any event, the defendant at that point is able to present his case for full consideration by a state court charged, as are the federal courts, to preserve the defendant's constitutional rights. Federal interference with this process would involve precisely the same concerns discussed in *Younger* and recited in the Court's opinion in this case.

* * *

* * * If the federal court finds that the threatened prosecution would depend upon a statute it judges unconstitutional, the State may decide to forgo prosecution of similar conduct in the future, believing the judgment persuasive. Should the state prosecutors not find the decision persuasive enough to justify forbearance, the successful federal plaintiff will at least be able to bolster his allegations of unconstitutionality in the state trial with a decision of the federal district court in the immediate locality. The state courts may find the reasoning convincing even though the prosecutors did not. Finally, of course, the state legislature may decide, on the basis of the federal decision, that the statute would be better amended or repealed. All these possible avenues of relief would be reached voluntarily by the States and would be completely consistent with the concepts of federalism discussed [in *Younger*]. * * *

NOTE ON STANDING AND THE RES JUDICATA EFFECT OF PRIOR JUDGMENTS

1. The Court in *Steffel* reached a unanimous judgment that the *Younger* doctrine does not forbid a declaratory judgment as to the validity of a criminal statute where no state prosecution is pending.

(a) Were the Harvard Law Review editors, quoted in the appellate opinion, not justified in concluding that the *Younger* concerns were equally applicable here? Did Justice Black make the mistake of choosing an inappropriate vehicle—the equitable notion of an adequate remedy at law—to carry his ideas, leaving the Court free in *Steffel* to apply the doctrinal vehicle in a literal fashion to find no adequate remedy at law?

(b) Did Congress tip the scales with the Declaratory Judgment Act? Footnote 18 makes a powerful argument which the Court cannot ignore, does it not?

(c) Was the Court unanimous because the real battle is to be fought on other issues—the ability of persons to obtain declaratory judgments and the value of such judgments when given? This note explores these two issues.

2. Justice Stewart found *Steffel* to be no significant erosion of *Younger* because such cases where plaintiffs can establish the necessary standing will be extremely rare. Is this not surely correct? A prospective federal plaintiff must violate the offending statute, or come so close to violating it, that he will draw a threat of prosecution from police, a threat which (in light of footnote 10) must remain alive throughout the course of the federal litigation. See City of Houston v. Hill, 482 U.S. 451, 107 S.Ct. 2502, 96 L.Ed.2d 398 (1987)

(standing established by history of multiple arrests under challenged ordinance followed by acquittals or dropped charges in state court).

(a) Is the federal plaintiff not at the mercy of police? Do they not have full power—by deciding whether to prosecute—to determine whether *Younger* applies? Are you thinking that the prospective federal plaintiff could run to the federal courthouse, before the police procured his indictment, and offset the *Younger* doctrine by filing his § 1983 complaint first? Read the *Hicks* case (and commentary) following this Note.

(b) Is the Court's ruling on standing consistent with the Declaratory Judgment Act, as disclosed by the latter's legislative history in footnote 18? Does the Court not force the federal plaintiff to eat the mushroom/toadstool in order to establish his standing? Compare American Machine & Metals, Inc. v. De Bothezat Impeller Co., 166 F.2d 535 (2d Cir. 1948) with International Longshoremen's and Warehousemen's Union, Local 37 v. Boyd, 347 U.S. 222, 74 S.Ct. 447, 98 L.Ed. 650 (1954). Should standing in constitutional cases be more restrictive than in ordinary contracts cases? Why?

3.   Justice Brennan's opinion for the Court in *Steffel* borrowed heavily from his earlier separate opinion in Perez v. Ledesma, 401 U.S. 82, 93, 91 S.Ct. 674, 681, 27 L.Ed.2d 701 (1971), a companion case to *Younger.* Are you persuaded that a declaratory judgment is indeed less intrusive than an injunction? Does your answer not depend on the worth or use of such a judgment?

(a) Is a declaratory judgment significantly milder relief because, at least until a follow-up injunction is issued, it is not backed by the court's contempt power? Is it a less intrusive form of relief because even if the court declares certain conduct, e.g., non-inciting speech, to be protected, prosecutors are left free to indict the federal plaintiff for activities outside the protected sphere, e.g., inciting speech?

(b) Did Brennan give up too much when he opined that a declaratory judgment has only "some" res judicata effect, and even that is uncertain? Compare Justices White's and Rehnquist's concurring opinions. Is White's declaratory judgment not in effect an injunction? Is Rehnquist's not a mere advisory opinion? Has Brennan tried to find middle ground where none exists?

4.   After *Steffel* the Court faced the interrelated issues of res judicata and injunctive relief in a somewhat different procedural posture in **Wooley v. Maynard**, 430 U.S. 705, 97 S.Ct. 1428, 51 L.Ed.2d 752 (1977). In that case a Jehovah's Witness, who had been thrice convicted in state court for obscuring the New Hampshire motto "Live Free or Die" on his automobile license plate, filed suit under § 1983 to have future prosecutions enjoined on the ground that forcing him to display the motto violated the First Amendment. The state court judgments, which had specifically considered and rejected Maynard's constitutional arguments, were final, and the jail sentence imposed had been served at the time of filing the federal complaint. Chief Justice Burger's rather cryptic opinion for the Court summarily dismissed the state's *Younger* argument by stating that here, as in *Steffel,* no state prosecution was pending at the time the federal complaint was filed. The Court even assented to the

entry of an injunction against further prosecutions rather than a declaratory judgment.

(a) Why did the Court treat this as a *Younger* case? Was it not rather an appropriate occasion to apply res judicata rules? The state court had fully adjudicated Maynard's constitutional claim, the judgments were final, and this suit was not a habeas corpus action in which res judicata rules do not apply. Should Maynard not have been barred from relitigating the issue? See 28 U.S.C.A. § 1738.See Section E of this Chapter. Is the state court judgment res judicata, but only as to prior acts by Maynard, not the future ones at issue in the § 1983 suit?

(b) Note that in this case the res judicata effect would run exactly the opposite of that discussed by Justices White and Rehnquist in *Steffel*—that is, federal courts were being asked to give res judicata effect to a state court judgment. Can Justice White, who joined the *Maynard* majority, have it both ways, denying res judicata effect to a state judgment but requiring that states give such effect to federal declaratory judgments? Can the Court give limited res judicata effect to both courts' judgments—such effect to state judgments as to *past* conduct (thus prohibiting collateral attack on the state's judgment) and such effect to federal declaratory judgments as to *future* conduct (that occurring after the federal judgment)?

(c) Of course much of the brouhaha about res judicata evaporates in the declaratory judgment context if a follow-up injunction is also granted; with no state proceedings there is no occasion for the federal plaintiff to plead his federal judgment in the state case. Noting that exceptional circumstances must be shown to justify an injunction, Chief Justice Burger found them present in *Maynard* (430 U.S. at 712, 97 S.Ct. at 1434):

> "We have such a situation here for, as we have noted, three successive prosecutions were undertaken against Mr. Maynard in the span of five weeks. This is quite different from a claim for federal equitable relief when a prosecution is threatened for the first time. The threat of repeated prosecutions in the future against both him and his wife, and the effect of such a continuing threat on their ability to perform the ordinary tasks of daily life which require an automobile, is sufficient to justify injunctive relief."

Does a declaratory judgment remain the preferred form of relief? Is this injunction really more intrusive than a declaratory judgment?

HICKS v. MIRANDA

Supreme Court of the United States, 1975.
422 U.S. 332, 95 S.Ct. 2281, 45 L.Ed.2d 223.

MR. JUSTICE WHITE delivered the opinion of the Court.

* * *

I

On November 23 and 24, 1973, pursuant to four separate warrants issued seriatim, the police seized four copies of the film "Deep Throat," each of which had been shown at the Pussycat Theatre in Buena Park, Orange County, Cal. On November 26 an eight-count criminal misdemeanor charge was filed in the Orange County Municipal Court against two employees of the theater, each film seized being the subject matter of two counts in the complaint. Also on November 26, the Superior Court of Orange County ordered appellees to show cause why "Deep Throat" should not be declared obscene, an immediate hearing being available to appellees, who appeared that day, objected on state-law grounds to the court's jurisdiction to conduct such a proceeding, purported to "reserve" all federal questions, and refused further to participate. Thereupon, on November 27 the Superior Court held a hearing, viewed the film, took evidence, and then declared the movie to be obscene and ordered seized all copies of it that might be found at the theater. This judgment and order were not appealed by appellees.

Instead, on November 29, they filed this suit in the District Court against appellants—four police officers of Buena Park and the District Attorney and Assistant District Attorney of Orange County. The complaint recited the seizures and the proceedings in the Superior Court, stated that the action was for an injunction against the enforcement of the California obscenity statute, and prayed for judgment declaring the obscenity statute unconstitutional, and for an injunction ordering the return of all copies of the film, but permitting one of the films to be duplicated before its return.

A temporary restraining order was requested and denied, the District Judge finding the proof of irreparable injury to be lacking and an insufficient likelihood of prevailing on the merits to warrant an injunction. He requested the convening of a three-judge court, however, to consider the constitutionality of the statute. Such a court was then designated on January 8, 1974.

Service of the complaint was completed on January 14, 1974, and answers and motions to dismiss, as well as a motion for summary judgment, were filed by appellants. Appellees moved for a preliminary injunction. None of the motions was granted and no hearings held, all of the issues being ordered submitted on briefs and affidavits. * * *

Meanwhile, on January 15, the criminal complaint pending in the Municipal Court had been amended by naming appellees as additional parties defendant and by adding four conspiracy counts, [but hearings and procedural wrangling delayed the trial].

On June 4, 1974, the three-judge court issued its judgment and opinion declaring the California obscenity statute to be unconstitutional for failure to satisfy the requirements of *Miller I* [Miller v. California, 413 U.S. 15, 93 S.Ct. 2607, 37 L.Ed.2d 419 (1973)] and ordering appellants to return to appellees all copies of "Deep Throat" which had been seized as well as to refrain from making any additional seizures. Appellants' claim that Younger v. Harris required dismissal of the case was rejected, the court holding that no criminal charges were pending in the state court against appellees and that in any event the pattern of search warrants and seizures demonstrated bad faith and harassment on the part of the authorities, all of which relieved the court from the strictures of Younger v. Harris, supra, and its related cases.

Appellants filed various motions for rehearing * * * calling the court's attention to * * * the dismissal on July 25, 1974, "for want of a substantial federal question" of the appeal in Miller v. California, 418 U.S. 915, 94 S.Ct. 3206, 41 L.Ed.2d 1158 (*Miller II*), from a judgment of the Superior Court, Appellate Department, Orange County, California, sustaining the constitutionality of the very California obscenity statute which the District Court had declared unconstitutional. * * *

On September 30, the three-judge court denied appellants' motions, reaffirmed its June 4 Younger v. Harris ruling and, after concluding it was not bound by the dismissal of *Miller II,* adhered to its judgment that the California statute was invalid under the Federal Constitution. * * *

* * *

The District Court committed error in reaching the merits of this case despite the appellants' insistence that it be dismissed under Younger v. Harris. When they filed their federal complaint, no state criminal proceedings were pending against appellees by name; but two employees of the theater had been charged and four copies of "Deep Throat" belonging to appellees had been seized, were being held, and had been declared to be obscene and seizable by the Superior Court. Appellees had a substantial stake in the state proceedings, so much so that they sought federal relief, demanding that the state statute be declared void and their films be returned to them. Obviously, their interests and those of their employees were intertwined; and, as we have pointed out, the federal action sought to interfere with the pending state prosecution. Absent a clear showing that appellees, whose lawyers also represented their employees, could not seek the return of their property in the state proceedings and see to it that their federal claims were presented there, the requirements of Younger v. Harris could not be avoided on the ground that no criminal prosecution was pending against appellees on the date the federal complaint was filed. The rule in Younger v. Harris is designed to "permit state courts to try state cases free from interference by federal courts," particularly where the party to the federal case may fully litigate his claim before the state court. Plainly, "[t]he same comity considerations apply," Allee v. Medrano, 416 U.S. 802, 831, 94 S.Ct. 2191, 2208, 40 L.Ed.2d 566 (Burger, C.J., concurring), where the interference is sought by some, such as appellees, not parties to the state case.

What is more, on the day following the completion of service of the complaint, appellees were charged along with their employees in Municipal Court. Neither Steffel v. Thompson, nor any other case in this Court has held that for Younger v. Harris to apply, the state criminal proceedings must be pending on the day the federal case is filed. Indeed, the issue has been left open; and we now hold that where state criminal proceedings are begun against the federal plaintiffs after the federal complaint is filed but before any proceedings of substance on the merits have taken place in the federal court, the principles of Younger v. Harris should apply in full force. Here, appellees were charged on January 15, prior to answering the federal case and prior to any proceedings whatsoever before the three-judge court. Unless we are to trivialize the principles of Younger v. Harris, the federal complaint should have been dismissed on the appellants' motion absent satisfactory proof of those extraordinary circumstances calling into play one of the limited exceptions to the rule of Younger v. Harris and related cases.

The District Court concluded that extraordinary circumstances had been shown in the form of official harassment and bad faith, but this was also error. The relevant findings of the District Court were vague and conclusory. There were references to the "pattern of seizure" and to "the evidence brought to light by the petition for rehearing"; and the unexplicated conclusion was then drawn that "regardless of the nature of any judicial proceeding," the police were bent on banishing "Deep Throat" from Buena Park. Yet each step in the pattern of seizures condemned by the District Court was authorized by judicial warrant or order; and the District Court did not purport to invalidate any of the four warrants, in any way to question the propriety of the proceedings in the Superior Court * * *. Absent at least some effort by the District Court to impeach the entitlement of the prosecuting officials to rely on repeated judicial authorization for their conduct, we cannot agree that bad faith and harassment were made out. Indeed, such conclusion would not necessarily follow even if it were shown that the state courts were in error on some one or more issues of state or federal law.

In the last analysis, it seems to us that the District Court's judgment rests almost entirely on its conclusion that the California obscenity statute was unconstitutional and unenforceable. But even assuming that the District Court was correct in its conclusion, the statute had not been so condemned in November 1973, and the District Court was not entitled to infer official bad faith merely because it—the District Court—disagreed with [a California appellate court decision upholding the statute]. Otherwise, bad faith and harassment would be present in every case in which a state statute is ruled unconstitutional, and the rule of Younger v. Harris would be swallowed up by its exception. The District Court should have dismissed the complaint before it and we accordingly reverse its judgment.

So ordered.

Judgment reversed.

MR. JUSTICE STEWART, with whom MR. JUSTICE DOUGLAS, MR. JUSTICE BRENNAN, and MR. JUSTICE MARSHALL join, dissenting.

* * *

In Steffel v. Thompson, the Court unanimously held that the principles of equity, comity, and federalism embodied in Younger v. Harris, and

Samuels v. Mackell, do not preclude a federal district court from entertaining an action to declare unconstitutional a state criminal statute when a state criminal prosecution is threatened but not pending at the time the federal complaint is filed. Today the Court holds that the *Steffel* decision is inoperative if a state criminal charge is filed at any point after the commencement of the federal action "before any proceedings of substance on the merits have taken place in the federal court." Any other rule, says the Court, would "trivialize" the principles of Younger v. Harris. I think this ruling "trivializes" *Steffel,* decided just last Term, and is inconsistent with those same principles of equity, comity, and federalism.

There is, to be sure, something unseemly about having the applicability of the *Younger* doctrine turn solely on the outcome of a race to the courthouse. The rule the Court adopts today, however, does not eliminate that race; it merely permits the State to leave the mark later, run a shorter course, and arrive first at the finish line. This rule seems to me to result from a failure to evaluate the state and federal interests as of the time the state prosecution was commenced.

* * *

A State has a vital interest in the enforcement of its criminal law, and this Court has said time and again that it will sanction little federal interference with that important state function. But there is nothing in our decision in *Steffel* that requires a State to stay its hand during the pendency of the federal litigation. If, in the interest of efficiency, the State wishes to refrain from actively prosecuting the criminal charge pending the outcome of the federal declaratory judgment suit, it may, of course, do so. But no decision of this Court requires it to make that choice.

The Court today, however, goes much further than simply recognizing the right of the State to proceed with the orderly administration of its criminal law; it ousts the federal courts from their historic role as the "primary reliances" for vindicating constitutional freedoms. This is no less offensive to "Our Federalism" than the federal injunction restraining pending state criminal proceedings condemned in Younger v. Harris. The concept of federalism requires "sensitivity to the legitimate interests of *both* State and National Governments." Younger v. Harris and its companion cases reflect the principles that the federal judiciary must refrain from interfering with the legitimate functioning of state courts. But surely the converse is a principle no less valid.

The Court's new rule creates a reality which few state prosecutors can be expected to ignore. It is an open invitation to state officials to institute state proceedings in order to defeat federal jurisdiction. One need not impugn the motives of state officials to suppose that they would rather prosecute a criminal suit in state court than defend a civil case in a federal forum. Today's opinion virtually instructs state officials to answer federal complaints with state indictments. * * *

* * *

NOTE ON Hicks AND LATER DEVELOPMENTS UNDER Younger

1. The federal defendants added Miranda as a party in the state criminal proceedings on the day following service on them of the federal complaint. At that time the federal district court had already heard and denied plaintiffs' motion for a temporary restraining order, and it had requested and received designation of a three-judge court.

(a) The Court held that its decision in *Steffel* is inapplicable if state proceedings are initiated before any "proceedings of substance" have begun in the federal suit. The Court does not explain the reasons for such a decision beyond noting that a contrary holding would "trivialize" the *Younger* doctrine. What reasons support *Hicks*?

(b) Justice Brennan joined Justice Stewart in arguing that *Hicks* "trivializes" *Steffel*. Is the argument persuasive? Compare Brennan's position on parallel proceedings here with his dissent in Preiser v. Rodriguez, sub-section G.1 supra. Are the positions consistent? How often do you think that the *Hicks* scenario occurs? If seldom, is this why it does not trivialize *Steffel*?

(c) What are "proceedings of substance"? Any in which the federal defendants have appeared? All which take place after filing of motions for summary judgment? All after the end of discovery? Should it not vary depending on how much energy the district court and parties have invested in the litigation and how near it is to judgment? Should the court of appeals review by an abuse-of-discretion standard?

(d) Is it not likely, absent a cumbersome grand jury indictment process, that much time will have elapsed between service of the federal complaint and initiation of state proceedings? Was Justice Stewart not correct when he argued that *Hicks* is an open invitation to prosecutors to file state criminal charges? Is this desirable? Assuming that the federal plaintiff has requested a declaratory judgment, is *Hicks* consistent with the Declaratory Judgment Act? See the Borchard statement in *Steffel* at n. 18 and paragraph 2(b) of the Note following *Steffel*.

2. As an alternative ground for its decision the Court noted that even though Miranda was not a named party to the state prosecution at the time of filing his § 1983 suit, he effectively controlled defense of the state charges, and therefore should have been considered a party to the pending prosecution and foreclosed from a federal forum under *Younger*. The notion at work here seems to be a variant of the longstanding res judicata rule of privity. See Restatement of Judgments, § 83–92 (1942); cf. Restatement (Second) of Judgments (declining use of label "privity" and describing relationships that bind one to judgment). Was the Court correct to import this idea into the *Younger* doctrine? How strictly should it be incorporated? The Court in *Hicks* points to "intertwined" interests and appearances by Miranda's lawyers in both cases. Would the first factor alone have been sufficient? See *Steffel* at n. 19. The second alone sufficient? See Doran v. Salem Inn, Inc., infra.

3. Could a federal plaintiff short-circuit the *Hicks* scenario by obtaining a preliminary injunction to halt initiation of state proceedings? Less than a week after it handed down *Hicks*, the Supreme Court decided **Doran v.**

Salem Inn, Inc., 422 U.S. 922, 95 S.Ct. 2561, 45 L.Ed.2d 648 (1975). There three "topless dancing" bars filed suit under § 1983 to enjoin enforcement of a city criminal ordinance banning bare-breasted dancing. A requested TRO was denied immediately, but after one of the bars ("M & L") resumed its topless revue and was charged with violating the ordinance, the district court heard plaintiffs' motion for a preliminary injunction against prosecution of any of them and granted it. Justice Rehnquist, writing for eight members of the Court, first distinguished among the plaintiffs, finding that "while respondents are represented by common counsel, and have similar business activities and problems, they are apparently unrelated in terms of ownership, control, and management." Looking at M & L alone, the Court applied the *Younger* doctrine for the reasons set out in *Hicks*. Since prosecutions were never commenced against the other two bars, the Court found them entitled to at least declaratory relief under *Steffel*. The opinion continued (422 U.S. at 930–31, 95 S.Ct. at 2567):

> "The District Court, however, did not grant declaratory relief to Salem and Tim–Rob, but instead granted them preliminary injunctive relief. Whether injunctions of future criminal prosecutions are governed by *Younger* standards is a question which we reserved in both *Steffel,* and Younger v. Harris. We now hold that on the facts of this case the issuance of a preliminary injunction is not subject to the restrictions of *Younger*. * * *
>
> "No state proceedings were pending against either Salem or Tim–Rob at the time the District Court issued its preliminary injunction. Nor was there any question that they satisfied the requirements for federal jurisdiction. As we have already stated they were assuredly entitled to declaratory relief and since we have previously recognized that '[o]rdinarily * * * the practical effect of [injunctive and declaratory] relief will be virtually identical,' *Samuels,* we think that Salem and Tim–Rob were entitled to have their claims for preliminary injunctive relief considered without regard to *Younger*'s restrictions. At the conclusion of a successful federal challenge to a state statute or local ordinance, a district court can generally protect the interests of a federal plaintiff by entering a declaratory judgment, and therefore the stronger injunctive medicine will be unnecessary. But prior to final judgment there is no established declaratory remedy comparable to a preliminary injunction; unless preliminary relief is available upon a proper showing, plaintiffs in some situations may suffer unnecessary and substantial irreparable harm. Moreover, neither declaratory nor injunctive relief can directly interfere with enforcement of contested statutes or ordinances except with respect to the particular federal plaintiffs, and the State is free to prosecute others who may violate the statute."

(a) Does *Doran* "trivialize" *Hicks*? If federal plaintiffs can rather quickly obtain a TRO or preliminary injunction against their prosecution, will that not effectively kill the prosecutor's power to turn a *Steffel*—type case into a *Hicks*—type case?

(b) In *Doran* no charges could have been filed against the two bars other than M & L because neither had violated the city ordinance. Does *Doran* work, then (note the quick filing of charges against M & L), only because the two bars established their standing without violating the city ordinance? If M & L had not offered itself as the sacrificial lamb (perhaps an inappropriate metaphor) to show the certainty of application of the statute, would M & L have had standing? Compare Boyle v. Landry, page 263 supra. If *Doran* represents a relaxation of standing rules, is it not a salutary development? See *Steffel*, n. 18.

(c) After reciting the language quoted above, Justice Rehnquist proceeded to determine whether the district court abused its discretion in issuing a preliminary injunction in this case. He suggested that although *Younger* did not apply as such, courts must be sensitive to the State's interest in enforcing its criminal laws, which "implicates the concerns for federalism which lie at the heart of *Younger*," and labeled the standard to be applied in balancing private and state interests a "stringent" one. Does this undercut what Rehnquist said earlier about the inapplicability of *Younger*? The Court found the issue here "a close one," but sustained the district court's finding of irreparable harm ("substantial loss of business and perhaps even bankruptcy") and likelihood of success on the merits. Do you think that the Court would find the requisite irreparable injury in a teacher's loss of classroom intellectual discussion occasioned by a prosecution threat for teaching Marxism? Loss of power to influence an election occasioned by threatened application of an anti-littering ordinance?

4. The Court in *Hicks* refused to infer bad faith from either the state's multiple seizures of film prints or the filing of the state charges immediately after service of the federal complaint.

(a) If a plaintiff can show that the state charges would not have been brought but for the plaintiff's federal suit, would that constitute "bad faith" to make *Younger* inapplicable? If your answer is no, does not *Hicks* simply become a judicially sanctioned removal procedure, running the opposite direction—federal to state court—from the normal removal statute? Cf. 28 U.S.C.A. § 1442.

(b) What is meant by the phrase "bad faith" as used in the exception to the *Younger* doctrine? See Cullen v. Fliegner, 18 F.3d 96, 103 (2d Cir.1994) (prior bad relations between plaintiff and state actor); Smith v. Hightower, 693 F.2d 359 (5th Cir.1982). Cases finding the exception present have been few, and it seems fair to say that this limitation on *Younger* is rather limited. See Fiss, *Dombrowski*, 86 YALE L.J. 1106, 1115 (1977). Might there be related concepts? Would a charge under a state statute pre-empted federal law be impermissible? See Woodfeathers, Inc. v. Washington County, 180 F.3d 1017 (9th Cir. 1999) (environmental law claimed to be pre-empted and unconstitutional).

(c) What is the source of the "bad faith" exception? Does it reflect nothing more than the ancient equitable notion that multiple wrongs, e.g., repeated trespasses, entitle a plaintiff to injunctive relief? Or does it reflect a notion that there is no valid state interest to balance against the plaintiff's constitutional interest when the state prosecution is in bad faith?

5. The other exception to the *Younger* doctrine, "extraordinary circumstances," such as a flagrantly unconstitutional statute, has also turned out to

be a loophole as tight as a noose. The Court has stressed that "such circumstances must be 'extraordinary' in the sense of creating an extraordinarily pressing need for immediate federal equitable relief, not merely in the sense of presenting a highly unusual factual situation." Kugler v. Helfant, 421 U.S. 117, 125, 95 S.Ct. 1524, 1531, 44 L.Ed.2d 15 (1975). There the Court denied relief to a judge claiming bias at the hands of his colleagues. But see Gibson v. Berryhill, 411 U.S. 564, 577, 93 S.Ct. 1689, 1697, 36 L.Ed.2d 488 (1973). And the notion of a "flagrantly" unconstitutional statute has been interpreted so strictly—one so " 'in every clause, sentence, paragraph, and in whatever manner and against whomever,' " Trainor v. Hernandez, 431 U.S. 434, 447, 97 S.Ct. 1911, 1920, 52 L.Ed.2d 486 (1977), that the exception built around that language also appears dead. Id., 431 U.S. at 462, 97 S.Ct. at 1927, 1928 (Stevens, J., dissenting); see Soifer & Macgill, *The* Younger *Doctrine: Reconstructing Reconstruction*, 55 TEX. L. REV. 1141, 1210 (1977). Why is it that the Supreme Court has so deeply interred the two exceptions to the *Younger* doctrine when its record as to when the doctrine applies has been such a wavering one?

6. Take this occasion to look back on the *Younger* principle from the initial decision through *Steffel, Hicks,* and *Doran.* Has the trail—far from reflecting any basic doctrinal considerations concerning "Our Federalism"—not simply followed at every turn traditional equitable principles? Indeed, when doctrinal considerations seemed to indicate one result, as in *Steffel* or *Doran,* has the court not largely molded the doctrine to fit the rules of equity? Should a line of decisions as important as those following *Younger,* have a firmer foundation? Or is equity precisely the right way to approach these problems?

(b) *Younger* and State Civil Proceedings

HUFFMAN v. PURSUE, LTD.
Supreme Court of the United States, 1975.
420 U.S. 592, 95 S.Ct. 1200, 43 L.Ed.2d 482.

MR. JUSTICE REHNQUIST delivered the opinion of the Court.

This case requires that we decide whether our decision in Younger v. Harris bars a federal district court from intervening in a state civil proceeding such as this when the proceeding is based on a statute believed by the District Court to be unconstitutional.

I

Appellants are the sheriff and prosecuting attorney of Allen County, Ohio. This case arises from their efforts to close the Cinema I Theatre, in Lima, Ohio. Under the management of both its current tenant, appellee Pursue, Ltd., and appellee's predecessor, William Dakota, the Cinema I has specialized in the display of films which may fairly be characterized as pornographic, and which in numerous instances have been adjudged obscene after adversary hearings.

Appellants sought to invoke the Ohio public nuisance statute, Ohio Rev.Code Ann. § 3767.01 et seq. (1971), against appellee. Section

3767.01(C) provides that a place which exhibits obscene films is a nuisance while § 3767.06 requires closure for up to a year of any place determined to be a nuisance. The statute also provides for preliminary injunctions pending final determination of status as a nuisance, for sale of all personal property used in conducting the nuisance, and for release from a closure order upon satisfaction of certain conditions (including a showing that the nuisance will not be reestablished).

Appellants instituted a nuisance proceeding in the Court of Common Pleas of Allen County against appellee's predecessor, William Dakota. During the course of the somewhat involved legal proceedings which followed, the Court of Common Pleas reviewed 16 movies which had been shown at the theater. The court rendered a judgment that Dakota had engaged in a course of conduct of displaying obscene movies at the Cinema I, and that the theater was therefore to be closed, pursuant to Ohio Rev.Code Ann. § 3767.06 (1971) * * *.

Appellee, Pursue, Ltd., had succeeded to William Dakota's leasehold interest in the Cinema I prior to entry of the state-court judgment. Rather than appealing that judgment within the Ohio court system, it immediately filed suit in the United States District Court for the Northern District of Ohio. The complaint was based on 42 U.S.C.A. § 1983 and alleged that appellants' use of Ohio's nuisance statute constituted a deprivation of constitutional rights under the color of state law. It sought injunctive relief and a declaratory judgment that the statute was unconstitutional and unenforceable. Since the complaint was directed against the constitutionality of a state statute, a three-judge court was convened. The District Court concluded that while the statute was not vague, it did constitute an overly broad prior restraint on First Amendment rights insofar as it permanently or temporarily prevented the showing of films which had not been adjudged obscene in prior adversary hearings. Cf. Near v. Minnesota ex rel. Olson, 283 U.S. 697, 51 S.Ct. 625, 75 L.Ed. 1357 (1931). Fashioning its remedy to match the perceived constitutional defect, the court permanently enjoined the execution of that portion of the state court's judgment that closed the Cinema I to films which had not been adjudged obscene. * * *

* * *

II

Younger and its companion cases considered the propriety of federal-court intervention in pending state criminal prosecutions. [The Court here recounted in detail the bases for its decision in such cases.]

III

The seriousness of federal judicial interference with state civil functions has long been recognized by this Court. We have consistently required that when federal courts are confronted with requests for such relief, they should abide by standards of restraint that go well beyond those of private equity jurisprudence. For example, Massachusetts State Grange v. Benton, 272 U.S. 525, 47 S.Ct. 189, 71 L.Ed. 387 (1926), involved an effort to enjoin the operation of a state daylight savings act. Writing for the Court, Mr. Justice Holmes cited Fenner v. Boykin, supra, and emphasized a rule that "should be very strictly observed," "that no injunction ought to issue against officers of a State clothed with authority to enforce the law in question, unless in a case reasonably free from doubt and when necessary to prevent great and irreparable injury."

Although Mr. Justice Holmes was confronted with a bill seeking an injunction against state executive officers, rather than against state judicial proceedings, we think that the relevant considerations of federalism are of no less weight in the latter setting. If anything, they counsel more heavily toward federal restraint, since interference with a state judicial proceeding prevents the state not only from effectuating its substantive policies, but also from continuing to perform the separate function of providing a forum competent to vindicate any constitutional objections interposed against those policies. Such interference also results in duplicative legal proceedings, and can readily be interpreted "as reflecting negatively upon the state courts' ability to enforce constitutional principles." Cf. Steffel v. Thompson * * *.

The component of *Younger* which rests upon the threat to our federal system is thus applicable to a civil proceeding such as this quite as much as it is to a criminal proceeding. *Younger* however, also rests upon the traditional reluctance of courts of equity, even within a unitary system, to interfere with a criminal prosecution. Strictly speaking, this element of *Younger* is not available to mandate federal restraint in civil cases. But whatever may be the weight attached to this factor in civil litigation involving private parties, we deal here with a state proceeding which in important respects is more akin to a criminal prosecution than are most civil cases. The State is a party to the Court of Common Pleas proceeding, and the proceeding is both in aid of and closely related to criminal statutes which prohibit the dissemination of obscene materials. Thus, an offense to the State's interest in the nuisance litigation is likely to be every bit as great as it would be were this a criminal proceeding. Similarly, while in this case the District Court's injunction has not directly disrupted Ohio's criminal justice system, it has disrupted that State's efforts to protect the very interests which underlie its criminal laws and to obtain compliance with precisely the standards which are embodied in its criminal laws.

IV

In spite of the critical similarities between a criminal prosecution and Ohio nuisance proceedings, appellee nonetheless urges that there is also a critical difference between the two which should cause us to limit *Younger* to criminal proceedings. This difference, says appellee, is that whereas a state-court criminal defendant may, after exhaustion of his state remedies, present his constitutional claims to the federal courts through habeas corpus, no analogous remedy is available to one, like appellee, whose constitutional rights may have been infringed in a state proceeding which cannot result in custodial detention or other criminal sanction.

A civil litigant may, of course, seek review in this Court of any federal claim properly asserted in and rejected by state courts. Moreover, where a final decision of a state court has sustained the validity of a state statute challenged on federal constitutional grounds, an appeal to this Court lies as a matter of right. 28 U.S.C.A. § 1257(2). Thus, appellee in this case was assured of eventual consideration of its claim by this Court. But quite apart from appellee's right to appeal had it remained in state court, we conclude that it should not be permitted the luxury of federal litigation of issues presented by ongoing state proceedings, a luxury which, as we have already explained, is quite costly in terms of the interests which *Younger* seeks to protect.

Appellee's argument, that because there may be no civil counterpart to federal habeas it should have contemporaneous access to a federal forum for its federal claim, apparently depends on the unarticulated major premise that every litigant who asserts a federal claim is entitled to have it decided on the merits by a federal, rather than a state, court. We need not consider the validity of this premise in order to reject the result which appellee seeks. Even assuming, *arguendo,* that litigants are entitled to a federal forum for the resolution of all federal issues, that entitlement is most appropriately asserted by a state litigant when he seeks to *relitigate* a federal issue adversely determined in *completed* state court proceedings.[18] We do not understand why the federal forum must be available prior to completion of the state proceedings in which the federal issue arises, and the considerations canvassed in *Younger* militate against such a result.

[The state court proceedings in this case had been completed, but the Court noted Pursue's failure to appeal and concluded] that a necessary concomitant of *Younger* is that a party in appellee's posture must exhaust his state appellate remedies before seeking relief in the District Court * * *.

Virtually all of the evils at which *Younger* is directed would inhere in federal intervention prior to completion of state appellate proceedings, just as surely as they would if such intervention occurred at or before trial. Intervention at the later stage is if anything more highly duplicative, since an entire trial has already taken place, and it is also a direct aspersion on the capabilities and good faith of state appellate courts. Nor, in these state-initiated nuisance proceedings, is federal intervention at the appellate stage any the less a disruption of the State's efforts to protect

---

18. We in no way intend to suggest that there is a right of access to a federal forum for the disposition of all federal issues, or that the normal rules of res judicata and judicial estoppel do not operate to bar relitigation in actions under 42 U.S.C.A. § 1983 of federal issues arising in state court proceedings. Cf. Preiser v. Rodriguez, 411 U.S. 475, 497, 93 S.Ct. 1827, 1840, 36 L.Ed.2d 439 (1973). Our assumption is made solely as a means of disposing of appellee's contentions without confronting issues which have not been briefed or argued in this case. [See the Court's later decision in Wooley v. Maynard, discussed in the Note on Standing and Res Judicata supra.]

interests which it deems important. Indeed, it is likely to be even more disruptive and offensive because the State has already won a nisi prius determination that its valid policies are being violated in a fashion which justifies judicial abatement.

Federal post-trial intervention, in a fashion designed to annul the results of a state trial, also deprives the States of a function which quite legitimately is left to them, that of overseeing trial court dispositions of constitutional issues which arise in civil litigation over which they have jurisdiction. We think this consideration to be of some importance because it is typically a judicial system's appellate courts which are by their nature a litigant's most appropriate forum for the resolution of constitutional contentions. Especially is this true when, as here, the constitutional issue involves a statute which is capable of judicial narrowing. In short, we do not believe that a State's judicial system would be fairly accorded the opportunity to resolve federal issues arising in its courts if a federal district court were permitted to substitute itself for the State's appellate courts. We therefore hold that *Younger* standards must be met to justify federal intervention in a state judicial proceeding as to which a losing litigant has not exhausted his state appellate remedies.[21]

* * * The judgment of the District Court is vacated and the cause is remanded for further proceedings consistent with this opinion.

It is so ordered.

MR. JUSTICE BRENNAN, with whom MR. JUSTICE DOUGLAS and MR. JUSTICE MARSHALL join, dissenting.

I dissent. The treatment of the state *civil* proceeding as one "in aid of and closely related to criminal statutes" is obviously only the first step toward extending to state *civil* proceedings generally the holding of Younger v. Harris * * *.

Younger v. Harris was basically an application, in the context of the relation of federal courts to pending state criminal prosecutions, of "the basic doctrine of equity jurisprudence that courts of equity * * * particularly should not act to restrain a criminal prosecution." "The maxim that equity will not enjoin a criminal prosecution summarizes centuries of weighty experience in Anglo–American law."

The tradition, however, has been quite the opposite as respects federal injunctive interference with pending state civil proceedings. Even though

---

21. By requiring exhaustion of state appellate remedies for the purposes of applying *Younger* we in no way undermine Monroe v. Pape. There we held that one seeking redress under 42 U.S.C.A. § 1983 for a deprivation of federal rights need not first initiate state proceedings based on related state causes of action. Monroe v. Pape had nothing to do with the problem presently before us, that of the deference to be accorded state proceedings which have already been initiated and which afford a competent tribunal for the resolution of federal issues. [In Wooley v. Maynard, supra, the federal plaintiff likewise had sought no appellate review of his constitutional claim, but the Court nevertheless entertained his § 1983 suit without requiring the exhaustion of appellate remedies. It distinguished *Huffman* on the ground that Maynard was not trying to annul the previous state court judgment but only prevent future prosecutions. 430 U.S. at 710–711, 97 S.Ct. at 1432–1434. Does *Wooley* effectively overrule *Huffman* on the exhaustion issue? See Fiss, *Dombrowski*, 86 YALE L.J. 1103, 1142 (1977).]

legislation as far back as 1793 has provided in "seemingly uncompromising language," Mitchum v. Foster, 407 U.S. 225, 233, 92 S.Ct. 2151, 2157, 32 L.Ed.2d 705 (1972), that a federal court "may not grant an injunction to stay proceedings in a State court" with specified exceptions, see 28 U.S.C.A. § 2283, the Court has consistently engrafted exceptions upon the prohibition. * * *

* * *

Even if the extension of Younger v. Harris to pending state civil proceedings can be appropriate in any case, and I do not think it can be,[2] it is plainly improper in the case of an action by a federal plaintiff, as in this case, grounded upon 42 U.S.C.A. § 1983. That statute serves a particular congressional objective long recognized and enforced by the Court. Today's extension will defeat that objective. This is true notwithstanding the possibility of review by this Court of state decisions for, "even when available by appeal rather than only by discretionary writ of certiorari [that possibility] is an inadequate substitute for the initial District Court determination * * * to which the litigant is entitled in the federal courts." * * * The extension today of Younger v. Harris to require exhaustion in an action under § 1983 drastically undercuts Monroe v. Pape and its numerous progeny—the mere filing of a complaint against a potential § 1983 litigant forces him to exhaust state remedies.

* * *

Note on the Extension of Younger to Civil Cases

1. If Justice Brennan is correct in his view that applying Younger to the civil area does not comport with traditional equity rules, is he not right in suggesting that the Court is here departing from its usual practice of preferring equity rules over doctrinal purity? Cf. paragraph 6 of the Note on Hicks, supra. What explains the Court's actions? In reading this Note, consider particularly whether the extension of Younger to the civil area represents especially a triumph for Justice Black's collateral notion in Younger that state courts ought to have the first opportunity to construe their own statutes in order to avoid constitutional issues.

2. Justice Brennan also argues that the unavailability of habeas corpus in the civil area means that Younger can no longer be considered simply a variant of the exhaustion doctrine—committing one to state remedies first but then allowing return to a federal forum via habeas corpus. In the civil setting Younger operates to exclude § 1983 plaintiffs altogether from their federal forum.

(a) Does the accuracy of Justice Brennan's remark depend upon how the Supreme Court develops its later decision in Wooley v. Maynard, discussed also in the Note on Standing and Res Judicata, Chapter 1G.4 supra? In

---

2. Abstention where authoritative resolution by state courts of ambiguities in a state statute is sufficiently likely to avoid or significantly modify federal questions raised by the statute is another matter. * * *

Wooley the Court permitted a challenge to future enforcement of a state statute even though the plaintiff had earlier lost on the same constitutional issue in defense of prior, final prosecutions in state court which the plaintiff did not seek to annul. On the face of the *Wooley* opinion the only importance attached to the plaintiff's desire not to annul the prior judgments was that that concession released him from *Huffman*'s demand that he have exhausted available appeals in state court. Does this leave open the possibility that a federal plaintiff can seek to annul a previous state judgment—in both civil cases and criminal cases involving no confinement (where habeas corpus is unavailable)—provided he exhausts his appellate remedies as required by *Huffman* before filing the § 1983 complaint? But see *Huffman,* at n.18. Would there be strong reasons for allowing such relitigation in the criminal context (such as suits for damages or to expunge records of convictions) even though not in ordinary civil litigation? See the Note on Standing and the Res Judicata Effect of Prior Judgments, paragraph 4, in this sub-section supra.

(b) If no relitigation beyond that recognized in *Wooley* is permitted, then the *Huffman*–type plaintiff will be forced to rely for his vindication purely on the U.S. Supreme Court's willingness to review a final state court judgment. Is Justice Rehnquist correct in stating that this safeguard is adequate? Congress has, since *Huffman*, amended the statute regulating Supreme Court review to make this class of cases fall within the Court's certiorari jurisdiction. See 28 U.S.C. § 1257 (as amended, 1988). Should that lead Justice Rehnquist to change his position?

(c) If relitigation of the type envisioned in paragraph (a), supra, is permitted, then *Younger* in the civil area still operates as an exhaustion of remedies doctrine, at least in those situations where some mechanism exists for allowing the state official to initiate a state proceeding. Does this undercut Monroe v. Pape? If not, is it because the occasions for this to occur appear few? If a state official files for a state court declaratory judgment as to the constitutionality of a school's attendance zones, for example, naming complaining school children and their parents as class defendants, would *Huffman* require a federal court in a subsequent § 1983 suit to stay its proceedings? No, because *Huffman* applies only to quasi-criminal proceedings?

3.   Following *Huffman* the Court extended *Younger* to a wider variety of civil cases.

(a) In **Juidice v. Vail**, 430 U.S. 327, 97 S.Ct. 1211, 51 L.Ed.2d 376 (1977), the state court defendants found to have federal standing had defaulted in ordinary debt actions and had later been held in contempt and jailed for failing to appear at a postjudgment deposition designed to discover their assets. Without appealing the issue in state court, they thereafter challenged the contempt citation in a § 1983 action. Since the state proceedings against them were still pending, the Court noted that their federal complaint should be dismissed if *Younger* applied, and it was held to apply (430 U.S. at 335–36, 97 S.Ct. at 1217–18):

"A State's interest in the contempt process, through which it vindicates the regular operation of its judicial system, * * * is surely an important interest. * * * Whether disobedience of a court-sanctioned subpoena, and the resulting process leading to a finding of contempt of court, is labeled civil, quasi-criminal, or criminal in nature, we think the salient fact is that federal court interference with the State's contempt process is an offense to the State's interest * * * likely to be every bit as great as it would be were this a criminal proceeding. *Huffman,* supra."

(b) **Trainor v. Hernandez**, 431 U.S. 434, 97 S.Ct. 1911, 52 L.Ed.2d 486 (1977), came down two months after *Juidice.* Illinois suspected Hernandez and spouse of defrauding the state of welfare funds and, with a choice under state law of proceeding criminally or civilly, chose the milder route of trying to recover the overpayments in a civil action in state court, attaching the Hernandez' assets. Rather than challenging the summary attachment procedures in the pending state proceeding, the defendants filed a suit under § 1983 in federal court, asking that all state welfare officials be enjoined from seeking such attachments. The Court framed the question presented to it very broadly[1] but answered it more narrowly,[2] 431 U.S. at 444:

"Both the suit and the accompanying writ of attachment were brought to vindicate important state policies such as safeguarding the fiscal integrity of those [welfare] programs. The state authorities also had the option of vindicating these policies through criminal prosecutions. Although, as in *Juidice,* the State's interest here is '[p]erhaps * * * not quite as important as is the State's interest in the enforcement of its criminal laws * * * or even its interest in the maintenance of a quasi-criminal proceeding * * *,' the principles of *Younger* and *Huffman* are broad enough to apply to interference by a federal court with an ongoing civil enforcement action such as this, brought by the State in its sovereign capacity."

(c) In **Pennzoil Co. v. Texaco, Inc.**, 481 U.S. 1, 107 S.Ct. 1519, 95 L.Ed.2d 1 (1987), Pennzoil obtained a $10.5 billion judgment against Texaco on state law grounds. State law required posting a similar sized bond to stay the judgment pending appeal, a prohibitively large sum even for Texaco. Texaco then filed suit in federal court under § 1983 seeking to have Texas' bond requirement declared unconstitutional. The Supreme Court refused to permit the suit on *Younger* grounds, holding that even though this was a civil case, important state interests were at stake as in *Juidice.* 481 U.S. at 13–14, 107 S.Ct. at 1527–28. The Court also emphasized the possibility of a state-court decision that would obviate the need for federal constitutional litigation. Justice Brennan dissented on the ground that only Pennzoil, not Texaco, had a great interest in the Texas proceedings. Id. at 19–20, 107 S.Ct. at 1530–31.

(d) Are *Juidice,* and *Trainor,* and *Pennzoil* significant extensions of *Huffman?* Is any pending state court proceeding where the state appears as plaintiff enough to oust the federal district court's jurisdiction in a subsequent § 1983 suit? Only if the State's suit is quasi-criminal or an "enforcement"

1. "[W]hen a suit is filed in a federal court challenging the constitutionality of a state law under the Federal Constitution and seeking to have state officers enjoined from enforcing it, should the federal court proceed to judgment when it appears that the State has already instituted proceedings in the state court to enforce the challenged statute against the federal plaintiff and the latter could tender and have his federal claims decided in the state court?" 431 U.S. at 440, 97 S.Ct. at 1916.

2. In a footnote the Court, after its broad statement of the issue, cautioned, "As in Juidice v. Vail, we have no occasion to decide whether *Younger* principles apply to all civil litigation." 431 U.S. at 445 n. 8, 97 S.Ct. at 1919 n. 8.

action parallel to a criminal sanction? Only when the state policies enforced in state court are fairly "important" ones? Reconsider paragraph 2(c) supra, especially recalling the possibility of a State or state official pursuing a declaratory judgment remedy. Would that case draw the Court's deference after *Trainor*? Cf. Moore v. Sims, 442 U.S. 415, 99 S.Ct. 2371, 60 L.Ed.2d 994 (1979).

4. Should *Huffman* also be extended to state administrative proceedings? In **Middlesex County Ethics Committee v. Garden State Bar Ass'n**, 457 U.S. 423, 102 S.Ct. 2515, 73 L.Ed.2d 116 (1982) (NO. 81–460), the Supreme Court held that *Younger* and *Huffman* applied to bar federal interference with a state bar disciplinary hearing conducted by an ethics committee.

(a) In *Middlesex County* a majority of the ethics committee members were lawyers and the process allowed the assertion of constitutional issues. Are those conditions necessary to receipt of deference under *Huffman*? See Amanatullah v. Colorado Bd. of Medical Examiners, 187 F.3d 1160 (10th Cir. 1999) (medical licensing review board).

(b) The Court also recognized the "the unique relationship between the [state] Supreme Court and the local ethics committee," a relationship which effectively gave the state court power to review all ethics decisions. Is any agency entitled to deference, provided judicial review of its decisions is readily available? See Amanatullah v. Colorado Bd. of Medical Examiners, supra.

(c) Has *Younger* any other possibility for other expansion? To protect legislative proceedings, for example? See New Orleans Public Serv., Inc. v. Council of New Orleans, 491 U.S. 350, 109 S.Ct. 2506, 105 L.Ed.2d 298 (1989). To protect the proceedings of specialized federal courts? See Schlesinger v. Councilman, 420 U.S. 738, 95 S.Ct. 1300, 43 L.Ed.2d 591 (1975).

4. How should the adjunct rules of *Younger* be applied in the civil setting? *Steffel* would presumably apply with equal force, because with no state court proceeding pending there is no state remedy for federal plaintiffs, but what should happen with the *Hicks, Doran,* and *Wooley* rules?

(a) Is the argument in support of *Hicks* less compelling in the civil area because races to the courthouse are a common and accepted phenomenon in civil suits? Or is it an even stronger argument here?

(b) Note that the Court in each of the cases extending *Younger* into the civil area did not simply forbid the federal district court to issue an injunction, it also ordered the complaints dismissed. Would it not be a better practice to forbid *preliminary* injunctions, i.e. overrule *Doran,* and allow both state and federal courts to take the case, with the first to reach judgment controlling? (This is the practice in normal duplicative civil litigation.) Why not?

(c) Should the *Wooley* case, permitting a federal suit after the state judgment is final, be extended into the civil area? Are the res judicata aspects of the case, ignored in the Court's opinion, stronger in the civil context? On the other hand, refusing to carry *Wooley* into this area would make application of *Younger* an iron-clad rule allocating cases to state courts, would it not? And would that not go far beyond even overruling the "no exhaustion" rule of Monroe v. Pape?

5. *Younger* began as a doctrine to limit federal injunctive interference with state court criminal processes. Even as it expanded to cover some civil proceedings, the Court has generally been careful not to extend it across-the-board to damages actions brought in federal court. In **Quackenbush v. Allstate Ins. Co.**, 517 U.S. 706, 116 S.Ct. 1712, 135 L.Ed.2d 1 (1996), the Court discussed several of its abstention doctrines, including the *Younger* line, and located their basis primarily in the federal courts' "equitable discretion," plus a wider group of cases permitting the federal courts "discretion" in issuing relief (primarily declaratory judgments).

(a) Should *Younger, Huffman*, and their relatives never apply to damages actions? Is res judicata a sufficient doctrine to protect the state's interest when only damages are sought? The *Quackenbush* Court held that stays of damages actions might be appropriate. See also Deakins v. Monaghan, 484 U.S. 193, 108 S.Ct. 523, 98 L.Ed.2d 529 (1988) (dismissal is improper). Is this unexceptional because courts generally have power to control the flow of cases on their dockets?

(b) Does the gist, if not the details, of *Quackenbush*, support this criticism of *Younger*: despite all its talk about high-minded principles of federalism, it has at almost every turn merely enforced traditional equitable concerns about making injunctions too readily available? Is *Younger* at heart a mundane traveler looking for a handsome coat?

(c) What quality in the *Younger* doctrine has made it so endearing to the Court? Its work in allocating decisions to more conservative state courts? Its tendency to reduce the federal caseload? Its efficiency in reducing duplicative litigation? Its respect for the state's interest in putting its own house in order? Its malleable ability to undermine, when thought necessary, Monroe v. Pape?

NATIONAL PRIVATE TRUCK COUNCIL, INC. v. OKLAHOMA TAX COMMISSION

Supreme Court of the United States, 1995.
515 U.S. 582, 115 S.Ct. 2351, 132 L.Ed.2d 509.

JUSTICE THOMAS delivered the opinion of the Court.

In the Oklahoma state courts, petitioners successfully challenged certain Oklahoma taxes as violating the "dormant" Commerce Clause. Although the Oklahoma Supreme Court ordered respondents to award refunds pursuant to state law, it also held that petitioners were not entitled to declaratory or injunctive relief under § 1983, and, accordingly, that they could not obtain attorney's fees under 42 U.S.C. § 1988(b) (1988 ed., Supp. V). Petitioners argue that this holding violates the Supremacy Clause, U.S. Const., Art. VI, cl. 2. We affirm.

I

[In 1983 Oklahoma imposed discriminatory taxes on certain truckers to retaliate against some states that had imposed discriminatory taxes on Oklahoma truckers. These were held unconstitutional by the Oklahoma

Supreme Court under the dormant Commerce Clause in the case below; subsequently the Supreme Court held that dormant Commerce Clause claims are generally cognizable under § 1983, but on remand the Oklahoma Supreme Court adhered to its decision to award only a tax refund, refusing to award any § 1983–based remedies, including attorneys fees.]

II

We have long recognized that principles of federalism and comity generally counsel that courts should adopt a hands-off approach with respect to state tax administration. Immediately prior to the enactment of § 1983, the Court articulated the reasons behind the reluctance to interfere:

> "It is upon taxation that the several States chiefly rely to obtain the means to carry on their respective governments, and it is of the utmost importance to all of them that the modes adopted to enforce the taxes levied should be interfered with as little as possible." Dows v. Chicago, 11 Wall. 108, 110, 20 L.Ed. 65 (1871).

Since the passage of § 1983, Congress and this Court repeatedly have shown an aversion to federal interference with state tax administration. [For example, the Tax Injunction Act of 1937, 28 U.S.C. § 1341, prohibits federal courts from enjoining the collection of any state tax "where a plain, speedy and efficient remedy may be had in the courts of such State." We have also held that this Act cannot be circumvented by the expedient of requesting a federal declaratory judgment rather than an injunction. As for state courts themselves, we have required them to enforce the Commerce Clause's prohibition on discriminatory taxes, McKesson Corp. v. Division of Alcoholic Beverages and Tobacco, Fla. Dept. of Business Regulation, 496 U.S. 18, 110 S.Ct. 2238, 110 L.Ed.2d 17 (1990), but we have given them flexibility in choosing the methods of enforcement, from before-levy injunctions to after-levy refunds. The remedy need only be "clear and certain." Finally, in Fair Assessment in Real Estate Assn., Inc. v. McNary, 454 U.S. 100, 116, 102 S.Ct. 177, 186, 70 L.Ed.2d 271 (1981), we held that these general principles cannot be circumvented by the expediency of requesting a federal court in a § 1983 suit to award damages equal to the taxes sought to be recovered.]

Seeking to overcome the longstanding federal reluctance to [permit federal courts to] interfere with state taxation, petitioners [have brought their § 1983 claim in state court.] For purposes of this case, we will assume without deciding that state courts generally must hear § 1983 suits. [But we hold today that § 1983 cannot cover this claim, whether presented in a state or federal court, because] Congress did not authorize injunctive or declaratory relief under § 1983 in state tax cases when there is an adequate remedy at law.[5]

---

5. Will v. Michigan Dept. of State Police, 491 U.S. 58, 68–69, 109 S.Ct. 2304, 2310–2311, 105 L.Ed.2d 45 (1989), already established that petitioners' claim for refunds against the State could not proceed under § 1983.

III

* * *

In determining whether Congress has authorized state courts to issue injunctive and declaratory relief in state tax cases, we must interpret § 1983 in light of the strong background principle against federal interference with state taxation. Given this principle, we hold that § 1983 does not call for either federal or state courts to award injunctive and declaratory relief in state tax cases when an adequate legal remedy exists. Petitioners do not dispute that Oklahoma has offered an adequate remedy in the form of refunds. Under these circumstances, the Oklahoma courts' denial of relief under § 1983 was consistent with the long line of precedent underscoring the federal reluctance to interfere with state taxation.

Our cases since *Dows* have uniformly concluded that federal courts cannot enjoin the collection of state taxes when a remedy at law is available. Until *Fair Assessment*, one could have construed these cases as concerning only the equitable powers of the federal courts. In *Fair Assessment*, however, the principle of noninterference with state taxation led us to construe § 1983 narrowly. We held that § 1983 does not permit federal courts to award damages in state tax cases when state law provides an adequate remedy. * * *

* * *

Just as *Fair Assessment* relied upon a background principle in interpreting § 1983 to preclude damages actions in tax cases brought in federal court, so we rely on the same principle in interpreting § 1983 to provide no basis for courts to award injunctive relief when an adequate legal remedy exists. Our interpretation is supported not only by the background principle of federal noninterference discussed in *Fair Assessment*, but also by the principles of equitable restraint discussed at length in that case. Whether a suit is brought in federal or state court, Congress simply did not authorize the disruption of state tax administration in this way.

* * * After all, an injunction issued by a state court pursuant to § 1983 is just as disruptive as one entered by a federal court.

* * *

The availability of an adequate legal remedy renders a declaratory judgment unwarranted as well. Cf. Samuels v. Mackell, (holding that prohibition against enjoining pending state criminal proceedings applies to granting of declaratory relief). Declaratory relief in state tax cases might throw tax administration "into disarray, and taxpayers might escape the ordinary procedural requirements imposed by state law." Perez v. Ledesma, 401 U.S. 82, 128, n. 17, 91 S.Ct. 674, 699, n. 17, 27 L.Ed.2d 701 (1971) (Brennan, J., concurring in part and dissenting in part). We simply do not read § 1983 to provide for injunctive or declaratory relief against a state tax, either in federal or state court, when an adequate legal remedy exists.[6]

* * *

Because petitioners had an adequate legal remedy, the Oklahoma courts could not have awarded either declaratory or injunctive relief against the state taxes under § 1983. It follows that when no relief can be awarded pursuant to § 1983, no attorney's fees can be awarded under § 1988. Accordingly, the judgment of the Oklahoma Supreme Court is

Affirmed.

JUSTICE KENNEDY, concurring. [Omitted.]

NOTE ON *Younger-LIKE DOCTRINES AND THEIR APPLICATION IN STATE COURTS*

1. Although the principle of non-interference in state tax collection began life as a limitation on federal judicial power, it mutated in *National Private Truck Council* to a principle which limited § 1983 itself, regardless of whether it is employed in federal or state court.

(a) It is clear, is it not, that the Court has simply read wholesale its rules limiting federal courts into § 1983? Notice the exception permitting suits, especially as it is elaborated in footnote 6. Does the Court even try to locate these principles in some language in § 1983? Has Justice Thomas' respect for statutory text deserted him in this case? Or is this a case like Pierson v. Ray, Chapter 1D.1 supra, where Congressional failure to overturn a hoary precedent signals that the precedent is retained in § 1983? What was that precedent?

(b) Is it so clear that the precedent forbids both federal and state interference with state tax collection? How does the Court try to persuade you that state judicial interference, when based on a federal claim under § 1983, is just as bad as federal judicial interference? Do you agree that the problems are the same?

2. To the extent that *National Private Truck Council* reads prudential principles developed for federal courts into § 1983, thus making them applicable in state court actions as well, it mirrors the Court's similar effort in Will v. Michigan Dept. of State Police, Chapter 1H.2 infra (reading federal-power-limiting sovereign immunity rules into § 1983, thus making them applicable in state as well as federal courts). Are such decisions raw assertions of

---

6. As our opinions reveal, there may be extraordinary circumstances under which injunctive or declaratory relief is available even when a legal remedy exists. For example, if the "enforcement of the tax would lead to a multiplicity of suits, or produce irreparable injury, [or] throw a cloud upon the title," equity might be invoked. As we have made clear, however, the multiplicity-of-suits rationale for permitting equitable relief extends only to those situations where there is a real risk of "numerous suits between the same parties, involving the same issues of law or fact." Matthews v. Rodgers, 284 U.S. 521, 530, 52 S.Ct. 217, 221, 76 L.Ed. 447 (1932). Thus, if a state court awards a refund to a taxpayer on the ground that the tax violates the Federal Constitution, but state tax authorities continue to impose the unconstitutional tax, injunctive and declaratory relief might then be appropriate. In such circumstances, the remedy might be thought to be "inadequate."

Supreme Court power over statutes? Or are they properly respectful opinions about state power? Perhaps both?

3. Should the Court take a cue from *National Private Truck Council* and read *Younger*'s comity principles into § 1983, thus making them also applicable in state-court actions under § 1983? Is *Younger*'s concern for federalism as much about Congressional non-interference as it is about federal judicial non-interference?

(a) If the *Younger* doctrine is read into § 1983, would Congress have power to overturn such a statutory construction of § 1983? Is it possible that the *Younger* doctrine is not only grounded in § 1983, but also in the Constitution? Cf. Alden v. Maine, 527 U.S. 706, 119 S.Ct. 2240, 144 L.Ed.2d 636 (1999) (federal sovereign-immunity limitations, once thought to limit federal judicial power, also limit Congressional power over the states). Reconsider an issue raised in the Note following *Younger*: what is the source of "our federalism" as the concept is developed in *Younger*?

(b) *National Private Truck Council* concerns only the very narrow issue of restrictions on state tax collection. Although it was unanimously decided, is it not likely that a similar attempt to read the *Younger* doctrine into § 1983 would meet some serious opposition on the Court? Or is *Younger* an equally narrow exception to § 1983 since it involves only criminal prosecutions?

H. SUITS AGAINST GOVERNMENTS

1. LOCAL GOVERNMENTS

(a) Liability

Recall that in **Monell v. Department of Social Services of the City of New York**, Chapter 1A supra, the Supreme Court held that local governmental units were "persons" within the meaning of § 1983. At the same time, however, the Court held that municipal and county governments were not automatically responsible for every act committed by a governmental employee, rejecting liability based on the respondeat superior doctrine. As the Court noted, 436 U.S. at 694, 98 S.Ct. at 2038:

> "[A] local government may not be sued under § 1983 for an injury inflicted solely by its employees or agents. Instead, it is when execution of a government's policy or custom, whether made by its lawmakers or by those whose edicts or acts may fairly be said to represent official policy, inflicts the injury that the government as an entity is responsible under § 1983."

Post–*Monell* cases have been concerned, therefore, with the circumstances under which an employee's acts—in *Monell*'s words—"may fairly be said to represent official policy," either customary policy or written policy.

CITY OF LOS ANGELES v. HELLER

Supreme Court of the United States, 1986.
475 U.S. 796, 106 S.Ct. 1571, 89 L.Ed.2d 806.

PER CURIAM.

[Heller sued police officer Bushey and his employer, the City of Los Angeles and its Police Commission, under § 1983. The district court bifurcated the trial, first considering the claim against the individual officer. Only issues of liability were tried; Bushey presented no affirmative defense. After the jury returned a verdict for the officer, the district court dismissed plaintiff's *Monell*-based claim against the municipal defendants. The Ninth Circuit reversed, but defendants petitioned the Supreme Court for review by certiorari.]

[The municipal entities] were sued only because they were thought legally responsible for Bushey's actions; if the latter inflicted no constitutional injury on respondent, it is inconceivable that the [municipal entities] could be liable to respondent.

* * * [N]either Monell v. New York City Department of Social Services nor any other of our cases authorizes the award of damages against a municipal corporation based on the actions of one of its officers when in fact the jury has concluded that the officer inflicted no constitutional harm. If a person has suffered no constitutional injury at the hands of the individual police officer, the fact that the department regulations might have *authorized* the use of constitutionally excessive force is quite beside the point.

The petition for certiorari is granted, and the judgment of the Court of Appeals is reversed and the case remanded for further proceedings consistent with this opinion.

It is so ordered.

JUSTICE BRENNAN took no part in the consideration or decision of this case.

JUSTICE MARSHALL dissents from the summary [manner of] disposition * * *.

JUSTICE STEVENS, with whom JUSTICE MARSHALL joins, dissenting. [Omitted.]

NOTE ON THE DERIVATIVE AND NON-DERIVATIVE NATURE OF LOCAL GOVERNMENT LIABILITY

1. *Heller* emphasizes in its brief per curiam disposition two considerations that have pervasively influenced the area of local government liability under § 1983. First, *Heller* holds that there can be no municipal liability without individual liability, that is, municipal liability is derivative of the liability of an individual real person's § 1983 liability.

(a) Are not governments legal fictions as much as corporations? A "government" never handed out a parking ticket, beat a citizen, or levied a tax.

Instead, a real person hands out parking tickets in the name of "government," a real person beats a fellow citizen in the name of "government," and a group of real persons asks for money in the name of "government." Is *Heller* not correct in emphasizing that the collective can only be responsible when some real person acting for the collective has behaved unconstitutionally? (If you disagree with the majority, is it because you believe that the responsible real persons might be other persons than just Officer Bushey? See paragraph 2 infra.)

(b) Is there a substantive policy goal also served by *Heller*'s approach? Will the necessity of finding a real person to be a constitutional violator prevent jury sympathy for plaintiffs? Why? By preventing juries from tagging "deep pocket" municipalities with liability unless they are also willing to tag individuals? Later cases implicitly hold that a plaintiff need not name a real person as defendant in order to recover against the city; all he must do is show that an individual real person committed a violation for which the city is responsible. Does this undercut *Heller*'s assumed substantive policy goal?

(c) Although the local government's liability is derivative, are not the municipality and the individual officer's interests in real conflict, sufficient so as to require separate legal representation? An officer would want to avoid all liability, but if he fears a finding of liability, it would be in his interest to claim that he had acted pursuant to official policy, would it not? That would make the city co-liable, and against whom would an efficient plaintiff's attorney seek to collect her judgment? Would not a single attorney representing both defendants have a conflict of interest? See Dunton v. County of Suffolk, 729 F.2d 903 (2d Cir.1984).

(d) If a local government and an official are both held liable under § 1983, liability is ordinarily joint and several, as in ordinary torts. See, e.g., DiSorbo v. Hoy, 343 F.3d 172 (2d Cir. 2003). May a court apportion damages between individual and governmental defendants? Cf. Missouri v. Jenkins (*Jenkins III*), 495 U.S. 33, 110 S.Ct. 1651, 109 L.Ed.2d 31 (1990) (approving apportionment of costs of injunctive relief between governmental defendants).

2. *Heller* also accentuates the idea of causation—that for a local government to be liable to a plaintiff under § 1983, its policy must have caused the plaintiff's harm. Thus, where a city's policy may be unconstitutional but the defendant officer has not behaved unconstitutionally, the policy did not cause the plaintiff's harm.

(a) Is this aspect of *Heller* an implied holding on the plaintiff's standing, a holding similar to that in the Court's decisions in City of Los Angeles v. Lyons, Chapter 1F.2 supra, and Boyle v. Landry, Chapter 1G.4 supra? If the plaintiff has suffered no constitutionally proscribed harm, then he stands, with respect to any unconstitutional policy, as a normal unaffected citizen, does he not?

(b) If the officer in *Heller* had behaved unconstitutionally, but was excused from liability because of qualified immunity, could the city have still been held liable? Yes, if the city's policy were unconstitutional? Yes, provided the city itself has no immunity?

3. Consider the four possible relations between city policy (constitutional or unconstitutional) and an officer's actions (constitutional or unconstitutional), listed below.

	city policy	officer's actions
i.	constitutional	constitutional
ii.	unconstitutional	constitutional
iii.	constitutional	unconstitutional
iv.	unconstitutional	unconstitutional

(a) In which situations, according to *Heller*, would municipal liability be impossible? Does not *Heller* control two of the lines on this list because the Court did not care to hear if the city policy was itself constitutional or unconstitutional?

(b) On the list above, would there always be liability on line iv? No, because that would be respondeat superior liability? No, because it would still be necessary to show that the officer-defendant was actually following the policy? Could there ever be liability on line iii? Yes, because a constitutional policy (issuing guns to police) might cause unconstitutional acts (misuse of the guns)? Would that amount to respondeat superior liability? (These issues will be discussed again after reading the *Canton* and *Bryan* cases later in this sub-Chapter.)

(c) On those lines where responsibility is theoretically possible, would you still need to know if there were an actual causal relation between the city policy and the officer's actions? If a city had a policy of shooting all fleeing felons, but it was not known to many street-level officers, would the city be responsible for an officer who shot a fleeing felon without probable cause?

4. What does it really mean to hold a local government liable under § 1983? What does it mean to have the "deep pocket" of the city pay a judgment? Who really pays such judgments? Should *Monell*'s liability rules be made with taxpayer responsibility in mind? What rules would force taxpayers to elect, or re-elect, only persons who observe constitutional rights? Should there be no local government liability in situations where taxpayers were in no position to prevent their leaders from misbehaving? Would that result in municipal liability only for unconstitutional actions by city lawmakers?

5. Despite *Heller*'s holding, later cases suggest that municipal liability is non-derivative in another sense: it cannot be based on respondeat superior, *Monell*, Chapter 1A supra, and therefore a "local governments are responsible only for their own illegal acts," Connick v. Thompson, ___ U.S. ___, 131 S.Ct. 1350, 179 L.Ed.2d 417 (2011). The suggestion is that the municipal government can only be held liable in circumstances where its authorized decision-makers have made it liable. Who are these people who *are* the city? In particular, focus on two major discrete attributional considerations. (At the

close of this section you will have the opportunity to decide whether these two considerations may be merged together to present a single unified theory of local government liability—or indeed whether there is not a third possible theory.)

(a) *Attribution Line #1.* First, what real persons may be deemed to be the city whenever they act to make policy? *Monell* held, for example, that New York City's regulation-writers make city policy, and most cases assume that local government legislators are policy-makers when they pass ordinances. See, e.g., Owen v. City of Independence, 445 U.S. 622, 100 S.Ct. 1398, 63 L.Ed.2d 673 (1980) (city council resolution). In these circumstances, the lawmakers are the "government," or their actions may be fairly attributable to the "government." What other persons exercise such power that they are city policymakers? (Does every decision by such a person make "policy"? Or are there ad hoc "non-policy" decisions that do not give rise to local government liability even when made by a city leader?)

(b) *Attribution Line #2.* Second, for those persons who are not at the policymaking level, under what circumstances might their acts be attributed to higher-up persons, persons who are deemed municipal policymakers (under the first consideration above)? *Monell* holds that respondeat superior doctrines cannot be read into § 1983, so that mere employment of a low-level officer does not make his policymaking superior (and thus the city) liable for the employee's misconduct. What kind of linkage must there be between the supervisor and the underling to support attribution of the underling's acts to the superior? See City of Oklahoma City v. Tuttle, infra.

PEMBAUR v. CITY OF CINCINNATI

Supreme Court of the United States, 1986.
475 U.S. 469, 106 S.Ct. 1292, 89 L.Ed.2d 452.

JUSTICE BRENNAN delivered the opinion of the Court, except as to Part II–B.

In Monell v. New York City Dept. of Social Services, the Court concluded that municipal liability under 42 U.S.C. § 1983 is limited to deprivations of federally protected rights caused by action taken "pursuant to official municipal policy of some nature...." The question presented is whether, and in what circumstances, a decision by municipal policymakers on a single occasion may satisfy this requirement.

I

Bertold Pembaur is a licensed Ohio physician and the sole proprietor of the Rockdale Medical Center, located in the city of Cincinnati in Hamilton County. Most of Pembaur's patients are welfare recipients who rely on government assistance to pay for medical care. During the spring of 1977, Simon Leis, the Hamilton County Prosecutor, began investigating charges that Pembaur fraudulently had accepted payments from state welfare agencies for services not actually provided to patients. A grand jury was convened, and the case was assigned to Assistant Prosecutor

William Whalen. In April, the grand jury charged Pembaur in a six-count indictment.

During the investigation, the grand jury issued subpoenas for the appearance of two of Pembaur's employees. When these employees failed to appear as directed, the prosecutor obtained capiases for their arrest and detention from the Court of Common Pleas of Hamilton County.[7] [When county sheriffs sought to enter a private part of Dr. Pembaur's clinic in order to find the two employees and take them into custody, the doctor blocked their way. The officers sought advice from prosecutor Whalen, who at the direction of the County Prosecutor Leis, instructed them to enter by force, saying "Go in and get them." Claiming that the entry was unconstitutional, Pembaur later filed this suit against several city and county officers and the governments themselves. By an odd coincidence, on the day following filing of Pembaur's case, the Supreme Court ruled that the Fourth Amendment bars such searches of a person's home or office, absent a warrant, even when the entry is to execute an arrest warrant for a third person. See Steagald v. United States, 451 U.S. 204, 101 S.Ct. 1642, 68 L.Ed.2d 38 (1981).]

Much of the testimony at the four-day trial concerned the practices of the Hamilton County police in serving capiases. Frank Webb, one of the Deputy Sheriffs present at the clinic on May 19, testified that he had previously served capiases on the property of third persons without a search warrant, but had never been required to use force to gain access. Assistant Prosecutor Whalen was also unaware of a prior instance in which police had been denied access to a third person's property in serving a capias and had used force to gain entry. Lincoln Stokes, the County Sheriff, testified that the Department had no written policy respecting the serving of capiases on the property of third persons and that the proper response in any given situation would depend upon the circumstances. He too could not recall a specific instance in which entrance had been denied and forcibly gained. Sheriff Stokes did testify, however, that it was the practice in his Department to refer questions to the County Prosecutor[8] for instructions under appropriate circumstances and that "it was the proper thing to do" in this case. The District Court awarded judgment to the defendants and dismissed the complaint in its entirety. [It reasoned that the individual defendants were entitled to qualified immunity because the law was unsettled at the time of the search. It held the governments free of liability because in its view the officers had not acted pursuant to "official policy." The Court of Appeals affirmed with respect to the individual defendants and split on the governments, reinstating the claim

---

7. A capias is a writ of attachment commanding a county official to bring a subpoenaed witness who has failed to appear before the court to testify and to answer for civil contempt. See Ohio Rev.Code Ann. § 2317.21 (1981).

8. Hamilton County Prosecutor Leis was not made a defendant because counsel for petitioner believed that Leis was absolutely immune. We express no view as to the correctness of this evaluation. Cf. Imbler v. Pachtman (leaving open the question of a prosecutor's immunity when he acts "in the role of an administrator or investigative officer rather than that of an advocate"). [Repositioned footnote.]

against the city but not the county. Pembaur sought review of the dismissal of the county.]

II

A

Our analysis must begin with the proposition that "Congress did not intend municipalities to be held liable unless action pursuant to official municipal policy of some nature caused a constitutional tort." Monell v. New York City Dept. of Social Services. As we read its opinion, the Court of Appeals held that a single decision to take particular action, although made by municipal policymakers, cannot establish the kind of "official policy" required by *Monell* as a predicate to municipal liability under § 1983.[6] * * * [E]xamination of the opinion in *Monell* clearly demonstrates that the Court of Appeals misinterpreted its holding.

Monell is a case about responsibility. In the first part of the opinion, we held that local government units could be made liable under § 1983 for deprivations of federal rights, overruling a contrary holding in Monroe v. Pape. In the second part of the opinion, we recognized a limitation on this liability and concluded that a municipality cannot be made liable by application of the doctrine of respondeat superior. In part, this conclusion rested upon the language of § 1983, which imposes liability only on a person who "subjects, or causes to be subjected" any individual to a deprivation of federal rights; we noted that this language "cannot easily be read to impose liability vicariously on government bodies solely on the basis of the existence of an employer-employee relationship with a tortfeasor." Primarily, however, our conclusion rested upon the legislative history, which disclosed that, while Congress never questioned its power to impose civil liability on municipalities for their own illegal acts, Congress did doubt its constitutional power to impose such liability in order to oblige municipalities to control the conduct of others. We found that, because of these doubts, Congress chose not to create such obligations in § 1983. Recognizing that this would be the effect of a federal law of respondeat superior, we concluded that § 1983 could not be interpreted to incorporate doctrines of vicarious liability.

The conclusion that tortious conduct, to be the basis for municipal liability under § 1983, must be pursuant to a municipality's "official policy" is contained in this discussion. The "official policy" requirement was intended to distinguish acts of the municipality from acts of employees of the municipality, and thereby make clear that municipal liability is

---

6. The opinion below also can be read as holding that municipal liability cannot be imposed for a single incident of unconstitutional conduct by municipal employees whether or not that conduct is pursuant to municipal policy. Such a conclusion is unsupported by either the language or reasoning of *Monell*, or by any of our subsequent decisions. As we explained last Term in Oklahoma City v. Tuttle, [which follows], once a municipal policy is established, "it requires only one application ... to satisfy fully *Monell*'s requirement that a municipal corporation be held liable only for constitutional violations resulting from the municipality's official policy." The only issue before us, then, is whether petitioner satisfied *Monell*'s requirement that the tortious conduct be pursuant to "official municipal policy."

limited to action for which the municipality is actually responsible. *Monell* reasoned that recovery from a municipality is limited to acts that are, properly speaking, acts "of the municipality"—that is, acts which the municipality has officially sanctioned or ordered.

With this understanding, it is plain that municipal liability may be imposed for a single decision by municipal policymakers under appropriate circumstances. No one has ever doubted, for instance, that a municipality may be liable under § 1983 for a single decision by its properly constituted legislative body—whether or not that body had taken similar action in the past or intended to do so in the future—because even a single decision by such a body unquestionably constitutes an act of official government policy. See, e.g., Owen v. City of Independence, 445 U.S. 622, 100 S.Ct. 1398, 63 L.Ed.2d 673 (1980) (city council passed resolution firing plaintiff without a pretermination hearing); Newport v. Fact Concerts, Inc., 453 U.S. 247, 101 S.Ct. 2748, 69 L.Ed.2d 616 (1981) (city council canceled license permitting concert because of dispute over content of performance). But the power to establish policy is no more the exclusive province of the legislature at the local level than at the state or national level. *Monell*'s language makes clear that it expressly envisioned other officials "whose acts or edicts may fairly be said to represent official policy," and whose decisions therefore may give rise to municipal liability under § 1983.

Indeed, any other conclusion would be inconsistent with the principles underlying § 1983. To be sure, "official policy" often refers to formal rules or understandings—often but not always committed to writing—that are intended to, and do, establish fixed plans of action to be followed under similar circumstances consistently and over time. That was the case in *Monell* itself, which involved a written rule requiring pregnant employees to take unpaid leaves of absence before such leaves were medically necessary. However, as in *Owen* and *Newport,* a government frequently chooses a course of action tailored to a particular situation and not intended to control decisions in later situations. If the decision to adopt that particular course of action is properly made by that government's authorized decisionmakers, it surely represents an act of official government "policy" as that term is commonly understood. More importantly, where action is directed by those who establish governmental policy, the municipality is equally responsible whether that action is to be taken only once or to be taken repeatedly. To deny compensation to the victim would therefore be contrary to the fundamental purpose of § 1983.

B

Having said this much, we hasten to emphasize that not every decision by municipal officers automatically subjects the municipality to § 1983 liability. Municipal liability attaches only where the decisionmaker possesses final authority to establish municipal policy with respect to the action ordered.[10] The fact that a particular official—even a policymaking official—has discretion in the exercise of particular functions does not, without more, give rise to municipal liability based on an exercise of that discretion. The official must also be responsible for establishing final government policy respecting such activity before the municipality can be held liable.[12] Authority to make municipal policy may be granted directly by a legislative enactment or may be delegated by an official who possesses such authority, and of course, whether an official had final policymaking authority is a question of state law. However, like other governmental entities, municipalities often spread policymaking authority among various officers and official bodies. As a result, particular officers may have authority to establish binding county policy respecting particular matters and to adjust that policy for the county in changing circumstances. To hold a municipality liable for actions ordered by such officers exercising their policymaking authority is no more an application of the theory of respondeat superior than was holding the municipalities liable for the decisions of the city councils in *Owen* and *Newport.* In each case municipal liability attached to a single decision to take unlawful action made by municipal policymakers. We hold that municipal liability under § 1983 attaches where—and only where—a deliberate choice to follow a course of action is made from among various alternatives by the official or officials responsible for establishing final policy with respect to the subject matter in question.

C

Applying this standard to the case before us, we have little difficulty concluding that the Court of Appeals erred in dismissing petitioner's claim against the county. The Deputy Sheriffs who attempted to serve the capiases at petitioner's clinic found themselves in a difficult situation. Unsure of the proper course of action to follow, they sought instructions from their supervisors. The instructions they received were to follow the orders of the County Prosecutor. The Prosecutor made a considered decision based on his understanding of the law and commanded the

---

10. Section 1983 also refers to deprivations under color of a state "custom or usage," and the Court in *Monell* noted accordingly that "local governments, like every other § 1983 'person,' . . . may be sued for constitutional deprivations visited pursuant to governmental 'custom' even though such a custom has not received formal approval through the body's official decisionmaking channels." A § 1983 plaintiff thus may be able to recover from a municipality without adducing evidence of an affirmative decision by policymakers if able to prove that the challenged action was pursuant to a state "custom or usage." Because there is no allegation that the action challenged here was pursuant to a local "custom," this aspect of *Monell* is not at issue in this case.

12. Thus, for example, the County Sheriff may have discretion to hire and fire employees without also being the county official responsible for establishing county employment policy. If this were the case, the Sheriff's decisions respecting employment would not give rise to municipal liability, although similar decisions with respect to law enforcement practices, over which the Sheriff is the official policymaker, would give rise to municipal liability. Instead, if county employment policy was set by the Board of County Commissioners, only that body's decisions would provide a basis for county liability. This would be true even if the Board left the Sheriff discretion to hire and fire employees and the Sheriff exercised that discretion in an unconstitutional manner; the decision to act unlawfully would not be a decision of the Board. However, if the Board delegated its power to establish final employment policy to the Sheriff, the Sheriff's decisions would represent county policy and could give rise to municipal liability.

officers forcibly to enter petitioner's clinic. That decision directly caused the violation of petitioner's Fourth Amendment rights.

Respondent argues that the County Prosecutor lacked authority to establish municipal policy respecting law enforcement practices because only the County Sheriff may establish policy respecting such practices. Respondent suggests that the County Prosecutor was merely rendering "legal advice" when he ordered the Deputy Sheriffs to "go in and get" the witnesses. Consequently, the argument concludes, the action of the individual Deputy Sheriffs in following this advice and forcibly entering petitioner's clinic was not pursuant to a properly established municipal policy.

We might be inclined to agree with respondent if we thought that the Prosecutor had only rendered "legal advice." However, the Court of Appeals concluded, based upon its examination of Ohio law, that both the County Sheriff and the County Prosecutor could establish county policy under appropriate circumstances, a conclusion that we do not question here. * * * The Sheriff testified that his Department followed this practice under appropriate circumstances and that it was "the proper thing to do" in this case. We decline to accept respondent's invitation to overlook this delegation of authority by disingenuously labeling the Prosecutor's clear command mere "legal advice." In ordering the Deputy Sheriffs to enter petitioner's clinic the County Prosecutor was acting as the final decisionmaker for the county, and the county may therefore be held liable under § 1983.

The decision of the Court of Appeals is reversed, and the case is remanded for further proceedings consistent with this opinion.

It is so ordered.

JUSTICE WHITE, concurring.

The forcible entry made in this case was not then illegal under federal, state, or local law. The City of Cincinnati frankly conceded that forcible entry of third-party property to effect otherwise valid arrests was standard operating procedure. * * * Vesting discretion in its officers to use force and its use in this case sufficiently manifested county policy to warrant reversal of the judgment below.

This does not mean that every act of municipal officers with final authority to effect or authorize arrests and searches represents the policy of the municipality. It would be different if Steagald v. United States had been decided when the events at issue here occurred, if the state constitution or statutes had forbade forceful entries without a warrant, or if there had been a municipal ordinance to this effect. Local law enforcement officers are expected to obey the law and ordinarily swear to do so when they take office. Where the controlling law places limits on their authority, they cannot be said to have the authority to make contrary policy. Had the sheriff or prosecutor in this case failed to follow an existing warrant requirement, it would be absurd to say that he was nevertheless executing county policy in authorizing the forceful entry in this case and even stranger to say that the county would be liable if the sheriff had secured a warrant and it turned out that he and the magistrate had mistakenly thought there was probable cause for the warrant. If deliberate or mistaken acts like this, admittedly contrary to local law, expose the county to liability, it must be on the basis of respondeat superior and not because the officers' acts represents local policy.

Such results would not conform to *Monell* and the cases following it. I do not understand the Court to hold otherwise * * *.

JUSTICE STEVENS, concurring in part and concurring in the judgment.

[The Court struggles to define the word "policy," but that word does not appear in the text of § 1983. In my view of § 1983,] both the broad remedial purpose of the statute and the fact that it embodied contemporaneous common law doctrine, including respondeat superior, require a conclusion that Congress intended that a governmental entity be liable for the constitutional deprivations committed by its agents in the course of their duties.[4]

[If we are free to look at policy concerns, they also support reading § 1983 to adopt respondeat superior liability.] Although I recognize that the County may provide insurance protection for its agents, I believe that the primary party against whom the judgment should run is the County itself. The County has the resources and the authority that can best avoid future constitutional violations and provide a fair remedy for those that have occurred in the past. Thus, even if "public policy" concerns should inform the construction of § 1983, those considerations, like the statute's remedial purpose and common law background, support a conclusion of County liability for the unconstitutional, axe-swinging entry in this case.

Because I believe that Parts I, II–A, and II–C are consistent with the purpose and policy of § 1983, as well as with our precedents, I join those parts of the Court's opinion and concur in the judgment.

JUSTICE O'CONNOR, concurring in part and concurring in the judgment.

For the reasons stated by Justice White, I agree that the municipal officers here were acting as policy makers within the meaning of Monell v. New York City Dept. of Social Services. * * *

Because, however, I believe that the reasoning of the majority goes beyond that necessary to decide the case, and because I fear that the standard the majority articulates may be misread to expose municipalities

---

4. Several commentators have concluded that the dicta in Monell v. New York City Dept. of Social Services regarding respondeat superior misreads the legislative history of § 1983. See, e.g., Blum, *From* Monroe *to* Monell: *Defining the Scope of Municipal Liability in Federal Courts*, 51 TEMP. L.Q. 409, 413, n. 15 (1978) ("The interpretation adopted by the Court with respect to the rejection of vicarious liability under § 1983 had been espoused prior to *Monell* by one author who drew a distinction between 'political' § 1983 cases, in which a city itself causes the constitutional violation, and 'constitutional tort' § 1983 cases, in which an attempt is made to impose vicarious liability on the city for the misconduct of its employees.... Although this view of § 1983 may represent a sensitive response to the fiscal plight of municipal corporations today, it should not be acknowledged as a legitimate interpretation of congressional intent in 1871").

to liability beyond that envisioned by the Court in *Monell*, I join only parts I and IIA of the Court's opinion and the judgment.

JUSTICE POWELL, with whom THE CHIEF JUSTICE and JUSTICE REHNQUIST join, dissenting.

*   *   *

* * * [The majority's] reasoning is circular: it contends that policy is what policymakers make, and policymakers are those who have authority to make policy.

* * * Thus, the Court's test for determining the existence of policy focuses only on whether a decision was made "by the official or officials responsible for establishing final policy with respect to the subject matter in question." In my view, the question whether official policy—in any normal sense of the term—has been made in a particular case is not answered by explaining who has final authority to make policy. The question here is not "could the county prosecutor make policy?" but rather, "did he make policy?" By focusing on the authority granted to the official under state law, the Court's test fails to answer the key federal question presented. The Court instead turns the question into one of state law. Under a test that focuses on the authority of the decisionmaker, the Court has only to look to state law for the resolution of this case. * * * Apparently that recitation of authority is all that is needed under the Court's test because no discussion is offered to demonstrate that the Sheriff or the Prosecutor actually used that authority to establish official county policy in this case.

Moreover, the Court's reasoning is inconsistent with *Monell*. Today's decision finds that policy is established because a policymaking official made a decision on the telephone that was within the scope of his authority. The Court ignores the fact that no business organization or governmental unit makes binding policy decisions so cavalierly. The Court provides no mechanism for distinguishing those acts or decisions that cannot fairly be construed to create official policy from the normal process of establishing an official policy that would be followed by a responsible public entity. Thus, the Court has adopted in part what it rejected in *Monell*: local government units are now subject to respondeat superior liability, at least with respect to a certain category of employees, i.e., those with final authority to make policy. * * *

In my view, proper resolution of the question whether official policy has been formed should focus on two factors: (i) the nature of the decision reached or the action taken, and (ii) the process by which the decision was reached or the action was taken.

Focusing on the nature of the decision distinguishes between policies and mere ad hoc decisions. Such a focus also reflects the fact that most policies embody a rule of general applicability. That is the tenor of the Court's statement in *Monell* that local government units are liable under § 1983 when the action that is alleged to be unconstitutional "implements or executes a policy statement, ordinance, regulation, or decision officially adopted and promulgated by that body's officers." The clear implication is that policy is created when a rule is formed that applies to all similar situations—a "governing principle [or] plan." Webster's New Twentieth Century Dictionary 1392 (2d ed. 1979).[6] When a rule of general applicability has been approved, the government has taken a position for which it can be held responsible.

Another factor indicating that policy has been formed is the process by which the decision at issue was reached. Formal procedures that involve, for example, voting by elected officials, prepared reports, extended deliberation or official records indicate that the resulting decisions taken "may fairly be said to represent official policy." * * *

Applying these factors to the instant case demonstrates that no official policy was formulated. * * * The Court's result today rests on the implicit conclusion that the Prosecutor's response—"go in and get them"—altered the prior case-by-case approach of the Department and formed a new rule to apply in all similar cases. Nothing about the Prosecutor's response to the inquiry over the phone, nor the circumstances surrounding the response, indicates that such a rule of general applicability was formed.

Similarly, nothing about the way the decision was reached indicates that official policy was formed. The prosecutor, without time for thoughtful consideration or consultation, simply gave an off-the-cuff answer to a single question. There was no process at all. The Court's holding undercuts the basic rationale of *Monell,* and unfairly increases the risk of liability on the level of government least able to bear it. I dissent.

NOTE ON GOVERNMENTAL RESPONSIBILITY FOR "POLICYMAKERS"

1. The Justices appear to agree that some set of persons beyond city council members can make policy for which a city would be responsible. Who are such persons?

(a) Note the curious lineup of votes in this case. A majority of Justices agrees in part II–C that Justice Brennan has correctly applied the test articulated in part II–B, but a majority does not actually agree to the test. Why did Justice Brennan lose Justices White and O'Connor?

(b) Is the test proposed in part II(B) a good one? Apparently in order to meet the test, an official must be (i) a final decisionmaker (ii) on the topic for which he acted. Is this test as easily applied as it appears? Consider footnote 12. Is it lucid enough to persuade you? See Williams v. Butler, 863 F.2d 1398 (8th Cir.1988) (en banc) (considering whether particular city judge has final authority over personnel decision involving court clerk).

2. A majority agrees in *Pembaur* that state law will supply the basis for determining who is a final decisionmaker. That decision was reconfirmed in

---

6. The focus on a rule of general applicability does not mean that more than one instance of its application is required. The local government unit may be liable for the first application of a duly constituted unconstitutional policy.

City of St. Louis v. Praprotnik, 485 U.S. 112, 108 S.Ct. 915, 99 L.Ed.2d 107 (1988). But the Court has shown some division over the issue raised in Justice Brennan's footnote 10 in *Pembaur*. To what extent can a plaintiff look behind state law to show that a particular officer was "the real decisionmaker" whose judgments should bind the city? Writing for four Justices in *Praprotnik,* Justice O'Connor explained the disagreement between herself and Justice Brennan, 485 U.S. at 125 n. 1, 108 S.Ct. at 925 n. 1:

"Unlike Justice Brennan, we would not replace [the state law] standard with a new approach in which state law becomes merely 'an appropriate starting point' for an 'assessment of a municipality's actual power structure,' [citing Brennan's opinion for three justices]. Municipalities cannot be expected to predict how courts or juries will assess their 'actual power structures,' and this uncertainty could easily lead to results that would be hard in practice to distinguish from the results of a regime governed by the doctrine of respondeat superior. It is one thing to charge a municipality with responsibility for the decisions of officials invested by law, or by a 'custom or usage' having the force of law, with policymaking authority. It would be something else, and something inevitably more capricious, to hold a municipality responsible for every decision that is perceived as 'final' through the lens of a particular factfinder's evaluation of the city's 'actual power structure.' "

(a) Is Justice O'Connor's approach too formalistic? Does Justice Brennan leave the city in peril as O'Connor charges? See Ware v. Unified Sch. Dist. No. 492, 902 F.2d 815, 818 (10th Cir.1990).

(b) Is O'Connor's own standard too imprecise? Note that while she refers first to written law, she also states that policy may be made "by a 'custom or usage' having the force of law." Does that not allow a plaintiff to go beyond written law? See Watson v. City of Kansas City, Kansas, 857 F.2d 690 (10th Cir.1988) (alleged custom of police not protecting against domestic violence).

(c) Is the adoption of state law, as either dispositive or as a starting point, for identifying policymakers a mistake? In *Praprotnik,* Justice O'Connor states that "we can be confident that state law (which may include valid local ordinances and regulations) will always direct a court to some official or body that has the responsibility for making law or setting policy in any given area of a local government's business," 485 U.S. at 125, 108 S.Ct. at 925. Is this true? Do municipalities create their power structures with clarity in anticipation of future § 1983 litigation? Or do they write ambiguous charters so as to diffuse governmental power?

(d) Is the question of final authority under state law a one of fact for the jury or one of law for the judge? See Jett v. Dallas Independent Sch. Dist., 491 U.S. 701, 109 S.Ct. 2702, 105 L.Ed.2d 598 (1989). If it is one of law when reference is made to written materials, is it also one of law when the allegation is that the policy is based on "custom or usage"? And the follow-up question, whether the identified officials actually made the decision that caused plaintiff's constitutional harm, is that a question of law or fact? See Mandel v. Doe, 888 F.2d 783 (11th Cir.1989).

3. Justices White and O'Connor added important caveats in *Pembaur* when they wrote that even a final policymaker's decision would not create

local government liability if the official violated local law, in effect acting outside the scope of his authority. See Carrero v. New York City Housing Auth., 890 F.2d 569, 576–77 (2d Cir.1989) (city not responsible for supervisor's sexual harassment where city had specific policy against sex discrimination).

(a) Is this approach consistent with the Court's ruling on action "under color of" law in Monroe v. Pape? *Monroe*'s ruling allows for the creation of individual liability for defendant officers who exceed or abuse their lawful authority. Under White's approach, the city itself could not be liable, at least not if it had a law specifically forbidding the abusive acts of the officer. Is this a good policy result? Would a wise city council simply adopt the following ordinance: "It is a violation of the policy of this city for any official to act in violation of the Constitution"?

(b) How do White and O'Connor conceive of municipal liability? Do they consider the issue solely one of remedy following a finding of a constitutional violation? Or are they asking over again the liability question, this time focusing on whether the city has sanctioned a constitutional violation? If the latter, do you agree that this is the preferred approach? See Schuck, *Municipal Liability Under Section 1983: Some Lessons from Tort Law and Organization Theory*, 77 GEO. L. J. 1753 (1989).

(c) Is Justice Stevens correct that the Court seriously distorted municipal liability by introducing the concept of official "policy"? See Schuck, supra, at 1772–79 (criticizing Court's focus on "policy"); Kramer and Sykes, *Municipal Liability Under Section 1983: A Legal and Economic Analysis*, 1987 SUP.CT. REV. 249, 287 (arguing in favor of strict liability for employees' acts).

4. In its later decision in **Bryan County v. Brown**, 520 U.S. 397, 117 S.Ct. 1382, 137 L.Ed.2d 626 (1997), the Court referred to *Pembaur* as an "easy case" because the policymaker himself had committed a constitutional violation when he authorized the search in question. Thus, "[no] questions of fault or causation arose." *Bryan County* involved a sheriff's nepotistic decision to hire a relative with a background of violent conduct; the relative later severely injured a motorist through use of excessive force. Although the sheriff was admittedly a policymaker, the Court overturned a jury's verdict finding the county liable for his single hiring decision. In her majority opinion, Justice O'Connor first noted that the hiring decision was not itself unconstitutional, and then she added, 520 U.S. at 406–12, 117 S.Ct. at 1389–92:

"Claims not involving an allegation that the municipal action itself violated federal law, or directed or authorized the deprivation of federal rights, present much more difficult problems of proof. That a plaintiff has suffered a deprivation of federal rights at the hands of a municipal employee will not alone permit an inference of municipal culpability and causation; the plaintiff will simply have shown that the *employee* acted culpably. . . .

* * * "Where a claim of municipal liability rests on a single decision, not itself representing a violation of federal law and not directing such a violation, the danger that a municipality will be held liable without fault is high. Because the decision necessarily governs a single case, there can

be no notice to the municipal decisionmaker, based on previous violations of federally protected rights, that his approach is inadequate. Nor will it be readily apparent that the municipality's action caused the injury in question, because the plaintiff can point to no other incident tending to make it more likely that the plaintiff's own injury flows from the municipality's action, rather than from some other intervening cause.

* * *

"As discussed above, a finding of culpability simply cannot depend on the mere probability that any officer inadequately screened will inflict any constitutional injury. Rather, it must depend on a finding that *this* officer was highly likely to inflict the *particular* injury suffered by the plaintiff. The connection between the background of the particular applicant and the specific constitutional violation alleged must be strong. . . ."

(a) *Bryan County* distinguishes between single acts of a policymaker in two contexts—where his own decision is unconstitutional and where his own decision is constitutional. Why is municipal liability easy to find in the latter context? Because the underling who enforces a policy is unimportant—the policymaker himself committed the constitutional violation?

(b) Does *Bryan County* imply that a local government could be held responsible for a policymaker's acts—even if they were constitutional—where there were multiple unconstitutional enforcement decisions by underlings? As you review the following case, try to formulate a guideline to distinguish those circumstances in which a policymaker has himself acted and those in which an underling has acted.

CITY OF OKLAHOMA CITY v. TUTTLE

Supreme Court of the United States, 1985.
471 U.S. 808, 105 S.Ct. 2427, 85 L.Ed.2d 791.

JUSTICE REHNQUIST announced the judgment of the Court, and delivered the opinion of the Court with respect to Part II, and an opinion with respect to Part III, in which THE CHIEF JUSTICE, JUSTICE WHITE, and JUSTICE O'CONNOR joined.

* * *

On October 4, 1980, Officer Julian Rotramel, a member of the Oklahoma City police force, shot and killed Albert Tuttle outside the We'll Do Club, a bar in Oklahoma City. Officer Rotramel, who had been on the force for 10 months, had responded to an all-points bulletin indicating that there was a robbery in progress at the Club. [While inside the club, Rotramel had detained Tuttle as a suspect; when Tuttle escaped Rotramel's grasp and ran outside, the officer chased him and upon finding him in a crouched position with hands near his boots, shot him.]

Respondent Rose Marie Tuttle is Albert Tuttle's widow, and the administratrix of his estate. She brought suit under § 1983 in the United States District Court, Western District of Oklahoma, against Rotramel and the city, alleging that their actions had deprived Tuttle of certain of his constitutional rights. [At the trial there was no evidence that Rotramel or another officer had ever been involved in a similar incident. Plaintiff] sought to hold the city liable under *Monell,* presumably on the theory that a municipal "custom or policy" had led to the constitutional violations. With respect to municipal liability the trial judge instructed the jury:

* * *

"Absent more evidence of supervisory indifference, such as acquiescence in a prior matter of conduct, official policy such as to impose liability ... under the federal Civil Rights Act cannot ordinarily be inferred from a single incident of illegality such as a first excessive use of force to stop a suspect; *but a single, unusually excessive use of force may be sufficiently out of the ordinary to warrant an inference that it was attributable to inadequate training or supervision amounting to 'deliberate indifference' or 'gross negligence' on the part of the officials in charge.* The city cannot be held liable for simple negligence. Furthermore, the plaintiff must show a causal link between the police misconduct and the adoption of a policy or plan by the defendant municipality." App. 42–44 (Emphasis supplied.)

[Based on this instruction the jury returned a verdict against the city for $1,500,000 in damages, which was affirmed on appeal over the city objection to the instruction. The Supreme Court agreed to review the instruction.]

* * *

By its terms, of course, [§ 1983] creates no substantive rights; it merely provides remedies for deprivations of rights established elsewhere. Here respondent's claim is that her husband was deprived of his life "without due process of law," in violation of the Fourteenth Amendment, or that he was deprived of his right to be free from the use of "excessive force in his apprehension"—presumably a right secured by the Fourth and Fourteenth Amendments. Having established a deprivation, however, respondent still must establish that the city was the "person" who "cause[d] [Tuttle] to be subjected" to the deprivation. * * *

* * *

* * * [T]he instruction given by the District Court allowed the jury to impose liability on the basis of such a single incident without the benefit of the additional evidence. The trial court stated that the jury could "infer," from "a single, unusually excessive use of force ... that it was attributable to inadequate training or supervision amounting to 'deliberate indifference' or 'gross negligence' on the part of the officials in charge."

We think this inference unwarranted; * * * the inference allows a § 1983 plaintiff to establish municipal liability without submitting proof of a single action taken by a municipal policymaker.

* * *

[There is a] wide difference between the municipal "policy" at issue in *Monell* and the "policy" alleged here. The "policy" of the New York City Department of Social Services that was challenged in *Monell* was a policy that by its terms compelled pregnant employees to take mandatory leaves of absence before such leaves were required for medical reasons; this policy in and of itself violated the constitutional rights of pregnant employees by reason of our decision in Cleveland Board of Education v. LaFleur, 414 U.S. 632, 94 S.Ct. 791, 39 L.Ed.2d 52 (1974). Obviously, it requires only one application of a policy such as this to satisfy fully *Monell's* requirement that a municipal corporation be held liable only for constitutional violations resulting from the municipality's official policy.

Here, however, the "policy" that respondent seeks to rely upon is far more nebulous, and a good deal further removed from the constitutional violation, than was the policy in *Monell*. To establish the constitutional violation in *Monell* no evidence was needed other than a statement of the policy by the municipal corporation, and its exercise; but the type of "policy" upon which respondent relies, and its causal relation to the alleged constitutional violation, are not susceptible to such easy proof. In the first place, the word "policy" generally implies a course of action consciously chosen from among various alternatives; it is therefore difficult in one sense even to accept the submission that someone pursues a "policy" of "inadequate training," unless evidence be adduced which proves that the inadequacies resulted from conscious choice—that is, proof that the policymakers deliberately chose a training program which would prove inadequate. And in the second place, some limitation must be placed on establishing municipal liability through policies that are not themselves unconstitutional, or the test set out in *Monell* will become a dead letter. Obviously, if one retreats far enough from a constitutional violation some municipal "policy" can be identified behind almost any such harm inflicted by a municipal official; for example, Rotramel would never have killed Tuttle if Oklahoma City did not have a "policy" of establishing a police force. But *Monell* must be taken to require proof of a city policy different in kind from this latter example before a claim can be sent to a jury on the theory that a particular violation was "caused" by the municipal "policy." At the very least there must be an affirmative link between the policy and the particular constitutional violation alleged.

Here the instructions allowed the jury to infer a thoroughly nebulous "policy" of "inadequate training" on the part of the municipal corporation from the single incident described earlier in this opinion, and at the same time sanctioned the inference that the "policy" was the cause of the incident. Such an approach provides a means for circumventing *Monell's* limitations altogether. Proof of a single incident of unconstitutional activity is not sufficient to impose liability under *Monell,* unless proof of the incident includes proof that it was caused by an existing, unconstitutional municipal policy, which policy can be attributed to a municipal policymaker. Otherwise the existence of the unconstitutional policy, and its origin, must be separately proved. But where the policy relied upon is not itself unconstitutional, considerably more proof than the single incident will be necessary in every case to establish both the requisite fault on the part of the municipality, and the causal connection between the "policy" and the constitutional deprivation. Under the charge upheld by the Court of Appeals the jury could properly have imposed liability on the city based solely upon proof that it employed a nonpolicymaking officer who violated the Constitution. The decision of the Court of Appeals is accordingly

Reversed.

JUSTICE POWELL took no part in the decision of this case.

JUSTICE BRENNAN, with whom JUSTICE MARSHALL and JUSTICE BLACKMUN join, concurring in part and concurring in the judgment.

* * *

A single police officer may grossly, outrageously, and recklessly misbehave in the course of a single incident. Such misbehavior may in a given case be fairly attributable to various municipal policies or customs, either those that authorized the police officer so to act or those that did not authorize but nonetheless were the "moving force," Polk County v. Dodson, 454 U.S. 312, 326, 102 S.Ct. 445, 454, 70 L.Ed.2d 509 (1981), or cause of the violation. In such a case, the city would be at fault for the constitutional violation. Yet it is equally likely that the misbehavior was attributable to numerous other factors for which the city may not be responsible; the police officer's own unbalanced mental state is the most obvious example. Cf. Brandon v. Holt, 469 U.S. 464, 466, 105 S.Ct. 873, 875, 83 L.Ed.2d 878 (1985). In such a case, the city itself may well not bear any part of the fault for the incident; there may have been nothing that the city could have done to avoid it. Thus, without some evidence of municipal policy or custom independent of the police officer's misconduct, there is no way of knowing whether the city is at fault. To infer the existence of a city policy from the isolated misconduct of a single, low-level officer, and then to hold the city liable on the basis of that policy, would amount to permitting precisely the theory of strict *respondeat superior* liability rejected in *Monell.*

JUSTICE STEVENS, dissenting.

[Justice Stevens' review of the legislative history, which he contended adopt common law rules of respondeat superior liability, is omitted.]

NOTE ON GOVERNMENTAL RESPONSIBILITY FOR THE ACTIONS OF NON-POLICYMAKING OFFICERS

1.   Justice Rehnquist concedes that when policymakers write laws, that single act may be enough to establish a city's liability for an officer's implementation of the law. But when non-policymakers' actions are at issue, says the plurality in *Tuttle,* the plaintiff can only prove municipal liability by establishing, at "the very least," that there was an official policy and that there was an "affirmative link" between the underling's actions and city

policy. How would Justice Rehnquist define "policy"? Is this a reprise of his position in the *Pembaur* case? Does his view of policy relate or tie to his view of an "affirmative link"?

2. The notion of an "affirmative link" can be found in earlier, in such cases as Polk County v. Dodson, 454 U.S. 312, 102 S.Ct. 445, 70 L.Ed.2d 509 (1981) (using similar phrase "moving force"). Assuming once again that local governments are legal fictions, see Note on the Derivative Nature of Local Government Liability, supra, Justice Rehnquist must mean an "affirmative link" between the underling and a policymaking official, must he not?

What is such an "affirmative link"? Consider the possible degrees of connection between a superior policymaking officer and an underling's actions.

(a) Are the following affirmative links:

(i) a supervisor "instructs" an underling to carry out an act;

(ii) a supervisor "conspires" with an underling to carry out an act, and the underling carries out the plan;

(iii) a supervisor "encourages" an underling to carry out an act without specifically ordering him to do it.

Assuming that *Pembaur* is rightly decided, why are these easy cases? Because the supervisor herself is liable and, under *Pembaur,* that makes the city liable? See Bryan County v. Brown, discussed in the preceding Note supra. Cf. Allee v. Medrano, 416 U.S. 802, 94 S.Ct. 2191, 40 L.Ed.2d 566 (1974) (supervisors responsible for officers' acts where there was a "single plan" by all defendants) (injunction); Lankford v. Gelston, 364 F.2d 197 (4th Cir.1966) (supervisors directed action) (injunction).

(b) Now consider a continuing list of connections with some less direct links between a policymaking official and an underling:

(iv) a supervisor "knew of and tacitly supported" the underling's independent decision to act (e.g., by praising underling before or afterward);

(v) a supervisor "knew of and condoned" an underling's act (e.g., by tolerating repeated acts without reprimand);

(vi) a supervisor actively sought not to know that underlings were committing unconstitutional acts (e.g., "Don't tell me; I don't want to know");

(vii) a supervisor "should have known" from a pattern of abuse that underlings were committing unconstitutional acts (e.g., reasonable prudent supervisor would have discovered acts);

(viii) a supervisor has a "duty" to know and be responsible for her underling's acts in certain rare areas in which the supervisor has a constitutional duty to act (e.g., supervisor does not know that underlings are failing to provide medical care to prisoners in violation of *Estelle*);

(ix) a supervisor has "respondeat superior" responsibility for all underlings at all times.

Monell explicitly rejects liability only for the last example. Why are the others more difficult to decide than the cases in subparagraph (a)? Because you wonder whether the supervisor "caused" the harm that underling imposed on the plaintiff? Some appellate courts find an affirmative link in some of these situations, usually ending with condonation, but not in others. Where would you draw the line? Compare Brown v. City of Ft. Lauderdale, 923 F.2d 1474 (11th Cir. 1991) ("must have known"), and McLin v. City of Chicago, 742 F.Supp. 994, 1002 (N.D.Ill. 1990) (supervisors "knew of the code of silence but failed to take steps to eliminate it"), with Jane Doe A by and through Jane Doe B v. Special Sch. Dist., 901 F.2d 642, 646 (8th Cir. 1990) (no liability where supervisors had no notice).

(c) What is the relationship between the "single-act/multiple-acts" dispute and the "affirmative links" disclosed above? Is a single act sufficient to prove municipal policy in situations (i)–(iii), but multiple acts by underlings are necessary in situations (iv) and (v)? See Calhoun v. Ramsey, 408 F.3d 375 (7th Cir. 2005); Gutierrez–Rodriguez v. Cartagena, 882 F.2d 553, 567 (1st Cir. 1989); Jones v. City of Chicago, 856 F.2d 985, 995–96 (7th Cir. 1988).

3. Most of the concepts in the *Tuttle* line of cases are taken from the law of supervisory responsibility, that is, cases concerning the personal liability of individual supervisors for their underlings' acts. See, e.g., Rizzo v. Goode, 423 U.S. 362, 96 S.Ct. 598, 46 L.Ed.2d 561 (1976) (rejecting respondeat superior liability for supervisors themselves). Later cases involving local government liability have likewise been read back into the law of supervisory liability. See, e.g., Greason v. Kemp, 891 F.2d 829 (11th Cir.1990).

(a) In **Ashcroft v. Iqbal**, ___ U.S. ___, 129 S.Ct. 1937, 173 L.Ed.2d 868 (2009), the plaintiff sued supervisor's for the acts of their underlings, roughly parallel to the issues presented here. Although the case primarily concerned pleading standards, the Court first discussed liability rules so that it could determine what needed to be pled. Said the Court, ___ U.S. at ___, 129 S.Ct. at 1949:

> "Respondent * * * argues that, under a theory of 'supervisory liability,' petitioners can be liable for 'knowledge and acquiescence in their subordinates' [constitutional violations in discrimination cases where intent is normally an element of the claim.] That is to say, respondent believes a supervisor's mere knowledge of his subordinate's discriminatory purpose amounts to the supervisor's violating the Constitution. We reject this argument. Respondent's conception of 'supervisory liability' is inconsistent with his accurate stipulation that petitioners may not be held accountable for the misdeeds of their agents. In a § 1983 suit * * *— where masters do not answer for the torts of their servants-the term 'supervisory liability' is a misnomer. Absent vicarious liability, each Government official, his or her title notwithstanding, is only liable for his or her own misconduct."

Should the list in subparagraph (b) supra be reconsidered following *Iqbal*? If so, where does *Iqbal* suggest that the line should be drawn?

(b) Several circuit courts have declined to apply *Iqbal*, adhering to apparently contrary circuit precedent. See, e.g., Starr v. Baca, 633 F.3d 1191 (9th Cir. 2011) (*Iqbal* does not overturn circuit's use of blanket "deliberate indifference standard for all prisoner claims against supervisors); Santiago v. Warminster Tp., 629 F.3d 121 (3d Cir. 2010) (noting *Iqbal* but following circuit precedent that a supervisor may be personally liable ... if he or she participated in violating the plaintiff's rights, directed others to violate them, or, as the person in charge, had knowledge of and acquiesced in his subordinates' violations").[1] Is the "deliberate indifference" standard adequate to state a claim against the supervisor for an independent constitutional violation?

(c) Is this cross-pollination between municipal and supervisory liability cases appropriate? When the constitutional violator is an underling rather than a policymaker, the local government cannot be held liable unless the underlings actions can be attributed to a policymaker. Are the supervisory liability cases relevant here because they already sufficiently describe when the acts of an underling may be attributed to a superior? Is the only unique issue for municipal liability that of whether the linked supervisor is a policymaker under *Pembaur*?

4. Is there a "grand unification theory" that explains both the *Pembaur* and *Tuttle* lines of cases? What themes do the two lines have in common? Is it causation? Who caused what?

(a) Is causation taken for granted in the *Pembaur* case? Why? Why is causation a more difficult issue in *Tuttle*? Justice Rehnquist appears to concede that it possible for a constitutionally permissible decision by a supervisor to cause a constitutional violation by an underling, but he appears to demand a greater showing of causation under such circumstances. Should he have made the concession? Why is a greater showing of causation necessary?

(b) As a practical matter, the various degrees of connection between underling and supervisor, discussed in ¶ 1 supra, have been eclipsed by developments in the *Canton* case, which follows. As you read that decision, ask how its analysis presents plaintiffs with a more appealing alternative than the search for an "affirmative link" as discussed in *Tuttle*.

CANTON v. HARRIS

Supreme Court of the United States, 1989.
489 U.S. 378, 109 S.Ct. 1197, 103 L.Ed.2d 412.

JUSTICE WHITE delivered the opinion of the Court.

In this case, we are asked to determine if a municipality can ever be liable under 42 U.S.C. § 1983 for constitutional violations resulting from its failure to train municipal employees. We hold that, under certain circumstances, such liability is permitted by the statute.

I

In April 1978, respondent Geraldine Harris was arrested by officers of the Canton Police Department. Harris was brought to the police station in

---

1. For similar pre-*Iqbal* decisions, see Graham v. Sauk Prairie Police Comm'n, 915 F.2d 1085, 1104 (7th Cir.1990); Bordanaro v. McLeod, 871 F.2d 1151, 1155 (1st Cir.1989); Cabrales v. County of Los Angeles, 864 F.2d 1454, 1461 (9th Cir. 1988). Cf. Atteberry v. Nocona General Hosp., 430 F.3d 245 (5th Cir. 2005) (supervisory liability).

a patrol wagon. When she arrived at the station, Harris was found sitting on the floor of the wagon. She was asked if she needed medical attention, and responded with an incoherent remark. After she was brought inside the station for processing, Mrs. Harris slumped to the floor on two occasions. Eventually, the police officers left Mrs. Harris lying on the floor to prevent her from falling again. No medical attention was ever summoned for Mrs. Harris. After about an hour, Mrs. Harris was released from custody, and taken by an ambulance (provided by her family) to a nearby hospital. There, Mrs. Harris was diagnosed as suffering from several emotional ailments; she was hospitalized for one week and received subsequent outpatient treatment for an additional year.

Some time later, Mrs. Harris commenced this action alleging many state law and constitutional claims against the city of Canton and its officials. Among these claims was one seeking to hold the city liable under 42 U.S.C. § 1983 for its violation of Mrs. Harris' right, under the Due Process Clause of the Fourteenth Amendment, to receive necessary medical attention while in police custody.

A jury trial was held on Mrs. Harris' claims. Evidence was presented that indicated that, pursuant to a municipal regulation,[2] shift commanders were authorized to determine, in their sole discretion, whether a detainee required medical care. In addition, testimony also suggested that Canton shift commanders were not provided with any special training (beyond first-aid training) to make a determination as to when to summon medical care for an injured detainee.

At the close of the evidence, the District Court submitted the case to the jury, which rejected all of Mrs. Harris' claims except one: her § 1983 claim against the city resulting from its failure to provide her with medical treatment while in custody. [The District Court and Court of Appeals upheld the judgments on a theory that the jury could have found that the city "failed to train" its officers. The Court of Appeals nevertheless remanded for a new trial based on more precise instructions. The Supreme Court granted the city's petition for writ of certiorari.]

* * *

III

* * * [O]ur first inquiry in any case alleging municipal liability under § 1983 is the question of whether there is a direct causal link between a municipal policy or custom, and the alleged constitutional deprivation. The inquiry is a difficult one; one that has left this Court deeply divided in a series of cases that have followed *Monell*; one that is the principal focus of our decision again today.

---

2. The city regulation in question provides that a police officer assigned to act as "jailer" at the City Police Station: "shall, when a prisoner is found to be unconscious or semi-unconscious, or when he or she is unable to explain his or her condition, or who complains of being ill, have such person taken to a hospital for medical treatment, with permission of his supervisor before admitting the person to City Jail."

A

Based on the difficulty that this Court has had defining the contours of municipal liability in these circumstances, petitioner urges us to adopt the rule that a municipality can be found liable under § 1983 only where "the policy in question [is] itself unconstitutional." * * * Under such an approach, the outcome here would be rather clear: we would have to reverse and remand the case with instructions that judgment be entered for petitioner. There can be little doubt that on its face the city's policy regarding medical treatment for detainees is constitutional. The policy states that the City Jailer "shall ... have [a person needing medical care] taken to a hospital for medical treatment, with permission of his supervisor...." It is difficult to see what constitutional guarantees are violated by such a policy.

Nor, without more, would a city automatically be liable under § 1983 if one of its employees happened to apply the policy in an unconstitutional manner, for liability would then rest on respondeat superior. The claim in this case, however, is that if a concededly valid policy is unconstitutionally applied by a municipal employee, the city is liable if the employee has not been adequately trained and the constitutional wrong has been caused by that failure to train. For reasons explained below, we conclude, as have all the Courts of Appeals that have addressed this issue, that there are limited circumstances in which an allegation of a "failure to train" can be the basis for liability under § 1983. Thus, we reject petitioner's contention that only unconstitutional policies are actionable under the statute.

B

Though we agree with the court below that a city can be liable under § 1983 for inadequate training of its employees, we cannot agree that the District Court's jury instructions on this issue were proper, for we conclude that the Court of Appeals provided an overly broad rule for when a municipality can be held liable under the "failure to train" theory. Unlike the question of whether a municipality's failure to train employees can ever be a basis for § 1983 liability—on which the Courts of Appeals have all agreed—there is substantial division among the lower courts as to what degree of fault must be evidenced by the municipality's inaction before liability will be permitted. We hold today that the inadequacy of police training may serve as the basis for § 1983 liability only where the failure to train amounts to deliberate indifference to the rights of persons with whom the police come into contact. This rule is most consistent with our admonition in *Monell* and Polk County v. Dodson, 454 U.S. 312, 326, 102 S.Ct. 445, 454, 70 L.Ed.2d 509 (1981), that a municipality can be liable under § 1983 only where its policies are the "moving force [behind] the constitutional violation." Only where a municipality's failure to train its employees in a relevant respect evidences a "deliberate indifference" to the rights of its inhabitants can such a shortcoming be properly thought of as a city "policy or custom" that is actionable under § 1983. As Justice Brennan's opinion in Pembaur v. Cincinnati, put it: "[M]unicipal liability under § 1983 attaches where—and only where—a deliberate choice to follow a course of action is made from among various alternatives" by city policy makers. See also Oklahoma City v. Tuttle (opinion of Rehnquist, J.). Only where a failure to train reflects a "deliberate" or "conscious" choice by a municipality—a "policy" as defined by our prior cases—can a city be liable for such a failure under § 1983.

Monell's rule that a city is not liable under § 1983 unless a municipal policy causes a constitutional deprivation will not be satisfied by merely alleging that the existing training program for a class of employees, such as police officers, represents a policy for which the city is responsible. That much may be true. The issue in a case like this one, however, is whether that training program is adequate; and if it is not, the question becomes whether such inadequate training can justifiably be said to represent "city policy." It may seem contrary to common sense to assert that a municipality will actually have a policy of not taking reasonable steps to train its employees. But it may happen that in light of the duties assigned to specific officers or employees the need for more or different training is so obvious, and the inadequacy so likely to result in the violation of constitutional rights, that the policymakers of the city can reasonably be said to have been deliberately indifferent to the need.[10] In that event, the failure to provide proper training may fairly be said to represent a policy for which the city is responsible, and for which the city may be held liable if it actually causes injury.

In resolving the issue of a city's liability, the focus must be on adequacy of the training program in relation to the tasks the particular officers must perform. That a particular officer may be unsatisfactorily trained will not alone suffice to fasten liability on the city, for the officer's shortcomings may have resulted from factors other than a faulty training program. It may be, for example, that an otherwise sound program has occasionally been negligently administered. Neither will it suffice to prove that an injury or accident could have been avoided if an officer had had better or more training, sufficient to equip him to avoid the particular injury-causing conduct. Such a claim could be made about almost any encounter resulting in injury, yet not condemn the adequacy of the program to enable officers to respond properly to the usual and recurring situations with which they must deal. And plainly, adequately trained officers occasionally make mistakes; the fact that they do says little about the training program or the legal basis for holding the city liable.

Moreover, for liability to attach in this circumstance the identified deficiency in a city's training program must be closely related to the

---

10. For example, city policy makers know to a moral certainty that their police officers will be required to arrest fleeing felons. The city has armed its officers with firearms, in part to allow them to accomplish this task. Thus, the need to train officers in the constitutional limitations on the use of deadly force, see Tennessee v. Garner, can be said to be "so obvious," that failure to do so could properly be characterized as "deliberate indifference" to constitutional rights.

It could also be that the police, in exercising their discretion, so often violate constitutional rights that the need for further training must have been plainly obvious to the city policy makers, who, nevertheless, are "deliberately indifferent" to the need.

ultimate injury. Thus in the case at hand, respondent must still prove that the deficiency in training actually caused the police officers' indifference to her medical needs. Would the injury have been avoided had the employee been trained under a program that was not deficient in the identified respect? Predicting how a hypothetically well-trained officer would have acted under the circumstances may not be an easy task for the factfinder, particularly since matters of judgment may be involved, and since officers who are well trained are not free from error and perhaps might react very much like the untrained officer in similar circumstances. But judge and jury, doing their respective jobs, will be adequate to the task.

To adopt lesser standards of fault and causation would open municipalities to unprecedented liability under § 1983. In virtually every instance where a person has had his or her constitutional rights violated by a city employee, a § 1983 plaintiff will be able to point to something the city "could have done" to prevent the unfortunate incident. Thus, permitting cases against cities for their "failure to train" employees to go forward under § 1983 on a lesser standard of fault would result in de facto respondeat superior liability on municipalities—a result we rejected in *Monell.* It would also engage the federal courts in an endless exercise of second-guessing municipal employee-training programs. This is an exercise we believe the federal courts are ill-suited to undertake, as well as one that would implicate serious questions of federalism. Cf. Rizzo v. Goode, 423 U.S. 362, 378–380, 96 S.Ct. 598, 46 L.Ed.2d 561 (1976).

Consequently, while claims such as respondent's—alleging that the city's failure to provide training to municipal employees resulted in the constitutional deprivation she suffered—are cognizable under § 1983, they can only yield liability against a municipality where that city's failure to train reflects deliberate indifference to the constitutional rights of its inhabitants.

* * *

V

Consequently, for the reasons given above, we vacate the judgment of the Court of Appeals and remand this case for further proceedings consistent with this opinion.

It is so ordered.

JUSTICE BRENNAN, concurring. [Omitted.]

JUSTICE O'CONNOR, with whom JUSTICE SCALIA and JUSTICE KENNEDY join, concurring in part and dissenting in part.

* * * My single point of disagreement with the majority is * * * a small one. Because I believe, as the majority strongly hints, that respondent has not and could not satisfy the fault and causation requirements we adopt today, I think it unnecessary to remand this case to the Court of Appeals for further proceedings. * * *

* * * Where a § 1983 plaintiff can establish that the facts available to city policymakers put them on actual or constructive notice that the particular omission is substantially certain to result in the violation of the constitutional rights of their citizens, the dictates of *Monell* are satisfied. * * *

In my view, it could be shown that the need for training was obvious in one of two ways. First, a municipality could fail to train its employees concerning a clear constitutional duty implicated in recurrent situations that a particular employee is certain to face. As the majority notes, see ante, n. 10, the constitutional limitations established by this Court on the use of deadly force by police officers present one such situation. The constitutional duty of the individual officer is clear, and it is equally clear that failure to inform city personnel of that duty will create an extremely high risk that constitutional violations will ensue. The claim in this case— that police officers were inadequately trained in diagnosing the symptoms of emotional illness—falls far short of the kind of "obvious" need for training that would support a finding of deliberate indifference to constitutional rights on the part of the city. [But this is not such an area. There is no Supreme Court precedent even addressing whether there is a duty to provide such care.]

Second, I think municipal liability for failure to train may be proper where it can be shown that policymakers were aware of, and acquiesced in, a pattern of constitutional violations involving the exercise of police discretion. In such cases, the need for training may not be obvious from the outset, but a pattern of constitutional violations could put the municipality on notice that its officers confront the particular situation on a regular basis, and that they often react in a manner contrary to constitutional requirements. The lower courts that have applied the "deliberate indifference" standard we adopt today have required a showing of a pattern of violations from which a kind of "tacit authorization" by city policymakers can be inferred. See, e.g., Fiacco v. City of Rensselaer, 783 F.2d 319, 327 (CA2 1986) (multiple incidents required for finding of deliberate indifference).

* * * [Here, plaintiff] presented no testimony from any witness indicating that there had been past incidents of "deliberate indifference" to the medical needs of emotionally disturbed detainees or that any other circumstance had put the city on actual or constructive notice of a need for additional training in this regard. * * * There is quite simply nothing in this record to indicate that the city of Canton had any reason to suspect that failing to provide this kind of training would lead to injuries of any kind, let alone violations of the Due Process Clause. * * *

* * * As the authors of the Ku Klux Klan Act themselves realized, the resources of local government are not inexhaustible. The grave step of shifting of those resources to particular areas where constitutional violations are likely to result through the deterrent power of § 1983 should certainly not be taken on the basis of an isolated incident. If § 1983 and the Constitution require the city of Canton to provide detailed medical and psychological training to its police officers, or to station paramedics at its jails, other city services will necessarily suffer, including those with far more direct implications for the protection of constitutional rights. Because respondent's evidence falls far short of establishing the high degree of fault on the part of the city required by our decision today, and because there is no indication that respondent could produce any new proof in this regard, I would reverse the judgment of the Court of Appeals and order entry of judgment for the city.

NOTE ON GOVERNMENTAL RESPONSIBILITY FOR
FAILURE TO TRAIN AND OTHER DUTIES

1. How should *Canton* be characterized in the way it allows liability for failure to train: as inviting local government liability through its open "deliberate indifference" standard? Or as constraining local government liability through the precise examples and limiting rules? Which approach would be better?

(a) Does "deliberate indifference" have any meaning outside the two contexts identified by Justice White in footnote 10 and by Justice O'Connor in her separate opinion? In what other ways might a city be deliberately indifferent to training? Is "deliberate indifference" here the same as "deliberate indifference" in Eighth Amendment cases, see Farmer v. Brennan, Chapter 1B.2 supra? Cf. Atteberry v. Nocona General Hosp., 430 F.3d 245 (5th Cir. 2005) (cross-citing in supervisory liability case).

(b) Notice how the tone of Justice White's opinion changes when he begins to talk about rule-bound limitations on liability. Does his opinion begin to lose consistency? How do you reconcile these statements: the "focus must be on adequacy of the training program," yet "it [will not] suffice to prove that an injury or accident could have been avoided if an officer had better or more training"? Does White mean minimal adequacy is the test, after which degrees of adequacy are irrelevant? What is the minimum?

(c) Are the issues presented in *Canton* ones of law or fact? How does Justice White evade the issue? Are you as confident as he that judge and jury working together can apply his test?

(d) Reconsider ¶ 3 of the previous Note in light of *Canton*'s adoption of the deliberate indifference standard. At least two recent precedents have declared that a local government or supervising official is responsible only for its or his "own" constitutional violations, *Iqbal*, discussed in ¶ 3 of the preceding Note, and Connick v. Thompson, discussed infra in this Note. In light of Canton, would it be accurate to say that deliberate indifference makes a violation? Is it a violation of constitutional law or § 1983? See Connick supra, ___ U.S. at ___, 131 S.Ct. at 1359: "local government may be liable under this section [1983] if the governmental body itself 'subjects' a person to a deprivation of rights or 'causes' a person 'to be subjected' to such deprivation."

2. Consider the two contexts mentioned in footnote 10 and in Justice O'Connor's separate opinion. What is their source? How will they be applied? In the Court's later decision in **Bryan County v. Brown**, 520 U.S. 397, 117 S.Ct. 1382, 137 L.Ed.2d 626 (1997), the Court explained these as necessary components in the process of establishing that the local government, rather than a mere employee, was at fault for the resulting constitutional violation. In *Bryan County* Justice O'Connor explained that in "failure to train" cases, there is no proof that the city leaders themselves have instructed or directed employees to commit constitutional violations and thus no proof that the city is directly responsible for those violations. The proof of repetitious acts or "obvious" problems thus are methods of proving the "fault" of the leaders and their "causation" of the ensuing acts of officers on the street. Alluding to the two contexts identified in footnote 10 in *Canton*, she continued, 520 U.S. at 407–09, 117 S.Ct. at 1390–91:

> "We concluded in *Canton* that an 'inadequate training' claim could be the basis for § 1983 liability in 'limited circumstances.' We spoke, however, of a deficient training 'program,' necessarily intended to apply over time to multiple employees. Existence of a 'program' makes proof of fault and causation at least possible in an inadequate training case. If a program does not prevent constitutional violations, municipal decision-makers may eventually be put on notice that a new program is called for. Their continued adherence to an approach that they know or should know has failed to prevent tortious conduct by employees may establish the conscious disregard for the consequences of their action—the 'deliberate indifference'—necessary to trigger municipal liability. In addition, the existence of a pattern of tortious conduct by inadequately trained employees may tend to show that the lack of proper training, rather than a one-time negligent administration of the program or factors peculiar to the officer involved in a particular incident, is the 'moving force' behind the plaintiff's injury." * * *

> "In leaving open in *Canton* the possibility that a plaintiff might succeed in carrying a failure-to-train claim [under the 'obviousness' standard] without showing a pattern of constitutional violations, we simply hypothesized that, in a narrow range of circumstances, a violation of federal rights may be a highly predictable consequence of a failure to equip law enforcement officers with specific tools to handle recurring situations. The likelihood that the situation will recur and the predictability that an officer lacking specific tools to handle that situation will violate citizens' rights could justify a finding that policymakers' decision not to train the officer reflected 'deliberate indifference' to the obvious consequence of the policymakers' choice—namely, a violation of a specific constitutional or statutory right. The high degree of predictability may also support an inference of causation—that the municipality's indifference led directly to the very consequence that was so predictable."

(a) In **Connick v. Thompson**, __ U.S. __, 131 S.Ct. 1350, 179 L.Ed.2d 417 (2011), the Court once again rejected a claim of municipal liability, this one based on a claimed institutional failure of the prosecutor's office to train his prosecutors not to commit *Brady* violations (failure to disclose exculpatory evidence, here a blood sample). It was conceded at trial that the office had never conducted a training program, although all prosecutors were aware of the *Brady* rule. The Court found no governmental liability because, though there had been four other *Brady* violations in the office over the years, none had involved situations similar to Thompson's, the non-disclosure of blood evidence. Thus, held the Court, the chief prosecutor as policymaker was not "on notice that specific training was necessary to avoid this constitutional violation." Was the Court demanding too much?

(b) Does the discussion in *Bryan County* make clear what is deemed "obvious" and what is not? In the *Bryan County* case the case rejected the argument that poor review in making hiring decisions could present an "obvious" risk of constitutional violations by those hired. The risk of liability based purely on a respondeat superior theory was too great, said the Court. Why is that? Because the topic of "hiring" affects all employees and might lead to too much liability? But is the same not also true of employee training, as in *Canton*? See Connick v. Thompson, supra (risk of Brady violations rejected because it also does not satisfy the obviousness test).

(c) What meets the obviousness test besides unconstitutional deadly use of force? Should municipalities train in race relations because it is obvious that racist decisionmaking would cause constitutional harm? Justice O'Connor argues that training to provide psychological care would not meet the obviousness test; would the same be true for training to provide medical care for serious, known medical needs? Training in the proper use of police dogs? See Kerr v. City of West Palm Beach, 875 F.2d 1546 (11th Cir.1989). Hiring of a nurse who injects patients with paralytic drugs? Cf. Atteberry v. Nocona General Hosp., 430 F.3d 245 (5th Cir. 2005) (supervisory liability).

3. Is *Canton* consistent with the *DeShaney* case, which generally recoils against the imposition of affirmative duties?

(a) The two cases were handed down within months of one another. Both involve the theme of judicially imposed ordering of municipal spending priorities. How could they have been decided contrary to one another? Is *Canton* severely limited by the *Heller* case—there can only be liability for failure to train where there is an underlying constitutional violation by an individual officer? Even if that is true, might there be some cases where determining a constitutional violation and determining local government liability call for the same inquiry? See Popham v. City of Talladega, 908 F.2d 1561 (11th Cir.1990) (phrases expressing liability standards may be the same, actual tests not).

(b) Even if *Heller* distinguishes *Canton* and *DeShaney,* is not *Canton* essentially like *DeShaney* in that it imposes liability costs on a new defendant, the city, for non-constitutional violations (given part III–A)? Is *Canton,* in this regard, some salve for the harms created by the earlier decision? Or is it an unwise retreat from a properly decided case?

(c) Is *Canton* consistent with the "under color of" law holding in Monroe v. Pape? Why do we have the rule that a pattern of action need not be shown to recover against an individual defendant, but must be shown (outside the obviousness context) against a municipality?

4. *Canton* deals with the failure to train officers in the police context. What is its future scope?

(a) Is there any reason to believe that *Canton*'s training duty will be restricted to police? Will local governments be required to train all their employees? How will a town of 2,000 people afford this cost? Will states begin to provide training to local government officials? Will *Canton* erode the power of local governments? If so, is that good or bad?

(b) Should *Canton* be extended to failure to supervise underlings after training has finished? Can failure to supervise be distinguished from failure to train? See Greason v. Kemp, 891 F.2d 829 (11th Cir. 1990).

5. What is the best policy decision, for or against local government liability?

(a) If local governments are strictly liable for all § 1983 violations by their employees, will that not induce them to watch employees carefully, thus having a great deterrent effect on violations? Would not local governments vigorously weed out rights violators? Too vigorously to suit employees? Alternatively, would strict liability for local governments leave individual officers with no disincentive to violate § 1983 because the employees would never need to fear personal liability?

(b) Does local government liability change the dynamics of § 1983 litigation by providing a "deep pocket" to pay judgments? Does that encourage "strike suits," ones brought only to obtain unfair settlements?

(c) Is the present system best because it leads both officers and governments to fear liability?

(b) Defenses to Local Government Liability

OWEN v. CITY OF INDEPENDENCE

Supreme Court of the United States, 1980.
445 U.S. 622, 100 S.Ct. 1398, 63 L.Ed.2d 673.

MR. JUSTICE BRENNAN delivered the opinion of the Court.

Monell v. New York City Dept. of Social Services overruled Monroe v. Pape insofar as *Monroe* held that local governments were not among the "persons" to whom 42 U.S.C. § 1983 applies and were therefore wholly immune from suit under the statute. *Monell* reserved decision, however, on the question whether local governments, although not entitled to an absolute immunity, should be afforded some form of official immunity in § 1983 suits. In this action brought by petitioner in the District Court for the Western District of Missouri, the Court of Appeals for the Eighth Circuit held that respondent city of Independence, Mo., "is entitled to qualified immunity from liability" * * *. We granted certiorari. We reverse.

I

[Owen had filed suit under § 1983 claiming that the circumstances of his discharge as police chief in 1972 violated his right to procedural due process. The city council had voted to discharge him for improprieties in office without giving him notice or hearing before or afterwards. It was conceded that the discharge took place prior to the Court's precedent-setting decision on procedural due process in Board of Regents v. Roth, 408 U.S. 564, 92 S.Ct. 2701, 33 L.Ed.2d 548 (1972).]

III

Because the question of the scope of a municipality's immunity from liability under § 1983 is essentially one of statutory construction, the starting point in our analysis must be the language of the statute itself. By its terms, § 1983 "creates a species of tort liability that on its face admits of no immunities." Imbler v. Pachtman. Its language is absolute and unqualified; no mention is made of any privileges, immunities, or defenses that may be asserted. Rather, the Act imposes liability upon "every person" who, under color of state law or custom, "subjects, or causes to be subjected, any citizen of the United States ... to the deprivation of any rights, privileges, or immunities secured by the Constitution and laws." And *Monell* held that these words were intended to encompass municipal corporations as well as natural "persons."

Moreover, the congressional debates surrounding the passage of § 1 of the Civil Rights Act of 1871—the forerunner of § 1983—confirm the expansive sweep of the statutory language. Representative Shellabarger, the author and manager of the bill in the House, explained in his introductory remarks [that the bill should be "liberally and beneficently construed."]

* * *

However, notwithstanding § 1983's expansive language and the absence of any express incorporation of common-law immunities, we have, on several occasions, found that a tradition of immunity was so firmly rooted in the common law and was supported by such strong policy reasons that "Congress would have specifically so provided had it wished to abolish the doctrine." Pierson v. Ray. [The Court reviewed the cases in Chapter 1D supra.]

In each of these cases, our finding of § 1983 immunity "was predicated upon a considered inquiry into the immunity historically accorded the relevant official at common law and the interests behind it." Imbler v. Pachtman. Where the immunity claimed by the defendant was well established at common law at the time § 1983 was enacted, and where its rationale was compatible with the purposes of the Civil Rights Act, we have construed the statute to incorporate that immunity. But there is no tradition of immunity for municipal corporations, and neither history nor policy supports a construction of § 1983 that would justify the qualified immunity accorded the city of Independence by the Court of Appeals. We hold, therefore, that the municipality may not assert the good faith of its officers or agents as a defense to liability under § 1983.[18]

A

Since colonial times, a distinct feature of our Nation's system of governance has been the conferral of political power upon public and municipal corporations for the management of matters of local concern. As *Monell* recounted, by 1871, municipalities—like private corporations—were treated as natural persons for virtually all purposes of constitutional and statutory analysis. In particular, they were routinely sued in both federal and state courts. Cf. Cowles v. Mercer County, 7 Wall. 118, 19 L.Ed. 86 (1869). Local governmental units were regularly held to answer in damages for a wide range of statutory and constitutional violations, as well as for common-law actions for breach of contract.[19]

* * *

Yet in the hundreds of cases from that era awarding damages against municipal governments for wrongs committed by them, one searches in vain for much mention of a qualified immunity [for a municipality based upon the good faith of its officers.] In the leading case of Thayer v. Boston, 36 Mass. 511, 515–516 (1837), for example, Chief Justice Shaw explained:

> "There is a large class of cases, in which the rights of both the public and of individuals may be deeply involved, in which it cannot be known at the time the act is done, whether it is lawful or not. The event of a legal inquiry in a court of justice, may show that it was unlawful. Still, if it was not known and understood to be unlawful at the time, if it was an act done by the officers having competent authority, either by express vote of the city government, or by the nature of the duties and functions with which they are charged, by their offices, to act upon the general subject matter, and especially if the act was done with an honest view to obtain for the public some

18. The governmental immunity at issue in the present case differs significantly from the official immunities involved in our previous decisions. In those cases, various government officers had been sued in their individual capacities, and the immunity served to insulate them from personal liability for damages. Here, in contrast, only the liability of the municipality itself is at issue, not that of its officers, and in the absence of an immunity, any recovery would come from public funds.

19. Primary among the constitutional suits heard in federal court were those based on a municipality's violation of the Contract Clause, and the courts' enforcement efforts often included "various forms of 'positive' relief, such as ordering that taxes be levied and collected to discharge federal-court judgments, once a constitutional infraction was found." Monell v. New York City Dept. of Social Services. Damages actions against municipalities for federal statutory violations were also entertained. See, e.g., Levy Court v. Coroner, 2 Wall. 501, 17 L.Ed. 851 (1865). In addition, state constitutions and statutes, as well as municipal charters, imposed many obligations upon the local governments, the violation of which typically gave rise to damages actions against the city. See generally Note, Streets, Change of Grade, Liability of Cities for, 30 Am.St.Rep. 835 (1893), and cases cited therein. With respect to authorized contracts—and even unauthorized contracts that are later ratified by the corporation—municipalities were liable in the same manner as individuals for their breaches. See generally 1 J. Dillon, Law of Municipal Corporations §§ 385, 394 (2d ed. 1873) (hereinafter Dillon). Of particular relevance to the instant case, included within the class of contract actions brought against a city were those for the wrongful discharge of a municipal employee, and where the claim was adjudged meritorious, damages in the nature of backpay were regularly awarded. See, e.g., Richardson v. School Dist. No. 10, 38 Vt. 602 (1866). * * *

lawful benefit or advantage, reason and justice obviously require that the city, in its corporate capacity, should be liable to make good the damage sustained by an individual in consequence of the acts thus done."

The *Thayer* principle was later reiterated by courts in several jurisdictions * * *. [The same approach was used by English courts. The 42d Congress recognized these precedents in its discussions.]

To be sure, there were two doctrines that afforded municipal corporations some measure of protection from tort liability. The first sought to distinguish between a municipality's "governmental" and "proprietary" functions; as to the former, the city was held immune, whereas in its exercise of the latter, the city was held to the same standards of liability as any private corporation. The second doctrine immunized a municipality for its "discretionary" or "legislative" activities, but not for those which were "ministerial" in nature. A brief examination of the application and the rationale underlying each of these doctrines demonstrates that Congress could not have intended them to limit a municipality's liability under § 1983.

The governmental-proprietary distinction owed its existence to the dual nature of the municipal corporation. On the one hand, the municipality was a corporate body, capable of performing the same "proprietary" functions as any private corporation, and liable for its torts in the same manner and to the same extent, as well. On the other hand, the municipality was an arm of the State, and when acting in that "governmental" or "public" capacity, it shared the immunity traditionally accorded the sovereign. [Yet even in this area the municipality lost its immunity if the state withdrew it.] Municipalities were therefore liable not only for their "proprietary" acts, but also for those "governmental" functions as to which the State had withdrawn their immunity. And, by the end of the 19th century, courts regularly held that in imposing a specific duty on the municipality either in its charter or by statute, the State had impliedly withdrawn the city's immunity from liability for the nonperformance or misperformance of its obligation. See, e.g., Weightman v. The Corporation of Washington, 1 Black 39, 50–52, 17 L.Ed. 52 (1862); Providence v. Clapp, 17 How. 161, 167–169, 15 L.Ed. 72 (1855). Thus, despite the nominal existence of an immunity for "governmental" functions, municipalities were found liable in damages in a multitude of cases involving such activities.

* * *

The second common-law distinction between municipal functions— that protecting the city from suits challenging "discretionary" decisions— was grounded * * * on a concern for separation of powers. A large part of the municipality's responsibilities involved broad discretionary decisions on issues of public policy—decisions that affected large numbers of persons and called for a delicate balancing of competing considerations. For a court or jury, in the guise of a tort suit, to review the reasonableness of the city's judgment on these matters would be an infringement upon the powers properly vested in a coordinate and coequal branch of government. In order to ensure against any invasion into the legitimate sphere of the municipality's policymaking processes, courts therefore refused to entertain suits against the city "either for the non-exercise of, or for the manner in which in good faith it exercises, discretionary powers of a public or legislative character." 2 [J.] Dillon, [The Law of Municipal Corporations] § 753, at 862 [(1869)].

* * *

Once again, an understanding of the rationale underlying the common-law immunity for "discretionary" functions explains why that doctrine cannot serve as the foundation for a good-faith immunity under § 1983. That common-law doctrine merely prevented courts from substituting their own judgment on matters within the lawful discretion of the municipality. But a municipality has no "discretion" to violate the Federal Constitution; its dictates are absolute and imperative. And when a court passes judgment on the municipality's conduct in a § 1983 action, it does not seek to second-guess the "reasonableness" of the city's decision nor to interfere with the local government's resolution of competing policy considerations. Rather, it looks only to whether the municipality has conformed to the requirements of the Federal Constitution and statutes.
* * *

In sum, we can discern no "tradition so well grounded in history and reason" that would warrant the conclusion that in enacting § 1 of the Civil Rights Act, the 42d Congress sub silentio extended to municipalities a qualified immunity based on the good faith of their officers. Absent any clearer indication that Congress intended so to limit the reach of a statute expressly designed to provide a "broad remedy for violations of federally protected civil rights," Monell v. New York City Dept. of Social Services, we are unwilling to suppose that injuries occasioned by a municipality's unconstitutional conduct were not also meant to be fully redressable through its sweep.

B

Our rejection of a construction of § 1983 that would accord municipalities a qualified immunity for their good-faith constitutional violations is compelled both by the legislative purpose in enacting the statute and by considerations of public policy. The central aim of the Civil Rights Act was to provide protection to those persons wronged by the " '[m]isuse of power, possessed by virtue of state law and made possible only because the wrongdoer is clothed with the authority of state law.' " Monroe v. Pape. By creating an express federal remedy, Congress sought to "enforce provisions of the Fourteenth Amendment against those who carry a badge of authority of a State and represent it in some capacity, whether they act in accordance with their authority or misuse it." Monroe v. Pape, supra.

How "uniquely amiss" it would be, therefore, if the government itself—"the social organ to which all in our society look for the promotion of liberty, justice, fair and equal treatment, and the setting of worthy norms and goals for social conduct"—were permitted to disavow liability for the injury it has begotten. A damages remedy against the offending party is a vital component of any scheme for vindicating cherished constitutional guarantees, and the importance of assuring its efficacy is only accentuated when the wrongdoer is the institution that has been established to protect the very rights it has transgressed. Yet owing to the qualified immunity enjoyed by most government officials, many victims of municipal malfeasance would be left remediless if the city were also allowed to assert a good-faith defense. Unless countervailing considerations counsel otherwise, the injustice of such a result should not be tolerated.[33]

Moreover, § 1983 was intended not only to provide compensation to the victims of past abuses, but to serve as a deterrent against future constitutional deprivations, as well. See Carey v. Piphus. The knowledge that a municipality will be liable for all of its injurious conduct, whether committed in good faith or not, should create an incentive for officials who may harbor doubts about the lawfulness of their intended actions to err on the side of protecting citizens' constitutional rights. Furthermore, the threat that damages might be levied against the city may encourage those in a policymaking position to institute internal rules and programs designed to minimize the likelihood of unintentional infringements on constitutional rights. Such procedures are particularly beneficial in preventing those "systemic" injuries that result not so much from the conduct of any single individual, but from the interactive behavior of several government officials, each of whom may be acting in good faith. Cf. Note, *Developments in the Law: Section 1983 and Federalism*, 90 HARV. L. REV. 1133, 1218–1219 (1977).[36]

Our previous decisions conferring qualified immunities [protects officials who enforce local law as constitutional law evolves. This consideration does not apply when] the damages award comes not from the official's pocket, but from the public treasury. It hardly seems unjust to require a municipal defendant which has violated a citizen's constitutional rights to compensate him for the injury suffered thereby. Indeed, Congress enacted § 1983 precisely to provide a remedy for such abuses of official power. See Monroe v. Pape. Elemental notions of fairness dictate that one who causes a loss should bear the loss.

---

33. The absence of any damages remedy for violations of all but the most "clearly established" constitutional rights could also have the deleterious effect of freezing constitutional law in its current state of development, for without a meaningful remedy aggrieved individuals will have little incentive to seek vindication of those constitutional deprivations that have not previously been clearly defined.

36. In addition, the threat of liability against the city ought to increase the attentiveness with which officials at the higher levels of government supervise the conduct of their subordinates. The need to institute system-wide measures in order to increase the vigilance with which otherwise indifferent municipal officials protect citizens' constitutional rights is, of course, particularly acute where the front line officers are judgment-proof in their individual capacities.

It has been argued, however, that revenue raised by taxation for public use should not be diverted to the benefit of a single or discrete group of taxpayers, particularly where the municipality has at all times acted in good faith. On the contrary, the accepted view is that stated in Thayer v. Boston—"that the city, in its corporate capacity, should be liable to make good the damage sustained by an [unlucky] individual, in consequence of the acts thus done." 36 Mass. at 515. After all, it is the public at large which enjoys the benefits of the government's activities, and it is the public at large which is ultimately responsible for its administration. Thus, even where some constitutional development could not have been foreseen by municipal officials, it is fairer to allocate any resulting financial loss to the inevitable costs of government borne by all the taxpayers, than to allow its impact to be felt solely by those whose rights, albeit newly recognized, have been violated. See generally 3 K. Davis, Administrative Law Treatise § 25.17 (1958 and Supp.1970); Michelman, *Property, Utility, and Fairness: Some Thoughts on the Ethical Foundations of "Just Compensation" Law*, 80 HARV. L. REV. 1165 (1967).[39]

[We also need not worry that monetary liability under § 1983 will over-deter local governments from performing their duties.] More important, though, is the realization that consideration of the municipality's liability for constitutional violations is quite properly the concern of its elected or appointed officials. Indeed, a decisionmaker would be derelict in his duties if, at some point, he did not consider whether his decision comports with constitutional mandates and did not weigh the risk that a violation might result in an award of damages from the public treasury. As one commentator aptly put it: "Whatever other concerns should shape a particular official's actions, certainly one of them should be the constitutional rights of individuals who will be affected by his actions. To criticize section 1983 liability because it leads decisionmakers to avoid the infringement of constitutional rights is to criticize one of the statute's raisons d'être."[41]

IV

In sum, our decision holding that municipalities have no immunity from damages liability flowing from their constitutional violations harmonizes well with developments in the common law and our own pronouncements on official immunities under § 1983. Doctrines of tort law have changed significantly over the past century, and our notions of governmental responsibility should properly reflect that evolution. No longer is individual "blameworthiness" the acid test of liability; the

---

39. Monell v. New York City Dept. of Social Services, indicated that the principle of loss-spreading was an insufficient justification for holding the municipality liable under § 1983 on a respondeat superior theory. Here of course, quite a different situation is presented [because liability has already been attributed to the city under *Monell*'s standards.] In this circumstance— when it is the local government itself that is responsible for the constitutional deprivation—it is perfectly reasonable to distribute the loss to the public as a cost of the administration of government, rather than to let the entire burden fall on the injured individual.

41. Note, *Developments in the Law: Section 1983 and Federalism*, 90 HARV. L. REV. 1133, 1224 (1977).

principle of equitable loss-spreading has joined fault as a factor in distributing the costs of official misconduct. We believe that today's decision, together with prior precedents in this area, properly allocates these costs among the three principals in the scenario of the § 1983 cause of action: the victim of the constitutional deprivation; the officer whose conduct caused the injury; and the public, as represented by the municipal entity. The innocent individual who is harmed by an abuse of governmental authority is assured that he will be compensated for his injury. The offending official, so long as he conducts himself in good faith, may go about his business secure in the knowledge that a qualified immunity will protect him from personal liability for damages that are more appropriately chargeable to the populace as a whole. And the public will be forced to bear only the costs of injury inflicted by the "execution of a government's policy or custom, whether made by its lawmakers or by those whose edicts or acts may fairly be said to represent official policy." Monell v. New York City Dept. of Social Services.

Reversed.

MR. JUSTICE POWELL, with whom THE CHIEF JUSTICE, MR. JUSTICE STEWART, and MR. JUSTICE REHNQUIST join, dissenting.

* * *

Because today's decision will inject constant consideration of § 1983 liability into local decisionmaking, it may restrict the independence of local governments and their ability to respond to the needs of their communities. Only this Term, we noted that the "point" of immunity under § 1983 "is to forestall an atmosphere of intimidation that would conflict with [officials'] resolve to perform their designated functions in a principled fashion." Ferri v. Ackerman, 444 U.S. 193, 203–204, 100 S.Ct. 402, 409, 62 L.Ed.2d 355 (1979). The Court now argues that local officials might modify their actions unduly if they face personal liability under § 1983, but that they are unlikely to do so when the locality itself will be held liable. This contention denigrates the sense of responsibility of municipal officers, and misunderstands the political process. Responsible local officials will be concerned about potential judgments against their municipalities for alleged constitutional torts. Moreover, they will be accountable within the political system for subjecting the municipality to adverse judgments. If officials must look over their shoulders at a strict municipal liability for unknowable constitutional deprivations, the resulting degree of governmental paralysis will be little different from that caused by fear of personal liability. Cf. Wood v. Strickland.[9]

* * *

---

9. The Court's argument is not only unpersuasive, but also is internally inconsistent. The Court contends that strict liability is necessary to "create an incentive for officials ... to err on the side of protecting citizens' constitutional rights." Yet the Court later assures us that such liability will not distort municipal decisionmaking because "[t]he inhibiting effect is significantly reduced, if not eliminated ... when the threat of personal liability is removed." Thus, the Court

The Court nevertheless suggests that, as a matter of social justice, municipal corporations should be strictly liable even if they could not have known that a particular action would violate the Constitution. After all, the Court urges, local governments can "spread" the costs of any judgment across the local population. The Court neglects, however, the fact that many local governments lack the resources to withstand substantial unanticipated liability under § 1983. Even enthusiastic proponents of municipal liability have conceded that ruinous judgments under the statute could imperil local governments. E.g., Note, *Damage Remedies Against Municipalities for Constitutional Violations*, 89 HARV. L. REV. 922, 958 (1976).[11] By simplistically applying the theorems of welfare economics and ignoring the reality of municipal finance, the Court imposes strict liability on the level of government least able to bear it. For some municipalities, the result could be a severe limitation on their ability to serve the public.

* * *

[Indeed, the 42d Congress acknowledged these same concerns when it rejected the Sherman Amendment, discussed in the *Monell* case.] Most significant, the opponents [of the amendment] objected to liability imposed without any showing that a municipality knew of an impending constitutional deprivation. Senator Sherman defended this feature of the amendment as a characteristic of Riot Acts long in force in England and this country. But Senator Stevenson argued against creating "a corporate liability for personal injury which no prudence or foresight could have prevented." [His view prevailed in the amended provision later adopted.]

These objections to the Sherman amendment apply with equal force to strict municipal liability under § 1983. Just as the 42d Congress refused to hold municipalities vicariously liable for deprivations that could not be known beforehand, this Court should not hold those entities strictly liable for deprivations caused by actions that reasonably and in good faith were thought to be legal. The Court's approach today, like the Sherman amendment, could spawn onerous judgments against local governments and distort the decisions of officers who fear municipal liability for their actions. Congress' refusal to impose those burdens in 1871 surely undercuts any historical argument that federal judges should do so now.

* * *

The Court's decision also runs counter to the common law in the 19th century, which recognized substantial tort immunity for municipal actions. E.g., 2 J. Dillon, Law of Municipal Corporations §§ 753, 764, pp. 862–863, 875–876 (2d ed. 1873); W. Williams, Liability of Municipal Corporations for Tort 9, 16 (1901). * * * It is inconceivable that a

---

apparently believes that strict municipal liability is needed to modify public policies, but will not have any impact on those policies anyway.

11. For example, in a recent case in Alaska, a jury awarded almost $500,000 to a policeman who was accused of "racism and brutality" and removed from duty without notice and an opportunity to be heard. Wayson v. City of Fairbanks, 22 ATLA L.Rep. 222 (Alaska Fourth Dist.Super.Ct.1979).

Congress thoroughly versed in current legal doctrines would have intended through silence to create the strict liability regime now imagined by this Court.[18] [Even the *Thayer* case, on which the majority relies, was later substantially restricted by Massachusetts courts and was finally repudiated in 1877.]

* * *

[Today's decision also disregards modern law: 90% of the states recognize an immunity under state law analogous to qualified immunity.] This disregard of precedent and policy is especially unfortunate because suits under § 1983 typically implicate evolving constitutional standards. A good-faith defense is much more important for those actions than in those involving ordinary tort liability. The duty not to run over a pedestrian with a municipal bus is far less likely to change than is the rule as to what process, if any, is due the busdriver if he claims the right to a hearing after discharge.

* * * As a result, local governments and their officials will face the unnerving prospect of crushing damages judgments whenever a policy valid under current law is later found to be unconstitutional. I can see no justice or wisdom in that outcome.

NOTE ON LIMITATIONS ON GOVERNMENTAL RESPONSIBILITY

1. As the *Owen* case indicates, the Supreme Court has refused to extend qualified immunity to local government units. Yet *Owen* was decided during the period when such immunity was considered to have a subjective component for testing good faith, in addition to the current component that focuses exclusively on the settled nature of constitutional law.

(a) Is *Owen* affected by the change to an objective test for qualified immunity? Are the factors relied upon by Justice Brennan equally applicable in light of an objective test?

(b) Does the resort to common law as of 1871 serve Justice Brennan well? Is Justice Powell right—there was no history of immunity because there was no history of liability? Recall the similar issue raised by Justice Scalia, in the context of immunity for individual officers, in the *Malley* case, discussed in Chapter 1D. Is Justice Powell correct in referring to Brennan's approach as "strict liability" for municipalities?

(c) *Owen* declines to extend an officer's qualified immunity to a local government. Does the opinion necessarily preclude an absolute immunity for local governments?

2. If there is no protective immunity for local governments, then such governments will be held liable for violations of both settled and changing constitutional law, whenever the *Monell* attribution standards are met. Are

---

18. * * * The Court takes some solace in the absence in the 19th century of a qualified immunity for local governments. That absence, of course, was due to the availability of absolute immunity for governmental and discretionary acts. There is no justification for discovering strict municipal liability in § 1983 when that statute was enacted against a background of extensive municipal immunity. * * * [Repositioned footnote.]

the *Monell* factors alone adequate to protect local government interests in avoiding damage judgments?

(a) Does *Monell*'s emphasis on "policy" sufficiently confine municipal liability to those situations where a considered choice was made, situations where decisionmakers had sufficient deliberative time to consider the evolving nature of constitutional law? Reconsider *Pembaur* in light of *Owen.*

(b) Is *Owen* itself a compromise in the greater scheme of things? Did the success of official immunity in protecting individual defendants leave unimmunized local government liability as the only real source of relief for plaintiffs? If so, is the trade off a good one? Who should bear the monetary cost of unconstitutional wrongdoing by city policymakers—the policymakers, the taxpayers, or the plaintiff? Does your answer change in the context of unsettled, evolving constitutional law?

(c) Was *Owen* compelled by the Court's decision in the *Lyons* case? If injunctive relief is barred when there is an adequate remedy at law, does it place pressure on the justices to allow damages remedies? Should the Court return to an era that emphasized remedial decrees and de-emphasized damage recoveries?

3. The year following *Owen,* in **City of Newport v. Fact Concerts, Inc.**, 453 U.S. 247, 101 S.Ct. 2748, 69 L.Ed.2d 616 (1981), the Supreme Court allayed some of the dissenters' concerns when it ruled that municipalities were immune from punitive damages awards. Following the technique employed in *Owen,* the Court looked at the common law existing in 1871 and determined that the "virtually unanimous" practice was to disallow such awards against local governments. 453 U.S. at 260–61, 101 S.Ct. at 2756–57. The Court reasoned on policy grounds that such an award " 'punishes' only the taxpayers, who took no part in the commission of the tort." Id. at 267.

(a) Justice Brennan dissented on a procedural ground, but he observed in a footnote that the majority had not sufficiently distinguished between punitive damages awards based on respondeat superior and those, as under § 1983, predicated on "official policy." He suggested that the "blameless taxpayer" rationale had no application to such official-policy cases. Do you agree?

(b) Can *Fact Concerts* be explained by a simpler maxim—"enough is enough"? Are compensatory damages enough to compensate the plaintiff? Enough to deter grossly negligent or malicious wrongdoing? Are punitive damages deterrent enough when they are awarded from an individual defendant alone?

4. Assume that you can rewrite § 1983's mix of individual and municipal liability rules, without regard to the common law as it existed in 1871. How would you draft the rules? Should the new law apportion damages between individuals and local governments? What mix of liability rules would maximize compensation and deterrence? Should such rules take account of "blameless taxpayers" or rely on cost-spreading without regard to fault?

2. STATE GOVERNMENTS AND THE ELEVENTH AMENDMENT

WILL v. MICHIGAN DEPT. OF STATE POLICE

Supreme Court of the United States, 1989.
491 U.S. 58, 109 S.Ct. 2304, 105 L.Ed.2d 45.

JUSTICE WHITE delivered the opinion of the Court.

This case presents the question whether a State, or an official of the State while acting in his or her official capacity, is a "person" within the meaning of 42 U.S.C. § 1983.

Petitioner Ray Will filed suit in Michigan Circuit Court alleging various violations of the United States and Michigan Constitutions as grounds for a claim under § 1983.

He alleged that he had been denied a promotion to a data systems analyst position with the Department of State Police for an improper reason, that is, because his brother had been a student activist and the subject of a "red squad" file maintained by respondent. Named as defendants were the Department of State Police and the Director of State Police in his official capacity, also a respondent here.

[The state courts found that plaintiff's constitutional rights had been violated, but refused to give relief against the state, holding that it was not a "person" under § 1983.]

Some courts, including the Michigan Supreme Court here, have construed our decision in Quern v. Jordan, 440 U.S. 332, 99 S.Ct. 1139, 59 L.Ed.2d 358 (1979), as holding by implication that a State is not a person under § 1983. See Smith v. Department of Pub. Health, 428 Mich. 540, 581, 410 N.W.2d 749, 767 (1987). *Quern* held that § 1983 does not override a State's Eleventh Amendment immunity, a holding that the concurrence suggested was "patently dicta" to the effect that a State is not a person, 440 U.S. at 350, 99 S.Ct. 1139, 59 L.Ed.2d 358 (Brennan, J., concurring in judgment).

Petitioner filed the present § 1983 action in Michigan state court, which places the question whether a State is a person under § 1983 squarely before us since the Eleventh Amendment does not apply in state courts. Maine v. Thiboutot, 448 U.S. 1, 9, n. 7, 100 S.Ct. 2502, 2507, n. 7, 65 L.Ed.2d 555 (1980). For the reasons that follow, we reaffirm today what we had concluded prior to *Monell* and what some have considered implicit in *Quern:* that a State is not a person within the meaning of § 1983.

We observe initially that if a State is a "person" within the meaning of § 1983, the section is to be read as saying that "every person, including a State, who, under color of any statute, ordinance, regulation, custom, or usage, of any State or Territory or the District of Columbia, subjects...." That would be a decidedly awkward way of expressing an intent to subject the States to liability. At the very least, reading the statute in this way is not so clearly indicated that it provides reason to depart from the often-expressed understanding that "in common usage, the term 'person' does not include the sovereign, [and] statutes employing the [word] are ordinarily construed to exclude it." Wilson v. Omaha Indian Tribe, 442 U.S. 653, 667, 99 S.Ct. 2529, 2537, 61 L.Ed.2d 153 (1979) [internal quotations omitted].

* * *

The language of § 1983 also falls far short of satisfying the ordinary rule of statutory construction that if Congress intends to alter the "usual constitutional balance between the States and the Federal Government," it must make its intention to do so "unmistakably clear in the language of the statute." Atascadero State Hospital v. Scanlon, 473 U.S. 234, 242, 105 S.Ct. 3142, 3147, 87 L.Ed.2d 171 (1985). *Atascadero* was an Eleventh Amendment case, but a similar approach is applied in other contexts. Congress should make its intention "clear and manifest" if it intends to pre-empt the historic powers of the States, Rice v. Santa Fe Elevator Corp., 331 U.S. 218, 230, 67 S.Ct. 1146, 1152, 91 L.Ed. 1447 (1947), or if it intends to impose a condition on the grant of federal moneys, Pennhurst State School and Hospital v. Halderman, 451 U.S. 1, 16, 101 S.Ct. 1531, 1539, 67 L.Ed.2d 694 (1981); South Dakota v. Dole, 483 U.S. 203, 207, 107 S.Ct. 2793, 2795, 97 L.Ed.2d 171 (1987). "In traditionally sensitive areas, such as legislation affecting the federal balance, the requirement of clear statement assures that the legislature has in fact faced, and intended to bring into issue, the critical matters involved in the judicial decision." United States v. Bass, 404 U.S. 336, 349, 92 S.Ct. 515, 523, 30 L.Ed.2d 488 (1971).

Our conclusion that a State is not a person within the meaning of § 1983 is reinforced by Congress' purpose in enacting the statute. Congress enacted § 1 of the Civil Rights Act of 1871, 17 Stat. 13, the precursor to § 1983, shortly after the end of the Civil War "in response to the widespread deprivations of civil rights in the Southern States and the inability or unwillingness of authorities in those States to protect those rights or punish wrongdoers." Felder v. Casey. Although Congress did not establish federal courts as the exclusive forum to remedy these deprivations, it is plain that "Congress assigned to the federal courts a paramount role" in this endeavor, Patsy v. Board of Regents of Florida, 457 U.S. 496, 503, 102 S.Ct. 2557, 2561, 73 L.Ed.2d 172 (1982).

Section 1983 provides a federal forum to remedy many deprivations of civil liberties, but it does not provide a federal forum for litigants who seek a remedy against a State for alleged deprivations of civil liberties. The Eleventh Amendment bars such suits unless the State has waived its immunity, Welch v. Texas Dept. of Highways and Public Transportation, 483 U.S. 468, 472–73, 107 S.Ct. 2941, 97 L.Ed.2d 389 (1987) (plurality opinion), or unless Congress has exercised its undoubted power under § 5 of the Fourteenth Amendment to override that immunity. That Congress, in passing § 1983, had no intention to disturb the States' Eleventh Amendment immunity and so to alter the Federal–State balance in that respect was made clear in our decision in *Quern*. Given that a principal purpose behind the enactment of § 1983 was to provide a federal forum for civil rights claims, and that Congress did not provide such a federal forum for civil rights claims against States, we cannot accept petitioner's argument that Congress intended nevertheless to create a cause of action against States to be brought in state courts, which are precisely the courts Congress sought to allow civil rights claimants to avoid through § 1983.

This does not mean, as petitioner suggests, that we think that the scope of the Eleventh Amendment and the scope of § 1983 are not separate issues. Certainly they are. But in deciphering congressional intent as to the scope of § 1983, the scope of the Eleventh Amendment is a consideration, and we decline to adopt a reading of § 1983 that disregards it.

Our conclusion is further supported by our holdings that in enacting § 1983, Congress did not intend to override well-established immunities or defenses under the common law. "One important assumption underlying the Court's decisions in this area is that members of the 42d Congress were familiar with common-law principles, including defenses previously recognized in ordinary tort litigation, and that they likely intended these common-law principles to obtain, absent specific provisions to the contrary." Newport v. Fact Concerts, Inc., 453 U.S. 247, 258, 101 S.Ct. 2748, 2755, 69 L.Ed.2d 616 (1981). The doctrine of sovereign immunity was a familiar doctrine at common law. "The principle is elementary that a State cannot be sued in its own courts without its consent." Railroad Co. v. Tennessee, 101 U.S. 337, 339, 25 L.Ed. 960 (1880). It is an "established principle of jurisprudence" that the sovereign cannot be sued in its own courts without its consent. Beers v. Arkansas, 61 U.S. (20 How.) 527, 529, 15 L.Ed. 991 (1858). We cannot conclude that § 1983 was intended to disregard the well-established immunity of a State from being sued without its consent.

The legislative history of § 1983 does not suggest a different conclusion.

* * *

Likewise, the Act of Feb. 25, 1871, § 2, 16 Stat. 431 (the "Dictionary Act"),[8] on which we relied in *Monell*, does not counsel a contrary conclusion here. As we noted in *Quern*, that Act, while adopted prior to § 1 of the Civil Rights Act of 1871, was adopted after § 2 of the Civil Rights Act of 1866, from which § 1 of the 1871 Act was derived. Moreover, we disagree with Justice Brennan that at the time the Dictionary Act was passed "the phrase 'bodies politic and corporate' was understood to include the States." Rather, an examination of authorities of the era

---

8. The Dictionary Act provided that "in all acts hereafter passed ... the word 'person' may extend and be applied to bodies politic and corporate ... unless the context shows that such words were intended to be used in a more limited sense." Act of Feb. 25, 1871, § 2, 16 Stat. 431.

suggests that the phrase was used to mean corporations, both private and public (municipal), and not to include the States. In our view, the Dictionary Act, like § 1983 itself and its legislative history, fails to evidence a clear congressional intent that States be held liable.

* * *

Petitioner asserts, alternatively, that state officials should be considered "persons" under § 1983 even though acting in their official capacities. In this case, petitioner named as defendant not only the Michigan Department of State Police but also the Director of State Police in his official capacity.

Obviously, state officials literally are persons. But a suit against a state official in his or her official capacity is not a suit against the official but rather is a suit against the official's office. Brandon v. Holt, 469 U.S. 464, 471, 105 S.Ct. 873, 877, 83 L.Ed.2d 878 (1985). As such, it is no different from a suit against the State itself. See, *e.g.,* Kentucky v. Graham, 473 U.S. 159, 165–166, 105 S.Ct. 3099, 3104–3105, 87 L.Ed.2d 114 (1985); *Monell,* supra, at 690, n. 55, 98 S.Ct., at 2035, n. 55. We see no reason to adopt a different rule in the present context, particularly when such a rule would allow petitioner to circumvent congressional intent by a mere pleading device.[10]

We hold that neither a State nor its officials acting in their official capacities are "persons" under § 1983. The judgment of the Michigan Supreme Court is affirmed.

It is so ordered.

JUSTICE BRENNAN, with whom JUSTICE MARSHALL, JUSTICE BLACKMUN, and JUSTICE STEVENS join, dissenting.

Because this case was brought in state court, the Court concedes, the Eleventh Amendment is inapplicable here. Like the guest who wouldn't leave, however, the Eleventh Amendment lurks everywhere in today's decision and, in truth, determines its outcome.

* * *

The idea that the word "persons" ordinarily excludes the sovereign can be traced to the "familiar principle that the King is not bound by any act of Parliament unless he be named therein by special and particular words." Dollar Savings Bank v. United States, 86 U.S. (19 Wall.) 227, 239, 22 L.Ed. 80 (1874). As this passage suggests, however, this interpretive principle applies only to "the enacting sovereign." United States v. California, 297 U.S. 175, 186, 56 S.Ct. 421, 425, 80 L.Ed. 567 (1936).

* * *

---

10. Of course a State official in his or her official capacity, when sued for injunctive relief, would be a person under § 1983 because "official-capacity actions for prospective relief are not treated as actions against the State." Kentucky v. Graham, 473 U.S., at 167, n. 14, 105 S.Ct., at 3106, n. 14; Ex parte Young, 209 U.S. 123, 159–160, 28 S.Ct. 441, 453–454, 52 L.Ed. 714 (1908). This distinction is "commonplace in sovereign immunity doctrine," L. Tribe, American Constitutional Law.

Both before and after the time when the Dictionary Act and § 1983 were passed, the phrase "bodies politic and corporate" was understood to include the States. See, *e.g.,* J. Bouvier, 1 A Law Dictionary Adapted to the Constitution and Laws of the United States of America 185 (11th ed., 1866).

* * *

The reason why States are "bodies politic and corporate" is simple: just as a corporation is an entity that can act only through its agents, "[t]he State is a political corporate body, can act only through agents, and can command only by laws." Poindexter v. Greenhow, 114 U.S. [270,] 288, 5 S.Ct. [903,] 912–913, 29 L.Ed.2d 185 (1885). See also Black's Law Dictionary 159 (5th ed. 1979) ("body politic or corporate": "[a] social compact by which the whole people covenants with each citizen, and each citizen with the whole people, that all shall be governed by certain laws for the common good"). As a "body politic and corporate," a State falls squarely within the Dictionary Act's definition of a "person."

* * *

To describe the breadth of the Court's holding is to demonstrate its unwisdom. If States are not "persons" within the meaning of § 1983, then they may not be sued under that statute regardless of whether they have consented to suit. Even if, in other words, a State formally and explicitly consented to suits against it in federal or state court, no § 1983 plaintiff could proceed against it because States are not within the statute's category of possible defendants.

This is indeed an exceptional holding. Not only does it depart from our suggestion in Alabama v. Pugh, 438 U.S. 781, 782, 98 S.Ct. 3057, 3058, 57 L.Ed.2d 1114 (1978), that a State could be a defendant under § 1983 if it consented to suit, but it also renders ineffective the choices some States have made to permit such suits against them. See, e.g., Della Grotta v. Rhode Island, 781 F.2d 343 (CA1 1986). I do not understand what purpose is served, what principle of federalism or comity is promoted, by refusing to give force to a State's explicit consent to suit.

* * *

JUSTICE STEVENS, dissenting. [Omitted.]

NOTE ON **Will** AND THE BACKGROUND OF ELEVENTH AMENDMENT JURISPRUDENCE

1. *Will* read into the language of § 1983 a somewhat complex set of rules derived directly from the Court's pre-existing Eleventh Amendment jurisprudence.[1] While those rules can be organized in several ways, see footnote 3 infra, they substantially provide as follows:

---

1. Later decisions from the Court ground these rules not only in the Eleventh Amendment but also in background constitutional considerations emanating from the text of the Constitution,

The General Rule. Suits against a state in its own name as well as suits against its officers, where the relief sought would impact on state programs, are barred in federal court. Thus, suits for injunctive relief against state officers asking them to perform an official function are barred, while suits against an officer for payment from his own pocket do not impact on the state and thus fall outside the General Rule. See Blatchford v. Native Village of Noatak, 501 U.S. 775, 111 S.Ct. 2578, 115 L.Ed.2d 686 (1991) (states and Indian tribes reciprocally immune from suit); Welch v. State Dept. of Highways, 483 U.S. 468, 107 S.Ct. 2941, 97 L.Ed.2d 389 (1987); In re Ayers, 123 U.S. 443, 8 S.Ct. 164, 31 L.Ed. 216 (1887).

The Young *Exception.* A suit against an officer alleging a violation of the federal Constitution is excepted from the General Rule, based upon the fiction that the officer is acting outside his authority, thus stripping his actions of the cloak of the state. Ex parte Young, 209 U.S. 123, 28 S.Ct. 441, 52 L.Ed. 714 (1908).[2]

Exception to the Exception. Even in suits alleging a federal constitutional violation, some relief is forbidden because it too seriously or retroactively impacts on the state treasury. See Edelman v. Jordan, excerpted later in this sub-section.[3]

(a) The *Will* opinion leading up to footnote 10 supports the General Rule, and footnote 10 adopts the Exceptions, correct? Note the authorities cited in footnote 10. What other reading can you give the footnote?

(b) If *Will* simply reads the Eleventh Amendment's complex rules into the word "person" in § 1983, does the result surprise you? Are you amazed that the single word "person" could have such a convoluted meaning? Or are you not surprised, for even though the Eleventh Amendment is phrased in terms of federal jurisdiction, it actually serves much more fundamental goals?

(c) The practical effect of *Will,* of course, is to protect states not only from federal court suits under § 1983, but also from such suits when they are filed in state court. Is *Will* thus a symmetrical counterpart to Howlett v. Rose, discussed in the Note on § 1983 in State Courts, Chapter 1E supra? Only if you think that the Eleventh Amendment is concerned with more than jurisdiction?

---

principally Article III, before Amendment 11 was added. See Alden v. Maine, 527 U.S. 706, 119 S.Ct. 2240, 144 L.Ed.2d 636 (1999); Henry Paul Monaghan, *The Sovereign Immunity "Exception,"* 110 HARV. L. REV. 102 (1996).

2. Compare Home Tel. and Tel. Co. v. City of Los Angeles, discussed in the Note on the Personal Liability Model for § 1983, supra, which held that acts outside the scope of one's state authority are nevertheless state action for Fourteenth Amendment purposes. Ex Parte Young holds the contrary for Eleventh Amendment purposes, an irony well recognized by constitutional scholars. Wright & Kane, Federal Courts § 48 (7th ed. 2011).

3. In Virginia Office for Protection and Advocacy v. Stewart, ___ U.S. ___, 131 S.Ct. 1632, 179 L.Ed.2d 675 (2011), the Court covered the same rules with these statements: 1) "States have retained their traditional immunity from suit"; 2) *Young* provides that "because an unconstitutional legislative enactment is 'void,' a state official who enforces that law 'comes into conflict with the superior authority of [the] Constitution,' and therefore is 'stripped of his official or representative character and is subjected in his person to the consequences of his individual conduct'"; but 3) the exception "does not apply 'when the state is the real, substantial party in interest,'" as when the "'judgment sought would expend itself on the public treasury or domain, or interfere with public administration'" rather than provide for "prospective" relief.

(d) Section 1983 cases against a state officer that seek injunctive relief rather than monetary payments from the state present no problem under *Will* or the traditional Eleventh Amendment rules. Why? Thus major staples of § 1983 litigation such as school desegregation suits and prison reform litigation survive the *Will* decision, do they not?

2. If *Will* effectively precludes in state court those § 1983 suits that would be barred by the Eleventh Amendment from federal court, what policy judgments support such a result? Granted that federal courts should not too much interfere with either federal or state treasuries for some important reasons (to be explored later), why should *state* courts be similarly restrained? Does the federal Congress have a valid interest in maintaining the restricted role of state courts? Is there a federal constitutional interest in restricting state courts? If a state wishes to override *Will,* may it provide a cause of action under state law for federal constitutional violations by the state?

3. The Eleventh Amendment notions that underlie *Will* have been under extremely vigorous attack in liberal and academic circles, principally on the ground that it perpetuates a mistaken interpretation of the amendment and leaves victims remediless. See Port Authority Trans–Hudson Corp. v. Feeney, 495 U.S. 299, 110 S.Ct. 1868, 109 L.Ed.2d 264 (1990) (Brennan, J., joined by Blackmun and Stevens, JJ., concurring); Jackson, *The Supreme Court, the Eleventh Amendment, and State Sovereign Immunity*, 98 YALE L. J. 1 (1988). But is this true? In **McKesson Corp. v. Division of Alcoholic Bev. & Tobacco**, 496 U.S. 18, 110 S.Ct. 2238, 110 L.Ed.2d 17 (1990), authored by Justice Brennan for a unanimous Court, the state of Florida had sought to avoid paying back unconstitutionally collected taxes. The Court ruled that due process requires that states provide repayment and that the Eleventh Amendment does not restrict the Court's ability to award such restitution on direct review of state-court judgments.

(a) Is *McKesson* consistent with *Will?* Do the cases show that the Supreme Court does not trust the lower courts—federal or state—to deal with state treasuries, but does trust itself? Does *McKesson* alleviate for plaintiffs the problems created by *Will,* at least with respect to constitutional claims? Are *McKesson* and *Will* easily reconciled: the constitutional principle served is federal constitutional supremacy, and the availability of a remedy in the Supreme Court is adequate to vindicate that interest? See Carlos Vazquez, *What Is Eleventh Amendment Immunity*, 106 YALE L.J. 1683 (1997).

(b) If § 1983 cannot be employed in state court because a state is not a covered "person," how can a plaintiff get to the Supreme Court in order to invoke *McKesson*? Is the route open only when state law provides a cause of action to the plaintiff? Must state law provide a remedy for all federal violations, or only for the property deprivations at issue in *McKesson* itself?

4. *Will* does not settle all matters, of course, because its footnote 10 does not spell out the line between permissible and impermissible official capacity suits. The Eleventh Amendment jurisprudence therefore remains pertinent. See the *Edelman* case, which follows the next Note.

NOTE ON NOMENCLATURE IN SUITS AGAINST GOVERNMENT OFFICERS:
"PERSONAL CAPACITY" AND "OFFICIAL CAPACITY"

1. The nomenclature in the area of sovereign immunity law, and to a related extent in the area of municipal liability under § 1983, has been dogged by substantial confusion among three doctrinal phrases, reviewed below, and their relationship to two phrases of art, "personal capacity suits" and "official capacity suits."

   (i) *Under color of law*: The original *Monroe* decision foresaw that there can be two distinctly different types of permissible § 1983 actions, those in which the officer obeyed state law while acting within his lawful authority and those in which the officer flouted state law while acting outside the limits of his state-law authority. In both circumstances the defendant is acting "under color of law." See Chapter 1C supra.

   (ii) *Official immunity*: An officer sued under § 1983 may assert a defense against damages liability called "official immunity," either absolute immunity or qualified immunity. See Chapter 1D supra.

   (iii) *Sovereign immunity*: States may assert a defense of sovereign immunity in § 1983 actions, and some suits against state officers will be deemed to be actions against the state even when the officer is the only named defendant. See ¶ 1 of the preceding Note. The sovereign immunity rules are also captured in the word "person" as used in § 1983, as discussed in the preceding *Will* case.

The confusion is usually predicated on this assumption by defendants: If I am being sued for action under color of law, then I must be a governmental officer, and therefore I must be able to claim official immunity or even sovereign immunity. If the assumption were true, no § 1983 suit could ever be successful because every case in which the plaintiff established that a defendant acted under color of law, a necessary element of every claim, there would exist one or the other defense. Of course, that cannot be true.

2. To a certain extent, the Court's tendency to use the phrases "personal capacity" and "official capacity" to describe different kinds of § 1983 actions has promoted the confusion among different doctrines. The Supreme Court eliminated most of the confusion in **Hafer v. Melo**, 502 U.S. 21, 112 S.Ct. 358, 116 L.Ed.2d 301 (1991), and **Kentucky v. Graham**, 473 U.S. 159, 105 S.Ct. 3099, 87 L.Ed.2d 114 (1985). Both cases involved suits against state-level officials under § 1983, with the plaintiff in *Kentucky* styling his suit as one against the defendant in his "personal capacity" and the plaintiff in *Hafer* styling his suit as one against the defendant in her "official capacity." Both cases discuss the interplay between the phrases and the concepts reviewed in ¶ 1 supra. The *Hafer* opinion, authored by Justice O'Connor announced the Court's approach, 502 U.S. at 25, 112 S.Ct. at 361–62:

   "In Kentucky v. Graham, the Court sought to eliminate lingering confusion about the distinction between personal-and official-capacity suits. We emphasized that official-capacity suits 'generally represent only another way of pleading an action against an entity of which an officer is an agent,' Id. (quoting Monell v. New York City Dept. of Social Services). Suits against state officials in their official capacity therefore should be treated as suits against the State. * * * [T]he only immunities available to the defendant in an official-capacity action are those that the governmental entity possesses.

"Personal-capacity suits, on the other hand, seek to impose individual liability upon a government officer for actions taken under color of state law [as that phrase is customarily used in § 1983 cases. Defendants in 'personal capacity' suits] may assert personal immunity defenses such as [qualified immunity]."

(a) The first step to eliminating confusion, continued the Court, is to de-link the "capacity" phrases and the concept of "under color of law": "the phrase 'acting in their official capacities' is best understood as a reference to the capacity in which the state officer is sued, not the capacity in which the officer inflicts the alleged injury," 502 U.S. at 26, 112 S.Ct. at 362. In other words, all injuries are inflicted by the officer acting by the power conferred by state law, and that use of power, whether proper or abusive, satisfies the "under color of law requirement," 502 U.S. at 28, 112 S.Ct. at 363.[1]

(b) What then do "personal capacity" and "official capacity" mean if they relate not to action "under color of law" but to "the capacity in which the officer is sued"? Kentucky v. Graham, supra, held that a personal capacity suit seeks to recover from the officer personally, while an official capacity suit seeks to recover from the government itself. Recovery from an officer personally or individually never implicates sovereign immunity because the relief impacts the officer's purse, not the state's. See ¶ 1 of the preceding Note.

(c) On the other hand, recovery from an officer in his official capacity, as the Court held in *Will*, is not always forbidden by sovereign immunity rules (or the definition of the word "person"). Injunctive relief is permitted to prevent ongoing constitutional violations, but damages claims at law are barred, for reasons discussed in the case following this Note.

3. What are the details of "personal capacity" suits? What follows if a pleader invokes the "personal capacity" language?

(a) As the passage from *Hafer* reveals, ¶ 2 supra, if the recovery is sought from the officer personally, that defendant may invoke the defenses available to any officer personally sued for damages, principally "official immunity." Cf. Chapter 1D supra. (Justice O'Connor's attempt in *Hafer* to re-label these as "personal immunities"—an apparent effort to make "personal capacity" congruent with "personal immunity"—has not endured, leaving us with the still-confusing idea that "official immunity" is invocable as a defense in "personal capacity" suits.)

---

1. "[Defendant's argument that 'personal capacity' suits are linked to action 'under color of law' and may only be brought when a defendant has violated state law] finds no support in the broad language of § 1983. To the contrary, it ignores our holding that Congress enacted § 1983 'to enforce provisions of the Fourteenth Amendment against those who carry a badge of authority of a State and represent it in some capacity, whether they act in accordance with their authority or misuse it.' Monroe v. Pape."

(b) Whether either of the two official immunities, absolute and qualified, actually bars any given "personal capacity" suit under § 1983 is determined by reference to the rules governing those immunities. These rules, see Chapter 1D supra, do not turn on the "personal" or "official" nature of a defendant's acts.

(c) "Personal capacity" suits are permitted regardless of whether the defendant violated state law or abused state law power. Cf. Kentucky v. Graham, supra (personal capacity action against a defendant who obeyed state law in posting Ten Commandments). This reinforces the basic notion in § 1983 jurisprudence that defendants must sometimes choose between obeying state law and obeying constitutional law. Fear of § 1983 liability induces them to make which choice? Official immunity excuses them from this predicament under what circumstances?

4. What are the details of "official capacity" suits? What follows if the pleader invokes the "official capacity" language?

(a) As noted in *Hafer*, ¶ 2 supra, a defendant in an "official capacity" suit may assert the defenses available to the governmental entity of which he is an officer, primarily sovereign immunity for state-level defendants. Since "official capacity" suits against an officer for damages payable by the state are barred by sovereign immunity (or *Will*'s definition of the word "person" in § 1983), the only viable "official capacity" claims are those for injunctive relief.

(b) The principal benefit to the plaintiff is that in an "official capacity" suit the case continues even if the named defendant dies or leaves office. *Hafer*, supra.[2] In effect, the suit is against the named officer as well as against any successor who also would enforce the same policies challenged in the § 1983 action. Similarly, after a favorable judgment, any injunctive decree would also run against the named defendant and any successors who might enforce the same policies. See Hutto v. Finney, 437 U.S. 678, 98 S.Ct. 2565, 57 L.Ed.2d 522 (1978) (attorneys fees and injunctive relief).[3]

(c) "Official capacity" suits, with the benefits discussed above, may only be pursued when it is alleged that the defendant has obediently enforced the state's policy, not when he has strayed from his limited state authority. Note the citation to *Monell* and its definition of policy in *Hafer*, footnote 1, supra. Why is it fair to continue a case against successors in office under such circumstances? Why would it be unfair to continue a case or an injunction against successors in office in "personal capacity" suits where there was no policy?

---

2. See 502 U.S. at 25, 112 S.Ct. at 361: "Indeed, when officials sued in [their official] capacity in federal court die or leave office, their successors automatically assume their roles in the litigation. See FED. R. CIV. PRO. 25(d)(1); FED. R. APP. PRO. 43(c)(1); this Court's Rule 35.3. Because the real party in interest in an official-capacity suit is the governmental entity and not the named official, 'the entity's policy or custom' must have played a part in the violation of federal law." *Graham* (quoting *Monell*)."

3. Does the continuation of suit and relief against successors in office show that "official capacity" actions against state officers are in fact suits against the state itself? Is *Ex Parte Young*'s idea that these are not suits against the state pure fiction? What policies support the fiction in injunctive cases? See the following case and Note.

5. Would it be better to abolish use of the phrases "official capacity" and "personal capacity" and instead require the plaintiff to name the real parties who would be bound by any judgment, the officer and the state? If this simplifying step were taken, how would the sovereign immunity rules, ¶ 1 in the preceding Note, need to be re-written to maintain the status quo? Under what circumstances would suits against a named "state" be permissible without violating the Eleventh Amendment?

6. The same phrases, "personal capacity" and "official capacity," are also used in cases involving local-government officers, which creates some further confusion because local governments can claim no Eleventh Amendment immunity. What roles do the phrases play in such circumstances? In **Brandon v. Holt**, 469 U.S. 464, 105 S.Ct. 873, 83 L.Ed.2d 878 (1985), the Supreme Court faced a § 1983 case in which a plaintiff had named a real-person officer as a defendant and not the officer's local government. The case had proceeded with the government attorneys defending the suit, and the usual *Monell* proofs of governmental policy had been tried, resulting in a judgment holding the local government liable. The Supreme Court held that plaintiff's use of the phrase "official capacity" was sufficient to put the local government on notice that it was the real party defendant.

(a) Would a judgment for the plaintiff have been affirmed if the plaintiff had used the "official immunity" phrase but had failed to present evidence of an official policy under *Monell*? The answer must be no, correct? So there is no actual advantage to using the phrase, is there? In the context of suits against state-level officers, the phrase "official capacity" helps to lubricate acceptance of highly complicated sovereign immunity rules, but in the context of suits against local governments is there any substantial reason for allowing use of these confusing phrases?

(b) Given the confusion over use of the phrases defining capacity, plaintiffs in both suits against state officers and suits against local officers routinely add the boilerplate language that "defendants are sued in both their personal and official capacities." Why is this a safe route for the plaintiff? Cf. FRCP 54(c) ("every final judgment shall grant the relief to the party in whose favor it is rendered is entitled, even if the party has not demanded such relief in the party's pleadings"). Does this safe route create a potential problem for plaintiffs under FRCP 11 (ethical pleading requirements)?

EDELMAN v. JORDAN

Supreme Court of the United States, 1974.
415 U.S. 651, 94 S.Ct. 1347, 39 L.Ed.2d 662.

MR. JUSTICE REHNQUIST delivered the opinion of the Court.

[Plaintiff Jordan's federal class action challenged Illinois' delay in providing public assistance to blind persons as a violation of equal protection and the federal Social Security Act, under which the state program was cooperatively conducted with substantial federal payments to the state. The district court found Illinois' practice to violate the Act and ordered future compliance and an award of all past benefits "wrongfully withheld" from class members. On appeal the Seventh Circuit rejected the state's contention that award of "retroactive benefits" intruded on the state's sovereign immunity under the Eleventh Amendment. The Supreme Court granted certiorari.]

While the [Eleventh] Amendment by its terms does not bar suits against a State by its own citizens, this Court has consistently held that an unconsenting State is immune from suits brought in federal courts by her own citizens as well as by citizens of another State. Hans v. Louisiana, 134 U.S. 1, 10 S.Ct. 504, 33 L.Ed. 842 (1890). It is also well established that even though a State is not named a party to the action, the suit may nonetheless be barred by the Eleventh Amendment. In Ford Motor Co. v. Department of Treasury, 323 U.S. 459, 65 S.Ct. 347, 89 L.Ed. 389 (1945), the Court said:

> "[W]hen the action is in essence one for the recovery of money from the state, the state is the real, substantial party in interest and is entitled to invoke its sovereign immunity from suit even though individual officials are nominal defendants." Id. at 464, 65 S.Ct., at 350.

Thus the rule has evolved that a suit by private parties seeking to impose a liability which must be paid from public funds in the state treasury is barred by the Eleventh Amendment. Great Northern Life Insurance Co. v. Read[, 322 U.S. 47, 64 S.Ct. 873, 88 L.Ed. 1121 (1944)]; Kennecott Copper Corp. v. State Tax Comm'n, 327 U.S. 573, 66 S.Ct. 745, 90 L.Ed. 862 (1946).

The Court of Appeals in this case, while recognizing that the *Hans* line of cases permitted the State to raise the Eleventh Amendment as a defense to suit by its own citizens, nevertheless concluded that the Amendment did not bar the award of retroactive payments of the statutory benefits found to have been wrongfully withheld. The Court of Appeals held that the above-cited cases, when read in light of this Court's landmark decision in Ex parte Young do not preclude the grant of such a monetary award in the nature of equitable restitution.

* * *

Ex parte Young was a watershed case in which this Court held that the Eleventh Amendment did not bar an action in the federal courts seeking to enjoin the Attorney General of Minnesota from enforcing a statute claimed to violate the Fourteenth Amendment of the United States Constitution. This holding has permitted the Civil War Amendments to the Constitution to serve as a sword, rather than merely as a shield, for those whom they were designed to protect. But the relief awarded in Ex parte Young was prospective only; the Attorney General of Minnesota was enjoined to conform his future conduct of that office to the requirement of the Fourteenth Amendment. Such relief is analogous to that awarded by the District Court in the prospective portion of its order under review in this case.

But the retroactive position of the District Court's order here, which requires the payment of a very substantial amount of money which that court held should have been paid, but was not, stands on quite a different footing. These funds will obviously not be paid out of the pocket of petitioner Edelman. * * *

[They] must inevitably come from the general revenues of the State of Illinois, and thus the award resembles far more closely the monetary award against the State itself, Ford Motor Co. v. Department of Treasury, supra, than it does the prospective injunctive relief awarded in Ex parte Young.

The Court of Appeals, in upholding the award in this case, held that it was permissible because it was in the form of equitable "restitution" instead of damages, and therefore capable of being tailored in such a way as to minimize disruptions of the state program of categorical assistance. But we must judge the award actually made in this case, and not one which might have been differently tailored in a different case, and we must judge it in the context of the important constitutional principle embodied in the Eleventh Amendment.[11]

We do not read Ex parte Young or subsequent holdings of this Court to indicate that any form of relief may be awarded against a state officer, no matter how closely it may in practice resemble a money judgment payable out of the state treasury, so long as the relief may be labeled "equitable" in nature. The Court's opinion in Ex parte Young hewed to no such line. Its citation of Hagood v. Southern, 117 U.S. 52, 6 S.Ct. 608, 29 L.Ed. 805 (1886), and In re Ayers, 123 U.S. 443, 8 S.Ct. 164, 31 L.Ed. 216 (1887), which were both actions against state officers for specific performance of a contract to which the State was a party, demonstrate that equitable relief may be barred by the Eleventh Amendment.

As in most areas of the law, the difference between the type of relief barred by the Eleventh Amendment and that permitted under Ex parte Young will not in many instances be that between day and night. The injunction issued in Ex parte Young was not totally without effect on the State's revenues, since the state law which the Attorney General was

---

11. It may be true, as stated by our Brother Douglas in dissent, that "[m]ost welfare decisions by federal courts have a financial impact on the States." But we cannot agree that such a financial impact is the same where a federal court applies Ex parte Young to grant prospective declaratory and injunctive relief, as opposed to an order of retroactive payments as was made in the instant case. * * *

This argument neglects the fact that where the State has a definable allocation to be used in the payment of public aid benefits, and pursues a certain course of action such as the processing of applications within certain time periods as did Illinois here, the subsequent ordering by a federal court of retroactive payments to correct delays in such processing will invariably mean there is less money available for payments for the continuing obligations of the public aid system.

As stated by Judge McGowan in Rothstein v. Wyman, 467 F.2d 226, 235 (CA2 1972):

"The second federal policy which might arguably be furthered by retroactive payments is the fundamental goal of congressional welfare legislation—the satisfaction of the ascertained needs of impoverished persons. * * * As time goes by, however, retroactive payments become compensatory rather than remedial; the coincidence between previously ascertained and existing needs becomes less clear."

enjoined from enforcing provided substantial monetary penalties against railroads which did not conform to its provisions. Later cases from this Court have authorized equitable relief which has probably had greater impact on state treasuries than did that awarded in Ex parte Young. In Graham v. Richardson, 403 U.S. 365, 91 S.Ct. 1848, 29 L.Ed.2d 534 (1971), Arizona and Pennsylvania welfare officials were prohibited from denying welfare benefits to otherwise qualified recipients who were aliens. In Goldberg v. Kelly, 397 U.S. 254, 90 S.Ct. 1011, 25 L.Ed.2d 287 (1970), New York City welfare officials were enjoined from following New York State procedures which authorized the termination of benefits paid to welfare recipients without prior hearing. But the fiscal consequences to state treasuries in these cases were the necessary result of compliance with decrees which by their terms were prospective in nature. State officials, in order to shape their official conduct to the mandate of the Court's decrees, would more likely have to spend money from the state treasury than if they had been left free to pursue their previous course of conduct. Such an ancillary effect on the state treasury is a permissible and often an inevitable consequence of the principle announced in Ex parte Young, supra.

But that portion of the District Court's decree which petitioner challenges on Eleventh Amendment grounds goes much further than any of the cases cited. It requires payment of state funds, not as a necessary consequence of compliance in the future with a substantive federal-question determination, but as a form of compensation to those whose applications were processed on the slower time schedule at a time when petitioner was under no court-imposed obligation to conform to a different standard. While the Court of Appeals described this retroactive award of monetary relief as a form of "equitable restitution," it is in practical effect indistinguishable in many aspects from an award of damages against the State. It will to a virtual certainty be paid from state funds, and not from the pockets of the individual state officials who were the defendants in the action. It is measured in terms of a monetary loss resulting from a past breach of a legal duty on the part of the defendant state officials.

* * *

The Court of Appeals held in the alternative that even if the Eleventh Amendment be deemed a bar to the retroactive relief awarded respondent in this case, the State of Illinois had waived its Eleventh Amendment immunity and consented to the bringing of such a suit by participating in the federal [public assistance] program. The Court of Appeals relied upon our holdings in Parden v. Terminal Ry. of Alabama State Docks Dept., 377 U.S. 184, 84 S.Ct. 1207, 12 L.Ed.2d 233 (1964), and Petty v. Tennessee–Missouri Bridge Comm'n, 359 U.S. 275, 79 S.Ct. 785, 3 L.Ed.2d 804 (1959) * * *. Parden involved a congressional enactment which by its terms authorized suit by designated plaintiffs against a general class of defendants which literally included States or state instrumentalities. Similarly, Petty v. Tennessee–Missouri Bridge Comm'n, supra, involved congressional approval, pursuant to the Compact Clause, of a compact between Tennessee and Missouri, which provided that each compacting State would have the power "to contract, to sue, and be sued in its own name." The question of waiver or consent under the Eleventh Amendment was found in those cases to turn on whether Congress had intended to abrogate the immunity in question, and whether the State by its participation in the program authorized by Congress had in effect consented to the abrogation of that immunity.

But in this case the threshold fact of congressional authorization to sue a class of defendants which literally includes States is wholly absent. * * * The Court of Appeals held that as a matter of federal law Illinois had "constructively consented" to this suit by participating in the federal AABD program and agreeing to administer federal and state funds in compliance with federal law. Constructive consent is not a doctrine commonly associated with the surrender of constitutional rights, and we see no place for it here. In deciding whether a State has waived its constitutional protection under the Eleventh Amendment, we will find waiver only where stated "by the most express language or by such overwhelming implications from the text as [will] leave no room for any other reasonable construction." Murray v. Wilson Distilling Co., 213 U.S. 151, 171, 29 S.Ct. 458, 464, 53 L.Ed. 742 (1909). * * *

The mere fact that a State participates in a program through which the Federal Government provides assistance for the operation by the State of a system of public aid is not sufficient to establish consent on the part of the State to be sued in the federal courts. * * *

The only language in the Social Security Act which purported to provide a federal sanction against a State which did not comply with federal requirements for the distribution of federal monies was found in former 42 U.S.C.A. § 1384 (now replaced by substantially similar provisions in 42 U.S.C.A. § 804), which provided for termination of future allocations of federal funds when a participating State failed to conform with federal law.[16] This provision by its terms did not authorize suit against anyone, and standing alone, fell far short of a waiver by a participating State of its Eleventh Amendment immunity.

Our Brother Marshall argues in dissent, and the Court of Appeals held, that although the Social Security Act itself does not create a private cause of action, the cause of action created by 42 U.S.C.A. § 1983, coupled with the enactment of the AABD program, and the issuance by HEW of regulations which require the States to make corrective payments after successful "fair hearings" and provide for federal matching funds to satisfy federal court orders of retroactive payments, indicate that Congress intended a cause of action for public aid recipients such as respondent. It is, of course, true that Rosado v. Wyman, 397 U.S. 397, 90 S.Ct. 1207, 25

---

16. HEW sought passage of a bill in the 91st Congress, H.R. 16311, § 407(a), which would have given it authority to require retroactive payments to eligible persons denied such benefits. The bill failed to pass the House of Representatives.

L.Ed.2d 442 (1970), held that suits in federal court under § 1983 are proper to secure compliance with the provisions of the Social Security Act on the part of participating States. But it has not heretofore been suggested that § 1983 was intended to create a waiver of a State's Eleventh Amendment immunity merely because an action could be brought under that section against state officers, rather than against the State itself. Though a § 1983 action may be instituted by public aid recipients such as respondent, a federal court's remedial power, consistent with the Eleventh Amendment, is necessarily limited to prospective injunctive relief, Ex parte Young, supra, and may not include a retroactive award which requires the payment of funds from the state treasury, Ford Motor Co. v. Department of Treasury, supra.

Respondent urges that since the various Illinois officials sued in the District Court failed to raise the Eleventh Amendment as a defense to the relief sought by respondent, petitioner is therefore barred[19] from raising the Eleventh Amendment defense in the Court of Appeals or in this Court. The Court of Appeals apparently felt the defense was properly presented, and dealt with it on the merits. We approve of this resolution, since it has been well settled since the decision in Ford Motor Co. v. Department of Treasury, supra, that the Eleventh Amendment defense sufficiently partakes of the nature of a jurisdictional bar so that it need not be raised in the trial court * * *.

* * *

Reversed and remanded.

[JUSTICES DOUGLAS, BRENNAN, MARSHALL, and BLACKMUN dissented on the ground that the state had waived its immunity through participation in the cooperative federal program. JUSTICE MARSHALL added (415 U.S. at 692, 94 S.Ct. at 1370):]

Absent any remedy which may act with retroactive effect, state welfare officials have everything to gain and nothing to lose by failing to comply with the congressional mandate that assistance be paid with reasonable promptness to all eligible individuals. This is not idle speculation without basis in practical experience. In this very case, for example, Illinois officials have knowingly violated since 1968 federal regulations on the strength of an argument as to its invalidity which even the majority deems unworthy of discussion. Without a retroactive-payment remedy, we are indeed faced with the spectre of a state, perhaps calculatingly, defying federal law and thereby depriving welfare recipients of the financial assistance Congress thought it was giving them.

---

19. Respondent urges that the State of Illinois has abolished its common-law sovereign immunity in its state courts, and appears to argue that suit in a federal court against the State may thus be maintained. Brief for Respondent 23. Petitioner contends that sovereign immunity has not been abolished in Illinois as to this type of case. Brief for Petitioner 31–36. Whether Illinois permits such a suit to be brought against the State in its own courts is not determinative of whether Illinois has relinquished its Eleventh Amendment immunity from suit in the federal courts. Chandler v. Dix, 194 U.S. 590, 591–592, 24 S.Ct. 766, 767, 48 L.Ed. 1129 (1904).

NOTE ON RELIEF NOT BARRED BY THE ELEVENTH AMENDMENT

1. What is it about prospective relief that makes it acceptable and retroactive relief unacceptable?

(a) Is the phrase "retroactive relief" merely shorthand for "damages"? Note that the Court in *Edelman* left intact the lower court's order requiring future payments of benefits. Are retroactive monetary awards more difficult for the state to accommodate—to plan for and include within the state budget—than prospective awards?

(b) Although some difficult later cases skew the line between retroactive and prospective relief for specific contexts outside the confines of § 1983, see Carlos Vazquez, *Night and Day:* Cour D'Alene, Breard, *and the Unraveling of the Prospective–Retrospective Distinction in Eleventh Amendment Immunity Doctrine*, 87 GEO. L.J. 1 (1998) (e.g., habeas corpus cases), can you think of any relief against a state that is retroactive and yet non-monetary? How about an order requiring transfer of land unconstitutionally taken by a state? Compare North Carolina v. Temple, 134 U.S. 22, 10 S.Ct. 509, 33 L.Ed. 849 (1890), with California v. Deep Sea Research, Inc., 523 U.S. 491, 118 S.Ct. 1464, 140 L.Ed.2d 626 (1998). Should *Edelman* be restricted to just damages awards and their equivalents? Just to damages awards?

2. Another aspect of **Milliken v. Bradley** (*Milliken II*), see Chapter 1F.2 supra, unanimously upheld against an Eleventh Amendment defense an award of injunctive relief despite its substantial cost to the state, specifically a required monetary contribution from the state to local school authorities to aid desegregation. The decree, said the Court, "fits squarely within the prospective compliance exception reaffirmed by *Edelman*." Is *Edelman*'s line between prospective and retrospective relief an illusory one in light of the simultaneous holding in *Milliken II* that the scope of the violation determines the scope of the remedy? Under this proportionality rule, does not even prospective injunctive relief effectively require compensation keyed to a prior wrong—just like retrospective damages?

(a) If the scope of the violation determines the scope of the remedy, will not an injunctive decree cost the defendant about as much as paying out a compensatory damages award? What is the difference—monetarily—between restructuring the state's educational program at a cost to it of $5.8 million (as in *Milliken II*) and simply awarding plaintiffs damages in the sum of $5.8 million? Is the amount of the award relevant? Should *Milliken II* have been decided differently if the required contribution been $150 million? $650 million? See Carlos Vazquez, *Night and Day*, supra (suggesting that one way to maintain the aversion to retrospective relief is to overturn *Milliken*).

(b) If the distinguishing characteristic between permissible and impermissible relief is not cost, what is it? Does the injunctive decree show the state more respect and leave the state with more options, or does the damages award? Is there not a respectable argument for the proposition that the flexibility inherent in equity power gives the federal courts much more discretionary power over state resources than they would ever have in a mere award of damages?

(c) Perhaps it could be argued that limiting relief to prospective injunctions leaves the state free to choose whether to continue the program at all; if it found the cost of operating a constitutionally sound program too expensive, the state could simply cease operations. But could the state cease to act so long as its prior inflictions of injury went unremedied? Could it close down schools, for example, and leave a generation of whites with their good educations and blacks with their inferior, segregated educations? Or would the state be free to cease only after remedying its wrong under federal court injunctive review? See Vazquez, supra. If the latter, how does the financial impact differ from a damages award?

3. In **Hutto v. Finney**, 437 U.S. 678, 98 S.Ct. 2565, 57 L.Ed.2d 522 (1978), the Court approved the award of attorneys fees as litigation costs ancillary to permissible injunctive relief. Would a TRO or preliminary injunction requiring the continuation of state program payments be considered prospective or ancillary under *Hutto*? If an attorneys-fee award is sometimes appropriate against a state, is an enhanced award to compensate for delay in payment barred? See Missouri v. Jenkins by Agyei, 491 U.S. 274, 109 S.Ct. 2463, 105 L.Ed.2d 229 (1989). How should courts treat an order to the state requiring it to notify all winners of prospective relief in federal court that they could file state-law claims for retrospective relief in state court? See Quern v. Jordan, 440 U.S. 332, 99 S.Ct. 1139, 59 L.Ed.2d 358 (1979), aff'g, 563 F.2d 873 (7th Cir.1977).

4. Can federal courts order even prospective relief when plaintiff prevails on a pendent state law claim? In **Pennhurst State School and Hosp. v. Halderman**, 465 U.S. 89, 104 S.Ct. 900, 79 L.Ed.2d 67 (1984), the plaintiff requested relief under both federal and state law, but the trial court awarded injunctive relief against the defendant officer only on the state law claim. The Court held such relief barred by sovereign immunity.

(a) Consult the Eleventh Amendment rules set out in the preceding Note. Of which rule did the plaintiffs run afoul? The dissenters in *Pennhurst* argued in favor of an additional aspect of the Exception, that when necessary to avoid deciding a difficult constitutional issue, the federal court could grant relief on the state law ground. This served the important traditional goal, they said, of discouraging unnecessary constitutional decisionmaking. Do you agree with them? Or was their proposed trade-off not worth the price it cost?

(b) Would the dissenters' approach have simply encouraged plaintiffs to bring pendent state law claims when they feared that sovereign immunity might limit success of their federal law claims? (This is not a rhetorical question.)

(c) *Pennhurst* presented a pendent state law claim; *Ex parte Young* presented federal constitutional claims. As discussed below, it is possible to bring suit under § 1983 for violation of certain federal *statutes*. See Chapter 1I infra. Would such suits be controlled by *Pennhurst* or *Ex parte Young*? Or by neither?

5. Congress has power, held the Court in **Fitzpatrick v. Bitzer**, 427 U.S. 445, 96 S.Ct. 2666, 49 L.Ed.2d 614 (1976), to abrogate states' Eleventh Amendment immunity, at least for state violations of the Fourteenth Amendment. Justice Rehnquist's opinion for the Court held that the Fourteenth

Amendment constituted a specific textual limitation on the States and that under § 5 of the Amendment Congress was given special legislative power to enforce the limitation. "We think," said the Court, 427 U.S. at 456, "that Congress may, in determining what is 'appropriate legislation' for the purpose of enforcing the provisions of the Fourteenth Amendment, provide for private suits against States or state officials which are constitutionally impermissible in other contexts."[1]

(a) Does *Fitzpatrick* effectively create a two-tier Eleventh Amendment, one as interpreted by courts, the other as legislated by Congress? See **United States v. Georgia**, 546 U.S. 151, 126 S.Ct. 877, 163 L.Ed.2d 650 (2006) (Americans with Disabilities Act abrogates sovereign immunity—but only for claims that also constitute Fourteenth Amendment violations). Does the Court treat other constitutional provisions similarly? See Nowak & Rotunda, Constitutional Law § 8.1 (7th ed. 2004) (discussing active and "dormant" commerce clause analyses). But should the Eleventh Amendment be different because it is a jurisdictional provision, and the Court has long resisted expansion of its constitutionally limited jurisdiction? See Marbury v. Madison, 5 U.S. (1 Cranch) 137, 2 L.Ed. 60 (1803).

(b) Should Congress amend § 1983 to provide for relief against states? For limited relief on the same grounds as relief is permitted against municipalities under *Monell*? Why should local governments pay for policy-based § 1983 violations and state governments not?

(c) Should Congress grant greater protection to state treasuries by limiting prospective relief available under § 1983 in official capacity suits? Can Congress do that?

6. In later cases the Supreme Court has restricted federal power to abrogate sovereign immunity by use of its powers under Article I, but these cases have no affect on Congress' power under the Fourteenth Amendment or on the Court's residual sovereign immunity rules as developed in *Edelman*. See, e.g., Alden v. Maine, 527 U.S. 706, 119 S.Ct. 2240, 144 L.Ed.2d 636 (1999) (discussing relations among the various doctrines). Now refocus on the residual sovereign immunity rules in *Edelman*: are they constitutional rules or equitable/prudential rules that the Court may alter based on the facts of individual cases? See Idaho v. Coeur d'Alene Tribe of Idaho, 521 U.S. 261, 117 S.Ct. 2028, 138 L.Ed.2d 438 (1997) (of five votes for sovereign immunity, two justices find principles of *Ex Parte Young* to be equitable rather than constitutional).[2]

NOTE ON THE DIVIDING LINE BETWEEN STATE AND LOCAL ENTITIES

1. Eleventh Amendment immunity applies only to state-level governmental entities, not to local governments. Lincoln County v. Luning, 133 U.S. 529, 10 S.Ct. 363, 33 L.Ed. 766 (1890); Stewart v. Baldwin County Bd. of

---

1. The abrogation must be clear and unambiguous. See Sossamon v. Texas, ___ U.S. ___, 131 S.Ct. 1651, 179 L.Ed.2d 700 (2011) (provision in Religious Land Use and Institutionalized Persons Act of 2000 for "appropriate relief against a government" is inadequate).

2. A related doctrine of waiver has been employed in some cases. See Lapides v. Board of Regents of University System of Georgia, 535 U.S. 613, 122 S.Ct. 1640, 152 L.Ed.2d 806 (2002) (state's removal of a § 1983 claim to federal court waives sovereign immunity).

Educ., 908 F.2d 1499, 1509 (11th Cir.1990) (Alabama school boards are not state-level entities and thus receive no Eleventh Amendment immunity).

(a) Given the liability that local governments must bear under *Monell* and the freedom from monetary liability that state-level entities receive under the Eleventh Amendment, there is great pressure on all governmental agencies to portray themselves as state-level entities. In most cases, such as *Will* and *Monell,* the results are easy because the defendant will be either a state governmental agency or a county or municipality.

(b) But with the expansion of governmental agencies at the state and even interstate level, how should all the interstitial agencies be treated? Should regional state junior colleges be treated differently from a state land-grant university?

2.   The interstitial tiers of state government—those between cities and counties that are deemed local and the State itself—may be sorted out, according to the Court in **Mt. Healthy City Sch. Dist. Bd. of Educ. v. Doyle**, 429 U.S. 274, 280, 97 S.Ct. 568, 572, 50 L.Ed.2d 471 (1977), by looking, "at least in part, [at] the nature of the entity created by state law." In **Port Authority Trans–Hudson Corp. v. Feeney**, 495 U.S. 299, 110 S.Ct. 1868, 109 L.Ed.2d 264 (1990), Justice Brennan's concurring opinion for three members of the Court suggested that the decision as to whether an entity was a state-level body should turn simply on whether the entity at issue was "an arm of the State," was "integrally related to the State," or was "the direct means by which the State acts, for instance a state agency."

(a) In *Mt. Healthy* the Court looked at the following aspects of the Ohio law creating school districts: (i) that the nomenclature of the Ohio Code described school districts as outside the word "State"; (ii) the sources of funding for the school districts, which was both through state and local levies; and (iii) the geographically local power of the entity. "On balance," concluded the Court, the local school board "is more like a county or city than it is like an arm of the state." Is this approach satisfactory?

(b) If state law is relevant, as the Court held in *Mt. Healthy,* could a state insulate its cities and counties, indeed all of its local subdivisions, by labeling all of them in the state code as state entities, suable only in state court? Cf. Chicot County v. Sherwood, 148 U.S. 529, 13 S.Ct. 695, 37 L.Ed. 546 (1893).

(c) Should courts look directly at state law, as in the *Pembaur* line of cases, section H supra (using state law to define policymaking officials)? Would it be better to say that state law is not binding as law but rather serves as evidence of how the state divides its power—and that a decision as to the consequences of that division is a question of federal law? See Auer v. Robbins, 519 U.S. 452, 117 S.Ct. 905, 137 L.Ed.2d 79 (1997) (unanimous) (local Board of Police Commissioners of St. Louis is not an arm of state of Missouri entitled to Eleventh Amendment immunity–governor appoints 80% of members but city is responsible for financial liabilities and state exercises no direct control over board). Cf. Wilson v. Garcia, section E supra (choice of state statute of limitation for § 1983 is a federal question); Moor v. Alameda County, 411 U.S. 693, 717–21, 93 S.Ct. 1785, 1799–1802, 36 L.Ed.2d 596 (1973) (treating parallel issue of subdivisions subject to suit as "citizens" under diversity jurisdiction).

3. A similar problem can arise with respect to individual officers of government, such as a prosecutor or even a judge. If a prosecutor is a local official, she may make policy for which a local government can be held liable, but if she is a state-level official there may be no liability at all because of sovereign immunity. In **McMillian v. Monroe County**, 520 U.S. 781, 117 S.Ct. 1734, 138 L.Ed.2d 1 (1997), Justice Rehnquist suggested that the outcome could be different in each state, depending on the history and structure of each state's government. His 5–4 majority found sheriffs in Alabama to be state-level officers.

(a) Despite the split in results, the technique used by the majority and the dissent appeared to be the same. Both groups found the nomenclature of state law (Alabama's constitution labeled sheriff's as "state" officers) not to be dispositive, though the majority gave it more weight, and each group looked instead at the actual powers conferred on the sheriffs and what authorities in turn controlled the sheriffs. Is this the correct approach? Or should state law be dispositive?

(b) How persuasive is the majority opinion, which emphasized Alabama's history of errant sheriffs and the state's desire to have them controlled by the legislature, which has power to remove them? How persuasive is the dissent, which emphasized that sheriff's are elected from local districts (counties) by voters and derive their funding from local governments? Is there a flaw in this area of jurisprudence? Should so much turn on the labels "state" and "local" when in fact many states adopt creative hybrids to meet their conceptions of good public policy?

(c) What other bodies might be deemed arms of the state in their respective state laws and constitutions? See Purcell ex rel. Estate of Morgan v. Toombs County, 400 F.3d 1313 (11th Cir. 2005) (Georgia sheriff); Benn v. First Judicial Dist. of Pa., 426 F.3d 233 (3d Cir. 2005) (Pennsylvania judge's judicial district; locally funded but a state office).

4. How should courts deal with the creations of interstate compacts or other interstate bodies? See Lake Country Estates, Inc. v. Tahoe Regional Planning Agency, 440 U.S. 391, 99 S.Ct. 1171, 59 L.Ed.2d 401 (1979).

I. EXPANSION AND CONTRACTION OF § 1983

MAINE v. THIBOUTOT

Supreme Court of the United States, 1980.
448 U.S. 1, 100 S.Ct. 2502, 65 L.Ed.2d 555.

MR. JUSTICE BRENNAN delivered the opinion of the Court.

The case presents two related questions arising under 42 U.S.C. §§ 1983 and 1988. Respondents brought this suit in the Maine Superior Court alleging that petitioners, the State of Maine and its Commissioner of Human Services, violated § 1983 by depriving respondents of welfare benefits to which they were entitled under the federal Social Security Act, specifically 42 U.S.C. § 602(a) (7). The petitioners present two issues: (1) whether § 1983 encompasses claims based on purely statutory violations of federal law, and (2) if so, whether attorney's fees under § 1988 may be awarded to the prevailing party in such an action.

I

Respondents, Lionel and Joline Thiboutot, are married and have eight children, three of whom are Lionel's by a previous marriage. The Maine Department of Human Services notified Lionel that, in computing the Aid to Families with Dependent Children (AFDC) benefits to which he was entitled for the three children exclusively his, it would no longer make allowance for the money spent to support the other five children, even though Lionel is legally obligated to support them. Respondents, challenging the State's interpretation of 42 U.S.C. § 602(a)(7), exhausted their state administrative remedies and then sought judicial review of the administrative action in the State Superior Court. By amended complaint, respondents also claimed relief under § 1983 for themselves and others similarly situated. The Superior Court's judgment enjoined petitioners from enforcing the challenged rule and ordered them to adopt new regulations, to notify class members of the new regulations, and to pay the correct amounts retroactively to respondents and prospectively to eligible class members.[1] The court, however, denied respondents' motion for attorney's fees. The Supreme Judicial Court of Maine, 405 A.2d 230 (1979), concluded that respondents had no entitlement to attorney's fees under state law, but were eligible for attorney's fees pursuant to the Civil Rights Attorney's Fees Awards Act of 1976, 90 Stat. 2641, 42 U.S.C. § 1988. We granted certiorari. 444 U.S. 1042, 100 S.Ct. 727, 62 L.Ed.2d 728 (1980). We affirm.

* * * The question before us is whether the phrase "and laws," as used in § 1983, means what it says, or whether it should be limited to some subset of laws. Given that Congress attached no modifiers to the phrase, the plain language of the statute undoubtedly embraces respondents' claim that petitioners violated the Social Security Act.

Even were the language ambiguous, however, any doubt as to its meaning has been resolved by our several cases suggesting, explicitly or implicitly, that the § 1983 remedy broadly encompasses violations of federal statutory as well as constitutional law. Rosado v. Wyman, 397 U.S. 397, 90 S.Ct. 1207, 25 L.Ed.2d 442 (1970), for example, "held that suits in federal court under § 1983 are proper to secure compliance with the provisions of the Social Security Act on the part of participating States." Edelman v. Jordan, 415 U.S. 651, 675, 94 S.Ct. 1347, 1362, 39 L.Ed.2d 662 (1974). Monell v. New York City Dept. of Social Services, as support for its conclusion that municipalities are "persons" under § 1983, reasoned that "there can be no doubt that § 1 of the Civil Rights Act [of 1871] was intended to provide a remedy, to be broadly construed, against all forms of official violation of federally protected rights." * * *

---

1. The State did not appeal the judgment against it.

[The jurisdictional counterpart to § 1983, 28 U.S.C. § 1343(3), contains no reference to "and laws," but only a narrower reference to laws "providing for equal rights." But the reference in the jurisdictional provision should not affect § 1983 itself. When Congress codified the 1871 Civil Rights Act in 1874, adding the "and laws" language that is found in § 1983 today, it broadened the scope of the original statute.]

* * * Congress was aware of what it was doing [when it codified § 1983 and added the "and laws" language], and the legislative history does not demonstrate that the plain language was not intended. Petitioners' arguments amount to the claim that had Congress been more careful, and had it fully thought out the relationship among the various sections, it might have acted differently. That argument, however, can best be addressed to Congress, which, it is important to note, has remained quiet in the face of our many pronouncements on the scope of § 1983. Cf. TVA v. Hill, 437 U.S. 153, 98 S.Ct. 2279, 57 L.Ed.2d 117 (1978).

Petitioners next argue that, even if this claim is within § 1983, Congress did not intend statutory claims to be covered by the Civil Rights Attorney's Fees Awards Act of 1976, which added the following sentence to 42 U.S.C. § 1988 (emphasis added):

"In *any action* or proceeding *to enforce* a provision of sections 1981, 1982, *1983,* 1985, and 1986 of this title, title IX of Public Law 92B318 [20 U.S.C. 1681 et seq.], or in any civil action or proceeding, by or on behalf of the United States of America, to enforce, or charging a violation of, a provision of the United States Internal Revenue Code, or title VI of the Civil Rights Act of 1964 [42 U.S.C. 2000d et seq.], the court, in its discretion, may allow the prevailing party, other than the United States, a reasonable attorney's fee as part of the costs."

Once again, given our holding [above], the plain language provides an answer. The statute states that fees are available in *any* § 1983 action. Since we hold that this statutory action is properly brought under § 1983, and since § 1988 makes no exception for statutory § 1983 actions, § 1988 plainly applies to this suit. [The legislative history of the quoted amendment to § 1988 is consistent with this interpretation. Moreover, no sovereign immunity concerns are implicated by an award of court costs, which includes attorneys fees.]

* * *

Affirmed.

MR. JUSTICE POWELL, with whom THE CHIEF JUSTICE and MR. JUSTICE REHNQUIST join, dissenting.

* * *

[The 1874 Congress, which revised the original language of § 1983 as found in the 1871 Civil Rights Act, intended to make no change in the substantive scope of the Act. The most plausible reading of their work is that they intended to have § 1983 cover all Fourteenth–Amendment-based rights, plus the then-existing federal statutory rights that related to equality. The "and laws" language was simply a way of noting that some existing statutes guaranteeing equality of rights were themselves based on the Fourteenth Amendment.]

[Moreover, the] Court's opinion does not consider the nature or scope of the litigation it has authorized. In practical effect, today's decision means that state and local governments, officers, and employees now may face liability whenever a person believes he has been injured by the administration of any federal-state cooperative program, whether or not that program is related to equal or civil rights.[11]

Even a cursory survey of the United States Code reveals that literally hundreds of cooperative regulatory and social welfare enactments may be affected. The States now participate in the enforcement of federal laws governing migrant labor, noxious weeds, historic preservation, wildlife conservation, anadromous fisheries, scenic trails, and strip mining. Various statutes authorize federal-state cooperative agreements in most aspects of federal land management. In addition, federal grants administered by state and local governments now are available in virtually every area of public administration. Unemployment, Medicaid, school lunch subsidies, food stamps, and other welfare benefits may provide particularly inviting subjects of litigation. Federal assistance also includes a variety of subsidies for education, housing, health care, transportation, public works, and law enforcement. Those who might benefit from these grants now will be potential § 1983 plaintiffs.

No one can predict the extent to which litigation arising from today's decision will harass state and local officials; nor can one foresee the number of new filings in our already overburdened courts. But no one can doubt that these consequences will be substantial. And the Court advances no reason to believe that any Congress—from 1874 to the present day—intended this expansion of federally imposed liability on state defendants.

* * *

Today's decision confers upon the courts unprecedented authority to oversee state actions that have little or nothing to do with the individual rights defined and enforced by the civil rights legislation of the Reconstruction Era. This result cannot be reconciled with the purposes for which § 1983 was enacted. It also imposes unequal burdens on state and federal officials in the joint administration of federal programs and may expose state defendants to liability for attorney's fees in virtually every case. If any Member of the 43d Congress had suggested legislation embodying these results, the proposal certainly would have been hotly debated. It is simply inconceivable that Congress, while professing a firm intention not to make substantive changes in the law, nevertheless intended to enact a major new remedial program by approving—without discus-

---

11. The only exception will be in cases where the governing statute provides an exclusive remedy for violations of its terms. See Adickes v. S. H. Kress & Co., 398 U.S. 144, 150–151, n. 5 (1970); cf. Great American Fed. S. & L. Assn. v. Novotny, 442 U.S. 366 (1979).

sion—the addition of two words to a statute adopted only three years earlier.

* * *

Moreover, until today this Court never had held that § 1983 encompasses all purely statutory claims. Past treatment of the subject has been incidental and far from consistent. The only firm basis for decision is the historical evidence, which convincingly shows that the phrase the Court now finds so clear was—and remains—nothing more than a shorthand reference to equal rights legislation enacted by Congress. To read "and laws" more broadly is to ignore the lessons of history, logic, and policy.

* * *

NOTE ON § 1983's "AND LAWS" LANGUAGE AND OTHER NON-FOURTEENTH-AMENDMENT CLAIMS

1. Why would plaintiffs want to invoke § 1983 to enforce standards found in other federal statutes? To obtain § 1983's clear cause of action, thus dispatching the necessity of implying a cause of action? To obtain § 1983's damage remedy when the other federal statute might only create injunctive or regulatory relief? To obtain § 1983's award of attorneys fees? But if Congress wrote all the other statutes without providing such remedies, is it not likely that it did not want such remedies for such statutes?

(a) Many, virtually all, of the cases upon which the majority relies in *Thiboutot,* such as King v. Smith, might equally well be rationalized as implied-causes-of-action cases, that is, cases where the Court implied a civil remedy for the other federal statute based on its history and purpose. Cf. Cort v. Ash, 422 U.S. 66, 95 S.Ct. 2080, 45 L.Ed.2d 26 (1975) (popular case of the era setting out standards for implying a claim). The implied cause of action, however, did not necessarily confer all the remedies available under § 1983, including attorneys fees. If that is so, does not the expansive reading of "and laws" retroactively amend a host of statutes to give them provisions Congress never intended them to have?

(b) Is there not a heart-warming irony in *Thiboutot?* Has Justice Brennan not temporarily become a committed literal textualist? And have not the "conservative" dissenters become committed contextualists who wish to look beyond the words of § 1983? Seeing the Justices caught in their own webs stirs a law student's soul, does it not?

2. The Term following the *Thiboutot* decision, the Supreme Court severely curtailed claims under § 1983's "and laws" language when it decided **Middlesex County Sewerage Auth. v. National Sea Clammers Ass'n**, 453 U.S. 1, 101 S.Ct. 2615, 69 L.Ed.2d 435 (1981). This rather unappetizingly named case, authored by Justice Powell, grafted two exceptions onto the *Thiboutot* decision, echoing footnote 11 in his *Thiboutot* dissent. He stated the exceptions as follows, 453 U.S. at 19:

"(i) whether Congress had foreclosed private enforcement of [the other] in th[at] enactment itself, and (ii) whether the statute at issue * * * was the kind that created enforceable "rights" under § 1983. [With respect to the first exception, when] the remedial devices provided in a particular act are sufficiently comprehensive, they may suffice to demonstrate Congressional intent to preclude the remedy of suits under § 1983."

(a) Why did *Middlesex* have the effect of virtually shutting off claims under the "and laws" provision? Most federal civil statutes probably fall into one of two mutually exclusive categories: they are either regulatory or funding statutes (which thus create no rights because they create no cause of action) or they provide for a proceeding or cause of action to enforce the statute's standards (which thus have their own enforcement scheme and become exclusive). Is this not a situation in which the two exceptions swallow the rule (perhaps an unfortunate metaphor given the name of the case)?

(b) In the years following *Middlesex* few lower court cases recognized claims under § 1983's "and laws" language, except for the very type of claim recognized in *Thiboutot* itself, welfare entitlement cases. Claims to enforce modern federal regulatory schemes, such as the Federal Water Pollution Control Act at issue in *Middlesex,* virtually dried up. See Boatowners and Tenants Association v. Port of Seattle, 716 F.2d 669 (9th Cir.1983).

3.   In 1987 the Court in counterpoint severely restricted the first of *Middlesex*'s two exceptions, thus once again opening the door to increased use of § 1983 to enforce standards found in other federal statutes. In **Wright v. City of Roanoke Redevelopment & Housing Auth.**, 479 U.S. 418, 107 S.Ct. 766, 93 L.Ed.2d 781 (1987), the Court reasoned that in order to foreclose a § 1983 claim under the first exception, the other federal statute's remedial scheme would need to be so comprehensive as to demonstrate that it was an "exclusive" remedy. *Wright* went on to hold that tenants could employ § 1983 to enforce their rights under the National Housing Act, even though it provided its own set of remedies.

(a) The Court fine-tuned *Wright* in **Golden State Transit Corp. v. City of Los Angeles**, 493 U.S. 103, 110 S.Ct. 444, 107 L.Ed.2d 420 (1989), the Court elaborated on *Wright* by clarifying its terms and assigning specific burdens to plaintiffs and defendants who would seek to use or avoid § 1983 when the claim enforced standard created by other federal statutes. Plaintiff, said the Court, must first show that the other federal law is one creating a "right," that is, that it "creates obligations binding on the governmental unit[,] rather [than merely] express[ing] a congressional preference for certain kinds of treatment." If plaintiff makes the required showing that a right is at stake, defendant may nevertheless turn back such a claim by showing that "Congress specifically foreclosed a remedy under § 1983" by providing an enforcement regime so comprehensive that parallel enforcement through § 1983 "would be inconsistent with Congress' carefully tailored scheme." 493 U.S. at 107, 110 S.Ct. at 449 (internal quotations omitted). In *Golden State* the Court sustained use of § 1983 to invoke implicit rights contained in the National Labor Relations Act, rights created when the NLRA pre-empted local law. (The city had intruded upon strike negotiations by requiring the taxi company to settle a strike as a condition of renewal of its city-granted franchise.) Are these concerns remote from, or essentially similar to, the original goals of § 1983?[1]

(b) More recent cases appear to have tightened *Golden State*'s standards, limiting the number of statutes which may be invoked under § 1983. As to the first factor, finding of a "right," in **Blessing v. Freestone**, 520 U.S. 329, 117 S.Ct. 1353, 137 L.Ed.2d 569 (1997), the Court unanimously held that there exists no § 1983 "and laws" action to enforce a state's "substantial compliance" with the "complex" federal command to seek child support from "deadbeat dads" under the Social Security Act. The burden on the plaintiff, said Justice O'Connor for the Court, is to "define with particularity" what rights are created for plaintiffs under complex regulatory statutes, something that cannot be done unless the federal statute unambiguously imposes a mandatory, binding obligation on the states. As to the second factor, the exclusiveness of the remedy available under the other statute, in **City of Rancho Palos Verdes v. Abrams**, 544 U.S. 113, 125 S.Ct. 1453, 161 L.Ed.2d 316 (2005), Justice Scalia's majority opinion rejected use of § 1983 to enforce admitted rights created by the Telecommunications Act of 1996, noting that the "provision of an express, private means of redress in the statute itself is *ordinarily* an indication that Congress did not intend to leave open a more expansive remedy under § 1983" (emphasis added). Although the Court refused to adopt an iron-clad rule, it noted that "the existence of a more restrictive private remedy for statutory violations [such as the quick deadlines for filing claims here] has been the dividing line between those cases in which we have held that an action would lie under § 1983 and those in which we have held that it would not." 520 U.S. at 121, 117 S.Ct. 1458. Do *Blessing* and *Palos Verdes* finally accomplish Justice Powell's goals from *Middlesex*? See Chapter 6D (limitations on judicially implied causes of action). Cf. Granite Rock Co. v. International Broth. of Teamsters, ___ U.S. ___, 130 S.Ct. 2847, 177 L.Ed.2d 567 (2010) (refusing to create tort rules even for implied claims under Labor Management Relations Act).

4. When § 1983 is used to enforce constitutional rights, some highly articulated rules enforce the Eleventh Amendment's concern for state sovereign immunity. See Chapter 1, supra. Presumably, these rules apply equally in "and laws" suits under § 1983, especially given the holding in Will v. Michigan State Department of Police that states are not statutory "persons" under § 1983. Does the *Thiboutot–Middlesex* line of cases apply only to local governments?[2]

(a) If these cases apply only to local governments, does that make Justice Brennan's all-inclusive approach more palatable? If yes, is that because you believe that local governments are less likely to obey, or less capable of obeying, federal statutory prescriptions?

1. Results were somewhat unpredictable in this period. Compare Wilder v. Virginia Hospital Ass'n, 496 U.S. 498, 110 S.Ct. 2510, 110 L.Ed.2d 455 (1990) (hospitals may sue state for damages because of interference with their fee rights under federal Boren Amendment) (5–4 vote), with Suter v. Artist M., 503 U.S. 347, 112 S.Ct. 1360, 118 L.Ed.2d 1 (1992) (Adoption Assistance and Child Welfare Act does not create right in child beneficiaries to sue under § 1983).

2. Although the state of Maine appears in the title of the *Thiboutot* case, the State did not take part in the Supreme Court. See note 1 in *Thiboutot*.

(b) Would Congress have power to amend § 1983's "and laws" language to subject states to liability? Presumably, any such legislation would be constitutionally grounded in whatever provision gave Congress the power to enact that underlying legislation enforced in the § 1983 action. Does Congress have constitutional authority under Article I to subject the states to liability for failure to obey federal statutes enacted under Article I? See Seminole Tribe of Florida v. Florida, 517 U.S. 44, 116 S.Ct. 1114, 134 L.Ed.2d 252 (1996) (Indian Gaming Regulatory Act, which requires states to negotiate compact with resident tribes to permit gaming and allows states to be sued if they violate duty, violates Eleventh Amendment because Congress has no authority under Commerce Clause to abrogate states' immunity from suit in federal courts); Alden v. Maine, 527 U.S. 706, 119 S.Ct. 2240, 144 L.Ed.2d 636 (1999) (sovereign immunity principles also bar Congress from subjecting states to suit in state courts; Congress lacks Article I, § 8 power to abrogate this immunity).

5. As a parallel to the "and laws" cases, the Court for the first time in 1991 approved the use of § 1983 to enforce rights existing in the Constitution but outside the Fourteenth Amendment, specifically a right to be free of state regulation under the "dormant" commerce clause. **Dennis v. Higgins**, 498 U.S. 439, 111 S.Ct. 865, 112 L.Ed.2d 969 (1991), involved a claim by a motor carrier that Nebraska had imposed taxes on it that effected an unconstitutional burden on interstate commerce. Justice White's opinion stressed that while Fourteenth Amendment concerns had been at the center of the passage of § 1983, its literal language applied to "any rights" arising under the Constitution, not just those grounded in the Fourteenth Amendment. And the Court pointed to a long course of jurisprudence that had established commerce-clause violations as not merely state intrusions upon federal interests but as impingements upon persons' "rights."

(a) Is *Dennis* the triumph of procedure over substance? Dormant commerce clause claims had long been brought in federal court as implied rights of action, so the only effect of permitting them under § 1983 was to bestow § 1983's entitlement to attorneys fees. 498 U.S. at 452, 111 S.Ct. at 873 (Kennedy, J., dissenting). Should that decision have been left more specifically to Congress?

(b) Even as it recognized dormant commerce clause suits as appropriate under § 1983, *Dennis* confirmed that every preemption claim based on a federal statute passed under the active commerce clause power would not create a § 1983 claim. 498 U.S. at 446, 111 S.Ct. at 870. This was necessary in order to maintain the "and laws" line of cases intact, was it not? If every statute passed under Art. I § 8 created rights, rights that were turned into constitutional rights via the Supremacy Clause, then § 1983 could be used to enforce all federal statutory rights, not only those approved under the *Golden State* test, correct? What are the constitutional implications of a rule that would have permitted such suits? See Florida Prepaid Postsecondary Education Expense Board v. College Savings Bank, 527 U.S. 627, 119 S.Ct. 2199, 144 L.Ed.2d 575 (1999) (Congress lacks power under Article I to subject states to patent infringement suits; it must also lack power under the Fourteenth Amendment to protect such an interest or else limits on Article I power would be meaningless).

(c) *Dennis* protects economic interests under the dormant commerce clause as part of § 1983's coverage of "rights ... secured by the Constitution." Are these rights different from Fourteenth–Amendment-based rights? Cf. Prudential Ins. Co. v. Benjamin, 328 U.S. 408, 66 S.Ct. 1142, 90 L.Ed. 1342 (1946) (Congress can render constitutional under active commerce clause power state actions that would otherwise be unconstitutional under the dormant commerce clause). What are statutory "rights"? What are "civil rights"?

NOTE ON THE ELASTICITIES OF § 1983 LITIGATION: SUPPLEMENTAL JURISDICTION AND IMPLIED REPEAL

1. "Supplemental Jurisdiction" is new nomenclature for a traditional idea. Despite the expansion of § 1983 to cover some other federal rights, discussed in the preceding Note, one of the enduring themes in the field is that § 1983 cannot be used to enforce purely state-created (state-law) claims. See Paul v. Davis, 424 U.S. 693, 96 S.Ct. 1155, 47 L.Ed.2d 405 (1976). Without a basis in § 1983, such state law claims cannot be brought to federal court, absent diversity of citizenship (or some other very limited federal jurisdictional basis). Nevertheless, the Court has long recognized that state law claims may be appended to any federal law claim properly within a federal court's federal question jurisdiction, under appropriate circumstances. See United Mine Workers v. Gibbs, 383 U.S. 715, 86 S.Ct. 1130, 16 L.Ed.2d 218 (1966). Federal suits under § 1983 provide a ready vehicle for such "pendent" claims.

(a) *Gibbs* provided that there is federal subject-matter jurisdiction over an entire case when the federal claim is a nonfrivolous part of the case; in this instance, the "case" is identified as all claims arising from the same "common nucleus of operative fact." 383 U.S. at 725, 86 S.Ct. at 1138. If the state-law claim is grounded in essentially the same underlying events as the federal (§ 1983) claim, then the federal court has jurisdictional power over both claims, state and federal. Thus most § 1983 suits, raising non-frivolous claims that focus on a specific transaction or event, may be used as a vehicle for raising in federal court state-law claims grounded in the same transaction or event. See Mendoza v. K–Mart, Inc., 587 F.2d 1052 (10th Cir. 1978) (assault and battery claims appended to § 1983 claim); Dunton v. County of Suffolk, 729 F.2d 903 (2d Cir.1984) (frivolous § 1983 claim cannot provide a basis for pendent jurisdiction).

(b) Once the court has established its jurisdictional power to hear a pendent claim, says *Gibbs*, 383 U.S. at 726, 86 S.Ct. at 1139, the district court has discretion to hear or not hear the pendent claim based upon perceived economies and fairness in trying all claims in one sitting.

(c) *Gibbs* was substantially codified in the Judicial Improvements Act of 1990, which created 28 U.S.C. § 1367, and its concept of pendent jurisdiction was merged with the related concept of ancillary jurisdiction to form "supplemental jurisdiction." Section 1367 also provides for so-called pendent-party jurisdiction, thus expanding on previous options by allowing plaintiffs to bring in additional parties who are involved in the same transaction. See Finley v.

United States, 490 U.S. 545, 109 S.Ct. 2003, 104 L.Ed.2d 593 (1989) (rejecting pendent party jurisdiction the year before legislative overruling in § 1367). (d) When state-law claims are joined with a § 1983 claim in state court, there is no occasion to discuss supplemental jurisdiction. The state court ordinarily simply hears the § 1983 suit as another count, section, or claim in its general jurisdiction. See Howlett v. Rose, discussed in the Note on § 1983 in State Courts, Chapter 1E supra.

2. Section 1983 may contract as well as expand. Specifically, Congress may pass new legislation covering sub-topics of constitutional rights; if the new legislation provides an exclusive remedy for the rights it encompasses, that statute will "impliedly repeal" or effectively pre-empt the § 1983 remedy. See Smith v. Robinson, 468 U.S. 992, 104 S.Ct. 3457, 82 L.Ed.2d 746 (1984) (Education of the Handicapped Act supplants § 1983 for procedural due process claims to educational opportunity for handicapped student; since EHA lacks attorneys fee award provision, no fee recoverable); Preiser v. Rodriguez, Chapter 1G supra (habeas corpus statute supplants § 1983 for some prisoners' complaints).

(a) Given the expansion of Congressional legislation protecting constitutional rights since 1964, see Chapters 5–8 infra, there is actually a good possibility that some new legislation may overlap with § 1983. How can courts determine when the overlap is so substantial that the newer legislation should be deemed to be exclusive? See Smith v. Robinson, supra (comprehensive nature of new statute's remedial scheme evidences Congress' desire that it be an exclusive remedy). The test appears to rely on factors similar to those employed in deciding the "and laws" cases, discussed in the preceding Note. See *Golden State,* 493 U.S. at 106, 110 S.Ct. at 448 (citing Smith v. Robinson).

(b) Would it be better for Congress to specify when it desires a remedy to be exclusive? Or is it satisfactory to note that if Congress disagrees with the Court's decision as to implied repeal, Congress may then amend its statute? See the Handicapped Children's Protection Act of 1986, 20 U.S.C. § 1415(e) (4) (statutorily overruling Smith v. Robinson).

3. When Congress enacts another statute that displaces part of § 1983 by providing an alternative remedy, must that remedy be as effective as § 1983? Is the full damages remedy under § 1983 constitutionally required? See Harris v. Garner, 190 F.3d 1279 (11th Cir. 1999) (Prison Litigation Reform Act displaces § 1983 and its limitation on recovery of damages for some emotional distress is constitutional).

4. Courts sometimes confuse two related but distinct issues: whether another statute is among the "and laws" which can be invoked in a § 1983 suit and whether the other law impliedly repeals or preempts § 1983. It is clear that § 1983 can coexist with another overlapping statute, each having a separate scope and offering a potential plaintiff an alternative claim. In Fitzgerald v. Barnstable School Committee, 555 U.S. 246, 129 S.Ct. 788, 172 L.Ed.2d 582 (2009), the Court held that the sex-equality provisions of Title IX of the Education Amendments of 1972, see Chapter 6A–D infra, do not preclude § 1983 claims against schools covered by the newer statute. How are these issues different from those applicable in the "and laws" discussion? See id. (cross-citing "and laws" cases). Lower courts have held that it is entirely possible that another statute may be exclusive unto itself and thus outside the

"and laws" language, without being so comprehensive that it supplants § 1983. See, e.g., Huebschen v. Department of Health, 716 F.2d 1167 (7th Cir.1983); Day v. Wayne County, 749 F.2d 1199 (6th Cir.1984) (§ 1983 claim for constitutional violation by state employer not repealed by Title VII; Title VII rights may not be enforced through "and laws" provision in § 1983). Since the dispositive question is congressional intent, not merely policy rationality, this is a perfectly plausible result, is it not?

PART TWO

SEMI-CONSTITUTIONAL STATUTES:
THE POWER OF CONGRESS TO
EXPAND CONSTITUTION-BASED
RIGHTS

∎ ∎ ∎

CHAPTER 2

SECTIONS 1981 AND 1982—PRIVATE RACIAL DISCRIMINATION AND THE THIRTEENTH AMENDMENT

■ ■ ■

A. THE PROCESS OF REBIRTH—AND A SUGGESTION OF LIMITS

General Introduction. This Chapter begins the study of several statutes that highlight a special phenomenon in civil rights law. Despite the dominant themes of constitutional law and judicial power contained in Part One, civil rights law is often a cooperative venture that requires Congress to play a strong role. In the Chapters that follow, constitutional law presents a baseline, but the statutes covered here go further, providing remedies that the Constitution alone does not contemplate. (The Thirteenth Amendment to the Constitution, for example, bars only "slavery," but Congress can go further and ban the modern relics of slavery, such as discrimination in property sales.) This, in turn, creates another problem not often seen in Part One—just how far can Congress go in adding to constitutional baselines? As we shall see in these Chapters, Congress has power to act and can play a strong role in expanding civil rights, but its power is not unlimited.

The first two statutes studied in Part Two have received very favorable treatment from the Supreme Court, and on the few occasions when the Court has not been expansive, Congress has overridden the Court to restore protection that the Court thought was not present in the statutes. Why has the Court been generally receptive to these statutes—because they cover racial discrimination and fall at the very core of traditional civil rights concerns? Because they cover such basic social needs as housing, employment, and participation in the American market economy? The second two statutes, after some early experimentation, have received much cooler receptions from the Court. Moreover, when Congress has made some minor efforts to go enact more expansive versions of these statutes, the Court has resisted. In fact, the Court even held some provisions of civil rights law unconstitutional—the first time that had happened in over 100 years. When can a statute designed to protect civil rights be unconstitutional?

Introduction to the Civil Rights Act of 1866 and Modern Sections 1981 and 1982. As was the case with section 1983, the statutes covered in Chapter Two also lay essentially dormant from the time of their passage in 1866 until their resuscitation in the 1960's. The reasons for that dormancy, however, were only partially related to the concerns that caused the original narrow interpretation of § 1983. The most decisive influence on the construction of these statutes was the Supreme Court's decision in **The Civil Rights Cases**, 109 U.S. 3, 3 S.Ct. 18, 27 L.Ed. 835 (1883), a decision that held unconstitutional a separate older civil rights act, that of 1875.[1] The central theme of that case—that the Fourteenth Amendment reaches only state action, and thus cannot support a statute outlawing private racial discrimination—demonstrably affected judicial interpretation of other civil rights statutes. In dicta in *The Civil Rights Cases*, for example, and other important decisions in the late nineteenth century, the Court interpreted §§ 1981 and 1982 as requiring state action. See id. at 16–17.[2] One can see the effect of the dicta in the rare reported opinions of the Twentieth Century that consistently assumed that such statutes as § 1981 only cover state actors. See, e.g., Kansas City v. Williams, 205 F.2d 47 (8th Cir. 1953); Valle v. Stengel, 176 F.2d 697 (3d Cir. 1949).

Yet, the Court's opinion in *The Civil Rights Cases* also discussed the Thirteenth Amendment as a source of congressional power to enact civil rights legislation. On one hand, it specifically held that proof of state action is not required in order to prevail under that amendment. See 109 U.S. at 20–21, 3 S.Ct. at 27–29. This view of the Thirteenth Amendment, assuming that it could be tied eventually to §§ 1981 and 1982, meant that at least some civil rights statutes could cover private persons in addition to state actors. Yet even as the case opened this door, it closed another. Although Congress could reach private actors, suggested the Court, it could only reach them on the topic specifically covered by the Thirteenth Amendment—"slavery and involuntary servitude." And as debilitating as racial restrictions on contracting and buying property might be, to the Nineteenth Century mind they simply were not synonymous with enslavement. See 109 U.S. at 21–24, 3 S.Ct. at 28–31 (racial discrimination in public accommodations not a "badge of slavery"; Court asks, "what has [racial discrimination] to do with the question of slavery?"). In fact, a notable decision of the late Nineteenth Century found that "mere person-

---

1. The Civil Rights Act of 1875, 18 Stat. 335, the last of the Reconstruction-era civil rights statutes, forbade private racial discrimination in places of public accommodation, such as hotels and theaters, and on public conveyances, such as trains. Although Republicans had not yet ceded the issue of civil rights, as they conclusively did following the disputed election of 1876, the heyday of Reconstruction had long since passed as of 1875. See K. Stampp, The Era of Reconstruction 186–215 (Vintage ed. 1967). It is likely that the 1875 act passed Congress not as a remedy for African–Americans, but as a personal testimonial to its recently deceased sponsor, Radical Republican Senator Charles Sumner. See id. at 139–41.

2. For other examples, see Yick Wo v. Hopkins, 118 U.S. 356, 369, 6 S.Ct. 1064, 30 L.Ed. 220 (1886); Virginia v. Rives, 100 U.S. (10 Otto) 313, 318, 25 L. Ed. 667 (1879).

al assaults," even when racially motivated and intended to interfere with contractual rights, were not within the scope of the Thirteenth Amendment. The Court explained that such conduct could not reduce an African–American "individual to a condition of slavery," and therefore fell outside Congress' power to legislate a remedy to the Thirteenth Amendment. Hodges v. United States, 203 U.S. 1, 18, 27 S.Ct. 6, 9, 51 L.Ed. 65 (1906).

Even as the Court authorized Congress to act, but not to act too far, it also maintained its concern for federalism. This theme, also sometimes seen in the cases decided under § 1983, led the Court occasionally to a narrow construction of civil rights statutes. See City of Memphis v. Greene, 451 U.S. 100, 101 S.Ct. 1584, 67 L.Ed.2d 769 (1981) (narrow construction of § 1982); Collins v. Hardyman, 341 U.S. 651, 71 S.Ct. 937, 95 L.Ed. 1253 (1951) (interpreting § 1985(3) so as not to "federalize" state tort law). This theme is often difficult to isolate, because it is frequently interwoven with the pair of related statutory and constitutional issues noted above.

JONES v. ALFRED H. MAYER CO.

Supreme Court of the United States, 1968.
392 U.S. 409, 88 S.Ct. 2186, 20 L.Ed.2d 1189.

MR. JUSTICE STEWART delivered the opinion of the Court.

In this case we are called upon to determine the scope and constitutionality of an Act of Congress, 42 U.S.C.A. § 1982, which provides that:

"All citizens of the United States shall have the same right, in every State and Territory, as is enjoyed by white citizens thereof to inherit, purchase, lease, sell, hold, and convey real and personal property."

On September 2, 1966, the petitioners filed a complaint in the District Court for the Eastern District of Missouri, alleging that the respondents had refused to sell them a home in the Paddock Woods community of St. Louis County for the sole reason that petitioner Joseph Lee Jones is a Negro. Relying in part upon § 1982, the petitioners sought injunctive and other relief.[1] The District Court sustained the respondents' motion to dismiss the complaint, and the Court of Appeals for the Eighth Circuit affirmed, concluding that § 1982 applies only to state action and does not reach private refusals to sell. We granted certiorari to consider the questions thus presented. For the reasons that follow, we reverse the judgment of the Court of Appeals. We hold that § 1982 bars *all* racial discrimination, private as well as public, in the sale or rental of property, and that the statute, thus construed, is a valid exercise of the power of Congress to enforce the Thirteenth Amendment.

---

1. To vindicate their rights under 42 U.S.C.A. § 1982, the petitioners invoked the jurisdiction of the District Court to award "damages or * * * equitable or other relief under any Act of Congress providing for the protection of civil rights * * *." 28 U.S.C.A. § 1343(4). In such cases, federal jurisdiction does not require that the amount in controversy exceed $10,000.

I.

At the outset, it is important to make clear precisely what this case does *not* involve. Whatever else it may be, 42 U.S.C.A. § 1982 is not a comprehensive open housing law. In sharp contrast to the Fair Housing Title (Title VIII) of the Civil Rights Act of 1968, Pub.L. 90–284, 82 Stat. 81, the statute in this case deals only with racial discrimination and does not address itself to discrimination on grounds of religion or national origin. * * *

Thus, although § 1982 contains none of the exemptions that Congress included in the Civil Rights Act of 1968, it would be a serious mistake to suppose that § 1982 in any way diminishes the significance of the law recently enacted by Congress. [The Court also noted that Congress was aware of the *Jones* litigation and found a need to pass the Fair Housing Act even should the Court construe § 1982 as reaching private discrimination.]

II.

This Court last had occasion to consider the scope of 42 U.S.C.A. § 1982 in 1948, in Hurd v. Hodge, 334 U.S. 24, 68 S. Ct. 847, 92 L. Ed. 1187. That case arose when property owners in the District of Columbia sought to enforce racially restrictive covenants against the Negro purchasers of several homes on their block. A federal district court enforced the restrictive agreements by declaring void the deeds of the Negro purchasers. * * *

The agreements in *Hurd* covered only two-thirds of the lots of a single city block, and preventing Negroes from buying or renting homes in that specific area would not have rendered them ineligible to do so elsewhere in the city. * * * Although the covenants could have been enforced without denying the general right of Negroes to purchase or lease real estate, the enforcement of those covenants would nonetheless have denied the Negro purchasers "the same right 'as is enjoyed by white citizens * * * to inherit, purchase, lease, sell, hold, and convey real and personal property.'" That result, this Court concluded, was prohibited by § 1982. To suggest otherwise, the Court said, "is to reject the plain meaning of language."

Hurd v. Hodge, supra, squarely held, therefore, that a Negro citizen who is denied the opportunity to purchase the home he wants "[s]olely because of [his] race and color," has suffered the kind of injury that § 1982 was designed to prevent. The basic source of the injury in *Hurd* was, of course, the action of private individuals—white citizens who had agreed to exclude Negroes from a residential area. But an arm of the Government—in that case, a federal court—had assisted in the enforcement of that agreement.[24] Thus Hurd v. Hodge, supra, did not present the question whether *purely* private discrimination, unaided by any action on

---

24. See Shelley v. Kraemer, 334 U.S. 1, 12, 68 S. Ct. 836, 841, 92 L. Ed. 1161.

the part of government, would violate § 1982 if its effect were to deny a citizen the right to rent or buy property solely because of his race or color.

* * * It is true that a dictum in *Hurd* said that § 1982 was directed only toward "governmental action," but neither *Hurd* nor any other case before or since has presented that precise issue for adjudication in this Court. Today we face that issue for the first time.

III.

We begin with the language of the statute itself. In plain and unambiguous terms, § 1982 grants to all citizens, without regard to race or color, "the same right" to purchase and lease property "as is enjoyed by white citizens." As the Court of Appeals in this case evidently recognized, that right can be impaired as effectively by "those who place property on the market" as by the State itself. For, even if the State and its agents lend no support to those who wish to exclude persons from their communities on racial grounds, the fact remains that, whenever property "is placed on the market for whites only, whites have a right denied to Negroes." So long as a Negro citizen who wants to buy or rent a home can be turned away simply because he is not white, he cannot be said to enjoy "the *same* right * * * as is enjoyed by white citizens * * * to * * * purchase [and] lease * * * real and personal property." 42 U.S.C.A. § 1982. (Emphasis added.)

On its face, therefore, § 1982 appears to prohibit *all* discrimination against Negroes in the sale or rental of property—discrimination by private owners as well as discrimination by public authorities. Indeed, even the respondents seem to concede that, if § 1982 "means what it says"—to use the words of the respondents' brief—then it must encompass every racially motivated refusal to sell or rent and cannot be confined to officially sanctioned segregation in housing. Stressing what they consider to be the revolutionary implications of so literal a reading of § 1982, the respondents argue that Congress cannot possibly have intended any such result. Our examination of the relevant history, however, persuades us that Congress meant exactly what it said.

IV.

In its original form, 42 U.S.C.A. § 1982 was part of § 1 of the Civil Rights Act of 1866. * * * To the Congress that passed the Civil Rights Act of 1866, it was clear that the right to do these things might be infringed not only by "State or local law" but also by "custom, or prejudice." Thus, when Congress provided in § 1 of the Civil Rights Act that the right to purchase and lease property was to be enjoyed equally throughout the United States by Negro and white citizens alike, it plainly meant to secure that right against interference from any source whatever, whether governmental or private.

Indeed, if § 1 had been intended to grant nothing more than an immunity from *governmental* interference, then much of § 2 would have made no sense at all.[32] For that section, which provided fines and prison terms for certain individuals who deprived others of rights "secured or protected" by § 1, was carefully drafted to exempt private violations of § 1 from the criminal sanctions it imposed. There would, of course, have been no private violations to exempt if the only "right" granted by § 1 had been a right to be free of discrimination by public officials. * * *

In attempting to demonstrate the contrary, the respondents rely heavily upon the fact that the Congress which approved the 1866 statute wished to eradicate the recently enacted Black Codes—laws which had saddled Negroes with "onerous disabilities and burdens, and curtailed their rights * * * to such an extent that their freedom was of little value * * *." Slaughter–House Cases, 16 Wall. 36, 70, 21 L. Ed. 394. The respondents suggest that the only evil Congress sought to eliminate was that of racially discriminatory laws in the former Confederate States. But the Civil Rights Act was drafted to apply throughout the country, and its language was far broader than would have been necessary to strike down discriminatory statutes.

That broad language, we are asked to believe, was a mere slip of the legislative pen. We disagree. For the same Congress that wanted to do away with the Black Codes *also* had before it an imposing body of evidence pointing to the mistreatment of Negroes by private individuals and unofficial groups, mistreatment unrelated to any hostile state legislation. * * *

Indeed, one of the most comprehensive studies then before Congress stressed the prevalence of private hostility toward Negroes and the need to protect them from the resulting persecution and discrimination. The report noted the existence of laws virtually prohibiting Negroes from owning or renting property in certain towns, but described such laws as "mere isolated cases," representing "the local outcroppings of a spirit * * * found to prevail everywhere"—a spirit expressed, for example, by lawless acts of brutality directed against Negroes who traveled to areas where they were not wanted. The report concluded that, even if anti-Negro legislation were "repealed in all the States lately in rebellion," equal treatment for the Negro would not yet be secured.

In this setting, it would have been strange indeed if Congress had viewed its task as encompassing merely the nullification of racist laws in the former rebel States. That the Congress which assembled in the Nation's capital in December 1865 in fact had a broader vision of the task before it became clear early in the session, when three proposals to

---

32. Section 2 provided:

"That any person who, *under color of any law, statute, ordinance, regulation, or custom,* shall subject, or cause to be subjected, any inhabitant of any State or Territory to the deprivation of any right secured or protected by this act, * * * shall be deemed guilty of a misdemeanor, and, on conviction, shall be punished by fine not exceeding one thousand dollars, or imprisonment not exceeding one year, or both, in the discretion of the court." (Emphasis added)

For the evolution of this provision into 18 U.S.C.A. § 242, see Screws v. United States, 325 U.S. 91, 98–99, 65 S. Ct. 1031, 1033–1034, 89 L. Ed. 1495.

invalidate discriminatory state statutes were rejected as "too narrowly conceived." From the outset it seemed clear at least to Senator Trumbull of Illinois, Chairman of the Judiciary Committee, that stronger legislation might prove necessary. * * *

* * *

On January 5, 1866, Senator Trumbull introduced the bill he had in mind—the bill which later became the Civil Rights Act of 1866. * * * Of course, Senator Trumbull's bill would, as he pointed out, "destroy all [the] discriminations" embodied in the Black Codes, but it would do more: It would affirmatively secure for all men, whatever their race or color, what the Senator called the "great fundamental rights":

> "the right to acquire property, the right to go and come at pleasure, the right to enforce rights in the courts, to make contracts, and to inherit and dispose of property."

As to those basic civil rights, the Senator said, the bill would "break down *all* discrimination between black men and white men."

That the bill would indeed have so sweeping an effect was seen as its great virtue by its friends and as its great danger by its enemies but was disputed by none. Opponents of the bill charged that it would not only regulate state laws but would directly "determine the persons who [would] enjoy * * * property within the States," threatening the ability of white citizens "to determine who [would] be members of [their] communit[ies] * * *." The bill's advocates did not deny the accuracy of those characterizations. Instead, they defended the propriety of employing federal authority to deal with "the white man * * * [who] would invoke the power of local prejudice" against the Negro. Thus, when the Senate passed the Civil Rights Act on February 2, 1866, it did so fully aware of the breadth of the measure it had approved.

[References to the House debates are omitted.]

Nor was the scope of the 1866 Act altered when it was re-enacted in 1870, some two years after the ratification of the Fourteenth Amendment. It is quite true that some members of Congress supported the Fourteenth Amendment "in order to eliminate doubt as to the constitutional validity of the Civil Rights Act as applied to the States." Hurd v. Hodge, 334 U.S. 24, 32–33, 68 S. Ct. 847, 852. But it certainly does not follow that the adoption of the Fourteenth Amendment or the subsequent readoption of the Civil Rights Act were meant somehow to *limit* its application to state action. * * *

Against this background, it would obviously make no sense to assume, without any historical support whatever, that Congress made a silent decision in 1870 to exempt private discrimination from the operation of the Civil Rights Act of 1866. "The cardinal rule is that repeals by implication are not favored." Posadas v. National City Bank, 296 U.S. 497, 503, 56 S.Ct. 349, 352, 80 L.Ed. 351. All Congress said in 1870 was that the 1866 law "is hereby re-enacted." That is all Congress meant.

As we said in a somewhat different setting two Terms ago, "We think that history leaves no doubt that, if we are to give [the law] the scope that its origins dictate, we must accord it a sweep as broad as its language." United States v. Price, 383 U.S. 787, 801, 86 S. Ct. 1152, 1160. "We are not at liberty to seek ingenious analytical instruments," ibid., to carve from § 1982 an exception for private conduct—even though its application to such conduct in the present context is without established precedent. And, as the Attorney General of the United States said at the oral argument of this case, "The fact that the statute lay partially dormant for many years cannot be held to diminish its force today."

V.

The remaining question is whether Congress has power under the Constitution to do what § 1982 purports to do: to prohibit all racial discrimination, private and public, in the sale and rental of property. Our starting point is the Thirteenth Amendment, for it was pursuant to that constitutional provision that Congress originally enacted what is now § 1982. * * *

As its text reveals, the Thirteenth Amendment "is not a mere prohibition of state laws establishing or upholding slavery, but an absolute declaration that slavery or involuntary servitude shall not exist in any part of the United States." Civil Rights Cases, 109 U.S. 3, 20, 3 S. Ct. 18, 28, 27 L. Ed. 835. It has never been doubted, therefore, "that the power vested in Congress to enforce the article by appropriate legislation," ibid., includes the power to enact laws "direct and primary, operating upon the acts of individuals, whether sanctioned by state legislation or not." Id., at 23, 3 S. Ct., at 30.

Thus, the fact that § 1982 operates upon the unofficial acts of private individuals, whether or not sanctioned by state law, presents no constitutional problem.

If Congress has power under the Thirteenth Amendment to eradicate conditions that prevent Negroes from buying and renting property because of their race or color, then no federal statute calculated to achieve that objective can be thought to exceed the constitutional power of Congress simply because it reaches beyond state action to regulate the conduct of private individuals. The constitutional question in this case, therefore, comes to this: Does the authority of Congress to enforce the Thirteenth Amendment "by appropriate legislation" include the power to eliminate all racial barriers to the acquisition of real and personal property? We think the answer to that question is plainly yes.

"By its own unaided force and effect," the Thirteenth Amendment "abolished slavery, and established universal freedom." Civil Rights Cases, 109 U.S. 3, 20, 3 S. Ct. 18, 28. Whether or not the Amendment *itself* did any more than that—a question not involved in this case—it is at least clear that the Enabling Clause of that Amendment empowered Congress to do much more. For that clause clothed "Congress with power

Rule → enabling Clause

to pass *all laws necessary and proper for abolishing all badges and incidents of slavery in the United States.* Ibid. (Emphasis added.)

Surely Senator Trumbull was right. Surely Congress has the power under the Thirteenth Amendment rationally to determine what are the badges and the incidents of slavery, and the authority to translate that determination into effective legislation. Nor can we say that the determination Congress has made is an irrational one. For this Court recognized long ago that, whatever else they may have encompassed, the badges and incidents of slavery—its "burdens and disabilities"—included restraints upon "those fundamental rights which are the essence of civil freedom, namely, the same right * * * to inherit, purchase, lease, sell and convey property, as is enjoyed by white citizens." Civil Rights Cases, 109 U.S. 3, 22, 3 S. Ct. 18, 29.[78] Just as the Black Codes, enacted after the Civil War to restrict the free exercise of those rights, were substitutes for the slave system, so the exclusion of Negroes from white communities became a substitute for the Black Codes. And when racial discrimination herds men into ghettos and makes their ability to buy property turn on the color of their skin, then it too is a relic of slavery.

Negro citizens, North and South, who saw in the Thirteenth Amendment a promise of freedom—freedom to "go and come at pleasure" and to "buy and sell when they please"—would be left with "a mere paper guarantee" if Congress were powerless to assure that a dollar in the hands of a Negro will purchase the same thing as a dollar in the hands of a white man. At the very least, the freedom that Congress is empowered to secure under the Thirteenth Amendment includes the freedom to buy whatever a white man can buy, the right to live wherever a white man can live. If Congress cannot say that being a free man means at least this much, then the Thirteenth Amendment made a promise the Nation cannot keep.

* * *

Reversed.

---

a. The Court later cited the test of McCulloch v. Maryland, 17 U.S. (4 Wheat.) 316, 4 L.Ed. 579 (1819): "Let the end be legitimate, let it be within the scope of the constitution, and all means which are appropriate, which are plainly adapted to that end, which are not prohibited, but consist with the letter and spirit of the constitution, are constitutional."

78. * * * In Hodges v. United States, 203 U.S. 1, 27 S. Ct. 6, 51 L. Ed. 65, a group of white men had terrorized several Negroes to prevent them from working in a sawmill. The terrorizers were convicted under 18 U.S.C.A. § 241 (then Revised Statutes § 5508) of conspiring to prevent the Negroes from exercising the right to contract for employment, a right secured by 42 U.S.C.A. § 1981 * * *.

This Court reversed the conviction. The majority recognized that "one of the disabilities of slavery, one of the indicia of its existence, was a lack of power to make or perform contracts." * * * Yet the majority said that "no mere personal assault or trespass or appropriation operates to reduce the individual to a condition of slavery," id. at 18, 27 S. Ct., at 9 and asserted that only conduct which actually enslaves someone can be subjected to punishment under legislation enacted to enforce the Thirteenth Amendment. * * *

The conclusion of the majority in *Hodges* rested upon a concept of congressional power under the Thirteenth Amendment irreconcilable with the position taken by every member of this Court in the *Civil Rights Cases* and incompatible with the history and purpose of the Amendment itself. Insofar as *Hodges* is inconsistent with our holding today, it is hereby overruled.

MR. JUSTICE HARLAN, whom MR. JUSTICE WHITE joins, dissenting.[b]

* * *

Like the Court, I began analysis of § 1982 by examining its language. * * * The Court finds it "plain and unambiguous" that this language forbids purely private as well as state-authorized discrimination. With all respect, I do not find it so. For me, there is an inherent ambiguity in the term "right," as used in § 1982. The "right" referred to may either be a right to equal status under the law, in which case the statute operates only against state-sanctioned discrimination, or it may be an "absolute right" enforceable against private individuals. To me, the words of the statute, taken alone, suggest the former interpretation, not the latter.

* * * And with deference I suggest that the language of § 2, taken alone, no more implies that § 2 "was carefully drafted to exempt private violations of § 1 from the criminal sanctions it imposed," than it does that § 2 was carefully drafted to enforce all of the rights secured by § 1.[c]

[The legislative history of the 1866 Act also cannot bear the weight that the Court attributes to it. Indeed, that history shows that earlier versions of the provisions, found in the Freedman's Bill and applicable to the southern states only, covered only state actors. It is implausible that the later 1866 Act, which was to apply nationally, would have remedies more expansive than those aimed at the former rebel states where discrimination was strongest. The] similar structure of the companion Freedmen's bill, drafted by the same hand and largely parallel in structure, would seem to confirm that the limitation to "state action" was deliberate.

* * *

On January 29, Senator Trumbull also uttered the first of several remarkably similar and wholly unambiguous statements which indicated that the bill was aimed only at "state action." He said:

> "[This bill] may be assailed as drawing to the Federal Government powers that properly belong to 'States'; but I apprehend, rightly considered, it is not obnoxious to that objection. *It will have no operation in any State where the laws are equal, where all persons have the same civil rights without regard to color or race. It will have no operation in the State of Kentucky when her slave code and all her laws discriminating between persons on account of race or color shall be abolished.*"[20]

* * *

The foregoing analysis of the language, structure, and legislative history of the 1866 Civil Rights Act shows, I believe, that the Court's

---

b. [Justice Douglas' concurring opinion is omitted.]

c. [Section 2 of the 1866 Act is quoted in footnote 32 of the majority opinion, supra.]

20. Cong. Globe, 39th Cong., 1st. Sess., 476 (Emphasis added).

thesis that the Act was meant to extend to purely private action is open to the most serious doubt, if indeed it does not render that thesis wholly untenable. Another, albeit less tangible, consideration points in the same direction. Many of the legislators who took part in the congressional debates inevitably must have shared the individualistic ethic of their time, which emphasized personal freedom and embodied a distaste for governmental interference which was soon to culminate in the era of laissez-faire. It seems to me that most of these men would have regarded it as a great intrusion on individual liberty for the Government to take from a man the power to refuse for personal reasons to enter into a purely private transaction involving the disposition of property, albeit those personal reasons might reflect racial bias. It should be remembered that racial prejudice was not uncommon in 1866, even outside the South. Although Massachusetts had recently enacted the Nation's first law prohibiting racial discrimination in public accommodations, Negroes could not ride within Philadelphia streetcars or attend public schools with white children in New York City. Only five States accorded equal voting rights to Negroes, and it appears that Negroes were allowed to serve on juries only in Massachusetts. Residential segregation was the prevailing pattern almost everywhere in the North. There were no state "fair housing" laws in 1866, and it appears that none had ever been proposed. In this historical context, I cannot conceive that a bill thought to prohibit purely private discrimination not only in the sale or rental of housing but in *all* property transactions would not have received a great deal of criticism explicitly directed to this feature. The fact that the 1866 Act received *no* criticism of this kind is for me strong additional evidence that it was not regarded as extending so far.

[In light of the recent enactment of the Civil Rights Act of 1968, Pub.L. 90–284, 82 Stat. 73, which contains a detailed code outlawing so much racial discrimination in housing and property sales, I would dismiss the writ of certiorari as improvidently granted.]

NOTE ON INTERPRETATION OF THE *1866 CIVIL RIGHTS ACT*

1.   The *Jones* case focuses on rather classical elements in interpreting the scope of the 1866 Civil Rights Act—statutory language, the structure of the legislation, and legislative history. Which side is more persuasive on each issue? Consider first the language of § 1982.

(a) Is the language of § 1982 ambiguous? Unambiguous? Unambiguous when one considers what phrase is omitted? What language found in § 1983 is missing in § 1982?

(b) Reconsider the full language of the 1866 Act by reading § 1982 together with its original sibling, § 1981. When the full list of prohibitions is read, has the state action concept subtly crept into the 1866 Act?

2.   Consider the structure of the 1866 Act. Does it indicate that there is an implicit state action requirement in § 1982? Note that a companion provision, § 2 in the original act, provided a criminal penalty for state actors

who violated the rights enumerated in §§ 1981 and 1982, both contained in § 1 of the original act.

(a) Does the existence of § 2's criminal remedy conclusively demonstrate that § 1 contains no state action requirement? What reply did Justice Harlan give?

(b) Consider the construction given to §§ 1 and 2 in **The Civil Rights Cases,** 109 U.S. 3, 16–17, 3 S.Ct. 18, 24–26, 27 L.Ed. 835 (1883). The Court there referred to § 1 as a "declaratory section" and § 2 as "the penal part by which the declaration is enforced, and which is the really effective part of the law." This holistic interpretation sees the entire statute as nothing but a criminal provision, § 2 being the procedural mechanism for enforcing the rights set out in § 1. Why is this Nineteenth Century interpretation plausible? Section 1982, when compared to § 1983, not only lacks a reference to conduct "under color of" law, it also lacks a reference to "action at law, suit in equity, or other proper proceeding for redress"; i.e., § 1982 lacks language indicating that it creates a civil cause of action. Does this reinforce the Court's dictum in The Civil Rights Cases?

(c) Whatever Congress may have intended by its structuring of the 1866 Act, the codifiers of the law in 1878 separated § 1 into its present separate provisions, §§ 1981 and 1982, and indicated that the provisions provided for civil remedies. Does this action support the Court's holding in *Jones*? The Court's view of the work of the revisers, used to deflect the argument against covering private discrimination, makes the reviser's work meaningless. Could the Court have used the revision to support its wider interpretation of the 1866 Act?

3. The Court's extensive discussion of the even more extensive legislative history of the 1866 Act has been considerably shortened in print here. Suffice it to say that there are no explicit statements by sponsors or opponents that directly answer the question of whether private acts of discrimination are covered. The majority and separate opinion do their best with implicit statements.

(a) How persuasive are the implicit statements quoted by the majority and Justice Harlan? Do the statements that Justice Harlan finds "wholly unambiguous" indicate anything more than Senator Trumbull's feeling that if states themselves protect blacks, they need have no fear of § 1982? Is the statement only unambiguous in light of the social assumptions of the Nineteenth Century? See ¶ 4 infra.

(b) In the single most direct statement concerning coverage of private discrimination, one opponent of the 1866 Act charged that it would require the selling of church pews, a common fundraising practice among churches at the time, to blacks who desired them. See Congr. Globe, 39th Cong., 1st Sess. 3146. Since churches are surely private actors, does this statement indicate coverage of private discrimination? Or should such a statement by an opponent—never answered by the proponents of the bill—be considered a mere scare tactic that cannot be taken seriously?

4. Should the general social ethic of the times be taken into account in interpreting a statute? Justice Harlan also relied on the "individualistic

ethic" of the time to show it extremely unlikely that members of Congress intended to undo the rampant discrimination prevalent in both North and South following the Civil War. Was Congress motivated by this ethic, or that of promoting freedom for ex-slaves?

(a) Is this a valid inquiry? Historians have discussed the same issue in detail. See K. Stampp, The Era of Reconstruction 1865–1877 (documenting the extreme negative shift in political attitudes toward blacks during the post war period); D. Donald, The Politics of Reconstruction 1863–1867 (statistical analysis of voting patterns suggests a slightly more conservative Reconstruction Congress). Is there one answer, several, or none to this historical inquiry concerning Congress' motives? Professor Donald, id. at 56, quotes California's Senator Conness regarding the 1867 Reconstruction Act: "I do not know exactly what is in controversy here, although I have been listening for some time. The arguments seem to be drawn so fine that it has almost passed from my perception."

(b) Assuming that courts should investigate legislative history, does it follow that judges are also competent to delve into 100–year-old legislative history? Are judges forced into such inquiries because of the lack of alternative routes to decision?

(c) Assuming that the Court was correct in its historical inquiry, should it nevertheless have left the unused statute in its century-long suspended animation? Especially in light of Congress' more detailed modern legislation? With such modern legislation only recently enacted, especially with such comprehensive and detailed coverage, why would the Court press ahead with a somewhat problematic interpretation of the older, simpler 1866 Civil Rights Act?

5. *Jones* holds that § 1982 covers private discrimination. Does it cover *only* private discrimination, or action taken "under color of" law as well? In other words, what is the relation between the 1866 Act and § 1983? In **Jett v. Dallas Independent School Dist.**, 491 U.S. 701, 109 S.Ct. 2702, 105 L.Ed.2d 598 (1989) (discussing part of 1866 Act codified in § 1981), a majority took the position that § 1983 provides the exclusive remedy for racial discrimination claims filed against government officials, thus displacing the 1866 Act.

(a) What difference does it make? In its prohibition of racial discrimination, is § 1983 narrower? Is the difference in the details, such as applicable statutes of limitations? See Goodman v. Lukens Steel Co., 482 U.S. 656, 107 S.Ct. 2617, 96 L.Ed.2d 572 (1987) (§ 1981, like § 1983, borrows state statute of limitations). Consider the extensive list of other sub-issues affecting § 1983, from remedies to immunities. Which, if any, would also apply to claims under the 1866 Act?

(b) Whatever might explain the result in *Jett*, Congress overrode the decision in the Civil Rights Act of 1991, § 102(a)(1), now codified as § 1981(c): "The rights protected by this section are protected against impairment by non-governmental discrimination and impairment under color of State law." What did Congress think it was accomplishing by adding § 1981 as a supplement to § 1983? (Was it just slapping the Court's wrists? Is this the first indication that Congress and the Court, even in modern times, are going to wrangle over who takes control of civil rights?)

NOTE ON THE TWO-TIER THIRTEENTH AMENDMENT

1. Two issues commonly arise in interpreting congressional power under the Thirteenth Amendment: (i) power to reach private actors and (ii) the power to reach topics beyond "slavery and involuntary servitude." The first of those issues had been settled for well over a century prior to the *Jones* decision. In 1884 the Court held that Congress has power under the Amendment to adopt "primary and direct" legislation controlling the behavior of private individuals. **The Civil Rights Cases**, 109 U.S. 3, 20, 23, 3 S.Ct. 18, 27, 30, 27 L.Ed. 835 (1883). The hotly debated statutory issue in *Jones,* whether Congress had intended to reach private action, raised hardly a whimper as a constitutional issue: Congress has such power to use if it so wishes. The remainder of this Note concerns the other issue involving the Thirteenth Amendment—the topical breadth of congressional power.

2. With a deft sleight of hand Justice Stewart makes it appear that *The Civil Rights Cases* announced the proposition that Congress has the power to eradicate the "badges and incidents of slavery." But a careful reading of that 1883 precedent shows that the quoted clause begins with the phrase "it is assumed that." Later the 1883 Court notes that it is only "[c]onceding" this proposition for purposes of argument. See 109 U.S. at 20–21, 3 S. Ct. at 27–29. Re-examine this issue: should Congress have power under § 2 of the Thirteenth Amendment to abolish not only slavery, but also the continuing social relics of slavery?

    (a) The Court in *Jones* interprets § 2 as a particularized version of the Necessary and Proper Clause, applicable to § 1 of the Thirteenth Amendment. It quotes the somewhat relaxed standard of review appropriate to Congressional action under Art. I, § 8. This approach is unexceptional, is it not?

    (b) Should you be bothered by the fact that the Court's approach creates a two-tier Constitution, one that has a facial scope that is enforced by the Court (abolition of "slavery and involuntary servitude") and an expansive scope that can be legislatively created by Congress? Is this really so unusual? Compare, for example, the Court's "dormant" (or "negative") and "active" Commerce Clause jurisprudence. See Nowak & Rotunda, CONSTITUTIONAL LAW, chapters 8 and 4 (7th ed. 2004). Is the Commerce Clause unique? Is the Thirteenth Amendment different from the Commerce Clause? See Tyler Pipe Industries v. Washington State Dept. of Revenue, 483 U.S. 232, 265, 107 S.Ct. 2810, 97 L.Ed.2d 199 (1987) (Scalia, J., dissenting in part) (taking the position that the Negative Commerce Clause is a mistake).[1]

3. Is it unusual to give Congress continuing authority to deal with the continuing social consequences of a problem, when it has power to deal with the original problem itself? Or should the power end when the original problem itself ends? Similar concerns were raised when Congress attempted to use its War Power under Art. I, § 8, not only to make war (World War II),

---

1. Justice Scalia later joined the majority position, considering himself bound by *stare decisis* to follow a practice with which he disagreed. See West Lynn Creamery v. Healy, 512 U.S. 186, 207, 114 S.Ct. 2205, 129 L.Ed.2d 157 (1994).

but also to deal with social dislocations caused by the war (a shortage of housing to be cured by rent control regulation). In **Woods v. Cloyd W. Miller Co.**, 333 U.S. 138, 68 S.Ct. 421, 92 L.Ed. 596 (1948), the Court rejected the contention that the War Power expired with the cessation of hostilities. The Court relied on similar decisions post-dating World War I, decisions upholding prohibition laws on the ground that they conserved cereals and grains left in short supply by the war.

(a) Does *Woods* show that *Jones* is in the mainstream of constitutional jurisprudence? Or does it show how easily this congressional power might be abused? Do you really think that Congress passed an anti-liquor law following World War I because it was concerned with grain shortages?

(b) If Congress has continuing authority to deal with the social consequences of war or slavery, when does that power end? Do you agree with the statement in The Civil Rights Cases, 109 U.S. at 25, that "[w]hen a man has emerged from slavery ... there must be some process in the course of his elevation when he takes the rank of mere citizen, and ceases to be the special favorite of the laws"? Can courts persuasively draw such lines? Cf. Grutter v. Bollinger, 539 U.S. 306, 123 S.Ct. 2325, 156 L.Ed.2d 304 (2003) (state's "race-conscious admissions policies [for higher education] must be limited" to "25 years" after approval of first such plan). Should Congress have a much longer time limit when devising remedies when they are, like § 1982, race-neutral? How long?

4. Assuming that Congress has power to deal with the "badges and incidents of slavery," and to deal with them in their evolving social context, how broad is this extensive power?

(a) In **The Civil Rights Cases**, 109 U.S. at 25, 3 S. Ct. at 31 (emphasis added), the Court held that "[mere discriminations on account of race or color [are] not regarded of badges of *slavery*" because white Americans practiced discrimination against freed blacks as well as against enslaved blacks. What is the constitutional problem with this reasoning? When Congress wishes to deal with harm to interstate commerce, for example, may it over-regulate, sweeping within its legislation, for the goal of administrative efficiency, some superficially similar situations that do not necessarily affect interstate commerce? See Mandeville Island Farms v. American Crystal Sugar Co., 334 U.S. 219, 236, 68 S.Ct. 996, 92 L.Ed. 1328 (1948). Or must it narrowly tailor its statute to the social facts? Cf. United States v. Lopez, 514 U.S. 549, 115 S.Ct. 1624, 131 L.Ed.2d 626 (1995) (legislation unconstitutional due to failure to make a convincing record of impact on interstate commerce).

(b) The narrow holding in *Jones* is that Congress might rationally conclude that racial discrimination in the sale of property is a relic of slavery. Given the reports before Congress in 1866, detailing discrimination against newly freed slaves in the South, this conclusion is virtually beyond doubt, is it not? Was housing discrimination occurring in 1965 also a relic of slavery? How do you know? (This is not a rhetorical question.) Compare Cassandra Jones Havard, *Democratizing Credit: Examining the Structural Inequities of Subprime Lending*, 56 SYRACUSE L. REV. 233 (2006) (residual racial effects in modern housing practices), with Peter Dreier, *America's Urban Crisis: Symp-*

toms, Causes, Solutions, 71 N.C. L. Rev. 1351 (1993) (noting that hyper-segregation of housing does not affect all blacks).

(c) Is virtually every topic related to race a social relic of slavery? Or do the "badges and incidents of slavery" comprise a short list of known harms essential to slavery? See The Civil Rights Cases, 109 U.S. at 21 22, 3 S. Ct. at 28–30 (1860's controls on hotel stays by African–Americans were not "incident" to slavery itself, but were "merely a means of preventing . . . escapes").

(d) As you may see from reading excerpts from *The Civil Rights Cases,* a considerable shift of judicial opinion had occurred concerning slavery between 1883 and 1968. What caused that change?

5.   Assuming that Congress has such broad power over slavery, including any matters relating to race, what exactly is included within the concept of slavery? *Jones* itself reached only a limited issue, holding that at least the Thirteenth Amendment empowers Congress to deal with the race-based slavery system that existed before Reconstruction in the South.

(a) Does the Thirteenth Amendment also give Congress power over all historically identifiable race-based systems of servitude, including the peonage system subjugating Mexican–Americans in Texas and the indentured system subjugating Asian–Americans in California? When in 1970 Congress extended § 1981 to cover all "persons" rather than all "citizens," Congress cited the need to protect Chinese immigrant laborers in California. Congr. Globe, 41st Cong., 2nd Sess., 3658 (remarks of Sen. Stewart). Does this show a somewhat contemporaneous understanding that the Thirteenth Amendment reaches additional slavery systems beyond that which harmed African–Americans? Does the power extend to all racial and ethnic discrimination, regardless of whether there existed a historical system of enslavement, on the theory that Congress has power over problems that present the same potential for harm as the historical slave systems?

(b) Does the Thirteenth Amendment also give Congress power over non-race-based discrimination, for example, gender/sex discrimination? On what theory—that the subjugation of women in the Nineteenth Century was similar to the subjugation of African–Americans? But is that true (or even demeaning to the experience of African–Americans)? When Congress extended the Fair Housing Act to cover sex discrimination, it explicitly relied upon its power under the Thirteenth Amendment. *Hearings on S. 1604 before the Senate Subcommittee on Housing and Urban Affairs* 431 93rd Cong., 1st Sess. (1973). Is the amendment constitutional?

(c) Does the Thirteenth Amendment also give Congress power over any "discrimination" Congress considers unfair, for example, that against tractor-trailer drivers who are required to maintain a slower speed in some states or to use alternative "truck routes"? That against large families seeking rental housing? See R. Schwemm, Housing Discrimination Law and Litigation, Chapter 6A–D (release 10, 2000).

6.   Is the question of Congressional power under the Thirteenth Amendment now somewhat academic, given the Court's expansion of the Commerce Clause power? See Chapter 3D infra.

B.   SECTION 1982 AND EQUAL PROPERTY RIGHTS

SULLIVAN v. LITTLE HUNTING PARK, INC.

Supreme Court of the United States, 1969.
396 U.S. 229, 90 S.Ct. 400, 24 L.Ed.2d 386.

Opinion of the Court by MR. JUSTICE DOUGLAS, announced by MR. JUSTICE BLACK.

* * *

Little Hunting Park, Inc. is a Virginia nonstock corporation organized to operate a community park and playground facilities for the benefit of residents in an area of Fairfax County, Virginia. A membership share entitles all persons in the immediate family of the shareholder to use the corporation's recreation facilities. Under the bylaws a person owning a membership share is entitled when he rents his home to assign the share to his tenant, subject to approval of the board of directors. Paul E. Sullivan and his family owned a house in this area and lived in it. Later he bought another house in the area and leased the first one to T.R. Freeman, Jr., an employee of the U.S. Department of Agriculture; and assigned his membership share to Freeman. The board refused to approve the assignment because Freeman was a Negro. Sullivan protested that action and was notified that he would be expelled from the corporation by the board. A hearing was accorded him and he was expelled, the board tendering him cash for his two shares.

Sullivan and Freeman sued under 42 U.S.C.A. §§ 1981, 1982 for injunctions and monetary damages. Since Freeman no longer resides in the area served by Little Hunting Park, Inc., his claim is limited solely to damages.

The trial court denied relief to each petitioner. We reverse those judgments.

* * *

The Virginia trial court rested on its conclusion that Little Hunting Park was a private social club. But we find nothing of the kind on this record. There was no plan or purpose of exclusiveness. It is open to every white person within the geographic area, there being no selective element other than race. See Daniel v. Paul, 395 U.S. 298, 301–302, 89 S. Ct. 1697, 1699–1700, 23 L.Ed.2d 318. * * *

In Jones v. Mayer Co., the complaint charged a refusal to sell petitioner a home because he was black. In the instant case the interest conveyed was a leasehold of realty coupled with a membership share in a nonprofit company organized to offer recreational facilities to owners and lessees of real property in that residential area. It is not material whether the membership share be considered realty or personal property, as

§ 1982 covers both. Section 1982 covers the right "to inherit, purchase, lease, sell, hold, and convey real and personal property." There is a suggestion that transfer on the books of the corporation of Freeman's share is not covered by any of those verbs. The suggestion is without merit. There has never been any doubt but that Freeman paid part of his $129 monthly rental for the assignment of the membership share in Little Hunting Park. The transaction clearly fell within the "lease." The right to "lease" is protected by § 1982 against the actions of third parties, as well as against the actions of the immediate lessor. Respondents' actions in refusing to approve the assignment of the membership share in this case was clearly an interference with Freeman's right to "lease." A narrow construction of the language of § 1982 would be quite inconsistent with the broad and sweeping nature of the protection meant to be afforded by § 1 of the Civil Rights Act of 1866, 14 Stat. 27, from which § 1982 was derived.

We turn to Sullivan's expulsion for the advocacy of Freeman's cause. If that sanction, backed by a state court judgment, can be imposed, then Sullivan is punished for trying to vindicate the rights of minorities protected by § 1982. Such a sanction would give impetus to the perpetuation of racial restrictions on property. That is why we said in Barrows v. Jackson, 346 U.S. 249, 259, 73 S. Ct. 1031, 1036, 97 L. Ed. 1586, that the white owner is at times "the only effective adversary" of the unlawful restrictive covenant. Under the terms of our decision in *Barrows,* there can be no question but that Sullivan has standing to maintain this action.

* * *

We held in Jones v. Alfred H. Mayer Co. that although § 1982 is couched in declaratory terms and provides no explicit method of enforcement, a federal court has power to fashion an effective equitable remedy. That federal remedy for the protection of a federal right is available in the state court, if that court is empowered to grant injunctive relief generally, as is the Virginia court. Va.Code Ann. § 8–610 (1957 Repl.Vol.).

Finally, as to damages, Congress, by 28 U.S.C.A. § 1343(4), created federal jurisdiction for "damages or * * * equitable or other relief under any Act of Congress providing for the protection of civil rights * * *." We reserved in Jones v. Alfred H. Mayer Co. the question of what damages, if any, might be appropriately recovered for a violation of § 1982.

We had a like problem in Bell v. Hood, 327 U.S. 678, 66 S. Ct. 773, 90 L. Ed. 939, where suit was brought against federal officers for alleged violations of the Fourth and Fifth Amendments. The federal statute did not in terms at least provide any remedy. We said:

"[W]here federally protected rights have been invaded, it has been the rule from the beginning that courts will be alert to adjust their remedies so as to grant the necessary relief. And it is also well settled that where legal rights have been invaded, and a federal statute provides for a general right to sue for such invasion, federal courts may use any available remedy to make good the wrong done." Id., at 684, 66 S. Ct., at 777.

The existence of a statutory right implies the existence of all necessary and appropriate remedies. As stated in Texas & Pacific R. Co. v. Rigsby, 241 U.S. 33, 39, 36 S. Ct. 482, 484, 60 L. Ed. 874:

> "A disregard of the command of the statute is a wrongful act and where it results in damage to one of the class for whose especial benefit the statute was enacted, the right to recover the damages from the party in default is implied * * *."

Compensatory damages for deprivation of a federal right are governed by federal standards, as provided by Congress in 42 U.S.C.A. § 1988, [text omitted]. This means, as we read § 1988, that both federal and state rules on damages may be utilized, whichever better serves the policies expressed in the federal statutes. Cf. Brazier v. Cherry, 5 Cir., 293 F.2d 401. The rule of damages, whether drawn from federal or state sources, is a federal rule responsive to the need whenever a federal right is impaired. We do not explore the problem further, as the issue of damages was not litigated below.

Reversed.

Mr. Justice Harlan, with whom The Chief Justice and Mr. Justice White join, dissenting.

Because Congress has not provided a comprehensive scheme for dealing with the kinds of discrimination found in this case, I think it very unwise as a matter of policy for the Court to use § 1982 as a broad delegation of power to develop a common law of forbidden racial discriminations. A comparison of 42 U.S.C.A. § 1982 with the new Fair Housing Law, and consideration of the Court's task in applying each, demonstrate to me the need for restraint, and the appropriateness of dismissing the writ in this case, now grounded solely on an alleged violation of § 1982.

* * *

By attempting to deal with the problem of discrimination in the provision of recreational facilities under § 1982, the Court is forced, in the context of a very vague statute, to decide what transactions involve "property" for purposes of § 1982. The majority states that "[i]t is not material whether the membership share [in Little Hunting Park] be considered realty or personal property, as § 1982 covers both." But examination of the opinion will show that the majority has failed to explain why the membership share is *either* real *or* personal property for purposes of § 1982. The majority's complete failure to articulate any standards for deciding what is property within the meaning of § 1982 is a fair indication of the great difficulties courts will inevitably confront if § 1982 is used to remedy racial discrimination in housing. And lurking in the background are grave constitutional issues should § 1982 be extended too far into some types of private discrimination.

* * *

Second, the majority has not explained what legal standard should determine Sullivan's rights under § 1982. The majority simply states that "Sullivan has standing to maintain this action" under § 1982, without even acknowledging that some standard is essential for this case to be ultimately decided.

One can imagine a variety of standards, each based on different legal conclusions as to the "rights" and "duties" created by § 1982, and each having very different remedial consequences. For example, does § 1982 give Sullivan a right to relief only for injuries resulting from Little Hunting Park's interference with *his* statutory duty to Freeman under § 1982? If so, what is Sullivan's duty to Freeman under § 1982? Unless § 1982 is read to impose a duty on Sullivan to *protest* Freeman's exclusion, he would be entitled to reinstatement under this standard only if the Board had expelled him for the simple act of assigning his share to Freeman.

As an alternative, Sullivan might be thought to be entitled to relief from those injuries that flowed from the Board's violation of *its* "duty" to Freeman under § 1982. Such a standard might suggest that Sullivan is entitled to damages that resulted from Little Hunting Park's initial refusal to accept the assignment to Freeman but again not to reinstatement. Or does the Court think that § 1982 gives Sullivan a right to relief from injuries that result from his "legitimate" protest aimed at convincing the Board to accept Freeman? If so, what protest activities were legitimate here? Most extreme would be a standard that would give Sullivan relief from injuries that were the result of *any* actions he took to protest the Board's initial refusal, irrespective of Sullivan's means of protest. * * *

* * *

NOTE ON THE SCOPE OF § 1982 AND WHO HAS "PROPERTY" RIGHTS

1.　What is the meaning of "property" as used in § 1982? What transactions are covered by the verbs used in the statute?

(a) Why was the interest in using the swimming pool a "property" interest covered by § 1982? Because it is incident to the leasehold? Because it is personal property? Is "property" to be defined by looking at state law, or is there a federal definition of property for § 1982?

(b) Consider the verbs used in § 1982: are there any transactions concerning property that are not covered? But are only transactions covered? Would a person have a right to continued quite enjoyment of her property without racial interference? Is the language of § 1982—the adjectives describing property and the verbs covering conveyance—broad enough to reach every transaction involving exchange of goods (as opposed to services)? Cf. Tillman v. Wheaton–Haven Recreation Ass'n, Inc., 410 U.S. 431, 93 S.Ct. 1090, 35 L.Ed.2d 403 (1973).

(c) If the renter in *Sullivan* had not been entitled to automatic entry to the club, but only consideration for entry, would there have been a claim under § 1982? Cf. Boy Scouts of America v. Dale, 530 U.S. 640, 120 S.Ct. 2446, 147 L.Ed.2d 554 (2000) (constitutional right of small selective groups to exclude others). Is there no privacy interest in the usual § 1982 case because the verbs apply to persons who are offering to or soliciting from the public?

2. In **City of Memphis v. Greene**, 451 U.S. 100, 101 S.Ct. 1584, 67 L.Ed.2d 769 (1981), Justice Stevens' opinion for the Court held that a city's closure of city streets from a black-populated area through a white-populated area implicated no property rights held by black homeowners. Can this be correct?

(a) The majority emphasized that the street closure had no adverse effect on black home values and merely required them to use an alternative street rather than the one they preferred. Is this an example of the "no-harm, no-foul" rule of law?

(b) If blacks had been directly affected in their enjoyment of their property—the ability to get home faster and enjoy their back yards—would there have been an effect on property? Cf. Shaare Tefila Congregation v. Cobb, infra.

3. In the usual case, as in Jones v. Alfred H. Mayer Co., a putative black buyer will sue a reluctant white seller. In *Sullivan* both parties desire the transaction, and it is a third party which exercises its veto power to reduce the buyer's right to naught. The peculiar construction of § 1982 makes it easy to declare this situation covered, does it not? Consider some related issues.

(a) Could a § 1982 action be maintained by a white person who charged that a black person refused to sell property because of race? In **Shaare Tefila Congregation v. Cobb**, 481 U.S. 615, 107 S.Ct. 2019, 95 L.Ed.2d 594 (1987), the Court construed § 1982 in parallel with § 1981 to cover "race" as the term was understood in 1866 at the time of the statute's adoption. (The case involved anti-Semitic slogans spray-painted on a synagogue.) If all races have a claim under § 1982, and if third-part interference with a lease is a violation of § 1982, what is the philosophical assumption underlying the statute—that integration is the American norm? Is that true? See Douglas S. Massey & Nancy A. Denton, AMERICAN APARTHEID (1993).

(b) Would § 1982 also reach a third party who burns a cross in the yard of a neighborhood's new black family? Beats the family? A more modern, and hopefully more realistic variation on this problem is that of harassment of fellow condo dwellers. In light of the decision in *Shaare Tefila*, consider Bloch v. Frischholz, 587 F.3d 771 (7th Cir. 2009) (discussing intentional discrimination under the Fair Housing Act), where plaintiffs sued their fellow condo owners for racial discrimination claiming that the condo association had selectively enforced a rule hallway decorations so as to prevent them from hanging a tradition Jewish mezuzah (prayer scroll or door box containing the prayer) at their door. The events took place long after the plaintiffs had bought the property. Is racial harassment of a person at their home automatically actionable under § 1982 or must it somehow affect property rights?

(c) Gentrification is the name given to the process of middle-class (often white) persons returning to buy homes in America's inner cities. See Allison D. Christians, *Note, Breaking the Subsidy Cycle: A Proposal for Affordable*

Housing, 32 COLUM. J.L. & SOC. PROBS. 131, 139–42 (1999). If a predominantly black neighborhood objects to such changing demographics, is it powerless to resist? Would any black renters or homeowner who refused to sublet or sell to a white buyer be violating § 1982? Is that good or bad? See J. Peter Byrne, *Two Cheers for Gentrification*, 46 How. L.J. 405 (2003).

4.   Even though the statute may cover the situation at issue in *Sullivan*, there remains the issue of who may maintain a suit for correction—and who gets the damages if such a suit is won. Why does Sullivan, the white homeowner, have a suit under § 1982, and should he receive compensation for Sullivan's losses? Is Justice Harlan's dissent sophistry, an academic's inability to see the necessities of the real world? Or has he found a critical flaw in Justice Douglas' reasoning?

(a) The Court held that Sullivan "has standing" to sue under § 1982. Is that the same as saying that he has a claim of his own? In **CBOCS West, Inc. v. Humphries**, 553 U.S. 442, 128 S.Ct. 1951, 170 L.Ed.2d 864 (2008), involving § 1983 but cross-citing Sullivan, the Court permitted plaintiff to bring his own suit under § 1981 for a claim of retaliation after he was discharged for complaining about the racist discharge of a co-worker. Does *CBOCS* make it clear that *Sullivan* concerns not just third-party standing but an independent claim for the affected third-party? It may be easy to see what the plaintiff's damages were in *CBOCS* (because the plaintiff had also been discharged), but what would be the damages for the white plaintiff in *Sullivan*? Can he recover only for his future loss of pool membership or also for the term when Freeman was not allowed to be a member? If the latter, should he be required share the windfall recovery with Freeman?

(b) In **Trafficante v. Metropolitan Life Ins. Co.**, 409 U.S. 205, 93 S.Ct. 364, 34 L.Ed.2d 415 (1972), the Court granted standing to existing tenants to sue under the Fair Housing Act of 1968, 42 U.S.C.A. § 3610(a), to redress the landlord's discrimination against blacks who desire to become tenants. Is that decision regarding standing even broader than *Sullivan*'s holding? Would homeowner Sullivan have been granted standing if Freeman had been rejected for club membership after renting some other house in the neighborhood? Compare Gladstone Realtors v. Village of Bellwood, 441 U.S. 91, 99 S.Ct. 1601, 60 L.Ed.2d 66 (1979) (town has standing under Fair Housing Act to sue real estate agents who "steer" prospective homeowners to racially designated neighborhoods), with Warth v. Seldin, 422 U.S. 490, 95 S.Ct. 2197, 45 L.Ed.2d 343 (1975) (no standing for Fourteenth Amendment based challenge to zoning practices). Should § 1982 be interpreted as eliminating prudential considerations of standing so that all who meet the Article III minimum standards (of an injury in fact which would be redressed if requested relief is granted) would be permitted to sue? Compare Friends of the Earth v. Laidlaw, 528 U.S. 167, 120 S.Ct. 693, 145 L.Ed.2d 610 (2000) (citizen suits by "persons having an interest which is or may be adversely affected," under terms of Clean Water Act, may include monetary awards as a deterrence to future misconduct; act is constitutional). If broad standing and monetary awards are appropriate for racial discrimination cases, under § 1982 or elsewhere, should the money go to the citizen-plaintiffs or to the government? See id.

(c) "Testers" are persons who offer themselves for transactions in order to test whether a prospective defendant will discriminate based on race. (Typically, two persons similarly situated except for race seek the same transaction, presenting the possibility for suits alleging racial bias.) Does a tester have standing to sue under § 1982? See Kyles v. J.K. Guardian Sec. Services, Inc. 222 F.3d 289 (7th Cir. 2000) (no standing for testers under § 1981). Why not?

5. The rules on relief under § 1982 are substantially the same as those already discussed regarding § 1983, see Chapter 1, Section E.1, supra, except, of course, that when private parties appear as the defendant the limitations on injunctive and monetary relief arising out of the governmental role of the defendant will not apply (e.g., official immunity, sovereign immunity, the rule of Rizzo v. Goode, etc.). See, e.g., Lee v. Southern Home Sites Corp., 429 F.2d 290 (5th Cir.1970).

(a) Should the usual equitable rules favoring damages apply in § 1982 cases? If a black buyer wants to buy and is rejected because of race, must he settle for the damages or can he get specific performance to compel the sale of "Whiteacre"?

(b) If damages are awarded, should they be limited to the financial loss incurred in buying or leasing more expensive property, or should there be other elements of damages? See Johnson v. Hale, 13 F.3d 1351 (9th Cir. 1994) (humiliation); Smith v. Sol D. Adler Realty Co., 436 F.2d 344, 350–51 (7th Cir.1970) (black and white plaintiffs; mental anguish).

6. Consider how the issues raised in this Note should be used to decide Walker v. Pointer, 304 F.Supp. 56 (N.D.Tex.1969): a young white couple claimed that their landlord summarily and nonjudicially evicted them from their apartment because they had invited black friends to visit them at the apartment. Have the plaintiffs stated a claim under § 1982? What is the appropriate remedy?

CLARK v. UNIVERSAL BUILDERS, INC.

United States Court of Appeals, Seventh Circuit, 1974.
501 F.2d 324.

SWYGERT, CHIEF JUDGE.

This appeal is from a grant of a directed verdict for defendants at the close of the plaintiffs' case in chief. Plaintiffs are a class of black citizens who purchased newly constructed houses in Chicago from defendants under land installment contracts during the period from 1958 to 1968. Defendants include the building contractor of the houses and the various land companies through which the houses were sold to plaintiffs. In the district court plaintiffs claimed that as a result of intense racial discrimination in Chicago and its metropolitan area there existed at all pertinent times a housing market for whites and a separate housing market for blacks, the latter confined to a relatively small geographical area in the central city. Plaintiffs contended that the demand among blacks for housing greatly exceeded the supply of housing available in the black market and that the defendants exploited this situation by building houses in or adjacent to black areas and selling the houses to plaintiffs at prices far in excess of the amounts which white persons paid for comparable residences in neighboring urban areas, and on onerous terms far less favorable than those available to white buyers of similar properties, all in violation of plaintiffs' rights under the Thirteenth and Fourteenth Amendments and under the Civil Rights Act of 1866. Plaintiffs' exploitation theory of liability was sustained by District Judge Hubert Will as stating a claim for relief under section 1982 of the Civil Rights Act of 1866. Accordingly, Judge Will denied defendants' motion to dismiss plaintiffs' complaint. Contract Buyers League v. F & F Investment, 300 F.Supp. 210 (1969), aff'd on other grounds, 420 F.2d 1191 (7th Cir.1970), cert. denied, Universal Builders, Inc. v. Clark, 400 U.S. 821, 91 S. Ct. 40, 27 L.Ed.2d 49 (1970). The case then went to trial before District Judge Joseph Sam Perry, and plaintiffs, pursuant to Judge Will's approval of their exploitation theory of liability under section 1982, presented evidence before a jury of defendants' alleged exploitation of the discriminatory housing situation prevalent in Chicago during the period 1958 through 1968. Upon completion of plaintiffs' case in chief, Judge Perry granted defendants' motion for directed verdict, holding in opposition to Judge Will's theory of the case that:

> * * * [C]ounsel for the plaintiffs have not painted a pretty picture of the defendants, but that picture is a picture of exploitation for profit, and not racial discrimination.

> * * *

> Nowhere in the six weeks' trial is there one scintilla of evidence that the defendants or any of them or their agents ever refused to sell to a white person or a black person or a nonwhite person any house or refused to sell one or the other at a higher or lower price, absolutely no positive evidence of discrimination in this record.

> * * *

> Accordingly, for want of any evidence in support of the complaint, the motion for a directed verdict by all of the defendants now on trial is hereby granted, and the complaint of all of the plaintiffs is hereby dismissed as to all of the defendants.

Under Judge Perry's theory of the case, absent evidence of defendants' sales of the same or similar housing to whites on more favorable terms and prices, namely, the traditional theory of racial discrimination, plaintiffs failed to make out a case of liability under section 1982.

* * *

[I]

At the outset we note that section 1982 is framed in broad yet clear language. It provides that:

> All citizens of the United States shall have the same right * * * as is enjoyed by white citizens thereof to * * * purchase * * * real * * * property.

Facially, therefore, the scope of section 1982 would appear to be rather far reaching; indeed such a reading of the statute is supported by the Supreme Court's interpretation of section 1982 in Jones v. Mayer Co. In that case the Court was confronted with questions as to the scope and constitutionality of section 1982. The plaintiff in that case, a black person, brought an action pursuant to section 1982 claiming that the defendants refused to sell him a house on the basis of his race. The district court dismissed the plaintiff's complaint, and the court of appeals affirmed, concluding that section 1982 applied only to state action and not private action. The Supreme Court rejected the argument for a narrow construction of section 1982, holding in broad language:

> [T]hat § 1982 bars *all* racial discrimination, private as well as public, in the sale or rental of property, and that the statute, thus construed, is a valid exercise of the power of Congress to enforce the Thirteenth Amendment. 392 U.S. 413, 88 S. Ct. 2189 [Emphasis in original].

The Court went on to note that section 1982 was an attempt by Congress to provide "that the right to purchase and lease property was to be enjoyed equally throughout the United States by Negro and white citizens alike" and that Congress "plainly meant to secure that right against interference from any source whatever, whether governmental or private." The Court concluded its analysis by stating that section 1982 must be accorded " 'a sweep as broad as its language.' " * * *

Clearly the Court's decision in Jones v. Mayer Co. does not, contrary to defendants' assertions, detract from plaintiffs' contention as to the scope of section 1982. Rather, the decision is support for plaintiffs' theory for in *Jones* the Court viewed section 1982 as a broad based instrument to be utilized in eliminating all discrimination and the effects thereof in the ownership of property. Accordingly, Jones v. Mayer Co. does not stand as an obstacle to plaintiffs' case, but supports it.

Defendants insist that section 1982 cannot be construed to encompass other than the traditional type of discrimination, that is, that defendants offered to sell to whites on more favorable terms and prices than to plaintiffs. Keeping in mind the Supreme Court's admonition in Lane v. Wilson, 307 U.S. 268, 275, 59 S. Ct. 872, 876, 83 L. Ed. 1281 (1939), that the Constitution and statutes promulgated in its enforcement nullify "sophisticated as well as simpleminded modes of discrimination," we reject defendants' notion of adherence to a strict, rigid, and traditional type of discrimination. We need not resort to a labeling exercise in categorizing certain activity as discriminatory and others as not of such character for section 1982 is violated if the facts demonstrate that defendants exploited a situation created by socioeconomic forces tainted by racial discrimination. Indeed, there is no difference in results between the traditional type of discrimination and defendants' exploitation of a discriminatory situation. Under the former situation blacks either pay excessive prices or are refused altogether from purchasing housing, while under the latter situation they encounter oppressive terms and exorbitant prices relative to the terms and prices available to white citizens for comparable housing.

To avoid this conclusion, defendants contend that even though the results obtained under both the traditional and exploitation theories are similar, they come about through significantly different means. Under the traditional theory a black man is denied the "same right" as a white man in that the seller offers to sell the same house to each but at different prices and terms due to the differences in race of the prospective buyer. It is defendants' position that they offered the plaintiffs the same terms and prices they would offer whites. Therefore it is asserted that plaintiffs had the same right as white citizens. This argument ignores current realities of racial psychology and economic practicalities. Defendants can find no justification for their actions in a claim that they would have sold on the same terms to those whites who elected to enter the black market and to purchase housing in the ghetto and segregated inner-city neighborhoods at exorbitant prices, far in excess of prices for comparable homes in the white market. It is no answer that defendants would have exploited whites as well as blacks. To accept defendants' contention would be tantamount to perpetuating a subterfuge behind which every slumlord and exploiter of those banished to the ghetto could hide by a simple rubric: The same property would have been sold to whites on the same terms.

Defendants urge that other sellers and not they were the active agents of discrimination. That is, blacks were excluded from the white market by other sellers who refused to sell to plaintiffs and that accordingly plaintiffs' action lies solely against those other owners and real estate operators and not the defendants. But, we repeat, defendants cannot escape the reach of section 1982 by proclaiming that they merely took advantage of a discriminatory situation created by others. We find repugnant to the clear language and spirit of the Civil Rights Act the claim that he who exploits and preys on the discriminatory hardship of a black man occupies a more protected status than he who created the hardship in the first instance. Moreover, defendants' actions prolong and perpetuate a system of racial residential segregation, defeating the assimilation of black citizens into full and equal participation in a heretofore all white society. Through the medium of exorbitant prices and severe, long-term land contract terms blacks are tied to housing in the ghetto and segregated inner-city neighborhoods from which they can only hope to escape someday without severe financial loss. By demanding prices in excess of the fair market value of a house and in excess of what whites pay for comparable housing, defendants extract from blacks resources much needed for other necessities of life, thereby reducing their standard of living and lessening their chances of escaping the vestiges of a system of slavery and oppression.[5] Indeed, defendants' activity encourages overt discrimination by others since it deflects or forestalls a frontal attack on such discrimination by offering the long-oppressed black an unattractive yet alternative choice to that of a confrontation for equal buyers' rights in a white neighborhood.

Defendants in effect contend that this is solely a matter of economics and not of discrimination. We cannot accept this contention for although the laws of supply and demand may function so as to establish a market level for the buyer in the black housing areas, it is clear that these laws are affected by a contrived market condition which is grounded in and fed upon by racial discrimination—that is, the available supply of housing is determined by the buyer's race. In other contexts the law has prevented sellers from charging whatever the market will bear when special circumstances have occasioned market shortages or superior bargaining positions. In such instances sellers were denied the opportunity to exploit others merely because the opportunity existed.

Contrary to the trial court's stance, the shortage of housing here was triggered not by an economic phenomenon but by a pattern of discrimination that has no place in our society.[6] Accordingly, neither prices nor profits—whether derived through well-intentioned, good-faith efforts or predatory and unethical practices—may reflect or perpetuate discrimination against black citizens. We agree with Judge Will's statement that "there cannot in this country be markets or profits based on the color of a man's skin." Contract Buyers League v. F & F Investment, 300 F.Supp. 210, 216 (N.D.Ill.1969). Price and profit differentials between individual buyers may be justified on a multitude of grounds; for example, the prospective purchaser's reputation or his financial position and potential earning power. But price or profit may not turn on whether the prospective buyer has dark or light pigmentation.

* * *

With respect to the standard of liability upon which a violation of the statute may be predicated within the factual context here depicted, we

---

5. Charging prices greater than white citizens pay for comparable housing means that blacks are required to dedicate a greater portion of their income to housing than white citizens; leaving less to spend on other necessary items such as education, medical care, food, clothing, home improvements and recreation. As a result, the exploitation of the dual housing market assists in the relegation of blacks to a continuing position of social inequality and inferiority while those who exploit the dual housing market enjoy the benefits of enormous wealth exacted from black citizens.

6. In analyzing the market shortage confronting plaintiffs the trial judge stated:

The same economic forces and the law of supply and demand create and destroy markets for building boom towns in time of war and dying ghost towns in time of peace. The same thing occurs in other economic phenomena, such as a gold rush, a uranium strike, a new highway, a railway or the St. Lawrence Waterway. One area is distressed; another is incremented by increased activity.

The "economic phenomena" referred to by the trial judge have nothing to do with the race of the persons involved; the financial impact upon the citizenry is the same regardless of their color. The impact of the phenomenon of racial discrimination, however, falls solely on the black citizenry.

hold that the benchmark for guiding a seller's conduct in the black market is reasonableness. * * * By demanding prices far in excess of a property's fair market value and far in excess of prices for comparable housing available to white citizens the seller ventures into the realm of unreasonableness. The statute does not mandate that blacks are to be sold houses at the exact same price and on the exact same terms as are available to white citizens. Reasonable differentials due to a myriad of permissible factors can be expected and are acceptable. But the statute does not countenance the efforts of those who would exploit a discriminatory situation under the guise of artificial differences.

* * *

We hold accordingly that plaintiffs state a claim under section 1982 since they allege that (1) as a result of racial residential segregation dual housing markets exist and (2) defendant sellers took advantage of this situation by demanding prices and terms unreasonably in excess of prices and terms available to white citizens for comparable housing. If the plaintiffs sustain the burden of proof on these elements they make out a *prima facie* case, whereupon, as recently made clear by the Supreme Court, the burden of proof shifts to the defendants "to articulate some legitimate, nondiscriminatory reason" for the price and term differential. McDonnell Douglas Corp. v. Green, 411 U.S. 792, 802, 93 S. Ct. 1817, 1824, 36 L.Ed.2d 668 (1973).

II

Having determined the substantive framework upon which an action may be brought pursuant to section 1982 we address ourselves to the correctness of the directed verdict entered in favor of the defendants at the close of plaintiffs' case in chief. * * *

There was sufficient evidence to establish, *prima facie,* the existence of dual housing markets in the Chicago metropolitan area as a result of racial residential segregation. Dr. Karl E. Taeuber, a professor of sociology, testified as an expert witness about the results of his extensive research on the dispersion of population in the city of Chicago. His statistical analysis indicated that Chicago was a highly segregated city and that there was a very high degree of residential segregation between whites and blacks. Moreover, despite the decrease of white population in the city accompanied by a rapid increase of the black population, the supply of new housing available to whites was much greater than that available to blacks. Also, during the pertinent time period the expanding suburban housing market was limited almost completely to whites. Dr. Taeuber testified that the main obstacle to the movement of blacks into the white areas of Chicago and suburban residential areas was the high degree of discrimination against blacks in the white market. As a result the supply of housing available to whites was far greater in both absolute and relative terms to the supply of new housing available to blacks.

Plaintiffs produced additional proof concerning the existence of dual housing markets through the testimony of another expert witness, Scott Tyler, a real estate broker and appraiser with many years of experience in the real estate business in Chicago. Significantly, defendants seemingly concede the existence of a dual housing market in Chicago. Nor do we think it beyond the strictures of judicial notice to observe that there exists in Chicago and its environs a high degree of racial residential segregation.[10]

We turn to the second element of the case, whether there was a sufficient *prima facie* showing of an unreasonable differential in price and sale terms between the housing sold or offered by defendants to plaintiffs and comparable housing available to whites. Expert witness Tyler's appraisals demonstrated that on the average the contract prices charged by defendants [to their black purchasers] exceeded the fair market value of [similar nearby] homes [available to whites] by $6,508, or 34.5 percent. Expert witness Hank was of the opinion that on the average defendants' prices exceeded fair market value by $4,209, or 20.6 percent. * * * Based on the foregoing we think a jury could reasonably reach the conclusion that defendants' price differential was unreasonably in excess of fair market value and prices available to white citizens for comparable housing. Accordingly, there was sufficient evidence on the price differential to send the case to the jury.

Turning to the issue of the reasonableness of the sale terms differential the evidence at trial indicated that defendants refused to sell other than on land contract to plaintiffs.[12] There was testimony to the effect that defendants refused to participate in any sales through a deed and mortgage arrangement despite the prospective buyer's ability to obtain mortgage financing. The evidence indicates that plaintiffs were of the equivalent economic status as many whites who routinely obtained mortgages to finance the purchase of houses and that a competing construction company in the black market sold the vast majority of its homes on deed and mortgage to blacks similarly situated economically to plaintiffs. Also, the evidence demonstrates that some plaintiffs made down payments of up to forty-five percent of the contract price—well above the amount needed to qualify for mortgages—and yet defendants refused to deal on terms other than contract. On the basis of this evidence it could reasonably be inferred that defendants utilized the contract method of sales to facilitate their exorbitant pricing practices and not because of significant differences between plaintiffs' economic status and that of whites similarly situated who were able to utilize mortgage financing. Hence, a jury could find that

10. A recent study by the Council on Municipal Performance indicates that of the thirty largest cities in the United States, Chicago is the second most segregated. See Vol. 1, No. 2 Municipal Performance Report, November 1973, at 16–18.

12. * * * Title to the real estate was retained by the land company until the entire amount of the deferred balance was satisfied. Upon default and repossession the land companies were permitted to retain the entire amount which the contract purchaser had paid on the property and any improvements.

the different treatment accorded plaintiffs by defendants' sales terms was discriminatory.

[The Court also held the defendants liable under a "traditional" view of § 1982 because they had developed separate housing tracts in black and white neighborhoods and had used a higher mark-up in setting prices in the black development.]

In summary, it is difficult as a *prima facie* matter to infer that the substantial disparity between the pricing practices of defendants in the black real estate market and the pricing practices in the white market was attributable to some factor other than the race of the buyers. Whether defendants afforded plaintiffs the "same right" to purchase housing as offered white buyers was, based on the foregoing evidence, an issue to be properly submitted to the jury.

[Reversed and remanded.]

Note on Predatory Pricing and Single-Race Victimization

1. In a portion of its opinion not reproduced here the *Clark* court held that a seller which operates in two markets, one white and one black, and charges higher prices in the black market violates § 1982 even under the "traditional" theory of liability. Is such a situation actually any different from that which the court treated under its "exploitation" theory, that of the builder who operates in only a black market but charges higher prices than a nominal competitor who operates in a white market?

(a) Does *Clark* impose a duty on those who deal with blacks to avoid taking advantage of socioeconomic conditions in black neighborhoods? If the "exploitation" theory is adopted, does § 1982 become an affirmative action statute: one must do more than avoid discriminatory thinking and indeed one must take prior discrimination into account and act so as to neutralize its continuing effects?

(b) The *Clark* opinion carefully speaks of a "prima facie" case. What does that mean operationally? What would rebut such a case? Under the exploitation theory is the ultimate issue still intentional racial discrimination? Cf. Village of Arlington Heights v. MHDC, Chapter 1B.5 supra.

2. Compare with *Clark* the Fifth Circuit's decision in **Love v. DeCarlo Homes, Inc.**, 482 F.2d 613 (5th Cir.1973), which presented strikingly similar facts, according to Judge Bell's opinion for the court:

"The alleged injury to plaintiffs stems from the fact that black citizens in 1963 were forced to buy houses in a limited geographic area because of residential racial segregation in the Dade County, Florida area. This residential racial segregation resulted in a scarcity of residential housing available to blacks. In plaintiffs' view, DeCarlo Homes exploited this scarcity to exact onerous and unlawful terms. The allegations presented in plaintiffs' complaint, if true, would presumably afford a basis for relief in the state courts in the form of seeking reformation of contract or actions for fraud and deceit or damages. The difficulty, however, with plaintiffs' bringing a civil rights suit in federal court is that the acts complained of do not fit within the traditional concept of racial discrimination.''

Plaintiffs in *Love* had proved that the same builder sold houses to whites in a different neighborhood on more favorable terms, but the court dismissed such proof because ''the houses in this predominantly white subdivision were not in a similar market costwise or with the differences attendant in the marginal risk of financing present.''

(a) Would the *Love* court have been satisfied only if white and black purchasers in the same subdivision had been extended different credit terms? In *Love* the sale price in the white neighborhood was higher than in the black development, though the other terms were more favorable. Id. at 615. Was that the defect in the plaintiffs' case? Was it a prima facie case but a rebutted one because of evidence that quality varied with price and other sales terms?

(b) Should the focus under § 1982 be racial motivation or differential treatment? Does the *Love* court demand proof of differential treatment: a seller violates § 1982 by treating blacks differently from the way it treats whites but not if it deals with blacks and mistreats them, even if the mistreatment is racially motivated? Does this cast new light on *Arlington Heights,* supra, because it shows that motivation is sometimes an easier standard to meet than that of differential treatment? Cf. Palmer v. Thompson, 403 U.S. 217, 91 S.Ct. 1940, 29 L.Ed.2d 438 (1971) (record showing discriminatory motivation in closing city's swimming pools irrelevant where both blacks and whites hurt by closings).

3. Since the *Clark* and *Love* cases were decided, the Supreme Court in **General Building Contractors Ass'n, Inc. v. Pennsylvania**, 458 U.S. 375, 102 S.Ct. 3141, 73 L.Ed.2d 835 (1982) (discussing part of § 1 of the 1866 Act now codified as § 1981), has interpreted the 1866 Civil Rights Act to reach only intentional discrimination, not impact-style discrimination. Does this holding overrule or undercut the older circuit decisions?

(a) Is the problem with the exploitation theory that one does not know whether a builder is taking advantage of persons because they are black or because they earn less, on average, than whites? If the owner of a chain of furniture stores decides to open a branch in an inner city neighborhood, predominantly populated by blacks, because he thinks that he can charge exorbitant interest rates in financing the sales of personal property to blacks, is he discriminating against his customers because they are African–Americans, or because they are poor? Indeed, is he ''discriminating'' against them at all?

(b) Section 1982 does not contain the word ''discriminate,'' but instead uses the comparative idea of treatment the ''same'' as ''white citizens.'' How should courts decide cases in which the defendant deals with a single racial group, a not unusual occurrence given segregated housing patterns in many cities, and victimizes that group? If a ''con artist'' sells the Brooklyn Bridge only to residents of an adjacent black neighborhood, is he dissimilarly treating the black citizens? Is he discriminating against them?

(c) Absent an intent element, would § 1982 federalize land fraud law involving minorities? Would that be a bad idea?

4. The "single-race victimization" problem looms large in one modern context—"predatory" or above-par financing for homes. See Robert Schwemm & Jeffery Taren, *Discretionary Pricing, Mortgage Discrimination, and the Fair Housing Act*, 45 HARV.CIV.RTS.-CIV.LIBS. L.REV. 375 (2010) (treating the issue under the Fair Housing Act). Would the differential pricing of financing violate § 1982? Cf. Sullivan, supra (what is the effect on "property"?).

(a) Does your answer depend on whether, after *General Building Contractors*, the predation is intentionally race-based? And how would a single plaintiff know that he had suffered such discrimination? How specific must his complaint state the problem? See Swanson v. Citibank, N.A., 614 F.3d 400 (7th Cir. 2010) (specificity of pleading requirements debated). If the complaint proceeds, what would a court do with this defense: "We targeted these homeowners because they were financially vulnerable, not because they were black?" Or, "We targeted their neighborhood because it was easy to make money there?" See Cox v. City of Dallas, Tex., 430 F.3d 734 (5th Cir. 2005) (illegal garbage dump allowed in minority area only through negligence).

(b) Is mortgage financing even covered by § 1982? Review the *Sullivan* case, supra. Is a mortgage part of one's "property"? Which of the transactional verbs in § 1982 is implicated by a mortgage or lending decision? Is the mortgage company a third party with obligations under § 1982? (Would § 1981 provide a remedy? See Chapter 2C infra.)

(c) The recession of 2007–09 had a devastating impact on racial minorities, especially African–Americans, lowering their net worth, on average, to about 5% of that of whites. Loss of jobs and homes contributed to this decline. See Mildred Wigfall Robinson, *The Current Economic Situation and its Impact on Gender, Race, and Class*, 14 J. GENDER RACE & JUST. 431 (2011). Is the problem of racial disparity and property and other assets so singular that mere antidiscrimination laws are inadequate? Are traditional civil rights laws simply irrelevant?

NOTE ON THE FAIR HOUSING ACT AND ITS RELATION TO § 1982

1. The Fair Housing Act of 1968, 42 U.S.C. § 3601 et seq., contains far more detailed and explicit prohibitions on discrimination, and other unlawful activity, than those contained in § 1982. It specifically outlaws blockbusting (inducing owners to sell based on representations of impending sales to minorities in the neighborhood), racial steering (inducing buyers to purchase property in neighborhoods of the same racial make-up), racially oriented advertising (advertisements and commercials that identify housing as for a particular race), and redlining (refusal to finance housing in certain areas because of race). See Robert Schwemm, Housing Discrimination Law and Litigation § 27.2 (revision 10, 2000).

(a) Should all of the acts made illegal under the Fair Housing Act also be deemed to be illegal under § 1982, at least so long as they were done with a racial motive? But the modern act contains at least four racially-relevant exceptions not found in § 1982, most notably a wide-ranging exemption for small owner-occupied rental apartment buildings (the so-called "Mrs. Murphy's Rooming House" exemption). See R. Schwemm, supra, at § 9.3. Since these exceptions were part of the political compromise necessary to obtain passage of the modern act, should they also be read into § 1982?

(b) Should courts alternatively interpret the modern legislation as having impliedly repealed § 1982? Jones v. Mayer held that the newer legislation's "enactment had no affect on § 1982," 392 U.S. at 416, 88 S. Ct. at 2190, and most courts have interpreted this as rejecting implied repeal. See Schwemm, supra, at § 27.2. Should Congress repeal § 1982 and require plaintiffs to use the modern housing discrimination law?

2.   Why would a plaintiff choose § 1982 over the Fair Housing Act, as the vehicle for a housing discrimination claim? Why would she choose the Fair Housing Act over § 1982?

(a) As noted above, the coverage of the two acts is not always parallel because of exceptions in the modern legislation. The modern law also applies only to "dwellings," not all real and personal property. See Phiffer v. Proud Parrot Motor Hotel, Inc., 648 F.2d 548, 550–51 (9th Cir.1980). But § 1982 is occasionally narrower; for example, it protects only "citizens," while the Fair Housing Act covers all "persons," thus including aliens who suffer racial discrimination. See, e.g., Robinson v. 12 Lofts Realty, Inc., 610 F.2d 1032, 1036 n. 9 (2d Cir.1979).

(b) Available remedies under the two statutes varied before 1988 amendments to the Fair Housing Act, which removed limitations on damages and attorneys fees and brought the new law more into alignment with § 1982. See R. Schwemm, supra, at § 27.2. Traditionally, the modern act has a shorter statute of limitations than that which would often apply in § 1982 actions, which, like § 1983, traditionally borrowed state personal injury limitations periods. See, Goodman v. Lukens Steel Co., 482 U.S. 656, 107 S.Ct. 2617, 96 L.Ed.2d 572 (1987) (§ 1981 case); Denny v. Hutchinson Sales Corp., 649 F.2d 816, 820 (10th Cir.1981) (§ 1982 case). Some change may have been effected by the 1991 Civil Rights Act, however. See Jones v. R.R. Donnelley & Sons Co., 541 U.S. 369, 124 S.Ct. 1836, 158 L.Ed.2d 645 (2004) (any post–1991 amendments to federal law might create new claims having a different limitations period).

(c) The Fair Housing Act covers at least some claims of impact discrimination in addition to intentional discrimination, see R. Schwemm, supra, at § 10.04, but there is a defense for necessary neutral rules paralleling concepts developed in employment discrimination law. See generally Chapter 7 infra.

(d) Finally, the Fair Housing Act also contains an affirmative action provision, requiring that local governments that receive federal housing grants must "affirmatively further" fair housing, 42 U.S.C. 3608. Should this provision be interpreted to require local governments to promote housing integration? See United States ex rel. Anti–Discrimination Center of Metro New York, Inc. v. Westchester County, New York, 668 F. Supp.2d 548 (S.D.N.Y. 2009) (False Claims Act suit challenges county's certification that it had met these goals).

3.   Substantial amendments to the Fair Housing Act, adopted in 1988, extend the act's concerns far beyond racial discrimination, primarily by protecting persons with "handicap[s]," 42 U.S.C. § 3602(h), and those who

suffer adversely because of their "family status." 42 U.S.C. § 3602(k). A previous amendment added sex discrimination soon after initial passage of the original act. Pub.L. 93–383, § 808, 88 Stat. 633, 729 (1974).

(a) Does the expansion of civil rights laws to cover other bases of discrimination necessarily weaken their focus on racial discrimination? Is racial discrimination the gravest problem in the civil rights arena, the problem requiring our singular efforts? Does mere discussion of whether other groups merit civil rights protection pit group against group, causing unnecessary fighting over who should be protected? Does that mean the issue should go undiscussed?

(b) If Congress is so willing to pass modern civil rights legislation, was it really socially necessary for the Court to resurrect § 1982? Reconsider Jones v. Mayer.

4. Despite their ready availability, and despite continuing reports of substantial racial discrimination in the sale and rental of housing, and substantial de facto segregation in neighborhood housing, both § 1982 and the Fair Housing Act are seldom litigated. See generally Kushner, *The Fair Housing Amendments Act of 1988: The Second Generation of Fair Housing,* 42 VAND. L. REV. 1049 (1989); R. Schwemm (ed.), The Fair Housing Act After Twenty Years, A Conference at Yale Law School (1988). Yet, despite the dearth of litigation, there is the widespread belief that housing discrimination, overt and residual remains. As Prof. Calmore has said, "In many ways, racism has simply overwhelmed fair housing." John O. Calmore, *Race/ism Lost and Found: The Fair Housing Act at Thirty,* 52 U. MIAMI L. REV. 1067 (1998) (also observing that since 1968 "segregation . . . has now become 'hypersegregation' ").

(a) Are Americans—primarily blacks and whites, but other racial groups as well—socialized to accept housing discrimination and segregation? Do we not care very much about segregation so long as good housing is available to all? Is it available to all? See Patrick A. Simmons, Fannie Mae Foundation, Census Note 7: Changes in Minority Homeownership During the 1990s (2001) (homeownership rates in 2000 were 72.4% for whites, 46.3% for African Americans, 45.7% for Hispanics, and 53.2% for Asians).

(b) Is housing segregation really not very much related to racial consciousness at all, but to ordinary migration patterns that have characterized settlement of many different nationality groups in the United States? Compare Paul Boudreaux, *An Individual Preference Approach to Suburban Racial Desegregation,* 27 FORDHAM URB. L.J. 533 (1999) ("traditional model [of institutionalized racism] cannot explain all the causes of segregation in housing"), with Sheryll D. Cashin, *Civil Rights in the New Decade: The Geography of Opportunity,* 31 CUMB. L. REV. 467 (2001) (greater enforcement of civil rights laws needed).

SECTION 1981 AND EQUAL CONTRACTING RIGHTS

1. THE RIGHT TO "MAKE AND ENFORCE" CONTRACTS

Following the Supreme Court's decision in Jones v. Mayer, the lower courts almost uniformly interpreted § 1981 as also covering private racial discrimination. See Waters v. Wisconsin Steel Works of International Harvester Co., 427 F.2d 476 (7th Cir.1970). For many African–Americans, the quest for property might be financially difficult,[1] but freedom in contracting is a daily concern—both in freely selling services to buying goods and services with hard-earned wages. Thus, it was not surprising that the Supreme Court soon confirmed that it too would interpret all of the 1866 Civil Rights Act, § 1981 as well as § 1982, to cover private acts of discrimination. See Johnson v. Railway Express Agency, Inc., 421 U.S. 454, 95 S.Ct. 1716, 44 L.Ed.2d 295 (1975) (holding employment contracting covered by § 1981).[2] As you can see in the case that follows, a rejuvenated § 1981, when joined with the reinvigorated § 1982, created a pair of powerful weapons in the fight against racial discrimination.

Yet the conflict has been more prolonged than one might expect. Whereas § 1982 protects property rights, § 1981 protects contracting rights and a string of additional rights related to equal participation in the judicial system. Does the topical coverage of § 1981 raise a range of problems not illuminated in *Jones*'s consideration of § 1982? When federal civil rights laws deal with the broad range of personal services that may be the subject of contracts, do they risk intruding upon privacy concerns or topics traditionally regulated by state law that are not present when only property transfers are at issue?

RUNYON v. McCRARY

Supreme Court of the United States, 1976.
427 U.S. 160, 96 S.Ct. 2586, 49 L.Ed.2d 415.

MR. JUSTICE STEWART delivered the opinion of the Court.

The principal issue presented by these consolidated cases is whether a federal law, namely, 42 U.S.C.A. § 1981, prohibits private schools from excluding qualified children solely because they are Negroes.

I

The respondents in No. 75–62, Michael McCrary and Colin Gonzales, are Negro children. By their parents, they filed a class action against the

---

1. See Patrick A. Simmons, Fannie Mae Foundation, Census Note 7: Changes in Minority Homeownership During the 1990s (2001) (homeownership rates as of last decennial census were 72.4% for whites, 46.3% for African Americans, 45.7% for Hispanics, and 53.2% for Asians).

2. As the Fourth Circuit stated in Young v. International Tel. & Tel. Co., 438 F.2d 757, 760 (3d Cir.1971): "Certainly the recently emancipated slaves had little or nothing other than their personal services about which to contract. If such contracts were not included [under § 1981], what was?"

petitioners in No. 75–62, Russell and Katheryne Runyon, who are the proprietors of Bobbe's School in Arlington, Va. Their complaint alleged that they had been prevented from attending the school because of the petitioners' policy of denying admission to Negroes, in violation of 42 U.S.C.A. § 1981 and Title II of the Civil Rights Act of 1964, 42 U.S.C.A. § 2000a et seq. They sought declaratory and injunctive relief and damages. On the same day Colin Gonzales, the respondent in No. 75–66, filed a similar complaint by his parents against the petitioner in No. 75–66, Fairfax–Brewster School, Inc., located in Fairfax County, Va. * * *

The suits were consolidated for trial. The findings of the District Court, which were left undisturbed by the Court of Appeals, were as follows. Bobbe's School opened in 1958 and grew from an initial enrollment of five students to 200 in 1972. A day camp was begun in 1967 and has averaged 100 children per year. The Fairfax–Brewster School commenced operations in 1955 and opened a summer day camp in 1956. A total of 223 students were enrolled at the school during the 1972–1973 academic year, and 236 attended the day camp in the summer of 1972. Neither school has ever accepted a Negro child for any of its programs.

In response to a mailed brochure addressed "resident" and an advertisement in the "Yellow Pages" of the telephone directory, Mr. and Mrs. Gonzales telephoned and then visited the Fairfax–Brewster School in May 1969. After the visit, they submitted an application for Colin's admission to the day camp. The school responded with a form letter, which stated that the school was "unable to accommodate [Colin's] application." Mr. Gonzales telephoned the school. Fairfax–Brewster's Chairman of the Board explained that the reason for Colin's rejection was that the school was not integrated. Mr. Gonzales then telephoned Bobbe's School, from which the family had also received in the mail a brochure addressed to "resident." In response to a question concerning that school's admissions policies, he was told that only members of the Caucasian race were accepted. In August 1972, Mrs. McCrary telephoned Bobbe's School in response to an advertisement in the telephone book. She inquired about nursery school facilities for her son, Michael. She also asked if the school was integrated. The answer was no.

Upon these facts, the District Court found that the Fairfax–Brewster School had rejected Colin Gonzales' application on account of his race and that Bobbe's School had denied both children admission on racial grounds. The court held that 42 U.S.C.A. § 1981 makes illegal the schools' racially discriminatory admissions policies. [The court of appeals affirmed.]

* * *

II

It is worth noting at the outset some of the questions that these cases do not present. They do not present any question of the right of a private social organization to limit its membership on racial or any other grounds. They do not present any question of the right of a private school to limit its student body to boys, to girls, or to adherents of a particular religious faith, since 42 U.S.C.A. § 1981 is in no way addressed to such categories of selectivity. They do not even present the application of § 1981 to private sectarian schools that practice *racial* exclusion on religious grounds. Rather, these cases present only two basic questions: whether § 1981 prohibits private, commercially operated, nonsectarian schools from denying admission to prospective students because they are Negroes, and, if so, whether that federal law is constitutional as so applied.

A. APPLICABILITY OF § 1981

It is now well established that § 1 of the Civil Rights Act of 1866, 14 Stat. 27, 42 U.S.C.A. § 1981, prohibits racial discrimination in the making and enforcement of private contracts.[8] See Johnson v. Railway Express Agency. Cf. Jones v. Alfred H. Mayer Co.

In *Jones* the Court held that the portion of § 1 of the Civil Rights Act of 1866 presently codified as 42 U.S.C.A. § 1982 prohibits private racial discrimination in the sale or rental of real or personal property. Relying on the legislative history of § 1, from which both § 1981 and § 1982 derive, the Court concluded that Congress intended to prohibit "all racial discrimination, private and public, in the sale * * * of property," and that this prohibition was within Congress' power under § 2 of the Thirteenth Amendment "rationally to determine what are the badges and the inci-

---

8. The historical note appended to the portion of the Civil Rights Act of 1866, presently codified in 42 U.S.C.A. § 1981, indicates that § 1981 is derived solely from § 16 of the Act of May 31, 1870, 16 Stat. 144. The omission from the historical note of any reference to § 18 of the 1870 Act, which re-enacted § 1 of the 1866 Act, or to the 1866 Act itself reflects a similar omission from the historical note that was prepared in connection with the 1874 codification of federal statutory law. The earlier note was appended to the draft version of the 1874 revision prepared by three commissioners appointed by Congress.

On the basis of this omission, at least one court has concluded, in an opinion that antedated Johnson v. Railway Express Agency, that § 1981 is based exclusively on the Fourteenth Amendment and does not, therefore, reach private action. Cook v. Advertiser Co., 323 F.Supp. 1212 (M.D.Ala.), aff'd on other grounds, 458 F.2d 1119 (CA5). But the holding in that case ascribes an inappropriate significance to the historical note presently accompanying § 1981, and thus implicitly to the earlier revisers' note.

The commissioners who prepared the 1874 draft revision were appointed pursuant to the Act of June 27, 1866, 14 Stat. 74, re-enacted by the Act of May 4, 1870, c. 72, 16 Stat. 96. They were given authority to "revise, simplify, arrange, and consolidate all statutes of the United States," Act of June 27, 1866, § 1, 14 Stat. 74, by "bring[ing] together all statutes and parts of statutes which, from similarity of subject, ought to be brought together, *omitting redundant or obsolete enactments * * *.*" § 2, 14 Stat. 75 (emphasis added). The commissioners also had the authority under § 3 of the Act of June 27, 1866, to "designate such statutes or parts of statutes as, in their judgment, ought to be repealed, with their reasons for such repeal." 14 Stat. 75.

It is clear that the commissioners did not intend to recommend to Congress, pursuant to their authority under § 3 of the Act of June 27, 1866, that any portion of § 1 of the Civil Rights Act of 1866 be repealed upon the enactment of the 1874 revision. When the commissioners were exercising their § 3 power of recommendation, they so indicated, in accordance with the requirements of § 3. See 1 Draft Revision of the United States Statutes, Title XXVI, §§ 8, 13 (1872). No indication of a recommended change was noted with respect to the section of the draft which was to become § 1981. It is thus most plausible to assume that the revisers omitted a reference to § 1 of the 1866 Act or § 18 of the 1870 Act either inadvertently or on the assumption that the relevant language in § 1 of the 1866 Act was superfluous in light of the closely parallel language in § 16 of the 1870 Act.

* * *

dents of slavery, and * * * to translate that determination into effective legislation.''

As the Court indicated in *Jones,* that holding necessarily implied that the portion of § 1 of the 1866 Act presently codified as 42 U.S.C.A. § 1981 likewise reaches purely private acts of racial discrimination. The statutory holding in *Jones* was that the "[1866] Act was designed to do just what its terms suggest: to prohibit all racial discrimination, whether or not under color of law, with respect to the rights enumerated therein—including the right to purchase or lease property." One of the "rights enumerated" in § 1 is "the same right * * * to make and enforce contracts * * * as is enjoyed by white citizens * * *." 14 Stat. 27. Just as in *Jones* a Negro's § 1 right to purchase property on equal terms with whites was violated when a private person refused to sell to the prospective purchaser solely because he was a Negro, so also a Negro's § 1 right to "make and enforce contracts" is violated if a private offeror refuses to extend to a Negro, solely because he is a Negro, the same opportunity to enter into contracts as he extends to white offerees.

* * *

It is apparent that the racial exclusion practiced by the Fairfax–Brewster School and Bobbe's Private School amounts to a classic violation of § 1981. The parents of Colin Gonzales and Michael McCrary sought to enter into contractual relationships with Bobbe's School for educational services. Colin Gonzales' parents sought to enter into a similar relationship with the Fairfax–Brewster School. Under those contractual relationships, the schools would have received payments for services rendered, and the prospective students would have received instruction in return for those payments. The educational services of Bobbe's School and the Fairfax–Brewster School were advertised and offered to members of the general public.[10] But neither school offered services on an equal basis to white and nonwhite students. As the Court of Appeals held, "there is ample evidence in the record to support the trial judge's factual determinations * * * [that] Colin [Gonzales] and Michael [McCrary] were denied admission to the schools because of their race." 515 F.2d, at 1086. The Court of Appeals' conclusion that § 1981 was thereby violated follows inexorably from the language of that statute, as construed in *Jones, Tillman,* and *Johnson.*

* * *

---

10. * * * Both Bobbe's School and the Fairfax–Brewster School advertised in the "Yellow Pages" of the telephone directory and both used mass mailings in attempting to attract students. As the Court of Appeals observed, these "schools are private only in the sense that they are managed by private persons and they are not direct recipients of public funds. Their actual and potential constituency, however, is more public than private. They appeal to the parents of all children in the area who can meet their academic and other admission requirements. This is clearly demonstrated in this case by the public advertisements." Id. at 1089.

The pattern of exclusion is thus directly analogous to that at issue in Sullivan v. Little Hunting Park, Inc., and Tillman v. Wheaton–Haven Recreation Assn., where the so-called private clubs were open to all objectively qualified whites—i.e., those living within a specified geographic area.

* * *

B. CONSTITUTIONALITY OF § 1981 AS APPLIED

The question remains whether § 1981, as applied, violates constitutionally protected rights of free association and privacy, or a parent's right to direct the education of his children.

1. Freedom of Association

In NAACP v. Alabama, 357 U.S. 449, [at 460,] 78 S. Ct. 1163, [at 1170–71,] 2 L.Ed.2d 1488, and similar decisions, the Court has recognized a First Amendment right "to engage in association for the advancement of beliefs and ideas * * *." That right is protected because it promotes and may well be essential to the "[e]ffective advocacy of both public and private points of view, particularly controversial ones" that the First Amendment is designed to foster. Ibid. See Buckley v. Valeo 424 U.S. 1, 15, 96 S. Ct. 612, 632–33, 46 L.Ed.2d 659; NAACP v. Button, 371 U.S. 415, 83 S. Ct. 328, 9 L.Ed.2d 405.

From this principle it may be assumed that parents have a First Amendment right to send their children to educational institutions that promote the belief that racial segregation is desirable, and that the children have an equal right to attend such institutions. But it does not follow that the *practice* of excluding racial minorities from such institutions is also protected by the same principle. As the Court stated in Norwood v. Harrison, 413 U.S. 455, [at 469–70,] 93 S. Ct. 2804, [at 2812–13,] 37 L.Ed.2d 723, "the Constitution * * * places no value on discrimination," and while "[i]nvidious private discrimination may be characterized as a form of exercising freedom of association protected by the First Amendment * * * it has never been accorded affirmative constitutional protections. And even some private discrimination is subject to special remedial legislation in certain circumstances under § 2 of the Thirteenth Amendment; Congress has made such discrimination unlawful in other significant contexts." In any event, as the Court of Appeals noted, "there is no showing that discontinuance of [the] discriminatory admission practices would inhibit in any way the teaching in these schools of any ideas or dogma." 515 F.2d at 1087.

2. Parental Rights

In Meyer v. Nebraska, 262 U.S. 390, [at 399,] 43 S. Ct. 625, [at 626–27,] 67 L. Ed. 1042, the Court held that the liberty protected by the Due Process Clause of the Fourteenth Amendment includes the right "to acquire useful knowledge, to marry, establish a home and bring up children," and, concomitantly, the right to send one's children to a private school that offers specialized training—in that case, instruction in the German language. In Pierce v. Society of Sisters, 268 U.S. 510, 45 S. Ct. 571, 69 L. Ed. 1070, the Court applied "the doctrine of Meyer v. Nebraska," to hold unconstitutional an Oregon law requiring the parent, guardian, or other person having custody of a child between 8 and 16 years of age to send that child to public school on pain of criminal liability. The Court thought it "entirely plain that the [statute] unreasonably interferes with the liberty of parents and guardians to direct the upbringing and education of children under their control." In Wisconsin v. Yoder, 406 U.S. 205, 92 S. Ct. 1526, 32 L.Ed.2d 15, the Court stressed the limited scope of *Pierce,* pointing out that it lent "no support to the contention that parents may replace state educational requirements with their own idiosyncratic views of what knowledge a child needs to be a productive and happy member of society" but rather "held simply that while a State may posit [educational] standards, it may not pre-empt the educational process by requiring children to attend public schools." Id. at 239, 92 S. Ct. at 1545 (White, J., concurring). And in Norwood v. Harrison, the Court once again stressed the "limited scope of *Pierce,*" which simply "affirmed the right of private schools to exist and to operate * * *."

It is clear that the present application of § 1981 infringes no parental right recognized in *Meyer, Pierce, Yoder,* or *Norwood.* No challenge is made to the petitioner schools' right to operate or the right of parents to send their children to a particular private school rather than a public school. Nor do these cases involve a challenge to the subject matter which is taught at any private school. Thus, the Fairfax–Brewster School and Bobbe's School * * * remain presumptively free to inculcate whatever values and standards they deem desirable. *Meyer* and its progeny entitle them to no more.

3.   The Right of Privacy

The Court has held that in some situations the Constitution confers a right of privacy. See Roe v. Wade, 410 U.S. 113, 152–153, 93 S. Ct. 705, 35 L.Ed.2d 147.

While the application of § 1981 to the conduct at issue here—a private school's adherence to a racially discriminatory admissions policy— does not represent governmental intrusion into the privacy of the home or a similarly intimate setting, it does implicate parental interests. These interests are related to the procreative rights protected in Roe v. Wade, supra. A person's decision whether to bear a child and a parent's decision concerning the manner in which his child is to be educated may fairly be characterized as exercises of familial rights and responsibilities. But it does not follow that because government is largely or even entirely precluded from regulating the child-bearing decision, it is similarly re- stricted by the Constitution from regulating the implementation of paren- tal decisions concerning a child's education.

The Court has repeatedly stressed that while parents have a constitu- tional right to send their children to private schools and a constitutional right to select private schools that offer specialized instruction, they have no constitutional right to provide their children with private school education unfettered by reasonable government regulation.[15] Indeed, the Court in *Pierce* expressly acknowledged "the power of the State reason-

---

15.   The *Meyer–Pierce–Yoder* "parental" right and the privacy right, while dealt with separate- ly in this opinion, may be no more than verbal variations of a single constitutional right.

ably to regulate all schools, to inspect, supervise and examine them, their teachers and pupils * * *." 268 U.S. at 534, 45 S. Ct., at 573.

Section 1981, as applied to the conduct at issue here, constitutes an exercise of federal legislative power under § 2 of the Thirteenth Amendment fully consistent with *Meyer, Pierce,* and the cases that followed in their wake. As the Court held in Jones v. Alfred H. Mayer Co., supra: "It has never been doubted * * * 'that the power vested in Congress to enforce [the Thirteenth Amendment] by appropriate legislation' * * * includes the power to enact laws 'direct and primary, operating upon the acts of individuals, whether sanctioned by State legislation or not.'"

The prohibition of racial discrimination that interferes with the making and enforcement of contracts for private educational services furthers goals closely analogous to those served by § 1981's elimination of racial discrimination in the making of private employment contracts[16] and, more generally, by § 1982's guarantee that "a dollar in the hands of a Negro will purchase the same thing as a dollar in the hands of a white man." 392 U.S., at 443, 88 S. Ct. at 2205.

* * *

For the reasons stated in this opinion, the judgment of the Court of Appeals is in all respects affirmed.

It is so ordered.

MR. JUSTICE POWELL, concurring.

* * *

Although the range of consequences suggested by the dissenting opinion go far beyond what we hold today, I am concerned that our decision not be construed more broadly than would be justified.

By its terms § 1981 necessarily imposes some restrictions on those who would refuse to extend to Negroes "the same right * * * to make and enforce contracts * * * as is enjoyed by white citizens." But our holding that this restriction extends to certain actions by private individuals does not imply the intrusive investigation into the motives of every refusal to contract by a private citizen that is suggested by the dissent. As the Court of Appeals suggested, some contracts are so personal "as to have a discernible rule of exclusivity which is inoffensive to § 1981." 515 F.2d 1082, 1088 (1975).

In Sullivan v. Little Hunting Park, supra, we were faced with an association in which "[t]here was no plan or purpose of exclusiveness." Participation was "open to every white person within the geographic area, there being no selective element other than race." See also Tillman v. Wheaton–Haven Recreation Assn., supra. In certain personal contractual

---

16. The Court has recognized in similar contexts the link between equality of opportunity to obtain an education and equality of employment opportunity. See McLaurin v. Oklahoma State Regents, 339 U.S. 637, 70 S. Ct. 851, 94 L. Ed. 1149; Sweatt v. Painter, 339 U.S. 629, 70 S. Ct. 848, 94 L. Ed. 1114.

relationships, however, such as those where the offeror selects those with whom he desires to bargain on an individualized basis, or where the contract is the foundation of a close association (such as, for example, that between an employer and a private tutor, babysitter, or housekeeper), there is reason to assume that, although the choice made by the offeror is selective, it reflects "a purpose of exclusiveness" other than the desire to bar members of the Negro race. Such a purpose, certainly in most cases, would invoke associational rights long respected.

The case presented on the record before us does not involve this type of personal contractual relationship. * * * A small kindergarten or music class, operated on the basis of personal invitations extended to a limited number of preidentified students, for example, would present a far different case.

I do not suggest that a "bright line" can be drawn that easily separates the type of contract offer within the reach of § 1981 from the type without. * * * [It is clear that] § 1981, as interpreted by our prior decisions, does reach certain acts of racial discrimination that are "private" in the sense that they involve no *state* action. But choices, including those involved in entering into a contract, that are "private" in the sense that they are not part of a commercial relationship offered generally or widely, and that reflect the selectivity exercised by an individual entering into a personal relationship, certainly were never intended to be restricted by the 19th century Civil Rights Acts. The open offer to the public generally involved in the cases before us is simply not a "private" contract in this sense. Accordingly, I join the opinion of the Court.

MR. JUSTICE STEVENS, concurring.

For me the problem in these cases is whether to follow a line of authority which I firmly believe to have been incorrectly decided.

Jones v. Alfred H. Mayer Co. and its progeny have unequivocally held that § 1 of the Civil Rights Act of 1866 prohibits private racial discrimination. There is no doubt in my mind that that construction of the statute would have amazed the legislators who voted for it. Both its language and the historical setting in which it was enacted convince me that Congress intended only to guarantee all citizens the same legal capacity to make and enforce contracts, to obtain, own, and convey property, and to litigate and give evidence. Moreover, since the legislative history discloses an intent not to outlaw segregated public schools at that time, it is quite unrealistic to assume that Congress intended the broader result of prohibiting segregated private schools. Were we writing on a clean slate, I would therefore vote to reverse.

* * *

[However, here the court must follow its precedents.] For even if *Jones* did not accurately reflect the sentiments of the Reconstruction Congress, it surely accords with the prevailing sense of justice today.

The policy of the Nation as formulated by the Congress in recent years has moved constantly in the direction of eliminating racial segregation in all sectors of society. This Court has given a sympathetic and liberal construction to such legislation. For the Court now to overrule *Jones* would be a significant step backwards, with effects that would not have arisen from a correct decision in the first instance. Such a step would be so clearly contrary to my understanding of the mores of today that I think the Court is entirely correct in adhering to *Jones*.

With this explanation, I join the opinion of the Court.

MR. JUSTICE WHITE, with whom MR. JUSTICE REHNQUIST joins, dissenting.

* * *

* * * On its face the statute gives "[a]ll persons" (plainly including Negroes) the *"same right* * * * to make * * * contracts * * * as is enjoyed by white citizens." (Emphasis added.) The words "right * * * enjoyed by white citizens" clearly refer to rights existing apart from this statute. Whites had at the time when § 1981 was first enacted, and have (with a few exceptions mentioned below) no right to make a contract with an unwilling private person, no matter what that person's motivation for refusing to contract. Indeed it is and always has been central to the very concept of a "contract" that there be "assent by the parties who form the contract to the terms thereof," Restatement of Contracts § 19(b) (1932); see also 1 S. Williston, Law of Contracts § 18(3) (3 ed., 1957). The right to make contracts, enjoyed by white citizens, was therefore always a right to enter into binding agreements only with willing second parties. Since the statute only gives Negroes the "same rights" to contract as is enjoyed by whites, the language of the statute confers no right on Negroes to enter into a contract with an unwilling person no matter what that person's motivation for refusing to contract. What is conferred by 42 U.S.C.A. § 1981 is the *right*—which was enjoyed by whites—"to make contracts" with other willing parties and to "enforce" those contracts in court. Section 1981 would thus invalidate any state statute or court-made rule of law which would have the effect of disabling Negroes or any other class of persons from making contracts or enforcing contractual obligations or otherwise giving less weight to their obligations than is given to contractual obligations running to whites. The statute by its terms does not require any private individual or institution to enter into a contract or perform any other act under any circumstances; and it consequently fails to supply a cause of action by respondent students against petitioner schools based on the latter's racially motivated decision not to contract with them.

* * *

NOTE ON THE OPPORTUNITY TO CONTRACT AND PRIVATE CHOICE

1. *Runyon* quickly reconfirmed what had been explicit in the Court's earlier consideration of § 1981—that it also covered private acts of discrimination and that the right to "make and enforce" contracts includes the

opportunity to enter into contracts, not simply the right to enforce contracts already made.

(a) Is the argument for applying § 1981 to private discrimination as strong as that for so interpreting § 1982? Note the Court's footnote 8. Are you persuaded?

(b) Note Justice White's dissent in *Runyon*. Would not that position effectively read a state action requirement back into § 1981? The majority essentially reads the right "to make ... contracts" on equal terms with whites to consist of a right to negotiate a contract without race being taken into account, so that if a white person would have made a contract with the plaintiff but for the consideration of race, his action is proscribed by § 1981. Justice White assumes that the white person is left free to refuse to negotiate a contract with a black person; a black person may simply enforce a contract without racial consideration playing a role. Does White place too much emphasis upon the right to "enforce" a contract, ignoring the right "to make" the contract?

2. In an ironic, indeed bizarre, twist of fate, the dissenters who had failed to restrict § 1981 in *Runyon* succeeded in narrowing the statute in **Patterson v. McLean Credit Union**, 491 U.S. 164, 109 S.Ct. 2363, 105 L.Ed.2d 132 (1989). Whereas the dissent in *Runyon* argued that § 1981 does not apply to contractual opportunity, in *Patterson* the majority held that the statute *only* applied to such pre-formation activity—not to subsequent performance under the contract. Justice Scalia's opinion first stated that considerations of stare decisis counseled against overturning *Runyon*'s holding regarding private discrimination, but then he wrote that § 1981 should be construed literally: since it covers only the right "to make and enforce" contracts, § 1981 "does not apply to conduct which occurs after the formation of a contract," and thus does not protect a black woman who alleged on-the-job racial harassment. 491 U.S. at 170, 109 S. Ct. at 2369.

(a) In an additional statement, the *Patterson* Court ruled that the other verb in § 1981, "to enforce," provides a claim for plaintiffs only when a private party so interferes with their right to seek redress under state contract law that the plaintiff has been unable "to enforce" his contractual rights. Threats and intimidation might give rise to such a claim, for example. Did the two halves of the Patterson interpretation of § 1981 leave the statute as an irrational fragment of law? Or did it properly coordinate federal and state law—giving federal law a role in ensuring the opportunity to contract, but then leaving evenhanded state contract law to solve post-formation problems?

(b) Under *Patterson*, would a restauranteur who agrees to serve blacks, but then intentionally provides bad service and poor food, be liable under § 1981? Could not an unwilling contractor avoid § 1981's proscriptions by simply agreeing to serve initially, then driving black customers away with his insolence? (There would presumably be state contract claims to be tried in such cases; do you trust them? Why(not)?)

(c) The **Civil Rights Act of 1991**, set out in the Appendix, legislatively overruled the *Patterson* decision with a new § 1981(b): "For purposes of [now § 1981(a)], the term 'make and enforce contracts' includes the making, performance, modification, and termination of contracts, and the enjoyment of all benefits, privileges, terms, and conditions of the contractual relationship."[17] Does the 1991 amendment eliminate all of *Patterson*'s influence on § 1981?

(d) The change made by the 1991 Act has special importance in light of another federal statute, see 28 U.S.C. § 1658(a), which created a uniform "catch-all" statute of limitations for all federal claims created after December 1, 1990. This means that any restored to or created in § 1981 by the 1991 Act are governed by the catch-all four-year statute of limitations. See Jones v. R.R. Donnelley & Sons Co., 541 U.S. 369, 124 S.Ct. 1836, 158 L.Ed.2d 645 (2004) (harassment and post-formation claims covered by new 4–year statute; any old claims remain covered by analogous state statute of limitations, as before). Cf. Goodman v. Lukens Steel Co., 482 U.S. 656, 660, 107 S.Ct. 2617, 96 L.Ed.2d 572 (1987) (method for finding most analogous state limitations statute). Are you confident that you can distinguish between pre-contract and post-contract claims?

3. Consider the interaction between the *Patterson* case and the Civil Rights Act of 1991 in light of Justice Stevens' concurring opinion in *Runyon*. To what extent should a Justice take into account current congressional thinking when she construes a statute? If she believes that her interpretation is correct, but that the current Congress would not follow it, should she hesitate?

(a) Consider Justice Stevens' specific opinion in *Runyon*. Has he announced a rule of statutory interpretation or a rule of political accommodation? If he truly thinks that the statute covers only state action but that Congress disagrees, should the proof not be in the pudding: he should have voted his conscience and allowed Congress to vote its views later? Is there not a risk that a Justice will guess wrong about what Congress would do?

(b) If one guesses about what the current Congress would want, how general or specific should the guess be? While the contemporary Congress, as Stevens noted, had passed several laws concerning private racial discrimination with respect to certain topics, it had never passed a statute barring all private racial discrimination. Indeed, it had specifically refused to pass such legislation regarding private education. Although Congress had supplemented several civil rights acts, it had on several occasions adopted legislation designed to slow desegregation of even public schools. See Abernathy, *Title VI and the Constitution: A Regulatory Model for Defining Discrimination*, 70 Geo. L.J. 1, 33–35 (1981). How good are Justices at knowing the unexpressed desires of Congress?

(c) On the other hand, does it not seem like an inordinate waste of time—and judicial-political capital—to fight for a statutory interpretation that a Justice certainly knows will be reversed? That may have been the case with Justice Scalia's opinion in the *Patterson* case, see ¶ 2 supra. If a Justice can foresee that his interpretation will be overturned, should he forebear? If it is an honestly held view, should the Justice similarly forebear?

---

17. The 1991 Act also created a new § "1981A," not to be confused with the original § 1981, which was re-labeled "1981(a)." Section 1981A is discussed in Chapter 7 infra.

4. Two constitutional issues can arise when Congress enacts legislation: the question of whether Congress has power to enact such legislation, see Note on Interpretation of the Thirteenth Amendment, following the *Jones* case (excerpted in subpart A of this Chapter), and the question of whether Congress has exceeded its power by infringing upon individual rights. *Runyon* raises the second issue.

(a) The Court rejects three constitutional rights that are allegedly infringed, and does so rather peremptorily, does it not? Do you agree with these dispositions? Does it bother you that in order to secure statutorily based rights the Court must narrowly construe constitutionally based rights? Is there no such confrontation in this case because commercial education was at issue? See the first paragraph in Section II of *Runyon*. Was the Court a bit too cavalier in its response to a constitutional claim of privacy?

(b) Note how Justice Powell attempts to solve through statutory interpretation some of the constitutional concerns related to privacy. Do you find his position persuasive? Or has he performed plastic surgery on § 1981, giving it a cleft it never should have had? Does the statutory word "contracts" exclude agreements between individual persons for personal benefits? See, e.g., Marvin v. Marvin, 18 Cal.3d 660, 557 P.2d 106, 134 Cal.Rptr. 815 (1976) (woman who lives with a man may sue him on oral contract promising to treat her as if she were a wife and giving her community property rights).

5. Can civil rights statutes designed to enforce accommodation for all Americans really be unconstitutional? Two cases decided after *Runyon* have struck down state-level civil rights laws because they infringed privacy rights. In **Hurley v. Irish–American Gay, Lesbian and Bisexual Group of Boston**, 515 U.S. 557, 115 S.Ct. 2338, 132 L.Ed.2d 487 (1995), the Supreme Court found unconstitutional Massachusetts' civil rights law as it had been applied to open Boston's St. Patrick's Day parade to gay and lesbian groups, a minority covered by the state law's public accommodations provisions. In **Boy Scouts of America v. Dale**, 530 U.S. 640, 120 S.Ct. 2446, 147 L.Ed.2d 554 (2000), the Court found New Jersey's Law Against discrimination unconstitutional as applied to the Boy Scouts' selection of scoutmasters.

(a) The Court's unanimous opinion in *Hurley* found that the state's enforcement of the law in this context unconstitutionally infringed on the parade organizers' free speech rights, in particular, the right to be free from being compelled to repeat or promote the speech of others. The Court's unanimity is perhaps traceable to a foolish statement by the state court in the case: "proper celebration ... requires diversity and inclusiveness" of all groups, it said. The Supreme Court held that this very prescription of what is orthodox violates the First Amendment. See West Virginia State Board of Education v. Barnette, 319 U.S. 624, 63 S.Ct. 1178, 87 L.Ed. 1628 (1943) (students may not be compelled by law to salute and pledge allegiance to the American flag): "[N]o official, high or petty, can prescribe what shall be orthodox in politics, nationalism, religion, or other matters of opinion or force citizens to confess ... their faith therein."[18]

---

18. If the statute at issue in *Hurley* had been a federal statute enforcing the Thirteenth Amendment, would it have been doubly unconstitutional because it also exceeded Congress'

(b) The *Boy Scouts* decision came on a closer 5–4 vote. There the Court held that the state law, by compelling the Scout's to take a homosexual despite their charter values forbidding it, would "unduly burden" the expressive associational rights of the group members. The Court added, 530 U.S. at 653:

> "That is not to say that an expressive association can erect a shield against antidiscrimination laws simply by asserting that mere acceptance of a member from a particular group would impair its message. But here Dale [is openly gay and a] gay rights activist. Dale's presence in the Boy Scouts would, at the very least, force the organization to send a message, both to the youth members and the world, that the Boy Scouts accepts homosexual conduct as a legitimate form of behavior. [when in fact its members oppose that message]."

(c) Civil rights statutes, even federal ones, are mere statutory enactments that clarify, extend, or enforce constitutional commands; they are not themselves of constitutional dimension. See Jones v. Alfred H. Mayer Co., excerpted earlier in this Chapter, and the Notes following it. So there is no doubt that they may, like any other statute, violate limits placed on Congress, correct? Could Congress constitutionally bestow the death penalty on all persons with racially offensive thoughts? Could it ban all racially offensive books?

(d) Should constitutional rights, which are otherwise broadly interpreted, be narrowly construed when they run up against civil rights laws? See, e.g., R.A.V. v. St. Paul, 505 U.S. 377, 112 S.Ct. 2538, 120 L.Ed.2d 305 (1992) (unanimously holding city's hate speech law unconstitutional). Does *Runyon*'s narrower ruling now look like it has been limited to its facts, a commercial school open to the public? It was once popular to argue that the constitutional law of speech and association should be loosened in order to recognize the special harms that speech can cause to minorities. See Mari Matsuda, *Public Response to Racist Speech: Considering the Victim's Story*, 87 MICH. L. REV. 2320 (1989) ("racist speech is best treated as a *sui generis* category" because of the harm minorities have suffered from racist speech). Why has the Court so decisively rejected that idea? Cf. Mark A. Graber, *Old Wine in New Bottles: The Constitutional Status of Unconstitutional Speech*, 48 VAND. L. REV. 349 (1995): "[I]n every age the leading proponents of various bans on certain ideas have insisted that the First Amendment does not fully protect the right to deny or criticize what their generation regards to be fundamental constitutional values."

6.   In light of the later *Hurley* and *Boy Scouts* decisions, would *Runyon* have presented a substantially more difficult constitutional issue if the school had been a truly selective private or church-related school? The Fifth Circuit faced the issue in **Brown v. Dade Christian Schools, Inc.**, 556 F.2d 310 (5th Cir.1977) (en banc). In that case an institution which the court described as a "sectarian school, located on the property of and receiving subsidies from the New Testament Baptist Church," but which advertised in the telephone book and enrolled students from outside the church's membership, denied

---

power to eliminate the badges and incidents of slavery? Is discrimination against persons based on their sexual orientation a badge of slavery? This issue will be discussed in Chapter 3 infra.

admission to two black students because of their race. The 13–member Court of Appeals split into three camps. Five, in an opinion by Judge Hill, affirmed the district court's finding that the racial exclusion was based on "social and political" policy rather than religious conviction, noting that although individual members may have felt racial fraternization to conflict with their religious beliefs, the evidence showed that the "corporate" church had not adopted that view as a religious tenet. Judges Goldberg and Brown also voted to affirm the district court's relief for the plaintiffs, although on quite different grounds. They objected to Judge Hill's "constrictive definition of religion," focused on the church members rather than the corporate church, and found the racial policy dictated by the members' perception of their potential "disobedience to God." Goldberg then balanced this right to religious freedom against the "congressional judgment manifested in § 1981" and "the Constitution itself," and found the government's interest in eradicating slavery overriding in light of the minor damage done to religion (the school would remain free to teach racial segregation). Finally, Judge Roney led six judges in agreeing with Goldberg that religion was at issue, but urging a remand to the district court to decide the constitutional issue thereby presented. (Judge Coleman, while joining the Roney opinion, strongly suggested that he would "absolutely separate" church and state and grant no relief since this school was a "[non-]commercial enterprise.")

(a) Which set of judges comes closest to capturing the themes later adopted by the Supreme Court in *Hurley* and *Boy Scouts*? How would you have resolved the case in light of the Court's later decisions?

(b) Test your willingness to apply neutral principles to all cases with this alternate view of the religious school. In Employment Division v. Smith, 494 U.S. 872, 110 S.Ct. 1595, 108 L.Ed.2d 876 (1990), the Supreme Court held that a state may apply general prohibitory laws (here, punishing use of hallucinogenic drugs) to all persons without making an exception for religious practitioners. Cf. Lyng v. Northwest Indian Cemetery Protective Ass'n, 485 U.S. 439, 108 S.Ct. 1319, 99 L.Ed.2d 534 (1988) (government may build road through tribal burial ground even though it interferes with tribal members' religious beliefs). Were these cases rightly decided? If so, would they support § 1981's application to church schools that racially discriminate? Only church schools?

(c) Section 1981 does not apply only to educational contracts, of course. So consider these same issues in other private contractual settings, e.g., social clubs, country clubs and private dues-paying membership clubs. Would § 1981 make liable country clubs and smaller groups that exclude black members? Only if the country club were willing to take the public position that it favored racial discrimination (just as the Boy Scouts opposed homosexuality)? Is this factor—somewhat like social pressure—what makes it unlikely that the *Hurley* and *Boy Scouts* cases will have a large impact on § 1981?

7. Consider Justice Powell's apparent respect for racially discriminatory decisions when made in some contexts, such as hiring a nanny for one's children. Is that just racism expressing itself? If it is, are we all racists? Consider these problems.

(a) Should there be some irreducible zone of privacy, of group association, where civil rights laws should not apply? Is there an actual social good to be appreciated in allowing persons to make some race-based decisions? States may not outlaw mixed-race marriages, Loving v. Virginia, 388 U.S. 1, 87 S.Ct. 1817, 18 L.Ed.2d 1010 (1967), but that case says noting about an individual's choice in marriage. Assume that you live in a state that still recognizes contracts to marry. Would a person's decision to withdraw from a marriage contract, based solely on newly recognized antipathy for her partner's racial group, violate § 1981?

(b) As we shall see below, § 1981 also applies to blacks who discriminate on the basis of race. Would a black woman, who listens to her family's entreaties not to marry a man of another race because "it will dilute our heritage and weaken our culture," be liability for violating § 1981? Cf. Alan Dershowitz, THE VANISHING AMERICAN JEW: IN SEARCH OF JEWISH IDENTITY FOR THE NEXT CENTURY (1997) (lamenting that intermarriage and assimilation may result in the loss of culture).

2. "CONTRACTS," "PERSONS," AND RELATED PROBLEMS: A ROLE FOR STATE LAW?

COOK v. ADVERTISER CO., INC.

United States Court of Appeals, Fifth Circuit, 1972.
458 F.2d 1119.

COLEMAN, CIRCUIT JUDGE:

May a Court exercise jurisdiction over the content and arrangement of the *society pages* of a newspaper? That is the real issue in this appeal. In a judgment dismissing the complaint, the District Court [Frank M. Johnson, Jr., Chief Judge] held in the negative, Cook v. Advertiser Company, 323 F.Supp. 1212 (M.D. Ala., 1971). We affirm.

One of the class action plaintiffs, Samuel G. Cook, a Negro, alleged that on May 18, 1970, he tendered the photo and wedding announcement of his fiancee, Miss Sherrie Ann Martin, of the same race, to the society editor and to the publisher of The Montgomery Advertiser, the only newspaper of any substantial circulation in the area, with the request that the story appear on the *society page* and "not the black page." The proposed restrictions were rejected; the story and the picture were never published. The wedding occurred on June 12, 1970.

On June 15, 1970 Cook and seven others filed a class action against the newspaper and its publisher, alleging that:

"The Advertiser publishes a society section in its Sunday edition where it prints bridal announcements and wedding stories and pictures. Stories and pictures appearing in this society section are accepted only from white people. All stories and pictures submitted by whites from Montgomery County are published in this society section. The Advertiser refuses to accept and print wedding stories from Negroes to appear in the society section. Wedding stories and pictures of Negro persons are accepted and printed outside the regular society section on a Negro news page."

[Cook's complaint claimed that the Advertiser's acquisition and use of material amounted to a contract, even though no fee was charged for publication, and that applying separate terms to blacks violated § 1981. He asked, in addition to a damage award, that the defendant be enjoined "from refusing to print the picture and story of his wedding" on its regular Society Page rather than the "Negro News" page.]

* * * Our analysis of the transactions between Cook and the Advertiser leads us to believe that they did not amount to a contract, implied or otherwise. It appears that the Advertiser generally wrote and published items on its society page, based on information furnished in questionnaires voluntarily filed by those who wanted an item published. There was never an agreement that every questionnaire, without exception, would result in a story on the society page. The newspaper received no pecuniary consideration from any person filing a questionnaire. There was no agreement to publish and there was no consideration received for any publication actually made. We have been cited no case which holds that such an arrangement constitutes a binding contract between the parties. Thus no § 1981 jurisdiction could arise under the right to contract.

Having determined that the method pursued by the Montgomery Advertiser for acquisition and use of material in its society pages did not constitute a standing offer which became a binding contract when material was submitted, we do not reach the second question presented, that is whether or not granting of the relief sought by the plaintiffs-appellants would be violative of the First Amendment to the Constitution of the United States as constituting an abridgment of freedom of the press.

The judgment appealed from is

Affirmed.

WISDOM, CIRCUIT JUDGE (concurring specially):

* * *

The plaintiff Cook argues that he was denied the same right to "make and enforce" a contract with the Advertiser as is enjoyed by white residents of Montgomery. Cook's argument is appealing. An applicant takes the time and the trouble to record in writing and deliver to the Advertiser information about his impending marriage. In return, the paper bears the expense of publishing the applicant's wedding announcement, thereby providing the applicant and his family with flattering and enjoyable publicity. Though no cash is exchanged, each side incurs a detriment and each side receives a benefit. One could say that the Advertiser has promulgated an offer for a unilateral contract, by communicating to the white residents of the Montgomery area that it will promise to print their announcements if they provide the necessary information. When the information is presented to the paper, a contract is formed, or so the argument might run; a promise is exchanged for performance.

Yet the argument proceeds from a mistaken premise. Not every exchange of conferred benefits creates a contract. In this case Cook cannot succeed in demonstrating the formation of a contract between the Advertiser and Montgomery residents simply because the residents provide the Advertiser with information and the Advertiser provides the residents with publicity. [I do not believe that failure to publish a white bride's photograph would support a suit for breach of contract. The promise, if any, is only a promise to consider publication within the newspaper's editorial discretion.]

* * *

NOTE ON THE MEANING OF "CONTRACTS"

1.   In **Scott v. Young**, 421 F.2d 143 (4th Cir.1970), a privately owned recreational facility excluded blacks from entering. Said the court (id. at 145): "The Timberlake proprietors bestow the right to admission in return for a fee. This is unquestionably a contract. Refusal to extend the same *contractual opportunity* to blacks is * * * a violation of * * * § 1981." (Emphasis added.) Is the *Cook* court's view inconsistent with *Scott*? Why was there no contract in *Cook*? Because it offered no contractual opportunity to anyone? What is a "contract"?

(a)   Was there no contract in *Cook* because under common law there was no "offer" which Cook "accepted"? Since the newspaper reserved to itself the power to decide what to print, was its action not an offer, but a solicitation of Cook's offer? If that view is adopted, could a shoe store not defeat the purpose of § 1981 by posting a sign at its entry saying, "The prices marked on our goods are not an offer to sell, but a solicitation for bids which the management, in its sole discretion, will decide whether to accept"?

(b)   Is the *Cook* circumstance not a contract because no money or other valuable consideration changed hands? Yet, did the newspaper not receive consideration of some real value when it accepted wedding announcements, material which not only attracts reader-purchasers but also advertisers of silver, china, and other wedding gifts?

2.   Was Judge Wisdom's opinion a better way to decide *Cook*? Or did he defer to the press based on First–Amendment concerns that do not exist? In **Pittsburgh Press Co. v. Pittsburgh Comm'n on Human Relations**, 413 U.S. 376, 93 S.Ct. 2553, 37 L.Ed.2d 669 (1973), a local ordinance banned both sex discrimination in employment and "help-wanted ads" classified by sex. The Supreme Court upheld the ordinance as applied to the advertisements, despite the press's argument that "the focus in this case must be upon the exercise of editorial judgment by the newspaper as to where to place the advertisement." The Court found this "judgmental discretion" insufficient to confer First Amendment protection in light of the illegal commercial activity which it induced. Finally, said Justice Powell, limiting his opinion for the Court, nothing in this decision "authorize[s] any restriction whatever, wheth-

er of content or layout, on stories or commentary originated by the *Pittsburgh Press*."

(a) Does *Pittsburgh Press* support or undermine Judge Wisdom's position in *Cook*? In another portion of his complaint, Cook challenged the Advertiser's practice of segregating obituary notices. The newspaper, which charged $20 to print such a notice, changed that practice immediately upon being sued, and the claim was dropped. Would the court of appeals have found the transactions regarding obituary notices to be contracts?

(b) Judge Wisdom found that the newspaper had given only a conditional promise to consider publication, and, he adds, this "is plainly so understood by the public." If the record below showed that the Advertiser published every white bride's picture in the Society Pages, and relegated every black bride's picture to the Black Page, would that undercut his view?

3. The majority in *Cook* cites not one case or authority for its decision. The concurring judge cites Corbin on Contracts, a staple of state law cases deciding contracts claims. What law should determine whether there is a contract in a § 1981 case—state contract law or a federalized version of "contracts" that would serve the special purposes of § 1981?

(a) One option would be the *Erie* model: have § 1981 adopt the test for contract used in the state where the federal court sits (and presumably, most often, the state where the "contract" was made). See Erie Railroad v. Tompkins, 304 U.S. 64, 58 S.Ct. 817, 82 L.Ed. 1188 (1938). Would state law fit § 1981's needs? If the right is the right to contract equally with all other persons, shouldn't the definition of contract be the same for all persons? Would adopting state law serve that purpose?

(b) Would a uniform federal definition be better? Does the phrase "contract" not simply define those situations in which, for a variety of reasons, the makers of law believe that justice requires enforcement of mutual promises or other just expectations? Cf. W. Friedman, Legal Theory 400–04 (1967) (Benthamite influence on contract notions); Calamari and Perillo, Contracts § 31–2 (1977). Is there a unique federal interest, related to racial equality, that would require a federal definition of "contract"? Under this view the shoe store owner in paragraph 2(a) supra, is covered under § 1981 regardless of whether he makes an offer or solicits offers under state law; rather, he is covered because he holds himself out to conduct human interactions which, when entered into, federal law deems enforceable as "contracts."

(c) Is the traditional idea of "contract" even irrelevant to most modern economic and social situations? Has society returned to an age when status—the informal accrual expectations—is more important than contracts? See Kessler, *Contracts of Adhesion—Some Thoughts about Freedom of Contract*, 43 Colum. L. Rev. 629, 640 (1943). See generally G. Gilmore, The Death of Contract (1974). Should "contracts" in § 1981 therefore be interpreted widely to accomplish the social goal of eradicating all racial discrimination with respect to any "status"? How does the case that follows affect your judgment on these issues?

DOMINO'S PIZZA, INC., v. McDONALD

Supreme Court of the United States, 2006.
546 U.S. 470, 126 S.Ct. 1246, 163 L.Ed.2d 1069.

Justice Scalia delivered the opinion of the Court.

We decide whether [an individual plaintiff who owns a corporation may sue for harm done to the corporation in violation of] 42 U.S.C. § 1981.

Respondent John McDonald, a black man, is the sole shareholder and president of JWM Investments, Inc. (JWM), a corporation organized under Nevada law. He sued petitioners (collectively Domino's) in the District Court for the District of Nevada, claiming violations of § 1981. The allegations of the complaint [stated that JWM signed a contract with Domino's to build four restaurants in Las Vegas that would be leased to Domino's for the purpose of operating its "fast food" business. Soon after the contracts were signed, Domino's employees in Nevada purposely tried to make JWM's business fail, refusing to perform as required under the contract between JWM and Domino's.]

At least in part because of the failed contracts, JWM filed for * * * bankruptcy. The trustee for JWM's bankruptcy estate initiated an adversary proceeding against Domino's for breach of contract. For whatever reason, the trustee chose not to assert a § 1981 claim alleging Domino's interference with JWM's right to make and enforce contracts. The breach of contract claim was settled for $45,000, and JWM gave Domino's a complete release. Consequently, no further claims arising out of the same episode could be pursued on JWM's behalf.[2] [Soon after,] McDonald filed the present § 1981 claim against Domino's in his personal capacity[, seeking damages for himself under § 1981. He claimed that Domino's had broken the contracts with JWM because of McDonald's race, harming McDonald personally by making him lose control of his closely held corporation. The district dismissed the complaint, but the Ninth Circuit reinstated it, observing that both the corporation and McDonald personally had suffered losses based on Domino's alleged racial discrimination. It permitted McDonald's separate claim to proceed. We reverse.]

II

Among the many statutes that combat racial discrimination, § 1981, originally § 1 of the Civil Rights Act of 1866, 14 Stat. 27, has a specific function. It protects the equal right of "[a]ll persons within the jurisdiction of the United States" to "make and enforce contracts" without respect to race. 42 U.S.C. § 1981(a). The statute currently defines "make

---

2. Since JWM settled its claims and is not involved in this case, we have no occasion to determine whether, as a corporation, it *could* have brought suit under § 1981. We note, however, that the Courts of Appeals to have considered the issue have concluded that corporations may raise § 1981 claims. See, *e.g.*, *Hudson Valley Freedom Theater, Inc. v. Heimbach*, 671 F.2d 702, 706 (C.A.2 1982).

and enforce contracts" to "includ[e] the making, performance, modification, and termination of contracts, and the enjoyment of all benefits, privileges, terms, and conditions of the contractual relationship." § 1981(b).

McDonald argues that the statute must be read to give him a cause of action because he "made and enforced contracts" for JWM.... We think not. The right to "make contracts" guaranteed by the statute was not the insignificant right to act as an agent for someone else's contracting–any more than it was the insignificant right to act as amanuensis in writing out the agreement, and thus to "make" the contract in that sense. Rather, it was the right—denied in some States to blacks, as it was denied at common law to children—to give and receive *contractual rights* on one's own behalf. Common usage alone is enough to establish this, but the text of the statute makes this common meaning doubly clear by speaking of the right to "make *and enforce*" contracts. When the Civil Rights Act of 1866 was drafted, it was well known that "[i]n general a mere agent, who has no beneficial interest in a contract which he has made on behalf of his principal, cannot support an action thereon." 1 S. Livermore, A Treatise on the Law of Principal and Agent 215 (1818).

Any claim brought under § 1981, therefore, must initially identify an impaired "contractual relationship," § 1981(b), under which the plaintiff has rights.[3] Such a contractual relationship need not already exist, because § 1981 protects the would-be contractor along with those who already have made contracts. We made this clear in Runyon v. McCrary, which subjected defendants to liability under § 1981 when, for racially-motivated reasons, they prevented individuals who *"sought to enter* into contractual relationships" from doing so (emphasis added). We have never retreated from what should be obvious from reading the text of the statute: Section 1981 offers relief when racial discrimination blocks the creation of a contractual relationship, as well as when racial discrimination impairs an existing contractual relationship, so long as the plaintiff has or would have rights under the existing or proposed contractual relationship.

* * *

McDonald's complaint does identify a contractual relationship, the one between Domino's and JWM. But it is fundamental corporation and agency law—indeed, it can be said to be the whole purpose of corporation and agency law—that the shareholder and contracting officer of a corporation has no rights and is exposed to no liability under the corporation's contracts. McDonald now makes light of the law of corporations and of

---

3. We say "under which the plaintiff has rights" rather than "to which the plaintiff is a party" because we do not mean to exclude the possibility that a third-party intended beneficiary of a contract may have rights under § 1981. See, *e.g.*, 2 Restatement (Second) of Contracts § 304, p. 448 (1979) ("A promise in a contract creates a duty in the promisor to any intended beneficiary to perform the promise, and the intended beneficiary may enforce the duty"). Neither do we mean to affirm that possibility. The issue is not before us here, McDonald having made no such claim.

agency—arguing, for instance, that because he "negotiated, signed, performed, and sought to enforce the contract," Domino's was wrong to
"insist that [the contract] somehow was not his 'own.'" Brief for Respondent 4. This novel approach to the law contradicts McDonald's own
experience. Domino's filed a proof of claim against JWM during its
corporate bankruptcy; it did *not* proceed against McDonald personally.
The corporate form and the rules of agency protected his personal assets,
even though he "negotiated, signed, performed, and sought to enforce"
contracts for JWM. The corporate form and the rules of agency similarly
deny him rights under those contracts.

As an alternative to ignoring corporation and agency law, McDonald
proposes a new test for § 1981 standing: Any person who is an "actual
target" of discrimination, and who loses some benefit that would otherwise have inured to him had a contract not been impaired, may bring a
suit. [This view is inconsistent with the text of § 1981, with its] explicit
statutory requirement that the plaintiff be the "perso[n]" whose "right
. . . to make and enforce contracts," § 1981(a), was "impair[ed],"
§ 1981(c), on account of race. * * *

* * *

McDonald resorts finally to policy arguments[, all of which address
unlikely scenarios.] The most important response, however, is that nothing in the text of § 1981 suggests that it was meant to provide an omnibus
remedy for *all* racial injustice. * * *

Reversed.

NOTE ON THE LAW APPLIED IN SECTION 1981 CASES

1. Justice Scalia's opinion for a unanimous Court appears to answer
some questions about § 1981 and to raise still others. First, consider the idea,
expressed near the end of the opinion, that § 1981 was not "meant to provide
an omnibus remedy for *all* racial injustice." This seems to suggest that,
whatever the scope of the word "contracts," it should not be manipulated to
reach many social relationships that are not covered by traditional notions of
contract. The idea of a federally developed set of relationships defined as
"contracts" appears to be dead.[1]

(a) Despite the reluctance to make § 1981 a remedy for a wide-ranging
set of social relationships, the Court seems to suggest that the definition of
"contractual relation" is federal. Do you agree? Does this still leave open the
issue of whether "contract" itself is to have a federal (albeit conventional)
meaning?

(b) Is Justice Powell's concurring opinion in *Runyon*, where he mused
that some "contracts" might be so private as to imply non-coverage under

---

1. Note that, as to a statute of limitations, § 1981 already uses two sources of law, depending
on whether the claim is for pre-contract or post-contract discrimination. One of them is federal.
See Jones v. R.R. Donnelley & Sons Co., 541 U.S. 369, 124 S.Ct. 1836, 158 L.Ed.2d 645 (2004)
(harassment and post-formation claims covered by new 4–year statute; any old claims remain
covered by analogous state statute of limitations, as before), discussed in the Note following the
Runyon case.

§ 1981, still viable? And Judge Wisdom's concurring opinion in *Cook*, is it still viable? Why, because both are narrowing views of contracts rather than expansive ones? Is that plausible? Fair?

(c) Deferring to state law might in fact create a "living" view of contracts as state law changes to meet modern needs. See, e.g., Marvin v. Marvin, 18 Cal.3d 660, 557 P.2d 106, 134 Cal.Rptr. 815 (1976) (California Supreme Court changes equitable rules to allow unmarried persons living together and having sexual relations to make enforceable contracts for property division). Do you like it better now?

2. The Court is somewhat ambiguous about the sources for interpreting the various common-law phrases used in § 1981. Consider the Court's treatment of the word "person," especially insofar as it relates to corporate law. On this issue, the Court noted that "it is fundamental corporation and agency law—indeed, it can be said to be the whole purpose of corporation and agency law—that the shareholder and contracting officer of a corporation has no rights and is exposed to no liability under the corporation's contracts."

(a) The Court's view is the modern American view, but it is not the only view—and indeed the United States only moved to a consensus on this issue in the early twentieth Century. See Janet Alexander, *Unlimited Shareholder Liability Through a Procedural Lens*, 106 HARV. L. REV. 387, 415 (1992) ("unlimited shareholder liability was the general American rule until the early nineteenth century"; by 1850 virtually all the states "had enacted statutes providing for limited liability," though not all switched to this position until early in the Twentieth Century). If a state were to change its corporate law to revert to shareholder liability, would the Court defer to that state's corporate law for claims arising in that state?

(b) Consider the Court's footnote 3 and the paragraph preceding it in the text. The text suggests that the Court might be defining "corporation" by looking at the law as it existed in the states in 1866, when § 1981 was originally adopted. (Compare the discussion of official immunity in Chapter 1D supra.) Footnote 3 suggests that modern law, perhaps the modern consensus of the states, might help define relationships covered by § 1981. Which view is better? Why?

3. Does the Court's decision suggest answers to the issues raised in Sullivan v. Little Hunting Park, and the Note following it in subpart A of this Chapter? That case allowed standing to a landlord who had rented his house to a person who later suffered discrimination—but it left unanswered the question of whether the landlord himself had a claim for damages.

(a) Viewed in contractual terms, would the landlord be a third-party who has "rights" that are violated when his tenant is the victim of racial discrimination? Only if the discrimination caused the landlord to lose the tenant? Only if the tenant later could not pay rent (perform under the contract) due to the discrimination?

(b) What circumstances might fit within the third-party exception discussed in *Domino's Pizza*'s footnote 3? If a company lost a contract because it had hired black workers, would the workers have a claim under § 1981? Would McDonald have had a claim if he had made a long-term contract between himself and JWM, which could not be performed due to the bankruptcy caused by Domino's racial discrimination? Was McDonald's problem that he tried to sue as the shareholder of JWM instead of as the employee?

3. "RACIAL" CLASSIFICATIONS AND THE FORCE OF HISTORY

McDONALD v. SANTA FE TRAIL TRANSPORTATION CO.

Supreme Court of the United States, 1976.
427 U.S. 273, 96 S.Ct. 2574, 49 L.Ed.2d 493.

MR. JUSTICE MARSHALL delivered the opinion of the Court.

Petitioners, L.N. McDonald and Raymond L. Laird, brought this action in the United States District Court for the Southern District of Texas seeking relief against Santa Fe Trail Transportation Co. (Santa Fe), and International Brotherhood of Teamsters Local 988 (Local 988), which represented Santa Fe's Houston employees, for alleged violations of the Civil Rights Act of 1866, 42 U.S.C.A. § 1981, and of Title VII of the Civil Rights Act of 1964, 42 U.S.C.A. § 2000e et seq., in connection with their discharge from Santa Fe's employment. * * *

I

[Plaintiffs claimed that their employer fired them because of race, specifically the imposition of sanctions, including discharge, in circumstances where similarly situation African–Americans would not have been discharged. The district court held that neither § 1981 nor Title VII, see Ch. 7 infra, covered claims by "white persons." The court of appeals affirmed. We reverse.]

II

Title VII of the Civil Rights Act of 1964 prohibits the discharge of "any individual" because of "such individual's race," § 703(a)(1), 42 U.S.C.A. § 2000e–2(a)(1). Its terms are not limited to discrimination against members of any particular race. Thus, although we were not there confronted with racial discrimination against whites, we described the Act in Griggs v. Duke Power Co., 401 U.S. 424, 431, 91 S. Ct. 849, 853, 28 L.Ed.2d 158 (1971), as prohibiting "[d]iscriminatory preference for *any* [racial] group, *minority or majority*" (emphasis added). * * *

We therefore hold today that Title VII prohibits racial discrimination against the white petitioners in this case upon the same standards as would be applicable were they Negroes and Jackson white.[8]

---

8. * * * Santa Fe disclaims that the actions challenged here were any part of an affirmative action program, see Brief for Respondent Santa Fe 19 n. 5, and we emphasize that we do not consider here the permissibility of such a program, whether judicially required or otherwise prompted. Cf. Brief for United States as *Amicus Curiae* 7 n. 5.

III

Title 42 U.S.C.A. § 1981 provides in pertinent part: "All persons within the jurisdiction of the United States shall have the same right in every State and Territory to make and enforce contracts * * * as is enjoyed by white citizens. * * * " We have previously held, where discrimination against Negroes was in question, that § 1981 affords a federal remedy against discrimination in private employment on the basis of race, and respondents do not contend otherwise. The question here is whether § 1981 prohibits racial discrimination in private employment against whites as well as nonwhites.

While neither of the courts below elaborated its reasons for not applying § 1981 to racial discrimination against white persons, respondents suggest two lines of argument to support that judgment. First, they argue that by operation of the phrase "as is enjoyed by white citizens," § 1981 unambiguously limits itself to the protection of nonwhite persons against racial discrimination. Second, they contend that such a reading is consistent with the legislative history of the provision, which derives its operative language from § 1 of the Civil Rights Act of 1866, Act of Apr. 9, 1866, c. 31, § 1, 14 Stat. 27. The 1866 statute, they assert, was concerned predominantly with assuring specified civil rights to the former Negro slaves freed by virtue of the Thirteenth Amendment, and not at all with protecting the corresponding civil rights of white persons.

We find neither argument persuasive. Rather, our examination of the language and history of § 1981 convinces us that § 1981 is applicable to racial discrimination in private employment against white persons.

First, we cannot accept the view that the terms of § 1981 exclude its application to racial discrimination against white persons. On the contrary, the statute explicitly applies to *"all* persons" (emphasis added), including white persons. While a mechanical reading of the phrase "as is enjoyed by white citizens" would seem to lend support to respondents' reading of the statute, we have previously described this phrase simply as emphasizing "the racial character of the rights being protected," Georgia v. Rachel, 384 U.S. 780, 791, 86 S. Ct. 1783, 1789, 16 L.Ed.2d 925 (1966). In any event, whatever ambiguity there may be in the language of § 1981 is clarified by an examination of the legislative history of § 1981's language as it was originally forged in the Civil Rights Act of 1866. It is to this subject that we now turn.

The bill ultimately enacted as the Civil Rights Act of 1866 was introduced by Senator Trumbull of Illinois as a "bill * * * to protect *all* persons in the United States in their civil rights * * * " (emphasis added), and was initially described by him as applying to "every race and color." Cong. Globe, 39th Cong., 1st Sess., 211 (1866) (hereinafter Cong. Globe). Consistent with the views of its draftsman,[17] and the prevailing view in

---

17. Cf. Cong. Globe 474:

the Congress as to the reach of its powers under the enforcement section of the Thirteenth Amendment, the terms of the bill prohibited any racial discrimination in the making and enforcement of contracts against whites as well as nonwhites[, covering all discrimination based on "race and color."].

While it is, of course, true that the immediate impetus for the bill was the necessity for further relief of the constitutionally emancipated former Negro slaves, the general discussion of the scope of the bill did not circumscribe its broad language to that limited goal. On the contrary, the bill was routinely viewed, by its opponents and supporters alike, as applying to the civil rights of whites as well as nonwhites[, as shown by Sen. Trumbull's explicit statement that "this bill applies to white men as well as black men."] * * *

It is clear, thus, that the bill, as it passed the Senate, was not limited in scope to discrimination against nonwhites. Accordingly, respondents pitch their legislative history argument largely upon the House's amendment of the Senate bill to add the "as is enjoyed by white citizens" phrase. * * *

Representative Wilson of Iowa, Chairman of the Judiciary Committee and the bill's floor manager in the House, proposed the addition of the quoted phrase immediately upon the introduction of the bill. The change was offered explicitly to technically "perfect" the bill, and was accepted as such without objection or debate. Id. at 1115.

That Wilson's amendment was viewed simply as a technical adjustment without substantive effect is corroborated by the structure of the bill as it then stood. Even as amended the bill still provided that "there shall be no discrimination in civil rights or immunities among citizens of the United States in any State or Territory of the United States on account of race, color, or previous condition of slavery." To read Wilson's amendment as excluding white persons from the particularly enumerated civil rights guarantees of the Act would contradict this more general language; and we would be unwilling to conclude, without further evidence, that in adopting the amendment without debate or discussion, the House so regarded it.[22]

* * * Finally, in later dialogue [during the debates] Wilson made quite clear that the purpose of his amendment was not to affect the Act's protection of white persons. Rather, he stated, "the reason for offering [the amendment] was this: it was thought by some persons that unless these qualifying words were incorporated in the bill, those rights might be

---

"I take it that any statute which is not equal to all, and which deprives any citizen of civil rights which are secured to other citizens, is an unjust encroachment upon his liberty; and is, in fact, a badge of servitude which, by the Constitution, is prohibited." (Emphasis added.) [sic]

22. The provision generally forbidding "discrimination in civil rights or immunities * * * on account of race, color, or previous condition of slavery" was ultimately struck from the statute in the House. * * * [T]he debates make clear that the ground for objection to that provision, and the reason for its ultimate omission, was the breadth of the terms "civil rights and immunities," beyond those specifically enumerated in the second half of § 1, rather than an antagonism to the principle of protection for every race. * * *

extended to all citizens, whether male or female, majors or minors.'' Cong. Globe, App. 157. Thus, the purpose of the amendment was simply "to emphasize the racial character of the rights being protected,'' Georgia v. Rachel, 384 U.S., at 791, 86 S. Ct. at 1789, 1790, not to limit its application to nonwhite persons.

* * *

The judgment of the Court of Appeals for the Fifth Circuit is reversed, and the case is remanded for further proceedings consistent with this opinion.

So ordered.

[A dissent by JUSTICE WHITE, joined by JUSTICE REHNQUIST, is omitted.]

ST. FRANCIS COLLEGE v. AL–KHAZRAJI

Supreme Court of the United States, 1987.
481 U.S. 604, 107 S.Ct. 2022, 95 L.Ed.2d 582.

JUSTICE WHITE delivered the opinion of the Court.

Respondent, a citizen of the United States born in Iraq, was an associate professor at St. Francis College, one of the petitioners here. In January 1978, he applied for tenure; the Board of Trustees denied his request on February 23, 1978. [He thereafter filed suit under § 1981, charging that he had been the victim of racial discrimination, but] the District Court ruled that § 1981 does not reach claims of discrimination based on Arabian ancestry. [The Court of Appeals for the Third Circuit reversed.]

* * *

Petitioners contend that respondent is a Caucasian and cannot allege the kind of discrimination § 1981 forbids. Concededly, McDonald v. Santa Fe Trail Transportation Co., held that white persons could maintain a § 1981 suit; but that suit involved alleged discrimination against a white person in favor of a black, and petitioner submits that the section does not encompass claims of discrimination by one Caucasian against another. We are quite sure that the Court of Appeals properly rejected this position. Petitioner's submission rests on the submission that all those who might be deemed Caucasians today were thought to be of the same race when § 1981 became law in the 19th century; and it may be that a variety of ethnic groups, including Arabs, are now considered to be within the Caucasian race.[4] The understanding of "race" in the 19th century, howev-

---

4. There is a common popular understanding that there are three major human races— Caucasoid, Mongoloid, and Negroid. Many modern biologists and anthropologists, however, criticize racial classifications as arbitrary and of little use in understanding the variability of human beings. It is said that genetically homogeneous populations do not exist and traits are not discontinuous between populations; therefore, a population can only be described in terms of relative frequencies of various traits. Clear-cut categories do not exist. The particular traits which have generally been chosen to characterize races have been criticized as having little biological significance. It has been found that differences between individuals of the same race are often

er, was different. Plainly, all those who might be deemed Caucasian today were not thought to be of the same race at the time § 1981 became law.

In the middle years of the 19th century, dictionaries commonly referred to race as a "continued series of descendants from a parent who is called the *stock*," N. Webster, An American Dictionary of the English Language 666 (New York 1830) (emphasis in original), "[t]he lineage of a family," N. Webster, 2 A Dictionary of the English Language 411 (New Haven 1841), or "descendants of a common ancestor," J. Donald, Chambers's Etymological Dictionary of the English Language 415 (London 1871). The 1887 edition of Webster's expanded the definition somewhat: "The descendants of a common ancestor; a family, tribe, people or nation, believed or presumed to belong to the same stock." N. Webster, Dictionary of the English Language (W. Wheeler ed. 1887). It was not until the 20th century that dictionaries began referring to the Caucasian, Mongolian and Negro races, 8 The Century Dictionary and Cyclopedia 4926 (1911), or to race as involving divisions of mankind based upon different physical characteristics. Webster's Collegiate Dictionary 794 (1916). Even so, modern dictionaries still include among the definitions of race as being "a family, tribe, people, or nation belonging to the same stock." Webster's Third New International Dictionary Mass.1870 (1971); Webster's Ninth New Collegiate Dictionary 969 (Springfield, Mass.1986).

Encyclopedias of the 19th century also described race in terms of ethnic groups, which is a narrower concept of race than petitioners urge. Encyclopedia Americana in 1858, for example, referred in 1854 to various races such as Finns, gypsies, Basques, and Hebrews. The 1863 version of the New American Cyclopaedia divided the Arabs into a number of subsidiary races, represented the Hebrews as of the Semitic race, and identified numerous other groups as constituting races, including Swedes, Norwegians, Germans, Greeks, Finns, Italians, Spanish, Mongolians, Russians, and the like. The Ninth edition of the Encyclopedia Britannica also referred to Arabs (1878), Jews (1881), and other ethnic groups such as Germans (1879), Hungarians (1880), and Greeks (1880), as separate races. These dictionary and encyclopedic sources are somewhat diverse, but it is clear that they do not support the claim that for the purposes of § 1981, Arabs, Englishmen, Germans and certain other ethnic groups are to be considered a single race. We would expect the legislative history of § 1981, which the Court held in Runyon v. McCrary had its source in the Civil Rights Act of 1866 [and an 1870 re-enactment] to reflect this common understanding, which it surely does. The debates are replete with refer-

greater than the differences between the "average" individuals of different races. These observations and others have led some, but not all, scientists to conclude that racial classifications are for the most part sociopolitical, rather than biological, in nature. S. Molnar, HUMAN VARIATION (2d ed. 1983); S. Gould, THE MISMEASURE OF MAN (1981); M. Banton & J. Harwood, THE RACE CONCEPT (1975); A. Montagu, MAN'S MOST DANGEROUS MYTH (1974); A. Montagu, STATEMENT ON RACE (1972); SCIENCE AND THE CONCEPT OF RACE (M. Mead, T. Dobzhansky, E. Tobach, & R. Light eds. 1968); A. Montagu, THE CONCEPT OF RACE (1964); R. Benedict, RACE AND RACISM (1942); Littlefield, Lieberman, & Reynolds, *Redefining Race: The Potential Demise of a Concept in Physical Anthropology*, 23 CURRENT ANTHROPOLOGY 641 (1982); *Proposals on the Biological Aspects of Race*, 17 INT'L S. SCI. J. 71 (1965); Washburn, *The Study of Race*, 65 AMERICAN ANTHROPOLOGIST 521 (1963).

ences to the Scandinavian races, Cong. Globe, 39th Cong., 1st Sess., 499 (1866) (remarks of Sen. Cowan), as well as the Chinese, id., at 523 (remarks of Sen. Davis), Latin, id. at 238 (remarks of Rep. Kasson during debate of home rule for the District of Columbia), Spanish, id. at 251 (remarks of Sen. Davis during debate of District of Columbia suffrage) and Anglo–Saxon races, id. at 542 (remarks of Rep. Dawson), Jews, ibid., Mexicans, see ibid., (remarks of Rep. Dawson), blacks, passim, and Mongolians, id. at 498 (remarks of Sen. Cowan), were similarly categorized. Gypsies were referred to as a race. Ibid., (remarks of Sen. Cowan). Likewise, the Germans:

> "Who will say that Ohio can pass a law enacting that no man of the German race ... shall ever own any property in Ohio, or shall ever make a contract in Ohio, or ever inherit property in Ohio, or ever come into Ohio to live, or even to work? If Ohio may pass such a law, and exclude a German citizen ... because he is of the German nationality or race, then may every other State do so." Id. at 1294 (Remarks of Sen. Shellabarger).

There was a reference to the Caucasian race, but it appears to have been referring to people of European ancestry. Id. at 523 (remarks of Sen. Davis).

The history of the 1870 Act reflects similar understanding of what groups Congress intended to protect from intentional discrimination. It is clear, for example, that the civil rights sections of the 1870 Act provided protection for immigrant groups such as the Chinese. This view was expressed in the Senate. Cong. Globe, 41st Cong., 2d Sess., 1536, 3658, 3808 (1870). In the House, Representative Bingham described § 16 of the Act, part of the authority for § 1981, as declaring "that the States shall not hereafter discriminate against the immigrant from China and in favor of the immigrant from Prussia, nor against the immigrant from France and in favor of the immigrant from Ireland." Id. at 3871.

Based on the history of § 1981, we have little trouble in concluding that Congress intended to protect from discrimination identifiable classes of persons who are subjected to intentional discrimination solely because of their ancestry or ethnic characteristics. Such discrimination is racial discrimination that Congress intended § 1981 to forbid, whether or not it would be classified as racial in terms of modern scientific theory.[5] The Court of Appeals was thus quite right in holding that § 1981, "at a minimum," reaches discrimination against an individual "because he or she is genetically part of an ethnically and physiognomically distinctive sub-grouping of homo sapiens." It is clear from our holding, however, that a distinctive physiognomy is not essential to qualify for § 1981 protection.

---

5. We note that under prior cases, discrimination by States on the basis of ancestry violates the Equal Protection Clause of the Fourteenth Amendment. Hernandez v. Texas, 347 U.S. 475, 479, 74 S. Ct. 667, 671, 98 L. Ed. 866 (1954); Oyama v. California, 332 U.S. 633, 646, 68 S. Ct. 269, 275, 92 L. Ed. 249 (1948); Hirabayashi v. United States, 320 U.S. 81, 100, 63 S. Ct. 1375, 1385, 87 L. Ed. 1774 (1943). See also, Hurd v. Hodge, 334 U.S. 24, 32, 68 S. Ct. 847, 851, 92 L. Ed. 1187 (1948).

If respondent on remand can prove that he was subjected to intentional discrimination based on the fact that he was born an Arab, rather than solely on the place or nation of his origin, or his religion, he will have made out a case under § 1981.

The judgment of the Court of Appeals is accordingly affirmed.

JUSTICE BRENNAN, concurring.

* * * * I write separately only to point out that the line between discrimination based on "ancestry or ethnic characteristics," and discrimination based on "place or nation of . . . origin," is not a bright one. It is true that one's ancestry—the ethnic group from which an individual and his or her ancestors are descended—is not necessarily the same as one's national origin—the country "where a person was *born,* or, more broadly, the country from which his or her ancestors *came.*" Espinoza v. Farah Manufacturing Company, 414 U.S. 86, 88, 94 S. Ct. 334, 38 L.Ed.2d 287 (1973) (emphasis added). Often, however, the two are identical as a factual matter: One was born in the nation whose primary stock is one's own ethnic group. Moreover, national origin claims have been treated as ancestry or ethnicity claims in some circumstances. For example, in the Title VII context, the terms overlap as a legal matter. See 29 C.F.R. § 1606.1 (1986) (emphasis added) (national origin discrimination "includ[es], but [is] not limited to, the denial of equal employment opportunity because of an individual's, or his or her ancestor's, place of origin; *or* because an individual has the physical, cultural, or linguistic characteristics of a national origin group"); Espinoza, supra, at 89, 94 S. Ct., at 337 (the deletion of the word ancestry from the final version of § 703 of Title VII of the Civil Rights Act of 1964, 42 U.S.C. § 2000e–2(e), "was not intended as a material change, . . . suggesting that the terms 'national origin' and 'ancestry' were considered synonymous"). I therefore read the Court's opinion to state only that discrimination based on *birthplace alone* is insufficient to state a claim under § 1981.

NOTE ON "RACIAL" GROUPS COVERED BY § 1981

1. In *McDonald* the Court construes § 1981 to cover whites as well as blacks. Had no legislative history been available, would Justice Marshall's argument have been nearly so strong?

(a) Can much of the legislative history be explained away in this manner: Congress knew that whites possessed the identified rights and therefore one could "break down all discrimination" by covering blacks alone? Consider another possible interpretation of § 1981's coverage of race: whites are covered, but only when they are the victims of discrimination against blacks. How can this be so? See Trafficante v. Metropolitan Life Ins. Co., 409 U.S. 205, 93 S.Ct. 364, 34 L.Ed.2d 415 (1972) ("standing to sue" based on desire for integrated relationships); Walker v. Pointer, 304 F.Supp. 56 (N.D.Tex. 1969) (white guest of black tenant).

(b) Was *McDonald* motivated by some modern conception that in order to be fair a non-discrimination statute must protect all races from discrimination, not simply the traditionally victimized races? See Crenshaw, *Race, Reform, and Retrenchment: Transformation, and Legitimation in Antidiscrimination Law,* 101 HARV. L. REV. 1331, 1368 (1988) (successful strategies in protecting black interests are those likely to be seen as fair by the national majority—and that is talk of equal rights). Is this not a modern idea, but one possessed by the 1866 Congress? Would a federal statute that protects only blacks run afoul the equal protection concerns read into the Due Process Clause of the Fifth Amendment? See Case Development, 20 HOW. L. J. 512, 523–24 (1977).

(c) Can a white person discriminate against another white person because of that person's race? Can a black person discriminate against another black person because of that person's race? How so? Can blacks ever be guilty of discrimination? Not against whites, but only against other races, such as Asians? See Claire Jean Kim, BITTER FRUIT: THE POLITICS OF BLACK-KOREAN CONFLICT IN NEW YORK CITY (2000) (discussing history of black-Haitian and Korean conflict in New York); Brandon Bosworth, Blacks Against Asians, in FrontPageMagazine.com (December 13, 2000), http://www.frontpagemag.com/Articles/ReadArticle.asp?ID=3408 (last visited March 23, 2006) (same issue from a conservative political perspective). Is to suggest that blacks cannot commit racial discrimination itself a stereotyping of African–Americans?

(d) What is the impact of these cases on affirmative action plans? In a concluding footnote in *Gratz v. Bollinger*, 539 U.S. 244, 123 S.Ct. 2411, 156 L.Ed.2d 257 (2003), the Court incorporated its affirmative-action jurisprudence into contracts covered by § 1981: "[W]ith respect to [the white plaintiff's claim under] § 1981, we have explained that the provision was 'meant, by its broad terms, to proscribe discrimination in the making or enforcement of contracts against, or in favor of, any race.'" Regarding the Court's rules of affirmative action, see Chapter 6E infra.

2. In *Al–Khazraji* the Court construes § 1981 to cover "at least" discrimination based on "ancestry or ethnic characteristics," thus covering many sub-groups often subsumed under a single racial label, such as "white" (or Caucasian). Had no legislative history been available, would Justice White's argument have been nearly so strong? With the legislative history, is there any doubt about the Court's conclusion? What are the limits of the holding?

(a) Presumably, if a plaintiff can find his group cited in the 1866 or 1870 debates, he is protected from such categorical discrimination, but what should courts do about a group not listed? Would discrimination against the following groups be covered: Afrikaners? Polynesians? "Dark-skinned" people?[6] Native–Americans?

(b) Would Al–Khazraji have been covered for discrimination against him as an Iraqi–American rather than as an Arab–American? If during the War in Iraq, a large U.S. airline refused to carry Iraqi citizens on its flights, would the persons refused service have a claim under § 1981? While § 1981 applies to "persons," not only "citizens," that means only that such non-citizens are also protected from racial discrimination, not from state-of-origin discrimina-

---

6. Note that § 1981 covers only "race," even as modified by the Supreme Court, and omits the word "color," which is also used in modern civil rights statutes. See Chapters 6–7 infra.

tion, correct? Or do you agree with Justice Brennan about the drawing of such a legal distinction?

(c) In the companion case to *Al–Khazraji,* **Shaare Tefila Congregation v. Cobb**, see the Note following Cook v. Advertiser, supra, the Court held that Jews were covered under § 1982 because they were considered a separate racial group at the time of passage of the 1866 Civil Rights Act. Would the plaintiffs in *Al–Khazraji* and *Shaare Tefila* have been covered if the discrimination had been directed toward them as religious adherents to Islam and Judaism? (Note: Not all Jews are adherents to the religion of Judaism, and not all Arabs subscribe to the Islamic religion.)

(d) Finally, in light of § 1981's coverage of "persons," consider alien-status situations: Is discrimination against persons because they are non-citizens covered by § 1981? Compare Bhandari v. First National Bank of Commerce, 829 F.2d 1343 (5th Cir.1987), with Guerra v. Manchester Terminal Corp., 498 F.2d 641 (5th Cir.1974). Of course, even if not covered because of alien status, aliens would be covered for racial discrimination. How bright are the lines between ethnicity, nationality, and alien-status?

3. Does the confluence of *McDonald* and *Al–Khazraji* have the effect of making African–Americans liable for their mistreatment of other ethnic groups? Suppose a group of blacks decided to drive a local Korean storeowner out of business. Would they be liable under § 1981? Cf. Park v. City of Atlanta, 120 F.3d 1157 (11th Cir.1997) (rioters destroy Korean storeowner's property).

(a) Notice that § 1981 applies to all "contracts," not just to sellers, vendors, or storeowners. (Title VII, by contrast (Chapter 7 infra), covers only discrimination by an employer against an employee, not vice versa). Is the refusal of a patron to give her business to a store also a refusal to "contract" based on race?

(b) Does it turn the Thirteenth Amendment and § 1981 on their heads to read them to limit black self-help and economic empowerment? Or should blacks, like all other racial or ethnic groups, be bound by the same rules regarding racial consciousness and action?

4. How far can the label "race" be stretched? Does § 1981 protect against some forms of group-based, though non-lineal, discrimination? Recall that "race" does not appear in the statute itself, but is derived from the notion of rights equal to those of "white citizens."

(a) If § 1981 covers ethnicity, does it cover the accents of language that relate to ethnicity, e.g., discrimination against a person with a Hawaiian accent? See Matsuda, *Voices of America: Accent, Antidiscrimination Law, and a Jurisprudence for the Last Reconstruction,* 100 YALE L.J. 1329 (1991).

(b) How strong is the argument for interpreting § 1981 to cover sex discrimination? Might it be said that women once possessed—still possess—rights inferior to those of "white citizens"? But consider the last quotation in *McDonald* (from Rep. Wilson). Does the Court's decisional technique in *Al–Khazraji*—tying the statute to its historical context—preclude coverage of sex discrimination?

(c) Should § 1981's coverage be tied to the groups receiving high-level scrutiny under equal protection analysis? Consider *Al–Khazraji's* footnote 5.

5. Whatever bases of discrimination it may cover, § 1981 covers only intentional discrimination, as the Court notes in *Al–Khazraji* and as it specifically held in **General Building Contractors Ass'n, Inc. v. Pennsylvania**, 458 U.S. 375, 102 S.Ct. 3141, 73 L.Ed.2d 835 (1982). The Court in *General Building Contractors* first explained that the Civil Rights Act of 1866 expresses concerns tied to the virtually simultaneous approval of the Fourteenth Amendment, which itself reaches only intentional discrimination. 458 U.S. at 384–86, 102 S. Ct. at 3146–48. Yet even considered alone and as grounded in the Thirteenth Amendment, the Court found a concern only with intentional harm, id. at 386–88:

> "In determining whether § 1981 reaches practices that merely result in a disproportionate impact on a particular class, or instead is limited to conduct motivated by a discriminatory purpose, we must be mindful of the 'events and passions of the time' in which the law was forged. The Civil War had ended in April 1865. The First Session of the Thirty-ninth Congress met on December 4, 1865, some six months after the preceding Congress had sent to the States the Thirteenth Amendment and just two weeks before the Secretary of State certified the Amendment's ratification. On January 5, 1866, Senator Trumbull introduced the bill that would become the 1866 Act.

> "The principal object of the legislation was to eradicate the Black Codes, laws enacted by Southern legislatures imposing a range of civil disabilities on freedmen. Most of these laws embodied express racial classifications, and although others, such as those penalizing vagrancy, were facially neutral, Congress plainly perceived all of them as consciously conceived methods of resurrecting the incidents of slavery. * * *

> * * *

> "The immediate evils with which the Thirty-ninth Congress was concerned simply did not include practices that were 'neutral on their face, and even neutral in terms of intent,' Griggs v. Duke Power Co. (Chapter 7A.1 infra, a case arising under the Civil Rights Act of 1964), but that had the incidental effect of disadvantaging blacks to a greater degree than whites. Congress instead acted to protect the freedmen from intentional discrimination by those whose object was 'to make their former slaves dependent serfs, victims of unjust laws, and debarred from all progress and elevation by organized social prejudices.' Cong. Globe, 39th Cong., 1st Sess., 1839 (1866) (Rep. Clarke). The supporters of the bill repeatedly emphasized that the legislation was designed to eradicate blatant deprivations of civil rights, clearly fashioned with the purpose of oppressing the former slaves. To infer that Congress sought to accomplish more than this would require stronger evidence in the legislative record than we have been able to discern."

(a) The Court later in its opinion referred to §§ 1981 and 1982 as the "legislative cousins of the Fourteenth Amendment." Id. at 389. Are you persuaded?

(b) If Congress were asked today to amend § 1981 to cover impact-style discrimination, should it do so? Recall that § 1981 covers all contracts, not simply those for employment. Is an impact or effects test more appropriate for narrowly targeted civil rights statutes, such as the employment discrimination provisions of Title VII of the Civil Rights Act of 1964?

(c) Although § 1981 covers only intentional discrimination, it also covers retaliation as a form of intentional discrimination. In CBOCS West, Inc. v. Humphries, 553 U.S. 442, 128 S.Ct. 1951, 170 L.Ed.2d 864 (2008), the plaintiff claimed that he had complained about the intentional racist treatment of a co-worker and was thereafter himself fired because of his complaint. Citing the Sullivan precedent, Chapter 2B supra, the Court treated the case as one of third-party standing and allowed the suit to go forward. *CBOCS* would only apply where the original party had a contractual relationship and where the complaint concerned racial mistreatment, correct?

6. In the 1990's it became increasingly popular to characterize black Americans as African–Americans, even though all such persons had not emigrated to the United States directly from Africa. Does this new emphasis on race as ethnicity ("African–American") rather than color ("black") merely bring the discussion of race full circle—back to where it was in 1866?

NOTE ON THIRTEENTH AMENDMENT POWER OVER NON-RACIAL ISSUES

1. One assumes that *McDonald* and *Al–Khazraji* were not decided in a vacuum and that the Court must have implicitly thought that its construction of § 1981 was constitutionally sound. What is the implicit constitutional holding of the two cases?

(a) In holding in *McDonald* that whites are covered by § 1981, has the Court given Congress greater power under § 2 of the Thirteenth Amendment than that of eradicating the relics of the historical institution of American race-based slavery? Even though whites were not themselves enslaved, might not Congress rationally determine that it was necessary to outlaw all racial discrimination in order to protect blacks—and all of American society—against lingering racist thinking inculcated by American slavery? In other words, is Congress' Thirteenth Amendment power focused on all "race-based" slavery?

(b) Can the holding in *Al–Khazraji* also be tied to other historical American slave systems, which included not only race-based slavery in the southern states but also peonage and "coolie" labor systems in Texas and California, that were based on ethnicity (Amerindian, Chicano, and Chinese workers)? See J. F. Bannon, INDIAN LABOR IN THE SPANISH INDIES (1966). Reconsider Congress' ideas toward race in 1866: if one conceives of the American slave institution as based in ethnicity-like conceptions of "race," then all ethnic discrimination also relates to the historical American race-based slavery system, does it not? Should one read these cases more broadly, as giving Congress power to deal with any other slavery or involuntary servitude that was like the historical American institutions?

2. Is Congress' power under § 2 of the Thirteenth Amendment limited to racial issues? It may seem remarkable now, but the Supreme Court as early

as 1911 had held that the Thirteenth Amendment gave Congress power to reach more than race-based slavery or involuntary servitude. In **Bailey v. State of Alabama**, 219 U.S. 219, 31 S.Ct. 145, 55 L.Ed. 191 (1911), the Court considered a state statute which required persons to serve out labor contracts or be jailed. It was attacked by a black man who alleged that the state's practice violated the Anti–Peonage Laws, now 18 U.S.C. §§ 1581–88, enacted pursuant to the Thirteenth Amendment. In agreeing with this contention the Court noted that "[w]e at once dismiss from consideration the fact that the plaintiff in error is a black man" for the state statute "makes no racial discrimination, and the record fails to show" any. 219 U.S. at 231, 31 S. Ct. at 147. Later the Court stated: "While the immediate concern was with African slavery, the Amendment was not limited to that. It was a charter of universal civil freedom for all persons, of whatever race, color or estate, under the flag." Id. at 240–41, 31 S. Ct. at 151. Does *Bailey* hold that Congress can cover *any* person or group with its Thirteenth Amendment power?

3. Recall that the *Bailey* case, supra, was decided during the period when the Court took a much narrower view of what constituted slavery, see Note on the Desirability of Resurrecting § 1982, ¶ 3, in Chapter 2A supra (actual enslavement standard). Even "involuntary servitude," a term which *Bailey* held to "have a 'larger meaning than slavery,' " was nevertheless severely restricted to "any state of bondage" or "control by which the personal service of one man is disposed of or coerced for another's benefit." 219 U.S. at 241, 31 S. Ct. at 151. To recognize Congress' power to reach any person in those circumstances was to admit only a minor Congressional power, was it not?

(a) Since Jones v. Mayer Co., and its progeny, however, the Court has also allowed Congress to reach and outlaw what that branch determines to be the "badges and incidents" of slavery, including disabilities in contracting for jobs, purchasing housing, or securing an education, conditions which fall considerably short of "actual enslavement." Standing alone, perhaps neither *Bailey*'s recognition of power to protect any person or group, nor *Jones* power to declare the modern disabilities which connote slavery gives Congress too much power, but do the two together not present Congress with greatly expanded power? Too much power?

(b) Considering the double power mentioned in the preceding subparagraph, could Congress ban all private sex discrimination? Discrimination against aged persons? Handicapped persons? Mistreatment of juveniles? If this prospect unsettles you, is it because you believe that states ought to be the repository of legislative power as to those issues? Which of the two Congressional powers—that in *Bailey* to aid all persons or that in *Jones* to define slavery—would you favor restricting? But is not each, alone, equally defensible and even necessary? Would you favor a dual standard which permitted Congress to aid any person as to actual enslavement, but only blacks or others institutionally and historically enslaved as to continuing "badges and incidents"? Was Congress acting within its Thirteenth Amendment power in 1974 when it extended the Fair Housing Act, 42 U.S.C.A. § 3601 et seq., to forbid sex discrimination? Cf. Bray v. Alexandria Women's Health Clinic, 506 U.S. 263, 113 S.Ct. 753, 122 L.Ed.2d 34 (1993) (suggesting that there is no Thirteenth Amendment power to protect women seeking an abortion).

4. In **United States v. Kozminski**, 487 U.S. 931, 108 S.Ct. 2751, 101 L.Ed.2d 788 (1988), the Court considered whether 28 U.S.C. § 241, which protects the Thirteenth Amendment right to be free from involuntary servitude, could be applied to a farmer who kept "two mentally retarded men ... in poor health, in squalid conditions, and in relative isolation" working on his farm. Citing seventy-year-old precedents, the Court noted that "the phrase 'involuntary servitude' was intended to extend 'to cover those forms of compulsory labor akin to African slavery ...,' " thus signifying "an intent to prohibit compulsion through physical coercion." 487 U.S. at 942, 108 S. Ct. at 2760. Since the prosecution in the case had based its case on the defendants' use of mere psychological coercion and "brainwashing," the Supreme Court threw out the conviction.

(a) The Court stated that the statute authorizing the criminal prosecution had only adopted rights existing on the face of the Thirteenth Amendment; that is, Congress had not used its power under § 2 to enforce the amendment in greater detail. If Congress passed a statute under § 2 specifically outlawing psychological coercion, would it be constitutional?

(b) The *Kozminski* Court also seemed troubled by any interpretation of the Thirteenth Amendment that would cover psychological coercion because that would "criminalize a broad range of day-to-day activity." The Court mentioned a parent's threatening withdrawal of affection in order to induce an adult offspring to work, or a political leader's charismatic persuading of volunteers to work for him without pay. Is the Court right? Does allowing the Thirteenth Amendment to reach these arguments "run the slavery argument into the ground"? The Civil Rights Cases, 109 U.S. 3, 24, 3 S.Ct. 18, 30, 27 L.Ed. 835 (1883).

CHAPTER 3

SECTION 1985(3): EQUAL SECURITY, CONSPIRACIES, AND DUAL CONSTITUTIONAL SOURCES

■ ■ ■

A. RESUSCITATION AND POSSIBILITIES

The Issues. The preceding chapter traced the development of Congressional power under the Thirteenth Amendment to enact legislation prohibiting private action constituting badges or incidents of slavery. While that development has gone far toward protecting from private infringement the core civil right to racial equality, §§ 1981 and 1982 cover only contracting and property transfers. As the Court emphasized in *Domino's Pizza v. McDonald*, Chapter 2C.2 supra, these statutes were not "meant to provide an omnibus remedy for *all* racial injustice." Nor do they cover any of the constitutional rights protected by § 1983—procedural due process, non-racial equal protection, and substantive due process rights such as freedom of speech and religion. And § 1983, which does cover those rights, protects only against deprivations caused by state—not private—actors. This chapter covers the search for a statute which would protect all constitutional rights (as § 1983 does) from private interference (as §§ 1981–1982 do).

The issue, however, is not merely one of statutory law, but also constitutional law—congressional power under the Constitution to enact such a statute. This presents a problem because most constitutional rights are considered to be derived from the Fourteenth Amendment—which itself reaches only state action, and thus presumptively limits Congress' remedial power to situations involving state action. To make matters more confusing, however, not all rights necessarily come from the Fourteenth Amendment: the rights to travel and to petition the federal government for redress of grievances, for example, may lie in other constitutional provisions. Is there an implied state-action limitation for those rights as well?

The twin search for a federal statute and Congressional power has met one recurring impediment, the assertion that legislative authority with respect to private actors rests with the states. This assertion reflects the traditional reading and philosophy of the Constitution, a reading which correctly observes that with few exceptions the Constitution speaks to the states or the federal government and not to private parties. Regulation of the normal affairs of private life is left to the states. Indeed, this philosophy of the federal government's role has garnered such keen support that it has itself been occasionally elevated to constitutional principle. In Erie Railroad Co. v. Tompkins, 304 U.S. 64, 58 S.Ct. 817, 82 L.Ed. 1188 (1938), for example, Justice Brandeis' opinion for the Court condemned the federal courts' assumption of power to announce state common law with the explicit statement that "[t]here is no federal general common law" and no constitutional power to make it. In short, the twin search for a federal statute and Congressional power has long been stymied by the recognition that every expansion of federal power necessarily contracts the previously rather exclusive power of the states.

The History. Even under the traditional philosophy there was one area in which federal power over private persons was easily recognized, and that was the situation in which the federal government sought to protect its own existence or promote those interests specifically allocated to the federal government under Article I. Thus, because the federal government had power to pass the homestead laws under Article I, it was also empowered to punish private persons who interfered with homesteaders,[1] and because it had constitutional power to hold federal prisoners in custody, it could punish private persons who sought to harm anyone in federal custody.[2] And, of course, Congress' Article I, Section 8 power over interstate commerce has often been used to enact legislation directly limiting some private persons' ability to take unfair advantage of their fellow citizens,[3] but there remained few civil rights laws that used this power, and they are severely restricted topically.[4] The search for a statute that would cover all constitutional rights—and protect them from private interference—continued.

One civil statute, 42 U.S.C.A. § 1985(3), and its criminal counterpart 18 U.S.C.A. § 241, seemed likely candidates. The criminal provision had been used in the late Nineteenth Century homesteading and federal prisoners cases mentioned above. The civil counterpart, 42 U.S.C. § 1985(3), demonstrably covered some private activity ("going in disguise on the highway") and gave civil rights advocates some cause for hope.

The *Guest* Case—An Opening. The first opening for development came in United States v. Guest, 383 U.S. 745, 86 S.Ct. 1170, 16 L.Ed.2d 239 (1966), reviewing a criminal prosecution under § 241. The majority held that the statute "incorporates no more than the Equal Protection

1. United States v. Waddell, 112 U.S. 76, 5 S.Ct. 35, 28 L.Ed. 673 (1884).

2. Logan v. United States, 144 U.S. 263, 12 S.Ct. 617, 36 L.Ed. 429 (1892).

3. See, e.g., National Labor Relations Bd. v. Jones & Laughlin Steel Corp., 301 U.S. 1, 57 S.Ct. 615, 81 L.Ed. 893 (1937) (National Labor Relations Act of 1935); United States v. Sullivan, 332 U.S. 689, 68 S.Ct. 331, 92 L.Ed. 297 (1948) (Federal Food, Drug, and Cosmetic Act of 1938).

4. See Part III of this book for examples.

Clause itself" and makes no attempt to go further to cover private action. But three justices, led by Justice Clark, added a single sentence their concurring opinion: "it is, I believe, both appropriate and necessary under the circumstances here to say that there now can be no doubt that the specific language of § 5 empowers the Congress to enact laws punishing all conspiracies—with or without state action—that interfere with Fourteenth Amendment rights." In addition, Justice Brennan, also leading a group of three justices, went into further detail supporting Congress' power under § 5, 383 U.S. at 784:

> "No one would deny that Congress could enact legislation directing state officials to provide Negroes with equal access to state schools, parks and other facilities owned or operated by the State. Nor could it be denied that Congress has the power to punish state officers who, in excess of their authority and in violation of state law, conspire to threaten, harass and murder Negroes for attempting to use these facilities. And I can find no principle of federalism nor word of the Constitution that denies Congress power to determine that in order adequately to protect the right to equal utilization of state facilities, it is also appropriate to punish other individuals—not state officers themselves and not acting in concert with state officers—who engage in the same brutal conduct for the same misguided purpose."

Although the majority in *Guest* refused to interpret § 241 to go further than the Fourteenth Amendment itself, a second majority—Justice Clark's three votes and Justice Brennan's three votes—announced that they would uphold at least some congressional legislation designed to apply Fourteenth Amendment rights, which normally require proof of state action, to private persons.[5] (In a further suggestion of congressional power, even the first (Court) majority held that Congress could legislate with respect to private persons interfering with the right to travel. This was because that right, of its own constitutional force, restrains private persons who would interfere with other private persons' right of interstate travel.)[6]

The possibility suggested in *Guest*—the three concurring votes added to the three dissenting votes, yielding an apparent six-vote majority for reaching private action under the Fourteenth Amendment—soon came to prominence in a case interpreting § 1985(3).[7]

---

5. Only Justice Harlan expressed open skepticism on this issue: "As a general proposition it seems to me very dubious that the Constitution was intended to create certain rights of private individuals as against other private individuals. The Constitutional Convention was called to establish a nation, not to reform the common law. Even the Bill of Rights, designed to protect personal liberties, was directed at rights against governmental authority, not other individuals." 383 U.S. at 771 (dissenting on this issue).

6. 383 U.S. at 759 n.17: "The right to interstate travel is a right that the Constitution itself guarantees, [and it] is a right secured against interference from any source whatever, whether governmental or private. In this connection, it is important to reiterate that the right to travel freely from State to State finds constitutional protection that is quite independent of the Fourteenth Amendment."

7. Years later, in Morrison v. United States, Chapter 3D infra, the Court would criticize the "3 + 3" argument as "simply not the way that reasoned constitutional adjudication proceeds." In the late 1960s, however, few thought to question the counting of votes. Should they have done so?

GRIFFIN v. BRECKENRIDGE

Supreme Court of the United States, 1971.
403 U.S. 88, 91 S.Ct. 1790, 29 L.Ed.2d 338.

MR. JUSTICE STEWART delivered the opinion of the Court.

[Griffin's complaint alleged that he and other black Mississippians were passengers traveling on "the federal, state, and local highways" of Mississippi with a Tennessee citizen when they were mistaken for civil rights workers and beaten by the defendants. Their subsequent complaint under § 1985(3) claimed that the defendants conspired "to prevent said plaintiffs and other Negro–Americans * * * from seeking the equal protection of the laws and from enjoying the equal rights, privileges, and immunities of citizens * * *, including but not limited to their rights to freedom of speech, movement, association and assembly; their right to petition their government for redress of their grievances; their rights to be secure in their persons and their homes; and their rights not to be enslaved nor deprived of life and liberty other than by due process of law." The district dismissed, relying on Collins v. Hardyman, 341 U.S. 651, 71 S.Ct. 937, 95 L.Ed. 1253 (1951), which in effect construed the above language of § 1985(3) as reaching only conspiracies under color of state law. The Court of Appeals for the Fifth Circuit affirmed. We reverse and remand.]

I

Collins v. Hardyman was decided 20 years ago. The complaint in that case alleged that the plaintiffs were members of a political club that had scheduled a meeting to adopt a resolution opposing the Marshall Plan, and to send copies of the resolution to appropriate federal officials; that the defendants conspired to deprive the plaintiffs of their rights as citizens of the United States peaceably to assemble and to equal privileges and immunities under the laws of the United States * * *. The Court held that this complaint did not state a cause of action under § 1985(3) [due to failure to allege any action by state officials. The Court made clear that it was not deciding a constitutional question, but was only construing the statute.]

* * *

II

Whether or not Collins v. Hardyman was correctly decided on its own facts is a question with which we need not here be concerned. But it is clear, in the light of the evolution of decisional law in the years that have passed since that case was decided, that many of the constitutional problems there perceived simply do not exist. Little reason remains, therefore, not to accord to the words of the statute their apparent meaning. * * *

III

We turn, then, to an examination of the meaning of § 1985(3). On their face, the words of the statute fully encompass the conduct of private persons. The provision speaks simply of "two or more persons in any State or Territory" who "conspire or go in disguise on the highway or on the premises of another." Going in disguise, in particular, is in this context an activity so little associated with official action and so commonly connected with private marauders that this clause could almost never be applicable under the artificially restrictive construction of *Collins*. And since the "going in disguise" aspect must include private action, it is hard to see how the conspiracy aspect, joined by a disjunctive, could be read to require the involvement of state officers.

The provision continues, specifying the motivation required "for the purpose of depriving, either directly or indirectly, any person or class of persons of the equal protection of the laws, or of equal privileges and immunities under the laws." This language is, of course, similar to that of § 1 of the Fourteenth Amendment, which in terms speaks only to the States, and judicial thinking about what can constitute an equal protection deprivation has, because of the Amendment's wording, focused almost entirely upon identifying the requisite "state action" and defining the offending forms of state law and official conduct. A century of Fourteenth Amendment adjudication has, in other words, made it understandably difficult to conceive of what might constitute a deprivation of the equal protection of the laws by private persons. Yet there is nothing inherent in the phrase that requires the action working the deprivation to come from the State. Indeed, the failure to mention any such requisite can be viewed as an important indication of congressional intent to speak in § 1985(3) of *all* deprivations of "equal protection of the laws" and "equal privileges and immunities under the laws," whatever their source.

The approach of this Court to other Reconstruction civil rights statutes in the years since *Collins* has been to "accord [them] a sweep as broad as [their] language." United States v. Price, 383 U.S. 787, 801, 86 S.Ct. 1152, 1160, 16 L.Ed.2d 267; Jones v. Alfred H. Mayer Co. Moreover, very similar language in closely related statutes has early and later received an interpretation quite inconsistent with that given to § 1985(3) in *Collins*. [The Court here noted that the criminal statutory analogue to § 1985(3), 18 U.S.C.A. § 241, had been held to apply to private persons in United States v. Harris, supra, and United States v. Williams, 341 U.S. 70, 71 S.Ct. 581, 95 L.Ed. 758 (1951).]

A like construction of § 1985(3) is reinforced when examination is broadened to take in its companion statutory provisions. There appear to be three possible forms for a state action limitation on § 1985(3)—that there must be action under color of state law, that there must be interference with or influence upon state authorities, or that there must be a private conspiracy so massive and effective that it supplants those authorities and thus satisfies the state action requirement. The Congress that passed the Civil Rights Act of 1871, 17 Stat. 13, § 2 of which is the parent of § 1985(3), dealt with each of these three situations in explicit terms in other parts of the same Act. An element of the cause of action established by the first section, now 42 U.S.C.A. § 1983, is that the deprivation complained of must have been inflicted under color of state law. To read any such requirement into § 1985(3) would thus deprive that section of all independent effect. As for interference with State officials, § 1985(3) itself contains another clause dealing explicitly with that situation.[8] And § 3 of the 1871 Act provided for military action at the command of the President should massive private lawlessness render state authorities powerless to protect the federal rights of classes of citizens, such a situation being defined by the Act as constituting a state denial of equal protection. 17 Stat. 14. Given the existence of these three provisions, it is almost impossible to believe that Congress intended, in the dissimilar language of the portion of § 1985(3) now before us, simply to duplicate the coverage of one or more of them.

The final area of inquiry into the meaning of § 1985(2) lies in its legislative history. As originally introduced in the 42d Congress, the section was solely a criminal provision outlawing certain conspiratorial acts done with intent "to do any act in violation of the rights, privileges, or immunities of another person * * *." Cong. Globe, 42d Cong., 1st Sess., App. 68 (1871). Introducing the bill, the House sponsor, Representative Shellabarger stressed that "the United States always has assumed to enforce, as against the States, *and also persons,* every one of the provisions of the Constitution." Id. at App. 69 (emphasis supplied). The enormous sweep of the original language led to pressures for amendment, in the course of which the present civil remedy was added. The explanations of the added language centered entirely on the animus or motivation that would be required, and there was no suggestion whatever that liability would not be imposed for purely private conspiracies. [One supporter pointedly commented, "I do not want to see [this measure] so amended that there shall be taken out of it the frank assertion of the power of the national Government to protect life, liberty, and property, irrespective of the act of the State." Id. at App. 141.]

* * *

It is thus evidence that all indicators—text, companion provisions, and legislative history—point unwaveringly to § 1985(3)'s coverage of private conspiracies. That the statute was meant to reach private action does not, however, mean that it was intended to apply to all tortious, conspiratorial interferences with the rights of others. For, though the supporters of the legislation insisted on coverage of private conspiracies, they were equally emphatic that they did not believe, in the words of Representative Cook, "that Congress has a right to punish an assault and battery when committed by two or more persons within a State." Id., at

---

8. [See the statutory language regarding "hindering the constituted authorities of any State."]

485. The constitutional shoals that would lie in the path of interpreting § 1985(3) as a general federal tort law can be avoided by giving full effect to the congressional purpose—by requiring, as an element of the cause of action, the kind of invidiously discriminatory motivation stressed by the sponsors of the limiting amendment [accepted by Representative Shellabarger.] The language requiring intent to deprive of *equal* protection, or *equal* privileges and immunities, means that there must be some racial, or perhaps otherwise class-based, invidiously discriminatory animus behind the conspirators' action.[9] The conspiracy, in other words, must aim at a deprivation of the equal enjoyment of rights secured by the law to all.[10]

IV

We return to the petitioners' complaint to determine whether it states a cause of action under § 1985(3) as so construed. To come within the legislation a complaint must allege that the defendants did (1) "conspire or go in disguise on the highway or on the premises of another" (2) "for the purpose of depriving, either directly or indirectly, any person or class of persons of the equal protection of the laws, or of equal privileges and immunities under the laws." It must then assert that one or more of the conspirators (3) did, or caused to be done, "any act in furtherance of the object of [the] conspiracy," whereby another was (4a) "injured in his person or property" or (4b) "deprived of having and exercising any right or privilege of a citizen of the United States."

The complaint fully alleges [a conspiracy and a motive to violate equal rights based on race, thus supporting the statute's first two requirements. The allegations of detentions and threats satisfy the third requirement, and the allegation of injury meets the fourth requirement.] The complaint, then, states a cause of action under § 1985(3). Indeed, the conduct here alleged lies so close to the core of the coverage intended by Congress that it is hard to conceive of wholly private conduct that would come within the statute if this does not. We must, accordingly, consider whether Congress had constitutional power to enact a statute that imposes liability under federal law for the conduct alleged in this complaint.

V

* * *

That § 1985(3) reaches private conspiracies to deprive others of legal rights can, of itself, cause no doubts of its constitutionality. It has long

---

9. We need not decide, given the facts of this case, whether a conspiracy motivated by invidiously discriminatory intent other than racial bias would be actionable under the portion of § 1985(3) before us. Cf. Cong. Globe, 42d Cong., 1st Sess., 567 (1871) (remarks of Sen. Edmunds).

10. The motivation requirement introduced by the word "equal" into the portion of § 1985(3) before us must not be confused with the test of "specific intent to deprive a person of a federal right made definite by decision or other rule of law" articulated by the plurality opinion in Screws v. United States, 325 U.S. 91, 103, 65 S.Ct. 1031, 1036, 89 L.Ed. 1495, for prosecutions under 18 U.S.C. § 242. Section 1985(3), unlike § 242, contains no specific requirement of "willfulness." Cf. Monroe v. Pape, 365 U.S. 167, 187, 81 S.Ct. 473, 484, 5 L.Ed.2d 492. The motivation aspect of § 1985(3) focuses not on scienter in relation to deprivation of rights but on invidiously discriminatory animus.

been settled that 18 U.S.C.A. § 241, a criminal statute [with a specific intent requirement], reaches wholly private conspiracies and is constitutional. E.g., In re Quarles, 158 U.S. 532, 15 S.Ct. 959, 39 L.Ed. 1080; Logan v. United States, 144 U.S. 263, 293–295, 12 S.Ct. 617, 626–627, 36 L.Ed. 429; United States v. Waddell, 112 U.S. 76, 77–81, 5 S.Ct. 35, 36–38, 28 L.Ed. 673; Ex parte Yarbrough, 110 U.S. 651, 4 S.Ct. 152, 28 L.Ed. 274. Our inquiry, therefore, need go only to identifying a source of congressional power to reach the private conspiracy alleged by the complaint in this case.

A

[First we consider the Thirteenth Amendment. Surely] there has never been any doubt of the power of Congress to impose liability on private persons under § 2 of that amendment, "for the amendment is not a mere prohibition of state laws establishing or upholding slavery, but an absolute declaration that slavery or involuntary servitude shall not exist in any part of the United States." Civil Rights Cases, 109 U.S. 3, 20, 3 S.Ct. 18, 28, 27 L.Ed. 835. See also Jones v. Alfred H. Mayer Co. Not only may Congress impose such liability, but the varieties of private conduct that it may make criminally punishable or civilly remediable extend far beyond the actual imposition of slavery or involuntary servitude. By the Thirteenth Amendment, we committed ourselves as a Nation to the proposition that the former slaves and their descendants should be forever free. To keep that promise, "Congress has the power under the Thirteenth Amendment rationally to determine what are the badges and the incidents of slavery, and the authority to translate that determination into effective legislation." Jones v. Alfred H. Mayer Co., supra, at 440, 88 S.Ct., at 2203. We can only conclude that Congress was wholly within its powers under § 2 of the Thirteenth Amendment in creating a statutory cause of action for Negro citizens who have been the victims of conspiratorial, racially discriminatory private action aimed at depriving them of the basic rights that the law secures to all free men.

B

Our cases have firmly established that the right of interstate travel is constitutionally protected, does not necessarily rest on the Fourteenth Amendment, and is assertable against private as well as governmental interference. United States v. Guest[, supra]. The "right to pass freely from state to state" has been explicitly recognized as "among the rights and privileges of national citizenship." That right, like other rights of national citizenship, is within the power of Congress to protect by appropriate legislation. E.g., United States v. Guest.

The complaint in this case alleges [that defendants sought to prevent] the petitioners and other Negroes from exercising their "rights to travel the public highways without restraint in the same terms as white citizens in Kemper County, Mississippi." Finally, the conspiracy was alleged to have been inspired by the respondents' erroneous belief that Grady, a

Tennessean, was a worker for Negro civil rights. Under these allegations it is open to the petitioners to prove at trial that they had been engaging in interstate travel or intended to do so, that their federal right to travel interstate was one of the rights meant to be discriminatorily impaired by the conspiracy, that the conspirators intended to drive out-of-state civil rights workers from the State, or that they meant to deter the petitioners from associating with such persons. * * *

C

In identifying these two constitutional sources of congressional power, we do not imply the absence of any other. More specifically, the allegations of the complaint in this case have not required consideration of the scope of the power of Congress under § 5 of the Fourteenth Amendment. By the same token, since the allegations of the complaint bring this cause of action so close to the constitutionally authorized core of the statute, there has been no occasion here to trace out its constitutionally permissible periphery.

* * *

Reversed and remanded.

NOTE ON THE RELATION BETWEEN Griffin AND Guest

1. Recall that Justice Brennan's separate opinion in *Guest* claimed that the statute there applied to private conduct and that Congress had constitutional power under the Fourteenth Amendment to reach such private conduct. Does *Griffin* mimic Justice Brennan's position in *Guest*? Or has the Court only practiced some fancy footwork to avoid a difficult constitutional issue?

(a) Does *Griffin* hold that § 1985(3) reaches Fourteenth Amendment rights when infringed by private parties? Does it provide a future possibility for holding this when it suggests that the statute (i) is meant to reach private action, and (ii) the only remaining issue is Congress' power to do so? Doesn't the "second majority" in *Guest* (Clark + Brennan, six votes) answer the second question for Fourteenth Amendment rights? In other words, does the method of decision adopted in *Griffin* suggest a future positive answer given the existence of *Guest*'s second majority?

(b) Why are the questions in subparagraph (a) so difficult to answer? Has Justice Stewart given the illusion of reading § 1985(3) as Brennan wanted § 241 read, without actually explicitly saying so? Why did Brennan not file a concurring opinion reaching the Fourteenth Amendment issue? Had the intervening decision in Jones v. Mayer Co., Chapter 2A supra, which, as *Griffin* shows, makes it possible to reach private racial discrimination under the Thirteenth Amendment, cooled the ardor Brennan showed in *Guest*? Did *Jones'* decision on the Thirteenth Amendment make it unnecessary to construe § 1985(3) to reach Fourteenth Amendment rights? Consider this question in reading section B of this Chapter.

2. How does the Court's construction of § 1985(3) cut it loose from apparent roots in the Fourteenth Amendment? What does the Court do with the statutory phrase "equal protection of the laws"?

(a) Are you persuaded that this phrase is unrelated to the concept of "state action"? Has a century and a half of constitutional law under the Fourteenth Amendment led us to link two phrases—equal protection and "state action"—that have no necessary link?

(b) What meaning does the Court ascribe to "equal protection of the laws"? As an animus requirement, what types of animus or motivations does it cover?

(c) Had the Court omitted any reference to "perhaps otherwise class-based invidiously discriminatory animus," wouldn't all constitutional problems have been solved? If the statute requires a racial animus, then it is always valid under the Thirteenth Amendment, is it not? Racial motivation in harming anyone based on race, so long as it could be seen as a relic of slavery, would fall within Congress' Thirteenth Amendment power, would it not? Did the Court bite off one issue too many?

3. Consider again the following two-stage characterization of the holding in *Griffin:* (i) as a matter of statutory construction the Court holds that § 1985(3) reaches all private conspiracies; (ii) then in every future case a trial court must ask whether there is a constitutional basis for Congress reaching any particular private conspiracy.

(a) If this is the appropriate reading of *Griffin,* does it not create a future unclear constitutional issue every time that § 1985(3) is applied in a new context? Why would the Court adopt a statutory interpretation that would create an on-going series of constitutional problems? Is it not a more customary practice to construe federal legislation so as to avoid difficult constitutional issues? (Or did the Court foresee no constitutional shoals because it fully expected *Guest*'s second majority to save future applications?)

(b) Has the majority artfully created a construct that allows it to deflect any pressure to continue developing § 1985(3)? After all, in the end, the only parts of the decision actually favorable to a power to reach private persons under the Fourteenth Amendment are some dictum about other animuses covered and speculation about how members of the Court might vote in future cases.

(c) Reconsider Justice Brennan's vote in *Guest,* which emphasized that the civil rights workers meant to use state facilities and were kept from those facilities by private actors. Would he find Fourteenth Amendment power in Congress to assist the workers if they had been entering a private home? Is that at least another case? (Recall also Justice Clark's summary sentence in *Guest*: might it not have future limits?)

B. THE YEARS OF EXPERIMENTATION

1. CONGRESSIONAL POWER UNDER THE FOURTEENTH AMENDMENT

ACTION v. GANNON

United States Court of Appeals, Eighth Circuit, 1971, en banc.
450 F.2d 1227.

HEANEY, CIRCUIT JUDGE.

We are asked to decide whether a United States District Court has jurisdiction to enjoin two organizations, the Black Liberation Front and Action, and their members, from continuing to disrupt the religious services of a predominantly white Catholic parish. [The disruptions occurred over a series of Sundays in 1969, as members of ACTION entered during church services and shouted amplified "notice and demands" to the congregation. Some ACTION members sat in the aisles until removed by police. The demands included a warning that the protestors would continue to disrupt services until their demands were met.[4]]

[Relying on § 1985(3), the District Judge entered a permanent injunction against the protests in order to protect the rights of the parishioners to free exercise of their religion. This appeal followed. We note that in the time since the trial court's decision, the Supreme Court has handed down its opinion in Griffin v. Breckenridge, holding that § 1985(3) reaches race-based private conspiracies.]

Griffin did not resolve the question of whether § 1985(3) can be constitutionally applied to the facts of this case. *Griffin* teaches (1) that we need not find the language of § 1985(3) constitutional in all its possible applications in order to uphold its facial constitutionality and its application to the facts of a particular case; (2) that § 1985(3) is not unconstitutional solely on the grounds that it reaches wholly private conspiracies; and (3) that a source of congressional power to reach the private conspiracy must be found in each case.

* * *

---

4. * * *"Ladies and Gentlemen of the church, ACTION's 'BLACK SUNDAYS,' phase two, are series of protest demonstrations. The demonstrations will last for a period of six months. "If you wish *not* to become involved, it would be best that you take a six month leave-of-absence from the church. ACTION's 'BLACK SUNDAYS' at this church will take place *without further warning*. If you're present, of course, you'll become involved—a very shocking experience! * * * "ACTION DEMANDS:

"1. ACTION demands that all properties, including slum property be made public.

"2. ACTION demands that the property owner (the church superior staff) make itself available to act as a non-profit bonding agency for all Black residents of St. Louis." * * *

"5. ACTION demands 75% of the 'monies take', annually, to be relinquished to ACTION for the purpose of financing energetic community base programs that are actively combating white racism in other areas, regardless of creed." * * *

"ACTION'S 'BLACK SUNDAYS' DEMONSTRATIONS WILL CEASE WHEN ALL DEMANDS ARE MET!!!!!"

It is quite clear that neither the Thirteenth Amendment nor the constitutional right to travel interstate can serve as a source of power here [as they did in *Griffin*]. But we think it equally clear that Congress had power to reach this conspiracy under §§ 1 and 5 of the Fourteenth Amendment. [The parishioners' religious rights are protected by the First Amendment, which has been incorporated into the Fourteenth Amendment's Due Process Clause. Although that amendment itself reaches only state actors, Congress may use its power under § 5 to go further—to reach private persons. See United States v. Guest.]

In *Guest,* six Justices—Warren, Black, Douglas, Clark, Brennan and Fortas—expressed the view that Congress has power under § 5 of the Fourteenth Amendment to punish private conspiracies that interfere with Fourteenth Amendment rights. [We also rely on scholars who have agreed that Congress can under § 5 protect against private action that would deny Fourteenth Amendment rights.[55]]

* * *

This interpretation of the Amendment would leave to Congress the question of the extent to which it desired to exercise its power under the Amendment subject, of course, to the limitation previously expressed in this opinion that it can only exercise its power with respect to rights protected by the Fourteenth Amendment. * * * *[a]

Brewer v. Hoxie School Dist. No. 46, 238 F.2d 91 (8th Cir.1956), arose from the school district's attempts to comply with Brown v. Board of Education. Without waiting for a complaint to be filed against them or for a court judgment against Arkansas' segregation law, school board officials moved voluntarily to open desegregated schools in the summer of 1955. When private individuals and groups allegedly conspired to disrupt the desegregated schools, the school district filed this suit to enjoin their activities. They predicated their case for federal injunctive relief primarily on the Constitution itself, and the appellate court agreed (id. at 99–100):

> "[Brown v. Board of Education held that segregation of public schools violates the Equal Protection Clause, and the plaintiff school board members are therefore under a constitutional duty to segregate their schools.] It follows as a necessary corollary that they have a federal right to be free from direct and deliberate interference with the performance of the constitutionally imposed duty. The right arises

---

55. See generally, *Federal Civil Action Against Private Individuals for Crimes Involving Civil Rights*, 74 YALE L. J. 1462, 1469, 1470 (1965); Frank and Munro, [*The Original Understanding of "Equal Protection of the Laws,"* 50 COLUM. L. REV. 131,] at 165 [(1950)]; * * * and J. ten Broek, [THE ANTI-SLAVERY ORIGINS OF THE FOURTEENTH AMENDMENT] 217 [(1951)].

a. [Judge Mehaffy concurred on the ground that the racial basis for ACTION's conduct brought the case within the Thirteenth Amendment, as in Griffin itself, making it unnecessary to reach the question of Congress' power to reach private actors under the Fourteenth Amendment.—Ed.]

by necessary implication from the imposition of the duty as clearly as though it had been specifically stated in the Constitution. In many cases the implied rights which have been upheld by the courts have been of far less importance than the right against being interfered with in obeying the Constitution which is here involved. [The Court here cited *Logan*, *Quarles*, and similar cases cited in the introduction to this Chapter.]

"The existence of a Constitutional duty presupposes a correlative Constitutional right in the person for whom the duty is to be exercised. Thus in Logan v. United States, the Supreme Court upheld what is now Title 18, United States Code, Section 241, as the basis for conviction of three men charged with mob violence against prisoners in the custody of a United States Marshal. The Court held that the prisoners, who were awaiting trial for an offense against the United States, had a federal right to be protected in their persons while in federal custody. The Court said that the existence of the duty on the part of the government to protect its prisoners 'implies a corresponding right of the prisoners to be so protected.'

"It is no less true, of course, that the existence of a Constitutional duty also presupposes a correlative right in the person upon whom the duty is imposed to be free from direct interference with its performance. * * *"

The *Brewer* Court found it unnecessary to deal seriously with § 1985(3), and noted only cryptically that the district court "was not in error" in relying on the statute as "additional support" for its decision.

In **Westberry v. Gilman Paper Co.**, 507 F.2d 206 (5th Cir.1975) (2–1 vote), Westberry filed suit under § 1985(3) alleging that the company and its officials conspired to kill him because of his activism on environmental issues, denying his Fourteenth Amendment right that his life and liberty would not be taken without due process of law. Judge Goldberg's opinion for a dividend panel reversed a district court dismissal of the complaint. After finding that § 1985(3) reached all private conspiracies, Judge Goldberg then acknowledged that, in obedience to *Griffin*, it would be necessary to find a source of constitutional power to reach the conspiracy charged in this case. He found it in the Fourteenth Amendment (id. at 211, 213–14):

"There are three reasons for believing that private discriminatory acts come within the purview of section 5 of the Fourteenth Amendment should Congress believe that a preclusion of such acts is helpful in insuring the effectuation of section 1. First, we find such an indication in the legislative history behind the Act. Second, we find such a conclusion expressed by a majority of the members of the Supreme Court sitting in United States v. Guest. Third, decisions in previous cases, allowing a cause of action, are difficult to distinguish from the case before us. [Lengthy discussion of the first two points is omitted.]

"Third, as Professor Cox has noted,[9] it is difficult to find a distinction between the power of Congress to regulate private interference with constitutionally protected rights in other instances and the Congressional power to prevent the sort of interference plaintiff alleges here. [One such case is Brewer v. Hoxie School Dist., which upheld judicial power to deal with individual activities aimed at preventing the state from performing its Fourteenth Amendment duties.]

"The *Brewer* [case differs] from the instant case in only one respect—the immediacy of the relationship between the state and the injured person. In criticizing a distinction based on this ground, Prof. Cox notes: 'In this view, the lynching of a Negro in the custody of the state might be made a federal offense, because of the relationship between the police officials and the prisoner, but the United States could not punish a homicide on Boston Common even though it resulted from racial prejudice, because there would be no relationship between the victim and the state.' 80 Harv. L. Rev at 116. A constitutional distinction cannot reasonably rest on the mere presence or absence of a non-injuring state representative if we are to retain the amendment's focus on protection of the victim. Once it is recognized that private actors may be curtailed to insure equal protection of the laws, Congress has the responsibility to determine at what point along the continuum of private activities it wishes to provide a cause of action...."

A Preliminary Essay With Chart: Against Whom Are Rights Assertable?

1. Rights—Against Whom?

The triumph of rational legal positivism in the first half of this century led us to reject the notion that either law or rights exist as a "brooding omnipresence"[1] in the sky, a "transcendental body"[2] of mystical privileges and capacities. Rather, prevailing legal philosophy posits, "law in the sense in which courts speak of it does not exist without some definite authority behind it,"[3] that is, government. Rights—such as freedom of speech or procedural due process or the right to be free from physical harm—are defined and

9. Cox, *Foreword: Constitutional Adjudication and the Promotion of Human Rights*, 80 Harv. L. Rev. 91, 108–121 (1966).

1. Guaranty Trust Co. v. York, 326 U.S. 99, 102, 65 S.Ct. 1464, 89 L.Ed. 2079 (1945).

2. Black & White Taxicab & Transfer Co. v. Brown & Yellow Taxicab & Transfer Co., 276 U.S. 518, 533, 48 S.Ct. 404, 408–409, 72 L.Ed. 681 (1928) (Holmes, J., dissenting).

3. Id.

maintained by government, and they are nothing less, or more, than the government's assurance of protection in one's decisions or activities. That assurance may be stated in statutes, common law or the governmental constitution.

Just as it no longer makes sense to us to think of rights as mere disembodied ideas, it is also inadequate to define rights only in terms of the holder. Instead a right defines and creates a relationship: not a right to use property, not even Person X's right to use property, but Person X's right to use property to the exclusion of Person Y. Since some rights run against substantially all other persons, they may delude us to believe that rights do not define a relation but inhere only in the holder, e.g., the right to be free from negligent acts or to be free from physical invasion of our bodies. But these rights themselves do not run against all persons,[4] and a moment's reflection will quickly bring to mind a wide range of rights which the holder may assert only against a narrow class: e.g., the right to be free from defective products[5] or the right of a traveler to demand food and lodging.[6]

The foregoing discussion is critical to an understanding of the nature of federal constitutional rights because it suggests that the rights created in that document may be more precisely circumscribed than is generally assumed. The Nineteenth Amendment, for example, provides that the right to vote regardless of sex may not be abridged "by the United States or by any State," thus establishing a right to vote in federal and state elections, a right assertable against government. The amendment says nothing to the Boy Scouts, Campfire Girls, or any other non-governmental entity which might discriminate in its election practices. The right created, the relation superintended, is that between an individual and government, not between two individuals, and the right defined is only that of the individual to be free from governmental restraint on the named topic.

Although most federal constitutional rights speak to the individual-government relation, a few speak as well to relations between two individuals. The Thirteenth Amendment, for example, does not simply protect an individual from governmentally imposed slavery, but states that no slavery "shall exist," suggesting that the framers intended to reach even the relation between two individuals, one of whom would enslave the other.

Two final observations are necessary. First, although the Constitution itself speaks to few private relations, it often authorizes Congress to pass legislation, as to a topic within its constitutional power, which would define rights among individuals. The commerce clause, for example, does not speak directly to private persons, but it empowers Congress to pass legislation with such an aim; this legislation thereafter speaks directly to private persons,

---

4. The government, for example, is not always forbidden to invade citizens' bodies. See Jacobson v. Massachusetts, 197 U.S. 11, 25 S.Ct. 358, 49 L.Ed. 643 (1905) (compulsory vaccination).

5. In general, only the manufacturer or seller is held strictly liable for defective products; no liability is assessed other sellers, such as private sale by one consumer to another. See Prosser, TORTS 676–82 (5th ed., Supp. 1988).

6. States recognizing such a right generally impose the obligation only upon innkeepers or similarly limited enterprises, and not upon all businesses open to the public. See Garifine v. Monmouth Park Jockey Club, 29 N.J. 47, 148 A.2d 1 (1959).

creating in one individual a right to be free from another individual's actions. Thus, although *federal constitutional* rights often run only against government, federal statutory rights often reach also individual violators, provided Congress has legislative authority to reach such acts. Second, the limited nature of federal constitutional rights should not induce one to believe that all rights are thereby limited, for states as the general repositories of governmental power remain competent to define rights among individuals, and indeed most of our daily-used rights spring from this source (e.g., freedom from negligence, defective products, physical abuse).

2.   The Chart of Rights—The Potential and Limits of Experimentation

With these fundamental principles in mind, consider the following Chart of Rights. Categories I and II are self-explanatory. Category III is designed to help you think more discriminatingly about the federal constitutional rights which should be assertable by one individual against another individual under § 1985(3).

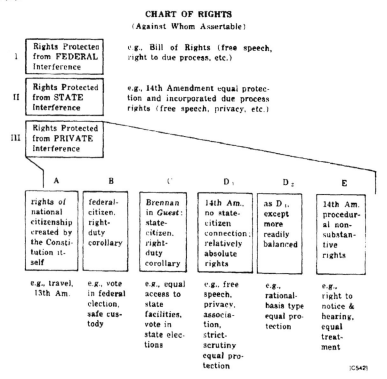

CHART OF RIGHTS
(Against Whom Assertable)

I	Rights Protected from FEDERAL Interference	e.g., Bill of Rights (free speech, right to due process, etc.)
II	Rights Protected from STATE Interference	e.g., 14th Amendment equal protection and incorporated due process rights (free speech, privacy, etc.)
III	Rights Protected from PRIVATE Interference	

A	B	C	D₁	D₂	E
rights of national citizenship created by the Constitution itself	federal-citizen, right-duty corollary	Brennan in *Guest*: state-citizen, right-duty corollary	14th Am., no state-citizen connection; relatively absolute rights	as D₁, except more readily balanced	14th Am. procedural non-substantive rights
e.g., travel, 13th Am.	e.g., vote in federal election, safe custody	e.g., equal access to state facilities, vote in state elections	e.g., free speech, privacy, association, strict-scrutiny equal protection	e.g., rational-basis type equal protection	e.g., right to notice & hearing, equal treatment

Boxes A–E, subsets of Category III, represent the gradually more inclusive, and more difficult to sustain, situations in which § 1985(3) might be employed.

Box A. The class consists of those few rights which the constitutional text, or the Court's version of that text, makes assertable against individuals. That § 1985(3) covers individuals' deprivation of these rights was established in Griffin v. Breckenridge, which listed the right to interstate travel and freedom from racial discrimination as illustrations of rights in this class.

Box B. This class accounts for the older cases to which you have seen repeated allusions (e.g., *Logan* and *Waddell*), which were prosecutions under what is now 18 U.S.C.A. § 241. These cases characteristically involved an individual who had some special relation with a federal program or official (as diagramed below in the discussion of Box C). No specific statute in each case defined the federal right, and therefore, in order to sustain convictions under § 241's statutory focus on individual rights, the Court had to construct a theory which would show that the individual who participated in the federal relationship had "rights." The Court's formulation posited that federal officers had a constitutional duty to carry out their orders and that any individual benefitting from the federal officers' performance of this duty thus had a "corollary right" to have this federal duty carried out. This "corollary right," the cases hold, is one which is assertable against third party individuals who would interfere with the "federal duty"—"individual right" relation.

Box C. Boxes A and B say nothing as to Fourteenth Amendment rights, rights which it is suggested in Boxes C–E should not be treated in the lump. Box C describes the situation which Justice Brennan found covered by § 241 (and presumably therefore by § 1985(3) as well) in *Guest*: an individual desires to participate in a state program or enter a state-owned building and is prevented from doing so by a third-party individual.

In order to decide whether you agree with Brennan consider the elements from which his argument might be derived:

Box B cases   Brewer v. Hoxie School Dist.

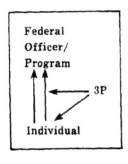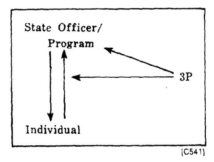

Brennan's opinion in *Guest* appears to build on two previously established and respected elements: the Box B cases and Brewer v. Hoxie School District, briefly excerpted supra. Both cases see "rights" as a relationship consisting of an individual right and a government duty. *Logan, Waddell,* etc. had established that federal power reaches private third parties (3P) who interfere with the right-duty relation ($\downarrow$ $\uparrow$) by harming the individual entitled to rights, at least when the relevant government is the federal government. *Brewer* might be seen as holding that federal power also extends to state-individual relations under the Fourteenth Amendment, at least where the third party (3P) individuals interfere with the duty of the state in the right-duty relation ($\downarrow$ $\uparrow$). Brennan may be seen as simply blending these elements and applying them to the new circumstance in Box C: (i) *Brewer*'s description of the Fourteenth Amendment as creating a right-duty relation between the individual and the state is married to (ii) the idea from the Box B cases that a third-party's interference with the private person also interferes with such a right-duty relationship.

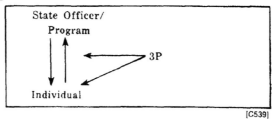

[C539]

Box D₁. This class consists of substantive due process (e.g., free speech) and strict-scrutiny equal protection rights under the Fourteenth Amendment where there is no individual-state relation as in Box C. Action v. Gannon is a good example, and diagraming it shows the difference between this situation and those in Box C:

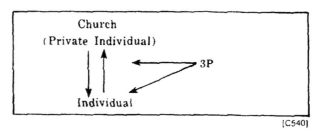

[C540]

So diagramed *Action* becomes a case in which a crucial Fourteenth Amendment element, state action, which existed in *Guest* at least in the sense that the state's Fourteenth Amendment duty was frustrated, is lacking. Of course, one could make the argument that the state has a duty to oversee and effectuate every Fourteenth Amendment right, and thus should be considered a partner in every exercise of free speech or equal access. That is Professor Cox's argument as described in the *Westberry* case (referring to a racial attack on Boston Common or a taking of property).

Box D₂. This describes the same situation as D₁ except the rights are those of ordinary due process and equal protection where the "rational basis" level of scrutiny would be applied. Note that even in Box D₁ the application of the usual standards of judicial review seems strained: how can a court ask if one private individual has a "compelling state interest" for discriminating against another individual? Cf. Roe v. Wade, 410 U.S. 113, 93 S.Ct. 705, 35 L.Ed.2d 147 (1973). When the level of scrutiny moves down to rational basis review, is the entire inquiry not skewed further? Can the open-ended and flexible standards developed for reviewing *governmental* actions toward individuals produce desirable results when the alleged violator is another individual?

Box E. This class consists of those further Fourteenth Amendment rights, also outside the duty-right relation, which are primarily procedural in nature, e.g., the procedural due process right to notice and a hearing. Cf. Westberry v. Gilman Paper Co., briefly excerpted earlier in this sub-chapter. These rights developed vis-a-vis government to provide procedural mechanisms to insure that bureaucracies would likely reach a correct decision in applying law (decisional criteria) to facts. Is this interest not largely non-existent in the context of individual decisionmaking? Or, put otherwise, would not most of us find it onerous in the extreme to exchange intuition and whimsy for rational decisionmaking in our daily affairs? Those pink pumps may not look good on you, but do you not have the liberty to purchase them foolishly, without notifying others and hearing their views?

NOTE ON THE EXPERIMENT: NATURE OF RIGHTS AND THE SCOPE OF § 1985(3)

1. Can all Fourteenth Amendment rights be diagramed as in Box C? Professor Archibald Cox in *Foreword: Constitutional Adjudication and the Promotion of Human Rights*, 80 HARV. L. REV 91 (1966) concluded yes. The state's relation with the plaintiff individual in *Guest* was quite immediate as he intended to enter a public building, but Professor Cox argued that the relation regarding other Fourteenth Amendment rights is essentially the same, though the distance between government and the individual is greater. Walking across a public park creates such a relation, said Cox; similarly, when a thief steals a horse, he takes property without just compensation in violation of the individual owner's Fourteenth–Amendment–based expectation that a state would be duty-bound to protect his property. Id. at 116–17. Do you agree?

(a) Professor Cox's construction, as noted in *Westberry*, reaches all Fourteenth–Amendment–based rights and has the effect of imposing a general duty on state officers to protect all citizens. This far-reaching theory appears to have been decisively rejected by the Supreme Court in DeShaney v. Winnebago County Dept. of Social Services, Chapter 1B.5 supra. See also Flagg Bros., Inc. v. Brooks, Chapter 1C supra. Is *Brewer* still good law after *DeShaney* because there the state government wanted to fulfill its duties and third parties were preventing it from doing so? Or is even *Brewer* itself no longer a plausible decision? Can Brennan's position in *Guest* be saved?

(b) If you concede that *DeShaney* must be followed (no affirmative duty on states to protect private persons under the Fourteenth Amendment), and yet you believe that Brennan's *Guest* view is also correct, can you rationalize the two views? Is the difference between the situations, as Cox suggests, merely one of degree—the varying closeness of the state-individual relation? As the relation between the individual and state grows closer and the facts more concrete, do our suspicions not proportionately grow because we think that the state could have prevented the private acts, but refused to do so? That the state shared the third parties' goals? Alternatively, could *Guest* be described as involving overt and actual individual-state relations—attendance at a courthouse—whereas the relation in the horse thief situation is only theoretical and rests upon the unilateral expectation of the individual alone?

2.   Assume that Cox is not correct and that one need not accept Congressional power to enforce all constitutional rights equally. Line-drawing would then be possible. As you move through the subsets of Box III, where would you draw the line to define the limit of Congressional power under the Fourteenth Amendment?

(a) Notice the same phenomenon here that we discussed regarding state action: the more one extends the safeguards of the Fourteenth Amendment to private individuals, the more restraint one places on individual liberty or freedom to make private choices. Recall how the protection of the parishioners' religious rights in *ACTION* seemed to threaten the defendants' free speech rights. Does approval through Box C strike the proper balance between the interest in extending safeguards and the interest in protecting free choice? Approval through Box D? Box E?

(b) Professor Cox ameliorates the effect of his argument in paragraph 1 by noting that though Congress would possess constitutional power to reach all private interference with Fourteenth Amendment rights, it would not exercise such power. Does Professor Cox effectively make these issues nonconstitutional, leaving them to Congress' political judgment, as noted in the *Westberry* case? Is that a preferable solution, or should the judiciary define more precise limits on congressional power?

3.   The need to balance plaintiff's and defendant's rights was highlighted in a part of the *ACTION* case not reproduced here, a part in which the appellate court narrowed the scope of the injunction so as to protect the parishioners' church observances without denying the protestors' speech rights. A similar issue arose in the 1990's when the Supreme Court considered cases involving injunctions based on state law against demonstrators at abortion clinics. In **Schenck v. Pro–Choice Network of Western NY**, 519 U.S. 357, 117 S.Ct. 855, 137 L.Ed.2d 1 (1997), Justice Rehnquist wrote for a unanimous Court that review stronger than mere "time-place-and-manner" analysis was necessary to protect demonstrators' residual free-speech rights, even assuming that their violent speech and protest were not constitutionally protected. The Court later divided over the precise application of these limits to restraints in the case, with some intriguing role reversals (as the usual liberals voted to uphold greater restrictions than the usual conservatives desired). Deciding that the state-law injunctions must be "content-neutral" and burden "no more speech than necessary to serve a significant governmental interest," the Court upheld a ban on demonstrating within 15 feet of the clinic entrance, but struck down a floating buffer zone that barred any demonstrator from approaching any patient. Even after so restricting the injunction, the Court stressed that the defendants' conduct here was "extraordinary" in duration and contemptuousness of pre-injunction law-enforcement efforts.[1]

---

1.   The *Schenck* case was one in a series of attempts by abortion-rights proponents to limit picketing at abortion clinics, with mixed results. The Supreme Court upheld a state criminal provision in Hill v. Colorado, 530 U.S. 703, 120 S.Ct. 2480, 147 L.Ed.2d 597 (2000) (law limiting approaching within eight feet of a person entering a health-care facility without person's consent). The Court, on the other hand, disapproved the use of federal RICO statutes to stop the protests. Scheidler v. National Organization for Women, Inc., 547 U.S. 9, 126 S.Ct. 1264, 164 L.Ed.2d 10 (2006) (unanimously holding that violence alone does not violate underlying federal laws).

(a) Does the *Schenck* case cause you second thoughts about extending § 1985(3) to cover private actors? Yes, because it would create more such confrontations between equally-important constitutional rights? No, because the Court can, as in *Schenck*, adequately adjust these competing rights?

(b) In *Schenck*, the injunctions, as reviewed by the Supreme Court, were grounded in state law. Would the plaintiffs have had a claim under § 1985(3)?

4. The Preliminary Essay with Chart asks you to consider the current controversy in light of modern sensibilities about the positive nature of rights. But perhaps this context is misleading and unfaithful to Congress' Nineteenth Century sensibilities.

(a) The modern construct is predicated upon the triumph of rational positivism, a revolution which had not occurred at the time of the Fourteenth Amendment's ratification, see Swift v. Tyson, 41 U.S. (16 Pet.) 1, 10 L.Ed. 865 (1842). If the framers thought that they were creating idealistic general rights with the Fourteenth Amendment, would that not induce you to believe that Congress under § 5 could enforce the right generally as to any infringement? Is the wording of the Fourteenth Amendment the stumbling block? Cf. Amend. XIII.

(b) Even assuming that the overall construct must be accepted, who is to say that Fourteenth Amendment rights do not fall under Box IIIA? Though the second sentence of Amendment XIV, clause 1, contains a reference to state action, the first sentence does not. Could the conferral of citizenship not be said to give to Congress power to define the rights of citizens, including rights assertable against other private persons? See Civil Rights Cases, 109 U.S. 3, 46–47, 3 S.Ct. 18, 46, 47, 27 L.Ed. 835 (1883) (Harlan, J., dissenting). How could such rights be identified? Cf. Karst, *Foreword: Equal Citizenship Under the Fourteenth Amendment*, 91 HARV. L. REV 1 (1977).

5. Note the historical context in which post-*Griffin* experimentation occurred in the 1960's and early 1970's. The predominant concern of all the scholars cited in *ACTION* and *Westberry* was racial discrimination, and leading cases usually involved racial discrimination, as in *ACTION*. (The same was true of the *Brewer* case in the 1950s.) This historical concern can now be resolved using the Thirteenth Amendment's dual coverage of (i) racial animus and (ii) private persons. In terms of the Chart of Rights, all racial cases easily fall within Box IIIA, where application of § 1985(3) creates no constitutional problems after the Court's decisions in *Griffin* and Jones v. Alfred H. Mayer Co., Chapter 2 supra. If one's civil rights agenda focuses primarily on racial discrimination, therefore, this entire issue of protecting Fourteenth Amendment rights from private interference evaporates. So who is pushing the argument? How strong is their claim to civil rights protection?

2. RACIAL—"AND PERHAPS OTHERWISE CLASS-BASED INVIDIOUSLY DISCRIMINATORY ANIMUS"

NOVOTNY v. GREAT AMERICAN FEDERAL SAVINGS AND LOAN ASS'N

United States Court of Appeals, Third Circuit, 1978, en banc.
584 F.2d 1235, rev'd on other grounds, 442 U.S.
366, 99 S.Ct. 2345, 60 L.Ed.2d 957 (1979).

ADAMS, CIRCUIT JUDGE.

[Novotny worked for the Great American Savings and Loan for several years, eventually joining the board of directors of the company. In that capacity, he allegedly discovered that other board members were engaging in a conspiracy to deny female employees equal rights at the company. He championed the cause of one woman in particular, and the debate became so heated that the board eventually fired Novotny. He then sued them under § 1985(3) and Title VII, see Chapter VII infra, but the district court dismissed both claims. We think that the case should be heard further based in the Supreme Court's decision in Griffin v. Breckenridge, which permitted claims based on "racial, or otherwise class based, invidiously discriminatory animus." The animus requirement has worked well as a "threshold requirement" for screening § 1985(3) cases at an early stage.[19]]

We need not determine here what classes other than those distinguished by race or gender may be within the ambit of § 1985(3). The Court in Frontiero v. Richardson[30] remarked: "Congress itself has concluded that classifications based upon sex are inherently invidious." And in discussing discrimination, the Court pointed out that sex, like race and national origin, is an immutable characteristic determined by the accident of birth and that the sex characteristic frequently bears no relation to ability to perform or contribute to society. Thus, to deprive members of a class founded on gender of equal protection or equal privileges and immunities without any justification is to act in an irrational and odious

---

19. E.g. Dacey v. Dorsey, 568 F.2d 275 (2d Cir.1978) (individual who sued bar association challenged failure of members of bar association to recuse themselves from his case; no class based discrimination alleged); Phillips v. Intl. Assn. of Bridge Workers, 556 F.2d 939 (9th Cir.1977) (dissident union members not a class); Morgan v. Odem, 552 F.2d 147 (5th Cir.1977) ("newcomers" not a class); McLellan v. Mississippi Power & Light Co., 545 F.2d 919 (5th Cir.1977) (en banc) (bankrupts not a class); Harrison v. Brooks, 519 F.2d 1358 (1st Cir.1975) (homeowners affected by zoning changes not a class); Arnold v. Tiffany, 487 F.2d 216 (9th Cir.1973) cert. denied 415 U.S. 984, 94 S.Ct. 1578, 39 L.Ed.2d 881 (1974) (newspaper dealers desiring to form a trade association not a class); Hughes v. Ranger Fuel Corp., 467 F.2d 6, 8–10 (4th Cir.1972) (company's action against environmentalists held a response to individual's actions, not class-based); Jacobson v. Industrial Foundation, 456 F.2d 258 (5th Cir.1972) (applicants for workman's compensation are not a class); Cf. Downs v. Sawtelle, 574 F.2d 1 (1st Cir.1978) slip op. (deaf may not be a class); See generally Note, *The Scope of Section 1985(3) Since Griffin v. Breckenridge*, 45 GEO.WASH.L.REV. 239, 252–58 (1976) (discussing cases); Note, *Private Conspiracies to Violate Civil Rights*, 90 HARV. L. REV 1721, 1727–29 (1977) (discussing cases).

30. 411 U.S. 677, 687, 93 S.Ct. 1764, 1771, 36 L.Ed.2d 583 (1973) (plurality opinion).

manner—hence, with an invidiously discriminatory animus [as described in *Griffin*].

The principle that individuals should not be discriminated against on the basis of traits for which they bear no responsibility makes discrimination against individuals on the basis of immutable characteristics repugnant to our system. The fact that a person bears no responsibility for gender, combined with the pervasive discrimination practiced against women, and the emerging rejection of sexual stereotyping as incompatible with our ideals of equality convince us that whatever the outer boundaries of the concept, an animus directed against women includes the elements of a "class-based invidiously discriminatory" motivation.

We therefore join the two circuits that have included sex discrimination within the categories of animus condemned by § 1985(3).[36]

[Reversed and remanded.]

NOTE ON CLASSES COVERED BY § 1985(3)

1. As the Supreme Court foresaw in *Griffin*, § 1985(3)'s reach into the realm of private actions runs the risk of having federal law displace ordinary state tort law. The Court defended the expansion into this realm by noting that § 1985(3) would only reach "unequal" deprivations of constitutional rights, interpreted by the Court as deprivations based upon "racial, or perhaps otherwise class-based, invidiously discriminatory animus." *Novotny* is a typical case from the ensuing "years of experimentation" when lower courts were trying to decide the limits of § 1985(3).

(a) Do you agree with *Novotny*'s conclusion that sex discrimination should be considered such an animus? Does the court suggest that the classes protected are the "suspect classes" of equal protection scrutiny? After Craig v. Boren, 429 U.S. 190, 97 S.Ct. 451, 50 L.Ed.2d 397 (1976) (mid-level scrutiny), and United States v. Virginia, 518 U.S. 515, 116 S.Ct. 2264, 135 L.Ed.2d 735 (1996) (demanding mid-level scrutiny), is sex such a classification? Note that the Third Circuit's reference to the "Court" in the *Frontiero* case is not entirely correct, as it admitted in footnote 30, because Justice Brennan's opinion represented only four votes on the Court.

(b) Early cases following *Griffin* toyed with the notion that almost any class could claim protection under § 1985(3); one court even seriously considered whether "middle class white families" constituted such a group. See Azar v. Conley, 456 F.2d 1382, 1386 & n. 5 (6th Cir.1972). Later cases, as *Novotny* shows in its footnote 19, have taken a much narrower view. What accounts for the change? Is it because once one passes "suspect classes" there is no clear guidepost as to what groups to include? Because open-ended

36. Conroy v. Conroy, 575 F.2d 175, at 177 (8th Cir.1978) (explicitly recognized a sex discrimination claim under § 1985(3)). And while in Cohen v. Illinois Inst. of Technology, 524 F.2d 818 (7th Cir.1975), cert. denied 425 U.S. 943 (1976) (Stevens, J.), the Seventh Circuit rejected a sex discrimination claim grounded directly on a violation of the Fourteenth Amendment because of a lack of what it regarded as the requisite state action, dicta in subsequent cases consistently list "sex" as a "class" cognizable under § 1985(3). Meiners v. Moriarity, 563 F.2d 343, 348 (7th Cir.1977).

expansion negates the very goal *Griffin* had in mind in constructing the animus requirement?

2. Why not simply restrict the animus requirement solely to race? This not only concentrates the statute on the historical problem of racial bias, it also conveniently eliminates any constitutional problems, since Congress has power under the Thirteenth Amendment to reach private actors. See Jones v. Alfred H. Mayer Co., Chapter 3A supra.

(a) It seems most plausible, in retrospect, that the *Griffin* Court used the phrase "race or perhaps otherwise class-based invidiously discriminatory animus" to permit future expansion of § 1985(3), if it should be necessary or appropriate. Now that you have seen the line-drawing problems involved in expansion, what is your judgment? Is coverage of sex discrimination, in light of the fact that women could not even vote at the time of adoption of § 1985(3), just one stretch too far?

(b) If you find it appropriate to expand § 1985(3) to cover sex discrimination, is it because there is no other federal statute that generally protects women against violence? Cf. Scheidler v. National Organization for Women, Inc., 547 U.S. 9, 126 S.Ct. 1264, 164 L.Ed.2d 10 (2006) (unanimously holding that violence alone does not violate RICO Act). Is it the Court's role to decide whether expansion of a statute is necessary? (Reserve this question for more consideration later.)

(c) Could the constitutional aspects of this knotty problem be solved by simply holding that sex discrimination is included within Congress' Thirteenth Amendment power? But that would require two stretches—one of the statutory language and another of the Thirteenth Amendment, as interpreted in Jones v. Alfred H. Mayer Co. Are you prepared to do that?

3. Revisit the issue of classes covered by § 1985(3) after reading section C of this Chapter infra. In several Supreme Court cases the Supreme Court never specifically rejected the coverage for women, Bray v. Alexandria Women's Health Clinic, section C infra, but it strongly suggested that the limit was somewhere near the line of race, perhaps including those who associate with persons of another race. See United Brotherhood of Carpenters and Joiners v. Scott, section C infra. The historical argument for this position seems relatively strong. Is there a non-historical argument for going further than history would go? Is it stronger than the historical argument?

C. THE END OF EXPERIMENTATION?

UNITED BROTHERHOOD OF CARPENTERS AND JOINERS v. SCOTT

Supreme Court of the United States, 1983.
463 U.S. 825, 103 S.Ct. 3352, 77 L.Ed.2d 1049.

JUSTICE WHITE, delivered the opinion of the Court.

This case concerns the scope of the cause of action made available by 42 U.S.C. § 1985(3) to those injured by conspiracies formed "for the purpose of depriving, either directly or indirectly, any person or class of persons of the equal protection of the laws, or of equal privileges and immunities under the laws."

I

A.A. Cross Construction Co., Inc. (Cross), contracted with the Department of the Army to construct the Alligator Bayou Pumping Station and Gravity Drainage Structure on the Taylor Bayou Hurricane Levee near Port Arthur, Tex. In accordance with its usual practice, Cross hired workers for the project without regard to union membership. [Some local residents and unions objected to this policy, and on January 17, 1975, a large group gathered to hold a pre-planned protest at the construction site. Several of the protestors entered the site and beat Cross employees and threatened them with continued violence unless non-union workers departed or joined the union. These acts delayed construction and caused Cross to default on its contract with the Army. Cross and two employees thereafter sued the unions and some union members under § 1985(3), winning judgments that were affirmed on appeal. Both courts found the class animus requirement met by proof of bias against non-union workers; both also rejected a requirement of state action for a claim based on the First Amendment.]

II

We do not disagree with the District Court and the Court of Appeals that there was a conspiracy, an act done in furtherance thereof, and a resultant injury to persons and property. Contrary to the Court of Appeals, however, we conclude that an alleged conspiracy to infringe First Amendment rights is not a violation of § 1985(3) unless it is proved that the State is involved in the conspiracy or that the aim of the conspiracy is to influence the activity of the State. We also disagree with the Court of Appeals' view that there was present here the kind of animus that § 1985(3) requires.

A

The Equal Protection Clause of the Fourteenth Amendment prohibits any State from denying any person the equal protection of the laws. The First Amendment, which by virtue of the Due Process Clause of the Fourteenth Amendment now applies to state governments and their officials, prohibits either Congress or a State from making any "law ... abridging the freedom of speech, ... or the right of the people peaceably to assemble." Had § 1985(3) in so many words prohibited conspiracies to deprive any person of the equal protection of the laws guaranteed by the Fourteenth Amendment or of freedom of speech guaranteed by the First Amendment, it would be untenable to contend that either of those provisions could be violated by a conspiracy that did not somehow involve

SEMI-CONSTITUTIONAL STATUTES
PT. 2

or affect a State. [State action is required to prove a violation of rights created by the Fourteenth Amendment.]

* * *

Griffin v. Breckenridge is not to the contrary. There we held that § 1985(3) reaches purely private conspiracies and, as so interpreted, was not invalid on its face or as there applied. [But that case involved a conspiracy that] was actionable because it was aimed at depriving the plaintiffs of rights protected by the Thirteenth Amendment and the right to travel guaranteed by the Federal Constitution. Section 1985(3) constitutionally can and does protect those rights from interference by purely private conspiracies.

Griffin did not hold that even when the alleged conspiracy is aimed at a right that is by definition a right only against state interference the plaintiff in a § 1985(3) suit nevertheless need not prove that the conspiracy contemplated state involvement of some sort. The complaint in *Griffin* alleged, among other things, a deprivation of First Amendment rights, but we did not sustain the action on the basis of that allegation and paid it scant attention. Instead, we upheld the application of § 1985(3) to private conspiracies aimed at interfering with rights constitutionally protected against private, as well as official, encroachment.

Neither is respondents' position helped by the assertion that even if the Fourteenth Amendment does not provide authority to proscribe exclusively private conspiracies, precisely the same conduct could be proscribed by the Commerce Clause. That is no doubt the case; but § 1985(3) is not such a provision, since it "provides no substantive rights itself" to the class conspired against. Great American Federal Savings & Loan Assn. v. Novotny, 442 U.S. 366, 372, 99 S.Ct. 2345, 2349, 60 L.Ed.2d 957 (1979). The rights, privileges, and immunities that § 1985(3) vindicates must be found elsewhere, and here the right claimed to have been infringed has its source in the First Amendment. Because that Amendment restrains only official conduct, to make out their § 1985(3) case, it was necessary for respondents to prove that the State was somehow involved in or affected by the conspiracy.

* * *

B

[As we specifically noted in *Griffin*, Congress added the animus requirement to § 1985(3) in order to prevent the statute from becoming a general federal remedy for "all tortious, conspiratorial interferences with the rights of others," based primarily on Congress' assumption that it lacked power to punish such simple assaults and batteries.]

* * *

Because the facts in *Griffin* revealed an animus against Negroes and those who supported them, a class-based, invidious discrimination which was the central concern of Congress in enacting § 1985(3), the Court expressly declined to decide "whether a conspiracy motivated by invidiously discriminatory intent other than racial bias would be actionable under the portion of § 1985(3) before us." 403 U.S. at 102, n. 9, 91 S.Ct., at 1798, n. 9. Both courts below answered that question; both held that the section not only reaches conspiracies other than those motivated by racial bias but also forbids conspiracies against workers who refuse to join a union. We disagree with the latter conclusion and do not affirm the former.

C

The Court of Appeals arrived at its result by first describing the Reconstruction-era Ku Klux Klan as a political organization that sought to deprive a large segment of the Southern population of political power and participation in the governance of those States and of the Nation. The Court of Appeals then reasoned that because Republicans were among the objects of the Klan's conspiratorial activities, Republicans in particular and political groups in general were to be protected by § 1985(3). Finally, because it believed that an animus against an economic group such as those who preferred nonunion association is "closely akin" to the animus against political association, the Court of Appeals concluded that the animus against nonunion employees in the Port Arthur area was sufficiently similar to the animus against a political party to satisfy the requirements of § 1985(3).

We are unpersuaded. In the first place, it is a close question whether § 1985(3) was intended to reach any class-based animus other than animus against Negroes and those who championed their cause, most notably Republicans. The central theme of the bill's proponents was that the Klan and others were forcibly resisting efforts to emancipate Negroes and give them equal access to political power. The predominant purpose of § 1985(3) was to combat the prevalent animus against Negroes and their supporters. The latter included Republicans generally, as well as others, such as Northerners who came South with sympathetic views towards the Negro. Although we have examined with some care the legislative history that has been marshaled in support of the position that Congress meant to forbid wholly non-racial, but politically motivated conspiracies, we find difficult the question whether § 1985(3) provided a remedy for every concerted effort by one political group to nullify the influence of or do other injury to a competing group by use of otherwise unlawful means. To accede to that view would go far toward making the federal courts, by virtue of § 1985(3), the monitors of campaign tactics in both state and federal elections, a role that the courts should not be quick to assume. If respondents' submission were accepted, the proscription of § 1985(3) would arguably reach the claim that a political party has interfered with the freedom of speech of another political party by encouraging the heckling of its rival's speakers and the disruption of the rival's meetings.

We realize that there is some legislative history to support the view that § 1985(3) has a broader reach. Senator Edmunds' statement on the floor of the Senate is the clearest expression of this view. He said that if a conspiracy were formed against a man "because he was a Democrat, if you please, or because he was a Catholic, or because he was a Methodist, or because he was a Vermonter, ... then this section could reach it." Cong. Globe, 42d Cong., 1st Sess., 567 (1871). The provision that is now § 1985(3), however, originated in the House[, and the animus requirement was also added there. In such circumstances, the isolated statement by Senator Edmunds cannot be given great weight.]

D

Even if the section must be construed to reach conspiracies aimed at any class or organization on account of its political views or activities, or at any of the classes posited by Senator Edmunds, we find no convincing support in the legislative history for the proposition that the provision was intended to reach conspiracies motivated by bias towards others on account of their *economic* views, status, or activities. Such a construction would extend § 1985(3) into the economic life of the country in a way that we doubt that the 1871 Congress would have intended when it passed the provision in 1871. [There is simply no persuasive evidence that the social problems that Congress faced included animus against persons based on their economic views.] * * * The animus was against Negroes and their sympathizers, and perhaps against Republicans as a class, but not against economic groups as such.

* * *

We thus cannot construe § 1985(3) to reach conspiracies motivated by economic or commercial animus. Were it otherwise, for example, § 1985(3) could be brought to bear on any act of violence resulting from union efforts to organize an employer or from the employer's efforts to resist it, so long as the victim merely asserted and proved that the conduct involved a conspiracy motivated by an animus in favor of unionization, or against it, as the case may be. The National Labor Relations Act, 29 U.S.C. § 151 *et seq.* addresses in great detail the relationship between employer, employee, and union in a great variety of situations, and it would be an unsettling event to rule that strike and picket-line violence must now be considered in the light of the strictures of § 1985(3). Moreover, if anti-union, antinonunion, or antiemployer biases represent the kinds of animus that trigger § 1985(3), there would be little basis for concluding that the statute did not provide a cause of action in a variety of other situations where one economic group is pitted against another, each having the intent of injuring or destroying the economic health of the other. We think that such a construction of the statute, which is at best only arguable and surely not compelled by either its language or legislative history, should be eschewed and that group actions generally resting on economic motivations should be deemed beyond the reach of § 1985(3). Economic and commercial conflicts, we think, are best dealt with by statutes, federal or state, specifically addressed to such problems, as well as by the general law proscribing injuries to persons and property. If we have misconstrued the intent of the 1871 Congress, or, in any event, if Congress now prefers to take a different tack, the Court will, of course, enforce any statute within the power of Congress to enact.

Accordingly, the judgment of the Court of Appeals is

Reversed.

JUSTICE BLACKMUN, with whom JUSTICE BRENNAN, JUSTICE MARSHALL, and JUSTICE O'CONNOR join, dissenting.

[The Court mistakenly ties § 1985(3) to the Fourteenth Amendment. Unlike § 1983, however, § 1985(3) contains no reference to rights protected by the Constitution. Instead, the federal interest is signified solely by the animus requirement. If the animus requirement is met, conspiracies that cause harm are covered, regardless of whether undertaken by private persons or state actors. The question in this case, therefore, is whether plaintiffs have met the animus requirement.]

II

As *Griffin* recognized, the words "equal protection of the laws" and "equal privileges and immunities" limit the types of actionable private conspiracies to those involving class-based animus. As an initial matter, the intended victims must be victims not because of any personal malice the conspirators have toward them, but because of their membership in or affiliation with a particular class. Cong. Globe, 42d Cong., 1st Sess., 702 (Apr. 14, 1871) (remarks of Sen. Edmunds); see *id.* at 567 (Apr. 11, 1871) (remarks of Sen. Edmunds). Moreover, the class must exist independently of the defendants' actions; that is, it cannot be defined simply as the group of victims of the tortious action. See Askew v. Bloemker, 548 F.2d 673, 678 (C.A.7 1976); Lopez v. Arrowhead Ranches, 523 F.2d 924, 928 (C.A.9 1975).

A

Aside from this initial rule of exclusion, however, the types of classes covered by the statute are far from clear. [Most statements made during the congressional debates show a concern with the Klan as a political organization which identified its victims by their politics.]

In my view, Congress intended to provide a federal remedy for all *classes* that seek to exercise their legal rights in unprotected circumstances similar to those of the victims of Klan violence. Instead of contemplating a list of actionable class traits, though, Congress had in mind a functional definition of the scope of § 2. As Representative Garfield stated in the debates, the chief danger was "a systematic maladministration of [the laws], or a neglect or refusal to enforce their provisions." Id. at App. 153 (Apr. 4, 1871). Congress did not require that a § 2 plaintiff allege a neglect on the part of state officers to enforce the laws equally. Instead, it took the view that whenever a conspiracy involved invidious animus toward a class of persons, the possibility of ineffective state enforcement was sufficient to support federal intervention. Id. at 485 (Apr. 5, 1871) (remarks of Rep. Cook).

B

This view of the scope of § 2 is corroborated by congressional statements of concern for another group subject to Klan violence: economic migrants. While the Klan's victims usually were Republicans, Congress extended protection to this group because of its tenuous position in the South. Reconstruction, although mainly a political program, see J. Randall & D. Donald, The Civil War and Reconstruction 592–600 (2d ed. 1961), also was an attempt to reorganize the economic life of the region. W. Du Bois, Black Reconstruction in America 345–353 (1962).

* * *

* * * The critical consideration is the 42d Congress' perception that the atrocities perpetrated by the Klan were injuring persons who, largely because of their political affiliation, were unable to demand protection from local law enforcement officials. Congress intended to provide a remedy to any class of persons, whose beliefs or associations placed them in danger of not receiving equal protection of the laws from local authorities. While certain class traits, such as race, religion, sex, and national origin, *per se* meet this requirement, other traits also may implicate the functional concerns in particular situations.

III

In the circumstances of this case, respondents are protected by § 2 and fall within this definition. Port Arthur, Tex., was a self-professed union town. Respondents were threatened because of petitioners' view that nonunion workers were encroaching into an area that petitioners desired to keep union dominated. The identity or individuality of each of the victims was irrelevant to the conspiracy; the victims were attacked because of their pre-existing nonunion association. The conspiracy was similar to the Klan conspiracies Congress desired to punish in enacting § 2. In this union town, the effectiveness of local law enforcement protection for nonunion workers was open to question. Petitioners intended to hinder a particular group in the exercise of their legal rights because of their membership in a specific class.

* * *

NOTE ON § 1985(3) AND THE STATUTORY ENFORCEMENT OF CONSTITUTIONAL NORMS

1. Consider first the dispositive issue decided in the *Carpenters* case, the scope of the phrase "racial or perhaps otherwise class-based invidiously discriminatory animus." What is the precise holding of the Court in *Carpenters*? That only blacks are covered? That certain economically defined groups are not covered? That racial groups and their supporters are covered?

(a) If § 1985(3) is confined to cases involving racial animus, all constitutional shoals disappear, do they not, because the Thirteenth Amendment supports its application to private parties and the Fourteenth its application to state actors?

(b) If § 1985(3) also extends to supporters of racial minorities, would that construction also be sustainable under the Thirteenth Amendment as applied to private parties? Yes, at least insofar as the supporters were championing the interests of racial minorities? See Sullivan v. Little Hunting Park, Chapter 2B supra.

(c) Although the Court strongly suggests in *Carpenters* that it may confine § 1985(3) to cases of race-based animus, should race be broadly construed here, as under the 1866 Civil Rights Act to cover all groups considered separate races at the time of passage of the 1871 Act? If a group defiles a synagogue and attacks its members because they dislike Jews, or attack a mosque because they dislike Arab–Americans, would the victims have a claim under § 1985(3)? Cf. Shaare Tefila Congregation v. Cobb, 481 U.S. 615, 107 S.Ct. 2019, 95 L.Ed.2d 594 (1987); St. Francis College v. Al–Khazraji, 481 U.S. 604, 107 S.Ct. 2022, 95 L.Ed.2d 582 (1987). Re-read the Note on "Racial" Groups Covered by § 1981, Chapter 2C supra.

2. With respect to coverage of private persons, the *Carpenters* Court appears to construe § 1985(3) as a non-substantive statute that only enforces norms found elsewhere: when the norms or rights are found in the Fourteenth Amendment, the statute requires proof of state action because the Fourteenth Amendment itself requires state action.

(a) Does this aspect of the Court's holding mean that § 1985(3) has the same coverage as its criminal law counterpart, 18 U.S.C. § 241, was given by the majority in the *Guest* case? Why does the Court seem disposed to restrict the statute to enforcing facially evident constitutional rights? Because it has no guideposts for what more Congress might have wanted? Because the Court itself wants no more?

(b) Does the Court in fact restrict § 1985(3) to pure state action situations—or does it leave room to go as far as *Brewer* and the Box C cases discussed in the previous Note? Note the Court's language in *Carpenters*: when a Fourteenth Amendment right is at issue, there is no violation of § 1985(3) "unless it is proved that the State is involved in the conspiracy *or that the aim of the conspiracy is to influence the activity of the State.*" (Emphasis added.) The Court later restates the test: plaintiff must "prove that the State was somehow involved in or *affected by* the conspiracy." (Emphasis added.) Does this language leave open the possibility of covering some private actors?

3. The Court's theory is that § 1985(3) itself creates no rights; it merely enforces the Amendments as it finds them, and so claims based on the Fourteenth Amendment require proof of state action, while any claim based on the Thirteenth Amendment—any race-based claim—can be pursued against private persons.[1] The Court's theory works well to harmonize *Carpen-*

---

1. The case cited to support this theory arose in a somewhat different context. As with § 1983, § 1985(3) contains an "and laws" provision that permits plaintiffs to enforce not only

ters with the Court's previous decision in *Griffin*, which had permitted race-based claims under the Thirteenth Amendment to be brought against private persons. But hasn't the Court overlooked one small problem? Isn't there a second constitutional issue in all Thirteenth Amendment cases—the issue of whether Congress can legislate against not only slavery, but also its "badges and incidents"? If § 1985(3) creates no rights, and is limited to enforcing constitutional rights as found in the Amendments themselves, why aren't even race-based claims limited to "slavery or involuntary servitude," the only topics covered by the Thirteenth Amendment itself?

(a) As the Court held in **United States v. Kozminski**, 487 U.S. 931, 108 S.Ct. 2751, 101 L.Ed.2d 788 (1988), on its face the Thirteenth Amendment reaches only physical coercion tending to enslave persons—not all intimidation. *Carpenters'* "no additional rights" theory would then lead to restriction of § 1985(3) only to cases of physical violence producing enslaving conditions. That was not what *Griffin* foresaw, is it?

(b) In order to save both the Court's theory and the apparent facial policy of § 1985(3), it seems necessary to argue that § 1985(3) takes rights as it finds them only with respect to the question of state action. The statute itself goes beyond the face of the Thirteenth Amendment by covering physical violence based on race because it is reasonable to view such violence as a relic of slavery. But this makes § 1985(3) a hybrid, on state action taking constitutional rights as it finds them but on other issues enforcing rights as enhanced by the statute itself. What indication is there that Congress actually wanted this result?

4. Notice Justice Brennan's dissenting opinion in *Carpenters*. It appears to go far beyond the position attributed to him in the Preliminary Essay with Chart supra. Using a functional test, he would apply § 1985(3) to any private activity that interferes with Fourteenth Amendment rights in a circumstance where it appears that the state has defaulted on customary role of protecting citizens.

(a) Is Brennan's opinion consistent with the *DeShaney* case's rejection of affirmative constitutional duties? (Note that *Carpenters* was decided six years before *DeShaney*.)

(b) Is Brennan's approach workable? Note the last paragraph of his opinion. Can the Court be expected to look, case-by-case, at local circumstances to determine if police or local officials favored one side of a dispute over another? Isn't this approach the discredited approach to "under color" of law originally offered by Justice Harlan in Monroe v. Pape, Chapter 1A supra?

(c) Is coverage of economic conflict a good use for § 1985(3)? A primary vehicle of the traditional civil rights movement has been the economic

---

rights based in the Constitution, but also some rights based in other federal statutes. The Court's decisions in this area reflect the same concerns already discussed with respect to § 1983. See Chapter 1l supra. Thus in **Great American Federal Savings & Loan Ass'n v. Novotny**, 442 U.S. 366, 99 S.Ct. 2345, 60 L.Ed.2d 957 (1979), cited in *Carpenters*, the Court refused to allow a plaintiff to use § 1985(3) as a vehicle for enforcing employment-discrimination rights found in Title VII of the Civil Rights Act of 1964, finding that the newer statute supplied a comprehensive enforcement scheme that precluded the parallel use of § 1985(3) to enforce the same rights. Since § 1985(3) applies only to conspiracies, however, it is seldom used to enforce rights found in other federal statutes.

boycott, and on some occasions supporters have resorted to violence during such activities. See NAACP v. Claiborne Hardware Co., 458 U.S. 886, 102 S.Ct. 3409, 73 L.Ed.2d 1215 (1982) (group and its leader cannot be held liable for violence not induced by group). Also reconsider an issue posed in another guise in Chapter 2: If an African–American group sponsors a boycott of a white-or Asian-owned store, with violence or threats as a part of the boycott, has the storeowner a claim under § 1985(3)? Cf. Federal Trade Commission v. Superior Court Trial Lawyers Ass'n, 493 U.S. 411, 110 S.Ct. 768, 107 L.Ed.2d 851 (1990); International Longshoremen's Ass'n v. Allied International, 456 U.S. 212, 102 S.Ct. 1656, 72 L.Ed.2d 21 (1982) (no First Amendment protection for coercive or non-political boycotts). How would Justice Brennan handle these cases?

BRAY v. ALEXANDRIA WOMEN'S HEALTH CLINIC

United States Supreme Court, 1993.
506 U.S. 263, 113 S.Ct. 753, 122 L.Ed.2d 34.

JUSTICE SCALIA delivered the opinion of the Court.

[Abortion clinics and organizations with members seeking abortions sued Operation Rescue and others under § 1985(3), seeking an injunction against demonstrations conducted at abortion clinics. The trial court enjoined the demonstrations, and the appellate court affirmed. We reverse.]

I

Our precedents establish that in order to prove a private conspiracy in violation of the first clause of § 1985(3), a plaintiff must show, inter alia, (1) that "some racial, or perhaps otherwise class-based, invidiously discriminatory animus [lay] behind the conspirators' action," Griffin v. Breckenridge, and (2) that the conspiracy "aimed at interfering with rights" that are "protected against private, as well as official, encroachment," Carpenters v. Scott. We think neither showing has been made in the present case.

A

We have not yet had occasion to resolve the "perhaps" [in Griffin v. Breckenridge insofar as it suggested that animuses beyond race might be covered]; only in *Griffin* itself have we addressed and upheld a claim under § 1985(3), and that case involved race discrimination. Respondents assert that there qualifies alongside race discrimination, as an "otherwise class-based, invidiously discriminatory animus" covered by the 1871 law, opposition to abortion. Neither common sense nor our precedents support this.

To begin with, we reject the apparent conclusion of the District Court (which respondents make no effort to defend) that opposition to abortion constitutes discrimination against the "class" of "women seeking abortion." Whatever may be the precise meaning of a "class" for purposes of

Griffin's speculative extension of § 1985(3) beyond race, the term unquestionably connotes something more than a group of individuals who share a desire to engage in conduct that the § 1985(3) defendant disfavors. Otherwise, innumerable tort plaintiffs would be able to assert causes of action under § 1985(3) by simply defining the aggrieved class as those seeking to engage in the activity the defendant has interfered with. This definitional ploy would convert the statute into the "general federal tort law" it was the very purpose of the animus requirement to avoid. . . . "Women seeking abortion" is not a qualifying class.

Respondents' contention, however, is that the alleged class-based discrimination is directed not at "women seeking abortion" but at women in general. We find it unnecessary to decide whether that is a qualifying class under § 1985(3), since the claim that petitioners' opposition to abortion reflects an animus against women in general must be rejected. * * * The record in this case does not indicate that petitioners' demonstrations are motivated by a purpose (malevolent or benign) directed specifically at women as a class; to the contrary, the District Court found that petitioners define their "rescues" not with reference to women, but as physical intervention " 'between abortionists and the innocent victims,' " and that "all [petitioners] share a deep commitment to the goals of stopping the practice of abortion and reversing its legalization" * * * *

[Some activities may of course be so closely linked to one group that discrimination against the activity may raise a presumption of discrimination against the group.] A tax on wearing yarmulkes is a tax on Jews. But opposition to voluntary abortion cannot possibly be considered such an irrational surrogate for opposition to (or paternalism towards) women. Whatever one thinks of abortion, it cannot be denied that there are common and respectable reasons for opposing it, other than hatred of or condescension toward (or indeed any view at all concerning) women as a class—as is evident from the fact that men and women are on both sides of the issue, just as men and women are on both sides of petitioners' unlawful demonstrations.

Respondents' case comes down, then, to the proposition that intent is legally irrelevant; that since voluntary abortion is an activity engaged in only by women, to disfavor it is ipso facto to discriminate invidiously against women as a class. Our cases do not support that proposition * * * [I]n Personnel Administrator of Mass. v. Feeney, [we] sustain[ed] against an Equal Protection Clause challenge a Massachusetts law giving employment preference to military veterans, a class which in Massachusetts was over 98% male. " 'Discriminatory purpose,' " we said, "implies more than intent as volition or intent as awareness of consequences. It implies that the decisionmaker . . . selected or reaffirmed a particular course of action at least in part 'because of,' not merely 'in spite of,' its adverse effects upon an identifiable group." The same principle applies to the "class-based, invidiously discriminatory animus" requirement of § 1985(3) * * *[4]

* * *

---

4. We think this principle applicable to § 1985(3) not because we believe that Equal Protection Clause jurisprudence is automatically incorporated into § 1985(3), but rather because it is

B

Respondents' federal claim fails for a second, independent reason: [they can prove no violation] of a right guaranteed against private impairment. See *Carpenters*. * * *

Respondents, like the courts below, rely upon the right to interstate travel—which we have held to be, in at least some contexts, a right constitutionally protected against private interference. See *Griffin*, supra. But all that respondents can point to by way of connecting petitioners' actions with that particular right is the District Court's finding that "[s]ubstantial numbers of women seeking the services of [abortion] clinics in the Washington Metropolitan area travel interstate to reach the clinics." That is not enough. [See] United States v. Guest. [It is not enough that the right to interstate travel be affected by defendants' conduct; the intent of the conspiracy must be to hinder interstate travel.]

* * *

The other right alleged by respondents to have been intentionally infringed is the right to abortion * * * Whereas, unlike the right of interstate travel, the asserted right to abortion was assuredly "aimed at" by the petitioners, deprivation of that federal right (whatever its contours) cannot be the object of a purely private conspiracy. In *Carpenters*, we rejected a claim that an alleged private conspiracy to infringe First Amendment rights violated § 1985(3). The statute does not apply, we said, to private conspiracies that are "aimed at a right that is by definition a right only against state interference," but applies only to such conspiracies as are "aimed at interfering with rights ... protected against private, as well as official, encroachment." There are few such rights[, and the] right to abortion is not among them. It * * * has been described in our opinions as one element of a more general right of privacy, see Roe v. Wade, or of Fourteenth Amendment liberty, [and thus applies only to state action].[16]

* * *

inherent in the requirement of a class-based animus, i.e., an animus based on class. We do not dispute Justice Stevens' observation that Congress "may offer relief from discriminatory effects," without evidence of intent. The question is whether it has done so, and if we are faithful to our precedents we must conclude that it has not * * *. In any event, the characteristic that formed the basis of the targeting here was not womanhood, but the seeking of abortion—so that the class the dissenters identify is the one we have rejected earlier: women seeking abortion. The approach of equating opposition to an activity (abortion) that can be engaged in only by a certain class (women) with opposition to that class leads to absurd conclusions. On that analysis, men and women who regard rape with revulsion harbor an invidious antimale animus. Thus, if state law should provide that convicted rapists must be paroled so long as they attend weekly counseling sessions; and if persons opposed to such lenient treatment should demonstrate their opposition by impeding access to the counseling centers; those protesters would, on the dissenters' approach, be liable under § 1985(3) because of their antimale animus.

16. Because of our disposition of this case, we need not address whether the District Court erred by issuing an injunction, despite the language in § 1985(3) authorizing only "an action for the recovery of damages occasioned by such injury or deprivation".... [Repositioned footnote]

The judgment of the Court of Appeals is reversed in part and vacated in part, and the case is remanded for further proceedings consistent with this opinion.

It is so ordered.

JUSTICE KENNEDY, concurring. [Omitted]

JUSTICE SOUTER, concurring in the judgment in part and dissenting in part.

* * *

[I join the Court's conclusion regarding § 1985(3) insofar as it discusses our precedents. Our precedents, however, cover only the "deprivations" clause in § 1985(3), and I would rule for the plaintiffs on the "prevention" (or "hindrance") clause. That clause also contains the phrase "equal protection of the laws," and we usually construe identical clauses identically in the same statute. But I would make an exception here. In the usual § 1985(3) case under the "deprivations" clause, construing "equal protection" to require a discriminatory animus prevents the statute from becoming a broad federal tort law.]

* * *

The prevention clause carries no such premonition of liability, however. Its most distinctive requirement, to prove a conspiratorial purpose to "preven[t] or hinde[r] the constituted authorities of any State or Territory from giving or securing ... the equal protection of the laws," is both an additional element unknown to the deprivation clause, and a significantly limiting condition. Private conspiracies to injure according to class or classification are not enough here; they must be conspiracies to act with enough force, of whatever sort, to overwhelm the capacity of legal authority to act evenhandedly in administering the law.

* * *

Equally inapposite to the prevention clause is the second *Griffin–Carpenters* deprivation clause limitation that where a conspiracy to deny equal protection would interfere with exercise of a federal constitutional right, it be a right "protected against private, as well as official encroachment." The justification for the Court's initial enquiry concerning rights protected by the Constitution against private action lay in its stated concern about the constitutional limits of congressional power to regulate purely private action. Once again, however, the reason that there is no arguable need to import the extratextual limitation from the deprivation clause into the prevention clause lies in the prevention clause's distinctive requirement that the purpose of a conspiracy actionable under its terms must include a purpose to accomplish its object by preventing or hindering officials in the discharge of their constitutional responsibilities. The conspirators' * * * act of frustrating or thwarting state officials in their exercise of the State's police power would amount simply to an extralegal

way of determining how that state power would be exercised. It would, in real terms, be the exercise of state power itself. To the degree that private conspirators would arrogate the State's police power to themselves to thwart equal protection by imposing what amounts to a policy of discrimination in place of the Constitution's mandate, their action would be tantamount to state action and be subject as such to undoubted congressional authority to penalize any exercise of state police power that would abridge the equal protection guaranteed by the Fourteenth Amendment.
* * * *17

JUSTICE STEVENS, with whom JUSTICE BLACKMUN joins, dissenting.

* * *

[T]he evidence establishes that petitioners engaged in a nationwide conspiracy; to achieve their goal they repeatedly occupied public streets and trespassed on the premises of private citizens in order to prevent or hinder the constituted authorities from protecting access to abortion clinics by women, a substantial number of whom traveled in interstate commerce to reach the destinations blockaded by petitioners. The case involves no ordinary trespass, nor anything remotely resembling the peaceful picketing of a local retailer. It presents a striking contemporary example of the kind of zealous, politically motivated, lawless conduct that led to the enactment of the Ku Klux Act in 1871 and gave it its name.

[Although the clear language of § 1985(3) appears to cover the situation in this case, *Griffin* requires additional proof of a class-based animus. I would hold that sex discrimination satisfies this requirement. I would further hold that under § 1985(3), unlike the Constitution's Equal Protection Clause, discriminatory effect alone is adequate to define a violation; there is no requirement of proof of intentional sex discrimination.] Congress may obviously offer statutory protections against behavior that the Constitution does not forbid, including forms of discrimination that undermine § 1985(3)'s guarantee of equal treatment under the law. Regardless of whether the examples of paternalistic discrimination given above involve a constitutional violation, as a matter of statutory construction it is entirely appropriate to conclude that each would satisfy the class-based animus requirement because none of them poses any danger of

---

17. The scope of this construction of the prevention clause is limited. It certainly would not forbid any conduct, unlike that at issue here, protected by the First Amendment. Nor would it reach even demonstrations that have only the incidental effect of overwhelming local police authorities, for the statute by its terms requires a "purpose" to "preven[t] or hinde[r] the constituted authorities of any State or Territory from giving or securing to all persons within such State or Territory the equal protection of the laws." Indeed, it would not necessarily reach even most types of civil disobedience that may be intended to overwhelm police by inviting multiple arrests, because the purpose of these is not ordinarily to discriminate against individuals on the basis of their exercise of an independently protected constitutional right. As to the lunch counter sit-in protests of the early 1960's, to which the Court refers, if the cases that made it to this Court are representative, these normally were not "mass" demonstrations, but rather led to the arrests of small groups of orderly students who refused to leave segregated establishments when requested to do so.... [Repositioned footnote]

converting § 1985(3) into a general tort law or creating concerns about the constitutionality of the statute.

* * *

JUSTICE O'CONNOR, with whom JUSTICE BLACKMUN joins, dissenting.

* * *

[I stand by the dissenting position I took in Carpenters v. Scott. The animus requirement can be met by proof of hostility to a class beyond race, such as the group of women seeking abortions in this case. They are] especially vulnerable to the threat of mob violence. The women seeking the clinics' services are not simply "the group of victims of the tortious action"; as was the case in *Carpenters*, petitioners' intended targets are clearly identifiable—by virtue of their affiliation and activities—before any tortious action occurs.

[I also agree with Justice Stevens that women are a class protected by § 1985(3) and that proof of discriminatory effect on them, not intentional discrimination, is adequate to state a claim, at least when the group targeted is composed exclusively of women. I also agree with Justice Souter that a claim can be made under the "prevention" or "hindrance" clause against private persons who interfere with state authorities. No proof of further state action is necessary.]

NOTE ON RESIDUAL ISSUES UNDER SECTION 1985(3)

1.   A bare 5–4 majority in *Bray* rejects the application of § 1985(3) to the actions of abortion protestors. First, the majority holds that the animus requirement in the statute requires the same proof of intent as in cases under the Equal Protection Clause. At least three dissenters reject this position.

(a) If *Carpenters* is correct and § 1985(3) enforces rights as they are found on the face of the constitution, then Fourteenth Amendment claims require proof of intentional animus, do they not? See Chapter 1B.5 supra. Even if they do not as a matter of constitutional law, does not the word "animus," implied from the statute in *Griffin*, strongly imply an intent to harm the class protected? Does not stare decisis favor the majority on this issue, as Justice Souter concedes?

(b) Justices Stevens, Blackmun, and O'Connor concede that animus is required but find the element met on these facts. All consider sex-based animus sufficient, but they divide on how that animus can be shown. How plausible is Justice Stevens' argument that Congress wanted to reach not only intentional conduct but also that having a disparate or differential impact? Would he apply such an impact test to race-based claims as well? If so, would not virtually every "conspiracy" to oppose any economic position have an adverse impact on blacks? See Chapter 1B.5 supra. Is the Libertarian Party a conspiracy in violation of § 1985(3) when it opposes taxes and government regulations, at least those that go to assisting blacks? Is the Republican Party such a conspiracy? Is the conservative Leadership Council of the Democratic

Party such a conspiracy?[1]

(c) Justice O'Connor tries to avoid the problems related to Justice Stevens' historically improbable effects test by arguing that an intent test is met if one realizes that the object of the conspiracy is a class composed exclusively of women. Was not that argument rejected in the constitutional context in Geduldig v. Aiello, 417 U.S. 484, 94 S.Ct. 2485, 41 L.Ed.2d 256 (1974) (pregnancy discrimination is not sex discrimination)? Does her argument, like Stevens', therefore also depend on the assumption that Congress wished in § 1985(3) to go beyond the face of the Constitution?

(d) The strong rhetoric in Justice Stevens' opinion suggests that he is deeply offended by the actions of Operation Rescue and thinks that they should be stopped. But isn't his argument for an effects test to protect women substantially implausible in light of the precedents? Isn't it extremely unlikely that the Reconstruction Congress wanted to protect women, much less protect women with a Constitution-supplementing effects test? When is it appropriate for a Justice to perform some surgery on a statute to reach a desired social goal? Why did Justice Stevens meekly give up the fight later, when he joined the majority in narrowly construing the federal RICO statute not to cover abortion protestors? See Scheidler v. National Organization for Women, Inc., 547 U.S. 9, 126 S.Ct. 1264, 164 L.Ed.2d 10 (2006) (unanimously holding that violence alone does not violate RICO Act).

2. The 5–4 majority in *Bray* also finds that since the abortion right is grounded in the Fourteenth Amendment, it requires proof of state action as in *Carpenters*. Is this just a restatement of *Carpenters'* holding, or does it go further?

(a) Did Justice Scalia omit from *Carpenters* the language alternatively permitting a plaintiff to show that "the State is involved in the conspiracy *or that the aim of the conspiracy is to influence the activity of the State*" (emphasis added)? Was the purpose of the conspiracy here to influence the activity of the state? If the answer is no, is it because under *DeShaney* the state had no constitutional duty to protect the women seeking abortions? Or is it because there was no proof that the state authorities were actually overwhelmed so that they could not act as they wished?

(b) Justice Stevens seems to realize the implications of his argument by distinguishing this case from "peaceful picketing of a local retailer," an apparent reference to NAACP v. Claiborne Hardware Co., 458 U.S. 886, 102 S.Ct. 3409, 73 L.Ed.2d 1215 (1982) (violence in black boycott that harmed storeowners was incidental by-product of "passionate" speech; protestors only exercising their free-speech rights) (per Stevens, J.). What makes the abortion protestors an "organized and violent mob" and the black protestors merely "passionate" advocates who incidentally induced violence? Does Justice Stevens' distinction turn appropriately on the facts of each case, or does it too easily allow a judge to apply her political views to the facts? Would Justice Stevens protect abortion protestors who did nothing more than repeatedly but

---

1. Note the similar issues that arise by applying an effects test to the right to travel. Under that approach, any putative plaintiff could transform her claim into a § 1985(3) case by recruiting supporters from out of state—whose rights to interstate travel would then be adversely affected by the ongoing confrontations. Is there a way to avoid this problem?

non-violently sit-in and disrupt an abortion clinic? What would Justice Stevens do if a group of black protestors blockaded abortion clinics on the ground that abortion was being promoted by whites as a method of genocide against blacks? Would that amount to a violation of § 1985(3)? Are some groups or rights superior to others? See Alan Phelps, *Picketing and Prayer: Restricting Freedom of Expression Outside Churches*, 85 CORNELL L. REV. 271 (1999).

3. Justice Souter offers an intriguing alternative approach. It notes that there is a second clause in § 1985(3), one that applies to persons who are "preventing or hindering the constituted authorities of any State or territory from giving or securing to all persons . . . the equal protection of the laws."

(a) Do you find persuasive Souter's argument that "equal protection of the laws" should have a different meaning in this clause, one not requiring proof of animus? He is right that there is little danger of replacing state tort laws, is he not? Even assuming no animus is required, is it obvious that conduct directed not at authorities but at private persons is covered? Could this provision simply cover the situation described in Brewer v. Hoxie School District, discussed earlier in this Chapter?

(b) Assuming that Souter's argument prevails, how large must the conspiracy be in order to "hinder" or "prevent" authorities from carrying out their law-enforcement goals? Is Souter's position the exact reverse of the problem Justice Brennan faced in his dissenting opinion in *Carpenters*? (Recall that Justice Brennan sought to show that local authorities were in league with the violent protestors; here Justice Souter apparently would require showing the opposite, that authorities who wanted to help were prevented from doing so.) Even though reversed, are the two problems similar because they are both questions of degree? (Does Justice Souter avoid the problem by automatically assuming that if the right was not protected by state police, then the right must have been functionally denied?)

(c) In **Kush v. Rutledge**, 460 U.S. 719, 103 S.Ct. 1483, 75 L.Ed.2d 413 (1983), the Court ruled that no animus requirement is needed in a § 1985(2) claim alleging interference with federal courts. Section 1985(2) has no "equal protection" language in the section covering interference with federal courts, but it does have such language in a second clause that is remarkably similar to the "hindering" clause in § 1985(3). Which way does *Kush* cut, for Justice Souter or against him?

D. THE DEATH OF CONSTITUTIONAL EXPERIMENTATION AND THE VIOLENCE AGAINST WOMEN ACT

MORRISON v. UNITED STATES
Supreme Court of the United States, 2000.
529 U.S. 598, 120 S.Ct. 1740, 146 L.Ed.2d 658.

CHIEF JUSTICE REHNQUIST delivered the opinion of the Court.

In these cases we consider the constitutionality of 42 U.S.C. § 13981, which provides a federal civil remedy for the victims of gender-motivated violence. The United States Court of Appeals for the Fourth Circuit, sitting en banc, struck down § 13981 because it concluded that Congress lacked constitutional authority to enact the section's civil remedy. Believing that these cases are controlled by our decisions in United States v. Lopez, 514 U.S. 549, 115 S.Ct. 1624, 131 L.Ed.2d 626 (1995), United States v. Harris, 106 U.S. 629, 1 S.Ct. 601, 27 L.Ed. 290 (1883), and the In re Civil Rights Cases, 109 U.S. 3, 3 S.Ct. 18, 27 L.Ed. 835 (1883), we affirm.

[Christy Brzonkala, a student at a state-operated university in Virginia, sued another student, Antonio Morrison, after he allegedly raped her and boasted about it to friends in a particularly crude fashion. Her claim relied on § 13891. She also sued the university and several of its officials because, although they had found Morrison responsible for the violence, they had refused to punish Morrison in any meaningful manner. That claim rested on another statute and is not before us for review.]

* * *

Section 13981 was part of the Violence Against Women Act of 1994, § 40302, 108 Stat. 1941–1942. It states that "[a]ll persons within the United States shall have the right to be free from crimes of violence motivated by gender." 42 U.S.C. § 13981(b). To enforce that right, subsection (c) declares:

"A person (including a person who acts under color of any statute, ordinance, regulation, custom, or usage of any State) who commits a crime of violence motivated by gender and thus deprives another of the right declared in subsection (b) of this section shall be liable to the party injured, in an action for the recovery of compensatory and punitive damages, injunctive and declaratory relief, and such other relief as a court may deem appropriate."

* * *

Every law enacted by Congress must be based on one or more of its powers enumerated in the Constitution. "The powers of the legislature are defined and limited; and that those limits may not be mistaken, or forgotten, the constitution is written." Marbury v. Madison, 1 Cranch 137, 176, 2 L.Ed. 60 (1803) (Marshall, C. J.). Congress explicitly identified the sources of federal authority on which it relied in enacting § 13981. It said that a "Federal civil rights cause of action" is established "[p]ursuant to the affirmative power of Congress ... under section 5 of the Fourteenth Amendment to the Constitution, as well as under section 8 of Article I of the Constitution." 42 U.S.C. § 13981(a). We address Congress' authority to enact this remedy under each of these constitutional provisions in turn.

II

[Section 13981 cannot be sustained under Congress' power over interstate commerce. See Chapter 5 infra.]

III

Because we conclude that the Commerce Clause does not provide Congress with authority to enact § 13981, we address petitioners' alternative argument that the section's civil remedy should be upheld as an exercise of Congress' remedial power under § 5 of the Fourteenth Amendment. As noted above, Congress expressly invoked the Fourteenth Amendment as a source of authority to enact § 13981.

The principles governing an analysis of congressional legislation under § 5 are well settled. Section 5 states that Congress may " 'enforce' by 'appropriate legislation' the constitutional guarantee that no State shall deprive any person of 'life, liberty, or property, without due process of law,' nor deny any person 'equal protection of the laws.' " City of Boerne v. Flores, 521 U.S. 507, 517, 117 S.Ct. 2157, 138 L.Ed.2d 624 (1997). Section 5 is "a positive grant of legislative power," Katzenbach v. Morgan, [Chapter 8 infra], that includes authority to "prohibit conduct which is not itself unconstitutional and [to] intrud[e] into 'legislative spheres of autonomy previously reserved to the States.' " Flores, supra; see also Kimel v. Florida Bd. of Regents, 528 U.S. 62, 81, 120 S.Ct. 631, 145 L.Ed.2d 522 (2000). However, "[a]s broad as the congressional enforcement power is, it is not unlimited." Oregon v. Mitchell, 400 U.S. 112, 128, 91 S.Ct. 260, 27 L.Ed.2d 272 (1970); see also Kimel, supra. In fact, as we discuss in detail below, several limitations inherent in § 5's text and constitutional context have been recognized since the Fourteenth Amendment was adopted.

Petitioners' § 5 argument is founded on an assertion that there is pervasive bias in various state justice systems against victims of gender-motivated violence. This assertion is supported by a voluminous congressional record. Specifically, Congress received evidence that many participants in state justice systems are perpetuating an array of erroneous stereotypes and assumptions. Congress concluded that these discriminatory stereotypes often result in insufficient investigation and prosecution of gender-motivated crime, inappropriate focus on the behavior and credibility of the victims of that crime, and unacceptably lenient punishments for those who are actually convicted of gender-motivated violence. See H.R. Conf. Rep. No. 103–711, at 385–386; S.Rep. No. 103–138, at 38, 41–55; S.Rep. No. 102–197, at 33–35, 41, 43–47. Petitioners contend that this bias denies victims of gender-motivated violence the equal protection of the laws and that Congress therefore acted appropriately in enacting a private civil remedy against the perpetrators of gender-motivated violence to both remedy the States' bias and deter future instances of discrimination in the state courts.

As our cases have established, state-sponsored gender discrimination violates equal protection unless it "serves important governmental objectives and . . . the discriminatory means employed are substantially related to the achievement of those objectives." United States v. Virginia, 518 U.S. 515, 533, 116 S.Ct. 2264, 135 L.Ed.2d 735 (1996). However, the language and purpose of the Fourteenth Amendment place certain limitations on the manner in which Congress may attack discriminatory conduct. These limitations are necessary to prevent the Fourteenth Amendment from obliterating the Framers' carefully crafted balance of power between the States and the National Government. Foremost among these limitations is the time-honored principle that the Fourteenth Amendment, by its very terms, prohibits only state action. "[T]he principle has become firmly embedded in our constitutional law that the action inhibited by the first section of the Fourteenth Amendment is only such action as may fairly be said to be that of the States. That Amendment erects no shield against merely private conduct, however discriminatory or wrongful." Shelley v. Kraemer, 334 U.S. 1, 13, and n. 12, 68 S.Ct. 836, 92 L.Ed. 1161 (1948).

Shortly after the Fourteenth Amendment was adopted, we decided two cases interpreting the Amendment's provisions, United States v. Harris, 106 U.S. 629, 1 S.Ct. 601, 27 L.Ed. 290 (1883), and the Civil Rights Cases, 109 U.S. 3, 3 S.Ct. 18, 27 L.Ed. 835 (1883). In *Harris,* the Court considered a challenge to § 2 of the Civil Rights Act of 1871. That section sought to punish "private persons" for "conspiring to deprive any one of the equal protection of the laws enacted by the State." We concluded that this law exceeded Congress' § 5 power because the law was "directed exclusively against the action of private persons, without reference to the laws of the State, or their administration by her officers." In so doing, we reemphasized our statement from Virginia v. Rives, 100 U.S. 313, 318, 25 L.Ed. 667 (1879), that " 'these provisions of the fourteenth amendment have reference to State action exclusively, and not to any action of private individuals.' "

We reached a similar conclusion in the *Civil Rights Cases.* In those consolidated cases, we held that the public accommodation provisions of the Civil Rights Act of 1875, which applied to purely private conduct, were beyond the scope of the § 5 enforcement power. 109 U.S., at 11, 3 S.Ct. 18 ("Individual invasion of individual rights is not the subject-matter of the [Fourteenth] [A]mendment"). See also, e.g., Romer v. Evans, 517 U.S. 620, 628, 116 S.Ct. 1620, 134 L.Ed.2d 855 (1996) ("[I]t was settled early that the Fourteenth Amendment did not give Congress a general power to prohibit discrimination in public accommodations"); Lugar v. Edmondson Oil Co., 457 U.S. 922, 936, 102 S.Ct. 2744, 73 L.Ed.2d 482 (1982) ("Careful adherence to the 'state action' requirement preserves an area of individual freedom by limiting the reach of federal law and federal judicial power"); United States v. Cruikshank, 92 U.S. 542, 554, 23 L.Ed. 588 (1875) ("The fourteenth amendment prohibits a state from depriving any person of life, liberty, or property, without due process of law; but this adds nothing to the rights of one citizen as against another. It simply furnishes an additional guaranty against any encroachment by the States upon the fundamental rights which belong to every citizen as a member of society").

* * *

Petitioners contend that two more recent decisions have in effect overruled this longstanding limitation on Congress' § 5 authority. They rely on United States v. Guest for the proposition that the rule laid down in the *Civil Rights Cases* is no longer good law. [The majority opinion in *Guest* reached no constitutional issues. Nevertheless, three] Members of the Court, in a separate opinion by Justice Brennan, expressed the view that the *Civil Rights Cases* were wrongly decided, and that Congress could under § 5 prohibit actions by private individuals. Three other Members of the Court, who joined the opinion of the Court, joined a separate opinion by Justice Clark which in two or three sentences stated the conclusion that Congress could "punis[h] all conspiracies—with or without state action—that interfere with Fourteenth Amendment rights." Justice Harlan, in another separate opinion, commented with respect to the statement by these Justices:

> "The action of three of the Justices who joined the Court's opinion in nonetheless cursorily pronouncing themselves on the far-reaching constitutional questions deliberately not reached in Part II seems to me, to say the very least, extraordinary." Id., at 762, n. 1, 86 S.Ct. 1170 (opinion concurring in part and dissenting in part).

* * *

To accept petitioners' argument, * * * one must add to the three Justices joining Justice Brennan's reasoned explanation for his belief that the *Civil Rights Cases* were wrongly decided, the three Justices joining Justice Clark's opinion who gave no explanation whatever for their similar view. This is simply not the way that reasoned constitutional adjudication proceeds. We accordingly have no hesitation in saying that it would take more than the naked dicta contained in Justice Clark's opinion, when added to Justice Brennan's opinion, to cast any doubt upon the enduring vitality of the *Civil Rights Cases* and *Harris*.

* * *

Petitioners alternatively argue that, unlike the situation in the *Civil Rights Cases,* here there has been gender-based disparate treatment by state authorities, whereas in those cases there was no indication of such state action. There is abundant evidence, however, to show that the Congresses that enacted the Civil Rights Acts of 1871 and 1875 had a purpose similar to that of Congress in enacting § 13981: There were state laws on the books bespeaking equality of treatment, but in the administration of these laws there was discrimination against newly freed slaves. * * *

But even if that distinction were valid, we do not believe it would save § 13981's civil remedy. For the remedy is simply not "corrective in its character, adapted to counteract and redress the operation of such prohibited [s]tate laws or proceedings of [s]tate officers." *Civil Rights Cases, supra.* Or, as we have phrased it in more recent cases, prophylactic legislation under § 5 must have a "congruence and proportionality between the injury to be prevented or remedied and the means adopted to that end." Florida Prepaid Postsecondary Ed. Expense Bd. v. College Savings Bank, 527 U.S. 627, 639, 119 S.Ct. 2199, 144 L.Ed.2d 575 (1999); *Flores*, supra. Section 13981 is not aimed at proscribing discrimination by officials which the Fourteenth Amendment might not itself proscribe; it is directed not at any State or state actor, but at individuals who have committed criminal acts motivated by gender bias.

In the present cases, for example, § 13981 visits no consequence whatever on any Virginia public official involved in investigating or prosecuting Brzonkala's assault. The section is, therefore, unlike any of the § 5 remedies that we have previously upheld. In Katzenbach v. Morgan, [Chapter 8 infra], Congress prohibited New York from imposing literacy tests as a prerequisite for voting because it found that such a requirement disenfranchised thousands of Puerto Rican immigrants who had been educated in the Spanish language of their home territory. That law, which we upheld, was directed at New York officials who administered the State's election law and prohibited them from using a provision of that law. In South Carolina v. Katzenbach, [Chapter 8 infra], Congress imposed voting rights requirements on States that, Congress found, had a history of discriminating against blacks in voting. The remedy was also directed at state officials in those States. Similarly, in Ex parte Virginia, 100 U.S. 339, 25 L.Ed. 676 (1879), Congress criminally punished state officials who intentionally discriminated in jury selection; again, the remedy was directed to the culpable state official.

Section 13981 is also different from these previously upheld remedies in that it applies uniformly throughout the Nation. Congress' findings indicate that the problem of discrimination against the victims of gender-motivated crimes does not exist in all States, or even most States. By contrast, the § 5 remedy upheld in Katzenbach v. Morgan, supra, was directed only to the State where the evil found by Congress existed, and in South Carolina v. Katzenbach, supra, the remedy was directed only to those States in which Congress found that there had been discrimination.

For these reasons, we conclude that Congress' power under § 5 does not extend to the enactment of § 13981.

IV

Petitioner Brzonkala's complaint alleges that she was the victim of a brutal assault. But Congress' effort in § 13981 to provide a federal civil remedy can be sustained neither under the Commerce Clause nor under § 5 of the Fourteenth Amendment. If the allegations here are true, no civilized system of justice could fail to provide her a remedy for the conduct of respondent Morrison. But under our federal system that remedy must be provided by the Commonwealth of Virginia, and not by the United States. The judgment of the Court of Appeals is

Affirmed.[b]

---

b. The concurring opinion of Justice Thomas and the dissenting opinion of Justice Souter, joined by Justices Stevens, Breyer, and Ginsburg (upholding the statute under the Commerce Clause), are omitted.

Justice BREYER, with whom Justice STEVENS joins, and with whom Justice SOUTER and Justice GINSBURG join as to Part I–A, dissenting.

I

[I would sustain § 13981 under the Commerce Clause. See Chapter 5 infra.]

II

Given my conclusion on the Commerce Clause question, I need not consider Congress' authority under § 5 of the Fourteenth Amendment. Nonetheless, I doubt the Court's reasoning rejecting that source of authority. The Court points out that in United States v. Harris and the *Civil Rights Cases* the Court held that § 5 does not authorize Congress to use the Fourteenth Amendment as a source of power to remedy the conduct of *private persons*. That is certainly so. The Federal Government's argument, however, is that Congress used § 5 to remedy the actions of *state actors,* namely, those States which, through discriminatory design or the discriminatory conduct of their officials, failed to provide adequate (or any) state remedies for women injured by gender-motivated violence—a failure that the States, and Congress, documented in depth. [Neither *Harris* nor the *Civil Rights Cases* involved such a claim of an underlying violation by state officials; the statutes in those cases were directed solely against private persons as a remedy for private wrongs.]

The Court responds directly to the relevant "state actor" claim by finding that the present law lacks " 'congruence and proportionality' " to the state discrimination that it purports to remedy. That is because the law, unlike federal laws prohibiting literacy tests for voting, imposing voting rights requirements, or punishing state officials who intentionally discriminated in jury selection, is not "directed . . . at any State or state actor."

But why can Congress not provide a remedy against private actors? Those private actors, of course, did not themselves violate the Constitution. But this Court has held that Congress at least sometimes can enact remedial "[l]egislation . . . [that] prohibits conduct which is not itself unconstitutional." *Flores*, supra; see also Katzenbach v. Morgan [Chapter 8 infra]; South Carolina v. Katzenbach, [Chapter 8 infra]. The statutory remedy does not in any sense purport to "determine what constitutes a constitutional violation." It intrudes little upon either States or private parties. It may lead state actors to improve their own remedial systems, primarily through example. It restricts private actors only by imposing liability for private conduct that is, in the main, already forbidden by state law. Why is the remedy "disproportionate"? And given the relation between remedy and violation—the creation of a federal remedy to substitute for constitutionally inadequate state remedies—where is the lack of "congruence"?

* * *

Note on Fourteenth Amendment Power to Control Private Persons

1. The primary thrust of the Court's opinion in *Morrison* repeats the truism that the Fourteenth Amendment on its face regulates only state action. See also Chapter 1C supra. About this there is no difference of opinion among the Justices. The real question is whether Congress may use its § 5 power to go beyond the face of the statute. In one respect, the majority admits that it may, citing cases to be discussed in Chapter 8 infra. These cases hold that once Congress finds a violation of the Amendment, it may as a remedy require states to undertake action that is not itself constitutionally required.

(a) The Court appears to restrict this remedial power under § 5 to the question of constitutional violations; it refuses to allow Congress to go beyond the state-action limit of the Fourteenth Amendment to reach private action as well. On what cases does the Court rely? Does their early vintage make them less reliable or more authoritative? (In a part of the opinion not excerpted here, the Court thought the latter because the Justices then on the Court had first-hand, contemporaneous knowledge of the circumstances of the adoption of the Amendment. Do you agree?)

(b) The Court also notes that modern legislation enforcing the Fourteenth Amendment, discussed in Chapter 8 infra, has always been directed at the very state officials who violated the Fourteenth Amendment. Is this a strong argument that there is a settled consensus that Congress may not go beyond the face of the Fourteenth Amendment to reach private activities? This remedy is novel, is it not? Is its sheer novelty what dooms it?

2. The government specifically invoked United States v. Guest in its brief, relying on the so-called "second majority" theory—the theory that Justice Brennan's three dissenting votes could be added to Justice Clark's three concurring votes, to make a six-vote majority in favor of power to reach private actors under § 5.

(a) How does the Court attack the "second majority" theory? Was it right to ignore Clark on the ground that he (obviously) had not given much thought to his dictum?

(b) Although he later took a more expansive view, Justice Brennan's original view in *Guest* had plausible support in precedent, albeit creatively used. See Preliminary Essay with Chart, supra. Even the later majority opinion in *Carpenters* left in place the idea that Congress could reach private persons in situations where state government had been "involved in" or "affected by" private conduct. Does the situation here fit within that language?

(c) Diagram the relationship between the plaintiff, the state, and the private person in this case, following the patterns discussed in the Chart of Rights, supra. Is this a situation where the plaintiff was trying to attend a state facility (the university) and was prevented by a third-party's interference? Or is the university irrelevant because this was just a private interaction as in ACTION v. Gannon with the state nowhere in the diagram—except for a discredited argument that the state always has an affirmative duty to protect all citizens? (Could the statute have been upheld as applied to such state-university settings but not as applied to other private settings?)

3. Justice Breyer's musings in Part II of his dissenting opinion take the view that Congress may cure state officials' Fourteenth Amendment violations by authorizing civil suits against private persons. (The majority found this remedy non-congruent because it visited a remedy on private persons who had not violated the Amendment and failed to visit a remedy on those state officials who had committed the violation.) Justice Breyer argued that there was congruence. Is the dispute between the Justices not about civil rights, but more broadly about federalism?

(a) What is the connection that Justice Breyer sees between § 13981's civil remedy (against private persons) and the purported violation (by state actors)? He states that the remedy against private persons "may lead state actors to improve their own remedial systems, primarily through example." Is the majority right to see this argument as an open-ended thesis that would validate any legislation against private actors? Did Breyer have a better argument, one based on the idea that a federal remedy might actually help states accomplish their goals? Can Congress help the states—when they request it—by punishing private persons who frustrate a state's attempts to enforce its own laws? Cf. Brewer v. Hoxie School Dist., excerpted earlier in this Chapter.

(b) Why—think the unthinkable here—would Congress have legislated a private remedy for violence against women when it found that states were failing to, or even promoting, violence against women? Why did it not adopt a criminal law punishing the offending state officials themselves? Was Congress just trying to legislate local tort laws, local laws regulating private behavior, and used the Fourteenth Amendment as a fig leaf to cover up its forbidden goal?

(c) If a state is failing to protect, even intentionally failing to protect, some or all of its citizens in violation of the Equal Protection Clause, may the federal government step in and replace the state? Or is Congress required to leave the state apparatus in place and control its failure to act? (Though Congress has no general "police power," does it have a default police power when a state has committed a constitutional violation? Does the default power include authority to make laws on all topics that a state would otherwise be authorized to make?)

(d) If Virginia had simply repealed its rape law, would the repeal have been unconstitutional under the Fourteenth Amendment? Would Congress have had authority to remedy the situation?

4. *Morrison* appears to leave the "second majority" theory from *Guest* in tatters, if not completely destroyed. What is lost if the theory dies?

(a) Congress retains power to act against state officials for any violation of the Fourteenth Amendment, including sex discrimination. For example, three years after *Morrison*, in **NEVADA DEPARTMENT OF HUMAN RESOURCES v. HIBBS**, 538 U.S. 721, 123 S.Ct. 1972, 155 L.Ed.2d 953 (2003) (per Rehnquist, J.), the Court upheld the Family and Medical Leave Act on the ground that its regulations of state employment practices was a reasonable remedy for a record of sex discrimination against women. The remedy applied to the offending states themselves.

(b) Congress after *Morrison* retains its power under § 2 of the Thirteenth Amendment to legislate remedies for slavery, including regulation of private persons who discriminate based on race. See Chapter 2 supra.

(c) Absent some other regulatory power (such as the Commerce Clause, Chapter 7 infra, or the Spending Power, Chapter 6, infra), Congress lacks power to reach non-race-based discrimination by private persons—unless the Thirteenth Amendment is held to reach such topics. Should it be?

CHAPTER 4

APPLYING THE OLDER CIVIL RIGHTS
STATUTES TO FEDERAL
OFFICIALS

■ ■ ■

A. STATUTORY CLAIMS

DISTRICT OF COLUMBIA v. CARTER

Supreme Court of the United States, 1973.
409 U.S. 418, 93 S.Ct. 602, 34 L.Ed.2d 613.

Mr. Justice Brennan delivered the opinion of the Court.

On February 12, 1969, respondent filed this civil action in the United States District Court for the District of Columbia alleging that in 1968 Police Officer John R. Carlson of the Metropolitan Police Department of the District of Columbia arrested him without probable cause and, while he was being held by two other officers, beat him with brass knuckles. The complaint alleged further that Carlson's precinct captain, the chief of police, and the District of Columbia each had negligently failed to train, instruct, supervise, and control Carlson with regard to the circumstances in which an arrest may be made and the extent to which various degrees of force may be used to effect an arrest. Respondent sought damages against each defendant upon several theories, including a common-law theory of tort liability and an action for deprivation of civil rights pursuant to 42 U.S.C.A. § 1983 * * *.

The District Court dismissed the complaint against all defendants without opinion. On appeal, the United States Court of Appeals for the District of Columbia Circuit reversed, holding that the allegations of the complaint were sufficient to state causes of action under both the common-law and federal statutory theories of liability. Carter v. Carlson, 144 U.S.App.D.C. 388, 447 F.2d 358 (D.C.Cir.1971). In sustaining respondent's claims under § 1983, the court held that "[a]cts under color of the law of the District of Columbia are under color of the law of a 'State or Territory' for the purpose of § 1983." We granted certiorari. For the reasons stated below, we hold that the District of Columbia is not a "State or Territory" within the meaning of § 1983. We therefore reverse the judgment of the

Court of Appeals insofar as that judgment sustained respondent's claims under § 1983.

I

Whether the District of Columbia constitutes a "State or Territory" within the meaning of any particular statutory or constitutional provision depends upon the character and aim of the specific provision involved. Indeed, such "[w]ords generally have different shades of meaning, and are to be construed if reasonably possible to effectuate the intent of the lawmakers; and this meaning in particular instances is to be arrived at, not only by a consideration of the words themselves, but by considering, as well, the context, the purposes of the law, and the circumstances under which the words were employed." Puerto Rico v. Shell Co. (P.R.), Ltd., 302 U.S. 253, 258, 58 S.Ct. 167, 169, 82 L.Ed. 235 (1937); Atlantic Cleaners & Dyers v. United States, 286 U.S. 427, 433, 52 S.Ct. 607, 608–609, 76 L.Ed. 1204 (1932).

The Court of Appeals' conclusion that the District of Columbia is a "State or Territory" for the purpose of § 1983 was premised almost exclusively upon this Court's earlier determination that "the District of Columbia is included within the phrase 'every State and Territory'" as employed in 42 U.S.C.A. § 1982. Hurd v. Hodge, 334 U.S. 24, 31, 68 S.Ct. 847, 851, 92 L.Ed. 1187 (1948). At first glance, it might seem logical simply to assume, as did the Court of Appeals, that identical words used in two related statutes were intended to have the same effect. Nevertheless, "[w]here the subject-matter to which the words refer is not the same in the several places where they are used, or the conditions are different, or the scope of the legislative power exercised in one case is broader than that exercised in another, the meaning well may vary to meet the purposes of the law * * *." Atlantic Cleaners & Dyers v. United States, supra, 286 U.S. at 433, 52 S.Ct., at 609. And the logic underlying the Court of Appeals' assumption breaks down completely where, as here, "there is such variation in the connection in which the words are used as reasonably to warrant the conclusion that they were employed * * * with different intent." Ibid.

Section 1982 * * * was enacted as a means to enforce the Thirteenth Amendment's proclamation that "[n]either slavery nor involuntary servitude * * * shall exist within the United States, or any place subject to their jurisdiction." See Jones v. Alfred H. Mayer Co. "As its text reveals, the Thirteenth Amendment 'is not a mere prohibition of state laws establishing or upholding slavery, but an absolute declaration that slavery or involuntary servitude shall not exist in any part of the United States.'" Civil Rights Cases, 109 U.S. 3, 20, 3 S.Ct. 18, 27–28, 27 L.Ed. 835 (1883). Thus, it cannot be doubted that the power vested in Congress to enforce this Amendment includes the power to enact laws of nationwide application.

Moreover, like the Amendment upon which it is based, § 1982 is not a "mere prohibition of state laws establishing or upholding" racial discrimination in the sale or rental of property but, rather, an "absolute" bar to *all* such discrimination, private as well as public, federal as well as state. Cf. Jones v. Alfred H. Mayer Co. With this in mind, it would be anomalous indeed if Congress chose to carve out the District of Columbia as the sole exception to an act of otherwise universal application. And this is all the more true where, as here, the legislative purposes underlying § 1982 support its applicability in the District. The dangers of private discrimination, for example, that provided a focal point of Congress' concern in enacting the legislation, were, and are, as present in the District of Columbia as in the States, and the same considerations that led Congress to extend the prohibitions of § 1982 to the Federal Government apply with equal force to the District, which is a mere instrumentality of that Government. Thus, in the absence of some express indication of legislative intent to the contrary, there was ample justification for the holding in *Hurd* that § 1982 was intended to outlaw racial discrimination in the sale or rental of property in the District of Columbia as well as elsewhere in the United States.

The situation is wholly different, however, with respect to § 1983. Unlike § 1982, which derives from the Civil Rights Act of 1866, § 1983 has its roots in § 1 of the Ku Klux Klan Act of 1871, Act of Apr. 20, 1871, § 1, 17 Stat. 13. This distinction has great significance, for unlike the 1866 Act, which was passed as a means to enforce the Thirteenth Amendment, the primary purpose of the 1871 Act was "to enforce the Provisions of the Fourteenth Amendment." 17 Stat. 13; see, e.g., Monroe v. Pape. And it has long been recognized that "[d]ifferent problems of statutory meaning are presented by two enactments deriving from different constitutional sources." Monroe v. Pape, supra.

In contrast to the reach of the Thirteenth Amendment, the Fourteenth Amendment has only limited applicability, the commands of the Fourteenth Amendment are addressed only to the State or to those acting under color of its authority. See, e.g., Civil Rights Cases, supra. The Fourteenth Amendment itself "erects no shield against merely private conduct, however discriminatory or wrongful."[8] Shelley v. Kraemer, 334 U.S. 1, 13, 68 S.Ct. 836, 842, 92 L.Ed. 1161 (1948). Similarly, actions of the Federal Government and its officers are beyond the purview of the Amendment. And since the District of Columbia is not a "State" within the meaning of the Fourteenth Amendment see Bolling v. Sharpe, 347 U.S. 497, 499, 74 S.Ct. 693, 694, 98 L.Ed. 884 (1954), neither the District nor its officers are subject to its restrictions.[9]

8. This is not to say, of course, that Congress may not proscribe purely private conduct under § 5 of the Fourteenth Amendment. See United States v. Guest, 383 U.S. 745, 762, 86 S.Ct. 1170, 1180, 16 L.Ed.2d 239 (1966) (Clark, J., concurring); id. at 782–784, 86 S.Ct., at 1190–1192 (Brennan, J., concurring and dissenting). * * *

9. Thus, unlike the situation with respect to § 1982 and the Thirteenth Amendment, inclusion of the District of Columbia in § 1983 cannot be subsumed under Congress' power to enforce the Fourteenth Amendment but, rather, would necessitate a wholly separate exercise of Congress' power to legislate for the District under Art. I, § 8, cl. 17.

Like the Amendment upon which it is based, § 1983 is of only limited scope. The statute deals only with those deprivations of rights that are accomplished under the color of the law of "any State or Territory." It does not reach purely private conduct and, with the exception of the Territories,[11] actions of the Federal Government and its officers are at least facially exempt from its proscriptions. Thus, unlike the situation presented in *Hurd,* the instant case does not involve a constitutional provision and related statute of universal applicability. This being so, the considerations that led to an expansive reading of § 1982 so as to include the District of Columbia simply do not apply with respect to § 1983. We must therefore examine the legislative history of § 1983 to determine whether the purposes for which the Act was adopted support a similarly broad construction.

II

* * *

Although there are threads of many thoughts running through the debates on the 1871 Act, it seems clear that § 1 of the Act, with which we are here concerned, was designed primarily in response to the unwillingness or inability of the state governments to enforce their own laws against those violating the civil rights of others. Thus, while the [Ku Klux] Klan itself provided the principal catalyst for the legislation, the remedy created in § 1 "was not a remedy against [the Klan] or its members but against those who representing a State in some capacity were *unable* or *unwilling* to enforce a state law." Monroe v. Pape (emphasis in original). * * *

To the Reconstruction Congress, the need for some form of federal intervention was clear. It was equally clear, however, that Congress had neither the means nor the authority to exert any direct control, on a day-to-day basis, over the actions of state officials. The solution chosen was to involve the federal judiciary. At the time this Act was adopted, it must be remembered, there existed no general federal-question jurisdiction in the lower federal courts. Rather, "Congress relied on the state courts to vindicate essential rights arising under the Constitution and federal laws." Zwickler v. Koota, 389 U.S. 241, 245, 88 S.Ct. 391, 394, 19 L.Ed.2d 444 (1967). With the growing awareness that this reliance had been misplaced, however, Congress recognized the need for original federal court jurisdiction as a means to provide at least indirect federal control over the unconstitutional actions of state officials. * * *

---

11. As initially enacted, § 1 of the 1871 Act applied only to action under color of the law of any "State." 17 Stat. 13. The phrase "or Territory" was added, without explanation, in the 1874 codification and revision of the United States Statutes at Large. Rev.Stat. § 1979 (1874). Since the Territories are not "States" within the meaning of the Fourteenth Amendment, see South Porto Rico Sugar Co. v. Buscaglia, 154 F.2d 96, 101 (C.A.1 1946); Anderson v. Scholes, 83 F.Supp. 681, 687 (Alaska 1949), this addition presumably was an exercise of Congress' power to regulate the Territories under Art. IV, § 3, cl. 2.

There was no need, however, to create federal court jurisdiction for the District of Columbia. Even prior to 1871, the courts of the District possessed general jurisdiction over both federal and local matters. Act of Mar. 3, 1863, c. 91, 12 Stat. 762. Thus, the jurisdictional aspects of § 1 of the 1871 Act were entirely superfluous with respect to the District. Moreover, while Congress was unable to exert any direct control over the actions of state officials, it was authorized under Art. I, § 8, cl. 17, of the Constitution to exercise plenary power over the District of Columbia and its officers. Indeed, "[t]he power of Congress over the District of Columbia includes all the legislative powers which a state may exercise over its affairs." Berman v. Parker, 348 U.S. 26, 31, 75 S.Ct. 98, 102, 99 L.Ed. 27 (1954). And since the District is itself the seat of the National Government, Congress was in a position to observe and, to a large extent, supervise the activities of local officials. Thus, the rationale underlying Congress' decision not to enact legislation similar to § 1983 with respect to federal officials—the assumption that the Federal Government could keep its own officers under control—is equally applicable to the situation then existing in the District of Columbia.

* * *

With this unique status of the District of Columbia in mind, and in the absence of any indication in the language, purposes, or history of § 1983 of a legislative intent to include the District within the scope of its coverage, the conclusion is compelled that the Court of Appeals erred in holding that the District of Columbia constitutes a "State or Territory" within the meaning of § 1983. Just as "[w]e are not at liberty to seek ingenious analytical instruments" to avoid giving a congressional enactment the broad scope its language and origins may require, United States v. Price, 383 U.S. [787], 801, 86 S.Ct., at 1160 so too are we not at liberty to recast this statute to expand its application beyond the limited reach Congress gave it. This is not to say, of course, that a claim, such as a possible claim against Officer Carlson, of alleged deprivation of constitutional rights is not litigable in the federal courts of the District. See Bivens v. Six Unknown Named Agents of Federal Bureau of Narcotics, 403 U.S. 388, 91 S.Ct. 1999, 29 L.Ed.2d 619 (1971); Bell v. Hood, 327 U.S. 678, 66 S.Ct. 773, 90 L.Ed. 939 (1946). But insofar as the judgment of the Court of Appeals sustaining respondent's claims rested on § 1983, that judgment must be, and is, reversed.

Judgment reversed.

NOTE ON LATER DEVELOPMENTS IN COVERAGE OF FEDERAL OFFICERS

1. *Carter*'s refusal to include the District of Columbia within the ambit of § 1983 lived a short life. In **Public Law 96–170**, § 1 (1979) Congress overrode the decision in legislation that created the current version of § 1983. District of Columbia officials favored the change, hoping that it would eventually gain adherents to the cause of statehood for the District.

(a) As applied to the District, are the rights being enforced derived from the Fourteenth Amendment or the Fifth? What is the source of Congress' power to legislate these remedies for these rights?

(b) With inclusion comes the related problem of governmental status: is the District of Columbia a state, and thus entitled to protection under *Will* and the Eleventh Amendment? Or is it a local government subject to liability under the line of cases? See O'Callaghan v. District of Columbia, 741 F.Supp. 273 (D.D.C.1990) (DC not a state; *Monell* applies). Compare Morgan v. District of Columbia, 824 F.2d 1049 (D.C. Cir.1987) (D.C. a municipality), with Sanders v. Washington Metropolitan Area Transit Authority, 819 F.2d 1151 (D.C. Cir.1987) (transit agency for D.C. metropolitan area enjoys Eleventh Amendment immunity and federal sovereign immunity). See generally Smith v. District of Columbia, 413 F.3d 86 (D.C. Cir. 2005) (treating the issue as settled and applying circuit precedent to determine municipal liability).

2.   As *Carter* indicates, the Court has long settled the issue of whether other federal officers are subject to suit under § 1983: those in the territories are; those in the central government and its agencies are not.

(a) The federal territories have always been covered under § 1983. Should they be treated as states or local governments for purposes of governmental liability? See Ngiraingas v. Sanchez, 495 U.S. 182, 110 S.Ct. 1737, 109 L.Ed.2d 163 (1990) (Territory of Guam not a "person" suable under § 1983; treated same as a state under *Will*).

(b) The central government and its agencies are not subject to the Fourteenth Amendment and lie outside the scope of § 1983. There is a method, however, for suing federal officers in virtually the same manner as § 1983 authorizes suits against state officers. Haynesworth v. Miller, 820 F.2d 1245 (D.C. Cir.1987) (adopting § 1983 standards for other constitutional claims against federal officials); see section B of this Chapter.

3.   Does Carter hold that federal officials nationwide are subject to suit under § 1982? Or that private persons within the District of Columbia fall under the statute's coverage? See Gautreaux v. Chicago Housing Auth., 503 F.2d 930, 931 (7th Cir.1974), afield sub nom. Hills v. Gautreaux, 425 U.S. 284, 96 S.Ct. 1538, 47 L.Ed.2d 792 (1976). Would it be easier to construe Thirteenth Amendment–based statutes as covering federal officials, on the ground that its commands affect not only the states but all governments and citizens?

(a) Given the dual nature of § 1985(3), as enforcer of both Thirteenth and Fourteenth Amendment rights, should it apply to federal officials? Apply to private persons in the District of Columbia? What rights would the plaintiff be invoking—those grounded in the Thirteenth and Fifth Amendments? The Bill of Rights generally? See Hobson v. Wilson, 737 F.2d 1 (D.C. Cir.1984) (yes for D.C. and federal officials); McCord v. Bailey, 636 F.2d 606 (D.C.Cir.1980) (§ 1985(2)).

(b) Even if §§ 1981, 1982, and 1985(3) have some application to federal officials, there remains the question of whether these statutes have been displaced by newer, specialized statutes that have their own exclusive remedial schemes. In **Brown v. General Services Administration**, 425 U.S. 820, 96 S.Ct. 1961, 48 L.Ed.2d 402 (1976), for example, the Court held that the

Equal Employment Opportunity Amendments of 1972 subjected federal agencies to employment discrimination suits under Title VII of the Civil Rights Act of 1964. This remedy was found to be exclusive, thus displacing whatever remedy might be available under § 1981.

(c) Section 1981 and Title VII co-exist as optional remedies when the defendant is a private employer. See Johnson v. Railway Express Agency, 421 U.S. 454, 95 S.Ct. 1716, 44 L.Ed.2d 295 (1975). Why would the Court adopt a different approach to claims against the federal government as employer? Why would it wish to see all claims channeled through one statute?

4. Should all Thirteenth Amendment–based civil rights statutes be amended to make clear that federal officers are included within their terms?

B. ALTERNATIVES TO THE OLDER STATUTES: DIRECT CONSTITUTIONAL CLAIMS

BIVENS v. SIX UNKNOWN NAMED AGENTS OF FEDERAL BUREAU OF NARCOTICS

Supreme Court of the United States, 1971.
403 U.S. 388, 91 S.Ct. 1999, 29 L.Ed.2d 619.

MR. JUSTICE BRENNAN delivered the opinion of the Court.

The Fourth Amendment provides that:

"The right of the people to be secure in their persons, houses, papers, and effects, against unreasonable searches and seizures, shall not be violated. * * *"

In Bell v. Hood, 327 U.S. 678, 66 S.Ct. 773, 90 L.Ed. 939 (1946), we reserved the question whether violation of that command by a federal agent acting under color of his authority gives rise to a cause of action for damages consequent upon his unconstitutional conduct. Today we hold that it does.

This case has its origin in an arrest and search carried out on the morning of November 26, 1965. Petitioner's complaint alleged that on that day respondents, agents of the Federal Bureau of Narcotics acting under claim of federal authority, entered his apartment and arrested him for alleged narcotics violations. The agents manacled petitioner in front of his wife and children, and threatened to arrest the entire family. They searched the apartment from stem to stern. Thereafter, petitioner was taken to the federal courthouse in Brooklyn, where he was interrogated, booked, and subjected to a visual strip search.

On July 7, 1967, petitioner brought suit in Federal District Court. In addition to the allegations above, his complaint asserted that the arrest and search were effected without a warrant, and that unreasonable force was employed in making the arrest; fairly read, it alleges as well that the arrest was made without probable cause. Petitioner claimed to have suffered great humiliation, embarrassment, and mental suffering as a result of the agents' unlawful conduct, and sought $15,000 damages from each of them. The District Court, on respondents' motion, dismissed the complaint on the ground, *inter alia,* that it failed to state a cause of action[, and the Court of Appeals affirmed]. We reverse.

I

Respondents do not argue that petitioner should be entirely without remedy for an unconstitutional invasion of his rights by federal agents. In respondents' view, however, the rights that petitioner asserts—primarily rights of privacy—are creations of state and not of federal law. Accordingly, they argue, petitioner may obtain money damages to redress invasion of these rights only by an action in tort, under state law, in the state courts. In this scheme the Fourth Amendment would serve merely to limit the extent to which the agents could defend the state law tort suit by asserting that their actions were a valid exercise of federal power: if the agents were shown to have violated the Fourth Amendment, such a defense would be lost to them and they would stand before the state law merely as private individuals. Candidly admitting that it is the policy of the Department of Justice to remove all such suits from the state to the federal courts for decision, respondents nevertheless urge that we uphold dismissal of petitioner's complaint in federal court, and remit him to filing an action in the state courts in order that the case may properly be removed to the federal court for decision on the basis of state law.

We think that respondents' thesis rests upon an unduly restrictive view of the Fourth Amendment's protection against unreasonable searches and seizures by federal agents, a view that has consistently been rejected by this Court. Respondents seek to treat the relationship between a citizen and a federal agent unconstitutionally exercising his authority as no different from the relationship between two private citizens. In so doing, they ignore the fact that power, once granted, does not disappear like a magic gift when it is wrongfully used. An agent acting—albeit unconstitutionally—in the name of the United States possesses a far greater capacity for harm than an individual trespasser exercising no authority other than his own. Cf. Amos v. United States, 255 U.S. 313, 317, 41 S.Ct. 266, 267–268, 65 L.Ed. 654 (1921); United States v. Classic, 313 U.S. 299, 326, 61 S.Ct. 1031, 1043, 85 L.Ed. 1368 (1941). Accordingly, as our cases make clear, the Fourth Amendment operates as a limitation upon the exercise of federal power regardless of whether the State in whose jurisdiction that power is exercised would prohibit or penalize the identical act if engaged in by a private citizen. * * *

First. Our cases have long since rejected the notion that the Fourth Amendment proscribes only such conduct as would, if engaged in by private persons, be condemned by state law. * * * Gambino v. United States, 275 U.S. 310, 48 S.Ct. 137, 72 L.Ed. 293 (1927) * * *.

Second. The interests protected by state laws regulating trespass and the invasion of privacy, and those protected by the Fourth Amendment's guarantee against unreasonable searches and seizures, may be inconsistent or even hostile. Thus, we may bar the door against an unwelcome private intruder, or call the police if he persists in seeking entrance. The availability of such alternative means for the protection of privacy may lead the State to restrict imposition of liability for any consequent trespass. A private citizen, asserting no authority other than his own, will not normally be liable in trespass if he demands, and is granted, admission to another's house. See W. Presser, THE LAW OF TORTS § 18, pp. 109–110 (3d ed., 1964); 1 F. Harper & F. James, The Law of Torts § 1.11 (1956). But one who demands admission under a claim of federal authority stands in a far different position. Cf. Amos v. United States, 255 U.S. 313, 317, 41 S.Ct. 266, 267–268, 65 L.Ed. 654 (1921). The mere invocation of federal power by a federal law enforcement official will normally render futile any attempt to resist an unlawful entry or arrest by resort to the local police; and a claim of authority to enter is likely to unlock the door as well. See Weeks v. United States, 232 U.S. 383, 386, 34 S.Ct. 341, 342, 58 L.Ed. 652 (1914); Amos v. United States, supra. "In such cases there is no safety for the citizen except in the protection of the judicial tribunals, for rights which have been invaded by the officers of the government, professing to act in its name. There remains to him but the alternative of resistance, which may amount to crime." United States v. Lee, 106 U.S. 196, 219, 1 S.Ct. 240, 259, 27 L.Ed. 171 (1882). Nor is it adequate to answer that state law may take into account the different status of one clothed with the authority of the Federal Government. For just as state law may not authorize federal agents to violate the Fourth Amendment, Weeks v. United States, supra; Ex parte Ayers, 123 U.S. 443, 507, 8 S.Ct. 164, 183–184, 31 L.Ed. 216 (1887), neither may state law undertake to limit the extent to which federal authority can be exercised. In re Neagle, 135 U.S. 1, 10 S.Ct. 658, 34 L.Ed. 55 (1890). * * *

Third. That damages may be obtained for injuries consequent upon a violation of the Fourth Amendment by federal officials should hardly seem a surprising proposition. Historically, damages have been regarded as the ordinary remedy for an invasion of personal interests in liberty. See Nixon v. Condon, 286 U.S. 73, 52 S.Ct. 484, 76 L.Ed. 984 (1932); Katz, *The Jurisprudence of Remedies: Constitutional Legality and the Law of Torts in* Bell v. Hood, 117 U.Pa.L.Rev. 1, 8–33 (1968). Of course, the Fourth Amendment does not in so many words provide for its enforcement by an award of money damages for the consequences of its violation. But "it is * * * well settled that where legal rights have been invaded, and a federal statute provides for a general right to sue for such invasion, federal courts may use any available remedy to make good the wrong done." Bell v. Hood, 327 U.S. at 684, 66 S.Ct., at 777 (footnote omitted.) The present case involves no special factors counseling hesitation in the absence of affirmative action by Congress. We are not dealing with a question of "federal fiscal policy," as in United States v. Standard Oil Co., 332 U.S. 301, 311, 67 S.Ct. 1604, 1609–1610, 91 L.Ed. 2067 (1947). In that case we refused to infer from the Government-soldier relationship that the United

States could recover damages from one who negligently injured a soldier and thereby caused the Government to pay his medical expenses and lose his services during the course of his hospitalization. Noting that Congress was normally quite solicitous where the federal purse was involved, we pointed out that "the United States [was] the party plaintiff to the suit. And the United States has power at any time to create the liability." Id. at 316, 67 S.Ct., at 1612; see United States v. Gilman, 347 U.S. 507, 74 S.Ct. 695, 98 L.Ed. 898 (1954). Nor are we asked in this case to impose liability upon a congressional employee for actions contrary to no constitutional prohibition, but merely said to be in excess of the authority delegated to him by the Congress. Wheeldin v. Wheeler, 373 U.S. 647, 83 S.Ct. 1441, 10 L.Ed.2d 605 (1963). Finally, we cannot accept respondents' formulation of the question as whether the availability of money damages is necessary to enforce the Fourth Amendment. For we have here no explicit congressional declaration that persons injured by a federal officer's violation of the Fourth Amendment may not recover money damages from the agents, but must instead be remitted to another remedy, equally effective in the view of Congress. The question is merely whether petitioner, if he can demonstrate an injury consequent upon the violation by federal agents of his Fourth Amendment rights, is entitled to redress his injury through a particular remedial mechanism normally available in the federal courts. * * * "The very essence of civil liberty certainly consists in the right of every individual to claim the protection of the laws, whenever he receives an injury." Marbury v. Madison, 1 Cranch 137, 163, 2 L.Ed. 60 (1803). Having concluded that petitioner's complaint states a cause of action under the Fourth Amendment, * * * we hold that petitioner is entitled to recover money damages for any injuries he has suffered as a result of the agents' violation of the Amendment.

* * *

Judgment reversed and case remanded.

MR. JUSTICE HARLAN, concurring in the judgment.

* * *

[T]he interest which Bivens claims—to be free from official conduct in contravention of the Fourth Amendment—is a federally protected interest. Therefore, the question of judicial *power* to grant Bivens damages is not a problem of the "source" of the "right"; instead, the question is whether the power to authorize damages as a judicial remedy for the vindication of a federal constitutional right is placed by the Constitution itself exclusively in Congress' hands.

The contention that the federal courts are powerless to accord a litigant damages for a claimed invasion of his federal constitutional rights until Congress explicitly authorizes the remedy cannot rest on the notion that the decision to grant compensatory relief involves a resolution of policy considerations not susceptible of judicial discernment. [We have, for example, implied damages remedies under federal statutes which lack an express provision for a cause of action. We have similarly implied injunctive remedies for constitutional violations, so there is nothing unique in the status of constitutional provisions that makes them inappropriate for implication of remedies.]

* * *

[The government's] arguments for a more stringent test to govern the grant of damages in constitutional cases seem to be adequately answered by the point that the judiciary has a particular responsibility to assure the vindication of constitutional interests such as those embraced by the Fourth Amendment. To be sure, "it must be remembered that legislatures are ultimate guardians of the liberties and welfare of the people in quite as great a degree as the courts." Missouri, Kansas & Texas R. Co. of Texas v. May, 194 U.S. 267, 270, 24 S.Ct. 638, 639, 48 L.Ed. 971 (1904). But it must also be recognized that the Bill of Rights is particularly intended to vindicate the interests of the individual in the face of the popular will as expressed in legislative majorities; at the very least, it strikes me as no more appropriate to await express congressional authorization of traditional judicial relief with regard to these legal interests than with respect to interests protected by federal statutes.

The question then, is, as I see it, whether compensatory relief is "necessary" or "appropriate" to the vindication of the interest asserted. In resolving that question, it seems to me that the range of policy considerations we may take into account is at least as broad as the range a legislature would consider with respect to an express statutory authorization of a traditional remedy. In this regard I agree with the Court that the appropriateness of according Bivens compensatory relief does not turn simply on the deterrent effect liability will have on federal official conduct. Damages as a traditional form of compensation for invasion of a legally protected interest may be entirely appropriate even if no substantial deterrent effects on future official lawlessness might be thought to result. Bivens, after all, has invoked judicial processes claiming entitlement to compensation for injuries resulting from allegedly lawless official behavior, if those injuries are properly compensable in money damages. I do not think a court of law—vested with the power to accord a remedy—should deny him his relief simply because he cannot show that future lawless conduct will thereby be deterred.

And I think it is clear that Bivens advances a claim of the sort that, if proved, would be properly compensable in damages. The personal interests protected by the Fourth Amendment are those we attempt to capture by the notion of "privacy"; while the Court today properly points out that the type of harm which officials can inflict when they invade protected zones of an individual's life are different from the types of harm private citizens inflict on one another, the experience of judges in dealing with private trespass and false imprisonment claims supports the conclusion that courts of law are capable of making the types of judgment concerning causation and magnitude of injury necessary to accord meaningful compensation for invasion of Fourth Amendment rights.

* * *

MR. CHIEF JUSTICE BURGER, dissenting.

I dissent from today's holding which judicially creates a damage remedy not provided for by the Constitution and not enacted by Congress. We would more surely preserve the important values of the doctrine of separation of powers—and perhaps get a better result—by recommending a solution to the Congress as the branch of government in which the Constitution has vested the legislative power. Legislation is the business of the Congress, and it has the facilities, and competence for that task—as we do not. * * *

* * *

MR. JUSTICE BLACK, dissenting.

In my opinion for the Court in Bell v. Hood, we did as the Court states, reserve the question whether an unreasonable search made by a federal officer in violation of the Fourth Amendment gives the subject of the search a federal cause of action for damages against the officers making the search. There can be no doubt that Congress could create a federal cause of action for damages for an unreasonable search in violation of the Fourth Amendment. Although Congress has created such a federal cause of action against *state* officials acting under color of state law, it has never created such a cause of action against federal officials. If it wanted to do so, Congress could, of course, create a remedy against federal officials who violate the Fourth Amendment in the performance of their duties. But the point of this case and the fatal weakness in the Court's judgment is that neither Congress nor the State of New York has enacted legislation creating such a right of action. For us to do so is, in my judgment, an exercise of power that the Constitution does not give us.

Even if we had the legislative power to create a remedy, there are many reasons why we should decline to create a cause of action where none has existed since the formation of our Government. The courts of the United States as well as those of the States are choked with lawsuits. The number of cases on the docket of this Court have reached an unprecedented volume in recent years. * * * Unfortunately, there have also been a growing number of frivolous lawsuits, particularly actions for damages against law enforcement officers whose conduct has been judicially sanctioned by state trial and appellate courts and in many instances even by this Court. * * * Of course, there are instances of legitimate grievances, but legislators might well desire to devote judicial resources to other problems of a more serious nature.

* * *

[JUSTICE BLACKMUN's dissenting opinion is omitted.]

NOTE ON DIRECT CONSTITUTIONAL CAUSES OF ACTION

1.   Consider the following syllogism: § 1983 is to 28 U.S.C.A. § 1343 as *Bivens* is to 28 U.S.C.A. § 1331. That is, the basis for original federal district court subject matter jurisdiction may vary with whether one presents a direct constitutional claim like *Bivens* or a § 1983 claim. The constitutional nature of the claim, however, remains the same.

(a)   At the time *Bivens* was decided, § 1331 authorized federal district courts to hear federal question claims only if the amount in controversy exceeded $10,000. That limitation has since been removed, allowing direct constitutional claims against federal officers into federal court on the same terms as § 1983 claims—regardless of the dollar amount at issue. Compare 28 U.S.C. § 1331 with 28 U.S.C. § 1343(3).

(b)   If the Court is willing to construe a grant of jurisdiction as also implying a cause of action, is § 1983 unnecessary, or even redundant? See Zehner v. Trigg, 133 F.3d 459 (7th Cir.1997). If § 1983 is narrower in some respect than the Fourteenth Amendment, can plaintiffs claim a direct, unlimited cause of action springing from the Amendment itself? See Turpin v. Mailet, 579 F.2d 152 (2d Cir.1978) (en banc) (pre-*Monell* decision sanctions direct constitutional claim against municipalities then exempt under § 1983). Is the only purpose of this fiction to avoid any statutory limitations in § 1983 itself (such as limitations on statutory liability for governments or availability of defenses)?

(c)   Should courts be able to create such causes of action when Congress has not acted? Is Congress' jurisdictional grant a slender reed upon which to build a judicial power to create substantive law? Cf. Textile Workers Union v. Lincoln Mills, 353 U.S. 448, 77 S.Ct. 912, 1 L.Ed.2d 972 (1957) (judge-made labor law created from jurisdictional grant). Is it easier for the Court to assume power in a case like *Bivens* because it is *constitutional* law that is at issue, the Court's traditional bailiwick since Marbury v. Madison? Cf. Wheeldin v. Wheeler, 373 U.S. 647, 650–52, 83 S.Ct. 1441, 10 L.Ed.2d 605 (1963) (refusal to create non-constitutional common law claim); see also Paul v. Davis, Chapter 1A supra.

2.   Note the government attorneys' representation in *Bivens* that they routinely remove all state-court suits against federal officials to federal court under 28 U.S.C.A. § 1442(a). If this practice is consistently followed, is the pertinent question not the availability of a federal forum but what law is applied?

(a)   Paragraph 1(c) above suggested that the Court snapped up some of Congress' power in *Bivens*. Was it not also state power upon which the Court intruded? If the government attorneys' position had been adopted, state law would have governed a plaintiff's claim even after removal, although the agents could use the legality of their actions under the Constitution as a defense. Are you persuaded of the need for federal (constitutional) law to govern not only defenses but also liability?

(b)   Is the desire for uniformity the strongest argument for *Bivens*? Would not such uniformity have been in the agents' interest, too? Or do the agents not achieve some uniformity under their removal scenario—states may never expect more of them than the Fourth Amendment permits, but may expect less?

3. Perhaps the pertinent issue in *Bivens* is not whether the Court has usurped either Congress' or the states' power to make law, but whether the Court is competent to create a *damage* remedy.

(a) Note Justice Harlan's concurring opinion in which he points to the "presumed availability of federal equitable relief" to vindicate constitutional rights. Why is the availability of injunctive relief presumed? Because there must be some remedy for the right created? Because federal courts—or at least the Supreme Court—must be able to order future compliance or its role as supreme arbiter is lost?

(b) If injunctive relief is available, is there any reason not to grant a damage remedy as well? Should not damages be a preferred remedy because they are less intrusive than an injunction, as the Court held in Los Angeles v. Lyons, Chapter 1F.2 supra?

(c) In the years soon after *Bivens*, the Court twice implied new direct constitutional claims, one in the *Passman* case, which follows this Note, and the other in Carlson v. Green, 446 U.S. 14, 100 S.Ct. 1468, 64 L.Ed.2d 15 (1980) (implied damage claim under the Eighth Amendment for federal prisoner). In the same period, during the late 1960's to 1980, the Court was also active in expanding (and setting) the contours of § 1983 as it applied to state officials, see Chapter 1B supra. Were *Bivens* and its subsequent iterations just an outgrowth of the Court's experience—or drive—in § 1983 cases?

4. Two important legacies remain from the *Bivens* decision, and each has greatly affected the subsequent manner in which the Court has considered direct constitutional claims. First, notice the subtle difference between the decisionmaking processes of the majority and Justice Harlan: whereas the majority seems to expect a direct constitutional claim to follow for all constitutional rights, Justice Harlan appears to consider a prudential judgment—an almost legislative judgment—to be necessary before any particular constitutional claim for damages can be recognized. The second legacy of *Bivens* is its acknowledgment that a direct constitutional claim might be displaced by legislation providing "another remedy, equally effective in the view of Congress." What did the Court mean?

DAVIS v. PASSMAN

Supreme Court of the United States, 1979.
442 U.S. 228, 99 S.Ct. 2264, 60 L.Ed.2d 846.

* * *

I

At the time this case commenced, respondent Otto E. Passman was a United States Congressman from the Fifth Congressional District of Louisiana. On February 1, 1974, Passman hired petitioner Shirley Davis as a deputy administrative assistant. Passman subsequently terminated her employment, effective July 31, 1974, writing Davis that, although she was an "able, energetic and a very hard worker," he had concluded "that it was essential that the understudy to my Administrative Assistant be a man."

Davis brought suit in the United States District Court for the Western District of Louisiana, alleging that Passman's conduct discriminated against her "on the basis of sex in violation of the United States Constitution and the Fifth Amendment thereto." Davis sought damages in the form of backpay.[11] * * *

[The Supreme Court found that the Fifth Amendment's equal-protection principles provided plaintiff with a right to be free from gender discrimination, a right which the lower courts had also acknowledged. The Court of Appeals, however, had refused to recognize a direct cause of action to enforce such a right.]

* * * The Court of Appeals reached this conclusion through the application of the criteria set out in Cort v. Ash, 422 U.S. 66, 95 S.Ct. 2080, 45 L.Ed.2d 26 (1975), for ascertaining whether a private cause of action may be implied from "a statute not expressly providing one." Id. at 78, 95 S.Ct., at 2088. The Court of Appeals used these criteria to determine that those in petitioner's position should not be able to enforce the Fifth Amendment's Due Process Clause, and that petitioner therefore

---

11. Respondent argues that the subject matter of petitioner's suit is nonjusticiable because judicial review of congressional employment decisions would necessarily involve a "lack of respect due coordinate branches of government." Baker v. Carr, 369 U.S. 186, 217, 82 S.Ct. 691, 710, 7 L.Ed.2d 663 (1962). We disagree. While we acknowledge the gravity of respondent's concerns, we hold that judicial review of congressional employment decisions is constitutionally limited only by the reach of the Speech or Debate Clause of the Constitution, Art. I, § 6, cl. 1. The Clause provides that Senators and Representatives, "for any Speech or Debate in either House, * * * shall not be questioned in any other Place." It protects Congressmen for conduct necessary to perform their duties "within the 'sphere of legitimate legislative activity.'" Eastland v. United States Servicemen's Fund, 421 U.S. 491, 501, 95 S.Ct. 1813, 1820, 44 L.Ed.2d 324 (1975). The purpose of the Clause is "to protect the integrity of the legislative process by insuring the independence of individual legislators." United States v. Brewster, 408 U.S. 501, 507, 92 S.Ct. 2531, 2535, 33 L.Ed.2d 507 (1972). Thus "[i]n the American governmental structure, the clause serves the * * * function of reinforcing the separation of powers so deliberately established by the Founders." United States v. Johnson, 383 U.S. 169, 178, 86 S.Ct. 749, 754, 15 L.Ed.2d 681 (1966). The Clause is therefore a paradigm example of "a textually demonstrable constitutional commitment of [an] issue to a coordinate political department." Baker v. Carr, supra, at 217, 82 S.Ct., at 710. Since the Speech or Debate Clause speaks so directly to the separation of powers concerns raised by respondent, we conclude that if respondent is not shielded by the Clause, the question whether his dismissal of petitioner violated her Fifth Amendment rights would, as we stated in Powell v. McCormack, 395 U.S. 486, 89 S.Ct. 1944, 23 L.Ed.2d 491 (1969), "require no more than an interpretation of the Constitution. Such a determination falls within the traditional role accorded courts to interpret the law, and does not involve a 'lack of respect due [a] coordinate branch of government,' nor does it involve an 'initial policy determination of a kind clearly for non-judicial discretion.' Baker v. Carr, 369 U.S. 186, at 217, 82 S.Ct. 691, at 710." 395 U.S., at 548–549, 89 S.Ct., at 1978.

The en banc Court of Appeals did not decide whether the conduct of respondent was shielded by the Speech or Debate Clause. In the absence of such a decision, we also intimate no view on this question. We note, however, that the Clause shields federal legislators with absolute immunity "not only from the consequences of litigation's results, but also from the burden of defending themselves." Dombrowski v. Eastland, 387 U.S. 82, 85, 87 S.Ct. 1425, 1427, 18 L.Ed.2d 577 (1967). Defenses based upon the Clause should thus ordinarily be given priority, since federal legislators should be exempted from litigation if their conduct is in fact protected by the Clause. [Repositioned footnote]

had no cause of action under the Amendment. This was error, for the question of who may enforce a *statutory* right is fundamentally different than the question of who may enforce a right that is protected by the Constitution.

Statutory rights and obligations are established by Congress, and it is entirely appropriate for Congress, in creating these rights and obligations, to determine in addition who may enforce them and in what manner.

[But constitutionally based rights are different.]

At least in the absence of "a textually demonstrable constitutional commitment of [an] issue to a coordinate political department," Baker v. Carr, supra, we presume that justiciable constitutional rights are to be enforced through the courts. And, unless such rights are to become merely precatory, the class of those litigants who allege that their own constitutional rights have been violated, and who at the same time have no effective means other than the judiciary to enforce these rights, must be able to invoke the existing jurisdiction of the courts for the protection of their justiciable constitutional rights. "The very essence of civil liberty," wrote Chief Justice Marshall in Marbury v. Madison, 5 U.S. 137, 163, 1 Cranch 137, 163, 2 L.Ed. 60 (1803), "certainly consists in the right of every individual to claim the protection of the laws, whenever he receives an injury. One of the first duties of government is to afford that protection." * * *

* * *

Although petitioner has a cause of action, her complaint might nevertheless be dismissed under Rule 12(b)(6) unless it can be determined that judicial relief is available. We therefore proceed to consider whether a damages remedy is an appropriate form of relief.

* * * *Bivens,* supra, holds that in appropriate circumstances a federal district court may provide relief in damages for the violation of constitutional rights if there are "no special factors counseling hesitation in the absence of affirmative action by Congress." Id. 403 U.S. at 396, 91 S.Ct., at 2005.

First, a damages remedy is surely appropriate in this case. "Historically, damages have been regarded as the ordinary remedy for an invasion of personal interests in liberty." *Bivens.* Relief in damages would be judicially manageable, for the case presents a focused remedial issue without difficult questions of valuation or causation. See id. (Harlan, J., concurring in judgment). Litigation under Title VII of the Civil Rights Act of 1964 has given federal courts great experience evaluating claims for backpay due to illegal sex discrimination. [See Chapter 7, infra.] Moreover, since respondent is no longer a Congressman, see n. 1, supra, equitable relief in the form of reinstatement would be unavailing. And there are available no other alternative forms of judicial relief. For Davis, as for *Bivens,* "it is damages or nothing." *Bivens,* supra. (Harlan, J., concurring in judgment).

Second, although a suit against a Congressman for putatively unconstitutional actions taken in the course of his official conduct does raise special concerns counseling hesitation, we hold that these concerns are coextensive with the protections afforded by the Speech or Debate Clause. See n. 11, supra. If respondent's actions are not shielded by the Clause, we apply the principle that "legislators ought generally to be bound by [the law] as are ordinary persons." Gravel v. United States, 408 U.S. 606, 615, 92 S.Ct. 2614, 2622, 33 L.Ed.2d 583 (1972). * * *

Third, there is in this case "no *explicit* congressional declaration that persons" in petitioner's position injured by unconstitutional federal employment discrimination "may not recover money damages from" those responsible for the injury. *Bivens,* supra, at 397. (Emphasis supplied.) The Court of Appeals apparently interpreted § 717 of Title VII of the Civil Rights Act of 1964, 86 Stat. 111, 42 U.S.C.A. § 2000e–16 [Chapter 7 infra], as an explicit congressional prohibition against judicial remedies for those in petitioner's position. When § 717 was added to Title VII to protect federal employees from discrimination, it failed to extend this protection to congressional employees such as petitioner who are not in the competitive service. See 42 U.S.C.A. § 2000e–16(a). There is no evidence, however, that Congress meant § 717 to foreclose alternative remedies available to those not covered by the statute. * * *

Finally, the Court of Appeals appeared concerned that, if a damages remedy were made available to petitioner, the danger existed "of deluging federal courts with claims * * *." 571 F.2d at 800. We do not perceive the potential for such a deluge. By virtue of 42 U.S.C.A. § 1983, a damages remedy is already available to redress injuries such as petitioner's when they occur under color of state law. Moreover, a plaintiff seeking a damages remedy under the Constitution must first demonstrate that his constitutional rights have been violated. We do not hold that every tort by a federal official may be redressed in damages. See Wheeldin v. Wheeler, 373 U.S. 647, 83 S.Ct. 1441, 10 L.Ed.2d 605 (1963). And, of course, were Congress to create equally effective alternative remedies, the need for damages relief might be obviated. See *Bivens,* supra. * * *

* * *

The judgment of the Court of Appeals is reversed and the case is remanded for further proceedings consistent with this opinion.

So ordered.

Mr. Chief Justice Burger, with whom Mr. Justice Powell and Mr. Justice Rehnquist join, dissenting.

I dissent because, for me, the case presents very grave questions of separation of powers, rather than Speech or Debate Clause issues, although the two have certain common roots. Congress could, of course, make *Bivens* type remedies available to its staff employees—and to other congressional employees—but it has not done so. On the contrary. Congress has historically treated its employees differently from the arrangements for other Government employees. Historically, staffs of Members have been considered so intimately a part of the policymaking and political process that they are not subject to being selected, compensated or tenured as others who serve the Government. The vulnerability of employment on congressional staffs derives not only from the hazards of elections but from the imperative need for loyalty, confidentiality and political compatibility—not to a political party, an institution, or an administration, but to the individual Member.

* * *

At this level of government—staff assistants of Members—long accepted concepts of separation of powers dictate, for me, that until Congress legislates otherwise as to employment standards for its own staffs, judicial power in this area is circumscribed. The Court today encroaches on that barrier. Cf. *Sinking Fund Cases,* 99 U.S. 700, 9 Otto 700, 718, 25 L.Ed. 496 (1878).

MR. JUSTICE POWELL, with whom THE CHIEF JUSTICE and MR. JUSTICE REHNQUIST join, dissenting.

Although I join the opinion of THE CHIEF JUSTICE, I write separately to emphasize that no prior decision of this Court justifies today's intrusion upon the legitimate powers of Members of Congress.

The Court's analysis starts with the general proposition that "the judiciary is clearly discernible as the primary means through which [constitutional] rights may be enforced," *ante,* at 13. It leaps from this generalization, unexceptionable itself, to the conclusion that individuals who have suffered an injury to a constitutionally protected interest, and who lack an "effective" alternative, "*must* be able to invoke the existing jurisdiction of the courts for the protection of their justiciable constitutional rights." Id. at 14 (emphasis supplied). Apart from the dubious logic of this reasoning, I know of no precedent of this Court that supports such an absolute statement of the federal judiciary's obligation to entertain private suits that Congress has not authorized. On the contrary, I have thought it clear that federal courts must exercise a principled discretion when called upon to infer a private cause of action directly from the language of the Constitution. In the present case, for reasons well summarized by THE CHIEF JUSTICE, principles of comity and separation of powers should require a federal court to stay its hand.

* * *

[JUSTICE STEWART'S opinion in favor of remanding the case for consideration of the applicability of the Speech or Debate Clause is omitted.]

NOTE ON LIMITS OF AND DEFENSES TO CONSTITUTIONAL CLAIMS

1. In the years immediately following *Bivens* lower federal courts received such claims hospitably. See Lehman, Bivens *and Its Progeny: The Scope of a Constitutional Cause of Action for Torts Committed by Government*

Officials, 4 HAST. CONST. L.Q. 531, 566–72 & nn. 226 & 229 (1977) (claims permitted under a variety of constitutional provisions). Yet even as it created another direct constitutional claim in *Passman,* the Court acknowledged that there might be limitations on its creation of damage claims and that there might be defenses to such claims. What is the source of law for such limitations and defenses?

2. The argument for a discretionary exception to *Bivens,* that is, a judicial power to decline to imply an automatic remedy for damages, finally won the Court's attention in **Chappell v. Wallace**, 462 U.S. 296, 103 S.Ct. 2362, 76 L.Ed.2d 586 (1983), in which the Court unanimously refused to authorize a *Bivens* suit by enlisted personnel who sued their commanding officers for racial discrimination in job assignments. The Court, speaking through Chief Justice Burger, stated that *Bivens* had always recognized an exception when "special factors" were present—here, control over the military and its command structure.

(a) What is the difference between the factors in *Passman* and those in *Chappell*? Had a private citizen claimed that military officers had discriminatorily taken property or used excessive force, would the special factors relied on in *Chappell* bar a constitutional damage claim?[1]

(b) Justice Powell's dissent in *Passman* is quite receptive to exceptions, echoing themes from Justice Harlan's opinion in *Bivens*. He argues that *Bivens*-type claims should only be created in the Court's "principled discretion," and that intrusion onto congressional staffing prerogatives counseled restraint in this case. Do you agree? If the restraint is based on "principle," what is the principle? Is it a constitutionally influenced—even if not specifically mandated—principle? Does even Justice Brennan in *Passman* admit that such discretionary factors might be appropriate to consider? What is there about the structure of his opinion that sends a signal to lower-court judges that they should seldom find these factors relevant? See Brown, *Letting Statutory Tails Wag Constitutional Dogs—Have the Bivens Dissenters Prevailed?,* 64 IND.L.REV. 263 (1989) (discussing difference between implied claims under statutes and those under Constitution).[2]

(c) In more recent years *Bivens* claims have met a warier Court, permits reflecting the movement toward greater reticence in implying claims generally. Cf. Chapter 6D.1 infra. In **Wilkie v. Robbins**, 551 U.S. 537, 127 S.Ct. 2588, 168 L.Ed.2d 389 (2007), the plaintiff claimed that officers of the Bureau of Land Management had harassed and intimidated him to force him to give the government a free easement, a claim the Court assumed would amount to a constitutional violation of his property rights. Reviewing its precedents and calling the *Bivens* damages remedy "not an automatic entitlement," the Court declared that such cases call for the "weighing reasons for and against the creation of a new cause of action, the way common law judges have always

---

1. Compare Collins v. Bender, 195 F.3d 1076 (9th Cir.1999) (*Bivens* claim for personnel actions not permitted, but claim for illegal search and seizure allowed because not a personnel action).

2. Is introduction of legislative discretion into *Bivens*-type cases subject to attack from a conservative direction? See Carlson v. Green, 446 U.S. 14, 31–54, 100 S.Ct. 1468, 1478–90, 64 L.Ed.2d 15 (1980) (Rehnquist, J., dissenting). Would the cure be to rule out discretion, or to stop implying any direct constitutional action for damages?

done." Ultimately, Justice Souter's majority opinion concluded that because some government inducement to grant an easement is legal and some is not, a claim should not be recognized because of "line-drawing difficulties." Justice Ginsburg's dissent noted that line-drawing is always a problem in law, but did not justify the six-year reign of harassment in this case. Who has the better argument on the merits? Could the plaintiff have sued for an injunction against the unconstitutional acts? If so, wouldn't the same "line-drawing difficulties" be present?

3. Creation of direct constitutional claims would also be greatly curtailed, as the Court noted in *Bivens,* if an otherwise-implied constitutional claim were displaced by legislation providing "another remedy, equally effective in the view of Congress." (*Passman* uses a shorter phrase, "equally effective alternative remedies.") Is this similar to the issue discussed earlier with respect to § 1983's "and laws" language? See the Note following Maine v. Thiboutot, Chapter 1I supra. Is it similar to the displacement of § 1983 by other more particularized statutes protecting constitutional rights? See the *Schweicker* case following this Note.

4. *Bivens*-type actions could also be restricted by recognition of countervailing defenses. Some of these are constitutionally based. The *Passman* decision referred to, but found inapplicable, the Speech or Debate Clause of Article I, § 6. There are also others.

(a) The scope of the Speech or Debate Clause as a constitutional defense was revisited shortly after *Passman* in **Hutchinson v. Proxmire**, 443 U.S. 111, 99 S.Ct. 2675, 61 L.Ed.2d 411 (1979), which confined the defense to "legislative activities" and held that defamatory press releases were not protected. *Hutchinson* involved a state-law defamation claim, but would its reasoning not be equally applicable to direct constitutional claims?

(b) In **Nixon v. Fitzgerald**, 457 U.S. 731, 102 S.Ct. 2690, 73 L.Ed.2d 349 (1982), the Court held that the President was absolutely immune from direct constitutional claims for damages. Although there is no explicit protection for the President that is equivalent to the Speech or Debate Clause, the Court based its decision again on constitutional considerations, alluding to our "constitutional tradition" and to the "President's unique status under the Constitution." In **Clinton v. Jones**, 520 U.S. 681, 117 S.Ct. 1636, 137 L.Ed.2d 945 (1997) (unanimous), the Court found such principles inapplicable to a claim not involving official functions of the presidential office. Do you agree?

(c) What other constitutional defenses might defeat a *Bivens*-type claim? See, e.g., the Note on Intent and Causation, Chapter 1B.5 supra.

5. The Court has found no constitutional basis for immunities for lower level federal officers, but it has constructed them nevertheless. In **Butz v. Economou**, 438 U.S. 478, 98 S.Ct. 2894, 57 L.Ed.2d 895 (1978), the Court held that official immunities, like those developed for use in § 1983 actions, were equally applicable to direct constitutional claims against federal officers. The trial court had authorized absolute immunity for federal discretionary officials, but the Court rejected that position. In deciding that federal officers were to receive immunities no greater than those of their peers in state government, the Court reasoned that to "create a system in which the Bill of

Rights monitors more closely the conduct of state officials than it does that of federal officials is to stand the constitutional design on its head."

(a) Did the Court in *Butz* overlook an even more fundamental issue: granted that federal officials should not receive more protection than state officials, why should they receive any immunity at all? Was not the theory of Pierson v. Ray that Congress intended in § 1983 to preserve common law immunities? Since these are implied constitutional claims, there is no possibility to attribute these defenses to Congress; is it not the Court itself which is legislating these immunities? (Recall that some of the cases read in Chapter 1 were in fact claims against federal officers. See, e.g., Harlow v. Fitzgerald, Chapter 1D.3 supra.)

(b) If the official immunities recognized in *Butz* came from judicial policymaking, do they not represent a triumph for the Harlan–Powell approach to judicially legislating the appropriateness of direct constitutional claims? (In retrospect, were the immunities developed for § 1983 cases not also judicially legislated?)

(c) Should exhaustion of administrative remedies be required as a prerequisite for *Bivens* claims against federal officials? See McCarthy v. Madigan, 503 U.S. 140, 112 S.Ct. 1081, 117 L.Ed.2d 291 (1992) (no for claims against prison officials).

6. A sovereign immunity defense, largely paralleling that created for state treasuries under the Eleventh Amendment, and read into § 1983 in Will v. Michigan, Chapter 1H.2 supra, has also been created to protect the federal treasury. The rules are summarized in **Larson v. Domestic & Foreign Commerce Corp.**, 337 U.S. 682, 69 S.Ct. 1457, 93 L.Ed. 1628 (1949), and discussed in Abernathy, *Sovereign Immunity in a Constitutional Government,* 10 Harv.C.R.–C.L.L.Rev. 322 (1975).

(a) Like state sovereign immunity cases, the law developed here allows suits against officers alleged to have violated federal constitutional rights. See Dugan v. Rank, 372 U.S. 609, 620–21, 83 S.Ct. 999, 10 L.Ed.2d 15 (1963).

(b) Nevertheless certain forms of relief are prohibited, specifically those calling for payments from the federal treasury or disposition of property claimed by the government. See Larson, supra at 691 n. 11. Is this exception coextensive with that recognized for states in Edelman v. Jordan, Chapter 1H.2 supra? Should it be?

(c) The Supreme Court in F.D.I.C. v. Meyer, 510 U.S. 471, 114 S.Ct. 996, 127 L.Ed.2d 308 (1994), held that a *Bivens* claim does not override this traditional immunity defense so as to permit suits against federal agencies., noting that "the purpose of *Bivens* is to deter *the officer*, not the agency" (emphasis in original). Therefore, a claim, if any, exists only against governmental officials. Does the Court have constitutional power to imply a remedy directly against governmental agencies? Are its rules in this area an exercise of constitutional power or statutory power? Or even interstitial statutory power?

SCHWEIKER v. CHILICKY

Supreme Court of the United States, 1988.
487 U.S. 412, 108 S.Ct. 2460, 101 L.Ed.2d 370.

JUSTICE O'CONNOR delivered the opinion of the Court.

This case requires us to decide whether the improper denial of Social Security disability benefits, allegedly resulting from violations of due process by government officials who administered the Federal Social Security program, may give rise to a cause of action for money damages against those officials. We conclude that such a remedy, not having been included in the elaborate remedial scheme devised by Congress, is unavailable.

[Plaintiffs had lost disability benefits due them under the federal Social Security Act, allegedly because of procedural due process violation in the termination of their previously awarded benefits. Federal officials had allegedly encouraged the denial of benefits through its "continuing disability review" (CDR) process, a complicated system of forcing beneficiaries to establish their eligibility repeatedly. Each plaintiff had actually sought and recovered a retroactive award of benefits under procedures made available by the Social Security Act itself, but the Act provided no damages for the emotional distress that the plaintiffs had suffered during their periods of lost benefits. The Court gave a very sympathetic description of the widespread economic and social distress that resulted from the defendants' alleged wrongdoing.]

Our more recent decisions have responded cautiously to suggestions that *Bivens* remedies be extended into new contexts. The absence of statutory relief for a constitutional violation, for example, does not by any means necessarily imply that courts should award money damages against the officers responsible for the violation. Thus, in Chappell v. Wallace, 462 U.S. 296, 103 S.Ct. 2362, 76 L.Ed.2d 586 (1983), we refused—unanimously—to create a *Bivens* action for enlisted military personnel who alleged that they had been injured by the unconstitutional actions of their superior officers and who had no remedy against the Government itself:

> "The special nature of military life—the need for unhesitating and decisive action by military officers and equally disciplined responses by enlisted personnel—would be undermined by a judicially created remedy exposing officers to personal liability at the hands of those they are charged to command * * * *"

* * *

Similarly, we refused—again unanimously—to create a *Bivens* remedy for a First Amendment violation "aris[ing] out of an employment relationship that is governed by comprehensive procedural and substantive provisions giving meaningful remedies against the United States." Bush v. Lucas, 462 U.S. 367, 368, 103 S.Ct. 2404, 2406, 76 L.Ed.2d 648 (1983). * * * The Court stressed that the case involved policy questions in an area that had received careful attention from Congress. Noting that the Legislature is far more competent than the Judiciary to carry out the necessary "balancing [of] governmental efficiency and the rights of employees," we refused to "decide whether or not it would be good policy to permit a federal employee to recover damages from a supervisor who has improperly disciplined him for exercising his First Amendment rights."

In sum, the concept of "special factors counseling hesitation in the absence of affirmative action by Congress" has proved to include an appropriate judicial deference to indications that congressional inaction has not been inadvertent. When the design of a government program suggests that Congress has provided what it considers adequate remedial mechanisms for constitutional violations that may occur in the course of its administration, we have not created additional *Bivens* remedies.

B

The administrative structure and procedures of the Social Security system, which affects virtually every American, "are of a size and extent difficult to comprehend." Richardson v. Perales, 402 U.S. 389, 399, 91 S.Ct. 1420, 1426, 28 L.Ed.2d 842 (1971). Millions of claims are filed every year under the Act's disability benefits programs alone, and these claims are handled under "an unusually protective [multi]-step process for the review and adjudication of disputed claims." Heckler v. Day, 467 U.S. 104, 106, 104 S.Ct. 2249, 2251, 81 L.Ed.2d 88 (1984).

[The Court described the various steps of administrative review available under the Social Security Act. These are supplemented by a right to judicial review in the federal district court. The Act specifically includes a right to assert constitutional complaints. Nevertheless, the Act provides only for retroactive benefits awards, not damages for any violations of statutory or constitutional rights.]

The case before us cannot reasonably be distinguished from Bush v. Lucas. Here, exactly as in *Bush,* Congress has failed to provide for "complete relief": respondents have not been given a remedy in damages for emotional distress or for other hardships suffered because of delays in their receipt of Social Security benefits. The creation of a *Bivens* remedy would obviously offer the prospect of relief for injuries that must now go unredressed. Congress, however, has not failed to provide meaningful safeguards or remedies for the rights of persons situated as respondents were. Indeed, the system for protecting their rights is, if anything, considerably more elaborate than the civil service system considered in *Bush.* The prospect of personal liability for official acts, moreover, would undoubtedly lead to new difficulties and expense in recruiting administrators for the programs Congress has established. Congressional competence at "balancing governmental efficiency and the rights of [individuals]," *Bush,* is no more questionable in the social welfare context than it is in the civil service context.

Congressional attention to problems that have arisen in the administration of CDR (including the very problems that gave rise to this case) has, moreover, been frequent and intense. See, *e.g.,* H.R.Rep. No. 98–618, pp. 2, 4 (1984); S.Rep. No. 98–466, pp. 10, 17–18 (1984), U.S. Code Cong. & Admin.News 1984, p. 3038. Congress itself required that the CDR program be instituted. Within two years after the program began, Congress enacted emergency legislation providing for the continuation of benefits even after a finding of ineligibility by a state agency. Less than two years after passing that law, and fully aware of the results of extensive investigations of the practices that led to respondents' injuries, Congress again enacted legislation aimed at reforming the administration of CDR; that legislation again specifically addressed the problem that had provoked the earlier emergency legislation. At each step, Congress chose specific forms and levels of protection for the rights of persons affected by incorrect eligibility determinations under CDR. At no point did Congress choose to extend to any person the kind of remedies that respondents seek in this lawsuit. Cf. 130 Cong.Rec. H1960–1961 (Mar. 27, 1984) (Rep. Perkins) (expressing regret that the bill eventually enacted as the 1984 Reform Act did not provide additional relief for persons improperly terminated during the early years of CDR). Thus, congressional unwillingness to provide consequential damages for unconstitutional deprivations of a statutory right is at least as clear in the context of this case as it was in *Bush.*

* * *

[W]e, declined in *Bush* " 'to create a new substantive legal liability ...' because we are convinced that Congress is in a better position to decide whether or not the public interest would be served by creating it." 462 U.S., at 390, 103 S.Ct., at 2417 (citation omitted). That reasoning applies as much, or more, in this case as it did in *Bush* itself.

* * *

In the end, respondents' various arguments are rooted in their insistent and vigorous contention that they simply have not been adequately recompensed for their injuries. They say, for example:

> "Respondents are disabled workers who were dependent upon their Social Security benefits when petitioners unconstitutionally terminated them. Respondents needed those benefits, at the time they were wrongfully withheld, to purchase food, shelter, medicine, and life's other necessities. The harm they suffered as a result bears no relation to the dollar amount of the benefits unjustly withheld from them. For the Government to offer belated restoration of back benefits in a lump sum and attempt to call it quits, after respondents have suffered deprivation for months on end, is not only to display gross insensitivity to the damage done to respondents' lives, but to trivialize the seriousness of petitioners' offense." Brief for Respondents 11.

We agree that suffering months of delay in receiving the income on which one has depended for the very necessities of life cannot be fully remedied by the "belated restoration of back benefits." The trauma to respondents, and thousands of others like them, must surely have gone beyond what anyone of normal sensibilities would wish to see imposed on innocent disabled citizens. Nor would we care to "trivialize" the nature of the wrongs alleged in this case. Congress, however, has addressed the problems created by state agencies' wrongful termination of disability benefits. Whether or not we believe that its response was the best response, Congress is the body charged with making the inevitable compromises required in the design of a massive and complex welfare benefits program. Cf. Dandridge v. Williams, 397 U.S. 471, 487, 90 S.Ct. 1153, 1162, 25 L.Ed.2d 491 (1970). Congress has discharged that responsibility to the extent that it affects the case before us, and we see no legal basis that would allow us to revise its decision.[3]

Because the relief sought by respondents is unavailable as a matter of law, the case must be dismissed. The judgment of the Court of Appeals to the contrary is therefore

Reversed.

JUSTICE STEVENS, concurring in part and concurring in the judgment. [Omitted]

JUSTICE BRENNAN, with whom JUSTICE MARSHALL and JUSTICE BLACKMUN join, dissenting.

* * *

I agree that in appropriate circumstances we should defer to a congressional decision to substitute alternative relief for a judicially created remedy. Neither the design of Title II's administrative review process, however, nor the debate surrounding its reform contain any suggestion that Congress meant to preclude recognition of a *Bivens* action for persons whose constitutional rights are violated by those charged with administering the program, or that Congress viewed this process as an adequate

---

3. The Solicitor General contends that Congress has explicitly precluded the creation of a *Bivens* remedy for respondents' claims. Cf. *Bivens.* His argument rests on 42 U.S.C. § 405(h) (1982 ed. Supp. III), which provides:

"The findings and decision of the Secretary after a hearing shall be binding upon all individuals who were parties to such hearing. No findings of fact or decision of the Secretary shall be reviewed by any person, tribunal, or governmental agency except as herein provided. No action against the United States, the Secretary, or any officer or employee thereof shall be brought under section 1331 or 1346 of title 28 to recover on any claim arising under [Title II]." Relying on Heckler v. Ringer, 466 U.S. 602, 614–616, 620–626, 104 S.Ct. 2013, 2021–2022, 2024–2028, 80 L.Ed.2d 622 (1984), and Weinberger v. Salfi, 422 U.S. 749, 756–762, 95 S.Ct. 2457, 2462–2465, 45 L.Ed.2d 522 (1975), the Solicitor General has previously argued that the third sentence of this provision prevents any exercise of general federal-question jurisdiction under § 1331. See Bowen v. Michigan Academy of Family Physicians, 476 U.S. 667, 679, 106 S.Ct. 2133, 2140, 90 L.Ed.2d 623 (1986). Without deciding the question, we noted that arguments could be made for and against the Solicitor General's position. We continue to believe that the exact scope of the third sentence's restriction on federal-question jurisdiction is not free from doubt; because we hold on other grounds that a *Bivens* remedy is precluded in this case, we need not decide whether § 405(h) would have the same effect.

substitute remedy for such violations. Indeed, Congress never mentioned, let alone debated, the desirability of providing a statutory remedy for such constitutional wrongs. Because I believe legislators of "normal sensibilities" would not wish to leave such traumatic injuries unrecompensed, I find it inconceivable that Congress meant by mere silence to bar all redress for such injuries.

* * *

Here, as the legislative history of the 1984 Reform Act makes abundantly clear, Congress did not attempt to achieve a delicate balance between the constitutional rights of Title II beneficiaries on the one hand, and administrative concerns on the other. Rather than fine-tuning "an elaborate remedial scheme that ha[d] been constructed step by step" over the better part of a century, Congress confronted a paralyzing breakdown in a vital social program, which it sought to rescue from near-total anarchy. * * *

* * *

At no point during the lengthy legislative debate, however, did any Member of Congress so much as hint that the substantive eligibility criteria, notice requirements, and interim payment provisions that would govern *future* disability reviews adequately redressed the harms that beneficiaries may have suffered as a result of the unconstitutional actions of individual state and federal officials in *past* proceedings, or that the constitutional rights of those unjustly deprived of benefits in the past had to be sacrificed in the name of administrative efficiency or any other governmental interest. The Court today identifies no legislative compromise, "inevitable" or otherwise, in which lawmakers expressly declined to afford a remedy for such past wrongs. Nor can the Court point to any legislator who suggested that state and federal officials should be shielded from liability for any unconstitutional acts taken in the course of administering the review program, or that exposure to liability for such acts would be inconsistent with Congress' comprehensive and carefully crafted remedial scheme.

Although the Court intimates that Congress consciously chose not to afford any remedies beyond the prospective protections set out in the 1984 Reform Act itself, the one legislator the Court identifies as bemoaning the Act's inadequate response to past wrongs argued only that the legislation should have permitted all recipients, including those whose benefits were terminated before December 31, 1984, to seek a redetermination of their eligibility under the new review standards. See 130 Cong.Rec. H1961 (Mar. 27, 1984) (remarks of Rep. Perkins). Neither this legislator nor any other, however, discussed the possibility or desirability of redressing injuries flowing from the temporary loss of benefits in those cases where the benefits were ultimately restored on administrative appeal. The possibility that courts might act in the absence of congressional measures was never even discussed, let alone factored into Congress' response to the emergency it faced.

* * *

NOTE ON CONGRESSIONAL DETERMINATION OF "EQUALLY ADEQUATE" ALTERNATIVE REMEDIES

1. *Schweiker* holds that a federal statute, in order to suffice as an alternative capable of displacing direct constitutional claims, need not provide all the relief that would otherwise be available from the *Bivens*-type claim. In judging whether an alternative is "equally adequate," the Court decides that a strong measure of deference is due to a Congress that "has provided what it considers to be adequate remedial mechanisms for constitutional violations."

(a) Does Congress receive deference in this situation because it actually considered damage remedies and refused to adopt them? Or because it so seriously studied remedies that we can be sure that its "inaction [in providing a full remedy] has not been inadvertent"? Put differently, does Congress receive deference only when it explicitly rules out a full remedy? Or deference also when it closely considers its remedy, even though it does not indicate a conscious choice of a limited remedy?

(b) Does the majority approach convert "the special factors exception [in]to an expansive loophole"? See Nichol, Bivens, Chilicky, *and Constitutional Damages Claims,* 75 U.VA.L.REV. 1117, 1149 (1989). Or is it just an exercise of discretion with which you may disagree? Is that the problem with discretion as a basis for lawmaking?

(c) Do you agree with Justice Brennan's approach? Should a congressional remedy only be deemed exclusive when Congress has explicitly indicated such a choice? He took that position in Carlson v. Green, 446 U.S. 14, 100 S.Ct. 1468, 64 L.Ed.2d 15 (1980), where he persuaded the Court to imply a damage remedy for a federal prisoner even though a remedy already existed under the federal Tort Claims Act. Why did he lose his majority in *Chilicky*?

(d) Is implication of a damages remedy especially troublesome whenever the remedy would control the actions of officials implementing a federal grant program? See Carpenter's Produce v. Arnold, 189 F.3d 686 (8th Cir.1999) (administrative remedies under disaster relief laws preclude implication of constitutional claim for damages for racial discrimination). Is it also a problem when the remedy would control a private grantee acting under color of federal law? See Correctional Services Corp. v. Malesko, 534 U.S. 61, 122 S.Ct. 515, 151 L.Ed.2d 456 (2001) (yes because plaintiffs will seek to recover from the entity, lessening the deterrent effect of a remedy on the individual wrongdoer).

2. Is Justice Brennan's opinion slightly disingenuous when he demands an explicit congressional alternative before he will abandon a *Bivens* action? Do you believe that Congress really left open the *Bivens* option in this case?

(a) Have the Court and Justice Brennan sandbagged themselves by their own past actions? Can the Court seriously condemn Congress for failing to provide complete damage remedies for all constitutional actions when the

Court itself has adopted several defenses that preclude damage remedies? Reconsider official immunities and sovereign immunity available to both state and federal officers and governments: if Congress' remedy is inadequate in this case, is not the Court's set of remedies inadequate every time one of these defenses results in the dismissal of a constitutional claim?

(b) On the other hand, the difficulty of determining whether a patchwork of other remedies constitutes an adequate alternative is demonstrated in **Wilkie v. Robbins**, 551 U.S. 537, 127 S.Ct. 2588, 168 L.Ed.2d 389 (2007), the landowner-harassment suit discussed in the previous Note. There the Court reviewed the various tort, administrative, and even criminal remedies available to the plaintiff for the multiple harassing actions occurring over a six-year period. It was ultimately unable to decide whether any one or a combination of these would have been effective in deterring the defendants campaign of "a thousand cuts." It ultimately avoided the issue by deciding the case on other grounds. Should indeterminism in the availability of a remedy cut the other way, so that only the certainty of an effective alternative precludes a *Bivens* suit?

(c) For a rare example of a situation where Congress has explicitly provided for an alternative remedy, see **Hui v. Castaneda**, ___ U.S. ___, 130 S.Ct. 1845, 176 L.Ed.2d 703 (2010). In that case, involving a claim against Public Health Service personnel, a unanimous Court held that an explicit provision in the Federal Tort Claims Act immunizing "any" PHS personnel from "claims" and making the FTCA "exclusive" explicitly barred a *Bivens* action. Of course, the FTCA remedy remained available.

3.   When Congress has provided virtually *any* remedy, is the Court institutionally incapable of challenging that decision because any contrary decision by the Court would look like arbitrary line-drawing? Compare Coleman v. Miller, 307 U.S. 433, 59 S.Ct. 972, 83 L.Ed. 1385 (1939) (opinion of Hughes, C.J.) (judges cannot decide whether constitutional amendment has grown too stale to be ratified because they lack standards to draw such lines), with Mahan v. Howell, 410 U.S. 315, 93 S.Ct. 979, 35 L.Ed.2d 320 (1973) (court will approve reapportionment variations of up to 16%, but strongly suggested this is the limit).

(a) In **Chappell v. Wallace**, 462 U.S. 296, 103 S.Ct. 2362, 76 L.Ed.2d 586 (1983) (also discussed in the previous Note), the Court explained that, in addition to the special considerations of military life, it would also take into account that federal statutes provided a comprehensive system of military justice. See 462 U.S. at 300–303. No remedy under that system provided specifically for the recovery of damages. Did it nevertheless provide an "equally effective" remedy?

(b) In a companion case decided the same day as *Chappell,* the Court also refused to create a direct constitutional claim for an aerospace engineer who claimed that his superiors had retaliated against him for exercising his free speech rights. **Bush v. Lucas**, 462 U.S. 367, 103 S.Ct. 2404, 76 L.Ed.2d 648 (1983). The Court pointed to the existence of an elaborate civil service system that provided administrative and judicial remedies for abuse of employees, including backpay awards. While it admitted that these were "not as completely effective" as a claim for damages, it nevertheless found them to be "clearly constitutionally adequate." 462 U.S. at 379 & n. 14, 103 S.Ct. at 2412 & n. 14. Should the Court defer to Congress on the adequacy of its alternative remedies?

(c) Was the problem in *Passman,* excerpted earlier in this sub-chapter, that Congress had provided absolutely no remedies for complaints against its members?

4. Is it fair to say that the period of *Bivens* activism is dead, and has been for some years? In **Correctional Services Corp. v. Malesko**, 534 U.S. 61, 122 S.Ct. 515, 151 L.Ed.2d 456 (2001), the Court refused to imply a *Bivens*-type remedy against private persons acting under color of federal law, overturning the Second Circuit's creation of a remedy for such claims. The Court relied, in part, on the availability of ordinary tort remedies in refusing to extend *Bivens.* What the Court said in reviewing its precedents, however, seemed far more important than the holding itself, 534 U.S. at 69–70:

"Since [1980] we have consistently refused to extend *Bivens* liability to any new context or new category of defendants. * * * "

"In 30 years of *Bivens* jurisprudence we have extended its holding only twice, to provide an otherwise nonexistent cause of action against individual officers alleged to have acted unconstitutionally, or to provide a cause of action for a plaintiff who lacked any alternative remedy for harms caused by an individual officer's unconstitutional conduct. Where such circumstances are not present, we have consistently rejected invitations to extend *Bivens* * * *."

(a) In retrospect, was the *Bivens–Passman–Carlson* trio of cases, decided in the decade from 1971–1980, itself an anomaly in an otherwise unbroken string of refusals to get involved in implying constitutional remedies? Is *Bivens* the exception and not the rule? See also ¶ 2 supra. Alternatively, was *Bivens* actually a great success? In the cases in which the Court later refused to imply a remedy, it was because Congress itself had created some alternative method for protecting constitutional rights. Are all these alternative remedies the sweet fruit of an "alternative dispute resolution" process? Are courts the only protectors of constitutional rights?

(b) But reconsider now the issue raised in the previous Note. *Bivens* may not apply because either (i) an alternative remedy is available or (ii) the Court decides in its common law discretion not to create a remedy. Should the second factor exist? What is a plaintiff to do if there is no alternative remedy and the Court decides not to offer a damages remedy? Does the assumption that a Constitution-based injunction is always available not become critical? Review *Bivens* supra.

(c) Even before the decision in *Correctional Services Corp.,* there was substantial evidence that *Bivens* was a shell, with little actual impact in terms of success for plaintiffs' litigators. See Cornelia T.L. Pillard, *Taking Fiction Seriously: The Strange Results of Public Officials' Individual Liability under* Bivens, 88 GEO. L. J. 65 (1999). Professor Pillard's review, id. at 65–66 found the following:

"*Bivens* has * * * proved to be a surreptitiously progovernment decision. Although it appears to provide a mechanism for remedying constitutional violations, its application has rarely led to damages recoveries. Government figures reflect that, out of approximately 12,000 *Bivens* claims filed between 1971 and 1985, *Bivens* plaintiffs actually obtained a judgment that was not reversed on appeal in only four cases."

Was the *Bivens* effort worth the results? Viewed through the lens of legal realism, did *Bivens* ever really exist?

5.   Should Congress draft a comprehensive statutory provision for protecting against constitutional violations? What should it say?

(a) Should a statute for federal constitutional violations mimic § 1983? Or are there many federal interests, such as the military or intelligence agencies that are too sensitive for challenge with damage actions? Cf. Tenet v. Doe, 544 U.S. 1, 125 S.Ct. 1230, 161 L.Ed.2d 82 (2005) (suits by spies against government to enforce terms of claimed spying contract are forbidden by century-old common-law rule disallowing such claims).

(b) In the absence of such a federal statute, how do *Bivens* actions—from implication of claims to defenses—differ from the law established under § 1983? See Rosen, *The* Bivens *Constitutional Tort: An Unfulfilled Promise,* 67 N. CAR. L. REV. 337 (1989) (cataloguing ways in which law under *Bivens* does not measure up to § 1983). Should *Bivens* claims be different because they implicate separation-of-powers concerns not present in § 1983 cases? Or are these concerns no greater than the federalism concerns that have affected § 1983?

PART THREE

SECOND RECONSTRUCTION AND BEYOND—THE CIVIL RIGHTS ACTS, 1964 TO PRESENT

■ ■ ■

TITLE II OF THE CIVIL RIGHTS ACT OF 1964—PUBLIC ACCOMMODATIONS AND CONGRESSIONAL POWER UNDER THE COMMERCE CLAUSE

■ ■ ■

HEART OF ATLANTA MOTEL, INC. v. UNITED STATES

Supreme Court of the United States, 1964.
379 U.S. 241, 85 S.Ct. 348, 13 L.Ed.2d 258.

MR. JUSTICE CLARK delivered the opinion of the Court.

* * *

1. The Factual Background and Contentions of the Parties.

The case comes here on admissions and stipulated facts. Appellant owns and operates the Heart of Atlanta Motel which has 216 rooms available to transient guests. The motel is located on Courtland Street, two blocks from downtown Peachtree Street. It is readily accessible to interstate highways 75 and 85 and state highways 23 and 41. Appellant solicits patronage from outside the State of Georgia through various national advertising media, including magazines of national circulation; it maintains over 50 billboards and highway signs within the State, soliciting patronage for the motel; it accepts convention trade from outside Georgia and approximately 75% of its registered guests are from out of State. Prior to passage of [Title II of the Civil Rights Act of 1964] the motel had followed a practice of refusing to rent rooms to Negroes, and it alleged that it intended to continue to do so. In an effort to perpetuate that policy this suit was filed[, claiming that the Act exceeded Congress' power under the Commerce Clause, Art. I, § 8, cl. 3.]

* * *

At the trial the appellant offered no evidence, submitting the case on the pleadings, admissions and stipulation of facts; however, appellees proved the refusal of the motel to accept Negro transients after the passage of the Act. The District Court sustained the constitutionality of the sections of the Act under attack (§§ 201(a), (b)(1) and (c)(1)) and issued a permanent injunction on the counterclaim of the appellees. It restrained the appellant from "[r]efusing to accept Negroes as guests in the motel by reason of their race or color" and from "[m]aking any distinction whatever upon the basis of race or color in the availability of the goods, services, facilities, privileges, advantages or accommodations offered or made available to the guests of the motel, or to the general public, within or upon any of the premises of the Heart of Atlanta Motel, Inc."

* * *

3. Title II of the Act.

This Title is divided into seven sections beginning with § 201(a) which provides that:

> "All persons shall be entitled to the full and equal enjoyment of the goods, services, facilities, privileges, advantages, and accommodations of any place of public accommodation, as defined in this section, without discrimination or segregation on the ground of race, color, religion, or national origin."

There are listed in § 201(b) four classes of business establishments, each of which "serves the public" and "is a place of public accommodation" within the meaning of § 201(a) "if its operations affect commerce, or if discrimination or segregation by it is supported by State action." The covered establishments are [hotels and lodging places, restaurants, places of entertainment, and all other establishments in which one of the above is located. Each of the four has its own test for "affecting commerce," the test for hotels being that they "affect commerce per se."]

4. Application of Title II to Heart of Atlanta Motel.

It is admitted that the operation of the motel brings it within the provisions of § 201(a) of the Act and that appellant refused to provide lodging for transient Negroes because of their race or color and that it intends to continue that policy unless restrained.

The sole question posed is, therefore, the constitutionality of the Civil Rights Act of 1964 as applied to these facts. The legislative history of the Act indicates that Congress based the Act on § 5 and the Equal Protection Clause of the Fourteenth Amendment as well as its power to regulate interstate commerce under Art. I, § 8, cl. 3, of the Constitution. [Finding the latter power adequate, we find it unnecessary to examine § 5 of the Fourteenth Amendment.] * * *

6. The Basis of Congressional Action.

While the Act as adopted carried no congressional findings the record of its passage through each house is replete with evidence of the burdens that discrimination by race or color places upon interstate commerce. See Hearings before Senate Committee on Commerce on S. 1732, 88th Cong.,

1st Sess.; S.Rep. No. 872, [88th Cong., 2d Sess.]; Hearings before Senate Committee on the Judiciary on S. 1731, 88th Cong., 1st Sess.; Hearings before House Subcommittee No. 5 of the Committee on the Judiciary on miscellaneous proposals regarding Civil Rights, 88th Cong., 1st Sess., ser. 4; H.R.Rep. No. 914, [88th Cong., 1st Sess.]. This testimony included the fact that our people have become increasingly mobile with millions of people of all races traveling from State to State; that Negroes in particular have been the subject of discrimination in transient accommodations, having to travel great distances to secure the same; that often they have been unable to obtain accommodations and have had to call upon friends to put them up overnight, S.Rep. No. 872, supra, at 14–22; and that these conditions had become so acute as to require the listing of available lodging for Negroes in a special guidebook which was itself "dramatic testimony to the difficulties" Negroes encounter in travel. Senate Commerce Committee Hearings, supra, at 692–694. These exclusionary practices were found to be nationwide, the Under Secretary of Commerce testifying that there is "no question that this discrimination in the North still exists to a large degree" and in the West and Midwest as well. Id. at 735, 744. This testimony indicated a qualitative as well as quantitative effect on interstate travel by Negroes. The former was the obvious impairment of the Negro traveler's pleasure and convenience that resulted when he continually was uncertain of finding lodging. As for the latter, there was evidence that this uncertainty stemming from racial discrimination had the effect of discouraging travel on the part of a substantial portion of the Negro community. Id. at 744. This was the conclusion not only of the Under Secretary of Commerce but also of the Administrator of the Federal Aviation Agency who wrote the Chairman of the Senate Commerce Committee that it was his "belief that air commerce is adversely affected by the denial to a substantial segment of the traveling public of adequate and desegregated public accommodations." Id. at 12–13. We shall not burden this opinion with further details since the voluminous testimony presents overwhelming evidence that discrimination by hotels and motels impedes interstate travel.

7. The Power of Congress Over Interstate Travel.

The power of Congress to deal with these obstructions depends on the meaning of the Commerce Clause. Its meaning was first enunciated 140 years ago by the great Chief Justice John Marshall in Gibbons v. Ogden, 9 Wheat. 1, 6 L.Ed. 23 (1824), in these words:

> " * * * * It is the power to regulate; that is, to prescribe the rule by which commerce is to be governed. This power, like all others vested in Congress, is complete in itself, may be exercised to its utmost extent, and acknowledges no limitations, other than are prescribed in the constitution. * * * If, as has always been understood, the sovereignty of Congress * * * is plenary as to those objects [specified in the Constitution], the power over commerce * * * is vested in Congress as absolutely as it would be in a single govern-

ment, having in its constitution the same restrictions on the exercise of the power as are found in the constitution of the United States. The wisdom and the discretion of Congress, their identity with the people, and the influence which their constituents possess at elections, are, in this, as in many other instances, as that, for example, of declaring war, the sole restraints on which they have relied, to secure them from its abuse. They are the restraints on which the people must often rely solely, in all representative governments. * * * "

In short, the determinative test of the exercise of power by the Congress under the Commerce Clause is simply whether the activity sought to be regulated is "commerce which concerns more States than one" and has a real and substantial relation to the national interest. Let us now turn to this facet of the problem.

That the "intercourse" of which the Chief Justice spoke included the movement of persons through more States than one was settled as early as 1849, in the Passenger Cases (Smith v. Turner), 7 How. 283, 12 L.Ed. 702, * * *. Nor does it make any difference whether the transportation is commercial in character. [Caminetti v. United States, 242 U.S. 470, 484–86, 37 S.Ct. 192, 194–195, 61 L.Ed. 442 (1917)]. * * *

* * *

The same interest in protecting interstate commerce which led Congress to deal with segregation in interstate carriers and the white-slave traffic has prompted it to extend the exercise of its power to gambling, Lottery Case (Champion v. Ames), 188 U.S. 321, 23 S.Ct. 321, 47 L.Ed. 492 (1903) [and at least thirteen other social problems covered by federal securities, antitrust, minimum wage, labor-union, crop-control, and other laws.]

That Congress was legislating against moral wrongs in many of these areas rendered its enactments no less valid. In framing Title II of this Act Congress was also dealing with what it considered a moral problem. But that fact does not detract from the overwhelming evidence of the disruptive effect that racial discrimination has had on commercial intercourse. It was this burden which empowered Congress to enact appropriate legislation, and, given this basis for the exercise of its power, Congress was not restricted by the fact that the particular obstruction to interstate commerce with which it was dealing was also deemed a moral and social wrong.

It is said that the operation of the motel here is of a purely local character. But, assuming this to be true "[i]f it is interstate commerce that feels the pinch, it does not matter how local the operation which applies the squeeze." United States v. Women's Sportswear Mfg. Ass'n, 336 U.S. 460, 464, 69 S.Ct. 714, 716, 93 L.Ed. 805 (1949). See National Labor Relations Board v. Jones & Laughlin Steel Corp., [301 U.S. 1, 57 S.Ct. 615, 81 L.Ed. 893 (1937)]. As Chief Justice Stone put it in United States v. Darby, [312 U.S. 100, 61 S.Ct. 451, 85 L.Ed. 609 (1941)]:

"The power of Congress over interstate commerce is not confined to the regulation of commerce among the states. It extends to those activities intrastate which so affect interstate commerce or the exercise of the power of Congress over it as to make regulation of them appropriate means to the attainment of a legitimate end, the exercise of the granted power of Congress to regulate interstate commerce. See McCulloch v. Maryland, 4 Wheat. 316, 421, 4 L.Ed. 579." 312 U.S. at 118, 61 S.Ct. at 459.

Thus the power of Congress to promote interstate commerce also includes the power to regulate the local incidents thereof, including local activities in both the States of origin and destination, which might have a substantial and harmful effect upon that commerce. One need only examine the evidence which we have discussed above to see that Congress may—as it has—prohibit racial discrimination by motels serving travelers, however "local" their operations may appear.

* * *

Affirmed.

MR. JUSTICE BLACK, concurring.

* * *

It requires no novel or strained interpretation of the Commerce Clause to sustain Title II as applied in either of these cases. At least since Gibbons v. Ogden, 9 Wheat. 1, 6 L.Ed. 23, decided in 1824 in an opinion by Chief Justice John Marshall, it has been uniformly accepted that the power of Congress to regulate commerce among the States is plenary, "complete in itself, may be exercised to its utmost extent, and acknowledges no limitations, other than are prescribed in the constitution." 9 Wheat. at 196. * * *

Furthermore, it has long been held that the Necessary and Proper Clause, Art. I, § 8, cl. 18, adds to the commerce power of Congress the power to regulate local instrumentalities operating within a single State if their activities burden the flow of commerce among the States. [Shreveport Case, Houston, E. & W.T.R. Co. v. United States, 234 U.S. 342, 353–354, 34 S.Ct. 833, 837, 58 L.Ed. 1341 (1914)] * * *.

MR. JUSTICE DOUGLAS, concurring.[a]

I.

Though I join the Court's opinions, I am somewhat reluctant here, as I was in Edwards v. People of State of California, 314 U.S. 160, 177, 62 S.Ct. 164, 168, 86 L.Ed. 119 to rest solely on the Commerce Clause. My reluctance is not due to any conviction that Congress lacks power to regulate commerce in the interests of human rights. It is rather my belief that the right of people to be free of state action that discriminates against them because of race, like the "right of persons to move freely from State

a. [Justice Goldberg concurred on similar grounds.]

to State" (Edwards v. People of State of California, supra, at 177, 62 S.Ct. at 169), "occupies a more protected position in our constitutional system than does the movement of cattle, fruit, steel and coal across state lines." Ibid. * * *

Hence I would prefer to rest on the assertion of legislative power contained in § 5 of the Fourteenth Amendment which states: "The Congress shall have power to enforce, by appropriate legislation, the provisions of this article"—a power which the Court concedes was exercised at least in part in this Act.

* * *

My [minority] opinion last Term in Bell v. State of Maryland, [set out in the Note on State Neutrality as Private Action, Chapter 1C supra] makes clear my position that the right to be free of discriminatory treatment (based on race) in places of public accommodation—whether intrastate or interstate—is a right guaranteed against state action by the Fourteenth Amendment and that state enforcement of the kind of trespass laws which Maryland had in that case was state action within the meaning of the Amendment.

* * *

KATZENBACH v. McCLUNG

Supreme Court of the United States, 1964.
379 U.S. 294, 85 S.Ct. 377, 13 L.Ed.2d 290.

[This companion case to *Heart of Atlanta* came to the Court on the government's appeal from a district court's injunction against application of Title II to Ollie's Barbecue, a small family-owned restaurant in Birmingham, Alabama, which catered to "family and white collar trade with a take-out service for Negroes." Located 11 blocks from the nearest interstate highway, the restaurant admitted that it came under the statutory commerce test prescribed for restaurants—a substantial portion of its food supplies, though bought locally, had been procured by the wholesaler from outside the state. The district court had found the statutory coverage of Ollie's Barbecue unconstitutional, but the Supreme Court reversed, stressing Congress' finding of facts.]

The record is replete with testimony of the burdens placed on interstate commerce by racial discrimination in restaurants. A comparison of per capita spending by Negroes in restaurants, theaters, and like establishments indicated less spending, after discounting income differences, in areas where discrimination is widely practiced. This condition, which was especially aggravated in the South, was attributed in the testimony of the Under Secretary of Commerce to racial segregation. See Hearings before the Senate Committee on Commerce on S. 1732, 88th Cong., 1st Sess., 695. This diminutive spending springing from a refusal to serve Negroes and their total loss as customers has, regardless of the absence of direct evidence, a close connection to interstate commerce. The fewer customers a restaurant enjoys the less food it sells and consequently the less it buys. S.Rep. No. 872, 88th Cong., 2d Sess., at 19; Senate Commerce Committee Hearings, at 207. In addition, the Attorney General testified that this type of discrimination imposed "an artificial restriction on the market" and interfered with the flow of merchandise. Id. at 18–19; also, on this point, see testimony of Senator Magnuson, 110 Cong.Rec. 7402–7403. In addition, there were many references to discriminatory situations causing wide unrest and having a depressant effect on general business conditions in the respective communities. See, e.g., Senate Commerce Committee Hearings, at 623–630, 695–700, 1384–1385.

Moreover there was an impressive array of testimony that discrimination in restaurants had a direct and highly restrictive effect upon interstate travel by Negroes. This resulted, it was said, because discriminatory practices prevent Negroes from buying prepared food served on the premises while on a trip, except in isolated and unkempt restaurants and under most unsatisfactory and often unpleasant conditions. This obviously discourages travel and obstructs interstate commerce for one can hardly travel without eating. Likewise, it was said that discrimination deterred professional, as well as skilled, people from moving into areas where such practices occurred and thereby caused industry to be reluctant to establish there. S.Rep. No. 872, supra, at 18–19.

We believe that this testimony afforded ample basis for the conclusion that established restaurants in such areas sold less interstate goods because of the discrimination, that interstate travel was obstructed directly by it, that business in general suffered and that many new businesses refrained from establishing there as a result of it. Hence the District Court was in error in concluding that there was no connection between discrimination and the movement of interstate commerce. The court's conclusion that such a connection is outside "common experience" flies in the face of stubborn fact.

It goes without saying that, viewed in isolation, the volume of food purchased by Ollie's Barbecue from sources supplied from out of state was insignificant when compared with the total foodstuffs moving in commerce. But, as our late Brother Jackson said for the Court in Wickard v. Filburn, 317 U.S. 111, 63 S.Ct. 82, 87 L.Ed. 122 (1942):

> "That [the] appellee's own contribution to the demand for wheat may be trivial by itself is not enough to remove him from the scope of federal regulation where, as here, his contribution, taken together with that of many others similarly situated, is far from trivial." At 127–128, 63 S.Ct. at 90.

We noted in *Heart of Atlanta Motel* that a number of witnesses attested to the fact that racial discrimination was not merely a state or regional problem but was one of nationwide scope. Against this background, we must conclude that while the focus of the legislation was on the individual restaurant's relation to interstate commerce, Congress appropriately considered the importance of that connection with the knowledge that the discrimination was but "representative of many others throughout the country, the total incidence of which if left unchecked may well become far-reaching in its harm to commerce." Polish National Alliance of U.S. v. National Labor Relations Board, 322 U.S. 643, 648, 64 S.Ct. 1196, 1199, 88 L.Ed. 1509 (1944).

* * *

The appellees contend that Congress has arbitrarily created a conclusive presumption that all restaurants meeting the criteria set out in the Act "affect commerce." Stated another way, they object to the omission of a provision for a case-by-case determination—judicial or administrative—that racial discrimination in a particular restaurant affects commerce.

But Congress' action in framing this Act was not unprecedented. In United States v. Darby, 312 U.S. 100, 61 S.Ct. 451, 85 L.Ed. 609 (1941), this Court held constitutional the Fair Labor Standards Act of 1938. There Congress determined that the payment of substandard wages to employees engaged in the production of goods for commerce, while not itself commerce, so inhibited it as to be subject to federal regulation. The appellees in that case argued, as do the appellees here, that the Act was invalid because it included no provision for an independent inquiry regarding the effect on commerce of substandard wages in a particular business. But the Court rejected the argument, observing that:

> "[Sometimes] Congress itself has said that a particular activity affects the commerce, as it did in the present Act, the Safety Appliance Act * * * and the Railway Labor Act * * *. In passing on the validity of legislation of the class last mentioned the only function of courts is to determine whether the particular activity regulated or prohibited is within the reach of the federal power." At 120–121, 61 S.Ct. at 460.

Here, as there, Congress has determined for itself that refusals of service to Negroes have imposed burdens both upon the interstate flow of food and upon the movement of products generally. Of course, the mere fact that Congress has said when particular activity shall be deemed to affect commerce does not preclude further examination by this Court. But where we find that the legislators, in light of the facts and testimony before them, have a rational basis for finding a chosen regulatory scheme necessary to the protection of commerce, our investigation is at an end. * * *

* * *

Reversed.

NOTE ON TITLE II AND CONGRESS' COMMERCE CLAUSE POWER

1. Title II has been little litigated in recent years because its goal has been widely achieved and because the resuscitation of §§ 1981 and 1982 has left the newer statute, with its notice-requirement and restrictive relief, in disfavor among plaintiffs. To what extent are Title II and §§ 1981 and 1982 coextensive in the topics or bases of discrimination covered? Which is wider?

(a) Sections 204(c) and (d) of Title II, 42 U.S.C.A. § 2000a–3(c) & (d), require plaintiffs to exhaust available state remedies for 30 days before initiating suit. If no such remedies are available, the court may stay an action and refer the plaintiff to the federal Community Relations Service for handling. As these above provisions suggest, the goal of the Title was to achieve voluntary compliance, a factor which also drove Congress to limit plaintiffs to "preventive relief," a phrase which the Court has indicated excludes damages. Newman v. Piggie Park Enterprises, Inc., 390 U.S. 400, 401–02, 88 S.Ct. 964, 965–67, 19 L.Ed.2d 1263 (1968). Should Congress expand the relief available? Except for remedy, do §§ 1981 and 1982 completely overlap Title II, making changes unnecessary?

(b) Section 207 of Title II provides that the "remedies provided in this [Title] shall be the exclusive means of enforcing the rights based on this [Title], but nothing in this [Title] shall preclude any individual or any State or local agency from asserting any right based on any other Federal or State law" or local ordinances. In **United States v. Johnson**, 390 U.S. 563, 88 S.Ct. 1231, 20 L.Ed.2d 132 (1968), the Court held that this provision precluded criminal prosecution under 18 U.S.C.A. § 241 of restaurant proprietors (who are subject to Title II) but not "outside hoodlums" (who are not). The Court read the exclusive-remedy provision as saving only proprietors by ensuring that there would be an advance determination of coverage for each individual restauranteur before punitive sanctions, such as contempt of court, could be applied. Does the *Johnson* case suggest that a suit under § 1985(3) might be brought against "outsiders"? See Chapter 3B supra.

2. The important legacy of Title II has been the Supreme Court decisions sustaining the use of Congress' commerce clause power to protect civil rights, a power also used to enact the most important provision of the 1964 Act, Title VII's prohibition on employment discrimination. (See Chapter 7 infra). How wide is that power? *Heart of Atlanta,* with its strong evidence of the defendant's catering to interstate traffic, presented the easiest factual situation which could have come before the Court.

(a) The traditional post–1937 prerequisite for the exercise of commerce clause power has been the showing of a nexus between the problem Congress wishes to correct and interstate commerce. Is *Heart of Atlanta* an easy case because factually the motel's catering to interstate commerce and refusing to serve blacks showed the commerce connection in sharp perspective? Notice that Title II covers all hotels, regardless of their individual impact on commerce. Can the statute be applied to a hotel serving no interstate travelers at all? Could the question be answered by referring to *McClung* and its invocation of the aggregation principle of Wickard v. Filburn? When there is no impact can Congress do any "totaling up"?

(b) Alternatively consider *McClung*'s invocation of the class legislation principle of United States v. Darby. See Perez v. United States, 402 U.S. 146, 152, 91 S.Ct. 1357, 1360, 1361, 28 L.Ed.2d 686 (1971); cf. Westfall v. United States, 274 U.S. 256, 259, 47 S.Ct. 629, 630, 71 L.Ed. 1036 (1927) (Holmes, J.: "When it is necessary in order to prevent an evil to make the law embrace more than the precise thing to be prevented it may do so.") Is the *Darby* rule applicable here? Is its conception of the commerce power too broad?

3. Given the tremendous expansion of interstate activities over the last several decades, the vast interrelation of markets in the United States, and the availability of the *Wickard* and *Darby* techniques noted above, is there any limit to Congress' power under the commerce clause? This paragraph discusses limits when Congress seeks to regulate private persons. (The next paragraph covers regulation of states.) With respect to private persons, the Supreme Court has created a substantial hurdle to continued federal regulation of intrastate activities that are claimed to have an effect on interstate commerce. In **United States v. Lopez**, 514 U.S. 549, 115 S.Ct. 1624, 131 L.Ed.2d 626 (1995), the Supreme Court struck down a federal statute regulating guns that had not themselves been shown to pass in interstate commerce, and in **United States v. Morrison**, 529 U.S. 598, 120 S.Ct. 1740, 146 L.Ed.2d 658 (2000), the Court used *Lopez*'s principles to strike down a federal statute (the Violence Against Women Act) regulating sex-based violence against women. (The latter case was the first to invalidate a modern federal civil rights statute.)

(a) In *Morrison*, the Court faced a statute that gave persons harmed by gender-motivated violence a remedy against the private persons who committed the violent acts, regardless of whether the persons had moved in interstate commerce. The government sought to justify the Act on the ground that such sex-based violence, or the cumulative effects of it, had a substantial affect on interstate commerce. Among several factors, the Court emphasized these: (i) the activity in question, violence, was itself "non-economic" or not necessarily related to economic activity; and (ii) the effects on interstate business were so attenuated that this "effects of crime" argument would validate any and all federal regulation—an unacceptable result given the to define federal power and protect reserved state police powers. Would these observations equally undercut Title II?

(b) The *Morrison* Court liberally sprinkled its decision with citations to *Heart of Atlanta* and *McClung*, and it noted that it was not undercutting or overturning those decisions, which remain in good standing. Can you rationalize the new decision with the older cases? Was the Court afraid to take on the older cases, or did it perhaps see no benefit from undertaking the fight given the ease of supporting Title II, as applied to race, under the Thirteenth Amendment?

(c) Are *Heart of Atlanta Motel* and *McClung* in fact much easier cases because the defendants' activities are "economic" and involve no traditional state functions, such as definition of interpersonal crimes or family status? And was there not a definitional requirement of interstate commerce in *McClung*? And aren't hotels, especially chain hotels that advertise interstate, also easily seen as connected to interstate commerce? Are the older cases not in fact easily distinguishable from *Morrison*?

4. The Court has more recently also limited Congress' ability to legislate directly to regulate states themselves under the Commerce Clause, at least in one major respect relevant here. In **Alden v. Maine**, 527 U.S. 706, 119 S.Ct. 2240, 144 L.Ed.2d 636 (1999), the Supreme Court held that even when Congress may otherwise have power to regulate states under the Commerce Clause, it lacks constitutional power to abrogate a state's immunity to suit—

either in federal or state court. In **Florida Prepaid Postsecondary Education Expense Board v. College Savings Bank,** 527 U.S. 627, 119 S.Ct. 2199, 144 L.Ed.2d 575 (1999), decided the same day, the Court ruled that states could be subjected to suit for their violations of the Fourteenth Amendment, but it held that alleged false advertising of a state-sponsored college-savings plan could not reasonably be seen as a violation of the Fourteenth Amendment. (This issue is treated in greater historical detail in Chapter 8 infra.)

(a) Do the *Alden* and *Florida Prepaid* cases represent any significant threat to traditional civil rights legislation? For the traditional grounds of discrimination covered by Title II—all high-level scrutiny categories under the Fourteenth Amendment, it would be unnecessary to use the Commerce Clause to regulate states (*Alden* inapplicable) and there would be undoubted power under the Fourteenth Amendment (*Florida Prepaid* inapplicable).

(b) The Court has already held that Congress can adopt legislation under the Fourteenth Amendment to expand the remedies for women. **Nevada Department of Human Resources v. Hibbs**, 538 U.S. 721, 123 S.Ct. 1972, 155 L.Ed.2d 953 (2003), involved the federal Family and Medical Leave Act, which generally required states to give both male and female employees leave after the birth of a child. Chief Justice Rehnquist's majority opinion upheld the statute, finding that by giving equal leave to men and women parents, it properly cured the long history of sex discrimination in state employment, especially the sex stereotypes created by state leave policies that applied only to women. As applied to states, therefore, the uncovered area between *Morrison* and *Hibbs* appears to be sex discrimination that is not a constitutional violation (e.g., no state action, lack of intentional discrimination). Is this a significant range of problems? Can any non-coverage be cured by use of the federal Spending Power, Chapter 6 infra?

(c) For other topics that have newly-acquired status of high-level protection under the Fourteenth Amendment, the issues raised in paragraph (b) seem equally relevant. **Lawrence v. Texas**, 539 U.S. 558, 123 S.Ct. 2472, 156 L.Ed.2d 508 (2003), would suggest congressional power to legislate protection for homosexual rights in the sense of sexual activity. But *Lawrence* was not an Equal Protection case. Can Congress legislate protection for sexual orientation outside the area of sexuality? Can Congress outlaw discrimination against state school teachers based on sexual orientation?

(d) Regarding disability discrimination, the picture is less clear. In **Board of Trustees of the University of Alabama v. Garrett**, 531 U.S. 356, 121 S.Ct. 955, 148 L.Ed.2d 866 (2001), the Court held that Congress may not impose higher-than-constitutional duties on states absent a historical record of irrational discrimination (—the lower standard applicable to state-sponsored disability classifications). The absence of a Fourteenth Amendment violation also led to a finding of no congressional power to abrogate state sovereign immunity. On the other hand, in **U.S. v. Georgia**, 546 U.S. 151, 126 S.Ct. 877, 163 L.Ed.2d 650 (2006), the Supreme Court held that to the extent that any violations of federal disability-protection statutes also state constitutional violations, they may proceed to trial and sovereign immunity is validly abrogated. Do the pair of cases suggest that some disability-protecting legislation aimed at the states is permissible and some is not?[1]

---

1. What other topics might fit the same pattern as disability discrimination? See Kimel v. Florida Bd. of Regents, 528 U.S. 62, 120 S.Ct. 631, 145 L.Ed.2d 522 (2000) (age discrimination). Are there others?

CHAPTER 6

TITLE VI AND ITS ANALOGUES—CIVIL RIGHTS AS A REGULATORY REGIME

■ ■ ■

Beginning with Title VI of the Civil Rights Act of 1964, 42 U.S.C.A. § 2000d, Congress passed a series of civil rights statutes designed to eradicate discrimination in the United States by ensuring that public and private programs receiving federal grants are operated in a non-discriminatory manner. Section 601 of the Act, 42 U.S.C.A. § 2000d, setting out the substantive coverage of Title VI, provided that

> "[n]o person in the United States shall, on the ground of race, color, or national origin, be excluded from participation in, be denied the benefits of, or be subjected to discrimination under any program or activity receiving Federal financial assistance."

Later enactments extended the non-discrimination principle to sex-based distinctions, age classifications, and those based on handicapped status.[1]

Title VI began as simply one more arrow in the quiver used to fight racial discrimination. But along the course of its development, it became, along with its analogues, a significant laboratory for the development of new civil rights tools, primarily an "effects test" and a broad array of regulatory standards for enforcing the test. These tools, first justified as appropriate for application to private decisions because the private persons had received public funding, were later extended in one significant statute—the Americans with Disabilities Act of 1990 (ADA)—to a broad group of citizens and state governments regardless of whether they receive federal funds. Title VI and the ADA, therefore, are important to the

---

1. The basic analogues prohibit discrimination based on *sex,* but only in certain educational programs (Title IX of the Educational Amendments of 1972, 20 U.S.C. § 1681 et seq.), *handicapped status* (§ 504 of the Rehabilitation Act of 1973, 29 U.S.C. § 794), and *age* (Title III of the Age Discrimination Act of 1975, 42 U.S.C. § 6102) [the only provision explicitly to rule out a private right of enforcement, 42 U.S.C. § 6104(e)].

This Chapter will typically use the nomenclature ("handicap," "sex," and "age") employed in the original statutes. This may result in some labeling confusion, however, because newer statutes protecting disabled persons use the term "disability" rather than "handicap." For purposes of statutory analysis the terms are usually congruent, and the terms will sometimes be used interchangeably when referring to principles applicable to multiple statutes.

discussion about civil rights policy because they offer a rich background discussion of tools and the justifications for using such tools.

This Chapter is organized around three rather complex themes that are common to Title VI (and its analogues) and the ADA. Section A treats the connection between Title VI and constitutional notions of equal protection. In particular, the statute does not make clear whether it proscribes only intentional discrimination or also the adverse effects of non-intentional discrimination. This problem is compounded by a relatively new element in civil rights law—the existence of a vast body of federal agency regulations that supplement Title VI. How much deference should courts give to these administrative standards, standards that Congress foresaw as having a highly political component? Social costs that may arise from using an impact test may appear more starkly here than in ordinary constitutional cases, because federal monetary grants superintended by Title VI are invariably designed to promote some other underlying social goal. These cases present the potential conflict between attainment of civil rights goals and attainment of other important social policies, from education to health care to the arts. If Title VI is read to adopt an effects test that increases the program recipient's costs, does that expense simply take funds from the underlying grant program?

Section B explores the complexity introduced into the equation by the ADA, which goes beyond the effects test of Title VI and invokes a more individuated "reasonable accommodation" test to protect the interests of disabled persons. This new test has the result of imposing an affirmative duty on some citizens to protect disabled or handicapped persons. Is that duty more justifiable when the obligated citizen has willingly received federal funding than when she has not? Moreover, the ADA imposes this duty only when there is a "disability," a term often assumed to have contours much less precise than traditional civil rights statutes protecting against race-or sex-based discrimination. Section B also explores the inter-relation between this vagueness and the affirmative duty imposed by the statute. Discussion of the "reasonable accommodation" test also requires students to confront the fact that accomplishing these social goals has social costs as well as social benefits. How should these costs be borne?

Sections C and D cover the methods of enforcing Title VI and its Spending Power analogues. Section C, which focuses on the sanction of terminating funding for discriminating grantees, raises statutory issues that induce discussion of the appropriate reach of Title VI and tests the thesis that civil rights regulation is fair to all citizens just because they receive some federal largesse. Given the extensive array of existing federal programs, virtually all Americans and the organizations with which they associate will be recipients of federal funds—from educational grants to farm subsidies to Social Security payments in retirement—and thus all are potentially subject to congressional control under the Spending Clause and Title VI. Is there a zone of personal or associational privacy into which Congress should not intrude, even though it may have constitutional power to do so? Administrative enforcement also creates problems for civil rights groups when it is invoked: termination costs the federal agency its leverage—the very connection to the recipient that initially gave it the power to demand civil rights compliance—and denies program benefits to the very groups they were designed to assist. Section D therefore explores whether litigation is a better alternative. Even when litigation is useful, it raises problems about the extent of liability that should be imposed, and those issues are also discussed in Section D.

A. DEFINING "DISCRIMINATION": THE INTENT—OR—EFFECTS CONTROVERSY

LAU v. NICHOLS

Supreme Court of the United States, 1974.
414 U.S. 563, 94 S.Ct. 786, 39 L.Ed.2d 1.

MR. JUSTICE DOUGLAS delivered the opinion of the Court.

The San Francisco, California, school system was integrated in 1971 as a result of a federal court decree, 339 F.Supp. 1315. See Lee v. Johnson, 404 U.S. 1215, 92 S.Ct. 14, 30 L.Ed.2d 19. The District Court found that there are 2,856 students of Chinese ancestry in the school system who do not speak English. Of those who have that language deficiency, about 1,000 are given supplemental courses in the English language. About 1,800, however, do not receive that instruction.

This class suit brought by non-English-speaking Chinese students against officials responsible for the operation of the San Francisco Unified School District seeks relief against the unequal educational opportunities, which are alleged to violate, inter alia, the Fourteenth Amendment. No specific remedy is urged upon us. Teaching English to the students of Chinese ancestry who do not speak the language is one choice. Giving instructions to this group in Chinese is another. There may be others. Petitioners ask only that the Board of Education be directed to apply its expertise to the problem and rectify the situation.

The District Court denied relief. The Court of Appeals affirmed, holding that there was no violation of the Equal Protection Clause of the Fourteenth Amendment or of § 601 of the Civil Rights Act of 1964, which excludes from participation in federal financial assistance, recipients of aid which discriminate against racial groups, 483 F.2d 791. One judge dissented. A hearing en banc was denied, two judges dissenting. Id. at 805.

We granted the petition for certiorari because of the public importance of the question presented, 412 U.S. 938, 93 S.Ct. 2786, 37 L.Ed.2d 397.

The Court of Appeals reasoned that "[e]very student brings to the starting line of his educational career different advantages and disadvantages caused in part by social, economic and cultural background, created and continued completely apart from any contribution by the school system," 483 F.2d at 797. Yet in our view the case may not be so easily decided. This is a public school system of California and § 71 of the California Education Code states that "English shall be the basic language of instruction in all schools." * * *

Moreover, § 8573 of the Education Code provides that no pupil shall receive a diploma of graduation from grade 12 who has not met the standards of proficiency in "English," as well as other prescribed subjects. Moreover, by § 12101 of the Education Code (Supp.1973) children between the ages of six and 16 years are (with exceptions not material here) "subject to compulsory full-time education."

Under these state-imposed standards there is no equality of treatment merely by providing students with the same facilities, textbooks, teachers, and curriculum; for students who do not understand English are effectively foreclosed from any meaningful education.

Basic English skills are at the very core of what these public schools teach. Imposition of a requirement that, before a child can effectively participate in the educational program, he must already have acquired those basic skills is to make a mockery of public education. We know that those who do not understand English are certain to find their classroom experiences wholly incomprehensible and in no way meaningful.

We do not reach the Equal Protection Clause argument which has been advanced but rely solely on § 601 of the Civil Rights Act of 1964, 42 U.S.C.A. § 2000d, to reverse the Court of Appeals.

That section bans discrimination based "on the ground of race, color, or national origin," in "any program or activity receiving Federal financial assistance." The school district involved in this litigation receives large amounts of federal financial assistance. The Department of Health, Education, and Welfare (HEW), which has authority to promulgate regulations prohibiting discrimination in federally assisted school systems, 42 U.S.C.A. § 2000d–1, in 1968 issued one guideline that "[s]chool systems are responsible for assuring that students of a particular race, color, or national origin are not denied the opportunity to obtain the education generally obtained by other students in the system." 33 Fed.Reg. 4955. In 1970 HEW made the guidelines more specific, requiring school districts that were federally funded "to rectify the language deficiency in order to open" the instruction to students who had "linguistic deficiencies," 35 Fed.Reg. 11595.

By § 602 of the Act HEW is authorized to issue Rules, regulations, and orders to make sure that recipients of federal aid under its jurisdiction conduct any federally financed projects consistently with § 601. HEW's regulations, 45 CFR 80.3(b)(1), specify that the recipients may not

> "(ii) Provide any service, financial aid, or other benefit to an individual which is different, or is provided in a different manner, from that provided to others under the program;

* * *

"(iv) Restrict an individual in any way in the enjoyment of any advantage or privilege enjoyed by others receiving any service, financial aid, or other benefit under the program."

Discrimination among students on account of race or national origin that is prohibited includes "discrimination * * * in the availability or use of any academic * * * or other facilities of the grantee or other recipient." Id., § 80.5(b).

Discrimination is barred which has that *effect* even though no purposeful design is present: a recipient "may not * * * utilize criteria or methods of administration which have the effect of subjecting individuals to discrimination" or have "the effect of defeating or substantially impairing accomplishment of the objectives of the program as respect individuals of a particular race, color, or national origin." Id., § 80.3(b)(2).

It seems obvious that the Chinese-speaking minority receive fewer benefits than the English-speaking majority from respondents' school system which denies them a meaningful opportunity to participate in the educational program—all earmarks of the discrimination banned by the regulations. In 1970 HEW issued clarifying guidelines, 35 Fed.Reg. 11595, which include the following:

"Where inability to speak and understand the English language excludes national origin-minority group children from effective participation in the educational program offered by a school district, the district must take affirmative steps to rectify the language deficiency in order to open its instructional program to these students."

"Any ability grouping or tracking system employed by the school system to deal with the special language skill needs of national origin-minority group children must be designed to meet such language skill needs as soon as possible and must not operate as an educational dead end or permanent track."

Respondent school district contractually agreed to "comply with title VI of the Civil Rights Act of 1964 * * * and all requirements imposed by or pursuant to the Regulation" of HEW (45 CFR pt. 80) which are "issued pursuant to that title * * *"and also immediately to "take any measures necessary to effectuate this agreement." The Federal Government has power to fix the terms on which its money allotments to the States shall be disbursed. Oklahoma v. United States Civil Service Commission, 330 U.S. 127, 142–143, 67 S.Ct. 544, 552–554, 91 L. ED. 794. Whatever may be the limits of that power, Steward Machine Co. v. Davis, 301 U.S. 548, 590, 57 S.Ct. 883, 892, 81 L. ED. 1279 et seq., they have not been reached here. Senator Humphrey, during the floor debates on the Civil Rights Act of 1964, said:[4]

---

4. 110 Cong.Rec. 6543 (Sen. Humphrey, quoting from President Kennedy's message to Congress, June 19, 1963).

"Simple justice requires that public funds, to which all taxpayers of all races contribute, not be spent in any fashion which encourages, entrenches, subsidizes, or results in racial discrimination."

We accordingly reverse the judgment of the Court of Appeals and remand the case for the fashioning of appropriate relief.

Reversed and remanded.

MR. JUSTICE WHITE concurs in the result.

MR. JUSTICE STEWART, with whom THE CHIEF JUSTICE and MR. JUSTICE BLACKMUN join, concurring in the result.

* * * [I]t is not entirely clear that § 601 of the Civil Rights Act of 1964, 42 U.S.C.A. § 2000d, standing alone, would render illegal the expenditure of federal funds on these schools. For that section provides that "[n]o person in the United States shall, on the ground of race, color, or national origin, be excluded from participation in, be denied the benefits of, or be subjected to discrimination under any program or activity receiving Federal financial assistance."

On the other hand, the interpretive guidelines published by the Office for Civil Rights of the Department of Health, Education, and Welfare in 1970, 35 Fed.Reg. 11595, clearly indicate that affirmative efforts to give special training for non-English-speaking pupils are required by Tit. VI as a condition to receipt of federal aid to public schools. * * *

The critical question is, therefore, whether the regulations and guidelines promulgated by HEW go beyond the authority of § 601.[2] Last Term, in Mourning v. Family Publications Service, Inc., 411 U.S. 356, 369, 93 S.Ct. 1652, 1661, 36 L.Ed.2d 318, we held that the validity of a regulation promulgated under a general authorization provision such as § 602 of Tit. VI "will be sustained so long as it is 'reasonably related to the purposes of the enabling legislation.'" I think the guidelines here fairly meet that test. Moreover, in assessing the purposes of remedial legislation we have found that departmental regulations and "consistent administrative construction" are "entitled to great weight." Trafficante v. Metropolitan Life Insurance Co., 409 U.S. 205, 210, 93 S.Ct. 364, 367, 34 L.Ed.2d 415; Griggs v. Duke Power Co., 401 U.S. 424, 433–434, 91 S.Ct. 849, 854–855, 28 L.Ed.2d 158; Udall v. Tallman, 380 U.S. 1, 85 S.Ct. 792, 13 L.Ed.2d 616. The Department has reasonably and consistently interpreted § 601 to require affirmative remedial efforts to give special attention to linguistically deprived children.

For these reasons I concur in the result reached by the Court.

MR. JUSTICE BLACKMUN, with whom THE CHIEF JUSTICE joins, concurring in the result.

* * *

---

2. The respondents do not contest the standing of the petitioners to sue as beneficiaries of the federal funding contract between the Department of Health, Education, and Welfare and the San Francisco Unified School District.

I merely wish to make plain that when, in another case, we are concerned with a very few youngsters, or with just a single child who speaks only German or Polish or Spanish or any language other than English, I would not regard today's decision, or the separate concurrence, as conclusive upon the issue whether the statute and the guidelines require the funded school district to provide special instruction. For me, numbers are at the heart of this case and my concurrence is to be understood accordingly.

NOTE ON EARLY REACTION TO AN EFFECTS TEST AND THE LIMITS OF CONSTITUTIONAL "TESTS"

1. Do you find persuasive Justice Douglas' argument that Title VI covers not only intentional discrimination but also neutral decisions having an adverse effect on racial minorities? Do the departmental regulations and Guidelines support him as much as he thinks? Section 602 of Title VI gives some authority to the agencies, and the legislative history discloses strong circumstantial evidence that Congress, unable to decide whether specifically to cover effects-type discrimination, dumped the problem into the laps of the agencies. A significant part of that compromise, however, was the requirement that the President personally approve any such regulations. See Charles Abernathy, *Title VI and the Constitution: A Regulatory Model for Defining "Discrimination,"* 70 GEO. L. J. 1, 47–48 (1981).

(a) Where in the administrative materials is the most explicit reference to adoption of an effects test? Is it in the Title VI "regulations," or in the informal "guidelines" issued by the agencies without presidential participation? Have the agencies exceeded the scope of the regulations in their more detailed "guidelines"? Has the government, from president to administrative bureaucracy, avoided the requirement in § 602 that the president accept personal political responsibility for interpreting Title VI?

(b) Do the agencies have the power under a new administration to rescind, with the president's approval, the previously adopted regulations? Or does the first adoption bind all future Presidents? Compare Rust v. Sullivan, set out in section C of this Chapter (new regulations adopted under Reagan administration significantly additionally restricted the ability of federally funded family planning clinics to advise about abortions; held, such regulations entitled to deference). Could a future administration rescind *Lau*'s effects test by amending the regulations implementing Title VI? Is *Lau* built on a reliable foundation?

2. The Court's decision in *Lau* came at a time of intense controversy over whether the Equal Protection Clause should be interpreted to ban only intentional discrimination or also effects-style (or impact-style) discrimination. See Chapter 1B.5 supra. *Lau,* therefore, may seem in retrospect to have been an attempt by the Court to avoid the unsettled constitutional issue by deciding the case on statutory and regulatory grounds. But its holding that Title VI deviated from constitutional law soon came under attack—from the left. In **Regents of the Univ. of California v. Bakke**, 438 U.S. 265, 98 S.Ct. 2733, 57 L.Ed.2d 750 (1978), a white applicant to medical school

challenged the university's program of reserving 16% of the places in its entering classes for blacks and other minorities. He claimed violations of the Equal Protection Clause and Title VI. Five members of the Court declined to follow the usual practice of deciding cases on narrow, statutory grounds because, they said, Title VI's provisions are coterminous with those of the Fourteenth Amendment's nondiscrimination principle. Justice Powell, speaking for himself alone, reviewed the legislative history of Title VI and found persuasive "evidence of the incorporation of a constitutional standard into Title VI," 438 U.S. at 286, 98 S.Ct. at 2746; he did not speak directly to the continued viability of *Lau* and its effects test, although his use of *Arlington Heights*'s formulation regarding intent, 438 U.S. at 318–19, 98 S.Ct. at 2763, suggests that he considered *Lau* to be superseded.[1] See also 438 U.S. at 308 n. 44, 98 S.Ct. at 2758 n. 44.

Justices Brennan, White, Marshall, and Blackmun filed an opinion stating somewhat enigmatically that "[w]e agree with Mr. Justice Powell that, as applied in the case before us, Title VI goes no further in prohibiting the use of race than the Equal Protection Clause," 438 U.S. at 325, 98 S.Ct. at 2767, and then proceeded to face the *Lau* precedent (438 U.S. at 351–52, 98 S.Ct. at 2780):

> "*Lau* is significant in two related respects. First, it indicates that in at least some circumstances agencies responsible for the administration of Title VI may require recipients who have not been guilty of any constitutional violations to depart from a policy of color-blindness and to be cognizant of the impact of their actions upon racial minorities. Secondly, *Lau* clearly requires that institutions receiving federal funds be accorded considerable latitude in voluntarily undertaking race-conscious action designed to remedy the exclusion of significant numbers of minorities from the benefits of federally funded programs. * * *"

> "We recognize that *Lau,* especially when read in light of our subsequent decision in Washington v. Davis, 426 U.S. 229, 96 S.Ct. 2040, 48 L.Ed.2d 597 (1976), which rejected the general proposition that governmental action is unconstitutional solely because it has a racially disproportionate impact, may be read as being predicated upon the view that, at least under some circumstances, Title VI proscribes conduct which might not be prohibited by the Constitution. Since we are now of the opinion, for the reasons set forth above, that Title VI's standard, applicable alike to public and private recipients of federal funds, is no broader than the Constitution's, we have serious doubts concerning the correctness of what appears to be the premise of that decision. * * *"[2]

---

1. On the constitutional issue, Justice Powell ruled that the racial discrimination against Bakke could not be justified under strict scrutiny because, although the university's program served the compelling governmental interest of fostering diversity in education, that goal could be achieved by less drastic means.

2. On the constitutional issue, Brennan's group applied middle-level scrutiny of the type used in sex-discrimination cases, see Craig v. Boren, 429 U.S. 190, 97 S.Ct. 451, 50 L.Ed.2d 397 (1976) (per Brennan, J.), and upheld the university's program because it furthered the important governmental objective of remedying general societal discrimination against minorities and did so in a manner substantially related to accomplishing that objective.

(a) Justice Powell's vote together with those of the four in Justice Brennan's group yielded a majority which viewed Title VI as coterminous with the Constitution in this case. Was Justice Brennan attempting to leave open the possibility that *Lau* might remain good law in another context? Is there an argument which would allow Brennan to have his cake and eat it, too—follow an effects test for proof of plaintiff's case but use the Court's constitutional standards for other aspects of Title VI? Could *Bakke* be distinguished in the future because it involved a suit by a white person rather than a member of a traditionally protected class? Because HEW guidelines permitted affirmative action, and it is the guidelines which are critical in construing Title VI? Compare the guidelines cited in *Lau*.

(b) Justice Stevens, joined by Chief Justice Burger and Justices Stewart and Rehnquist, applied the language of Title VI literally and found that since Bakke had been "excluded from" school based on his race, Title VI was violated. He found no need to rule whether Title VI's standard differed from that of the Constitution. If one reads *Lau* as holding that Title VI may require more of the states than the Constitution alone demands, does Stevens' opinion say that Congress may also demand that they do less than the Constitution permits? Does that amount to a diminution of constitutional rights? Cf. Katzenbach v. Morgan, Chapter 7A infra and the Note following that case.

(c) Justice Brennan replied to Justice Stevens' dissent by arguing that Congress intended no fixed meaning for Title VI but meant it to be a flexible, growing statute, changing as our conceptions of equal protection mature. Is this desire to construe Title VI flexibly predicated on the belief—or myth—that the nation is on a path leading inexorably to expansion of freedoms? Can there not be contractions as well? Is one group's expansion, as shown by Justice Stevens' opinion, another's contraction?

(d) If Title VI was intended to be a flexible, growing statute, as Brennan suggested, in whose hands was it to flex—the courts' or those of the executive branch officials who would promulgate regulations under § 602? What would have happened in *Bakke* if HEW had promulgated regulations clearly forbidding preferential admissions? Would Brennan and Powell have deferred to the regulations even though they would be willing to construe the Constitution itself to permit such programs?

3. Though many of the grantees covered by Title VI are governmental bodies, the statute applies to all grantees, including private parties. See Grove City College v. Bell, Chapter 6C infra. Assuming that Title VI at least covers intentional discrimination, the same discriminatory conduct barred by the Constitution, can these constitutional norms of equal protection be applied, without change, to private parties?

(a) In constitutional law some racial discrimination is permitted—that which serves a compelling state interest. See Nowak & Rotunda, CONSTITUTIONAL LAW § 14.3 (7th ed. 2004). Can equivalent private discrimination be excused if there is a "compelling private interest"? Or is it meaningless to talk in such terms because a governmental interest is, by definition, a collectively derived interest, with the connotation of an overriding public interest that such a decision implies?

(b) Would it be better to construe Title VI as flatly proscribing all intentional race-based decision making? But that would make it more comprehensive than constitutional law, would it not? Would that interpretation then outlaw all affirmative action programs by grantees? Should Title VI be interpreted as flatly outlawing intentional race-based discrimination, but only that practiced against racial minorities, not affirmative action programs designed to help minorities?

(c) Should Title VI be interpreted to allow a "compelling state interest" defense for governmental grantees but not private grantees? Does anything in the statute or regulations authorize this distinction between grantees?

(d) With respect to governmental grantees and intentional discrimination, what does Title VI add to constitutional law? Anything? Only an enforcement stick—the threat of loss of funding?

4. Assuming that Title VI also outlaws effects-style discrimination, the issues in the previous paragraph remain relevant, albeit in a different guise. Does Title VI or the implementing regulations recognize any defense to effects-style discrimination? Or is every racially neutral practice that disproportionately effects racial minorities forbidden by Title VI? If it is true, as the Court assumed in the Equal Protection cases on this issue, see Chapter 1B.5 supra, that there are many demographic and financial differences between whites, blacks, and other minorities as groups, then will not a great many grantee decisions cause adverse effects for blacks and minorities? Is it not therefore desirable to have some defense for such claims?

(a) If the school board's practice of operating schools from 9 A.M. to 3 P.M. has an adverse impact on a particular minority group, because those children need more educational time or their parents cannot find late afternoon child care, would the 9–to–3 school day be illegal under Title VI, absent some defense? Would a 9–to–6 day be any less illegal? Would a school system's decision to assign classic books, such as those about Huckleberry Finn and Tom Sawyer which contain racially offensive words for blacks, have an adverse effect on blacks in violation of *Lau*? See Monteiro v. Tempe Union High School Dist., 158 F.3d 1022 (9th Cir.1998) (discussing Huck Finn and the possibility that other books might have an adverse affect on other minority groups).

(b) If a grantee requires children to pay for lunches or uniforms or field trips during the program, would such requirements all violate Title VI (absent some defense) in a community where minority families earn less than white families? Cf. Powell v. Ridge, 189 F.3d 387 (3d Cir. 1999) (educational funding practices challenged for Pennsylvania public schools). Does Title VI require "racial socialism"? Is it a "black reparations" statute? Should this result be avoided by adding a defense to effects-type claims?

(c) Considering the vast scope of federal grants to state and local governments, does Title VI's effects test have the potential for effectively overturning the constitutional rules that federal courts will remedy only state action that is intentionally discriminatory against minorities? Could Title VI be used to attack neutral police practices having a discriminatory effect on blacks and Hispanics? See Burton v. City of Belle Glade, 178 F.3d 1175 (11th Cir.1999) (housing agency's actions). Cf. Ferguson v. City of Charleston, S.C., 186 F.3d 469 (4th Cir.1999) (law enforcement potential).

(d) Regarding language minorities, is every state program that is operated in English a presumptive violation of Title VI? See Sandoval v. Hagan, 197 F.3d 484 (11th Cir.1999) (drivers' license test in English only violates Title VI), rev'd on other grounds, see subpart C of this Chapter infra.

5. Presumably, the remedy for an effects-type violation would be to remove the differential effect on racial minorities. For the specific issue raised in *Lau*, minority language education, how should the differential effect of English-only education be eliminated? Consider the two most obvious choices: (i) special English-as-a-Second-Language (ESL) courses, followed by mainstreaming the minority students in ordinary classes taught in English, and (ii) direct instruction in the primary, home language of the student throughout the school years (i.e., math in Mandarin Chinese, science in Mandarin Chinese, etc.).

(a) What interest groups would tend to prefer each approach? Why? Consider the largest language minority in the United States, Spanish-speakers. Should groups supporting such persons prefer ESL and mainstreaming because it maximizes the integration of such persons into American society and gives them the best opportunity to enjoy the economic benefits of U.S. society? Or should such groups support instruction in Spanish so as to preserve the Spanish-language culture and promote political cohesion among Spanish-speakers?

(b) Which course would or should members of society at large prefer? Which would "liberals" or "conservatives" prefer, Republicans or Democrats, urban dwellers or rural dwellers? Does Title VI dictate a solution to this issue, or should local governments be permitted to choose any remedy, provided it works in eliminating the illegal differential effect?

(c) Consider the number of variations possible because of the number of potential minority languages in the U.S. Should "Ebonics" be considered a language so that those urban blacks who speak it will be taught differently?[3] Should the Ebonics-speakers be segregated into classes for only Ebonics-speakers? If a local government or school board in a predominantly Spanish-speaking area of Texas adopts Spanish as the language of instruction for area schools, would English-speakers have a claim under Title VI and *Lau*?

(d) Could similar issues arise under other Title VI analogues? See Cohen v. Brown University, 101 F.3d 155 (1st Cir.1996) (integration or equal segregated status for women's sports teams under Title IX).

6. Some have proposed that Title VI itself be used, or that its principles be adapted for use, to bring about "environmental justice," that is the correction of widespread social practices that result in minorities living near environmentally unsafe facilities. See Sheila Foster, *Justice from the Ground*

---

3. Ebonics is the name given to the organized English dialect spoken by some black Americans. Regarding proposals, primarily in California, to recognize it as a language of instruction in schools, see Lori Olszewski, Oakland Parent Calls for Boycott of Schools: Ebonics Champion Says Blacks Aren't Being Taught, S.F. Chron., June 26, 1997, at A17; Editorial, Mainstream English Is the Key: Official Status for Black English Won't Cure Educational Problems, L.A. Times, Dec. 22, 1996, at M4.

Up: Distributive Inequities, Grassroots Resistance, and the Transformative Politics of the Environmental Justice Movement, 86 CALIF. L. REV. 775 (1998). In Chester Residents Concerned for Quality Living v. Seif, 132 F.3d 925 (3d Cir.1997), the Third Circuit ruled that Title VI can be used to challenge adverse impacts on a minority community occasioned by the state's grant of more dumping permits in a predominantly black city than it authorized for surrounding predominantly white areas. It remanded the case for trial.

(a) Could plaintiffs challenge an individual permit decision that adversely affects a minority community, or would they need to await a series of decisions and determine whether the collective pattern of permits had an adverse effect on their community? If an individual permitting decision can be challenged, then every permit in or near a minority community would be presumptively invalid, would it not? If plaintiffs must await a pattern of decisions, how many permits are needed to notice a pattern?

(b) Is Title VI's effects test necessarily a group remedy for accumulated social injustices? Under the effects test, could an individual black student claim that re-configured bus routes adversely affected him? Would we need to know how the routes affected all black students riding school buses? Or should all grantee-schools be required to meet the needs of each individual black student?

GUARDIANS ASSOCIATION v. CIVIL SERVICE COMMISSION OF THE CITY OF NEW YORK

Supreme Court of the United States, 1983.
463 U.S. 582, 103 S.Ct. 3221, 77 L.Ed.2d 866.

JUSTICE WHITE announced the judgment of the Court and delivered the following opinion, in Parts I, III, IV and V of which JUSTICE REHNQUIST joins.

The threshold issue before the Court is whether the private plaintiffs in this case need to prove discriminatory intent to establish a violation of Title VI of the Civil Rights Act of 1964, 42 U.S.C. § 2000d, *et seq.,* and administrative implementing regulations promulgated thereunder. I conclude, as do four other Justices, in separate opinions, that the Court of Appeals erred in requiring proof of discriminatory intent.[4] However, I conclude that the judgment below should be affirmed on other grounds, because, in the absence of proof of discriminatory animus, compensatory relief should not be awarded to private Title VI plaintiffs; unless discriminatory intent is shown, declaratory and limited injunctive relief should be

---

4. The five of us reach the conclusion that the Court of Appeals erred by different routes. Justice Stevens, joined by Justice Brennan and Justice Blackmun, reasons that, although Title VI itself requires proof of discriminatory intent, the administrative regulations incorporating a disparate impact standard are valid.

Justice Marshall would hold that, under Title VI itself, proof of disparate impact discrimination is all that is necessary. I agree with Justice Marshall that discriminatory animus is not an essential element of a violation of Title VI. I also believe that the regulations are valid, even assuming *arguendo* that Title VI, in and of itself, does not proscribe disparate impact discrimination. Part II, *infra.*

the only available private remedies for Title VI violations. There being four other Justices who would affirm the judgment of the Court of Appeals, that judgment is accordingly affirmed.

[The Civil Service Commission, a recipient of federal funds, used a facially neutral employment test that disproportionately excluded blacks and Hispanics from consideration for hiring by the police department. Plaintiffs sought compensatory remedies for the wages they would have earned had they been hired. The trial court ruled for the plaintiffs, but the Court of Appeals reversed, finding that plaintiffs must prove intentional discrimination in order to prevail under Title VI.]

II

[The Court of Appeals thought that our decisions in *Bakke* overruled our decision in *Lau*, but I see the cases as reconcilable. Although "Title VI does not of its own force proscribe unintentional racial discrimination," the opinions of the concurring Justices in *Lau* make clear that the gist of our holding was this: while it "was not at all clear that Title VI, standing alone, would prohibit unintentional discrimination, [its] implementing regulations, which explicitly forbade impact discrimination, were valid because not inconsistent with the purposes of Title VI."] The upshot of Justice Stewart's opinion was that those charged with enforcing Title VI had sufficient discretion to enforce the statute by forbidding unintentional as well as intentional discrimination. Nothing that was said in *Bakke* is to the contrary. [I am convinced that Stewart and the fellow concurring Justices correctly interpreted Title VI.]

* * *

Although the Court of Appeals erred in construing Title VI, it does not necessarily follow that its judgment should be reversed. As an alternative ground for affirmance, respondents defend the judgment on the basis that there is no private right of action available under Title VI that will afford petitioners the [compensatory] relief that they seek. I agree that the relief * * * is unavailable to them under Title VI, at least where no intentional discrimination has been proved, as is the case here.

* * *

Affirmed.[27]

JUSTICE MARSHALL, dissenting.[a]

* * *

---

27. Despite the numerous opinions, the views of at least five Justices on two issues are identifiable. The dissenters, Justices Brennan, Marshall, Blackmun, and Stevens, join with me to form a majority for upholding the validity of the regulations incorporating a disparate-impact standard. A different majority, however, would not allow compensatory relief in the absence of proof of discriminatory intent. Justice Rehnquist and I reach this conclusion directly. Justice Powell, joined by the Chief Justice, believe that no private relief should ever be granted under Title VI under any circumstances. Justice O'Connor would hold that all relief should be denied unless discriminatory intent is proven. It follows from the views of these three latter Justices that no compensatory relief should be awarded if discriminatory animus is not shown.

a. [The concurring opinions are omitted. See footnote 27 of the majority opinion.—Ed.]

If we were required to decide the issue presented by this case in the absence of a persuasive administrative interpretation of the statute, I would hold, in accordance with the view expressed in *Bakke,* that Title VI requires proof of discriminatory intent, even though this holding would entail overruling Lau v. Nichols. But the case comes to us against the background of administrative regulations that have uniformly and consistently interpreted the statute to prohibit programs that have a discriminatory impact and that cannot be justified on nondiscriminatory grounds. [Congress and our cases have accepted these regulations]

* * *

The legislative history of Title VI fully confirms that Congress intended to delegate to the Executive Branch substantial leeway in interpreting the meaning of discrimination under Title VI. See Abernathy, *Title VI and the Constitution: A Regulatory Model for Defining "Discrimination,"* 70 GEO. L. J. 1, 20–39 (1981). The word "discrimination" was nowhere defined in Title VI. Instead, Congress authorized executive departments and agencies to adopt regulations with the antidiscrimination principle of § 601 of the Act "as a general criterion to follow." Civil Rights: Hearings on H.R. 7152 Before the House Comm. on the Judiciary, 88th Cong., 1st Sess. 2740 (1963) (testimony of Attorney General Kennedy). Congress willingly conceded "[g]reat powers" to the executive branch in defining the reach of the statute. Id. at 1520 (statement of Rep. Cellar, Chairman of the House Judiciary Committee). Indeed, the significance of the administrative role in the statutory scheme is underscored by the fact that Congress required the President to approve all Title VI regulations.

In the face of a reasonable and contemporaneous administrative construction that has been consistently adhered to for nearly 20 years, originally permitted and subsequently acquiesced in by Congress, and expressly adopted by this Court in *Lau,* I would hold that Title VI bars practices that have a discriminatory impact and cannot be justified on legitimate grounds.[15]

[Moreover, I see no reason to limit relief available after a finding of effects-type discrimination. I therefore dissent.]

JUSTICE STEVENS, with whom JUSTICE BRENNAN and JUSTICE BLACKMUN join, dissenting.

[After *Bakke,* proof of intentional discrimination is required to state a claim under Title VI. But a separate case may be brought for violation of Title VI's implementing regulations.] Significantly, those regulations do more than merely prohibit grant recipients from administering the funds

---

15. Proof of the disproportionate racial impact of a program or activity is, of course, not the end of the case. Rather a prima facie showing of discriminatory impact shifts the burden to the recipient of federal funds to demonstrate a sufficient nondiscriminatory justification for the program or activity. See Bryan v. Koch, 627 F.2d 612, 623 (C.A.2 1980) (Kearse, J., concurring in part and dissenting in part). In this case, respondents failed to provide an adequate justification.

I also agree with Justice White that the administrative regulations are valid even assuming *arguendo* that Title VI itself does not proscribe disparate impact discrimination.

with a discriminatory purpose; they require recipients to administer the grants in a manner that has no racially discriminatory *effects*.

This Court has repeatedly upheld the validity of those regulations and their "effects" standard. Lau v. Nichols. The reason is that Title VI explicitly authorizes "[e]ach Federal department and agency which is empowered to extend Federal financial assistance ... to effectuate the provisions of section 601 ... by issuing rules, regulations, or orders of general applicability which shall be consistent with achievement of the objectives of the statute authorizing the financial assistance...." 78 Stat. 252, 42 U.S.C. § 2000d–1. Nothing in the regulations is inconsistent with any of the statutes authorizing the disbursement of the grants that the respondent received.

* * *

NOTE ON THE EVOLVED EFFECTS TEST AND BALANCING SOCIAL COSTS

1. Some Justices in the *Guardians* case take the position that Title VI forbids only intentional discrimination and therefore provides no remedy, damages or otherwise, for effects-style discrimination. Some Justices take the position that Title VI forbids both types of discrimination and provides a damage remedy for both. Justice White's dispositive, Solomonic vote finds that both types are covered by Title VI, but that a damage remedy is available only for intentional discrimination. (Review Justice White's footnote 27.) A majority therefore confirms that Title VI bars impact-style discrimination.

(a) Should Justice White's opinion be read as an attempt to mitigate the costs of remedying disparate effects by limiting monetary recoveries for violations? Even if it is a good compromise, is his compromise position persuasive? Is there any reason to believe that Congress intended the result he advocates?

(b) The concurring Justices who rely on *Bakke* in its interpretation of Title VI have a strong position, do they not? Didn't Justice Brennan see this issue coming in *Bakke*? Was he focusing too much on the short-term desire to win in that case and too little on maintaining what had been won in *Lau*?

(c) Are those Justices who favor an effects test merely repeating the majority position in *Lau*? Justice Marshall's dissenting opinion seems to be different from Stevens': how so? Would Marshall permit a change in the regulations, or does he see them as freezing the correct interpretation of Title VI? Would Stevens permit change?

(d) Despite the fractured nature of the Court in *Guardians*, and the rapid departure of many of the pivotal Justices in the case, later opinions generally treated its overall result with respect, and Justice White's position proved to be remarkably durable. See Davis v. Monroe County Bd. of Educ., 526 U.S. 629, 119 S.Ct. 1661, 143 L.Ed.2d 839 (1999) (citing *Guardians* for the principle that damages are recoverable under Title VI analogues only for "intentional conduct that violates the clear terms of the statute" itself) (5–4 vote); Gebser v. Lago Vista Independent School Dist., 524 U.S. 274, 118 S.Ct. 1989, 141 L.Ed.2d 277 (1998) (*Guardians* held that "the relief in an action under Title VI alleging unintentional discrimination should be prospective only") (5–4 vote).[1] Lower courts, see infra, follow *Guardians*'s effects test, albeit also attaching Justice Marshall's balancing defense.

2. While the Supreme Court and federal appellate courts have continued to follow an effects test for Title VI, at least as to prospective injunctive relief, lower courts have also incorporated Justice Marshall's view, set out in footnote 15 of his *Guardians* opinion, that there must be substantive limits or countervailing defenses that ensure that not every discriminatory effect is a per se violation. Is Justice Marshall's footnote 15 itself a compromise position?

(a) Lower courts typically interpret Title VI's effects test to mimic that used under Title VII, see Chapter 7A infra, thus permitting defendants to excuse an adverse effect on minorities in some circumstances. The balancing process is described in **Powell v. Ridge**, 189 F.3d 387, 393 (3d Cir. 1999) (collecting cases): "Thus, a plaintiff in a Title VI disparate [effects] suit bears the initial burden of establishing * * * that a facially neutral practice has resulted in a racial disparity. If the plaintiff meets that burden, then the defendant must establish a 'substantial legitimate justification' [for the facially neutral practice]. Once the defendant meets its rebuttal burden, the plaintiff must then establish either that the defendant overlooked an equally effective alternative with less discriminatory effects or that the proffered justification is no more than a pretext for racial discrimination." What is a "substantial legitimate justification"? Doesn't this test look remarkably like Title VII's "disparate impact test"? Have the appellate courts followed *Guardians* or—realistically—Griggs v. Duke Power Co.?

(b) Under Title VII, the apparent source for the lower courts' test for Title VI, this balancing test has evolved from the statute itself and it's use of the "effects" language (albeit with support from EEOC "Guidelines"). See Chapter 7A supra. Now re-read *Lau*: can you find any suggestion in the statute that an effects test was intended by Congress? That it was left to federal regulators to decide? If the latter, is there any indication whatsoever in the regulations that an affirmative, balancing defense is available? Have lower courts borrowed from Title VII because they should—or just because it is there?

3. The most difficult and problematic claims of justification for adverse impacts involve resource allocations or costs issues. In a parallel context, in **Olmstead v. L.C. ex rel. Zimring**, 527 U.S. 581, 119 S.Ct. 2176, 144 L.Ed.2d 540 (1999) (involving mental health care services and a claim of discrimination under similar statutes), a dispositive plurality ruled that, in the context of providing treatment to individual persons, the cost defense could be used to justify delays but not denials of treatment. Other Justices would have provided more leeway to state planners to consider costs. Should the "cost defense" apply to Title VI cases involving claims of adverse effects?

---

1. As late as 1992 the Court suggested that Title VI's prohibitions are only coextensive with those of the Constitution, see United States v. Fordice, 505 U.S. 717, 732 n. 7, 112 S.Ct. 2727, 2737 n. 7, 120 L.Ed.2d 575 (1992), citing the separate opinions in *Guardians*. In any event, the cases quoted in the text seem to mark the evolution toward current acceptance of Justice White's opinion in *Guardians*, at least by a 5–4 majority on the Court.

4. Finally, consider the possibility that Title VI has two different effects tests—one general test that allows for balancing and another in which the balancing has already been done by the regulators when they adopt a per se guideline. *Olmstead*, discussed in the immediately preceding paragraph, would be an example of the first type of balancing: absent specific regulatory standards, the Court itself must balance one set of social goals (eliminating racial effects in the context of Title VI) against another social goal (such as preserving program resources, providing better schools, etc.). Lau v. Nichols would be an example of the specific effects test enforcing agency balancing: the agency has already determined that instruction is English only has an adverse effect on minorities that cannot be justified by any grantee interests, and all the court must do is enforce the agency guideline as written.

(a) Which category of effects test would be easier for courts to enforce?

(b) Which effects test is more consistent with the majority position in *Guardians* and *Lau* suggesting that Title VI gave extra authority to federal agencies? Why would extra authority be given to agencies—because they have expertise that judges do not?

NOTE ON LEGAL REALISM AND THE EFFECTS TEST OVER TIME

1. A review of the circuit court decisions enforcing *Lau* and *Guardians* in the federal appellate courts finds a stark division of cases along the lines suggested in the last paragraph of the previous Note. See Charles Abernathy, *Legal Realism and the Failure of the "Effects" Test for Discrimination*, 94 GEO. L. J. 267 (2006). While there were remarkably few cases in the years between *Lau* and 2001, when litigation of effects claims ended, see subpart C of this Chapter infra, the pattern of results is unmistakable.

2. Consider first some sample cases involving strict agency guidelines that fairly predictably pre-determine outcomes. Consider how you would decide the following cases.

(a) In Larry P. v. Riles, 793 F.2d 969 (9th Cir. 1984), involved use of an IQ test to place students in special classes for mentally disabled students; the test resulted in over-assignment of minorities to such classes by a wide margin. Specific federal grant criteria required that placement tests be validated before use in assigning students, and the ones in use had not been validated. What result?

(b) Sandoval v. Hagan, 197 F.3d 484 (11th Cir. 1999), rev'd on other grounds as discussed infra, Alabama offered driving licenses only to persons who could pass a test offered in English. Non–English speakers who were disproportionately excluded sued. Regulations like those seen in *Lau* forbade the state's practice. What result?

(c) Did courts in either case need to undertake an independent evaluation or balancing of the respective social policies that were at issue for plaintiffs and defendants? (Are you suspicious that both cases involved intentional discrimination?)

3. Now consider some sample cases involving no specific guidelines, cases in which the courts were required to balance the interest in preventing adverse effects on minorities against some other competing social goal.

(a) In Debra P. v. Turlington, 730 F.2d 1405 (11th Cir. 1984), Florida hired an outside consultant who sought to formulate a literacy test to ensure that all high school students could read at a minimal level before graduation; special classes helped to assure passage and students could re-take the test, and black passage rates improved, but the test disproportionately failed African–American students. What result?[1]

(b) In NAACP v. Medical Center, Inc., 657 F.2d 1322 (3d Cir. 1981) (en banc), an inner-city hospital with aging facilities and languishing programs wanted to move much of its operations to the suburbs, where it could attract more paying customers and build new facilities more efficiently. Because of often-seen demographics in eastern U.S. cities, the move would have an adverse effect on blacks, even with some ameliorative programs designed to keep some services in the inner-city area. What result?[2]

(c) In Latinos Unidos de Chelsea en Accion (LUCHA) v. Secretary of Housing and Urban Development, 799 F.2d 774 (1st Cir. 1986), Hispanic renters challenged a dilapidated urban mini-city's plan to reduce subsidies to renters in order to spend disproportionately more of its federal housing grant to aid homeowners, who were mostly white. This would have increased the city's tax base and stabilized a deteriorating city; other programs did not disproportionately adversely affect Hispanics. What result?[3]

(d) In New York Urban League v. New York, 71 F.3d 1031 (2d Cir. 1995), users of local transit challenged new fare schedules that raised their transit prices more than prices were raised for suburban commuters entering the city by rail. Urban users were disproportionately minorities; both urban and commuter transit systems were already heavily subsidized. What result?[4]

(e) In Ferguson v. City of Charleston, 186 F.3d 469 (4th Cir. 1999), rev'd on other grounds, 532 U.S. 67, 121 S.Ct. 1281, 149 L.Ed.2d 205 (2001), the city hospital required involuntary testing of all mothers of new-born babies for cocaine in order to provide specialized care to such mothers (including treatment) and their babies. The program yielded proportionately more black mothers who were then subject to treatment and potential prosecution for drug crimes. What result?

---

1. See Georgia State Conference of NAACP v. Georgia, 775 F.2d 1403 (11th Cir. 1985) (use of objective tests for special education assignments; assignments resulted in racial disparities, but record showed remarkable progress of students so assigned); Quarles v. Oxford Mun. Separate Sch. Dist., 868 F.2d 750 (5th Cir. 1989) (advance-placement classes in university town disproportionately populated by white students). See also United States v. LULAC, 793 F.2d 636 (5th Cir. 1986) (qualifying test for entering teacher-training programs challenged for racially disparate effects, where test required only basic skills necessary for learning material in the course).

2. See Bryan v. Koch, 627 F.2d 612 (2d Cir. 1980) (closure of one of many NYC hospitals disproportionately makes care more difficult for minorities, though study shows closed facility to be the least utilized and most difficult to maintain); Elston v. Talladega County Bd. of Educ., 997 F.2d 1394 (11th Cir. 1993) (closure of school in black neighborhood and reassignment of students to new consolidate school farther from homes).

3. See City of Chicago v. Lindley, 66 F.3d 819 (7th Cir. 1995) (city sues to gain more of state's old-age assistance for its residents, who are disproportionately black, shifting funding from rural residents).

4. See New York City Environmental Justice Alliance v. Giuliani, 214 F.3d 65 (2d Cir. 2000) (city's program of selling off excess property to raise money for public housing and urban renewal, including sale of urban garden plots used by plaintiffs, is challenged because of its adverse effect on minorities).

(f) Are these cases considerably more difficult to decide than those mentioned in paragraph 2 supra? Why?

4. Now consider the actual results in the cases decided on the merits, after balancing, in the years between *Lau* and 2001.

(a) Plaintiffs won both of the cases discussed in paragraph 2. The specific regulatory guidance from federal agencies was dispositive in both cases. Outcomes were assisted by strong records suggesting possible intentional discrimination against minorities.

(b) Plaintiffs lost every appellate case in which open-ended balancing by the courts was needed. In fact, of the 35 judges to sit to hear such cases, from the liberal lions of the old Eleventh Circuit to modern conservative Republicans, only two judges ever dissented from rulings for grantees—and one of those was on a procedural mechanism, not on the merits of the balance to be struck. Why were judges so overwhelmingly opposed to second-guessing grantee decisions that had no provable disparate intent and only a disproportionate effect?

5. In Abernathy, *Legal Realism and the Failure of the "Effects" Test for Discrimination*, paragraph 1 supra, the author found five strong themes running through these cases: (i) judges acknowledged the legitimacy of the grantee interest in its neutral [non-intentionally discriminatory] practices; (ii) judges often perceived the existence of a zero-sum game that made it necessary for judges to choose abstractly based on who was more "worthy"; (iii) judges saw the adverse effects as not casually related to the grantees' conduct but as a lingering manifestation of others' discrimination in the past; (iv) judges often saw the benefits to be gained by plaintiffs as short-term rewards, whereas society would benefit from a longer-term view; and (v) judges show a lack of self-confidence in their ability to manage the balancing to choose a defendable result, one not based on purely normative personal values.

(a) As we shall see in Chapter 7A infra, the similar "disparate effects" test used for Title VII has also produced, at least in more recent years, no large number of pro-plaintiff decisions. Is the effects test just too amorphous—a balancing of "apples and oranges" that is inevitable value-laden? Does that suggest why judges are much more accepting of cases involving specific agency guidelines with criteria to guide their decisions? Are these exactly the kinds of decisions for which there should be political accountability? (If you think not, is it because you think the political organs will not make the decisions you prefer? But isn't this statute a political judgment?)

(b) Would it have been better for Congress to adopt a series of "mini-Title VI" statutes, each addressing a different topic and indicating with per se rules what is forbidden by grantees? Alternately, would it have been better for agency officials to draft many more specific guidelines indicating to judges how they should rule? What kind of guideline would you have written for each of the circumstances mentioned in paragraph 3 supra? How these social issues even too difficult for agency officials—bureaucrats—to decide?

(c) Are these problems of social balancing too difficult for politicians, too? Is there any social mechanism for discussing and building a consensus about how to decide these problems? Is the discussion occurring during ordinary political campaigns?

6. As discussed in subpart C of this Chapter, the Supreme Court finally put a stop to all plaintiff-initiated litigation of effects-based Title VI claims in **Alexander v. Sandoval**, 532 U.S. 275, 121 S.Ct. 1511, 149 L.Ed.2d 517 (2001), holding that there is no explicit or implied right of action for such claims. (Plaintiff-initiated claims for intentional discrimination remain viable.)

(a) *Lau*-type claims are now no longer available as a matter of plaintiff-initiated, § 1983–style litigation, even when the relief sought is only equitable as in *Guardians*. Does *Sandoval* essentially reverse both *Lau* and *Guardians* by making repeats of those cases impossible?

(b) Given the history of decisions discussed in this Note, did plaintiffs lose anything when *Sandoval* was decided? No, because they were not winning any cases anyway? Yes, because they lose the chance for future evolution of judicial thinking? Yes, because they lose the opportunity to present effects-type claims in situations where there is a specific agency guideline to inform judicial decisions?

(c) *Sandoval* leaves open the possibility of agency enforcement under § 602, 42 U.S.C. § 2000d–1 (by termination of the grant or "any other means" authorized by law). Apparently, the effects test may still be enforced in agency proceedings, which are themselves reviewable in court as provided by § 2000d–1. Does this mean that these issues will eventually return to the courts? Will they be easier to decide at that point because of the application of agency expertise or political acumen to the problems?

(d) If agency enforcement becomes robust, will Title VI be workable? Title VI's effects test necessarily lessens the value of a federal grant by a value equal to the cost of eliminating the (by definition) unintentional adverse effect on some minorities of the neutral operational practices that would otherwise be used to administer the federal grant. Would a prospective grantee be wise to calculate whether the grant would result in a net value worth accepting the grant with civil-rights strings attached? If a grantee loses a suit under Title VI, would it be wise to re-think whether it wishes to avoid future grant applications?

B. DEFINING "DISCRIMINATION": "REASONABLE ACCOMMODATION" FOR DISABLED PERSONS

While the effects test of Title VI seems destined to operate at the demographic group level, disability law has developed a similar principle that is applied to individual "disabled" or "handicapped" persons. In part, as revealed in the following cases, the attention to individual circumstances has been justified by the variable nature of disabilities: whereas minority status has been treated by civil rights laws as an on-off switch (minority or non-minority), disability and appropriate responses to it, have been conceived by the statutes as a rheostat (a sliding switch which recognizes degrees of disability and needed responses, as a sliding light switch would create degrees of illumination or darkness). As you read the following materials, try to decide whether disability and minority status are really such different conditions. Also consider the impulse that leads to civil rights protection for minorities versus disabled persons: in what respect are both the victims of "discrimination"? (Section 504, as discussed in this subpart, parallels Title VI by covering federal grantees. The Americans With Disabilities Act (ADA) applies regardless of the receipt of federal funding and covers discrimination in three major topical areas, "employment (Title I of the Act), public services (Title II), and public accommodations (Title III)," PGA Tour, Inc. v. Martin, 532 U.S. 661, 121 S.Ct. 1879, 149 L.Ed.2d 904 (2001).)

SCHOOL BOARD OF NASSAU COUNTY v. ARLINE

Supreme Court of the United States, 1987.
480 U.S. 273, 107 S.Ct. 1123, 94 L.Ed.2d 307.

JUSTICE BRENNAN delivered the opinion of the Court.

Section 504 of the Rehabilitation Act of 1973, 87 Stat. 394, as amended, 29 U.S.C. § 794 (Act), prohibits a federally funded state program from discriminating against a handicapped individual solely by reason of his or her handicap. This case presents the questions whether a person afflicted with tuberculosis, a contagious disease, may be considered a "handicapped individual" within the meaning of § 504 of the Act, and, if so, whether such an individual is "otherwise qualified" to teach elementary school.

I

From 1966 until 1979, respondent Gene Arline taught elementary school in Nassau County, Florida. She was discharged in 1979 after suffering a third relapse of tuberculosis within two years. After she was denied relief in state administrative proceedings, she brought suit in federal court, alleging that the School Board's decision to dismiss her because of her tuberculosis violated § 504 of the Act.

[At trial it was disclosed that the school board first suspended Ms. Arline with pay for almost a year, then discharged her when she continued to test positive for tuberculosis. The school board admitted that there was no wrongdoing on Ms. Arline's part; she was discharged solely because she had a contagious disease. The district court held that contagious diseases were not handicaps covered under § 504, but the Court of Appeals reversed.]

II

In enacting and amending the Act, Congress enlisted all programs receiving federal funds in an effort "to share with handicapped Americans the opportunities for an education, transportation, housing, health care, and jobs that other Americans take for granted." 123 Cong.Rec. 13515 (1977) (statement of Sen. Humphrey). To that end, Congress not only increased federal support for vocational rehabilitation, but also addressed the broader problem of discrimination against the handicapped by including § 504, an antidiscrimination provision patterned after Title VI of the Civil Rights Act of 1964.[5] Section 504 of the Rehabilitation Act reads in pertinent part:

> "No otherwise qualified handicapped individual in the United States, as defined in section 706(7) of this title, shall, solely by reason of his handicap, be excluded from participation in, be denied the benefits of, or be subjected to discrimination under any program or activity receiving Federal financial assistance ..." 29 U.S.C. § 794.

Rule

In 1974 Congress expanded the definition of "handicapped individual" for use in § 504 to read as follows:

> "[A]ny person who (i) has a physical or mental impairment which substantially limits one or more of such person's major life activities, (ii) has a record of such an impairment, or (iii) is regarded as having such an impairment." 29 U.S.C. § 706(7)(B).

def.

The amended definition reflected Congress' concern with protecting the handicapped against discrimination stemming not only from simple prejudice, but from "archaic attitudes and laws" and from "the fact that the American people are simply unfamiliar with and insensitive to the difficulties confront[ing] individuals with handicaps." S.Rep.No. 93–1297, p. 50 (1974), U.S.Code Cong. & Admin.News 1974, p. 6400. * * *

In determining whether a particular individual is handicapped as defined by the Act, the regulations promulgated by the Department of Health and Human Services are of significant assistance. * * * The regulations are particularly significant here because they define two critical terms used in the statutory definition of handicapped individual. "Physical impairment" is defined as follows:

> "[A]ny physiological disorder or condition, cosmetic disfigurement, or anatomical loss affecting one or more of the following body systems: neurological; musculoskeletal; special sense organs; respiratory, including speech organs; cardiovascular; reproductive, digestive, genitourinary; hemic and lymphatic; skin; and endocrine." 45 CFR § 84.3(j)(2)(I) (1985).

def.

In addition, the regulations define "major life activities" as:

> "functions such as caring for one's self, performing manual tasks, walking, seeing, hearing, speaking, breathing, learning, and working. § 84.3(j)(2)(ii).

def.

---

5. Congress' decision to pattern § 504 after Title VI is evident in the language of the statute, compare 29 U.S.C. § 794 with 42 U.S.C. § 2000d, and in the legislative history of § 504, see, e.g., S.Rep.No. 93–1297, pp. 39–40 (1974), U.S.Code Cong. & Admin.News 1974, p. 6373; S.Rep.No. 95–890, p. 19 (1978). Cf. tenBroek & Matson, The Disabled and the Law of Welfare, 54 Cal. L. Rev. 809, 814–815 and nn. 21–22 (1966) (discussing theory and evidence that "negative attitudes and practices toward the disabled resemble those commonly attached to 'underprivileged ethnic and religious minority groups' "). * * *

III

Within this statutory and regulatory framework, then, we must consider whether Arline can be considered a handicapped individual. According to the testimony of [Arline's expert] Dr. McEuen, Arline suffered tuberculosis "in an acute form in such a degree that it affected her respiratory system," and was hospitalized for this condition.

Arline thus had a physical impairment as that term is defined by the regulations, since she had a "physiological disorder or condition . . . affecting [her] . . . respiratory [system]." 45 CFR § 84.3(j)(2)(I) (1985). This impairment was serious enough to require hospitalization, a fact more than sufficient to establish that one or more of her major life activities were substantially limited by her impairment. Thus, Arline's hospitalization for tuberculosis in 1957 suffices to establish that she has a "record of . . . impairment" within the meaning of 29 U.S.C. § 706(7)(B)(ii), and is therefore a handicapped individual.

Petitioners concede that a contagious disease may constitute a handicapping condition to the extent that it leaves a person with "diminished physical or mental capabilities," Brief for Petitioners 15, and concede that Arline's hospitalization for tuberculosis in 1957 demonstrates that she has a record of a physical impairment, see Tr. of Oral Arg. 52–53. Petitioners maintain, however, Arline's record of impairment is irrelevant in this case, since the School Board dismissed Arline not because of her diminished physical capabilities, but because of the threat that her relapses of tuberculosis posed to the health of others.

We do not agree with petitioners that, in defining a handicapped individual under § 504, the contagious effects of a disease can be meaningfully distinguished from the disease's physical effects on a claimant in a case such as this. Arline's contagiousness and her physical impairment each resulted from the same underlying condition, tuberculosis. It would be unfair to allow an employer to seize upon the distinction between the effects of a disease on others and the effects of a disease on a patient and use that distinction to justify discriminatory treatment.[7]

Nothing in the legislative history of § 504 suggests that Congress intended such a result. That history demonstrates that Congress was as concerned about the effect of an impairment on others as it was about its effect on the individual. Congress extended coverage, in 29 U.S.C. § 706(7)(B)(iii), to those individuals who are simply "regarded as having"

---

7. The United States argues that it is possible for a person to be simply a carrier of a disease, that is, to be capable of spreading a disease without having a "physical impairment" or suffering from any other symptoms associated with the disease. The United States contends that this is true in the case of some carriers of the Acquired Immune Deficiency Syndrome (AIDS) virus. From this premise the United States concludes that discrimination solely on the basis of contagiousness is never discrimination on the basis of a handicap. The argument is misplaced in this case, because the handicap here, tuberculosis, gave rise both to a physical impairment *and* to contagiousness. This case does not present, and we therefore do not reach, the questions whether a carrier of a contagious disease such as AIDS could be considered to have a physical impairment, or whether such a person could be considered, solely on the basis of contagiousness, a handicapped person as defined by the Act.

a physical or mental impairment. The Senate Report provides as an example of a person who would be covered under this subsection "a person with some kind of visible physical impairment which in fact does not substantially limit that person's functioning." S.Rep.No. 93–1297, p. 64 (1974). Such an impairment might not diminish a person's physical or mental capabilities, but could nevertheless substantially limit that person's ability to work as a result of the negative reactions of others to the impairment.

Allowing discrimination based on the contagious effects of a physical impairment would be inconsistent with the basic purpose of § 504, which is to ensure that handicapped individuals are not denied jobs or other benefits because of the prejudiced attitudes or the ignorance of others. By amending the definition of "handicapped individual" to include not only those who are actually physically impaired, but also those who are regarded as impaired and who, as a result, are substantially limited in a major life activity, Congress acknowledged that society's accumulated myths and fears about disability and disease are as handicapping as are the physical limitations that flow from actual impairment. Few aspects of a handicap give rise to the same level of public fear and misapprehension as contagiousness. Even those who suffer or have recovered from such noninfectious diseases as epilepsy or cancer have faced discrimination based on the irrational fear that they might be contagious. The Act is carefully structured to replace such reflexive reactions to actual or perceived handicaps with actions based on reasoned and medically sound judgments: the definition of "handicapped individual" is broad, but only those individuals who are both handicapped *and* otherwise qualified are eligible for relief. The fact that *some* persons who have contagious diseases may pose a serious health threat to others under certain circumstances does not justify excluding from the coverage of the Act *all* persons with actual or perceived contagious diseases. Such exclusion would mean that those accused of being contagious would never have the opportunity to have their condition evaluated in light of medical evidence and a determination made as to whether they were "otherwise qualified."

* * *

IV

The remaining question is whether Arline is otherwise qualified for the job of elementary school teacher. To answer this question in most cases, the District Court will need to conduct an individualized inquiry and make appropriate findings of fact. Such an inquiry is essential if § 504 is to achieve its goal of protecting handicapped individuals from deprivations based on prejudice, stereotypes, or unfounded fear, while giving appropriate weight to such legitimate concerns of grantees as avoiding exposing others to significant health and safety risks. The basic factors to be considered in conducting this inquiry are well established.[17]

---

17. "An otherwise qualified person is one who is able to meet all of a program's requirements in spite of his handicap." Southeastern Community College v. Davis, 442 U.S. 397, 406, 99 S.Ct.

In the context of the employment of a person handicapped with a contagious disease, we agree with *amicus* American Medical Association that this inquiry should include:

> "[findings of] facts, based on reasonable medical judgments given the state of medical knowledge, about (a) the nature of the risk (how the disease is transmitted), (b) the duration of the risk (how long is the carrier infectious), (c) the severity of the risk (what is the potential harm to third parties) and (d) the probabilities the disease will be transmitted and will cause varying degrees of harm." Brief for American Medical Association as *Amicus Curiae* 19.

In making these findings, courts normally should defer to the reasonable medical judgments of public health officials.[18] The next step in the "otherwise-qualified" inquiry is for the court to evaluate, in light of these medical findings, whether the employer could reasonably accommodate the employee under the established standards for that inquiry. See supra, note 17.

Because of the paucity of factual findings by the District Court, we, like the Court of Appeals, are unable at this stage of the proceedings to resolve whether Arline is "otherwise qualified" for her job. The District Court made no findings as to the duration and severity of Arline's condition, nor as to the probability that she would transmit the disease. Nor did the court determine whether Arline was contagious at the time she was discharged, or whether the School Board could have reasonably accommodated her.[19] Accordingly, the resolution of whether Arline was otherwise qualified requires further findings of fact.

* * *

Affirmed.

CHIEF JUSTICE REHNQUIST, with whom JUSTICE SCALIA joins, dissenting.

2361, 2367, 60 L.Ed.2d 980 (1979). In the employment context, an otherwise qualified person is one who can perform "the essential functions" of the job in question. 45 CFR § 84.3(k) (1985). When a handicapped person is not able to perform the essential functions of the job, the court must also consider whether any "reasonable accommodation" by the employer would enable the handicapped person to perform those functions. Ibid. Accommodation is not reasonable if it either imposes "undue financial and administrative burdens" on a grantee, Southeastern Community College v. Davis, supra, at 412, or requires "a fundamental alteration in the nature of [the] program" id., at 410. See 45 CFR § 84.12(c) (1985) (listing factors to consider in determining whether accommodation would cause undue hardship); 45 CFR pt. 84, App. A, p. 315 (1985) ("where reasonable accommodation does not overcome the effects of a person's handicap, or where reasonable accommodation causes undue hardship to the employer, failure to hire or promote the handicapped person will not be considered discrimination").

18. This case does not present, and we do not address, the question whether courts should also defer to the reasonable medical judgments of private physicians on which an employer has relied.

19. Employers have an affirmative obligation to make a reasonable accommodation for a handicapped employee. Although they are not required to find another job for an employee who is not qualified for the job he or she was doing, they cannot deny an employee alternative employment opportunities reasonably available under the employer's existing policies. See n. 17, supra; 45 CFR § 84.12 and App. A, pp. 315–316 (1985).

In Pennhurst State School and Hospital v. Halderman, 451 U.S. 1, 101 S.Ct. 1531, 67 L.Ed.2d 694 (1981), this Court made clear that, where Congress intends to impose a condition on the grant of federal funds, "it must do so unambiguously." * * *

Our decision in *Pennhurst* was premised on the view that federal legislation imposing obligations only on recipients of federal funds is "much in the nature of a contract," [with recipients agreeing to aid handicapped persons in exchange for receipt of the federal funds that subject them to § 504's standards].

The legitimacy of this *quid pro quo* rests on whether recipients of federal funds voluntarily and knowingly accept the terms of the exchange. There can be no knowing acceptance unless Congress speaks "with a clear voice" in identifying the conditions attached to the receipt of funds.

The requirement that Congress unambiguously express conditions imposed on federal moneys is particularly compelling in cases such as this where there exists longstanding state and federal regulation of the subject matter. From as early as 1796, Congress has legislated directly in the area of contagious diseases. Congress has also, however, left significant leeway to the States, which have enacted a myriad of public health statutes designed to protect against the introduction and spread of contagious diseases. When faced with such extensive regulation, this Court has declined to read the Rehabilitation Act expansively. See Alexander v. Choate, 469 U.S. 287, 105 S.Ct. 712, 83 L.Ed.2d 661 (1985). Absent an expression of intent to the contrary, "Congress . . . 'will not be deemed to have significantly changed the federal-state balance.' "

Applying these principles, I conclude that the Rehabilitation Act cannot be read to support the result reached by the Court. The record in this case leaves no doubt that Arline was discharged because of the contagious nature of tuberculosis, and not because of any diminished physical or mental capabilities resulting from her condition. Thus, in the language of § 504, the central question here is whether discrimination on the basis of contagiousness constitutes discrimination "by reason of . . . handicap." Because the language of the Act, regulations, and legislative history are silent on this issue, the principles outlined above compel the conclusion that contagiousness is not a handicap within the meaning of § 504. It is therefore clear that the protections of the Act do not extend to individuals such as Arline.

* * *

Preliminary Note on the Analytical and Theoretical Elements in Disability Law

1. Section 504 works as a two-step statute. First, in order to gain protection a person must be deemed handicapped. Second, provided one is handicapped, grantees must reasonably accommodate that person's handicaps on an individual basis. (The more recent Americans with Disabilities Act of

1990, 42 U.S.C. § 12111 et seq., substitutes the word "disability" for "handicap," at the request of groups representing persons benefitted by such legislation. See S. Rep. No. 116, 101st Cong., 1st Sess., 21 (1989).)[1]

2. *Defining Handicap/Disability.* Notice the detail in the definition of protected persons here as compared to Title VI, which essentially leaves "race" and "color" undefined. What is the decisionmaking process for determining whether a particular circumstance causes a person to possess a statutorily defined "handicap"? And why is such a detailed decisionmaking process necessary?

(a) The statute sets out three circumstances that define a handicapped person: "[A]ny person who (i) has a physical or mental impairment which substantially limits one or more of such person's major life activities, (ii) has a record of such an impairment, or (iii) is regarded as having such an impairment." Are persons in categories (ii) and (iii) in fact impaired in any way? Why should such persons be protected? Even if category (ii) can be rationalized as continued protection for a person formerly disabled, how can category (iii) be justified?

(b) Focusing exclusively on the primary definition of "handicap" (category (i) in the preceding sub-paragraph), is that definition too broad, at least as supplemented by regulatory definitions of "mental or physical impairment" and "major life activity"? Who is not handicapped under this definition? In Daley v. Koch, 892 F.2d 212 (2d Cir.1989) (collecting cases), the court faced a claim by a postal employee who alleged that he had been discharged because of his handicap—"poor judgment, irresponsible behavior, and poor impulse control." The court held that these were not handicaps under the act, but is this result so clear? Were these not "mental impairments"? Did they not affect a "major life activity," that is, "working"? In Pack v. Kmart Corp., 166 F.3d 1300 (10th Cir.1999), an employee claimed that depression rendered her unable to sleep and concentrate, thus making her disabled. Was she?

(c) As the *Daley* case suggests, one may be impaired by degrees, and the definition of "handicapped" does not attach until some level of seriousness is reached. Guidelines adopted to illuminate similar definitions in the ADA stress that impairments must place a person outside the "normal" range before he will be deemed disabled. EEOC Interpretive Guidance on Title I of the Americans with Disabilities Act, 29 C.F.R. Part 1630 Appendix (1999) (commenting on § 1630.2(h): " 'impairment' does not include physical characteristics such as eye color, hair color, left-handedness, or height, weight or muscle tone that are within 'normal' range and are not the result of a physiological disorder"). See Pack v. Kmart Corp., 166 F.3d 1300 (10th Cir. 1999) (disabled compared to "average person"). What is "normal"? What is outside the range of the "average person"? (Reserve judgment on this approach until after reading the next principal case, which casts further light on the issue.)

---

1. For some clarity of analysis and historical accuracy, this Note primarily uses the nomenclature of the act under discussion, though the comparability of the two statutory definitions makes complete consistency impossible. Use of the terms "disability" and "disabled" therefore predominates.

(d) How persuasive is the Court's holding that contagious diseases are handicaps? Are you surprised that the legislative history is not clear about this? Should the relative silence indicate that infectious diseases are not intuitively "handicaps" they way most other disabilities are? What about influenza or the common cold—are they impairments? Is a broken limb? See EEOC Interpretive Guidance, supra (commenting on § 1630.2(j)) ("chronic impairments of short duration [ ] are usually not disabilities," nor are "broken limbs, sprained joints, concussions, appendicitis, and influenza"). Why? Is Justice Scalia correct in arguing that ambiguity should favor non-coverage in all such situations?

3. *Non-discrimination for Actually Qualified Persons.* At step #2 of analysis, once a person is determined to be "handicapped," she is only guaranteed equal, non-discriminatory treatment if she is "otherwise qualified." Consider footnote 17's statement of parameters for establishing someone's qualification: (i) one who can in fact meet all requirements, such as performing essential job functions; (ii) one unable to perform all functions but who can be reasonably accommodated. In this paragraph, consider the first category—those who can perform the job as it currently exists. What employer could reasonably oppose hiring a person who can in fact perform all the currently existing demands of the job? Consider the interplay between the definitions in step #1 and this first group of persons at step #2—those persons actually qualified.

(a) Recall the second and third definitions of "handicap" discussed in ¶ 1 supra—the definition that protects persons who have only a history of handicap or who are merely deemed to be handicapped when they in fact are not. Will not such persons always win at step #2 because they will in fact be qualified because they have no disability that prevents them from performing the job at issue? (Is the only issue in such cases the factual one of whether the person is indeed qualified?)

(b) Recall the first definition of "handicapped" in ¶ 1—the definition that protects persons who are actually impaired in some substantial way. If the disability that these persons possess is irrelevant to their job (a wheelchair bound person performing as an attorney, for example), such persons will also be qualified for the job as it currently exists, correct? These persons are, in effect, impaired in ways irrelevant to their jobs.

(c) With respect to the persons identified in this paragraph, are § 504 and the ADA simply pro-production, pro-rationality statutes that maximize the labor supply by rationalizing decisions about ability to work? If that is so, the only problematic group consists of those who are in fact impaired under the definitions in ¶ 1, yet are unable to perform the currently existing job as described in this paragraph. These persons benefit from the alternative protection at step #2—the requirement of "reasonable accommodation" that imposes an affirmative duty on grantees or employers to make reasonable changes in their employment practices in order to make the job one that the handicapped person can perform.

4. *Accommodation for Persons Not Actually Qualified for the Job as It Currently Exists.* What is "reasonable accommodation"? What is the scope of the duty to accommodate? In **Southeastern Community College v. Davis,**

442 U.S. 397, 99 S.Ct. 2361, 60 L.Ed.2d 980 (1979), the plaintiff, diagnosed as having a severe hearing disability, was denied admission to nursing school because her disability would make it too difficult for her to participate in classes and clinics or to work and communicate effectively as a nurse following graduation. The Court discussed her argument for admission, 442 U.S. at 407, 99 S.Ct. at 2368:

> "Respondent contends nevertheless that § 504, properly interpreted compels Southeastern to undertake affirmative action that would dispense with the need for effective oral communication. First, it is suggested that respondent can be given individual supervision by faculty members whenever she attends patients directly. Moreover, certain required courses might be dispensed with altogether for respondent. It is not necessary, she argues, that Southeastern train her to undertake all the tasks a registered nurse is licensed to perform. Rather, it is sufficient to make § 504 applicable if respondent might be able to perform satisfactorily some of the duties of a registered nurse or to hold some of the positions available to a registered nurse.

> "Respondent finds support for this argument in portions of the HEW regulations [set out in 45 CFR pt. 84]. In particular, a provision applicable to postsecondary educational programs requires covered institutions to make 'modifications' in their programs to accommodate handicapped persons, and to provide 'auxiliary aids' such as sign-language interpreters. Respondent argues that this regulation imposes an obligation to ensure full participation in covered programs by handicapped individuals and, in particular, requires Southeastern to make the kind of adjustments that would be necessary to permit her safe participation in the nursing program.

> "We note first that on the present record it appears unlikely respondent could benefit from any affirmative action that the regulation reasonably could be interpreted as requiring. Section 84.44(d)(2), for example, explicitly excludes 'devices or services of a personal nature' from the kinds of auxiliary aids a school must provide a handicapped individual. Yet the only evidence in the record indicates that nothing less than close, individual attention by a nursing instructor would be sufficient to ensure patient safety if respondent took part in the clinical phase of the nursing program. * * * Such a fundamental alteration in the nature of a program is far more than the 'modification' the regulation requires.

> "Moreover, an interpretation of the regulations that required the extensive modifications necessary to include respondent in the nursing program would raise grave doubts about their validity. If these regulations were to require substantial adjustments in existing programs beyond those necessary to eliminate discrimination against otherwise qualified individuals, they would do more than clarify the meaning of § 504. Instead, they would constitute an unauthorized extension of the obligations imposed by the statute."

(a) What is an "undue hardship"? How does one decide when administrative or financial burdens have become "undue"? Does this call for "sliding scale" review? Note that when Congress adopted the Americans With Disabilities Act of 1990, Pub.L. 101–336, 104 Stat. 327, codified at 42 U.S.C. § 12101 et seq., which extensively applies to employment, it appeared to adopt precisely such a balancing approach. See 42 U.S.C. § 12111(10). What should happen in Ms. Arline's case on remand from the Supreme Court? Is her employment more important than the risk of disease to her students? Does it matter how great that risk is? Is any risk too great given that children are involved?[2]

(b) Assume that a police officer seeks to be accommodated by reassignment to another job outside the police department; is that a reasonable accommodation? Would it still be reasonable if the officer sought to retain the higher salary from the former job which he could not perform? Compare Davoll v. Webb, 194 F.3d 1116 (10th Cir.1999) (reassignment is not a per se hardship; individual consideration necessary), with Myers v. Hose, 50 F.3d 278, 284 (4th Cir.1995) (transfer not required if employee cannot be accommodated in present position). Could an employee on leave reasonably ask that a job be held open for him indefinitely? See Watkins v. J & S Oil Co., Inc., 164 F.3d 55 (1st Cir.1998). Should courts follow the approach in religious accommodation cases heard under Title VII, Chapter 7B.2 infra, and require little more than minimal accommodation from volunteers? See, e.g., Trans World Airlines, Inc. v. Hardison, 432 U.S. 63, 97 S.Ct. 2264, 53 L.Ed.2d 113 (1977).

(c) Assume that learning-disabled students who remain in high school beyond the usual four years wish to continue to compete in varsity athletics; is a request to state officials to waive the usual limits on varsity sports a reasonable accommodation? See Washington v. Indiana High School Athletic Ass'n, Inc., 181 F.3d 840 (7th Cir.1999) (preliminary injunction awarded plaintiff).

5. *Accommodation and Balancing (continued).* In **PGA Tour, Inc. v. Martin**, 532 U.S. 661, 121 S.Ct. 1879, 149 L.Ed.2d 904 (2001), the Court accepted that a professional golfer with an atrophied leg was disabled, and the PGA agreed that allowing a golf cart to be used, instead of walking the course, as all other players are required to do, would be a reasonable accommodation—except for one factor. Allowing the cart would "fundamentally alter" the nature of the sport.[3] The (PGA) took the position that riding in a cart would give Martin an unfair advantage over other golfers who were required to risk fatigue while walking the course for several hours, and famed pro Jack Nicklaus testified that "fatigue" affects the game and is a part of determining winners in the sport. The trial judge rejected that view, noting that walking expended little energy and that Martin's disability added a compensating fatigue in his own personal situation. The Supreme Court agreed, 532 U.S. at 682–87, 121 S.Ct. at 1895–96:

> "In theory, a modification of petitioner's golf tournaments might constitute a fundamental alteration in two different ways. It might alter such an essential aspect of the game of golf that it would be unacceptable even

---

2. See Roberts v. Progressive Independence, Inc., 183 F.3d 1215 (10th Cir.1999) (reasonable accommodation is a jury issue). Do you agree?

3. "[Discrimination includes] a failure to make reasonable modifications in policies, practices, or procedures, when such modifications are necessary to afford such goods, services, facilities, privileges, advantages, or accommodations to individuals with disabilities, *unless the entity can demonstrate that making such modifications would fundamentally alter the nature* of such goods, services, facilities, privileges, advantages, or accommodations." 42 U.S.C. § 12182(b)(2)(A)(ii).

if it affected all competitors equally; changing the diameter of the hole from three to six inches might be such a modification. Alternatively, a less significant change that has only a peripheral impact on the game itself might nevertheless give a disabled player, in addition to access to the competition as required by Title III, an advantage over others and, for that reason, fundamentally alter the character of the competition. We are not persuaded that a waiver of the walking rule for Martin would work a fundamental alteration in either sense [because ancient and some modern rules show that walking has not always been fundamental to the game of golf.]''

* * *

"The force of petitioner's argument [that elite, professional golf requires walking is] mitigated by the fact that golf is a game in which it is impossible to guarantee that all competitors will play under exactly the same conditions or that an individual's ability will be the sole determinant of the outcome. For example, changes in the weather may produce harder greens and more head winds for the tournament leader than for his closest pursuers. A lucky bounce may save a shot or two. Whether such happenstance events are more or less probable than the likelihood that a golfer afflicted with [a disability] would one day qualify for the * * * PGA TOUR, they at least demonstrate that pure chance may have a greater impact on the outcome of elite golf tournaments than the fatigue resulting from the enforcement of the walking rule."

(a) Should courts make these kinds of decisions? If Martin had been disabled by atrophied arm, would the Court have required that he be allowed to use a smaller, lighter-weight ball that could fly farther with his weakened stroke? May a person disabled by the existence of small hands ask for the accommodation—a virtually no-cost accommodation—of being allowed to use a smaller basketball? May a field-goal kicker in professional football disabled with a delicate foot, request the accommodation of being allowed to use a lead toe in his kicking boot? How much lead? (Does Justice Stevens seem to distinguish between outdoor sports affected by the weather and indoor ones that are not?)

(b) Justice Stevens seems to treat the issues as equivalent to an "on-off" switch, subject to categorical "yes or no" answers as to whether an accommodation is reasonable or whether it "fundamentally" alters the game. Is it not more likely that issues are relevant by degree? And who decides whether the degree of relevance is adequate or not? If football were still played with no helmets, would use of a helmet to protect a weakened head "fundamentally alter" the game? May a disabled participant in rugby, where no helmets are used today, reasonably request to be allowed to use one?

(c) In the *Martin* case, the Court relied on expert testimony to show that the energy expended by walking the golf course is the equivalent in calories to one "Big Mac." The Court in *Arline* also suggested that experts should help courts decide theses medical questions. Are the issues ones purely of expertise, or do they also require a normative judgment? A mixed factual and normative judgment? (If you were willing to permit helmets for rugby or a lead-protected toe for football kickers, how hard may the helmet be? How much lead is allowed the kicker? Enough to protect the disabled person? Do you need to consider potential harm to other players as well as potential unfairness?)

6. In response to criticism that courts were ill-prepared to answer these types of questions, the majority in *Martin* issued this reply, 532 U.S. at 689, 121 S.Ct. at 1897: "[P]etitioner's questioning of the ability of courts to apply the reasonable modification requirement to athletic competition is a complaint more properly directed to Congress, which drafted the ADA's coverage broadly, than to us. [Any attempt to avoid decision] renders the word 'fundamentally' largely superfluous, because it treats the alteration of any rule governing an event at a public accommodation to be a fundamental alteration."

(a) Assuming sports are covered, this position seems unassailable, does it not? If there is a culprit here, it is Congress, is it not? Whereas the balancing dilemma created by Title VI was of the Court's own making, see subpart A of this Chapter supra, here Congress has demanded that courts play this role.

(b) On the other hand, the issue here may be one of coverage. Just as coverage of infectious diseases created the problem for balancing in *Arline*, coverage of sports makes the for a difficult issue for courts to decide in *Martin*. How strong is the argument that the sports tournaments, as opposed to sports facilities for public use, are places of "public accommodation" under the ADA? See 42 U.S.C. § 12181(7) (defining the term to include "a gymnasium, health spa, bowling alley, golf course, or other place of exercise or recreation"). Was the phrase intended to protect only patrons or also the professional performers at such places?

(c) Congress has in the ADA added a defense that permits restaurants and others employing "food handlers" to exclude them from employment in some circumstances. See 42 U.S.C.A. § 12113. Should the exclusion be categorical? Should it apply to other situations involving infectious diseases? Should sports be excluded from coverage?

7. What is the relation between an effects test (such as in Title VI) and an accommodation requirement? Is the latter a substitute for the former? A supplement? In **Alexander v. Choate**, 469 U.S. 287, 105 S.Ct. 712, 83 L.Ed.2d 661 (1985), the Court appeared to be unable to decide whether § 504 adopted an effects test in addition to its accommodation requirement. The plaintiffs claimed that Tennessee's practice of limiting the days-per-year for which it would pay for poor people sent to hospitals under the Medicaid program, constituted discrimination against handicapped persons in violation of § 504. The plaintiffs did not argue that the plan was adopted intentionally to harm their class, but rather that since handicapped persons needed more hospital stays than non-handicapped persons, a limitation on visits would have the effect of discriminating against the class. The Court rejected the argument, 469 U.S. at 295, 105 S. CT. at 717:

> "Discrimination against the handicapped was perceived by Congress to be most often the product, not of invidious animus, but rather of thoughtlessness and indifference—of benign neglect. Thus, Representative Vanik, introducing the predecessor to § 504 in the House, described the treatment of the handicapped as one of the country's "shameful oversights," which caused the handicapped to live among society "shunt-

ed aside, hidden, and ignored." 117 Cong.Rec. 45974 (1971). Similarly, Senator Humphrey, who introduced a companion measure in the Senate, asserted that "we can no longer tolerate the invisibility of the handicapped in America...." 118 Cong.Rec. 525–526 (1972). And Senator Cranston, the Acting Chairman of the Subcommittee that drafted § 504, described the Act as a response to "previous societal neglect." 119 Cong.Rec. 5880, 5883 (1973). See also 118 Cong.Rec. 526 (1972) (statement of cosponsor Sen. Percy) (describing the legislation leading to the 1973 Act as a national commitment to eliminate the "glaring neglect" of the handicapped). Federal agencies and commentators on the plight of the handicapped similarly have found that discrimination against the handicapped is primarily the result of apathetic attitudes rather than affirmative animus.

* * *

"At the same time, the position urged by respondents—that we interpret § 504 to reach all action disparately affecting the handicapped—is also troubling. Because the handicapped typically are not similarly situated to the nonhandicapped, respondents' position would in essence require each recipient of federal funds first to evaluate the effect on the handicapped of every proposed action that might touch the interests of the handicapped, and then to consider alternatives for achieving the same objectives with less severe disadvantage to the handicapped. The formalization and policing of this process could lead to a wholly unwieldy administrative and adjudicative burden. See *Note, Employment Discrimination Against the Handicapped and Section 504 of the Rehabilitation Act: An Essay on Legal Evasiveness*, 97 HARV. L. REV. 997, 1008 (1984) (describing problems with pure disparate impact model in context of employment discrimination against the handicapped). Had Congress intended § 504 to be a National Environmental Policy Act for the handicapped, requiring the preparation of "Handicapped Impact Statements" before any action was taken by a grantee that affected the handicapped, we would expect some indication of that purpose in the statute or its legislative history. Yet there is nothing to suggest that such was Congress' purpose. Thus, just as there is reason to question whether Congress intended § 504 to reach only intentional discrimination, there is similarly reason to question whether Congress intended § 504 to embrace all claims of disparate-impact discrimination.

"Any interpretation of § 504 must therefore be responsive to two powerful but countervailing considerations—the need to give effect to the statutory objectives and the desire to keep § 504 within manageable bounds. Given the legitimacy of both of these goals and the tension between them, we decline the parties' invitation to decide today that one of these goals so overshadows the other as to eclipse it."

(a) The Court subsequently decided that whatever effects test might be appropriate for § 504, it was not violated by Tennessee's action because it would not deny handicapped persons "meaningful access" to health care. 469 U.S. at 306, 105 S. CT. at 723. Was this an evasion?

(b) The Court at the same time reaffirmed its adoption of an accommodation principle for § 504. See 469 U.S. at 308, 105 S.Ct. at 724. Does the accommodation principle not require the same attentiveness by the defendant as an effects test would? At least when an individual brought his problem to the defendant's attention, the defendant would be required to consider accommodation, would it not?

(c) In light of *Arline*'s demand for "individualized inquir[ies]," is a class-based effects test workable under § 504? Do § 504 and the ADA effectively trade an effects test for the far greater benefit of "reasonable accommodation"? See Christine Jolls, *Antidiscrimination and Accommodation*, 115 HARV. L. REV. 642 (2001) (comparing antidiscrimination and accommodation principles).

(d) As a matter of social policy, would an individualized accommodation test be more appropriate for Title VI than the effects test presently adopted? Would it help African–Americans more? Would it generate less racial consciousness or more? Which is preferable?

NOTE ON THE THEORETICAL ELEMENTS IN DISABILITY LAW

1. Why do disabled persons receive protection under "civil rights" laws? Why do other groups? In *Arline*'s footnote 2, statutes protecting handicapped persons are said to be justified on the basis of analogizing the treatment of such persons to the treatment of African–Americans. In this paragraph, consider some more detailed possibilities. First, one could posit an Equality and Rationality Model that deems all persons protected because "we are the same," and discrimination is therefore irrational. Other models will be discussed below. In other words, we consider in this Note the political and social motivations for passing different civil rights statutes might themselves be different.

(a) Though it is quite likely that white support for the black civil rights movement contained many elements of the Charity Model, see Taylor Branch, PARTING THE WATERS: AMERICA IN THE KING YEARS, 1954–1963 at 803–09 (1988), judicial decisions in the modern civil rights era have consistently justified civil rights protection for African–Americans by reference to the Equality Model, arguing that blacks and whites are the same and that discrimination against black persons is not simply a hateful act, but ultimately an irrational one because all persons are the same. See Brown v. Board of Education, 347 U.S. 483, 74 S.Ct. 686, 98 L.Ed. 873 (1954) (segregation "inherently" unequal). Cf. United States v. Virginia, 518 U.S. 515, 116 S.Ct. 2264, 135 L.Ed.2d 735 (1996): "Supposed 'inherent differences' are no longer accepted as a ground for race or national origin classifications": while there are "[p]hysical differences between men and women," such differences are "cause for celebration, but not for denigration of the members of either sex or for artificial constraints on an individual's opportunity."[1]

---

1. Indeed, the concept has proved to be so strong that it has occasionally marked an outer boundary for traditional race-based civil rights concepts, a reason for refusing to provide even more protections for African–Americans. See, e.g., City of Richmond v. J.A. Croson Co., Chapter 7D infra (affirmative action limited because all Americans are minorities of some kind and all have a racial identification).

(b) Now consider the persons identified in ¶ 3 of the previous Note—"actually qualified persons." This includes those persons who are not in fact currently disabled but have a history of such or are mistakenly regarded as disabled. It also includes disabled persons whose disability is irrelevant to their job or program activity. The Equality and Rationality Model also justifies protection for these persons, does it not? Since these persons can in fact perform the same, with respect to relevant job or program activities, as a non-disabled person, they are "the same," and dissimilar treatment of them would be irrational, would it not?

(c) Can the Equality and Rationality Model justify protection for other disabled persons, persons who by definition cannot perform the same as non-disabled persons? Note that the ADA declares a non-discrimination principle, then separately defines discrimination to require the same treatment and also accommodation. Is this an admission that persons needing accommodation are not being treating the same as non-disabled persons? (Would a wealth-disabled person who cannot perform a job due to inadequate education receive accommodation under the ADA? Does this show that disabled persons who need accommodation are receiving a benefit not usually accorded others?)

2. Consider a second model that would justify protection for persons not covered above, a Charity Model. The Charity Model could justify protection for those persons who are in fact disabled and whose disability requires that the job be changed to accommodate them. The accommodation could be seen as charity given to mostly deserving persons, persons who through bad luck or circumstance find themselves disabled (where but for good fortune others in society might find themselves).

(a) Note the exclusions from coverage in all or parts of the ADA, which by definition rules that certain persons will not be deemed disabled even if they otherwise meet the test for "disabled": "(1) transvestism, transsexualism, pedophilia, exhibitionism, voyeurism, gender identity disorders not resulting from physical impairments, or other sexual behavior disorders; (2) compulsive gambling, kleptomania, or pyromania; or (3) psychoactive substance use disorders resulting from current illegal use of drugs," 42 U.S.C.A. § 12211. See also 42 U.S.C.A. §§ 12114, 12208 (other specialty exclusions). Do the topics on this list suggest that Congress had in mind some concept of the "deserving" disabled?

(b) Disability-rights advocates reject a charity-based rationale for protections, often with some vehemence. See Chai Feldblum, *The Moral Rhetoric of Legislation*, 72 N.Y.U. L. REV. 992 (1997). Why? For the same reasons that many Americans reject or avoid becoming recipients of charity? Does charity necessarily imply that the recipient is of lower status? Does it imply that in the American social setting?

3. Consider other possible models justifying protection for disabled persons, including an Insurance Model. Under this model, the social cost-sharing that reasonable accommodation involves can be seen not as an act of charity, but as an act of self-protection—as insurance—should any person become disabled in the future. The social cost-sharing is not done to benefit others so much as to benefit oneself in the event of future need.

(a) Does the Insurance Model explain the broad bi-partisan support that accompanied passage of the ADA? If one expects to benefits, even contingently, from a program in the future, then it is more like Social Security than charity, is it not? Does the Insurance Model also explain why legislators would be attracted to a very broad definition of "disability"? After all, if the insurance policy has narrow coverage, then protection will not be there for the policyholder in the future, correct? Doesn't self-interest compel the policyholder—the citizen—to support a broad legislative definition of disability?

(b) What other models might justify protection for disabled persons entitled to accommodation? Would you support an Insurance Model, which justifies the accommodation as an insurance reimbursement for those who have had the bad luck of suffering a disability? Might one argue for a Readjustment of Power Model, one which sees prior society as physically structured by the powerful in ways that unthinkingly limits others? Do § 504 and the ADA simply bring us back to a fairer baseline of opportunity?

(c) If § 504 and the ADA are justified on the Insurance Model, it might be rational to see both statutes as part of a broader system of social security, one that provides direct payments to some quite disabled persons (who cannot be accommodated) and indirect benefits (through accommodation, especially in employment) payable from federal grantees under § 504 or other businesses or governments (under the ADA). In **Cleveland v. Policy Management Systems Corp.**, 526 U.S. 795, 119 S.Ct. 1597, 143 L.Ed.2d 966 (1999), the Court faced the question of whether a declaration of disability and request for social-security-type disability payments disentitles the requestor to protection when she later sues an employer claiming that she should have been accommodated. What result? Should Congress re-write the statutes to make the programs interlock so that everyone falls into one category of protection or the other?

(d) Adoption of the ADA was promoted, in part, on the cost-savings that would be accomplished from putting disabled people back to work. Does this suggest that it might be rational to conduct a cost-benefit study to determine if certain types of disabilities cost more than they save? Should the same analysis be done for individual disabled persons seeking employment accommodations?

4. Now consider whether § 504 and the ADA accomplish civil rights goals in the fundamental sense of helping most those who suffer from the most discrimination. Recall the two-step analysis for determining coverage: a person must first show that she is disabled and only then may she claim the benefits of accommodation unless there is an undue hardship.

(a) Is it not likely that the person who most easily satisfies the Court at step #1 will be the person least likely to be accommodated without undue hardship at step #2. In the *Arline* case, if Ms. Arline is extremely contagious and can easily pass her disease to her students, can she be easily accommodated on remand? If a golfer as in the *Martin* case has an extreme disability, such as quadriplegia, is there any alteration to the game of golf that can be made to accommodate him? In the *Davis* case, there was no accommodation possible for a student who was so severely disabled that she could not benefit from the program, even in an altered condition. Do these disability-protecting civil rights statutes protect least those who need it most? See Zukle v. Regents of University of California, 166 F.3d 1041 (9th Cir.1999) (no accommodation at medical school for student with such pronounced learning disability that she scored in the bottom 5% of all test-takers).

(b) Is it not likely that the person with the least disability—or no current disability at all, but is regarded as disabled or has a history of disability—will be the most easily accommodated person? For some, in fact, no accommodation will even be necessary because they are equal in ability. Do these statutes protect most those who need it least?

(c) What justifies these apparently perverse or anomalous results? Which Model discussed above lends itself to explaining these results? Are there other models that explain these statutes? See, e.g., John J. Donohue III, *Employment Discrimination Law in Perspective: Three Concepts of Equality*, 92 Mich. L. Rev. 2583 (1994) (developing models based on the law and economics movement).

5. Finally consider the two different ways in which § 504 and the ADA readjust relationships or require cost-sharing or transfer of costs. Are they like other civil rights statutes?

(a) To the extent that these statutes require accommodation that is paid for by the employer or program grantee, they may be said to require readjustment of costs between institutions and individuals, a kind of vertical readjustment of costs. Third parties—other individuals—appear not to be directly affected. (But is this true? If an employer's costs are increased by having to accommodate one employee, will not less money remain to pay the wages of the other employees? Does the answer depend not on how much the employer has available, but the labor supply or the elasticity of wages?)

(b) Regardless of how one decides the foregoing issue, there seems to be something different about Ms. Arline's case: if she is restored to teaching in the classroom, the persons who must "pay" for her accommodation are her students who now risk catching her disease. Similarly, in the *Martin* case, if the PGA accommodates Martin, the persons who "pay" are the other professional golfers who now may be beaten because of the advantage Mr. Martin has derived from riding in a golf cart. In other words, the cost-sharing is horizontal between program beneficiaries or employees or other private individuals, not vertically between the powerful and the disabled. Are these civil rights statutes therefore more difficult to justify?

(c) Should § 504 and the ADA be amended to rule out horizontal cost-sharing? Do other civil rights statutes also involve horizontal cost-shifting? See, e.g., Chapter 6E and 7D infra (affirmative action).

6. Re-examine these issues in the context of the next principal case, involving AIDS. It involves the so-called "direct threat" exception to "reasonable accommodation." Does it merely restate the reasonable accommodation test in another context?

BRAGDON v. ABBOTT

Supreme Court of the United States, 1998.
524 U.S. 624, 118 S.Ct. 2196, 141 L.Ed.2d 540 (1998).

JUSTICE KENNEDY delivered the opinion of the Court.

We address in this case the application of the Americans with Disabilities Act of 1990 (ADA),[2] 42 U.S.C. § 12101 et seq., to persons infected with the human immunodeficiency virus (HIV). We granted certiorari to review, first, whether HIV infection is a disability under the ADA when the infection has not yet progressed to the so-called symptomatic phase; and, second, whether * * * respondent's infection with HIV posed no direct threat to the health and safety of her treating dentist.

I

[Respondent Abbott, infected with HIV but without "most serious symptoms," sought dental care from Petitioner Bragdon in 1994. The dentist conducted an examination, found a cavity, and informed the patient that because of her HIV infection he wanted to fill the cavity at a hospital where extra services would be available in case of need. The hospital would charge for its services, but the dentist offered to perform his work without increased fee. The patient declined and later brought this suit under a section of the ADA that provides: "No individual shall be discriminated against on the basis of disability in the full and equal enjoyment of the goods, services, facilities, privileges, advantages, or accommodations of any place of public accommodation by any person who ... operates a place of public accommodation." § 12182(a). The term "public accommodation" is defined to include the "professional office of a health care provider." § 12181(7)(F). Another section states:

"Nothing in this subchapter shall require an entity to permit an individual to participate in or benefit from the goods, services, facilities, privileges, advantages and accommodations of such entity where such individual poses a direct threat to the health or safety of others." § 12182(b)(3). The lower courts found for the plaintiff on all pertinent issues.]

II

[We first review the ruling that respondent's HIV infection constituted a disability under the first definition in the ADA: "a physical or mental impairment that substantially limits one or more of the major life activities of such individual * * *."] The ADA's definition of disability is drawn almost verbatim from the definition of "handicapped individual" included in the Rehabilitation Act of 1973, 29 U.S.C. § 706(8)(B) (1988 ed.), and the definition of "handicap" contained in the Fair Housing Amendments

---

2. [The ADA contains several titles that protect disabled persons in a variety of contexts. The most important are employment (the majority of litigated cases), transportation, and public accommodations. See the Appendix.] [Note by editor.]

Act of 1988, 42 U.S.C. § 3602(h)(1) (1988 ed.). Congress' repetition of a well-established term carries the implication that Congress intended the term to be construed in accordance with pre-existing regulatory interpretations. In this case, Congress did more than suggest this construction; it adopted a specific statutory provision in the ADA directing as follows:

> "Except as otherwise provided in this chapter, nothing in this chapter shall be construed to apply a lesser standard than the standards applied under [§ 504] of the Rehabilitation Act of 1973 or the regulations issued by Federal agencies pursuant to such title." 42 U.S.C. § 12201(a).

The directive requires us to construe the ADA to grant at least as much protection as provided by the regulations implementing the Rehabilitation Act.

1

The first step in the inquiry under subsection (A) requires us to determine whether respondent's condition constituted a physical impairment[, and thus we turn to the protective standards under § 504, as set out in the *Arline* case.] In issuing these regulations, HEW decided against including a list of disorders constituting physical or mental impairments, out of concern that any specific enumeration might not be comprehensive. 42 Fed.Reg. 22685 (1977), reprinted in 45 CFR pt. 84, App. A, p. 334 (1997). The commentary accompanying the regulations, however, contains a representative list of disorders and conditions constituting physical impairments, including "such diseases and conditions as orthopedic, visual, speech, and hearing impairments, cerebral palsy, epilepsy, muscular dystrophy, multiple sclerosis, cancer, heart disease, diabetes, mental retardation, emotional illness, and . . . drug addiction and alcoholism." Ibid. [HIV infection is understandably not on the list because it had not yet been identified when the list was made, but its characteristics fit the regulatory definition.]

The disease follows a predictable and, as of today, an unalterable course. Once a person is infected with HIV, the virus invades different cells in the blood and in body tissues. Certain white blood cells, known as helper T-lymphocytes or CD4+ cells, are particularly vulnerable to HIV. The virus attaches to the CD4 receptor site of the target cell and fuses its membrane to the cell's membrane. HIV is a retrovirus, which means it uses an enzyme to convert its own genetic material into a form indistinguishable from the genetic material of the target cell. The virus' genetic material migrates to the cell's nucleus and becomes integrated with the cell's chromosomes. Once integrated, the virus can use the cell's own genetic machinery to replicate itself. Additional copies of the virus are released into the body and infect other cells in turn. Young, The Replication Cycle of HIV–1, in The AIDS Knowledge Base, pp. 3.1–2 to 3.1–7 (P. Cohen, M. Sande, & P. Volberding eds., 2d ed.1994) (hereinafter AIDS Knowledge Base); Folks & Hart, The Life Cycle of Human Immunodeficiency Virus Type 1, in AIDS: Etiology, Diagnosis, Treatment and Prevention 29–39 (V. DeVita et al. eds., 4th ed.1997) (hereinafter AIDS: Etiology); Greene, Molecular Insights into HIV–1 Infection, in The Medical Management of AIDS 18–24 (M. Sande & P. Volberding eds., 5th ed.1997) (hereinafter Medical Management of AIDS). Although the body does produce antibodies to combat HIV infection, the antibodies are not effective in eliminating the virus. [Medical citations omitted.]

The virus eventually kills the infected host cell [and spreads throughout the blood. It later enters] its asymptomatic phase. The term is a misnomer, in some respects, for clinical features persist throughout, including lymphadenopathy, dermatological disorders, oral lesions, and bacterial infections. Although it varies with each individual, in most instances this stage lasts from 7 to 11 years. The virus now tends to concentrate in the lymph nodes, though low levels of the virus continue to appear in the blood. [Medical citations omitted.] It was once thought the virus became inactive during this period, but it is now known that the relative lack of symptoms is attributable to the virus' migration from the circulatory system into the lymph nodes. [Medical citations omitted.] [The medical community defines "AIDS" as existing when the patient's CD4+ count drops below a certain level, and typical symptoms at this stage include pneumocystis carinii pneumonia, Kaposi's sarcoma, and non-Hodgkins lymphoma, and increased bouts of fever, weight loss, fatigue, lesions, nausea, and diarrhea. Death follows. (Extensive medical citations omitted.)]

In light of the immediacy with which the virus begins to damage the infected person's white blood cells and the severity of the disease, we hold it is an impairment from the moment of infection * * *

2

The statute is not operative, and the definition not satisfied, unless the impairment affects a major life activity. Respondent's claim throughout this case has been that the HIV infection placed a substantial limitation on her ability to reproduce and to bear children.... We have little doubt that had different parties brought the suit they would have maintained that an HIV infection imposes substantial limitations on other major life activities. [But we granted certiorari on the issue of whether "reproduction is a major life activity," and we now turn to that issue.]

We have little difficulty concluding that it is. As the Court of Appeals held, "[t]he plain meaning of the word 'major' denotes comparative importance" and "suggest[s] that the touchstone for determining an activity's inclusion under the statutory rubric is its significance." Reproduction falls well within the phrase "major life activity." Reproduction and the sexual dynamics surrounding it are central to the life process itself.

While petitioner concedes the importance of reproduction, he claims that Congress intended the ADA only to cover those aspects of a person's life which have a public, economic, or daily character[, but nothing in the statute suggests such a limitation. Moreover, as] we have noted, the ADA must be construed to be consistent with regulations issued to implement the Rehabilitation Act. See 42 U.S.C. § 12201(a).... These regulations are contrary to petitioner's attempt to limit the meaning of the term "major" to public activities. The inclusion of activities such as caring for one's self and performing manual tasks belies the suggestion that a task must have a public or economic character in order to be a major life activity for purposes of the ADA. On the contrary, the Rehabilitation Act regulations support the inclusion of reproduction as a major life activity, since reproduction could not be regarded as any less important than working and learning. Petitioner advances no credible basis for confining major life activities to those with a public, economic, or daily aspect. In the absence of any reason to reach a contrary conclusion, we agree with the Court of Appeals' determination that reproduction is a major life activity for the purposes of the ADA.

3

The final element of the disability definition in subsection (A) is whether respondent's physical impairment was a substantial limit on the major life activity she asserts. The Rehabilitation Act regulations provide no additional guidance. 45 CFR pt. 84, App. A, p. 334 (1997).

Our evaluation of the medical evidence leads us to conclude that respondent's infection substantially limited her ability to reproduce in two independent ways. First, a woman infected with HIV who tries to conceive a child imposes on the man a significant risk of becoming infected. The cumulative results of 13 studies collected in a 1994 textbook on AIDS indicates that 20% of male partners of women with HIV became HIV-positive themselves, with a majority of the studies finding a statistically significant risk of infection. Osmond & Padian, Sexual Transmission of HIV, in AIDS Knowledge Base 1.9–8, and tbl. 2; see also Haverkos & Battjes, Female-to-Male Transmission of HIV, 268 JAMA 1855, 1856, tbl. (1992) (cumulative results of 16 studies indicated 25% risk of female-to-male transmission). (Studies report a similar, if not more severe, risk of male-to-female transmission. See, e.g., Osmond & Padian, AIDS Knowledge Base 1.9–3, tbl. 1, 1.9–6 to 1.9–7.)

Second, an infected woman risks infecting her child during gestation and childbirth, i.e., perinatal transmission. Petitioner concedes that women infected with HIV face about a 25% risk of transmitting the virus to their children. Published reports available in 1994 confirm the accuracy of this statistic. [Medical citations omitted.]

Petitioner points to evidence in the record suggesting that antiretroviral therapy can lower the risk of perinatal transmission to about 8%, [citing studies, some of them challenged by the patient]. We need not resolve this dispute in order to decide this case, however. It cannot be said as a matter of law that an 8% risk of transmitting a dread and fatal disease to one's child does not represent a substantial limitation on reproduction.

The Act addresses substantial limitations on major life activities, not utter inabilities. Conception and childbirth are not impossible for an HIV victim but, without doubt, are dangerous to the public health. This meets the definition of a substantial limitation. The decision to reproduce carries economic and legal consequences as well. There are added costs for antiretroviral therapy, supplemental insurance, and long-term health care for the child who must be examined and, tragic to think, treated for the infection. The laws of some States, moreover, forbid persons infected with HIV from having sex with others, regardless of consent. [Six state codes cited.]

In the end, the disability definition does not turn on personal choice. When significant limitations result from the impairment, the definition is met even if the difficulties are not insurmountable. For the statistical and other reasons we have cited, of course, the limitations on reproduction may be insurmountable here. Testimony from the respondent that her HIV infection controlled her decision not to have a child is unchallenged. In the context of reviewing summary judgment, we must take it to be true * * *. Respondent's HIV infection is a physical impairment which substantially limits a major life activity, as the ADA defines it * * *.

* * *

III

[We also granted certiorari on the issue of whether courts should defer to a doctor's medical judgment in deciding these kinds of cases.] Again, we begin with the statute. Notwithstanding the protection given respondent by the ADA's definition of disability, petitioner could have refused to treat her if her infectious condition "pose[d] a direct threat to the health or safety of others." 42 U.S.C. § 12182(b)(3). The ADA defines a direct threat to be "a significant risk to the health or safety of others that cannot be eliminated by a modification of policies, practices, or procedures or by the provision of auxiliary aids or services." Ibid. * * *

The ADA's direct threat provision stems from the recognition in School Bd. of Nassau City. v. Arline of the importance of prohibiting discrimination against individuals with disabilities while protecting others from significant health and safety risks, resulting, for instance, from a contagious disease. In Arline, the Court reconciled these objectives by construing the Rehabilitation Act not to require the hiring of a person who posed "a significant risk of communicating an infectious disease to others."] n. 16. Congress amended the Rehabilitation Act and the Fair Housing Act to incorporate the language. See 29 U.S.C. § 706(8)(D) (excluding individuals who "would constitute a direct threat to the health or safety of other individuals"); 42 U.S.C. § 3604(f)(9) (same). It later relied on the same language in enacting the ADA. See 28 CFR pt. 36, App. B, p. 626 (1997) (ADA's direct threat provision codifies Arline). Because few, if any, activities in life are risk free, Arline and the ADA do not ask whether a risk exists, but whether it is significant. Arline, supra.

[The existence, or nonexistence, of a significant risk must be determined from the standpoint of the person who refuses the treatment or accommodation, and the risk assessment must be based on medical or other objective evidence. *Arline*, supra.] As a health care professional, petitioner had the duty to assess the risk of infection based on the objective, scientific information available to him and others in his profession. His belief that a significant risk existed, even if maintained in good faith, would not relieve him from liability. To use the words of the question presented, petitioner receives no special deference simply because he is a health care professional. * * *

Our conclusion that courts should assess the objective reasonableness of the views of health care professionals without deferring to their individual judgments does not answer the implicit assumption in the question presented, whether petitioner's actions were reasonable in light of the available medical evidence. In assessing the reasonableness of petitioner's actions, the views of public health authorities, such as the U.S. Public Health Service, CDC, and the National Institutes of Health, are of special weight and authority. Arline, supra; 28 CFR pt. 36, App. B, p. 626 (1997). The views of these organizations are not conclusive, however. A health care professional who disagrees with the prevailing medical consensus may refute it by citing a credible scientific basis for deviating from the accepted norm. See W. Keeton, D. Dobbs, R. Keeton, & D. Owen, Prosser and Keeton on Law of Torts § 32, p. 187 (5th ed.1984).

We have reviewed so much of the record as necessary to illustrate the application of the rule to the facts of this case. For the most part, the Court of Appeals followed the proper standard in evaluating the petitioner's position and conducted a thorough review of the evidence. Its rejection of the District Court's reliance on the Marianos affidavits [concerning cases of transmission of HIV in dental offices] was a correct application of the principle that petitioner's actions must be evaluated in light of the available, objective evidence. The record did not show that CDC had published the conclusion set out in the affidavits at the time petitioner refused to treat respondent. [Nor is the dentist's offer to treat the patient in a hospital pertinent, given the facts that he had no medical privileges at a hospital and none nearby offered the safety measures he wanted to use.]

We are concerned, however, that the Court of Appeals might have placed mistaken reliance upon two other sources. In ruling no triable issue of fact existed on this point, the Court of Appeals relied on the 1993 CDC Dentistry Guidelines and the 1991 American Dental Association Policy on HIV. This evidence is not definitive. As noted earlier, the CDC Guidelines recommended certain universal precautions which, in CDC's view, "should reduce the risk of disease transmission in the dental environment." [Medical citations omitted.] ... In our view, the Guidelines do not necessarily contain implicit assumptions conclusive of [the risk posed in this case]. The Guidelines set out CDC's recommendation that the universal precautions are the best way to combat the risk of HIV transmission. They do not assess the level of risk.

Nor can we be certain, on this record, whether the 1991 American Dental Association Policy on HIV carries the weight the Court of Appeals attributed to it. The Policy does provide some evidence of the medical community's objective assessment of the risks posed by treating people infected with HIV in dental offices [by noting that there is "little risk of transmission" and that "patients may be safely treated in private dental offices."] We note, however, that the Association is a professional organization, which, although a respected source of information on the dental profession, is not a public health authority. It is not clear the extent to which the Policy was based on the Association's assessment of dentists' ethical and professional duties in addition to its scientific assessment of the risk to which the ADA refers. Efforts to clarify dentists' ethical obligations and to encourage dentists to treat patients with HIV infection with compassion may be commendable, but the question under the statute is one of statistical likelihood, not professional responsibility. Without more information on the manner in which the American Dental Association formulated this Policy, we are unable to determine the Policy's value in evaluating whether petitioner's assessment of the risks was reasonable as a matter of law.

* * *

There are reasons to doubt whether petitioner advanced evidence sufficient to raise a triable issue of fact on the significance of the risk. Petitioner relied on two principal points: First, he asserted that the use of high-speed drills and surface cooling with water created a risk of airborne HIV transmission. The study on which petitioner relied was inconclusive, however, determining only that "[f]urther work is required to determine whether such a risk exists." Johnson & Robinson, Human Immunodeficiency Virus–1 (HIV–1) in the Vapors of Surgical Power Instruments, 33 J. of Medical Virology 47, 47 (1991) * * *. Scientific evidence and expert testimony must have a traceable, analytical basis in objective fact * * *.

Second, petitioner argues that, as of September 1994, CDC had identified seven dental workers with possible occupational transmission of HIV. See U.S. Dept. of Health and Human Services, Public Health Service, CDC, HIV/AIDS Surveillance Report, vol. 6, no. 1, p. 15, tbl. 11 (Mid-year ed. June 1994). These dental workers were exposed to HIV in the course of their employment, but CDC could not determine whether HIV infection had resulted. It is now known that CDC could not ascertain whether the seven dental workers contracted the disease because they did not present themselves for HIV testing at an appropriate time after their initial exposure. Gooch et al., Percutaneous Exposures to HIV–Infected Blood Among Dental Workers Enrolled in the CDC Needlestick Study, 126 J. American Dental Assn. 1237, 1239 (1995). It is not clear on this record, however, whether this information was available to petitioner in September 1994. If not, the seven cases might have provided some, albeit not necessarily sufficient, support for petitioner's position. Standing alone, we doubt it would meet the objective, scientific basis for finding a significant risk to the petitioner.

[These factual issues and the question of whether summary judgment is appropriate based on them can be decided on remand.] The determination of the Court of Appeals that respondent's HIV infection was a disability under the ADA is affirmed. The judgment is vacated, and the case is remanded for further proceedings consistent with this opinion.

It is so ordered.

[Concurring opinions omitted.]

CHIEF JUSTICE REHNQUIST, with whom JUSTICE SCALIA and JUSTICE THOMAS join, and with whom JUSTICE O'CONNOR joins as to Part II, concurring in the judgment in part and dissenting in part.

[The parties do not dispute that positive HIV-status is a "physical impairment."] According to the Court, the next question is "whether reproduction is a major life activity." That, however, is only half of the relevant question. As mentioned above, the ADA's definition of a "disability" requires that the major life activity at issue be one "of such individual." § 12102(2)(A). The Court truncates the question, perhaps because there is not a shred of record evidence indicating that, prior to becoming infected with HIV, respondent's major life activities included reproduction (assuming for the moment that reproduction is a major life activity at all) [for there is no evidence she was considering reproduction.] Indeed, when asked during her deposition whether her HIV infection had in any way impaired her ability to carry out any of her life functions, respondent answered "No." * * *

But even aside from the facts of this particular case, the Court is simply wrong in concluding as a general matter that reproduction is a "major life activity." [A dictionary definition suggests that "major" as used here refers to "comparative importance."] No one can deny that reproductive decisions are important in a person's life. But so are decisions as to who to marry, where to live, and how to earn one's living. Fundamental importance of this sort is not the common thread linking the statute's listed activities. The common thread is rather that the activities are repetitively performed and essential in the day-to-day existence of a normally functioning individual. They are thus quite different from the series of activities leading to the birth of a child.

[It is argued that] reproduction must be a major life activity because regulations issued under the ADA define the term "physical impairment" to include physiological disorders affecting the reproductive system. If reproduction were not a major life activity, they argue, then it would have made little sense to include the reproductive disorders in the roster of physical impairments. This argument is simply wrong. There are numerous disorders of the reproductive system, such as dysmenorrhea and endometriosis, which are so painful that they limit a woman's ability to engage in major life activities such as walking and working. And, obviously, cancer of the various reproductive organs limits one's ability to engage in numerous activities other than reproduction.

But even if I were to assume that reproduction is a major life activity of respondent, I do not agree that an asymptomatic HIV infection "substantially limits" that activity. The record before us leaves no doubt that those so infected are still entirely able to engage in sexual intercourse, give birth to a child if they become pregnant, and perform the manual tasks necessary to rear a child to maturity * * *. [That HIV infection is fatal in the future is also irrelevant for the ADA requires that the disability must be limiting in the present, not the future.] Respondent's argument, taken to its logical extreme, would render every individual with a genetic marker for some debilitating disease "disabled" here and now because of some possible future effects * * *.

II

* * *

I agree with the Court that "the existence, or nonexistence, of a significant risk must be determined from the standpoint of the person who refuses the treatment or accommodation," as of the time that the decision refusing treatment is made. I disagree with the Court, however, that "[i]n assessing the reasonableness of petitioner's actions, the views of public health authorities ... are of special weight and authority." [In litigation between private parties,] the credentials of the scientists employed by the public health authority, and the soundness of their studies, must stand on their own. [*Arline* held only that public health officials deserved deference; it did not hold that other health professionals' judgment should be ignored.]

Applying these principles here, it is clear to me that petitioner has presented more than enough evidence to avoid summary judgment on the "direct threat" question. In June 1994, the Centers for Disease Control and Prevention published a study identifying seven instances of possible transmission of HIV from patients to dental workers. While it is not entirely certain whether these dental workers contracted HIV during the course of providing dental treatment, the potential that the disease was transmitted during the course of dental treatment is relevant evidence. One need only demonstrate "risk," not certainty of infection. See *Arline*, supra (" 'the probabilities the disease will be transmitted' " is a factor in assessing risk). [I therefore agree that the case should be remanded for trial.]

NOTE ON DEFINING "DISABILITY" AND THE ADA AMENDMENTS OF 2008

1. *Bragdon* concludes that HIV infection constitutes a disability from the moment of infection. Or does it?

(a) While finding that AIDS is a physical impairment from the moment of HIV infection, before symptomatic AIDS has appeared, the Court holds that it results in a statutory disability only because it additionally limits a major life activity—reproduction. This means that the plaintiff HIV-infected woman was disabled because of the disease's affect on her procreational choices. Does Chief Justice Rehnquist make a valid point when he notes that there is no proof that the plaintiff was in fact procreationally active or wanted to procreate? Do you read the majority opinion as turning on whether plaintiff wanted to have children or wanted to have sex? Is sex a major life activity?

(b) Given the possibility of transmission of HIV between males and female partners, would a heterosexual non-HIV-infected male also be disabled because his choices about procreation would also be limited?

(c) Homosexual activity is not likely to lead to procreation, and thus the rationale employed in *Bragdon* does not readily apply to protect HIV-infected homosexuals. If *Bragdon* can be read to cover sex choices, does it then cover homosexuals? What other life activities, apart from sex-related activities, might be considered sufficiently major to lead to recognition of a disability in the context of non-heterosexuals? Are all of these activities affected from the moment of infection with HIV? Is it possible that heterosexuals are deemed disabled from the moment of HIV infection, but homosexuals become disabled only at a later phase? Review *Bragdon*'s medical descriptions of the progressive nature of HIV infection. If sex is a major life activity, are homosexuals affected from the moment of infection because knowing that one is infected will affect future sexual activity?

(d) *Bragdon* appears to hold that an impairment may exist even when a claimant's choices are only limited, not just when they are completely foreclosed. Is that aspect of the decision inconsistent with the cases discussed in the following paragraphs? Do the following cases, moreover, support Chief Justice Rehnquist's dissenting demand that the individual claimant show that her life activities were actually restricted?

2. In **Sutton v. United Air Lines, Inc.**, 527 U.S. 471, 119 S.Ct. 2139, 144 L.Ed.2d 450 (1999), twin-sister pilots sued the airline because it refused to hire them as pilots due to their severe, but eyeglass-correctable, myopia. The Court, with only Justices Stevens and Breyer dissenting, held that sight impairment can be a disability under the ADA, but the determination of impairment "should be made with reference to measures that mitigate the individual's impairment, including, in this instance, eyeglasses and contact lenses." Rejecting a contrary position adopted by administrative agency regulations as inconsistent with the statute itself, the Court ruled that any impairment must actually and presently exist for that particular individual in order to limit a major life activity—a circumstance not present if the impairment is correctable for the specific claimant. Justice O'Connor sought further to justify the Court's position, 119 S.Ct. at 2147–49:

> "The agency['s] approach would often require courts and employers to speculate about a person's condition and would, in many cases, force them to make a disability determination based on general information about how an uncorrected impairment usually affects individuals, rather than on the individual's actual condition. For instance, under this view, courts would almost certainly find all diabetics to be disabled, because if they failed to monitor their blood sugar levels and administer insulin,

they would almost certainly be substantially limited in one or more major life activities. A diabetic whose illness does not impair his or her daily activities would therefore be considered disabled simply because he or she has diabetes. Thus, the guidelines approach would create a system in which persons often must be treated as members of a group of people with similar impairments, rather than as individuals. This is contrary to both the letter and the spirit of the ADA. * * *

"Finally, and critically, findings enacted as part of the ADA require the conclusion that Congress did not intend to bring under the statute's protection all those whose uncorrected conditions amount to disabilities. Congress found that "some 43,000,000 Americans have one or more physical or mental disabilities * * *." § 12101(a)(1). [That figure, based on widespread studies, is consistent with a definition of impairment that uses a "functional approach" focusing on the claimant's actual ability to work. The petitioners' definition would result in at least 160 million Americans being labeled disabled, a result clearly at odds with Congress' understanding of the scope of disability.]"

"Because it is included in the ADA's text, the finding that 43 million individuals are disabled gives content to the ADA's terms, specifically the term "disability." Had Congress intended to include all persons with corrected physical limitations among those covered by the Act, it undoubtedly would have cited a much higher number of disabled persons in the findings. That it did not is evidence that the ADA's coverage is restricted to only those whose impairments are not mitigated by corrective measures."

(a) Is it simply common sense that a person who has readily correctable eyesight is not really impaired in any meaningful way?[1] Is that what the Court or Congress thought? Why should a person who can put on glasses or contact lenses—and correct her own problem, as most in society do—be deemed impaired, when the consequence of being labeled disabled is that others must care for her? Is the affirmative duty of reasonable accommodation that the ADA imposes on others leading the Court to restrict the group of persons who can benefit from that affirmative duty? Does the Court consider the ADA's assistance for disabled people to be un-American socialism? Or just unworkable?

(b) Regardless of whether the Sutton sisters were actually disabled, were they not "regarded as" disabled by their employer, thus entitling them to coverage under the "regarded-as" definition of disability? Sutton's 7–2 majority also rejected this claim, 119 S.Ct. at 2150: "an employer is free to decide that physical characteristics or medical conditions that do not rise to the level of an impairment—such as one's height, build, or singing voice—are preferable to others, just as it is free to decide that some limiting, but not

---

1. In Albertsons, Inc. v. Kirkingburg, infra, the Court extended its holding to cover those impairments for which the body itself makes natural corrections. There it suggested that a person with a vision impairment in one eye should not be deemed impaired because the brain compensates by mentally filling-in the picture that it expects to receive from the non-functional eye: "We see no principled basis for distinguishing between measures undertaken with artificial aids [as in Sutton] and measures undertaken, whether consciously or not, with the body's own systems." 527 U.S. at 555.

substantially limiting, impairments make individuals less than ideally suited for the job." Is this just another way of saying that the applicants fell within the normal range of seeing ability (as corrected) and that employers are free to choose the more-qualified among the normal within running afoul of the ADA? In other words, does the ADA cover only the *dis*abled, not the *less* able? See Albertsons, Inc. v. Kirkinburg, infra: "While the Act 'addresses substantial limitations on major life activities, not utter inabilities,' *Bragdon*, it concerns itself only with limitations that are in fact substantial." 527 U.S. at 565.

(c) Does it follow from the majority opinion that every correctable disability will leave the otherwise-disabled person without protection? Does the issue then turn on whether the claimant remains impaired even after mitigation of the impairment? Does a wheelchair-user become non-disabled because he has a wheelchair? After *Sutton*, does the answer depend on whether she remains impaired in life activity despite the wheelchair?

3. Other cases decided the same day as *Sutton* cemented its rejection of a broad approach to the ADA that would have defined broad swaths of society as "disabled" who could benefit from "reasonable accommodation." **Murphy v. United Parcel Service**, 527 U.S. 516, 119 S.Ct. 2133, 144 L.Ed.2d 484 (1999), involved a person with hypertension who could, with medication, perform most "life activities"—except "work." The Court ruled that "[w]hen the life activity under consideration is that of working, the statutory phrase 'substantially limits' requires at a minimum, that plaintiffs allege they are unable to work in a broad class of jobs." The plaintiff, who lost his job as a DOT-certified mechanic, was admittedly qualified to hold many other mechanic positions, and thus lost his suit. **Albertson's, Inc. v. Kirkingburg**, 527 U.S. 555, 119 S.Ct. 2162, 144 L.Ed.2d 518 (1999), involved a truck driver who lost his job after it was discovered that he had monocular vision, a condition placing him below minimum Department of Transportation regulations for certification as a driver. The Court decided that the DOT rules prevail.

(a) Even as the *Albertson's* case showed the power of collateral regulations to affect civil rights cases, the *Sutton* and *Murphy* cases manifested a growing judicial concern with regulations adopted for enforcement of the ADA itself. In *Sutton*, in particular, Justice O'Connor pointedly noted that although the statute gave divided authority to several departments and agencies to implement specific provisions of the Act, there was no power granted to any body to interpret the generally applicable provisions of the ADA: "Most notably, no agency has been delegated authority to interpret the term 'disability.' " 527 U.S. at 479.[2] Nevertheless, in **Chevron U.S.A. Inc. v. Echazabal**, 536 U.S. 73, 122 S.Ct. 2045, 153 L.Ed.2d 82 (2002), the Court upheld EEOC regulations that extended the "direct threat" defense to cover not only dangers to others but also dangers to the disabled person himself. Is *Chevron* another example of the narrowing of the ADA and § 504? Do all of the cases discussed in this Note carry a similar theme—the need to narrow coverage of some impairments because of the horizontal costs that they impose on innocent third parties? Should disability statutes show some concern for those

---

2. At several places in these opinions the Court also specifically declines to decide whether the less formal guidelines (or "Interpretive Guidance") are entitled to deference from courts. See id. at 2146.

who might be harmed by accommodations given persons the Court perceives as myopic pilots in *Sutton*, a hypertensive truck driver in *Murphy*, or a one-eyed truck driver in *Alberston's*? (Is there any horizontal cost-shifting when the person harmed by the direct threat is the disabled person himself?)

(b) A hallmark of much modern federal legislation has been the writing of statutes that adopt general principles that are then supplemented quite substantially by regulations which carry the real details of the law. See, e.g., Southern New England Telephone Co. v. Federal Communications Commission, 525 U.S. 366, 119 S.Ct. 721, 142 L.Ed.2d 835 (1999) (major telecommunications reform legislation implemented by regulation). Should this legislative approach be used for civil rights legislation? Is it enough for Congress to decide that Americans want to provide more help and assistance to disabled persons? Or should Congress be required to state in some detail the circumstances in which the protection will be provided? Is the problem that intentional discrimination may be easily prohibited, with few exceptions and social tradeoffs, but that regulation of effects-type discrimination or reasonable accommodation involve minute individualized tradeoffs that are beyond the scope of broad legislation? If they are beyond the scope of general legislation, should they be deemed beyond the scope of law generally?

(c) Civil rights advocates have generally supported the model of general legislation supplemented by detailed regulations and guidelines, based on some broad confidence that regulation-writers and guidelines-drafters will be quite sympathetic to their positions. Is the price of victory the loss of a broad-based discussion of the actual tradeoffs involved in implementing civil rights goals? See Sheila Foster, *Justice from the Ground Up: Distributive Inequities, Grassroots Resistance, and the Transformative Politics of the Environmental Justice Movement*, 86 Calif. L. Rev. 775 (1998) (arguing for political action and a wider social discussion). Does *Chevron* show that regulation-writing can contract coverage as well as expand it?

4. Finally, in **Toyota Motor Manufacturing, Kentucky, Inc. v. Williams**, 534 U.S. 184, 122 S.Ct. 681, 151 L.Ed.2d 615 (2002), the Court more directly faced the issue of whether work itself is a major life activity. The case involved a woman who claimed that carpal tunnel syndrome, developed on the job, prevented her from performing her the tasks of her position, even though she testified that she could perform other tasks at the factory. The appellate court found her disabled because unable to perform the major life activity of "manual tasks." Justice O'Connor's unanimous opinion for the Court reversed, finding it error to focus on "only a limited class of manual tasks" instead of "tasks that are of central importance to most people's daily lives." The Court noted that "the manual tasks in question must be central to daily life," and the impairment "permanent or long-term."

(a) The Court noted that the preamble to the ADA stated that approximately "43,000,000 Americans" have one or more disabilities, and it thus shied away from an interpretation of the Act that would produce a "number of disabled Americans [that] would surely have been much higher." Do you agree?

(b) Is there some inherent tension in § 504 and the ADA? It seems that if everyone is to be insured under the disability statutes, so that there will be widespread support from everyone who might become dependent on it, but at the same time it cannot become so broad that everyone is simultaneously paying for each other's impairments. Can the Court find a happy medium through defining the word "disability"?

(c) Are § 504 and the ADA different from all or most other civil rights statutes because they protect no identifiable minority? Are they different because they do not protect against any fixed identification (e.g., race or gender) as the other statutes do? Is that the source of the problem seen in the *Toyota* case? Is the demand that the impairment be "permanent or long-term" an attempt to identify a stable minority, a stable protected class?

5. Following the cases cited above, Congress passed and President Bush signed the **ADA Amendments Act of 2008**, Pub. L. 110–325, 122 Stat. 3553 (2008). Rejecting *Sutton* and *Toyota* by name, the Act specifically adding to "work" to the category of major life activities and defining "regarded as impaired" to include "an actual or perceived physical or mental impairment whether or not the impairment limits or is perceived to limit a major life activity." Does the 2008 Act mean that the Court must now do what it was attempting to avoid–proceed to the second step of deciding which accommodations are "reasonable"?

(a) The 2008 Amendments also provided that an "impairment that is episodic or in remission is a disability if it would substantially limit a major life activity when active" and that a "determination of whether an impairment substantially limits a major life activity shall be made without regard to the ameliorative effects of mitigating measures" such as medications or technological aids. If a person is disabled "without regard to" use of disability-relieving aids, is the employer or program required to provide these aids as reasonable accommodation? If so, does the Act effectively declare that the person remains disabled even after receiving the assistance? Would it be reasonable to require an employer to pay for accommodations for the duration of employment?

(b) The 2008 Act provided, however, that the "ameliorative effects of the mitigating measures of *ordinary eyeglasses or contact lenses* shall be considered in determining whether an impairment substantially limits a major life activity" (emphasis added). Why are ordinary eyeglasses and contact lenses not to be considered? Are such impairments so "normal" that they are not "impairments" at all? Are these not disabilities simply because Congress says they are not? Consider some original provisions of the ADA: excluded are current users of illegal drugs, §§ 12114, 12210 (deemed not "qualified individuals" unless rehabilitated), psychotics suffering due to "current" drug abuse, § 12211(b)(3) [psychosis arising from previous illegal drug use not textually excluded]; homosexuals and bisexuals, § 12211(a) (such traits declared not to be impairments, thus not disabilities); practitioners of transvestism, transsexualism, pedophilia, etc. § 12211(b)(1) (declared not covered without explanation); compulsive gamblers, kleptomaniacs, pyromaniacs, § 12211(b)(2) (same). Is it clear why some supporters of excluded groups would agree to exclusion under the ADA even though they do not consider the group's behavior aberrant?

(c) If definitional exclusions are set at a somewhat distant boundary, and if inclusions are now defined quite broadly, is almost everything that limits a person for a greater than temporary period now a "disability"? If so, Congress has charged the courts with making law, has it not, under the guise of deciding which accommodations are "reasonable"?

NOTE ON SHIFTING SOCIAL COSTS TO THIRD PARTIES AND THE EFFECTIVENESS OF DISABILITY LAW

1. The classic modern civil rights statute increases the freedom of citizens by restricting the power of social institutions. See sub-part A of this Chapter; Chapter 7 infra. In the process, as discussed in the preceding two Notes, these statutes may shift some costs to these large institutions. Section 504 and the ADA, on the other hand, may also transfer social costs from one individual to another. The accommodation that an employer must provide for a disabled employee or beneficiary can have substantial collateral consequences for other employees. As introduced in the Note following the *Arline* case, § 504 and the ADA appear to have significant potential for transferring costs to third parties. This Note faces that issue directly.

2. In **US Airways, Inc. v. Barnett**, 535 U.S. 391, 122 S.Ct. 1516, 152 L.Ed.2d 589 (2002), an employee was found to be disabled, and transfer to another job was deemed a reasonable accommodation. When he was later "bumped" from that job by a more senior employee, he sued claiming that he should have been accommodated by being allowed to avoid the usual seniority rules. The Court held that absent unusual circumstances, the existence of the seniority system barred accommodation of the type requested here and that the very existence of the system would entitle the employer to summary judgment. (Only two Justices voted to set aside the seniority system.) In the course of his majority opinion, Justice Breyer observed the following, 535 U.S. at 400–01, 122 S.Ct. at 1522–23:

"[A] demand for an effective accommodation could prove unreasonable because of its impact, not on business operations, but on fellow employees—say because it will lead to dismissals, relocations, or modification of employee benefits to which an employer, looking at the matter from the perspective of the business itself, may be relatively indifferent. [It is therefore not "undue hardship to the employer that should be the touchstone of accommodation, but whether" the accommodation is independently "reasonable."]

"Neither does the statute's primary purpose require Barnett's special reading. The statute seeks to diminish or to eliminate the stereotypical thought processes, the thoughtless actions, and the hostile reactions that far too often bar those with disabilities from participating fully in the Nation's life, including the workplace. These objectives demand unprejudiced thought and reasonable responsive reaction on the part of employers and fellow workers alike. They will sometimes require affirmative conduct to promote entry of disabled people into the workforce. They do not, however, demand action beyond the realm of the reasonable."

(a) If the contrary rule were adopted, one requiring co-worker to forego their seniority rights for a disabled employee, who would bear the "cost" of the disabled person's accommodation?

(b) How do you interpret the second quoted paragraph's language about "reasonable responsive action on the part of employers and fellow workers alike"? What is the antecedent of "they" in the next sentence? Is the requirement one that also applies to "fellow workers"? If so, how is that consistent with the Court's actual holding insulating most seniority systems from challenge? Must fellow workers volunteer to accommodate a disabled worker in all employment relations except those relating to seniority?

(c) In the course of holding that avoidance of seniority systems is not ordinarily a reasonable accommodation, the Court supported its decision by noting, 535 U.S. at 404–05, that "[m]ost important for present purposes, to require the typical employer to show more than the existence of a seniority system might well undermine the employees' expectations of consistent, uniform treatment [and would] substitute a complex case-specific 'accommodation' decision made by management for the more uniform, impersonal operation of seniority rules. Such management decision making, with its inevitable discretionary elements, would involve a matter of the greatest importance to employees [and] it might well take place fairly often[, making it inconsistent with the ADA's assumption that accommodation would not protect vast numbers of people regularly]." Are seniority systems the only employment practices that offer uniform rules on which employees might rely? Isn't Justice Breyer's observation true of many situations in employment?

3. Even some accommodation that appears to affect only the employer, transferring costs from the disabled individual to the employer, might on closer examination involve horizontal cost transfers. Should courts closely scrutinize such cases to avoid possible effects on third parties?

(a) For example, in Roberts v. Progressive Independence, Inc., 183 F.3d 1215 (10th Cir.1999), an employee of a disability rights organization, who suffered from cerebral palsy and used a wheelchair and personal care attendants, was ordered to attend a business meeting in another city; he requested that a personal care attendant known to him accompany him at company expense (in order to provide for his hygiene needs and supervise his travel in the absence of a wheelchair aboard the plane). The court found for the plaintiff. Who bears the expense of the judgment? If the employer has a travel budget, as most companies do, what happens to the travel plans of other employees after this plaintiff travels to Miami with an assistant for three days?

(b) Reasonable accommodation virtually by definition costs something. Whether it is $25 to raise a desk to accommodate a person in a wheelchair or $15,000 to alter transportation vehicles at a university. See United States v. Board of Trustees, 908 F.2d 740, 750–51 (11th Cir.1990) (lift-equipped bus service; cost of $15,000 to provide service deemed not an undue burden given university's $1.2 million budget). Do these costs necessarily reduce the wage pool available to other employees or the social benefits available to other students? Does any money spent on reasonable accommodation reduce that sum total of money available for other uses? Should the corporate defendant just make up the difference by foregoing some profits? Who pays that cost?

4.   The decisions in *Bragdon* and *Arline* highlight a more tangible cost to third parties that arises in the context of disabilities based on infectious diseases.[1] The risk of disease is a risk borne by other employees or program participants, not by the corporate shareholders, correct?

(a) *Bragdon* candidly recognizes that the risk need not be zero in order for a plaintiff to recover: "Because few, if any, activities in life are risk free, *Arline* and the ADA do not ask whether a risk exists, but whether it is significant." How great must the risk be in order to be significant? What happens to a fellow employee, a doctor, or another program participant if the court permits a minor risk—and the third party thereafter is infected?

(b) In *Arline* the plaintiff had tuberculosis. Assume that transmission is difficult, resulting in perhaps only one possibility of infection per 100,000 close interactions. The teacher has three such interactions with each of her 33 students each day for the ten days her disease is active, or 1,000 interactions. If the infection risk is 1%, is that too great a risk for these schoolchildren to bear? If the risk could be lowered further by having the children wear masks, should that be required? How should *Arline* be decided on remand? See Arline v. School Bd. of Nassau County, 692 F.Supp. 1286 (M.D. Fla. 1988) (reinstatement to job ordered).

(c) Does *Bragdon* provide any clues as to statistics of acceptable risk? In discussing whether HIV infection is a substantial limitation on the plaintiff, the Court notes that she herself runs at least "an 8% risk of transmitting a dread and fatal disease to [her] child" if she becomes pregnant. This is determined to be a sufficient risk to her to constitute a substantial limit on her procreational activities. Would an 8% risk of infection to the dentist constitute a significant risk justifying his refusal to provide services to the HIV-infected patient? In other words, should the risk-bearing rules be the same for both claimant and health-care provider?

(d) In *Bragdon* the patient posed a risk to the health-care provider. In Estate of Mauro v. Borgess Medical Center, 137 F.3d 398 (6th Cir.1998), the hospital discharged an HIV-infected health-care worker. Should the analysis be the same as in *Bragdon*?

5.   The Court in both *Bragdon* and *Arline* tries to solve the problem of risk assessment by directing trial courts to health-care professionals. But as the *Bragdon* Court notices, some professional medical organizations can have a political element in their decisionmaking. Even assuming that courts defer only to the scientific judgment of medical authorities concerning disease transmission and infection risk, does that solve the problem?

---

1.   Analytically, the *Arline* case involves the question of accommodation following a finding that the plaintiff is disabled. The "direct threat" determination, on the other hand, is analytically part of the determination whether a person is "qualified" for the job. Should this affect a court's analysis? See Estate of Mauro v. Borgess Medical Center, 137 F.3d 398 (6th Cir.1998): "The 'direct threat' standard applied in the Americans With Disabilities Act is based on the same standard as 'significant risk' applied by the Rehabilitation Act. Our analysis under both Acts thus merges into one question: Did [plaintiff's] activities as a surgical technician * * * pose a direct threat or significant risk to the health or safety of others?"

(a) Medical studies regarding the risks of infection typically note the possibility of disease transmission (anecdotal evidence) and/or statistical evidence concerning the number of transmissions per contact. Occasionally, as in *Bragdon*, a normative judgment is added. See, e.g., Centers for Disease Control, U.S. Dep't of Health & Human Servs., Recommendations for Preventing Transmission of Human Immunodeficiency Virus and Hepatitis B Virus to Patients During Exposure–Prone Invasive Procedures, 40 Morbidity & Mortality Weekly Report, 1, 3–4 (July 12, 1991) ("small" risk of infection). The professional observations regarding disease transmission methods and rates presumably fall within a medical professional's expertise, but does the normative judgment about the degree of risk? Is one person's "small" risk another's "great" risk?

(b) Assume that on remand the dentist in *Bragdon* is required to treat HIV-infected patients; despite the low risk, he becomes infected from one of these patients. Is that fair? Has he waived any claim to privacy and protection from disease by offering his health services to the public? If one of the schoolchildren in *Arline* is infected when the teacher returns to the classroom, is that fair? Has the student waived her claim to privacy by going to public school? If this is unfair, do the infected third parties have a remedy? Against whom?

(c) *Bragdon* appears to discuss risk by starting at the low end of the scale; a person of low risk is otherwise qualified despite the risk. Yet the EEOC regulations appear to start at the other end of the spectrum, requiring that claimants be accommodated unless they pose a high risk. See 29 C.F.R. § 1630.2(r) (1996): "An employer [may not discharge an infectious employee] merely because of a slightly increased risk. The risk can only be considered when it poses a significant risk, i.e. high probability, of substantial harm...." In other words, third parties are required to accept middling risks that do not reach a level of "high probability" of "substantial harm." Should the statute work the opposite way around? Should persons be required to accept only insignificant risks? How does § 1630.2(r) (2011) avoid this issue?

6. Is risk assessment always a matter of statistics? The *Arline* Court says that the reasonable-accommodation decision focuses on several factors, only one of which is risk. The ADA's "direct threat" provision, adapted from *Arline* (as noted in *Bragdon*), may also consider other factors, such as the ability to attenuate the risk. Are some risks non-quantifiable?

(a) In LaChance v. Duffy's Draft House, Inc., 146 F.3d 832 (11th Cir. 1998), an epileptic person, who suffered from seizures that left him dazed but not unconscious, was fired from his job as a cook after having two seizures on his first night at work. The employer claimed that the employee could not perform the job safely and posed a danger to others because of the need of cooks to use knives and hot cooking devices. No evidence of statistical risk was offered. How should the court rule?

(b) In Myers v. Hose, 50 F.3d 278 (4th Cir.1995), an insulin-dependent diabetic schoolbus driver lost his job after also suffering a heart attack and hypertension. Can he keep his job? Should he be allowed an open-ended period to correct his diet, reducing his disease symptoms, so that he can return to work?

(c) The above cases involved non-infectious diseases, and judgments were awarded the defendants. Does the ADA give more protection to persons with infectious diseases than to persons with non-infectious diseases? Should the statute operate the opposite way?

7. Review the cases in the preceding Note. Was the ADA Amendments Act of 2008 a mistake? Would it be better to define some conditions as non-disabilities in order to avoid the subjectivity and cost transfers associated with determining "reasonable accommodations" and "direct threats"? Does your answer depend on whether you think that judges are good at balancing social costs? Are better than nothing?

8. To the extent that the ADA or other disability laws require accommodation and shift some costs to institutions or to third-party individuals (such as co-workers or schoolchildren), the statute operates to solve the social problem of lack of opportunities or civic participation for disabled persons by imposing some costs on others. Would alternative methods better serve this goal?

(a) Each employer that provides accommodation must pay the cost of the accommodation, even though all of society benefits by employing the disabled worker. Similarly, an employer with no disabled employees pays nothing, free-riding on the social good done by the neighboring employer. Should the employer with a disabled employee receive a tax credit for serving this public good? Conversely, should there be a limit on the amount that any one employer is required to pay each year for accommodation, with all over that amount paid from public funds?[2]

(b) In **Cleveland v. Policy Management Systems Corp.**, 526 U.S. 795, 119 S.Ct. 1597, 143 L.Ed.2d 966 (1999), the Court held that Social Security's definitions for disability, which entitle claimants to public financial support, do not necessarily dovetail with definitions under the ADA. Thus a person who has applied for Social Security benefits on the ground that she is disabled from working is not estopped from suing her employer under the ADA. A person may both satisfy the ADA and be entitled to public benefits. Should Congress amend the two laws to make them more congruent? Would the public be better served by having an integrated system that automatically gives social security benefits to anyone not able to prevail on their disability claims under § 504 or the ADA?

(c) The presumption in the disability rights statutes generally has favored integration of disabled persons. See Ruth Colker, *The Disability Integration Presumption: Thirty Years Later*, 154 U. Pa. L. Rev. 789 (2006) (discussing problems with the assumption in the context of mainstreaming students in education). Are the actual results under the ADA and § 504 harder to square with a presumption of integration? If so, why?

9. Given the complexity of analysis under § 504 and the ADA, can one say that disabled persons have a "right" not to be subjected to discrimina-

---

2. The employer or other institution that is covered under § 504 because of receipt of federal grants might deduct compliance from the amount of the underlying grant and might even opt to apply for no more grants. But those covered under the ADA because they engage in commerce have no opt-out choices and no grants against which to deduct compliance.

tion? Are modern civil rights statutes just like all other legislation, a matter of interest-group politics, not "rights"?

(a) Some courts have observed that substantial numbers of disability cases are being filed by the same small group of repetitive claimants, resulting in an abuse of the litigation system for these laws. See, e.g., Molski v. Mandarin Touch Restaurant, 359 F. Supp.2d 924, 926 (C.D. Cal.2005) (one plaintiff "filed more than 400 federal lawsuits" in fewer than ten years; second plaintiff filed 36 suits; lawyer's firm "filed at least 223" such cases); Brother v. Tiger Partner, LLC, 331 F. Supp.2d 1368, 1369 (M.D. Fla. 2004) ("at least fifty-four" suits filed by same plaintiff and attorney); Rodriguez v. Investco, L.L.C., 305 F.Supp.2d 1278, 1281 n.10 (M.D. Fla. 2004) (579 cases filed in three years by five organizations and their members). Are these litigants and attorneys pursuing valuable goals by invoking disability claims, or do these cases show that there is only a narrow interest group, or perhaps even a few attorneys, committed to these statutes? Cf. http://archive.calbar.ca. gov/*Archive.aspx?articleId=94653&categoryId=94594&month=1& year=2009 (*Molski* attorney barred from filing suits for his frequent client; and disciplined by state bar); http://www.calbarjournal.com/January2011/Top Headlines/TH7.aspx (second attorney disbarred). On the other hand, is it possible that the statutes are under-enforced because of the reluctance of most plaintiffs to sue? See Ruth Colker, THE DISABILITY PENDULUM: THE FIRST DECADE OF THE AMERICANS WITH DISABILITIES ACT 188 (2005).

(b) Do you think that § 504 and the ADA have increased integration of long-term disabled persons into the economy and society, or has it resulted in a net loss of involvement of disabled persons? See Michael Waterstone, *The Untold Story of the Rest of the Americans with Disabilities Act*, 59 VAND. L. REV. 1807 (2005); Samuel R. Bagenstos, *Has the Americans with Disabilities Act Reduced Employment for People with Disabilities?*, 25 BERKELEY J. EMP. LAB. L. 527 (2004). Thomas DeLeire, an economist who studies the effects of disability laws, determined in *The Wage and Employment Effects of the Americans with Disabilities Act*, 35 J. OF HUMAN RESOURCES 694 (2000), that the enactment of the ADA caused an immediate "dramatic" 7% drop in the employment of disabled persons that has lasted a decade or more and resulted in no overall increase in wages for such persons. Why?

C. THE REACH OF TITLE VI AND ITS ANALOGUES

Title VI of the Civil Rights Act of 1964, together with its best-known analogues, Title IX of the Education Amendments of 1972 and § 504 of the 1973 Rehabilitation Act, condition the receipt of federal program grants on the willingness of the recipient to abjure certain discrimination (race, sex in some educational circumstances, and handicap). Although the prior sections of this Chapter have focused on litigation, the textually prominent enforcement mechanism for noncompliance is the termination of the grant, "but such termination ... shall be limited to the particular political entity, or part thereof, or other recipient [found to have discriminated] and shall be limited in its effect to the particular program, or part thereof, in which such non-compliance has been found." 42 U.S.C. § 2000d–1 (1980), 20 U.S.C. § 1682 (1980). Cf. 29 U.S.C. § 795 (1980) ("program or activity" language in original § 504).[1]

The legislative history of Title VI strongly suggested that Congress meant "program" to mean a specific federal grant program, and the Fifth Circuit so held in a part of the *Taylor County* case not reprinted in this book.[2] Why would Congress so limit the sanction? What should be the proper scope of Congress' concern when it attaches conditions to the money it spends?

BOARD OF PUBLIC INSTRUCTION OF TAYLOR COUNTY v. FINCH

United States Court of Appeals, Fifth Circuit, 1969.
414 F.2d 1068.

Before Bell and Goldberg, Circuit Judges, and Atkins, District Judge.

Goldberg, Circuit Judge:

Nominally, this case involves a challenge to the validity of an order by the Department of Health, Education and Welfare (HEW) terminating the payment of federal funds to the Board of Public Instruction of Taylor County, Florida, for violating Title VI of the Civil Rights Act of 1964. Underlying this challenge, however, is a broader question concerning the character and reach of the limitations which Congress has placed upon the power of an administrative agency to cut off federal funds and the Congressional policy behind such limitations.

The facts of this case are undisputed. [The school board maintained segregated schools, but began to dismantle them after passage of the 1964 Civil Rights Act. HEW, which provided federal grants to the district, demanded faster desegregation. The board failed to meet these demands.]

[Following a hearing, HEW terminated all funds earmarked for Taylor County under the three different federal grant programs that had previously sent money there.] The record shows that none of the findings of the HEW hearing examiner or of the HEW Reviewing Authority are programmatically oriented, at least if the term "program" is understood to refer to the individual grant statutes under which aid was given to the Taylor County School District. It is also plain on the face of the order entered by HEW that the termination of federal funds is not "limited in its effect" to one or more of the federally financed activities described in the grant statutes, but extends to "any classes of Federal financial assistance arising under *any Act of Congress.* * * *" [Emphasis added.]

1. The older versions of the various statutes are given for reasons that will become clear later.

2. See 414 F.2d at 1077. The best source for legislative history of Title VI is the extensive reported hearings in the House of Representatives. See Hearings Before Subcommittee No. 5, Committee on the Judiciary, House of Representatives, 88th Cong., 1st Sess. (1963). The final explanation of the "particular program" language can be found in 110 Cong.Rec. 7061–62 (1964).

Petitioner asks us to vacate the HEW order as a plain violation of the statute.

* * *

The facts of the present case make it impossible for this court to determine whether or not petitioner has been prejudiced by HEW's failure to make findings of fact tailored to particular federal programs. Three separate and distinct federal programs are here involved. One concerns federal aid for the education of children of low income families; one involves grants for supplementary educational centers; the third provides special grants for the education of adults who have not received a college education. Each of the programs has a different objective; each requires a separate plan and separate administrative approval; and each has an individual provision for appellate review. Under these circumstances it is not possible to say on the basis of segregation of faculty and students that all programs in the schools in Taylor County are constitutionally defective. It is perfectly possible that the federal grant for supplementary educational centers would have been used for a facility entirely separate from the rest of the school system. It is also possible that the grant for adult educational classes supported a program that was administered in an entirely desegregated manner even if the elementary and high school classes were not. HEW's failure to make findings of fact on these issues has deprived this court of the means with which to properly discharge its reviewing function. In order to affirm HEW's action, we would have to assume, contrary to the express mandate of 42 U.S.C.A. § 2000d–1, that defects in one part of a school system automatically infect the whole. Such an assumption in disregard of statutory requirements is inconsistent with both fundamental justice and with our judicial responsibilities. * * *

The action of HEW in the proceedings below was clearly disruptive of the legislative scheme. The legislative history of 42 U.S.C.A. § 2000d–1 (§ 602 of the Act) indicates a Congressional purpose to avoid a punitive as opposed to a therapeutic application of the termination power. The procedural limitations placed on the exercise of such power were designed to insure that termination would be "pinpoint(ed) * * * to the situation where discriminatory practices prevail." 1964 U.S.Code Cong. & Adm. News, p. 2512. As said by Senator Long during the Senate debate:

> "Proponents of the bill have continually made it clear that it is the intent of Title VI not to require wholesale cutoffs of Federal Funds from all Federal programs in entire States, but instead to require a careful case-by-case application of the principle of nondiscrimination to those particular activities which are actually discriminatory or segregated." 110 Cong.Rec. 7103 (1964).

It is important to note that the purpose of limiting the termination power to "activities which are actually discriminatory or segregated" was not for the protection of the political entity whose funds might be cut off, but for the protection of the innocent beneficiaries of programs *not* tainted by discriminatory practices. The very nature of such a purpose indicates that more than just the rights of one political entity are here involved. The termination of federal funds affects the lives of persons not represented in the administrative proceedings below. For their protection, we may not regard the limitations on the termination power as mere procedural niceties peripheral to the purposes of the Act. Congressional history indicates that limiting the scope of the termination power was integral to the legislative scheme. 100 Cong.Rec. 7063. * * *

* * *

The order entered by HEW in the instant case is vacated, and the cause remanded to that agency for further proceedings not inconsistent with this opinion.

GROVE CITY COLLEGE v. BELL

Supreme Court of the United States, 1984.
465 U.S. 555, 104 S.Ct. 1211, 79 L.Ed.2d 516.

JUSTICE WHITE delivered the opinion of the Court.

Section 901(a) of Title IX of the Education Amendments of 1972, 86 Stat. 373, 20 U.S.C. § 1681(a), prohibits sex discrimination in "any education program or activity receiving Federal financial assistance," and § 902 directs agencies awarding most types of assistance to promulgate regulations to ensure that recipients adhere to that prohibition. Compliance with departmental regulations may be secured by termination of assistance "to the particular program, or part thereof, in which ... noncompliance has been ... found" or by "any other means authorized by law." § 902, 20 U.S.C. § 1682.

This case presents several questions concerning the scope and operation of these provisions and the regulations established by the Department of Education. We must decide, first, whether Title IX applies at all to Grove City College, which accepts no direct assistance but enrolls students who receive federal grants that must be used for educational purposes. If so, we must identify the "education program or activity" at Grove City that is "receiving Federal financial assistance" and determine whether federal assistance to that program may be terminated solely because the College violates the Department's regulations by refusing to execute an Assurance of Compliance with Title IX. Finally, we must consider whether the application of Title IX to Grove City infringes the First Amendment rights of the College or its students.

I

Petitioner Grove City College is a private, coeducational, liberal arts college that has sought to preserve its institutional autonomy by consistently refusing state and federal financial assistance. Grove City's desire to avoid federal oversight has led it to decline to participate, not only in direct institutional aid programs, but also in federal student assistance programs under which the College would be required to assess students' eligibility and to determine the amounts of loans, work-study funds, or grants they should receive. Grove City has, however, enrolled a large number of students who receive Basic Educational Opportunity Grants (BEOG's), 20 U.S.C. § 1070a (1982 ed.), under the Department of Education's Alternate Disbursement System (ADS).[5]

[When requested by the Department to execute an "Assurance of Compliance" with Title IX's proscriptions, the college refused and instituted this declaratory judgment action to clarify its status under the statute. The trial court ruled for the college, but was reversed on appeal.]

II

In defending its refusal to execute the Assurance of Compliance required by the Department's regulations, Grove City first contends that neither it nor any "education program or activity" of the College receives any federal financial assistance within the meaning of Title IX by virtue of the fact that some of its students receive BEOG's and use them to pay for their education. We disagree.

* * *

[T]he language of § 901(a) contains no hint that Congress perceived a substantive difference between direct institutional assistance and aid received by a school through its students. The linchpin of Grove City's argument that none of its programs receives any federal assistance is a perceived distinction between direct and indirect aid, a distinction that finds no support in the text of § 901(a). Nothing in § 901(a) suggests that Congress elevated form over substance by making the application of the nondiscrimination principle dependent on the manner in which a program or activity receives federal assistance. There is no basis in the statute for the view that only institutions that themselves apply for federal aid or receive checks directly from the Federal Government are subject to regulation.

* * *

* * * Title IX was patterned after Title VI of the Civil Rights Act of 1964. The drafters of Title VI envisioned that the receipt of student aid funds would trigger coverage, and, since they approved identical language, we discern no reason to believe that the Congressmen who voted for Title

---

5. The Secretary, in his discretion, has established two procedures for computing and disbursing BEOG's. Under the Regular Disbursement System (RDS), the Secretary estimates the amount that an institution will need for grants and advances that sum to the institution, which itself selects eligible students, calculates awards, and distributes the grants by either crediting students' accounts or issuing checks. 34 CFR §§ 690.71–690.85 (1983). Most institutions whose students receive BEOG's participate in the RDS, but the ADS is an option made available by the Secretary to schools that wish to minimize their involvement in the administration of the BEOG program. Institutions participating in the program through the ADS must make appropriate certifications to the Secretary, but the Secretary calculates awards and makes disbursements directly to eligible students. 34 CFR §§ 690.91–690.96 (1983).

IX intended a different result. [Administrative regulations are consistent with this view. 40 Fed.Reg. 24137 (1975).]

* * *

With the benefit of clear statutory language, powerful evidence of Congress' intent, and a longstanding and coherent administrative construction of the phrase "receiving Federal financial assistance," we have little trouble concluding that Title IX coverage is not foreclosed because federal funds are granted to Grove City's students rather than directly to one of the College's educational programs. There remains the question, however, of identifying the "education program or activity" of the College that can properly be characterized as "receiving" federal assistance through grants to some of the students attending the College.

III

An analysis of Title IX's language and legislative history led us to conclude in North Haven Board of Education v. Bell, [456 U.S. 512, 521, 102 S.Ct. 1912, 1918, 72 L.Ed.2d 299 (1982),] that "an agency's authority under Title IX both to promulgate regulations and to terminate funds is subject to the program-specific limitations of §§ 901 and 902." Although the legislative history contains isolated suggestions that entire institutions are subject to the nondiscrimination provision whenever one of their programs receives federal assistance, we cannot accept the Court of Appeals' conclusion that in the circumstances present here Grove City itself is a "program or activity" that may be regulated in its entirety.
* * *

If Grove City participated in the BEOG program through the RDS, we would have no doubt that the "education program or activity receiving Federal financial assistance" would not be the entire College; rather, it would be its student financial aid program. RDS institutions receive federal funds directly, but can use them only to subsidize or expand their financial aid programs and to recruit students who might otherwise be unable to enroll. In short, the assistance is earmarked for the recipient's financial aid program. Only by ignoring Title IX's program-specific language could we conclude that funds received under the RDS, awarded to eligible students, and paid back to the school when tuition comes due represent federal aid to the entire institution.

We see no reason to reach a different conclusion merely because Grove City has elected to participate in the ADS. Although Grove City does not itself disburse students' awards, BEOG's clearly augment the resources that the College itself devotes to financial aid. As is true of the RDS, however, the fact that federal funds eventually reach the College's general operating budget cannot subject Grove City to institution-wide coverage. Grove City's choice of administrative mechanisms, we hold, neither expands nor contracts the breadth of the "program or activity"— the financial aid program—that receives federal assistance and that may be regulated under Title IX.

To the extent that the Court of Appeals' holding that BEOG's received by Grove City's students constitute aid to the entire institution rests on the possibility that federal funds received by one program or activity free up the College's own resources for use elsewhere, the Court of Appeals' reasoning is doubly flawed. First, there is no evidence that the federal aid received by Grove City's students results in the diversion of funds from the College's own financial aid program to other areas within the institution. Second, and more important, the Court of Appeals' assumption that Title IX applies to programs receiving a larger share of a school's own limited resources as a result of federal assistance earmarked for use elsewhere within the institution is inconsistent with the program-specific nature of the statute. Most federal educational assistance has economic ripple effects throughout the aided institution, and it would be difficult, if not impossible, to determine which programs or activities derive such indirect benefits. Under the Court of Appeals' theory, an entire school would be subject to Title IX merely because one of its students received a small BEOG or because one of its departments received an earmarked federal grant. This result cannot be squared with Congress' intent.

The Court of Appeals' analogy between student financial aid received by an educational institution and nonearmarked direct grants provides a more plausible justification for its holding, but it too is faulty. Student financial aid programs, we believe, are *sui generis*. In neither purpose nor effect can BEOG's be fairly characterized as unrestricted grants that institutions may use for whatever purpose they desire. The BEOG program was designed, not merely to increase the total resources available to educational institutions, but to enable them to offer their services to students who had previously been unable to afford higher education. * * * In that sense, student financial aid more closely resembles many earmarked grants.

We conclude that the receipt of BEOG's by some of Grove City's students does not trigger institution-wide coverage under Title IX. In purpose and effect, BEOG's represent federal financial assistance to the College's own financial aid program, and it is that program that may properly be regulated under Title IX.

[Given our present interpretation of Title IX, the college may be asked to execute an Assurance of Compliance limited to its financial aid program.]

V

Grove City's final challenge to the Court of Appeals' decision—that conditioning federal assistance on compliance with Title IX infringes First Amendment rights of the College and its students—warrants only brief consideration. Congress is free to attach reasonable and unambiguous conditions to federal financial assistance that educational institutions are not obligated to accept. E.g., Pennhurst State School and Hospital v. Halderman, 451 U.S. 1, 17, 101 S.Ct. 1531, 1539, 67 L.Ed.2d 694 (1981).

Grove City may terminate its participation in the BEOG program and thus avoid the requirements of § 901(a). Students affected by the Department's action may either take their BEOG's elsewhere or attend Grove City without federal financial assistance. Requiring Grove City to comply with Title IX's prohibition of discrimination as a condition for its continued eligibility to participate in the BEOG program infringes no First Amendment rights of the College or its students.

Accordingly, the judgment of the Court of Appeals is

Affirmed.

[Concurring opinions by JUSTICES POWELL, O'CONNOR, STEVENS, and CHIEF JUSTICE REHNQUIST are omitted.]

JUSTICE BRENNAN, with whom JUSTICE MARSHALL joins, concurring in part and dissenting in part.

[The consistent administrative interpretation of Title VI had placed the burden on recipients to show that deficiencies in one part of its program would not affect programs receiving federal assistance; otherwise the proscriptions of Title VI were deemed to apply to the entire institution.]

It must have been clear to the Congress enacting Title IX, therefore, that the administrative interpretation of that statute would follow a similarly expansive approach. Nothing in the legislative history suggests otherwise; and "[i]t is always appropriate to assume that our elected representatives, like other citizens, know the law."

* * *

NOTE ON THE *"CORRECTNESS"* OF Grove City AND Its Legislative Reversal

1. The first part of *Grove City* holds that indirect payments to universities, by students' assignment of their federal grants to the schools they attend, brings Title IX responsibility upon the school. The legislative history strongly supports this result, does it not? But consider the policy implications of broadly covering the indirect recipients of federal funds: with approximately 40% of all federal spending going for transfer payments to individuals, and with approximately 20% of the gross national product being cycled through the federal treasury, a very sizeable portion of American society receives federal funds indirectly. Does extending federal control to the indirect recipients of federal funds give the central government too much power over citizens' daily lives?

(a) Title IX operates only in the sphere of educational funding where the ultimate recipients of federal funds are institutions. Does this lessen any concern with privacy interests? Should there be no concern over privacy interests: after all, the recipient has gone to the public for money, has he not? If one takes public money, should one forfeit privacy, or not?

(b) Although it was unclear at the time of Title VI's passage, it is now rather settled that a recipient of federal funds is not a state actor, correct? See

Rendell–Baker v. Kohn and Blum v. Yaretsky, discussed in Chapter 1C supra. To that extent, Title VI and its analogues are not constitutionally compelled, correct? So the issue here is only one of public policy, correct?

2. Now consider the second part of *Grove City* as well as the *Taylor County* case. Are the cases rightly decided when they restrict funding termination to the "particular program[s] or part thereof" that has received federal money?

(a) The principle that the courts invoke comes directly from the statute, does it not? Is your disagreement with the principle or with how the courts apply the principle?

(b) The panel that decided *Taylor County* consisted of two of the most liberal judges on the old Fifth Circuit. Do you agree with their spirited defense of the particular program limitation? Is their concern with discriminating recipients or the harm done to innocent program beneficiaries? Do you agree with Judge Goldberg that blameless beneficiaries of programs should continue to receive their benefits, even though some other aspects of the recipient's activity may run afoul of Title VI's non-discrimination command?

(c) In another part of the *Taylor County* decision the court noted that the particular-program limitation would not apply if collateral programs were "infected by a 'discriminatory environment' created by other programs." Is this proviso significantly broader than *Grove City* because it notes the possibility that one program's defects might infect other programs? Is the problem with *Grove City* the majority's inability to see that the particular grants at issue, funds supplied to the school as tuition, affected the entire school?

3. With respect to funding termination in whole or in part, consider also the tactical issue. Assume that your only goal is maximum compliance with your grant conditions (here, civil rights compliance plus getting program dollars to intended beneficiaries). Will complete termination give you more leverage over the recipient or less?

(a) If your only sanction is complete termination, do you not run the risk that the recipient will simply walk away from the grant, especially if its compliance costs are high? On the other hand might you be able to secure prompt compliance by threatening a recipient with the intolerable loss of large grants on which it has come to rely? As a practical matter, which recipients are likely to submit to pressure and which are not?

(b) An unpublished study conducted for the Department of Health, Education and Welfare in the middle 1970's suggested that the threat of funding termination worked less rationally than one might expect. Agency negotiators had little interest in funding termination as a sanction for isolated, non-systematic discrimination, and politics (especially from federal politicians representing large urban school districts) affected some outcomes. Memorandum on Alternative Civil Rights Sanctions and Enforcement Processes, Dep't of HEW (1977). How does this information affect your tactical judgment?

(c) Should the funding sanction be dropped as unworkable? Is it an inherent problem because Title VI operates through the Spending Power? Should Title VI be re-written to base it on the commerce clause (like the

Americans with Disabilities Act) or on the Fourteenth Amendment (for state entities), thus making the receipt of federal funds irrelevant? Or are its controls only appropriate because a grantee has taken public funds?

4. Immediately following the decision in *Grove City* Senator Hatfield introduced S. 2363, 98th Cong., 2d Sess. It provided in a single sentence that "section 901(a) of the Education Amendments of 1972, relating to the prohibition on sex discrimination, is amended by striking out "education program or activity," and inserting in lieu thereof "educational program, activity, and institution" Did this amendment cure the problem of the "particular program" language by making it clear that an institution was covered as a whole? The amendment languished for over two years without action. A notably more complex bill passed in 1987. **The Civil Rights Restoration Act of 1987**, which ultimately passed and reversed *Grove City*, provides that it "is necessary to restore the prior consistent and long-standing executive branch interpretation and broad institution-wide application" of Title VI and its analogues. Pub.L. 100–259, § 2(2), 102 Stat. 28. To that end, new sections were adopted for each statute that substantially tracked those added to Title VI, 42 U.S.C. § 2000d–4(a):

> "For the purposes of this title, the term "program or activity" and the term "program" mean all of the operations of—
>
> (1)(A) a department, agency, special purpose district, or other instrumentality of a State or of a local government; or (B) the entity of such State or local government that distributes such assistance and each such department or agency (and each other State or local government entity) to which the assistance is extended, in the case of assistance to a State or local government;
>
> (2)(A) a college, university, or other postsecondary institution, or a public system of higher education; or (B) a local educational agency (as defined in section 198(a)(10) of the Elementary and Secondary Education Act of 1965), system of vocational education, or other school system;
>
> (3)(A) an entire corporation, partnership, or other private organization, or an entire sole proprietorship—
>
>> (i) if assistance is extended to such corporation, partnership, private organization, or sole proprietorship as a whole; or
>>
>> (ii) which is principally engaged in the business of providing education, health care, housing, social services, or parks and recreation; or
>
> (B) the entire plant or other comparable, geographically separate facility to which Federal financial assistance is extended, in the case of any other corporation, partnership, private organization, or sole proprietorship; or
>
> (4) any other entity which is established by two or more of the entities described in paragraph (1), (2), or (3);
>
> any part of which is extended Federal financial assistance."

(a) Why is the provision so detailed? Why was it more difficult than first appeared to identify when an entire grantee would be covered?

(b) What grantees are not covered in whole by the 1987 amendment? What is the effect of leaving the former language concerning "particular program[s], or part thereof" in place? Does the amendment overturn *Taylor County* as well as *Grove City?* See Radcliff v. Landau, 883 F.2d 1481, 1483 (9th Cir.1989): "Receipt of federal financial assistance by any student or portion of a school thus subjects the entire school to Title VI coverage."

5. In addition to its other sections, the Restoration Act also added a provision (§ 7) entitled "Rule of Construction," 102 Stat. 31: "Nothing in the Amendments made by this Act shall be construed to extend the application of the Acts so amended to ultimate beneficiaries of Federal financial assistance excluded from coverage before the enactment of this Act."

(a) If non-discrimination is a laudable principle, why should not ultimate beneficiaries also be required to observe it? Is this provision an acknowledgment of privacy concerns discussed in the previous Note?

(b) Is your grandmother a "recipient" of federal funds when she receives her social security check each month? Is she bound by Title VI's non-discrimination command, including its effects test? Is there anything in Title VI that suggests that she would not be covered?

RUMSFELD v. FORUM FOR ACADEMIC AND INSTITUTIONAL RIGHTS, INC.

Supreme Court of the United States, 2006.
547 U.S. 47, 126 S.Ct. 1297, 164 L.Ed.2d 156.

CHIEF JUSTICE ROBERTS delivered the opinion of the Court.

When law schools began restricting the access of military recruiters to their students because of disagreement with the Government's policy on homosexuals in the military, Congress responded by enacting the Solomon Amendment. See 10 U.S.C.A. § 983 (Supp.2005). That provision specifies that if any part of an institution of higher education denies military recruiters access equal to that provided other recruiters, the entire institution would lose certain federal funds. The law schools responded by suing, alleging that the Solomon Amendment infringed their First Amendment freedoms of speech and association. The District Court disagreed but was reversed by a divided panel of the Court of Appeals for the Third Circuit, which ordered the District Court to enter a preliminary injunction against enforcement of the Solomon Amendment. We granted certiorari.

I

Respondent Forum for Academic and Institutional Rights, Inc. (FAIR), is an association of law schools and law faculties. Its declared mission is "to promote academic freedom, support educational institutions in opposing discrimination and vindicate the rights of institutions of higher education." FAIR members have adopted policies expressing their opposition to discrimination based on, among other factors, sexual orientation. They would like to restrict military recruiting on their campuses because they object to the policy Congress has adopted with respect to homosexuals in the military. See 10 U.S.C. § 654.[6] The Solomon Amendment, however, forces institutions to choose between enforcing their nondiscrimination policy against military recruiters in this way and continuing to receive specified federal funding.

[The Solomon Amendment, as amended, requires universities that receive of federal funds not to treat military recruiters differently from the way the school treats other outside recruiters. FAIR argues that the Solomon Amendment thereby restricts its speech and associational rights because it forces law schools to choose between their rights and their federal funding. The trial court denied preliminary relief, but the Third Circuit, by a 2–1 vote, reversed. We in turn reverse the appellate court.]

* * *

III

The Constitution grants Congress the power to "provide for the common Defence," "[t]o raise and support Armies," and "[t]o provide and maintain a Navy." Art. I, § 8, cls. 1, 12–13. Congress' power in this area "is broad and sweeping," and there is no dispute in this case that it includes the authority to require campus access for military recruiters. That is, of course, unless Congress exceeds constitutional limitations on its power in enacting such legislation. See Rostker v. Goldberg, 453 U.S. 57, 67, 101 S.Ct. 2646, 69 L.Ed.2d 478 (1981). But the fact that legislation that raises armies is subject to First Amendment constraints does not mean that we ignore the purpose of this legislation when determining its constitutionality; as we recognized in *Rostker,* "judicial deference . . . is at its apogee" when Congress legislates under its authority to raise and support armies.

Although Congress has broad authority to legislate on matters of military recruiting, it nonetheless chose to secure campus access for military recruiters indirectly, through its Spending Clause power. The Solomon Amendment gives universities a choice: Either allow military recruiters the same access to students afforded any other recruiter or forgo certain federal funds. Congress' decision to proceed indirectly does not reduce the deference given to Congress in the area of military affairs. Congress' choice to promote its goal by creating a funding condition deserves at least as deferential treatment as if Congress had imposed a mandate on universities.

Congress' power to regulate military recruiting under the Solomon Amendment is arguably greater because universities are free to decline the federal funds. In Grove City College v. Bell, 465 U.S. 555, 575–576,

---

6. Under this policy, a person generally may not serve in the Armed Forces if he has engaged in homosexual acts, stated that he is a homosexual, or married a person of the same sex. Respondents do not challenge that policy[, the so-called "Don't Ask, Don't Tell" policy adopted by the Clinton Administration,] in this litigation.

104 S.Ct. 1211, 79 L.Ed.2d 516 (1984), we rejected a private college's claim that conditioning federal funds on its compliance with Title IX of the Education Amendments of 1972 violated the First Amendment. We thought this argument "warrant[ed] only brief consideration" because "Congress is free to attach reasonable and unambiguous conditions to federal financial assistance that educational institutions are not obligated to accept." We concluded that no First Amendment violation had occurred—without reviewing the substance of the First Amendment claims—because Grove City could decline the Government's funds. *Id.*, at 575–576, 104 S.Ct. 1211.

Other decisions, however, recognize a limit on Congress' ability to place conditions on the receipt of funds. We recently held that " 'the government may not deny a benefit to a person on a basis that infringes his constitutionally protected . . . freedom of speech even if he has no entitlement to that benefit.' " United States v. American Library Assn., Inc., 539 U.S. 194, 210, 123 S.Ct. 2297, 156 L.Ed.2d 221 (2003). Under this principle, known as the unconstitutional conditions doctrine, the Solomon Amendment would be unconstitutional if Congress could not directly require universities to provide military recruiters equal access to their students.

This case does not require us to determine when a condition placed on university funding goes beyond the "reasonable" choice offered in *Grove City* and becomes an unconstitutional condition. It is clear that a funding condition cannot be unconstitutional if it could be constitutionally imposed directly. See Speiser v. Randall, 357 U.S. 513, 526, 78 S.Ct. 1332, 2 L.Ed.2d 1460 (1958). Because the First Amendment would not prevent Congress from directly imposing the Solomon Amendment's access requirement, the statute does not place an unconstitutional condition on the receipt of federal funds.

A

The Solomon Amendment neither limits what law schools may say nor requires them to say anything. Law schools remain free under the statute to express whatever views they may have on the military's congressionally mandated employment policy, all the while retaining eligibility for federal funds. See Tr. of Oral Arg. 25 (Solicitor General acknowledging that law schools "could put signs on the bulletin board next to the door, they could engage in speech, they could help organize student protests"). As a general matter, the Solomon Amendment regulates conduct, not speech. It affects what law schools must *do*—afford equal access to military recruiters—not what they may or may not *say*.

Nevertheless, the Third Circuit concluded that the Solomon Amendment violates law schools' freedom of speech in a number of ways. * * * We consider each issue in turn.[4]

---

4. The Court of Appeals also held that the Solomon Amendment violated the First Amendment because it compelled law schools to subsidize the Government's speech "by putting

1

Some of this Court's leading First Amendment precedents have established the principle that freedom of speech prohibits the government from telling people what they must say. In West Virginia Bd. of Ed. v. Barnette, 319 U.S. 624, 642, 63 S.Ct. 1178, 87 L.Ed. 1628 (1943), we held unconstitutional a state law requiring schoolchildren to recite the Pledge of Allegiance and to salute the flag. And in Wooley v. Maynard, 430 U.S. 705, 717, 97 S.Ct. 1428, 51 L.Ed.2d 752 (1977), we held unconstitutional another that required New Hampshire motorists to display the state motto—"Live Free or Die"—on their license plates.

The Solomon Amendment does not require any similar expression by law schools. [There are some incidental statements that accommodating the recruiters might entail.] This sort of recruiting assistance, however, is a far cry from the compelled speech in *Barnette* and *Wooley*. The Solomon Amendment, unlike the laws at issue in those cases, does not dictate the content of the speech at all, which is only "compelled" if, and to the extent, the school provides such speech for other recruiters. There is nothing in this case approaching a Government-mandated pledge or motto that the school must endorse.

The compelled speech to which the law schools point is plainly incidental to the Solomon Amendment's regulation of conduct, and "it has never been deemed an abridgment of freedom of speech or press to make a course of conduct illegal merely because the conduct was in part initiated, evidenced, or carried out by means of language, either spoken, written, or printed." Giboney v. Empire Storage & Ice Co., 336 U.S. 490, 502, 69 S.Ct. 684, 93 L.Ed. 834 (1949). Congress, for example, can prohibit employers from discriminating in hiring on the basis of race. The fact that this will require an employer to take down a sign reading "White Applicants Only" hardly means that the law should be analyzed as one regulating the employer's speech rather than conduct. Compelling a law school that sends scheduling e-mails for other recruiters to send one for a military recruiter is simply not the same as forcing a student to pledge allegiance, or forcing a Jehovah's Witness to display the motto "Live Free or Die," and it trivializes the freedom protected in *Barnette* and *Wooley* to suggest that it is.

2

Our compelled-speech cases are not limited to the situation in which an individual must personally speak the government's message. We have also in a number of instances limited the government's ability to force one speaker to host or accommodate another speaker's message. See Hurley v.

---

demands on the law schools' employees and resources." [But these] accommodations the law schools must provide to military recruiters are minimal, are not of a monetary nature, and are extended to all employers recruiting on campus, not just the Government. [Moreover, the compelled-speech doctrine applies only when one must subsidize speech by another private person; it does not apply to the Government's speech, as we recently held in Johanns v. Livestock Marketing Assn., 544 U.S. 550, 559, 125 S.Ct. 2055, 161 L.Ed.2d 896 (2005).] The military recruiters' speech is clearly Government speech.

Irish–American Gay, Lesbian and Bisexual Group of Boston, Inc., 515 U.S. 557, 566, 115 S.Ct. 2338, 132 L.Ed.2d 487 (1995) (state law cannot require a parade to include a group whose message the parade's organizer does not wish to send); Miami Herald Publishing Co. v. Tornillo, 418 U.S. 241, 258, 94 S.Ct. 2831, 41 L.Ed.2d 730 (1974) (right-of-reply statute violates editors' right to determine the content of their newspapers). Relying on these precedents, the Third Circuit concluded that the Solomon Amendment unconstitutionally compels law schools to accommodate the military's message "[b]y requiring schools to include military recruiters in the interviews and recruiting receptions the schools arrange."

The compelled-speech violation in each of our prior cases, however, resulted from the fact that the complaining speaker's own message was affected by the speech it was forced to accommodate. The expressive nature of a parade was central to our holding in *Hurley*, 515 U.S., at 568, 115 S.Ct. 2338 ("Parades are . . . a form of expression, not just motion, and the inherent expressiveness of marching to make a point explains our cases involving protest marches"). We concluded that because "every participating unit affects the message conveyed by the [parade's] private organizers," a law dictating that a particular group must be included in the parade "alter[s] the expressive content of th[e] parade." As a result, we held that the State's public accommodation law, as applied to a private parade, "violates the fundamental rule of protection under the First Amendment, that a speaker has the autonomy to choose the content of his own message." *Id.,* at 573, 115 S.Ct. 2338. [This was also true in our other earlier decisions.]

In this case, accommodating the military's message does not affect the law schools' speech, because the schools are not speaking when they host interviews and recruiting receptions. Unlike a parade organizer's choice of parade contingents, a law school's decision to allow recruiters on campus is not inherently expressive. Law schools facilitate recruiting to assist their students in obtaining jobs. A law school's recruiting services lack the expressive quality of a parade, a newsletter, or the editorial page of a newspaper; its accommodation of a military recruiter's message is not compelled speech because the accommodation does not sufficiently interfere with any message of the school.

The schools respond that if they treat military and nonmilitary recruiters alike in order to comply with the Solomon Amendment, they could be viewed as sending the message that they see nothing wrong with the military's policies, when they do. We rejected a similar argument in PruneYard Shopping Center v. Robins, 447 U.S. 74, 100 S.Ct. 2035, 64 L.Ed.2d 741 (1980). In that case, we upheld a state law requiring a shopping center owner to allow certain expressive activities by others on its property. We explained that there was little likelihood that the views of those engaging in the expressive activities would be identified with the owner, who remained free to disassociate himself from those views and who was "not . . . being compelled to affirm [a] belief in any governmentally prescribed position or view." *Id.,* at 88, 100 S.Ct. 2035.

The same is true here. Nothing about recruiting suggests that law schools agree with any speech by recruiters, and nothing in the Solomon Amendment restricts what the law schools may say about the military's policies. We have held that high school students can appreciate the difference between speech a school sponsors and speech the school permits because legally required to do so, pursuant to an equal access policy. Board of Ed. of Westside Community Schools (Dist.66) v. Mergens, 496 U.S. 226, 250, 110 S.Ct. 2356, 110 L.Ed.2d 191 (1990) (plurality opinion); accord, *id.*, at 268, 110 S.Ct. 2356 (Marshall, J., concurring in judgment); see also Rosenberger v. Rector and Visitors of Univ. of Va., 515 U.S. 819, 841, 115 S.Ct. 2510, 132 L.Ed.2d 700 (1995) (attribution concern "not a plausible fear"). Surely students have not lost that ability by the time they get to law school.

3

Having rejected the view that the Solomon Amendment impermissibly regulates *speech,* we must still consider whether the expressive nature of the *conduct* regulated by the statute brings that conduct within the First Amendment's protection. In *O'Brien,* we recognized that some forms of " 'symbolic speech' " were deserving of First Amendment protection. 391 U.S., at 376, 88 S.Ct. 1673. But we rejected the view that "conduct can be labeled 'speech' whenever the person engaging in the conduct intends thereby to express an idea." *Ibid.* Instead, we have extended First Amendment protection only to conduct that is inherently expressive. In Texas v. Johnson, 491 U.S. 397, 406, 109 S.Ct. 2533, 105 L.Ed.2d 342 (1989), for example, we applied *O'Brien* and held that burning the American flag was sufficiently expressive to warrant First Amendment protection.

[The recruiting conduct regulated by the Solomon Amendment is not inherently expressive.] An observer who sees military recruiters interviewing away from the law school has no way of knowing whether the law school is expressing its disapproval of the military, all the law school's interview rooms are full, or the military recruiters decided for reasons of their own that they would rather interview someplace else. [Only the speech accompanying the law school's practices makes the point that the schools oppose military policy affecting homosexuals, and that indicates that the conduct itself is not expressive.] We have held that "an incidental burden on speech is no greater than is essential, and therefore is permissible under *O'Brien,* so long as the neutral regulation promotes a substantial government interest that would be achieved less effectively absent the regulation." United States v. Albertini, 472 U.S. 675, 689, 105 S.Ct. 2897, 86 L.Ed.2d 536 (1985). The Solomon Amendment clearly satisfies this requirement. Military recruiting promotes the substantial Government interest in raising and supporting the Armed Forces—an objective that would be achieved less effectively if the military were forced to recruit on less favorable terms than other employers. The Court of Appeals' proposed alternative methods of recruiting are beside the point. The issue is not whether other means of raising an army and providing for a navy might be adequate. That is a judgment for Congress, not the courts. See U.S. Const., Art. I, § 8, cls. 12–13; *Rostker,* 453 U.S., at 64–65, 101 S.Ct. 2646. It suffices that the means chosen by Congress add to the effectiveness of military recruitment. Accordingly, even if the Solomon Amendment were regarded as regulating expressive conduct, it would not violate the First Amendment under *O'Brien.*

B

* * * We have recognized a First Amendment right to associate for the purpose of speaking, which we have termed a "right of expressive association." See, e.g., Boy Scouts of America v. Dale, 530 U.S. 640, 644, 120 S.Ct. 2446, 147 L.Ed.2d 554 (2000). The reason we have extended First Amendment protection in this way is clear: The right to speak is often exercised most effectively by combining one's voice with the voices of others. See Roberts v. United States Jaycees, 468 U.S. 609, 622, 104 S.Ct. 3244, 82 L.Ed.2d 462 (1984). If the government were free to restrict individuals' ability to join together and speak, it could essentially silence views that the First Amendment is intended to protect. *Ibid.*

FAIR argues that the Solomon Amendment violates law schools' freedom of expressive association. According to FAIR, law schools' ability to express their message that discrimination on the basis of sexual orientation is wrong is significantly affected by the presence of military recruiters on campus and the schools' obligation to assist them. [But in *Dale* we noted that forced acceptance of a homosexual scoutmaster would "significantly affect" the Scouts' expression of disapproval of homosexuality.]

The Solomon Amendment, however, does not similarly affect a law school's associational rights. To comply with the statute, law schools must allow military recruiters on campus and assist them in whatever way the school chooses to assist other employers. Law schools therefore "associate" with military recruiters in the sense that they interact with them. But recruiters are not part of the law school. Recruiters are, by definition, outsiders who come onto campus for the limited purpose of trying to hire students—not to become members of the school's expressive association. This distinction is critical. Unlike the public accommodations law in *Dale,* the Solomon Amendment does not force a law school " 'to accept members it does not desire.' " *Id.,* at 648, 120 S.Ct. 2446 (quoting *Roberts, supra,* at 623, 104 S.Ct. 3244). The law schools *say* that allowing military recruiters equal access impairs their own expression by requiring them to associate with the recruiters, but just as saying conduct is undertaken for expressive purposes cannot make it symbolic speech, see *supra,* at 1310–1311, so too a speaker cannot "erect a shield" against laws requiring access "simply by asserting" that mere association "would impair its message." 530 U.S., at 653, 120 S.Ct. 2446.

* * *

The Solomon Amendment [does not diminish the attractiveness of membership in law school communities so as to hinder the schools' ability to get out its message.] Students and faculty are free to associate to voice their disapproval of the military's message; nothing about the statute affects the composition of the group by making group membership less desirable. The Solomon Amendment therefore does not violate a law school's First Amendment rights. A military recruiter's mere presence on campus does not violate a law school's right to associate, regardless of how repugnant the law school considers the recruiter's message.

* * *

In this case, FAIR has attempted to stretch a number of First Amendment doctrines well beyond the sort of activities these doctrines protect. The law schools object to having to treat military recruiters like other recruiters, but that regulation of conduct does not violate the First Amendment. To the extent that the Solomon Amendment incidentally affects expression, the law schools' effort to cast themselves as just like the schoolchildren in *Barnette,* the parade organizers in *Hurley,* and the Boy Scouts in *Dale* plainly overstates the expressive nature of their activity and the impact of the Solomon Amendment on it, while exaggerating the reach of our First Amendment precedents.

Because Congress could require law schools to provide equal access to military recruiters without violating the schools' freedoms of speech or association, the Court of Appeals erred in holding that the Solomon Amendment likely violates the First Amendment. We therefore reverse the judgment of the Third Circuit and remand the case for further proceedings consistent with this opinion.

It is so ordered.

JUSTICE ALITO took no part in the consideration or decision of this case.

NOTE ON THE CONSTITUTIONAL LIMITS OF FEDERAL FUNDING DECISIONS

1. As the *FAIR* decision demonstrates, funding termination is a neutral tool that neither promotes nor protects activities often engaged in by traditional civil rights groups. Congress may attach conditions to its grants in order to prevent a wide range of "discrimination"—from race-based discrimination to discrimination against military recruiters.

(a) As the Court's unanimous decision makes clear, the Court sees the arguments raised by the law professors in *FAIR* as essentially the same type of frivolous arguments that could be raised by racial discriminators who might seek to resist traditional civil rights laws on the ground that their acts of discrimination were "speech" or "expressive conduct" or an associational right. You would reject FAIR's argument out-of-hand had it been made by a racial discriminator resisting Title VI, would you not? See Runyon v. McCrary, Chapter 2C.1 supra (rejecting similar speech and associational claims in the context of § 1981 and a private school resisting enrollment of black children). Are you prepared to reconsider that case?

(b) Is it tempting to argue that homosexual-protecting speech is the right kind of speech and black-harming speech is not? That argument as to what is the truly correct message to convey was decisively rejected by a unanimous Court in Hurley v. Irish–American Gay, Lesbian and Bisexual Group of Boston, Inc., discussed in *FAIR*. Is it tempting to argue that government has a "compelling state interest" in alleviating discrimination but not in permitting it to continue? Was that argument also rejected in *Hurley*, at least implicitly?

(c) Note the somewhat dismissive tone of the Court's unanimous opinion: "Compelling a law school that sends scheduling e-mails for other recruiters to send one for a military recruiter is simply not the same as forcing a student to pledge allegiance, * * * and it trivializes the [First Amendment] to suggest that it is"; "FAIR has attempted to stretch a number of First Amendment doctrines well beyond the sort of activities these doctrines protect." Is it clear that one cannot take government money, conditioned on performing an action, then claim that performing the action violates its speech interest in opposing the action? Is that why the Court was unanimous?

(d) If you object to the result in *FAIR*, is your real dispute with the Solomon Amendment rather than with the Court's free speech doctrines? Should Congress as a general proposition resist the temptation to use its Spending power to place conditions on private grantees? Can freedom be better maximized by simply leaving fewer grantees regulated by Congress' Spending Power conditions?

2. In **Rust v. Sullivan**, 500 U.S. 173, 111 S.Ct. 1759, 114 L.Ed.2d 233 (1991), the Court by a 5–4 vote upheld a federal law that conditioned receipt of federal funds on not promoting abortion as a means of family planning. The plaintiffs claimed that their speech rights and fundamental right regarding abortion had been infringed, but the Court found the argument unpersuasive, ruling that "unequal subsidization" of viewpoints and personal practices is no constitutional violation because the government has a free hand in promoting its own preferred practices and views. [Note the similarity to the later-developed "government speech" doctrine discussed in *FAIR*'s footnote 4.]

(a) The Court explained in *Rust* that the "Government can, without violating the Constitution, selectively fund a program to encourage certain activities it believes to be in the public interest, without at the same time funding an alternate program which seeks to deal with the problem in another way. In so doing, the Government has not discriminated on the basis of viewpoint; it has merely chosen to fund one activity to the exclusion of the other." Is there no discrimination, as the Court later explained in *FAIR*, because a funding recipient is always free to reject the grant?

(b) Was *Rust* a closer case because the government's acknowledged special interest in maintaining the military and national security were not at stake? If the military's "Don't Ask, Don't Tell" policy had been a policy developed for employees of the Department of Agriculture and the Solomon Amendment had guaranteed non-discriminatory treatment for recruitment of agriculture employees, do you think the result would have been different?

3. The Court reiterated the approach adopted in *Rust* in **National Endowment for the Arts v. Finley**, 524 U.S. 569, 118 S.Ct. 2168, 141 L.Ed.2d 500 (1998), a case involving a federal statute that limited arts grants by the National Endowment for the Arts by requiring funders to take "decency and respect for the diverse beliefs" of citizens into account in awarding grants. While the Court admitted that the "First Amendment certainly has application in the subsidy context," the 8–1 majority found no problems because the provision denied funding to no particular artist and thus interfered with no particular artistic expression. More importantly, the Court noted that the grants were awarded selectively based on vague criteria—a perfectly permissible process because government may allocate competitive funding on bases that would violate free-speech rules were direct regulation involved. Government enjoys "wide latitude" in deciding what to subsidize.

(a) Given *Rust* and *Finley*, would it be difficult to perceive a circumstance in which a grantee could challenge a funding denial on constitutional grounds, absent outright proof of some impermissible motivation in making individual actual grant selections? Is *FAIR* more about the power of government to choose what it will subsidize—how it will spend the taxpayer's dollar—than it is about speech or the military?

(b) Might it be possible that some regulations adopted under Title VI would be deemed unconstitutional because of the demands made on grantees? Assume, for example, that government regulations required race-based selection policies by grantees. Might these be unconstitutional? See Lutheran Church—Missouri Synod v. F.C.C., 141 F.3d 344 (D.C.Cir.1998) (FCC affirmative-action regulations unconstitutional as applied to license holder). Cf. Regents of the Univ. of California v. Bakke, Chapter 6A supra (particular affirmative action program unconstitutional and violation of Title VI).

4. As with all federal legislation, those controlling the award of grants may be unconstitutional for two reasons: that they violate restrictions on governmental power (such as the First Amendment) or that they exceed the power allocated to the federal government under the Spending Power of Article I, § 8. The *FAIR*, *Rust,* and *Finley* cases concern the first issue. The remainder of this Note concerns the second.[1] In the spending context the issue has traditionally been framed as one of whether the federal funding law unconstitutionally exceeds federal authority and intrudes onto state authority. Whether the grantee is a private or state entity, the issue has traditionally been the same—and it has been treated with little seriousness since the 1930's. The Court quickly disposed of the issue in Lau v. Nichols, set out in subpart A of this Chapter:

> "The Federal Government has power to fix the terms on which its money allotments to the States shall be disbursed. Oklahoma v. United States Civil Serv. Comm., 330 U.S. 127, 142–43, 67 S.Ct. 544, 552–54, 91 L.Ed. 794 (1947). Whatever may be the limits of that power, Steward

---

1. This Note covers only the issue of federal power to enact legislation. Additional issues arise in sub-chapter D, infra, when litigation is chosen as the method of enforcement.

Machine Co. v. Davis, 301 U.S. 548, 590, 57 S.Ct. 883, 892, 81 L.Ed. 1279 (1937) * * *, they have not been reached here."

(a) In the *Oklahoma* and *Davis* cases, cited in *Lau*, the Court did not doubt that Congress through its spending (or taxing) power might seek to affect affairs which were otherwise beyond its Article I powers. Rather the cases were devoted to states' contentions that Congress had exercised the power in violation of the Tenth Amendment by "destroying or impairing the autonomy of the states." *Davis,* 301 U.S. at 548, 57 S.Ct. at 883. The Court found no such coercion. Does direct federal intervention in local decisionmaking, as envisioned by the regulations cited in *Lau*, pose a greater threat of coercion? Cf. *Oklahoma*, 330 U.S. 127, 143–44, 67 S.Ct. at 554.

(b) Why has the Court given such short constitutional shrift to arguments opposing conditions on federal grants? The Court's opinion in *Davis*, supra, 301 U.S. at 589–90, 57 S.Ct. at 891, 892, points to "robust common sense which assumes the freedom of the will as a working hypothesis." Is it true today that states can turn down federal housing, education or transportation aid? Can private universities turn down similar grants?

(c) Should the Court's inquiry into the limits of the spending power focus on whether there is an adequate nexus between the condition imposed and the goal Congress seeks to accomplish with its grant program? Cf. *Oklahoma*, 330 U.S. at 143, 67 S.Ct. at 553, 554 (limit on political activity by state employees administering programs receiving federal grants leads to better administration of programs). Do the conditions imposed by Title VI and its analogues rationally relate to the goals of major federal grant programs for improving education, constructing research facilities or housing, and providing health care? If so, is it because we presume that part of the federal goal is to maximize participation in the programs by all members of the public? Did the Solomon Amendment also promote greater opportunities (even if not maximize them)? Even if you find no such nexus, is it not possible for Congress to promote two interests with one grant—increased housing and increased participation by blacks, women, handicapped and aged persons? See Central State University v. American Assoc. of University Professors, 526 U.S. 124, 119 S.Ct. 1162, 143 L.Ed.2d 227 (1999) (legislature may pursue two independent, even potentially contradictory, goals simultaneously without running afoul rationality scrutiny); New Orleans v. Dukes, 427 U.S. 297, 96 S.Ct. 2513, 49 L.Ed.2d 511 (1976) (same).

5. Even with the justices committed to more state independence (through reinvigoration of the Tenth Amendment) the Court has remained skeptical of state attacks on federal statutes adopted under the Spending Power, statutes that operate by offering grants or contracts to state and private entities. In **South Dakota v. Dole**, 483 U.S. 203, 107 S.Ct. 2793, 97 L.Ed.2d 171 (1987), Chief Justice Rehnquist's majority opinion for the Court upheld a federal statute that conditioned states' receipt of federal highway funding on their agreement to raise their alcohol-consumption ages to 21. The opinion stressed the deference due Congress in deciding whether the grants (and restrictions included in them) were for the general welfare.

(a) The only significant restriction that the Court has placed on Congressional action under the Spending Clause is the demand that Congress be explicit in subjecting the states to restrictions. Thus in **Pennhurst State School and Hospital v. Halderman**, 451 U.S. 1, 101 S.Ct. 1531, 67 L.Ed.2d 694 (1981), the Court held that due to statutory ambiguity the Developmentally Disabled Assistance and Bill of Rights Act could not be read to create any substantive rights to "appropriate treatment" for mentally disabled persons. Justice Rehnquist's majority opinion observed that the theory underlying the Spending Power is essentially one of contract. He added, 451 U.S. at 17, 101 S.Ct. at 1540:

> "The legitimacy of Congress' power to legislate under the spending power thus rests on whether the State voluntarily and knowingly accepts the terms of the "contract." There can, of course, be no knowing acceptance if a State is unaware of the conditions or is unable to ascertain what is expected of it. Accordingly, if Congress intends to impose a condition on the grant of federal moneys, it must do so unambiguously. By insisting that Congress speak with a clear voice, we enable the States to exercise their choice knowingly, cognizant of the consequences of their participation."

Is the statement in Title VI sufficiently clear to survive *Pennhurst*? Is Title VI's adverse-effects test sufficiently clearly legislated to survive under *Pennhurst*? If it were not so clear originally, is it clear now after the cases discussed in Chapter 6A? Compare Bennett v. Kentucky Dept. of Ed., 470 U.S. 656, 665–666, 105 S.Ct. 1544, 84 L.Ed.2d 590 (1985) (rejecting claim of insufficient notice under *Pennhurst*; Congress need not "specifically identif[y] and proscrib[e]" each condition in the legislation).

(b) *Pennhurst* involved states accepting federal grants. Should its safeguard apply also to private entities receiving federal funds?

6.   The Americans with Disabilities Act involves slightly different issues concerning Congressional power, because unlike Title VI and § 504, it is based largely on the Commerce Clause rather than the Spending Power. As Commerce Clause legislation, the ADA presents issues analogous to those raised in **Reno v. Condon**, 528 U.S. 141, 120 S.Ct. 666, 145 L.Ed.2d 587 (2000), a case in which the Court upheld the Driver's Privacy Protection Act (DPPA), a federal law restricting the ability of the states to disclose a driver's personal information without the driver's consent. Enacted under the Commerce Clause power, the statute was upheld (after noting that it regulated material in interstate commerce) despite a Tenth Amendment challenge. Chief Justice Rehnquist's opinion for a unanimous Court stated that the federal law merely required alteration of state activities and did not actually require state officials to administer federal statutes.

(a) Do you believe that the ADA also merely requires alteration of state activities, not state administration of federal duties?

(b) Could the ADA be justified as legislation designed to implement the Fourteenth Amendment? Board of Trustees of University of Alabama v. Garrett, 531 U.S. 356, 121 S.Ct. 955, 148 L.Ed.2d 866 (2001) (no).

7. Constitutional law marks only the permissible outer boundary of legislation. Does *Rust* raise your concern that the Spending Clause power is a two-edged sword: the rights Congress creates one political season may be quite different from the "civil rights" statutorily created in a different political season? Similarly, regulations adopted in one administration might differ from those adopted in another.

(a) Should Title VI be amended to permit private affirmative action programs undertaken by non-governmental grantees? Cf. Grutter v. Bollinger, subpart E of this Chapter infra (such programs permitted on limited terms for limited duration). Assuming that affirmative action may be limited for governmental bodies because of their constitutional roles, see City of Richmond v. J.A. Croson Co., Chapter 7D infra, does that mean that private entities should be similarly disabled? Is the best public policy that which governs private entities least? Would experimentation in affirmative action by private entities be appropriate even if governmental experimentation is not?

(b) A substantial number of Americans receive public assistance to attend university. Can—should—Congress demand a life-long assurance of no race-based, sex-based, or disability-based discrimination in exchange for receipt of the grant? Note the existing exclusive in Title VI for programs of "guaranty or insurance" and the non-coverage in the Civil Rights Restoration Act of discrimination by "ultimate beneficiaries." Does Title VI already contain some very wide loopholes that show Congress' unwillingness to attach strings to all federal money?

D. ENFORCEMENT BY PRIVATELY-INITIATED LITIGATION

The previous sub-chapter developed themes in modern disability legislation that grew in fertile ground prepared by Title VI's adverse-effects test. In this sub-chapter we return to Title VI and its pure analogues adopted under the Spending Power. (The ADA, though its substantive provisions draw on § 504 (a Title VI analogue), was adopted primarily under Congress Commerce Clause power. It has specific methods of litigation patterned after Title VII of the 1964 Act, and thus avoids the concerns discussed in this sub-chapter.) In some respects, our earlier discussions assumed that Title VI and its analogues are enforced by litigation initiated by harmed beneficiaries of the various Acts—as we saw in cases such as *Lau* and *Guardians* in sub-Chapter A. This sub-chapter examines the litigation remedy more closely, including the constitutional and policy issues it raises.

The first sub-part concerns the decision to use litigation as a remedy for Title VI. The second sub-part concerns the parties who may be subjected to liability through litigation. Most of the cases in the latter subpart arise under Title IX of the Educational Amendments of 1972, 20 U.S.C. § 1681 et seq., and involve intentional discrimination in education.

1. AN IMPLIED CAUSE OF ACTION FOR PROGRAM BENEFICIARIES

CANNON v. UNIVERSITY OF CHICAGO

Supreme Court of the United States, 1979.
441 U.S. 677, 99 S.Ct. 1946, 60 L.Ed.2d 560.

MR. JUSTICE STEVENS delivered the opinion of the Court.

Petitioner's complaints allege that her applications for admission to medical school were denied by the respondents because she is a woman. Accepting the truth of those allegations for the purpose of its decision, the Court of Appeals held that petitioner has no right of action against respondents that may be asserted in a federal court. 559 F.2d 1063. We granted certiorari to review that holding.

* * *

The Court of Appeals quite properly devoted careful attention to this question of statutory construction. As our recent cases—particularly Cort v. Ash, 422 U.S. 66, 95 S.Ct. 2080, 45 L.Ed.2d 26—demonstrate, the fact that a federal statute has been violated and some person harmed does not automatically give rise to a private cause of action in favor of that person. Instead, before concluding that Congress intended to make a remedy available to a special class of litigants, a court must carefully analyze the four factors that *Cort* identifies as indicative of such an intent. Our review of those factors persuades us, however, that the Court of Appeals reached the wrong conclusion and that petitioner does have a statutory right to pursue her claim that respondents rejected her application on the basis of her sex. After commenting on each of the four factors, we shall explain why they are not overcome by respondents' countervailing arguments.

I

First, the threshold question under *Cort* is whether the statute was enacted for the benefit of a special class of which the plaintiff is a member. That question is answered by looking to the language of the statute itself. [Here it is clear to us that Title IX protects a specific class in much the same way as the Voting Rights Act and other civil rights statutes for which we have implied remedies for private plaintiffs.]

Second, the *Cort* analysis requires consideration of legislative history. We must recognize, however, that the legislative history of a statute that does not expressly create or deny a private remedy will typically be equally silent or ambiguous on the question. Therefore, in situations such as the present one "in which it is clear that federal law has granted a class of persons certain rights, it is not necessary to show an intention to *create* a private cause of action, although an explicit purpose to *deny* such cause of action would be controlling." *Cort,* supra, 422 U.S. at 82, 95 S.Ct., at 2090 (emphasis in original). But this is not the typical case. Far from evidencing any purpose to *deny* a private cause of action, the history of Title IX rather plainly indicates that Congress intended to create such a remedy.

Title IX was patterned after Title VI of the Civil Rights Act of 1964. [At least a dozen federal appellate courts implied a remedy for violation of Title VI since soon after its adoption, and Congress was aware of those decisions when it enacted similar language in Title IX. The second *Cort* factor also favors the plaintiffs.].

Third, under *Cort,* a private remedy should not be implied if it would frustrate the underlying purpose of the legislative scheme. On the other hand, when that remedy is necessary or at least helpful to the accomplishment of the statutory purpose, the Court is decidedly receptive to its implication under the statute.

Title IX, like its model Title VI, sought to accomplish two related, but nevertheless somewhat different, objectives. First, Congress wanted to avoid the use of federal resources to support discriminatory practices; second, it wanted to provide individual citizens effective protection against those practices. Both of these purposes were repeatedly identified in the debates on the two statutes.

The first purpose is generally served by the statutory procedure for the termination of federal financial support for institutions engaged in discriminatory practices. That remedy is, however, severe and often may not provide an appropriate means of accomplishing the second purpose if merely an isolated violation has occurred. In that situation, the violation might be remedied more efficiently by an order requiring an institution to accept an applicant who had been improperly excluded. Moreover, in that kind of situation it makes little sense to impose on an individual, whose only interest is in obtaining a benefit for herself, or on HEW, the burden of demonstrating that an institution's practices are so pervasively discriminatory that a complete cutoff of federal funding is appropriate. The award of individual relief to a private litigant who has prosecuted her own suit is not only sensible but is fully consistent with—and in some cases even necessary to—the orderly enforcement of the statute.

The Department of Health, Education and Welfare, which is charged with the responsibility for administering Title IX, perceives no inconsistency between the private remedy and the public remedy.[41] On the contrary, the agency takes the unequivocal position that the individual remedy will provide effective assistance to achieving the statutory purposes. The agency's position is unquestionably correct.[42]

---

41. * * * [W]e are not persuaded that individual suits are inappropriate in advance of exhaustion of administrative remedies. Because the individual complainants cannot assure themselves that the administrative process will reach a decision on their complaints within a reasonable time, it makes little sense to require exhaustion. See 3 K. Davis, Administrative Law Treatise § 20.01, at 57 (1958).

42. In its submissions to this Court, as well as in other public statements, HEW has candidly admitted that it does not have the resources necessary to enforce Title IX in a substantial number of circumstances:

Fourth, the final inquiry suggested by *Cort* is whether implying a federal remedy is inappropriate because the subject matter involves an area basically of concern to the States. No such problem is raised by a prohibition against invidious discrimination of any sort, including that on the basis of sex. Since the Civil War, the Federal Government and the federal courts have been the " '*primary* and powerful reliances' " in protecting citizens against such discrimination. Steffel v. Thompson, 415 U.S. 452, 464, 94 S.Ct. 1209, 1218, 39 L.Ed.2d 505 (emphasis in original), quoting F. Frankfurter & J. Landis, The Business of the Supreme Court 65 (1928). Moreover, it is the expenditure of federal funds that provides the justification for this particular statutory prohibition. There can be no question but that this aspect of the *Cort* analysis supports the implication of a private federal remedy.

In sum, there is no need in this case to weigh the four *Cort* factors; all of them support the same result. Not only the words and history of Title IX, but also its subject matter and underlying purposes, counsel implication of a cause of action in favor of private victims of discrimination.

*   *   *

IV

When Congress intends private litigants to have a cause of action to support their statutory rights, the far better course is for it to specify as much when it creates those rights. But the Court has long recognized that under certain limited circumstances the failure of Congress to do so is not inconsistent with an intent on its part to have such a remedy available to the persons benefitted by its legislation. Title IX presents the atypical situation in which *all* of the circumstances that the Court has previously identified as supportive of an implied remedy are present. We therefore conclude that petitioner may maintain her lawsuit, despite the absence of any express authorization for it in the statute.

The judgment of the Court of Appeals is reversed and the case is remanded for further proceedings consistent with this opinion.

[Other opinions omitted.]

NOTE ON PRIVATE ENFORCEMENT OF *TITLE VI* AND *ITS SPENDING-POWER ANALOGUES*

1.   Are you persuaded by Justice Stevens' opinion? Which part is most convincing? Congress' knowledge that lower courts had already implied a claim for enforcement of Title VI? Was it the support of the agencies that eliminated any controversy? Consider whether the litigation remedy solves or accentuates problems previously noted regarding Title VI's statutory scheme (the same one adopted for Title IX).

"As a practical matter, HEW cannot hope to police all federally funded education programs, and even if administrative enforcement were always feasible, it often might not redress individual injuries. An implied private right of action is necessary to ensure that the fundamental purpose of Title IX, the elimination of sex discrimination in federally funded education programs, is achieved." Reply Brief for the Federal Respondents, at 6. * * *

(a) Do not direct private actions by-pass that agency expertise? Was the Court wrong not to require exhaustion of federal administrative remedies in such suits? Does the practice of referring to experts under the *Arline* case, sub-chapter B supra, provide an alternative approach? Is there no expertise that is relevant in cases of intentional discrimination? Is expertise relevant in "effects" cases?

(b) The funding sanction under Title VI was criticized by liberal judges in the *Taylor County* case because termination harms not only the grantee but also the intended program beneficiaries. Do private suits solve the problem of the relative ineffectiveness of the funding sanction? Or do private suits magnify the problem by draining grant money away from the federally funded program that has been sued?

2. Although the Court in *Cannon* implied a private cause of action for violations of Title IX and, by implication, Title VI, the Court in **Guardians Ass'n v. Civil Service Comm'n of the City of New York**, sub-chapter A supra, held by a fractured vote that damage remedies were recoverable only in cases involving intentional discrimination, not in those involving discriminatory effects. Justice White, casting the dispositive vote and joined by only a single other justice, explained his position, 463 U.S. at 596, 103 S.Ct. at 3229:

> "Thus, the Court has more than once announced that in fashioning remedies for violations of Spending Clause statutes by recipients of federal funds, the courts must recognize that the recipient has "alternative choices of assuming the additional costs" of complying with what a court has announced is necessary to conform to federal law or "of not using federal funds" and withdrawing from the federal program entirely. Although a court may identify the violation and enjoin its continuance or order recipients of federal funds prospectively to perform their duties incident to the receipt of federal money, the recipient has the option of withdrawing and hence terminating the prospective force of the injunction."

(a) Does the *Guardians* decision respond to the concerns raised in the Note following the *Lau* case, sub-chapter A supra, regarding the monetary cost to grantees of an effects test? Does *Guardians* in practice mean that grantees will only be required to cure discriminatory effects after a judgment against them? Does this remove all incentives to comply with the effects test? Alternatively, could the monetary impact of effects-based judgments be avoided altogether by simply restricting *Cannon*'s implied remedy to cases of alleged intentional discrimination, thus making funding termination the exclusive remedy for effects-test violations?

(b) Could *Guardians* be supported by the view that effects-type discrimination is not as objectionable as intentional discrimination? Would you agree?

(c) Does the *Guardians* holding apply to Title IX or to § 504? See subsection D.2 of this Chapter infra. If these statutes provide a damage remedy for intentional discrimination, do they displace (i.e., impliedly repeal) § 1983 as to such claims? See Fitzgerald v. Barnstable School Committee, 555 U.S. 246, 129 S.Ct. 788, 172 L.Ed.2d 582 (2009) (no, both remedies available; Title IX). What is the actual impact then of implying a remedy under Title VI and its analogues? Is it useful only for claims based on effects-type discrimination? See Alexander v. Sandoval, which follows this Note infra.

3. Although *Cannon* implies a private right of action to enforce at least some Title VI claims, the Supreme Court later held that states retained their Eleventh Amendment immunity in suits against them under Title VI's § 504 analogue. In that case, **Atascadero State Hospital v. Scanlon**, 473 U.S. 234, 105 S.Ct. 3142, 87 L.Ed.2d 171 (1985), the Court reasoned that Congress had not explicitly abrogated the states' immunity, thus leaving intact the usual rule against retroactive monetary awards payable from the state treasury. See the Note following the *Will* case, Chapter 1H.2 supra. The following year Congress apparently made its desires clear and overrode *Atascadero*. See Pub.L. 99–506, 100 Stat. 1845, codified at 42 U.S.C. § 2000d–7; Brennan v. Stewart, 834 F.2d 1248 (5th Cir.1988) (statute overrules decision). Is that the way you read § 2000d–7?

(a) How does the Court know what Congress wants when Congress has not been clear? Congress has not overturned *Cannon,* but has reversed *Grove City* (sub-chapter C), *Atascadero* (apparently), and at least one other decision restricting remedies under a federal funding statute. See Smith v. Robinson, 468 U.S. 992, 104 S.Ct. 3457, 82 L.Ed.2d 746 (1984) (attorneys fees unavailable in suit under Handicapped Children's Protection Act of 1986), legislatively reversed by Pub.L. 99–372, 100 Stat. 796, codified at 20 U.S.C. § 1415. Is this a minuet between Court and Congress? Was the Court out of step with Congress' statutory wishes? Or was each succeeding Congress in the 1980s simply further disposed toward civil rights compliance than previous sessions of Congress?

(b) Assuming that Congress specifically abrogated state immunity to suit under § 504, has it the constitutional power to do so? The answer is complex because Congress has power to regulate racial and gender discrimination directly under the Fourteenth Amendment, where it also has power to abrogate state sovereign immunity. See Fitzpatrick v. Bitzer, Chapter 7B.3 infra. (Presumably, after *FAIR*, the same would apply even when Congress indirectly protects against discrimination against high-scrutiny groups under the Spending Power.) When Congress legislates to protect a group receiving only low-level scrutiny, it can claim no authority under the Fourteenth Amendment. See Chapter 5 supra; Board of Trustees of University of Alabama v. Garrett, 531 U.S. 356, 121 S.Ct. 955, 148 L.Ed.2d 866 (2001) (no power to demand higher protection for disabilities, which receive only rational basis scrutiny; no power to apply ADA's reasonable accommodation principle to the states or to abrogate state immunity regarding such claims). See also Kimel v. Florida Bd. of Regents, 528 U.S. 62, 72–73, 120 S.Ct. 631, 145 L.Ed.2d 522 (2000) (age discrimination follows the same pattern).

(c) The Court generally has not permitted abrogation of state immunity by use of Congress' powers listed in Article I, see College Savings Bank v. Florida Prepaid Postsecondary Ed. Expense Bd., 527 U.S. 666, 669–670, 119 S.Ct. 2219, 144 L.Ed.2d 605 (1999); Seminole Tribe of Fla. v. Florida, 517 U.S. 44, 54, 116 S.Ct. 1114, 134 L.Ed.2d 252 (1996), though it has not specifically ruled on the Spending Power. Can the U.S. government sue on its contract with the state grantees in such cases?

4. Finally consider whether private plaintiffs can bring suit under Title VI to force the federal agencies to enforce Title VI more vigorously. In **Adams v. Richardson**, 480 F.2d 1159 (D.C. Cir.1973), the court overseeing most federal compliance efforts upheld such suits, noting that while the Department of Health, Education and Welfare had much discretion in how to enforce the statute, it could not abdicate its enforcement duties entirely.

(a) On remand plaintiffs' attorneys became heavily involved in monitoring HEW's enforcement efforts, and the district court set specific time-tables for processing individual complaints. See Adams v. Mathews, 536 F.2d 417, 418 (D.C. Cir.1976) (no review). In 1974 HEW received and approved the state-wide desegregation plans for eight states' universities, but on plaintiffs' motion for further relief the district court found that "such plans did not meet important desegregation requirements and have failed to achieve significant progress toward higher education desegregation." Adams v. Califano, 430 F.Supp. 118, 119 (D.D.C.1977). Were the district court's actions on remand inconsistent with the 1972 appellate decision? Did the appellate rationale not foreclose the district court's action?

(b) In the 1977 opinion, the district court noted that HEW admitted that its 1974 guidelines and plans "lacked 'standards of clarity and specificity,'" "haven't worked," and that the Department must "get about the business of changing them or altering them." 430 F.Supp. at 120. Was HEW inviting continued court supervision? Why did it do so? Might it have increased HEW's bargaining leverage during voluntary negotiations with grantees to point to the court order?

(c) In the 1960's Alabama officials reportedly asked federal officials to place them under court orders rather than voluntarily end segregation. Without the appearance of being compelled by the court to act, said the Alabamians, it would be politically impossible to make any desegregation efforts.[1] Was that the situation in *Adams* in 1977?

(d) Should judicial supervision of agency enforcement continue? Or has the grand scope of intervention gone too far? See Women's Equity Action League v. Cavazos, 906 F.2d 742 (D.C. Cir.1990) (per Ginsburg, J.) (role of the courts has reached a "terminal point"). Was it the success of *Cannon* that made the Court think that the *Adams* approach was no longer necessary?

ALEXANDER v. SANDOVAL

United States Supreme Court, 2001.
532 U.S. 275, 121 S.Ct. 1511, 149 L.Ed.2d 517 (2001).

JUSTICE SCALIA delivered the opinion of the Court.

This case presents the question whether private individuals may sue to enforce disparate-impact regulations promulgated under Title VI of the Civil Rights Act of 1964. [The lower court invalidated Alabama's requirement that driver's license examinees take a test in English, finding that the requirement had a disparate effect or impact on ethnic minorities, in violation of federal regulations adopted pursuant to 42 USC § 602. We reverse.]

---

1. See Comment, Race Quotas, 8 HARV. CIV. RIGHTS–CIV. LIB. L. REV. 128, 146 n. 102 (1973).

II

Although Title VI has often come to this Court, it is fair to say (indeed, perhaps an understatement) that our opinions have not eliminated all uncertainty regarding its commands. For purposes of the present case, however, it is clear from our decisions, from Congress's amendments of Title VI, and from the parties' concessions that three aspects of Title VI must be taken as given. First, private individuals may sue to enforce § 601 of Title VI and obtain both injunctive relief and damages. In Cannon v. University of Chicago the Court held that a private right of action existed to enforce Title IX of the Education Amendments of 1972, [analogizing to Title VI's § 601]. Congress has since ratified *Cannon's* holding. Section 1003 of the Rehabilitation Act Amendments of 1986, expressly abrogated States' sovereign immunity against suits brought in federal court to enforce Title VI and provided that in a suit against a State "remedies (including remedies both at law and in equity) are available . . . to the same extent as such remedies are available . . . in the suit against any public or private entity other than a State," § 2000d–7(a)(2). It is thus beyond dispute that private individuals may sue to enforce § 601.

Second, it is similarly beyond dispute—and no party disagrees—that § 601 prohibits only intentional discrimination. [A majority of the Justices in the *Bakke* case held that Title VI itself bans only such discrimination as is also forbidden by the Fourteenth Amendment, and therefore what] we said in Alexander v. Choate is true today: "Title VI itself directly reach[es] only instances of intentional discrimination."

Third, we must assume for purposes of deciding this case that regulations promulgated under § 602 of Title VI may validly proscribe activities that have a disparate impact on racial groups, even though such activities are permissible under § 601. Though no opinion of this Court has held that, five Justices in Guardians voiced that view of the law at least as alternative grounds for their decisions, and dictum in Alexander v. Choate is to the same effect. These statements are in considerable tension with the rule of *Bakke* and *Guardians* that § 601 forbids only intentional discrimination, but petitioners have not challenged the regulations here. We therefore assume for the purposes of deciding this case that the [federal] regulations proscribing activities that have a disparate impact on the basis of race are valid.

Respondents assert that the issue in this case, like the first two described above, has been resolved by our cases. To reject a private cause of action to enforce the disparate-impact regulations, they say, we would "[have] to ignore the actual language of *Guardians* and *Cannon*." Brief for Respondents 13. The language in *Cannon* to which respondents refer does not in fact support their position * * *. But in any event, this Court is bound by holdings, not language. *Cannon* was decided on the assumption that the University of Chicago had intentionally discriminated against petitioner. It therefore *held* that Title IX created a private right of action to enforce its ban on intentional discrimination, but had no occasion to consider whether the right reached regulations barring disparate-impact discrimination. [No other case actually reached and decided the issue of whether there exists a private right to enforce Title VI's disparate-impact regulations.]

Nor does it follow straightaway from the three points we have taken as given that Congress must have intended a private right of action to enforce disparate-impact regulations. We do not doubt that regulations applying § 601's ban on intentional discrimination are covered by the cause of action to enforce that section. Such regulations, if valid and reasonable, authoritatively construe the statute itself, and it is therefore meaningless to talk about a separate cause of action to enforce the regulations apart from the statute. A Congress that intends the statute to be enforced through a private cause of action intends the authoritative interpretation of the statute to be so enforced as well. The many cases that respondents say have "assumed" that a cause of action to enforce a statute includes one to enforce its regulations illustrate (to the extent that cases in which an issue was not presented can illustrate anything) only this point; each involved regulations of the type we have just described, as respondents conceded at oral argument. Our decision in Lau v. Nichols falls within the same category. The Title VI regulations at issue in *Lau*, similar to the ones at issue here, forbade funding recipients to take actions which had the effect of discriminating on the basis of race, color, or national origin. Unlike our later cases, however, the Court in *Lau* interpreted § 601 itself to proscribe disparate-impact discrimination, saying that it "rel[ied] solely on § 601 . . . to reverse the Court of Appeals," and that the disparate-impact regulations simply "[made] sure that recipients of federal aid . . . conduct[ed] any federally financed projects consistently with § 601." * * *

We must face now the question avoided by *Lau*, because we have since rejected *Lau*'s interpretation of § 601 as reaching beyond intentional discrimination. It is clear now that the disparate-impact regulations do not simply apply § 601—since they indeed forbid conduct that § 601 permits—and therefore clear that the private right of action to enforce § 601 does not include a private right to enforce these regulations. That right must come, if at all, from the independent force of § 602. As stated earlier, we assume for purposes of this decision that § 602 confers the authority to promulgate disparate-impact regulations; the question remains whether it confers a private right of action to enforce them. If not, we must conclude that a failure to comply with regulations promulgated under § 602 that is not also a failure to comply with § 601 is not actionable.

Implicit in our discussion thus far has been a particular understanding of the genesis of private causes of action. Like substantive federal law itself, private rights of action to enforce federal law must be created by Congress. The judicial task is to interpret the statute Congress has passed to determine whether it displays an intent to create not just a private right but also a private remedy. Statutory intent on this latter point is determinative. Without it, a cause of action does not exist and courts may not create one, no matter how desirable that might be as a policy matter, or how compatible with the statute. "Raising up causes of action where a statute has not created them may be a proper function for common-law courts, but not for federal tribunals."

Respondents would have us revert in this case to the understanding of private causes of action that held sway 40 years ago when Title VI was enacted. That understanding is captured by the Court's statement in J.I. Case Co. v. Borak, 377 U.S. 426, 433, 84 S.Ct. 1555, 12 L.Ed.2d 423 (1964), that "it is the duty of the courts to be alert to provide such remedies as are necessary to make effective the congressional purpose" expressed by a statute. We abandoned that understanding in Cort v. Ash, 422 U.S. 66, 78, 95 S.Ct. 2080, 45 L.Ed.2d 26 (1975)—which itself interpreted a statute enacted under the *ancien regime*—and have not returned to it since * * *. Having sworn off the habit of venturing beyond Congress's intent, we will not accept respondents' invitation to have one last drink * * *.

We therefore begin (and find that we can end) our search for Congress's intent with the text and structure of Title VI. Section 602 authorizes federal agencies "to effectuate the provisions of [§ 601] * * * by issuing rules, regulations, or orders of general applicability." 42 U.S.C. § 2000d–1. It is immediately clear that the "rights-creating" language so critical to the Court's analysis in *Cannon* of § 601 is completely absent from § 602. Whereas § 601 decrees that "[n]o person ... shall ... be subjected to discrimination," 42 U.S.C. § 2000d, the text of § 602 provides that "[e]ach Federal department and agency ... is authorized and directed to effectuate the provisions of [§ 601]," 42 U.S.C. § 2000d–1. Far from displaying congressional intent to create new rights, § 602 limits agencies to "effectuat[ing]" rights already created by § 601. And the focus of § 602 is twice removed from the individuals who will ultimately benefit from Title VI's protection. Statutes that focus on the person regulated rather than the individuals protected create "no implication of an intent to confer rights on a particular class of persons." Section 602 is yet a step further removed: it focuses neither on the individuals protected nor even on the funding recipients being regulated, but on the agencies that will do the regulating * * *. So far as we can tell, this authorizing portion of § 602 reveals no congressional intent to create a private right of action.

Nor do the methods that § 602 goes on to provide for enforcing its authorized regulations manifest an intent to create a private remedy; if anything, they suggest the opposite. Section 602 empowers agencies to enforce their regulations either by terminating funding to the "particular program, or part thereof," that has violated the regulation or "by any other means authorized by law," 42 U.S.C. § 2000d–1. No enforcement action may be taken, however, "until the department or agency concerned has advised the appropriate person or persons of the failure to comply with the requirement and has determined that compliance cannot be secured by voluntary means." *Ibid.* And every agency enforcement action is subject to judicial review. § 2000d–2. If an agency attempts to terminate program funding, still more restrictions apply. * * * Whatever these elaborate restrictions on agency enforcement may imply for the private enforcement of rights created *outside* of § 602 [in § 601], they tend to contradict a congressional intent to create privately enforceable rights through § 602 itself. The express provision of one method of enforcing a substantive rule suggests that Congress intended to preclude others * * *.

Both the Government and respondents argue that the *regulations* contain rights-creating language and so must be privately enforceable, see Brief for United States 19–20; Brief for Respondents 31, but that argument skips an analytical step. Language in a regulation may invoke a private right of action that Congress through statutory text created, but it may not create a right that Congress has not. Touche Ross & Co. v. Redington, 442 U.S., at 577, n. 18, 99 S.Ct. 2479 ("[T]he language of the statute and not the rules must control"). Thus, when a statute has provided a general authorization for private enforcement of regulations, it may perhaps be correct that the intent displayed in each regulation can determine whether or not it is privately enforceable. But it is most certainly incorrect to say that language in a regulation can conjure up a private cause of action that has not been authorized by Congress. Agencies may play the sorcerer's apprentice but not the sorcerer himself.

* * *

The judgment of the Court of Appeals is reversed.

It is so ordered.

JUSTICE STEVENS, with whom JUSTICE SOUTER, JUSTICE GINSBURG, and JUSTICE BREYER join, dissenting.

* * * In separate lawsuits spanning several decades, we have endorsed an action identical in substance to the one brought in this case, [citing *Lau, Cannon, Guardians*]. Giving fair import to our language and our holdings, every Court of Appeals to address the question has concluded that a private right of action exists to enforce the rights guaranteed both by the text of Title VI and by any regulations validly promulgated pursuant to that Title, and Congress has adopted several statutes that appear to ratify the status quo * * *.

The majority acknowledges that *Cannon* is binding precedent with regard to both Title VI and Title IX, but seeks to limit the scope of its holding to cases involving allegations of intentional discrimination. The distinction the majority attempts to impose is wholly foreign to *Cannon*'s text and reasoning. The opinion in *Cannon* consistently treats the question presented in that case as whether a private right of action exists to enforce "Title IX" (and by extension "Title VI"), and does not draw any distinctions between the various types of discrimination outlawed by the operation of those statutes. Though the opinion did not reach out to affirmatively preclude the drawing of every conceivable distinction, it could hardly have been more clear as to the scope of its holding: A private right of action exists for "victims of *the* prohibited discrimination." Not some of the prohibited discrimination, but all of it.

* * *

Our fractured decision in Guardians Assn. v. Civil Serv. Comm'n of New York City reinforces the conclusion that this issue is effectively settled. While the various opinions in that case took different views as to the spectrum of relief available to plaintiffs in Title VI cases, a clear majority of the Court expressly stated that private parties may seek injunctive relief against governmental practices that have the effect of discriminating against racial and ethnic minorities. As this case involves just such an action, its result ought to follow naturally from *Guardians*.

NOTE ON THE DECLINE OF PRIVATE ENFORCEMENT OF THE EFFECTS TEST

1. As discussed in the Note on Legal Realism and the Effects Test Over Time, subpart A of this Chapter supra, there is some reason to question whether ending judicial enforcement of the effects test robbed plaintiffs of any significant advantage. Before the decision in *Sandoval*, judicial enforcement of the effects test had been spotty at best, limited primarily to situations where explicit agency guidelines informed judges exactly how to strike the balance between grantee interests and the disparate effect of neutral program practices.

(a) Is keeping a private right of action for cases involving specific regulations or guidelines a sufficient justification for upholding a private right of action for effects-based claims. If there are explicit agency rules already on the books, cannot the agency be expected to enforce those rules in agency proceedings? See *Board of Instruction of Taylor County v. Finch*, subpart B of this Chapter supra; Cannon v. University of Chicago, supra, n.42 (agency without resources to enforce Title VI). Do you also worry that politics might affect the agency's resolution of a case? Re-read § 602: are politics supposed to influence cases? Only regulation drafting, not specific cases?

(b) The Court's *Sandoval* decision was part of a larger effort by the Court to reverse the 1970's-era practice of readily implying private rights to sue from regulatory statutes that contained no explicit authorization for private suits. (Note Justice Scalia's reference in *Sandoval* to the *"ancien regime"* and his statement that "[h]aving sworn off the habit of venturing beyond Congress's intent, we will not accept respondents' invitation to have one last drink.") In retrospect, the Court's experience under § 1983 may have made it willing to imply private remedies—and thus judicially enforce in ordinary litigation—for many other civil rights statutes that were silent as to judicial enforcement. Was § 1983's influence on Title VI and its Spending–Power analogues too strong? Are judicially enforced private rights of action unsuited to statutes that build primarily on an administrative regime?

(c) Since the 1980's, the Court has also restricted implication of direct constitutional private rights of action, see Chapter 4B supra; Correctional Services Corporation v. Malesko, 534 U.S. 61, 122 S.Ct. 515, 151 L.Ed.2d 456 (2001). The rationale has usually been that the existence of a congressionally specified statutory remedy, whether judicial or administrative, makes implication of a judicial remedy unnecessary—or even an invasion of Congress' prerogative to choose remedies. Is that essentially the same rationale used in *Sandoval*?

(d) Unlike § 504 and Title VI, the ADA specifically authorizes private enforcement actions. Does it show that mixed administrative-judicial enforcement can work? Does the fact that Title VI is a Spending Power statute, with federal control tied to federal grants and contracts, make it different from the ADA? If so, is it because of the underlying competition in most Spending Power statutes between accomplishment of competing goals, programmatic goals and civil rights goals?

2. By leaving in place *Cannon*'s private right of action for claims of intentional discrimination, *Sandoval* creates two categories—claims of intentional discrimination pursuable by private litigation and claims of discriminatory effects for which there is no such private right to sue. This makes it necessary to determine into which category any particular type of claims falls.

(a) In **Jackson v. Birmingham Board of Education**, 544 U.S. 167, 125 S.Ct. 1497, 161 L.Ed.2d 361 (2005), the Court was required to decide whether retaliation claims under Title IX fit the intent classification or the effects classification. Justice O'Connor's opinion for a bare 5–4 majority decided it was the latter, 544 U.S. at 173–74, 125 S.Ct. at 1504:

> "More than 25 years ago, in *Cannon*, we held that Title IX implies a private right of action to enforce its prohibition on intentional sex discrimination. In subsequent cases, we have defined the contours of that right of action[, citing primarily sexual harassment cases to be discussed in the next sub-part of this Chapter]. In all of these cases, we relied on the text of Title IX, which, subject to a list of narrow exceptions not at issue here, broadly prohibits a funding recipient from subjecting any person to 'discrimination' 'on the basis of sex.' 20 U.S.C. § 1681. Retaliation against a person because that person has complained of sex discrimination is another form of intentional sex discrimination encompassed by Title IX's private cause of action. Retaliation is, by definition, an intentional act. It is a form of 'discrimination' because the complainant is being subjected to differential treatment. Moreover, retaliation is discrimination 'on the basis of sex' because it is an intentional response to the nature of the complaint: an allegation of sex discrimination."

(b) *Jackson* indicates that sexual harassment claims also retain a private right of action, but there remains open for discussion at least one other notable class of Title IX cases, those involving a claim of equal access to programs, especially sports activities. See Cohen v. Brown University, 101 F.3d 155 (1st Cir.1996) (equal access for women to sports via separate women's teams). Are these cases necessarily intentional discrimination claims because the schools have segregated male-female sports teams, and therefore have classified intentionally by sex?

3. Finally, consider the somewhat related issue of extra-territorial application of America's civil rights laws. Should the Court imply or enforce a private right of action against defendants whose conduct occurs outside the land territory of the United States? Should it imply an action against foreign

entities, for example cruise ships, that are in U.S. territorial waters? In **Spector v. Norwegian Cruise Line Ltd.**, 545 U.S. 119, 125 S.Ct. 2169, 162 L.Ed.2d 97 (2005), the Court considered a passenger's claim that a foreign-owned vessel had failed to comply with the ADA's requirements of accessibility for disabled persons. The appellate court had adopted a blanket rule against application of U.S. law to ships temporarily in U.S., citing a string of Supreme Court precedents. A fractured Court reversed, with the plurality noting, 545 U.S. at 130–32, 125 S. Ct. at 2177–79:

> "This Court has long held that general statutes are presumed to apply to conduct that takes place aboard a foreign-flag vessel in United States territory if the interests of the United States or its citizens, rather than interests internal to the ship, are at stake. See *Cunard S. S. Co.* v. *Mellon,* 262 U.S. 100, 127, 43 S.Ct. 504, 67 L.Ed. 894 (1923) (holding that the general terms of the National Prohibition Act apply to foreign-flag ships in United States waters because "[t]here is in the act no provision making it inapplicable" to such ships). The general rule that United States statutes apply to foreign-flag ships in United States territory is subject only to a narrow exception. Absent a clear statement of congressional intent, general statutes may not apply to foreign-flag vessels insofar as they regulate matters that involve only the internal order and discipline of the vessel, rather than the peace of the port. * * * This exception to the usual presumption, however, does not extend beyond matters of internal order and discipline. [To the extent that the ADA imposes requirements that do not affect internal order of discipline, it may be applied to foreign vessels.]"

(a) In a subsequent passage, Justice Kennedy's narrow plurality opinion noted that "[c]ruise ships flying foreign flags of convenience offer public accommodations and transportation services to over 7 million United States residents annually, departing from and returning to ports located in the United States." 545 U.S. at 132, 125 S. Ct. at 2178. Is the better basis for decision in *Spector* the simple observation that U.S. law should be presumed to apply when cruise lines intentionally serve the U.S. market and derive revenue here? Should any vessel that knowingly picks up a passenger in American waters be required to follow U.S. antidiscrimination law in dealing with passengers?

(b) The problem with a broad rule, of course, is that compliance with ADA accessibility standards could potentially cost cruise lines millions of dollars. There is also the possibility of conflicting national rules, e.g., design rules required by the law of other nations, that would make it impossible for shipowners to comply with all local laws. Should the remedy implied in *Spector* apply only to non-discrimination of the intentional variety, with no obligation for reasonable accommodation? (Note the potential similarity to the *Cannon–Sandoval* line of cases that imply suits for intentional discrimination but not ones for effects-based claims. The four dissenters in *Spector,* echoing themes from *Sandoval,* would have exempted all maritime operations from coverage, and they accused the plurality of "creative" "fine-tuning" of the ADA to achieve not Congress' goals but their own. See 545 U.S. at 158, 125 S.Ct. at 2193.)

(c) In an apparent response to concerns expressed in the preceding sub-paragraph, the *Spector* plurality went on to hold that any "requirement [that] could mandate a permanent and significant alteration of a physical feature of the ship—that is, an element of basic ship design and construction[,—] would interfere with the internal affairs of foreign ships [because they would implicate] fundamental issues of ship design and construction, and it might be impossible for a ship to comply with all the requirements different jurisdictions might impose." 545 U.S. at 135, 125 S.Ct. at 2180. A majority was gained when Justice Kennedy added that the ADA's exemptions might not even require any alterations in the case of cruise ships because of the potential expense involved. Should these issues always be decided by explicit Congressional statements because of the potential effect on international affairs? Title I of the ADA, covering employment, contains a detailed statement about the potential extra-territorial application of only to its provisions, see 42 U.S.C. § 12112(c)(1); which way should that fact cut in *Spector*'s case under Title II of the ADA, which contains no similar language?

(d) In what other civil-rights contexts can these issues arise? See EEOC v. Arabian American Oil Co., 499 U.S. 244, 260, 111 S.Ct. 1227, 113 L.Ed.2d 274 (1991) (no application of Title VII to U.S. workers of U.S. companies operating abroad). Congress thereafter amended Title VII to spell out in detail how and where its commands would apply in the international context. See 42 U.S.C. § 2000e–1(b). Are values found in American civil rights laws so universal or so worthy and important that they should be applied extra-territorially whenever there is authority to do so? Or would that be American cultural imperialism?

2.   LIABILITY OF GRANTEES WHEN EMPLOYEES OR PROGRAM PARTICIPANTS DISCRIMINATE

DAVIS v. MONROE COUNTY BOARD OF EDUCATION

United States Supreme Court, 1999.
526 U.S. 629, 119 S.Ct. 1661, 143 L.Ed.2d 839.

JUSTICE O'CONNOR delivered the opinion of the Court.

Petitioner brought suit against the Monroe County Board of Education and other defendants, alleging that her fifth-grade daughter had been the victim of sexual harassment by another student in her class. Among petitioner's claims was a claim for monetary and injunctive relief under Title IX of the Education Amendments of 1972 (Title IX), 86 Stat. 373, as amended, 20 U.S.C. § 1681 et seq. The District Court dismissed petitioner's Title IX claim on the ground that "student-on-student," or peer, harassment provides no ground for a private cause of action under the statute. The Court of Appeals for the Eleventh Circuit, sitting en banc, affirmed. We consider here whether a private damages action may lie against the school board in cases of student-on-student harassment. We conclude that it may, but only where the funding recipient acts with deliberate indifference to known acts of harassment in its programs or activities. Moreover, we conclude that such an action will lie only for harassment that is so severe, pervasive, and objectively offensive that it effectively bars the victim's access to an educational opportunity or benefit.

I

[The plaintiff's daughter suffered a prolonged period of sexual harassment from a fellow student during half of her year in fifth grade at a public school receiving federal financial assistance. The conduct included attempts "to touch [the child's] breasts and genital area" and "vulgar statements such as 'I want to get in bed with you' and 'I want to feel your boobs.'" The repeated incidents were allegedly repeatedly reported to the teacher, but nothing was done, and the harassment continued and increased. The daughter's grades dropped, and she later wrote a suicide note. Other victims and incidents were brought to the school authorities' attention, but the teacher failed to intervene except to tell the harasser to stop—and to tell the victim that she was the "only one complaining." The parent later filed a complaint in federal court under Title IX, but it was dismissed. The Eleventh Circuit affirmed.]

II

Title IX provides, with certain exceptions not at issue here, that

> "[n]o person in the United States shall, on the basis of sex, be excluded from participation in, be denied the benefits of, or be subjected to discrimination under any education program or activity receiving Federal financial assistance." 20 U.S.C. § 1681(a).

[A]

* * *

[Since the school board has admitted that sexual harassment can constitute intentional discrimination, we turn to the question of] whether a district's failure to respond to student-on-student harassment in its schools can support a private suit for money damages. See Gebser v. Lago Vista Independent School Dist., 524 U.S. 274, 283, 118 S.Ct. 1989, 141 L.Ed.2d 277 (1998) [where we approved, under limited circumstances, a claim for damages under Title IX for teacher-on-student harassment]. This Court has indeed recognized an implied private right of action under Title IX, see Cannon v. University of Chicago, supra, and we have held that money damages are available in such suits, Franklin v. Gwinnett County Public Schools, 503 U.S. 60, 112 S.Ct. 1028, 117 L.Ed.2d 208 (1992). Because we have repeatedly treated Title IX as legislation enacted pursuant to Congress' authority under the Spending Clause, however, see, e.g., Gebser v. Lago Vista Independent School Dist., supra; see also Guardians Assn. v. Civil Serv. Comm'n of New York City (Title VI), private damages actions are available only where recipients of federal funding had adequate notice that they could be liable for the conduct at issue. When Congress acts pursuant to its spending power, it generates legislation "much in the nature of a contract: in return for federal funds, the States agree to comply with federally imposed conditions." Pennhurst State School and Hospital v. Halderman, 451 U.S. 1, 17, 101 S.Ct. 1531, 67 L.Ed.2d 694 (1981). In interpreting language in spending legislation, we thus "insis[t] that Congress speak with a clear voice," recognizing that "[t]here can, of course, be no knowing acceptance [of the terms of the putative contract] if a State is unaware of the conditions [imposed by the legislation] or is unable to ascertain what is expected of it." Ibid.

Invoking Pennhurst, respondents urge that Title IX provides no notice that recipients of federal educational funds could be liable in damages for harm arising from student-on-student harassment. Respondents contend, specifically, that the statute only proscribes misconduct by grant recipients, not third parties [because the school district has little or no control over third parties].

We agree with respondents that a recipient of federal funds may be liable in damages under Title IX only for its own misconduct. * * *

We disagree with respondents' assertion, however, that petitioner seeks to hold the Board liable for [the harassing student's] actions instead of its own. Here, petitioner attempts to hold the Board liable for its own decision to remain idle in the face of known student-on-student harassment in its schools. In Gebser, we concluded that a recipient of federal education funds may be liable in damages under Title IX where it is deliberately indifferent to known acts of sexual harassment by a teacher. * * *

Accordingly, [in Gebser we avoided agency principles of strict liability and] declined the invitation to impose liability under what amounted to a negligence standard—holding the district liable for its failure to react to teacher-student harassment of which it knew or should have known. Rather, we concluded that the district could be liable for damages only where the district itself intentionally acted in clear violation of Title IX by remaining deliberately indifferent to acts of teacher-student harassment of which it had actual knowledge. * * * By employing the "deliberate indifference" theory already used to establish municipal liability under § 1983, see City of Canton v. Harris, 489 U.S. 378, 109 S.Ct. 1197, 103 L.Ed.2d 412 (1989), we concluded in Gebser that recipients could be liable in damages only where their own deliberate indifference effectively "cause[d]" the discrimination. The high standard imposed in Gebser sought to eliminate any "risk that the recipient would be liable in damages not for its own official decision but instead for its employees' independent actions."

* * *

[The school board can be held liable under a "deliberate indifference" standard for student-on-student harassment as much as for teacher-on-student harassment.] This is not to say that the identity of the harasser is irrelevant. On the contrary, both the "deliberate indifference" standard and the language of Title IX narrowly circumscribe the set of parties whose known acts of sexual harassment can trigger some duty to respond on the part of funding recipients. Deliberate indifference makes sense as a theory of direct liability under Title IX only where the funding recipient has some control over the alleged harassment. A recipient cannot be directly liable for its indifference where it lacks the authority to take remedial action.

[There are other safeguards against over-zealous enforcement against school boards.] The statute's plain language confines the scope of prohibited conduct based on the recipient's degree of control over the harasser and the environment in which the harassment occurs. If a funding recipient does not engage in harassment directly, it may not be liable for damages unless its deliberate indifference "subject[s]" its students to harassment. That is, the deliberate indifference must, at a minimum, "cause [students] to undergo" harassment or "make them liable or vulnerable" to it. Random House Dictionary of the English Language 1415 (1966) (defining "subject" as "to cause to undergo the action of something specified; expose" or "to make liable or vulnerable; lay open; expose"). Moreover, because the harassment must occur "under" "the operations of" a funding recipient, see 20 U.S.C. § 1681(a); § 1687 (defining "program or activity"), the harassment must take place in a context subject to the school district's control.

These factors combine to limit a recipient's damages liability to circumstances wherein the recipient exercises substantial control over both the harasser and the context in which the known harassment occurs. Only then can the recipient be said to "expose" its students to harassment or "cause" them to undergo it "under" the recipient's programs. We agree with the dissent that these conditions are satisfied most easily and most obviously when the offender is an agent of the recipient. We rejected the use of agency analysis in *Gebser*, however, and we disagree that the term "under" somehow imports an agency requirement into Title IX. As noted above, the theory in *Gebser* was that the recipient was directly liable for its deliberate indifference to discrimination. * * * *

Where, as here, the misconduct occurs during school hours and on school grounds—the bulk of [the harassing child's] misconduct, in fact, took place in the classroom—the misconduct is taking place "under" an "operation" of the funding recipient. In these circumstances, the recipient retains substantial control over the context in which the harassment occurs. More importantly, however, in this setting the Board exercises significant control over the harasser. * * * We thus conclude that recipients of federal funding may be liable for "subject[ing]" their students to discrimination where the recipient is deliberately indifferent to known acts of student-on-student sexual harassment and the harasser is under the school's disciplinary authority.

* * *

We stress that our conclusion here—that recipients may be liable for their deliberate indifference to known acts of peer sexual harassment— does not mean that recipients can avoid liability only by purging their schools of actionable peer harassment or that administrators must engage in particular disciplinary action. We thus disagree with respondents' contention that, if Title IX provides a cause of action for student-on-student harassment, "nothing short of expulsion of every student accused of misconduct involving sexual overtones would protect school systems from liability or damages." See Brief for Respondents 16. Likewise, the dissent erroneously imagines that victims of peer harassment now have a Title IX right to make particular remedial demands. In fact, as we have previously noted, courts should refrain from second guessing the disciplinary decisions made by school administrators.

School administrators will continue to enjoy the flexibility they require [unless their reaction to a well-founded complaint of harassment] is clearly unreasonable in light of the known circumstances. * * * In an appropriate case, there is no reason why courts, on a motion to dismiss, for summary judgment, or for a directed verdict, could not identify a response as not "clearly unreasonable" as a matter of law.

* * *

B

The requirement that recipients receive adequate notice of Title IX's proscriptions also bears on the proper definition of "discrimination" in the context of a private damages action. We have elsewhere concluded that sexual harassment is a form of discrimination for Title IX purposes and that Title IX proscribes harassment with sufficient clarity to satisfy Pennhurst's notice requirement and serve as a basis for a damages action. See Gebser v. Lago Vista Independent School Dist. Having previously determined that "sexual harassment" is "discrimination" in the school context under Title IX, [and we now reiterate in the context of peer harassment that liability arises only for conduct] that is so severe, pervasive, and objectively offensive that it can be said to deprive the victims of access to the educational opportunities or benefits provided by the school.

The most obvious example of student-on-student sexual harassment capable of triggering a damages claim would thus involve the overt, physical deprivation of access to school resources. Consider, for example, a case in which male students physically threaten their female peers every day, successfully preventing the female students from using a particular school resource—an athletic field or a computer lab, for instance. District administrators are well aware of the daily ritual, yet they deliberately ignore requests for aid from the female students wishing to use the resource. The district's knowing refusal to take any action in response to such behavior would fly in the face of Title IX's core principles, and such deliberate indifference may appropriately be subject to claims for monetary damages. It is not necessary, however, to show physical exclusion to demonstrate that students have been deprived by the actions of another student or students of an educational opportunity on the basis of sex. Rather, a plaintiff must establish sexual harassment of students that is so severe, pervasive, and objectively offensive, and that so undermines and detracts from the victims' educational experience, that the victim-students are effectively denied equal access to an institution's resources and opportunities. Cf. Meritor Savings Bank, FSB v. Vinson, [discussed in Chapter 7B.2 infra].

* * *

C

Applying this standard to the facts at issue here, we conclude that the Eleventh Circuit erred in dismissing petitioner's complaint. Petitioner alleges that her daughter was the victim of repeated acts of sexual harassment by [a peer] over a 5–month period, and there are allegations in support of the conclusion that [the] misconduct was severe, pervasive, and objectively offensive [with a concrete impact on her grades in school]. The complaint also suggests that petitioner may be able to show both actual knowledge and deliberate indifference on the part of the Board, which made no effort whatsoever either to investigate or to put an end to the harassment.

On this complaint, we cannot say "beyond doubt that [petitioner] can prove no set of facts in support of [her] claim which would entitle [her] to relief." Conley v. Gibson, 355 U.S. 41, 45–46, 78 S.Ct. 99, 2 L.Ed.2d 80 (1957). Accordingly, the judgment of the United States Court of Appeals for the Eleventh Circuit is reversed, and the case is remanded for further proceedings consistent with this opinion.

It is so ordered.

JUSTICE KENNEDY, with whom THE CHIEF JUSTICE, JUSTICE SCALIA, and JUSTICE THOMAS join, dissenting.

* * *

[There are serious problems with the majority's over-reliance on the theory that the school district here has "subjected" the student to discrimination. "Subjected" connotes action "authorized or in accordance with" school board desires. That may be true of teacher-student harassment because the teacher is part of the school authority, but it can never be true of students, who are not authorized to act for the school board. Even DOE took this position for the first 25 years after passage of Title IX, as its interpretive regulations held schools responsible only for those to whom they had delegated power. See 34 CFR § 106.51(a)(3) (1998).]

* * *

[Of course, much adolescent behavior is inappropriate and offensive to others as such young people explore their place in society. But one must question whether labeling such conduct "harassment" is useful—or that it was ever intended by Congress.] The difficulties schools will encounter in identifying peer sexual harassment are already evident in teachers' manuals designed to give guidance on the subject. For example, one teachers' manual on peer sexual harassment suggests that sexual harassment in kindergarten through third grade includes a boy being "put down" on the playground "because he wants to play house with the girls" or a girl being "put down because she shoots baskets better than the boys." Minnesota Dept. of Education, Girls and Boys Getting Along: Teaching Sexual Harassment Prevention in the Elementary Classroom 65 (1993). Yet another manual suggests that one student saying to another, "You look nice" could be sexual harassment, depending on the "tone of voice," how the student looks at the other, and "who else is around." N. Stein & L. Sjostrom, Flirting or Hurting? A Teacher's Guide on Student-to-Student Sexual Harassment in Schools (Grades 6 through 12) 14 (1994). Blowing a kiss is also suspect. Ibid. This confusion will likely be compounded once the sexual-harassment label is invested with the force of federal law, backed up by private damages suits.

* * *

The cost of defending against peer sexual harassment suits alone could overwhelm many school districts, [and] school liability in one peer sexual harassment suit could approach, or even exceed, the total federal funding of many school districts. Petitioner, for example, seeks damages of $500,000 in this case. Respondent school district received approximately $679,000 in federal aid in 1992–1993. The school district sued in *Gebser* received only $120,000 in federal funds a year. Indeed, the entire 1992–1993 budget of that district was only $1.6 million.

* * *

The prospect of unlimited Title IX liability will, in all likelihood, breed a climate of fear that encourages school administrators to label even the most innocuous of childish conduct sexual harassment. It would appear to be no coincidence that, not long after the DOE issued its proposed policy guidance warning that schools could be liable for peer sexual harassment in the fall of 1996, a North Carolina school suspended a 6–year–old boy who kissed a female classmate on the cheek for sexual harassment, on the theory that "[u]nwelcome is unwelcome at any age." Los Angeles Times, Sept. 25, 1996, p. A11. A week later, a New York school suspended a second-grader who kissed a classmate and ripped a button off her skirt. Buffalo News, Oct. 2, 1996, p. A16. The second grader said that he got the idea from his favorite book "Corduroy," about a bear with a missing button. Ibid. School administrators said only, "We were given guidelines as to why we suspend children. We follow the guidelines." Ibid.

* * *

A school faced with a peer sexual harassment complaint in the wake of the majority's decision may well be beset with litigation from every side.

One student's demand for a quick response to her harassment complaint will conflict with the alleged harasser's demand for due process. Another student's demand for a harassment-free classroom will conflict with the alleged harasser's claim to a mainstream placement under the Individuals with Disabilities Education Act or with his state constitutional right to a continuing, free public education. On college campuses, and even in secondary schools, a student's claim that the school should remedy a sexually hostile environment will conflict with the alleged harasser's claim that his speech, even if offensive, is protected by the First Amendment. In each of these situations, the school faces the risk of suit, and maybe even multiple suits, regardless of its response. [These potential conflicts can be avoided by simply enforcing the statute as written, which gives no indication that Congress intended to cover peer harassment as opposed to teacher-on-student harassment.]

NOTE ON GRANTEE LIABILITY FOR FAILURE TO REMEDY OTHERS' DISCRIMINATION

1. The *Davis* decision builds on two important precedents. In the first case, **Franklin v. Gwinnett County Public Schools**, 503 U.S. 60, 112 S.Ct. 1028, 117 L.Ed.2d 208 (1992), a unanimous Court held that the implied cause of action recognized in the *Cannon* case includes a damages remedy. Noting that when a cause of action is implied, "we presume the availability of all appropriate remedies unless Congress has expressly indicated otherwise," the Court specifically relied on its decision in the *Guardians* case, noting that "a clear majority expressed the view that damages were available under Title VI in an action seeking remedies for an intentional violation." 503 U.S. at 69–70, 112 S.Ct. at 1034–35. Since Title IX is modeled on Title VI, and since the case involved an allegation of intentional discrimination, the Court considered the issue of the availability of a damages remedy to be an easy one. See also Consolidated Rail Corp. v. Darrone, 465 U.S. 624, 104 S.Ct. 1248, 79 L.Ed.2d 568 (1984) (retroactive monetary remedy also available in suit under § 504 for intentional discrimination based on handicap).

(a) The *Franklin* case involved a claim of intentional discrimination by a teacher employed at a school. The Court did not consider the issue of whether the school was being held liable for the teacher's intentionally discriminatory acts or its own. The opinion, however, follows *Guardians* by noting that the relevant acts in question were not simply "intentional" but "intentionally discriminatory." How does *Davis* change that focus?

(b) The *Davis* Court notes that it is not holding the board liable for the harassing student's actions, but only for its own actions. The student's acts were considered "intentionally discriminatory," but were the school board's actions also "intentionally discriminatory" or only "intentional"? If intentional, it is the school board's intention to do what? To be discriminatory against young girls? To be more focused on smooth administration than education? To be risk-averse? Are these latter intents sex-based discrimination? Cf. Personnel Administrator v. Feeney, discussed in the Note on Intent and Causation, Chapter 1B.5 supra (intentional discrimination covers only situation where defendant chose "a particular course at least in part 'because of,' not merely 'in spite of,' its adverse effect" on women).

(c) *Davis* slides past the difficult issue of whether the school board has acted "intentionally discriminatorily" by relying on the "subjected to discrimination" language in Title IX. Is this type of liability more like "intentional discrimination" for which damages would be recoverable under *Guardians*, or is it more like the "adverse-effects" type of liability for which damages may not be recovered under Title VI and its analogues? Should the Court have discussed this issue more clearly, especially in light of its admission that remedies should be implied in Spending Clause statutes only where there is clear notice of such liability?

2.   The second precedent on which *Davis* relies is **Gebser v. Lago Vista Independent School Dist.**, 524 U.S. 274, 283, 118 S.Ct. 1989, 141 L.Ed.2d 277 (1998), was the first to discuss whether school boards could be held liable in a damages action under Title IX when their employees acted intentionally discriminatorily. Facing a claim of teacher-student harassment[1], Justice O'Connor's majority opinion announced the principle on which she relied in *Davis*—that school boards are not vicariously liable for their employees' acts, but only for their own "deliberate indifference" to reports of discrimination of which they had "actual knowledge." The majority admitted that its decision was policy-based, and not statutorily commanded: "Because the private right of action under Title IX is judicially implied, we have a measure of latitude to shape a sensible remedial scheme that best comports with the statute." 118 S.Ct. at 1996. The Court found support for its notice requirement consistent with the regulatory enforcement system in the statute, compare § 602 in Title VI, which specifically permits remedial action only after notice.

(a) The *Gebser* case focused almost entirely on the issue of "actual notice," and contains no discussion or justification for the "deliberate indifference" test that would apply had the school authorities received actual notice. It was apparently only dictum since the required notice had not been received. Does that mean that no precedent actually supported the result in *Davis*?

(b) Justice O'Connor's *Gebser* opinion was joined by those Justices who dissented in *Davis*; similarly, the dissenters in *Gebser* were those Justices who joined her in *Davis*. How stable is the law developed in the two cases? Does the law reflect solely Justice O'Connor's idiosyncratic views? Or is it the centrist, if minimal, position of an actual majority of the Justices?

(c) If the law in this area is highly influenced by the Justices and involves some measure of policymaking by the Justices, why not draw the line after *Gebser*, which involved only employees? Is there not a bright line between employees, whom the school authorities can control directly by discharge, and students, whom schools (through high school) must accept and over whom they may only theoretically exercise supervision? Is the majority's "control" test as easily applied as Justice O'Connor suggests? Is ponytail-tugging on the

---

1.   For over a year the teacher engaged in sexual intercourse with the eighth-grade (later ninth-grade) student, often during school hours. No parental or student complaint was ever lodged with school authorities, and the situation was discovered only when a police officer discovered the two having sex and arrested the teacher. The school board thereafter discharged the teacher and state authorities revoked his teaching certification. 524 U.S. at 277; 118 S.Ct. at 1993.

walk home from school within the school's control? Is the boy who harasses girls in the park after school, but who is a perfect little gentleman at school, within the school's control? Assume that a school chooses to take students to a museum or restaurant or spring-break trip to Washington, D.C. Are the providers of services encountered along the way in the control of the school because the board chose the vendors and could have insisted on no-harassment terms in their contracts? Would such extensive coverage really be objectionable?

3. Now consider the principal holdings in *Davis* itself. First, the school board may be held liable, says the Court, for its own conduct of deliberate indifference toward actual reports of student-on-student sexual harassment.

(a) What is the source of the "deliberate indifference" standard? The citation to *Canton* appears to make clear that it is the version of the test that is used in determining § 1983 liability of municipalities, not the constitutional test used in Eighth Amendment and other litigation. See Chapter 1B.3–4 supra.[2] So what does "deliberate indifference" mean?

(b) Is the "deliberate indifference" standard a red herring that diverts attention from the critical issue in *Davis*—that of whether the school board, after it receives actual notice, has responded "in a manner that is not clearly unreasonable"? How should this language be interpreted? Consider this view: If the goal is to ensure that all students actually receive the benefits of the educational program, it might not be unreasonable in many contexts (the blown kiss, for example) simply to tell the victim to "be a strong girl and ignore him" or to tell the harasser to "be nicer and more sensitive"; in other cases, warnings or expulsion might be warranted. Do you agree? If so, should school authorities receive substantial deference in deciding which case, in light of the personalities of the actual students involved, deserves which response? How would such deference be enforced, by a jury or by a judge? If it is by a jury, is there any assurance of deference actually being given?

4. School boards need only respond if the conduct that has occurred is "sexual harassment." Are you satisfied that the Court has adequately defined what constitutes harassment? Although the Court refuses to adopt the agency principles of Title VII for determining grantee liability under Title IX, it does adopt by reference the employment title's definition of harassment. As you will see in Chapter 7, that is a somewhat amorphous, contextual test. Is that test appropriate for the Title IX context?

(a) Title IX applies to certain educational programs, and therefore the harassment standard adopted in *Davis* effectively treats harassment in education the same as harassment in employment. Are the two contexts similar? Does the juvenile nature of the peers in the educational context make a difference?[3]

---

2. Presumably, however, the separate "actual knowledge" standard from *Davis* replicates one critical aspect of the constitutional test. See Farmer v. Brennan, Chapter 1B.2 supra.

3. In the higher education context, presumably students are more mature. Should that lead to a stronger stand against harassment because males are more mature or a lesser stand because women are stronger and more mature (and thus able to care more for themselves)? Or is maturity irrelevant?

(b) The federal regulations barring peer sexual harassment, as disclosed in the dissenting opinion in *Davis*, came 25 years following the adoption of the statute. Had societal attitudes toward sexual harassment changed in the time between 1972, the year of Richard Nixon's first election as President, and 1997, the year of the Monica Lewinsky affair during the Clinton administration? If so, would it not be better to have Congress consciously legislate the standards that should be used in the educational context rather than have them adopted by the Court and bureaucrats in Washington? Or is it perfectly proper to allow the statute to evolve in the hands of federal administrators as society changes?

5. Now consider the overall impact of the *Davis* decision. In Justice O'Connor's view educational authorities who receive actual notice of sexual harassment in school will be induced to take "not clearly unreasonable" responses to those complaints, thus assuring open participation in programs (primarily for girls and women) without regard to sex. In the dissent's view, the *Davis* decision will lead to federal intrusion in sensitive local educational decisions and turn what are essentially child-raising issues into litigational issues for federal courts.

(a) Which prediction is probably more accurate? Are the political dynamics of local government such that school boards will continue to enjoy the deference that Justice O'Connor wants them to receive? After ten years of life with the *Davis* decision, should it be open to revision based on which predictions proved correct, or would *stare decisis* prevent that?

(b) Assuming that reading a crystal ball is a difficult proposition, what would risk-averse school authorities do in response to the *Davis* decision? Justice Kennedy sees a related problem of over-deterrence, as school boards steer far clear of the entire problem, He links publication of DOE harassment policies with subsequent zero-tolerance decisions in local school districts. Assuming some connection, will *Davis* accentuate the drive toward zero tolerance of any potential sexual harassment? Is a six-year-old's kiss "sexual harassment"? Might a local school board treat it as such in fear of a suit by the kissed-child's parents?

(c) Title IX applies to the school boards in these cases only because they receive federal funds, often quite small sums that are dwarfed by the damages claims made by plaintiffs. Will school districts simply decline federal grants in order to escape potential liability under Title IX? If so, that would render *Davis* totally ineffective, would it not?[4] Or would the half of all parents who have girls in public schools demand that school boards not forsake their children?

6. Finally, consider whether the *Davis* decision creates a potential future conflict among civil rights groups. Cf. Note on Private Enforcement of Title VI and Its Spending–Power Analogues, ¶ 4, supra (potential competition in administrative enforcement).

(a) Justice Kennedy argues that severe sex harassers, who are mentally impaired, may have a claim to accommodation under disability laws that will

---

4. Could liability under § 1983 take the place of Title IX? Re-read § 1983. What language in the older statute is the same as that found relevant to Title IX liability in *Davis*?

conflict with the harassed student's claim under Title IX. He sees this as putting school boards in a difficult position where they are unlikely to be able to satisfy both claimants. Do you agree? Or is this just an attempt to pit one civil-rights community against another?

(b) A potentially more plausible argument for conflict among civil rights constituencies might juxtapose Title IX to the coverage of racial discrimination and harassment under Title VI. If you believe that young black males are subjected to greater school discipline than are young whites, is it not possible that many young white girls will have their claims more sympathetically (and aggressively) resolved when the harasser is a black male? If school boards adopt zero-tolerance policies, will those policies fall more heavily on young black males? Cf. Fuller v. Decatur Public School Bd. of Educ. School Dist. 61, 78 F.Supp.2d 812 (C.D.Ill.2000) (Jesse Jackson leads a widely publicized crusade for reinstatement of black students expelled from school for violating zero-tolerance policy regarding fighting at sports events; claims dismissed).[5]

E. AFFIRMATIVE ACTION AND TITLE VI

We began this Chapter with a consideration of Title VI's "effects test" and its interaction with the various Justices' attitudes toward affirmative action. In **Regents of the Univ. of California v. Bakke**, 438 U.S. 265, 98 S.Ct. 2733, 57 L.Ed.2d 750 (1978), the Court divided four-four on the question of whether Title VI permits affirmative action based on race. One lone figure, courtly Justice Powell, disposed of the case by holding that Title VI permits some but not all affirmative action. In the years that followed, the Court moved on to determined, increasingly, that the Constitution bars most affirmative action, at least unless the program is based on the actor's own likely prior violation. See City of Richmond v. J.A. Croson Co., Chapter 7D infra. In 2003, history turned again to the *Bakke* position, oddly seeming to repeat itself, as Justice O'Connor picked up Justice Powell's mantle.

GRUTTER v. BOLLINGER

Supreme Court of the United States, 2003.
539 U.S. 306, 123 S.Ct. 2325, 156 L.Ed.2d 304.

JUSTICE O'CONNOR delivered the opinion of the Court.

This case requires us to decide whether the use of race as a factor in student admissions by the University of Michigan Law School (Law School) is unlawful. [Like most elite law schools Michigan uses admissions criteria—LSAT scores and undergraduate grade-point averages—that would ordinarily lead to little representation of minorities in their classes,

---

5. Also consider a much more incendiary and problem-laden argument: community attitudes toward the permissible level of sexual banter may vary by geographic community and ethnic group. (Notice that all the Supreme Court cases in this area arose in southern school districts with substantial minority populations.) Will white school administrators use *Davis* to impose "white values" on black students? Conversely, are school administrators responding inadequately to black girls' claims of sexual harassment?

especially "groups which have been historically discriminated against, like African–Americans, Hispanics and Native Americans." Expressing a desire for a more diverse student body, not just racially diverse, but diverse in many social ways, the Law School developed an admissions system that looked at more factors, including race, with the hope that the more diverse student body would encourage fellow students to learn from each other. Although no student was admitted unless expected to do well enough to graduate, the Law School frankly admitted that "soft variables" such as race or enthusiasm of recommendations could trump hard predictive indicators such as the LSAT to ensure an applicant's admission. It also admitted that it sought a "critical mass" of each minority to ensure that such students would feel free to speak in class, without also feeling an obligation to speak as a minority representative. A white woman rejected under the system challenged it as a violation of the Equal Protection Clause, Title VI, and § 1981. After a trial judgment in her favor was reversed on appeal, the Supreme Court granted certiorari to review the issue of whether such a race-conscious program was permissible.]

Since this Court's splintered decision in *Bakke,* Justice Powell's opinion announcing the judgment of the Court has served as the touchstone for constitutional analysis of race-conscious admissions policies. Public and private universities across the Nation have modeled their own admissions programs on Justice Powell's views on permissible race-conscious policies. See, *e.g.,* Brief for Judith Areen et al. as *Amici Curiae* 12–13 (law school admissions programs employ "methods designed from and based on Justice Powell's opinion in *Bakke*"); Brief for Amherst College et al. as *Amici Curiae* 27 ("After *Bakke,* each of the *amici* (and undoubtedly other selective colleges and universities as well) reviewed their admissions procedures in light of Justice Powell's opinion * * * and set sail accordingly"). We therefore discuss Justice Powell's opinion in some detail.

Justice Powell began by stating that "[t]he guarantee of equal protection cannot mean one thing when applied to one individual and something else when applied to a person of another color. If both are not accorded the same protection, then it is not equal." In Justice Powell's view, when governmental decisions "touch upon an individual's race or ethnic background, he is entitled to a judicial determination that the burden he is asked to bear on that basis is precisely tailored to serve a compelling governmental interest." Under this exacting standard, only one of the interests asserted by the university survived Justice Powell's scrutiny.

First, Justice Powell rejected an interest in " 'reducing the historic deficit of traditionally disfavored minorities in medical schools and in the medical profession' " as an unlawful interest in racial balancing. Second, Justice Powell rejected an interest in remedying societal discrimination because such measures would risk placing unnecessary burdens on innocent third parties "who bear no responsibility for whatever harm the beneficiaries of the special admissions program are thought to have suffered." Third, Justice Powell rejected an interest in "increasing the number of physicians who will practice in communities currently underserved," concluding that even if such an interest could be compelling in some circumstances the program under review was not "geared to promote that goal."

Justice Powell approved the university's use of race to further only one interest. "the attainment of a diverse student body." With the important proviso that "constitutional limitations protecting individual rights may not be disregarded," Justice Powell grounded his analysis in the academic freedom that "long has been viewed as a special concern of the First Amendment." Justice Powell emphasized that nothing less than the " 'nation's future depends upon leaders trained through wide exposure' to the ideas and mores of students as diverse as this Nation of many peoples." In seeking the "right to select those students who will contribute the most to the 'robust exchange of ideas,' " a university seeks "to achieve a goal that is of paramount importance in the fulfillment of its mission." Both "tradition and experience lend support to the view that the contribution of diversity is substantial."

Justice Powell was, however, careful to emphasize that in his view race "is only one element in a range of factors a university properly may consider in attaining the goal of a heterogeneous student body." For Justice Powell, "[i]t is not an interest in simple ethnic diversity, in which a specified percentage of the student body is in effect guaranteed to be members of selected ethnic groups," that can justify the use of race. Rather, "[t]he diversity that furthers a compelling state interest encompasses a far broader array of qualifications and characteristics of which racial or ethnic origin is but a single though important element."

* * *

[Today "we endorse Justice Powell's view that student body diversity is a compelling state interest that can justify the use of race in university admissions," at least when the means are narrowly tailored to achieve that goal.]

The Law School's educational judgment that such diversity is essential to its educational mission is one to which we defer. The Law School's assessment that diversity will, in fact, yield educational benefits is substantiated by respondents and their *amici*. Our scrutiny of the interest asserted by the Law School is no less strict for taking into account complex educational judgments in an area that lies primarily within the expertise of the university. Our holding today is in keeping with our tradition of giving a degree of deference to a university's academic decisions, within constitutionally prescribed limits [, citing cases giving only rational basis review to constitutional claims by students that university administrators had treated them unfairly].

We have long recognized that, given the important purpose of public education and the expansive freedoms of speech and thought associated with the university environment, universities occupy a special niche in our constitutional tradition. In announcing the principle of student body diversity as a compelling state interest, Justice Powell invoked our cases recognizing a constitutional dimension, grounded in the First Amendment, of educational autonomy: "The freedom of a university to make its own judgments as to education includes the selection of its student body." From this premise, Justice Powell reasoned that by claiming "the right to select those students who will contribute the most to the 'robust exchange of ideas,'" a university "seek[s] to achieve a goal that is of paramount importance in the fulfillment of its mission." Our conclusion that the Law School has a compelling interest in a diverse student body is informed by our view that attaining a diverse student body is at the heart of the Law School's proper institutional mission, and that "good faith" on the part of a university is "presumed" absent "a showing to the contrary."

As part of its goal of "assembling a class that is both exceptionally academically qualified and broadly diverse," the Law School seeks to "enroll a 'critical mass' of minority students." Brief for Respondents Bollinger et al. 13. The Law School's interest is not simply "to assure within its student body some specified percentage of a particular group merely because of its race or ethnic origin." That would amount to outright racial balancing, which is patently unconstitutional. Richmond v. J.A. Croson Co. Rather, the Law School's concept of critical mass is defined by reference to the educational benefits that diversity is designed to produce [such as, promoting cross-racial understanding by breaking down racial stereotypes and preparing students for the increasingly diverse society in which they will work.]

These benefits are not theoretical but real, as major American businesses have made clear that the skills needed in today's increasingly global marketplace can only be developed through exposure to widely diverse people, cultures, ideas, and viewpoints. Brief for 3M et al. as *Amici Curiae* 5; Brief for General Motors Corp. as *Amicus Curiae* 3–4. What is more, high-ranking retired officers and civilian leaders of the United States military assert that, "[b]ased on [their] decades of experience," a "highly qualified, racially diverse officer corps * * * is essential to the military's ability to fulfill its principle mission to provide national security." Brief for Julius W. Becton, Jr. et al. as *Amici Curiae* 27. The primary sources for the Nation's officer corps are the service academies and the Reserve Officers Training Corps (ROTC), the latter comprising students already admitted to participating colleges and universities. *Id.,* at 5. At present, "the military cannot achieve an officer corps that is *both* highly qualified *and* racially diverse unless the service academies and the ROTC used limited race-conscious recruiting and admissions policies." *Ibid.* (emphasis in original) * * *.

* * *

[Michigan Law School's admission system also satisfies the "narrow tailoring" component of strict scrutiny because it does not make race a dispositive selection criterion.] As Justice Powell made clear in *Bakke,* truly individualized consideration demands that race be used in a flexible, nonmechanical way. It follows from this mandate that universities cannot establish quotas for members of certain racial groups or put members of those groups on separate admissions tracks. Nor can universities insulate applicants who belong to certain racial or ethnic groups from the competition for admission. Universities can, however, consider race or ethnicity more flexibly as a "plus" factor in the context of individualized consideration of each and every applicant.

We are satisfied that the Law School's admissions program, like the Harvard plan described by Justice Powell, does not operate as a quota. Properly understood, a "quota" is a program in which a certain fixed number or proportion of opportunities are "reserved exclusively for certain minority groups." Richmond v. J.A. Croson Co. Quotas " 'impose a fixed number or percentage which must be attained, or which cannot be exceeded,' and "insulate the individual from comparison with all other candidates for the available seats." *Bakke,* supra. In contrast, "a permissible goal * * * require[s] only a good-faith effort * * * to come within a range demarcated by the goal itself," and permits consideration of race as a "plus" factor in any given case while still ensuring that each candidate "compete[s] with all other qualified applicants," Johnson v. Transportation Agency, Santa Clara Cty., [principal text, page 807]. [The desire to attain a "critical mass" of each minority group is not inconsistent with this goal, provided it does not degenerate into a "rigid quota," and keeping track of admitted students with "daily reports" of number of minority admittees is also permissible so long as each applicant continues to receive "individualized consideration."]

* * *

Here, the Law School engages in a highly individualized, holistic review of each applicant's file, giving serious consideration to all the ways an applicant might contribute to a diverse educational environment. The Law School affords this individualized consideration to applicants of all races. There is no policy, either *de jure* or *de facto,* of automatic acceptance or rejection based on any single "soft" variable. Unlike the program at issue in Gratz v. Bollinger, [discussed in the Note, infra], the Law School awards no mechanical, predetermined diversity "bonuses" based on race or ethnicity. Like the Harvard plan, the Law School's admissions policy "is flexible enough to consider all pertinent elements of diversity in light of the particular qualifications of each applicant, and to place them on the same footing for consideration, although not necessarily according them the same weight." *Bakke,* supra (opinion of Powell, J.). [Although a university is required to consider other alternatives to achieve its diversity goals, it need not "exhaust" such options, and we defer to its "good faith consideration" the viability of such alternatives.]

* * *

We are mindful, however, that "[a] core purpose of the Fourteenth Amendment was to do away with all governmentally imposed discrimination based on race."Accordingly, race-conscious admissions policies must be limited in time. ["Sunset provisions" and "periodic reviews" of the necessity of affirmative action plans can meet this durational requirement, and universities "should draw on the most promising aspects of the[] race-neutral alternatives" already used by other universities experimenting with reduced reliance on race-conscious plans.]

We take the Law School at its word that it would "like nothing better than to find a race-neutral admissions formula" and will terminate its race-conscious admissions program as soon as practicable. It has been 25 years since Justice Powell first approved the use of race to further an interest in student body diversity in the context of public higher education. Since that time, the number of minority applicants with high grades and test scores has indeed increased. We expect that 25 years from now, the use of racial preferences will no longer be necessary to further the interest approved today.

In summary, the Equal Protection Clause does not prohibit the Law School's narrowly tailored use of race in admissions decisions to further a compelling interest in obtaining the educational benefits that flow from a diverse student body. Consequently, petitioner's statutory claims based on Title VI and 42 U.S.C. § 1981 also fail. See *Bakke* (opinion of Powell, J.) ("Title VI * * * proscribe[s] only those racial classifications that would violate the Equal Protection Clause or the Fifth Amendment"); General Building Contractors Assn., Inc. v. Pennsylvania, [Chapter 2C supra] (the prohibition against discrimination in § 1981 is co-extensive with the Equal Protection Clause). The judgment of the Court of Appeals for the Sixth Circuit, accordingly, is affirmed * * *.

JUSTICE GINSBURG, with whom JUSTICE BREYER joins, concurring.

[I have serious reservations about whether the twenty-five-year limit on affirmative action that Justice O'Connor envisions can be achieved. This number appears to be based on the correlation with the twenty-five years since the *Bakke* decision. But it] was only 25 years before *Bakke* that this Court declared public school segregation unconstitutional, a declaration that, after prolonged resistance, yielded an end to a law-enforced racial caste system, itself the legacy of centuries of slavery. See Brown v. Board of Education. [The continuing racial discrimination in America, especially visible in still-segregated schools, shows that the need for affirmative action may well survive for decades to come.] * * *. From today's vantage point, one may hope, but not firmly forecast, that over the next generation's span, progress toward nondiscrimination and genuinely equal opportunity will make it safe to sunset affirmative action.

JUSTICE SCALIA, with whom JUSTICE THOMAS joins, concurring in part and dissenting in part.

* * * Unlike a clear constitutional holding that racial preferences in state educational institutions are impermissible, or even a clear anticonstitutional holding that racial preferences in state educational institutions are OK, today's *Grutter–Gratz* split double header seems perversely de-

signed to prolong the controversy and the litigation * * *. (Tempting targets, one would suppose, will be those universities that talk the talk of multiculturalism and racial diversity in the courts but walk the walk of tribalism and racial segregation on their campuses—through minority-only student organizations, separate minority housing opportunities, separate minority student centers, even separate minority-only graduation ceremonies.) And still other suits may claim that the institution's racial preferences have gone below or above the mystical *Grutter*-approved "critical mass." Finally, litigation can be expected on behalf of minority groups intentionally short changed in the institution's composition of its generic minority "critical mass." I do not look forward to any of these cases. The Constitution proscribes government discrimination on the basis of race, and state-provided education is no exception.

JUSTICE THOMAS, with whom JUSTICE SCALIA joins * * *, concurring in part and dissenting in part.

Frederick Douglass, speaking to a group of abolitionists almost 140 years ago, delivered a message lost on today's majority:

"[I]n regard to the colored people, there is always more that is benevolent, I perceive, than just, manifested towards us. What I ask for the negro is not benevolence, not pity, not sympathy, but simply *justice*. The American people have always been anxious to know what they shall do with us * * *. I have had but one answer from the beginning. Do nothing with us! Your doing with us has already played the mischief with us. Do nothing with us! If the apples will not remain on the tree of their own strength, if they are worm-eaten at the core, if they are early ripe and disposed to fall, let them fall! * * * And if the negro cannot stand on his own legs, let him fall also. All I ask is, give him a chance to stand on his own legs! Let him alone! * * * [Y]our interference is doing him positive injury." What the Black Man Wants: An Address Delivered in Boston, Massachusetts, on 26 January 1865, reprinted in 4 The Frederick Douglass Papers 59, 68 (J. Blassingame & J. McKivigan eds.1991) (emphasis in original).

Like Douglass, I believe blacks can achieve in every avenue of American life without the meddling of university administrators. Because I wish to see all students succeed whatever their color, I share, in some respect, the sympathies of those who sponsor the type of discrimination advanced by the University of Michigan Law School (Law School). The Constitution does not, however, tolerate institutional devotion to the status quo in admissions policies when such devotion ripens into racial discrimination. Nor does the Constitution countenance the unprecedented deference the Court gives to the Law School, an approach inconsistent with the very concept of "strict scrutiny."

* * *

[The truth is that the Law School seeks to have its cake and eat it too: it wants to keep its elitist reliance on LSAT scores, but then also seeks to correct their racially exclusionary results.] Having decided to use the LSAT, the Law School must accept the constitutional burdens that come with this decision. The Law School may freely continue to employ the LSAT and other allegedly merit-based standards in whatever fashion it likes. What the Equal Protection Clause forbids, but the Court today allows, is the use of these standards hand-in-hand with racial discrimination. An infinite variety of admissions methods are available to the Law School. Considering all of the radical thinking that has historically occurred at this country's universities, the Law School's intractable approach toward admissions is striking * * *.

CHIEF JUSTICE REHNQUIST, with whom JUSTICE SCALIA, JUSTICE KENNEDY, and JUSTICE THOMAS join, dissenting.

* * * In practice, the Law School's program bears little or no relation to its asserted goal of achieving "critical mass." Respondents explain that the Law School seeks to accumulate a "critical mass" of *each* underrepresented minority group. ("The Law School's * * * current policy * * * provide[s] a special commitment to enrolling a 'critical mass' of 'Hispanics' "). But the record demonstrates that the Law School's admissions practices with respect to these groups differ dramatically and cannot be defended under any consistent use of the term "critical mass."

From 1995 through 2000, the Law School admitted between 1,130 and 1,310 students. Of those, between 13 and 19 were Native American, between 91 and 108 were African–Americans, and between 47 and 56 were Hispanic. If the Law School is admitting between 91 and 108 African–Americans in order to achieve "critical mass," thereby preventing African–American students from feeling "isolated or like spokespersons for their race," one would think that a number of the same order of magnitude would be necessary to accomplish the same purpose for Hispanics and Native Americans * * *. In order for this pattern of admission to be consistent with the Law School's explanation of "critical mass," one would have to believe that the objectives of "critical mass" offered by respondents are achieved with only half the number of Hispanics and one-sixth the number of Native Americans as compared to African–Americans. [The record consistently shows that Michigan accepts black students under the same circumstances where it rejects Hispanics and Native–Americans.]

These statistics have a significant bearing on petitioner's case. Respondents have *never* offered any race-specific arguments explaining why significantly more individuals from one underrepresented minority group are needed in order to achieve "critical mass" or further student body diversity. They certainly have not explained why Hispanics, who they have said are among "the groups most isolated by racial barriers in our country," should have their admission capped out in this manner. True, petitioner is neither Hispanic nor Native American. But the Law School's disparate admissions practices with respect to these minority groups demonstrate that its alleged goal of "critical mass" is simply a sham. Petitioner may use these statistics to expose this sham, which is the basis for the Law School's admission of less qualified underrepresented minorities in preference to her. Surely strict scrutiny cannot permit these sort of disparities without at least some explanation.

Only when the "critical mass" label is discarded does a likely explanation for these numbers emerge. [The statistics clearly show that the number of each admitted minority correlates not with critical mass but with the number of applicants from each group.] For example, in 1995, when 9.7% of the applicant pool was African–American, 9.4% of the admitted class was African–American. By 2000, only 7.5% of the applicant pool was African–American, and 7.3% of the admitted class was African–American. This correlation is striking * * *. The tight correlation between the percentage of applicants and admittees of a given race, therefore, must result from careful race based planning by the Law School. It suggests a formula for admission based on the aspirational assumption that all applicants are equally qualified academically, and therefore that the proportion of each group admitted should be the same as the proportion of that group in the applicant pool * * *.

JUSTICE KENNEDY, dissenting.

* * * The Court's refusal to apply meaningful strict scrutiny will lead to serious consequences. By deferring to the law schools' choice of minority admissions programs, the courts will lose the talents and resources of the faculties and administrators in devising new and fairer ways to ensure individual consideration. Constant and rigorous judicial review forces the law school faculties to undertake their responsibilities as state employees in this most sensitive of areas with utmost fidelity to the mandate of the Constitution. Dean Allan Stillwagon, who directed the Law School's Office of Admissions from 1979 to 1990, explained the difficulties he encountered in defining racial groups entitled to benefit under the School's affirmative action policy. He testified that faculty members were "breathtakingly cynical" in deciding who would qualify as a member of underrepresented minorities. An example he offered was faculty debate as to whether Cubans should be counted as Hispanics: One professor objected on the grounds that Cubans were Republicans. Many academics at other law schools who are "affirmative action's more forthright defenders readily concede that diversity is merely the current rationale of convenience for a policy that they prefer to justify on other grounds." Schuck, *Affirmative Action: Past, Present, and Future*, 20 YALE L. & POL'Y REV. 1, 34 (2002) (citing Levinson, *Diversity*, 2 U. PA. J. CONST. L. 573, 577–578 (2000); Rubenfeld, *Affirmative Action*, 107 YALE L.J. 427, 471 (1997)). This is not to suggest the faculty at Michigan or other law schools do not pursue aspirations they consider laudable and consistent with our constitutional traditions. It is but further evidence of the necessity for scrutiny that is real, not feigned, where the corrosive category of race is a factor in decisionmaking. Prospective students, the courts, and the public can demand that the State and its law schools prove their process is fair and constitutional in every phase of implementation * * *.

NOTE ON AFFIRMATIVE ACTION BY EDUCATIONAL GRANTEES

1. In the original *Bakke* decision, four Justices voted to strike down the school race-based admissions plan on statutory grounds, four voted to uphold it under mid-level constitutional scrutiny, and only Justice Powell gave it strict scrutiny. See subpart A of this Chapter supra. In *Grutter*, the entire Court, at least superficially, agrees with Powell's framework, using strict scrutiny as the basis for review.[1] A 5–4 majority finds, again imitating Justice Powell in *Bakke*, that student-body diversity is a compelling state interest.

(a) Diversity is accepted as a compelling state interest largely because it is deemed related to the First–Amendment interest of educators in controlling their classrooms. Presumably, the interest is therefore compelling not only because it is important in some social sense, but also because it represents a constitutional interest as significant as that enshrined in the Equal Protection Clause. Do you agree? Is control over what the audience hears—what the students learn—an inherent part of what the speaker—the teacher—has to say?

(b) According to the majority, the permissible diversity is not simply racial diversity; rather racial diversity must be part of a wider search for a more inclusive diversity that touches on many factors relevant to student selection. Does this make racial diversity more palatable, or does it highlight how racial diversity is more pernicious than other forms of diversity? Is there something paradoxical in Michigan's inclusion of blacks in law classrooms for the purpose of showing non-blacks that blacks are not all the same? Or is it perfectly rational because the racial stereotypes in non-blacks' heads can only be overcome by choosing blacks to demonstrate this?

(c) Does the compelling interest recognized by the majority limit affirmative action programs to educational institutions, or at least educational environments? Is *Grutter* a one-topic exception, permitting race-based affirmative action only in education? If so, what practical considerations appear to justify such an approach?

2. While recognizing educational diversity as an acceptable goal, the Court rejects the goals of remedying the historical deficit of minorities in education (called "racial balancing"), curing "societal discrimination" caused by others than the school itself, and promoting more professionals who would serve their own communities. Do you agree that these are unacceptable goals? Why does the Court reject them, just as Justice Powell rejected them in *Bakke*?

(a) Unlike the goal of educational diversity, these rejected goals would presumably apply across the board to many activities that a government or federal grantee might pursue, from education to housing or even welfare assistance. Is it the breadth of affirmative action that would be permitted that

---

1. In Gratz v. Bollinger, ¶ 4 infra, Justices Ginsburg and Breyer state their belief that conduct designed to remedy racial discrimination against historically subjugated groups should not be treated the same as conduct designed to perpetuate it. They nevertheless agree that what they call "close review" is necessary to separate beneficial from harmful programs.

makes these goals impermissible for the majority? Does this reinforce the idea that *Grutter* is a one-of-a-kind case, restricted to education?

(b) Does the rejection of these alternative goals tell us something about why diversity is an acceptable goal? About why the Court defines acceptable diversity so broadly? Consider this argument: All of the rejected goals focus on race as such and make some basic assumptions about who minorities are and what minority group members will do or say once the educational process is ended. The Court's broad definition of diversity—as more than racial diversity—makes no assumption about race, and indeed makes the assumption that there is no stereotypical minority person. Does the diversity goal break down stereotypes in the long run while the goals reinforce such stereotypes?

3.   The principal dispute between the majority and the dissenters appears to focus on the question of whether Michigan Law School is indeed conducting a search for diversity in its classes or whether it has only undertaken a disguised program of racial balancing. This in turn raises the question of the amount of credence or deference one is willing to give to the Michigan faculty and educators generally.

(a) Justice O'Connor pointedly notes that educational administrators and teachers deserve deference in setting university goals and in pursuing them in good faith. Is her reliance on cases adopting rational-basis review for generic constitutional claims appropriate when she has admitted that high-level review is needed? Or is the deference here a defensible extension of the same deference that was given to prison guards in Whitley v. Albers, Chapter 1B.2 supra (also an O'Connor opinion) or prison administrators in Turner v. Safley, Chapter 1B.2 supra? (Is there a political dilemma here for politically oriented justices: if one likes deference to prison guards, one is probably against deference to educators, and vice versa, correct? Should neither receive deference?)

(b) Chief Justice Rehnquist makes a very powerful showing, using statistical analysis, that Michigan's actual system bears little relation to "critical mass" and high correlation with proportional selection or racial balancing. Justice Kennedy also notes the rather crass and racist discussions that apparently preceded adoption of the affirmative action plan. Do they persuade you that educators should not be trusted and that Michigan's plan in particular fails the *Bakke* test?

(c) Do you believe that the Michigan administrators were really seeking a "critical mass" of each minority group? Isn't it odd, as Chief Justice Rehnquist notes, that "critical mass" for blacks is so much higher than it is for Hispanics or Native Americans? Would it be more honest for the university to admit that critical mass is a proportional concept? But does that then make it forbidden "racial balancing"?

4.   In **Gratz v. Bollinger**, 539 U.S. 244, 123 S.Ct. 2411, 156 L.Ed.2d 257 (2003), handed down the same day as *Grutter*, the Court struck down a race-based undergraduate admissions system used by Michigan. The undergraduate program used a "bonus point" system that also was claimed to promote "diversity"; it resulted in the admission of "virtually ... every qualified applicant" who is black, Hispanic, or Native American. Whites and others were subjected to a demanding process that was selective. Only a few

athletes and minorities received individualized consideration. Justice O'Connor, whose fifth vote upheld the Michigan Law program, here doomed the Michigan undergraduate program. Chief Justice Rehnquist's majority opinion ruled that the undergraduate plan failed to give individualized consideration to each applicant in such a way as to put all applicants into competition for all seats, as required by Justice Powell in *Bakke*.

(a) What is the real defect in the undergraduate selection process—that it gives blacks so many points that all such applicants are automatically accepted, or merely that it uses a point system and automatic selection by point totals (rather than individualized consideration)? For Justice O'Connor, it was apparently more the latter than the former: "*Grutter* requires ... consideration of each applicant's individualized qualifications, including the contribution each individual's race or ethnic identity will make to the diversity of the student body, taking into account diversity within and among all racial and ethnic groups." Does that mean that point systems, as discussed and approved by Justice Powell in *Bakke*, are now only permissible if they are non-automatic and lead to further individualized review? Does O'Connor mean to say that the points can get a black applicant into the consideration pool but cannot be used to guarantee admission?

(b) Think realistically: can large state universities afford to invest the resources necessary to make the individualized decisions required by *Gratz*? Is *Grutter* an ephemeral victory for affirmative action because only small elite schools, often graduate schools, can afford the process it envisions? Or could a university easily evade *Gratz* by hiring ten students who superficially review those applicants in the point-eligible pool, individually considering and rubber-stamping most black candidates? Is Michigan's undergraduate admissions program just a more honest and less elite version of the law school process?

(c) Is the overt honesty of the Michigan undergraduate program its fatal flaw? Consider this argument: race-based plans are fundamentally inconsistent with American aspirations, and when it is necessary to have them, their operation must be pushed underground—made difficult but tolerated, acknowledged but diminished in discussion, so that what is valuable in the long run prevails over what is necessary in the short-term. Is that an adequate justification for Justice O'Connor's *Grutter–Gratz* decision? Is the problem with Ginsburg and Souter, the only two justices to uphold both undergraduate and law school plans, that they want to force U.S. society to eat crow?

(d) Do you agree with Justice Scalia that the difficulty in distinguishing between acceptable and unacceptable plans will foment more litigation in the future? Will the difficulty of enforcing O'Connor's distinction keep on the front burner the racial issue that she wants pushed to the rear of the stove?

5. Justice Thomas (proud descendant of slaves), joined by Justice Scalia (devout Catholic offspring of Italian–American immigrants), strikes a resounding anti-elitist chord in *Grutter*, viewing the university as a patronizing collection of scholars who need to rely on race only because they so firmly want to keep their elitist LSAT and other exclusionary selection criteria.

(a) Is Thomas correct in thinking that race-based admissions is an issue only for elite schools? A great number of schools accept all applicants deemed minimally qualified (perhaps even some not qualified, provided they have tuition money or loan proceeds). Such schools, by definition, have student bodies that reflect racially the composition of their applicant pools. Which way does this fact cut? Should elite schools also be permitted to achieve such results? Or does every race-based program at a selective school merely have the effect of moving some black student up in the educational hierarchy while moving some white student down?

(b) In rejecting what he characterizes as the patronizing attitude of race-based affirmative action in admissions, Thomas also seems to emphasize an issue raised by Rehnquist and Kennedy—that such programs pit racial groups against one another, sometimes even minority against minority. Is the Michigan Law plan defective for not including women and gays/lesbians/bisexuals? Defective because it sets the "critical mass" for Native Americans so much lower than that for blacks? (The intra-minority rivalry dims if one notices that each group receives admission proportional to applications, but doesn't that undermine the rationale that admissions are based on a need for "critical mass" rather than racial balancing?)

6. The *Grutter* majority demands that race-based, diversity-seeking programs be time limited. Do you find this defensible? Because this is "voluntary" affirmative action, may the state's voters decide before the 25 years have expired that they want no more affirmative action?

(a) Consider this view: Analytically, one could easily see how race-based plans founded on a desire to remedy past discrimination would be time-limited: when the past wrong is remedied, the programs would end because they no longer serve the remedial goal. But the desire for diversity is unconnected to past wrongs and appears enduring: no matter how rosy the future, educators would have an interest in ensuring diversity in their classrooms so that no chance under-admission of blacks would ever occur. Now re-consider O'Connor's diversity rationale: is the diversity that she recognizes really disconnected from past and present racial discrimination? Does she recognize as legitimate the racial interest in diversity only insofar as it is necessary to populate a classroom of non-stereotypical persons? When the stereotypes end, then does the rationale end?

(b) Is twenty-five years a sufficient time for programs to continue, or do you agree with Ginsburg that it may take much longer than that? But doesn't Ginsburg have a potential problem: won't such plans create an expectation or entitlement to favored status that will be difficult to terminate in the future? Is this not a problem because the plans are only voluntarily undertaken by the majority? No, because educational elites are not the majority?

(c) Three years following *Grutter*, Michigan's voters by an almost 2–1 majority amended the state constitution to forbid the program approved in *Grutter*. Moreover, the initiative broadly forbade future racial preferences throughout state government. See M.C.L.A. Const. Art. 1, § 26 (2006). Is it unconstitutional to limit voluntary affirmative action? Compare Hunter v. Erickson, 393 U.S. 385, 89 S.Ct. 557, 21 L.Ed.2d 616 (1969) (local government charter amendment requiring prior voter approval of fair housing legislation that would benefit minorities unconstitutional), with Coalition for Economic Equity v. Wilson, 110 F.3d 1431 (9th Cir.1997) (California Proposition 209, barring affirmative action in the state and adopted in reaction to existing plans, is not unconstitutional). Is a government or grantee that begins an affirmative action program obliged to continue it? Until when—the end of Justice O'Connor's twenty-five year period?

7.   The Court in both *Grutter* and *Gratz* interprets the Equal Protection Clause, then extends its result to Title VI and § 1981. This has the practical effect of extending the announced rules from governmental entities to private schools, especially private schools receiving federal grants. See Runyon v. McCrary, Chapter 2C supra; Note on the Correctness of *Grove City* and Its Legislative Reversal of sub-part C of this Chapter supra. Should Title VI (and § 1981) be amended to permit private institutions greater range to experiment in admissions? Should they be repealed altogether, as applied to educational institutions, to permit more experimentation in that area?

CHAPTER 7

TITLE VII AND ITS ANALOGUES—
EMPLOYMENT DISCRIMINATION

■ ■ ■

Title VII, perhaps together with the Voting Rights Act of 1965, has become the most profound and enduring piece of civil rights legislation passed by Congress in this century. Just as the Voting Rights Act provided American minorities with leverage to shape their public lives through the vote, Title VII provided a means for building the private side of life, through both wages and the prestige which comes from increased exercise of managerial responsibility. This Title has also assumed great importance because it is the first piece of major civil rights legislation to protect the rights of women, and that protection has reverberated throughout our society.[1] The success of Title VII in promoting equality for minorities and women derives largely from techniques which have made it possible to eradicate not only overt acts of intentional discrimination, but also the subtler, more arbitrary forms of decisionmaking which have had an adverse impact on minorities and women seeking jobs. Those techniques, their use and limits, and the Court's role in reshaping Title VII into such a sophisticated piece of legislation occupy our attention at the beginning of this Chapter.

Title VII, however, protects not only blacks, women, and ethnic minorities, but also whites, men, and ethnic majorities (pluralities). Indeed, it protects *all persons* who suffer discrimination on one of the classificatory bases named in the statute.[2] In McDonald v. Santa Fe Trail Transportation Co., Chapter 2C supra, the Court wrote that "Title VII prohibits racial discrimination against [white persons] upon the same

---

1. In racial matters the Court had taken the initiative in expanding civil rights, deciding Brown v. Board of Educ. a decade before Congress passed the Civil Rights Act of 1964. But in the area of sex discrimination exactly the opposite was true: Title VII gave women certain statutory rights almost a decade before the Court interpreted the Constitution to provide an effective restraint on unequal treatment of women. See Reed v. Reed, 404 U.S. 71, 92 S.Ct. 251, 30 L.Ed.2d 225 (1971); Frontiero v. Richardson, 411 U.S. 677, 93 S.Ct. 1764, 36 L.Ed.2d 583 (1973).

2. Title VII has spawned analogues that cover *age discrimination* (Age Discrimination in Employment Act, 29 U.S.C. § 621 et seq.), and *discrimination against persons with disabilities* (Americans With Disabilities Act, 42 U.S.C. § 12101 et seq.) (—while the "reasonable accommo-dations" test builds on § 504, the entities covered mimics other title in the 1964 Act, and the litigational rules build principally on Title VII).

standards as would be applicable were they Negroes," and that equality of protection has raised ironic problems in the award of judicial relief as court orders remedying discrimination against blacks often have a collateral adverse impact on white employees. The second major focus of this Chapter will be the courts' efforts to adjust remedies under Title VII so as to take account of the diverse and sometimes divisive interests which can arise in a case of employment discrimination.

Finally, the courts' efforts to tailor relief in employment cases lead naturally to consideration of employers' efforts to remedy such problems through their own affirmative action programs. Should employers have the same flexibility as courts when they wish voluntarily to remedy black unemployment, or is Title VII violated by such efforts? This problem will draw our attention in a concluding section which will also accentuate the central theme of the Chapter: Can the Court play as active a role in reshaping modern civil rights legislation as it did with the older legislation studied in Part I of this book? What factors suggest that it should or should not play such a role?

A. "DISCRIMINATION" PROSCRIBED: STANDARDS AND DEFENSES

The Supreme Court has recognized two distinct types of claims which may arise under Title VII—claims of "disparate treatment" and those of "disparate impact," International Bhd. of Teamsters v. United States, 431 U.S. 324, 335 n. 15, 97 S.Ct. 1843, 1854, n. 15, 52 L.Ed.2d 396 (1977):

> " 'Disparate treatment' * * * is the most easily understood type of discrimination. The employer simply treats some people less favorably than others because of their race, color, religion, sex, or national origin. Proof of discriminatory motive is critical, although it can in some situations be inferred from the mere fact of differences in treatment. See, e.g., Village of Arlington Heights v. Metropolitan Housing Dev. Corp., [Ch. 1B.5 supra]. Undoubtedly disparate treatment was the most obvious evil Congress had in mind when it enacted Title VII. See, e.g., 110 Cong.Rec. 13088 (1964) (remarks of Sen. Humphrey) ('What the bill does * * * is simply to make it an illegal practice to use race as a factor in denying employment. It provides that men and women shall be employed on the basis of their qualifications, not as Catholic citizens, not as Protestant citizens, not as Jewish citizens, not as colored citizens, but as citizens of the United States').

> "Claims of disparate treatment may be distinguished from claims that stress 'disparate impact.' The latter involve employment practices that are facially neutral in their treatment of different groups but that in fact fall more harshly on one group than another and cannot be justified by business necessity. Proof of discriminatory

motive, we have held, is not required under a disparate impact theory. Compare, e.g., Griggs v. Duke Power Co., [which follows].''

Although disparate treatment (i.e., intentional discrimination) cases may be more "easily understood" than those involving disparate impact (i.e., unjustified discriminatory effect), the Court's chronological development of the two paradigm types of litigation came in the reverse order, and that is the order in which we shall study them. As you read this section keep in mind two tensions that may exist in the real world of litigation. First, because of cross-pollination, the ideas developed for proving discrimination under Title VII often are adopted in other areas. See, e.g., Chapter 6A supra (intent and similar "effects" tests under Title VI). At the same time, statute-to-statute variations mean that occasionally specific concerns in a related statute may displace the template that Title VII generally offers. See, e.g., Smith v. City of Jackson, 544 U.S. 228, 125 S.Ct. 1536, 161 L.Ed.2d 410 (2005) (Age Discrimination in Employment Act differs with respect to proving impact claims).

1. DISPARATE IMPACT: THE *GRIGGS* MODEL

GRIGGS v. DUKE POWER CO.

Supreme Court of the United States, 1971.
401 U.S. 424, 91 S.Ct. 849, 28 L.Ed.2d 158.

MR. CHIEF JUSTICE BURGER delivered the opinion of the Court.

We granted the writ in this case to resolve the question whether an employer is prohibited by the Civil Rights Act of 1964, Title VII, from requiring a high school education or passing of a standardized general intelligence test as a condition of employment in or transfer to jobs when (a) neither standard is shown to be significantly related to successful job performance, (b) both requirements operate to disqualify Negroes at a substantially higher rate than white applicants, and (c) the jobs in question formerly had been filled only by white employees as part of a longstanding practice of giving preference to whites.

Congress provided, in Title VII of the Civil Rights Act of 1964, for class actions for enforcement of provisions of the Act and this proceeding was brought by a group of incumbent Negro employees against Duke Power Company. All the petitioners are employed at the Company's Dan River Steam Station, a power generating facility located at Draper, North Carolina. At the time this action was instituted, the Company had 95 employees at the Dan River Station, 14 of whom were Negroes; 13 of these are petitioners here.

The District Court found that prior to July 2, 1965, the effective date of the Civil Rights Act of 1964, the Company openly discriminated on the basis of race in the hiring and assigning of employees at its Dan River plant. The plant was organized into five operating departments: (1) Labor, (2) Coal Handling, (3) Operations, (4) Maintenance, and (5) Laboratory and Test. Negroes were employed only in the Labor Department where the highest paying jobs paid less than the lowest paying jobs in the other four "operating" departments in which only whites were employed. Promotions were normally made within each department on the basis of job seniority. Transferees into a department usually began in the lowest position.

In 1955 the Company instituted a policy of requiring a high school education for initial assignment to any department except Labor, and for transfer from the Coal Handling to any "inside" department (Operations, Maintenance, or Laboratory). When the Company abandoned its policy of restricting Negroes to the Labor Department in 1965, completion of high school also was made a prerequisite to transfer from Labor to any other department. From the time the high school requirement was instituted to the time of trial, however, white employees hired before the time of the high school education requirement continued to perform satisfactorily and achieve promotions in the "operating" departments. Findings on this score are not challenged.

The Company added a further requirement for new employees on July 2, 1965, the date on which Title VII became effective. To qualify for placement in any but the Labor Department it became necessary to register satisfactory scores on two professionally prepared aptitude tests, as well as to have a high school education. Completion of high school alone continued to render employees eligible for transfer to the four desirable departments from which Negroes had been excluded if the incumbent had been employed prior to the time of the new requirement. In September 1965 the Company began to permit incumbent employees who lacked a high school education to qualify for transfer from Labor or Coal Handling to an "inside" job by passing two tests—the Wonderlic Personnel Test, which purports to measure general intelligence, and the Bennett Mechanical Comprehension Test. Neither was directed or intended to measure the ability to learn to perform a particular job or category of jobs. The requisite scores used for both initial hiring and transfer approximated the national median for high school graduates.[3]

The District Court had found that while the Company previously followed a policy of overt racial discrimination in a period prior to the Act, such conduct had ceased. The District Court also concluded that Title VII was intended to be prospective only and, consequently, the impact of prior inequities was beyond the reach of corrective action authorized by the Act.

The Court of Appeals was confronted with a question of first impression, as are we, concerning the meaning of Title VII. After careful analysis a majority of that court concluded that a subjective test of the employer's intent should govern, particularly in a close case, and that in this case there was no showing of a discriminatory purpose in the adoption of the

---

3. The test standards are thus more stringent than the high school requirement, since they would screen out approximately half of all high school graduates.

diploma and test requirements. On this basis, the Court of Appeals concluded there was no violation of the Act.

* * *

The objective of Congress in the enactment of Title VII is plain from the language of the statute. It was to achieve equality of employment opportunities and remove barriers that have operated in the past to favor an identifiable group of white employees over other employees. Under the Act, practices, procedures, or tests neutral on their face, and even neutral in terms of intent, cannot be maintained if they operate to "freeze" the status quo of prior discriminatory employment practices.

The Court of Appeals' opinion, and the partial dissent, agreed that, on the record in the present case, "whites register far better on the Company's alternative requirements" than Negroes.[6] 420 F.2d 1225, 1239 n. 6. This consequence would appear to be directly traceable to race. Basic intelligence must have the means of articulation to manifest itself fairly in a testing process. Because they are Negroes, petitioners have long received inferior education in segregated schools and this Court expressly recognized these differences in Gaston County v. United States, 395 U.S. 285, 89 S.Ct. 1720, 23 L.Ed.2d 309 (1969). There, because of the inferior education received by Negroes in North Carolina, this Court barred the institution of a literacy test for voter registration on the ground that the test would abridge the right to vote indirectly on account of race. Congress did not intend by Title VII, however, to guarantee a job to every person regardless of qualifications. In short, the Act does not command that any person be hired simply because he was formerly the subject of discrimination, or because he is a member of a minority group. Discriminatory preference for any group, minority or majority, is precisely and only what Congress has proscribed. What is required by Congress is the removal of artificial, arbitrary, and unnecessary barriers to employment when the barriers operate invidiously to discriminate on the basis of racial or other impermissible classification.

Congress has now provided that tests or criteria for employment or promotion may not provide equality of opportunity merely in the sense of the fabled offer of milk to the stork and the fox. On the contrary, Congress has now required that the posture and condition of the job-seeker be taken into account. It has—to resort again to the fable—provided that the vessel in which the milk is proffered be one all seekers can use. The Act proscribes not only overt discrimination but also practices that are fair in form, but discriminatory in operation. The touchstone is business necessi-

---

6. In North Carolina, 1960 census statistics show that, while 34% of white males had completed high school, only 12% of Negro males had done so. U.S. Bureau of the Census, U.S. Census of Population: 1960, Vol. 1, Characteristics of the Population, pt. 35, Table 47.

Similarly, with respect to standardized tests, the EEOC in one case found that use of a battery of tests, including the Wonderlic and Bennett tests used by the Company in the instant case, resulted in 58% of whites passing the tests, as compared with only 6% of the blacks. Decision of EEOC, CCH Empl. Prac. Guide, ¶ 17,304.53 (Dec. 2, 1966). See also Decision of EEOC 70–552, CCH Empl. Prac. Guide, ¶ 6139 (Feb. 19, 1970).

ty. If an employment practice which operates to exclude Negroes cannot be shown to be related to job performance, the practice is prohibited.

On the record before us, neither the high school completion requirement nor the general intelligence test is shown to bear a demonstrable relationship to successful performance of the jobs for which it was used. Both were adopted, as the Court of Appeals noted, without meaningful study of their relationship to job-performance ability. Rather, a vice president of the Company testified, the requirements were instituted on the Company's judgment that they generally would improve the overall quality of the work force.

The evidence, however, shows that employees who have not completed high school or taken the tests have continued to perform satisfactorily and make progress in departments for which the high school and test criteria are now used. The promotion record of present employees who would not be able to meet the new criteria thus suggests the possibility that the requirements may not be needed even for the limited purpose of preserving the avowed policy of advancement within the Company. In the context of this case, it is unnecessary to reach the question whether testing requirements that take into account capability for the next succeeding position or related future promotion might be utilized upon a showing that such long-range requirements fulfill a genuine business need. In the present case the Company has made no such showing.

The Court of Appeals held that the Company had adopted the diploma and test requirements without any "intention to discriminate against Negro employees." We do not suggest that either the District Court or the Court of Appeals erred in examining the employer's intent; but good intent or absence of discriminatory intent does not redeem employment procedures or testing mechanisms that operate as "built-in headwinds" for minority groups and are unrelated to measuring job capability.

The Company's lack of discriminatory intent is suggested by special efforts to help the undereducated employees through Company financing of two-thirds the cost of tuition for high school training. But Congress directed the thrust of the Act to the *consequences* of employment practices, not simply the motivation. More than that, Congress has placed on the employer the burden of showing that any given requirement must have a manifest relationship to the employment in question.

The facts of this case demonstrate the inadequacy of broad and general testing devices as well as the infirmity of using diplomas or degrees as fixed measures of capability. History is filled with examples of men and women who rendered highly effective performance without the conventional badges of accomplishment in terms of certificates, diplomas, or degrees. Diplomas and tests are useful servants, but Congress has mandated the commonsense proposition that they are not to become masters of reality.

The Company contends that its general intelligence tests are specifically permitted by § 703(h) of the Act.[8] That section authorizes the use of "any professionally developed ability test" that is not "designed, intended *or used* to discriminate because of race * * *." (Emphasis added.)

The Equal Employment Opportunity Commission, having enforcement responsibility, has issued guidelines interpreting § 703(h) to permit only the use of job-related tests.[9] The administrative interpretation of the Act by the enforcing agency is entitled to great deference. See, e.g., United States v. City of Chicago, 400 U.S. 8, 91 S.Ct. 18, 27 L.Ed.2d 9 (1970). Since the Act and its legislative history support the Commission's construction, this affords good reason to treat the guidelines as expressing the will of Congress.

Section 703(h) was not contained in the House version of the Civil Rights Act but was added in the Senate during extended debate. For a period, debate revolved around claims that the bill as proposed would prohibit all testing and force employers to hire unqualified persons simply because they were part of a group formerly subject to job discrimination. Proponents of Title VII sought throughout the debate to assure the critics that the Act would have no effect on job-related tests. [The Court explained that § 703(h) was added only to provide further assurance on the point, Congress rejecting an amendment which would have permitted testing unrelated to job skills.]

Nothing in the Act precludes the use of testing or measuring procedures; obviously they are useful. What Congress has forbidden is giving these devices and mechanisms controlling force unless they are demonstrably a reasonable measure of job performance. Congress has not commanded that the less qualified be preferred over the better qualified simply because of minority origins. Far from disparaging job qualifications as such, Congress has made such qualifications the controlling factor, so that race, religion, nationality, and sex become irrelevant. What Congress has commanded is that any tests used must measure the person for the job and not the person in the abstract.

The judgment of the Court of Appeals is, as to that portion of the judgment appealed from, reversed.

---

8. Section 703(h) applies only to tests. It has no applicability to the high school diploma requirement.

9. EEOC Guidelines on Employment Testing Procedures, issued August 24, 1966, provide:

"The Commission accordingly interprets 'professionally developed ability test' to mean a test which fairly measures the knowledge or skills required by the particular job or class of jobs which the applicant seeks, or which fairly affords the employer a chance to measure the applicant's ability to perform a particular job or class of jobs. The fact that a test was prepared by an individual or organization claiming expertise in test preparation does not, without more, justify its use within the meaning of Title VII."

The EEOC position has been elaborated in the new Guidelines on Employee Selection Procedures, 29 CFR 1607, 35 Fed.Reg. 12333 (Aug. 1, 1970). These guidelines demand that employers using tests have available "data demonstrating that the test is predictive of or significantly correlated with important elements of work behavior which comprise or are relevant to the job or jobs for which candidates are being evaluated." Id. at § 1607.4(c).

MR. JUSTICE BRENNAN took no part in the consideration or decision of this case.

NOTE ON THE BASIS FOR Griggs AND ITS EARLY ENFORCEMENT

1. As you read this Note and the cases in this section, ask whether Title VII protects groups or individuals. What signal does the *Griggs* decision send? A mixed one?

2. *Griggs* does not outlaw all employment tests any more than it outlaws all employment tests that have a disparate impact on blacks: what it does ban are those employment tests that have a disparate impact on blacks and cannot be justified ("validated") by the employer as "job-related." Is there any basis in the statute for the Court's holding?

(a) Notice the statutory language of prohibition in § 703(a). Is there any indication that employer practices having only a disparate impact or effect are banned? Is there any indication that they are not banned? See also the relief provision of Title VII, § 706(g), 42 U.S.C.A. § 2000e–5(g) (using the word "intentionally," but not the word "discrimination").[1]

(b) Now consider § 703(j) which provides that "[n]othing in this [title] shall be interpreted to require any employer" to grant a preference to any group because of an "imbalance" between the race of persons hired "in comparison with" those in the community or workforce. Is the *Griggs* rule not based on such a comparison? Is the operation of the *Griggs* rule a "preference"?

(c) The Court makes much of § 703(h), but does it authorize the *Griggs* rule or simply not forbid it? Critical to the Court's argument is its interpretation of the word "used," which it reads as "having the effect of." Would it have been equally plausible to read the word in conjunction with "designed" and "intended" so that it meant "intentionally used" or "used purposefully"?

3. In light of the issues raised in paragraph 2, is it not likely that the Court, rather than Congress, legislated the *Griggs* rule? [Note that Congress did not specifically enact the *Griggs* approach until 1991, then apparently in an effort to prevent the Court from backing away.] See Lewis v. City of Chicago, ___ U.S. ___, 130 S.Ct. 2191, 176 L.Ed.2d 967 (2010) (discussing effect of 1991 Civil Rights Act).

(a) Why would the Court have adopted a rebuttable effects test under Title VII when it had avoided doing so under the Equal Protection Clause? Was it because Title VII was a statute and Congress could undo the Court's rule if it proved unworkable or unwise? Because Title VII involves a narrowly defined subject-matter, employment, as compared to the full range of issues arising under equal protection?

(b) In its later decision in **Watson v. Fort Worth Bank & Trust**, 487 U.S. 977, 991, 108 S.Ct. 2777, 101 L.Ed.2d 827 (1988), the Court for the first time located a justification for *Griggs* in Title VII's text. According to the

---

1. Recall the similar confusion almost thirty years later over the word "intentional" as developed in the Court's decisions under Title IX, particularly in the *Davis* case, Chapter 6D supra.

Court, in defining prohibited conduct Title VII proscribes "employer's practices [that] may be said to 'adversely affect [an individual's] status as an employee, because of such individual's race, color, religion, sex, or national origin.' 42 U.S.C. § 2000e–2(a)(2)." Read the full section as noted in the Appendix. Are you persuaded? (Why did it take the Court 17 years to find and cite this section?)

4. The Court has noted that the *Griggs* analysis inherently calls for the use of "comparative statistics," **Dothard v. Rawlinson**, 433 U.S. 321, 329–30, 97 S.Ct. 2720, 2726–27, 53 L.Ed.2d 786 (1977), which look at the differential impact of any neutral employment criterion on the racial group affected (e.g., blacks and whites in *Griggs*, men and women in *Dothard*). Because the statistical analysis here may differ from that used in some disparate treatment cases, see subsection A.2 of this Chapter infra, consider how the statistical proof operates.

(a) Note that in *Griggs* the Court does not ask broadly whether the racial make-up of the company's workforce mirrors that of the community; instead the Court focuses on how the neutral rule at issue filters out blacks and whites in disproportionate numbers. This differential is the "disparate [or disproportionate] impact" that starts *Griggs'* analysis. The process is graphically represented as follows:

```
                              N
Black Potential Hires    —>   E        —>  Blacks Who
        (100)            —>   U            Passed (10)
                              T   R
White Potential Hires    —>   R   U    —>  Whites Who
        (1000)           —>   A   L        Passed (600)
                              L   E
```

In this sample, the neutral rule excludes 90 of 100 blacks for an exclusionary rate of 90%. The neutral rule excludes 400 whites for a rate of 40%. The appropriate comparative statistics are 90% versus 40%: the neutral rule thus has a disparate impact on blacks.

(b) As the Supreme Court held in **Wards Cove Packing Co. v. Atonio**, 490 U.S. 642, 109 S.Ct. 2115, 104 L.Ed.2d 733 (1989), discussed in other respects infra, the appropriate comparison is between competitors for the same jobs. Thus it is irrelevant to disparate impact analysis that there may be more whites in high-level jobs and more blacks in low-level jobs: the question for *Griggs* purposes is whether a neutral rule disparately impacts those competing for the same job. 490 U.S. at 659, 109 S.Ct. at 2126. See Garrison v. Gambro, Inc., 428 F.3d 933 (10th Cir. 2005) (applicants for jobs in workplace reorganization); Paige v. California, 291 F.3d 1141 (9th Cir. 2002) (appropriate pool depends on facts and is a question of fact for purposes of review).[2]

---

2. The *Griggs* Court used general population data to show the impact of the high-school diploma requirement, apparently on the thesis that the requirement affected everyone in the

(c) How great must the disparity between black and white exclusionary rates be in order to satisfy the *Griggs* test? Is the question one for subjective judicial appraisal or is it subject to expert analysis? See Ricci v. DeStefano, ___ U.S. ___, 129 S.Ct. 2658, 2678, 174 L.Ed.2d 490 (2009) (alluding to, but not requiring use of, EEOC's 80% rules—if minority selection is less than 80% of highest-performing groups, disparity assumed). See Isabel v. City of Memphis, 404 F.3d 404 (6th Cir. 2005) (approving a variety of approaches, some in conflict). Is there a particular problem when the number of workers to be compared is quite small? See Garrison v. Gambro, Inc., supra (18 total hires from fewer than 100 eligible): O'Regan v. Arbitration Forums, Inc., 246 F.3d 975 (7th Cir. 2001) (85 employees, four employees adversely affected, all women).

5. Once a plaintiff has shown the disparate impact of a neutral hiring practice, what obligation falls on the employer? What is "business necessity"? If an employer's good faith is irrelevant, does that mean that "business necessity" is unrelated to intentional discrimination? The Court appears to be asking whether the employer's neutral rule so serves its business goals that its importance outweighs its disproportionate impact. Is that how you read the case? If so, how can courts do this balancing? Where should the line be drawn?

6. Post–*Griggs* cases split along several discernible lines, especially after the later 1970's. Consider the following approaches to "business necessity":

(a) *Scored Tests.* In **Albemarle Paper Co. v. Moody**, 422 U.S. 405, 95 S.Ct. 2362, 45 L.Ed.2d 280 (1975), the Court faced multi-factor scored tests similar to that used in *Griggs*. After noting the proof of disparate impact, the Court required the employer to show through the analysis of experts in testing that the particular test used correlated with actual job performance for each particular job. It rejected subjective employer evaluations. Justice Blackmun, in a separate opinion, voiced the concern that the cost of requirements would make it impossible to validate a scored test, eliminating the defense for such tests and effectively ruling out their future use for ordinary jobs, 422 U.S. at 449, 95 S.Ct. at 2387, and this is the most often-seen result. See, e.g., United States v. City of Chicago, 549 F.2d 415 (7th Cir.1977). Only tests prepared and validated for particular jobs, usually professional jobs, have survived this scrutiny. See, e.g., Berkman v. City of New York, 812 F.2d 52 (2d Cir.1987). Tests for teachers and the like are rarely if ever rejected, despite some internal inconsistencies and errors. See, e.g., Association of Mexican–American Educators v. State of California, 231 F.3d 572 (9th Cir. 2000) (en banc). Some complain that these results show a blue-collar bias, a refusal to enforce *Griggs* strictly for professional jobs. See Bartholet, *Application of Title VII to Jobs in High Places,* 95 HARV.L.REV. 947, 952 (1982).

state. But that is, of course, untrue because some large number of persons seeking employment may have dropped out of high school voluntarily and others may be retired and no longer seeking retirement. Modern cases, both those involving disparate impact and disparate treatment, seek to identify the class of persons affected with much greater particularity. See, e.g., *Wards Cove*, which follows this Note ("otherwise-qualified applicants"); Hazelwood School Dist. v. United States, 433 U.S. 299, 307–08, 97 S.Ct. 2736, 2741, 53 L.Ed.2d 768 (1977) (school teachers, not general population, defines "relevant labor market").

(b) *Single-factor Tests and Safety*. In **New York City Transit Auth. v. Beazer**, 440 U.S. 568, 99 S.Ct. 1355, 59 L.Ed.2d 587 (1979), the Court upheld a neutral rule that prohibited methadone-users[3] from working for the transit authority. Although the Court held that the rule had not been shown to have a disproportionate impact on minorities, it went on in a footnote to express the opinion that, in any event, the company could justify its rule based on its safety concerns, even though only 25% of jobs were "safety-sensitive." 440 U.S. at 587 n. 31, 99 S.Ct. at 1366 n. 31. Is a neutral rule that serves its goal (here, safety) a "business necessity" when it only relates to one-quarter of the company's jobs? Should it have been deemed validated only for those jobs?

(c) The full range of decisions, especially those in the lower courts, is too broad to capture in a single Note. Virtually all focus on two issues: (i) what is the employer's goal and is it important; and (ii) how well does the neutral rule accomplish that goal? For a discussion of these older cases, see Shulman & Abernathy, The Law of Equal Employment Opportunity § 2.05 (1990). The first inquiry is seldom dispositive, for the employer's interest is in safety or efficiency, both routinely deemed important. The second inquiry, as shown in the cases above, is the difficult one. Should courts mimic high-level scrutiny under constitutional law, and demand a compelling employer interest pursued by the least drastic means? Or is some type of "mid-level" scrutiny more appropriate?[4]

WARDS COVE PACKING CO., INC. v. ATONIO

Supreme Court of the United States, 1989.
490 U.S. 642, 109 S.Ct. 2115, 104 L.Ed.2d 733.

Justice White delivered the opinion of the Court.

Title VII of the Civil Rights Act of 1964, 42 U.S.C. § 2000e–2(a) makes it an unfair employment practice for an employer to discriminate against any individual with respect to hiring or the terms and condition of employment because of such individual's race, color, religion, sex, or national origin; or to limit, segregate or classify his employees in ways that would adversely affect any employee because of the employee's race, color, religion, sex, or national origin. Griggs v. Duke Power Co. construed Title VII to proscribe "not only overt discrimination but also practices that are fair in form but discriminatory in practice." Under this basis for liability, which is known as the "disparate impact" theory and which is involved in this case, a facially neutral employment practice may be deemed violative of Title VII without evidence of the employer's subjective intent to discriminate that is required in a "disparate treatment" case.

---

3. Methadone is a heroin substitute that controls the physical symptoms of addiction without providing heroin's psychoactive effect. It is used in a program to wean heroin users from their addiction. The effectiveness of the drug and of the treatment programs vary, with some patients resuming their use of heroin.

4. The third option, review by analogy to rational basis scrutiny, has been rejected by the Court, Washington v. Davis, 426 U.S. 229, 247, 96 S.Ct. 2040, 48 L.Ed.2d 597 (1976), probably because such scrutiny virtually always results in validation and thus serves no "balancing" function.

I

The claims before us are disparate-impact claims, involving the employment practices of petitioners, two companies that operate salmon canneries in remote and widely separated areas of Alaska. The canneries operate only during the salmon runs in the summer months. * * * During the off season, the companies employ only a small number of individuals at their headquarters in Seattle and Astoria, Oregon, plus some employees at the winter shipyard in Seattle. * * *

Jobs at the canneries are of two general types: "cannery jobs" on the cannery line, which are unskilled positions; and "noncannery jobs," which fall into a variety of classifications. Most noncannery jobs are classified as skilled positions. Cannery jobs are filled predominantly by nonwhites, Filipinos and Alaska Natives. * * * Noncannery jobs are filled with predominantly white workers, who are hired during the winter months from the companies' offices in Washington and Oregon. Virtually all of the noncannery jobs pay more than cannery positions. The predominantly white noncannery workers and the predominantly nonwhite cannery employees live in separate dormitories and eat in separate mess halls.

In 1974, respondents, a class of nonwhite cannery workers who were (or had been) employed at the canneries, brought this Title VII action against petitioners. Respondents alleged that a variety of petitioners' hiring/promotion practices—e.g., nepotism, a rehire preference, a lack of objective hiring criteria, separate hiring channels, a practice of not promoting from within—were responsible for the racial stratification of the work force, and had denied them and other nonwhites employment as noncannery workers on the basis of race. Respondents also complained of petitioners' racially segregated housing and dining facilities.

[The district court refused to subject these "subjective hiring" criteria to disparate impact analysis, but the Court of Appeals reversed and directed that the district court consider both the plaintiffs' proof of disparate impact as well as defendants' proof of business necessity under *Griggs.*]

II

In holding that respondents had made out a prima facie case of disparate impact, the court of appeals relied solely on respondents' statistics showing a high percentage of nonwhite workers in the cannery jobs and a low percentage of such workers in the noncannery positions.

[The Court rejected this proof as inadequate for the reasons discussed in the preceding Note. The Court added that proof that minorities were not represented at each level of jobs proportionately with their population percentage was also irrelevant for another reason.]

Such a result cannot be squared with our cases or with the goals behind the statute. The Court of Appeals' theory, at the very least, would mean that any employer who had a segment of his work force that was— for some reason—racially imbalanced, could be haled into court and forced to engage in the expensive and time-consuming task of defending the "business necessity" of the methods used to select the other members of his work force. The only practicable option for many employers will be to adopt racial quotas, insuring that no portion of his work force deviates in racial composition from the other portions thereof; this is a result that Congress expressly rejected in drafting Title VII. See 42 U.S.C. § 2000e–2(j).

The Court of Appeals' theory would "leave the employer little choice ... but to engage in a subjective quota system of employment selection. This, of course, is far from the intent of Title VII." Albemarle Paper Co. v. Moody, (Blackmun, J., concurring in judgment).

* * *

III

Since the statistical disparity relied on by the Court of Appeals did not suffice to make out a prima facie case, any inquiry by us into whether the specific challenged employment practices of petitioners caused that disparity is pretermitted, as is any inquiry into whether the disparate impact that any employment practice may have had was justified by business considerations.[9] Because we remand for further proceedings, however, on whether a prima facie case of disparate impact has been made in defensible fashion in this case, we address two other challenges petitioners have made to the decision of the Court of Appeals.

A

First is the question of causation in a disparate-impact case. The law in this respect was correctly stated by Justice O'Connor's opinion last Term in Watson v. Fort Worth Bank & Trust, [487 U.S. 977, 108 S.Ct. 2777, 101 L.Ed.2d 827 (1988)]:

> "[W]e note that the plaintiff's burden in establishing a prima facie case goes beyond the need to show that there are statistical disparities in the employer's work force. The plaintiff must begin by identifying the specific employment practice that is challenged.... Especially in cases where an employer combines subjective criteria with the use of more rigid standardized rules or tests, the plaintiff is in our view responsible for isolating and identifying the specific employment practices that are allegedly responsible for any observed statistical disparities."

[The Court noted that the appellate court below had permitted plaintiffs to offer statistical evidence about the total effect of all hiring,

---

9. As we understand the opinions below, the specific employment practices were challenged only insofar as they were claimed to have been responsible for the overall disparity between the number of minority cannery and noncannery workers. The Court of Appeals did not purport to hold that any specified employment practice produced its own disparate impact that was actionable under Title VII. * * *

that is a single " 'set of cumulative comparative statistics as evidence of disparate impact of each and all' " of the challenged hiring practices.]

Our disparate-impact cases have always focused on the impact of *particular* hiring practices on employment opportunities for minorities. Just as an employer cannot escape liability under Title VII by demonstrating that, "at the bottom line," his work force is racially balanced (where particular hiring practices may operate to deprive minorities of employment opportunities), see Connecticut v. Teal, 457 U.S. [440], a Title VII plaintiff does not make out a case of disparate impact simply by showing that, "at the bottom line," there is racial *imbalance* in the work force. As a general matter, a plaintiff must demonstrate that it is the application of a specific or particular employment practice that has created the disparate impact under attack. Such a showing is an integral part of the plaintiff's prima facie case in a disparate-impact suit under Title VII.

Here, respondents have alleged that several "objective" employment practices (*e.g.*, nepotism, separate hiring channels, rehire preferences), as well as the use of "subjective decision making" to select noncannery workers, have had a disparate impact on nonwhites. Respondents base this claim on statistics that allegedly show a disproportionately low percentage of nonwhites in the at-issue positions. However, even if on remand respondents can show that nonwhites are underrepresented in the at-issue jobs in a manner that is acceptable under the standards set forth in Part II, supra, this alone will *not* suffice to make out a prima facie case of disparate impact. Respondents will also have to demonstrate that the disparity they complain of is the result of one or more of the employment practices that they are attacking here, specifically showing that each challenged practice has a significantly disparate impact on employment opportunities for whites and nonwhites. To hold otherwise would result in employers being potentially liable for "the myriad of innocent causes that may lead to statistical imbalances in the composition of their work forces." Watson v. Fort Worth Bank & Trust, supra.

Some will complain that this specific causation requirement is unduly burdensome on Title VII plaintiffs. But liberal civil discovery rules give plaintiffs broad access to employers' records in an effort to document their claims. Also, employers falling within the scope of the Uniform Guidelines on Employee Selection Procedures, 29 CFR § 1607.1 *et seq.* (1988), are required to "maintain ... records or other information which will disclose the impact which its tests and other selection procedures have upon employment opportunities of persons by identifiable race, sex, or ethnic group[s.]" See § 1607.4(A). This includes records concerning "the individual components of the selection process" where there is a significant disparity in the selection rates of whites and nonwhites. See § 1607.4(C). Plaintiffs as a general matter will have the benefit of these tools to meet their burden of showing a causal link between challenged employment practices and racial imbalances in the work force; respondents presumably took full advantage of these opportunities to build their case before the trial in the District Court was held.

Consequently, on remand, the courts below are instructed to require, as part of respondents' prima facie case, a demonstration that specific elements of the petitioners' hiring process have a significantly disparate impact on nonwhites.

B

If, on remand, respondents meet the proof burdens outlined above, and establish a prima facie case of disparate impact with respect to any of petitioners' employment practices, the case will shift to any business justification petitioners offer for their use of these practices. This phase of the disparate-impact case contains two components: first, a consideration of the justifications an employer offers for his use of these practices; and second, the availability of alternate practices to achieve the same business ends, with less racial impact. We consider these two components in turn.

(1)

Though we have phrased the query differently in different cases, it is generally well-established that at the justification stage of such a disparate impact case, the dispositive issue is whether a challenged practice serves, in a significant way, the legitimate employment goals of the employer. The touchstone of this inquiry is a reasoned review of the employer's justification for his use of the challenged practice. A mere insubstantial justification in this regard will not suffice, because such a low standard of review would permit discrimination to be practiced through the use of spurious, seemingly neutral employment practices. At the same time, though, there is no requirement that the challenged practice be "essential" or "indispensable" to the employer's business for it to pass muster: this degree of scrutiny would be almost impossible for most employers to meet, and would result in a host of evils we have identified above.

In this phase, the employer carries the burden of producing evidence of a business justification for his employment practice. The burden of persuasion, however, remains with the disparate-impact plaintiff. * * * This rule conforms with the usual method for allocating persuasion and production burdens in the federal courts, see Fed.Rule Evid. 301, and more specifically, it conforms to the rule in disparate-treatment cases that the plaintiff bears the burden of disproving an employer's assertion that the adverse employment action or practice was based solely on a legitimate neutral consideration. See Texas Dept. of Community Affairs v. Burdine, [Chapter 7A.2 infra]. We acknowledge that some of our earlier decisions can be read as suggesting otherwise. But to the extent that those cases speak of an employers' "burden of proof" with respect to a legitimate business justification defense, they should have been understood to mean an employer's production—but not persuasion—burden. The persuasion burden here must remain with the plaintiff, for it is he who must prove that it was "because of such individual's race, color," etc., that he was denied a desired employment opportunity. See 42 U.S.C. § 2000e–2(a).

(2)

Finally, if on remand the case reaches this point, and respondents cannot persuade the trier of fact on the question of petitioners' business necessity defense, respondents may still be able to prevail. To do so, respondents will have to persuade the factfinder that "other tests or selection devices, without a similarly undesirable racial effect, would also serve the employer's legitimate [hiring] interest[s];" by so demonstrating, respondents would prove that "[petitioners were] using [their] tests merely as a 'pretext' for discrimination." Albemarle Paper Co., supra. If respondents, having established a prima facie case, come forward with alternatives to petitioners' hiring practices that reduce the racially-disparate impact of practices currently being used, and petitioners refuse to adopt these alternatives, such a refusal would belie a claim by petitioners that their incumbent practices are being employed for nondiscriminatory reasons.

Of course, any alternative practices which respondents offer up in this respect must be equally effective as petitioners' chosen hiring procedures in achieving petitioners' legitimate employment goals. Moreover, "[f]actors such as the cost or other burdens of proposed alternative selection devices are relevant in determining whether they would be equally as effective as the challenged practice in serving the employer's legitimate business goals." Watson, supra. (O'Connor, J.). "Courts are generally less competent than employers to restructure business practices," Furnco Construction Corp. v. Waters, 438 U.S. 567, 578, 98 S.Ct. 2943, 2950, 57 L.Ed.2d 957 (1978); consequently, the judiciary should proceed with care before mandating that an employer must adopt a plaintiff's alternate selection or hiring practice in response to a Title VII suit.

IV

For the reasons given above, the judgment of the Court of Appeals is reversed, and the case is remanded for further proceedings consistent with this opinion.

It is so ordered.

JUSTICE STEVENS, with whom JUSTICE BRENNAN, JUSTICE MARSHALL, and JUSTICE BLACKMUN join, dissenting.

* * *

* * * Our opinions always have emphasized that in a disparate impact case the employer's burden is weighty. "The touchstone," the Court said in *Griggs*, "is business necessity." Later, we held that prison administrators had failed to "rebu[t] the prima facie case of discrimination by showing that the height and weight requirements are ... essential to effective job performance," Dothard v. Rawlinson. I am thus astonished to read that the "touchstone of this inquiry is a reasoned review of the employer's justification for his use of the challenged practice.... [T]here is no requirement that the challenged practice be ... 'essential.' " This casual—almost summary—rejection of the statutory construction that developed in the wake of *Griggs* is most disturbing. I have always believed that the *Griggs* opinion correctly reflected the intent of the Congress that enacted Title VII. Even if I were not so persuaded, I could not join a rejection of a consistent interpretation of a federal statute. Congress frequently revisits this statutory scheme and can readily correct our mistakes if we misread its meaning.

Also troubling is the Court's apparent redefinition of the employees' burden of proof in a disparate impact case. No prima facie case will be made, it declares, unless the employees " 'isolat[e] and identif[y] the specific employment practices that are allegedly responsible for any observed statistical disparities.' " This additional proof requirement is unwarranted. It is elementary that a plaintiff cannot recover upon proof of injury alone; rather, the plaintiff must connect the injury to an act of the defendant in order to establish prima facie that the defendant is liable. Although the causal link must have substance, the act need not constitute the sole or primary cause of the harm. Thus in a disparate impact case, proof of numerous questionable employment practices ought to fortify an employee's assertion that the practices caused racial disparities. Ordinary principles of fairness require that Title VII actions be tried like "any lawsuit." Cf. USPS Board of Governors v. Aikens, 460 U.S. 711, 714, n. 3, 103 S.Ct. 1478, 1481, n. 3, 75 L.Ed.2d 403 (1983). The changes the majority makes today, tipping the scales in favor of employers, are not faithful to those principles.

JUSTICE BLACKMUN, with whom JUSTICE BRENNAN and JUSTICE MARSHALL join, dissenting. [Omitted]

NOTE ON Wards Cove AND THE CIVIL RIGHTS ACT OF 1991

1. How is the plaintiffs' challenge in *Wards Cove* different from that of the plaintiffs in *Griggs*? *Griggs* considered a particular employment test and the statistical data related to the exclusionary effect of that single test. *Wards Cove* and similar cases are often called "subjective" employment cases because the "tests" under challenge are either subjective judgments of hiring officers ("I wanted eager salespeople") or multi-faceted judgments that cannot easily be separated into their constituent parts ("I hired clerks who could research and write well and get along with others in the office"). In either case, because of the amorphous nature of the hiring decisions, no statistics can be readily gathered except as to the bottom-line impact of the overall hiring process. Thus, in all such cases the plaintiff presents comparative statistical analysis of the overall hiring results—which typically show a racial imbalance in the workforce, thus leading some to call these "bottom line" cases.

(a) The Court rejects "bottom-line" analysis. What does it find flawed about the technique? Its inducement to use quotas? Its inability to show that any particular hiring factor caused the bottom-line results? Its imprecision—it makes the employer responsible for social ills (e.g., fewer educational opportunities for minorities) that the employer never caused?

(b) In **Connecticut v. Teal**, 457 U.S. 440, 102 S.Ct. 2525, 73 L.Ed.2d 130 (1982), the Court rejected a defendant's attempt to use bottom-line analysis as a defense. The employer's scored test had produced a disproportionate impact on blacks, an effect it sought to cure by adding back a sufficient number of blacks to the hiring process so that the overall hiring results showed a racial balance. Justice Brennan's opinion held the test illegal nevertheless. Is the dissenters' position in *Wards Cove* inconsistent with the position most of them took as a majority in *Teal*? (Some of the *Wards Cove* majority dissented in *Teal;* have they been consistent?)

(c) Does bottom-line analysis place too great a burden on employers, thus inducing them to manipulate their hiring to produce balanced workforces? What makes the burden great? The cost of showing business necessity for each subjective standard claimed to cause the imbalance? The sheer inability to make such a showing, regardless of cost? (How does one justify that she needs to hire "eager" sales clerks?) Is it the laziness of employers that could lead to quotas—because it is easier to adopt a quota than to rationalize employment practices?

(d) If bottom-line analysis produces manipulated hiring that results in "balanced" workforces, what is wrong with that? Is it intentional discrimination? Is it affirmative action in disguise?

(e) If bottom-line analysis places too great a burden on employers, does *Wards Cove*'s approach place too great a burden on plaintiffs? How will they isolate and identify, then gather comparative statistics about, each hiring practice they want to challenge? Does *Wards Cove* effectively hold that such practices should not be attacked through impact analysis? Should these cases be tried under disparate treatment analysis, because they really involve subtle intentional discrimination? Do plaintiffs want to use impact analysis because they are afraid they cannot prove intentional discrimination?

2. The dissenters in *Wards Cove* accuse the majority of changing the rules on bottom-line analysis. Is that so? Or did the majority simply refuse to go along with the application of *Griggs* to a new situation? Were the dissenters arguing for an expansion of *Griggs*?

(a) Is rightness in this area to be measured by what helps minorities? By what the Court thinks is wise or traditional social policy?

(b) Should the Court focus on Congress' intent, since this is, after all, a statute they are interpreting? What is the Court to do if Congress has been silent? Does the Court have the freedom to shape the statute's contours here as it did in its § 1983 jurisprudence? Is Title VII different because the concerns are non-constitutional (at least with respect to disparate impact discrimination)? Recall the Court's creation, in Chapter 6D supra, of implied (and frankly judicially determined) remedies under Title IX; is Title VII different because the remedies here are statutorily prescribed rather than implied?

3. *Wards Cove* not only confined *Griggs* and disparate impact analysis to identifiable employment practices, it also fine-tuned or changed the "business necessity" defense.

(a) What is the transactional difference between a production burden and a persuasion burden? The production burden alone will require the employer to put on evidence regarding its business justification, right? The persuasion burden operates only to break ties in the evidence, Fleming James et al., CIVIL PROCEDURE § 7.6 (5th ed. 2001). Thus after *Wards Cove*, when the evidence as to business justification is in equipoise, the plaintiff loses rather than the defendant. Is that such a great change?

(b) Assuming that disparate impact analysis calls for courts to balance adverse impact on minorities against the business interests of employers, what arguments favor the Court's position? Are courts simply incapable of making such choices? Do they lack judicially manageable standards? Recall the similar issue that arose under Title VI, Chapter 6A supra, where the Court approved regulations adopting an effects test—but never declared the scope of any justification for adverse effects. Was the Court scared off the problem there for the same reasons it was afraid here—its inability to balance apples (civil rights goals) and oranges (business goals)?[1]

(c) Consider the consequences of judicial error in holding, for example, that a masters degree is unnecessary for a medical technician's job, or that an experience requirement is unnecessary to be a police officer. Is the Court afraid of the social costs it might impose on individuals? Or is it afraid that this type of judicial review will ruin the market economy? Would such review be *Lochner*izing[2] under the guise of civil rights enforcement? Or is this kind of judicial review different because statutory enforcement is at issue, and Congress is always free to change Title VII if the Court proves to be a poor decisionmaker?

(d) The Court permits plaintiffs, even if they fail to prove lack of business justification, to show that alternative, less-exclusionary neutral rules were available to the employer. Does this ameliorate the impact of its business necessity decision? No, because the alternative must be "equally effective" and courts must remember to be deferential?

4. **The Civil Rights Act of 1991 and *Wards Cove*.** Two years after the decision in *Wards Cove,* Congress amended Title VII in response to several Court decisions. See Civil Rights Act of 1991, Pub.L. 102–166, 105 Stat. 1071 (1991), set out in the Appendix. To what extent does the 1991 Act overturn *Wards Cove*?

(a) With respect to a plaintiff's duty to identify "particular" employment practices, section 105 of the 1991 Act excuses compliance if "the elements of [an employer's] decisionmaking process are not capable of separation for analysis." Does this overturn *Wards Cove*'s approach to "bottom line" analysis?[3]

---

1. To the extent that the Court has considered possible justifications under Title VI, recall Justice Marshall's separate opinion in *Guardians*, Chapter 6A supra, footnote 15 of which permitted a grantee to excuse its adverse effects by offering a "sufficient nondiscriminatory justification." Is that test so different from the one used by the majority in *Wards Cove*?

2. See Lochner v. New York, 198 U.S. 45, 25 S.Ct. 539, 49 L.Ed. 937 (1905); Nowak & Rotunda, CONSTITUTIONAL LAW § 11.3 (2004) (reviewing Court's practice of examining constitutionality of economic regulations during the early twentieth century).

3. Section 106 of the 1991 Act outlaws "race norming" of test scores in order to produce non-statistically-disparate racial results. Does this provision confirm the result in the *Teal* case, supra?

(b) With respect to "business necessity," § 105 (when read in tandem with definitional provisions in § 104) indisputably changes the persuasion burden back to the employer. Yet whether § 105 provides a new definition of the defense is less clear: it applies if the employer shows that "the challenged practice is job related for the position in question and consistent with business necessity." The original preamble to the 1991 Act declared its intent to overrule *Wards Cove,* but the final version declares only an intent to "codify the concept[ ] of 'business necessity' []enunciated [] in *Griggs* [] prior to *Wards Cove.*" Since the *Wards Cove* majority claims that its decision is consistent with *Griggs*—that is, that there is no change—how should § 105 be interpreted? Does it overturn *Wards Cove*?[4]

(c) With respect to consideration of an employer's alternative selection criteria, § 105 also declares that the concept is to be interpreted "in accordance with the law as it existed" prior to *Wards Cove* (with its emphasis on "equally effective" alternatives). Does this weaken *Wards Cove*? How so?

(d) The thesis of the original supporters of the 1991 Act was that the Court had erroneously decided *Wards Cove* and that Congress could respond adequately by simply turning back the clock to the pre-*Wards Cove* law. Do you agree? Review the preceding Note: was the pre-existing law as favorable to plaintiffs as the original sponsors of the 1991 Act assumed?

5. More than two decades after passage of the 1991 Act, the Supreme Court remains silent on most of the interpretational issues that it posed regarding disparate impact. Early decisions held major provisions of the Act non-retroactive, and the other issues have not been raised. See Landgraf v. USI Film Products, 511 U.S. 244, 266, 114 S.Ct. 1483, 1497, 128 L.Ed.2d 229. (1994) (§ 102's provision for compensatory and punitive damages in cases of intentional discrimination not retroactive because it would impose a new legal rule on completed prior conduct; such retroactivity requires a "clear statement" of Congressional intent); Rivers v. Roadway Exp., Inc., 511 U.S. 298, 114 S.Ct. 1510, 128 L.Ed.2d 274 (1994) (amendments to § 1981 not retroactive).

(a) Federal appellate courts have found three issues regarding the relation between *Wards Cove* and the 1991 Act to be easy. First, there appears to be no provision in the Act that overturns *Wards Cove* insofar as it requires analysis to focus on persons competing for the same jobs (rather than a comparison of low-level and high-level jobs). See Bullington v. United Air Lines, Inc., 186 F.3d 1301, 1313 (10th Cir.1999); Atonio v. Wards Cove Packing Co., Inc., 10 F.3d 1485 (9th Cir.1993) (remand of principal case): "Nothing in the 1991 Act, however, modifies the central holding of Wards Cove that a disparate impact case cannot be established on the basis of a statistical disparity between the cannery work force and [other] noncannery * * * jobs." Second, courts have found no trouble deciding that § 105 shifts the burden of persuasion back to the defendant, overturning *Wards Cove.* See Lanning v. Southeastern Pennsylvania Transp. Authority (SEPTA), 181 F.3d 478 (3d Cir. 1999). Third, if alternatives are to be considered after the

---

4. In an extraordinarily unusual step, § 105(b) explicitly restricts the legislative history that may be consulted in interpreting § 105 to one memorandum in the record, which is relatively more favorable to maintaining the status quo on this issue. See the Appendix.

business necessity defense succeeds, the production and persuasion burdens are on the plaintiff. See International Broth. of Elec. Workers v. Mississippi Power & Light Co., 442 F.3d 313 (5th Cir. 2006) (declaring that the intent of the 1991 Act was to codify pre-*Wards Cove* practices).

(b) The first opinion to give significant attention to the precise issue of whether the 1991 Act altered the business necessity defense was the Third Circuit's decision in Lanning v. Southeastern Pennsylvania Transp. Authority (SEPTA), 181 F.3d 478, 488–90 (3d Cir. 1999) (2–1 decision). Although noting the difficulty of its task (based on unavailability of dispositive legislative history and on the fact that following adoption of the 1991 Act, both proponents and opponents of the *Wards Cove* test had claimed victory), the court decided that the 1991 Act required it to ignore *Wards Cove* and return to the pre–1989 precedents regarding business necessity, which it read as non-deferential toward employers. More recently, in Maldonado v. City of Altus, 433 F.3d 1294 (10th Cir. 2006), the court viewed the 1991 Act as "impos[ing] a heavier burden on plaintiffs" in proving disparate impact, but it returned to pre-*Wards Cove* precedents to determine business necessity. See also Isabel v. City of Memphis, 404 F.3d 404 (6th Cir. 2005).

(c) On the issue of isolating and identifying specific factors that have harmed the plaintiff's group, courts overwhelmingly continue to enforce *Wards Cove* itself, probably because the 1991 Act codifies this practice except when factors are incapable of separation. See paragraph 4(a) supra; Farrell v. Butler University, 421 F.3d 609 (7th Cir. 2005) (factors unique to individual plaintiff irrelevant; factors must impact all members of the group).

(d) The Supreme Court itself has not considered the mechanics of disparate impact claims is recent years, mirroring a general decline in Title–VII-based disparate impact litigation. The only disparate impact claims involved analogues to Title VII that have peculiarities not applicable to Title VII. Chevron U.S.A. Inc. v. Echazabal, 536 U.S. 73, 122 S.Ct. 2045, 153 L.Ed.2d 82 (2002), upheld an EEOC regulation that slightly expanded the scope of the business necessity defense in the context of disability cases involving potential dangers to co-workers or the employee himself. In **Smith v. City of Jackson**, 544 U.S. 228, 125 S.Ct. 1536, 161 L.Ed.2d 410 (2005), an odd-bedfellows majority led by Justices Stevens and Scalia upheld disparate impact claims for age discrimination cases, but found no valid claim. The Court somewhat obliquely referred to the 1991 Act as "modify[ing] the Court's holding in *Wards Cove*" and "expand[ing] the coverage of Title VII," but then it noted that the 1991 Act had not amended the ADEA. Therefore, the Court proceeded to apply "*Wards Cove*'s pre–1991 interpretation of Title VII," including its holding regarding subjective hiring. What would the 1991 Act require of Title VII claims?

6. Was adoption of the disparate impact test for employment discrimination a policy mistake? Even the strongest adherents of the theory admit that it has a "checkered history" and, after the first successes against obvious and entrenched systems, it has produced exceptionally few winning cases for plaintiffs. See Charles A. Sullivan, *Disparate Impact: Looking Past the* Desert Palace *Mirage*, 47 WM. & MARY L. REV. 911 (2005) (arguing for a reinvigoration

of disparate impact litigation, but admitting that "[d]evelopments in the courts since the 1991 Amendments have not been propitious").

(a) Professor Michael Selmi, in *Was the Disparate Impact Theory a Mistake?*, 53 UCLA L. REV. 701 (2006), argues that "[o]utside of the original context in which the theory arose, namely written employment tests, the disparate impact theory has produced no substantial social change and there is no reason to think that extending the theory to other contexts would have produced meaningful reform." Indeed, the experience with the disparate impact theory under Title VII is almost as uniformly ineffective for plaintiffs as it has been under Title VI. See Chapter 6 infra. If the disparate impact theory gives law professors an admirable basis for theorizing, but no practical results for plaintiffs, as Professor Selmi argues, what good is it?

(b) In *Ricci v. DeStefano*, Chapter 7D infra, the majority rejected a city's attempt to abandon its testing program (even though the city claimed that it was dumping the test results because of their disparate impact) because it not only saw the action as an attempt to promote racial balancing, but also because it seemed to see some value in the evenhandedness or neutrality of testing itself. An expert testifying for the city presented a widely held view among academics who study the area—that tests inherently and virtually always produce disparate impacts on blacks and other minorities. If this research is accurate, which way does it cut? Is testing itself always racist? Is it racists to think that testing is always racist? Is testing sometimes valuable even when it produces racially disparate results? When it is more valuable than the disparate results produced? Is it strange that there is in fact no consensus about which employment tests or practices are worth less? Do we need not a theory but a discussion of these details?

NOTE ON SUBJECTIVE HIRING, CLASS ACTIONS, AND THE WAL-MART CASE

1. Superficially, the Court's decision in **Wal-Mart Stores, Inc. v. Dukes**, ___ U.S. ___, 131 S.Ct. 2541, 180 L.Ed.2d 374 (2011), appears to limit class actions made in employment discrimination cases under Title VII. But it may have implications for Title VII's definitions of liability, at least at the practical level of litigation. The plaintiffs's innovative, hybrid claim against Wal-Mart charged that the company devolved employment decisionmaking to the store level, giving managers wide discretion that was used locally in an intentionally discriminatory manner against women (disparate treatment). In order to sue the company as a whole, the plaintiffs then alleged (i) that by using this system the company gave effect to an employment practice having an adverse effect on women (disparate impact) and (ii) that by maintaining the system with knowledge of its effects, they had committed intentional discrimination (further disparate treatment). In essence, the "corporate culture" made "every woman at the company the victim of one common discriminatory practice."

(a) The central part of the Court's opinion rejected class certification for the claims on the ground that all members's claims did not relate to "common facts," as required by FRCP 23. See Chapter 7C infra. It is how the Court treated the plaintiffs's legal theory that we turn our attention here.

(b) The Court's discussion on what makes claims "common" appears to mirror its treatment of a similar issue in *Wards Cove* and *Watson v. Fort Worth Bank & Trust*, as discussed in *Wards Cove*. There the Court noted that disparate impact cases "begin by identifying the specific employment practice that is challenged." Compare that language with *Wal-Mart*, ___ U.S. at ___, 131 S.Ct. at 2551:

> "Commonality requires the plaintiff to demonstrate that the class members 'have suffered the same injury.' This does not mean merely that they have all suffered a violation of the same provision of law. Title VII, for example, can be violated in many ways—by intentional discrimination, or by hiring and promotion criteria that result in disparate impact, and by the use of these practices on the part of many different superiors in a single company. Quite obviously, the mere claim by employees of the same company that they have suffered a Title VII injury, or even a disparate-impact Title VII injury, gives no cause to believe that all their claims can productively be litigated at once. Their claims must depend upon a common contention—for example, the assertion of discriminatory bias on the part of the same supervisor. That common contention, moreover, must be of such a nature that it is capable of classwide resolution—which means that determination of its truth or falsity will resolve an issue that is central to the validity of each one of the claims in one stroke."

Does *Wal-Mart*'s holding imply that the practice or policy subject to analysis under disparate impact must be similarly precisely defined?

(c) Justice Ginsburg's opinion, dissenting on this issue, found the claim to be supportable under *Ft. Worth Bank & Trust*, which she claimed also showed "commonality" of claims, ___ U.S. at ___, 131 S.Ct. at 2564–65:

> The District Court's identification of a common question, whether Wal-Mart's pay and promotions policies gave rise to unlawful discrimination, was hardly infirm. The practice of delegating to supervisors large discretion to make personnel decisions, uncontrolled by formal standards, has long been known to have the potential to produce disparate effects. Managers, like all humankind, may be prey to biases of which they are unaware. The risk of discrimination is heightened when those managers are predominantly of one sex, and are steeped in a corporate culture that perpetuates gender stereotypes.

> * * * *

> Aware of "the problem of subconscious stereotypes and prejudices," we held that the employer's "undisciplined system of subjective decisionmaking" was an "employment practic[e]" that "may be analyzed under the disparate impact approach." [Watson v. Ft. Worth Bank & Trust]. See also Wards Cove Packing Co. v. Atonio.

Did *Watson* and *Wards Cove* hold what Justice Ginsburg says they held? Did she omit some critical component of their holdings? In another part of her opinion Justice Ginsburg pointed out that women were broadly represented in lower levels of employment at Wal-Mart, but underrepresented at higher levels. Is this comparison relevant to a claim of disparate impact after *Wards Cove*?

2.   Assume that the practice of delegating authority is itself an "identifiable" employment practice about which one can gather information that shows that women receive less pay and fewer promotions than men. According to disparate impact analysis, the next step would be to ask whether Wal-Mart has a business necessity for the practice. Assume that Wal-Mart replies, "we are the largest employer in the United States; we are too big to manage centrally and must leave discretion to local managers." Under the 1991 Civil Rights Act, does that reason satisfy the business necessity test?

(a) Wal-Mart's spectacular success as a retailer might suggest that it has made some good decisions about managing the company and that these decisions contribute to the company's success and growth, does it not? See Secrets of Wal-Mart's Success, http://www.pbs.org/wgbh/pages/frontline/shows/walmart/secrets/ (last visited June 21, 2011) (Wal-Mart is #1 retailer since 2002; exerts central control over purchasing but has decentralized control over ordering, etc. at each store; low-cost workforce with much turnover is key to keeping labor costs low). Is that a sufficient showing? Wal-Mart hires a half-million workers each year due to its high turnover rate. Does the need to hire so many employees justify its practice of devolving hiring authority to the store level?

(b) If the business necessity test is met, how can the plaintiffs show the existence of a workable alternative that would have a less exclusionary impact on women? What alternatives exist? What would be their impact? Does the information in ¶ 2(a) suggest that no other alternative is as efficient as what Wal-Mart has chosen?

(c) Disparate impact claims ask court to weigh the interest of the employer in maintaining its practices against the affected group's interest in avoiding practices with a disproportionately adverse impact. Is that a balance that no tests created by the Supreme Court can strike? Is the history of disparate impact analysis simply a broad ruse designed to avoid the admission that there is no scientific answer, only a value judgment that may or may not be mistaken? Compare the similar issues raised in Chapter 6A concerning Title VI's similar effects test.

3.   Is the claim in *Wal-Mart* in reality a claim of disparate treatment, that is, intentional sex discrimination? Should "subjective hiring" claims be treated exclusively as disparate treatment claims?

(a) A substantial portion of the *Wal-Mart* plaintiffs's proof consisted of an attempt to show that "gender bias suffused Wal–Mart's company culture" (according to Justice Ginsburg) or that "uniform 'corporate culture' permits bias" (majority opinion). Is this not a disparate treatment claim—intentional sex discrimination? One of the plaintiff's experts conducted a regression analysis, see section 2(a) of this Chapter, which follows, that concluded that the differential in pay and promotion at Wal-Mart could be explained by no other factor than sex or gender differences between employees. Is this not a claim of intentional sex discrimination?

(b) Justice Ginsburg's concurring and dissenting seemed to imply that subjective hiring is suspect because an employer has "not developed precise and formal criteria for evaluating candidates" but has instead "relied instead on the subjective judgment of supervisors." Should Title VII require, or be interpreted to require, that all employers adopt such standards? Is this practical? What objective standards should be used for selecting the very best managers? Lawyers? Law professors? Law students? Do objective criteria for judging success exist?

2. DISPARATE TREATMENT—INTENTIONAL DISCRIMINATION

(a) Proof of Intent

As stated in the *Teamsters* footnote at the beginning of this Chapter, disparate treatment is nothing more than old-fashioned intentional discrimination. There are defenses sometimes available in such cases, see section B infra, but the initial hurdle for plaintiffs in every disparate treatment case is to prove that the defendant intentionally acted against her because of race, sex, etc. That is often a daunting task.

The simplest manner for proving intentional discrimination is by direct evidence. Occasionally the employer will facially classify by gender, for example, hoping to rely on a defense. That facial classification is intentional discrimination. No additional bad motive need be proved. See International Union, UAAAIW v. Johnson Controls, Inc., set out in section B.1 of this Chapter, infra. On other occasions it may be possible to prove even covert intent through live witnesses or documents, such as testimony that an employer confessed to an associate that he no longer wished to hire blacks or women. See Perry v. Woodward, 199 F.3d 1126 (10th Cir.1999) (Hispanic workers); Bell v. Birmingham Linen Service, 715 F.2d 1552 (11th Cir.1983) (black workers). Such cases are probably rare. See Cooper v. Southern Co., 390 F.3d 695, 724 n.15 (11th Cir. 2004): "Direct evidence is evidence which itself proves the existence of discrimination and does not require inference or interpretation, as for example a frank admission from a manager that he refused to hire an applicant because he was black or because she was female. As would be expected, such direct evidence is encountered only infrequently...."[1]

When direct evidence is unavailable, as in the vast majority of cases, plaintiffs must rely on circumstantial evidence. Circumstantial evidence may come in several guises, see Coffman v. Indianapolis Fire Dept., 578 F.3d 559 (7th Cir. 2009) (sex discrimination), but the Supreme Court has developed two "prima facie case" analyses to guide trial courts in their consideration of such evidence. One prima facie case controls individual

---

1. Are courts too demanding of what constitutes direct evidence? See Canady v. Wal–Mart Stores, Inc., 440 F.3d 1031 (8th Cir. 2006) ("What's up, my nigga?" not direct evidence because it does not directly relate to employment decision; no hostile work environment either). The Supreme Court seems to disagree. See Ash v. Tyson Foods, Inc., 546 U.S. 454, 126 S.Ct. 1195, 163 L.Ed.2d 1053 (2006) ("boy" directed at black employee may be proof of intentional discrimination depending on context and not per se benign).

disparate treatment claims, the other class claims. These are used in the vast majority of cases involving circumstantial evidence.

TEXAS DEPARTMENT OF COMMUNITY AFFAIRS v. BURDINE

Supreme Court of the United States, 1981.
450 U.S. 248, 101 S.Ct. 1089, 67 L.Ed.2d 207.

JUSTICE POWELL delivered the opinion of the Court.

This case requires us to address again the nature of the evidentiary burden placed upon the defendant in an employment discrimination suit brought under Title VII of the Civil Rights Act of 1964, 42 U.S.C. § 2000e *et seq.* The narrow question presented is whether, after the plaintiff has proved a prima facie case of discriminatory treatment, the burden shifts to the defendant to persuade the court by a preponderance of the evidence that legitimate, nondiscriminatory reasons for the challenged employment action existed.

I

[Plaintiff claimed that she had been denied a promotion and was later discharged because she was a woman. The district court ruled against her, but the Court of Appeals reversed.]

II

In McDonnell Douglas Corp. v. Green, 411 U.S. 792, 93 S.Ct. 1817, 36 L.Ed.2d 668 (1973), we set forth the basic allocation of burdens and order of presentation of proof in a Title VII case alleging discriminatory treatment. First, the plaintiff has the burden of proving by the preponderance of the evidence a prima facie case of discrimination. Second, if the plaintiff succeeds in proving the prima facie case, the burden shifts to the defendant "to articulate some legitimate, nondiscriminatory reason for the employee's rejection." Id. at 802. Third, should the defendant carry this burden, the plaintiff must then have an opportunity to prove by a preponderance of the evidence that the legitimate reasons offered by the defendant were not its true reasons, but were a pretext for discrimination. Id. at 804.

The nature of the burden that shifts to the defendant should be understood in light of the plaintiff's ultimate and intermediate burdens. The ultimate burden of persuading the trier of fact that the defendant intentionally discriminated against the plaintiff remains at all times with the plaintiff. See Board of Trustees of Keene State College v. Sweeney, 439 U.S. 24, 25, n. 2 (1978); id. at 29 (Stevens, J., dissenting). See generally 9 J. Wigmore, Evidence § 2489 (3d ed.1940) (the burden of persuasion "never shifts"). The *McDonnell Douglas* division of intermediate evidentiary burdens serves to bring the litigants and the court expeditiously and fairly to this ultimate question.

The burden of establishing a prima facie case of disparate treatment is not onerous. The plaintiff must prove by a preponderance of the evidence that she applied for an available position for which she was qualified, but was rejected under circumstances which give rise to an inference of unlawful discrimination.[2] The prima facie case serves an important function in the litigation: it eliminates the most common nondiscriminatory reasons for the plaintiff's rejection. As the Court explained in Furnco Construction Corp. v. Waters, 438 U.S. 567, 577 (1978), the prima facie case "raises an inference of discrimination only because we presume these acts, if otherwise unexplained, are more likely than not based on the consideration of impermissible factors." Establishment of the prima facie case in effect creates a presumption that the employer unlawfully discriminated against the employee. If the trier of fact believes the plaintiff's evidence, and if the employer is silent in the face of the presumption, the court must enter judgment for the plaintiff because no issue of fact remains in the case.[3]

The burden that shifts to the defendant, therefore, is to rebut the presumption of discrimination by producing evidence that the plaintiff was rejected, or someone else was preferred, for a legitimate, nondiscriminatory reason. The defendant need not persuade the court that it was actually motivated by the proffered reasons. It is sufficient if the defendant's evidence raises a genuine issue of fact as to whether it discriminated against the plaintiff.[4] To accomplish this, the defendant must clearly set forth, through the introduction of admissible evidence, the

---

2. In *McDonnell Douglas, supra,* we described an appropriate model for a prima facie case of racial discrimination. The plaintiff must show:

"(i) that he belongs to a racial minority; (ii) that he applied and was qualified for a job for which the employer was seeking applicants; (iii) that, despite his qualifications, he was rejected; and (iv) that, after his rejection, the position remained open and the employer continued to seek applicants from persons of complainant's qualifications." 411 U.S. at 802.

We added, however, that this standard is not inflexible, as "[t]he facts necessarily will vary in Title VII cases, and the specification above of the prima facie proof required from respondent is not necessarily applicable in every respect in differing factual situations." Id. at 802, n. 13.

In the instant case, it is not seriously contested that respondent has proved a prima facie case. She showed that she was a qualified woman who sought an available position, but the position was left open for several months before she finally was rejected in favor of a male, Walz, who had been under her supervision.

3. The phrase "prima facie case" not only may denote the establishment of a legally mandatory, rebuttable presumption, but also may be used by courts to describe the plaintiff's burden of producing enough evidence to permit the trier of fact to infer the fact at issue. 9 J. Wigmore, Evidence § 2494 (3d ed.1940). *McDonnell Douglas* should have made it apparent that in the Title VII context we use "prima facie case" in the former sense.

4. This evidentiary relationship between the presumption created by a prima facie case and the consequential burden of production placed on the defendant is a traditional feature of the common law. "The word 'presumption' properly used refers only to a device for allocating the production burden." F. James & G. Hazard, Civil Procedure § 7.9, p. 255 (2d ed.1977) (footnote omitted). See Fed. Rule Evid. 301. See generally 9 J. Wigmore, Evidence § 2491 (3d ed.1940). Cf. J. Maguire, Evidence, Common Sense and Common Law 185–186 (1947). Usually, assessing the burden of production helps the judge determine whether the litigants have created an issue of fact to be decided by the jury. In a Title VII case, the allocation of burdens and the creation of a presumption by the establishment of a prima facie case is intended progressively to sharpen the inquiry into the elusive factual question of intentional discrimination.

reasons for the plaintiff's rejection.[5] The explanation provided must be legally sufficient to justify a judgment for the defendant. If the defendant carries this burden of production, the presumption raised by the prima facie case is rebutted,[6] and the factual inquiry proceeds to a new level of specificity. Placing this burden of production on the defendant thus serves simultaneously to meet the plaintiff's prima facie case by presenting a legitimate reason for the action and to frame the factual issue with sufficient clarity so that the plaintiff will have a full and fair opportunity to demonstrate pretext. The sufficiency of the defendant's evidence should be evaluated by the extent to which it fulfills these functions.

The plaintiff retains the burden of persuasion. She now must have the opportunity to demonstrate that the proffered reason was not the true reason for the employment decision. This burden now merges with the ultimate burden of persuading the court that she has been the victim of intentional discrimination. She may succeed in this either directly by persuading the court that a discriminatory reason more likely motivated the employer or indirectly by showing that the employer's proffered explanation is unworthy of credence. See McDonnell Douglas, 411 U.S. at 804–805.

III

* * *

The [appellate] court placed the burden of persuasion on the defendant apparently because it feared that "[i]f an employer need only *articulate*—not prove—a legitimate, nondiscriminatory reason for his action, he may compose fictitious, but legitimate, reasons for his actions." Turner v. Texas Instruments, Inc., supra, at 1255 (emphasis in original). We do not believe, however, that limiting the defendant's evidentiary obligation to a burden of production will unduly hinder the plaintiff. First, as noted above, the defendant's explanation of its legitimate reasons must be clear and reasonably specific. See Loeb v. Textron, Inc., 600 F.2d 1003, 1011–1012, n. 5 (C.A.1 1979). This obligation arises both from the necessity of rebutting the inference of discrimination arising from the prima facie case and from the requirement that the plaintiff be afforded "a full and fair opportunity" to demonstrate pretext. Second, although the defendant does not bear a formal burden of persuasion, the defendant nevertheless retains an incentive to persuade the trier of fact that the employment decision was lawful. Thus, the defendant normally will attempt to prove

---

5. An articulation not admitted into evidence will not suffice. Thus, the defendant cannot meet its burden merely through an answer to the complaint or by argument of counsel.

6. See generally J. Thayer, Preliminary Treatise on Evidence 346 (1898). In saying that the presumption drops from the case, we do not imply that the trier of fact no longer may consider evidence previously introduced by the plaintiff to establish a prima facie case. A satisfactory explanation by the defendant destroys the legally mandatory inference of discrimination arising from the plaintiff's initial evidence. Nonetheless, this evidence and inferences properly drawn therefrom may be considered by the trier of fact on the issue of whether the defendant's explanation is pretextual. Indeed, there may be some cases where the plaintiff's initial evidence, combined with effective cross-examination of the defendant, will suffice to discredit the defendant's explanation.

the factual basis for its explanation. Third, the liberal discovery rules applicable to any civil suit in federal court are supplemented in a Title VII suit by the plaintiff's access to the Equal Employment Opportunity Commission's investigatory files concerning her complaint. See EEOC v. Associated Dry Goods Corp., 449 U.S. 590 (1981). Given these factors, we are unpersuaded that the plaintiff will find it particularly difficult to prove that a proffered explanation lacking a factual basis is a pretext. We remain confident that the *McDonnell Douglas* framework permits the plaintiff meriting relief to demonstrate intentional discrimination.

* * *

NOTE ON THE PRIMA FACIE CASE FOR INDIVIDUAL CLAIMS

1. What must plaintiff prove in order to raise an inference of discrimination? What must the defendant show in response?

(a) Given the four factors used under *McDonnell Douglas*, will every minority member who is minimally qualified for a job for which he is not hired be able to establish a prima facie case of discrimination?[1] Is the rationale given in the *Furnco* case appropriate for blue collar jobs only? Does the plaintiff need to show also that the defendant was aware of the plaintiff's race or even knew what his race was? See Woodman v. WWOR–TV, Inc., 411 F.3d 69 (2d Cir. 2005) (no ADEA prima facie case absent proof that employer knew plaintiff's age). Since Title VII covers all discrimination, not just that against minorities or women, can a male use *McDonnell Douglas* in bringing a claim of sex discrimination? See Hague v. Thompson Distribution Co., 436 F.3d 816 (7th Cir. 2006) (additional "background circumstances" required); Woods v. Perry, 375 F.3d 671 (8th Cir. 2004) (usual employer would not discriminate against majority).[2]

(b) Note how the employer in response need not show the importance of his reason for rejecting the plaintiff. It need only be a fact-based reason. As the Supreme Court emphasized in **Raytheon Co. v. Hernandez**, 540 U.S. 44, 124 S.Ct. 513, 157 L.Ed.2d 357 (2003) (ADA analogue), at this stage in disparate treatment analysis, there no balancing of the importance of the employer's reason permitted; factual existence of the offered reason is the only open question. Some courts have held that even a mistaken reason qualifies, since Title VII forbids discrimination, not mistakes. See Schoenfeld v. Babbitt, 168 F.3d 1257 (11th Cir.1999) (paperwork mistakes and bureaucratic foul-ups); Turner v. Texas Instruments, Inc., 555 F.2d 1251, 1256–57 & n. 6 (5th Cir.1977) (factual mistakes), overruled on other grounds, Burdine v. Texas Dept. of Community Affairs, 647 F.2d 513 (5th Cir.1981). How is this different from the business necessity showing required under disparate impact analysis? Is the difference in approach appropriate because the issue in

---

1. See Walker v. Mortham, 158 F.3d 1177 (11th Cir.1998) (plaintiffs need not prove that they were "equally" or "better" qualified than hired whites).

2. Are there any "special circumstances" where the *McDonnell Douglas* factors would not raise an inference of discrimination for one otherwise entitled to it? See Coghlan v. American Seafoods Co. LLC., 413 F.3d 1090 (9th Cir. 2005) ("same actor inference" weakens plaintiff's claim where same person who fired plaintiff is the one who earlier hired him).

disparate treatment analysis is purely one of fact, not an implicit balancing of civil rights goals and business goals? Is it simply too easy under *Burdine* for the employer to lie?

(c) What reasons fail to satisfy *Burdine*'s demand for a legitimate non-discriminatory reason? Mere denials of intent to discriminate? Would a "subjective reason" suffice (e.g., "I did not like her personality")? Or is that the equivalent of a mere denial? See Conner v. Fort Gordon Bus Co., 761 F.2d 1495 (11th Cir.1985).

(d) What would constitute proof of "pretext"? Is pretext another way of saying "catch the employer in a lie"? See Reeves v. Sanderson Plumbing Products, Inc., 530 U.S. 133, 120 S.Ct. 2097, 147 L.Ed.2d 105 (2000) (proof of non-performance on job countered with evidence of accurate performance); Ash v. Tyson Foods, Inc., 546 U.S. 454, 126 S.Ct. 1195, 163 L.Ed.2d 1053 (2006) (proof of qualifications superior to those of white persons chosen). Can the employer avoid the trap by manufacturing eccentric reasons for rejecting an employee? On the other hand, will it sometimes be too easy to cast doubt even upon an employer's valid reason—because few people, even employers, consistently follow the neutral standards on which they usually rely?

2.   After an inference of discrimination is raised, what is the transactional meaning of the different burdens allocated in *Burdine*? Consider what should happen at trial in each of the following sets of scenarios:

(a) (i) Plaintiff offers no evidence of one of the *McDonnell Douglas* factors or evidence that is not credible for any reasonable factfinder; defendant moves to dismiss. (See *Burdine*'s description of *McDonnell Douglas* and the text at footnote 6.)

(ii) Plaintiff offers some believable evidence of each such factor; defendant moves to dismiss. (See *Burdine*'s text near footnote 7.)

(b) (i) After plaintiff's acceptable proof, defendant offers no proof of a legitimate non-discriminatory reason; is judgment required for plaintiff? (See *Burdine*'s footnote 7.) Such cases should be extremely rare after *Burdine*, correct?

(ii) After plaintiff's acceptable proof, defendant offers testimony of a legitimate non-discriminatory reason; plaintiff offers evidence of pretext; is judgment required for either party? Although *Burdine* suggested an answer here, see the last paragraph in § II of *Burdine*, the Supreme Court gave a direct answer in **Reeves v. Sanderson Plumbing Products, Inc.**, 530 U.S. 133, 120 S.Ct. 2097, 147 L.Ed.2d 105 (2000) (ADEA case applying *Burdine* test), indicating that such cases go to the jury or judge sitting as factfinder. The circumstantial evidence arising from the prima facie case, together with proof that the employer's response may be a lie, is adequate to support a judgment for the plaintiff—but does not require it.

According to *Reeves*, supra, in cases in which each party offers evidence on all issues (scenario (b)(ii)), the prima facie case rules simply organize the evidence, leaving the case to be decided on credibility of the witnesses or weight of the evidence. Do the rules do little beyond inducing parties to present all such evidence? Is that all they should do?

3. The degree to which the factfinder is free to decide each individual case was vividly illustrated in **St. Mary's Honor Center v. Hicks**, 509 U.S. 502, 113 S.Ct. 2742, 125 L.Ed.2d 407 (1993). In that case the plaintiff, a supervisor at a half-way house who lost his job allegedly because of his race, met his initial burden under *Burdine*, and the employer offered two nondiscriminatory reasons in rebuttal (severity and number of rules violations on the job). The judge sitting as factfinder disbelieved that the two reasons motivated the plaintiff's discharge, but based on all the evidence (including that blacks sat on the disciplinary review committee) he refused to rule for the plaintiff because he remained unconvinced that racial discrimination, rather than mere personal animosity, was the actual reason for the discharge. The Court of Appeals reversed, holding that disbelief of the defense's rebuttal reasons automatically entitled the plaintiff to a judgment in his favor. Justice Scalia's fiery opinion for a 5–4 majority reversed that holding, emphasizing that traditionally the burden-of-production issue only determines whether a party has enough evidence to get to the jury, not what the jury must find, 509 U.S. at 509–24, 113 S.Ct. at 2748–2756:

> "[T]he burden-of-production determination necessarily precedes the credibility-assessment stage. At the close of the defendant's case, the court is asked to decide whether an issue of fact remains for the trier of fact to determine. None does if, on the evidence presented, (1) any rational person would have to find the existence of the facts [required of plaintiff under *McDonnell Douglas*], and (2) the defendant has failed to meet its burden of production [by submitting evidence which, "if true," would satisfy its rebuttal burden]. In that event, the court must award judgment to the plaintiff as a matter of law under Federal Rule of Civil Procedure 50(a)(1) (in the case of jury trials) or Federal Rule of Civil Procedure 52(c) (in the case of bench trials). If the defendant has failed to sustain its burden but reasonable minds could differ as to whether a preponderance of the evidence establishes the [plaintiff's facts under *McDonnell Douglas*], then a question of fact does remain, which the trier of fact will be called upon to answer.[3]

> "If, on the other hand, the defendant has succeeded in carrying its burden of production, the *McDonnell Douglas* framework—with its presumptions and burdens—is no longer relevant. To resurrect it later, after the trier of fact has determined that what was "produced" to meet the burden of production is not credible, flies in the face of our holding in Burdine that to rebut the presumption "[t]he defendant need not persuade the court that it was actually motivated by the proffered reasons." The presumption, having fulfilled its role of forcing the defendant to come forward with some response, simply drops out of the picture. The defendant's "production" (whatever its persuasive effect) having been made, the trier of fact proceeds to decide the ultimate question: whether

---

3. * * * As a practical matter, however, and in the real-life sequence of a trial, the defendant feels the "burden" not when the plaintiff's prima facie case is proved, but as soon as evidence of it is introduced. The defendant then knows that its failure to introduce evidence of a nondiscriminatory reason will cause judgment to go against it unless the plaintiff's prima facie case is held to be inadequate in law or fails to convince the factfinder. It is this practical coercion which causes the *McDonnell Douglas* presumption to function as a means of "arranging the presentation of evidence," Watson v. Fort Worth Bank & Trust. [Footnote by the Court—ed.]

plaintiff has proven "that the defendant intentionally discriminated against [him]" because of his race. The factfinder's disbelief of the reasons put forward by the defendant (particularly if disbelief is accompanied by a suspicion of mendacity) may, together with the elements of the prima facie case, suffice to show intentional discrimination. Thus, rejection of the defendant's proffered reasons will permit the trier of fact to infer the ultimate fact of intentional discrimination, and * * * "[n]o additional proof of discrimination is required [to support a finding for the plaintiff. But such a determination is only permitted, not required, because Title VII forbids discrimination, not lying.]"

* * *

"Title VII does not award damages against employers who cannot prove a nondiscriminatory reason for adverse employment action, but only against employers who are proven to have taken adverse employment action by reason of (in the context of the present case) race. That the employer's proffered reason is unpersuasive, or even obviously contrived, does not necessarily establish that the plaintiff's proffered reason of race is correct. That remains a question for the factfinder to answer, subject, of course, to appellate review—which should be conducted on remand in this case under the "clearly erroneous" standard of Federal Rule of Civil Procedure 52(a), see, e.g., Anderson v. Bessemer City, 470 U.S. 564, 573–576, 105 S.Ct. 1504, 1511–1513, 84 L.Ed.2d 518 (1985)."

(a) Consider, in light of the *St. Mary's* and *Reeves* decisions, the more sophisticated scenarios that could be added to those set out in ¶ 2 supra. First, assume a new line (c)(i) with the following scenario: Plaintiff presents evidence which if believed would satisfy the *McDonnell Douglas* factors, and defendant presents evidence which if believed would satisfy his need to show a legitimate non-discriminatory reason; no evidence of pretext is submitted. Can the defendant get an automatic judgment, or does the plaintiff get to have the factfinder decide the case?

(b) Now consider an alternative scenario, that in *St. Mary's* itself, where the factfinder disbelieves the defendant, but is permitted to rule for him nevertheless if he believes that there was in fact no discrimination. Does this not place every plaintiff in danger of losing even after they have shown all possible circumstantial evidence in their favor? Is this fair? Are both Scenarios (c)(i) and (c)(ii) equally fair because both put the parties equally at the mercy of the witnesses and the factfinder? Is the *St. Mary's* case, paradoxically, a pro-plaintiff case? If Justice Scalia is to be believed, then a jury may believe that actual discrimination exists whenever a plaintiff proves a mere prima facie case—thus subjecting the employer to trial and potential judgment in every case where only that evidence is offered, correct?

(c) Assuming that the factfinder is a judge, as traditionally was the case under Title VII, how do you think that most factfinders would rule in Scenarios (c)(i) and (c)(ii)? How likely is it that a judge would rule against an employer who has lied, unless there is other evidence in the record, as in *St. Mary's*, suggesting an absence of discrimination? How likely is it that a judge as factfinder would rule in favor of the plaintiff when all he has offered is evidence under *McDonnell Douglas* that was met by a plausible reason for not employing the plaintiff?

4. Title VII cases have traditionally been tried without a jury, see the Note on Discretionary Relief, section C of this Chapter, infra, but the Civil Rights Act of 1991 makes all employment-related disparate treatment claims for damages triable by jury. See Civil Rights Act of 1991, § 102(c), set out in the Appendix and codified at 42 U.S.C. § 1981A.[2] How do the *Burdine* rules operate in the context of juries?

(a) The classic view of production burdens is that they only guide the judge's determination as to whether a case should go to the jury. See F. James, Jr., G. Hazard, Jr., and J. Leubsdorf, CIVIL PROCEDURE ¶ 7.15 (2001). Should a judge never say the phrase "burden of production" in charging the jury in a Title VII case? Consider this view: "If the plaintiff puts on no believable evidence of the *McDonnell Douglas* factors, he must suffer an adverse judgment as a matter of law under FRCP 50(a) (formerly called a 'directed verdict'). Similarly, if the defendant offers no evidence of a believable non-discriminatory reason, it must sufferer an adverse judgment as a matter of law under FRCP 50(a). If both parties offer all the evidence foreseen in *Burdine*, then nothing is said about production burdens and the jury is simply charged to find if there was intentional racial discrimination present, with plaintiff bearing the persuasion burden on this issue." Is this the correct view, or are plaintiff and defendant entitled also to instructions reflecting the scenarios discussed in paragraph 3(a–b) supra? See Farley v. Nationwide Mut. Ins. Co., 197 F.3d 1322 (11th Cir.1999).[3]

(b) If the fully tried case leaves factfinding authority with the jury, how do you think that juries will rule in most cases? Will they be more pro-plaintiff in age discrimination cases under the ADEA? How will juries likely behave in cases of racial and sex discrimination? Does the answer to the latter question turn on the demographics of the jury or the political views of the jury venire? If predominantly black juries (in large cities) are more likely to rule for plaintiffs in racial discrimination cases, and if predominantly non-minority juries are more likely to rule for defendants in racial discrimination cases, will Title VII help least those who need it most and most those who may need it least? Would a risk-averse employer be wise to re-locate to a region having few minorities?

(c) How should the *Burdine–St. Mary's* rules interplay with summary judgment standards? If a defendant submits a proper affidavit disclosing a non-discriminatory reason, and plaintiff files no counter affidavit, is the employer entitled to summary judgment? Or does the issue of credibility of the employer's reason remain for trial after *St. Mary's*? See Cornwell v. Electra Cent. Credit Union, 439 F.3d 1018 (9th Cir. 2006) ("[M]any of our cases state that a plaintiff may defeat a defendant's motion for summary

2. Race-based disparate treatment claims for damages were already available to plaintiffs under § 1981. See Chapter 2 supra.

3. In other words, is plaintiff entitled to an instruction that if the jury believes his evidence and does not believe the defendant's reasons, that is sufficient evidence to permit a verdict for plaintiff, provided the jury believes there was actual discrimination present? Is defendant entitled to an instruction that even if the jury disbelieves its offered reasons, the jury may nevertheless rule for the defendant if it believes that there was no actual discrimination present?

judgment by offering proof that the employer's legitimate, nondiscriminatory reason is actually a pretext for racial discrimination"; failure to present such evidence results in summary judgment against plaintiff); Combs v. Plantation Patterns, 106 F.3d 1519, 1538 (11th Cir.1997) (discussing circuit conflicts over the circumstances in which plaintiff may avoid a summary judgment when defendant files an affidavit offering non-discriminatory reasons). See generally Celotex Corp. v. Catrett, 477 U.S. 317, 106 S.Ct. 2548, 91 L.Ed.2d 265 (1986) (discussing summary judgment in non-employment context).

(d) Do the *Burdine–St. Mary's* rules, whether in the context of judge or jury as a factfinder, assume that intentional racial discrimination is not the norm in American society and that each case must be judged on its own facts? Do you agree? If intentional racial discrimination is not the norm, does the "clearly erroneous" standard of appellate review (or "any evidence" standard for juries) nevertheless devolve too much discretion on trial court judges and juries, leaving them free to make eccentric judgments? See Hopkins v. Price Waterhouse, 920 F.2d 967, 982 (D.C. Cir.1990) (Henderson, J., concurring) (trial court's refusal to believe offered reason of plaintiff's personality faults, despite uncontested proof that she "screamed obscenities" at fellow employee, reluctantly sustained); Sheehan v. Purolator, Inc., 839 F.2d 99, 105 (2d Cir.1988) (finding of no discrimination despite admission of sex stereotyping reluctantly sustained).

INTERNATIONAL BROTHERHOOD OF TEAMSTERS v. UNITED STATES

Supreme Court of the United States, 1977.
431 U.S. 324, 97 S.Ct. 1843, 52 L.Ed.2d 396.

MR. JUSTICE STEWART delivered the opinion of the Court.

This litigation brings here several important questions under Title VII of the Civil Rights Act of 1964. The issues grow out of alleged unlawful employment practices engaged in by an employer [T.I.M.E.–D.C.] and a union. The employer is a common carrier of motor freight with nationwide operations, and the union represents a large group of its employees. [The government filed two suits consolidated under this decision, one for discrimination against blacks and the other for discrimination against Spanish-surnamed persons.]

The central claim in both lawsuits was that the company had engaged in a pattern or practice of discriminating against minorities in hiring so-called line drivers. Those Negroes and Spanish-surnamed persons who had been hired, the Government alleged, were given lower paying, less desirable jobs as servicemen or local city drivers, and were thereafter discriminated against with respect to promotions and transfers.[4] * * *

---

4. *Line drivers,* also known as over-the-road drivers, engage in long-distance hauling between company terminals. They compose a separate bargaining unit at T.I.M.E.–D.C. Other distinct bargaining units include *servicemen,* who service trucks, unhook tractors and trailers, and perform similar tasks; and *city operations,* composed of dockmen, hostlers, and city drivers who pick up and deliver freight within the immediate area of a particular terminal. All of these employees were represented by the petitioner International Brotherhood of Teamsters.

The cases went to trial and the District Court found that the Government had shown "by a preponderance of the evidence that T.I.M.E.–D.C. and its predecessor companies were engaged in a plan and practice of discrimination in violation of Title VII * * *." [The court of appeals affirmed this finding.]

* * *

II

In this Court the company and the union contend that their conduct did not violate Title VII in any respect, asserting * * * that the evidence introduced at trial was insufficient to show that the company engaged in a "pattern or practice" of employment discrimination. * * *

A

Consideration of the question whether the company engaged in a pattern or practice of discriminatory hiring practices involves controlling legal principles that are relatively clear. The Government's theory of discrimination was simply that the company, in violation of § 703(a) of Title VII, regularly and purposefully treated Negroes and Spanish-surnamed Americans less favorably than white persons. The disparity in treatment allegedly involved the refusal to recruit, hire, transfer, or promote minority group members on an equal basis with white people, particularly with respect to line-driving positions. The ultimate factual issues are thus simply whether there was a pattern or practice of such disparate treatment and, if so, whether the differences were "racially premised." McDonnell Douglas Corp. v. Green.

As the plaintiff, the Government bore the initial burden of making out a prima facie case of discrimination. And, because it alleged a system-wide pattern or practice of resistance to the full enjoyment of Title VII rights, the Government ultimately had to prove more than the mere occurrence of isolated or "accidental" or sporadic discriminatory acts. It had to establish by a preponderance of the evidence that racial discrimination was the company's standard operating procedure—the regular rather than the unusual practice.[16]

We agree with the District Court and the Court of Appeals that the Government carried its burden of proof. As of March 31, 1971, shortly after the Government filed its complaint alleging system-wide discrimination, the company had 6,472 employees. Of these, 314 (5%) were Negroes and 257 (4%) were Spanish-surnamed Americans. Of the 1,828 line drivers, however, there were only 8 (0.4%) Negroes and 5 (0.3%) Spanish-surnamed persons, and all of the Negroes had been hired after the litigation had commenced. With one exception—a man who worked as a

---

16. The "pattern or practice" language in § 707(a) of Title VII, was not intended as a term of art, and the words reflect only their usual meaning. Senator Humphrey explained:

"[A] pattern or practice would be present only where the denial of rights consists of something more than an isolated, sporadic incident, but is repeated, routine, or of a generalized nature. * * *"

line driver at the Chicago terminal from 1950 to 1959—the company and its predecessors *did not employ a Negro on a regular basis as a line driver until 1969.* And, as the Government showed, even in 1971 there were terminals in areas of substantial Negro population where all of the company's line drivers were white.[17] A great majority of the Negroes (83%) and Spanish-surnamed Americans (78%) who did work for the company held the lower-paying city operations and serviceman jobs, whereas only 39% of the nonminority employees held jobs in those categories.

The Government bolstered its statistical evidence with the testimony of individuals who recounted over 40 specific instances of discrimination. Upon the basis of this testimony the District Court found that "[n]umerous qualified black and Spanish-surnamed American applicants who sought line-driving jobs at the company over the years had their requests ignored, were given false or misleading information about requirements, opportunities, and application procedures, or were not considered and hired on the same basis that whites were considered and hired." Minority employees who wanted to transfer to line-driver jobs met with similar difficulties.

The company's principal response to this evidence is that statistics can never in and of themselves prove the existence of a pattern or practice of discrimination, or even establish a prima facie case shifting to the employer the burden of rebutting the inference raised by the figures. But, as even our brief summary of the evidence shows, this was not a case in which the Government relied on "statistics alone." The individuals who testified about their personal experiences with the company brought the cold numbers convincingly to life.

In any event, our cases make it unmistakably clear that "[s]tatistical analyses have served and will continue to serve an important role" in cases in which the existence of discrimination is a disputed issue. Mayor of Philadelphia v. Educational Equality League, 415 U.S. 605, 620, 94 S.Ct. 1323, 1333, 39 L.Ed.2d 630. See also McDonnell Douglas Corp. v. Green. Cf. Washington v. Davis, [Chapter 1B.5 supra]. We have repeatedly approved the use of statistical proof, where it reached proportions comparable to those in this case, to establish a prima facie case of racial discrimination in jury selection cases, see, e.g., Turner v. Fouche, 396 U.S. 346, 359, 90 S.Ct. 532, 539, 24 L.Ed.2d 567 (1970) [; cf. Chapter 1B.5 supra]. Statistics are equally competent in proving employment discrimination.[20] We caution only that statistics are not irrefutable; they come in

---

17. In Atlanta, for instance, Negroes composed 22.35% of the population in the surrounding metropolitan area and 51.31% of the population in the city proper. The company's Atlanta terminal employed 57 line drivers. All were white. In Los Angeles, 10.84% of the greater metropolitan population and 17.88% of the city population were Negro. But at the company's two Los Angeles terminals there was not a single Negro among the 374 line drivers. The proof showed similar disparities in San Francisco, Denver, Nashville, Chicago, Dallas, and at several other terminals.

20. Petitioners argue that statistics, at least those comparing the racial composition of an employer's work force to the composition of the population at large, should never be given

infinite variety and, like any other kind of evidence, they may be rebutted. In short, their usefulness depends on all of the surrounding facts and circumstances.

* * *

The District Court and the Court of Appeals, on the basis of substantial evidence, held that the Government had proved a prima facie case of systematic and purposeful employment discrimination, continuing well beyond the effective date of Title VII. The company's attempts to rebut that conclusion[23] were held to be inadequate.[24] For the reasons we have summarized, there is no warrant for this Court to disturb the findings of the District Court and the Court of Appeals on this basic issue.

* * *

[Vacated and remanded on other grounds.]

---

decisive weight in a Title VII case because to do so would conflict with § 703(j) of the Act, 42 U.S.C.A. § 2000e–2(j). That section provides:

> "Nothing contained in this subchapter shall be interpreted to require any employer * * * to grant preferential treatment to any individual or to any group because of the race * * * or national origin of such individual or group on account of an imbalance which may exist with respect to the total number or percentage of persons of any race * * * or national origin employed by any employer * * * in comparison with the total number or percentage of persons of such race * * * or national origin in any community, State, section, or other area, or in the available work force in any community, State, section, or other area."

The argument fails in this case because the statistical evidence was not offered or used to support an erroneous theory that Title VII requires an employer's work force to be racially balanced. Statistics showing racial or ethnic imbalance are probative in a case such as this one only because such imbalance is often a telltale sign of purposeful discrimination; absent explanation, it is ordinarily to be expected that nondiscriminatory hiring practices will in time result in a work force more or less representative of the racial and ethnic composition of the population in the community from which employees are hired. Evidence of longlasting and gross disparity between the composition of a work force and that of the general population thus may be significant even though § 703(j) makes clear that Title VII imposes no requirement that a work force mirror the general population. See, e.g., United States v. Sheet Metal Workers Local 36, 416 F.2d 123, 127 n. 7 (C.A.8 [1969]). * * *

23. The company's narrower attacks upon the statistical evidence—that there was no precise delineation of the areas referred to in the general population statistics, that the Government did not demonstrate that minority populations were located close to terminals or that transportation was available, that the statistics failed to show what portion of the minority population was suited by age, health, or other qualifications to hold trucking jobs, etc.—are equally lacking in force. At best, these attacks go only to the accuracy of the comparison between the composition of the company's work force at various terminals and the general population of the surrounding communities. They detract little from the Government's further showing that Negroes and Spanish-surnamed Americans who were hired were overwhelmingly excluded from line-driver jobs. * * *

In any event, fine tuning of the statistics could not have obscured the glaring absence of minority line drivers. As the Court of Appeals remarked, the company's inability to rebut the inference of discrimination came not from a misuse of statistics but from "the inexorable zero." 517 F.2d at 315. [Repositioned footnote.]

24. The company's evidence, apart from the showing of recent changes in hiring and promotion policies, consisted mainly of general statements that it hired only the best qualified applicants. But "affirmations of good faith in making individual selections are insufficient to dispel a prima facie case of systematic exclusion." Alexander v. Louisiana, 405 U.S. 625, 632, 92 S.Ct. 1221, 1226, 31 L.Ed.2d 536. * * *

NOTE ON THE PRIMA FACIE CASE FOR CLASS CLAIMS

1. In **Bazemore v. Friday**, 478 U.S. 385, 106 S.Ct. 3000, 92 L.Ed.2d 315 (1986), the Supreme Court unanimously held that the same organization of proof as used in the *Teamsters* case would also apply to class claims of disparate treatment. 478 U.S. at 397–98, 106 S.Ct. at 3007–08. Consider initially the showing required of the plaintiffs, statistical proof that their class is under-represented in the employer's hiring.[1]

(a) Is this the kind of bottom-line proof rejected in the *Wards Cove* case, section A of this Chapter, supra? If so, why would such proof be acceptable here? Because it only raises an inference of intentional discrimination, one that can be rebutted? See E.E.O.C. v. Joe's Stone Crab, Inc., 220 F.3d 1263 (11th Cir. 2000) (discussing difference between purpose of statistics in disparate impact and disparate treatment cases).

(b) Why does such statistical proof raise an inference of discrimination? Footnote 20 appears to rely on the statistical concept of random selection: if all hires were randomly drawn from among applicants, one would expect the percentage of blacks actually hired to be roughly the same as the percentage of blacks in the applicant pool.[2] If the percentages are noticeably different, one should be suspicious—and in American society, that means suspicious that racial considerations have infected the decisionmaking process. Is this any different from the reason that an inference arises in individual disparate treatment cases? See the *Burdine* case supra (discussing *Furnco Construction Co. v. Waters*).[3]

2. The employer must respond to the prima facie proof, says Justice Stewart, by offering more than mere denials that it intentionally discriminated. See footnote 24. What type of proof would satisfy the Court?

(a) In an individual disparate treatment case, an employer gives a legitimate non-discriminatory reason for not hiring the individual plaintiff, but an employer cannot ordinarily do that in class cases because of the volume of decisions. Thus the defendant must resort itself to statistical proof, ordinarily, to show that some other factor, or set of factors, is also consistent with the statistical results. See, e.g., Croker v. Boeing Co., 662 F.2d 975 (3d Cir.1981) (en banc) (apparent underrepresentation of blacks also consistent with hiring more experienced workers, rebutting inference of intentional discrimination).

---

1. It is sometimes possible to prove a class disparate-treatment claim by use of direct evidence, just as in an individual disparate treatment claim. See, e.g., Alexander v. Local 496, Laborers' Intern. Union of North America, 177 F.3d 394 (6th Cir.1999) (union admittedly granted waivers to whites, permitting their employment without experience, and denied the same waivers to blacks). *Teamsters'* model for proving illegal intent circumstantially need not be used in such cases.

2. *Teamsters'* focus on population-based data would find a chilly reception in most more recent decisions, and its focus on simple comparisons rather than multiple-regressions would probably be deemed a bit quaint. See Caridad v. Metro–North Commuter Railroad, 191 F.3d 283 (2d Cir.1999) (multiple regression analysis of actual job decisions controls for and thus is designed to exclude, possible explanations for any disparity). Why are population-based analyses less reliable? Because general population data do not reflect any possible differentials in qualifications (from skills to age distribution) of those actually available for work? Should courts presume that all racial, ethnic, and sex-based populations have the same job-related demographics?

3. Is there something special about the "inexorable zero," is it just another example of statistical proof? See generally, Note, The "Inexorable Zero," 117 HARV. L. REV. 1215 (2004) (noting that some courts attach special meaning to the zero, while others consider the zero important only if it comports with generally accepted statistical methods of analysis).

Is this burden too great? Or is it only commensurate with the cost a plaintiff must bear to establish the inference initially?

(b) Does *Teamsters'* focus on statistics, and a defendant's subsequent statistical defense, focus courts' attention too much on racial ratios? In footnote 20 in *Teamsters* the Court states that its approach does not run afoul § 703(j). Do you agree? But without statistical proofs, how will plaintiffs be able to prove discrimination when there is no "smoking gun," no direct evidence of intent to discriminate?

3. If only an inference of intentional discrimination arises from the statistical proof, what evidentiary burdens are created by the *Teamsters* case? In **Bazemore v. Friday**, supra, the Court held that the burdens in class cases also parallel those developed in *Burdine* for individual cases. Review of the trial court's factfinding is also by the same clearly erroneous standard as used in individual disparate treatment cases. 478 U.S., at 398–400, 106 S.Ct., at 3007–09.

(a) Does *Teamsters'* focus on statistics, when joined with *Bazemore's* evidentiary burdens, mean that trial in these cases will be a battle among statistical experts? And will appellate review be distant at best? Compare Munoz v. Orr, 200 F.3d 291 (5th Cir.2000) (evidence from plaintiff's expert rejected for admission, affirmed as not clearly erroneous for both disparate impact and disparate treatment claims), with Caridad v. Metro–North Commuter Railroad, 191 F.3d 283 (2d Cir.1999) (judgment regarding experts reversed and class certification ordered in disparate treatment case).

(b) Will this permit trial judges to roll their eyes at the blur of statistics and rule virtually as they see fit? See Bazemore, 478 U.S., at 403–04 & n. 15, 106 S.Ct., at 3010–11 & n. 15. Cf. Kumho Tire Co., Ltd. v. Carmichael, 526 U.S. 137, 119 S.Ct. 1167, 1176, 143 L.Ed.2d 238 (1999) (general power to rule on expert testimony gives some leeway to the trial judge). In the preceding Note, it was suggested that perhaps highly localized decisionmaking, laxly reviewed on appeal, may be appropriate for individual disparate treatment cases. Is the same true for class cases?

(c) In response to the rigors of statistical trials, some circuits appear to have raised the bar for plaintiffs to avoid summary judgment. See, e.g., Morgan v. United Parcel Service of America, Inc., 380 F.3d 459 (8th Cir. 2004): "Typically in a case like this one, plaintiffs will offer statistical evidence of disparities between protected and unprotected employees who are otherwise similarly situated[, and in] defense, employers attempt to show that the plaintiffs' 'proof is either inaccurate or insignificant.' To be legally sufficient, the plaintiffs' statistical evidence 'must show a disparity of treatment, *eliminate the most common nondiscriminatory explanations of the disparity, and thus permit the inference that, absent other explanation, the disparity more likely than not resulted from illegal discrimination"* (emphasis added). Does this approach require the plaintiff both to prove a prima facie case and disprove any rebuttal, even before it is offered? Under *Burdine*, in an individual disparate treatment case, a plaintiff can probably avoid summary judgment without proof of pretext; why should the rule be different here? Because the plaintiff must show that discrimination is the general practice and not an isolated one?

(d) How should the availability of jury trials and damage remedies under the **Civil Rights Act of 1991** affect use of the *Teamsters* model? Is *Teamsters* unworkable for juries? Are class-wide damages inappropriate for jury trial? See Cooper v. Southern Co., 390 F.3d 695 (11th Cir. 2004) (class claims for damages are difficult to certify); Allison v. Citgo Petroleum Corp., 151 F.3d 402 (5th Cir.1998) (2–1 decision).

4. The Court's decision in **Wal-Mart Stores, Inc. v. Dukes**, ___ U.S. ___, 131 S.Ct. 2541, 180 L.Ed.2d 374 (2011), appears to limit class claims made on a disparate treatment theory. Plaintiffs's 1.5 million-member class action claimed that Wal-Mart vested local managers with discretion to set wages and make promotions and that local managers engaged in sex discrimination in the exercise of this discretion; upper management's knowledge and tolerance of the situation, plaintiffs claimed, amounted to disparate treatment. As reported by Justice Scalia, ___ U.S. at 131, 2548 S.Ct. at ___, the plaintiffs "claim that the discrimination to which they have been subjected is common to all Wal–Mart's female employees [and that the company's] strong and uniform 'corporate culture' permits bias against women to infect, perhaps subconsciously, the discretionary decisionmaking of each one of Wal–Mart's thousands of managers—thereby making every woman at the company the victim of one common discriminatory practice." The Court rejected class certification under FRCP 23, ___ U.S. at ___, 131 S.Ct. at 2551, noting that

> Quite obviously, the mere claim by employees of the same company that they have suffered a Title VII injury, * * * gives no cause to believe that all their claims can productively be litigated at once. Their claims must depend upon a common contention—for example, the assertion of discriminatory bias on the part of the same supervisor. That common contention, moreover, must be of such a nature that it is capable of classwide resolution—which means that determination of its truth or falsity will resolve an issue that is central to the validity of each one of the claims in one stroke.

(a) On the precise issue of Wal-Mart's practices, the Court ruled that the company's policy of pushing decisions to a lower level where managers would make different decisions on many different bases negated a finding of common factors affecting every decision. Indeed, the Court went so far as to presume that devolving decisionmaking to local managers was non-discriminatory policy. Does *Wal–Mart* effectively restrict class actions to local stores, where the class would consist of those women harmed by a local manager's common acts of sex discrimination?

(b) Perhaps more significantly for disparate treatment cases, the *Wal-Mart* Court also rejected use of Rule 23(b) class actions to recover backpay when not incidental to injunctive relief. Rule 23(b) is only available when a defendant has acted "on grounds that apply generally to the class," and the Court held that classwide backpay claims are impermissible for broad reasons: "It does not authorize class certification when each individual class member would be entitled to a different injunction or declaratory judgment [or] an individualized [monetary] award." Does *Wal–Mart* doom all (large) class actions for disparate treatment because all damages awards would be different?

5. Although most cases involve primary claims of disparate treatment relating to terms and conditions of employment, Title VII also covers one other major category of disparate treatment claims, those for retaliation. See 42 U.S.C. § 2000e–3(a) (prohibiting "discriminat[ion] against" an employee or job applicant who has "made a charge, testified, assisted, or participated in" a Title VII proceeding or investigation). In recent years the Supreme Court has interpreted this provision quite broadly. In Burlington Northern & Santa Fe Railway Co. v. White, 548 U.S. 53, 126 S.Ct. 2405, 165 L.Ed.2d 345(2006), the Court held that the anti-retaliation section covers even minor sanctions that otherwise might not be actionable under Title VII's primary provisions because the retaliation section covers not just employment but actions intended to punish workers for making claims. Moreover, in Crawford v. Metropolitan Government of Nashville and Davidson County, 555 U.S. 271, 129 S.Ct. 846, 172 L.Ed.2d 650 (2009), the Court held that the anti-retaliation section protected even statements made during an internal investigation by the employer concerning conduct by other employees. Finally, in Thompson v. North American Stainless, LP, 562 U.S. ___, 131 S.Ct. 863, 178 L.Ed.2d 694 (2011), the Court approved an employee's claim based on his allegation that he had been fired to retaliate against his fiancee's filing of a Title VII complaint; he was a "person aggrieved" by an attempt to punish his fiancee. As Professor Zerht has pointed out, Lynn Ridgeway Zehrt, *Retaliation's Changing Landscape*, 20 GEO. MASON U. CIV. RTS. L.J. 143 (2010), the Court has broadened its view of actionable retaliation claims along a long statutory arc.[4] What explains this generous view of these claims of disparate treatment?

(b) Defenses

PRICE WATERHOUSE v. HOPKINS

Supreme Court of the United States, 1989.
490 U.S. 228, 109 S.Ct. 1775, 104 L.Ed.2d 268.

JUSTICE BRENNAN announced the judgment of the Court and delivered an opinion, in which JUSTICE MARSHALL, JUSTICE BLACKMUN, and JUSTICE STEVENS join.

[When the partners at Price Waterhouse, an accounting firm, deferred her for partnership and later refused to make her an offer, Ms. Hopkins sued under Title VII for intentional sex discrimination. She was supported by partners in her local office, primarily based on her work in securing a $25 million contract with the State Department, but overall reviews of her work were mixed. "The partners in Hopkins' office praised her character as well as her accomplishments, describing her in their joint statement as 'an outstanding professional' who had a 'deft touch,' a 'strong character, independence and integrity.'" But several partners complained that Hopkins had an abrasive personality, especially with staff members working under her.]

---

4. Cf. CBOCS West, Inc. v. Humphries, 553 U.S. 442, 128 S.Ct. 1951, 170 L.Ed.2d 864 (2008) (§ 1981 can also be used for retaliation claims); Gomez–Perez v. Potter, 553 U.S. 474, 128 S.Ct. 1931, 170 L.Ed.2d 887 (2008) (ADEA covers retaliation claims).

There were clear signs, though, that some of the partners reacted negatively to Hopkins' personality because she was a woman. One partner described her as "macho" (Defendant's Exh. 30); another suggested that she "overcompensated for being a woman" (Defendant's Exh. 31); a third advised her to take "a course at charm school" (Defendant's Exh. 27). Several partners criticized her use of profanity; in response, one partner suggested that those partners objected to her swearing only "because it[']s a lady using foul language." Tr. 321. Another supporter explained that Hopkins "ha[d] matured from a tough-talking somewhat masculine hard-nosed mgr to an authoritative, formidable, but much more appealing lady ptr candidate." Defendant's Exh. 27. But it was the man who, as Judge Gesell found, bore responsibility for explaining to Hopkins the reasons for the Policy Board's decision to place her candidacy on hold who delivered the *coup de grace*: in order to improve her chances for partnership, Thomas Beyer advised, Hopkins should "walk more femininely, talk more femininely, dress more femininely, wear make-up, have her hair styled, and wear jewelry." 618 F.Supp. at 1117.

Dr. Susan Fiske, a social psychologist and Associate Professor of Psychology at Carnegie–Mellon University, testified at trial that the partnership selection process at Price Waterhouse was likely influenced by sex stereotyping. * * * According to Fiske, Hopkins' uniqueness (as the only woman in the pool of candidates) and the subjectivity of the evaluations made it likely that sharply critical remarks such as these were the product of sex stereotyping—although Fiske admitted that she could not say with certainty whether any particular comment was the result of stereotyping. * * *

[Although the trial court held that "abrasiveness" was a legitimate concern for the firm, he] went on to decide, however, that some of the partners' remarks about Hopkins stemmed from an impermissibly cabined view of the proper behavior of women, and that Price Waterhouse had done nothing to disavow reliance on such comments. He held that Price Waterhouse had unlawfully discriminated against Hopkins on the basis of sex by consciously giving credence and effect to partners' comments that resulted from sex stereotyping. Noting that Price Waterhouse could avoid equitable relief by proving by clear and convincing evidence that it would have placed Hopkins' candidacy on hold even absent this discrimination, the judge decided that the firm had not carried this heavy burden. [The Court of Appeals affirmed.]

II

The specification of the standard of causation under Title VII is a decision about the kind of conduct that violates that statute. According to Price Waterhouse, an employer violates Title VII only if it gives decisive consideration to an employee's gender, race, national origin, or religion in making a decision that affects that employee. On Price Waterhouse's theory, even if a plaintiff shows that her gender played a part in an employment decision, it is still her burden to show that the decision would have been different if the employer had not discriminated. In Hopkins' view, on the other hand, an employer violates the statute whenever it allows one of these attributes to play any part in an employment decision. Once a plaintiff shows that this occurred, according to Hopkins, the employer's proof that it would have made the same decision in the absence of discrimination can serve to limit equitable relief but not to avoid a finding of liability. We conclude that, as often happens, the truth lies somewhere in-between.

* * *

Congress' intent to forbid employers to take gender into account in making employment decisions appears on the face of the statute. In now-familiar language, the statute forbids an employer to "fail or refuse to hire or to discharge any individual, or otherwise to discriminate with respect to his compensation, terms, conditions, or privileges of employment," or to "limit, segregate, or classify his employees or applicants for employment in any way which would deprive or tend to deprive any individual of employment opportunities or otherwise adversely affect his status as an employee, *because of* such individual's . . . sex." 42 U.S.C. §§ 2000e–2(a)(1), (2) (emphasis added). We take these words to mean that gender must be irrelevant to employment decisions. To construe the words "because of" as colloquial shorthand for "but-for causation," as does Price Waterhouse, is to misunderstand them.

But-for causation is a hypothetical construct. In determining whether a particular factor was a but-for cause of a given event, we begin by assuming that that factor was present at the time of the event, and then ask whether, even if that factor had been absent, the event nevertheless would have transpired in the same way. The present, active tense of the operative verbs of § 703(a)(1) ("to fail or refuse"), in contrast, turns our attention to the actual moment of the event in question, the adverse employment decision. The critical inquiry, the one commanded by the words of § 703(a)(1), is whether gender was a factor in the employment decision *at the moment it was made*. Moreover, since we know that the words "because of" do not mean "*solely* because of," we also know that Title VII meant to condemn even those decisions based on a mixture of legitimate and illegitimate considerations. When, therefore, an employer considers both gender and legitimate factors at the time of making a decision, that decision was "because of" sex and the other, legitimate considerations—even if we may say later, in the context of litigation, that the decision would have been the same if gender had not been taken into account.

* * *

To say that an employer may not take gender into account is not, however, the end of the matter, for that describes only one aspect of Title VII. The other important aspect of the statute is its preservation of an employer's remaining freedom of choice. We conclude that the preservation of this freedom means that an employer shall not be liable if it can prove that, even if it had not taken gender into account, it would have come to the same decision regarding a particular person. The statute's maintenance of employer prerogatives is evident from the statute itself and from its history, both in Congress and in this Court.

* * *

* * * We think these principles require that, once a plaintiff in a Title VII case shows that gender played a motivating part in an employment decision, the defendant may avoid a finding of liability[10] only by proving that it would have made the same decision even if it had not allowed gender to play such a role. This balance of burdens is the direct result of Title VII's balance of rights.

Our holding casts no shadow on *Burdine,* in which we decided that, even after a plaintiff has made out a prima facie case of discrimination under Title VII, the burden of persuasion does not shift to the employer to show that its stated legitimate reason for the employment decision was the true reason. [*Burdine* concerned analysis of whether intentional discrimination is present. The instant issue comes after such intent has been proved. *Burdine* also implicates a search for only one true intention, whereas here there are two claimed motivations—forbidden sex discrimination and a claim of concern for office interactions.]

In deciding as we do today, we do not traverse new ground. We have in the past confronted Title VII cases in which an employer has used an illegitimate criterion to distinguish among employees, and have held that it is the employer's burden to justify decisions resulting from that practice. When an employer has asserted that gender is a bona fide occupational qualification within the meaning of § 703(e), for example, we have assumed that it is the employer who must show why it must use gender as a criterion in employment. See Dothard v. Rawlinson, 433 U.S. 321, 332–37, 97 S.Ct. 2720, 2728–2730, 53 L.Ed.2d 786 (1977). * * *

---

10. Hopkins argues that once she made this showing, she was entitled to a finding that Price Waterhouse had discriminated against her on the basis of sex; as a consequence, she says, the partnership's proof could only limit the relief she received. She relies on Title VII's § 706(g), which permits a court to award affirmative relief when it finds that an employer "has intentionally engaged in or is intentionally engaging in an unlawful employment practice," and yet forbids a court to order reinstatement of, or backpay to, "an individual ... if such individual was refused ... employment or advancement or was suspended or discharged *for any reason other than* discrimination on account of race, color, religion, sex, or national origin." 42 U.S.C. § 2000e–5(g) (emphasis added). * * *

Without explicitly mentioning this portion of § 706(g), we have in the past held that Title VII does not authorize affirmative relief for individuals as to whom, the employer shows, the existence of systemic discrimination had no effect. See Franks v. Bowman Transportation Co., 424 U.S. 747, 772, 96 S.Ct. 1251, 1268, 47 L.Ed.2d 444 (1976); Teamsters v. United States, 431 U.S. 324, 367–71, 97 S.Ct. 1843, 1870–1873, 52 L.Ed.2d 396 (1977). These decisions suggest that the proper focus of § 706(g) is on claims of systemic discrimination, not on charges of individual discrimination. Cf. NLRB v. Transportation Management Corp., 462 U.S. 393, 103 S.Ct. 2469, 76 L.Ed.2d 667 (1983) (upholding the National Labor Relations Board's identical interpretation of § 10(c) of the National Labor Relations Act, 29 U.S.C. § 160(c), which contains language almost identical to § 706(g)).

We have reached a similar conclusion in other contexts where the law announces that a certain characteristic is irrelevant to the allocation of burdens and benefits. [See] Mt. Healthy City School Dist. Board of Education v. Doyle, 429 U.S. 274, 97 S.Ct. 568, 50 L.Ed.2d 471 (1977) [discussed in the Note on Intent and Causation, Chapter 1B.5 supra].
* * *

* * *

We have, in short, been here before. Each time, we have concluded that the plaintiff who shows that an impermissible motive played a motivating part in an adverse employment decision has thereby placed upon the defendant the burden to show that it would have made the same decision in the absence of the unlawful motive. Our decision today treads this well-worn path.

* * *

The courts below held that an employer who has allowed a discriminatory impulse to play a motivating part in an employment decision must prove by clear and convincing evidence that it would have made the same decision in the absence of discrimination. We are persuaded that the better rule is that the employer must make this showing by a preponderance of the evidence.

Conventional rules of civil litigation generally apply in Title VII cases, see, e.g., United States Postal Service Bd. of Governors v. Aikens, 460 U.S. 711, 716, 103 S.Ct. 1478, 1482, 75 L.Ed.2d 403 (1983) (discrimination not to be "treat[ed] ... differently from other ultimate questions of fact"), and one of these rules is that parties to civil litigation need only prove their case by a preponderance of the evidence. See, e.g., Herman & MacLean v. Huddleston, 459 U.S. 375, 390, 103 S.Ct. 683, 691, 74 L.Ed.2d 548 (1983). * * *

* * *

We hold that when a plaintiff in a Title VII case proves that her gender played a motivating part in an employment decision, the defendant may avoid a finding of liability only by proving by a preponderance of the evidence that it would have made the same decision even if it had not taken the plaintiff's gender into account. Because the courts below erred by deciding that the defendant must make this proof by clear and convincing evidence, we reverse the Court of Appeals' judgment against Price Waterhouse on liability and remand the case to that court for further proceedings.

It is so ordered.

JUSTICE WHITE, concurring in the judgment.

In my view, to determine the proper approach to causation in this case, we need look only to the Court's opinion in Mt. Healthy City School

District Bd. of Ed. v. Doyle, 429 U.S. 274, 97 S.Ct. 568, 50 L.Ed.2d 471 (1977). * * *

* * *

It is not necessary to get into semantic discussions on whether the *Mt. Healthy* approach is "but for" causation in another guise or creates an affirmative defense on the part of the employer to see its clear application to the issues before us in this case. As in *Mt. Healthy,* the District Court found that the employer was motivated by both legitimate and illegitimate factors. And here, as in *Mt. Healthy,* and as the Court now holds, Hopkins was not required to prove that the illegitimate factor was the only, principal, or true reason for the petitioner's action. Rather, as Justice O'Connor states, her burden was to show that the unlawful motive was a *substantial* factor in the adverse employment action. * * *

I agree with Justice Brennan that applying this approach to causation in Title VII cases is not a departure from and does not require modification of the Court's holdings in Texas Dept. of Community Affairs v. Burdine, and McDonnell Douglas Corp. v. Green. The Court has made clear that "mixed motive" cases, such as the present one, are different from pretext cases such as *McDonnell Douglas* and *Burdine.* In pretext cases, "the issue is whether either illegal or legal motives, but not both, were the 'true' motives behind the decision." NLRB v. Transportation Management Corp., 462 U.S. 393, 400, n. 5, 103 S.Ct. 2469, 2473, n. 5, 76 L.Ed.2d 667 (1983). In mixed motive cases, however, there is no one "true" motive behind the decision. Instead, the decision is a result of multiple factors, at least one of which is legitimate. It can hardly be said that our decision in this case is a departure from cases that are "inapposite." * * *

* * *

JUSTICE O'CONNOR, concurring in the judgment.

I agree with the plurality that on the facts presented in this case, the burden of persuasion should shift to the employer to demonstrate by a preponderance of the evidence that it would have reached the same decision concerning Ann Hopkins' candidacy absent consideration of her gender. I further agree that this burden shift is properly part of the liability phase of the litigation. I thus concur in the judgment of the Court. * * *

* * *

[However], I disagree with the plurality's dictum that the words "because of" do not mean "but-for" causation; manifestly they do. See Sheet Metal Workers v. EEOC, 478 U.S. 421, 499, 106 S.Ct. 3019, 3062, 92 L.Ed.2d 344 (1986) (White, J., dissenting) ("[T]he general policy under Title VII is to limit relief for racial discrimination in employment practices to actual victims of the discrimination"). We should not, and need not, deviate from that policy today. The question for decision in this case is what allocation of the burden of persuasion on the issue of causation best conforms with the intent of Congress and the purposes behind Title VII.

The evidence of congressional intent as to which party should bear the burden of proof on the issue of causation is considerably less clear. No doubt, as a general matter, Congress assumed that the plaintiff in a Title VII action would bear the burden of proof on the elements critical to his or her case. As the dissent points out, the interpretative memorandum submitted by sponsors of Title VII indicates that "the plaintiff, *as in any civil case,* would have the burden of proving that discrimination had occurred." 110 Cong.Rec. 7214 (1964) (emphasis added). But in the area of tort liability, from whence the dissent's "but-for" standard of causation is derived, the law has long recognized that in certain "civil cases" leaving the burden of persuasion on the plaintiff to prove "but-for" causation would be both unfair and destructive of the deterrent purposes embodied in the concept of duty of care. Thus, in multiple causation cases, where a breach of duty has been established, the common law of torts has long shifted the burden of proof to multiple defendants to prove that their negligent actions were not the "but-for" cause of the plaintiffs injury. See e.g., Summers v. Tice, 33 Cal.2d 80, 84–87, 199 P.2d 1, 3–4 (1948). The same rule has been applied where the effect of a defendant's tortious conduct combines with a force of unknown or innocent origin to produce the harm to the plaintiff. See Kingston v. Chicago & N.W.R. Co., 191 Wis. 610, 616, 211 N.W. 913, 915 (1927) ("Granting that the union of that fire [caused by defendant's negligence] with another of natural origin, or with another of much greater proportions, is available as a defense, the burden is on the defendant to show that ... the fire set by him was not the proximate cause of the damage"). See also 2 J. Wigmore, Select Cases on the Law of Torts, § 153, p. 865 (1912) ("When two or more persons by their acts are possibly the sole cause of a harm, or when two or more acts of the same person are possibly the sole cause, and the plaintiff has introduced evidence that one of the two persons, or one of the same person's two acts, is culpable, then the defendant has the burden of proving that the other person, or his other act, was the sole cause of the harm").

* * *

Where an individual disparate treatment plaintiff has shown by a preponderance of the evidence that an illegitimate criterion was a *substantial* factor in an adverse employment decision, the deterrent purpose of the statute has clearly been triggered. More importantly, as an evidentiary matter, a reasonable factfinder could conclude that absent further explanation, the employer's discriminatory motivation "caused" the employment decision. The employer has not yet been shown to be a violator, but neither is it entitled to the same presumption of good faith concerning its employment decisions which is accorded employers facing only circumstantial evidence of discrimination. Both the policies behind the statute, and the evidentiary principles developed in the analogous area of causation in the law of torts, suggest that at this point the employer may be required to convince the factfinder that, despite the smoke, there is no fire.

* * *

J<small>USTICE</small> K<small>ENNEDY</small>, with whom the C<small>HIEF</small> J<small>USTICE</small> and J<small>USTICE</small> S<small>CALIA</small> join, dissenting.

* * *

Our decisions confirm that Title VII is not concerned with the mere presence of impermissible motives; it is directed to employment decisions that result from those motives. The verbal formulae we have used in our precedents are synonymous with but-for causation. Thus we have said that providing different insurance coverage to male and female employees violates the statute by treating the employee " 'in a manner which but-for that person's sex would be different.' " Newport News Shipbuilding & Dry Dock Co. v. EEOC, 462 U.S. 669, 683, 103 S.Ct. 2622, 2631, 77 L.Ed.2d 89 (1983). We have described the relevant question as whether the employment decision was "based on" a discriminatory criterion, Teamsters v. United States, or whether the particular employment decision at issue was "made on the basis of" an impermissible factor, Cooper v. Federal Reserve Bank of Richmond, 467 U.S. 867, 875, 104 S.Ct. 2794, 2799, 81 L.Ed.2d 718 (1984).

* * *

The plurality [describes] the employer's showing as an "affirmative defense." This is nothing more than a label, and one not found in the language or legislative history of Title VII.

* * *

[A burden-shifting regime already exists under *Burdine*, and today's decision adds another burden-shifting device with different rules. This will cause needless confusion, especially in cases involving a jury trial.]

I do not believe the minor refinement in Title VII procedures accomplished by today's holding can justify the difficulties that will accompany it. Rather, I "remain confident that the *McDonnell Douglas* framework permits the plaintiff meriting relief to demonstrate intentional discrimination." *Burdine,* 450 U.S., at 258, 101 S.Ct., at 1096. Although the employer does not bear the burden of persuasion under *Burdine,* it must offer clear and reasonably specific reasons for the contested decision, and has every incentive to persuade the trier of fact that the decision was lawful. * * * In sum, the *Burdine* framework provides a "sensible, orderly way to evaluate the evidence in light of common experience as it bears on the critical question of discrimination," and it should continue to govern the order of proof in Title VII disparate treatment cases.

* * *

NOTE ON DEFENSES TO INTENTIONAL DISCRIMINATION

1. There are other textually demonstrable defenses to proven intentional discrimination under Title VII, e.g., the BFOQ ("bona fide occupational qualification") defense to intentional sex discrimination, discussed in section B.1 infra, but the mixed-motive defense is arguably more important because it is widely litigated and applies across the board to all claims. Despite the plurality's rather ethereal discussion of different theoretical bases of liability, a solid six-person majority agrees on the practical result: the mixed-motive or *Mt. Healthy* defense applies also in Title VII disparate treatment cases.

(a) Should analysis under Title VII be different because it has a statutory definition for discrimination? Do you agree with the dissent's argument that the statute makes intent a single issue for the plaintiff? Is this intuitively a single issue because both intent and mixed-motive bear on the issue of causation?

(b) Is the mixed-motive defense intuitively a separate issue because the defendant is, by admission at this stage of the case, already a wrongdoer— some intentional discrimination has been found? Is *Price Waterhouse* another example of the "bad man" theory of law—that law should be made to ensnare wrongdoers and prevent their evasions?

(c) If the *Price Waterhouse* defense turns on the already-established wrongdoing of the employer, is it not important to ensure that wrongdoing has been more than insubstantial? In other words, if an employer has mixed motives, is it important that the impermissible motive has been more than a de minimis element in the employer's decision?

2. Compare the Court's holding in *Price Waterhouse* with its decision in the *Wards Cove* case, section A of this Chapter, supra. Why does the Court treat a second, alternative motive as an affirmative defense, with a new burden-of-persuasion allocation?

3. Transactionally, how does the mixed-motive defense relate to the analytical method adopted for individual disparate treatment claims under *Burdine*? Assume that a plaintiff presents evidence of qualification sufficient to raise an inference of discrimination, then the employer responds with two presentations: first, it failed to hire plaintiff because of a legitimate non-discriminatory reason, and second, even if an illegal intent did creep into its decisionmaking, it nevertheless would not in any event have hired the plaintiff for the same non-discriminatory reason.

(a) What burden falls on the employer for the first presentation? For the second? If an employer is unable to show that it lacked a discriminatory motive when it has no persuasion burden, is it likely to prevail on the mixed-motive defense where it does bear that burden?

(b) Tactically, is an employer better advised to pretermit one presentation or the other? While inconsistent pleading is permitted, apparently inconsistent factual presentations undermine one's credibility before a factfinder, do they not?

(c) Why should there be any defense for mixed motives in a Title VII case? Do you agree with the plurality that the statutory language implies a causation-based defense?

4. The mixed-motive defense excuses the employer from liability, as noted in *Price Waterhouse* (calling it an "affirmative defense") when it had at the time of the original decision a separate and independent motivation for acting against the plaintiff. In the later case of **McKennon v. Nashville Banner Pub. Co.**, 513 U.S. 352, 115 S.Ct. 879, 130 L.Ed.2d 852 (1995), the Court unanimously recognized a more limited defense for "after-acquired evidence," that is information discovered after the original decision that could have excuse the decision had it been known at the time of the original decision. Thus the plaintiff's misconduct in removing confidential materials from the office, only discovered after she was discharged, could operate as a defense against her even though it could not have motivated her employer's discharge of her. In recognizing the defense, the Court limited its effect to that of precluding important monetary relief (such as reinstatement and backpay) after the date such evidence was discovered.

(a) What is the justification for the "after-acquired evidence" defense? Is it, like *Price Waterhouse* (and *Mt. Healthy*) essentially a recognition of what has "caused" the plaintiff's harm? Is it a rule about proximate cause?

(b) Does *McKennon* seriously weaken *Price Waterhouse*? Does it not allow every discriminator to cut its losses by hiring a private investigator to dig up dirt on the plaintiff after she files suit, thus limiting her recovery? Will plaintiffs be deterred from suing because they know that going to court will invite defendants to start researching their backgrounds?

(c) Although called a limited defense against certain relief, is not that relief exactly what the plaintiff would ordinarily want? If the defendant acts quickly, little or no damages will have accrued by the time the after-acquired evidence is discovered, right? Who wins under *McKennon*, the plaintiff's attorney because she will recover her fees since the plaintiff will technically win her claim?

5. In a bit of irony, Congress concluded that Justice Brennan's opinion in *Price Waterhouse* was an example of the conservative Supreme Court's evisceration of Title VII, and in § 107 of the **Civil Rights Act of 1991** it overrode that decision. Now the mixed-motive defense operates only to limit monetary relief and reinstatement, leaving declaratory judgments and attorneys fees available to the plaintiff who has otherwise won on the merits.

(a) Why should the plaintiff receive no monetary award when the mixed-motive defense is successfully proved? Would any monetary award be an undeserved windfall? Even if it is, would it not deter future intentionally discriminatory conduct by the defendant? Does § 107 try to steer a middle course that might accomplish both the goal of preventing windfalls and deterring further misconduct? (Or did Congress act for the less noble, but practical, purpose of preserving attorneys fees for a lawyer after his client's apparently winnable case is blown up by unforeseen assertion of the mixed-motive defense?)

(b) What is the relation between the mixed-motive defense and the "after-acquired evidence" defense in light of § 107? Does one limit relief from the moment the original decision was made and the other only from the moment information was acquired? Other than timing, is the impact of the two defenses the same? Should Congress bar use of the after-acquired-evidence defense?

6. After passage of the 1991 Act, the Supreme Court has twice faced cases that required interpretation of the mixed-motive provision in § 107. Both favored plaintiffs.

(a) How should the mixed-motive defense interact with the prima facie case rules of *Burdine*? Some circuits held that Title VII requires "direct evidence" of discrimination in order for the plaintiff to benefit from § 107; circumstantial evidence under Burdine was deemed inadequate to shift the burden to defendant under § 107. The Supreme Court rejected this approach in **Desert Palace, Inc. v. Costa**, 539 U.S. 90, 123 S.Ct. 2148, 156 L.Ed.2d 84 (2003). After *Desert Palace*, how should a trial judge instruct the jury to prevent confusion on the similar defense issues of "some legitimate nondiscriminatory reason" (production burden only for defendant) and "mixed-motive" (production and persuasion burdens)? Does the mixed-motive defense apply to other claims under Title VII, such as retaliation claims? See Porter v. Natsios, 414 F.3d 13 (D.C. Cir. 2005) (noting that all circuits say no, allowing it as a complete defense to liability).

(b) Most mixed-motive cases may be described as "horizontal"—a decisionmaker considers a range of bases for acting, one of the competing or complementary factors being a forbidden animus. In **Staub v. Proctor Hosp.**, ___ U.S. ___, 131 S.Ct. 1186, 179 L.Ed.2d 144 (2011), the Court found § 107 to be relevant also in "vertical" decisionmaking contexts, those in which such animus may be found at one or more of several levels of a multi-level process. Can an employer be held liable when a lower-level decisionmaker is motivated by a forbidden animus, but his supervisors, even though they ratify his decision, are not? The case, which arose under an analogue to Title VII that adopts § 107's terms, involved an employee discharged when a lower supervisor, motivated by discriminatory animus, set in motion a chain of events that resulted in his discharge in a decision made at a higher level. Justice Scalia's obscure opinion for the Court found that the statutory language authorized a finding of liability where the underling intended the result to be caused by his animus (e.g., the employee's discharge) and the result was effectuated further up the chain of command. Of course, an employer might yet prevail by proving an independent reason for the discharge at the higher level. How could the higher supervisor show the independence of her decision?

B. SPECIAL PROBLEMS AND EXTENDED ANALYSIS

1. SEX DISCRIMINATION CASES: THE BFOQ DEFENSE; PREGNANCY CLASSIFICATIONS

ROSENFELD v. SOUTHERN PACIFIC CO.

United States Court of Appeals, Ninth Circuit, 1971.
444 F.2d 1219.

Before CHAMBERS, HAMLEY and KILKENNY, CIRCUIT JUDGES.

HAMLEY, CIRCUIT JUDGE:

Leah Rosenfeld brought this action against Southern Pacific Company pursuant to * * * Title VII of the Civil Rights Act of 1964 (Act). Plaintiff, an employee of the company, alleged that in filling the position of agent-telegrapher at Thermal, California, in March, 1966, Southern Pacific discriminated against her solely because of her sex, by assigning the position to a junior male employee.

* * *

The court permitted the State of California to intervene because of its interest in defending the validity of the state's labor laws. [The district court entered judgment generally favorable to the plaintiff and this appeal followed.]

On the merits, Southern Pacific argues that it is the company's policy to exclude women, generically, from certain positions. The company restricts these job opportunities to men for two basic reasons: (1) the arduous nature of the work-related activity renders women physically unsuited for the jobs; (2) appointing a woman to the position would result in a violation of California labor laws and regulations which limit hours of work for women and restrict the weight they are permitted to lift. Positions such as that of agent-telegrapher at Thermal fall within the ambit of this policy. The company concludes that effectuation of this policy is not proscribed by Title VII of the Civil Rights Act due to the exception created by the Act for those situations where sex is a "bona fide occupational qualification."

While the agent-telegrapher position at Thermal is no longer in existence, the work requirements which that position entailed are illustrative of the kind of positions which are denied to female employees under the company's labor policy described above. During the harvesting season, the position may require work in excess of ten hours a day and eighty hours a week.[6] The position requires the heavy physical effort involved in

---

6. It was, indeed, this opportunity to earn overtime pay that made this position attractive to plaintiff.

climbing over and around boxcars to adjust their vents, collapse their bunkers and close and seal their doors. In addition, the employee must lift various objects weighing more than twenty-five pounds and, in some instances, more than fifty pounds.

* * *

There is therefore no doubt that the type of discrimination against women broadly prohibited by Title VII occurs under Southern Pacific's personnel policy. However, appellants contend that section 703(e) of the Act, 42 U.S.C.A. § 2000e–2(e), provides specific authority for Southern Pacific's described employment policy. This subsection reads:

"(e) Notwithstanding any other provision of this subchapter, (1) it shall not be an unlawful employment practice for an employer to hire and employ employees, * * * on the basis of his religion, sex, or national origin in those certain instances where religion, sex, or national origin is a bona fide occupational qualification reasonably necessary to the normal operation of that particular business or enterprise, * * * "

* * *

* * * The Equal Employment Opportunity Commission (Commission) has interpreted the particular exception to some extent in its published Guidelines. In pertinent part, the Guidelines provide that:

"(a) The Commission believes that the bona fide occupational qualification exception as to sex should be interpreted narrowly. * * *

"(i) The Commission will find that the following situations do not warrant the application of the bona fide occupational qualification exception:

* * *

"(ii) The refusal to hire an individual based on stereotyped characterizations of the sexes. Such stereotypes include, for example, that men are less capable of assembling intricate equipment; that women are less capable of aggressive salesmanship. The principle of non-discrimination requires that individuals be considered on the basis of individual capacities and not on the basis of any characteristics generally attributed to the group.

* * *

"(2) Where it is necessary for the purpose of authenticity or genuineness, the Commission will consider sex to be a bona fide occupational qualification, e.g., an actor or actress." 29 CFR 1604.1.

In the case before us, there is no contention that the sexual characteristics of the employee are crucial to the successful performance of the job, as they would be for the position of a wet-nurse, nor is there a need for authenticity or genuineness, as in the case of an actor or actress. 29 CFR 1604.1(a)(2). Rather, on the basis of a general assumption regarding the physical capabilities of female employees, the company attempts to raise a commonly accepted characterization of women as the "weaker sex" to the level of a BFOQ. The personnel policy of Southern Pacific here in question is based on "characteristics generally attributed to the group" of exactly the same type that the Commission has announced should not be the basis of an employment decision. 29 CFR 1604.1(a)(1)(ii). Based on the legislative intent and on the Commission's interpretation, sexual characteristics, rather than characteristics that might, to one degree or another, correlate with a particular sex, must be the basis for the application of the BFOQ exception. See Developments in the Law—Title VII, 84 Harv.L.Rev. 1109, 1178–79 (1971). Southern Pacific has not, and could not allege such a basis here, and section 703(e) thus could not exempt its policy from the impact of Title VII. There was no error in the granting of summary judgment on this issue.

The premise of Title VII, the wisdom of which is not in question here, is that women are now to be on equal footing with men. Weeks v. Southern Bell Tel. & Tel. Co., 408 F.2d 228, 236 (5th Cir.1969). The footing is not equal if a male employee may be appointed to a particular position on a showing that he is physically qualified, but a female employee is denied an opportunity to demonstrate personal physical qualification. Equality of footing is established only if employees otherwise entitled to the position, whether male or female, are excluded only upon a showing of individual incapacity. See Bowe v. Colgate–Palmolive Co., 416 F.2d 711, 718 (7th Cir.1969). This alone accords with the Congressional purpose to eliminate subjective assumptions and traditional stereotyped conceptions regarding the physical ability of women to do particular work. * * *

But the company points out that, apart from its intrinsic merit, its policy is compelled by California labor laws. * * *

[The employer, however, claims that its men-only classification is required by California's liberal protective legislation for women. The EEOC,] created by the provisions of Title VII of the Act, through its published Guidelines and Policy Statements has, albeit after considerable hesitation, taken the position that state "protective" legislation, of the type in issue here, conflicts with the policy of non-discrimination manifested by Title VII of the Act [and is overridden under the Supremacy Clause. We agree.]

* * *

Affirmed.

[JUDGE CHAMBERS' dissenting opinion, maintaining that the case had become moot, is omitted.]

NOTE ON THE BFOQ DEFENSE

1. In the courts of appeals, the *Rosenfeld* decision vied for legitimacy with an early Fifth Circuit pronouncement, Weeks v. Southern Bell Tel. &

Tel. Co., 408 F.2d 228 (5th Cir.1969). In *Weeks* a woman had been denied the job of "switchman" because it regularly required lifting 30–lb. loads, an activity the company labeled "strenuous" and which the district court found to be the basis for a BFOQ. Judge Johnson's decision for the appellate court reversed, framing the BFOQ defense more narrowly: "an employer has the burden of proving that he had * * * a factual basis for believing, that all or substantially all women would be unable to perform safely and efficiently the duties of the job involved." Id. at 235.

(a) How different is the *Weeks* standard from that adopted in *Rosenfeld*? Which is more consistent with the Act? With the EEOC Guidelines?

(b) The district court in Bowe v. Colgate–Palmolive Co., 272 F.Supp. 332, 365 (S.D.Ind.1967), rev'd in part, 416 F.2d 711 (7th Cir.1969), held that "[g]enerally recognized physical capabilities and physical limitations of the sexes may be made the basis for occupational qualification in generic terms." The *Weeks* court rejected this BFOQ test because it would allow "the exception * * * [to] swallow the rule." 408 F.2d at 235. Do you agree? If *Bowe* allows the exception to swallow the rule, does *Rosenfeld* allow the rule to swallow the exception?

(c) If you choose *Rosenfeld*'s rule over that of the *Weeks* case, is it because you believe that all persons should be treated as individuals? But if Congress wanted individualized treatment, why did it draft the BFOQ exception? Does *Rosenfeld* say that all persons must be treated as individuals? In light of the EEOC Guidelines, how would you decide the case of a woman who sued her employer after being discharged as a department-store Santa Claus following complaints from parents and children who wanted a "real" Santa? See "Santa Cites Sex Bias in Her Firing," Wash. Post, A10, col. 1 (August 21, 1999).

2. The Supreme Court faced the BFOQ issue in **Dothard v. Rawlinson**, 433 U.S. 321, 97 S.Ct. 2720, 53 L.Ed.2d 786 (1977), a suit in which a woman sought a job as guard in an all-male maximum security prison and was turned down because of her sex. The position required "continual close physical proximity to inmates." After noting that appellate courts had relied on varying "verbal formulation[s]," Justice Stewart's opinion for a divided Court concluded that the "BFOQ exception was in fact meant to be an extremely narrow exception"—but nevertheless found it met on the facts before the Court (433 U.S. at 334–36, 97 S.Ct. at 2729–30):

> "The environment in Alabama's penitentiaries is a peculiarly inhospitable one for human beings of whatever sex. Indeed, a federal district court has held that the conditions of confinement in the prisons of the State, characterized by 'rampant violence' and a 'jungle atmosphere,' are constitutionally intolerable. Pugh v. Locke, 406 F.Supp. 318, 325 (M.D.Ala). The record in the present case shows that because of inadequate staff and facilities, no attempt is made in the four maximum security male penitentiaries to classify or segregate inmates according to their offense or level of dangerousness—a procedure that, according to expert testimony, is essential to effective penalogical administration. Consequently, the estimated 20% of the male prisoners who are sex offenders are scattered throughout the penitentiaries' dormitory facilities.

"In this environment of violence and disorganization, it would be an oversimplification to characterize Regulation 204 as an exercise in 'romantic paternalism.' In the usual case, the argument that a particular job is too dangerous for women may appropriately be met by the rejoinder that it is the purpose of Title VII to allow the individual woman to make that choice for herself. More is at stake in this case, however, than an individual woman's decision to weigh and accept the risks of employment in a 'contact' position in a maximum security male prison.

"The essence of a correctional counselor's job is to maintain prison security. A woman's relative ability to maintain order in a male, maximum security, unclassified penitentiary of the type Alabama now runs could be directly reduced by her womanhood. There is a basis in fact for expecting that sex offenders who have criminally assaulted women in the past would be moved to do so again if access to women were established within the prison. There would also be a real risk that other inmates, deprived of a normal heterosexual environment, would assault women guards because they were women.[22] * * *

" * * * The likelihood that inmates would assault a woman because she was a woman would pose a real threat not only to the victim of the assault but also to the basic control of the penitentiary and protection of its inmates and the other security personnel. The employee's very womanhood would thus directly undermine her capacity to provide the security that is the essence of a correctional counselor's responsibility.[23]"

(a) Is *Dothard* one of those unusual cases where two wrongs make a right? Or was there a second factor that the Court should have discussed—the interest of prisoners in avoiding the presence of women? If the roles had been reversed, if men had sought jobs in a women's prison, how would you have rules in the case? See Everson v. Michigan Dept. of Corrections, 391 F.3d 737 (6th Cir. 2004) (BFOQ established, following suggestion that "appraisals need not be based on objective, empirical evidence, and common sense and deference to experts in the field may be used"). Can you reconcile your positions on *Dothard* and *Everson*?

(b) Does the *Dothard* holding tend to confirm the *Rosenfeld* test or the *Weeks* test? See Everson v. Michigan Dept. of Corrections, supra: "[T]he BFOQ defense has not been reduced to a single, universally-applicable test. The 'all or substantially all' and 'impossible or highly impractical' standards are, to use the language of *Dothard*, 'formulations' of the 'reasonable necessity' requirement, not hard-and-fast rules of law." Do you agree?

3. Modern Supreme Court decisions on sex discrimination in the Equal Protection context state that there are "[p]hysical differences between men

---

22. The record contains evidence of an attack on a female clerical worker in an Alabama prison, and of an incident involving a woman student who was taken hostage during a visit to one of the maximum security institutions. [Footnote by the Court.]

23. Alabama's penitentiaries are evidently not typical. The appellees' two experts testified that in a normal, relatively stable maximum security prison—characterized by control over the inmates, reasonable living conditions, and segregation of dangerous offenders—women guards could be used effectively and beneficially. Similarly, an *amicus* brief filed by the State of California attests to that State's success in using women guards in all-male penitentiaries. [Footnote by the Court; repositioned.]

and women" and that the sexes are not "fungible." United States v. Virginia, 518 U.S. 515, 116 S.Ct. 2264, 135 L.Ed.2d 735 (1996) (per Ginsburg, J.). Title VII's recognition of a BFOQ defense apparently adopts the same view. So the issue may ultimately turn on identifying the ways in which men and women relevantly differ. One difference may be that recognized in *Dothard*: men and women are different as sex objects. Thus, sex is a BFOQ in a jungle-like prison not because women generally are weaker than men, a mere stereotype, but because all women are sexually women. Do you prefer the "sex as sexiness" definition of BFOQ? Or is *Dothard* exactly wrong: sex as such cannot be a BFOQ or else any case can survive scrutiny?

(a) Can sex—being female—be a BFOQ for models for *Playboy*? For television commercials? For airline cabin attendants? In **Diaz v. Pan American World Airways**, 442 F.2d 385 (5th Cir.1971), the court ruled that Pan Am could not hire only female stewardesses, despite passenger preference for them. The decisive issue, said the court, is not whether female companionship makes a trip more pleasurable,[1] but whether sex differences directly relate to the "*essence* of the business operation" (emphasis in original). The Court ruled against the airline. But would the result be the same for Playboy Airlines or Hooters Airlines? See http://www.hootersair.com/, last visited April 2, 2006 (featuring a young woman in a revealing outfit). Hooters Air lasted but a few years, apparently unable to attract sufficient passengers, at least a sufficient number who enjoyed sexual innuendos while flying. See http://www.usatoday.com/travel/flights/2006-04-18-hooters-air_x.htm (last visited June 22, 2011). Should the market determine whether sex sells an airline seat? See http://www.airlinequality.com/Forum/hooters.htm (positive reviews from customers for "professionalism") (last visited June 20, 2011).

(b) Would the "essence" test cover permit the exclusive hiring of males as dancers for "Chippendales" troupe of near-nude male dancers? Of women as *Playboy* models? Women as Playboy "bunnies" at sex-themed restaurants? Are these different from Hooters Air because the predominant product is sex? Is it?

(c) Should sexual properties—potential sexiness desired or avoided—sometimes be the basis of a BFOQ? Is there a privacy right which might come into play at some point? See Everson v. Michigan Dept. of Corrections, supra (women's prison); Healey v. Southwood Psychiatric Hosp., 78 F.3d 128 (3d Cir. 1996) (sex a BFOQ in hiring counselors to match sex of patients previously suffering sex abuse and in need of therapy); Sibley Memorial Hospital v. Wilson, 488 F.2d 1338, 1342 (D.C. Cir.1973) (customer preference served in choice of attending nurses). Should courts say, in Victorian fashion, that sex cannot be a BFOQ when sexual desires would be served but can be a BFOQ if such desires would be denied?

(d) Are differential grooming regulations for men and women supported by a BFOQ? Are they not even a violation at all if everyone can reasonable meet the standard applied to him or her? See Jespersen v. Harrah's Operating Co., Inc., 392 F.3d 1076 (9th Cir. 2004) (make-up requirement for women); Willingham v. Macon Tel. Pub. Co., 507 F.2d 1084 (5th Cir. 1975) (en banc) (hair length for men).

---

1. The court appeared to assume that airline passengers were generally males.

4. Alternatively, can non-sexual properties provide a basis for a BFOQ? In **Western Air Lines, Inc. v. Criswell**, 472 U.S. 400, 105 S.Ct. 2743, 86 L.Ed.2d 321 (1985), the Court adopted the interpretation of BFOQ developed in sex discrimination cases and repeatedly referred to the idea that a BFOQ defense is appropriate only when the classification is a "proxy" for other non-discriminatory factors. See 472 U.S. at 414, 105 S.Ct. at 2751.

(a) What did the Court mean to suggest by using the word "proxy"? That sex or age itself is never relevant unless it is a reflection of other characteristics that are relevant? Does this concept help or hurt women? Is it consistent with the views expressed by Justice Ginsburg in U.S. v. Virginia, supra?

(b) The *Criswell* Court noted that a BFOQ defense would be appropriate when it is " 'impossible or highly impractical' to deal with [the excluded class] on an individualized basis," 472 U.S. at 414, 105 S.Ct. at 2751. Under this view would an NFL football team be permitted to exclude women from trying out for the team on the ground that virtually no woman could possibly be an NFL football player? If you think that "individualized treatment" is required in every circumstance, haven't you just eliminated the BFOQ defense from Title VII? It must permit some sex-based classifications, must it not?

5. Should Title VII be amended to remove the BFOQ exception? To enlarge it?

(a) Note that the BFOQ exception does not apply to racial discrimination. Why would Congress have adopted the exception for sex, religion, and national origin, but not race? Because it thought that race could never be a legitimate hiring criterion, but the others sometimes might be? Is race never relevant in employment? In Ferrill v. Parker Group, Inc., 168 F.3d 468 (11th Cir. 1999), the employer hired only black persons to conduct "push polls" and other "get-out-the vote" efforts by telephone. The "calling is race-matched, such that black voters are called by black [] employees who use the 'black' script, while white voters are called by white [] employees who use a different, 'white' script." Is this a violation of Title VII? Regardless of whether if it works to produce the results that clients want?

(b) To what extent have our opinions about the relevancy of sex to job performance changed in the years since the passage of Title VII? Are these changes not related to our changing views of the social roles of men and women? Can Title VII accommodate these changing views? Consider these issues in the pregnancy cases that follow this Note.

GENERAL ELECTRIC CO. v. GILBERT

Supreme Court of the United States, 1976.
429 U.S. 125, 97 S.Ct. 401, 50 L.Ed.2d 343.

MR. JUSTICE REHNQUIST delivered the opinion of the Court.

Petitioner, General Electric Company, provides for all of its employees a disability plan which pays weekly nonoccupational sickness and accident benefits. Excluded from the plan's coverage, however, are disabilities arising from pregnancy. Respondents, on behalf of a class of women employees, brought this action seeking, *inter alia,* a declaration that this exclusion constitutes sex discrimination in violation of Title VII * * *.

[Evidence introduced at trial showed that, while not a "disease" or "accident," ordinary pregnancy usually has a disabling effect for several weeks and that 10% of such pregnancies are complicated by actual diseases. Yet even with pregnancy excluded from plan coverage, female employees recovered an average of $82 (1970) to $113 (1971) per worker per year, while males recovered only $46 (1970) to $62 (1971) per worker per year. The district court also found that the cost of including pregnancy benefits would be "large," but undeterminable in advance. These statistics, however, were not found to justify exclusion of pregnancy from an otherwise comprehensive health plan.]

Between the date on which the District Court's judgment was rendered and the time this case was decided by the Court of Appeals, we decided Geduldig v. Aiello, 417 U.S. 484, 94 S.Ct. 2485, 41 L.Ed.2d 256 (1974), where we rejected a claim that a very similar disability program established under California law violated the Equal Protection Clause of the Fourteenth Amendment because that plan's exclusion of pregnancy disabilities represented sex discrimination. The majority of the Court of Appeals felt that *Geduldig* was not controlling because it arose under the Equal Protection Clause of the Fourteenth Amendment, and not under Title VII, 519 F.2d at 666–67. The dissenting opinion disagreed with the majority as to the impact of *Geduldig,* 519 F.2d at 668–69. We granted certiorari to consider this important issue in the construction of Title VII.

II

Section 703(a)(1) provides in relevant part that it shall be an unlawful employment practice for an employer

" * * * to discriminate against any individual with respect to his compensation, terms, conditions, or privileges of employment, because of such individual's race, color, religion, sex, or national origin," 42 U.S.C.A. § 2000e–2.

While there is no necessary inference that Congress, in choosing this language, intended to incorporate into Title VII the concepts of discrimination which have evolved from court decisions construing the Equal Protection Clause of the Fourteenth Amendment, the similarities between the congressional language and some of those decisions surely indicates that the latter are a useful starting point in interpreting the former. Particularly in the case of defining the term "discrimination," which Congress has nowhere in Title VII defined, those cases afford an existing body of law analyzing and discussing that term in a legal context not wholly dissimilar from the concerns which Congress manifested in enacting Title VII. We think, therefore, that our decision in Geduldig v. Aiello, supra, dealing with a strikingly similar disability plan, is quite relevant in determining whether or not the pregnancy exclusion did discriminate on the basis of sex. * * *

* * *

[In *Geduldig* the Court noted that the state's insurance program did not] "exclude anyone from benefit eligibility because of gender but merely removes one physical condition—pregnancy—from the list of compensable disabilities. While it is true that only women can become pregnant, it does not follow that every legislative classification concerning pregnancy is a sex-based classification * * *.

"The lack of identity between the excluded disability and gender as such under this insurance program becomes clear upon the most cursory analysis. The program divides potential recipients into two groups—pregnant women and nonpregnant persons. While the first group is exclusively female, the second includes members of both sexes." 417 U.S. at 496–497, n. 20, 94 S.Ct. at 2492.

The quoted language from *Geduldig* leaves no doubt that our reason for rejecting appellee's equal protection claim in that case was that the exclusion of pregnancy from coverage under California's disability benefits plan was not in itself discrimination based on sex.

* * *

The instant suit was grounded on Title VII rather than the Equal Protection Clause, and our cases recognize that a prima facie violation of Title VII can be established in some circumstances upon proof that the *effect* of an otherwise facially neutral plan or classification is to discriminate against members of one class or another. [See *Griggs*. But here there is not even a showing of a gender-based effect.]

* * * As in *Geduldig,* supra, we start from the indisputable baseline that "[t]he fiscal and actuarial benefits of the program * * * accrue to members of both sexes," 417 U.S. at 497 n. 20, 94 S.Ct., at 2492. We need not disturb the findings of the District Court to note that there is neither a finding, nor was there any evidence which would support a finding, that the financial benefits of the Plan "worked to discriminate against any definable group or class in terms of the aggregate risk protection derived by that group or class from the program," id. at 496, 94 S.Ct., at 2492. * * * As there is no proof that the package is in fact worth more to men than to women, it is impossible to find any gender-based discriminatory effect in this scheme simply because women disabled as a result of pregnancy do not receive benefits; that is to say, gender-based discrimination does not result simply because an employer's disability benefits plan is less than all inclusive.[17] For all that appears, pregnancy-related disabili-

---

17. Absent proof of different values, the cost to "insure" against the risks is, in essence, nothing more than extra compensation to the employees, in the form of fringe benefits. If the employer were to remove the insurance fringe benefits and, instead, increase wages by an amount equal to the cost of the "insurance," there would clearly be no gender-based discrimination, even though a female employee who wished to purchase disability insurance that covered all risks would have to pay more than would a male employee who purchased identical disability insurance, due to the fact that her insurance had to cover the "extra" disabilities due to pregnancy. While respondents seem to acknowledge that the failure to provide any benefit plan at all would not constitute sex-based discrimination in violation of Title VII, see note 18, infra, they illogically also suggest that the present scheme does violate Title VII because

ties constitute an *additional* risk, unique to women, and the failure to compensate them for this risk does not destroy the presumed parity of the benefits, accruing to men and women alike, which results from the facially even-handed *inclusion* of risks. To hold otherwise would endanger the common-sense notion that an employer who has no disability benefits program at all does not violate Title VII even though the "underinclusion" of risks impacts, as a result of pregnancy-related disabilities, more heavily upon one gender than upon the other.[18] Just as there is no facial gender-based discrimination in that case, so, too, there is none here.

* * *

Reversed.[a]

NOTE ON THE MEANING OF "SEX": THE PREGNANCY DISCRIMINATION ACT AND ITS LIMITS

1.　Congress promptly reversed the Court's decision in *Gilbert,* adopting the **Pregnancy Discrimination Act (PDA)** in 1978, Pub.L. 95–555, 92 Stat. 2076. It amended the statutory definitional provisions, § 2000e, as follows:

"(k) The terms 'because of sex' or 'on the basis of sex' include, but are not limited to, because of or on the basis of pregnancy, childbirth, or related medical conditions; and women affected by pregnancy, childbirth, or related medical conditions shall be treated the same for all employment-related purposes, including receipt of benefits under fringe benefit programs, as other persons not so affected but similar in their ability or inability to work, and nothing in section 2000e–2(h) of this title shall be interpreted to permit otherwise. This subsection shall not require an employer to pay for health insurance benefits for abortion, except where the life of the mother would be endangered if the fetus were carried to term, or except where medical complications have arisen from an abortion: *Provided,* That nothing herein shall preclude an employer from providing abortion benefits or otherwise affect bargaining agreements in regard to abortion."

(a)　A coalition of family-oriented groups and traditional supporters of women's rights supported passage of the PDA. Does its simple political

---

"A female must spend her own money to buy a personal disability policy covering pregnancy disability if she wants to be fully insured against a period of disability without income, whereas a male without extra expenditure is fully insured by GE against every period of disability." Supplemental Brief for Martha Gilbert *et al.* on Reargument, at 11. Yet, in both cases—the instant case and the case where there is no disability coverage at all—the ultimate result is that a woman who wished to be fully insured would have to pay an incremental amount over her male counterpart due solely to the possibility of pregnancy-related disabilities. Title VII's proscription on discrimination does not require, in either case, the employer to pay that incremental amount. The District Court was wrong in assuming, as it did, 375 F.Supp. at 383, that Title VII's ban on employment discrimination necessarily means that "greater economic benefit[s]" must be required to be paid to one sex or the other because of their differing roles in "the scheme of human existence."

18.　Respondents tacitly admit that this situation would not violate Title VII. They acknowledge that "GE had no obligation to establish any fringe benefit program." * * *

a.　In light of subsequent statutory changes, the two concurring and three dissenting opinions are omitted.—Ed.

promise to help women undercut long-term goals of equal respect for women in the workplace? Does the amendment reinforce the stereotype that sex, at least so far as women are concerned, is ineluctably connected to childbearing and child raising?

(b) The most fundamental issue underlying the PDA is a rather simple one: what is "sex" or gender? What characteristics make men and women different? Reproductive anatomy is an obvious difference, but are there others? Body strength? Math prowess or intuitive reasoning abilities? Hair length and dressing styles? This Note examines not only the PDA, but other potential differences between men and women that repeat the same underlying controversy.

2. Does a state law that gives pregnant women more protection than men run afoul of the PDA? In **California Federal Savings & Loan Ass'n v. Guerra**, 479 U.S. 272, 107 S.Ct. 683, 93 L.Ed.2d 613 (1987), an employer claimed that a state law that required a mandatory leave, with right to rehiring, to pregnant women conflicted with the PDA and was therefore pre-empted under the Constitution's Supremacy Clause. The Court rejected the claim, finding that the PDA did not forbid a preference for such women. Justice Marshall's opinion for the Court explained, 479 U.S. at 284–85, 289, 107 S.Ct. at 691–92, 693:

> "Petitioners argue that the language of the federal statute itself unambiguously rejects California's "special treatment" approach to pregnancy discrimination, thus rendering any resort to the legislative history unnecessary. They contend that the second clause of the PDA forbids an employer to treat pregnant employees any differently than other disabled employees. Because' "[t]he purpose of Congress is the ultimate touchstone" of the pre-emption inquiry, however, we must examine the PDA's language against the background of its legislative history and historical context. As to the language of the PDA, "[i]t is a 'familiar rule, that a thing may be within the letter of the statute and yet not within the statute, because not within its spirit, nor within the intention of its makers.'" Steelworkers v. Weber. [section D infra].

> "It is well established that the PDA was passed in reaction to this Court's decision in General Electric Co. v. Gilbert[, which it was designed to override]. * * *

> "Rather than imposing a limitation on the remedial purpose of the PDA, we believe that the second clause was intended to overrule the holding in *Gilbert* and to illustrate how discrimination against pregnancy is to be remedied. ("The meaning of the first clause is not limited by the specific language in the second clause, which explains the application of the general principle to women employees"). Accordingly, subject to certain limitations,[17] we agree with the Court of Appeals' conclusion that Congress intended the PDA to be "a floor beneath which pregnancy

---

17. For example, a State could not mandate special treatment of pregnant workers based on stereotypes or generalizations about their needs and abilities. [Footnote by the Court]

disability benefits may not drop—not a ceiling above which they may not rise.''

* * *

"By 'taking pregnancy into account,' California's pregnancy disability-leave statute allows women, as well as men, to have families without losing their jobs.''

(a) Do you agree with the Court's reasoning? If Congress had intended preferential, rather than equal, treatment for women, could it have found a better way of expressing that idea than in the second sentence of the PDA? See Justice White's dissenting opinion, 479 U.S. at 298, 107 S.Ct. at 698 (noting that the second sentence "could not be clearer").

(b) Justice White also noted the argument that "this construction of the PDA represents a resurgence of the 19th–century protective legislation which perpetuated sex-role stereotypes and which impeded women in their efforts to take their rightful place in the workplace." 479 U.S. at 300, 107 S.Ct. at 700. Among *amici* in the Court, who would have made such an argument? Do you suspect that there may have been a split among women's rights advocates as to whether to support the plaintiff in *Guerra*?

(c) Should men sometimes subsidize women in order to promote "equality" of results? Is that the goal of the PDA as interpreted in *Guerra*? Is that why the Court analogizes to affirmative action?

3. Was the PDA a technical and policy mistake? Would it have been better to not define pregnancy as commensurate with sex, but instead treat it as a neutral rule having a disparate impact on women? Would disparate impact analysis on many occasions produce decisions as favorable to women as those under the PDA? In **Nashville Gas Co. v. Satty**, 434 U.S. 136, 98 S.Ct. 347, 54 L.Ed.2d 356 (1977), Justice Rehnquist again wrote for the majority in a case raising the pregnancy issue. The gas company not only denied sick pay to pregnant women but also terminated all accrued seniority when a woman took pregnancy leave. The Court struck down the seniority rule, but generally sustained the sick pay practice. Speaking first to the seniority rule, the Court distinguished *Gilbert* as a case in which the employer declined to cure an additional risk of women (434 U.S. at 142–43, 98 S.Ct. at 351–52):

> "Here, by comparison, petitioner has not merely refused to extend to women a benefit that men cannot and do not receive, but has imposed on women a substantial burden that men need not suffer. The distinction between benefits and burdens is more than one of semantics. We held in *Gilbert* that § 703(a)(1) did not require that greater economic benefits be paid to one sex or the other "because of their different roles in the scheme of existence," *Gilbert,* supra. But that holding does not allow us to read § 703(a)(2) to permit an employer to burden female employees in such a way as to deprive them of employment opportunities because of their different role.

> "Recognition that petitioner's facially neutral seniority system does deprive women of employment opportunities because of their sex does not end the inquiry under § 703(a)(2) of Title VII. If a company's business necessitates the adoption of particular leave policies, Title VII does not

prohibit the company from applying these policies to all leaves of absence, including pregnancy leaves; Title VII is not violated even though the policies may burden female employees. *Griggs,* supra. But we agree with the District Court in this case that since there was no proof of any business necessity adduced with respect to the policies in question, that court was entitled to 'assume no justification exists.'

"The sick pay provisions were upheld on the basis of *Gilbert,* the Court again noting, as in the earlier case, that since there was no shown discriminatory effect on women in terms of payments or job opportunities, there was no occasion to decide whether such a showing would invalidate pregnancy exclusion in a sick-pay plan."

(a) Is pregnancy sometimes related to sex and sometimes not? Is the PDA's approach preferable because of the inconsistent results that might have followed had *Satty* not been overturned along with *Gilbert* by the PDA?

(b) Was the PDA unnecessary because *Gilbert* was simply wrongly decided? In cases prior to *Gilbert,* the Court had ruled that exclusion of women from jobs because of "sex plus" another characteristic, such as having school-age children under one's care, was intentional sex discrimination. See, e.g., Phillips v. Martin Marietta Corp., 400 U.S. 542, 91 S.Ct. 496, 27 L.Ed.2d 613 (1971). Is pregnancy such a situation? Because classification by pregnancy is by definition classification of "sex plus" pregnancy? But see AT & T Corp. v. Hulteen, ___ U.S. ___, 129 S.Ct. 1962, 173 L.Ed.2d 898 (2009) (PDA not retroactive; company's refusal to make its retirement plan retroactive to give benefits to pregnant women for work done prior to PDA's passage is not a decision based on "pregnancy").

4. Is pregnancy the only area in which persons might find it difficult to decide whether a particular classification so closely coincides with "sex" that it is in fact a "sex" classification? What are "sex" classifications? The PDA, which only deals with this issue regarding pregnancy, provides no certain answers. Are other amendments to Title VII necessary?

(a) If an employer has a policy of hiring only single females, can a married female claim that this constitutes sex discrimination under Title VII? See Stroud v. Delta Air Lines, 544 F.2d 892 (5th Cir.1977). Is it sex discrimination because you are certain that the employer is selling sexual attractiveness by employing single females? Can some women complain when others are the workplace beneficiaries of sexual imagery or sex stereotyping?

(b) Are differential grooming regulations for men and women facial sex discrimination under Title VII? See Willingham v. Macon Telegraph Pub. Co., 507 F.2d 1084 (5th Cir.1975) (en banc).

(c) Are there morphological differences between men and women beyond reproductive differences? Consider height and weight as a reflection of "being in good shape." May an employer seeking persons "in good shape" (e.g., exercise trainers) establish differential height-weight guidelines for men and women? Or is this facial sex discrimination? See Jarrell v. Eastern Air Lines, Inc., 430 F.Supp. 884 (E.D.Va.1977).

5. Consider the modern "potty issue" that may present parallels most similar to pregnancy: because of traditional differences in dress and hygienic

practices between most men and most women, men and women use bathroom facilities in a different manner.

(a) If an employer provides only unsanitary facilities suitable for use only while standing, is that facial sex discrimination? Or a neutral rule having a disparate impact? Neither? See Lynch v. Freeman, 817 F.2d 380 (6th Cir. 1987)

(b) Assume that it can be shown that women take more time in public restrooms than do men (a somewhat debatable proposition). If an employer provides only equal access for women employees (equal numbers of facilities per female and male employee), is that facial sex discrimination because this ineluctably disadvantages women employees? Compare Personnel Administrator of Massachusetts v. Feeney, Chapter 1B.5 supra, with Men's Room Trip Opens Door to Women's Rights, Chicago Tribune, Jul. 29, 1990, at 5 (insufficient facilities for women at public concert leads to prosecution for woman's use of men's restroom). Does Title VII require an employer to meet the equal (time-calculated) needs of men and women? Would your answer depend on whether women's hypothesized extra demand occurs because of physical differences between men and women or because of socially determined differences (e.g., attire)? If you would cover even the latter, are you admitting that even some social differences between men and women are "relevant"? Was that your position in the *Rosenfeld* case, set out earlier in this section?

(c) If men and women are different in some demographic respect, may an employer classify directly based on sex? In **City of Los Angeles, Dept. of Water and Power v. Manhart**, 435 U.S. 702, 98 S.Ct. 1370, 55 L.Ed.2d 657 (1978), the Court held such classification, in the context of differential retirement benefits, to constitute facial disparate treatment by sex. Would classification by other factors that are proxies for sex—height, weight, blood pressure—also constitute facial sex discrimination?

6. The central issue presented by *General Electric* and the PDA can arise under other civil rights statutes as well—indeed can arise whenever a statute identifies a certain characteristic of humans. Consider "age" discrimination, for example. In Smith v. City of Jackson, 544 U.S. 228, 125 S.Ct. 1536, 161 L.Ed.2d 410 (2005), the Court held that classification of employees by seniority and rank was not "age" discrimination even though one must move up the seniority list as one ages. Furthermore, in Kentucky Retirement Systems v. EEOC, 554 U.S. 135, 128 S.Ct. 2361, 171 L.Ed.2d 322 (2008), the Court held that discrimination based on retirement status is not "age" discrimination because "age and pension status remain "analytically distinct" concepts." Aren't these two cases just like general Electric, but with no PDA to "correct" them? Don't all civil rights statutes present the same problem? Is discrimination based on skin color "race" discrimination? (How does Title VII surmount this issue—with a mini-equivalent to the PDA?)

7. Do these issues relate to the question of "what is sex" or to that of "what is equality"? Are the two questions different? Consider the following case.

INTERNATIONAL UNION, UAAAIW
v. JOHNSON CONTROLS, INC.

Supreme Court of the United States, 1991.
499 U.S. 187, 111 S.Ct. 1196, 113 L.Ed.2d 158.

JUSTICE BLACKMUN delivered the opinion of the Court.

In this case we are concerned with an employer's gender-based fetal-protection policy. May an employer exclude a fertile female employee from certain jobs because of its concern for the health of the fetus the woman might conceive?

I

Respondent Johnson Controls, Inc., manufactures batteries. In the manufacturing process, the element lead is a primary ingredient. Occupational exposure to lead entails health risks, including the risk of harm to any fetus carried by a female employee.

[Johnson Controls initially followed a practice of warning women employees against the potential lead danger, but later it decided to exclude all "women who are pregnant or who are capable of bearing children" from specific jobs where high levels of lead contamination had been documented. Women who had lost jobs or undergone sterilization in order to keep preferred jobs brought this suit under Title VII, alleging discrimination because of their sex. The district court ruled against them and was affirmed on appeal.]

III

The bias in Johnson Controls' policy is obvious. Fertile men, but not fertile women, are given a choice as to whether they wish to risk their reproductive health for a particular job. Section 703(a) of the Civil Rights Act of 1964, 78 Stat. 255, as amended, 42 U.S.C. § 2000e–2(a), prohibits sex-based classifications in terms and conditions of employment, in hiring and discharging decisions, and in other employment decisions that adversely affect an employee's status. Respondent's fetal-protection policy explicitly discriminates against women on the basis of their sex. The policy excludes women with childbearing capacity from lead-exposed jobs and so creates a facial classification based on gender. Respondent assumes as much in its brief before this Court.

Nevertheless, the Court of Appeals assumed, as did the two appellate courts who already had confronted the issue, that sex-specific fetal-protection policies do not involve facial discrimination. These courts analyzed the policies as though they were facially neutral, and had only a discriminatory effect upon the employment opportunities of women. Consequently, the courts looked to see if each employer in question had established that its policy was justified as a business necessity. The business necessity standard is more lenient for the employer than the statutory BFOQ defense. * * *

* * * This Court faced a conceptually similar situation in Phillips v. Martin Marietta Corp., 400 U.S. 542 (1971), and found sex discrimination because the policy established "one hiring policy for women and another for men—each having pre-school-age children." Id. at 544. Johnson Controls' policy is facially discriminatory because it requires only a female employee to produce proof that she is not capable of reproducing.

Our conclusion is bolstered by the Pregnancy Discrimination Act of 1978 (PDA), 92 Stat. 2076, 42 U.S.C. § 2000e(k), in which Congress explicitly provided that, for purposes of Title VII, discrimination "on the basis of sex" includes discrimination "because of or on the basis of pregnancy, childbirth, or related medical conditions."[3] "The Pregnancy Discrimination Act has now made clear that, for all Title VII purposes, discrimination based on a woman's pregnancy is, on its face, discrimination because of her sex." Newport News Shipbuilding & Dry Dock Co. v. EEOC, 462 U.S. 669, 684 (1983). * * *

* * * Moreover, the absence of a malevolent motive does not convert a facially discriminatory policy into a neutral policy with a discriminatory effect. Whether an employment practice involves disparate treatment through explicit facial discrimination does not depend on why the employer discriminates but rather on the explicit terms of the discrimination. In *Martin Marietta, supra,* the motives underlying the employers' express exclusion of women did not alter the intentionally discriminatory character of the policy. Nor did the arguably benign motives lead to consideration of a business necessity defense. The question in that case was whether the discrimination in question could be justified under § 703(e) as a BFOQ. The beneficence of an employer's purpose does not undermine the conclusion that an explicit gender-based policy is sex discrimination under § 703(a) and thus may be defended only as a BFOQ.

* * *

IV

Under § 703(e)(1) of Title VII, an employer may discriminate on the basis of "religion, sex, or national origin in those certain instances where religion, sex, or national origin is a bona fide occupational qualification reasonably necessary to the normal operation of that particular business or enterprise." 42 U.S.C. § 2000e–2(e)(1). We therefore turn to the question whether Johnson Controls' fetal-protection policy is one of those "certain instances" that come within the BFOQ exception.

The BFOQ defense is written narrowly, and this Court has read it narrowly. See, e.g., Dothard v. Rawlinson, 433 U.S. 321, 332–37 (1977).

---

3. The Act added subsection (k) to § 701 of the Civil Rights Act of 1964 and reads in pertinent part:

"The terms 'because of sex' or 'on the basis of sex' [in Title VII] include, but are not limited to, because of or on the basis of pregnancy, childbirth, or related medical conditions; and women affected by pregnancy, childbirth, or related medical conditions shall be treated the same for all employment-related purposes . . . as other persons not so affected but similar in their ability or inability to work. . . ."

We have read the BFOQ language of § 4(f) of the Age Discrimination in Employment Act of 1967 (ADEA), 81 Stat. 603, as amended, 29 U.S.C. § 623(f)(1), which tracks the BFOQ provision in Title VII, just as narrowly. See Western Air Lines, Inc. v. Criswell, 472 U.S. 400 (1985). Our emphasis on the restrictive scope of the BFOQ defense is grounded on both the language and the legislative history of § 703.

The wording of the BFOQ defense contains several terms of restriction that indicate that the exception reaches only special situations. The statute thus limits the situations in which discrimination is permissible to "certain instances" where sex discrimination is "reasonably necessary" to the "normal operation" of the "particular" business. Each one of these terms—certain, normal, particular—prevents the use of general subjective standards and favors an objective, verifiable requirement. But the most telling term is "occupational"; this indicates that these objective, verifiable requirements must concern job-related skills and aptitudes.

* * *

Johnson Controls argues that its fetal-protection policy falls within the so-called safety exception to the BFOQ. Our cases have stressed that discrimination on the basis of sex because of safety concerns is allowed only in narrow circumstances. In Dothard v. Rawlinson this Court indicated that danger to a woman herself does not justify discrimination. We there allowed the employer to hire only male guards in contact areas of maximum-security male penitentiaries only because more was at stake than the "individual woman's decision to weigh and accept the risks of employment." We found sex to be a BFOQ inasmuch as the employment of a female guard would create real risks of safety to others if violence broke out because the guard was a woman. * * *

Similarly, some courts have approved airlines' layoffs of pregnant flight attendants at different points during the first five months of pregnancy on the ground that the employer's policy was necessary to ensure the safety of passengers. See Harriss v. Pan American World Airways, Inc., 649 F.2d 670 (C.A.9 1980); Burwell v. Eastern Air Lines, Inc., 633 F.2d 361 (C.A.4 1980), cert. denied, 450 U.S. 965 (1981); Condit v. United Air Lines, Inc., 558 F.2d 1176 (C.A.4 1977).

[And in our decision in *Criswell,* supra, we considered the safety of passengers—persons who were as necessary to the operation of the employer's business as were the inmates in *Dothard.* There we] stressed that in order to qualify as a BFOQ, a job qualification must relate to the "essence," *Dothard,* or to the "central mission of the employer's business," *Criswell.*

* * *

[Moreover, t]he PDA's amendment to Title VII contains a BFOQ standard of its own: unless pregnant employees differ from others "in their ability or inability to work," they must be "treated the same" as other employees "for all employment-related purposes." 42 U.S.C.

§ 2000e(k). This language clearly sets forth Congress' remedy for discrimination on the basis of pregnancy and potential pregnancy. Women who are either pregnant or potentially pregnant must be treated like others "similar in their ability ... to work." Ibid. In other words, women as capable of doing their jobs as their male counterparts may not be forced to choose between having a child and having a job.

* * *

The legislative history confirms what the language of the Pregnancy Discrimination Act compels. Both the House and Senate Reports accompanying the legislation indicate that this statutory standard was chosen to protect female workers from being treated differently from other employees simply because of their capacity to bear children. See Amending Title VII, Civil Rights Act of 1964, S.Rep. No. 95–331, pp. 4–6 (1977).

This history counsels against expanding the BFOQ to allow fetal-protection policies. The Senate Report quoted above states that employers may not require a pregnant woman to stop working at any time during her pregnancy unless she is unable to do her work. Employment late in pregnancy often imposes risks on the unborn child, see Chavkin, Walking a Tightrope: Pregnancy, Parenting, and Work, in Double Exposure 196, 196–202 (W. Chavkin ed.1984), but Congress indicated that the employer may take into account only the woman's ability to get her job done. See Becker, From *Muller v. Oregon* to Fetal Vulnerability Policies, 53 U.Chi. L.Rev. 1219, 1255–56 (1986). With the PDA, Congress made clear that the decision to become pregnant or to work while being either pregnant or capable of becoming pregnant was reserved for each individual woman to make for herself.

* * *

V

We have no difficulty concluding that Johnson Controls cannot establish a BFOQ. Fertile women, as far as appears in the record, participate in the manufacture of batteries as efficiently as anyone else. Johnson Controls' professed moral and ethical concerns about the welfare of the next generation do not suffice to establish a BFOQ of female sterility. * * *

Nor can concerns about the welfare of the next generation be considered a part of the "essence" of Johnson Controls' business. Judge Easterbrook in this case pertinently observed: "It is word play to say that 'the job' at Johnson [Controls] is to make batteries without risk to fetuses in the same way 'the job' at Western Air Lines is to fly planes without crashing." 886 F.2d at 913.

Johnson Controls argues that it must exclude all fertile women because it is impossible to tell which women will become pregnant while working with lead. This argument is somewhat academic in light of our conclusion that the company may not exclude fertile women at all; it perhaps is worth noting, however, that Johnson Controls has shown no "factual basis for believing that all or substantially all women would be unable to perform safely and efficiently the duties of the job involved." Weeks v. Southern Bell Tel. & Tel. Co., 408 F.2d 228, 235 (C.A.5 1969), quoted with approval in *Dothard,* 433 U.S. at 333. Even on this sparse record, it is apparent that Johnson Controls is concerned about only a small minority of women. Of the eight pregnancies reported among the female employees, it has not been shown that any of the babies have birth defects or other abnormalities. * * *

VI

A word about tort liability and the increased cost of fertile women in the workplace is perhaps necessary. One of the dissenting judges in this case expressed concern about an employer's tort liability and concluded that liability for a potential injury to a fetus is a social cost that Title VII does not require a company to ignore. It is correct to say that Title VII does not prevent the employer from having a conscience. The statute, however, does prevent sex-specific fetal-protection policies. These two aspects of Title VII do not conflict.

* * * It is worth noting that OSHA gave the problem of lead lengthy consideration and concluded that "there is no basis whatsoever for the claim that women of childbearing age should be excluded from the workplace in order to protect the fetus or the course of pregnancy." 43 Fed.Reg. 52952, 52966 (1978). Instead, OSHA established a series of mandatory protections which, taken together, "should effectively minimize any risk to the fetus and newborn child." Id. at 52966. See 29 CFR § 1910.125(k)(ii) (1989). Without negligence, it would be difficult for a court to find liability on the part of the employer. If, under general tort principles, Title VII bans sex-specific fetal-protection policies, the employer fully informs the woman of the risk, and the employer has not acted negligently, the basis for holding an employer liable seems remote at best.

Although the issue is not before us, the concurrence observes that "it is far from clear that compliance with Title VII will preempt state tort liability." The cases relied upon by the concurrence to support its prediction, however, are inapposite. For example, in California Federal S. & L. Assn. v. Guerra, 479 U.S. 272 (1987), we considered a California statute that expanded upon the requirements of the PDA and concluded that the statute was not pre-empted by Title VII because it was not inconsistent with the purposes of the federal statute and did not require an act that was unlawful under Title VII. Here, in contrast, the tort liability that the concurrence fears will punish employers for *complying* with Title VII's clear command. When it is impossible for an employer to comply with both state and federal requirements, this Court has ruled that federal law pre-empts that of the States. See, *e.g.,* Florida Lime & Avocado Growers, Inc. v. Paul, 373 U.S. 132, 142–143 (1963).

* * *

* * * Because Johnson Controls has not argued that it faces any costs from tort liability, not to mention crippling ones, the pre-emption question is not before us. We therefore say no more than that the concurrence's speculation appears unfounded as well as premature.

The tort-liability argument reduces to two equally unpersuasive propositions. First, Johnson Controls attempts to solve the problem of reproductive health hazards by resorting to an exclusionary policy. Title VII plainly forbids illegal sex discrimination as a method of diverting attention from an employer's obligation to police the workplace. Second, the spectre of an award of damages reflects a fear that hiring fertile women will cost more. The extra cost of employing members of one sex, however, does not provide an affirmative Title VII defense for a discriminatory refusal to hire members of that gender. Indeed, in passing the PDA, Congress considered at length the considerable cost of providing equal treatment of pregnancy and related conditions, but made the "decision to forbid special treatment of pregnancy despite the social costs associated therewith." Arizona Governing Committee v. Norris, 463 U.S. 1073, 1084, n. 14 (1983) (opinion of Marshall, J.).

We, of course, are not presented with, nor do we decide, a case in which costs would be so prohibitive as to threaten the survival of the employer's business. We merely reiterate our prior holdings that the incremental cost of hiring women cannot justify discriminating against them.

* * *

JUSTICE WHITE, with whom THE CHIEF JUSTICE and JUSTICE KENNEDY join, concurring in part and concurring in the judgment.

For the fetal protection policy involved in this case to be a BFOQ, * * * the policy must be "reasonably necessary" to the "normal operation" of making batteries, which is Johnson Controls' "particular business." Although that is a difficult standard to satisfy, nothing in the statute's language indicates that it could *never* support a sex-specific fetal protection policy.[1]

On the contrary, a fetal protection policy would be justified under the terms of the statute if, for example, an employer could show that exclusion of women from certain jobs was reasonably necessary to avoid substantial tort liability. Common sense tells us that it is part of the normal operation of business concerns to avoid causing injury to third parties, as well as to

---

1. The Court's heavy reliance on the word "occupational" in the BFOQ statute is unpersuasive. *Any* requirement for employment can be said to be an occupational qualification, since "occupational" merely means related to a job. See Webster's Third New International Dictionary 1560 (1976). Thus, Johnson Controls' requirement that employees engaged in battery manufacturing be either male or non-fertile clearly is an "occupational qualification." The issue, of course, is whether that qualification is "reasonably necessary to the normal operation" of Johnson Controls' business. It is telling that the Court offers no case support, either from this Court or the lower Federal Courts, for its interpretation of the word "occupational."

employees, if for no other reason than to avoid tort liability and its substantial costs.

* * *

Dothard and *Criswell* make clear that avoidance of substantial safety risks to third parties is *inherently* part of both an employee's ability to perform a job and an employer's "normal operation" of its business. * * *

On the facts of this case, for example, protecting fetal safety while carrying out the duties of battery manufacturing is as much a legitimate concern as is safety to third parties in guarding prisons (*Dothard*) or flying airplanes (*Criswell*).

Dothard and *Criswell* also confirm that costs are relevant in determining whether a discriminatory policy is reasonably necessary for the normal operation of a business. In *Dothard,* the safety problem that justified exclusion of women from the prison guard positions was largely a result of inadequate staff and facilities. If the cost of employing women could not be considered, the employer there should have been required to hire more staff and restructure the prison environment rather than exclude women. Similarly, in *Criswell* the airline could have been required to hire more pilots and install expensive monitoring devices rather than discriminate against older employees. The BFOQ statute, however, reflects "Congress' unwillingness to require employers to change the very nature of their operations." Price Waterhouse v. Hopkins, 490 U.S. 228, 242 (1989) (plurality opinion).

The Pregnancy Discrimination Act (PDA), 42 U.S.C. § 2000e(k), contrary to the Court's assertion, *ante,* at 15, did not restrict the scope of the BFOQ defense. The PDA was only an amendment to the "Definitions" section of Title VII, 42 U.S.C. § 2000e, and did not purport to eliminate or alter the BFOQ defense. Rather, it merely clarified Title VII to make it clear that pregnancy and related conditions are included within Title VII's antidiscrimination provisions. As we have already recognized, "the purpose of the PDA was simply to make the treatment of pregnancy consistent with general Title VII principles." Arizona Governing Committee for Tax Deferred Annuity and Deferred Compensation Plans v. Norris, 463 U.S. 1073, 1085, n. 14 (1983).

* * *

II

Despite my disagreement with the Court concerning the scope of the BFOQ defense, I concur in reversing the Court of Appeals because [here the company made no showing that there was a substantial risk to third parties or that its costs were significantly increased by allowing women to work in exposed positions under its previous less-restrictive policy. The employer also failed equally to consider the risk of lead to males.]

JUSTICE SCALIA, concurring in the judgment.

I generally agree with the Court's analysis[.] By reason of the Pregnancy Discrimination Act, it would not matter if all pregnant women placed their children at risk in taking these jobs, just as it does not matter if no men do so. As Judge Easterbrook put it in his dissent below, "Title VII gives parents the power to make occupational decisions affecting their families. A legislative forum is available to those who believe that such decisions should be made elsewhere."

NOTE ON PREGNANCY AND THE *BFOQ* DEFENSE

1. *Johnson Controls* confirms that facial classification by pregnancy is disparate treatment, thus implicating only the BFOQ defense, not the business justification defense of disparate impact analysis.[1] In **Steelworkers v. Weber**, section D of this Chapter, infra, however, the Court appeared to hold that an affirmative action program that facially classified by race was not automatically intentional discrimination; only if there was an additional stigma placed on blacks or an intolerable burden placed on whites was intentional discrimination held to be at issue.

(a) Are *Johnson Controls* and *Weber* consistent? Is this aspect of *Johnson Controls* consistent with the *Guerra* case, discussed in the preceding Note? (Compare the minority opinions in *Johnson Controls* with the majority opinion in *Guerra*: which shows a more patronizing attitude toward women?)

(b) If affirmative action based on race is to be upheld, why is it necessary to insist that such programs are not really facially racially discriminatory? Because there is no BFOQ defense for race, as there is for the other classifications covered by Title VII?

2. Do you agree with the majority's interpretation of the PDA as having its own special BFOQ provisions for pregnancy-based classifications? Is that what the Court actually holds?

(a) How is the pregnancy-based BFOQ different from the ordinary BFOQ provision? Does the Court hold that safety is relevant in ordinary BFOQ contexts, but not in the PDA context?

(b) Would an employer's concern for pregnancy and its effect on customers or co-workers never meet the Court's BFOQ test? May an employer discharge an unwed pregnant woman from employment where her job entails serving as a role model for teenage females? Is that intentional sex discrimination for which there is no pregnancy-related BFOQ? See Chambers v. Omaha Girls Club, Inc., 834 F.2d 697 (8th Cir.1987).

3. Is it a wise public policy choice to read Title VII as leaving the choice of working during pregnancy primarily to women? Is this case really about reproductive choice?

(a) Under the Court's abortion decisions, it would presumably be permissible for a state to regulate a woman's decision to abort her fetus during (at least) the third trimester. See Roe v. Wade, 410 U.S. 113, 163, 93 S.Ct. 705, 732, 35 L.Ed.2d 147 (1973) (serving the interest in potential life). Does

---

1. Absent the PDA, would an employer's regulation of abortion among its employees constitute intentional sex discrimination under the *Gilbert* case?

Johnson Controls allow her to make an unfettered choice during that period? Should a woman be permitted to subject her fetus to harm in the workplace under circumstances where a late-term abortion would result?

(b) Are the public policy considerations different here because it is an employer that is attempting to regulate choice, not the state?

(c) Is this case bad policy because it lowers the health standards of all workers? Are women equal when they have an equal right to be forced economically to choose higher-paying jobs that hurt their health? Have women "come a long way," in the parlance of one contemporary advertisement, when they have the equal right to buy health problems previously restricted to men? Or is the best way to better treatment for all to make certain that all are treated equally?

(d) Are men the victims of the employer's policy in *Johnson Controls*? Are they discriminated against because they are not excluded from unhealthy jobs?

4. The Court seems to suggest, but stops short of holding, that Title VII displaces state tort law that might impose tort liability on the employer who allows women to work in dangerous occupations. Has judicial politics made strange bedfellows in *Johnson Controls*?

(a) Should Title VII override state tort law to relieve the employer of the dilemma of potentially conflicting liabilities? Is there in fact an unavoidable conflict? Does the answer depend on whether the state law at issue imposes strict liability or only fault-based liability? Was this part of the Court's opinion a necessary element for obtaining the vote of some justices in the majority?

(b) Does the victory for plaintiffs in *Johnson Controls* demonstrate the new political alliances that may be formed in controversial civil rights cases? Among the dissenters on the lower court were well-known free-market conservative judges: is there not a *laissez-faire* feel to the Court's opinion? But, if present, this is a strange variant, is it not, for the decision disables the *employer* from interfering with the rational, self-interested workplace decisions of employees?

2. SEXUAL HARASSMENT

ONCALE v. SUNDOWNER OFFSHORE SERVICES, INC.

Supreme Court of the United States, 1998.
523 U.S. 75, 118 S.Ct. 998, 140 L.Ed.2d 201.

JUSTICE SCALIA delivered the opinion of the Court.

This case presents the question whether workplace harassment can violate Title VII's prohibition against "discriminat[ion] ... because of ... sex," 42 U.S.C. § 2000e–2(a)(1), when the harasser and the harassed employee are of the same sex.

I

The District Court having granted summary judgment for respondent, we must assume the facts to be as alleged by petitioner Joseph Oncale.

The precise details are irrelevant to the legal point we must decide, and in the interest of both brevity and dignity we shall describe them only generally. In late October 1991, Oncale was working for respondent Sundowner Offshore Services on a Chevron U.S. A., Inc., oil platform in the Gulf of Mexico. He was employed as a roustabout on an eight-man crew which included respondent [co-workers, two of whom had supervisory authority.] On several occasions, Oncale was forcibly subjected to sex-related, humiliating actions against him * * * in the presence of the rest of the crew. [Two co-workers] also physically assaulted Oncale in a sexual manner, and [one] threatened him with rape.

[Oncale filed a claim under Title VII alleging that he felt coerced to have sex and left the job based on such fear, but it was dismissed because the court held that male-on-male harassment is not "sex" discrimination. The Fifth Circuit affirmed.]

II

Title VII of the Civil Rights Act of 1964 provides, in relevant part, that "[i]t shall be an unlawful employment practice for an employer ... to discriminate against any individual with respect to his compensation, terms, conditions, or privileges of employment, because of such individual's race, color, religion, sex, or national origin." We have held that this not only covers "terms" and "conditions" in the narrow contractual sense, but "evinces a congressional intent to strike at the entire spectrum of disparate treatment of men and women in employment." Meritor Savings Bank, FSB v. Vinson, 477 U.S. 57, 64, 106 S.Ct. 2399, 2404, 91 L.Ed.2d 49 (1986). "When the workplace is permeated with discriminatory intimidation, ridicule, and insult that is sufficiently severe or pervasive to alter the conditions of the victim's employment and create an abusive working environment, Title VII is violated." Harris v. Forklift Systems, Inc., 510 U.S. 17, 21, 114 S.Ct. 367, 370, 126 L.Ed.2d 295 (1993).

Title VII's prohibition of discrimination "because of ... sex" protects men as well as women, and in the related context of racial discrimination in the workplace we have rejected any conclusive presumption that an employer will not discriminate against members of his own race. "Because of the many facets of human motivation, it would be unwise to presume as a matter of law that human beings of one definable group will not discriminate against other members of that group." Castaneda v. Partida, 430 U.S. 482, 97 S.Ct. 1272, 51 L.Ed.2d 498 (1977). In Johnson v. Transportation Agency, Santa Clara Cty., 480 U.S. 616, 107 S.Ct. 1442, 94 L.Ed.2d 615 (1987), a male employee claimed that his employer discriminated against him because of his sex when it preferred a female employee for promotion. Although we ultimately rejected the claim on other grounds, we did not consider it significant that the supervisor who made that decision was also a man. If our precedents leave any doubt on the question, we hold today that nothing in Title VII necessarily bars a claim of discrimination "because of ... sex" merely because the plaintiff and the defendant (or the person charged with acting on behalf of the defendant) are of the same sex.

Courts have had little trouble with that principle in cases like *Johnson*, where an employee claims to have been passed over for a job or promotion. But when the issue arises in the context of a "hostile environment" sexual harassment claim, the state and federal courts have taken a bewildering variety of stances. Some, like the Fifth Circuit in this case, have held that same-sex sexual harassment claims are never cognizable under Title VII. Other decisions say that such claims are actionable only if the plaintiff can prove that the harasser is homosexual (and thus presumably motivated by sexual desire). Still others suggest that workplace harassment that is sexual in content is always actionable, regardless of the harasser's sex, sexual orientation, or motivations.

We see no justification in the statutory language or our precedents for a categorical rule excluding same-sex harassment claims from the coverage of Title VII. As some courts have observed, male-on-male sexual harassment in the workplace was assuredly not the principal evil Congress was concerned with when it enacted Title VII. But statutory prohibitions often go beyond the principal evil to cover reasonably comparable evils, and it is ultimately the provisions of our laws rather than the principal concerns of our legislators by which we are governed. Title VII prohibits "discriminat[ion] ... because of ... sex" in the "terms" or "conditions" of employment. Our holding that this includes sexual harassment must extend to sexual harassment of any kind that meets the statutory requirements.

Respondents and their amici contend that recognizing liability for same-sex harassment will transform Title VII into a general civility code for the American workplace. But that risk is no greater for same-sex than for opposite-sex harassment, and is adequately met by careful attention to the requirements of the statute. Title VII does not prohibit all verbal or physical harassment in the workplace; it is directed only at "discriminat[ion] ... because of ... sex." We have never held that workplace harassment, even harassment between men and women, is automatically discrimination because of sex merely because the words used have sexual content or connotations. "The critical issue, Title VII's text indicates, is whether members of one sex are exposed to disadvantageous terms or conditions of employment to which members of the other sex are not exposed." Harris, supra, at 25, 114 S.Ct. at 372 (Ginsburg, J., concurring).

Courts and juries have found the inference of discrimination easy to draw in most male-female sexual harassment situations, because the challenged conduct typically involves explicit or implicit proposals of sexual activity; it is reasonable to assume those proposals would not have been made to someone of the same sex. The same chain of inference would be available to a plaintiff alleging same-sex harassment, if there were credible evidence that the harasser was homosexual. But harassing conduct need not be motivated by sexual desire to support an inference of discrimination on the basis of sex. A trier of fact might reasonably find such discrimination, for example, if a female victim is harassed in such sex-specific and derogatory terms by another woman as to make it clear that the harasser is motivated by general hostility to the presence of women in the workplace. A same-sex harassment plaintiff may also, of course, offer direct comparative evidence about how the alleged harasser treated members of both sexes in a mixed-sex workplace. Whatever evidentiary route the plaintiff chooses to follow, he or she must always prove that the conduct at issue was not merely tinged with offensive sexual connotations, but actually constituted "discrimina[tion] ... because of ... sex."

And there is another requirement that prevents Title VII from expanding into a general civility code: As we emphasized in *Meritor* and *Harris*, the statute does not reach genuine but innocuous differences in the ways men and women routinely interact with members of the same sex and of the opposite sex. The prohibition of harassment on the basis of sex requires neither asexuality nor androgyny in the workplace; it forbids only behavior so objectively offensive as to alter the "conditions" of the victim's employment. "Conduct that is not severe or pervasive enough to create an objectively hostile or abusive work environment—an environment that a reasonable person would find hostile or abusive—is beyond Title VII's purview." *Harris*. We have always regarded that requirement as crucial, and as sufficient to ensure that courts and juries do not mistake ordinary socializing in the workplace—such as male-on-male horseplay or intersexual flirtation—for discriminatory "conditions of employment."

We have emphasized, moreover, that the objective severity of harassment should be judged from the perspective of a reasonable person in the plaintiff's position, considering "all the circumstances." *Harris*. In same-sex (as in all) harassment cases, that inquiry requires careful consideration of the social context in which particular behavior occurs and is experienced by its target. A professional football player's working environment is not severely or pervasively abusive, for example, if the coach smacks him on the buttocks as he heads onto the field—even if the same behavior would reasonably be experienced as abusive by the coach's secretary (male or female) back at the office. The real social impact of workplace behavior often depends on a constellation of surrounding circumstances, expectations, and relationships which are not fully captured by a simple recitation of the words used or the physical acts performed. Common sense, and an appropriate sensitivity to social context, will enable courts and juries to distinguish between simple teasing or roughhousing among members of the same sex, and conduct which a reasonable person in the plaintiff's position would find severely hostile or abusive.

III

Because we conclude that sex discrimination consisting of same-sex sexual harassment is actionable under Title VII, the judgment of the

Court of Appeals for the Fifth Circuit is reversed, and the case is remanded for further proceedings consistent with this opinion.

It is so ordered.

JUSTICE THOMAS, concurring.

I concur because the Court stresses that in every sexual harassment case, the plaintiff must plead and ultimately prove Title VII's statutory requirement that there be discrimination "because of . . . sex."

NOTE ON THE DEFINITIONS OF "SEXUAL" AND "HARASSMENT"

1. Although the precise issue raised in *Oncale* is whether same-sex harassment can violate Title VII, the Court takes some time and care in defining what constitutes harassment itself. Consider the precedents on which it builds in this area. In **Meritor Savings Bank, FSB v. Vinson**, 477 U.S. 57, 106 S.Ct. 2399, 91 L.Ed.2d 49 (1986), the Court for the first time held that harassment could constitute discrimination under Title VII. The case involved an assumedly consensual sexual relationship between a supervisor (male) and a subordinate (female) that later turned bad, but with no " 'tangible loss' of an 'economic character' " for the subordinate. Justice Rehnquist's majority opinion noted that there were two possible kinds of harassment—that which was enforced by monetary awards or denials (so-called "quid pro quo" harassment because favors were demanded for money or benefits) and that which was enforced by making work conditions so difficult as to punish an undesired employee (so-called "hostile environment" harassment). This case involved the second type, and essentially the employer sought to exclude such claims from coverage by arguing that Title VII could not be violated where there was only a "non-economic injury." The Court rejected the argument, noting that such harassment impacts the "terms and conditions" of employment and is thus actionable.

(a) In only one paragraph did the Court turn its attention to the specific definition of harassment. It stated that conduct is harassing if it is "sufficiently severe or pervasive to alter the conditions of [the victim's] employment" (brackets in original), 477 U.S. at 67, 106 S.Ct. at 2406. This observation, like the Court's holding regarding the irrelevance of "non-economic loss," also focuses on the "conditions of employment." The existence or not of an economic loss would have been a bright-line rule for detecting whether terms of employment had changed; once that bright line is rejected, is there any other line for detecting when harassment is severe enough to alter the conditions of employment? Does not any unwanted sex-talk, no matter how minor, alter the conditions of employment based on sex? Why does the Court emphasize the severity of harassment? See Valentine–Johnson v. Roche, 386 F.3d 800 (6th Cir. 2004) (woman who had filed previous EEO complaints now complains that new boss (i) "put his arm around her while walking down the hall" and (ii) on another occasion was "standing too close to her"; no harassment).

(b) The employer in *Meritor* also sought to defend the action by noting that the sexual contact had been consensual, but the Court struck this defense in favor of a more ambiguous approach. "The gravamen of any sexual harassment claim is that the alleged sexual advances were 'unwelcome [and] not whether her actual participation in sexual intercourse was voluntary.' " The Court held that plaintiff's "sexually provocative speech or dress" could be relevant evidence in deciding whether the advances were welcome. Do you agree? What is the difference between "welcome[ness]" and voluntariness, given the evidence that may be relevant? Does use of suggestive language with one co-worker indicate that an employee will welcome sexy talk with others? See Swentek v. USAIR, 830 F.2d 552 (4th Cir.1987) (no). Does a prior relationship indicate receptiveness to a continuing relationship? See Gilooly v. Missouri Dept. of Health and Senior Services, 421 F.3d 734 (8th Cir. 2005) (male charges that former lover became "overly dependent" and hovered about him; held, no affect on terms of employment); Shrout v. Black Clawson Co., 689 F.Supp. 774 (S.D.Ohio 1988) (employee with prior consensual sexual relationship with supervisor has affirmative duty to warn him that acts are no longer welcome).

2. In its second precedent defining harassment, **Harris v. Forklift Systems, Inc.**, 510 U.S. 17, 114 S.Ct. 367, 126 L.Ed.2d 295 (1993), the Court faced a case in which a supervisor made sexual innuendoes and played immature sexual games with women employees (such as asking them to retrieve coins from his pocket). The lower courts found the case a close one and ultimately dismissed on the ground that plaintiff suffered no affect on her "psychological well-being." Justice O'Connor's opinion reversed this judgment, holding that the *Meritor* standard for an "abusive or hostile environment" does not focus alone on severity of the loss, but rather "takes a middle path between ... conduct that is merely offensive and [conduct causing] a tangible economic injury." The standard has two components: (i) on a "subjective[]" basis the conduct must be perceived as abusive by the victim, and (ii) the conduct, viewed in its entire context,[1] must on an "objective[]" basis create "an environment that a reasonable person would find hostile." Under this standard, "Title VII comes into play before the harassing conduct leads to a nervous breakdown" because conduct may be harassing when it "detract[s] from employees' job performance," or discourages them from remaining on the job, or keeps them from advancement in their careers.

(a) Is it clear after *Harris* that the relevant objective minimum measure of harassment is not the objectively "reasonable woman" but the objectively "reasonable person"? Do men's and women's expectations vary regarding what is "reasonable" sexual interaction in the workplace?[2] If the judges in sexual harassment cases are mostly male (or even self-confident females), will a "male" definition of what is harassment be enforced? See, e.g., Weiss v. Coca–Cola Bottling Co. of Chicago, 990 F.2d 333, 337 (7th Cir.1993) (claim that supervisor repeatedly asked about employee's personal life, told her how beautiful she was, asked her for dates, called her a dumb blonde, put his hand

---

1. In reviewing all of the circumstances, said the Court, one must consider such factors as "the frequency of the discriminatory conduct; its severity; whether it is physically threatening or humiliating, or a mere offensive utterance; and whether it unreasonably interferes with an employee's work performance," 510 U.S. at 23, 114 S.Ct. at 371.

2. Note Justice Scalia's statement in *Oncale* that there exist "genuine but innocuous differences in the ways men and women routinely interact with members of the same sex and of the opposite sex." Recall Justice Ginsburg's admonition in U.S. v. Virginia, discussed in the previous Note, that the sexes are not "fungible."

on her shoulder at least six times, placed "I love you" signs in her work area, and tried to kiss her once at a bar and twice at work are not actionable harassment); "inquiries about what color bra [complainant] was wearing, [offender's] suggestive tone of voice when asking her whether he could 'make a house call'" and "the one occasion when he pulled back her tank top with his fingers were lamentably inappropriate," but not sexually harassing. Do you agree?

(b) How do you think that the *Harris* case should have been decided on its facts on remand? Is it possible (focusing on the subjective inquiry) that some of the affected women were harassed and some not? Could a court (focusing only on the objective inquiry) determine that none was harassed?

3. Against the background of the *Meritor* and *Harris* cases, consider whether Justice Scalia's majority opinion in *Oncale* changes the definition of actionable harassment.

(a) In his concurring opinion in *Harris*, Justice Scalia criticized the majority opinion, saying that it "does not seem to me a very clear standard" and "lets virtually unguided juries decide" what is harassment. He nevertheless joined the majority because he saw "no alternative" approach to the problem. Does *Oncale* continue his acquiescence? Does *Oncale* change nothing?

(b) What is the cumulative impact of Justice Scalia's musings that "horseplay or intersexual flirtation" or "simple teasing or roughhousing" are not harassment? Do they help the analysis by providing an innocuous counterpoint against which to measure illegal acts? Does the admonition to use "[c]ommon sense and an appropriate sensitivity to social context" help matters?

(c) Justice O'Connor in *Harris* admitted that her combined subjective-objective inquiry is not a "mathematically precise test." Would a more precise test be desirable? Recall the similar issues discussed in Chapter 6 regarding sexual harassment in education. See Chapter 6D supra. Will the fluidity of the definition of harassment lead employers to adopt a zero tolerance policy for sexual discussions and inter-gender contact in the office? Would that be that a good thing? Or in modern society where other social institutions are in decline and work hours seem always to be lengthening, is the workplace a social institution where many men and women develop their social lives? Do those social lives need some toleration of sex-based exploration in the development of intimate human relationships?

4. Lower courts, while taking all the circumstances into account, as admonished in *Harris*, see ¶ 2 supra and accompanying footnote, usually emphasize two factors—the pervasiveness and the severity of the objectionable conduct. In other words, assuming a victim is subjectively offended (as all plaintiffs presumably are), an objective conclusion of harassment will be more possible when the conduct is either more pervasive, more severe, or both. See, e.g., Jensen v. Potter, 435 F.3d 444 (3d Cir. 2006) such minor incidents as a "loud and frightening clap" and spilling coffee on car can show hostility if there is "pounding regularity"; Morris v. Oldham County Fiscal Court, 201 F.3d 784 (6th Cir.2000) (four non-severe incidents cannot be harassment; summary judgment for employer).

(a) As one might expect, cases involving physical violence are usually treated as easy cases. See, e.g., Paroline v. Unisys Corp., 879 F.2d 100 (4th Cir.1989) ("unwanted sexual touchings and innuendo escalating to assault and battery"). Why? Other cases marking the required degree of severity or pervasiveness range over quite a broad spectrum, with some apparently conflicting decisions. Compare Volk v. Coler, 845 F.2d 1422, 1438–39 (7th Cir.1988) (numerous date requests, sexual touching, references to plaintiff as "babe," "women's lib[ber]," and "queer" are sufficiently severe and pervasive to state claim), with Holland v. Jefferson National Life Ins. Co., 883 F.2d 1307 (7th Cir.1989) (pre-*Harris*: saying that job required "big boobs" and sitting on employer's face is inadequate). Some cases hold or suggest that lack of severity can be made up by increasing pervasiveness, and vice-versa, see Paroline v. Unisys Corp., supra; Smith v. First Union Nat. Bank, supra. Is it nevertheless implicit that some interactions are so benign that no amount of repetition would make them actionable as harassment? See Wilkie v. Department of Health and Human Services, 638 F.3d 944 (8th Cir. 2011) (spreading of rumor that plaintiff was having an affair is neither severe nor pervasive enough to be harassing) (collecting cases); Cross v. Prairie Meadows Racetrack and Casino, Inc., 615 F.3d 977 (8th Cir. 2010) (four discrete incidents over two years—grabbing ponytail, brushing hand across breast to clean shirt, angry response to more-than-friendship proposal, and spreading rumor of participation in oral sex are insufficient). Do you think that these cases were correctly decided?

(b) Are the questions as to what constitutes severity and pervasiveness always jury questions? See Reeves v. C.H. Robinson Worldwide Inc., 594 F.3d 798 (11th Cir. 2010) (jury question when plaintiff overheard co-workers use words "whore," "bitch," etc., and vulgar discussions of other women's breasts, nipples, and buttocks, and one coworker used a pornographic image of a woman as his computer wallpaper); Beardsley v. Webb, 30 F.3d 524, 530 (4th Cir.1994) (whether harassment was sufficiently severe or pervasive is "quintessentially a question of fact" for the jury). Or are they only questions of fact when within the range of what judges deem to be objectively covered by Title VII? See *Wilkie*, supra (using phrase "as a matter of law" to dismiss claim); Mendoza v. Borden, Inc., 195 F.3d 1238 (11th Cir.1999) (awarding judgment as a matter of law in a case involving "(1) one instance in which [supervisor told employee] 'I'm getting fired up'; (2) one occasion in which [he] rubbed his hip against [her] hip while touching her shoulder and smiling; (3) two instances in which [he] made a sniffing sound while looking at [her] groin area and one instance of sniffing without looking at her groin; and (4) [his] 'constant' following and staring at Mendoza in a 'very obvious fashion' "; collecting numerous cases claimed to show a minimum standard to go to the jury). Do you think that jurors would be more or less likely to find harassment than judges are? (Would they be more likely to find sex harassment than racial harassment?)

5. Now consider the *Oncale* Court's ruling that "because of sex" in Title VII includes discrimination by any person that is motivated by the gender of the victim, even when the harasser is of the same sex.

(a) Why is the assumption of sex-based motivation easy, according to the Court, when the harasser and victim are of different sex or gender? Because, as the Court says, such harassment involves "explicit or implicit proposals of sexual activity"? Is that remark too easy and even misleading—do demeaning words directed at women in the workplace relate to "sexual activity" or to the harasser's objection to social roles being undertaken by women? When the harassment is across gender lines, should it matter that the topic or the means of harassment is sexual activity?

(b) The *Oncale* opinion states that the same reasons that make it easy to identify "sexual" harassment in cross-gender cases of harassment also make it easy to identify "sexual" harassment if "the harasser was homosexual." Is it also true when the victim is homosexual and the harasser is heterosexual? Would a heterosexual harasser of a homosexual victim have been motivated by "explicit or implicit proposals of sexual activity"—or because he objected to the sexual orientation of the victim? See Hopkins v. Baltimore Gas and Elec. Co., infra (discrimination because of sexual orientation only). Does *Oncale* protect heterosexuals from harassment by homosexuals but not homosexuals from harassment by heterosexuals?[3]

(c) Assuming that both the harassers and the victim in *Oncale* were heterosexuals, how likely is it that the plaintiff can establish that the harassment was because of his sex? Is it not very unlikely that in most such cases the harassers were opposed to the presence of men (that is, themselves) in the workforce? Is it not more likely that sexuality was the means of harassing the victim, but not the end? Is harassment not motivated by sex of the victim but by means of sexual innuendo actionable? See Hopkins v. Baltimore Gas and Elec. Co., 77 F.3d 745, 751–52 (4th Cir.1996); McWilliams v. Fairfax County Bd. of Supervisors, 72 F.3d 1191, 1196 (4th Cir.1996) (harassment because of "the victim's known or believed prudery, or shyness, or other form of vulnerability to sexually-focused speech or conduct" is not "sex" harassment).[4]

(d) Sexual harassment claims are essentially claims of intentional discrimination, and several cases hold that harassing remarks that are not intended as sex-based remarks are not actionable. See, e.g., Hopkins v. Baltimore Gas and Elec. Co., supra. Is this not the same issue raised by the *General Electric* case, discussed in the previous sub-section of this Chapter? When are words sufficiently related to one sex group that the use of them constitutes "sex" harassment? See Pucino v. Verizon Wireless Communications, Inc., 618 F.3d 112 (2d Cir. 2010) (use of the word "bitch" is not always sexually degrading; depends on context). If an office continually plays rap songs that mention "bitches" and "ho's," does that constitute harassment based on "sex"?

---

3. Paradoxically, does a very high demand for severity and pervasiveness, which gives women less protection in the harassment context, leave homosexuals with more protection (that is, less reason to fear being charged with harassment)? See Morgan v. Massachusetts Gen. Hosp., 901 F.2d 186, 193 (1st Cir.1990) (no Title VII liability where male plaintiff claimed that male co-worker stood behind him and bumped into him while he mopped, "peeped" at him in restroom, and asked him to dance at Christmas party).

4. What other theories might be available to show "sex" discrimination rather than "sexual orientation" discrimination? Is discrimination against gay men because they are "effeminate" "sex" discrimination because it presumes sex-based roles? Cf. Price Waterhouse v. Hopkins, Chapter 7A.2(b) supra; Schroer v. Billington, 525 F.Supp.2d 58 (D.D.C., 2007) ("sex stereotyping" claim accepted from "male-to-female transsexual").

6. This Note has separated the definitions of "harassment" and "sex." Is that misleading? Is there something unique about "sexual harassment" as a whole entity, and is it that uniqueness that makes these cases more difficult than a case involving race-based harassment?

(a) Reconsider the cases in ¶ 3 that hold that the events were not sufficiently pervasive or serious to constitute harassment. Could they also be seen as holdings that the harassment that occurred was not "because of sex"? Would the same decisions have been made if the harassment was based on the race of the employee?

(b) As revealed in *Oncale*, the Court's decisions in the sexual harassment area have built on the (few) earlier decisions involving racial harassment. Was that a mistake? Or is that the correct approach? In its later opinion in Faragher v. City of Boca Raton, discussed in the succeeding Note, the Court cited with approval the statement that "a lack of racial sensitivity does not, alone, amount to actionable [racial] harassment." Does that view also account for the many decisions against plaintiffs in the sexual harassment area? Should harassment laws be interpreted to require such sensitivity?

7. Who has standing to complain about sexual harassment?

(a) If one woman in the office willingly engages in sex and gains promotions, are the other women in the office victims of sexual harassment or discrimination? See Drinkwater v. Union Carbide Corp., 904 F.2d 853 (3d Cir.1990) (only if sex permeates the office environment). Do you agree? If other women in the office are victims, are men in the office also victims of the harassment? Alternatively, if none of the women feels subjectively harassed (i.e., the supervisor's actions are not unwelcome), do the men lose their standing to sue?

(b) Can men sue when women are the victims of a hostile-environment harassment, or is the harm in sexually offensive environments only to women? See Anjelino v. New York Times Co., 200 F.3d 73 (3d Cir.1999) (discussing possible theories of standing for men when women are harassed).

(c) In light of ¶ 5(b), does the standing issue relate to the *Oncale* Court's concern that Title VII not be turned into a "general civility code"? If both men and women have standing, will that tend to encourage complaints? Will it tend to push offices toward prohibiting any discussion of sex or any expression of physical tenderness among employees, even when women might feel comfortable in the environment? Does it tend to push Title VII toward prohibiting "sexiness" in addition to sex discrimination? (Is such a distinction real?)

(d) The issues raised in this paragraph often arise in cases of claimed retaliation when one person objects to harassment in the office, then allegedly suffers from retaliation because of the complaint. Is a claim of retaliation actionable under Title VII when a hostile environment is at issue? See Jensen v. Potter, 435 F.3d 444 (3d Cir. 2006) (per Alito, J.) (permitting such claims but noting circuit split). Cf. Crawford v. Metropolitan Government of Nashville and Davidson County, 555 U.S. 271, 129 S.Ct. 846, 172 L.Ed.2d 650 (2009) (broad view of retaliation standing in underlying harassment case). See generally Note on the Prima Facie Case for Class Claims, ¶ 5, in Chapter 7A.2(a) supra (discussing major expansions in retaliation claims).

8. In the vast majority of Title VII cases, an illegal employment decision by a supervisor will automatically lead to the employer's liability because the employer gives effect to the supervisor's decision by implementing it (denying employment, lowering wages, etc.). See Burlington Industries, Inc. v. Ellerth, following this Note. Consider how sexual harassment cases might be different.

(a) In so-called quid-pro-quo harassment cases, where the supervisor gives or withholds benefits in exchange for sexual favors, should automatic employer liability result because the employer gives effect to the supervisor's decision by implementing or denying a promotion, a salary increase, etc.? Do such cases really involve "harassment"? Are they not simply ordinary cases of differential pay or promotions based on sex of the victim?

(b) In so-called hostile-environment harassment cases, the supervisor has created an abusive work environment, but there has been no tangible change in pay or status implemented by the company hierarchy. Should such claims also result in automatic liability for the employer? See the following case.

BURLINGTON INDUSTRIES, INC. v. ELLERTH

Supreme Court of the United States, 1998.
524 U.S. 742, 118 S.Ct. 2257, 141 L.Ed.2d 633.

JUSTICE KENNEDY delivered the opinion of the Court.

We decide whether, under Title VII of the Civil Rights Act of 1964, an employee who refuses the unwelcome and threatening sexual advances of a supervisor, yet suffers no adverse, tangible job consequences, can recover against the employer without showing the employer is negligent or otherwise at fault for the supervisor's actions.

I

[Plaintiff Ellerth, a salesperson, claimed sexual harassment at the hands of her supervisor's supervisor, a "mid-level manager" in a company with 22,000 employees with 50 facilities in the U.S. The supervisor, one Slowik, had "authority to make hiring and promotion decisions subject to the approval of his supervisor, who signed the paperwork," but he was " 'not amongst the decision-making or policy-making hierarchy.' " The supervisor made sexually oriented suggestions to Ellerth but he never actually made an adverse employment decision against her; in fact, he promoted her.]

During her tenure at Burlington, Ellerth did not inform anyone in authority about Slowik's conduct, despite knowing Burlington had a policy against sexual harassment. In fact, she chose not to inform her immediate supervisor (not Slowik) because " 'it would be his duty as my supervisor to report any incidents of sexual harassment [to Slowik].' " On one occasion, she told Slowik a comment he made was inappropriate.

[Ellerth filed a Title VII suit for sex discrimination against Burlington. Although finding Slowik's conduct severe and pervasive enough to constitute harassment, the trial court rules that Burlington could not be held liable for "hostile-environment" claims (as opposed to "quid-pro-quo" claims) unless it knew or should have known of the supervisor's harassing conduct. A fractured Seventh Circuit majority reversed. Certiorari was granted.]

II

* * * Cases based on threats which are carried out are referred to often as quid pro quo cases, as distinct from bothersome attentions or sexual remarks that are sufficiently severe or pervasive to create a hostile work environment. The terms quid pro quo and hostile work environment are helpful, perhaps, in making a rough demarcation between cases in which threats are carried out and those where they are not or are absent altogether, but beyond this are of limited utility.

* * *

"Quid pro quo" and "hostile work environment" do not appear in the statutory text. The terms appeared first in the academic literature, see C. MacKinnon, SEXUAL HARASSMENT OF WORKING WOMEN (1979), [and later] found their way into decisions of the Courts of Appeals.

In Meritor [Savings Bank, FSB v. Vinson we used the terms, but for] a specific and limited purpose. There we considered whether the conduct in question constituted discrimination in the terms or conditions of employment in violation of Title VII. We assumed, and with adequate reason, that if an employer demanded sexual favors from an employee in return for a job benefit, discrimination with respect to terms or conditions of employment was explicit. Less obvious was whether an employer's sexually demeaning behavior altered terms or conditions of employment in violation of Title VII. We distinguished between quid pro quo claims and hostile environment claims, and said both were cognizable under Title VII, though the latter requires harassment that is severe or pervasive. [Thus we have used the terms as aids in defining a violation, but we have not used them in discussing the separate issue of an employer's liability for a supervisor's harassment. We agree that Ellerth's claim in this case, because it involved unfulfilled threats that created a hostile environment was properly classified as a "hostile environment" claim for purposes of analyzing whether it stated a claim.]

[After a determination of a violation has been made], however, the factors we discuss below, and not the categories quid pro quo and hostile work environment, will be controlling on the issue of vicarious liability [of the employer for the supervisor's acts]. That is the question we must resolve.

III

We must decide, then, whether an employer has vicarious liability when a supervisor creates a hostile work environment by making explicit threats to alter a subordinate's terms or conditions of employment, based on sex, but does not fulfill the threat. We turn to principles of agency law, for the term "employer" is defined under Title VII to include "agents." 42 U.S.C. § 2000e(b); see *Meritor*. In express terms, Congress has directed federal courts to interpret Title VII based on agency principles. Given such an explicit instruction, we conclude a uniform and predictable standard must be established as a matter of federal law. We rely "on the general common law of agency, rather than on the law of any particular State, to give meaning to these terms." The resulting federal rule, based on a body of case law developed over time, is statutory interpretation pursuant to congressional direction * * *.

As *Meritor* acknowledged, the Restatement (Second) of Agency (1957) (hereinafter Restatement), is a useful beginning point for a discussion of general agency principles. Since our decision in *Meritor*, federal courts have explored agency principles, and we find useful instruction in their decisions, noting that "common-law principles may not be transferable in all their particulars to Title VII." The EEOC has issued Guidelines governing sexual harassment claims under Title VII, but they provide little guidance on the issue of employer liability for supervisor harassment. See 29 CFR § 1604.11(c) (1997) (vicarious liability for supervisor harassment turns on "the particular employment relationship and the job functions performed by the individual").

[A: Restatement § 219(1)]

Section 219(1) of the Restatement sets out a central principle of agency law:

> "A master is subject to liability for the torts of his servants committed while acting in the scope of their employment."

An employer may be liable for both negligent and intentional torts committed by an employee within the scope of his or her employment. Sexual harassment under Title VII presupposes intentional conduct. While early decisions absolved employers of liability for the intentional torts of their employees, the law now imposes liability where the [supervisory] employee's "purpose, however misguided, is wholly or in part to further the master's business." W. Keeton, D. Dobbs, R. Keeton, & D. Owen, Prosser and Keeton on Law of Torts § 70, p. 505 (5th ed.1984) (hereinafter Prosser and Keeton on Torts). In applying scope of employment principles to intentional torts, however, it is accepted that "it is less likely that a willful tort will properly be held to be in the course of employment and that the liability of the master for such torts will naturally be more limited." F. Mechem, Outlines of the Law of Agency § 394, p. 266 (P. Mechem 4th ed., 1952). The Restatement defines conduct, including an intentional tort, to be within the scope of employment when "actuated, at least in part, by a purpose to serve the [employer]," even if it is forbidden by the employer. Restatement §§ 228(1)(c), 230. For example, when a salesperson lies to a customer to make a sale, the tortious conduct is within the scope of employment because it benefits the employer by increasing sales, even though it may violate the employer's policies. See Prosser and Keeton on Torts § 70, at 505–506.

As Courts of Appeals have recognized, a supervisor acting out of gender-based animus or a desire to fulfill sexual urges may not be actuated by a purpose to serve the employer. The harassing supervisor often acts for personal motives, motives unrelated and even antithetical to the objectives of the employer. Cf. Mechem, supra, § 368 ("for the time being [the supervisor] is conspicuously and unmistakably seeking a personal end"); see also Restatement § 235, Illustration 2 (tort committed while "[a]cting purely from personal ill will" not within the scope of employment); § 235, Illustration 3 (tort committed in retaliation for failing to pay the employee a bribe not within the scope of employment). There are instances, of course, where a supervisor engages in unlawful discrimination with the purpose, mistaken or otherwise, to serve the employer. E.g., Sims v. Montgomery County Comm'n, 766 F.Supp. 1052, 1075 (M.D.Ala.1990) (supervisor acting in scope of employment where employer has a policy of discouraging women from seeking advancement and "sexual harassment was simply a way of furthering that policy"). [But the] * * * general rule is that sexual harassment by a supervisor is not conduct within the scope of employment.

[B: RESTATEMENT § 219(2)]

* * * In limited circumstances, agency principles impose liability on employers even where employees commit torts outside the scope of employment. The principles are set forth in the much-cited § 219(2) of the Restatement:

"(2) A master is not subject to liability for the torts of his servants acting outside the scope of their employment, unless:

"(a) the master intended the conduct or the consequences, or

"(b) the master was negligent or reckless, or

"(c) the conduct violated a non-delegable duty of the master, or

"(d) the servant purported to act or to speak on behalf of the principal and there was reliance upon apparent authority, or he was aided in accomplishing the tort by the existence of the agency relation."

Subsection (a) addresses direct liability, where the employer acts with tortious intent, and indirect liability, where the agent's high rank in the company makes him or her the employer's alter ego. None of the parties contend Slowik's rank imputes liability under this principle. There is no contention, furthermore, that a nondelegable duty is involved. See § 219(2)(c). So, for our purposes here, subsections (a) and (c) can be put aside.

[Subsection 219(2)(b): "Employer's Negligence"]

* * * Under subsection (b), an employer is liable when the tort is attributable to the employer's own negligence. § 219(2)(b). Thus, although

a supervisor's sexual harassment is outside the scope of employment because the conduct was for personal motives, an employer can be liable, nonetheless, where its own negligence is a cause of the harassment. An employer is negligent with respect to sexual harassment if it knew or should have known about the conduct and failed to stop it. Negligence sets a minimum standard for employer liability under Title VII; but *Ellerth* seeks to invoke the more stringent standard of vicarious liability.

[SUBSECTION 219(2)(d): "APPARENT AUTHORITY"]

Subsection 219(2)(d) concerns vicarious liability for intentional torts committed by an employee when the employee uses apparent authority (the apparent authority standard), or when the employee "was aided in accomplishing the tort by the existence of the agency relation" (the aided in the agency relation standard). * * *

As a general rule, apparent authority is relevant where the agent purports to exercise a power which he or she does not have, as distinct from where the agent threatens to misuse actual power. Compare Restatement § 6 (defining "power") with § 8 (defining "apparent authority"). In the usual case, a supervisor's harassment involves misuse of actual power, not the false impression of its existence. Apparent authority analysis therefore is inappropriate in this context * * *. When a party seeks to impose vicarious liability based on an agent's misuse of delegated authority, the Restatement's aided in the agency relation rule, rather than the apparent authority rule, appears to be the appropriate form of analysis.

[SUBSECTION 219(d): "AIDED-IN-THE-AGENCY-RELATION"]

We turn to the aided in the agency relation standard. In a sense, most workplace tortfeasors are aided in accomplishing their tortious objective by the existence of the agency relation: Proximity and regular contact may afford a captive pool of potential victims. See Gary v. Long, 59 F.3d 1391, 1397 (C.A.D.C.1995). Were this to satisfy the aided in the agency relation standard, an employer would be subject to vicarious liability not only for all supervisor harassment, but also for all co-worker harassment, a result enforced by neither the EEOC nor any court of appeals to have considered the issue. The aided in the agency relation standard, therefore, requires the existence of something more than the employment relation itself.

At the outset, we can identify a class of cases where, beyond question, more than the mere existence of the employment relation aids in commission of the harassment: when a supervisor takes a tangible employment action against the subordinate. Every Federal Court of Appeals to have considered the question has found vicarious liability when a discriminatory act results in a tangible employment action. * * * Although few courts have elaborated how agency principles support this rule, we think it reflects a correct application of the aided in the agency relation standard.

* * * The concept of a tangible employment action appears in numerous cases in the Courts of Appeals discussing claims involving race, age,

and national origin discrimination, as well as sex discrimination. Without endorsing the specific results of those decisions, we think it prudent to import the concept of a tangible employment action for resolution of the vicarious liability issue we consider here. A tangible employment action constitutes a significant change in employment status, such as hiring, firing, failing to promote, reassignment with significantly different responsibilities, or a decision causing a significant change in benefits.

When a supervisor makes a tangible employment decision, there is assurance the injury could not have been inflicted absent the agency relation. A tangible employment action in most cases inflicts direct economic harm. As a general proposition, only a supervisor, or other person acting with the authority of the company, can cause this sort of injury. A co-worker can break a co-worker's arm as easily as a supervisor, and anyone who has regular contact with an employee can inflict psychological injuries by his or her offensive conduct. But one co-worker (absent some elaborate scheme) cannot dock another's pay, nor can one co-worker demote another. Tangible employment actions fall within the special province of the supervisor. The supervisor has been empowered by the company as a distinct class of agent to make economic decisions affecting other employees under his or her control.

* * *

Whether the agency relation aids in commission of supervisor harassment which does not culminate in a tangible employment action is less obvious * * *.

Although *Meritor* suggested the limitation on employer liability stemmed from agency principles, the Court acknowledged other considerations might be relevant as well. For example, Title VII is designed to encourage the creation of antiharassment policies and effective grievance mechanisms. Were employer liability to depend in part on an employer's effort to create such procedures, it would effect Congress' intention to promote conciliation rather than litigation in the Title VII context, and the EEOC's policy of encouraging the development of grievance procedures. To the extent limiting employer liability could encourage employees to report harassing conduct before it becomes severe or pervasive, it would also serve Title VII's deterrent purpose. * * * As we have observed, Title VII borrows from tort law the avoidable consequences doctrine, and the considerations which animate that doctrine would also support the limitation of employer liability in certain circumstances.

In order to accommodate the agency principles of vicarious liability for harm caused by misuse of supervisory authority, as well as Title VII's equally basic policies of encouraging forethought by employers and saving action by objecting employees, we adopt the following holding in this case and in Faragher v. Boca Raton, [see the following Note], also decided today. An employer is subject to vicarious liability to a victimized employee for an actionable hostile environment created by a supervisor with immediate (or successively higher) authority over the employee. When no tangible employment action is taken, a defending employer may raise an affirmative defense to liability or damages, subject to proof by a preponderance of the evidence, see Fed. Rule Civ. Proc. 8(c). The defense comprises two necessary elements: (a) that the employer exercised reasonable care to prevent and correct promptly any sexually harassing behavior, and (b) that the plaintiff employee unreasonably failed to take advantage of any preventive or corrective opportunities provided by the employer or to avoid harm otherwise. While proof that an employer had promulgated an anti-harassment policy with complaint procedure is not necessary in every instance as a matter of law, the need for a stated policy suitable to the employment circumstances may appropriately be addressed in any case when litigating the first element of the defense. And while proof that an employee failed to fulfill the corresponding obligation of reasonable care to avoid harm is not limited to showing any unreasonable failure to use any complaint procedure provided by the employer, a demonstration of such failure will normally suffice to satisfy the employer's burden under the second element of the defense. No affirmative defense is available, however, when the supervisor's harassment culminates in a tangible employment action, such as discharge, demotion, or undesirable reassignment.

[The case is remanded for further consideration.]

It is so ordered.

JUSTICE THOMAS, with whom JUSTICE SCALIA joins, dissenting.

The Court today manufactures a rule that employers are vicariously liable if supervisors create a sexually hostile work environment, subject to an affirmative defense that the Court barely attempts to define. This rule applies even if the employer has a policy against sexual harassment, the employee knows about that policy, and the employee never informs anyone in a position of authority about the supervisor's conduct. As a result, employer liability under Title VII is judged by different standards depending upon whether a sexually or racially hostile work environment is alleged. The standard of employer liability should be the same in both instances: An employer should be liable if, and only if, the plaintiff proves that the employer was negligent in permitting the supervisor's conduct to occur. * * *

NOTE ON EMPLOYER LIABILITY FOR SEXUAL HARASSMENT

1. The Court holds that there may not be employer liability for every supervisory act of sexual harassment. Rather, whether the employer is responsible for a supervisor's actions will turn on the application of "agency principles." The Court is candid in admitting that it is creating these rules itself based on its independent reading of agency doctrine developed elsewhere, primarily in the Restatement of Agency.[1] The Court then quickly

---

1. In Kolstad v. American Dental Ass'n, 527 U.S. 526, 119 S.Ct. 2118, 144 L.Ed.2d 494 (1999), the Court specifically refused to apply agency principles found in the Restatement after finding

dismisses three possible bases for attributing a supervisor's action to the employer.

(a) First, the Court holds that liability will ordinarily not attach under § 219(1) because a harassing supervisor promotes his own goals, is not actuated by the purpose of serving the employer, and thus cannot be said to be acting within the scope of his employment. Do you agree?

(b) Second, the Court also holds that § 219(2)(a) cannot apply here because Ellerth seeks to use principles of strict liability rather than negligence. Liability under the negligence rule would attach only if the employer "knew or should have known about the conduct and failed to stop it". Why did Ellerth not argue this point? Was it because she had never reported the supervisor's conduct to his superiors? Notice the relationship between this point and the affirmative defense later created by the Court: will that affirmative defense also apply to an argument of liability under § 219(2)(a) because unless the plaintiff complains the employer cannot know (nor should it have known) about the harassment? Is an argument based on § 219(2)(a) still potentially open, or is it dead as a practical matter?

(c) Finally, the Court rejects liability under § 219(2)(d)'s "apparent authority" language, noting that harassing supervisors typically do not project authority they lack, but rather misuse their actual authority. Can you think of any circumstance where a supervisor might make his employer liable under this section? Would a low-level supervisor be covered here if he claimed authority to fire a female employee and extracted sexual favors from her in exchange for not acting on the threats? But is it fair to hold employers responsible for low-level supervisors to whom they give no actual power while excusing them from liability for supervisors who actually have power? If you think this is a problem, should it be corrected by having the Court-created affirmative defense also apply to liability determined under this principle?

2. The Court ultimately finds that liability can attach in this case based on a fourth agency doctrine, the other principle in § 219(2)(d) that makes an employer liable when an employee has been aided in his harassment by the existence of the employment relation. The Court immediately notes that, despite the apparent clarity of the language of § 219(2)(d), something more than the employment relation itself is needed to attach liability to the employer under this principle. Initially the Court finds this "something more" in the concept of a "tangible loss" caused by the supervisor's decision, and when this is found, the employer, without more, is strictly liable, with no apparent defense of the kind discussed infra.

(a) Who are person's with power to impose a "tangible loss," and what constitutes a "tangible employment action"? In **Pennsylvania State Police v. Suders**, 542 U.S. 129, 124 S.Ct. 2342, 159 L.Ed.2d 204 (2004), the Supreme Court considered a claim by a woman that she had not only been subjected to a hostile-environment harassment, but that it had been so intolerable that she had been forced to quit ("constructively discharged"). Referring to such cases as "mixed claims," Justice Ginsburg's majority

that they would lead to "perverse" results undercutting the goals of Title VII. Note the defense created in *Burlington Industries* and discussed infra. Is it also a departure from principles otherwise found in the Restatement?

opinion found that constructive discharge alone is not a "tangible employment action"; only if joined with another action that meets the test will constructive discharge result in strict liability. This is because "[a]bsent 'an official act of the enterprise' as the last straw, the employer ordinarily would have no particular reason to suspect that a resignation is not the typical kind daily occurring in the work force."

(b) Why is vicarious employer liability appropriate in cases of tangible losses? Is it fair to say that a supervisor is "aided" by his agency relationship with the employer (thus making the employer vicariously liable under § 219(2)(d)) only when the employer has seen fit to invest him with actual power to cause economic losses to employees? In other words, is power the key? Or does *Pennsylvania State Police* suggest that notice is the key concept? Are the supervisors of supervisors put on constructive notice that their may be a problem only when there is formality of company action? Is the key concept formality itself, with the formality of discharge indicating to courts that the full resources of the employer are behind the adverse employment decision?[2]

(c) What decisions qualify as "tangible employment actions"? See Lutkewitte v. Gonzales, 436 F.3d 248 (D.C. Cir. 2006) (none found in (i) supervisor's directive that employee accompany him on business trip, (ii) submission to sex for fear of losing job, or (iii) receipt of benefits after compliance with demand for sexual favors). Note the apparently similar issue that can arise in cases alleging retaliation, where a plaintiff must show that an "adverse employment" action has been taken to punish her for complaining. There, however, the Court has taken a much more lenient view toward actionable losses. See Burlington Northern & Santa Fe Railway Co. v. White, 548 U.S. 53, 126 S.Ct. 2405, 165 L.Ed.2d 345(2006) (lesser sanctions not amounting to changes in terms or conditions of employment actionable for retaliation claim). What explains the difference?

3. As the Court described its actions later in *Pennsylvania State Police*, supra, § 219(2)(d) has no application, and the Court creates its own rules for liability when there has been no "tangible employment action." In such cases, there is also employer liability, but subject to the affirmative defense that it has acted reasonably (ordinarily provable by showing that it had a functioning complaint process in place) and the employee has not (ordinarily provable by showing that the employee failed to use that process).

(a) What is the source of this defense? Does it come from § 219(2)(d)? Or was the Court right to admit later that it created this defense and appended it to the Restatement principles? How does the Court justify having done this?

(b) What is the scope of the defense recognized? The burdens of production and persuasion, see section A.2 of this Chapter, supra, are both on the employer, correct? Ferraro v. Kellwood Co, 440 F.3d 96 (2d Cir. 2006) (proof that complainant failed to use a presumptively adequate in-house review

---

2. In *Pennsylvania State Police*, the Court said: "Absent such an official act [of discharge], the extent to which the supervisor's misconduct has been aided by the agency relation * * * is less certain. That uncertainty, our precedent establishes, justifies affording the employer the chance to establish, through the *Ellerth/Faragher* affirmative defense, that it should not be held vicariously liable." 542 U.S. at 148–49, 124 S.Ct. at 2355.

system carries the defendant's burden; resentment of employer's action on one prior complaint by another employee is not counter-proof of reasonableness of failure to use the system). Given the Court's statements about the ordinary application of this defense, what will every risk-averse employer do following this decision? If the defense results in sending most complaints of sexual harassment, at least those involving no "tangible loss," to in-house remediation, is that a good thing? Will the defense lead to protracted future litigation about whether the system is a sham or actually works?[3]

(c) Even when an employer has a review process, does there always remain the factual question of whether it in fact works? Is whether it works irrelevant if the plaintiff has failed to use it? McPherson v. City of Waukegan, 379 F.3d 430 (7th Cir. 2004) ("employer cannot be considered to have knowledge of sexual harassment 'unless the employee makes a concerted effort to inform the employer that a problem exists' ").

4. In a companion case decided the same day, **Faragher v. City of Boca Raton**, 524 U.S. 775, 118 S.Ct. 2275, 141 L.Ed.2d 662 (1998), Justice Souter's opinion for the Court added a few details to the *Burlington Industries* decision, this time in the context of a life guard who has suffered pervasive discrimination from co-workers and supervisors who made sexist remarks about her.

(a) In dictum, Justice Souter explained that sexual harassment by a company president would result in automatic vicarious liability for the employer because he is "indisputably within that class of an employer organization's officials who may be treated as the organization's proxy." On what agency principle is this idea based? See Restatement § 219(2)(a), as discussed briefly in *Burlington Industries* (referring to "high officials" who are the "alter ego" of the company). Who are such officials? Cf. Pembaur v. City of Cincinnati, Chapter 1H.1 supra. Would the affirmative defense recognized in *Burlington Industries* also apply to this basis for imputing liability to the company? See Dearth v. Collins, 441 F.3d 931 (11th Cir. 2006) (sole shareholder of corporation is not himself liable; *Ellerth* defense applies).

(b) Justice Souter also undertook a more detailed discussion of the affirmative defense created by the Court in *Burlington Industries*. He justified it as being drawn from the general legal "duty [on victims] 'to use such means as are reasonable under the circumstances to avoid or minimize the damages' that result from violations of the statute." He added that "no award against a liable employer should reward a plaintiff for what her own efforts could have avoided." Do you agree with this rationale? Does it view women as strong and capable of protecting themselves? Would a contrary decision have been patronizing to women or just more realistic about who has power in the modern workplace? Is the rationale correct because it treats all employees who might be harassed—both men and women—equally, or it that idea unrealistic also?

---

3. Compare the similar issues raised in the educational context and discussed in Chapter 6D supra. If the in-house process can be challenged, should it be judged by whether it actually correctly decided given cases on their facts? By whether it provided relief for the situation discovered? Or merely by whether it did not act unreasonably in dealing with the harassment uncovered?

(c) Would many harassed persons ever invoke an in-house complaint process? Would invocation forever mark them as complainers and inhibit their chances of promotion or other advancement? (But is this also true for filing suit directly under Title VII? Would not harassed persons contemplating a judicial remedy also fear that future prospective employers would not hire them based on their previous complaints?)

5. Move from the analytical basis for these decisions and consider their transactional results and real-world impact. Consider especially that the cases find liability only for actions by supervisors, not by co-workers.

(a) For a large group, perhaps the vast majority, of sexual harassment cases that do not involve "tangible employment actions," risk-averse employers will be able to defeat vicarious liability by showing the existence of their in-house system for processing sexual harassment complaints. Although *Ellerth* is couched as a decision about employer liability, not what constitutes a violation, is it not effectively a decision about liability as such? If so, does it effectively overrule *Meritor*, discussed in the preceding Note, by making it impossible to win against an employer when there has been no "tangible loss."[4] Could this result be avoided by making the supervisor personally liable under Title VII? Does Title VII permit that? See Dearth v. Collins, supra (discussing circuit cases and rejecting liability).

(b) If only supervisors make the employer liable under *Ellerth*, who is a supervisor? See Higbee v. Sentry Ins. Co., 440 F.3d 408 (7th Cir. 2006) (noting conflict in the circuits over breadth of the term "supervisor"). What rules apply to peer harassment, when one worker harasses a co-worker? Is it not actionable at all? Is it actionable, but only if a supervisor does nothing, converting it to supervisory harassment? Will other standards from the Restatement apply? See Pennsylvania State Police, supra, 542 U.S. at 143 n.6, 124 S.Ct. at 2352 n.6 ("*Ellerth* and *Faragher* expressed no view on the employer liability standard for co-worker harassment. Nor do we."); Arrieta–Colon v. Wal–Mart Puerto Rico, Inc., 434 F.3d 75 (1st Cir. 2006) (when "harassment is by a non-supervisory co-worker, the employer is liable only if the plaintiff can show that the employer 'knew or should have known of the charged ... harassment and failed to implement prompt and appropriate action' "). If the *Arrieta–Colon* standard is the law, how is it different from *Ellerth*?

6. Questions similar to those presented in *Ellerth* can arise outside the context of sexual harassment. A common one concerns employer responsibility in the context of a multi-layer supervisory system where one level sets in motion an adverse employment decision for discriminatory motives, but the final layer of decisionmaker acts without such a motive. In **Staub v. Proctor Hosp.**, ___ U.S. ___, 131 S.Ct. 1186, 179 L.Ed.2d 144 (2011), in a rather chatty and somewhat obscure opinion by Justice Scalia, the Court held that the "mixed-motive" provision in the statute (liability where discriminatory

---

4. Although the Court states that it must at the liability phase lay aside the distinction between "quid-pro-quo" cases and "hostile-environment" cases used at the violations-determination stage, is not the Court's later distinction between "tangible employment decisions" and mere threatening environments not a near-replication of the same ideas? How are they not different? Is there any "hostile-environment" case at the violations stage that can be labeled as involving a "tangible employment decision" at the liability stage? Re-read the Court's latter definition.

animus is "a motivating factor for the employer's action") guided its decision, although it appeared to mix together some agency principles as well, 131 S.Ct. at 1192:

"Animus and responsibility for the adverse action can both be attributed to the earlier [supervisor] if the [final] adverse action is the intended consequence of that agent's discriminatory conduct. So long as the [earlier supervisor] intends, for discriminatory reasons, that the adverse action occur, he has the scienter required to be liable under USERRA. And it is axiomatic under tort law that the exercise of judgment by the [final] decisionmaker does not prevent the earlier [supervisor's] action (and hence the earlier [supervisor's] discriminatory animus) from being the proximate cause of the harm."

(a) The Court noted that under the mixed-motive provision at issue, the burden of proving an intervening and independent motive resided with the employer.[5] How different is this from *Ellerth*'s approach for sexual harassment? Note also that after adoption of the 1991 Act, the defense only limits relief; it does not foreclose all liability. How is that different from *Ellerth*'s system?

(b) Would Title VII be better served by the enactment of specific rules for employer responsibility for the acts of supervisors and co-workers?

3. RELIGIOUS DISCRIMINATION: THE ACCOMMODATION REQUIREMENT

ANSONIA BOARD OF EDUCATION v. PHILBROOK

Supreme Court of the United States, 1986.
479 U.S. 60, 107 S.Ct. 367, 93 L.Ed.2d 305.

CHIEF JUSTICE REHNQUIST delivered the opinion of the Court.

Petitioner Ansonia Board of Education has employed respondent Ronald Philbrook since 1962 to teach high school business and typing classes in Ansonia, Connecticut. In 1968, Philbrook was baptized into the Worldwide Church of God. The tenets of the church require members to refrain from secular employment during designated holy days, a practice that has caused respondent to miss approximately six school days each year. We are asked to determine whether the employer's efforts to adjust respondent's work schedule in light of his beliefs fulfills its obligation under § 701(j) of the Civil Rights Act of 1964, 42 U.S.C. § 2000e(j), to "reasonably accommodate to an employee's ... religious observance or practice without undue hardship on the conduct of the employer's business."[1]

* * *

---

5. Staub arose under an anologue to Title VII, the Uniformed Services Employment and Reemployment Rights Act (USERRA), 38 U.S.C. § 4311, which protects against discrimination against members of the armed services on terms similar to those found in Title VII, including the provision regarding "a motivating factor" for discrimination. See section A.2(b) supra in this Chapter and its discussion of the "mixed-motive" defense in the 1991 Civil Rights Act, § 107.

1. The reasonable accommodation duty was incorporated into the statute, somewhat awkwardly, in the definition of religion. Title VII's central provisions make it an unlawful employ-

[The school district allowed employees to take, at their own discretion, three days of personal leave for religious observances. Since Philbrook wished to take more than that number he could do so only with a loss of pay. He offered to use some ordinary holidays for leave or to hire a substitute if the school board would give him more leave time, but the board refused. He sued, claiming that he had not been accommodated as required by § 701(j).]

As we noted in our only previous consideration of § 701(j), its language was added to the 1972 amendments on the floor of the Senate with little discussion. Trans World Airlines, Inc. v. Hardison, 432 U.S. 63, 74, n. 9, 97 S.Ct. 2264, 2271, n. 9, 53 L.Ed.2d 113 (1977). See 118 Cong.Rec. 705–706 (1972). In *Hardison*, supra, at 84, 97 S.Ct. at 2276, we determined that an accommodation causes "undue hardship" whenever that accommodation results in "more than a *de minimis* cost" to the employer.

* * * The employer in *Hardison* simply argued that all conceivable accommodations would result in undue hardship, and we agreed.

* * *

* * * [T]he Court of Appeals assumed that the employer had offered a reasonable accommodation of Philbrook's religious beliefs. This alone, however, was insufficient in that court's view to allow resolution of the dispute. The court observed that the duty to accommodate "cannot be defined without reference to undue hardship." It accordingly determined that the accommodation obligation includes a duty to accept "the proposal the employee prefers unless that accommodation causes undue hardship on the employer's conduct of his business." * * *

We find no basis in either the statute or its legislative history for requiring an employer to choose any particular reasonable accommodation. By its very terms the statute directs that any reasonable accommodation by the employer is sufficient to meet its accommodation obligation. The employer violates the statute unless it "demonstrates that [it] is unable to reasonably accommodate ... an employee's ... religious observance or practice without undue hardship on the conduct of the employer's business." Thus, where the employer has already reasonably accommodated the employee's religious needs, the statutory inquiry is at an end. The employer need not further show that each of the employee's alternative accommodations would result in undue hardship. As *Hardison* illustrates,

ment practice for an employer "to fail or refuse to hire or to discharge any individual, or otherwise to discriminate against any individual with respect to his compensation, terms, conditions, or privileges of employment, because of such individual's ... religion ...," § 703(a)(1), 42 U.S.C. § 2000e–2(a)(1), or "to limit, segregate, or classify his employees ... in any way which would deprive or tend to deprive any individual of employment opportunities or otherwise adversely affect his status as an employee, because of such individual's ... religion...." § 703(a)(2), 42 U.S.C. § 2000e–2(a)(2). Section 701(j), 42 U.S.C. § 2000e(j), was added in 1972 to illuminate the meaning of religious discrimination under the statute. It provides that "[t]he term 'religion' includes all aspects of religious observance and practice, as well as belief, unless an employer demonstrates that he is unable to reasonably accommodate to an employee's or prospective employee's religious observance or practice without undue hardship on the conduct of the employer's business."

the extent of undue hardship on the employer's business is at issue only where the employer claims that it is unable to offer any reasonable accommodation without such hardship. Once the Court of Appeals assumed that the school board had offered to Philbrook a reasonable alternative, it erred by requiring the board to nonetheless demonstrate the hardship of Philbrook's alternatives.

* * *

The remaining issue in the case is whether the school board's leave policy constitutes a reasonable accommodation of Philbrook's religious beliefs. Because both the District Court and the Court of Appeals applied what we hold to be an erroneous view of the law, neither explicitly considered this question. We think that there are insufficient factual findings as to the manner in which the collective bargaining agreement has been interpreted in order for us to make that judgment initially. We think that the school board policy in this case, requiring respondent to take unpaid leave for holy day observance that exceeded the amount allowed by the collective-bargaining agreement, would generally be a reasonable one. * * *

But unpaid leave is not a reasonable accommodation when paid leave is provided for all purposes *except* religious ones. A provision for paid leave "that is part and parcel of the employment relationship may not be doled out in a discriminatory fashion, even if the employer would be free ... not to provide the benefit at all." Such an arrangement would display a discrimination against religious practices that is the antithesis of reasonableness.

[Reversed and remanded for further fact-finding.]

JUSTICE MARSHALL, concurring in part and dissenting in part. [Omitted]

JUSTICE STEVENS, concurring in part and dissenting in part. [Omitted]

NOTE ON THE ACCOMMODATION PRINCIPLE

1. In *Ansonia* the Court requires no more than "de minimis" accommodation by the employer. What satisfies this burden?

(a) In the *Hardison* case, discussed in *Ansonia,* the Court indicated that a call to co-workers to volunteer to substitute for the plaintiff would satisfy the duty to accommodate. What is the equivalent accommodation in *Ansonia?* Allowing the employee to take off without pay?

(b) If no accommodation imposes only de minimis costs, then no accommodation is necessary, correct? Is every change in standard operating procedure a cost greater than de minimis? Does not allowing an employee to take leave without pay entail some costs for the employer, e.g., in finding a replacement or altering work schedules? Was the accommodation offered by the school board unnecessary under § 701(j)?

(c) Is the accommodation requirement of § 701(j) illusory? Does it have substance because at least it requires the employer to grant the plaintiff to use alternative leave without religious restrictions? But the general anti-discrimination command of Title VII would forbid that as intentional discrimination, would it not? If so, what does § 701(j) add?

2. Are the post–PDA cases discussed in the preceding subsection in fact accommodation cases? Notice how the PDA parallels § 701(j) in its amendment of the definitional section of Title VII. See *Ansonia*'s footnote 1. Would it be better to acknowledge frankly that the PDA cases rest on the principle that men, or society generally, must accommodate the special needs of pregnant women workers? But would this not undercut the purity of the argument that Title VII aims for "equal" treatment of men and women?

3. Why is the accommodation principle so narrowly construed in *Ansonia*? Does the Court fear that by allowing government to accommodate religion, it is running the risk of having government establish religion? Would an accommodation principle that required some citizens (employers) to support the religious observances of other citizens (employees) violate the Establishment Clause? This aspect of religious accommodation steps into a long-simmering constitutional controversy that pits equal treatment against accommodation. Compare See Sherbert v. Verner, 374 U.S. 398, 83 S.Ct. 1790, 10 L.Ed.2d 965 (1963) (denial of state unemployment benefits to sabbatarian; accommodation required), with Employment Division v. Smith, 494 U.S. 872, 110 S.Ct. 1595, 108 L.Ed.2d 876 (1990) (use of peyote for religious observance; equal treatment under general law is constitutional).

(a) In **Board of Education of Westside Community Schools v. Mergens**, 496 U.S. 226, 110 S.Ct. 2356, 110 L.Ed.2d 191 (1990), the Court upheld provisions of the Equal Access Act, 20 U.S.C. §§ 2071–74, which required that schools that open their facilities to noncurriculum-related student groups generally must also provide facilities to religiously oriented student groups. The Court rejected an Establishment Clause attack. Does *Mergens* support the constitutionality of a wider reading for § 701(j)? No, because *Mergens* only involved non-discrimination, the same principle recognized at the minimal core of *Ansonia*? Yes, because the Equal Access Act, like a broader reading of § 701(j) imposed costs on one party to aid another's religion? (Note that the Equal Access Act, however, is tied to receipt of federal funding.)

(b) More recently, inn **Cutter v. Wilkinson**, 544 U.S. 709, 125 S.Ct. 2113, 161 L.Ed.2d 1020 (2005), the Supreme Court upheld provisions of the Religious Land Use and Institutionalized Persons Act (RLUIPA) that provided prison inmates with greater protection than the Court itself had required as a matter of constitutional law. Declaring that "[o]ur decisions recognize that 'there is room for play in the joints' between the Clauses, some space for legislative action neither compelled by the Free Exercise Clause nor prohibited by the Establishment Clause," and yet also that " '[a]t some point, accommodation may devolve into an unlawful fostering of religion,' " the Court decided that RLUIPA successfully ran the gauntlet. Why? Because of its political compromise between Senators Hatch and Kennedy that protected both mega-churches and prisoners? Because "courts must take adequate account of the burdens a requested accommodation may impose on nonbeneficiaries"? See 544 U.S. at 720, 125 S.Ct. at 2121.

(c) Considering the *Mergens* and *Cutter* decisions, may Congress amend Title VII to require greater religious accommodation, see paragraph 4 infra, without violating the Establishment Clause? See Michael Paisne, *Boerne Supremacy: Congressional Responses to* City of Boerne v. Flores, *And the Scope of Congress's Article I Powers*, 105 COLUM. L. REV. 537 (2005); Kevin S. Schawrtz, *Applying Section 5:* Tennessee v. Lane *and Judicial Conditions on the Congressional Enforcement Power*, 114 YALE L.J. 1133 (2005). Cf. Christian Legal Soc. Chapter of Univ. of Cal., Hastings College of Law v. Martinez, 561 U.S. 130 S.Ct 2971 (2010) (policy requiring officially sanctioned student groups to open membership and leadership eligibility to all students, including those who disagree with group's religious beliefs, does not violate right of free speech or free exercise of religion).

4. The **Americans With Disabilities Act (ADA)**, 42 U.S.C. § 12101 et seq., the Title VII analogue (and part Title VI analogue) that covers discrimination against persons with disabilities, also contains an accommodation requirement. Modeled on the accommodation principle of the Rehabilitation Act of 1973, see the *Arline* and *Bragdon* cases, Chapter 6B supra, the ADA would require that qualified individuals be accommodated when it is possible to do so without undue hardship. See 42 U.S.C. §§ 12111(8), 12112(a). The Act particularly defines its terms, § 12111(9–10): "The term 'reasonable accommodation' may include—* * * (B) job restructuring, part-time or modified work schedules, reassignment to a vacant position, acquisition or modification of equipment or devices, appropriate adjustment or modifications of examinations, training materials or policies, the provision of qualified readers or interpreters, and other similar accommodations for individuals with disabilities."

(a) Does not the ADA provide a substantially more pro-plaintiff accommodation principle compared to that seen in Title VII's § 701(j)?

(b) The constitutional issues discussed above have no application to the ADA because the First Amendment protects only against the establishment of religion, not against the establishment of other preferences, correct? But the same arguments arise in the guise of public policy: is it wise or fair to have one sector of employers or employees subsidize another through imposition of accommodation duties? Or is this nothing more than an indirect tax to aid disabled persons?

5. Should an accommodation requirement be added to Title VII to assist African–Americans? Would that be demeaning because it would suggest that such persons cannot otherwise succeed? Is an accommodation requirement demeaning to religious adherents? To disabled persons? Are these questions difficult to answer because logic and labels are not as pertinent as values and attitudes?

4. SUITS AGAINST GOVERNMENTAL ENTITIES

FITZPATRICK v. BITZER

Supreme Court of the United States, 1976.
427 U.S. 445, 96 S.Ct. 2666, 49 L.Ed.2d 614.

MR. JUSTICE REHNQUIST delivered the opinion of the Court.

In the 1972 Amendments to Title VII of the Civil Rights Act of 1964, Congress, acting under § 5 of the Fourteenth Amendment, authorized federal courts to award money damages in favor of a private individual against a state government found to have subjected that person to employment discrimination on the basis of "race, color, religion, sex, or national origin."[2] The principal question presented by these cases is whether, as against the shield of sovereign immunity afforded the State by the Eleventh Amendment, Edelman v. Jordan, [Chapter 1H supra,] Congress has the power to authorize federal courts to enter such an award against the State as a means of enforcing the substantive guarantees of the Fourteenth Amendment. The Court of Appeals for the Second Circuit held that the effect of our decision in *Edelman* was to foreclose Congress' power. We granted certiorari to resolve this important constitutional question. We reverse.

* * *

[The plaintiffs were retired male employees of the State of Connecticut who claimed that the government's retirement benefits plan discriminated against them on the basis of sex. The lower courts agreed but refused to grant retroactive benefit awards, labeling them monetary awards. The issues of whether Title VII had been violated and whether the Act, as a statutory matter, permitted such relief were not presented in the Supreme Court.]

* * *

Our analysis begins where *Edelman* ended, for in this Title VII case the "threshold fact of congressional authorization," id. at 672, 94 S.Ct., at 1360, to sue the State as employer is clearly present. * * * [T]he Eleventh Amendment defense is asserted in the context of legislation passed pursuant to Congress' authority under § 5 of the Fourteenth Amendment.[9]

As ratified by the States after the Civil War, that Amendment quite clearly contemplates limitations on their authority. * * * The substantive provisions are by express terms directed at the States. Impressed upon

---

2. As relevant here, the definition of "person" in § 701(a) of the 1964 Act, 78 Stat. 253, 42 U.S.C.A. § 2000e(a), was amended by § 2(1) of the Equal Employment Opportunity Act of 1972 (hereinafter the 1972 Amendments), 86 Stat. 103, 42 U.S.C.A. § 2000e(a), to include "governments, governmental agencies, [and] political subdivisions."

9. There is no dispute that in enacting the 1972 Amendments to Title VII to extend coverage to the States as employers, Congress exercised its power under § 5 of the Fourteenth Amendment. See, e.g., H.R.Rep. No. 92–238, p. 19 (1971); S.Rep. No. 92–415, pp. 10–11 (1971).

them by those provisions are duties with respect to their treatment of private individuals. Standing behind the imperatives is Congress' power to "enforce" them "by appropriate legislation."

The impact of the Fourteenth Amendment upon the relationship between the Federal Government and the States, and the reach of congressional power under § 5, were examined at length by this Court in Ex parte State of Virginia, 100 U.S. 339, 25 L.Ed. 676 (1879). * * *

Ex parte State of Virginia's early recognition of this shift in the federal-state balance has been carried forward by more recent decisions of this Court. See, e.g., South Carolina v. Katzenbach, 383 U.S. 301, 308, 86 S.Ct. 803, 808, 15 L.Ed.2d 769 (1966) [set out in Chapter 8A infra].

* * *

It is true that none of these previous cases presented the question of the relationship between the Eleventh Amendment and the enforcement power granted to Congress under § 5 of the Fourteenth Amendment. But we think that the Eleventh Amendment, and the principle of state sovereignty which it embodies, see Hans v. Louisiana, 134 U.S. 1, 10 S.Ct. 504, 33 L.Ed. 842 (1890), are necessarily limited by the enforcement provisions of § 5 of the Fourteenth Amendment. In that section Congress is expressly granted authority to enforce "by appropriate legislation" the substantive provisions of the Fourteenth Amendment, which themselves embody significant limitations on state authority. When Congress acts pursuant to § 5, not only is it exercising legislative authority that is plenary within the terms of the constitutional grant, it is exercising that authority under one section of a constitutional Amendment whose other sections by their own terms embody limitations on state authority. We think that Congress may, in determining what is "appropriate legislation" for the purpose of enforcing the provisions of the Fourteenth Amendment, provide for private suits against States or state officials which are constitutionally impermissible in other contexts.[11]

* * *

Reversed.

MR. JUSTICE BRENNAN, concurring in the judgment.

* * * Congressional authority to enact the provisions of Title VII at issue in this case is found in the Commerce Clause, Art. I, § 8, cl. 3, and in § 5 of the Fourteenth Amendment, two of the enumerated powers granted Congress in the Constitution. I remain of the opinion that "because of its surrender, no immunity exists that can be the subject of a congressional declaration or a voluntary waiver."

I therefore concur in the judgment of the Court.

---

11. Apart from their claim that the Eleventh Amendment bars enforcement of the remedy established by Title VII in this case, respondent state officials do not contend that the substantive provisions of Title VII as applied here are not a proper exercise of congressional authority under § 5 of the Fourteenth Amendment.

MR. JUSTICE STEVENS, concurring in the judgment.

In my opinion the commerce power is broad enough to support federal legislation regulating the terms and conditions of state employment and, therefore, provides the necessary support for the 1972 Amendments to Title VII, even though Congress expressly relied on § 5 of the Fourteenth Amendment. But I do not believe plaintiffs proved a violation of the Fourteenth Amendment, and because I am not sure that the 1972 Amendments were "needed to secure the guarantees of the Fourteenth Amendment," see Katzenbach v. Morgan, 384 U.S. 641, 651, 86 S.Ct. 1717, 1724, 16 L.Ed.2d 828 [set out in Chapter 8A infra], I question whether § 5 of that Amendment is an adequate reply to Connecticut's Eleventh Amendment defense. I believe the defense should be rejected for a different reason.

* * *

The holding in *Edelman* does not necessarily require the same result in this case; this award will not be paid directly from the state treasury, but rather from two separate and independent pension funds. [The state will need to replenish these funds because of our judgment, but that is only a prospective impact, not a retroactive payment barred by *Edelman*.]

NOTE ON UNDERLYING CONSIDERATIONS AFFECTING COVERAGE OF STATE GOVERNMENTS

1. As footnote 2 of Justice Rehnquist's opinion in *Fitzpatrick* reveals, state and local governments were excluded from coverage in the original 1964 version of Title VII, but Congress lifted that statutory immunity in 1972. Congress claimed power to act under § 5 of the Fourteenth Amendment, legislating to eradicate the violation of state and local employee's rights to equal protection.

(a) The theory advanced by Justice Rehnquist in *Fitzpatrick* was not a new one. A law review article appearing in 1908 acknowledged the possibility that the specific wording of the Fourteenth Amendment might have superseded the Eleventh when equal protection or due process claims were at issue, but the author proposed the fiction later adopted by the Court in Ex parte *Young* as a preferable way of dealing with the issue. See Guthrie, *The Eleventh Article of Amendment to the Constitution of the United States*, 8 COLUM.L.REV. 183, 189 (1908) (suits against officers permissible). Why, after over 100 years of avoiding decision on whether the Fourteenth Amendment overruled the Eleventh, did the Court finally choose this theory in *Fitzpatrick*? Was it because Congress had seldom, if ever, subjected the states to suits for monetary liability prior to 1972?

(b) Note the concurring opinions' reliance on the Commerce Clause as a ground for federal power to regulate the states. Justice Rehnquist uses the Fourteenth. What is the essential ingredient in the Fourteenth Amendment, according to Justice Rehnquist, that may be missing in the Commerce Clause?

(c) Does Justice Rehnquist's argument not lead to a schizophrenic Eleventh Amendment: it has one meaning when Congress is silent and another when Congress decides against immunity? Does this give Congress effective power to make constitutional law? Is this so strange, given our history of a two-level Commerce Clause that has a dormant (judicially-enforced) element and an active (Congressionally-enforced) element? Note the same issues that arise under the Thirteenth Amendment, Chapter 2 supra.

(d) Although Congress may legislate an abrogation of the states' sovereign immunity, it must do so unambiguously in the text of its legislation. See Atascadero State Hosp. v. Scanlon, 473 U.S. 234, 105 S.Ct. 3142, 87 L.Ed.2d 171 (1985) (original version of Rehabilitation Act protecting handicapped persons insufficiently clear to abrogate states' immunity). What interests are served by the "clear statement" rule in this context? See Dellmuth v. Muth, 491 U.S. 223, 227, 109 S.Ct. 2397, 2400, 105 L.Ed.2d 181 (1989) (Education of the Handicapped Act fails clear statement test).

2. The *Fitzpatrick* concurrences' views regarding the Commerce Clause were eventually rejected, or severely limited, in a series of cases in the late 1990's. Although it remains unclear whether Congress can substantively regulate the states by use of its Article I, § 8 powers,[1] a consistent 5–4 majority has rejected the proposition that Congress can use those powers to subject the States to suit—in either federal or state courts. In **Seminole Tribe of Florida v. Florida**, 517 U.S. 44, 116 S.Ct. 1114, 134 L.Ed.2d 252 (1996), the Court ruled that Congress may not use its Article I, § 8 powers to abrogate the states' sovereign immunity (under the Eleventh Amendment and related doctrines) from suit in federal court, thus restricting *Fitzpatrick's* operation to those constitutional provisions that give Congress explicit power to regulate states. In **Alden v. Maine**, 527 U.S. 706, 119 S.Ct. 2240, 144 L.Ed.2d 636 (1999), involving a claim by state workers under the federal wages-and-hours law, the Court read *Seminole Tribe* to bar any similar Congressional power to subject states to suit under federal statutes in their own courts.

3. After *Seminole Tribe* and *Alden*, *Fitzpatrick* takes on a critical importance. If Congress can only regulate the states and subject them to suits (i.e., abrogate their sovereign immunity) through use of its Fourteenth Amendment power, then the Court must decide how broad that power is. In **Florida Prepaid Postsecondary Education Expense Board v. College Savings Bank**, 527 U.S. 627, 119 S.Ct. 2199, 144 L.Ed.2d 575 (1999), the Court in a 5–4 opinion by Chief Justice Rehnquist rejected the argument that Congress can legislate under § 5 of the Fourteenth Amendment to cure state violations of federal patent law. In order to have such power, held the Court, the legislation must be remedial of some constitutional violation covered by the Fourteenth Amendment's Equal Protection Clause or Due Process Clause. In **City**

---

1. Compare Printz v. United States, 521 U.S. 898, 117 S.Ct. 2365, 138 L.Ed.2d 914 (1997) (federal government cannot require state executive officials to use state resources to implement federal statute), and College Savings Bank v. Florida Prepaid Postsecondary Education Expense Board, 527 U.S. 666, 119 S.Ct. 2219, 144 L.Ed.2d 605 (1999) (state's participation in for-profit activity regulated by federal statute adopted under Commerce Clause does not operate as a constructive waiver of state's sovereign immunity to suit), with in Reno v. Condon, 528 U.S. 141, 120 S.Ct. 666, 145 L.Ed.2d 587 (2000) (federal statute restricting the ability of the states to disclose a driver's personal information, enacted under the Commerce Clause power, regulated commercial activity and does not run afoul of Tenth Amendment because it merely alters state activities and does not actually require state officials to administer federal statutes). See generally Chapter 5 supra.

of Boerne v. Flores, 521 U.S. 507, 117 S.Ct. 2157, 138 L.Ed.2d 624 (1997), the Court struck down the Religious Freedom Restoration Act (RFRA), finding that its provision of high-level scrutiny for religious topics found by the Court to merit no protection, was an impermissible statutory attempt to override constitutional law. As the Court later explained, Congress may impose remedies for what are constitutional violations, but it may not by statute change what are constitutional violations. See Morrison v. United States, Chapter 3 supra.

(a) To the extent that Congress has legislated under Title VII and related statutes to bar intentional discrimination against suspect classifications receiving higher-level scrutiny (e.g., racial and ethnic groups and women), *Fitzpatrick* appears to support the legislation. Other classifications, however, e.g., age, see Massachusetts Board of Retirement v. Murgia, 427 U.S. 307, 96 S.Ct. 2562, 49 L.Ed.2d 520 (1976) (per curiam), ordinarily receive only low-level scrutiny and are for practical purposes not protected by the Equal Protection Clause. When Congress outlaws discrimination against those groups, as it did in the Age Discrimination in Employment Act (ADEA), is it remedying a constitutional violation? Or is it declaring conduct illegal that is not itself a constitutional violation? If it is the latter, then is not the ADEA unconstitutional under *Florida Prepaid* insofar as it subjects states to suit in federal courts? In **Kimel v. Florida Board of Regents**, 528 U.S. 62, 120 S.Ct. 631, 145 L.Ed.2d 522 (2000), the Court held that Congress lacks power to abrogate state immunity from suit for ADEA violations under § 5, noting that age "is not a suspect classification," and therefore rational state judgments about age are not constitutional violations which Congress may remedy under the Fourteenth Amendment. Even with its BFOQ defense for age, see ¶ 5 of the Note on BFOQ Defense, section B.1 of this Chapter, supra, said the Court, the ADEA nevertheless covered far more than what the Court would hold unconstitutional, and therefore it could not be deemed remedial of constitutional violations under *Florida Prepaid*. Is the result in *Kimel* a foregone conclusion given *Florida Prepaid*?

(b) A related issue arises even with respect to legislation protecting against racial discrimination (or other classifications receiving high-level scrutiny). As discussed in Chapter 1B.5, supra, such classifications violate the Equal Protection Clause only when they are intentional. Title VII, on the other hand, covers both intentional discrimination and impact-style discrimination. See Griggs v. Duke Power Co., set out in section A of this Chapter, supra. Does subjecting state employers to an impact test for racial discrimination avoid the holding in *Florida Prepaid* and *Kimel*? No, because impact-style discrimination is not itself a constitutional violation? See City of Boerne v. Flores, supra. Yes, because the impact test is a remedy for earlier intentional discrimination? Cf. City of Rome v. United States, 446 U.S. 156, 100 S.Ct. 1548, 64 L.Ed.2d 119 (1980) ("effects" test under Voting Rights Act may be viewed as a remedy for earlier intentional discrimination, which is itself a constitutional violation). See generally, Nevada Department of Human Resources v. Hibbs, 538 U.S. 721, 123 S.Ct. 1972, 155 L.Ed.2d 953 (2003) (stating issue and upholding Family and Medical Leave Act); Richard A. Primus, *Equal Protection and Disparate Impact: Round Three*, 117 HARV. L. REV. 493 (2003).

(c) In **Board of Trustees of University of Alabama v. Garrett**, 531 U.S. 356, 121 S.Ct. 955, 148 L.Ed.2d 866 (2001), the Court held that, absent a separate constitutional violation, the Fourteenth Amendment does not require reasonable accommodation of disabled persons and that therefore Congress lacks authority under the Fourteenth Amendment to require states to make reasonable accommodations. The Court overturned Congress's purported effort to abolish state sovereign immunity. Cf. Chapter 3D (extent of Fourteenth Amendment power).[2] Does *Fitzpatrick* leave more "states's rights" intact than first appears?

4. The Eleventh Amendment immunizes only states and state-level entities and has no application to local governments. See the Note on the Dividing Line Between State and Local Entities, Chapter 1H.2 supra. If Congress can assuredly bar and subject to suit all intentional discrimination based on race or sex practiced by state-level entities, and can also reach all impact-style discrimination by local governments, is the practical effect of the restrictive cases discussed above relatively small? Does it depend on which level of government you think is more capable of committing violations of Title VII? Which forms of discrimination most affect or bother you?

BROWN v. GENERAL SERVICES ADMINISTRATION

Supreme Court of the United States, 1976.
425 U.S. 820, 96 S.Ct. 1961, 48 L.Ed.2d 402.

MR. JUSTICE STEWART delivered the opinion of the Court.

[Having twice been passed over for promotions despite a rating of "highly qualified," Brown filed an internal agency complaint alleging that he was not promoted because of his race. The agency and reviewing authority denied relief, and Brown thereafter filed suit under Title VII and, inter alia, § 1981. The lower courts declined to hear his case under either statute, ruling that his claim under Title VII was barred for failure to conform to procedural requirements and that it provided his exclusive remedy.]

The primary question in this litigation is not difficult to state: Is § 717 of the Civil Rights Act of 1964, as added by § 11 of the Equal Employment Opportunity Act of 1972, 42 U.S.C.A. § 2000e–16, the exclusive individual remedy available to a federal employee complaining of job-related racial discrimination? But the question is easier to state than it is to resolve. Congress simply failed explicitly to describe § 717's position in the constellation of antidiscrimination law. We must, therefore, infer congressional intent in less obvious ways. As Mr. Chief Justice Marshall once wrote for the Court: "Where the mind labours to discover the design of the legislature, it seizes everything from which aid can be derived * * *." United States v. Fisher, 2 Cranch 358, 386 (1805).

---

2. The Supreme Court has held, City of Cleburne v. Cleburne Living Center, 473 U.S. 432, 105 S.Ct. 3249, 87 L.Ed.2d 313 (1985), that disability classifications receive only low-level scrutiny. If the ADA happened to overlap with a fundamental right, such as the right of access to courts, would it's higher requirement be constitutional as applied to that right? See Tennessee v. Lane, 541 U.S. 509, 124 S.Ct. 1978, 158 L.Ed.2d 820 (2004) (yes).

Title VII of the Civil Rights Act of 1964 forbids employment discrimination based on race, color, religion, sex, or national origin. 42 U.S.C.A. §§ 2000e–2, 2000e–3. Until it was amended in 1972 by the Equal Employment Opportunity Act, however, Title VII did not protect federal employees. 42 U.S.C.A. § 2000e(b). Although federal employment discrimination clearly violated both the Constitution, Bolling v. Sharpe, 347 U.S. 497, 74 S.Ct. 693, 98 L.Ed. 884 (1954), and statutory law, 5 U.S.C.A. § 7151, before passage of the 1972 Act, the effective availability of either administrative or judicial relief was far from sure. Charges of racial discrimination were handled parochially within each federal agency. * * *

If administrative remedies were ineffective, judicial relief from federal employment discrimination was even more problematic before 1972. Although an action seeking to enjoin unconstitutional agency conduct would lie, it was doubtful that backpay or other compensatory relief for employment discrimination was available at the time that Congress was considering the 1972 Act. For example, in Gnotta v. United States, 415 F.2d 1271, the Court of Appeals for the Eighth Circuit had held in 1969 that there was no jurisdictional basis to support the plaintiff's suit alleging that the Corps of Engineers had discriminatorily refused to promote him. * * *

Concern was evinced during the hearings before the committees of both Houses over the apparent inability of federal employees to engage the judicial machinery in cases of alleged employment discrimination. See, *e.g.,* Hearings on S. 2515 *et al.* before the Subcommittee on Labor of the Senate Committee on Labor and Public Welfare, 92d Cong., 1st Sess., 296, 301, 308, 318 (1971); Hearings on H.R. 1746 before the General Subcommittee on Labor of the House Committee on Education and Labor, 92d Cong., 1st Sess., 320, 322, 385–86, 391–92 (1971). Although there was considerable disagreement over whether a civil action would lie to remedy agency discrimination, the committees ultimately concluded that judicial review was not available at all or, if available, that some forms of relief were foreclosed. Thus, the Senate Report observed: "The testimony of the Civil Service Commission notwithstanding, the committee found that an aggrieved Federal employee does not have access to the courts. In many cases, the employee must overcome a U.S. Government defense of sovereign immunity or failure to exhaust administrative remedies with no certainty as to the steps required to exhaust such remedies. Moreover, the remedial authority of the Commission and the courts has also been in doubt." S.Rep.No. 92–415, p. 16 (1971). Similarly, the House Committee stated: "There is serious doubt that court review is available to the aggrieved Federal employee. Monetary restitution or back pay is not attainable. In promotion situations, a critical area of discrimination, the promotion is often no longer available." H.R.Rep. No. 92–238, p. 25 (1971), U.S.Code Cong. & Admin.News 1972, p. 2160.

The conclusion of the committees was reiterated during floor debate. Senator Cranston, coauthor of the amendment relating to federal employment, asserted that it would, "[f]or the first time, permit Federal employees to sue the Federal Government in discrimination cases * * *." 118

Cong.Rec. 4929 (1972). Senator Williams, sponsor and floor manager of the bill, stated that it "provides, for the first time, to my knowledge, for the right of an individual to take his complaint to court." Id. at 4922.

The legislative history thus leaves little doubt that Congress was persuaded that federal employees who were treated discriminatorily had no effective judicial remedy. And the case law suggests that that conclusion was entirely reasonable. Whether that understanding of Congress was in some ultimate sense incorrect is not what is important in determining the legislative intent in amending the 1964 Civil Rights Act to cover federal employees. For the relevant inquiry is not whether Congress correctly perceived the then state of the law, but rather what its perception of the state of the law was.

This unambiguous congressional perception seems to indicate that the congressional intent in 1972 was to create an exclusive, preemptive administrative and judicial scheme for the redress of federal employment discrimination. We need not, however, rest our decision upon this inference alone. For the structure of the 1972 amendment itself fully confirms the conclusion that Congress intended it to be exclusive and pre-emptive.

* * *

The balance, completeness, and structural integrity of § 717 are inconsistent with the petitioner's contention that the judicial remedy afforded by § 717(c) was designed merely to supplement other putative judicial relief. His view fails, in our estimation, to accord due weight to the fact that unlike these other supposed remedies, § 717 does not contemplate merely judicial relief. Rather, it provides for a careful blend of administrative and judicial enforcement powers. Under the petitioner's theory, by perverse operation of a type of Gresham's law, § 717, with its rigorous administrative exhaustion requirements and time limitations, would be driven out of currency were immediate access to the courts under other, less demanding statutes permissible. The crucial administrative role that each agency together with the Civil Service Commission was given by Congress in the eradication of employment discrimination would be eliminated "by the simple expedient of putting a different label on [the] pleadings." Preiser v. Rodriguez, [Chapter 1G.1 supra]. It would require the suspension of disbelief to ascribe to Congress the design to allow its careful and thorough remedial scheme to be circumvented by artful pleading.

The petitioner relies upon our decision in Johnson v. Railway Express Agency, 421 U.S. 454, 95 S.Ct. 1716, 44 L.Ed.2d 295 (1975), for the proposition that Title VII did not repeal pre-existing remedies for employment discrimination. In *Johnson* the Court held that in the context of *private employment* Title VII did not pre-empt other remedies. But that decision is inapposite here. In the first place, there were no problems of sovereign immunity in the context of the *Johnson* case. Second, the holding in *Johnson* rested upon the explicit legislative history of the 1964 Act which " 'manifests a congressional intent to allow an individual to pursue independently his rights under both Title VII and other applicable state and federal statutes.' " 421 U.S., at 459, 95 S.Ct., at 1719, 44 L.Ed.2d, at 301. * * *

There is no such legislative history behind the 1972 amendments. Indeed, as indicated above, the congressional understanding was precisely to the contrary.

* * *

Affirmed.

MR. JUSTICE MARSHALL took no part in the consideration or decision of this case.

MR. JUSTICE STEVENS, with whom MR. JUSTICE BRENNAN joins, dissenting. * * *

As the legislative history discussed in Chandler v. Roudebush, 425 U.S. 840, 96 S.Ct. 1949, 48 L.Ed.2d 416 demonstrates, Congress intended federal employees to have the same rights available to remedy racial discrimination as employees in the private sector. Since the law is now well settled that victims of racial discrimination in the private sector have a choice of remedies and are not limited to Title VII, federal employees should enjoy parallel rights. * * *

The fact that Congress incorrectly assumed that federal employees would have no judicial remedy if § 717 had not been enacted undermines rather than supports the Court's conclusion that Congress intended to repeal or amend laws that it did not think applicable. Indeed, the General Subcommittee on Labor of the House Committee on Education and Labor rejected an amendment which would have explicitly provided that § 717 would be the exclusive remedy for federal employees. In sum, the legislative history of § 717 discloses a clear intent to provide federal employees with rights that parallel those available to employees in the private sector, no evidence of an intention to make the remedy exclusive, and the rejection of an amendment which would have so provided.

The burden of persuading us that we should interpolate such an important provision into a complex, carefully drafted statute is a heavy one. Since that burden has not been met, I would simply read the statute as Congress wrote it.

NOTE ON UNDERLYING CONSIDERATIONS AFFECTING COVERAGE OF THE FEDERAL GOVERNMENT

1. Since it has long been settled that the federal government may waive its sovereign immunity and consent to suit,[1] the constitutional problems discussed in the preceding Note, regarding Title VII's coverage of states, did not arise when Congress extended the statute to cover the federal government. Or did they simply emerge in a different guise?

---

1. See United States v. Sherwood, 312 U.S. 584, 61 S.Ct. 767, 85 L.Ed. 1058 (1941).

(a) How persuasive is Justice Stewart's opinion for the Court? Were the two points on which he relies—the ineffectiveness or nonexistence of prior remedies and the comprehensiveness of administrative remedies—not equally applicable in the context of private suits, where the Court has permitted § 1981 to coexist with Title VII (and indeed even revived the former)? See Chapter 2B supra. Was not Justice Stewart's jump from Congress' doubt about availability of prior remedies to the conclusion that Congress *intended* Title VII to be exclusive a non sequitur? Was the second point regarding implied exclusiveness convincingly rebutted in Justice Stevens' dissenting opinion?

(b) Can the majority's disposition of the case rather be explained as resting on unarticulated assumptions? That when the federal government waives its sovereign immunity it is entitled to substantial procedural devices to channel and limit the impact of such a waiver? That it is better to channel all claims through a statute explicitly waiving sovereign immunity than to decide unnecessarily whether sovereign immunity would apply at all under other non-waiver statutes such as § 1981?

(c) Given the Court's decision in Davis v. Passman, Chapter 4 supra, would Congress be well-advised to expand the coverage of Title VII to include all federal employees, forcing all through the administrative exhaustion requirements?

2. Although the Court in *Brown* moved firmly to shut off avenues other than Title VII, it also acted the same day to insure that under Title VII covered employees would receive judicial attention to their claims that would be as detailed as that accorded private litigants. In **Chandler v. Roudebush**, 425 U.S. 840, 96 S.Ct. 1949, 48 L.Ed.2d 416 (1976), the Court reversed a Ninth Circuit decision restricting federal employees suing under Title VII to the limited judicial review ordinarily accorded administrative decisions. The Court found § 717's provision of a "civil action" to indicate the contrary: Congress "faced a choice between record review of agency action based on traditional appellate standards and trial *de novo* of Title VII claims. The Senate committee selected trial *de novo* as the proper means for resolving the claims of federal employees," and the full Congress adopted that view. 425 U.S. at 861, 96 S.Ct. at 1960.

(a) Do *Brown* and *Chandler* together give covered federal employees a remedy as effective as that accorded state employees in the 1972 Amendments to Title VII? Do the provisions of Title VII in the Civil Rights Act of 1991 (making damages recoverable) provide even greater remedies, perhaps equivalent to those granted state employees under § 1983 and private employees under § 1981?

(b) Is it possible that the administrative remedies available under Title VII actually put federal employees in a better position than private employees? Title VII permits the EEOC itself to award remedies only in cases against federal agencies, and following the adoption of the Civil Rights Act of 1991 (providing a jury trial and damages for intentional discrimination under Title VII), the EEOC began to assess damage awards against federal agencies. The Court upheld the EEOC's power to do so in **West v. Gibson**, 527 U.S. 212, 119 S.Ct. 1906, 144 L.Ed.2d 196 (1999). Justice Breyer's opinion for a 5–4 majority found the power in the explicit words of § 717, which allowed the EEOC to award "appropriate remedies"; this phrase was broad enough, said the Court, to include remedies added later by the 1991 Act. The dissent found no waiver of sovereign immunity.

3. Although the Court has not found constitutional limits on waiver of federal sovereign immunity, it has nevertheless, in determining whether civil rights statutes have waived federal sovereign immunity, applied the "clear statement" rule that is also used in state sovereign immunity cases, discussed in the preceding Note. In **Lane v. Pena**, 518 U.S. 187, 116 S.Ct. 2092, 135 L.Ed.2d 486 (1996), for example, the Court found that Congress had not clearly waived federal sovereign immunity for claims of handicap discrimination against federal agencies under § 504.

(a) What interests are served by the clear statement rule in the context of federal sovereign immunity if there is no constitutional dimension to the issue as there is in Eleventh Amendment cases? Does the rule serve separation-of-powers interests, by keeping the courts from legislating too readily? Why have a special rule limiting judicially implied remedies in this context? Does the rule do nothing more than protect against too lightly spending federal money?

(b) The Court has applied the clear statement rule with some attention to detail, ruling in **Library of Congress v. Shaw**, 478 U.S. 310, 106 S.Ct. 2957, 92 L.Ed.2d 250 (1986), that Title VII's waiver of immunity, although permitting suits generally, did not permit the specific award of pre-judgment interest to successful plaintiffs. Is *Shaw* consistent with *Lane*? Congress can always overrule a judicial finding that its waiver is insufficiently specific by simply adopting more explicit legislation. See, e.g., Civil Rights Act of 1991, § 114 in the Appendix (overruling *Shaw*). Does this possibility dispose you to find fewer waivers or more? In other words, whom should inertia favor?

C. RELIEF

ALBEMARLE PAPER CO. v. MOODY

Supreme Court of the United States, 1975.
422 U.S. 405, 95 S.Ct. 2362, 45 L.Ed.2d 280.

MR. JUSTICE STEWART delivered the opinion of the Court.

[The district court found segregation in jobs but refused to enjoin the use of unvalidated tests or order backpay for those black workers who had suffered discrimination. A divided Fourth Circuit reversed. The Supreme Court granted certiorari, and framed the issue early in its opinion: "When employees or applicants for employment have lost the opportunity to earn wages because an employer has engaged in an unlawful discriminatory employment practice, what standards should a federal district court follow in deciding whether to award or deny backpay?"]

Whether a particular member of the plaintiff class should have been awarded any backpay and, if so, how much, are questions not involved in this review. The equities of individual cases were never reached. Though at least some of the members of the plaintiff class obviously suffered a loss of wage opportunities on account of Albermarle's unlawfully discriminatory system of job seniority, the District Court decided that *no* backpay should be awarded to *anyone* in the class. The court declined to make such an award on two stated grounds: the lack of "evidence of bad faith noncompliance with the Act," and the fact that "the defendants would be substantially prejudiced" by an award of backpay that was demanded contrary to an earlier representation and late in the progress of the litigation. * * *

* * *

The petitioners contend that the statutory scheme provides no guidance, beyond indicating that backpay awards are within the district court's discretion. We disagree. It is true that backpay is not an automatic or mandatory remedy; like all other remedies under the Act, it is one which the courts "may" invoke. The scheme implicitly recognizes that there may be cases calling for one remedy but not another, and—owing to the structure of the federal judiciary—these choices are, of course, left in the first instance to the district courts. However, such discretionary choices are not left to a court's "inclination, but to its judgment; and its judgment is to be guided by sound legal principles." United States v. Burr, 25 F.Cas. No. 14,692d, pp. 30, 35 (CC Va.1807) (Marshall, C.J.). The power to award backpay was bestowed by Congress, as part of a complex legislative design directed at a historic evil of national proportions. A court must exercise this power "in light of the large objectives of the Act," Hecht Co. v. Bowles, 321 U.S. 321, 331, 64 S.Ct. 587, 592, 88 L.Ed. 754 (1944). That the court's discretion is equitable in nature, see Curtis v. Loether, 415 U.S. 189, 197, 94 S.Ct. 1005, 1010, 39 L.Ed.2d 260 (1974), hardly means that it is unfettered by meaningful standards or shielded from thorough appellate review. In Mitchell v. Robert DeMario Jewelry, 361 U.S. 288, 292, 80 S.Ct. 332, 335, 4 L.Ed.2d 323 (1960), this Court held, in the face of a silent statute, that district courts enjoyed the "historic power of equity" to award lost wages to workmen unlawfully discriminated against under § 17 of the Fair Labor Standards Act of 1938, 52 Stat. 1069, as amended, 29 U.S.C.A. § 217 (1958 ed.). The Court simultaneously noted that "the statutory purposes [leave] little room for the exercise of discretion not to order reimbursement." 361 U.S. at 296, 80 S.Ct. at 337.

It is true that "[e]quity eschews mechanical rules * * * [and] depends on flexibility." Holmberg v. Armbrecht, 327 U.S. 392, 396, 66 S.Ct. 582, 584, 90 L.Ed. 743 (1946). But when Congress invokes the Chancellor's conscience to further transcendent legislative purposes, what is required is the principled application of standards consistent with those purposes and not "equity [which] varies like the Chancellor's foot."[10] Important national goals would be frustrated by a regime of discretion that "produce[d] different results for breaches of duty in situations that cannot be differen-

10. Eldon, L.C., in Gee v. Pritchard. 2 Swans. *403, *414, 36 Eng.Rep. 670, 674 (1818).

tiated in policy." Moragne v. States Marine Lines, 398 U.S. 375, 405, 90 S.Ct. 1772, 1790, 26 L.Ed.2d 339 (1970).

The District Court's decision must therefore be measured against the purposes which inform Title VII. As the Court observed in Griggs v. Duke Power Co., the primary objective was a prophylactic one:

> "It was to achieve equality of employment opportunities and remove barriers that have operated in the past to favor an identifiable group of white employees over other employees."

Backpay has an obvious connection with this purpose. If employers faced only the prospect of an injunctive order, they would have little incentive to shun practices of dubious legality. It is the reasonably certain prospect of a backpay award that "provide[s] the spur or catalyst which causes employers and unions to self-examine and to self-evaluate their employment practices and to endeavor to eliminate, so far as possible, the last vestiges of an unfortunate and ignominious page in this country's history." United States v. N.L. Industries, Inc., 479 F.2d at 354, 379 (CA8 1973).

It is also the purpose of Title VII to make persons whole for injuries suffered on account of unlawful employment discrimination. This is shown by the very fact that Congress took care to arm the courts with full equitable powers. For it is the historic purpose of equity to "secur[e] complete justice," Brown v. Swann, 10 Pet. 497, 503, 9 L.Ed. 508 (1836). * * *

The "make whole" purpose of Title VII is made evident by the legislative history. The backpay provision was expressly modeled on the backpay provision of the National Labor Relations Act. Under that Act, "[m]aking the workers whole for losses suffered on account of an unfair labor practice is part of the vindication of the public policy which the Board enforces." Phelps Dodge Corp. v. NLRB, 313 U.S. 177, 197, 61 S.Ct. 845, 854, 85 L.Ed. 1271 (1941). We may assume that Congress was aware that the Board, since its inception, has awarded backpay as a matter of course—not randomly or in the exercise of a standardless discretion, and not merely where employer violations are peculiarly deliberate, egregious, or inexcusable. Furthermore, in passing the Equal Employment Opportunity Act of 1972, Congress considered several bills to limit the judicial power to award backpay. These limiting efforts were rejected, and the backpay provision was re-enacted substantially in its original form. A Section-by-Section Analysis introduced by Senator Williams to accompany the Conference Committee Report on the 1972 Act strongly reaffirmed the "make whole" purpose of Title VII:

> The provisions of this subsection are intended to give the courts wide discretion exercising their equitable powers to fashion the most complete relief possible. In dealing with the present section 706(g) the courts have stressed that the scope of relief under that section of the Act is intended to make the victims of unlawful discrimination whole, and that the attainment of this objective rests not only upon the

elimination of the particular unlawful employment practice complained of, but also requires that persons aggrieved by the consequences and effects of the unlawful employment practice be, so far as possible, restored to a position where they would have been were it not for the unlawful discrimination. 118 Cong.Rec. 7168 (1972).

As this makes clear, Congress' purpose in vesting a variety of "discretionary" powers in the courts was not to limit appellate review of trial courts, or to invite inconsistency and caprice, but rather to make possible the "fashion[ing] [of] the most complete relief possible."

It follows that, given a finding of unlawful discrimination, backpay should be denied only for reasons which, if applied generally, would not frustrate the central statutory purposes of eradicating discrimination throughout the economy and making persons whole for injuries suffered through past discrimination.[14] The courts of appeals must maintain a consistent and principled application of the backpay provision, consonant with the twin statutory objectives, while at the same time recognizing that the trial court will often have the keener appreciation of those facts and circumstances peculiar to particular cases.

The District Court's stated grounds for denying backpay in this case must be tested against these standards. The first ground was that Albemarle's breach of Title VII had not been in "bad faith." This is not a sufficient reason for denying backpay. Where an employer *has* shown bad faith—by maintaining a practice which he knew to be illegal or of highly questionable legality—he can make no claims whatsoever on the Chancellor's conscience. But, under Title VII, the mere absence of bad faith simply opens the door to equity; it does not depress the scales in the employer's favor. If backpay were awardable only upon a showing of bad faith, the remedy would become a punishment for moral turpitude, rather than a compensation for workers' injuries. * * *

The District Court also grounded its denial of backpay on the fact that the respondents initially disclaimed any interest in backpay, first asserting their claim five years after the complaint was filed.

* * * To deny backpay because a *particular* cause has been prosecuted in an eccentric fashion, prejudicial to the other party, does not offend the broad purposes of Title VII. This is not to say, however, that the District Court's ruling was necessarily correct. Whether the petitioners were in fact prejudiced, and whether the respondents' trial conduct was excusable, are questions that will be open to review by the Court of Appeals, if the District Court, on remand, decides again to decline to make any award of backpay. But the standard of review will be the familiar one of whether the District Court was "clearly erroneous" in its factual findings and whether it "abused" its traditional discretion to locate "a just result" in light of the circumstances peculiar to the case, Langnes v. Green, 282 U.S. 531, 541, 51 S.Ct. 243, 247, 75 L.Ed. 520 (1931). On these

---

14. It is necessary, therefore, that if a district court does decline to award backpay, it carefully articulate its reasons.

issues of procedural regularity and prejudice, the "broad aims of Title VII" provide no ready solution.

[Vacated and remanded.]

[JUSTICE POWELL did not participate. JUSTICE MARSHALL'S concurring opinion, that of CHIEF JUSTICE BURGER dissenting on this issue, and JUSTICE BLACKMUN'S opinion concurring in the judgment are omitted.]

MR. JUSTICE REHNQUIST, concurring.

I join the opinion of the Court. The manner in which 42 U.S.C.A. § 2000e–5(g) is construed has important consequences not only as to the circumstances under which backpay may be awarded, but also as to the method by which any such award is to be determined.

* * *

* * * [T]o the extent that an award of backpay is thought to flow as a matter of course from a finding of wrongdoing, and thereby becomes virtually indistinguishable from an award for damages, the question (not raised by any of the parties, and therefore quite properly not discussed in the Court's opinion), of whether either side may demand a jury trial under the Seventh Amendment becomes critical. We said in Curtis v. Loether, 415 U.S. 189, 197, 94 S.Ct. 1005, 1010, 39 L.Ed.2d 260 (1974), in explaining the difference between the provision for damages under § 812 of the Civil Rights Act of 1968, 82 Stat. 88, 42 U.S.C.A. § 3612, and the authorization for the award of backpay which we treat here:

> In Title VII cases, also, the courts have relied on the fact that the decision whether to award back-pay is committed to the discretion of the trial judge. There is no comparable discretion here: if a plaintiff proves unlawful discrimination and actual damages, he is entitled to judgment for that amount. * * * Whatever may be the merit of the 'equitable' characterization in Title VII cases, there is surely no basis for characterizing the award of compensatory and punitive damages here as equitable relief. (Footnote omitted.)

* * *

To the extent, then, that the District Court retains substantial discretion as to whether or not to award backpay notwithstanding a finding of unlawful discrimination, the nature of the jurisdiction which the court exercises is equitable, and under our cases neither party may demand a jury trial. To the extent that discretion is replaced by awards which follow as a matter of course from a finding of wrongdoing, the action of the court in making such awards could not be fairly characterized as equitable in character, and would quite arguably be subject to the provisions of the Seventh Amendment.

* * *

NOTE ON DISCRETIONARY RELIEF, THE RIGHT TO JURY TRIAL, AND TITLE VII'S ADDED DAMAGES REMEDY

1. The Court in *Albemarle Paper* found "twin goals" in Title VII against which a discretionary award of backpay must be measured.

(a) How were the twin goals discovered? Are not deterrence and compensation the twin goals of almost all statutes creating civil enforcement actions?

(b) What considerations compel the Court to tighten the discretionary standards under Title VII, removing the ordinary rule of minimal review of trial judges' exercises of discretion? Is the Court trying to insure more favorable relief for employees? Or does it simply fear the lack of uniformity which would arise under the traditional equity standard? Both?

(c) After identifying the twin goals of Title VII, the Court asks whether the district court's reasons for denying backpay would frustrate either goal. Is this the critical aspect of the decision? Is it so clear that good faith should be ruled out as frustrating the Act's goals? Does the language of the Act help on this point? See 42 U.S.C. § 2000e–12(b).

2. Why did the Court, or at least its more liberal members, not go all the way and make backpay awards automatic? Did the statute preclude this? Or would such a move have raised other problems?

(a) Justice Rehnquist suggests that converting backpay into an automatic damage remedy would have run the risk of converting Title VII's equitable, non-jury suits into cases at law, thus requiring a jury trial by virtue of the Seventh Amendment to the Constitution. Was the Court trying to pursue a middle course, wringing out enough discretion to make backpay recoveries more likely and more effective, but retaining enough to make the suits equitable and avoid jury trial?

(b) Has the Court achieved a middle course? Or has it for most practical purposes made backpay automatic, absent eccentric prosecution of an individual suit? If the latter, what aspect of the decision achieves that result? The breadth of the identified statutory goals? The rejection of good faith as a ground for denying backpay?

(c) Now that the 1991 Amendments to Title VII permit damages remedies, see paragraph 4 infra, is the presumption of equitable relief still valid? Only if the only relief sought is equitable? If damages will compensate the plaintiff completely, is any equitable remedy appropriate? See Miles v. Indiana, 387 F.3d 591 (7th Cir. 2004) ("preferred remedy" is to restore plaintiff to job, even after damages award, but frontpay may be substituted for promotion if "awarding a promotion [would] create hostility or friction in the work environment"). Do you agree?

(d) Are some persons, such a illegal or undocumented immigrants, excluded from *Albemarle Paper*'s presumption of backpay? See Hoffman Plastic Compounds, Inc. v. N.L.R.B., 535 U.S. 137, 122 S.Ct. 1275, 152 L.Ed.2d 271 (2002) (no backpay in NLRA cases involving unions).

3. Should jury trials be discretionary in civil rights cases? In **Curtis v. Loether**, 415 U.S. 189, 94 S.Ct. 1005, 39 L.Ed.2d 260 (1974), a black woman

who charged that she had suffered racial discrimination in violation of § 804(a) of the Fair Housing Act of 1968, 42 U.S.C.A. § 3604(a), filed suit under § 812, 42 U.S.C.A. § 3612. The district court entered a preliminary injunction, dissolved prior to trial, and at a bench trial awarded $250 in punitive damages over the defendants' objection that they deserved a jury trial. The appellate court reversed and the Supreme Court agreed, rejecting the argument that the Seventh Amendment applies only to suits at common law and not Congressional enactments: Justice Marshall's opinion for a unanimous court concluded that the Amendment applied to all suits of a legal rather than maritime or equitable nature, and concluded (415 U.S. at 195–96, 94 S.Ct. at 1009):

> "We think it is clear that a damages action under § 812 is an action to enforce 'legal rights' within the meaning of our Seventh Amendment decisions. A damages action under the statute sounds basically in tort— the statute merely defines a new legal duty, and authorizes the courts to compensate a plaintiff for the injury caused by the defendant's wrongful breach. As the Court of Appeals noted, this cause of action is analogous to a number of tort actions recognized at common law. More important, the relief sought here—actual and punitive damages—is the traditional form of relief offered in the courts of law."

(a) The *Loether* Court confided that it was "not oblivious to the force of petitioner's policy arguments," 415 U.S. at 198, 94 S.Ct. at 1010, arguments which Judge (later Justice) Stevens characterized in his appellate opinion as ones that "probably favor denial of the right" to jury trial. Rogers v. Loether, 467 F.2d 1110, 1123 (7th Cir.1972). What are those policy arguments? Are they not the same arguments which prompted Congress in Title VII, and the Court in *Albemarle Paper* to make backpay a discretionary equitable remedy?

(b) Is a jury trial necessary when a backpay claim is joined with a request for equitable relief? Judge (later Attorney General) Bell's opinion for the court in Harkless v. Sweeny Independent School Dist., 427 F.2d 319, 324 (5th Cir.1970), held that a jury trial was unnecessary when a teacher sued under § 1983 for backpay and an injunction requiring reinstatement: "Back pay is merely an element of the equitable remedy of reinstatement." Do you agree? See Miles v. Indiana, 387 F.3d 591 (7th Cir. 2004) (civil jury trial on damages followed by judicial consideration of equitable relief).

4. The Civil Rights Act of 1991, section 102, now provides a remedy in damages for most violations of Title VII and its analogues. It does this not by amending Title VII directly, but by the circuitous route of adding a damages remedy for intentional discrimination after § 1981 for all plaintiffs who were otherwise covered by Title VII. See 42 U.S.C. § 1981A. There are rolling limits on the amount of damages, varying with the size of the defendant employer. The provision preserves the right to jury trial when damages are requested.

(a) Why did Congress choose the circuitous route of creating a new § 1981A? Why not amend Title VII itself, or even amend § 1981 itself (which already covers intentional racial discrimination)? Was Congress trying artfully to conceal the fact that its new provision effectively capped damages for women, while leaving them uncapped for blacks? See § 102(b)(4) (providing that limits enacted in this provision shall not be "construed to limit the scope of, or the relief available under," § 1981).

(b) In light of the policy reasons for avoiding jury trials in Title VII cases, as discussed above, when will a plaintiff choose to sue for damages? Will the prospective composition of the jury affect her judgment? Is it fair that a plaintiff can in effect determine whether she will have a jury trial by picking the type of remedy she wants? In what types of cases will the new amendment be most helpful? In what types of cases did plaintiffs previously go remediless because they had suffered no loss of pay? See section B.2 of this Chapter, supra (sexual harassment cases involving hostile environment and no tangible loss). If there has been no tangible loss, for what may damages be awarded—humiliation? See § 102(b)(3) (listing some compensable losses, including "other nonpecuniary losses").

(c) Because of the rolling caps on compensatory damages under § 1981A, it becomes necessary to distinguish between uncapped equitable remedies and capped damages recoveries. In Pollard v. E.I. du Pont de Nemours & Co., 532 U.S. 843, 121 S.Ct. 1946, 150 L.Ed.2d 62 (2001), the Court held that "frontpay" (wages paid between judgment and regaining the job, see the Note following the next principal case) is a form of equitable remedy not subject to the cap. Is "backpay" subject to the cap? Is it an easier issue to decide than frontpay or more difficult?

(d) The 1991 Act also provides for punitive damages. In **Kolstad v. American Dental Ass'n**, 527 U.S. 526, 119 S.Ct. 2118, 144 L.Ed.2d 494 (1999), a divided Court held that the 1991 Act authorized punitive damages only when there has been shown "malice or reckless indifference" to plaintiff's rights, fewer than all cases of intentional discrimination. Recognizing that employers can only be attributed a motive based on their supervisors' motives, the Court also held that "agency principles" would limit a punitive damages award when employers make a "good faith effort" to comply with the Act, citing Burlington Industries, Inc. v. Ellerth, section B.2 of this Chapter, supra. How likely is it that an employer with a knowledgeable human relations staff will pay punitive damages under *Kolstad*?

5. The ability to choose either a damages remedy under the 1991 Act or backpay under the original Act may have been severely compromised by the Court's later decision in **Wal-Mart Stores, Inc. v. Dukes**, ___ U.S. ___, 131 S.Ct. 2541, 180 L.Ed.2d 374 (2011), reversing the Ninth Circuit's somewhat aggressive view that FRCP 23(b) was available in a mammoth 1.5–million-member class action for damages at the retailer's 3,400 stores nationwide. Justice Scalia's majority opinion concluded that "claims for backpay were improperly certified under [Rule] 23(b)(2) [in cases where] the monetary relief is not incidental to the injunctive or declaratory relief" because "[p]ermitting the combination of individualized and classwide relief in a (b)(2) class is" impermissible. Does this effectively limit Title VII suits for monetary relief to backpay in cases where the monetary relief would be some form of liquidated, non-individualistic damages?[15]

15. Justice Ginsburg's concurring and dissenting opinion agreed that the class was improperly certified under Rule 23(b), but would have remanded for consideration of certification under Rule

(a) The quintessential Rule 23(b) decisions from the early days of Title VII, authored by some of the old lions of the Fifth Circuit, had enjoined overt and company-wide or factory-wide discriminatory practices and policies that had been used to perpetuate pre-Act discrimination at mass employers in southern states. See, e.g., Pettway v. American Cast Iron Pipe Co., 494 F.2d 211 (5th Cir. 1974) (per Tuttle, J.); United States v. Georgia Power Co., 474 F.2d 906 (5th Cir. 1973) (per Tuttle, J.). As a practical matter, however, it proved impossible to hold mini-trials to determine the backpay of all class members, and settlements creating a pool of money to be paid too claimants was ordinarily adopted. See, e.g., United States v. City of Jackson, Miss., 519 F.2d 1147 (5th Cir. 1975). Such a course of action would also have been the only practical remedy in *Wal-Mart*, would it not? How does this affect your appreciation of the Court's decision?

(b) The *Wal-Mart* Court did not forbid all class-wide claims for monetary relief, instead holding that "individualized monetary claims belong in Rule 23(b)(3) [with its attendant protective mechanisms for the class members]—predominance, superiority, mandatory notice, and the right to opt out." The risk, according to the Court, was that the named class members—or more realistically, their attorneys—might make strategic decisions that "place at risk potentially valid claims for monetary relief" by class members. (Note that a successful class action would extinguish all claims by class members.) Is *Wal-Mart* actually protective of the majority of class members who are not named plaintiffs?

(c) Realizing that individual trials would be impractical, the Ninth Circuit devised a scheme of holding selected demonstration trials, with the ratio of victories for plaintiffs (and amount of backpay awarded) then being used to calculate the total potential damages; this sum would be divided among remaining class members. The Court rejected this novel method as a violation of Wal-Mart's right to an individualized opportunity to present a defense to each claim. Do mass class actions potentially violate the rights of both plaintiffs and defendants?

FRANKS v. BOWMAN TRANSPORTATION CO., INC.

Supreme Court of the United States, 1976.
424 U.S. 747, 96 S.Ct. 1251, 47 L.Ed.2d 444.

MR. JUSTICE BRENNAN delivered the opinion of the Court.

This case presents the question whether identifiable applicants who were denied employment because of race after the effective date and in violation of Title VII of the Civil Rights Act of 1964, 78 Stat. 253, as amended, 42 U.S.C.A. § 2000e et seq., may be awarded seniority status retroactive to the dates of their employment applications.[1]

Petitioner Franks brought this class action in the United States District Court for the Northern District of Georgia against his former

---

23(b)(3). The majority also rejected that approach, for reasons discussed in subsection A.1 of this Chapter.

1. Petitioners also alleged an alternative claim for relief for violations of 42 U.S.C.A. § 1981. In view of our decision we have no occasion to address that claim.

employer, respondent Bowman Transportation Co., and his unions, the International Union of District 50, Allied and Technical Workers of the United States and Canada, and its local, No. 13600, alleging various racially discriminatory employment practices in violation of Title VII. Petitioner Lee intervened on behalf of himself and others similarly situated alleging racially discriminatory hiring and discharge policies limited to Bowman's employment of over-the-road (OTR) truck drivers. Following trial, the District Court found that Bowman had engaged in a pattern of racial discrimination in various company policies, including the hiring, transfer, and discharge of employees, and found further that the discriminatory practices were perpetrated in Bowman's collective-bargaining agreement with the unions. The District Court certified the action as a proper class action under Fed.Rule Civ.Proc. 23(b)(2), and of import to the issues before this Court, found that petitioner Lee represented all black applicants who sought to be hired or to transfer to OTR driving positions prior to January 1, 1972. In its final order and decree, the District Court subdivided the class represented by petitioner Lee into a class of black nonemployee applicants for OTR positions prior to January 1, 1972 (class 3), and a class of black employees who applied for transfer to OTR positions prior to the same date (class 4).

[The district court entered a general injunction against discrimination and specifically ordered Bowman to notify members of both subclasses 3 and 4 of a right to "priority consideration" for future OTR jobs. It declined to award seniority status retroactive to the date of discrimination. The plaintiffs appealed seeking further relief, and the Fifth Circuit ordered that such seniority be given to members of subclass 4, employees applying to transfer to OTR, but it too declined to give seniority to subclass 3, non-employees who had sought OTR jobs but had never been hired by the company.]

II

In affirming the District Court's denial of seniority relief to the class 3 group of discriminates, the Court of Appeals held that the relief was barred by § 703(h) of Title VII, 42 U.S.C.A. § 2000e–2(h). We disagree. Section 703(h) provides in pertinent part:

> Notwithstanding any other provision of this title, it shall not be an unlawful employment practice for an employer to apply different standards of compensation, or different terms, conditions, or privileges of employment pursuant to a bona fide seniority or merit system * * * provided that such differences are not the result of an intention to discriminate because of race, color, religion, sex, or national origin * * *.

The Court of Appeals reasoned that a discriminatory refusal to hire "does not affect the bona fides of the seniority system. Thus, the differences in the benefits and conditions of employment which a seniority system accords to older and newer employees is protected [by § 703(h)] as 'not an unlawful employment practice.'" 495 F.2d at 417. Significantly, neither Bowman nor the unions undertake to defend the Court of Appeals' judgment on that ground. It is clearly erroneous.

The black applicants for OTR positions composing class 3 are limited to those whose applications were put in evidence at the trial. The underlying legal wrong affecting them is not the alleged operation of a racially discriminatory seniority system but of a racially discriminatory hiring system. Petitioners do not ask for modification or elimination of the existing seniority system, but only an award of the seniority status they would have individually enjoyed under the present system but for the illegal discriminatory refusal to hire. It is this context that must shape our determination as to the meaning and effect of § 703(h).

On its face, § 703(h) appears to be only a definitional provision; as with the other provisions of § 703, subsection (h) delineates which employment practices are illegal and thereby prohibited and which are not. Section 703(h) certainly does not expressly purport to qualify or proscribe relief otherwise appropriate under the remedial provisions of Title VII, § 706(g), 42 U.S.C.A. § 2000e–5(a), in circumstances where an illegal discriminatory act or practice is found. Further, the legislative history of § 703(h) plainly negates its reading as limiting or qualifying the relief authorized under § 706(g).

[Sponsors of the original bill assured the Senate that "Title VII would have no effect on seniority rights existing at the time it takes effect." The final Dirksen–Mansfield substitute bill for the first time used the language now in § 703(h), but Senator Humphrey, who participated in drafting the compromise, stated that the provision was not designed to alter the general meaning of Title VII but to "clarif[y] its present intent and effect." Accordingly,] it is apparent that the thrust of the section is directed toward defining what is and what is not an illegal discriminatory practice in instances in which the post-Act operation of a seniority system is challenged as perpetuating the effects of discrimination occurring prior to the effective date of the Act. There is no indication in the legislative materials that § 703(h) was intended to modify or restrict relief otherwise appropriate once an illegal discriminatory practice occurring after the effective date of the Act is proved—as in the instant case, a discriminatory refusal to hire. * * * We therefore hold that the Court of Appeals erred in concluding that, as a matter of law, § 703(h) barred the award of seniority relief to the unnamed class 3 members.

III

There remains the question whether an award of seniority relief is appropriate under the remedial provisions of Title VII, specifically, § 706(g). * * * Last Term's Albemarle Paper Co. v. Moody, consistently with the congressional plan, held that one of the central purposes of Title VII is "to make persons whole for injuries suffered on account of unlawful employment discrimination." To effectuate this "make whole" objective, Congress in § 706(g) vested broad equitable discretion in the federal courts to "order such affirmative action as may be appropriate, which may include, but is not limited to, reinstatement or hiring of employees, with or without back pay * * *, or any other equitable relief as the court deems appropriate." The legislative history supporting the 1972 amendments of § 706(g) of Title VII affirms the breadth of this discretion. "The provisions of [§ 706(g)] are intended to give the courts wide discretion exercising their equitable powers to fashion the most complete relief possible. * * * [T]he Act is intended to make the victims of unlawful employment discrimination whole, and * * * the attainment of this objective * * * requires that persons aggrieved by the consequences and effects of the unlawful employment practice be, so far as possible, restored to a position where they would have been were it not for the unlawful discrimination." Section-by-Section Analysis of H.R. 1746, accompanying the Equal Employment Opportunity Act of 1972—Conference Report, 118 Cong.Rec. 7166, 7168 (1972). This is emphatic confirmation that federal courts are empowered to fashion such relief as the particular circumstances of a case may require to effect restitution, making whole insofar as possible the victims of racial discrimination in hiring.[21] Adequate relief may well be denied in the absence of a seniority remedy slotting the victim in that position in the seniority system that would have been his had he been hired at the time of his application. It can hardly be questioned that ordinarily such relief will be necessary to achieve the "make-whole" purposes of the Act.

Seniority systems and the entitlements conferred by credits earned thereunder are of vast and increasing importance in the economic employment system of this Nation. S. Slichter, J. Healy, & E. Livernash, The Impact of Collective Bargaining on Management 104–115 (1960). Seniority principles are increasingly used to allocate entitlements to scarce benefits among competing employees ("competitive status" seniority) and to compute noncompetitive benefits earned under the contract of employment ("benefit" seniority). Ibid. We have already said about "competitive status" seniority that it "has become of overriding importance, and one of its major functions is to determine who gets or who keeps an available job." Humphrey v. Moore, 375 U.S. 335, 346–47, 84 S.Ct. 363, 370, 11 L.Ed.2d 370, 380 (1964). "More than any other provision of the collective[-bargaining] agreement * * * seniority affects the economic security of the individual employee covered by its terms." Aaron, *Reflections on the Legal Nature and Enforceability of Seniority Rights*, 75 HARV. L. REV. 1532, 1535 (1962). "Competitive status," seniority also often plays a broader role in

---

21. It is true that backpay is the only remedy specifically mentioned in § 706(g). But to draw from this fact and other sections of the statute any implicit statement by Congress that seniority relief is a prohibited, or at least less available, form of remedy is not warranted. Indeed, any such contention necessarily disregards the extensive legislative history underlying the 1972 amendments to Title VII. The 1972 amendments added the phrase speaking to "other equitable relief" in § 706(g). The Senate Report manifested an explicit concern with the "earnings gap" presently existing between black and white employees in American society. S.Rep. No. 92–415, p. 6 (1971). The Reports of both Houses of Congress indicated that "rightful place" was the intended objective of Title VII and the relief accorded thereunder. Ibid. H.R.Rep. No. 92–238, p. 4 (1971), U.S.Code Cong. & Admin.News 1972, p. 2137. As indicated, infra, rightful-place seniority, implicating an employee's *future* earnings, job security, and advancement prospects, is absolutely essential to obtaining this congressionally mandated goal. * * *

modern employment systems, particularly systems operated under collective-bargaining agreements [because of the many privileges linked to seniority].

Seniority standing in employment with respondent Bowman, computed from the departmental date of hire, determines the order of layoff and recall of employees. Further, job assignments for OTR drivers are posted for competitive bidding and seniority is used to determine the highest bidder. As OTR drivers are paid on a per-mile basis, earnings are therefore to some extent a function of seniority. Additionally, seniority computed from the company date of hire determines the length of an employee's vacation and pension benefits. Obviously merely to require Bowman to hire the class 3 victim of discrimination falls far short of a "make whole" remedy.[27] A concomitant award of the seniority credit he presumptively would have earned but for the wrongful treatment would also seem necessary in the absence of justification for denying that relief. Without an award of seniority dating from the time when he was discriminatorily refused employment, an individual who applies for and obtains employment as an OTR driver pursuant to the District Court's order will never obtain his rightful place in the hierarchy of seniority according to which these various employment benefits are distributed. He will perpetually remain subordinate to persons who, but for the illegal discrimination, would have been in respect to entitlement to these benefits his inferiors.

The Court of Appeals apparently followed this reasoning in holding that the District Court erred in not granting seniority relief to class 4 Bowman employees who were discriminatorily refused transfer to OTR positions. Yet the class 3 discriminatees in the absence of a comparable seniority award would also remain subordinated in the seniority system to the class 4 discriminatees. The distinction plainly finds no support anywhere in Title VII or its legislative history. Settled law dealing with the related "twin" areas of discriminatory hiring and discharges violative of the National Labor Relations Act, 29 U.S.C.A. § 151 et seq., provides a persuasive analogy. "[I]t would indeed be surprising if Congress gave a remedy for the one which it denied for the other." Phelps Dodge Corp. v. NLRB, 313 U.S. 177, 187, 61 S.Ct. 845, 849, 85 L.Ed. 1271, 1279 (1941). For courts to differentiate without justification between the classes of discriminatees "would be a differentiation not only without substance but in defiance of that against which the prohibition of discrimination is directed." Id. at 188, 61 S.Ct., at 850, 85 L.Ed., at 1280.

Similarly, decisions construing the remedial section of the National Labor Relations Act, § 10(c), 29 U.S.C.A. § 160(c)—the model for § 706(g),—make clear that remedies constituting authorized "affirmative action" include an award of seniority status, for the thrust of "affirmative

---

27. Further, at least in regard to "benefit"-type seniority such as length of vacation leave and pension benefits in the instant case, any general bar to the award of retroactive seniority for victims of illegal hiring discrimination serves to undermine the mutually reinforcing effect of the dual purposes of Title VII; it reduces the restitution required of an employer at such time as he is called upon to account for his discriminatory actions perpetrated in violation of the law. See Albemarle Paper Co. v. Moody.

action" redressing the wrong incurred by an unfair labor practice is to make "the employees whole, and thus restor[e] the economic status quo that would have obtained but for the company's wrongful [act]." NLRB v. Rutter–Rex Mfg. Co., 396 U.S. 258, 263, 90 S.Ct. 417, 420, 24 L.Ed.2d 405, 411 (1969). * * * Plainly the "affirmative action" injunction of § 706(g) has no lesser reach in the district courts. "Where racial discrimination is concerned, 'the [district] court has not merely the power but the duty to render a decree which will so far as possible eliminate the discriminatory effects of the past as well as bar like discrimination in the future.' " *Albemarle Paper*, supra.

IV

We are not to be understood as holding that an award of seniority status is requisite in all circumstances. * * *

* * *

We read the District Court's reference to the lack of evidence regarding a "vacancy, qualification, and performance" for every individual member of the class as an expression of concern that some of the unnamed class members (unhired black applicants whose employment applications were summarized in the record) may not in fact have been actual victims of racial discrimination. That factor will become material however only when those persons reapply for OTR positions pursuant to the hiring relief ordered by the District Court. Generalizations concerning such individually applicable evidence cannot serve as a justification for the denial of relief to the entire class. Rather, at such time as individual class members seek positions as OTR drivers, positions for which they are presumptively entitled to priority hiring consideration under the District Court's order,[31] evidence that particular individuals were not in fact victims of racial discrimination will be material. But petitioners here have carried their burden of demonstrating the existence of a discriminatory hiring pattern and practice by the respondents and, therefore, the burden will be upon respondents to prove that individuals who reapply were not in fact victims of previous hiring discrimination. Cf. McDonnell Douglas Corp. v. Green, [supra.][32] Only if this burden is met may retroactive seniority—if otherwise determined to be an appropriate form of relief

---

31. The District Court order is silent as to whether applicants for OTR positions who were previously discriminatorily refused employment must be presently qualified for those positions in order to be eligible for priority hiring under that order. The Court of Appeals, however, made it plain that they must be. We agree.

32. Thus Bowman may attempt to prove that a given individual member of class 3 was not in fact discriminatorily refused employment as an OTR driver in order to defeat the individual's claim to seniority relief as well as any other remedy ordered for the class generally. Evidence of a lack of vacancies in OTR positions at the time the individual application was filed, or evidence indicating the individual's lack of qualification for the OTR positions—under nondiscriminatory standards *actually applied* by Bowman to individuals who were in fact hired—would of course be relevant. It is true, of course, that obtaining the third category of evidence with which the District Court was concerned—what the individual discriminatee's job performance would have been but for the discrimination—presents great difficulty. No reason appears, however, why the victim rather than the perpetrator of the illegal act should bear the burden of proof on this issue.

under the circumstances of the particular case—be denied individual class members.

* * *

With reference to the problems of fairness or equity respecting the conflicting interests of the various groups of employees, the relief which petitioners seek is only seniority status retroactive to the date of individual application, rather than some form of arguably more complete relief.[36] No claim is asserted that nondiscriminatee employees holding OTR positions they would not have obtained but for the illegal discrimination should be deprived of the seniority status they have earned. It is therefore clear that even if the seniority relief petitioners seek is awarded, most if not all discriminatees who actually obtain OTR jobs under the court order will not truly be restored to the actual seniority that would have existed in the absence of the illegal discrimination. Rather, most discriminatees even under an award of retroactive seniority status will still remain subordinated in the hierarchy to a position inferior to that of a greater total number of employees than would have been the case in the absence of discrimination. Therefore, the relief which petitioners seek, while a more complete form of relief than that which the District Court accorded, in no sense constitutes "complete relief." Rather, the burden of the past discrimination in hiring is with respect to competitive status benefits divided among discriminatee and nondiscriminatee employees under the form of relief sought. The dissent criticizes the Court's result as not sufficiently cognizant that it will "directly implicate the rights and expectations of perfectly innocent employees." We are of the view, however, that the result which we reach today—which, standing alone, establishes that a sharing of the burden of the past discrimination is presumptively necessary—is entirely consistent with any fair characterization of equity jurisdiction, particularly when considered in light of our traditional view that "[a]ttainment of a great national policy * * * must not be confined within narrow canons for equitable relief deemed suitable by chancellors in ordinary private controversies." Phelps Dodge Corp. v. NLRB, 313 U.S. at 188, 61 S.Ct., at 850, 85 L.Ed., at 1280.

* * *

Accordingly, the judgment of the Court of Appeals affirming the District Court's denial of seniority relief to class 3 is reversed, and the case is remanded to the District Court for further proceedings consistent with this opinion.

---

36. Another countervailing factor in assessing the expected impact on the interests of other employees actually occasioned by an award of the seniority relief sought is that it is not probable in instances of class-based relief that all of the victims of the past racial discrimination in hiring will actually apply for and obtain the prerequisite hiring relief. Indeed, in the instant case, there appear in the record the rejected applications of 166 black applicants who claimed at the time of application to have had the necessary job qualifications. However, the Court was informed at oral argument that only a small number of those individuals have to this date actually been hired pursuant to the District Court's order ("five, six, seven, something in that order"), Tr. of Oral Arg. 23, although ongoing litigation may ultimately determine more who desire the hiring relief and are eligible for it. Id. at 15.

It is so ordered.

Reversed and remanded.

MR. JUSTICE STEVENS took no part in the consideration or decision of this case.

MR. CHIEF JUSTICE BURGER, concurring in part and dissenting in part.

I agree generally with Mr. Justice Powell * * *.

I would stress that the Court today does not foreclose claims of employees who might be injured by this holding from securing equitable relief on their own behalf.

MR. JUSTICE POWELL, with whom MR. JUSTICE REHNQUIST joins, concurring in part and dissenting in part.

[JUSTICE POWELL stated that he joined the "precise holding" of Part II of the Court's opinion.]

Although I am in accord with much of the Court's discussion in Parts III and IV, I cannot accept as correct its basic interpretation of § 706(g) as virtually requiring a district court, in determining appropriate equitable relief in a case of this kind, to ignore entirely the equities that may exist in favor of innocent employees. Its holding recognizes no meaningful distinction, in terms of the equitable relief to be granted, between "benefit"-type seniority and "competitive"-type seniority. The Court reaches this result by taking an absolutist view of the "make whole" objective of Title VII, while rendering largely meaningless the discretionary authority vested in district courts by § 706(g) to weigh the equities of the situation. Accordingly, I dissent from Parts III and IV.

NOTE ON SENIORITY SYSTEMS, STALE CLAIMS, AND COURT-ORDERED AFFIRMATIVE ACTION

1. In the first part of its *Franks* opinion the Court held that § 703(h) does not bar relief intruding on a seniority system when a violation of Title VII has otherwise been proved. If § 703(h) is directed toward substantive definitions of liability rather than relief, what is its scope? The Court answered that question the term following *Franks*. **International Brotherhood of Teamsters v. United States**, 431 U.S. 324, 97 S.Ct. 1843, 52 L.Ed.2d 396 (1977), involved an attempt to remedy pre-Act discrimination on the theory that it was "perpetuated" after Title VII's effective date by a company seniority system.[1] Justice Stewart's majority opinion noted that ordinarily under the *Griggs* doctrine the company's seniority system would present a prima facie violation of Title VII because of its disproportionate impact in excluding blacks and other minorities and " 'freez[ing] the status quo of prior discriminatory employment practices.' " But, said the Court,

---

1. The part of *Teamsters* reproduced in section A.2 of this Chapter, supra, deals with proved *post-Act* discrimination arising from company actions apart from the conduct of a seniority system. The Court had no trouble concluding that § 703(h) presented no obstacle to a relief decree intruding on the seniority system and designed to cure such post-Act discrimination, citing *Franks*. 431 U.S. at 347, 97 S.Ct. at 1860–61.

"both the literal terms of § 703(h) and the legislative history of Title VII demonstrate that Congress considered this very effect of many seniority systems and extended a measure of immunity to them." The Court continued (431 U.S. at 353–54, 97 S.Ct. at 1863–64):

"To be sure, § 703(h) does not immunize all seniority systems. It refers only to 'bona fide' systems, and a proviso requires that any differences in treatment not be 'the result of an intention to discriminate because of race * * * or national origin * * *.' But our reading of the legislative history compels us to reject the Government's broad argument that no seniority system that tends to perpetuate pre-Act discrimination can be 'bona fide.' To accept the argument would require us to hold that a seniority system becomes illegal simply because it allows the full exercise of the pre-Act seniority rights of employees of a company that discriminated before Title VII was enacted. It would place an affirmative obligation on the parties to the seniority agreement to subordinate those rights in favor of the claims of pre-Act discriminatees without seniority. The consequence would be a perversion of the congressional purpose. We cannot accept the invitation to disembowel § 703(h) by reading the words 'bona fide' as the Government would have us do. Accordingly, we hold that an otherwise neutral, legitimate seniority system does not become unlawful under Title VII simply because it may perpetuate pre-Act discrimination. Congress did not intend to make it illegal for employees with vested seniority rights to continue to exercise those rights, even at the expense of pre-Act discriminatees."

(a) Is *Teamsters* consistent with *Franks*? Compelled by *Franks*? See Justice Marshall's dissenting opinion, 431 U.S. at 377, 97 S.Ct. at 1875 (appellate cases and EEOC interpretations unanimously contrary).

(b) Will *Teamsters* have substantially diminished practical impact as time passes?

2. The Court has often used a similar immunization concept to prohibit revival of time-barred claims. Handed down on the same day as *Teamsters*, **United Air Lines, Inc. v. Evans**, 431 U.S. 553, 97 S.Ct. 1885, 52 L.Ed.2d 571 (1977), concerned a plaintiff's challenge to the company's seniority system as one which perpetuated an incident of post-Act discrimination for which she had failed to file a timely charge: the "perpetuated" discrimination provided the basis for the new timely charge. Justice Stevens rejected the argument by noting that "United was entitled to treat the past act as lawful" after expiration of the original statute of limitations. His opinion for the Court next turned to the issue of whether the seniority system itself was a violation of Title VII. The system, he found "is neutral in its operation," and that factor invokes the terms of § 703(h) (431 U.S. at 559–60, 97 S.Ct. at 1890).

(a) The Court relied in Evans in **Ledbetter v. Goodyear Tire & Rubber Co., Inc.**, 550 U.S. 618, 127 S.Ct. 2162, 167 L.Ed.2d 982 (2007), where it rejected a woman's claim that time-barred acts of intentional sex discrimination had been given new life when her employer relied on her past employment history in determining her current pay. Calling the case "basically the same as" *Evans*, the Court held that each act of prior discrimination constituted a discrete action which became time barred; further reliance on the effects of the prior acts, without proof that the reliance was itself intentionally discriminatory, did not create a new claim. Congress almost immediately overrode the *Ledbetter* decision by amending Title VII's statute of limitations. See 42 U.S.C. § 2000e–5(3)(A).[2] Which approach is preferable as a matter of policy? Such late-arising claims will necessarily require proof of intentional discrimination at the time of the original decisions, some years or decades earlier. How can such cases be proved? Should there be a limit to how far back plaintiff can go in order to protect employers from the accrual of massive liabilities? See 42 U.S.C. § 2000e–5(3)(B) (two years).

(b) Regarding seniority systems, does the *Evans* decision effectively preclude use of the *Griggs* doctrine when it is a seniority system which is claimed to have a discriminatory impact? See *Teamsters,* supra, 431 U.S. at 353 n. 38, 97 S.Ct. at 1863 n. 38. To the extent that *Evans* may be read to bar claims of disparate treatment, Congress overrode that decision even prior to *Ledbetter,* adopting essentially the same formulation used in overriding *Ledbetter.* See 42 U.S.C. § 2000e–5(e)(2).

3.   The two decisions noted above, of course, speak only to the occasions when a seniority system is directly challenged; *Franks* continues to govern when other practices are the focus of successful litigation and the only issue is whether to grant relief invading the seniority ranking. Was *Franks* rightly decided on its own terms?

(a) The Court in *Franks* followed the *Albemarle Paper Co.* construct to find a presumption in favor of rightful-place seniority awards. How persuasive is the dissent's argument that more discretion is needed? How could uniformity be assured?

(b) The argument between Justice Powell and the majority seems, perhaps facetiously, to turn largely on whether one perceives whites who won jobs during the years of discrimination against blacks as "perfectly innocent employees" or "arguably innocent employees." Is Justice Brennan right when he says that seniority awards do not constitute "complete relief" but "a sharing of the burden" between discriminatees and current employees? Why? Because current employees get to keep seniority, the enrichment they received as a by-product of the company's discrimination?

(c) Chief Justice Burger suggested that "front pay," in lieu of instatement to a job, could adequately compensate the black employee by paying him for all the present and future disadvantages of lack of seniority. Would such compensation be adequate, or is there any element of status and pride which needs to be served? If frontpay is awarded, For how many years may a plaintiff receive frontpay? See Biondo v. City of Chicago, 382 F.3d 680 (7th Cir. 2004) (12 years of frontpay exceeds district court's equitable discretion).[3]

---

2. "(3)(A) For purposes of this section, an unlawful employment practice occurs, with respect to discrimination in compensation in violation of this subchapter, when a discriminatory compensation decision or other practice is adopted, when an individual becomes subject to a discriminatory compensation decision or other practice, or when an individual is affected by application of a discriminatory compensation decision or other practice, including each time wages, benefits, or other compensation is paid, resulting in whole or in part from such a decision or other practice."

3. Does the availability of frontpay as an equitable remedy make the full scope of equitable relief coextensive with the damages remedy available under the Civil Rights Act of 1991, 42 U.S.C. § 1981A? Since frontpay is a prospective monetary award with some similarities to

(d) To the extent that an incumbent employee must share seniority with a newly slotted black person and may lose seniority if blacks are placed above him, should the *incumbent* receive front pay? See McAleer v. American Tel. & Tel. Co., 416 F.Supp. 435 (D.D.C.1976).

4. Is the system envisioned by the Court for identifying, hiring, and granting seniority to black class members a workable one?

(a) How does the *Franks* Court perceive the mechanics of the system? Will its actual operation, given the allocation of burdens of proof, be to grant a probationary job to every class member? Was *Franks* an easy case because all class members had filed applications and were identified?[4] Compare the similar issue discussed with respect to backpay in ¶ 5 of the previous Note (discussing the *Wal-Mart* case). Is it realistic to believe that there can be mini-trials for each class member? What will happen if the employer cannot meet its evidentiary burden with respect to sufficient claimants—so that more claimants win than there were positions open in the past?

(b) Although *Franks* speaks to the issue of whether a discriminatee can get seniority, it does not say when the person will get a job. No worker is displaced when seniority is awarded; can a court displace incumbents to make room for discriminatees? Make discriminatees wait for job openings? The Court faced these issues in a comparable situation in its "pattern or practice" decision in **Teamsters**, supra. In that case the Court appeared to reconsider the scope of discretion granted the trial court, at least on the issue of carrying out the seniority mandate of *Franks* (431 U.S. at 372–76, 97 S.Ct. at 1873–75):

> [A]fter the victims have been identified and their rightful place determined, the District Court will again be faced with the delicate task of adjusting the remedial interests of discriminatees and the legitimate expectations of other employees innocent of any wrongdoing. [The district court had permitted some laid-off workers to be rehired before discriminatees were rehired.] Although not directly controlled by the Act, the extent to which the legitimate expectations of nonvictim employees should determine when victims are restored to their rightful place is limited by basic principles of equity. In devising and implementing remedies under Title VII, no less than in formulating any equitable decree, a court must draw on the qualities of mercy and practicality [that] have made equity the instrument for nice adjustment and reconciliation between the public interest and private needs as well as between competing private claims. Especially when immediate implementation of an equitable remedy threatens to impinge upon the expectations of innocent parties, the courts must 'look to the practical realities and necessities inescapably involved in reconciling competing interests, in order to deter-

damages, should frontpay be limited to the amount of the damages cap in § 1981A? See Pollard v. E.I. du Pont de Nemours & Co., 532 U.S. 843, 121 S.Ct. 1946, 150 L.Ed.2d 62 (2001) (no).

4. In *Teamsters,* supra, the Court extended *Franks* to cover nonapplicants because a "consistently enforced discriminatory policy can surely deter job applications from those who are aware of it," but, unlike *Franks'* scheme for applicants, it required the nonapplicant to shoulder the burden of showing that he was qualified and would have applied but for the company's practice. See 431 U.S. at 362–76, 97 S.Ct. at 1868–75.

mine the special blend of what is necessary, what is fair, and what is workable. (internal quotations omitted)

Has the *Albemarle–Franks* presumption in favor of relief for plaintiffs finally lost its force?

5. Does the holding in *Franks* lead ineluctably to court-ordered quotas? The Court faced the issue of whether and under what circumstances a trial court may impose quota-based hiring standards as a remedy in **United States v. Paradise**, 480 U.S. 149, 107 S.Ct. 1053, 94 L.Ed.2d 203 (1987). In a divided judgment, four members of the Court (Justices Brennan, Marshall, Blackmun, and Stevens) took the view that district courts enjoy broad equitable discretion in deciding whether to impose racial hiring quotas as a cure for prior discrimination, provided that certain safeguards are taken to protect the interests of whites. Justice Powell decided that factors like those applicable in voluntary affirmative action cases, see section D of this Chapter, infra, are pertinent also to court-awarded relief. Four Justices took the view that quotas may only be used where they are necessary and constitute the least drastic means for ending the former discrimination.

(a) Why did no justice in *Paradise* argue for application of the *Albemarle Paper–Franks* standard that would have presumptively authorized quotas in many cases? Does the Court's failure to so act undercut the rationale of *Franks,* because neither instatement with seniority nor quotas is explicitly mentioned in Title VII's relief provisions?

(b) Are quotas or other numerically based orders of relief substantially different from the relief ordered in *Franks*? Different enough that they should be judged by a different standard? Reconsider *Franks* after reading the section D, which follows.

D. AFFIRMATIVE ACTION, SETTLEMENTS, AND THE TENSION IN TITLE VII

1. VOLUNTARY AFFIRMATIVE ACTION AND QUOTAS OR GOALS

UNITED STEELWORKERS OF AMERICA v. WEBER

Supreme Court of the United States, 1979.
443 U.S. 193, 99 S.Ct. 2721, 61 L.Ed.2d 480.

MR. JUSTICE BRENNAN delivered the opinion of the Court.

Challenged here is the legality of an affirmative action plan—collectively bargained by an employer and a union—that reserves for black employees 50% of the openings in an in-plant craft training program until the percentage of black craft workers in the plant is commensurate with the percentage of blacks in the local labor force. The question for decision is whether Congress, in Title VII of the Civil Rights Act of 1964 as amended, 42 U.S.C.A. § 2000e, left employers and unions in the private sector free to take such race-conscious steps to eliminate manifest racial imbalances in traditionally segregated job categories. We hold that Title VII does not prohibit such race-conscious affirmative action plans.

I

[The union and its employer, Kaiser Aluminum & Chemical Corporation (Kaiser), agreed in 1974 to a collective-bargaining agreement that contained "an affirmative action plan designed to eliminate conspicuous racial imbalances in Kaiser's then almost exclusively white craft work forces." The numerical goals for black hiring were supplemented with training programs for prospective hires. The specific plant at issue in this case had followed a practice of hiring only persons with skilled craft experience for craft jobs; against a history of black exclusion from such jobs, the experience requirement led to few blacks being offered skilled jobs (1.83% of craft jobs in an area where the workforce was 39% black). Under the agreement 50% of openings for training for skilled jobs went to blacks. Some blacks with less seniority were chosen over some whites with more seniority, and one of those whites, Weber, thereafter filed this suit under Title VII. The trial judge invalidated the plan, and the Fifth Circuit affirmed.]

II

We emphasize at the outset the narrowness of our inquiry. Since the Kaiser–USWA plan does not involve state action, this case does not present an alleged violation of the Equal Protection Clause of the Constitution. Further, since the Kaiser–USWA plan was adopted voluntarily, we are not concerned with what Title VII requires or with what a court might order to remedy a past proven violation of the Act. The only question before us is the narrow statutory issue of whether Title VII *forbids* private employers and unions from voluntarily agreeing upon bona fide affirmative action plans that accord racial preferences in the manner and for the purpose provided in the Kaiser–USWA plan. That question was expressly left open in McDonald v. Santa Fe Trail Trans. Co., [set out in Chapter 2C.3 supra,] which held, in a case not involving affirmative action, that Title VII protects whites as well as blacks from certain forms of racial discrimination.

Respondent argues that Congress intended in Title VII to prohibit all race-conscious affirmative action plans. Respondent's argument rests upon a literal interpretation of §§ 703(a) and (d) of the Act. Those sections make it unlawful to "discriminate * * * because of * * * race" in hiring and in the selection of apprentices for training programs. * * *

Respondent's argument is not without force. But it overlooks the significance of the fact that the Kaiser–USWA plan is an affirmative action plan voluntarily adopted by private parties to eliminate traditional patterns of racial segregation. In this context respondent's reliance upon a literal construction of §§ 703(a) and (d) and upon *McDonald* is misplaced. It is a "familiar rule, that a thing may be within the letter of the statute and yet not within the statute, because not within its spirit, nor within the intention of its makers." Holy Trinity Church v. United States, 143 U.S. 457, 459, 12 S.Ct. 511, 512, 36 L.Ed. 226 (1892). * * *

Congress' primary concern in enacting the prohibition against racial discrimination in Title VII of the Civil Rights Acts of 1964 was with "the plight of the Negro in our economy." 110 Cong.Rec. 6548 (remarks of Sen. Humphrey). Before 1964, blacks were largely relegated to "unskilled and semi-skilled jobs." Id. at 6548 (remarks of Sen. Humphrey); id. at 7204 (remarks of Sen. Clark), id. at 7279–7280 (remarks of Sen. Kennedy). Because of automation the number of such jobs was rapidly decreasing. See 110 Cong.Rec., at 6548 (remarks of Sen. Humphrey); id. at 7204 (remarks of Sen. Clark). As a consequence "the relative position of the Negro worker [was] steadily worsening. In 1947 the non-white unemployment rate was only 64 percent higher than the white rate; in 1962 it was 124 percent higher." Id. at 6547 (remarks of Sen. Humphrey). See also id. at 7204 (remarks of Sen. Clark). Congress considered this a serious social problem. As Senator Clark told the Senate:

> "The rate of Negro unemployment has gone up consistently as compared with white unemployment for the past 15 years. This is a social malaise and a social situation which we should not tolerate. That is one of the principal reasons why this bill should pass." Id. at 7220.

* * *

It plainly appears from the House Report accompanying the Civil Rights Act that Congress did not intend wholly to prohibit private and voluntary affirmative action efforts as one method of solving this problem. The Report provides:

> "No bill can or should lay claim to eliminating all of the causes and consequences of racial and other types of discrimination against minorities. There is reason to believe, however, that national leadership provided by the enactment of Federal legislation dealing with the most troublesome problems *will create an atmosphere conducive to voluntary or local resolution of other forms of discrimination.*" H.R.Rep. No. 914, 88th Cong., 1st Sess. (1963), at 18. (Emphasis supplied.)

Given this legislative history, we cannot agree with respondent that Congress intended to prohibit the private sector from taking effective steps to accomplish the goal that Congress designed Title VII to achieve. The very statutory words intended as a spur or catalyst to cause "employers and unions to self-examine and to self-evaluate their employment practices and to endeavor to eliminate, so far as possible, the last vestiges of an unfortunate and ignominious page in this country's history," Albemarle v. Moody, 422 U.S. 405, 418, 95 S.Ct. 2362, 2372, 45 L.Ed.2d 280 (1975), cannot be interpreted as an absolute prohibition against all private, voluntary, race-conscious affirmative action efforts to hasten the elimination of such vestiges.[4] * * *

---

4. The problem that Congress addressed in 1964 remains with us. In 1962 the nonwhite unemployment rate was 124% higher than the white rate. See 110 Cong.Rec. 6547 (remarks of

Our conclusion is further reinforced by examination of the language and legislative history of § 703(j) of Title VII. Opponents of Title VII raised two related arguments against the bill. First, they argued that the Act would be interpreted to *require* employers with racially imbalanced work forces to grant preferential treatment to racial minorities in order to integrate. Second, they argued that employers with racially imbalanced work forces would grant preferential treatment to racial minorities, even if not required to do so by the Act. See 110 Cong.Rec. 8618–19 (remarks of Sen. Sparkman). Had Congress meant to prohibit all race-conscious affirmative action, as respondent urges, it easily could have answered both objections by providing that Title VII would not require or *permit* racially preferential integration efforts. But Congress did not choose such a course. Rather Congress added § 703(j) which addresses only the first objection. The section provides that nothing contained in Title VII "shall be interpreted to *require* any employer * * * to grant preferential treatment * * * to any group because of the race * * * of such * * * group on account of" a de facto racial imbalance in the employer's work force. * * *

The reasons for this choice are evident from the legislative record. Title VII could not have been enacted into law without substantial support from legislators in both Houses who traditionally resisted federal regulation of private business. Those legislators demanded as a price for their support that "management prerogatives and union freedoms * * * be left undisturbed to the greatest extent possible." H.R.Rep. No. 914, 88th Cong., 1st Sess., Pt. 2 (1963), at 29. Section 703(j) was proposed by Senator Dirksen to allay any fears that the Act might be interpreted in such a way as to upset this compromise. The section was designed to prevent § 703 of Title VII from being interpreted in such a way as to lead to undue "Federal Government interference with private businesses because of some Federal employee's ideas about racial balance or imbalance." 110 Cong.Rec. at 14314 (remarks of Sen. Miller). Clearly, a prohibition against all voluntary, race-conscious, affirmative action efforts would disserve these ends.[7] * * *

* * *

We therefore hold that Title VII's prohibition in §§ 703(a) and (d) against racial discrimination does not condemn all private, voluntary, race-conscious affirmative action plans.

Sen. Humphrey). In 1978 the black unemployment rate was 129% higher. See Monthly Labor Review, U.S. Department of Labor, Bureau of Labor Statistics 78 (Mar.1979).

7. Respondent argues that our construction of § 703 conflicts with various remarks in the legislative record. See, e.g., 110 Cong.Rec. 7213 (Sens. Clark and Case); id. at 7218 (Sens. Clark and Case); id., at 6549 (Sen. Humphrey); id. at 8921 (Sen. Williams). We do not agree. In Senator Humphrey's words, these comments were intended as assurances that Title VII would not allow establishment of systems "to *maintain* racial balance in employment." Id. at 11848. They were not addressed to temporary, voluntary, affirmative action measures undertaken to eliminate manifest racial imbalance in traditionally segregated job categories. * * * [repositioned footnote—ed.]

III

We need not today define in detail the line of demarcation between permissible and impermissible affirmative action plans. It suffices to hold that the challenged Kaiser–USWA affirmative action plan falls on the permissible side of the line. The purposes of the plan mirror those of the statute. Both were designed to break down old patterns of racial segregation and hierarchy. Both were structured to "open employment opportunities for Negroes in occupations which have been traditionally closed to them." 110 Cong. Rec. 6548 (remarks of Sen. Humphrey).[8]

At the same time the plan does not unnecessarily trammel the interests of the white employees. The plan does not require the discharge of white workers and their replacement with new black hires. Cf. McDonald v. Santa Fe Trail Trans. Co., supra. Nor does the plan create an absolute bar to the advancement of white employees; half of those trained in the program will be white. Moreover, the plan is a temporary measure; it is not intended to maintain racial balance, but simply to eliminate a manifest racial imbalance. Preferential selection of craft trainees at the Gramercy plant will end as soon as the percentage of black skilled craft workers in the Gramercy plant approximates the percentage of blacks in the local labor force.

* * *

Reversed.

MR. JUSTICE POWELL and MR. JUSTICE STEVENS took no part in the consideration or decision of this case.

MR. JUSTICE BLACKMUN, concurring.

While I share some of the misgivings expressed in Mr. Justice Rehnquist's dissent, concerning the extent to which the legislative history of Title VII clearly supports the result the Court reaches today, I believe that additional considerations, practical and equitable, only partially perceived, if perceived at all, by the 88th Congress, support the conclusion reached by the Court today, and I therefore join its opinion as well as its judgment.

* * *

[Kaiser's previous use of unvalidated selection criteria for skilled jobs was an "arguable" violation of *Griggs*.] See Parson v. Kaiser Aluminum & Chemical Corp., 575 F.2d 1374, 1389 (C.A.5 1978), cert. denied, 441 U.S. 968, 99 S.Ct. 2417, 60 L.Ed.2d 1073 (1979). The parties [agree] that after critical reviews from the Office of Federal Contract Compliance, Kaiser and the Steelworkers established the training program in question here and modeled it along the lines of a Title VII consent decree later entered for the steel industry. See United States v. Allegheny–Ludlum Industries, Inc., 517 F.2d 826 (C.A.5 1975). [This attempt to satisfy black demands, however, only led to this suit by disaffected whites. Judge Wisdom in

---

8. See n. 1, supra. This is not to suggest that the freedom of an employer to undertake race-conscious affirmative action efforts depends on whether or not his effort is motivated by fear of liability under Title VII.

dissent below argued that Kaiser should be released from liability for affirmative action where it has committed an "arguable violation."]

The "arguable violation" theory has a number of advantages. It responds to a practical problem in the administration of Title VII not anticipated by Congress. It draws predictability from the outline of present law, and closely effectuates the purpose of the Act. Both Kaiser and the United States urge its adoption here. Because I agree that it is the soundest way to approach this case, my preference would be to resolve this litigation by applying it and holding that Kaiser's craft training program meets the requirement that voluntary affirmative action be a reasonable response to an "arguable violation" of Title VII.

II

The Court, however, declines to consider the narrow "arguable violation" approach and adheres instead to an interpretation of Title VII that permits affirmative action by an employer whenever the job category in question is "traditionally segregated." * * *

"Traditionally segregated job categories," where they exist, sweep far more broadly than the class of "arguable violations" of Title VII. The Court's expansive approach is somewhat disturbing for me because, as Mr. Justice Rehnquist points out, the Congress that passed Title VII probably thought it was adopting a principle of non-discrimination that would apply to blacks and whites alike. While setting aside that principle can be justified where necessary to advance statutory policy by encouraging reasonable responses as a form of voluntary compliance that mitigates "arguable violations," discarding the principle of nondiscrimination where no countervailing statutory policy exists appears to be at odds with the bargain struck when Title VII was enacted.

MR. CHIEF JUSTICE BURGER, dissenting. [Omitted]

MR. JUSTICE REHNQUIST, with whom THE CHIEF JUSTICE joins, dissenting.

In a very real sense, the Court's opinion is ahead of its time: it could more appropriately have been handed down five years from now, in 1984, a year coinciding with the title of a book from which the Court's opinion borrows, perhaps subconsciously[. The Court's willingness to use the same words but to insist that they now mean something different parallels a famous speech from George Orwell's *1984*.]

The operative sections of Title VII prohibit racial discrimination in employment *simpliciter*. Taken in its normal meaning, and as understood by all Members of Congress who spoke to the issue during the legislative debates, this language prohibits a covered employer from considering race when making an employment decision, whether the race be black or white. [We confirmed this recognition in McDonald v. Santa Fe Trail Trans. Co, holding, based on] "uncontradicted legislative history" that "Title VII prohibits racial discrimination against the white petitioners in this case

upon the same standards as would be applicable were they Negroes
* * *."

* * *

Quite simply, Kaiser's racially discriminatory admission quota is flatly
prohibited by the plain language of Title VII[, which bars "discriminate
against any individual because of his race, color, religion, sex, or national
origin."] In most cases, "[l]egislative history * * * is more vague than the
statute we are called upon to interpret." United States v. Public Utilities
Comm'n, 345 U.S. 295, 321, 73 S.Ct. 706, 720, 97 L.Ed. 1020 (1953)
(Jackson, J., concurring). Here, however, the legislative history of Title
VII is as clear as the language of §§ 703(a) and (d), and it irrefutably
demonstrates that Congress meant precisely what it said in §§ 703(a) and
(d)—that *no* racial discrimination in employment is permissible under
Title VII, not even preferential treatment of minorities to correct racial
imbalance. [Sen. Humphrey, the floor manager of Title VII promised that
it would not empower the EEOC or courts to require racial balance.
Senator Kuchel, another supporter, explicitly declared of Title VII: "Employers and labor organizations could not discriminate *in favor of or
against* a person because of his race, his religion, or his national origin. In
such matters * * * the bill now before us * * * is color-blind." A few days
later Senate supporters Clark and Case explicitly declared that "any
deliberate attempt to maintain a racial balance, whatever such a balance
may be, would involve a violation of title VII because maintaining such a
balance would require an employer to hire or to refuse to hire on the basis
of race." They added that an employer "would not be obliged—*or indeed
permitted*—to fire whites in order to hire Negroes, *or to prefer Negroes for
future vacancies, or, once Negroes are hired, to give them special seniority
rights at the expense of the white workers hired earlier.*"]

Thus with virtual clairvoyance the Senate's leading supporters of
Title VII anticipated precisely the circumstances of this case and advised
their colleagues that the type of minority preference employed by Kaiser
would violate Title VII's ban on racial discrimination. To further accentuate the point, Senator Clark introduced another memorandum dealing
with common criticisms of the bill, including the charge that racial quotas
would be imposed under Title VII. The answer was simple and to the
point: "Quotas are themselves discriminatory."

* * *

NOTE ON Weber AND THE TRANSITION TO Johnson

1.　In **McDonald v. Santa Fe Trail Transportation Co.**, 427 U.S.
273, 96 S.Ct. 2574, 49 L.Ed.2d 493 (1976), the Court reversed lower court
holdings that Title VII does not cover discrimination against white employees,[1] instead interpreting the Act to prohibit "racial discrimination against

---

1.　Recall the Court's parallel holding, Chapter 2C.3 supra, that 42 U.S.C.A. § 1981 also
reached discrimination against whites in making employment contracts.

[white persons] upon the same standards as would be applicable were they Negroes." Justice Marshall justified the decision of a unanimous Court (427 U.S. at 279–80, 96 S.Ct. at 2578–79):

> "Title VII of the Civil Rights Act of 1964 prohibits the discharge of 'any individual' because of 'such individual's race,' § 703(a)(1), 42 U.S.C.A. § 2000e–2(a)(1). Its terms are not limited to discrimination against members of any particular race. * * * This conclusion is in accord with uncontradicted legislative history to the effect that Title VII was intended to 'cover white men and white women and all Americans,' 110 Cong.Rec. 2578 (1964) (remarks of Rep. Celler), and create an 'obligation not to discriminate against whites,' id. at 7218 (memorandum of Sen. Clark). See also id. at 7213 (memorandum of Sens. Clark and Case); id. at 8912 (remarks of Sen. Williams). * * * "

(a) Is the decision in *Weber* consistent with that in *Santa Fe*? How should the earlier case be interpreted now? As holding whites protected except when a countervailing interest of promoting black interests is demonstrated? See paragraph 5 below.

(b) Is the "arguable violation" rationale, discussed by Justice Blackmun, an effort to eliminate the seeming contradiction between *Santa Fe* and *Weber* by showing that affirmative action should be viewed as curing past discrimination against blacks, not as causing present discrimination against whites? As Justice Blackmun noted, appellate courts such as the Fifth Circuit had upheld quota-like remedies for hiring in cases of persistent racial discrimination. The theory seems to be that surely an employer can settled a case before judgment on terms similar to what a court could order after judgment. Therefore, racial consciousness is necessary only as a cure; it is not an independent violation. Cf. Chapter 1F.2 (discussing the *Milliken* case and the permissibility of otherwise extra-constitutional remedies).

2. In Part III of the majority opinion Justice Brennan noted that Kaiser's plan appropriately balances the interests of white and black workers. Is this emphasis on groups of employees consistent with such Title VII decisions as **City of Los Angeles, Dep't of Water v. Manhart**, 435 U.S. 702, 98 S.Ct. 1370, 55 L.Ed.2d 657 (1978)? When in that case the employer sought to justify its sex-based pension plan with statistics showing that women as a group lived longer than men as a group, the Court replied that the "statute makes it unlawful to discriminate against any individual[; the] statute's focus on the individual is unambiguous."

(a) Is group-focused thinking acceptable in *Weber* because, unlike the practice at issue in *Manhart,* the group label is indeed relevant to an employment decision? In *Manhart* sex-grouping provided an inexact and unpredictable method for predicting longevity, but in *Weber* is race relevant to the employer's program because race itself had been the basis of prior denial of job opportunities? But this is just the "arguable violations" rationale, the theory not adopted in *Weber*, is it not?

(b) Is group-focused thinking equally unacceptable in *Weber* because it is as much a generalization here as in *Manhart*—there is no assurance that any preferred individual black person was in fact a victim of prior discrimination?

Compare the Court's handling of the same issue in the context of judicially ordered relief under Title VII, discussed in the previous Note.

(c) If one conceives of the prior discrimination against blacks as "general societal discrimination" against all blacks, cf. Regents v. Bakke, see Note on Early Reaction to the Effects Test, Chapter 6A supra, then the idea of unharmed "individual" blacks loses force, does it not? Does *Weber* signal victory under Title VII for the concept which Justices Brennan, White, Marshall, and Blackmun promoted under Title VI in *Bakke*? Is the permissibility to adopt quotas for "traditionally segregated jobs" just another way of saying that an employer may adopt affirmative action to cure the "societal discrimination" caused by other employers?

3. Which argument do you find more persuasive, Justice Brennan's for the majority or Justice Rehnquist's in dissent? Has one legislated while the other has been true to Congress' desires? Which one is which?

(a) Does not Justice Rehnquist's dissenting opinion seem much more conceptually tight and well-documented? The text seems superficially unambiguous, as even Justice Brennan admits. (Who has the stronger argument with respect to § 703(j)?) And notice Justice Rehnquist's use of legislative history as compared to Justice Brennan? Who has the more persuasive quotations? Is Justice Brennan's argument for a "spirit" distinct from the text adequately proven?

(b) Alternatively, has Justice Rehnquist become lost in his concepts while the majority is concerned with the real-world functioning of Title VII? Would Rehnquist's view not place an employer between Scylla and Charybdis, "between a rock and a hard place"? An employer guilty of past discrimination must ordinarily award retroactive seniority to blacks as well as restore backpay, see section C of this Chapter, supra, a prospect which the company might wish to avoid by granting blacks lesser affirmative action before a Title VII suit is instituted. Would not Justice Rehnquist's view make it impossible for a company to settle in advance of suit because to do so would violate white employees' rights under Title VII, subjecting it to a suit by white employees? See Justice Blackmun's concurring opinion. But does Justice Brennan adopt this "arguable violations" argument?

(c) Is Justice Rehnquist's argument so compelling even on its own conceptual terms? His argument depends, does it not, on a static view of society: the employer in 1964 ceases discrimination and begins to hire in a completely color-blind manner. But what of the employer that ceases discrimination in 1979 or later? What happens to all the black employees who suffered post-Act discrimination under Justice Rehnquist's construct? Does this show that his concern is not with employers' voluntary affirmative action plans but with any kind of non-color-blind affirmative action, even court-ordered relief in cases of proved discrimination? Is his opinion in *Weber* consistent with the one which he joined in Franks v. Bowman Transportation Co., section C of this Chapter? Would Justice Rehnquist need to adopt the "arguable violations" theory in order to maintain consistency?

4. Although the Court never specifically reversed the *Weber* holding, support for its approach slowly ebbed on the Court until it reached only a plurality status in **Johnson v. Transportation Agency**, 480 U.S. 616, 107

S.Ct. 1442, 94 L.Ed.2d 615 (1987). That case involved a hiring goal for women in jobs in the male-dominated transportation department for a California county. The employer sought to justify the goal under *Weber,* and five Justices approved. Justice Brennan specifically noted that affirmative action was not restricted to curing the employer's own prior discrimination. 480 U.S. at 630 n. 8, 107 S.Ct. at 1451 n. 8. Justice O'Connor, however, expressed a desire to reconsider *Weber* and observed that the Court had expanded the case too broadly by permitting affirmative action programs in cases lacking evidence of the employer's own prior discrimination. She added that while she would not require that an employer admit to prior discrimination in order to justify an affirmative action program, it would need to present statistical proof sufficient to raise the inference that it had committed such discrimination, citing the statistical prima facie case used in *Teamsters,* section A.2(a) of this Chapter, supra. 480 U.S. at 651, 107 S.Ct. at 1462. Justice White noted that he also had always understood *Weber*'s "traditionally segregated jobs" language to indicate jobs that the employer itself had systematically segregated. 480 U.S. at 657, 107 S.Ct. at 1465. Justices Scalia and Rehnquist gave the same reading to *Weber.* 480 U.S. at 658, 107 S.Ct. at 1465.

(a) Is Justice O'Connor's position just a variation on the "arguable violation" theory discussed in *Weber* by Justice Blackmun? Is it different from that considered by Justice Blackmun because it would require actual evidence to support the arguable violation? What dilemma is posed for the employer by this approach—double liability to whites and blacks? How so?

(b) If the "arguable violation" theory deters employers from undertaking as many affirmative action programs, is that a problem, as Justice Blackmun assumes, or is it a blessing, as the new Justices seem to think in *Johnson*? Should employers be somewhat inhibited from adopting quotas or goals? Why, because they are themselves discriminatory? Because they are imprecise?

5. Two years later the Court returned to the issue of affirmative-action quotas and goals in the *Croson* case, which follows. Although a constitutional law case, how does it affect the continuing vitality of *Weber*?

CITY OF RICHMOND v. J.A. CROSON CO.

Supreme Court of the United States, 1989.
488 U.S. 469, 109 S.Ct. 706, 102 L.Ed.2d 854.

JUSTICE O'CONNOR announced the judgment of the Court and delivered the opinion of the Court with respect to Parts I, III–B, and IV, an opinion with respect to Part II, in which THE CHIEF JUSTICE and JUSTICE WHITE join, and an opinion with respect to Parts III–A and V, in which THE CHIEF JUSTICE, JUSTICE WHITE and JUSTICE KENNEDY join.

In this case, we confront once again the tension between the Fourteenth Amendment's guarantee of equal treatment to all citizens, and the use of race-based measures to ameliorate the effects of past discrimination on the opportunities enjoyed by members of minority groups in our society.

I

[The company challenged the city's program for setting aside approximately 30% of its construction contracts for letting to Minority Business Enterprises (MBEs)—firms owned by "minority group members," that is "[c]itizens of the United States who are Blacks, Spanish-speaking, Orientals, Indians, Eskimos, or Aleuts." The city's black population totaled 50%; its minority construction contractors had won less than 1% of the city's prime construction contracts in the preceding five years. The city's programs permitted exceptions but none was made for the Croson Co., and it lost a contract to supply plumbing fixtures to a higher-bidding black contractor. The district court ruled for the city, but the court of appeals reversed.]

II

The Equal Protection Clause of the Fourteenth Amendment provides that "[N]o State shall ... deny to *any person* within its jurisdiction the equal protection of the laws" (emphasis added). As this Court has noted in the past, the "rights created by the first section of the Fourteenth Amendment are, by its terms, guaranteed to the individual. The rights established are personal rights." Shelley v. Kraemer, 334 U.S. 1, 22, 68 S.Ct. 836, 846, 92 L.Ed. 1161 (1948). The Richmond Plan denies certain citizens the opportunity to compete for a fixed percentage of public contracts based solely upon their race. To whatever racial group these citizens belong, their "personal rights" to be treated with equal dignity and respect are implicated by a rigid rule erecting race as the sole criterion in an aspect of public decisionmaking. * * *

Classifications based on race carry a danger of stigmatic harm. Unless they are strictly reserved for remedial settings, they may in fact promote notions of racial inferiority and lead to a politics of racial hostility. [We therefore subject all racial classifications, regardless of their origins, to "heightened scrutiny." This is particularly appropriate here because the legislative majority in Richmond is African–American; its affirmative action plans advantages the majority's own race.]

* * *

In Wygant [v. Jackson Board of Education], 476 U.S. 267, 106 S.Ct. 1842, 90 L.Ed.2d 260 (1986), four Members of the Court applied heightened scrutiny to a race-based system of employee layoffs [that sought to preserve a number of less senior black teachers so that they could act as "role models" for black schoolchildren]. Justice Powell, writing for the plurality, drew the distinction between "societal discrimination" which is an inadequate basis for race-conscious classifications, and the type of identified discrimination that can support and define the scope of race-based relief. [The plurality reiterated] the view expressed by Justice Powell in Bakke that "[s]ocietal discrimination, without more, is too amorphous a basis for imposing a racially classified remedy."

* * *

[III]

B

We think it clear that the factual predicate offered in support of the Richmond Plan [cannot be accepted]. Like the "role model" theory employed in *Wygant,* a generalized assertion that there has been past discrimination in an entire industry provides no guidance for a legislative body to determine the precise scope of the injury it seeks to remedy. It "has no logical stopping point." "Relief" for such an ill-defined wrong could extend until the percentage of public contracts awarded to MBEs in Richmond mirrored the percentage of minorities in the population as a whole.

* * *

These defects are readily apparent in this case. The 30% quota cannot in any realistic sense be tied to any injury suffered by anyone. The District Court relied upon five predicate "facts" in reaching its conclusion that there was an adequate basis for the 30% quota: (1) the ordinance declares itself to be remedial; (2) several proponents of the measure stated their views that there had been past discrimination in the construction industry; (3) minority businesses received .67% of prime contracts from the city while minorities constituted 50% of the city's population; (4) there were very few minority contractors in local and state contractors' associations; and (5) in 1977, Congress made a determination that the effects of past discrimination had stifled minority participation in the construction industry nationally. Supp.App. 163–167.

None of these "findings," singly or together, provide the city of Richmond with a "strong basis in evidence for its conclusion that remedial action was necessary." Wygant, 476 U.S. at 277, 106 S.Ct., at 1848 (plurality opinion). There is nothing approaching a prima facie case of a constitutional or statutory violation by *anyone* in the Richmond construction industry. [The attempt to show that blacks are grossly underrepresented in contracting fails because the city has used only general population data; when special qualifications are required, such as to run a business, a prima facie case must begin by identifying the pool of persons with the special qualification. Hazelwood School Dist. v. United States, 433 U.S. 299, 307–08, 97 S.Ct. 2736, 2741, 53 L.Ed.2d 768 (1977) [a Title–VII-based disparate treatment case-ed.] See also Mayor v. Educational Equality League, 415 U.S. 605, 620, 94 S.Ct. 1323, 1333, 39 L.Ed.2d 630 (1974) ("[T]his is not a case in which it can be assumed that all citizens are fungible for purposes of determining whether members of a particular class have been unlawfully excluded").]

* * *

The foregoing analysis applies only to the inclusion of blacks within the Richmond set-aside program. There is *absolutely no evidence* of past discrimination against Spanish-speaking, Oriental, Indian, Eskimo, or Aleut persons in any aspect of the Richmond construction industry. The

District Court took judicial notice of the fact that the vast majority of "minority" persons in Richmond were black. Supp.App. 207. It may well be that Richmond has never had an Aleut or Eskimo citizen. The random inclusion of racial groups that, as a practical matter, may never have suffered from discrimination in the construction industry in Richmond, suggests that perhaps the city's purpose was not in fact to remedy past discrimination.

* * *

IV

As noted by the court below, it is almost impossible to assess whether the Richmond Plan is narrowly tailored to remedy prior discrimination since it is not linked to identified discrimination in any way. We limit ourselves to two observations in this regard.

First, there does not appear to have been any consideration of the use of race-neutral means to increase minority business participation in city contracting. See United States v. Paradise, 480 U.S. 149, 171, 107 S.Ct. 1053, 1067, 94 L.Ed.2d 203 (1987) ("In determining whether race-conscious remedies are appropriate, we look to several factors, including the efficacy of alternative remedies").

* * *

Second, the 30% quota cannot be said to be narrowly tailored to any goal, except perhaps outright racial balancing. It rests upon the "completely unrealistic" assumption that minorities will choose a particular trade in lockstep proportion to their representation in the local population. See Sheet Metal Workers v. EEOC, 478 U.S. 421, 494, 106 S.Ct. 3019, 3060, 92 L.Ed.2d 344 (1986) [a Title VII case] (O'Connor, J., concurring in part and dissenting in part) ("[I]t is completely unrealistic to assume that individuals of one race will gravitate with mathematical exactitude to each employer or union absent unlawful discrimination").

* * *

V

Nothing we say today precludes a state or local entity from taking action to rectify the effects of identified discrimination within its jurisdiction. If the city of Richmond had evidence before it that non-minority contractors were systematically excluding minority businesses from subcontracting opportunities it could take action to end the discriminatory exclusion. Where there is a significant statistical disparity between the number of qualified minority contractors willing and able to perform a particular service and the number of such contractors actually engaged by the locality or the locality's prime contractors, an inference of discriminatory exclusion could arise. See Bazemore v. Friday, 478 U.S. at 398, 106 S.Ct., at 3008; Teamsters v. United States. Under such circumstances, the city could act to dismantle the closed business system by taking appropriate measures against those who discriminate on the basis of race or other illegitimate criteria. In the extreme case, some form of narrowly tailored racial preference might be necessary to break down patterns of deliberate exclusion.

* * *

Affirmed.

Justice Stevens, concurring in part and concurring in the judgment. [Omitted]

Justice Kennedy, concurring in part and concurring in the judgment. [Omitted]

Justice Scalia, concurring in the judgment.

* * *

In his final book, Professor Bickel wrote:

> "[A] racial quota derogates the human dignity and individuality of all to whom it is applied; it is invidious in principle as well as in practice. Moreover, it can easily be turned against those it purports to help. The history of the racial quota is a history of subjugation, not beneficence. Its evil lies not in its name, but in its effects: a quota is a divider of society, a creator of castes, and it is all the worse for its racial base, especially in a society desperately striving for an equality that will make race irrelevant." Bickel, The Morality of Consent, at 133.

Those statements are true and increasingly prophetic. Apart from their societal effects, however, which are "in the aggregate disastrous," id. at 134, it is important not to lose sight of the fact that even "benign" racial quotas have individual victims, whose very real injustice we ignore whenever we deny them enforcement of their right not to be disadvantaged on the basis of race.

* * *

Justice Marshall, with whom Justice Brennan and Justice Blackmun join, dissenting.

It is a welcome symbol of racial progress when the former capital of the Confederacy acts forthrightly to confront the effects of racial discrimination in its midst. In my view, nothing in the Constitution can be construed to prevent Richmond, Virginia, from allocating a portion of its contracting dollars for businesses owned or controlled by members of minority groups. Indeed, Richmond's set-aside program is indistinguishable in all meaningful respects from—and in fact was patterned upon—the federal set-aside plan which this Court upheld in Fullilove v. Klutznick, 448 U.S. 448, 100 S.Ct. 2758, 65 L.Ed.2d 902 (1980).

* * *

[T]he majority's criticisms of individual items of Richmond's evidence rest on flimsy foundations. First, the majority wants Richmond to prove a statistical disparity with more precise data than that based on population numbers, but we have not required that where, as here, the disparity is so great (.67% of contracts v. 50% of population). Moreover, here the disparity is further reinforced because it results from a prior history of discrimination with a continuing effect.]

* * *

JUSTICE BLACKMUN, with whom JUSTICE BRENNAN joins, dissenting. [Omitted]

NOTE ON THE EVOLVED VIEW OF AFFIRMATIVE ACTION AND QUOTAS

1. Has Justice O'Connor's position in the *Johnson* case finally prevailed in *Croson*, at least as the minimally acceptable standard for reviewing affirmative action cases?[1] Has the Court tied together Equal Protection principles and Title VII principles for purposes of analyzing affirmative action programs?

(a) On what cases does Justice O'Connor rely in *Croson* to prove her point about permissible predicates for remedies? Are they not the same Title VII cases on which she relied in *Johnson*? See the Note preceding the *Croson* case, supra. Has she not reprised the "arguable violations" theory (as built around the statistical prima facie case) of Title VII analysis? See also Rutherglen & Ortiz, *Affirmative Action Under the Constitution: From Confusion to Convergence*, 35 U.C.L.A.L.REV. 467 (1988). Is this the correct approach? See Fried, *Affirmative Action after* City of Richmond v. J.A. Croson Co.: *A Response to the Scholars' Statement*, 99 YALE L.J. 155 (1989).

(b) Compare the separation of statutory and constitutional concepts here with the similar controversy under Title VI. See the Note on Early Reaction to an Effects Test, Chapter 6A supra. Is there any consistency to the Justices' positions on the issue of separating statutory and constitutional doctrines? Is there consistency in the policy results that each tries to achieve? Does that mean that the former issue is less important than the latter?

2. Justice O'Connor's position, and that discussed by Justice Blackmun in *Weber*, can be found in early publications, where it is put forward as a "liberal" doctrine that would sustain quotas in cases of egregious wrongdoing. See, e.g., *Comment, Race Quotas*, 8 HARV.C.R.–C.L.L.REV. 128 (1973). How is it that the notion came to be regarded as a "conservative" one by 1989?

(a) Is Justice O'Connor's "arguable violations" approach actually a centrist position between the *Weber* majority (which would approve most quotas for "traditionally segregated jobs" and as cures for "societal discrimination") and Justice Scalia's adamant opposition to any group-wide, race-based relief? Does *Croson* tighten up the *Johnson* approach when it demands that an

---

1. *Croson*'s heightened scrutiny was later adopted by the Court in Shaw v. Reno, 509 U.S. 630, 113 S.Ct. 2816, 125 L.Ed.2d 511 (1993) (affirmative action in reapportionment), and Adarand Constructors, Inc. v. Pena, 515 U.S. 200, 115 S.Ct. 2097, 132 L.Ed.2d 158 (1995) (federal affirmative action program for MBEs).

affirmative action program be undertaken only as a last resort when other remedies are ineffective? Is Justice O'Connor's position still fairly labelable as an "arguable violations" approach?

(b) Consider the "arguable violations" approach and the "traditional segregated jobs" approach from the view of one wishing to adopt an affirmative action program. What is the monetary cost of complying with *Weber*'s test? (How long would it take for a law student to conduct the research to make the showing made in *Weber*'s footnote 1?) What is the cost of complying with the demand for a statistical prima facie case as used in *Teamsters*, section A.2.a of this Chapter, supra? (How much would an expert charge to collect the data and run the regression analyses necessary to make such a showing?) Is the "arguable violations" theory simply too expensive for anyone to use?

(c) Has Justice O'Connor actually tightened up the "arguable violations" theory by demanding a "strong basis in evidence" for the claimed violation? Note the ambiguity in her section "V"; has she escalated "arguable" violation to "almost certainly proved"? How much evidence of past discrimination should be required before an affirmative action plan can be initiated? See Concrete Works of Colorado, Inc. v. City and County of Denver, 540 U.S. 1027, 124 S.Ct. 556, 157 L.Ed.2d 449 (2003) (Scalia, J., dissenting from denial of certiorari) (noting split in the circuits over toughness of approaches to evidence, requiring pervasive former discrimination or "some").

3.   The "traditionally segregated jobs test" in *Weber* would permit an employer to cure an imbalance caused by others, a position also taken by the dissenters in *Croson*. What is wrong with that in Justice O'Connor's view?

(a) Is she afraid that curing others' discrimination might become a pretext for curing what is not discrimination at all? Why do minorities not have as high an employment rate as whites? Is it because of discrimination or other social factors?

(b) Does Justice O'Connor worry that quotas may take on a life of their own? That persons benefitted may begin to look at them as a current entitlement rather than as a cure for past discrimination? Do quotas or goals hurt the long-term achievement of equality because they increase racial consciousness in the short-term? Is it a necessary price to pay?

(c) Do affirmative action programs in fact help those who have been the victims of past discrimination? Is that another reason for O'Connor's concern? Does the arguable violation theory ameliorate that concern by making it more likely that the persons benefitted by an affirmative action program are those actually victimized in the past? See generally, W. Wilson, THE TRULY DISADVANTAGED: THE INNER CITY, THE UNDERCLASS, AND PUBLIC POLICY (1989).

4.   In **Grutter v. Bollinger**, 539 U.S. 306, 123 S.Ct. 2325, 156 L.Ed.2d 304 (2003), a slim 5–4 majority upheld race-based affirmative action in admissions to universities. Justice O'Connor's majority opinion applied strict scrutiny and found it satisfied. First, she wrote that an educational institution has a substantial interest in seeking diversity in its student body (based on the interest in exposing all students to many different views). Second, she found that an affirmative action plan that did not use a strict quota, but

which merely gave an extra advantage in competitive admissions to blacks and other minorities, was an acceptable means for promoting the interest in diversity. Though opposing strict numerical quotas, she also permitted schools to keep an eye on the total number of minorities admitted, reasoning that a university would need a "critical mass" (minimum number) of minority students in order to make it likely that any of them would stay in school, or feel free to speak in white-dominated classes. (The same day, the Court struck down an undergraduate admissions program that it interpreted to give an automatic preference to all minority applicants.[2])

(a) Is it settled after *Grutter* that the only acceptable affirmative action is in education, or related fields where the actors undertaking the affirmative action plan would have a First–Amendment interest in seeking diversity? Can affirmative action in employment be constitutionally undertaken by the federal government, using its power under § 5 of the Fourteenth Amendment? See Adarand Constructors, Inc. v. Pena, 515 U.S. 200, 115 S.Ct. 2097, 132 L.Ed.2d 158 (1995) (federal government subject to same strict scrutiny as states).

(b) In the *Wygant* case, involving teachers, the Court rejected the "role model" theory to justify affirmative action. Does *Grutter*'s approval of the diversity rationale and the supporting "critical mass" theory revive it? For students only, not for teachers? Is it acceptable to view students as role models for each but unacceptable to view teachers as role models for students? If so, why?

(c) Voluntary affirmative action is subject to negation: a company may decide against continuing or voters may act to overturn even legislatively mandate affirmative action. Three years following *Grutter*, Michigan's voters by an almost 2–1 majority amended the state constitution to forbid the program approved in *Grutter*. Moreover, the initiative broadly forbade future racial preferences throughout state government. See M.C.L.A. Const. Art. 1, § 26 (2006). Is it unconstitutional to limit voluntary affirmative action? Compare Hunter v. Erickson, 393 U.S. 385, 89 S.Ct. 557, 21 L.Ed.2d 616 (1969) (local government charter amendment requiring prior voter approval of fair housing legislation that would benefit minorities unconstitutional), with Coalition for Economic Equity v. Wilson, 110 F.3d 1431 (9th Cir.1997) (California Proposition 209, barring affirmative action in the state and adopted in reaction to existing plans, is not unconstitutional). Is a return to "neutrality"—no permission for affirmative action—discriminatory? Or is "neutrality" non-neutral? Are state and local governments constitutionally required to leave open the opportunity for any level of government to adopt an affirmative action program? Cf. Rumsfeld v. Forum for Academic and Fundamental Rights, Inc, Chapter 6C supra (Court rejects argument Congress must allow schools to adopt anti-discrimination rules for sexual orientation, despite federal law protecting military recruiters from discrimination).

---

2. In Gratz v. Bollinger, 539 U.S. 244, 123 S.Ct. 2411, 156 L.Ed.2d 257 (2003), decided the same day as *Grutter*, Justice O'Connor switched her vote and made a five-person majority that struck down a different admissions plan that automatically admitted blacks in order to meet a strict minimum enrollment goal. In other words, four Justices voted to forbid both plans, and four voted to uphold both plans. Only Justice O'Connor changed her vote to divide the results in the two cases. Justice Alito has since replaced Justice O'Connor on the Court.

5. In **Parents Involved in Community Schools v. Seattle School Dist. No. 1**, 551 U.S. 701, 127 S.Ct. 2738, 168 L.Ed.2d 508 (2006), Justice Roberts' opinion for the Court seemed to construe *Grutter* narrowly. With respect to any interest in curing prior discrimination, the Court specifically held that this rationale only applied when the affirmative action plan (here in school assignments) cured the adopter's own prior intentional discrimination; curing racial imbalance is insufficient. Second, any acceptable interest in diversity must encompass not race alone but "all factors that may contribute to student body diversity"; thus a plan that promotes only racial mixing is unacceptable under this rationale.

(a) Does the diversity rationale, even as diluted, have a future outside the educational arena? Can employer's seek diversity? Certainly, many large corporations in a wide variety of traditional product fields openly publicize their interest in racial and other diversity. See, e.g., http://www.merck.com/about/how-we-operate/diversity/employee-diversity.html (last visited June 24, 2011) (Merck Pharmaceuticals: "Diversity and inclusion are an integral part of our corporate culture and efforts to become a more customer-focused, high-performance organization"); http://www.cargill.com/careers/why-cargill/employee-diversity/index.jsp (Cargill agribusiness conglomerate: "great debates [that lead to 'great decisions'] are shaped by people that bring a variety of perspectives [and so having] the diversity that's necessary for the quality of debate to be at the highest possible level is clearly a business imperative").

(b) Would such diversity in employment reinforce stereotypes? See Ferrill v. Parker Group, Inc., 168 F.3d 468 (11th Cir.1999) (electoral consulting group conducting "push poll," fake poll designed through artful wording to encourage persons to vote in a desired manner, hired blacks to read black scripts and whites to read white scripts); Wittmer v. Peters, 87 F.3d 916 (7th Cir.1996) (state prison program of the "boot camp" variety for young offenders sought to limit hiring of camp officers to blacks, reflecting camp population); Patrolmen's Benev. Ass'n of City of New York, Inc. v. City of New York, 74 F.Supp.2d 321 (S.D.N.Y.1999) (city's plan to put black officers in district in order to reassure citizens in minority neighborhoods challenged by black officers; found violative of Title VII).

(c) Would your position on affirmative action in employment be affected by a consideration of why companies adopted diversity goals? Of whether it actually works to accomplish the representational goals or integration goals that its backers seek? See, e.g., Frank Dobbin, Alexandra Kalev, and Erin Kelly, *Diversity Management in Corporate America*, 6 CONTEXTS 21–27 (2007) (complex answers); COLOR LINES passim (John D. Skrentny, ed. 2001) (collection).

6. In **Ricci v. DeStefano**, sub-section E.2 infra, the Court conclusively decided that its constitutional jurisprudence would be applied to Title VII. Specifically, it held that *Croson*'s standard for reviewing affirmative action plans also applies to settlement of putative claims.

(a) *Croson*, as extended by *Ricci*, seems to overrule *Weber* as a practical matter, even though the Court does not say so in either case. Can you think of any thesis that might preserve *Weber*'s "traditionally segregated jobs" test?

(b) Reconsider also United States v. Paradise, discussed in ¶ 5 of the Note on Seniority Systems [Etc.], in Chapter 7D supra. Should judges be required to comply with the *Croson–Ricci* standards in ordering quota-based relief after a proven violation? Do all cases involving court-ordered relief automatically satisfy *Croson* because, by definition, there has been an actual prior violation, not just an arguable violation? See *Coalition for Economic Equity v. Wilson,* 110 F.3d 1431 (9th Cir.1997) (*Croson* applied, met).

2.   SETTLEMENTS AND THE TENSION IN TITLE VII

As the affirmative action cases demonstrate, courts have perceived some apparent tension within Title VII, as necessarily race-based cures for prior discrimination confront the statute's prohibition on race-based decisionmaking. This same perception of tension also appears in other contexts, most notably in the settlement of putative claims, especially those based on the disparate impact theory of liability. This arises from a paradox: as disparate impact analysis has separated itself from disparate treatment analysis, establishing itself as an independent basis for liability apart from intentional discrimination, proof of disparate impact tells us nothing about the (prior) existence of actual intentional discrimination. Can an employer undertake a race-based voluntary remedy in the absence of a disparate treatment violation—in the absence of intentional discrimination? More fundamentally, is the very theory and practice of disparate impact analysis a violation of disparate treatment principles?

RICCI v. DESTEFANO

Supreme Court of the United States, 2009
___ U.S. ___, 129 S.Ct. 2658, 174 L.Ed.2d 490

JUSTICE KENNEDY delivered the opinion of the Court.

In the fire department of New Haven, Connecticut—as in emergency-service agencies throughout the Nation—firefighters prize their promotion to and within the officer ranks. An agency's officers command respect [and higher salaries]. Aware of the intense competition for promotions, New Haven, like many cities, relies on objective examinations to identify the best qualified candidates.

[This litigation results from an examination, given in 2003, for promotions to lieutenant or captain. Viewing the results as discriminatory, the city threw them out. White and Hispanic firefighters who would have been promoted absent cancellation of the results then sued the city for racial discrimination in violation of Title VII and the U.S. Constitution. The city defended on the ground that use of the results would have made it liable black firefighters because of the test's disparate impact. The district court sided with the city, finding that the refusal to certify the results did not constitute intentional discrimination against whites. The Second Circuit affirmed in a brief one-paragraph order.]

We conclude that race-based action like the City's in this case is impermissible under Title VII unless the employer can demonstrate a strong basis in evidence that, had it not taken the action, it would have been liable under the disparate-impact statute. The respondents, we further determine, cannot meet that threshold standard. As a result, the City's action in discarding the tests was a violation of Title VII. In light of our ruling under the statutes, we need not reach the question whether respondents' actions may have violated the Equal Protection Clause.

I

[Industrial/Organizational Solutions, Inc. (IOS), a company specialized in the field, prepared the test. It developed the written part after a lengthy process of identifying "the tasks, knowledge, skills, and abilities that are essential for the lieutenant and captain positions," specifically reviewing New Haven's practices and interviewing its incumbent officers. At every stage of the process, IOS "oversampled minority firefighters to ensure that the results—which IOS would use to develop the examinations—would not unintentionally favor white candidates." The resultant job analyses were also used to create training manuals to prepare candidates for the test. This written portion of the test contained 100 multiple-choice questions written below the 10th-grade level. IOS developed the oral examination in a similar process, creating several hypotheticals that would be used to test a candidates command skills and other relevant abilities. Three-member panels, chosen from higher firefighting professionals outside the state, were trained to administer the oral exam. Two of the three members of each panel were minorities. After a final score was generated from the test, the city's civil service rules required that one of the top three scorers for each job level must be hired for each open position.]

Candidates took the examinations in November and December 2003. Seventy-seven candidates completed the lieutenant examination—43 whites, 19 blacks, and 15 Hispanics. Of those, 34 candidates passed—25 whites, 6 blacks, and 3 Hispanics. Eight lieutenant positions were vacant at the time of the examination. As the rule of three operated, this meant that the top 10 candidates were eligible for an immediate promotion to lieutenant. All 10 were white. Subsequent vacancies would have allowed at least 3 black candidates to be considered for promotion to lieutenant.

Forty-one candidates completed the captain examination—25 whites, 8 blacks, and 8 Hispanics. Of those, 22 candidates passed–16 whites, 3 blacks, and 3 Hispanics. Seven captain positions were vacant at the time of the examination. Under the rule of three, 9 candidates were eligible for an immediate promotion to captain–7 whites and 2 Hispanics.

[City officials told IOS that they were concerned about the results, and IOS offered to submit a validation study of the test, but the city attorney and Civil Service Board (CSB) declined to receive it. Instead CSB held a series of public meetings and hearings. At these gatherings, IOS defended its test and was supported by a Homeland Security official and former fire department captain from Michigan, "who is black," who supported the relevance of the exam questions. Opposing IOS were two major critics. One Hornsby, employed by a competitor to IOS, declined to review IOS's test in detail; he admitted that IOS had prepared "reasonably good test[s]" but went on to suggest that changing some details, such as testing locations, might have produced a less disparate impact on minorities. A Professor Helms, an expert in "race and culture as they influence performance on tests," declined to review the specific examination but noted that the results in New Haven were consistent with results usually produced by use of written tests in American society. She closed by saying that regardless of the content of the test, it would have produced "a disparity between blacks and whites, Hispanics and whites." At their final meeting, CSB deadlocked at 2–2, with one member abstaining, resulting in failure to certify the test results.]

II

A

* * *

[As originally enacted, Title VII's "principal" provision barred only disparate treatment. We later interpreted the Act in some cases to bar neutral criteria having an unjustified disparate impact. *Griggs*; *Albemarle Paper Co. v. Moody*. The 1991 Civil Rights Act codified these cases, including their three-step test for analyzing disparate impact. See 42 U.S.C. §§ 2000e–2(k)(1)(A) and (C).]

B

Our analysis begins with this premise: The City's actions would violate the disparate-treatment prohibition of Title VII absent some valid defense. All the evidence demonstrates that the City chose not to certify the examination results because of the statistical disparity based on race— *i.e.*, how minority candidates had performed when compared to white candidates. As the District Court put it, the City rejected the test results because "too many whites and not enough minorities would be promoted were the lists to be certified." 554 F.Supp.2d, at 152. Without some other justification, this express, race-based decisionmaking violates Title VII's command that employers cannot take adverse employment actions because of an individual's race. See § 2000e–2(a)(1).

* * *

We consider, therefore, whether the purpose to avoid disparate-impact liability excuses what otherwise would be prohibited disparate-treatment discrimination. [Petitioners argue that] avoiding unintentional discrimination cannot justify intentional discrimination. That assertion, however, ignores the fact that, by codifying the disparate-impact provision in 1991, Congress has expressly prohibited both types of discrimination. We must interpret the statute to give effect to both provisions where possible.

[Their back-up position, that there must be an actual violation of the disparate-impact provision in order to justify a defense for disparate treatment, also goes too far because it would, as a practical matter, prevent "voluntary compliance" with Title VII's disparate impact provisions.]

At the opposite end of the spectrum, respondents and the Government assert that an employer's good-faith belief that its actions are necessary to comply with Title VII's disparate-impact provision should be enough to justify race-conscious conduct. But the original, foundational prohibition of Title VII bars employers from taking adverse action "because of ... race." § 2000e–2(a)(1). And when Congress codified the disparate-impact provision in 1991, it made no exception to disparate-treatment liability for actions taken in a good-faith effort to comply with the new, disparate-impact provision in subsection (k). Allowing employers to violate the disparate-treatment prohibition based on a mere good-faith fear of disparate-impact liability would encourage race-based action at the slightest hint of disparate impact [and could easily lead to] a *de facto* quota system * * *, *Watson [v. Ft. Worth Bank & Trust]*. Even worse, an employer could discard test results (or other employment practices) with the intent of obtaining the employer's preferred racial balance. That operational principle could not be justified, for Title VII is express in disclaiming any interpretation of its requirements as calling for outright racial balancing. § 2000e–2(j). The purpose of Title VII "is to promote hiring on the basis of job qualifications, rather than on the basis of race or color." *Griggs*.

In searching for a standard that strikes a more appropriate balance, we note that this Court has considered cases similar to this one, albeit in the context of the Equal Protection Clause of the Fourteenth Amendment. The Court has held that certain government actions to remedy past racial discrimination—actions that are themselves based on race—are constitutional only where there is a " 'strong basis in evidence' " that the remedial actions were necessary. *Richmond v. J.A. Croson Co.*; Wygant [v. Jackson Bd. of Ed., 476 U.S. 267, 290, 106 S.Ct. 1842, 90 L.Ed.2d 260 (1986) (plurality opinion). These precedents saw this test as the best way to resolve the] tension between eliminating segregation and discrimination on the one hand and doing away with all governmentally imposed discrimination based on race on the other.

The same interests are at work in the interplay between the disparate-treatment and disparate-impact provisions of Title VII. Congress has imposed liability on employers for unintentional discrimination in order to rid the workplace of "practices that are fair in form, but discriminatory in operation." *Griggs*. But it has also prohibited employers from taking adverse employment actions "because of" race. § 2000e–2(a)(1). Applying the strong-basis-in-evidence standard to Title VII gives effect to both the disparate-treatment and disparate-impact provisions [in the context of voluntary compliance.] It limits [employer] discretion to cases in which there is a strong basis in evidence of disparate-impact liability, but it is not so restrictive that it allows employers to act only when there is a provable, actual violation.

* * *

If an employer cannot rescore a test based on the candidates' race, § 2000e–2(*l*), then it follows *a fortiori* that it may not take the greater step of discarding the test altogether to achieve a more desirable racial distribution of promotion-eligible candidates—absent a strong basis in evidence that the test was deficient and that discarding the results is necessary to avoid violating the disparate-impact provision. Restricting an employer's ability to discard test results (and thereby discriminate against qualified candidates on the basis of their race) also is in keeping with Title VII's express protection of bona fide promotional examinations. See § 2000e–2(h) ("[N]or shall it be an unlawful employment practice for an employer to give and to act upon the results of any professionally developed ability test provided that such test, its administration or action upon the results is not designed, intended or used to discriminate because of race").

* * *

C

The City argues that, even under the strong-basis-in-evidence standard, its decision to discard the examination results was permissible under Title VII. That is incorrect. Even if respondents were motivated as a subjective matter by a desire to avoid committing disparate-impact discrimination, the record makes clear there is no support for the conclusion that respondents had an objective, strong basis in evidence to find the tests inadequate, with some consequent disparate-impact liability in violation of Title VII.

[The exam used in this case had a disproportionate impact on blacks and Hispanics and "compelled" the city "to take a look" at the examination to determine if there was forbidden disparate impact.] The problem for [the city] is that a prima facie case of disparate-impact liability—essentially, a threshold showing of a significant statistical disparity and nothing more—is far from a strong basis in evidence that the City would have been liable under Title VII had it certified the results. That is because the City could be liable for disparate-impact discrimination only if the examinations were not job related and consistent with business necessity, or if there existed an equally valid, less-discriminatory alternative that served the City's needs but that the City refused to adopt. § 2000e–2(k)(1)(A), (C). We conclude there is no strong basis in evidence to establish that the test was deficient in either of these respects. * * *

There is no genuine dispute that the examinations were job-related and consistent with business necessity. The City's assertions to the contrary are "blatantly contradicted by the record." [The CSB record itself shows that IOS conducted "pains-taking analyses" of job qualifications that took care to overrepresent minorities. And the only person to examine the test questions themselves—the Homeland Security official who was black and who also had firefighting experience—found them to be relevant for both exams. Even Hornsby, the IOS competitor who criticized IOS for some details, admitted that "the exams 'appea[r] to be ... reasonably good' and recommended that the CSB certify the results." Moreover, although IOS was contractually obligated to give the city a study of the exams' validity, the city pointedly refused even to request it.]

Respondents also lacked a strong basis in evidence of an equally valid, less-discriminatory testing alternative that the City, by certifying the examination results, would necessarily have refused to adopt. [Re-balancing the written scores and oral scores to emphasize the latter] would have allowed the City to consider two black candidates for then-open lieutenant positions and one black candidate for then-open captain positions. [But CSB had no evidence that the balance used was arbitrary and no evidence to show that alternative] weighting would be an equally valid way to determine whether candidates possess the proper mix of job knowledge and situational skills to earn promotions. [Another option, altering selection rules to consider more than the top three candidates would have violated "Title VII's prohibition of adjusting test results on the basis of race. § 2000e–2(l)."]

On the record before us, there is no genuine dispute that the City lacked a strong basis in evidence to believe it would face disparate-impact liability if it certified the examination results. In other words, there is no evidence—let alone the required strong basis in evidence—that the tests were flawed because they were not job-related or because other, equally valid and less discriminatory tests were available to the City. Fear of litigation alone cannot justify an employer's reliance on race to the detriment of individuals who passed the examinations and qualified for promotions. The City's discarding the test results was impermissible under Title VII, and summary judgment is appropriate for petitioners on their disparate-treatment claim.

* * *

It is so ordered.

JUSTICE SCALIA, concurring.

I join the Court's opinion in full, but write separately to observe that its resolution of this dispute merely postpones the evil day on which the Court will have to confront the question: Whether, or to what extent, are the disparate-impact provisions of Title VII of the Civil Rights Act of 1964 consistent with the Constitution's guarantee of equal protection? The question is not an easy one. See generally Primus, Equal Protection and Disparate Impact: Round Three, 117 Harv. L.Rev. 493 (2003).

The difficulty is this: Whether or not Title VII's disparate-treatment provisions forbid "remedial" race-based actions when a disparate-impact violation would *not* otherwise result—the question resolved by the Court today—it is clear that Title VII not only permits but affirmatively *requires* such actions when a disparate-impact violation *would* otherwise result. But if the Federal Government is prohibited from discriminating on the basis of race, *Bolling v. Sharpe,* 347 U.S. 497, 500, 74 S.Ct. 693, 98 L.Ed. 884 (1954), then surely it is also prohibited from enacting laws mandating that third parties-*e.g.,* employers, whether private, State, or municipal-discriminate on the basis of race. * * *

JUSTICE ALITO, with whom JUSTICE SCALIA and JUSTICE THOMAS join, concurring.

[I join the majority opinion and write only in reply to the dissent's claim that the majority has misrepresented the factual record. Contrary to the dissent's suggestion that the city seriously tried to resolve its problem, the record shows the contrary. An African–American leader, a Rev. Kimber, joined with his political ally, Mayor DeStefano, to ensure that the test results would be thrown out. Rev. Kimber had played an important role in the mayor's campaigns and had been appointed in return to be Chairman of the city's Board of Fire Commissioners, a position he resigned after threatening not to hire recruits who "just have too many vowels in their name[s]." He remained on the board, however, and "retained 'a direct line to the mayor,'" using his contacts to "collud[e]" with the mayor and his staff to have the test results rejected. The record also disclosed political and racial considerations influenced the mayor's actions.]

Taking into account all the evidence in the summary judgment record, a reasonable jury could find the following. Almost as soon as the City disclosed the racial makeup of the list of firefighters who scored the highest on the exam, the City administration was lobbied by an influential community leader to scrap the test results, and the City administration decided on that course of action before making any real assessment of the possibility of a disparate-impact violation. To achieve that end, the City administration concealed its internal decision but worked—as things turned out, successfully—to persuade the CSB that acceptance of the test results would be illegal and would expose the City to disparate-impact liability. * * * Taking this view of the evidence, a reasonable jury could easily find that the City's real reason for scrapping the test results was not a concern about violating the disparate-impact provision of Title VII but a simple desire to please a politically important racial constituency. [It would have been impossible to conclude on this record, as the lower court did and as the dissent argues here, that the city acted in a good faith effort to settle a valid claim against the city.]

Petitioners are firefighters who seek only a fair chance to move up the ranks in their chosen profession. In order to qualify for promotion, they made personal sacrifices. Petitioner Frank Ricci, who is dyslexic, found it necessary to "hir[e] someone, at considerable expense, to read onto audiotape the content of the books and study materials." * * * Petitioner Benjamin Vargas, who is Hispanic, had to "give up a part-time job," and his wife had to "take leave from her own job in order to take care of their three young children while Vargas studied." * * *

The dissent grants that petitioners' situation is "unfortunate" and that they "understandably attract this Court's sympathy." But "sympathy" is not what petitioners have a right to demand. What they have a right to demand is evenhanded enforcement of the law—of Title VII's prohibition against discrimination based on race. And that is what, until today's decision, has been denied them.

JUSTICE GINSBURG, with whom JUSTICE STEVENS, JUSTICE SOUTER, and JUSTICE BREYER join, dissenting.

* * *

By order of this Court, New Haven, a city in which African–Americans and Hispanics account for nearly 60 percent of the population, must today be served—as it was in the days of undisguised discrimination—by a fire department in which members of racial and ethnic minorities are rarely seen in command positions. [Moreover, the] Court's recitation of the facts leaves out important parts of the story. Firefighting is a profession in which the legacy of racial discrimination casts an especially long shadow. In extending Title VII to state and local government employers in 1972, Congress took note of a U.S. Commission on Civil Rights (USCCR) report finding racial discrimination in municipal employment even "more pervasive than in the private sector." H.R.Rep. No. 92–238, p. 17 (1971). * * *

The city of New Haven (City) was no exception. In the early 1970's, African–Americans and Hispanics composed 30 percent of New Haven's population, but only 3.6 percent of the City's 502 firefighters. The racial disparity in the officer ranks was even more pronounced: "[O]f the 107 officers in the Department only one was black, and he held the lowest rank above private." *Firebird Soc. of New Haven, Inc. v. New Haven Bd. of Fire Comm'rs,* 66 F.R.D. 457, 460 (Conn.1975). [Following a settlement in this 1975 case, New Haven's "litigation-induced" efforts produced some results, but as compared to "New Haven's population," blacks and Hispanics remain underrepresented at the officer level.] It is against this backdrop of entrenched inequality that the promotion process at issue in this litigation should be assessed.

[The record is also replete with evidence that other cities have altered their exams in ways the have avoided these continuing, disparate results. This shows that other less discriminatory alternatives were available to New Haven. In fact, although the majority describes New Haven's test as "painstakingly" developed, its use of oral and written questions is little more than adherence to a formula developed in union contracts years earlier. Experts appearing at hearings recounted by the Court expressed these misgivings to the CSB, and it was entitled to rely on them.[3]]

---

3. Never mind the flawed tests New Haven used and the better selection methods used elsewhere, Justice ALITO's concurring opinion urges. Overriding all else, racial politics, fired up

Neither Congress' enactments nor this Court's Title VII precedents (including the now-discredited decision in *Wards Cove*) offer even a hint of "conflict" between an employer's obligations under the statute's disparate-treatment and disparate-impact provisions. Standing on an equal footing, these twin pillars of Title VII advance the same objectives: ending workplace discrimination and promoting genuinely equal opportunity. [Contrary to the majority's position, there is no conflict between them.]

In codifying the *Griggs* and *Albemarle* instructions, Congress declared unambiguously that selection criteria operating to the disadvantage of minority group members can be retained only if justified by business necessity. In keeping with Congress' design, employers who reject such criteria due to reasonable doubts about their reliability can hardly be held to have engaged in discrimination "because of" race. A reasonable endeavor to comply with the law and to ensure that qualified candidates of all races have a fair opportunity to compete is simply not what Congress meant to interdict. I would therefore hold that an employer who jettisons a selection device when its disproportionate racial impact becomes apparent does not violate Title VII's disparate-treatment bar automatically or at all, subject to this key condition: The employer must have good cause to believe the device would not withstand examination for business necessity.

* * *

NOTE ON THE TENSION BETWEEN DISPARATE IMPACT AND DISPARATE TREATMENT

1. At its most fundamental level, *Ricci* merely holds that *Croson*'s rules for voluntary affirmative action also govern settlements, at least when those settlements have been made because the employer notices racially problematic results based on disparate impact analysis. What both cases have in common is that both involve intentional acts of discrimination—the desire to act based on race of potential or present employees.

(a) The *Ricci* majority treated the case as obviously one of intentional racial discrimination—disparate treatment—because the city's conduct was motivated by the race of the persons who passed the test. The trial court seemed to think that all claims of disparate treatment must go through the three steps of the individual prima facie case discussed in *Burdine*, Chapter 7A.2(a). See 554 F.Supp.2d 142, 152 (D.Conn. 2006). This was clearly an error, was it not? See Chapter 7A.2(a) supra (prima facie case only for covert discrimination); City of Los Angeles, Dep't of Water v. Manhart, 435 U.S. 702, 98 S.Ct. 1370, 55 L.Ed.2d 657 (1978) (facial discrimination requires no additional proof of improper motive). The district court also opined that even if racial politics had been one motivating factor in the city's decision, it would not render the overall decision intentionally discriminatory. This was also

---

by a strident African–American pastor, were at work in New Haven. See ante, at 2665–2668. Even a detached and disinterested observer, however, would have every reason to ask: Why did such racially skewed results occur in New Haven, when better tests likely would have produced less disproportionate results? [repositioned footnote—Ed.]

error, was it not? See Chapter 7A.2(b) supra (if intentional discrimination is "a" factor, burden of proof switches to employer to show it would have made the same decision anyway).

(b) The trial court also suggested that there was no disparate treatment of whites because the city's decision was race-neutral: "[A]ll the test results were discarded, no one was promoted, and firefighters of every race will have to participate in another selection process to be considered for promotion." 554 F.Supp.2d at 158. This view seems to be consistent with Palmer v. Thompson, 403 U.S. 217, 91 S.Ct. 1940, 29 L.Ed.2d 438 (1971) (city's decision to close all swimming pools rather than ceasing to segregate them is constitutional because it treats blacks and whites equally—no one gets to use the pools). But *Palmer* is one of the most reviled cases from the original civil rights era. If it was wrongly decided, then surely the district court also erred on this ground, did it not?

(c) Is the basic assumption of *Ricci* that all bases of racial discrimination should be treated the same, so that what would be race-based if directed against blacks is also race-based when directed against whites? Does Justice Ginsburg disagree with that basic premise?

2. Having found intentional racial discrimination (disparate treatment), the Court then structures its inquiry to determine whether there is a legal excuse for the otherwise-illegal discrimination. The dissent takes a similar approach. What is the majority willing to accept? What is the dissent willing to accept?

(a) The majority and dissent seem to be in agreement that mere proof of disparate impact alone—a racial impact—would not justify a race-based settlement. Why not? Because that would be, or would lead to, racial balancing prohibited by the Act?[1] But it would promote settlements, would it not? Does Justice Ginsburg in effect admit that "voluntary compliance" and "settlement" are not the same thing?

(b) The majority presents what it describes as a moderate position, one that allows settlements and voluntary compliance but only when there is a "strong basis in evidence" that shows that there has been a prior violation. Does this accomplish the majority's goal of giving effect to both of Title VII's goals, (cure of) disparate impact discrimination and (steady enforcement against) disparate treatment discrimination? The Court notes that when Title VII was amended in 1991, no defense was added for "good-faith" settlements to claims of disparate impact. But it is equally true that Congress added no defense for settlements that meet the "strong basis in evidence" test. If the Court can create one test and call it a defense, can it not create the other just as easily? Did Congress approve either the majority's or the dissent's tests?

(c) Is the dissent's "good faith" test too generous to local governments, especially ones that might practice racial politics? Justice Alito's unusually

---

1. Despite her rejection of disparate impact alone as sufficient, in her opening description of the case Justice Ginsburg comes unusually close to suggesting that racial balance is to be expected. Notice her comparative statistics that use raw population percentages rather than qualified potential applicants for hiring or promotion. The Court has long rejected the idea that public employee workforces should mirror the population they serve. See Hazelwood School Dist. v. United States, 433 U.S. 299, 97 S.Ct. 2736, 53 L.Ed.2d 768 (1977).

personal recounting of the activities of Rev. Kimber (including ad hominem details not included in this text) included a reference to the minister's claims that the city was hiring too many persons with "too many vowels" in their names, a statement widely believed to be an anti-Italian–American slur. See "Alito's Opinion Notes Kimber's Heavy Hand," New Haven Register (June 30, 2009), http://www.nhregister.com/articles/2009/06/30/news/new_haven/a1–neboisericci.txt?viewmode=2 (last visited July 1, 2011). Is he simply arguing that minorities may also commit racial discrimination? Is Justice Ginsburg just being practical—of course, most voluntary affirmative action plans and settlements will come in cities with large minority populations?

3.   The Court's reliance on *Croson* strongly suggests that the "strong basis in evidence" test is the spiritual and historical successor to the "arguable violations" test from the 1970s and 1980s, discussed in section D.1 of this Chapter supra. But the application of law to fact may reveal more details about legal doctrine. Does the Court's application of its rule to the facts in New Haven suggest that it wants to see something more than an "arguable" violation? That it wants to see an almost certain violation?

(a) According to the Court, New Haven could not prevail because "there is no evidence—let alone the required strong basis in evidence—that the tests were flawed." Do you agree? Was the problem that city authorities had refused to receive IOS's proffered validation study for the tests? That none of the witnesses opposed to the tests had actually reviewed them? That the proposed alternatives to IOS's tests were only theoretical, with no proof that they actually would have produced less disparate results or could have met the city's needs to identify qualified candidates? Why didn't the city try to provide this evidence?

(b) Is the practical effect of *Ricci*, as shown by application of its test to the facts, that it raises the costs for any employer that wishes to settle putative claims by throwing out test results. Wouldn't the cost of doing all the things that the Court wanted be about equal to defending a disparate impact suit brought by African–Americans?

(c) Is the problem with Justice Ginsburg's approach that it reduces the costs to virtually zero? Notice that the only evidence that there may be acceptable alternatives comes from Mr. Hornsby, a competitor who did not review the tests, and Professor Helms, who testified that all tests produced disparate results (also without reviewing the tests at issue). Is Justice Ginsburg's approach simply a reprise of the "societal discrimination" argument made by Justice Brennan in *Weber*?

(d) Consider the even-longer-term implications of *Ricci*. Doesn't the decision simply encourage employers to avoid use of scored tests altogether because they may find themselves in a lawsuit regardless of whether they keeps the results or discard them? If Professor Helms is correct in saying that all scored tests will produce racially disparate results, will not every use of a test lead to a potential lawsuit?

4.   The majority frankly admits that its "strong basis in evidence" test originated in constitutional law, and it justifies borrowing the test on the ground that the underlying tension that it resolved in equal protection cases is the same tension that it helps resolve in Title VII cases: it permits some

remedies while limiting any impulse to adopt quotas freely. It also frankly admits that its resolution of the case on these grounds makes it unnecessary to reach plaintiff's constitutional claims.

(a) In a part of her opinion not reproduced above, Justice Ginsburg sharply disputed the majority's approach, arguing that in "construing Title VII," constitutional doctrines of equal protection are "of limited utility" because they cover only intentional discrimination (disparate treatment). She argued that the affirmative action cases like *Croson* are "particularly inapt" because in them race was the "decisive factor," not just one of many affecting the employer's decision. 129 S.Ct. at 2700–01. Do you agree? How is settlement like or not like an ordinary voluntary affirmative action plan? Compare the facts in *Weber*, for example, with those in *Ricci*: did not the company and union agree to the plan in *Weber*, at least in part, because they feared being sued for discrimination against African–Americans? Even under Justice Ginsburg's view of the case, is that not the same in *Ricci*? Is the pertinent difference in *Ricci* the avoidance of the use of numerical goals or quotas?

(b) Justice Scalia, at the other end of the spectrum from Justice Ginsburg, joins her in the view that Title VII and the Constitution may not be coterminous. But he notes that non-congruence means that Title VII's disparate impact test may actually be unconstitutional under the disparate treatment test of the Constitution. How strong is the argument? There may be some sad irony here. A long-sought goal of civil rights advocates, achieved in the 1991 Amendments to Title VII, was to free impact analysis from any suggestion that it was merely a mechanism for proving intentional discrimination—to establish impact analysis as an independent, free-standing provision for which proof of intentional discrimination is irrelevant. But separating it so successfully means that impact analysis can require a race-based remedy even when there admittedly has been no prior race-based intentional discrimination. Doesn't that violate *Croson*? Note the similar issue that arises under the Voting Rights Act. See Chapter 8B infra.

(c) The majority, having ruled for the plaintiffs on statutory grounds, studiously avoids any constitutional issues. Yet the majority's adoption of constitutional principles to guide Title VII may also produce an irony here. If the "strong basis in fact" test satisfactorily resolves the tensions impact and treatment analysis within Title VII, does it not also satisfactorily resolve the tensions between the Constitution (disparate treatment) and Title VII (disparate impact)? Has the majority's test saved Title VII's disparate impact test?

CHAPTER 8

VOTING RIGHTS ACT OF 1965— DISCRIMINATION IN VOTING

■ ■ ■

A. CONGRESS' CONSTITUTIONAL POWER

SOUTH CAROLINA v. KATZENBACH

Supreme Court of the United States, 1966.
383 U.S. 301, 86 S.Ct. 803, 15 L.Ed.2d 769.

MR. CHIEF JUSTICE WARREN delivered the opinion of the Court.

By leave of the Court, South Carolina has filed a bill of complaint, seeking a declaration that selected provisions of the Voting Rights Act of 1965 violate the Federal Constitution, and asking for an injunction against enforcement of these provisions by the Attorney General. Original jurisdiction is founded on the presence of a controversy between a State and a citizen of another State under Art. III, § 2, of the Constitution. * * * [Several states participated in the case as friends of the Court.[1]]

* * *

I.

The constitutional propriety of the Voting Rights Act of 1965 must be judged with reference to the historical experience which it reflects. Before enacting the measure, Congress explored with great care the problem of racial discrimination in voting. The House and Senate Committees on the Judiciary each held hearings for nine days and received testimony from a total of 67 witnesses. More than three full days were consumed discussing the bill on the floor of the House, while the debate in the Senate covered 26 days in all. At the close of these deliberations, the verdict of both chambers was overwhelming. The House approved the bill by a vote of 328–74, and the measure passed the Senate by a margin of 79–18.

---

1. States supporting South Carolina: Alabama, Georgia, Louisiana, Mississippi, and Virginia. States supporting the Attorney General: California, Illinois, and Massachusetts, joined by Hawaii, Indiana, Iowa, Kansas, Maine, Maryland, Michigan, Montana, New Hampshire, New Jersey, New York, Oklahoma, Oregon, Pennsylvania, Rhode Island, Vermont, West Virginia, and Wisconsin. [Footnote by the Court.]

Two points emerge vividly from the voluminous legislative history of the Act contained in the committee hearings and floor debates. First: Congress felt itself confronted by an insidious and pervasive evil which had been perpetuated in certain parts of our country through unremitting and ingenious defiance of the Constitution. Second: Congress concluded that the unsuccessful remedies which it had prescribed in the past would have to be replaced by sterner and more elaborate measures in order to satisfy the clear commands of the Fifteenth Amendment. We pause here to summarize the majority reports of the House and Senate Committees, which document in considerable detail the factual basis for these reactions by Congress. See H.R.Rep. No. 439, 89th Cong., 1st Sess., 8–16 (hereinafter cited as House Report); S.Rep. No. 162, pt. 3, 89th Cong., 1st Sess., 3–16, U.S.Code Congressional and Administrative News, p. 2437 (hereinafter cited as Senate Report).

The Fifteenth Amendment to the Constitution was ratified in 1870. Promptly thereafter Congress passed the Enforcement Act of 1870, which made it a crime for public officers and private persons to obstruct exercise of the right to vote. The statute was amended in the following year to provide for detailed federal supervision of the electoral process, from registration to the certification of returns. As the years passed and fervor for racial equality waned, enforcement of the laws became spotty and ineffective, and most of their provisions were repealed in 1894. The remnants have had little significance in the recently renewed battle against voting discrimination.

Meanwhile, beginning in 1890, the States of Alabama, Georgia, Louisiana, Mississippi, North Carolina, South Carolina, and Virginia enacted tests still in use which were specifically designed to prevent Negroes from voting.[9] Typically, they made the ability to read and write a registration qualification and also required completion of a registration form. These laws were based on the fact that as of 1890 in each of the named States, more than two-thirds of the adult Negroes were illiterate while less than one-quarter of the adult whites were unable to read or write. At the same time, alternate tests were prescribed in all of the named States to assure that white illiterates would not be deprived of the franchise. These included grandfather clauses, property qualifications, "good character" tests, and the requirement that registrants "understand" or "interpret" certain matter.

9. The South Carolina Constitutional Convention of 1895 was a leader in the widespread movement to disenfranchise Negroes. Key, Southern Politics, 537–539. Senator Ben Tillman frankly explained to the state delegates the aim of the new literacy test: "[T]he only thing we can do as patriots and as statesmen is to take from [the 'ignorant blacks'] every ballot that we can under the laws of our national government." He was equally candid about the exemption from the literacy test for persons who could "understand" and "explain" a section of the state constitution:

"There is no particle of fraud or illegality in it. It is just simply showing partiality, perhaps, [laughter,] or discriminating." He described the alternative exemption for persons paying state property taxes in the same vein: "By means of the $300 clause you simply reach out and take in some more white men and a few more colored men." Journal of the Constitutional Convention of the State of South Carolina 464, 469, 471 (1895). Senator Tillman was the dominant political figure in the state convention, and his entire address merits examination.

The course of subsequent Fifteenth Amendment litigation in this Court demonstrates the variety and persistence of these and similar institutions designed to deprive Negroes of the right to vote. Grandfather clauses were invalidated in Guinn v. United States, 238 U.S. 347, 35 S.Ct. 926, 59 L.Ed. 1340, and Myers v. Anderson, 238 U.S. 368, 35 S.Ct. 932, 59 L.Ed. 1349. Procedural hurdles were struck down in Lane v. Wilson, 307 U.S. 268, 59 S.Ct. 872, 83 L.Ed. 1281. The white primary was outlawed in Smith v. Allwright, 321 U.S. 649, 64 S.Ct. 757, 88 L.Ed. 987, and Terry v. Adams, 345 U.S. 461, 73 S.Ct. 809, 97 L.Ed. 1152. Improper challenges were nullified in United States v. Thomas, 362 U.S. 58, 80 S.Ct. 612, 4 L.Ed.2d 535. Racial gerrymandering was forbidden by Gomillion v. Lightfoot, 364 U.S. 339, 81 S.Ct. 125, 5 L.Ed.2d 110. Finally, discriminatory application of voting tests was condemned in Schnell v. Davis, 336 U.S. 933, 69 S.Ct. 749, 93 L.Ed. 1093; Alabama v. United States, 371 U.S. 37, 83 S.Ct. 145, 9 L.Ed.2d 112, and Louisiana v. United States, 380 U.S. 145, 85 S.Ct. 817, 13 L.Ed.2d 709.

According to the evidence in recent Justice Department voting suits, the latter strategem is now the principal method used to bar Negroes from the polls. Discriminatory administration of voting qualifications has been found in all eight Alabama cases, in all nine Louisiana cases, and in all nine Mississippi cases which have gone to final judgment. Moreover, in almost all of these cases, the courts have held that the discrimination was pursuant to a widespread "pattern or practice." White applicants for registration have often been excused altogether from the literacy and understanding tests or have been given easy versions, have received extensive help from voting officials, and have been registered despite serious errors in their answers.[12] Negroes, on the other hand, have typically been required to pass difficult versions of all the tests, without any outside assistance and without the slightest error.[13] The good-morals requirement is so vague and subjective that it has constituted an open invitation to abuse at the hands of voting officials. Negroes obliged to obtain vouchers from registered voters have found it virtually impossible to comply in areas where almost no Negroes are on the rolls.

In recent years, Congress has repeatedly tried to cope with the problem by facilitating case-by-case litigation against voting discrimination [including authorization for suits by the Attorney General and expansion of relief.]

---

12. A white applicant in Louisiana satisfied the registrar of his ability to interpret the state constitution by writing, "FRDUM FOOF SPETGH." United States v. State of Louisiana, D.C., 225 F.Supp. 353, 384. A white applicant in Alabama who had never completed the first grade of school was enrolled after the registrar filled out the entire form for him. United States v. Penton, D.C., 212 F.Supp. 193, 210–211.

13. In Panola County, Mississippi, the registrar required Negroes to interpret the provision of the state constitution concerning "the rate of interest on the fund known as the 'Chickasaw School Fund.'" United States v. Duke, 5 Cir., 332 F.2d 759, 764. In Forrest County, Mississippi, the registrar rejected six Negroes with baccalaureate degrees, three of whom were also Masters of Arts. United States v. Lynd, 5 Cir., 301 F.2d 818, 821.

Despite the earnest efforts of the Justice Department and of many federal judges, these new laws have done little to cure the problem of voting discrimination. According to estimates by the Attorney General during hearings on the Act, registration of voting-age Negroes in Alabama rose only from 14.2% to 19.4% between 1958 and 1964; in Louisiana it barely inched ahead from 31.7% to 31.8% between 1956 and 1965; and in Mississippi it increased only from 4.4% to 6.4% between 1954 and 1964. In each instance, registration of voting-age whites ran roughly 50 percentage points or more ahead of Negro registration.

The previous legislation has proved ineffective for a number of reasons. Voting suits are unusually onerous to prepare, sometimes requiring as many as 6,000 man-hours spent combing through registration records in preparation for trial. Litigation has been exceedingly slow, in part because of the ample opportunities for delay afforded voting officials and others involved in the proceedings. Even when favorable decisions have finally been obtained, some of the States affected have merely switched to discriminatory devices not covered by the federal decrees or have enacted difficult new tests designed to prolong the existing disparity between white and Negro registration. Alternatively, certain local officials have defied and evaded court orders or have simply closed their registration offices to freeze the voting rolls. The provision of the 1960 law authorizing registration by federal officers has had little impact on local maladministration because of its procedural complexities.

* * *

II.

[Sections 2 and 3 of the Act apply nationwide to bar intentional use of voting tests to discriminate on the basis of race and give courts extraordinary remedial powers in enforcement suits brought by the Attorney General, including power to appoint registrars, suspend the tests, and subject future changes in voting laws to the approval of the court or Attorney General. "The heart of the Act," however, is a "complex scheme of stringent remedies" in §§ 4 and 5 "aimed at areas where voting discrimination has been flagrant." In such jurisdictions, identified by a coverage formula discussed below, voting tests are automatically suspended without a prior judicial finding of discrimination. The Attorney General is empowered to appoint voting registrars in such areas, and the jurisdictions are also required to submit all changes in voting laws to the Attorney General or federal court in Washington, D.C.]

The remedial sections of the Act assailed by South Carolina automatically apply to any State, or to any separate political subdivision such as a county or parish, for which two findings have been made: (1) the Attorney General has determined that on November 1, 1964, it maintained a "test or device," and (2) the Director of the Census has determined that less than 50% of its voting-age residents were registered on November 1, 1964, or voted in the presidential election of November 1964. These findings are not reviewable in any court and are final upon publication in the Federal Register. § 4(b). As used throughout the Act, the phrase "test or device" means any requirement that a registrant or voter must "(1) demonstrate the ability to read, write, understand, or interpret any matter, (2) demonstrate any educational achievement or his knowledge of any particular subject, (3) possess good moral character, or (4) prove his qualifications by the voucher of registered voters or members of any other class." § 4(c).

Statutory coverage of a State or political subdivision under § 4(b) is terminated if the area obtains a declaratory judgment from the District Court for the District of Columbia, determining that tests and devices have not been used during the preceding five years to abridge the franchise on racial grounds. * * *

[South Carolina, Alabama, Alaska, Georgia, Louisiana, Mississippi, Virginia, 26 counties in North Carolina, and three counties in Arizona, one county in Hawaii, and one county in Idaho are currently covered. As a consequence of being brought under coverage, South Carolina's literacy test was suspended, federal voting examiners were appointed for two counties, and recently adopted voting changes extending the closing hours of polls became subject to the Attorney General's prior approval.]

III.

These provisions of the Voting Rights Act of 1965 are challenged on the fundamental ground that they exceed the powers of Congress and encroach on an area reserved to the States by the Constitution. South Carolina and certain of the *amici curiae* also attack specific sections of the Act for more particular reasons. [Arguments that the Act violates the state's right to due process and is a bill of attainder are insubstantial, since these clauses protect persons, not states.]

* * *

The ground rules for resolving this question [of Congressional power] are clear. The language and purpose of the Fifteenth Amendment, the prior decisions construing its several provisions, and the general doctrines of constitutional interpretation, all point to one fundamental principle. As against the reserved powers of the States, Congress may use any rational means to effectuate the constitutional prohibition of racial discrimination in voting. Cf. our rulings last Term, sustaining Title II of the Civil Rights Act of 1964, in Heart of Atlanta Motel v. United States, [Chapter 5 supra,] and Katzenbach v. McClung, [Chapter 5 supra]. We turn now to a more detailed description of the standards which govern our review of the Act.

Section 1 of the Fifteenth Amendment declares that "[t]he right of citizens of the United States to vote shall not be denied or abridged by the United States or by any State on account of race, color, or previous condition of servitude." This declaration has always been treated as self-executing and has repeatedly been construed, without further legislative specification, to invalidate state voting qualifications or procedures which are discriminatory on their face or in practice. [Numerous citations omitted.]

South Carolina contends that the cases cited above are precedents only for the authority of the judiciary to strike down state statute and procedures—that to allow an exercise of this authority by Congress would be to rob the courts of their rightful constitutional role. On the contrary, § 2 of the Fifteenth Amendment expressly declares that "Congress shall have power to enforce this article by appropriate legislation." By adding this authorization, the Framers indicated that Congress was to be chiefly responsible for implementing the rights created in § 1. "It is the power of Congress which has been enlarged. Congress is authorized to *enforce* the prohibitions by appropriate legislation. Some legislation is contemplated to make the [Civil War] amendments fully effective." Ex parte Virginia, 100 U.S. 339, 345, 25 L.Ed. 676. Accordingly, in addition to the courts, Congress has full remedial powers to effectuate the constitutional prohibition against racial discrimination in voting.

Congress has repeatedly exercised these powers in the past, and its enactments have repeatedly been upheld. * * * On the rare occasions when the Court has found an unconstitutional exercise of these powers, in its opinion Congress had attacked evils not comprehended by the Fifteenth Amendment. See United States v. Reese, 92 U.S. 214, 23 L.Ed. 563; James v. Bowman, 190 U.S. 127, 23 S.Ct. 678, 47 L.Ed. 979.

The basic test to be applied in a case involving § 2 of the Fifteenth Amendment is the same as in all cases concerning the express powers of Congress with relation to the reserved powers of the States. Chief Justice Marshall laid down the classic formulation, 50 years before the Fifteenth Amendment was ratified:

> "Let the end be legitimate, let it be within the scope of the constitution, and all means which are appropriate, which are plainly adapted to that end, which are not prohibited, but consist with the letter and spirit of the constitution, are constitutional." McCulloch v. Maryland, 4 Wheat. 316, 421, 4 L.Ed. 579.

* * *

IV.

Congress exercised its authority under the Fifteenth Amendment in an inventive manner when it enacted the Voting Rights Act of 1965. First: The measure prescribes remedies for voting discrimination which go into effect without any need for prior adjudication. This was clearly a legitimate response to the problem, for which there is ample precedent under other constitutional provisions. See Katzenbach v. McClung. Congress had found that case-by-case litigation was inadequate to combat widespread and persistent discrimination in voting, because of the inordinate amount of time and energy required to overcome the obstructionist tactics invariably encountered in these lawsuits. After enduring nearly a century of systematic resistance to the Fifteenth Amendment, Congress might well decide to shift the advantage of time and inertia from the perpetrators of the evil to its victims. The question remains, of course, whether the specific remedies prescribed in the Act were an appropriate means of combatting the evil, and to this question we shall presently address ourselves.

Second: The Act intentionally confines these remedies to a small number of States and political subdivisions which in most instances were familiar to Congress by name. This, too, was a permissible method of dealing with the problem. Congress had learned that substantial voting discrimination presently occurs in certain sections of the country, and it knew no way of accurately forecasting whether the evil might spread elsewhere in the future. In acceptable legislative fashion, Congress chose to limit its attention to the geographic areas where immediate action seemed necessary. See Salsburg v. State of Maryland, 346 U.S. 545, 550–54, 74 S.Ct. 280, 282–285, 98 L.Ed. 281. The doctrine of the equality of States, invoked by South Carolina, does not bar this approach, for that doctrine applies only to the terms upon which States are admitted to the Union, and not to the remedies for local evils which have subsequently appeared. See Coyle v. Smith, 221 U.S. 559, 31 S.Ct. 688, 55 L.Ed. 853, and cases cited therein.

Coverage Formula

We now consider the related question of whether the specific States and political subdivisions within § 4(b) of the Act were an appropriate target for the new remedies. South Carolina contends that the coverage formula is awkwardly designed in a number of respects and that it disregards various local conditions which have nothing to do with racial discrimination. These arguments, however, are largely beside the point. Congress began work with reliable evidence of actual voting discrimination in a great majority of the States and political subdivisions affected by the new remedies of the Act. The formula eventually evolved to describe these areas was relevant to the problem of voting discrimination, and Congress was therefore entitled to infer a significant danger of the evil in the few remaining States and political subdivisions covered by § 4(b) of the Act. No more was required to justify the application to these areas of Congress' express powers under the Fifteenth Amendment.

To be specific, the new remedies of the Act are imposed on three States—Alabama, Louisiana, and Mississippi—in which federal courts have repeatedly found substantial voting discrimination. Section 4(b) of the Act also embraces two other States—Georgia and South Carolina—plus large portions of a third State—North Carolina—for which there was more fragmentary evidence of recent voting discrimination mainly adduced by the Justice Department and the Civil Rights Commission. All of these areas were appropriately subjected to the new remedies. In identifying past evils, Congress obviously may avail itself of information from any probative source. See Heart of Atlanta Motel v. United States, supra.

The areas listed above, for which there was evidence of actual voting discrimination, share two characteristics incorporated by Congress into the coverage formula: the use of tests and devices for voter registration, and a voting rate in the 1964 presidential election at least 12 points below the national average. Tests and devices are relevant to voting discrimination because of their long history as a tool for perpetrating the evil; a low voting rate is pertinent for the obvious reason that widespread disenfranchisement must inevitably affect the number of actual voters. Accordingly, the coverage formula is rational in both practice and theory. It was therefore permissible to impose the new remedies on the few remaining States and political subdivisions covered by the formula, at least in the absence of proof that they have been free of substantial voting discrimination in recent years. * * * *

[The legislation is not subject to attack on grounds of underinclusiveness.] It is irrelevant that the coverage formula excludes certain localities which do not employ voting tests and devices but for which there is evidence of voting discrimination by other means. * * * Legislation need not deal with all phases of a problem in the same way, so long as the distinctions drawn have some basis in practical experience. See Williamson v. Lee Optical Co., 348 U.S. 483, 488–89, 75 S.Ct. 461, 464–465, 99 L.Ed. 563. * * *

[Nor is the Act overbroad, for it] provides for termination of special statutory coverage at the behest of States and political subdivisions in which the danger of substantial voting discrimination has not materialized during the preceding five years. Despite South Carolina's argument to the contrary, Congress might appropriately limit litigation under this provision to a single court in the District of Columbia, pursuant to its constitutional power under Art. III, § 1, to "ordain and establish" inferior federal tribunals. See Bowles v. Willingham, 321 U.S. 503, 510–12, 64 S.Ct. 641, 645, 646, 88 L.Ed. 892; Yakus v. United States, 321 U.S. 414, 427–31, 64 S.Ct. 660, 668, 670, 88 L.Ed. 834; Lockerty v. Phillips, 319 U.S. 182, 63 S.Ct. 1019, 87 L.Ed. 1339. * * *

South Carolina contends that these termination procedures are a nullity because they impose an impossible burden of proof upon States and political subdivisions entitled to relief. As the Attorney General pointed out during hearings on the Act, however, an area need do no more than submit affidavits from voting officials, asserting that they have not been guilty of racial discrimination through the use of tests and devices during the past five years, and then refute whatever evidence to the contrary may be adduced by the Federal Government. Section 4(d) further assures that an area need not disprove each isolated instance of voting discrimination in order to obtain relief in the termination proceedings. The burden of proof is therefore quite bearable, particularly since the relevant facts relating to the conduct of voting officials are peculiarly within the knowledge of the States and political subdivisions themselves.

The Act bars direct judicial review of the findings by the Attorney General and the Director of the Census which trigger application of the coverage formula. We reject the claim by Alabama as *amicus curiae* that this provision is invalid because it allows the new remedies of the Act to be imposed in an arbitrary way. The Court has already permitted Congress to withdraw judicial review of administrative determinations in numerous cases involving the statutory rights of private parties. For example, see United States v. California Eastern Line, 348 U.S. 351, 75 S.Ct. 419, 99 L.Ed. 383; Switchmen's Union v. National Mediation Bd., 320 U.S. 297, 64 S.Ct. 95, 88 L.Ed. 61. In this instance, the findings not subject to review consist of objective statistical determinations by the Census Bureau and a routine analysis of state statutes by the Justice Department. These functions are unlikely to arouse any plausible dispute, as South Carolina apparently concedes. In the event that the formula is improperly applied, the area affected can always go into court and obtain termination of coverage under § 4(b), provided of course that it has not been guilty of voting discrimination in recent years. This procedure serves as a partial substitute for direct judicial review.

Suspension of Tests

We now arrive at consideration of the specific remedies prescribed by the Act for areas included within the coverage formula. South Carolina assails the temporary suspension of existing voting qualifications, reciting the rule laid down by Lassiter v. Northampton County Bd. of Elections, 360 U.S. 45, 79 S.Ct. 985, 3 L.Ed.2d 1072, that literacy tests and related devices are not in themselves contrary to the Fifteenth Amendment. In that very case, however, the Court went on to say, "Of course a literacy test, fair on its face, may be employed to perpetuate that discrimination which the Fifteenth Amendment was designed to uproot." Id. at 53, 79 S.Ct. at 991. The record shows that in most of the States covered by the Act, including South Carolina, various tests and devices have been instituted with the purpose of disenfranchising Negroes, have been framed in such a way as to facilitate this aim, and have been administered in a discriminatory fashion for many years. Under these circumstances, the Fifteenth Amendment has clearly been violated. See Louisiana v. United States, 380 U.S. 145, 85 S.Ct. 817, 13 L.Ed.2d 709.

The Act suspends literacy tests and similar devices for a period of five years from the last occurrence of substantial voting discrimination. This was a legitimate response to the problem, for which there is ample precedent in Fifteenth Amendment cases. Ibid. Underlying the response was the feeling that States and political subdivisions which had been allowing white illiterates to vote for years could not sincerely complain about "dilution" of their electorates through the registration of Negro illiterates. Congress knew that continuance of the tests and devices in use at the present time, no matter how fairly administered in the future, would freeze the effect of past discrimination in favor of unqualified white registrants. Congress permissibly rejected the alternative of requiring a complete re-registration of all voters, believing that this would be too harsh on many whites who had enjoyed the franchise for their entire adult lives.

Review of New Rules

The Act suspends new voting regulations pending scrutiny by federal authorities to determine whether their use would violate the Fifteenth Amendment. This may have been an uncommon exercise of congressional power, as South Carolina contends, but the Court has recognized that exceptional conditions can justify legislative measures not otherwise appropriate. See Home Bldg. & Loan Ass'n v. Blaisdell, 290 U.S. 398, 54 S.Ct. 231, 78 L.Ed. 413 [payment moratoriums on debt enacted during the Great Depression do not violate Contracts Clause]. Congress knew that some of the States covered by § 4(b) of the Act had resorted to the extraordinary stratagem of contriving new rules of various kinds for the sole purpose of perpetuating voting discrimination in the face of adverse federal court decrees. Congress had reason to suppose that these States might try similar maneuvers in the future in order to evade the remedies for voting discrimination contained in the Act itself. Under the compulsion of these unique circumstances, Congress responded in a permissibly decisive manner.

* * *

Federal Examiners

[The Court upheld appointment of federal examiners to replace local examiners based on the evidence that local examiners had repeatedly disobeyed federal court orders to comply with the Fifteenth Amendment.]

The bill of complaint is dismissed.

MR. JUSTICE BLACK, concurring and dissenting.

[Though I agree that most of the Act is constitutional, § 5's provision subjecting some state's voting changes to review by Washington, presents a problem. Here Congress has] exercised its power under § 2 of the Fifteenth Amendment through the adoption of means that conflict with the most basic principles of the Constitution. As the Court says the limitations of the power granted under § 2 are the same as the limitations imposed on the exercise of any of the powers expressly granted Congress by the Constitution. The classic formulation of these constitutional limitations was stated by Chief Justice Marshall when he said in McCulloch v. State of Maryland, "Let the end be legitimate, let it be within the scope of the constitution, and all means which are appropriate, which are plainly adapted to that end, *which are not prohibited, but consist with the letter and spirit of the constitution,* are constitutional." (Emphasis added.) Section 5, by providing that some of the States cannot pass state laws or adopt state constitutional amendments without first being compelled to beg federal authorities to approve their policies, so distorts our constitutional structure of government as to render any distinction drawn in the

Constitution between state and federal power almost meaningless. * * * Moreover, it seems to me that § 5 which gives federal officials power to veto state laws they do not like is in direct conflict with the clear command of our Constitution that "The United States shall guarantee to every State in this Union a Republican Form of Government." I cannot help but believe that the inevitable effect of any such law which forces any one of the States to entreat federal authorities in faraway places for approval of local laws before they can become effective is to create the impression that the State or States treated in this way are little more than conquered provinces. * * *

* * *

NOTE ON CONGRESSIONAL POWER TO REMEDY CONSTITUTIONAL VIOLATIONS

1. South Carolina's argument that only the Judiciary Branch has power to enforce the Fifteenth Amendment is clearly untenable, is it not? Aside from the explicit wording of § 2 of the Amendment, consider Congress' ordinary exercise of its other constitutional powers over interstate commerce, coinage of money, or taxing. Are those powers initially exercised by Congress through judicial process? Has not Congress sometimes created administrative authorities to exercise enforcement authority, with only later review in the courts on the affected party's initiative? See, e.g., Federal Trade Commission Act, 15 U.S.C.A. § 45; Federal Reserve Act, 12 U.S.C.A. § 221 et seq. Is the 1965 Voting Rights Act different?

2. Note the Court's citation of Gibbons v. Ogden and McCulloch v. Maryland as the proper authorities by which to test Congress' action under the Fifteenth Amendment.

(a) *Gibbons* involved the use of Congress' substantive power under Article I, § 8, to regulate interstate commerce. Must not one read carefully *Gibbons'* phrase that the power is "complete in itself * * * and acknowledges no limitations"? That power, like any granted by the Constitution, is plenary only over the named topic, is it not, not over "evils not comprehended by the" Commerce Clause, Fifteenth Amendment, or other source of substantive power? See James v. Bowman (cited in *South Carolina*), 190 U.S. at 139 (no Fifteenth Amendment power to reach private actors who disenfranchise persons for reasons other than race).

(b) The *McCulloch* case sustained Congressional power under several clauses (including the Necessary and Proper Clause) of Article I, § 8, to establish the Bank of the United States. The Necessary and Proper Clause was held not to confer substantive powers but to empower Congress to choose the means to carry out the enumerated substantive powers of Article I, § 8: therefore, though Congress had no enumerated power to establish a bank, it could choose creation of a bank as a means for effectuating its substantive power to coin money and pay federal debts. Can any means be chosen? Any one rationally related to carrying out an enumerated power? Any one not specifically prohibited elsewhere in the Constitution?

3. In **Lassiter v. Northampton County Bd. of Elections**, 360 U.S. 45, 79 S.Ct. 985, 3 L.Ed.2d 1072 (1959), cited in *South Carolina,* the Court refused to find all literacy tests per se violative of the Fifteenth Amendment, although it noted that tests intentionally used to discriminate would be found unconstitutional. When Congress outlawed literacy tests in 1965 was it without power to do so because its attack was directed at an "evil not comprehended by the Fifteenth Amendment"? See *Gibbons,* supra. Yes, because the Act outlawed tests per se, and tests do not per se violate the Amendment? No, because the Act only suspended discriminatorily used tests, and such intentional misuse does violate the Amendment?

(a) The Court notes in *South Carolina* that Congress had before it substantial evidence of discriminatory use of voting tests, much of it in the form of court opinions finding under *Lassiter* that tests had been intentionally discriminatorily used. Does that make the question of Congress' power an easy one? Would the issue have been more difficult if courts had previously found no violations and Congress turned up the fact through its own investigations? If Congress found only random violations? If Congress conducted no investigations? See Oregon v. Mitchell, 400 U.S. 112, 131–34, 144–47, 216–17, 231–36, 282–84, 91 S.Ct. 260, 268–69, 274–76, 310–11, 318–21, 343–44, 27 L.Ed.2d 272 (1970) (extension of literacy test ban nationwide unanimously upheld).

(b) In light of the necessarily broad and unparticularized nature of Congress' fact-finding abilities, was it crucial that Congress provide a "bail-out" mechanism by which jurisdictions can prove themselves free of discrimination and escape the automatic coverage provisions of §§ 4 and 5? If a jurisdiction had not intentionally used its test to discriminate on the basis of race, would Congress lack Fifteenth Amendment power over its test? Or must the Court necessarily permit imprecision in legislation? Note the Court's rejection of underinclusiveness and overinclusiveness arguments against the Act. Does that suggest the bailout was unnecessary? Cf. Westfall v. United States, 274 U.S. 256, 259, 47 S.Ct. 629, 630, 71 L.Ed. 1036 (1927) (Holmes, J.: "[W]hen it is necessary in order to prevent an evil to make the law embrace more than the precise thing to be prevented it may do so."). When Congress extended the literacy test ban nationwide in 1970, it adopted no bailout provision. See 42 U.S.C.A. § 1973aa; Oregon v. Mitchell, supra, 400 U.S. at 283–284, 91 S.Ct. at 343–44 (Stewart, J., concurring).

4. Assuming that Congress has substantive power to enforce the Fifteenth Amendment, did the means chosen present graver constitutional problems under the *McCulloch* test? The suspension of tests, use of federal examiners, and preclearance of voting changes appear rationally related to curing the historical evils discovered by Congress and reported by the Court. But were such means, especially preclearance, barred because they were forbidden by the Constitution?

(a) Is Justice Black's dissent persuasive in its argument of a core of reserved state power? What is the constitutional source for this proposition, the Tenth Amendment? Or is it a non-textual "state's right"?

(b) Is Justice Black's dissent undercut by the Court's still later decision in **Fitzpatrick v. Bitzer**, Chapter 7B.4 supra? Citing the explicit coverage of states in § 1 of the Fourteenth Amendment, the Court there permitted Congress to act under § 5 to abrogate state sovereign immunity otherwise preserved by the Eleventh Amendment. If Congress can rely on such language in the Fourteenth Amendment to override states' rights guaranteed by the Eleventh Amendment, can it not rely on the same language in the Fifteenth Amendment to override states' rights guaranteed by the Tenth Amendment? Or should the Tenth Amendment remain as an unabrogatable core safeguard against Congressional inroads on the "independent existence" of states?

(c) Is it reasonably certain that all the provisions of the 1965 Act were "remedial" in the sense that they cured historically extant problems of unconstitutional state action in restricting the right to vote bases on race? If that is true, and if it is true that the Fifteenth Amendment textually covers state actors and gives remedial powers to Congress, is there any argument left against the Act?

5. The 1965 Voting Rights Act is regarded by many as the most effective piece of legislation passed during the Second Reconstruction of the 1960s in securing general equality and respect for black Americans. Why? See Chandler Davidson, *Voting Rights the Second Time Around: Happy Ending, or Prologue to a Third Try?*, 4 ELECTION L.J. 212 (2005), reviewing Richard M. Valelly, THE TWO RECONSTRUCTIONS: THE STRUGGLE FOR BLACK ENFRANCHISEMENT (2004) (arguing that "radical liberals" promoted both the First Reconstruction of 1865 and the Second Reconstruction of 1965, but only the second was successful, largely due to black self-protection through registering and voting). Does the success of the Act undermine the argument for its continuance?

(a) In 2006 Congress extended § 5's preclearance requirements for 25 more years until 2032, 72 years after the original adoption of the 1965 Voting Rights Act. See PL 109–246, 120 Stat 577 (2006), 42 U.S.C. 1973l(e). Cf. Grutter v. Bollinger, Chapter 6E supra (25 years after 2003 is projected time limit for affirmative action to remedy past discrimination). Has the partisan argument for the Act (that it leads to more black districts but also more Republican districts, see section B.1 infra) become more powerful than the remedial argument for it?

(b) In **Northwest Austin Mun. Utility Dist. No. One v. Holder**, ___ U.S. ___, 129 S.Ct. 2504, 174 L.Ed.2d 140 (2009), an otherwise minor case of statutory construction, the Court justified its pro-covered-jurisdiction view by claiming a need to avoid potential constitutional infirmities arising from a broader view. Newly appointed Chief Justice Roberts wrote, ___ U.S. at ___, 129 S.Ct. at 2511–12:

"The historic accomplishments of the Voting Rights Act are undeniable. When it was first passed, unconstitutional discrimination was rampant [but today] the registration gap between white and black voters is in single digits in the covered States; in some of those States, blacks now register and vote at higher rates than whites. Similar dramatic improvements have occurred for other racial minorities. {And minority candidates hold office at unprecedented levels.]

These improvements are no doubt due in significant part to the Voting Rights Act itself, and stand as a monument to its success. Past success alone, however, is not adequate justification to retain the preclearance requirements. See Issacharoff, Is Section 5 of the Voting Rights Act a Victim of Its Own Success? 104 Colum. L.Rev. 1710 (2004). It may be that these improvements are insufficient and that conditions continue to warrant preclearance under the Act. But the Act imposes current burdens and must be justified by current needs.''

Should the Voting Rights Act be seen as a temporary fixture for remedying unusual discrimination or as a permanent fixture of American political life?

KATZENBACH v. MORGAN

Supreme Court of the United States, 1966.
384 U.S. 641, 86 S.Ct. 1717, 16 L.Ed.2d 828.

Mr. Justice Brennan delivered the opinion of the Court.

These cases concern the constitutionality of § 4(e) of the Voting Rights Act of 1965.[1] That law, in the respects pertinent in these cases, provides that no person who has successfully completed the sixth primary grade in a public school in, or a private school accredited by, the Commonwealth of Puerto Rico in which the language of instruction was other than English shall be denied the right to vote in any election because of his inability to read or write English. Appellees, registered voters in New York City, brought this suit to challenge the constitutionality of § 4(e) insofar as it *pro tanto* prohibits the enforcement of the election laws of New York requiring an ability to read and write English as a condition of voting. Under these laws many of the several hundred thousand New York City residents who have migrated there from the Commonwealth of Puerto Rico had previously been denied the right to vote, and appellees attack § 4(e) insofar as it would enable many of these citizens to vote.[3] [The

---

1. The full text of § 4(e) is as follows:

"(1) Congress hereby declares that to secure the rights under the fourteenth amendment of persons educated in American-flag schools in which the predominant classroom language was other than English, it is necessary to prohibit the States from conditioning the right to vote of such persons on ability to read, write, understand, or interpret any matter in the English language.

"(2) No person who demonstrates that he has successfully completed the sixth primary grade in a public school in, or a private school accredited by, any State or territory, the District of Columbia, or the Commonwealth of Puerto Rico in which the predominant classroom language was other than English, shall be denied the right to vote in any Federal, State, or local election because of his inability to read, write, understand, or interpret any matter in the English language, except that in States in which State law provides that a different level of education is presumptive of literacy, he shall demonstrate that he has successfully completed an equivalent level of education in a public school in, or a private school accredited by, any State or territory, the District of Columbia, or the Commonwealth of Puerto Rico in which the predominant classroom language was other than English." 79 Stat. 439, 42 U.S.C.A. § 1973b(e).

3. This limitation on appellees' challenge to § 4(e), and thus on the scope of our inquiry, does not distort the primary intent of § 4(e). The measure was sponsored in the Senate by Senators Javits and Kennedy and in the House of Representatives by Gilbert and Ryan, all of New York, for the explicit purpose of dealing with the disenfranchisement of large segments of the Puerto Rican population in New York. Throughout the congressional debate it was repeatedly acknowledged that § 4(e) had particular reference to the Puerto Rican population in New York. That situation was the almost exclusive subject of discussion. See 111 Cong.Rec. 11028, 11060–74, 15666, 16235–45, 16282–83, 19192–201, 19375–78; see also Voting Rights, Hearings before Subcommittee No. 5 of the House Committee on the Judiciary on H.R. 6400, 89th Cong., 1st Sess., 100–01, 420–21, 508–17 (1965). The Solicitor General informs us in his brief to this Court,

District Court for the District of Columbia struck down the provision.] We reverse. We hold that, in the application challenged in these cases, § 4(e) is a proper exercise of the powers granted to Congress by § 5 of the Fourteenth Amendment and that by force of the Supremacy Clause, Article VI, the New York English literacy requirement cannot be enforced to the extent that it is inconsistent with § 4(e).

Under the distribution of powers effected by the Constitution, the States establish qualifications for voting for state officers, and the qualifications established by the States for voting for members of the most numerous branch of the state legislature also determine who may vote for United States Representatives and Senators, Art. I, § 2; Seventeenth Amendment; Ex parte Yarbrough, 110 U.S. 651, 663, 4 S.Ct. 152, 28 L.Ed. 274. But, of course, the States have no power to grant or withhold the franchise on conditions that are forbidden by the Fourteenth Amendment, or any other provision of the Constitution. Such exercises of state power are no more immune to the limitations of the Fourteenth Amendment than any other state action. The Equal Protection Clause itself has been held to forbid some state laws that restrict the right to vote.[6]

The Attorney General of the State of New York argues that an exercise of congressional power under § 5 of the Fourteenth Amendment that prohibits the enforcement of a state law can only be sustained if the judicial branch determines that the state law is prohibited by the provisions of the Amendment that Congress sought to enforce. More specifically, he urges that § 4(e) cannot be sustained as appropriate legislation to enforce the Equal Protection Clause unless the judiciary decides—even with the guidance of a congressional judgment—that the application of the English literacy requirement prohibited by § 4(e) is forbidden by the Equal Protection Clause itself. We disagree. Neither the language nor history of § 5 supports such a construction. As was said with regard to § 5 in Ex parte Com. of Virginia, 100 U.S. 339, 345, 25 L.Ed. 676: "It is the power of Congress which has been enlarged. Congress is authorized to *enforce* the prohibitions by appropriate legislation. Some legislation is contemplated to make the amendments fully effective." A construction of § 5 that would require a judicial determination that the enforcement of the state law precluded by Congress violated the Amendment, as a condition of sustaining the congressional enactment, would depreciate both congressional resourcefulness and congressional responsibility for implementing the Amendment. It would confine the legislative power in this context to the insignificant role of abrogating only those state laws that the judicial branch was prepared to adjudge unconstitutional, or of

that in all probability the practical effect of § 4(e) will be limited to enfranchising those educated in Puerto Rican schools. He advises us that, aside from the schools in the Commonwealth of Puerto Rico, there are no public or parochial schools in the territorial limits of the United States in which the predominant language of instruction is other than English and which would have generally been attended by persons who are otherwise qualified to vote save for their lack of literacy in English.

6. Harper v. Virginia Board of Elections, 383 U.S. 663, 86 S.Ct. 1079, 16 L.Ed.2d 169; Reynolds v. Sims, 377 U.S. 533, 84 S.Ct. 1362, 12 L.Ed.2d 506.

merely informing the judgment of the judiciary by particularizing the "majestic generalities" of § 1 of the Amendment. See Fay v. People of State of New York, 332 U.S. 261, 282–84, 67 S.Ct. 1613, 1624–25, 91 L.Ed. 2043.

Thus our task in this case is not to determine whether the New York English literacy requirement [satisfies] the Equal Protection Clause. [We upheld general literacy requirements in Lassiter v. Northampton County Bd. of Election, 360 U.S. 45, 79 S.Ct. 985, 3 L.Ed.2d 1072, but that was in the context of an Equal Protection challenge against them, and thus that case is inapposite. The question for us today is not] whether the judiciary would find that the Equal Protection Clause itself nullifies New York's English literacy requirement [but whether Congress can] prohibit the enforcement of the state law by legislating under § 5 of the Fourteenth Amendment[.] In answering this question, our task is limited to determining whether such legislation is, as required by § 5, appropriate legislation to enforce the Equal Protection Clause.

By including § 5 the draftsmen sought to grant to Congress, by a specific provision applicable to the Fourteenth Amendment, the same broad powers expressed in the Necessary and Proper Clause, Art. I, § 8, cl. 18. The classic formulation of the reach of those powers was established by Chief Justice Marshall in McCulloch v. Maryland. [The Court quoted the same passage excerpted in the *South Carolina* case.] * * *

[As we held in South Carolina v. Katzenbach, the appropriate test in the context of judging a Congressional statute is that adopted in the *McCulloch* case.] We therefore proceed to the consideration whether § 4(e) is "appropriate legislation" to enforce the Equal Protection Clause, that is, under the McCulloch v. Maryland standard, whether § 4(e) may be regarded as an enactment to enforce the Equal Protection Clause, whether it is "plainly adapted to that end" and whether it is not prohibited by but is consistent with the "letter and spirit of the constitution."[10]

[First, § 4(e) may be seen as remedial of rights of Puerto Ricans who have emigrated to New York.] More specifically, § 4(e) may be viewed as a measure to secure for the Puerto Rican community residing in New York nondiscriminatory treatment by government—both in the imposition of voting qualifications and the provision or administration of governmental services, such as public schools, public housing and law enforcement.

Section 4(e) may be readily seen as "plainly adapted" to furthering these aims of the Equal Protection Clause. The practical effect of § 4(e) is to prohibit New York from denying the right to vote to large segments of its Puerto Rican community. Congress has thus prohibited the State from

---

10. Contrary to the suggestion of the dissent, § 5 does not grant Congress power to exercise discretion in the other direction and to enact "statutes so as in effect to dilute equal protection and due process decisions of this Court." We emphasize that Congress' power under § 5 is limited to adopting measures to enforce the guarantees of the Amendment; § 5 grants Congress no power to restrict, abrogate, or dilute these guarantees. Thus, for example, an enactment authorizing the States to establish racially segregated systems of education would not be—as required by § 5—a measure "to enforce" the Equal Protection Clause since that clause of its own force prohibits such state laws.

denying to that community the right that is "preservative of all rights." Yick Wo v. Hopkins, 118 U.S. 356, 370, 6 S.Ct. 1064, 1071, 30 L.Ed. 220. This enhanced political power will be helpful in gaining nondiscriminatory treatment in public services for the entire Puerto Rican community.[11] Section 4(e) thereby enables the Puerto Rican minority better to obtain "perfect equality of civil rights and the equal protection of the laws." It was well within congressional authority to say that this need of the Puerto Rican minority for the vote warranted federal intrusion upon any state interests served by the English literacy requirement. It was for Congress, as the branch that made this judgment, to assess and weigh the various conflicting considerations—the risk or pervasiveness of the discrimination in governmental services, the effectiveness of eliminating the state restriction on the right to vote as a means of dealing with the evil, the adequacy or availability of alternative remedies, and the nature and significance of the state interests that would be affected by the nullification of the English literacy requirement as applied to residents who have successfully completed the sixth grade in a Puerto Rican school. It is not for us to review the congressional resolution of these factors. It is enough that we be able to perceive a basis upon which the Congress might resolve the conflict as it did. There plainly was such a basis to support § 4(e) in the application in question in this case. Any contrary conclusion would require us to be blind to the realities familiar to the legislators.

[Second, even if we consider only the topic of voting itself, the Act is nevertheless valid.] We are told that New York's English literacy requirement originated in the desire to provide an incentive for non-English speaking immigrants to learn the English language and in order to assure the intelligent exercise of the franchise. Yet Congress might well have questioned, in light of the many exemptions provided, and some evidence suggesting that prejudice played a prominent role in the enactment of the requirement,[14] whether these were actually the interests being served. Congress might have also questioned whether denial of a right deemed so precious and fundamental in our society was a necessary or appropriate means of encouraging persons to learn English, or of furthering the goal of an intelligent exercise of the franchise. Finally, Congress might well have concluded that as a means of furthering the intelligent exercise of the franchise, an ability to read or understand Spanish is as effective as ability

11. Cf. James Everard's Breweries v. Day, [265 U.S. 545, 44 S.Ct. 628, 68 L.Ed. 1174 (1924),] which held that, under the Enforcement Clause of the Eighteenth Amendment, Congress could prohibit the prescription of intoxicating malt liquor for medicinal purposes even though the Amendment itself only prohibited the manufacture and sale of intoxicating liquors for beverage purposes. Cf. also the settled principle applied in the Shreveport Case (Houston, E. & W.T.R. Co. v. United States, 234 U.S. 342, 34 S.Ct. 833, 58 L.Ed. 1341), and expressed in United States v. Darby, 312 U.S. 100, 118, 61 S.Ct. 451, 459, 85 L.Ed. 609, that the power of Congress to regulate interstate commerce "extends to those activities intrastate which so affect interstate commerce or the exercise of the power of Congress over it as to make regulation of them appropriate means to the attainment of a legitimate end * * *." Accord, Heart of Atlanta Motel v. United States, 379 U.S. 241, 258, 85 S.Ct. 348, 358, 13 L.Ed.2d 258.

14. [The Court quoted the sponsor's statement that "[m]ore precious even than the forms of government are the mental qualities of our race" which must be preserved by limiting new immigrants' right to vote.]

to read English for those to whom Spanish-language newspapers and Spanish-language radio and television programs are available to inform them of election issues and governmental affairs.[16] Since Congress undertook to legislate so as to preclude the enforcement of the state law, and did so in the context of a general appraisal of literacy requirements for voting, see State of South Carolina v. Katzenbach, supra, to which it brought a specially informed legislative competence,[17] it was Congress' prerogative to weigh these competing considerations. Here again, it is enough that we perceive a basis upon which Congress might predicate a judgment that the application of New York's English literacy requirement to deny the right to vote to a person with a sixth grade education in Puerto Rican schools in which the language of instruction was other than English constituted an invidious discrimination in violation of the Equal Protection Clause.

There remains the question whether the congressional remedies adopted in § 4(e) constitute means which are not prohibited by, but are consistent "with the letter and spirit of the constitution." [The only argument against the statute in this regard is that it is underinclusive for failing to protect even more non-English speakers. We held in South Carolina v. Katzenbach that such underinclusiveness is permissible. More exacting scrutiny is unnecessary since this statute does not deny rights; it expands them. As we have said before,] "reform may take one step at a time, addressing itself to the phase of the problem which seems most acute to the legislative mind," Williamson v. Lee Optical Co., 348 U.S. 483, 489, 75 S.Ct. 461, 465, 99 L.Ed. 563.

Guided by these principles, we are satisfied that appellees' challenge to this limitation in § 4(e) is without merit. In the context of the case before us, the congressional choice to limit the relief effected in § 4(e) may, for example, reflect Congress' greater familiarity with the quality of instruction in American-flag schools, a recognition of the unique historic relationship between the Congress and the Commonwealth of Puerto Rico, an awareness of the Federal Government's acceptance of the desirability of the use of Spanish as the language of instruction in Commonwealth schools, and the fact that Congress has fostered policies encouraging migration from the Commonwealth to the States. * * *

We therefore conclude that § 4(e), in the application challenged in this case, is appropriate legislation to enforce the Equal Protection Clause and that the judgment of the District Court must be and hereby is reversed.

---

16. See, e.g., 111 Cong.Rec. 11060–11061, 15666, 16235. The record in this case includes affidavits describing the nature of New York's two major Spanish-language newspapers, one daily and one weekly, and its three full-time Spanish-language radio stations and affidavits from those who have campaigned in Spanish-speaking areas.

17. See, e.g., 111 Cong.Rec. 11061 (Senator Long of Louisiana and Senator Young), 11064 (Senator Holland), drawing on their experience with voters literate in a language other than English. See also an affidavit from Representative Willis of Louisiana expressing the view that on the basis of his thirty years' personal experience in politics he has "formed a definite opinion that French-speaking voters who are illiterate in English generally have as clear a grasp of the issues and an understanding of the candidates, as do people who read and write the English language."

Reversed.

MR. JUSTICE DOUGLAS joins the Court's opinion except for the discussion of the question whether the congressional remedies adopted in § 4(e) constitute means which are not prohibited by, but are consistent with "the letter and spirit of the constitution." On that question, he reserves judgment until such time as it is presented by a member of the class against which that particular discrimination is directed.

MR. JUSTICE HARLAN, whom MR. JUSTICE STEWART joins, dissenting.

* * *

* * * Although § 5 most certainly does give to the Congress wide powers in the field of devising remedial legislation to effectuate the Amendment's prohibition on arbitrary state action, I believe the Court has confused the issue of how much enforcement power Congress possesses under § 5 with the distinct issue of what questions are appropriate for congressional determination and what questions are essentially judicial in nature.

When recognized state violations of federal constitutional standards have occurred, Congress is of course empowered by § 5 to take appropriate remedial measures to redress and prevent the wrongs. But it is a judicial question whether the condition with which Congress has thus sought to deal is in truth an infringement of the Constitution, something that is the necessary prerequisite to bringing the § 5 power into play at all. [Since English literacy requirements do not violate the Constitution, I do not see how there can be "remedial" power under § 5.]

* * * In State of South Carolina v. Katzenbach, decided earlier this Term, we held certain remedial sections of this Voting Rights Act of 1965 constitutional under the Fifteenth Amendment, which is directed against deprivations of the right to vote on account of race. In enacting those sections of the Voting Rights Act the Congress made a detailed investigation of various state practices that had been used to deprive Negroes of the franchise. [Courts had declared the practices covered by the Act to be constitutional violations, and there was voluminous evidence before Congress that these and more violations existed and needed an effective remedy.]

Section 4(e), however, presents a significantly different type of congressional enactment. The question here is not whether the statute is appropriate remedial legislation to cure an established violation of a constitutional command, but whether there has in fact been an infringement of that constitutional command[.] That question is one for the judicial branch ultimately to determine. * * * In effect the Court reads § 5 of the Fourteenth Amendment as giving Congress the power to define the *substantive* scope of the Amendment. * * *

I do not mean to suggest in what has been said that a legislative judgment of the type incorporated in § 4(e) is without any force whatsoever. Decisions on questions of equal protection and due process are based not on abstract logic, but on empirical foundations. To the extent "legislative facts" are relevant to a judicial determination, Congress is well equipped to investigate them, and such determinations are of course entitled to due respect. In State of South Carolina v. Katzenbach, supra, such legislative findings were made to show that racial discrimination in voting was actually occurring. Similarly, in Heart of Atlanta Motel, Inc. v. United States, [Chapter 5 supra], and Katzenbach v. McClung, [Chapter 5 supra], this Court upheld Title II of the Civil Rights Act of 1964 under the Commerce Clause. There again the congressional determination that racial discrimination in a clearly defined group of public accommodations did effectively impede interstate commerce was based on "voluminous testimony," which had been put before the Congress and in the context of which it passed remedial legislation.

But no such factual data provide a legislative record supporting § 4(e)[9] by way of showing that Spanish-speaking citizens are fully as capable of making informed decisions in a New York election as are English-speaking citizens. Nor was there any showing whatever to support the Court's alternative argument that § 4(e) should be viewed as but a remedial measure designed to cure or assure against unconstitutional discrimination of other varieties, e.g., in "public schools, public housing and law enforcement," to which Puerto Rican minorities might be subject in such communities as New York. There is simply no legislative record supporting such hypothesized discrimination of the sort we have hitherto insisted upon when congressional power is brought to bear on constitutionally reserved state concerns. See Heart of Atlanta Motel, supra; State of South Carolina v. Katzenbach, supra.

* * *

To deny the effectiveness of this congressional enactment is not of course to disparage Congress' exertion of authority in the field of civil rights; it is simply to recognize that the Legislative Branch like the other branches of federal authority is subject to the governmental boundaries set by the Constitution. * * *

NOTE ON CONGRESSIONAL POWER TO CHANGE THE SUBSTANTIVE SCOPE OF THE CONSTITUTION

1.   Insofar as *Morgan* holds that Congress enacted § 4(e) to cure discrimination in public schools, housing, and law enforcement, it is of the same "remedial" genre as South Carolina v. Katzenbach, the previous principal case, and holds that the Fourteenth Amendment like the Fifteenth gives Congress "necessary and proper" power to cure violations of the Equal Protection Clause.[1]

---

9. There were no committee hearings or reports referring to this section, which was introduced from the floor during debate on the full Voting Rights Act. See 111 Cong.Rec. 11027, 15666, 16234.

1. The means approved in *South Carolina* involved an immediate connection between harm and cure: discriminatory testing met by suspension of tests and evasion of decrees through

(a) The *McCulloch* test applicable to Congressional enactments mimics the rational basis test used for low-level review of state legislation under the Equal Protection and Due Process Clauses, as seen in the Court's cross citation to such cases in the *South Carolina* and *Morgan* opinions. Such review has been traditionally viewed as toothless, primarily because it yields to high degrees of overinclusiveness and underinclusiveness. See John Nowak and Ronald Rotunda, CONSTITUTIONAL LAW §§ 14.2–14.3 (8th ed. 2009). Does this level of review give Congress ample remedial power to deal with any problem that has been declared a constitutional violation?

(b) Does the test, as applied in *Morgan*, give Congress too much power? Notice how deferential the review is, for the Court does not ask whether Congress actually thought that there was governmental discrimination against Puerto Ricans in New York or that Congress actually thought that voting might cure any such violations if they existed. Instead, the Court assumes that Congress wants these goals and has deliberately chosen these statutory means to achieve those goals.[2] Does this not make all legislation automatically valid? Will not reviewing courts always think of rational explanations for what Congress has done, not irrational explanations? Does not this level of review allow Congress to hide its real—perhaps unconstitutional—motives? See Fitzgerald v. Racing Ass'n of Central Iowa, 539 U.S. 103, 123 S.Ct. 2156, 156 L.Ed.2d 97 (2003) (widely varying tax rates upheld after asking if "there is a plausible policy reason for the classification [and] the legislative facts on which the classification is apparently based rationally may have been considered to be true by the governmental decisionmaker"). What do you think really motivated Congress to enfranchise the affected Puerto Ricans living in New York?

(c) Review the *Northwest Austin* case, discussed in ¶ 5 of the preceding Note (constitutional limits of even remedial legislation). Does it signal that a Court majority is now prepared to end the deferential review of statutes said to be "remedial"?

2. It is *Morgan*'s second rationale for upholding § 4(e) that has created the most debate. Under this part of the Court's opinion, Justice Brennan

---

changes in laws met by requiring preclearance of changes. Is the remedy in *Morgan* more removed? Too much removed? Obvious "bootstrapping"? Cf. United States v. Darby, 312 U.S. 100, 119–22, 61 S.Ct. 451, 459–61, 85 L.Ed. 609 (1941) (power to prohibit interstate shipment gives power to control intrastate production which may be shipped).

How far may *Morgan*'s remedial rationale be pushed? Can Congress appoint a Puerto Rican mayor for the City of New York in order to cure discrimination in public housing, schools, and law enforcement? Compare Justice Black's dissenting opinion in *South Carolina* and paragraph 4 of the preceding Note. Should Congress be required to choose "less drastic" means or "substantially related" means, rather than merely "rational" means, when it seeks to cure Fourteenth Amendment violations? But would that not emasculate Congressional power? Compare Kramer v. Union Free School Dist. No. 15, 395 U.S. 621, 89 S.Ct. 1886, 23 L.Ed.2d 583 (1969), with McDonald v. Board of Election Commissioners, 394 U.S. 802, 89 S.Ct. 1404, 22 L.Ed.2d 739 (1969).

2. Note Justice Brennan's choice of words: § 4(e) "may be viewed" as a remedy for such other discrimination. Such language was characteristic of the cases conjuring state goals to satisfy the rational basis test under equal protection, a practice later avoided in some cases. It was a topic of some debate in the late 1960s and early 1970s. See G. Gunther, *Forward—In Search of Evolving Doctrine on a Changing Court: A Model for a Newer Equal Protection*, 86 HARV. L. REV. 1 (1972). Should such articulation of goals also be required of Congress when it exercises its "necessary and proper" powers?

notes that, even apart from the rationale of curing assumed discrimination against Puerto Ricans in provision of government services, § 4(e) may be sustained as an exercise of a Congressional power to make the determination as to whether New York's reasons for its English literacy requirement justifies the harm it causes Puerto Rican residents. The Court says that it need not find the New York law unconstitutional; it need only ask whether Congress might rationally have thought so. It is this aspect of *Morgan* which led Justice Harlan to charge that the majority had confused the issues of what is a violation (a question for the Court) with the question of what are proper remedies for such violations (a question for Congress).[3] Do you read Justice Brennan's opinion on this issue as holding that Congress has power under § 5 to change the substantive scope of the Fourteenth Amendment?

(a) Justice Brennan's opinion for the Court turns largely on Congress' ability as fact-finder, its "specially informed legislative competence." Is Justice Brennan's argument a bit hollow, considering that Congress held no hearings and made no factual findings? Or is he emphasizing a different kind of competence—a special normative competence based on Congress' political acumen? But is not that judgment, even if political, the type of "political" judgment that is for courts under *Marbury v. Madison*? Does Justice Harlan deny Congress either a factfinding role or a normative role? But he sees the normative role as more restricted, does he not?

(b) Are judicial interpretations of the Equal Protection Clause not powerfully shaped by the Court's aversion to intruding into legislative concerns? Just as the political question and justiciability doctrines explicitly separate the Court from legislative policymaking, the rational basis test and middle-level scrutiny also appear to give great leeway to legislative judgments because the Court is unsure of both the state's true interest and its own ability to balance the competing policy interests when they are known. See Fitzgerald v. Racing Ass'n of Central Iowa, supra ("plausible" justifications acceptable because actual reasons for legislation may be complex and contradictory—just the type for legislators to forge compromises to serve); Railway Express Agency v. New York, 336 U.S. 106, 69 S.Ct. 463, 93 L.Ed. 533 (1949) (advertising bans and exemptions). If the Court waters down its constitutional tests because of institutional limitations on fact-finding and interest-balancing that are inherent in the Judicial Branch, should the Federal Legislative Branch which does not suffer those infirmities be precluded from more vigorously searching out and balancing competing interests? But does that give power to Congress to declare anything unconstitutional? Does strict scrutiny, as enforced by the Court, already protect citizens from dissembling legislatures? See City of Richmond v. J.A. Croson Co., Chapter 7D supra (strict scrutiny smokes out forbidden legislative motives).

(c) If the judiciary is less competent than legislative bodies in fact-finding and interest-balancing, to which legislative body should the Court defer—the state legislature or Congress? The latter because of the Supremacy Clause? But would that not greatly diminish state authority? Is the Court needed as a

---

3. How does New York's argument, adopted by Justice Harlan, differ from that offered by the state in *South Carolina*?

less well-qualified but nevertheless neutral arbiter between the competing politicians?

3. Is Justice Harlan's conception of the Supreme Court as ultimate arbiter of the Constitution—*Marbury v. Madison* and all that—a romantic view of a world that never was? The Court's jurisprudence has many areas in which doctrine has created a two-level Constitution, one level at which the Court enforces minimal norms and another level where Congress can legislate more specific norms that the Court itself would not adopt. See Nowak & Rotunda, supra, § 8.1 (dormant and active Commerce Clause cases); Prudential Ins. Co. v. Benjamin, 328 U.S. 408, 66 S.Ct. 1142, 90 L.Ed. 1342 (1946) (Congress may under commerce power authorize states to do what Court held beyond their power under the dormant Commerce Clause); Wickard v. Filburn, 317 U.S. 111, 63 S.Ct. 82, 87 L.Ed. 122 (1942) (economic conflicts at issue in Commerce Clause cases "are wisely left under our system [to the] more flexible and responsible legislative process [in Congress because they] rarely lend themselves to judicial resolution"). Are civil-rights issues different?

(a) See the cases cited in the Court's footnote 11. Also recall Jones v. Mayer Co. and the cases on §§ 1981 and 1982 in Chapter 2 supra. Under the Thirteenth Amendment the Court has allowed Congress wide leeway to define the "badges and incidents of slavery." Is that not the power to declare constitutional law and to make an Amendment more precise and detailed than the Court would interpret it? Can Jones v. Mayer Co. and the Thirteenth Amendment be distinguished because the issue covered there—racial slavery—is much narrower than those arising under the Fourteenth—equal protection and due process on all topics? But see the Note on Interpretation of the Thirteenth Amendment, Chapter 2A supra (noting possible breadth in interpreting power over slavery).

(b) Must not Brennan's constitutional approach maintain the power of the Court to declare constitutional *minimums* which Congress may not reduce? If Congress exercised its § 5 power to extend due process rights where the Court had previously held none to exist, would *Morgan* sanction the legislation? If it found that a right previously recognized was not so fundamental after all, could it overturn the Court's decision? See Saenz v. Roe, 526 U.S. 489, 119 S.Ct. 1518, 143 L.Ed.2d 689 (1999) (right to travel renders states' durational residency requirements for receipt of welfare payments unconstitutional and federal statute cannot authorize states to use them).

(c) Justice Brennan tries to allay readers' fears with footnote 10, often called the "ratchet footnote" because, like the tool of the same name, it permits turning in only one direction. Does it provide a satisfactory answer? If Congress can expand rights but not contract them, how are we to recognize what is an expansion and what is a contraction? Could Congress, for example, expand the Fourteenth Amendment by giving rights to fetuses?[4]

---

4. See the S. 158, 97th Cong., 1st Sess., 127 (1981) ("Human Life Statute"): "The Congress finds that the life of each human being begins at conception [and] Congress further finds that the Fourteenth Amendment to the Constitution of the United States protects all human beings. [On] the basis of these finds, and in the exercise of the powers of the Congress, including its power

4. In successive voting rights cases in the early 1970s the Court immediately signaled some reservations, treating the expansive second rationale in Katzenbach v. Morgan as a poor relative.

(a) In **Oregon v. Mitchell**, 400 U.S. 112, 91 S.Ct. 260, 27 L.Ed.2d 272 (1970), the Court considered Congress' extension of the Voting Rights Act to forbid age discrimination against would-be voters aged 18 to 20 in both federal and state elections. Justice Brennan again put forward the *Morgan* rationale, but it drew only four votes.[5] Justice Harlan presented a refined version of his dissent in *Morgan* which also stressed legislative history to show that the Fourteenth Amendment did not comprehend state suffrage laws. Justice Stewart (who dissented in *Morgan*), joined by Chief Justice Burger and Justice Blackmun, took the position that "neither the *Morgan* case, nor any other case upon which the Government relies, establishes [a] congressional power [to change the substantive scope of the Constitution], even assuming that all those cases were rightly decided." Justice Black, who had joined the majority in *Morgan,* held that so much power as Congress had under § 5 extended only to protecting against racial discrimination.[6]

(b) In **City of Rome v. United States**, 446 U.S. 156, 100 S.Ct. 1548, 64 L.Ed.2d 119 (1980), the Court rejected the city's argument that the preclearance provisions of the Voting Rights Act were unconstitutional. Section 5's "effects test," claimed the city, exceeded the Constitution's intent test, see City of Mobile v. Bolden, 446 U.S. 55, 100 S.Ct. 1490, 64 L.Ed.2d 47 (1980). Justice Marshall's opinion for the Court observed that the adoption of a statutory effects test, in the context of proved prior discrimination in the covered jurisdictions, comprised merely a remedy for such prior intentional discrimination. 446 U.S. at 181, 100 S.Ct. at 1563. Does *Rome* indicate that although the line between *South Carolina* and *Morgan* may be great as an intellectual matter, Congress can with creativity avoid the controversy?

(c) In its 1975 Amendments to the Voting Rights Act of 1969, Congress extended protection to "language minorities" who had previously suffered discrimination in voting, and it ordered that guilty covered jurisdictions provide voting materials in the language of "the applicable minority group." 42 U.S.C.A. § 1973(f). Is the provision constitutional? Would your answer change if you discovered that Congress had defined discrimination as failure to provide non-English language ballots to "language minorities"? See id., § 1973(f)(3). In 1982 Congress extended the Voting Rights Act into the twenty-first century and added a new provision that allowed nationwide

---

under section 5 of the Fourteenth Amendment to the Constitution of the United States, the Congress hereby recognizes that for the purpose of enforcing the obligation of the States under the Fourteenth amendment not to deprive persons of life without due process of law, each human life exists from conception, without regard to race, sex, age, health, defect, or condition of dependency, and for this purpose 'person' includes all human beings." See generally Stephen H. Galebach, *A Human Life Statute,* 7 HUMAN LIFE REV. 3 (1981).

5. Justice Brennan's opinion was joined by Justices White and Marshall. Justice Douglas wrote separately but relied on the same ground. Justice Brennan asserted that Congress might reasonably find that the reasons put forward by states did not justify denial of the vote to persons aged 18–20.

6. The Court divided equally on the ultimate issue of whether Congress could enfranchise 18-year-olds in both federal and state elections, with Justice Black breaking the tie by permitting Congress to set the standard for federal elections but not those of the states. Congress thereafter passed, and the states promptly ratified, the Twenty-sixth Amendment.

challenges to voting practices that had the "results" of discriminating against minorities. See Thornburg v. Gingles, section B of this Chapter, infra. Since the new provision extends nationwide, not simply to the jurisdictions having a history of discrimination, does it fall outside *Rome*'s rationale?

5. Whatever was left of *Morgan*'s second rationale was finally and definitively rejected by the Court in a case involving not voting but religious discrimination. That case considered the Religious Freedom Restoration Act (RFRA), a statute that attempted to overturn Supreme Court decisions that gave less protection under the Free Exercise Clause to religious adherents than they adherents wanted. By legislative declaration, it substituted the more protective "compelling state interest test."[7] When a church seeking exemption from some local zoning laws invoked the Act, the Supreme Court struck it down in **City of Boerne v. Flores**, 521 U.S. 507, 117 S.Ct. 2157, 138 L.Ed.2d 624 (1997) (6–3 vote), finding that it exceeded Congress' powers under § 5 of the Fourteenth Amendment. Justice Kennedy's majority opinion reviewed the voting cases discussed earlier in this Note, then continued, 521 U.S. at 519–29, 117 S.Ct. at 2164–68 (all brackets in original):

> "Congress' power under § 5 however, extends only to "enforc[ing]" the provisions of the Fourteenth Amendment. The Court has described this power as "remedial," South Carolina v. Katzenbach. The design of the Amendment and the text of § 5 are inconsistent with the suggestion that Congress has the power to decree the substance of the Fourteenth Amendment's restrictions on the States. Legislation which alters the meaning of the Free Exercise Clause cannot be said to be enforcing the Clause. Congress does not enforce a constitutional right by changing what the right is. It has been given the power "to enforce," not the power to determine what constitutes a constitutional violation. Were it not so, what Congress would be enforcing would no longer be, in any meaningful sense, the "provisions of [the Fourteenth Amendment]."

> "While the line between measures that remedy or prevent unconstitutional actions and measures that make a substantive change in the governing law is not easy to discern, and Congress must have wide latitude in determining where it lies, the distinction exists and must be observed. There must be a congruence and proportionality between the injury to be prevented or remedied and the means adopted to that end. Lacking such a connection, legislation may become substantive in operation and effect. History and our case law support drawing the distinction, one apparent from the text of the Amendment.

* * *

---

7. The statute, 42 U.S.C. § 2000bb, cited the Court's decision in Employment Division v. Smith, 494 U.S. 872, 110 S.Ct. 1595, 108 L.Ed.2d 876 (1990), in which, narrowly interpreting precedents requiring accommodation of religion, Justice Scalia's opinion had upheld general state anti-drug laws and has refused to require the state to accommodate the religious exercise of smoking peyote. The Court specifically rejected use of a "compelling state interest test" in such circumstances, but RFRA claimed to set that decision aside, finding that "the compelling interest test as set forth in prior Federal court rulings is a workable test for striking sensible balances between religious liberty and competing prior governmental interests" and providing that "Government shall not substantially burden a person's exercise of religion even if the burden results from a rule of general applicability."

"Any suggestion that Congress has a substantive, non-remedial power under the Fourteenth Amendment is not supported by our case law. In Oregon v. Mitchell, a majority of the Court concluded Congress had exceeded its enforcement powers by enacting legislation lowering the minimum age of voters from 21 to 18 in state and local elections. The five Members of the Court who reached this conclusion explained that the legislation intruded into an area reserved by the Constitution to the States. Four of these five were explicit in rejecting the position that § 5 endowed Congress with the power to establish the meaning of constitutional provisions.

"There is language in our opinion in Katzenbach v. Morgan which could be interpreted as acknowledging a power in Congress to enact legislation that expands the rights contained in § 1 of the Fourteenth Amendment. This is not a necessary interpretation, however, or even the best one. [*Morgan* can be sustained by reading it only to involve remedial legislation.]

"If Congress could define its own powers by altering the Fourteenth Amendment's meaning, no longer would the Constitution be "superior paramount law, unchangeable by ordinary means." It would be "on a level with ordinary legislative acts, and, like other acts, ... alterable when the legislature shall please to alter it." Marbury v. Madison. Under this approach, it is difficult to conceive of a principle that would limit congressional power."

(a) Turning to the issue of whether RFRA could be considered "remedial," the Court undertook an extensive review of the legislative record, 521 U.S. at 530, 117 S.Ct. at 2169: "A comparison between RFRA and the Voting Rights Act is instructive[, for in] contrast to the record which confronted Congress and the judiciary in the voting rights cases, RFRA's legislative record lacks examples of modern instances of generally applicable laws passed because of religious bigotry." The Court found this dispositive. Does this show that the modern Court has adopted Justice Harlan's position in *Morgan*, including his demand for extensive factfinding that will enable judicial review of whether a statute is truly remedial?[8]

(b) Subsequent cases have adopted the *Boerne* approach and applied it to other areas, including a statute that claimed to promote Due Process rights and one claiming expansion of Equal Protection coverage. See Florida Prepaid Postsecondary Education Expense Board v. College Savings Bank, 527 U.S. 627, 119 S.Ct. 2199, 144 L.Ed.2d 575 (no § 5 power to protect property interests in patents; no legislative record of state's failure to provide due process protection for such patents); Kimel v. Florida Board of Regents, 528 U.S. 62, 120 S.Ct. 631, 145 L.Ed.2d 522 (2000) (no Congressional power under

---

8. After the Court invalidated the RFRA Congress passed a narrower version that, serving political interests, provided limited protection for prisoner's religious rights and greater land use by churches. See Religious Land Use and Institutionalized Persons Act of 2000 (RLUIPA), 42 U.S.C. § 2000cc (citing Spending Clause and Commerce Clause powers). It has been upheld as essentially consistent with the Court's constitutional rulings. See Cutter v. Wilkinson, 544 U.S. 709, 125 S.Ct. 2113, 161 L.Ed.2d 1020 (2005). More recently, however, the Court has determined that the statute does not abrogate state sovereign immunity. See Sossamon v. Texas, ___ U.S. ___, 131 S.Ct. 1651, 179 L.Ed.2d 700 (2011).

§ 5 to increase demands on states regarding age discrimination in employment). Are the provisions of the Voting Rights Act that protect "language minorities," see ¶ 5(c) supra, now vulnerable? If Congress enacted legislation protecting the voting rights of disabled persons, would it be upheld under § 5?

6. In historical context, Justice Brennan's *Morgan* rationale seems remarkably similar to his position in United States v. Guest, where he stated that Congress should be allowed to go beyond the state-action limits of the Fourteenth Amendment to cover private persons as well. See Chapter 3 supra.

(a) Both *Morgan* and *Guest* were decided within ten weeks of each other in the spring of 1966, some two years before the Court would hold that Congress has power to reach beyond actual enslavement to solve modern social problems—caused by private actors—that are the remnants of slavery. See Jones v. Alfred H. Mayer Co., Chapter 2A supra. Were the cases an overresponse to their times or an experiment that failed? If the latter, why did it fail?

(b) In **United States v. Morrison**, 529 U.S. 598, 120 S.Ct. 1740, 146 L.Ed.2d 658 (2000), the Court rejected the *Guest* theory, and pairing it with *City of Boerne*, supra, means that *Morgan* and *Guest* both died within three years of each other after thirty years of near-dormancy. Why were the concepts so little used? Why did they finally die in the late Twentieth Century?

(c) The modern approaches used in *Boerne* and *Morrison* still leave some substantial congressional power to enact remedies for court-declared constitutional standards. In **Nevada Department of Human Resources v. Hibbs**, 538 U.S. 721, 123 S.Ct. 1972, 155 L.Ed.2d 953 (2003), involving the federal Family and Medical Leave Act's requirement for leave at the birth of a child, Chief Justice Rehnquist's majority opinion upheld the statute. The majority was persuaded that the long history of sex discrimination in state employment, especially the sex stereotypes created by state leave policies that applied only to women. justified the provision as a cure for the prior discrimination. Recall that *Morrison* struck down a remedy applied to private persons after a finding of state-sponsored discrimination. Is *Hibbs* adequate power for a hardworking Congress that is willing to make a record of prior discrimination against any high-scrutiny class?[9]

---

9. The Court has also held that Congress may legislate to protect "fundamental rights" protected by the Fourteenth Amendment. See Tennessee v. Lane, 541 U.S. 509, 124 S.Ct. 1978, 158 L.Ed.2d 820 (2004) (protect access to the courts for disabled persons). Does this give Congress some wider power in the area of voting? See Kramer v. Union Free School Dist. No. 15, 395 U.S. 621, 89 S.Ct. 1886, 23 L.Ed.2d 583 (1969) (right is to an equal vote, but that covers more than racial distinctions).

B. COVERAGE AND ENFORCEMENT— REGIONALLY PRECLEARED "EFFECTS," NATIONWIDE "RESULTS"

1. SECTION 5 AND "PRECLEARANCE"— INTENT AND EFFECTS

GEORGIA v. UNITED STATES

Supreme Court of the United States, 1973.
411 U.S. 526, 93 S.Ct. 1702, 36 L.Ed.2d 472.

MR. JUSTICE STEWART delivered the opinion of the Court.

The Attorney General of the United States brought this suit under § 12(d) of the Voting Rights Act of 1965 as amended, 42 U.S.C.A. § 1973j(d), to enjoin the State of Georgia from conducting elections for its House of Representatives under the 1972 legislative reapportionment law. A three-judge District Court in the Northern District of Georgia agreed that certain aspects of the reapportionment law came within the ambit of § 5 of the Act, 42 U.S.C.A. § 1973(c), and that the State, which is subject to the provisions of § 5,[1] had not obtained prior clearance from either the Attorney General or the District Court for the District of Columbia. Accordingly, and without reaching the question whether the reapportionment plan had the purpose or effect of "denying or abridging the right to vote on account of race or color," 42 U.S.C.A. § 1973c, the District Court issued the requested injunction. The State brought this appeal. We noted probable jurisdiction, staying enforcement of the District Court judgment pending disposition of the appeal.

Following the 1970 Census, the Georgia Legislature set out to reapportion its State House of Representatives, State Senate, and federal congressional electoral districts. [Georgia submitted its reapportionment plan to the Attorney General, pursuant to § 5, but he objected to several of its features.] The objection letter cited the combination of multimember districts, numbered posts, majority run-off elections, and the extensive departure from the State's prior policy of adhering to county lines. On the basis of these changes, plus particular changes in the structure of potential black majority single-member districts, the Attorney General was "unable to conclude that the plan does not have a discriminatory racial effect on voting." The letter stated that the Attorney General therefore felt obligated to "interpose an objection to changes submitted by these reapportionment plans."

The State Legislature immediately enacted a new reapportionment plan and repealed its predecessor. [The Attorney General rejected this plan for similar reasons, noting that while he did not specifically find a discriminatory purpose or effect, he was unable to conclude, based on the evidence submitted, that the plan would not have such a purpose or effect.]

---

1. A State is subject to § 5 if it qualifies under § 4(b), * * *. It is stipulated that Georgia is covered under § 4(b).

When the Georgia Legislature resolved that it would take no further steps to enact a new plan, the Attorney General brought the present lawsuit.

The State of Georgia claims that § 5 is inapplicable to the 1972 House plan, both because the Act does not reach "reapportionment" and because the 1972 plan does not constitute a change from procedures "in force or effect on November 1, 1964." If applicable, the Act is claimed to be unconstitutional as applied. The State also challenges two aspects of the Attorney General's conduct of the § 5 objection procedure, claiming, first, that the Attorney General cannot object to a state plan without finding that it in fact has a discriminatory purpose or effect, and, second, that the Attorney General's objection to the 1971 plan was not made within the 60–day time period allowed for objection under the Act.

I

Despite the fact that multimember districts, numbered posts, and a majority runoff requirement were features of Georgia election law prior to November 1, 1964, the changes that followed from the 1972 reapportionment are plainly sufficient to invoke § 5 if that section of the Act reaches the substance of those changes. Section 5 is not concerned with a simple inventory of voting procedures, but rather with the reality of changed practices as they affect Negro voters. It seems clear that the extensive reorganization of voting districts and the creation of multimember districts in place of single-member districts in certain areas amounted to substantial departures from the electoral state of things under previous law. The real question is whether the substance of these changes undertaken as part of the state reapportionment are "standards, practices, or procedures with respect to voting" within the meaning of § 5.

* * *

The applicability of § 5 to election law changes such as those enacted by Georgia in its 1972 plan was all but conclusively established by the opinion of this Court in Allen v. State Board of Elections, 393 U.S. 544, 89 S.Ct. 817, 22 L.Ed.2d 1. The *Allen* opinion, dealing with four companion cases, held that § 5 applied to a broad range of voting law changes, and was constitutional as applied. With respect to the reach of § 5, we held that "[t]he legislative history on the whole supports the view that Congress intended to reach any state enactment which altered the election law of a covered State in even a minor way." Id. at 566, 89 S.Ct., at 832. One of the companion cases, Fairley v. Patterson, involved a claim that a change from district to at-large voting for county supervisor was a change in a "standard, practice, or procedure with respect to voting." The challenged procedure was held to be covered by § 5. We noted that "[t]he right to vote can be affected by a dilution of voting power as well as by an absolute prohibition on casting a ballot. See Reynolds v. Sims, 377 U.S. 533, 555, 84 S.Ct. 1362, 1378, 12 L.Ed.2d 506 (1964)." Id. at 569, 89 S.Ct., at 833. In holding that § 5 reached voting law changes that threatened to dilute Negro voting power, and in citing Reynolds v. Sims, we implicitly recognized the applicability of § 5 to similar but more sweeping election law changes arising from the reapportionment of state legislatures. 393

U.S. at 565–66, 583–86, 89 S.Ct., at 831–832, 840–842 (Harlan, J., concurring and dissenting).

Had Congress disagreed with the interpretation of § 5 in *Allen,* it had ample opportunity to amend the statute. After extensive deliberations in 1970 on bills to extend the Voting Rights Act, during which the *Allen* case was repeatedly discussed, the Act was extended for five years, without any substantive modification of § 5. Pub.L. 91–285, 84 Stat. 314, 315. We can only conclude, then, that *Allen* correctly interpreted the congressional design when it held that "the Act gives a broad interpretation to the right to vote, recognizing that voting includes 'all action necessary to make a vote effective.' "

Another measure of the decisiveness with which *Allen* controls the present case is the actual practice of covered States since the *Allen* case was decided. Georgia, for example, submitted its 1971 plan to the Attorney General because it clearly believed that plan was covered by § 5. * * *

In the present posture of this case, the question is not whether the redistricting of the Georgia House, including extensive shifts from single-member to multimember districts, in fact had a racially discriminatory purpose or effect. The question, rather, is whether such changes have the potential for diluting the value of the Negro vote and are within the definitional terms of § 5. It is beyond doubt that such a potential exists, cf. Whitcomb v. Chavis, 403 U.S. 124, 141–44, 91 S.Ct. 1858, 1867–1869, 29 L.Ed.2d 363. In view of the teaching of *Allen,* reaffirmed in Perkins v. Matthews, 400 U.S. 379, 91 S.Ct. 431, 27 L.Ed.2d 476, we hold that the District Court was correct in deciding that the changes enacted in the 1972 reapportionment plan for the Georgia House of Representatives were within the ambit of § 5 of the Voting Rights Act. And for the reasons stated at length in South Carolina v. Katzenbach, 383 U.S. at 308–337, 86 S.Ct., at 808–823, we reaffirm the Act is a permissible exercise of congressional power under § 2 of the Fifteenth Amendment.

II

By way of implementing the performance of his obligation to pass on state submissions under § 5, the Attorney General has promulgated and published in the Federal Register certain administrative regulations, 28 CFR Part 51[, as authorized by 5 U.S.C.A. § 301, the statute generally conferring power on department heads to make in-house rules.]

In 28 CFR 51.19, the Attorney General has set forth the standards to be employed in deciding whether or not to object to a state submission. The regulation states that the burden of proof is on the submitting party, and that the Attorney General will refrain from objecting only if his review of the material submitted satisfies him that the proposed change does not have a racially discriminatory purpose or effect. * * *

* * * [T]he appellants in effect attack the legitimacy of the regulation described above in contending that the Attorney General is without power

to object unless he has actually found that the changes contained in a submission have a discriminatory purpose or effect.

* * *

It is well established that in a declaratory judgment action under § 5, the plaintiff State has the burden of proof.[9] What the Attorney General's regulations do is to place the same burden on the submitting party in a § 5 objection procedure. Though the choice of language in the objection letter sent to the State of Georgia was not a model of precision, in the context of the promulgated regulations the letter surely notified the State with sufficient clarity that it had not sustained its burden of proving that the proposed changes were free of a racially discriminatory effect. It is not necessary to hold that this allocation of the burden of proof by the Attorney General was his only possible choice under the Act, in order to find it a reasonable means of administering his § 5 obligation. Any less stringent standard might well have rendered the formal declaratory judgment procedure a dead letter by making available to covered States a far smoother path to clearance. The Attorney General's choice of a proof standard was thus at least reasonable and consistent with the Act, and we hold that his objection pursuant to that standard was lawful and effective.

* * *

For the foregoing reasons, the judgment of the District Court is affirmed. Since, however, elections were conducted under the disputed 1972 plan by reason of this Court's stay order, it would be inequitable to require new elections at this time.

The case is remanded to the District Court with instructions that any future elections under the Georgia House reapportionment plan be enjoined unless and until the State, pursuant to § 5 of the Voting Rights Act, tenders to the Attorney General a plan to which he does not object, or obtains a favorable declaratory judgment from the District Court for the District of Columbia.

Affirmed and remanded with instructions.

MR. CHIEF JUSTICE BURGER, concurring in the result. [Omitted]

MR. JUSTICE WHITE, with whom MR. JUSTICE POWELL and MR. JUSTICE REHNQUIST join, dissenting.

* * *

I agree that in the light of our prior cases and congressional reenactment of § 5, that section must be held to reach state reapportionment statutes. Contrary to the Court, however, it is my view that the Attorney

---

9. The very effect of § 5 was to shift the burden of proof with respect to racial discrimination in voting. Rather than requiring affected parties to bring suit to challenge every changed voting practice, States subject to § 5 were required to obtain prior clearance before proposed changes could be put into effect. The burden of proof is on "the areas seeking relief." South Carolina v. Katzenbach, 383 U.S. 301, 335, 86 S.Ct. 803, 822, 15 L.Ed.2d 769.

General did not interpose an objection contemplated by § 5 and that there was therefore no barrier to the March 9 reapportionment going into effect.

* * *

* * * [I]t is not untoward to insist that the Attorney General not object to the implementation of the change until and unless he has reason to believe that the amendment has the prohibited purpose or effect. He should not be able to object by simply saying that he cannot make up his mind or that the evidence is in equipoise.

MR. JUSTICE POWELL, dissenting.

* * * It is indeed a serious intrusion, incompatible with the basic structure of our system, for federal authorities to compel a State to submit its legislation for *advance* review. As a minimum, assuming the constitutionality of the Act, the Attorney General should be required to comply with it explicitly and to invoke its provisions only when he is able to make an affirmative finding rather than an ambivalent one.

NOTE ON STRICT ENFORCEMENT OF THE PRECLEARANCE REQUIREMENT

1. The vast array of state organs that use or regulate voting for participation in government has created some interesting questions regarding which entities of government must comply with § 5. The Court has strictly enforced the preclearance test.

(a) In **United States v. Board of Comm'rs of Sheffield**, 435 U.S. 110, 98 S.Ct. 965, 55 L.Ed.2d 148 (1978), the city claimed that it was not covered by § 5 because it did not register voters—that was done by the county. Justice Brennan's majority opinion rejected the argument, holding the city covered because it was located within a jurisdiction (Alabama) which was itself covered. Is the result compelled by the wording of the coverage formula in § 4(b)? By the practical consideration that a contrary rule would allow a covered jurisdiction to "achieve through its instrumentalities what it could not do itself without preclearance"? 435 U.S. at 139, 98 S.Ct. at 983 (Powell, J., concurring).

(b) In **Lopez v. Monterey County**, 525 U.S. 266, 119 S.Ct. 693, 142 L.Ed.2d 728 (1999), the local government was a covered entity under § 5, but the entire state was not. The state made changes in voting practices that the local government was then required to implement. The Court held the changes subject to preclearance when implemented. How is this case different from *Sheffield*? Are not the concerns with evasion quite different?

(c) Consider other possible scenarios. If the entity sued is a school board or other special body rather than a general governmental unit, does *Sheffield* apply? See Dougherty County, Georgia, Bd. of Educ. v. White, 439 U.S. 32, 99 S.Ct. 368, 58 L.Ed.2d 269 (1978) (preclearance of school board rule requiring employee running for public office to take unpaid leave). Are state judicial elections covered by § 5? See Clark v. Roemer, 500 U.S. 646, 111 S.Ct. 2096, 114 L.Ed.2d 691 (1991). Are political parties covered in the creation of their party voting rules? See Morse v. Republican Party of Virginia, 517 U.S. 186, 116 S.Ct. 1186, 134 L.Ed.2d 347 (1996).

2. Just as the Court has liberally construed what jurisdictions are covered by the 1965 Act, it has also, as the *Georgia* case illustrates, consistently required that even minor changes in election rules must be submitted for preclearance if they "have the potential for diluting" black voting rights, a standard which in practice requires submission of any rule change even tangentially related to voting. See Dougherty County, Georgia, Bd. of Educ. v. White, supra.

(a) Why has the Court so consistently and forcefully enforced the preclearance requirement? How great is the intrusion into state interests: does the preclearance requirement invalidate state practices or simply require that they be suspended and scrutinized? Was that the hidden question in *Georgia*?

(b) If you look upon preclearance as a significant federal intrusion, would you not want to tighten the standards by which the Attorney General must review § 5 submissions so that actual disapprovals after review are fewer? Does that not account for the dissenters' position in *Georgia*?

(c) Do you agree with the Court's decision in *Georgia* to refuse to require new elections? Is that decision consistent with the otherwise strict enforcement of § 5? Should the Court have stayed the lower court's injunction against elections? Does the Court's action not sanction a violation of § 5? See Berry v. Doles, 438 U.S. 190, 98 S.Ct. 2692, 57 L.Ed.2d 693 (1978).

3. In **Connor v. Johnson**, 402 U.S. 690, 691, 91 S.Ct. 1760, 1761–62, 29 L.Ed.2d 268 (1971), the Court summarily held that a reapportionment plan adopted by decree of a federal district court in litigation arising under the Fourteenth Amendment and Reynolds v. Sims, 377 U.S. 533, 84 S.Ct. 1362, 12 L.Ed.2d 506 (1964), "is not within the reach of Section 5 of the Voting Rights Act" and need not be submitted for preclearance under § 5. Why? Because federal courts are not covered entities of a state?

(a) When a federal court finds a constitutional violation under *Reynolds*'s "one person—one vote" rule, it proceeds to, as required, work with state legislators in crafting an acceptable plan. Should it review the offered plan under § 5 to ensure that it does not have a discriminatory effect? Should it do so if the court created the plan without suggestions from state legislators? See Abrams v. Johnson, 521 U.S. 74, 117 S.Ct. 1925, 138 L.Ed.2d 285 (1997) (review plan under § 5).

(b) Is *Connor*'s impact only on venue—it decides which federal district court will review a plan for validity under § 5? Does that violate the Act's goal of building an expertise about voting cases in the rusted federal courts in the nation's capital?

4. The bailout provision—the mechanism by which jurisdictions may seek relief from compliance with § 5—is worded slightly differently from the coverage formula, but the Court has interpreted it to have a congruent scope. In **Northwest Austin Mun. Utility Dist. No. One v. Holder**, ___ U.S. ___, 129 S.Ct. 2504, 174 L.Ed.2d 140 (2009), the Court pointedly noted that it had stretched the interpretation of covered entities in the *Sheffield* case and proceeded to determine that any entity individually covered could also seek an

individual bailout. Together with some technical changes adopted in 1982, this means that local governments, even those within wholly covered states, can seek to bailout for purposes of submitting their local changes, and several have done so. See Voting Rights Act: Section 5 of the Act–History, Scope, and Purpose: Hearing Before the Subcommittee on the Constitution of the House Committee on the Judiciary, 109th Cong., 1st Sess., 2599–2834 (2005) (bailouts listed with details).

5. The Court's decision in *Georgia* and this Note deal primarily with the question of what must be precleared (and the connection between covered jurisdictions and those that may seek bailouts), with the Court only briefly touching the issue of the standard by which the submitted issue will be judged. That issue is discussed in greater detail in the case and Note which follow.

CITY OF RICHMOND, VIRGINIA v. UNITED STATES

Supreme Court of the United States, 1975.
422 U.S. 358, 95 S.Ct. 2296, 45 L.Ed.2d 245.

MR. JUSTICE WHITE delivered the opinion of the Court.

Under § 5 of the Voting Rights Act of 1965, a State or subdivision thereof subject to the Act may not enforce any change in "any voting qualification or prerequisite to voting" unless such change has either been approved by the Attorney General or that officer has failed to act within 60 days after submission to him, or unless in a suit brought by such State or subdivision the United States District Court for the District of Columbia has issued its declaratory judgment that such change "does not have the purpose and will not have the effect of denying or abridging the right to vote on account of race or color * * *." Perkins v. Matthews, 400 U.S. 379, 91 S.Ct. 431, 27 L.Ed.2d 476 (1971), held that § 5 reaches the extension of a city's boundaries through the process of annexation. Here, the city of Richmond annexed land formerly in Chesterfield County, and the issue is whether the city in its declaratory judgment action brought in the District Court for the District of Columbia has carried its burden of proof of demonstrating that the annexation had neither the purpose nor the effect of denying or abridging the right to vote of the Richmond Negro community on account of its race or color.

I

[The 1969 annexation of unincorporated land in Chesterfield County, overwhelmingly populated by whites, changed the City from 52% blacks to 42% blacks. Black representation, as measured by election of candidates supported by Crusade for Voters of Richmond, a black civic organization, was unchanged, three of nine on the city council in both the 1968 and 1970 elections, under the existing system of "at-large" districts.]

Shortly thereafter, City of Petersburg v. United States, 354 F.Supp. 1021 (1972), was decided by the United States District Court for the District of Columbia. There, the District Court held invalid an annexation by a Virginia city, where at-large council elections were the rule both before and after the annexation, but indicated that approval could be had "on the condition that modifications calculated to neutralize to the extent possible any adverse effect upon the political participation of black voters are adopted, i.e., that the plaintiff shift from an at-large to a ward system of electing its city councilmen." Id. at 1031. We affirmed that judgment. 410 U.S. 962, 93 S.Ct. 1441, 35 L.Ed.2d 698 (1973).

Thereafter, Richmond developed and submitted to the Attorney General various plans for establishing councilmanic districts in the city. With some modifications, to which the city council agreed, the Attorney General indicated approval of one of these plans. This was a nine-ward proposal under which four of the wards would have substantial black majorities, four wards substantial white majorities, and the ninth a racial division of approximately 59% white and 41% black. The city and the Attorney General submitted this plan to the District Court for the District of Columbia in the form of a consent judgment. The intervenors opposed it, and the District Court referred the case to a Special Master[, who ruled against the City.]

The District Court, 376 F.Supp. 1344 (1974), essentially accepted the findings and conclusions of the Special Master except for his recommendation with respect to deannexation. Based on the Special Master's findings the District Court concluded that the city's "1970 changes in its election practices following upon the annexation were discriminatory in purpose and effect and thus violative of Section 5's substantive standards as well as the section's procedural command that prior approval be obtained from the Attorney General or this court." Id. at 1352. The District Court went on to hold that the invidious racial purpose underlying the annexation had not been eliminated since no "objectively verifiable, legitimate purpose for annexation" had been shown and since the ward plan does not effectively eliminate or sufficiently compensate for the dilution of the black voting power resulting from the annexation. Id. at 1353–1354. Furthermore, in fashioning the ward system, the city had not, the court held, minimized the dilution of black voting power to the greatest possible extent, relying for this conclusion on another ward plan presented by intervenors which would have improved the chance that Negroes would control five out of the nine wards. The annexation could not be approved, therefore, because it also had the forbidden effect of denying the right to vote of the Negro community in Richmond.

* * *

II

We deal first with whether the annexation involved here had the effect of denying or abridging the right to vote within the contemplation of § 5 of the Voting Rights Act.

Perkins v. Matthews, supra, held that changes in city boundaries by annexation have sufficient potential for denying or abridging the right to vote on account of race or color that prior to becoming effective they must have the administrative or judicial approval required by § 5. But it would be difficult to conceive of any annexation that would not change a city's racial composition at least to some extent; and we did not hold in *Perkins* that every annexation effecting a reduction in the percentage of Negroes in the city's population is prohibited by § 5. [*Perkins* required preclearance; we deal here with the different issue of what answer should be given when that preclearance review is conducted.]

In City of Petersburg v. United States, supra, the city sought a declaratory judgment that a proposed annexation satisfied the standards of § 5. Councilmen were elected at large; Negroes made up more than half the population, but less than half the voters; and the area to be annexed contained a heavy white majority. A three-judge District Court for the District of Columbia, although finding no evidence of a racially discriminatory purpose, held that in the context of at-large elections, the annexation would have the effect of denying the right to vote because it would create or perpetuate a white majority in the city and, positing racial voting which was found to be prevalent, it would enhance the power of the white majority totally to exclude Negroes from the city council. The court held, however, that a reduction of a racial group's relative political strength in the community does not always deny or abridge the right to vote within the meaning of § 5:

> "If the view of the *Diamond* intervenors concerning what constitutes a denial or abridgment in annexation cases were to prevail, no court could ever approve any annexation in areas covered by the Voting Rights Act if there were a history of racial bloc-voting in local elections for any office and if the racial balance were to shift in even the smallest degree as a result of the annexation. It would not matter that the annexation was essential for the continued economic health of a municipality or that it was favored by citizens of all races; because if the demographic makeup of the surrounding areas were such that any annexation would produce a shift of majority strength from one race to another, a court would be required to disapprove it without even considering any other evidence, and the municipality would be effectively locked into its original boundaries. This Court cannot agree that this was the intent of Congress when it enacted the Voting Rights Act." 354 F.Supp. at 1030 (footnote omitted).

The court went on to hold that the effect on the right to vote forbidden by § 5, which had been found to exist in the case, could be cured by a ward plan for electing councilmen in the enlarged city:

> "The Court concludes then, that this annexation, insofar as it is a mere boundary change and not an expansion of an at-large system, is not the kind of discriminatory change which Congress sought to prevent; but it also concludes, in accordance with the Attorney General's findings, that this annexation can be approved only on the condition that modifications calculated to neutralize to the extent

possible any adverse effect upon the political participation of black voters are adopted, i.e., that the plaintiff shift from an at-large to a ward system of electing its city councilmen." Id. at 1031.

* * *

Petersburg was correctly decided. On the facts there presented, the annexation of an area with a white majority, combined with at-large councilmanic elections and racial voting, created or enhanced the power of the white majority to exclude Negroes totally from participation in the governing of the city through membership on the city council. We agreed, however, that that consequence would be satisfactorily obviated if at-large elections were replaced by a ward system of choosing councilmen. It is our view that a fairly designed ward plan in such circumstances would not only prevent the total exclusion of Negroes from membership on the council but would afford them representation reasonably equivalent to their political strength in the enlarged community.

We cannot accept the position that such a single-member ward system would nevertheless have the effect of denying or abridging the right to vote because Negroes would constitute a lesser proportion of the population after the annexation than before and, given racial bloc voting, would have fewer seats on the city council. If a city having a ward system for the election of a nine-man council annexes a largely white area, the wards are fairly redrawn, and as a result Negroes have only two rather than the four seats they had before, these facts alone do not demonstrate that the annexation has the effect of denying or abridging the right to vote. As long as the ward system fairly reflects the strength of the Negro community as it exists after the annexation, we cannot hold, without more specific legislative directions, that such an annexation is nevertheless barred by § 5. It is true that the black community, if there is racial bloc voting, will command fewer seats on the city council; and the annexation will have effected a decline in the Negroes' relative influence in the city. But a different city council and an enlarged city are involved after the annexation. Furthermore, Negro power in the new city is not undervalued, and Negroes will not be underrepresented on the council.

As long as this is true, we cannot hold that the effect of the annexation is to deny or abridge the right to vote. To hold otherwise would be either to forbid all such annexations or to require, as the price for approval of the annexation, that the black community be assigned the same proportion of council seats as before, hence perhaps permanently overrepresenting them and underrepresenting other elements in the community, including the nonblack citizens in the annexed area. We are unwilling to hold that Congress intended either consequence in enacting § 5.

We are also convinced that the annexation now before us, in the context of the ward system of election finally proposed by the city and then agreed to by the United States, does not have the effect prohibited by § 5. The findings on which this case was decided and is presented to us were that the postannexation population of the city was 42% Negro as compared with 52% prior to annexation. The nine-ward system finally submitted by the city included four wards each of which had a greater than a 64% black majority. Four wards were heavily white. The ninth had a black population of 40.9%. In our view, such a plan does not undervalue the black strength in the community after annexation; and we hold that the annexation in this context does not have the effect of denying or abridging the right to vote within the meaning of § 5. To the extent that the District Court rested on a different view, its judgment cannot stand.

III

The foregoing principles should govern the application of § 5 insofar as it forbids changes in voting procedures having the effect of denying or abridging the right to vote on the grounds of race or color. But the section also proscribes changes that are made with the purpose of denying the right to vote on such grounds. The District Court concluded that when the annexation eventually approved in 1969 took place, it was adopted by the city with a discriminatory racial purpose, the precise purpose prohibited by § 5 * * *.

* * *

Accepting the findings of the Master in the District Court that the annexation, as it went forward in 1969, was infected by the impermissible purpose of denying the right to vote based on race through perpetuating white majority power to exclude Negroes from office through at-large elections, we are nevertheless persuaded that if verifiable reasons are now demonstrable in support of the annexation, and the ward plan proposed is fairly designed, the city need do no more to satisfy the requirements of § 5. We are also convinced that if the annexation cannot be sustained on sound, nondiscriminatory grounds, it would be only in the most extraordinary circumstances that the annexation should be permitted on condition that the Negro community be permanently overrepresented in the governing councils of the enlarged city. We are very doubtful that those circumstances exist in this case; for, as far as this record is concerned, Chesterfield County was and still is quite ready to receive back the annexed area, to compensate the city for its capital improvements, and to resume governance of the area. It would also seem obvious that if there are no verifiable economic or administrative benefits from the annexation that would accrue to the city, its financial or other prospects would not be worsened by de-annexation.

We need not determine this matter now, however; for if, as we have made clear, the controlling factor in this case is whether there are now objectively verifiable, legitimate reasons for the annexation, we agree with the United States that further proceedings are necessary to bring up to date and reassess the evidence bearing on the issue. * * *

* * *

IV

We have held that an annexation reducing the relative political strength of the minority race in the enlarged city as compared with what it was before the annexation is not a statutory violation as long as the post-annexation electoral system fairly recognizes the minority's political potential. If this is so, it may be asked how it could be forbidden by § 5 to have the purpose and intent of achieving only what is a perfectly legal result under that section and why we need remand for further proceedings with respect to purpose alone. The answer is plain, and we need not labor it. An official action, whether an annexation or otherwise, taken for the purpose of discriminating against Negroes on account of their race has no legitimacy at all under our Constitution or under the statute. Section 5 forbids voting changes taken with the purpose of denying the vote on the grounds of race or color. Congress surely has the power to prevent such gross racial slurs, the only point of which is "to despoil colored citizens, and only colored citizens, of their theretofore enjoyed voting rights." Gomillion v. Lightfoot, 364 U.S. 339, 347, 81 S.Ct. 125, 130, 5 L.Ed.2d 110 (1960). Annexations animated by such a purpose have no credentials whatsoever; for "[a]cts generally lawful may become unlawful when done to accomplish an unlawful end * * *." Western Union Telegraph Co. v. Foster, 247 U.S. 105, 114, 38 S.Ct. 438, 439, 62 L.Ed. 1006 (1918). An annexation proved to be of this kind and not proved to have a justifiable basis is forbidden by § 5, whatever its actual effect may have been or may be.

The judgment of the District Court is vacated and the case is remanded to that court for further proceedings consistent with this opinion.

So ordered.

MR. JUSTICE POWELL took no part in the consideration or decision of this case.

MR. JUSTICE BRENNAN, with whom MR. JUSTICE DOUGLAS and MR. JUSTICE MARSHALL join, dissenting.

* * *

In my view, the flagrantly discriminatory purpose with which Richmond hastily settled its Chesterfield County annexation suit in 1969 compelled the District Court to deny Richmond the declaratory judgment. The record is replete with statements by Richmond officials which prove beyond question that the predominant (if not the sole) motive and desire of the negotiators of the 1969 settlement was to acquire 44,000 additional white citizens for Richmond, in order to avert a transfer of political control to what was fast becoming a black-population majority. * * *

Having succeeded in this patently discriminatory enterprise, Richmond now argues that it can purge the taint of its impermissible purpose by dredging up supposed objective justifications for the annexation and by replacing its practice of at-large councilmanic elections with a ward-voting system. * * * I have grave difficulty with the idea that the taint of an illegal purpose can, under § 5, be dispelled by the sort of *post hoc* rationalization which the city now offers.

* * *

The second prong of any § 5 inquiry is whether the voting change under consideration will have the effect of denying or abridging the right to vote on account of race or color. [Justice Brennan recited the statistics indicating a drop in black population from 52% to 42% (45% to 37% voting age population) as a result of annexation. This obvious "dilution," he said, cannot be cured by simply giving blacks proportional representation "within the post-annexation community."]

* * *

Today's decision seriously weakens the protection so emphatically accorded by the Act. Municipal politicians who are fearful of losing their political control to emerging black voting majorities are today placed on notice that their control can be made secure as long as they can find concentrations of white citizens into which to expand their municipal boundaries. Richmond's black population, having finally begun to approach an opportunity to elect responsive officials and to have a significant voice in the conduct of its municipal affairs, now finds its voting strength reduced by a plan which "guarantees" four seats on the City Council but which makes the elusive fifth seat more remote than it was before. The Court would offer, as consolation, the fact that blacks will enjoy a fair share of the voting power available under a ward system operating within the boundaries of the postannexation community; but that same rationale would support a plan which added far greater concentrations of whites to the city and reduced black voting strength to the equivalent of three seats, two seats, or even fractions of a seat. The reliance upon postannexation fairness of representation is inconsistent with what I take to be the fundamental objective of § 5, namely, the protection of *present* levels of voting effectiveness for the black population.

It may be true, as the Court suggests, that this interpretation would effectively preclude some cities from undertaking desperately needed programs of expansion and annexation. Certainly there is nothing in § 5 which suggests that black voters could or should be given a disproportionately high share of the voting power in a post-annexation community; where the racial composition of an annexed area is substantially different from that of the annexing area, it may well be impossible to protect preannexation black voting strength without invidiously diluting the voting strength of other racial groups in the community. I see no reason to assume that the "demographics" of the situation are such that this would be an insuperable problem for all or even most cities covered by the Act; but in any event, if there is to be a "municipal hardship" exception for annexations vis-à-vis § 5, that exception should originate with Congress and not with the courts.

* * *

NOTE ON STANDARDS APPLIED IN PRECLEARANCE SUITS

1. In a preclearance suit brought in the United States District Court for the District of Columbia, the plaintiff covered jurisdiction must show that its proposed change in voting practices neither has the purpose nor will have the effect of abridging the right to vote on account of race. The issue of intent or purpose is not discussed at length in *City of Richmond,* but presumably it has the same meaning ascribed to the terms in Village of Arlington Heights v. Metropolitan Housing Dev. Corp., Chapter 1B.5 supra. But cf. PL 109–246, § 5 120 Stat 577 (2006) (VRA Amendments of 2006) ("'(c) The term 'purpose' in [preclearance sections] shall include any discriminatory purpose").

(a) Unlike *Arlington Heights* and equal protection cases, the burden of proof here rests on the governmental entity to prove lack of discriminatory intent. Can that be done? How?

(b) The principal issue regarding intent in *City of Richmond* is not whether the city intentionally discriminated but whether it has purged itself of the motive by showing, as Justice Brennan calls it, a "post hoc rationalization." It is clear, is it not, that the majority would allow the city to excuse itself not only by showing that nondiscriminatory factors were considered at the time of annexation but also by proving that such factors exist later at the trial date? Is this the same approach as was approved in *Arlington Heights'* footnote 24? See the Note on Intent and Causation, Chapter 1B.5 supra. Is it the same as that used in Title VII cases? See Chapter 7A.2.b supra (especially the Note on Defenses to Intentional Discrimination and its discussion of variations on the mixed-motive defense). Why does the Court feel it necessary to allow later-developed reasons in the voting context but not in the employment or § 1983 context?[1]

(c) The 2006 Amendments to the Voting Rights Act contained a provision, § 5, "striking 'does not have the purpose and will not have the effect' and inserting 'neither has the purpose nor will have the effect' of discriminating." Does this slight change overrule *Richmond*'s allowance of post-hoc rationalizations?

2. On the issue of effect, majority and dissent agree that a diminution of black voting power constitutes a prohibited discriminatory effect; they disagree on whether diminution is to be measured against pre-annexation or post-annexation voting strength.

(a) Does the majority's choice of measurement make the effects test practically meaningless? Will it not, as Justice Brennan argues, allow a city government to decimate black voting power by lowering the ratio of blacks to whites through annexation of white neighborhoods? Why does the majority believe that its position is necessary?

(b) Why does the majority reject Brennan's appraisal of the situation? Is it because they cannot accept the alternative remedies that would follow—

---

1. Compare Miller v. Johnson, 515 U.S. 900, 115 S.Ct. 2475, 132 L.Ed.2d 762 (1995) (in order to prevail on claim of race-based affirmative action in redistricting, plaintiff must show not merely that race was "a" factor in the process, but the "predominant" factor). This is also different from the Title VII approach, is it not? Do the two variations, one favoring the plaintiff and one the defendant, balance each other?

either post-annexation "over-representation" of blacks or prohibition against annexation? Given the characteristics of most American urban areas, would not every annexation in a covered jurisdiction have a discriminatory effect under Brennan's test, regardless of sound reasons for the annexation? Would Brennan's test have the undesirable effect of freezing a city's boundaries, locking it into the same desperate situation as land-locked urban cores that are surrounded by small towns? Cf. Edward Glaeser, Bulldozing America's Shrinking Cities, NY Times, June 16, 2009, accessed online at http://economix.blogs.nytimes.com/2009/06/16/bulldozing-americas-shrinking-cities/ (last visited July 6, 2011). Alternatively, does Justice Brennan's test freeze into place minority control of fast-growing southern and western cities? See id. Is that good or bad?

(c) If the majority's ruling responds to the special problem of urban demographics, should its gloss on "intent" and "effect" be limited to annexation suits? Should the ruling also apply to reapportionment cases? Across the board to all voting situations?

(d) The problem of growing cities is matched in modern American life by declining cities, those whose population has dramatically declined due to changing economic fortunes. How would *Richmond* apply to such cities, assuming one is subject to preclearance? Is your opinion colored by the Court's later decision in the *Beer* case, infra?

3. The general effects test as used in § 5 has led to one rather precise test, the non-retrogression rule adopted in **Beer v. United States**, 425 U.S. 130, 96 S.Ct. 1357, 47 L.Ed.2d 629 (1976). This was a preclearance suit brought by the city of New Orleans to obtain approval for its redistricting plan for councilmanic elections. At the time of suit blacks comprised 45% of the city's population and resided primarily in an east-to-west strip through the city. In a districting plan predating the passage of the 1965 Act, leaders carved north-south bands across the city, so that whites constituted a pronounced majority in each of five districts; two additional council members were elected at-large. No blacks won election under this plan. The 1970 plan continued the same north-south pattern of earlier years and gave blacks a voting majority in one district. Bloc-voting patterns suggested that only one black person would be elected to the seven-member council, far below blacks' 45% population percentage, and for this reason both the Attorney General and district court disapproved the plan. The Supreme Court rejected their views, Justice Stewart's majority opinion declaring that any diluent effect on black voting power should be measured by comparison with *prior* voting power not projected current power (425 U.S. at 140–41, 96 S.Ct. at 1363–64):

> "By prohibiting the enforcement of a voting-procedure change until it has been demonstrated to the United States Department of Justice or to a three-judge federal court that the change does not have a discriminatory effect, Congress desired to prevent States from 'undo[ing] or defeat[ing] the rights recently won' by Negroes. H.R.Rep. No. 91–397, p. 8. Section 5 was intended 'to insure that [the gains thus far achieved in minority political participation] shall not be destroyed through new [discriminatory] procedures and techniques.' S.Rep. No. 94–295, p. 19.

"When it adopted a 7–year extension of the Voting Rights Act in 1975, Congress explicitly stated that 'the standard [under § 5] can only be fully satisfied by determining on the basis of the facts found by the Attorney General [or the District Court] to be true whether the ability of minority groups to participate in the political process and to elect their choices to office is *augmented, diminished, or not affected by the change affecting voting * * *.*' H.R.Rep. No. 94–196, p. 60 (emphasis added).[12] In other words the purpose of § 5 has always been to insure that no voting-procedure changes would be made that would lead to a retrogression in the position of racial minorities with respect to their effective exercise of the electoral franchise.

"It is thus apparent that a legislative reapportionment that enhances the position of racial minorities with respect to their effective exercise of the electoral franchise can hardly have the 'effect' of diluting or abridging the right to vote on account of race within the meaning of § 5. We conclude, therefore, that such an ameliorative new legislative apportionment cannot violate § 5 unless the new apportionment itself so discriminates on the basis of race or color as to violate the Constitution."

(a) Is the Court's decision in *Beer* consistent with *City of Richmond*? Does one measure dilution against present power, the other against the past? Does footnote 12 show that the Court is trying to have it both ways? Is Justice Brennan, who dissented in *Beer,* equally guilty of inconsistency? Is there only one principle in § 5—non-retrogression—that can be applied differently in different contexts?

(b) Can *Beer*'s non-retrogression serve as a floor below which black representation cannot go? In **Abrams v. Johnson**, 521 U.S. 74, 117 S.Ct. 1925, 138 L.Ed.2d 285 (1997), the Court reviewed a Georgia redistricting plan under § 5. It maintained one black district even after Georgia's population growth had entitled it to an extra seat in Congress, thus reducing black representation from 1 of 10 districts to 1 of 11. The Court rejected the argument that this violated *Beer*'s principle: "Under that logic, each time a State with a majority-minority district was allowed to add one new district because of population growth, it would have to be majority-minority. This the Voting Rights Act does not require." So is *Beer* hollow?[13] Or does its principle simply not apply at the state level for congressional seats?

(c) In its later decision in **Georgia v. Ashcroft**, 539 U.S. 461, 123 S.Ct. 2498, 156 L.Ed.2d 428 (2003), the Court described the non-retrogression principle as follows: "Section 5 of the Voting Rights Act 'has a limited substantive goal: to insure that no voting-procedure changes would be made that would lead to a retrogression in the position of racial minorities with respect to their effective exercise of the electoral franchise.' Thus, a plan that merely preserves 'current minority voting strength' is entitled to § 5 preclearance. Indeed, a voting change with a discriminatory but nonretrogressive

---

12. Cf. Mr. Justice Brennan's dissenting opinion in City of Richmond v. United States, supra, at 388: "I take to be the fundamental objective of § 5 * * * the protection of *present* levels of voting effectiveness for the black population." (Emphasis in original.) [Footnote by the Court.]

13. What should happen in the reverse-*Abrams* situation where a state loses a congressional seat? See Branch v. Smith, 538 U.S. 254, 123 S.Ct. 1429, 155 L.Ed.2d 407 (2003) (demonstrating the problem).

purpose or effect does not violate § 5. * * * '[P]reclearance under § 5 affirms nothing but the absence of backsliding.' " Is this a shortcoming or an accomplishment? See John C. Jeffries, Jr. & Daryl J. Levinson, *The Non–Retrogression Principle in Constitutional Law*, 86 CAL. L. REV. 1211 (1998) (forbidding new evils is a shortcoming). Is the glass half-empty or half-full?

(d) The 2006 Amendments to the Voting Rights Act claimed to overturn Georgia v. Ashcroft in § 5 with cryptic language denying preclearnace for any change "that has the purpose of or will have the effect of diminishing the ability of any citizens * * * to elect their preferred candidates." Is this language sufficient to show an intent to require further creation of minority districts? See Nathaniel Persily. *The Promise and Pitfalls of the New Voting Rights Act*, 117 Yale L.J. 174 (2007) (unanimous Senate adoption and near-unanimous House adoption masked serious, opposing interpretations of language purporting to change the non-retrogression principle); David L. Epstein & Sharyn O'Halloran, *The Paradox of Retrogression in the New VRA: Comment on Persily*, 117 Yale L.J. Pocket Part 245 (2008), http://thepocketpart. org/2008/05/06/epsteinohalloran.html (competing interpretations would serve different goals). If the 2006 Amendments are interpreted to require increased minority representation in all cases, would it be an unconstitutional mandatory affirmative action plan? Cf. City of Richmond v. Croson, Chapter 7D supra; Grutter v. Bollinger, Chapter 6E supra See also ¶ 4 infra.

4. If a state undertakes racially conscious districting designed to increase black voting power, it is subject to strict scrutiny. Shaw v. Reno, 509 U.S. 630, 113 S.Ct. 2816, 125 L.Ed.2d 511 (1993). Can the necessity of complying with § 5 provide the compelling state interest that would provide a defense? In **Bush v. Vera**, 517 U.S. 952, 116 S.Ct. 1941, 135 L.Ed.2d 248 (1996), Texas sought to excuse its race-based districting on this ground, but the Court declined to accept the invitation to craft such a defense, noting that § 5 had adopted a non-retrogression principle, see *Beer* supra, not a demand for maximized black representation. Any action, therefore, that "seeks to justify not maintenance, but substantial augmentation," is not required by § 5. This makes any asserted defense based on compliance irrelevant.

(a) Does *Bush*'s interpretation of *Beer* mean that § 5 can never be relied upon to justify a black-maximizing, race-conscious districting plan?

(b) Does the non-retrogression principle itself violate strict scrutiny because it is not narrowly tailored? Is the *Beer* principle necessary to prevent violations of minority voting rights?

5. *Beer* and *Bush* involved retrogression as the defining principle for § 5's effects test. Does "retrogression" play any role in applying § 5's intent test? The Court discussed this issue in **Reno v. Bossier Parish School Bd.**, 528 U.S. 320, 120 S.Ct. 866, 145 L.Ed.2d 845 (2000). In that case the covered entity sought preclearance of a new districting plan that did not cause retrogression as compared to the existing plan, but failed to create as many black districts as were theoretically possible under a competing plan offered by the NAACP. When the plaintiff sought preclearance, the federal government admitted that there was no "retrogressive effect" under *Beer* because such retrogression is measured against the existing plan, not proposed future plans. See ¶ 3 supra. The trial court found as a matter of fact that if there

were intentional discrimination, it had no retrogressive effect. The Supreme Court, Justice Scalia writing the opinion, therefore described the case as involving "discriminatory but nonretrogressive intent," thus connecting the retrogression principle not only to the effects element but also the intent element of § 5. Then the Court made its ruling: "the 'purpose' prong of § 5 covers only retrogressive dilution," and thus the absence of retrogression not only clears the plaintiff of charges of a discriminatory effect, it also requires that it be cleared of charges of discriminatory intent. Intent unfulfilled by a retrogressive effect, said the Court, is no violation of § 5, 528 U.S. at 335, 120 S.Ct. at 871:

> "[We have previously noted] the limited meaning that [§ 5] preclearance has in the vote-dilution context. It does not represent approval of the voting change; it is nothing more than a determination that the voting change is no more dilutive than what it replaces, and therefore cannot be stopped in advance under the extraordinary burden-shifting procedures of § 5, but must be attacked through the normal means of a [plaintiff-initiated suit]. As we have repeatedly noted, in vote-dilution cases § 5 prevents nothing but backsliding, and preclearance under § 5 affirms nothing but the absence of backsliding."

(a) Is Justice Scalia's opinion in *Reno* nothing more than a fancy application of the *Mount Healthy* mixed motive defense? See footnote 21 in *Arlington Heights*, Chapter 1B.5 supra; Note on Intent and Causation, Chapter 1B.5 supra; Burton v. City of Belle Glade, 178 F.3d 1175 (11th Cir. 1999) (refusal to annex predominantly black area; plaintiffs must show challenged "decision or act had a discriminatory purpose and effect").

(b) Justice Scalia admitted, 528 U.S. at 330, 120 S.Ct. at 873, that the Court's decision in *City of Richmond*

> "created a discontinuity between the effect and purpose prongs of § 5. We regard that, however, as nothing more than an ex necessitate limitation upon the effect prong in the particular context of annexation—to avoid the invalidation of all annexations of areas with a lower proportion of minority voters than the annexing unit. The case certainly does not stand for the proposition that the purpose and effect prongs have fundamentally different meanings * * *. The approved effect of the redistricting in *Richmond*, and the hypothetically disapproved purpose, were both retrogressive. We found it necessary to make an exception to normal retrogressive-effect principles, but not to normal retrogressive-purpose principles, in order to permit routine annexation. That sheds little light upon the issue before us here."

Recall that in *Richmond* the Court permitted post hoc reasons to excuse a discriminatory purpose; here the Court focuses on the retrogressive effect as measured against the pre-change status quo. Is this the "discontinuity" to which he is referring? If it is, then does not *Reno* limit the possibility of post hoc justifications to the annexation context? Is that not a good thing?

(c) The 2006 Amendments also express an intent to overturn Reno v. Bossier Parish. If so interpreted, would this provision exceed Congress' power under the Fifteenth and Fourteenth Amendments? Is the limited scope of the non-retrogression principle all that makes it constitutional acceptable? See section A of this Chapter supra (power to alter scope of constitution rejected); Northwest Austin Mun. Utility Dist. No. One v. Holder, ___ U.S. ___, 129 S.Ct. 2504, 174 L.Ed.2d 140 (2009) (narrow interpretation of preclearance provision required to avoid potential unconstitutionality).

6. Congress renewed the preclearance and some related provisions of the Voting Rights Act in 2006, extending its "sunset" time to 2032. Is renewal good policy?

(a) Professor Michael Pitts, a former Justice Department attorney for voting rights enforcement, notes that "big picture trends" are running against all aspects of the Voting Rights Act, Michael J. Pitts, *Congressional Enforcement of Affirmative Democracy Through Section 2 of The Voting Rights Act*, 25 N. ILL. U. L. REV. 185 (2005). He speaks primarily of policy options in the constitutional sense:

"First, the Court has embarked upon a federalism revolution that has provided state and local governments with much greater protection from the reach of Congress. Second, the Court has exhibited a general distaste for race-based remedies, as evidenced by the shift toward a strict nondiscrimination view of equal protection [and intentional discrimination]. These two big-picture trends converge with the Court's adoption of the congruence and proportionality doctrine [in *City of Boerne* that seems] to protect state and local governments from federal interference * * *. In practice, the doctrine protects these federalism and separation of powers values by requiring Congress to amass a compelling factual record of constitutional violations by state and local governments before enacting a remedy that provides more protection for citizens against these governmental entities than the Court would provide under the Constitution standing alone."

The Democrats in Congress thought that they had amassed such a record in support of the 2006 Amendments, but Republicans, who voted unanimously in the House in support of the plan, saw no such massive record of continued racial discrimination in voting. Indeed, the Roberts Court has described the Voting Rights Act as a major success story that has eliminated most of the problems of 1965, see *Northwest Austin*, supra. Echoing Prof. Pitts, the Court in that case also saw the gains as coming at the expense of significant federalism interests. Does your constitutional calculus of whether the damage is worth further gains turn on what those gains might be. What should they be?

(b) Is § 5 good social policy? Professor Samuel Issacharoff, in *Is Section 5 of the Voting Rights Act a Victim of its Own Success?*, 104 COLUM. L. REV. 1710 (2004), argues that extension of § 5 is debatably good policy, even if one's social goal is to maximize black representation, because of the

"changed political environment that has eroded the preconditions for the success of section 5 of the Voting Rights Act. The emerging conclusion is that section 5 has served its purposes and may now be impeding the type of political developments that could have been only a distant aspiration when the VRA was passed in 1965. [Moreover,] the combination of an administratively complex standard [from the cases] together with the strengthened world of partisan competition has called into question the continued utility of administrative preclearance * * *.''

At what point does one declare victory and leave the field? Is § 5 still a necessary "bargaining chip" for blacks to use in leveraging their minority status into meaningful power? See Pamela S. Karlan, Georgia v. Ashcroft *and the Retrogression of Retrogression*, 3 ELECTION L.J. 21 (2004). See Michael J. Pitts, *Let's Not Call the Whole Thing off Just Yet: a Response to Samuel Issacharoff's Suggestion to Scuttle Section 5 of the Voting Rights Act*, 84 NEB. L. REV. 605 (2005) (Issacharoff focuses too much on legislative and congressional districting and misses the important work § 5 does at the level of local governments).

(c) Is § 5 good political policy? Prof. Grant Hayden, in *The Supreme Court and Voting Rights: A More Complete Exit Strategy*, 83 N.C. L. REV. 949 (2005) argues that much of the Supreme Court's pro-plaintiff activism in voting cases has harmed minority interests, and he singles out majority-minority districts created through § 5 (and § 2, as discussed infra) as chief culprits:

> "The principal drawback was that such districts seemed to have the unintended side effect of helping the Republican Party[, and they] did so because the minority voters needed to create majority-minority districts had to come from somewhere, and that somewhere was the adjoining districts[, thus diluting or black power in those districts. This made it] more likely that, instead of a white Democrat, they would elect a white Republican. [As a result], minority voting rights advocates have to make a choice between increasing the number of minority officeholders and increasing the number of Democrats * * *."

Do you agree with Professor Hayden? If the Voting Rights Act is seen as a vehicle favoring one party, can it enjoy broad support? Was § 5 more of a success because it broke the political monopoly of the old Democratic Party? See Richard H. Pildes, *The Constitutionalization of Democratic Politics*, 118 HARV. L. REV. 28 (2004) (arguing that Voting Rights Act broke monopoly status of Democrats and opened politics in the South—and serves as a good example for how courts can mediate entrenchment of political parties). See also Michael J. Pitts, *Let's Not Call the Whole Thing Off Just Yet*, supra (arguing that sufficient political controls are in place to minimize partisan use of § 5). Can one separate race and partisan politics? Consider the issues raised in the next principal case, including the phenomenon of racial bloc voting.

2. THE "RESULTS" TEST IN AMENDED § 2

THORNBURG v. GINGLES

Supreme Court of the United States, 1986.
478 U.S. 30, 106 S.Ct. 2752, 92 L.Ed.2d 25.

JUSTICE BRENNAN announced the judgment of the Court and delivered the opinion of the Court with respect to Parts I, II, III–A, III–B, IV–A, and V, and an opinion with respect to Part III–C, in which JUSTICE MARSHALL, JUSTICE BLACKMUN, and JUSTICE STEVENS join, and an opinion with respect to Part IV–B, in which JUSTICE WHITE joins.

This case requires that we construe for the first time § 2 of the Voting Rights Act of 1965, as amended June 29, 1982. 42 U.S.C. § 1973. The specific question to be decided is whether the three-judge District Court, convened in the Eastern District of North Carolina pursuant to 28 U.S.C. § 2284(a) and 42 U.S.C. § 1973c, correctly held that the use in a legislative redistricting plan of multimember districts in five North Carolina legislative districts violated § 2 by impairing the opportunity of black voters "to participate in the political process and to elect representatives of their choice." § 2(b), 96 Stat. 134.

I

* * *

* * * The amendment was largely a response to this Court's plurality opinion in *Mobile v. Bolden,* 446 U.S. 55, 100 S.Ct. 1490, 64 L.Ed.2d 47 (1980), which had declared that, in order to establish a violation either of § 2 or of the Fourteenth or Fifteenth Amendments, minority voters must prove that a contested electoral mechanism was intentionally adopted or maintained by state officials for a discriminatory purpose. Congress substantially revised § 2 to make clear that a violation could be proved by showing discriminatory effect alone and to establish as the relevant legal standard the "results test," applied by this Court in *White v. Regester,* 412 U.S. 755, 93 S.Ct. 2332, 37 L.Ed.2d 314 (1973), and by other federal courts before *Bolden, supra.* S.Rep. No. 97–417, 97th Cong.2nd Sess. 28 (1982), U.S.Code Cong. & Admin.News 1982, pp. 177, 205 (hereinafter S.Rep.). [section 2 provides in part that a violation of the "results test" is]

"* * * established if, based on the totality of circumstances, it is shown that the political processes leading to nomination or election in the State or political subdivision are not equally open to participation by members of a class of citizens protected by subsection (a) in that its members have less opportunity than other members of the electorate to participate in the political process and to elect representatives of their choice. The extent to which members of a protected class have been elected to office in the State or political subdivision is one circumstance which may be considered: *Provided,* That nothing in this section establishes a right to have members of a protected class elected in numbers equal to their proportion in the population". Codified at 42 U.S.C. § 1973.

The Senate Judiciary Committee majority Report accompanying the bill that amended § 2, elaborates on the circumstances that might be probative of a § 2 violation, noting the following "typical factors":

"1.   the extent of any history of official discrimination in the state or political subdivision that touched the right of the members of the minority group to register, to vote, or otherwise to participate in the democratic process;

2.   the extent to which voting in the elections of the state or political subdivision is racially polarized;

3. the extent to which the state or political subdivision has used unusually large election districts, majority vote requirements, anti-single shot provisions, or other voting practices or procedures that may enhance the opportunity for discrimination against the minority group;

4. if there is a candidate slating process, whether the members of the minority group have been denied access to that process;

5. the extent to which members of the minority group in the state or political subdivision bear the effects of discrimination in such areas as education, employment and health, which hinder their ability to participate effectively in the political process;

6. whether political campaigns have been characterized by overt or subtle racial appeals;

7. the extent to which members of the minority group have been elected to public office in the jurisdiction.

"Additional factors that in some cases have had probative value as part of plaintiffs' evidence to establish a violation are: 'whether there is a significant lack of responsiveness on the part of elected officials to the particularized needs of the members of the minority group [and] whether the policy underlying the state or political subdivision's use of such voting qualification, prerequisite to voting, or standard, practice or procedure is tenuous.' " S.Rep., at 28–29, U.S.Code Cong. & Admin.News 1982, pp. 206–207.

The District Court applied the "totality of the circumstances" test set forth in § 2(b) to appellees' statutory claim, and, relying principally on the factors outlined in the Senate Report, held that the redistricting scheme violated § 2 because it resulted in the dilution of black citizens' votes in all seven disputed districts. * * *

* * *

II

Section 2 and Vote Dilution Through Use of Multimember Districts

* * *

Appellees contend that the legislative decision to employ multimember, rather than single-member, districts in the contested jurisdictions dilutes their votes by submerging them in a white majority, thus impairing their ability to elect representatives of their choice.

The essence of a § 2 claim is that a certain electoral law, practice, or structure interacts with social and historical conditions to cause an inequality in the opportunities enjoyed by black and white voters to elect their preferred representatives. This Court has long recognized that multimember districts and at-large voting schemes may " 'operate to minimize or cancel out the voting strength of racial [minorities in] the voting population.' " Burns v. Richardson, 384 U.S. 73, 88, 86 S.Ct. 1286,

16 L.Ed.2d 376 (1966) (quoting Fortson v. Dorsey, 379 U.S. 433, 439, 85 S.Ct. 498, 501, 13 L.Ed.2d 401 (1965)). See also Rogers v. Lodge, 458 U.S. 613, 617, 102 S.Ct. 3272, 3275, 73 L.Ed.2d 1012 (1982); White v. Regester, 412 U.S. at 765, 93 S.Ct., at 2339; Whitcomb v. Chavis, 403 U.S. 124, 143, 91 S.Ct. 1858, 1869, 29 L.Ed.2d 363 (1971). The theoretical basis for this type of impairment is that where minority and majority voters consistently prefer different candidates, the majority, by virtue of its numerical superiority, will regularly defeat the choices of minority voters. See, e.g., Grofman, ALTERNATIVES, IN REPRESENTATION AND REDISTRICTING ISSUES 113–114. Multimember districts and at-large election schemes, however, are not *per se* violative of minority voters' rights. S.Rep., at 16. Cf. Rogers v. Lodge, supra, 458 U.S. at 617, 102 S.Ct., at 3275; *Regester*, supra, 412 U.S. at 765, 93 S.Ct., at 2339; *Whitcomb*, supra, 403 U.S. at 142, 91 S.Ct., at 1868. Minority voters who contend that the multimember form of districting violates § 2, must prove that the use of a multimember electoral structure operates to minimize or cancel out their ability to elect their preferred candidates. See, e.g., S.Rep. at 16.

While many or all of the factors listed in the Senate Report may be relevant to a claim of vote dilution through submergence in multimember districts, unless there is a conjunction of the following circumstances, the use of multimember districts generally will not impede the ability of minority voters to elect representatives of their choice. Stated succinctly, bloc voting majority must *usually* be able to defeat candidates supported by a politically cohesive, geographically insular minority group.

These circumstances are necessary preconditions for multimember districts to operate to impair minority voters' ability to elect representatives of their choice for the following reasons. First, the minority group must be able to demonstrate that it is sufficiently large and geographically compact to constitute a majority in a single-member district. If it is not, as would be the case in a substantially integrated district, the *multimember form* of the district cannot be responsible for minority voters' inability to elect its candidates. Second, the minority group must be able to show that it is politically cohesive. If the minority group is not politically cohesive, it cannot be said that the selection of a multimember electoral structure thwarts distinctive minority group interests. Third, the minority must be able to demonstrate that the white majority votes sufficiently as a bloc to enable it—in the absence of special circumstances, such as the minority candidate running unopposed, usually to defeat the minority's preferred candidate. In establishing this last circumstance, the minority group demonstrates that submergence in a white multimember district impedes its ability to elect its chosen representatives.

Finally, we observe that the usual predictability of the majority's success distinguishes structural dilution from the mere loss of an occasional election.

III[.] Racially–Polarized Voting

* * *

B[.] THE DEGREE OF BLOC VOTING THAT IS LEGALLY SIGNIFICANT UNDER § 2

The Senate Report states that the "extent to which voting in the elections of the state or political subdivision is racially polarized," S.Rep. at 29, U.S.Code Cong. & Admin.News 1982, p. 206, is relevant to a vote dilution claim. Because, as we explain below, the extent of bloc voting necessary to demonstrate that a minority's ability to elect its preferred representatives is impaired varies according to several factual circumstances, the degree of bloc voting which constitutes the threshold of legal significance will vary from district to district. Nonetheless, it is possible to state some general principles and we proceed to do so.

The purpose of inquiring into the existence of racially polarized voting is twofold: to ascertain whether minority group members constitute a politically cohesive unit and to determine whether whites vote sufficiently as a bloc usually to defeat the minority's preferred candidates. Thus, the question whether a given district experiences legally significant racially polarized voting requires discrete inquiries into minority and white voting practices. A showing that a significant number of minority group members usually vote for the same candidates is one way of proving the political cohesiveness necessary to a vote dilution claim, and, consequently, establishes minority bloc voting within the context of § 2. And, in general, a white bloc vote that normally will defeat the combined strength of minority support plus white "crossover" votes rises to the level of legally significant white bloc voting. The amount of white bloc voting that can generally "minimize or cancel," S.Rep., at 28, U.S. Code Cong. & Admin.News 1982, p. 205, black voters' ability to elect representatives of their choice, however, will vary from district to district according to a number of factors, including the nature of the allegedly dilutive electoral mechanism; the presence or absence of other potentially dilutive electoral devices, such as majority vote requirements, designated posts, and prohibitions against bullet voting; the percentage of registered voters in the district who are members of the minority group; the size of the district; and, in multimember districts, the number of seats open and the number of candidates in the field. See, e.g., Jones, *The Impact of Local Election Systems on Black Political Representation*, 11 URB. AFF. Q. 345 (1976); United States Commission on Civil Rights, The Voting Rights Act: Unfulfilled Goals 38–41 (1981). Because loss of political power through vote dilution is distinct from the mere inability to win a particular election, *Whitcomb,* 403 U.S. at 153, 91 S.Ct., at 1874, a pattern of racial bloc voting that extends over a period of time is more probative of a claim that a district experiences legally significant polarization than are the results of a single election. * * *

As must be apparent, the degree of racial bloc voting that is cognizable as an element of a § 2 vote dilution claim will vary according to a variety of factual circumstances. Consequently, there is no simple doctrinal test for the existence of legally significant racial bloc voting. However, the foregoing general principles should provide courts with substantial guidance in determining whether evidence that black and white voters generally prefer different candidates rises to the level of legal significance under § 2.

* * *

We conclude that the District Court's approach, which tested data derived from three election years in each district, and which revealed that blacks strongly supported black candidates, while, to the black candidates' usual detriment, whites rarely did, satisfactorily addresses this facet of the proper legal standard.

C[.] Evidence of Racially Polarized Voting

* * *

[W]e reject appellants' argument that racially polarized voting refers to voting patterns that are in some way *caused by race,* rather than to voting patterns that are merely *correlated with the race of the voter,* is that the reasons black and white voters vote differently have no relevance to the central inquiry of § 2. By contrast, the correlation between race of voter and the selection of certain candidates is crucial to that inquiry.

Both § 2 itself and the Senate Report make clear that the critical question in a § 2 claim is whether the use of a contested electoral practice or structure results in members of a protected group having less opportunity than other members of the electorate to participate in the political process and to elect representatives of their choice. See, e.g., S.Rep., at 2, 27, 28, 29, n. 118, 36. As we explained, supra, multimember districts may impair the ability of blacks to elect representatives of their choice where blacks vote sufficiently as a bloc as to be able to elect their preferred candidates in a black majority, single-member district and where a white majority votes sufficiently as a bloc usually to defeat the candidates chosen by blacks. It is the *difference* between the choices made by blacks and whites—not the reasons for that difference—that results in blacks having less opportunity than whites to elect their preferred representatives. Consequently, we conclude that under the "results test" of § 2, only the correlation between race of voter and selection of certain candidates, not the causes of the correlation, matters.

* * *

IV

North Carolina and the United States maintain that the District Court failed to accord the proper weight to the success of some black candidates in the challenged districts. * * *

Section 2(b) provides that "[t]he extent to which members of a protected class have been elected to office . . . is one circumstance which may be considered." 42 U.S.C. § 1973(b). The Senate Committee Report also identifies the extent to which minority candidates have succeeded as a pertinent factor. S.Rep., at 29. However, the Senate Report expressly states that "the election of a few minority candidates does not 'necessarily foreclose the possibility of dilution of the black vote,'" noting that if it did, "the possibility exists that the majority citizens might evade [§ 2] by manipulating the election of a 'safe' minority candidate." Id. at 29, n. 115, U.S.Code Cong. & Admin.News 1982, p. 207, quoting Zimmer v. McKeithen, 485 F.2d 1297, 1307 (C.A.5 1973) (en banc), aff'd sub nom. East Carroll Parish School Board v. Marshall, 424 U.S. 636, 96 S.Ct. 1083, 47 L.Ed.2d 296 (1976) (per curiam). The Senate Committee decided, instead, to "'require an independent consideration of the record.'" S.Rep., at 29, n. 115, U.S.Code Cong. & Admin.News 1982, p. 207. The Senate Report also emphasizes that the question whether "the political processes are 'equally open' depends upon a searching practical evaluation of the 'past and present reality.'" Id. at 30, U.S.Code Cong. & Admin.News 1982, p. 208 (footnote omitted). Thus, the language of § 2 and its legislative history plainly demonstrate that proof that some minority candidates have been elected does not foreclose a § 2 claim. ["Sustained success" of black candidates, on the other hand, is inconsistent with a claim of vote dilution under § 2.]

V

Ultimate Determination of Vote Dilution

Finally, appellants and the United States dispute the District Court's ultimate conclusion that the multimember districting scheme at issue in this case deprived black voters of an equal opportunity to participate in the political process and to elect representatives of their choice.

* * *

We reaffirm our view that the clearly-erroneous test of Rule 52(a) is the appropriate standard for appellate review of a finding of vote dilution. As both amended § 2 and its legislative history make clear, in evaluating a statutory claim of vote dilution through districting, the trial court is to consider the "totality of the circumstances" and to determine, based "upon a searching practical evaluation of the 'past and present reality,'" S.Rep. at 30, U.S.Code Cong. & Admin.News 1982, p. 208 (footnote omitted), whether the political process is equally open to minority voters. "'This determination is peculiarly dependent upon the facts of each case,'" and requires "an intensely local appraisal of the design and impact" of the contested electoral mechanisms. The fact that amended § 2 and its legislative history provide legal standards which a court must apply to the facts in order to determine whether § 2 has been violated does not alter the standard of review. * * *

* * *

Affirmed in part and reversed in part.

JUSTICE WHITE, concurring.

JUSTICE BRENNAN states in Part III–C that the crucial factor in identifying polarized voting is the race of the voter and that the race of the candidate is irrelevant. Under this test, there is polarized voting if the majority of white voters vote for different candidates than the majority of the blacks, regardless of the race of the candidates. I do not agree. Suppose an eight-member multimember district that is 60% white and 40% black, the blacks being geographically located so that two safe black single-member districts could be drawn. Suppose further that there are six white and two black Democrats running against six white and two black Republicans. Under Justice Brennan's test, there would be polarized voting and a likely § 2 violation if all the Republicans, including the two blacks, are elected, and 80% of the blacks in the predominantly black areas vote Democratic. I take it that there would also be a violation in a single-member district that is 60% black, but enough of the blacks vote with the whites to elect a black candidate who is not the choice of the majority of black voters. This is interest-group politics rather than a rule hedging against racial discrimination. I doubt that this is what Congress had in mind in amending § 2 as it did, and it seems quite at odds with the discussion in Whitcomb v. Chavis, 403 U.S. 124, 149–60, 91 S.Ct. 1858, 1872–1878, 29 L.Ed.2d 363 (1971). Furthermore, on the facts of this case, there is no need to draw the voter/candidate distinction. * * *

JUSTICE O'CONNOR, with whom THE CHIEF JUSTICE, JUSTICE POWELL, and JUSTICE REHNQUIST join, concurring in the judgment.

* * *

In construing this compromise legislation, we must make every effort to be faithful to the balance Congress struck. This is not an easy task. We know that Congress intended to allow vote dilution claims to be brought under § 2, but we also know that Congress did not intend to create a right to proportional representation for minority voters. There is an inherent tension between what Congress wished to do and what it wished to avoid, because any theory of vote dilution must necessarily rely to some extent on a measure of minority voting strength that makes some reference to the proportion between the minority group and the electorate at large. In addition, several important aspects of the "results" test had received little attention in this Court's cases or in the decisions of the Courts of Appeals employing that test on which Congress also relied. Specifically, the legal meaning to be given to the concepts of "racial bloc voting" and "minority voting strength" had been left largely unaddressed by the courts when § 2 was amended.

* * *

[Justice Brennan's position on] vote dilution, taken in conjunction with the Court's standard for measuring undiluted minority voting strength, creates what amounts to a right to *usual, roughly* proportional representation on the part of sizable, compact, cohesive minority groups. If, under a particular multimember or single-member district plan, qualified minority groups usually cannot elect the representatives they would be likely to elect under the most favorable single-member districting plan, then § 2 is violated. Unless minority success under the challenged electoral system regularly approximates this rough version of proportional representation, that system dilutes minority voting strength and violates § 2.

* * *

As shaped by the Court today, then, the basic contours of a vote dilution claim require no reference to most of the *"Zimmer* factors" that were developed by the Fifth Circuit to implement *White's* results test and which were highlighted in the Senate Report. S.Rep. at 28–29; see Zimmer v. McKeithen, 485 F.2d 1297 (C.A.5 1973) (en banc), aff'd sub nom. East Carroll Parish School Board v. Marshall, 424 U.S. 636, 96 S.Ct. 1083, 47 L.Ed.2d 296 (1976) (per curiam). [These are the same factors set out at the beginning of the majority opinion, citing the Senate Committee Report on § 2.]

In my view, the Court's test for measuring minority voting strength and its test for vote dilution, operating in tandem, come closer to an absolute requirement of proportional representation than Congress intended when it codified the results test in § 2. It is not necessary or appropriate to decide in this case whether § 2 requires a uniform measure of undiluted minority voting strength in every case, nor have appellants challenged the standard employed by the District Court for assessing undiluted minority voting strength. [The facts of this case show that all the factors were met, and thus the issue of proportional representation need not be finally resolved, as Justice Brennan has sought to do.]

NOTE ON § 2 AND ITS *"RESULTS"* TEST

1. Section 2 of the Voting Rights Act differs from § 5 in three important respects. First, § 2 applies nationwide, while § 5 applies only to certain "covered jurisdictions" presumptively guilty of prior discrimination in voting. Second, as noted in Reno v. Bossier Parish School Bd., discussed in the previous Note, § 5 and preclearance work to retard some change; § 2 works to require change from the status quo. Finally, § 5 uses an intent and effects test, while § 2 uses a "results" test. This Note concentrates on the third of these differences.[1]

2. As noted by Justice O'Connor, the text of § 2 requires courts to cut a fine line between eliminating practical barriers that result in impeding minority voting power while not going so far as to create a right to proportional representation. Justice Brennan attempts to distinguish between the results test and a more aggressive effects test by stating that § 2 requires a host of factors to be considered and requires an appraisal of the "totality of the circumstances." In the context of challenges in multi-member districts, as here, he boils them down to three, often called the *"Gingles* factors": (i) size and compactness, (ii) political cohesiveness, and (iii) white bloc voting.

(a) Why is size/compactness relevant? Is it based on practicality—unless the minority is sufficiently large and geographically compact, there is no way

---

1. Jurisdictions that are subject to § 5 must independently comply with both § 2 and § 5; compliance with § 2 does not automatically ensure compliance with § 5. See Georgia v. Ashcroft, 539 U.S. 461, 123 S.Ct. 2498, 156 L.Ed.2d 428 (2003).

to create an ordinary single-member district, and no reason to do so because no minority could win in one? Assuming geographic compactness of the minority group, if the governing body has five at-large members, what percentage of voters would need to be black in order to satisfy this factor? One-fifth of all voters? One-half of one-fifth (plus one) because a black candidate would only need half the votes to win in one district? See Abrams v. Johnson, infra (assumption that 50% needed, relied on by district court, affirmed as not clearly erroneous).

(b) Why is political cohesiveness relevant? Is this based in practicality—with no political cohesiveness, there is also no chance of minority victory? Or is it more theoretical—without cohesiveness there is no "black consciousness" and therefore little or no need to protect the group's interest based on race?

(c) Why is white bloc voting relevant? Is this also practical—without it blacks probably can win elections by building coalitions? Or is it more theoretical—without "white consciousness" there is no racism to overcome? Rare is the case where all blacks vote for the black candidate and all whites vote for the white candidate. So how much less than 100% bloc voting would still permit a finding of bloc-voting? Does Justice Brennan say? See Abrams v. Johnson, infra (proof that "average percentage of whites voting for black candidates across Georgia ranged from 22% to 38%, and the average percentage of blacks voting for white candidates ranged from 20% to 23%," when joined with showing that blacks had won elections in some districts with as much as 23% white support, required affirmance of trial court's judgment that there was insufficient bloc voting).

(d) Is there substantial tension between factors (ii) and (iii)? Do not the *Gingles* factors presume that black bloc voting is a good thing and white bloc voting is not? Note the statistics from Abrams in the preceding sub-paragraph: does it not show that blacks bloc-voted even more than whites? If blacks can vote as a bloc to protect their interests, why cannot whites? Because they are the majority? Does § 2 of the Voting Rights Act protect only blacks (and minorities), or does it protect everyone from racial discrimination? Note the similar issues raised under Title VII, Chapter 7D supra, and § 1981, Chapter 2C.3 supra (all individuals covered for racial discrimination).

(e) Although the Court in *Gingles* describes its factors as applicable in challenges to multi-member districts (that demand single-member districts), are the factors also relevant to redistricting for legislative and Congressional districts? See Growe v. Emison, 507 U.S. 25, 113 S.Ct. 1075, 122 L.Ed.2d 388 (1993) (state redistricting using *Gingles*); Abrams v. Johnson, infra (Congressional districting). But see Voinovich v. Quilter, 507 U.S. 146, 113 S.Ct. 1149, 122 L.Ed.2d 500 (1993) (§ 2 may be violated by "district packing" of minorities as well as by dilution among districts). Cf. Chisom v. Roemer, 501 U.S. 380, 111 S.Ct. 2354, 115 L.Ed.2d 348 (1991) (judicial elections).

3. Justice Brennan closes with the observation that § 2 essentially gives factfinding and law-application competence to trial judges who will be reviewed by the clearly erroneous standard of FRCP 52.

(a) Does this protect him from the charge that his approach will always require proportional race-based representation? But does it not also mean that the outcome of cases may be highly variable depending on local circumstances? Compare the similar issues raised with respect to court-order affirmative action, Chapter 7D supra (Justice Brennan favors discretion). Is that exactly what § 2 intends? Does that mean that Congress saw black exclusion from practical power as a local and variable problem rather than a systemic problem?

(b) Where all *Gingles* factors are present, would a judgment against the plaintiffs be overturned as clearly erroneous? Can a decision *for* the plaintiffs be overturned? See Johnson v. De Grandy, 512 U.S. 997, 114 S.Ct. 2647, 129 L.Ed.2d 775 (yes, *Gingles* factors are not dispositive; overall totality of the circumstances is). Is the Supreme Court the ultimate guardian of § 2?

4. Only after the *Gingles* decision did the Court develop its modern affirmative action jurisprudence, see City of Richmond v. J.A. Croson Co., Chapter 7D supra. As a part of this development, the Court also ruled that race-based affirmative action to maximize black representation is also unconstitutional in **Shaw v. Reno**, 509 U.S. 630, 113 S.Ct. 2816, 125 L.Ed.2d 511 (1993). Justice O'Connor, author of the dissent in *Gingles*, wrote for the 5–4 majority. Would you expect a decline in the Court's support for *Gingles* after *Shaw*?

(a) In **Johnson v. De Grandy**, 512 U.S. 997, 114 S.Ct. 2647, 129 L.Ed.2d 775 (1994), Justice Souter wrote for the majority in a case in which Hispanics had majorities in districts which, if they could field winning candidates, would have given them representation reflective of their relative voting strength. The Court held that "no violation of § 2 can be found here, where, in spite of continuing discrimination and racial bloc voting, minority voters form effective voting majorities in a number of districts roughly proportional to the minority voters' respective shares in the voting-age population." Does this mark an accentuation under § 2 for the proportionality idea that *Shaw* overruled in the constitutional context? Is *Johnson* acceptable because it focuses on majorities of potential voters, not on actual elected representatives?

(b) In **Holder v. Hall**, 512 U.S. 874, 114 S.Ct. 2581, 129 L.Ed.2d 687 (1994), a much divided Court ruled that a challenge to an unusual county legislative setup—one representative for the entire county government—could not be challenged under § 2. The plurality ruled that there was no baseline reasonable alternative against which to measure the plan; two more votes came from justices who held that challenges to the very size of governmental bodies do not involve a challenge to a voting practice, and thus fall outside § 2. Does *Holder* preclude challenges to local charters that adopt a "county manager" form of government? If a county has a council and a single executive, does *Holder* bar a claim that § 2 should require co-executives so that minorities can participate in government?

(c) In **Abrams v. Johnson**, 521 U.S. 74, 117 S.Ct. 1925, 138 L.Ed.2d 285 (1997), Justice Kennedy wrote for the majority. Assuming, without deciding that a need to comply with § 2 might satisfy strict scrutiny under *Shaw*, the Court nevertheless held that no plausible violation based on the *Gingles* factors was possible on the facts of the case. Had a violation been found under the results test, would that have been a defense under *Shaw*? Is a § 2 violation the same thing as a constitutional violation, meaning that a state would then have a "remedial" rationale sufficient to meet strict scrutiny? Would the plan still need to be "narrowly drawn" to correct only *constitutional* violations?

5. As one might expect in modern America, the bi-polar division of voting power discussed in *Gingles* gives way to competition between many ethnic minorities in many parts of the country. See, e.g., Johnson v. De Grandy, supra; Growe v. Emison, supra; Glenn D. Magpantay, *Two Steps Forward, One Step Back, and a Side Step: Asian Americans and the Federal Help America Vote Act*, 10 ASIAN PAC. AM. L.J. 31 (2005) (Asian–Americans as a fast-growing minority with special voting concerns). How should the Court treat these multi-ethnic claims?

(a) Should the Court assume a "rainbow coalition" and put minorities together for measuring size/compactness and bloc voting? Should it look at the specific facts to determine if the minorities vote together (e.g., blacks and Hispanics) or one minority with the majority (e.g., whites and Hispanics), then treat the assembled groups as competitors? Might whites be the protected minority in some areas? See Note, *The Ties That Bind: Coalitions and Governance under Section 2 of the Voting Rights Act*, 117 HARV. L. REV. 2621 (2004) (arguing that coalition-building is more important to politics than representation of one's own group interests).

(b) Does § 2 create the potential of pitting minority against minority in a zero-sum political contest? If blacks obtain a district under § 2, might that rob Hispanics of the chance to have their district? If minorities live in adjacent but separate communities, or together in a mixed community, will it not be very difficult to carve out districts that are both majority-black and majority-Hispanic, especially if the "compactness" requirement includes a regular, ungerrymandered shape? Cf. Bush v. Vera, 517 U.S. 952, 116 S.Ct. 1941, 135 L.Ed.2d 248 (such compactness and non-"bizarreness" of shape required; African–American and Hispanic districts at issue).

6. Immigration and other demographic changes are rapidly producing an America composed of a majority of persons who today are labeled minorities. How should § 2 and Congress respond to these changes?

(a) Is § 2 perverse? Consider this argument: since § 2 protects more cohesive groups who vote (or are outvoted) as a bloc, it appears to protect only those who are on the verge of winning political power anyway; it leaves unprotected those who are the least politically powerful. Do you agree? Or should such less powerful groups lose—that is what politics is all about? (But if losing is just politics, does that not undercut the rationale of adopting § 2?)

(b) Should § 2 be repealed? Cf. Grant Hayden, *The Supreme Court and Voting Rights: A More Complete Exit Strategy*, 83 N.C. L. REV. 949 (2005) (noting problems caused by the section). Would repeal force minorities to coalesce, to build coalitions, sometimes along ethnic line and sometimes along other lines? Would that be a preferable approach to § 2's protection for traditional minorities? If you oppose this idea, is it because you fear that new minorities may displace blacks, whose concerns will once again go unaddressed?

(c) Is § 2 unconstitutional because its "results" test is not curative of a constitutional violation as measured by the Fifteenth Amendment's prohibition of intentional discrimination? Does it lack "congruence and proportionality" because its nationwide remedy exceeds the localized historical problem of suppression of black voters in the South? In striking down the federal Violence Against Women Act on this ground, **United States v. Morrison**, 529 U.S. 598, 120 S.Ct. 1740, 146 L.Ed.2d 658 (2000), the Court noted that its nationwide scope exceeded the areas in which prior violations had been shown, 529 U.S. at 626–27, 120 S.Ct. at 1759:

> "[The VAWA] is also different from these previously upheld remedies in that it applies uniformly throughout the Nation [even though] Congress' findings indicate that the problem of discrimination against the victims of gender-motivated crimes does not exist in all States, or even most States. By contrast, the § 5 remedy upheld in Katzenbach v. Morgan was directed only to the State where the evil found by Congress existed, and in South Carolina v. Katzenbach the remedy was directed only to those States in which Congress found that there had been discrimination."

Is § 2 a threat to federalism? See Michael J. Pitts, *Congressional Enforcement of Affirmative Democracy Through Section 2 of The Voting Rights Act*, 25 N. ILL. U. L. REV. 185 (2005) (arguing no because black voting is exceptional). Do you agree? Is § 2 only constitutional as applied to African–Americans?

APPENDIX

CIVIL RIGHTS STATUTES

■ ■ ■

A. UNITED STATES CODE PROVISIONS
20 U.S.C.

§ 1681. [Education Amendments, Title IX:] Sex

(a) Prohibition against discrimination; exceptions

No person in the United States shall, on the basis of sex, be excluded from participation in, be denied the benefits of, or be subjected to discrimination under any education program or activity receiving Federal financial assistance, except that:

(1) Classes of educational institutions subject to prohibition

in regard to admissions to educational institutions, this section shall apply only to institutions of vocational education, professional education, and graduate higher education, and to public institutions of undergraduate higher education. . . .

(3) Educational institutions of religious organizations with contrary religious tenets

this section shall not apply to an educational institution which is controlled by a religious organization if the application of this subsection would not be consistent with the religious tenets of such organization. . . .

(5) Public educational institutions with traditional and continuing admissions policy

in regard to admissions this section shall not apply to any public institution of undergraduate higher education which is an institution that traditionally and continually from its establishment has had a policy of admitting only students of one sex;

(6) Social fraternities or sororities; voluntary youth service organizations this section shall not apply to membership practices—

(A) of a social fraternity or social sorority which is exempt from taxation under section 501(a) of Title 26, the active membership of which consists primarily of students in attendance at an institution of higher education, or

(B) of the Young Men's Christian Association, Young Women's Christian Association, Girl Scouts, Boy Scouts, Camp Fire Girls, and voluntary youth service organizations which are so exempt, the membership of which has traditionally been limited to persons of one sex and principally to persons of less than nineteen years of age;

(7) Boy or Girl conferences this section shall not apply to—

(A) any program or activity of the American Legion undertaken in connection with the organization or operation of any Boys State conference, Boys Nation conference, Girls State conference, or Girls Nation conference; or

(B) any program or activity of any secondary school or educational institution specifically for ... the promotion of any Boys State conference, Boys Nation conference, Girls State conference, or Girls Nation conference; or ... the selection of students to attend any such conference;

(8) Father-son or mother-daughter activities at educational institutions

this section shall not preclude father-son or mother-daughter activities at an educational institution, but if such activities are provided for students of one sex, opportunities for reasonably comparable activities shall be provided for students of the other sex; and

(9) Institution of higher education scholarship awards in "beauty" pageants

this section shall not apply with respect to any scholarship or other financial assistance awarded by an institution of higher education to any individual because such individual has received such award in any pageant in which the attainment of such award is based upon a combination of factors related to the personal appearance, poise, and talent of such individual and in which participation is limited to individuals of one sex only, so long as such pageant is in compliance with other nondiscrimination provisions of Federal law. . . .

(c) "Educational institution" defined

For purposes of this chapter an educational institution means any public or private preschool, elementary, or secondary school, or any institution of vocational, professional, or higher education, except that in the case of an educational institution composed of more than one school, college, or department which are administratively separate units, such term means each such school, college, or department.

29 U.S.C.

§ 794. Nondiscrimination under Federal grants and programs [Rehabilitation Act of 1973]

(a) Promulgation of rules and regulations

No otherwise qualified individual with a disability in the United States ... shall, solely by reason of her or his disability, be excluded from the participation in, be denied the benefits of, or be subjected to discrimination under any program or activity receiving Federal financial assistance or under any program or activity conducted by any Executive agency or by the United States Postal Service. The head of each such agency shall promulgate such regulations as may be necessary to carry out the amendments to this section made by the Rehabilitation, Comprehensive Services, and Developmental Disabilities Act of 1978. Copies of any proposed regulation shall be submitted to appropriate authorizing committees of the Congress, and such regulation may take effect no earlier than the thirtieth day after the date on which such regulation is so submitted to such committees. . . .

(d) Standards used in determining violation of section

The standards used to determine whether this section has been violated in a complaint alleging employment discrimination under this section shall be the standards applied under title I of the Americans with Disabilities Act of 1990 (42 U.S.C. 12111 et seq.) and the provisions of sections 501 through 504, and 510, of the Americans with Disabilities Act of 1990 (42 U.S.C. 12201 to 12204 and 12210), as such sections relate to employment.

42 U.S.C.

§ 1973. [Voting Rights]

(a) No voting qualification or prerequisite to voting or standard, practice, or procedure shall be imposed or applied by any State or political subdivision in a manner which results in a denial or abridgement of the right of any citizen of the United States to vote on account of race or color, or in contravention of the guarantees set forth in section 1973b(f)(2) of this title, as provided in subsection (b) of this section. [Amended 1982]

(b) A violation of subsection (a) of this section is established if, based on the totality of circumstances, it is shown that the political processes leading to nomination or election in the State or political subdivision are not equally open to participation by members of a class of citizens protected by subsection (a) of this section in that its members have less opportunity than other members of the electorate to participate in the political process and to elect representatives of their choice. The extent to which members of a protected class have been elected to office in the State or political subdivision is one circumstance which may be considered: Provided, That nothing in this section establishes a right to have members of a protected class elected in numbers equal to their proportion in the population. [Amended 1982]

§ 1973b. Suspension of the use of tests or devices in determining eligibility to vote

(a) Action by State or political subdivision for declaratory judgment. . . .

(1) To assure that the right of citizens of the United States to vote is not denied or abridged on account of race or color, no citizen shall be denied the right to vote in any Federal, State, or local election because of his failure to comply with any test or device in any State with respect to which the determinations have been made under the first two sentences of subsection (b) of this section or in any political subdivision of such State (as such subdivision existed on the date such determinations were made with respect to such State), though such determinations were not made with respect to such subdivision as a separate unit, or in any political subdivision with respect to which such determinations have been made as a separate unit, unless the United States District Court for the District of Columbia issues a declaratory judgment under this section. No citizen shall be denied the right to vote in any Federal, State, or local election because of his failure to comply with any test or device in any State with respect to which the determinations have been made under the third sentence of subsection (b) of this section or in any political subdivision of such State (as such subdivision existed on the date such determinations were made with respect to such State), though such determinations were not made with respect to such subdivision as a separate unit, or in any political subdivision with respect to which such determinations have been made as a separate unit, unless the United States District Court for the District of Columbia issues a declaratory judgment under this section. A declaratory judgment under this section shall issue only if such court determines that during the ten years preceding the filing of the action, and during the pendency of such action—

(A) no such test or device has been used within such State or political subdivision for the purpose or with the effect of denying or abridging the right to vote on account of race or color or (in the case of a State or subdivision seeking a declaratory judgment under the second sentence of this subsection) in contravention of the guarantees of subsection (f)(2) of this section;

(B) no final judgment of any court of the United States, other than the denial of declaratory judgment under this section, has determined that denials or abridgements of the right to vote on account of race or color have occurred anywhere in the territory of such State or political subdivision or (in the case of a State or subdivision seeking a declaratory judgment under the second sentence of this subsection) that denials or abridgements of the right to vote in contravention of the guarantees of subsection (f)(2) of this section have occurred anywhere in the territory of such State or subdivision and no consent decree, settlement, or agreement has been entered into resulting in any abandonment of a voting practice challenged on such grounds; and no declaratory judgment under this section shall be entered during the pendency of an action commenced before the filing of an action under this section and alleging such denials or abridgements of the right to vote; . . .

(E) the Attorney General has not interposed any objection (that has not been overturned by a final judgment of a court) and no declaratory judgment has been denied under section 1973c of this title, with respect to any submission by or on behalf of the plaintiff or any governmental unit within its territory under section 1973c of this title, and no such submissions or declaratory judgment actions are pending. . . .

(8) The provisions of this section shall expire at the end of the twenty-five-year period following the effective date of the amendments made by the Fannie Lou Hamer, Rosa Parks, Coretta Scott King, César E. Chávez, Barbara C. Jordan, William C. Velásquez, and Dr. Hector P. Garcia Voting Rights Act Reauthorization and Amendments Act of 2006.

(b) Required factual determinations necessary to allow suspension of compliance with tests . . .

The provisions of subsection (a) of this section shall apply in any State or in any political subdivision of a State which (1) the Attorney General determines maintained on November 1, 1964, any test or device, and with respect to which (2) the Director of the Census determines that less than 50 per centum of the persons of voting age residing therein were registered on November 1, 1964, or that less than 50 per centum of such persons voted in the presidential election of November 1964. On and after August 6, 1970, in addition to any State or political subdivision of a State determined to be subject to subsection (a) of this section pursuant to the previous sentence, the provisions of subsection (a) of this section shall apply in any State or any political subdivision of a State which (i) the Attorney General determines maintained on November 1, 1968, any test or device, and with respect to which (ii) the Director of the Census determines that less than 50 per centum of the persons of voting age residing therein were registered on November 1, 1968, or that less than 50 per centum of such persons voted in the presidential election of November 1968. On and after August 6, 1975, in addition to any State or political subdivision of a State determined to be subject to subsection (a) of this section pursuant to the previous two sentences, the provisions of subsection (a) of this section shall apply in any State or any political subdivision of a State which (i) the Attorney General determines maintained on November 1, 1972, any test or device, and with respect to which (ii) the Director of the Census determines that less than 50 per centum of the citizens of voting age were registered on November 1, 1972, or that less than 50 per centum of such persons voted in the Presidential election of November 1972.

A determination or certification of the Attorney General or of the Director of the Census under this section or under section 1973f or 1973k of this title shall not be reviewable in any court and shall be effective upon publication in the Federal Register.

(c) "Test or device" defined

The phrase "test or device" shall mean any requirement that a person as a prerequisite for voting or registration for voting (1) demonstrate the ability to read, write, understand, or interpret any matter, (2) demonstrate any educational achievement or his knowledge of any particular subject, (3) possess good moral character, or (4) prove his qualifications by the voucher of registered voters or members of any other class. . . .

(e) Completion of requisite grade level of education in American-flag schools in which the predominant classroom language was other than English

(1) Congress hereby declares that to secure the rights under the fourteenth amendment of persons educated in American-flag schools in which the predominant classroom language was other than English, it is necessary to prohibit the States from conditioning the right to vote of such persons on ability to read, write, understand, or interpret any matter in the English language.

(2) No person who demonstrates that he has successfully completed the sixth primary grade in a public school in, or a private school accredited by, any State or territory, the District of Columbia, or the Commonwealth of Puerto Rico in which the predominant classroom language was other than English, shall be denied the right to vote in any Federal, State, or local election because of his inability to read, write, understand, or interpret any matter in the English language, except that in States in which State law provides that a different level of education is presumptive of literacy, he shall demonstrate that he has successfully completed an equivalent level of education in a public school in, or a private school accredited by, any State or territory, the District of Columbia, or the Commonwealth of Puerto Rico in which the predominant classroom language was other than English.

(f) Congressional findings of voting discrimination against language minorities; prohibition of English-only elections; other remedial measures

(1) The Congress finds that voting discrimination against citizens of language minorities is pervasive and national in scope. Such minority citizens are from environments in which the dominant language is other than English. In addition they have been denied equal educational opportunities by State and local governments, resulting in severe disabilities and continuing illiteracy in the English language. The Congress further finds that, where State and local officials conduct elections only in English, language minority citizens are excluded from participating in the electoral process. In many areas of the country, this exclusion is aggravated by acts of physical, economic, and political intimidation. The Congress declares that, in order to

enforce the guarantees of the fourteenth and fifteenth amendments to the United States Constitution, it is necessary to eliminate such discrimination by prohibiting English-only elections, and by prescribing other remedial devices.

(2) No voting qualification or prerequisite to voting, or standard, practice, or procedure shall be imposed or applied by any State or political subdivision to deny or abridge the right of any citizen of the United States to vote because he is a member of a language minority group.

(3) In addition to the meaning given the term under subsection (c) of this section, the term "test or device" shall also mean any practice or requirement by which any State or political subdivision provided any registration or voting notices, forms, instructions, assistance, or other materials or information relating to the electoral process, including ballots, only in the English language, where the Director of the Census determines that more than five per centum of the citizens of voting age residing in such State or political subdivision are members of a single language minority. With respect to subsection (b) of this section, the term "test or device", as defined in this subsection, shall be employed only in making the determinations under the third sentence of that subsection. . . .

§ 1973c. Alteration of voting qualifications and procedures; [Preclearance]

(a) Whenever a State or political subdivision with respect to which the prohibitions set forth in section 1973b(a) of this title based upon determinations made under the first sentence of section 1973b(b) of this title are in effect shall enact or seek to administer any voting qualification or prerequisite to voting, or standard, practice, or procedure with respect to voting different from that in force or effect on November 1, 1964, or whenever a State or political subdivision with respect to which the prohibitions set forth in section 1973b(a) of this title based upon determinations made under the second sentence of section 1973b(b) of this title are in effect shall enact or seek to administer any voting qualification or prerequisite to voting, or standard, practice, or procedure with respect to voting different from that in force or effect on November 1, 1968, or whenever a State or political subdivision with respect to which the prohibitions set forth in section 1973b(a) of this title based upon determinations made under the third sentence of section 1973b(b) of this title are in effect shall enact or seek to administer any voting qualification or prerequisite to voting, or standard, practice, or procedure with respect to voting different from that in force or effect on November 1, 1972, such State or subdivision may institute an action in the United States District Court for the District of Columbia for a declaratory judgment that such qualification, prerequisite, standard, practice, or procedure neither has the purpose nor will have the effect of denying or abridging the right to vote on account of race or color, or in contravention of the guarantees set forth in section 1973b(f)(2) of this title, and unless and until the court enters such judgment no person shall be denied the right to vote for failure to comply with such qualification, prerequisite, standard, practice, or procedure: Provided, That such qualification, prerequisite, standard, practice, or procedure may be enforced without such proceeding if the qualification, prerequisite, standard, practice, or procedure has been submitted by the chief legal officer or other appropriate official of such State or subdivision to the Attorney General and the Attorney General has not interposed an objection within sixty days after such submission, or upon good cause shown, to facilitate an expedited approval within sixty days after such submission, the Attorney General has affirmatively indicated that such objection will not be made. Neither an affirmative indication by the Attorney General that no objection will be made, nor the Attorney General's failure to object, nor a declaratory judgment entered under this section shall bar a subsequent action to enjoin enforcement of such qualification, prerequisite, standard, practice, or procedure. In the event the Attorney General affirmatively indicates that no objection will be made within the sixty-day period following receipt of a submission, the Attorney General may reserve the right to reexamine the submission if additional information comes to his attention during the remainder of the sixty-day period which would otherwise require objection in accordance with this section. Any action under this section shall be heard and determined by a court of three judges in accordance with the provisions of section 2284 of Title 28 and any appeal shall lie to the Supreme Court.

(b) Any voting qualification or prerequisite to voting, or standard, practice, or procedure with respect to voting that has the purpose of or will have the effect of diminishing the ability of any citizens of the United States on account of race or color, or in contravention of the guarantees set forth in section 1973b(f)(2) of this title, to elect their preferred candidates of choice denies or abridges the right to vote within the meaning of subsection (a) of this section.

(c) The term "purpose" in subsections (a) and (b) of this section shall include any discriminatory purpose. [2006 Amendment]

(d) The purpose of subsection (b) of this section is to protect the ability of such citizens to elect their preferred candidates of choice. [2006 Amendment]

§ 1981. Equal rights under the law

(a) Statement of equal rights

All persons within the jurisdiction of the United States shall have the same right in every State and Territory to make and enforce contracts, to sue, be parties, give evidence, and to the full and equal benefit of all laws and proceedings for the security of persons and property as is enjoyed by white citizens, and shall be subject to like punishment, pains, penalties, taxes, licenses, and exactions of every kind, and to no other.

(b) "Make and enforce contracts" defined

For purposes of this section, the term "make and enforce contracts" includes the making, performance, modification, and termination of contracts, and the enjoyment of all benefits, privileges, terms, and conditions of the contractual relationship.

(c) Protection against impairment

The rights protected by this section are protected against impairment by nongovernmental discrimination and impairment under color of State law.

§ 1981A. Damages in cases of intentional discrimination in employment

(a) Right of recovery

(1) ... In an action brought by a complaining party under section 706 or 717 of the Civil Rights Act of 1964 [42 U.S.C. §§ 2000e–5 or 2000e–16] against a respondent who engaged in unlawful intentional discrimination (not an employment practice that is unlawful because of its disparate impact) prohibited under section 703, 704, or 717 of the Act [42 U.S.C. §§ 2000e–2, 2000e–3, or 2000e–16], and provided that the complaining party cannot recover under section 1981 of this title, the complaining party may recover compensatory and punitive damages as allowed in subsection (b) of this section, in addition to any relief authorized by section 706(g) of the Civil Rights Act of 1964, from the respondent. [Under § 2 this remedy shall also apply to claims brought under the Americans With disabilities Act, provided that damages are not recoverable when the employer has made "good faith efforts" to accommodate an employee.]

(b) Compensatory and punitive damages

(1) ... A complaining party may recover punitive damages under this section against a respondent (other than a government, government agency or political subdivision) if the complaining party demonstrates that the respondent engaged in a discriminatory practice or discriminatory practices with malice or with reckless indifference to the federally protected rights of an aggrieved individual.

(2) ... Compensatory damages awarded under this section shall not include backpay, interest on backpay, or any other type of relief authorized under section 706(g) of the Civil Rights Act of 1964 [42 U.S.C. § 2000e–5(g)].

(3) ... The sum of the amount of compensatory damages awarded under this section for future pecuniary losses, emotional pain, suffering, inconvenience, mental anguish, loss of enjoyment of life, and other nonpecuniary losses, and the amount of punitive damages awarded under this section, shall not exceed, for each complaining party—

(A) in the case of a respondent who has more than 14 and fewer than 101 employees in each of 20 or more calendar weeks in the current or preceding calendar year, $50,000;

(B) in the case of a respondent who has more than 100 and fewer than 201 employees in each of 20 or more calendar weeks in the current or preceding calendar year, $100,000; and

(C) in the case of a respondent who has more than 200 and fewer than 501 employees in each of 20 or more calendar weeks in the current or preceding calendar year, $200,000; and

(D) in the case of a respondent who has more than 500 employees in each of 20 or more calendar weeks in the current or preceding calendar year, $300,000. . . .

(c) Jury trial

If a complaining party seeks compensatory or punitive damages under this section—

(1) any party may demand a trial by jury; and

(2) the court shall not inform the jury of the limitations described in subsection (b)(3) of this section. . . .

§ 1982.   Property rights of citizens

All citizens of the United States shall have the same right, in every State and Territory, as is enjoyed by white citizens thereof to inherit, purchase, lease, sell, hold, and convey real and personal property.

§ 1983.   Civil action for deprivation of rights

Every person who, under color of any statute, ordinance, regulation, custom, or usage, of any State or Territory or the District of Columbia, subjects, or causes to be subjected, any citizen of the United States or other person within the jurisdiction thereof to the deprivation of any rights, privileges, or immunities secured by the Constitution and laws, shall be liable to the party injured in an action at law, suit in equity, or other proper proceeding for redress, except that in any action brought against a judicial officer for an act or omission taken in such officer's judicial capacity, injunctive relief shall not be granted unless a declaratory decree was violated or declaratory relief was unavailable. For the purposes of this section, any Act of Congress applicable exclusively to the District of Columbia shall be considered to be a statute of the District of Columbia.

§ 1985.   Conspiracy to interfere with civil rights

. . . .

(2) Obstructing justice; intimidating party, witness, or juror

If two or more persons in any State or Territory conspire to deter, by force, intimidation, or threat, any party or witness in any court of the United States from attending such court, or from testifying to any matter pending therein, freely, fully, and truthfully, or to injure such party or witness in his person or property on account of his having so attended or testified, or to influence the verdict, presentment, or indictment of any grand or petit juror in any such court, or to injure such juror in his person or property on account of any verdict, presentment, or indictment lawfully assented to by him, or of his being or having been such juror; or if two or more persons conspire for the purpose of impeding, hindering, obstructing, or defeating, in any manner, the due course of justice in any State or Territory, with intent to deny to any citizen the equal protection of the laws, or to injure him or his property for lawfully enforcing, or attempting to enforce, the right of any person, or class of persons, to the equal protection of the laws;

(3) Depriving persons of rights or privileges

If two or more persons in any State or Territory conspire or go in disguise on the highway or on the premises of another, for the purpose of depriving, either directly or indirectly, any person or class of persons of the equal protection of the laws, or of equal privileges and immunities under the laws; or for the purpose of preventing or hindering the constituted authorities of any State or Territory from giving or securing to all persons within such State or Territory the equal protection of the laws; or if two or more persons conspire to prevent by force, intimidation, or threat, any citizen who is lawfully entitled to vote, from giving his support or advocacy in a legal manner, toward or in favor of the election of any lawfully qualified person as an elector for President or Vice President, or as a Member of Congress of the United States; or to injure any citizen in person or property on account of such support or advocacy; in any case of conspiracy set forth in this section, if one or more persons engaged therein do, or cause to be done, any act in furtherance of the object of such conspiracy, whereby another is injured in his person or property, or deprived of having and exercising any right or privilege of a citizen of the United States, the party so injured or deprived may have an action for the recovery of damages occasioned by such injury or deprivation, against any one or more of the conspirators.

§ 1988. Proceedings in vindication of civil rights

(a) Applicability of statutory and common law

The jurisdiction in civil and criminal matters conferred on the district courts ... for the protection of all persons in the United States in their civil rights, and for their vindication, shall be exercised and enforced in conformity with the laws of the United States, so far as such laws are suitable to carry the same into effect; but in all cases where they are not adapted to the object, or are deficient in the provisions necessary to furnish suitable remedies and punish offenses against law, the common law, as modified and changed by the constitution and statutes of the State wherein the court having jurisdiction of such civil or criminal cause is held, so far as the same is not inconsistent with the Constitution and laws of the United States, shall be extended to and govern the said courts in the trial and disposition of the cause, and, if it is of a criminal nature, in the infliction of punishment on the party found guilty.

(b) Attorney's fees

In any action or proceeding to enforce a provision of sections 1981, 1981a, 1982, 1983, 1985, and 1986 of this title, title IX of Public Law 92– 318 [20 U.S.C. § 1681 et seq.] [or] title VI of the Civil Rights Act of 1964 [42 U.S.C. § 2000d et seq.], . . . the court, in its discretion, may allow the prevailing party, other than the United States, a reasonable attorney's fee as part of the costs, except that in any action brought against a judicial officer for an act or omission taken in such officer's judicial capacity such officer shall not be held liable for any costs, including attorney's fees, unless such action was clearly in excess of such officer's jurisdiction.

(c) Expert fees

In awarding an attorney's fee under subsection (b) of this section in any action or proceeding to enforce a provision of section 1981 or 1981a of this title, the court, in its discretion, may include expert fees as part of the attorney's fee.

§ 1997e. Suits by prisoners

(a) Applicability of administrative remedies

No action shall be brought with respect to prison conditions under section 1983 of this title, or any other Federal law, by a prisoner confined in any jail, prison, or other correctional facility until such administrative remedies as are available are exhausted. . .

(c) Dismissal . . .

> (2) In the event that a claim is, on its face, frivolous, malicious, fails to state a claim upon which relief can be granted, or seeks monetary relief from a defendant who is immune from such relief, the court may dismiss the underlying claim without first requiring the exhaustion of administrative remedies.

§ 2000a. [Title II:] Prohibition against discrimination [in] public accommodation

(a) Equal access

All persons shall be entitled to the full and equal enjoyment of the goods, services, facilities, privileges, advantages, and accommodations of any place of public accommodation, as defined in this section, without discrimination or segregation on the ground of race, color, religion, or national origin.

(b) Establishments affecting interstate commerce [etc.]

Each of the following establishments which serves the public is a place of public accommodation within the meaning of this subchapter if its operations affect commerce, or if discrimination or segregation by it is supported by State action:

(1) any inn, hotel, motel, or other establishment which provides lodging to transient guests, other than an establishment located within a building which contains not more than five rooms for rent or hire and which is actually occupied by the proprietor of such establishment as his residence;

(2) any restaurant, cafeteria, lunchroom, lunch counter, soda fountain, or other facility principally engaged in selling food for consumption on the premises, including, but not limited to, any such facility located on the premises of any retail establishment; or any gasoline station;

(3) any motion picture house, theater, concert hall, sports arena, stadium or other place of exhibition or entertainment; and

(4) any establishment (A)(i) which is physically located within the premises of any establishment otherwise covered by this subsection, or (ii) within the premises of which is physically located any such covered establishment, and (B) which holds itself out as serving patrons of such covered establishment.

(c) Operations affecting commerce; criteria; "commerce" defined

The operations of an establishment affect commerce within the meaning of this subchapter if (1) it is one of the establishments described in paragraph (1) of subsection (b) of this section; (2) in the case of an establishment described in paragraph (2) of subsection (b) of this section, it serves or offers to serve interstate travelers or a substantial portion of the food which it serves, or gasoline or other products which it sells, has moved in commerce; (3) in the case of an establishment described in paragraph (3) of subsection (b) of this section, it customarily presents films, performances, athletic teams, exhibitions, or other sources of entertainment which move in commerce; and (4) in the case of an establishment described in paragraph (4) of subsection (b) of this section, it is physically located within the premises of, or there is physically located within its premises, an establishment the operations of which affect commerce within the meaning of this subsection. For purposes of this section, "commerce" means travel, trade, traffic, commerce, transportation, or communication among the several States, or between the District of Columbia and any State, or between any foreign country or any territory or possession and any State or the District of Columbia, or between points in the same State but through any other State or the District of Columbia or a foreign country.

(d) Support by State action

Discrimination or segregation by an establishment is supported by State action within the meaning of this subchapter if such discrimination or segregation (1) is carried on under color of any law, statute, ordinance, or regulation; or (2) is carried on under color of any custom or usage required or enforced by officials of the State or political subdivision thereof; or (3) is required by action of the State or political subdivision thereof.

(e) Private establishments

The provisions of this subchapter shall not apply to a private club or other establishment not in fact open to the public, except to the extent that the facilities of such establishment are made available to the customers or patrons of an establishment within the scope of subsection (b) of this section.

§ 2000d.   [Title VI: Discrimination] under Federally assisted programs on ground of race, color, or national origin

No person in the United States shall, on the ground of race, color, or national origin, be excluded from participation in, be denied the benefits of, or be subjected to discrimination under any program or activity receiving Federal financial assistance.

§ 2000d–1.   [Title VI:] Federal authority ... rules and regulations; [etc.]

Each Federal department and agency which is empowered to extend Federal financial assistance to any program or activity, by way of grant, loan, or contract other than a contract of insurance or guaranty, is authorized and directed to effectuate the provisions of section 2000d of this title with respect to such program or activity by issuing rules, regulations, or orders of general applicability which shall be consistent with achievement of the objectives of the statute authorizing the financial assistance in connection with which the action is taken. No such rule, regulation, or order shall become effective unless and until approved by the President. Compliance with any requirement adopted pursuant to this section may be effected (1) by the termination of or refusal to grant or to continue assistance under such program or activity to any recipient as to whom there has been an express finding on the record, after opportunity for hearing, of a failure to comply with such requirement, but such termination or refusal shall be limited to the particular political entity, or part thereof, or other recipient as to whom such a finding has been made and, shall be limited in its effect to the particular program, or part thereof, in which such noncompliance has been so found, or (2) by any other means authorized by law: Provided, however, That no such action shall be taken until the department or agency concerned has advised the appropriate person or persons of the failure to comply with the requirement and has determined that compliance cannot be secured by voluntary means. In the case of any action terminating, or refusing to grant or continue, assistance because of failure to comply with a requirement imposed pursuant to this section, the head of the Federal department or agency shall file with the committees of the House and Senate having legislative jurisdiction over the program or activity involved a full written report of the circumstances and the grounds for such action. No such action shall become effective until thirty days have elapsed after the filing of such report.

§ 2000d-4a. [Title VI:] "Program or activity" and "program" defined [CR Restoration Act]

For the purposes of this subchapter, the term "program or activity" and the term "program" mean all of the operations of—

(1)(A) a department, agency, special purpose district, or other instrumentality of a State or of a local government; or

(B) the entity of such State or local government that distributes such assistance and each such department or agency (and each other State or local government entity) to which the assistance is extended, in the case of assistance to a State or local government;

(2)(A) a college, university, or other postsecondary institution, or a public system of higher education; or

(B) a local educational agency (as defined in section 7801 of Title 20), system of vocational education, or other school system;

(3)(A) an entire corporation, partnership, or other private organization, or an entire sole proprietorship—

(i) if assistance is extended to such corporation, partnership, private organization, or sole proprietorship as a whole; or

(ii) which is principally engaged in the business of providing education, health care, housing, social services, or parks and recreation; or

(B) the entire plant or other comparable, geographically separate facility to which Federal financial assistance is extended, in the case of any other corporation, partnership, private organization, or sole proprietorship; or

(4) any other entity which is established by two or more of the entities described in paragraph (1), (2), or (3);

any part of which is extended Federal financial assistance.

§ 2000d-7. [Title VI:] Civil rights remedies equalization

(a) General provision

(1) A State shall not be immune under the Eleventh Amendment of the Constitution of the United States from suit in Federal court for a violation of section 504 of the Rehabilitation Act of 1973 [29 U.S.C. § 794], title IX of the Education Amendments of 1972 [20 U.S.C. § 1681 et seq.], ... title VI of the Civil Rights Act of 1964 [42 U.S.C. § 2000d et seq.], or the provisions of any other Federal statute prohibiting discrimination by recipients of Federal financial assistance.

(2) In a suit against a State for a violation of a statute referred to in paragraph (1), remedies (including remedies both at law and in

equity) are available for such a violation to the same extent as such remedies are available for such a violation in the suit against any public or private entity other than a State. . . .

§ 2000e.   [Title VII: Employment Discrimination:] Definitions

For the purposes of this subchapter—

. . .

(b) The term "employer" means a person engaged in an industry affecting commerce who has fifteen or more employees for each working day in each of twenty or more calendar weeks in the current or preceding calendar year, and any agent of such a person, but such term does not include (1) the United States, a corporation wholly owned by the Government of the United States, an Indian tribe, or any department or agency of the District of Columbia subject by statute to procedures of the competitive service (as defined in section 2102 of Title 5), or (2) a bona fide private membership club (other than a labor organization) which is exempt from taxation under section 501(c) of Title 26, except that during the first year after March 24, 1972, persons having fewer than twenty-five employees (and their agents) shall not be considered employers. . . .

(f) The term "employee" means an individual employed by an employer, except that the term "employee" shall not include any person elected to public office in any State or political subdivision of any State by the qualified voters thereof, or any person chosen by such officer to be on such officer's personal staff, or an appointee on the policy making level or an immediate adviser with respect to the exercise of the constitutional or legal powers of the office. The exemption set forth in the preceding sentence shall not include employees subject to the civil service laws of a State government, governmental agency or political subdivision. With respect to employment in a foreign country, such term includes an individual who is a citizen of the United States.

(g) The term "commerce" means trade, traffic, commerce, transportation, transmission, or communication among the several States; or between a State and any place outside thereof; or within the District of Columbia, or a possession of the United States; or between points in the same State but through a point outside thereof.

(h) The term "industry affecting commerce" means any activity, business, or industry in commerce or in which a labor dispute would hinder or obstruct commerce or the free flow of commerce and includes any activity or industry "affecting commerce" within the meaning of the Labor–Management Reporting and Disclosure Act of 1959, and further includes any governmental industry, business, or activity. . . .

(j) The term "religion" includes all aspects of religious observance and practice, as well as belief, unless an employer demonstrates that he is unable to reasonably accommodate to an employee's or prospective employee's religious observance or practice without undue hardship on the conduct of the employer's business.

(k) The terms "because of sex" or "on the basis of sex" include, but are not limited to, because of or on the basis of pregnancy, childbirth, or related medical conditions; and women affected by pregnancy, childbirth, or related medical conditions shall be treated the same for all employment-related purposes, including receipt of benefits under fringe benefit programs, as other persons not so affected but similar in their ability or inability to work, and nothing in section 2000e–2(h) of this title shall be interpreted to permit otherwise. This subsection shall not require an employer to pay for health insurance benefits for abortion, except where the life of the mother would be endangered if the fetus were carried to term, or except where medical complications have arisen from an abortion: Provided, That nothing herein shall preclude an employer from providing abortion benefits or otherwise affect bargaining agreements in regard to abortion.... [Pregnancy Discrimination Act]

(m) The term "demonstrates" means meets the burdens of production and persuasion. [1991 Amendment]

§ 2000e–2.   [Title VII:] Unlawful employment practices

(a) Employer practices

It shall be an unlawful employment practice for an employer—

(1) to fail or refuse to hire or to discharge any individual, or otherwise to discriminate against any individual with respect to his compensation, terms, conditions, or privileges of employment, because of such individual's race, color, religion, sex, or national origin; or

(2) to limit, segregate, or classify his employees or applicants for employment in any way which would deprive or tend to deprive any individual of employment opportunities or otherwise adversely affect his status as an employee, because of such individual's race, color, religion, sex, or national origin. . . . .

(e) Businesses or enterprises with [bona fide occupational qualifications]

Notwithstanding any other provision of this subchapter, (1) it shall not be an unlawful employment practice for an employer to hire and employ employees, for an employment agency to classify, or refer for employment any individual, for a labor organization to classify its membership or to classify or refer for employment any individual, or for an employer, labor organization, or joint labor-management committee controlling apprenticeship or other training or retraining programs to admit or employ any individual in any such program, on the basis of his religion, sex, or national origin in those certain instances where religion, sex, or national origin is a bona fide occupational qualification reasonably necessary to the normal operation of that particular business or enterprise, and

(2) it shall not be an unlawful employment practice for a school, college, university, or other educational institution or institution of learning to hire and employ employees of a particular religion if such school, college, university, or other educational institution or institution of learning is, in whole or in substantial part, owned, supported, controlled, or managed by a particular religion or by a particular religious corporation, association, or society, or if the curriculum of such school, college, university, or other educational institution or institution of learning is directed toward the propagation of a particular religion. . . .

(h) Seniority or merit system. . . .

Notwithstanding any other provision of this subchapter, it shall not be an unlawful employment practice for an employer to apply different standards of compensation, or different terms, conditions, or privileges of employment pursuant to a bona fide seniority or merit system, or a system which measures earnings by quantity or quality of production or to employees who work in different locations, provided that such differences are not the result of an intention to discriminate because of race, color, religion, sex, or national origin, nor shall it be an unlawful employment practice for an employer to give and to act upon the results of any professionally developed ability test provided that such test, its administration or action upon the results is not designed, intended or used to discriminate because of race, color, religion, sex or national origin. It shall not be an unlawful employment practice under this subchapter for any employer to differentiate upon the basis of sex in determining the amount of the wages or compensation paid or to be paid to employees of such employer if such differentiation is authorized by the provisions of section 206(d) of Title 29.

(i) Businesses or enterprises extending preferential treatment to Indians

Nothing contained in this subchapter shall apply to any business or enterprise on or near an Indian reservation with respect to any publicly announced employment practice of such business or enterprise under which a preferential treatment is given to any individual because he is an Indian living on or near a reservation.

(j) Preferential treatment [and] existing number or percentage imbalance

Nothing contained in this subchapter shall be interpreted to require any employer, employment agency, labor organization, or joint labor-management committee subject to this subchapter to grant preferential treatment to any individual or to any group because the race, color, religion, sex, or national origin of such individual or group on account of an imbalance which may exist with respect to the total number or percentage of persons of any race, color, religion, sex, or national origin employed by any employer, referred or classified for employment by any employment agency or labor organization, admitted to membership or classified by any labor organization, or admitted to, or employed in, any apprenticeship or other training program, in comparison with the total number or percentage of persons of such race, color, religion, sex, or national origin in any community, State, section, or other area, or in the available work force in any community, State, section, or other area.

(k) Burden of proof in disparate impact cases [1991 Amendment]

(1)(A) An unlawful employment practice based on disparate impact is established under this subchapter only if—

(i) a complaining party demonstrates that a respondent uses a particular employment practice that causes a disparate impact on the basis of race, color, religion, sex, or national origin and the respondent fails to demonstrate that the challenged practice is job related for the position in question and consistent with business necessity; or

(ii) the complaining party makes the demonstration described in subparagraph (C) with respect to an alternative employment practice and the respondent refuses to adopt such alternative employment practice.

(B)(i) With respect to demonstrating that a particular employment practice causes a disparate impact as described in subparagraph (A)(i), the complaining party shall demonstrate that each particular challenged employment practice causes a disparate impact, except that if the complaining party can demonstrate to the court that the elements of a respondent's decisionmaking process are not capable of separation for analysis, the decisionmaking process may be analyzed as one employment practice.

(ii) If the respondent demonstrates that a specific employment practice does not cause the disparate impact, the respondent shall not be required to demonstrate that such practice is required by business necessity.

(C) The demonstration referred to by subparagraph (A)(ii) shall be in accordance with the law as it existed on June 4, 1989, with respect to the concept of "alternative employment practice".

(2) A demonstration that an employment practice is required by business necessity may not be used as a defense against a claim of intentional discrimination under this subchapter.

(3) Notwithstanding any other provision of this subchapter, a rule barring the employment of an individual who currently and knowingly uses or possesses a controlled substance, as defined in schedules I and II of section 102(6) of the Controlled Substances Act (21 U.S.C. 802(6)), other than the use or possession of a drug taken under the supervision of a licensed health care professional, or any other use or possession authorized by the Controlled Substances Act [21 U.S.C. § 801 et seq.] or any other provision of Federal law, shall be considered an unlawful employment practice under this subchapter only if such rule is adopted or applied with an intent to discriminate because of race, color, religion, sex, or national origin.

(l) Prohibition of discriminatory use of test scores

It shall be an unlawful employment practice for a respondent, in connection with the selection or referral of applicants or candidates for employment or promotion, to adjust the scores of, use different cutoff scores for, or otherwise alter the results of, employment related tests on the basis of race, color, religion, sex, or national origin. [1991 Amendment]

(m) Impermissible consideration of race, color, religion, sex, or national origin. . . .

Except as otherwise provided in this subchapter, an unlawful employment practice is established when the complaining party demonstrates that race, color, religion, sex, or national origin was a motivating factor for any employment practice, even though other factors also motivated the practice. . . . [1991 Amendment]

§ 2000e–5. [Title VII:] Enforcement provisions

· · · ·

(g) Injunctions; appropriate affirmative action; equitable relief; accrual of back pay; reduction of back pay; limitations on judicial orders

(1) If the court finds that the respondent has intentionally engaged in or is intentionally engaging in an unlawful employment practice charged in the complaint, the court may enjoin the respondent from engaging in such unlawful employment practice, and order such affirmative action as may be appropriate, which may include, but is not limited to, reinstatement or hiring of employees, with or without back pay (payable by the employer, employment agency, or labor organization, as the case may be, responsible for the unlawful employment practice), or any other equitable relief as the court deems appropriate. Back pay liability shall not accrue from a date more than two years prior to the filing of a charge with the Commission. Interim earnings or amounts earnable with reasonable diligence by the person or persons discriminated against shall operate to reduce the back pay otherwise allowable. . . .

(2)˙ . . . (B) On a claim in which an individual proves a violation under section 2000e–2(m) of this title and a respondent demonstrates that the respondent would have taken the same action in the absence of the impermissible motivating factor, the court—

> (i) may grant declaratory relief, injunctive relief (except as provided in clause (ii)), and attorney's fees and costs demonstrated to be directly attributable only to the pursuit of a claim under section 2000e–2(m) of this title; and

> (ii) shall not award damages or issue an order requiring any admission, reinstatement, hiring, promotion, or payment, described in subparagraph (A). [1991 Amendment]. . . .

(k) Attorney's fee; liability of Commission and United States for costs

In any action or proceeding under this subchapter the court, in its discretion, may allow the prevailing party, other than the Commission or the United States, a reasonable attorney's fee (including expert fees) as part of the costs, and the Commission and the United States shall be liable for costs the same as a private person.

§ 2000e–16. [Title VII:] Employment by Federal Government

(a) Discriminatory practices prohibited; employees or applicants for employment subject to coverage

All personnel actions affecting employees or applicants for employment (except with regard to aliens employed outside the limits of the United States) in military departments as defined in section 102 of Title 5, in executive agencies as defined in section 105 of Title 5 (including employees and applicants for employment who are paid from nonappropriated funds), in the United States Postal Service and the Postal Rate Commission, in those units of the Government of the District of Columbia having positions in the competitive service, and in those units of the judicial branch of the Federal Government having positions in the competitive service, in the Smithsonian Institution, and in the Government Printing Office, the Government Accountability Office, and the Library of Congress shall be made free from any discrimination based on race, color, religion, sex, or national origin. . . .

(c) Civil action by employee or applicant for employment for redress of grievances; [etc.]

Within 90 days of receipt of notice of final action taken by a department, agency, or unit referred to in subsection (a) of this section, or by the Equal Employment Opportunity Commission upon an appeal from a decision or order of such department, agency, or unit on a complaint of discrimination based on race, color, religion, sex or national origin, brought pursuant to subsection (a) of this section, Executive Order 11478 or any succeeding Executive orders, or after one hundred and eighty days from the filing of the initial charge with the department, agency, or unit or with the Equal Employment Opportunity Commission on appeal from a decision or order of such department, agency, or unit until such time as final action may be taken by a department, agency, or unit, an employee or applicant for employment, if aggrieved by the final disposition of his complaint, or by the failure to take final action on his complaint, may file a civil action as provided in section 2000e–5 of this title, in which civil action the head of the department, agency, or unit, as appropriate, shall be the defendant. . . .

§ 12101. [Americans With Disabilities Act] Findings and purpose

(a) Findings

The Congress finds that—

(1) physical or mental disabilities in no way diminish a person's right to fully participate in all aspects of society, yet many people

with physical or mental disabilities have been precluded from doing so because of discrimination; others who have a record of a disability or are regarded as having a disability also have been subjected to discrimination;

(2) historically, society has tended to isolate and segregate individuals with disabilities, and, despite some improvements, such forms of discrimination against individuals with disabilities continue to be a serious and pervasive social problem;

(3) discrimination against individuals with disabilities persists in such critical areas as employment, housing, public accommodations, education, transportation, communication, recreation, institutionalization, health services, voting, and access to public services;

(4) unlike individuals who have experienced discrimination on the basis of race, color, sex, national origin, religion, or age, individuals who have experienced discrimination on the basis of disability have often had no legal recourse to redress such discrimination;

(5) individuals with disabilities continually encounter various forms of discrimination, including outright intentional exclusion, the discriminatory effects of architectural, transportation, and communication barriers, overprotective rules and policies, failure to make modifications to existing facilities and practices, exclusionary qualification standards and criteria, segregation, and relegation to lesser services, programs, activities, benefits, jobs, or other opportunities;

(6) census data, national polls, and other studies have documented that people with disabilities, as a group, occupy an inferior status in our society, and are severely disadvantaged socially, vocationally, economically, and educationally;

(7) the Nation's proper goals regarding individuals with disabilities are to assure equality of opportunity, full participation, independent living, and economic self-sufficiency for such individuals; and

(8) the continuing existence of unfair and unnecessary discrimination and prejudice denies people with disabilities the opportunity to compete on an equal basis and to pursue those opportunities for which our free society is justifiably famous, and costs the United States billions of dollars in unnecessary expenses resulting from dependency and nonproductivity.

(b) Purpose

It is the purpose of this chapter—

(1) to provide a clear and comprehensive national mandate for the elimination of discrimination against individuals with disabilities;

(2) to provide clear, strong, consistent, enforceable standards addressing discrimination against individuals with disabilities;

(3) to ensure that the Federal Government plays a central role in enforcing the standards established in this chapter on behalf of individuals with disabilities; and

(4) to invoke the sweep of congressional authority, including the power to enforce the fourteenth amendment and to regulate commerce, in order to address the major areas of discrimination faced day-to-day by people with disabilities.

§ 12102. [Americans With Disabilities Act: General] Definitions

As used in this chapter . . .

(1) Disability

The term "disability" means, with respect to an individual—

(A) a physical or mental impairment that substantially limits one or more major life activities of such individual;

(B) a record of such an impairment; or

(C) being regarded as having such an impairment (as described in paragraph (3)).

(2) Major life activities

(A) In general

For purposes of paragraph (1), major life activities include, but are not limited to, caring for oneself, performing manual tasks, seeing, hearing, eating, sleeping, walking, standing, lifting, bending, speaking, breathing, learning, reading, concentrating, thinking, communicating, and working.

(B) Major bodily functions

For purposes of paragraph (1), a major life activity also includes the operation of a major bodily function, including but not limited to, functions of the immune system, normal cell growth, digestive, bowel, bladder, neurological, brain, respiratory, circulatory, endocrine, and reproductive functions.

(3) Regarded as having such an impairment [2008 Amendment]

For purposes of paragraph (1)(C):

(A) An individual meets the requirement of "being regarded as having such an impairment" if the individual establishes that he or she has been subjected to an action prohibited under this chapter because of an actual or perceived physical or mental impairment whether or not the impairment limits or is perceived to limit a major life activity.

(B) Paragraph (1)(C) shall not apply to impairments that are transitory and minor. A transitory impairment is an impairment with an actual or expected duration of 6 months or less.

(4) Rules of construction regarding the definition of disability [2008 Amendment]

The definition of "disability" in paragraph (1) shall be construed in accordance with the following:

(A) The definition of disability in this chapter shall be construed in favor of broad coverage of individuals under this chapter, to the maximum extent permitted by the terms of this chapter.

(B) The term "substantially limits" shall be interpreted consistently with the findings and purposes of the ADA Amendments Act of 2008.

(C) An impairment that substantially limits one major life activity need not limit other major life activities in order to be considered a disability.

(D) An impairment that is episodic or in remission is a disability if it would substantially limit a major life activity when active.

(E)(i) The determination of whether an impairment substantially limits a major life activity shall be made without regard to the ameliorative effects of mitigating measures such as—

(I) medication, medical supplies, equipment, or appliances, low-vision devices (which do not include ordinary eyeglasses or contact lenses), prosthetics including limbs and devices, hearing aids and cochlear implants or other implantable hearing devices, mobility devices, or oxygen therapy equipment and supplies;

(II) use of assistive technology;

(III) reasonable accommodations or auxiliary aids or services; or

(IV) learned behavioral or adaptive neurological modifications.

(ii) The ameliorative effects of the mitigating measures of ordinary eyeglasses or contact lenses shall be considered in determining whether an impairment substantially limits a major life activity. . . .

§ 12111. [ADA Title I: Employment] Definitions

As used in this subchapter: . . .

(2) Covered entity

The term "covered entity" means an employer, employment agency, labor organization, or joint labor-management committee.

(3) Direct threat

The term "direct threat" means a significant risk to the health or safety of others that cannot be eliminated by reasonable accommodation. . . . .

(8) Qualified individual with a disability

The term "qualified individual" means an individual who, with or without reasonable accommodation, can perform the essential functions of the employment position that such individual holds or desires. For the purposes of this subchapter, consideration shall be given to the employer's judgment as to what functions of a job are essential, and if an employer has prepared a written description before advertising or interviewing applicants for the job, this description shall be considered evidence of the essential functions of the job.

(9) Reasonable accommodation

The term "reasonable accommodation" may include—

(A) making existing facilities used by employees readily accessible to and usable by individuals with disabilities; and

(B) job restructuring, part-time or modified work schedules, reassignment to a vacant position, acquisition or modification of equipment or devices, appropriate adjustment or modifications of examinations, training materials or policies, the provision of qualified readers or interpreters, and other similar accommodations for individuals with disabilities.

(10) Undue hardship

(A) In general

The term "undue hardship" means an action requiring significant difficulty or expense, when considered in light of the factors set forth in subparagraph (B).

(B) Factors to be considered

In determining whether an accommodation would impose an undue hardship on a covered entity, factors to be considered include—

(i) the nature and cost of the accommodation needed under this chapter;

(ii) the overall financial resources of the facility or facilities involved in the provision of the reasonable accommodation; the number of persons employed at such facility; the effect on expenses and resources, or the impact otherwise of such accommodation upon the operation of the facility;

(iii) the overall financial resources of the covered entity; the overall size of the business of a covered entity with respect to the number of its employees; the number, type, and location of its facilities; and

(iv) the type of operation or operations of the covered entity, including the composition, structure, and functions of the workforce of such entity; the geographic separateness, administrative, or fiscal relationship of the facility or facilities in question to the covered entity.

§ 12112. [ADA Title I: Employment] Discrimination

(a) General rule

No covered entity shall discriminate against a qualified individual with a disability because of the disability of such individual in regard to job application procedures, the hiring, advancement, or discharge of employees, employee compensation, job training, and other terms, conditions, and privileges of employment.

(b) Construction

As used in subsection (a) of this section, the term "discriminate" includes—

(1) limiting, segregating, or classifying a job applicant or employee in a way that adversely affects the opportunities or status of such applicant or employee because of the disability of such applicant or employee;

(2) participating in a contractual or other arrangement or relationship that has the effect of subjecting a covered entity's qualified applicant or employee with a disability to the discrimination prohibited by this subchapter (such relationship includes a relationship with an employment or referral agency, labor union, an organization providing fringe benefits to an employee of the covered entity, or an organization providing training and apprenticeship programs);

(3) utilizing standards, criteria, or methods of administration—

(A) that have the effect of discrimination on the basis of disability; or

(B) that perpetuate the discrimination of others who are subject to common administrative control;

(4) excluding or otherwise denying equal jobs or benefits to a qualified individual because of the known disability of an individual with whom the qualified individual is known to have a relationship or association;

(5)(A) not making reasonable accommodations to the known physical or mental limitations of an otherwise qualified individual with a disability who is an applicant or employee, unless such covered entity can demonstrate that the accommodation would impose an undue hardship on the operation of the business of such covered entity; or

(B) denying employment opportunities to a job applicant or employee who is an otherwise qualified individual with a disability, if such denial is based on the need of such covered entity to make reasonable accommodation to the physical or mental impairments of the employee or applicant;

(6) using qualification standards, employment tests or other selection criteria that screen out or tend to screen out an individual with a disability or a class of individuals with disabilities unless the standard, test or other selection criteria, as used by the covered entity, is shown to be job-related for the position in question and is consistent with business necessity; and

(7) failing to select and administer tests concerning employment in the most effective manner to ensure that, when such test is administered to a job applicant or employee who has a disability that impairs sensory, manual, or speaking skills, such test results accurately reflect the skills, aptitude, or whatever other factor of such applicant or employee that such test purports to measure, rather than reflecting the impaired sensory, manual, or speaking skills of such employee or applicant (except where such skills are the factors that the test purports to measure). . . .

§ 12113. [ADA Title I: Employment] Defenses

(a) In general

It may be a defense to a charge of discrimination under this chapter that an alleged application of qualification standards, tests, or selection criteria that screen out or tend to screen out or otherwise deny a job or benefit to an individual with a disability has been shown to be job-related and consistent with business necessity, and such performance cannot be accomplished by reasonable accommodation, as required under this subchapter.

(b) Qualification standards

The term "qualification standards" may include a requirement that an individual shall not pose a direct threat to the health or safety of other individuals in the workplace. . . .

(3) Construction

Nothing in this chapter shall be construed to preempt, modify, or amend any State, county, or local law, ordinance, or regulation applicable to food handling which is designed to protect the public health from individuals who pose a significant risk to the health or safety of others, which cannot be eliminated by reasonable accommodation, pursuant to the list of infectious or communicable diseases and the modes of transmissability published by the Secretary of Health and Human Services.

§ 12114. [ADA Title I: Employment] Illegal use of drugs and alcohol

(a) Qualified individual with a disability

For purposes of this subchapter, the term "qualified individual with a disability" shall not include any employee or applicant who is currently engaging in the illegal use of drugs, when the covered entity acts on the basis of such use. . . .

§ 12117. [ADA/Title I: Employment] Enforcement

(a) Powers, remedies, and procedures

The powers, remedies, and procedures set forth in sections 2000e–4, 2000e–5, 2000e–6, 2000e–8, and 2000e–9 of this title shall be the powers, remedies, and procedures this subchapter provides to the [Equal Employment Opportunity] Commission, to the Attorney General, or to any person alleging discrimination on the basis of disability in violation of any provision of this chapter, or regulations promulgated under section 12116 of this title, concerning employment.

§ 12181. [ADA Title III: Public Accommodations] Definitions

As used in this subchapter:

. . .

(7) Public accommodation

The following private entities are considered public accommodations for purposes of this subchapter, if the operations of such entities affect commerce—

(A) an inn, hotel, motel, or other place of lodging, except for an establishment located within a building that contains not more than five rooms for rent or hire and that is actually occupied by the proprietor of such establishment as the residence of such proprietor;

(B) a restaurant, bar, or other establishment serving food or drink;

(C) a motion picture house, theater, concert hall, stadium, or other place of exhibition or entertainment;

(D) an auditorium, convention center, lecture hall, or other place of public gathering;

(E) a bakery, grocery store, clothing store, hardware store, shopping center, or other sales or rental establishment;

(F) a laundromat, dry-cleaner, bank, barber shop, beauty shop, travel service, shoe repair service, funeral parlor, gas station, office of an accountant or lawyer, pharmacy, insurance office, professional office of a health care provider, hospital, or other service establishment;

(G) a terminal, depot, or other station used for specified public transportation;

(H) a museum, library, gallery, or other place of public display or collection;

(I) a park, zoo, amusement park, or other place of recreation;

(J) a nursery, elementary, secondary, undergraduate, or postgraduate private school, or other place of education;

(K) a day care center, senior citizen center, homeless shelter, food bank, adoption agency, or other social service center establishment; and

(L) a gymnasium, health spa, bowling alley, golf course, or other place of exercise or recreation. . . .

(9) Readily achievable

The term "readily achievable" means easily accomplishable and able to be carried out without much difficulty or expense. In determining whether an action is readily achievable, factors to be considered include—

(A) the nature and cost of the action needed under this chapter;

(B) the overall financial resources of the facility or facilities involved in the action; the number of persons employed at such facility; the effect on expenses and resources, or the impact otherwise of such action upon the operation of the facility;

(C) the overall financial resources of the covered entity; the overall size of the business of a covered entity with respect to the number of its employees; the number, type, and location of its facilities; and

(D) the type of operation or operations of the covered entity, including the composition, structure, and functions of the workforce of such entity; the geographic separateness, administrative or fiscal relationship of the facility or facilities in question to the covered entity. . . .

§ 12182. [ADA Title III: Public Accommodations] Prohibition of discrimination . . .

(a) General rule

No individual shall be discriminated against on the basis of disability in the full and equal enjoyment of the goods, services, facilities, privileges, advantages, or accommodations of any place of public accommodation by any person who owns, leases (or leases to), or operates a place of public accommodation.

(b) Construction

(1) General prohibition

(A) Activities

(i) Denial of participation

It shall be discriminatory to subject an individual or class of individuals on the basis of a disability or disabilities of such individual or class, directly, or through contractual, licensing, or other arrangements, to a denial of the opportunity of the individual or class to participate in or benefit from the goods, services, facilities, privileges, advantages, or accommodations of an entity.

(ii) Participation in unequal benefit

It shall be discriminatory to afford an individual or class of individuals, on the basis of a disability or disabilities of such individual or class, directly, or through contractual, licensing, or other arrangements with the opportunity to participate in or benefit from a good, service, facility, privilege, advantage, or accommodation that is not equal to that afforded to other individuals.

(iii) Separate benefit

It shall be discriminatory to provide an individual or class of individuals, on the basis of a disability or disabilities of such individual or class, directly, or through contractual, licensing, or other arrangements with a good, service, facility, privilege, advantage, or accommodation that is different or separate from that provided to other individuals, unless such action is necessary to provide the individual or class of individuals with a good, service, facility, privilege, advantage, or accommodation, or other opportunity that is as effective as that provided to others. . . .

(2) Specific prohibitions

(A) Discrimination

For purposes of subsection (a) of this section, discrimination includes—

(i) the imposition or application of eligibility criteria that screen out or tend to screen out an individual with a disability or any class of individuals with disabilities from fully and equally enjoying any goods, services, facilities, privileges, advantages, or accommodations, unless such criteria can be shown to be necessary for the provision of the goods, services, facilities, privileges, advantages, or accommodations being offered;

(ii) a failure to make reasonable modifications in policies, practices, or procedures, when such modifications are necessary to afford such goods, services, facilities, privileges, advantages, or accommodations to individuals with disabilities, unless the entity can demonstrate that making such modifications would fundamentally alter the nature of such goods, services, facilities, privileges, advantages, or accommodations;

(iii) a failure to take such steps as may be necessary to ensure that no individual with a disability is excluded, denied services, segregated or otherwise treated differently than other individuals because of the absence of auxiliary aids and services, unless the entity can demonstrate that taking such steps would fundamentally alter the nature of the good, service, facility, privilege, advantage, or accommodation being offered or would result in an undue burden;

(iv) a failure to remove architectural barriers, and communication barriers that are structural in nature, in existing facilities, and transportation barriers in existing vehicles and rail passenger cars used by an establishment for transporting individuals (not including barriers that can only be removed through the retrofitting of vehicles or rail passenger cars by the installation of a hydraulic or other lift), where such removal is readily achievable; and

(v) where an entity can demonstrate that the removal of a barrier under clause (iv) is not readily achievable, a failure to make such goods, services, facilities, privileges, advantages, or accommodations available through alternative methods if such methods are readily achievable. . . .

(3) Specific construction

Nothing in this subchapter shall require an entity to permit an individual to participate in or benefit from the goods, services, facilities, privileges, advantages and accommodations of such entity where such individual poses a direct threat to the health or safety of others. The term "direct threat" means a significant risk to the health or safety of others that cannot be eliminated by a modification of policies, practices, or procedures or by the provision of auxiliary aids or services. . . .

§ 12208.   [Miscellaneous:] Transvestites.

For the purposes of this Act, the term "disabled" or "disability" shall not apply to an individual solely because that individual is a transvestite.

B.   THE CIVIL RIGHTS ACT OF 1991

The Civil Rights Act of 1991

PL 102–166, November 21, 1991, 105 Stat 1071

An Act to amend the Civil Rights Act of 1964 to strengthen and improve Federal civil rights laws, to provide for damages in cases of intentional employment discrimination, to clarify provisions regarding disparate impact actions, and for other purposes.

Be it enacted by the Senate and House of Representatives of the United States of America in Congress assembled, . . .

§ 2.   Findings.

The Congress finds that—

(1) additional remedies under Federal law are needed to deter unlawful harassment and intentional discrimination in the workplace;

(2) the decision of the Supreme Court in Wards Cove Packing Co. v. Atonio, 490 U.S. 642 (1989) has weakened the scope and effectiveness of Federal civil rights protections; and

(3) legislation is necessary to provide additional protections against unlawful discrimination in employment.

§ 3.   Purposes.

The purposes of this Act are—

(1) to provide appropriate remedies for intentional discrimination and unlawful harassment in the workplace;

(2) to codify the concepts of "business necessity" and "job related" enunciated by the Supreme Court in Griggs v. Duke Power Co., 401 U.S. 424, 91 S.Ct. 849, 28 L.Ed.2d 158 (1971), and in the other Supreme Court decisions prior to Wards Cove Packing Co. v. Atonio, 490 U.S. 642, 109 S.Ct. 2115, 104 L.Ed.2d 733 (1989);

(3) to confirm statutory authority and provide statutory guidelines for the adjudication of disparate impact suits under title VII of the Civil Rights Act of 1964 (42 U.S.C. 2000e et seq.); and

(4) to respond to recent decisions of the Supreme Court by expanding the scope of relevant civil rights statutes in order to provide adequate protection to victims of discrimination.

§ 101. Prohibition Against All Racial Discrimination in the Making and Enforcement of Contracts.

Section 1977 of the Revised Statutes (42 U.S.C. 1981) is amended—

(1) by inserting "(a)" before "All persons within"; and

(2) by adding at the end the following new subsections:

"(b) For purposes of this section, the term 'make and enforce contracts' includes the making, performance, modification, and termination of contracts, and the enjoyment of all benefits, privileges, terms, and conditions of the contractual relationship.

"(c) The rights protected by this section are protected against impairment by nongovernmental discrimination and impairment under color of State law."

§ 102. Damages in Cases of Intentional Discrimination.

The Revised Statutes are amended by inserting after section 1977 (42 U.S.C.1981) the following new section:

"SEC. 1977A. DAMAGES IN CASES OF INTENTIONAL DISCRIMINATION IN EMPLOYMENT." [See new § 1981A in selected provisions of Title 42 *supra*.]

§ 104. Definitions.

Section 701 of the Civil Rights Act of 1964 (42 U.S.C. 2000e) is amended by adding at the end the following new subsections: ...

"(m) The term 'demonstrates' means meets the burdens of production and persuasion...."

§ 105. Burden of Proof in Disparate Impact Cases.

(a) Section 703 of the Civil Rights Act of 1964 (42 U.S.C. 2000e–2) is amended by adding at the end of the following new subsection:

"(k)(1)(A) An unlawful employment practice based on disparate impact is established under this title only if—

"(i)3a complaining party demonstrates that a respondent uses a particular employment practice that causes a disparate impact on the basis of race, color, religion, sex, or national origin and the respondent fails to demonstrate that the challenged practice is job related for the position in question and consistent with business necessity; or

"(ii) the complaining party makes the demonstration described in subparagraph (C) with respect to an alternative employment practice and the respondent refuses to adopt such alternative employment practice.

"(B)(i) With respect to demonstrating that a particular employment practice causes a disparate impact as described in subparagraph (A)(i), the complaining party shall demonstrate that each particular challenged employment practice causes a disparate impact, except that if the complaining party can demonstrate to the court that the elements of a respondent's decisionmaking process are not capable of separation for analysis, the decisionmaking process may be analyzed as one employment practice.

"(ii) If the respondent demonstrates that a specific employment practice does not cause the disparate impact, the respondent shall not be required to demonstrate that such practice is required by business necessity.

"(C) The demonstration referred to by subparagraph (A)(ii) shall be in accordance with the law as it existed on June 4, 1989, with respect to the concept of 'alternative employment practice'.

"(2) A demonstration that an employment practice is required by business necessity may not be used as a defense against a claim of intentional discrimination under this title. . . ."

(b) No statements other than the interpretive memorandum appearing at Vol. 137 Congressional Record S 15276 (daily ed. Oct. 25, 1991) shall be considered legislative history of, or relied upon in any way as legislative history in construing or applying, any provision of this Act that relates to Wards Cove—Business necessity/cumulation/alternative business practice.

§ 106. Prohibition Against Discriminatory Use of Test Scores.

Section 703 of the Civil Rights Act of 1964 (42 U.S.C. 2000e–2) (as amended by section 105) is further amended by adding at the end the following new subsection:

"(1) It shall be an unlawful employment practice for a respondent, in connection with the selection or referral of applicants or candidates for employment or promotion, to adjust the scores of, use different cutoff scores for, or otherwise alter the results of, employment related tests on the basis of race, color, religion, sex, or national origin."

§ 107. Clarifying Prohibition Against Impermissible [Actions]

(a) IN GENERAL.—Section 703 of the Civil Rights Act of 1964 (42 U.S.C. 2000e–2) (as amended by sections 105 and 106) is further amended by adding at the end the following new subsection:

"(m) Except as otherwise provided in this title, an unlawful employment practice is established when the complaining party demonstrates that race, color, religion, sex, or national origin was a motivating factor for any employment practice, even though other factors also motivated the practice."

(b) ENFORCEMENT PROVISIONS.—Section 706(g) of such Act (42 U.S.C. 2000e–5(g)) is amended—

(1) by designating the first through third sentences as paragraph (1);

(2) by designating the fourth sentence as paragraph (2)(A) and indenting accordingly; and

(3) by adding at the end the following new subparagraph:

"(B) On a claim in which an individual proves a violation under section 703(m) and a respondent demonstrates that the respondent would have taken the same action in the absence of the impermissible motivating factor, the court—

"(i) may grant declaratory relief, injunctive relief (except as provided in clause (ii)), and attorney's fees and costs demonstrated to be directly attributable only to the pursuit of a claim under section 703(m); and

"(ii) shall not award damages or issue an order requiring any admission, reinstatement, hiring, promotion, or payment, described in subparagraph (A)."....

§ 109. Protection of Extraterritorial Employment.

(a) DEFINITION OF EMPLOYEE.—Section 701(f) of the Civil Rights Act of 1964 (42 U.S.C. 2000e(f)) and section 101(4) of the Americans with Disabilities Act of 1990 (42 U.S.C. 12111(4)) are each amended by adding at the end the following: "With respect to employment in a foreign country, such term includes an individual who is a citizen of the United States."

(b) EXEMPTION.—[This prohibition shall not apply to an employer's practices] "with respect to an employee in a workplace in a foreign country if compliance with such section would cause such employer to violate the law of the foreign country in which such workplace is located."....

§ 116. Lawful Court–Ordered Remedies, Affirmative Action, and Conciliation Agreements not Affected.

Nothing in the amendments made by this title shall be construed to affect court-ordered remedies, affirmative action, or conciliation agreements, that are in accordance with the law....

†